THE COMPLETE GOLDEN DAWN
SYSTEM OF MAGIC

Some Other Titles From New Falcon Publications

Aleister Crowley's Illustrated Goetia
Taboo: Sex, Religion & Magick
Sex Magic, Tantra & Tarot: The Way of the Secret Lover
 By Christopher S. Hyatt, Ph.D., and Lon Milo DuQuette
Ask Baba Lon
 By Lon Milo DuQuette
Enochian World of Aleister Crowley
 By Lon Milo DuQuette and Aleister Crowley,
 Edited by David Cherubim
Cosmic Trigger 1
Cosmic Trigger 2
Cosmic Trigger 3
Coincidance
The Earth Will Shake
Email to the Universe
Nature's God
Prometheus Rising
TSOG: The Thing that Ate the Constitution
Wilhelm Reich in Hell
The Widow's Son
The Walls Came Tumbling Down
Sex, Drugs & Magick
Quantum Psychology
 By Robert Anton Wilson
Info-Psychology
The Intelligence Agents
Neuropolitique
What Does WoMan Want?
 By Timothy Leary, Ph.D.
Healing Energy, Prayer and Relaxation
The Complete Golden Dawn System of Magic
The Golden Dawn Audio CDs
What You Should Know About The Golden Dawn
The Eye in the Triangle: An Interpretation of Aleister Crowley
 By Israel Regardie
Rebellion, Revolution and Religiousness
 By Osho
The Dream Illuminati
The Illuminati of Immortality
 By Wayne Saalman
Monsters & Magical Sticks
 By Steven Heller, Ph.D. & Terry Steele
An Insider's Guide to Robert Anton Wilson
 Eric Wagner
Shaping Formless Fire
 By Stephen Mace
Aleister Crowley and the Treasure House of Images
 By J.F.C. Fuller, Aleister Crowley, David Cherubim,
 Lon Milo DuQuette and Nancy Wasserman

Please visit our website at http://www.newfalcon.com

ISRAEL REGARDIE

Born November 17, 1907 — Died March 10, 1985

THE COMPLETE GOLDEN DAWN SYSTEM OF MAGIC

BY

ISRAEL REGARDIE

**FOREWORD
BY
DAVID CHERUBIM**

NEW FALCON PUBLICATIONS
LAS VEGAS, NEVADA, U.S.A.

First Paperback Edition 2013

The paper used in this publication meets the minimum requirements of the American National Standard for Permanence of Paper for Printed Library Materials Z39.48-1984

Address all inquiries to:

NEW FALCON PUBLICATIONS
9550 S. Eastern Avenue, Suite 253
Las Vegas, NV 89123

website: http://www.newfalcon.com
email: info@newfalcon.com

MASTER TABLE OF CONTENTS

INTRODUCTORY SECTION

VOLUME TABLE OF CONTENTS

TABLE OF CONTENTS

VOLUME ONE
THE MAGICAL ALPHABET

IMPORTANT TABLES AND ILLUSTRATIONS

VOLUME TWO
THE IMPORTANCE OF DIVINATION

IMPORTANT TABLES AND ILLUSTRATIONS

VOLUME THREE
THE CORE OF THE TRADITION

IMPORTANT TABLES AND ILLUSTRATIONS

VOLUME FOUR
BASIC TECHNIQUES

IMPORTANT TABLES AND ILLUSTRATIONS

VOLUME FIVE
MAGICAL FUNDAMENTALS

IMPORTANT TABLES AND ILLUSTRATIONS

VOLUME SIX
OUTER ORDER RITUALS AND COMMENTARIES

IMPORTANT TABLES AND ILLUSTRATIONS

VOLUME SEVEN
RITUALS OF THE R.R. ET A.C. WITH THOSE OF
WAITE'S FELLOWSHIP

IMPORTANT TABLES AND ILLUSTRATIONS

VOLUME EIGHT
OTHER ORDER RITUALS AND MAGICAL DOCTRINES

IMPORTANT TABLES AND ILLUSTRATIONS

VOLUME NINE
THE TAROT

IMPORTANT TABLES AND ILLUSTRATIONS

VOLUME TEN
THE ENOCHIAN SYSTEM

IMPORTANT TABLES AND ILLUSTRATIONS

VOLUME ELEVEN
APPENDICES

ACKNOWLEDGMENTS

It gives me great pleasure to thank the following for their generosity and courtesy as follows:

Mr. Carr P. Collins Jr., for giving me free access to his vast collection of Golden Dawn manuscripts, many dated before the turn of the century. And who on two occasions visited England to bring me back a complete set of Golden Dawn documents for the express purpose of writing this book; The late Gerald Yorke for giving Carr Collins copies of a complete set of all the Golden Dawn documents ranging from Neophyte to Adeptus Minor issued to Frater De Profundis ad Lucem (Mr. Leigh F. Gardner), circa 1894-1896; Robert A. Gilbert, (now writing a biography of A.E. Waite) for his gift of two rituals from Waite's Fellowship of the Rosy Cross; Francis King for permission to use lengthy excerpts from his books *Ritual Magic in England* and *The Rebirth of Magic*; Gerald Suster for his contribution of a critique of Ellic Howe's book on the Golden Dawn; Thomas Head, Ph.D., who wrote the learned introduction to the Enochian system; Ms. Patricia Monocris for her Ritual "Requiescat in Pace"; Mr. Larry Epperson for his ritual on the Evocation of the Spirit Chassan to visible appearance; Edwin Steinbrecher for permission to quote at large from his *Inner Guide Meditation;* Ithell Colquhoun for the portrait of Mathers painted by Moina Mathers, the background of which I had lightened to bring his face more clearly into the foreground; Stuart R. Kaplan for his kind permission to quote from his *Encyclopedia of Tarot* and to use some cards of the *Golden Dawn Tarot* (U.S. Game Systems); Dr. Robert Wang for the photograph of his model of the Tree of Life projected into a sphere; Hans Nintzel for the use of his essay on Alchemy; Mr. Neville Armstrong of Spearman Ltd. (England) for his permission to use the portrait of McGregor Mathers and that of Dr. Wynn Westcott; Finally to the Wizard Book Shelf for permission to quote from their edition of *The Zohar* translated by Nurho de Manhar (San Diego, Calif. 1978), and to Victor A. Endersby for the quote from *The Hall of Mirrors.*

Finally I would like to express my deepest gratitude to the staff of Falcon Press and in particular S.L. Slaughter for his artistic work and persistence, Kris Morgan for her contribution of the Rose Cross, the Ring and the Disc, and the Seven Palaces of Holiness; Corey Hogan for his never ending determination and guidance in seeing that production proceeded on schedule, and Christopher S. Hyatt both for his help in editing, his original contribution of ideas and his never ending "push" to insure that all went as well as possible.

A NOTE ON STYLE

In addition to the official and unofficial documents of the Order in this book, there are a number of papers and articles contributed by various authors. What has to be noted about all these documents is a difference of style in writing and of spelling out some of the basic terms used in the Qabalah and Magic. It was my original intention to render style and spelling uniform in this book, but upon more prolonged reflection I have decided to let the individuality of each author speak for himself. As a result the reader will note that there are discrepancies here and there where the most basic technical names are used. For example, Sephirah is often spelled without the final letter. Of course this is minor, but at the same time it is symptomatic of a trend which may prove confusing if he neglects this warning. In other words do not pay too much attention to the trivialities of style, set, and spelling but rather try to grasp what each writer is attempting to say. On the whole we have tried to remain faithful to each writer's wishes and intent even to such a degree as to include some of their lesser errors and arrogances.

PERSISTENCE AND DETERMINATION

Over the years I have been asked over and over again what are the most important qualities that a student should possess in approaching the Great Work. Other than normal intelligence and emotional stability, I find two other qualities which are essential for success. They are best summed up in the following quotation by Calvin Coolidge:

Nothing in the world can take the place of persistence.

Talent will not; nothing is more common than unsuccessful men with talent.

Genius will not; unrewarded genius is almost a proverb.

Education will not; the world is full of educated derelicts.

Persistence and determination alone are omnipotent.

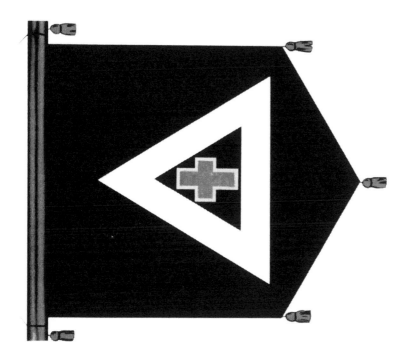

BANNER OF THE EAST

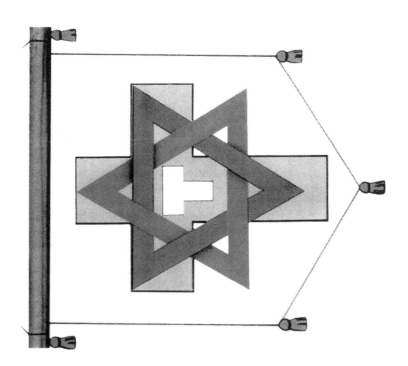

BANNER OF THE WEST

TREE OF LIFE IN A SPHERE

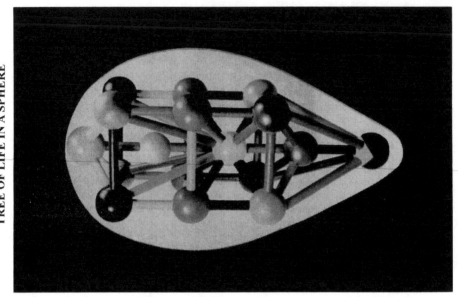

QABALISTIC TREE OF LIFE

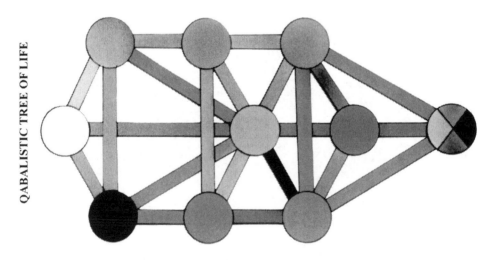

KERUB OF FIRE

KERUB OF AIR

KERUB OF WATER

KERUB OF EARTH

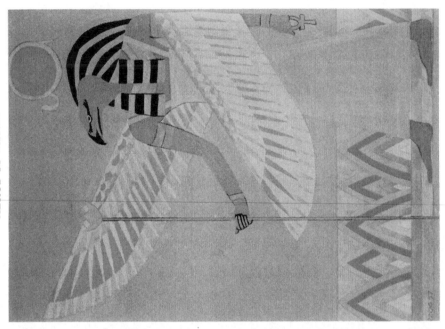

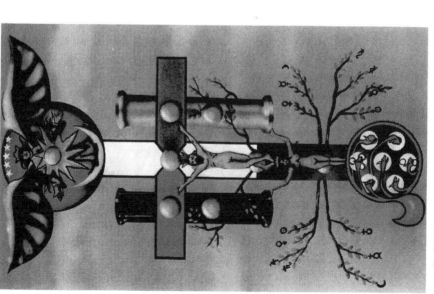

GARDEN OF EDEN BEFORE THE FALL

GARDEN OF EDEN AFTER THE FALL

THE HIGHER AND DIVINE GENIUS
(ON THE LID OF THE PASTOS)

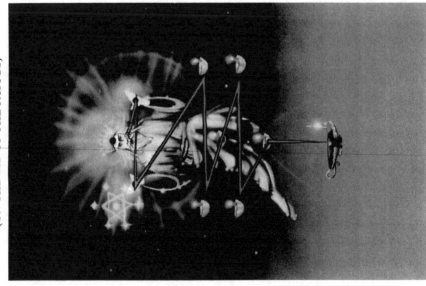

RESTORATION (ON THE LID OF THE PASTOS)

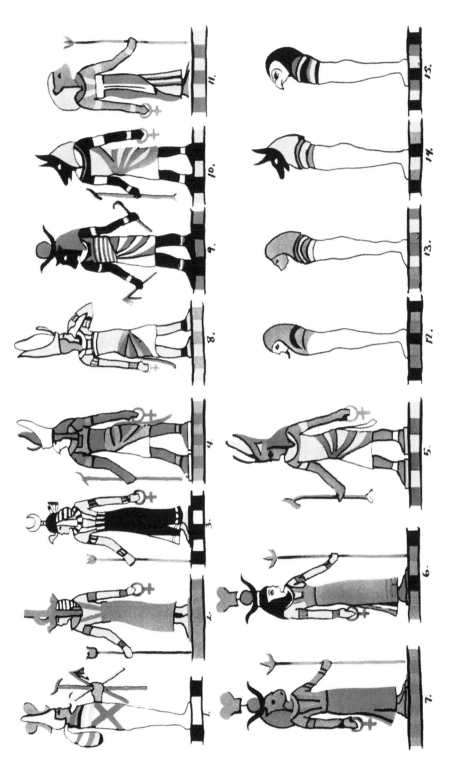

GOD FORMS

ENOCHIAN CHESS PIECES (FIRE)

ENOCHIAN CHESS PIECES (AIR)

FOREWORD

By
David Cherubim

*"Initiation is the preparation for immortality. Man is only
potentially immortal. Immortality is acquired when the
purely human part of him becomes allied to that spiritual
essence which was never created, was never born, and shall
never die. It is to effect this spiritual bond with the highest that
the Golden Dawn owes all its rituals and practical magical work."*

Israel Regardie

It is with great honor and joy that I am writing a Foreword to one of the most important and influential books of all time in the field of the *Magick Art*. This book, *The Complete Golden Dawn System of Magic,* is one of the greatest contributions to the Great Work in published form, a priceless gem of Occult Knowledge for students, neophytes and adepts of the *Magick Art*.

Before Israel Regardie passed away into the Infinite,[1] he asked his close friend and student, the late Christopher S. Hyatt,[2] to carry on and preserve his invaluable work. To this end, Dr. Hyatt devoted so much of his time and energy, selflessly and profusely, as witnessed by myself and others.

Besides carrying on the torch of Israel Regardie through the continuation of the Golden Dawn, and the establishment of the *Israel Regardie Foundation,* Dr. Hyatt also published some of Regardie's most important works, including this book, *The Complete Golden Dawn System of Magic*, which is, unquestionably, Israel Regardie's *Magnum Opus.*

---

[1] Israel Regardie (born Francis Israel Regudy in London, England on November 17th, 1907 and died on March 10th, 1985 in Sedona, Arizona) was one of the most influential Adepts of the Golden Dawn. He was also a dedicated writer, chiropractor and therapist. It was his main ambition to preserve and perpetuate the teachings and work of the Hermetic Order of the Golden Dawn and Aleister Crowley.

[2] Christopher S. Hyatt, Ph.D. (born Alan Ronald Miller in Chicago, Illinois on July 12th, 1943 and died on February 9th, 2008 in Scottsdale, Arizona) was the primary founder of New Falcon Publications. He was also the main founder of the *Israel Regardie Foundation.* He was an Adept of the Golden Dawn, trained in both psycho-physiology and clinical psychology, and he practiced as a Psychotherapist for many years. Today he is known as a world-famous author of a wide variety of books on Psychology, Sex, Tantra, Tarot, Self-transformation and Western Magic. Dr. Hyatt had more influence in making public and promoting the works of Aleister Crowley than is generally recognized today, and the same is true of Dr. Hyatt's mentor and close friend, Israel Regardie. If it were not for these two illustrious Adepts of the Golden Dawn, neither Crowley nor Thelema would be as well-known and accepted as they are today.

The first edition of this book was published in 1984 by Falcon Press (New Falcon Publications) in association with the *Israel Regardie Foundation.* Dr. Hyatt not only published this book, but he also helped Regardie edit it, a most arduous task in and of itself. The material in this book is an improved version of the influential and inspiring material that was contained in Regardie's original four-volume Golden Dawn set that revolutionized the Occult world.[3]

This new edition of the book, published almost 30 years after the original, is the first edition to be published in paperback form, making it accessible to a larger audience of readers by a major reduction in cost. This is a significant spiritual service. A paperback edition of this book should prove to be a major contribution to the preservation and perpetuation of the magical teachings and work of the Golden Dawn and Israel Regardie.

This paperback edition of the book contains five magical rituals by Israel Regardie from the archives of the *Israel Regardie Foundation.* These inspired and efficacious rituals, based on Golden Dawn magical techniques, have never been published before in book form. They are called the Pentagram Rituals of Air, Fire, Water, Earth and Spirit.

This paperback edition of the book also contains two articles ("The Re-Awakening of Osiris: Reclaiming the God of Reintegration in the Golden Dawn System" and "Consecration of a Lunar Talisman") by two highly respected modern-day Adepts of the Golden Dawn, Chic and Tabatha Cicero, who have devoted so much time, energy and love to the continuation of the Golden Dawn and the works of Israel Regardie.

This edition of the book also contains two previous articles by two other Golden Dawn Adepts and friends of mine, Lon Milo DuQuette and the late S. Jason Black (David P. Wilson), both of whom I first encountered in Los Angeles on separate occasions in 1985 at Baphomet Lodge, O.T.O., in Los Angeles (Wilson at an O.T.O. initiation and DuQuette at an O.T.O. Gnostic Mass), and both of whom, like myself, worked so closely with the late Dr. Hyatt (who, beside being an Adept of the Golden Dawn, was also a IX° member of the O.T.O., as was Regardie). This edition of the book also contains another previous article by Dr. Jack Willis, who was Regardie's personal student.

Now Israel Regardie (November 17th, 1907 – March 10th, 1985) met with the Golden Dawn magician Aleister Crowley (October 12th, 1875 – December 1st, 1947) in Paris, France on October 12th, 1928 to become his personal secretary and student (he also became Crowley's Confidential Agent and a IX° member of Crowley's O.T.O.).[4] On October 28th, 1930, Regardie took the Oath of the Probationer in Crowley's Order of the A.·. A.·. (*Astron Argon*). The Order of the A.·. A.·. was Crowley's reformulated and advanced version of the system of the Golden Dawn. He even maintained the name of the Golden Dawn (*Aurora Aurea*) for the Outer Order.[5]

---

[3] *The Golden Dawn: An Account of the Teachings, Rites, and Ceremonies of the Hermetic Order of the Golden Dawn,* by Israel Regardie (Chicago, IL: The Aries Press, 1937–1940).

[4] See the sixth revised edition of "*What you should know about the Golden Dawn,*" by Israel Regardie (New Falcon Publications, 1993) for a copy of a letter from Crowley dated June 12th, 1930, introducing Regardie as his Secretary and Confidential Agent; for a copy of Regardie's signed A.·. A.·. Probationer Oath; and for a copy of a Postcard from Crowley (729) sent to Regardie, addressing Regardie as a IX° initiate of the O.T.O. (Ordo Templi Orientis).

[5] In *An Interview with Israel Regardie: His Final Thoughts and Views* (Falcon Press, 1985), Israel Regardie stated the following about Aleister Crowley and the Golden Dawn, and his esteemed relation thereto: "They have left indelible marks on my life and my career if I want to use that term, but certainly on my personal life. Crowley first, and The Golden Dawn, second. On the other hand, I cannot separate Crowley from The Golden Dawn, because *Crowley was The Golden Dawn, and The Golden Dawn was Crowley.* Crowley, was, to use one of my earlier cliches, a graduate without honor from the Golden Dawn. He took the Golden Dawn

Then in January of 1933, shortly after severing with Crowley, Regardie, like his magical mentor, joined the Golden Dawn (or, more appropriately, an offshoot of the Order called the *Stella Matutina*) at Hermes Temple in Bristol with the Neophyte Motto Frater *Ad Majorem Adonai Gloriam.*[6] (In the book, "The Eye in the Triangle" [New Falcon Publications], Regardie states that he retained this same Neophyte Motto for his 5=6 Adept degree, the Adeptus Minor Grade.) Regardie resigned as an Adept from Hermes Temple of the *Stella Matutina* on December 5th, 1934.

Many years later Israel Regardie and Christopher S. Hyatt joined forces in the Great Work. Dr. Hyatt personally trained under Regardie, and he inevitably became Regardie's magical heir, continuing the Regardie lineage of the Golden Dawn in association with the *Israel Regardie Foundation* which was originally established by Dr. Hyatt to carry on Regardie's name and work. Dr. Hyatt was also one of the founders of the *Thelemic Order of the Golden Dawn.*[7]

Dr. Hyatt passed away into the Infinite on February 9th, 2008. Almost three years later, I determined to revive the *Israel Regardie Foundation.*[8] When I was asked by New Falcon Publications[9] to write a Foreword for this new edition of *The Complete Golden Dawn System of Magic*, I recognized it as an important opportunity to do the Great Work of the foundation, to help preserve and perpetuate the teachings of Israel Regardie and the Golden Dawn, and to carry on the important work of Dr. Hyatt in this regard.[10]

The Complete Golden Dawn System of Magic was Israel Regardie's last book, the final token of his True Will. Through this book he bequeathed to us the means to carry on the *Great Work* of the Golden Dawn which, in a nutshell, is Initiation. By its teachings, rituals and initiation ceremonies, the work of the Golden Dawn is to initiate and prepare us to "become more than human" or, in other terms, to "attain the Knowledge and Conversation of the Holy Guardian Angel." Such is the sublime work of Illumination or Enlightenment as described in magical terms.

---

teaching and transformed some of it, used other bits of it literally, but still it was all based on the Golden Dawn, even though he gave his Order another name, the A.A. So I felt very much at home in the Golden Dawn, and really had no problem absorbing the material, sailing through it very, very rapidly just as Crowley had many years earlier."

[6] A phrase meaning, "To the greater glory of my Lord."

[7] On the Vernal Equinox of 1990 e.v., David Cherubim and Christopher S. Hyatt inaugurated the *Thelemic Order of the Golden Dawn*, and they acted as the ruling Chiefs of the Order. Dr. Hyatt was a Chief of the Order until David Cherubim became the sole Chief on December 4th, 1994 e.v. The official website for *the Thelemic Order of the Golden Dawn* is at: http://www.thelemicgoldendawn.net.

[8] The *Israel Regardie Foundation* operates in association with the *Thelemic Order of the Golden Dawn* and the *Aleister Crowley Foundation* which was founded by David Cherubim in the US in 1998 e.v. to perpetuate the teachings of *Aleister Crowley*. The official website for the *Israel Regardie Foundation* is at: http://www.israelregardiefoundation.net. The official website for the *Aleister Crowley Foundation* is at: http://www.aleistercrowleyfoundation.net.

[9] After Dr. Hyatt's passing, his biological son Michael Miller became the President and CEO of New Falcon Publications. Michael is actively and successfully engaged in carrying on the publishing work of his father.

[10] Christopher S. Hyatt (*Frater Adonai Achad*) initiated David Cherubim (*Frater Aurora Aurea*) as an Adept in the Golden Dawn (or more accurately in the Second Order called the *Rosae Rubeae et Aureae Crucis*) on March 10th, 1990 e.v., five years after Regardie's death (March 10th, 1985 e.v.), to carry on Regardie's lineage of the Golden Dawn; and on April 13th, 1990 e.v., David Cherubim received certification from Dr. Hyatt for the grades of the Second Order (*Adeptus Minor, Adeptus Major and Adeptus Exemptus*), and he was also chartered by Dr. Hyatt on this same day to operate a Temple of the Golden Dawn in association with the *Israel Regardie Foundation*. He also became one of the Chief Officers of the *Israel Regardie Foundation* and a Chief Officer (Cancellarius) of the *Hermetic Temple and Order of the Golden Dawn*.

Like Aleister Crowley's prodigious periodical called *The Equinox* (in which Crowley published, for the first time, the Golden Dawn rituals of initiation, breaking his oaths of secrecy to the Golden Dawn, as did Regardie), *The Complete Golden Dawn System of Magic* was given to the world by Israel Regardie to preserve for us the Sacred Tradition, so that a new Renaissance might in due season rekindle the Hidden Light.

In Regardie's own inimitable words: "One of the things that has always rattled me is human secrecy. So long as this body of knowledge remains locked up in one or more human being's brains, it runs the risk of being lost to mankind forever. It needs to be put in book form to be distributed all over the world, so that if some type of cataclysm occurred someone, somewhere, would be able to rediscover this material and once more make it available. So long as a few books can be found tucked away somewhere, this knowledge cannot be lost. So therefore in writing *The Complete Golden Dawn System of Magic* my intention was to make it as complete as possible, hoping that Falcon Press (with new leaders at its helm) would make certain that this had the widest possible distribution. Thus, in the event that there was a major calamity, and Western civilization as we know it was destroyed in the Northern hemisphere, there would be dozens or hundreds of sets of this teaching distributed in the Southern hemisphere. Then this form of occult knowledge, this particular rendition of being 'brought to the Light,' would endure for another thousand years or so."[11]

Lastly, to you, the dear reader and practitioner of the invaluable material contained in this monumental book on the *Magick Art* of the Golden Dawn, I wish to say: May you realize and accomplish the *Great Work*, and attain the QUINTESSENCE, the Stone of the Philosophers, the Summum Bonum, True Wisdom, and Perfect Happiness!

David Cherubim
Israel Regardie Foundation
Los Angeles, CA, USA
March 10th, 2013 e.v.

---

[11] From *An Interview with Israel Regardie: His Final Thoughts and Views* (Phoenix, AZ: Falcon Press, 1985)

INTRODUCTION

HISTORY OF THE GOLDEN DAWN

THE EARLY YEARS

By
Israel Regardie[1]

"The Order of the Golden Dawn," narrates the history lecture of that Order, "is an Hermetic Society whose members are taught the principles of Occult Science and the Magic of Hermes. During the early part of the second half of last century, several eminent Adepti and Chiefs of the Order in France and England died, and their death caused a temporary dormant condition of Temple work.

"Prominent among the Adepti of our Order and of public renown, were Eliphas Levi the greatest of modern French magi; Ragon, the author of several books of occult lore; Kenneth M. Mackenzie, author of the famous and learned Masonic Encyclopaedia: and Frederick Hockley possessed of the power of vision in the crystal, and whose manuscripts are highly esteemed. These and other contemporary Adepti of this Order received their knowledge and power from predecessors of equal and even of greater eminence. They received indeed and have handed down to us their doctrine and system of Theosophy and Hermetic Science and the higher Alchemy from a long series of practised investigators whose origin is traced to the Fratres Roseae Crucis of Germany, which association was founded by one Christian Rosenkreutz about the year 1398 A.D. ...

"The Rosicrucian revisval of Mysticism was but a new development of the vastly older wisdom of the Qabalistic Rabbis and of that very ancient secret knowledge, the Magic of the Egyptians, in which the Hebrew Pentateuch tells you that Moses, the founder of the Jewish system was 'learned', that is, in which he had been initiated." In a slender but highly informative booklet entitled *Data of the History of the Rosicrucians* published in 1916 by the late Dr. William Wynn Westcott, we find the following brief statement: "In 1887 by permission of S.D.A. [Anna Sprengel] a continental Rosicrucian Adept, the Isis-Urania Temple of Hermetic Students of the G.D. was formed to give instruction in the mediaeval Occult sciences. Fratres M.E.V. [William Robert Woodman] with S.A. [Dr. Wynn Westcott] and S.R.M.D. [S.L. MacGregor Mathers] became the chiefs, and the latter wrote the rituals

---

[1] Originally published in *My Rosicrucian Adventure* (1936) which was revised and republished as *What You Should Know About the Golden Dawn* (Falcon Press, 1983)

in modern English from old Rosicrucian mss. (the property of S.A.) supplemented by his own literary researches."

In these two statements is narrated the beginning of the Hermetic Order of the Golden Dawn —an organisation which has exerted a greater influence on the development of Occultism since its revival in the last quarter of the 19th century than most people can realise. There can be little or no doubt that the Golden Dawn is, or rather was until very recently, the sole depository of magical knowledge, the only Occult Order of any real worth that the West in our time has known, and a great many other occult organisations owe what little magical knowledge is theirs to leakages issuing from that Order and from its renegade members.

The membership of the Golden Dawn was recruited from every circle, and it was represented by dignified professions as well as by all the arts and sciences, to make but little mention of the trades and business occupations. It included physicians, psychologists, clergymen, artists and philosophers; and normal men and women, humble and unknown, from every walk of life have drawn inspiration from its font of wisdom, and undoubtedly many would be happy to recognise and admit the enormous debt they owe to it.

As an organisation, it preferred always to shroud itself in an impenetrable cloak of mystery. Its teaching and methods of instruction were stringently guarded by various penalties attached to the most awe-inspiring obligations in order to ensure that secrecy. So well have these obligations with but one or two exceptions been kept that the general public knows next to nothing about the Order, its teaching, or the extent and nature of its membership. Though this book will touch upon the teaching of the Golden Dawn, concerning its membership as a whole the writer will have nothing to say, except perhaps to repeat what may already be more or less well-known. For instance, it is common knowledge that W.B. Yeats, Arthur Machen and, if rumour may be trusted, the late Arnold Bennett were at one time among its members, together with a good many other writers and artists.

With regard to the names given in Dr. Westcott's statement it is necessary that we bestow to them some little attention in order to unravel, so far as may be possible, the almost inextricable confusion which has characterised every previous effort to detail the history of the Order. M.E.V. was the motto chosen by Dr. William Robert Woodman, an eminent Freemason of the last century. Sapere Aude and Non Omnis Moriar were the two mottos used by Dr. Westcott, an antiquarian, scholar, and coroner by profession. S.R.M.D. or S. Rhiogail Ma Dhream was the motto of S.L. MacGregor Mathers, the translator of *The Greater Key of King Solomon*, the *Book of the Sacred Magic of Abramelin the Mage*, and *The Qabalah Unveiled*, which latter consisted of certain portions of the Zohar prefixed by an introduction of high erudition. He also employed the Latin motto Deo Duce Comite Ferro. S.D.A. was the abbreviation of the motto Sapiens Dom-inabitur Astris chosen by a Fräulein Anna Sprengel of Nüremberg, Germany. Such were the actors on this occult stage, this the *dramatis personae* in the background of the commencement of the Order. More than any other figures who may later have prominently figured in its government and work, these are the four outstanding figures publicly involved in the English foundation of what came to be known as The Hermetic Order of the Golden Dawn.

How the actual beginning came to pass is not really known. Or rather, because of so many conflicting stories and legends the truth is impossible to discover. At any rate, so far as England is concerned, without a doubt we must seek for its origins in the Societas Rosicruciana in Anglia. This was an organisation formulated in 1865 by eminent Freemasons, some of them claiming Rosicrucian initiation from continental authorities. Amongst those who claimed such initiation was one Kenneth Mackenzie, a Masonic scholar and encyclopaedist, who had received his at the hands of a Count Apponyi in Austria. The objects of this Society, which confined its membership to Freemasons in good standing, was "to afford mutual aid and encouragement in working out the great problems of Life, and in discovering the secrets of nature; to facilitate the study of the systems of philosophy founded upon the Kaballah and the doctrines of Hermes Trismegistus." Dr. Westcott also remarks that to-day its Fratres "are concerned in the study and administration of medicines, and in their manufacture upon old lines; they also teach and practise the curative effects of coloured light, and cultivate mental processes which are believed to induce spiritual enlightenment and extended powers of the human senses, especially in the directions of clairvoyance and clairaudience."

The first Chief of this Society, its Supreme Magus so-called, was one Robert Wentworth Little, who is said to have rescued some old rituals from a certain Masonic storeroom, and it was from certain of those papers that the Society's rituals were elaborated. He died in 1878, and in his stead was appointed Dr. William R. Woodman. Both Dr. Westcott and MacGregor Mathers were prominent and active members of this body. In fact, the former became Supreme Magus upon Woodman's death, the office of junior Magus being conferred upon Mathers. One legend has it that one day Westcott discovered in his library a series of cipher manuscripts, and in order to decipher them he enlisted the aid of MacGregor Mathers. It is said that this library was that of the Societas Rosicruciana in Anglia, and it is likewise asserted that those cipher manuscripts were among the rituals and documents originally rescued by Robert Little from Freemason's Hall. Yet other accounts have it that Westcott found the manuscripts on a bookstall in Farringdon Street. Further apocryphal legends claim that they were found in the library of books and manuscripts inherited from the mystic and clairvoyant, Frederick Hockley who died in 1885. Whatever the real origin of these mysterious cipher manuscripts, when eventually deciphered with the aid of MacGregor Mathers, they were alleged to have contained the address of Fräulein Anna Sprengel who purported to be a Rosicrucian Adept, in Nüremberg. Here was a discovery which, naturally, not for one moment was neglected. Its direct result was a lengthy correspondence with Fräulein Sprengel, culminating in the transmission of authority to Woodman, Westcott and Mathers, to formulate in England a semi-public occult organisation which was to employ an elaborate magical ceremonial, Qabalistic teaching, and a comprehensive scheme of spiritual training. Its foundation was designed to include both men and women on a basis of perfect equality in contradistinction to the policy of the Societas Rosicruciana in Anglia which was comprised wholly of Freemasons. Thus, in 1887, the Hermetic Order of the Golden Dawn was established. Its first English Temple, Isis-Urania, was opened in the following year.

There is a somewhat different version as to its origin, having behind it the authority of Frater F.R. the late Dr. Felkin, who was the Chief of the Stella Matutina as well as a member of the Societas Rosicruciana. According to his account, and the following words are substantially his own, prior to 1880 members of the Rosicrucian Order on the Continent selected with great care their own candidates whom they thought suitable for personal instruction. For these pupils they were each individually responsible, the pupils thus selected being trained by them in the theoretical traditional knowledge now used in the Outer Order. After some three or more years of intensive private study they were presented to the Chiefs of the Order, and if approved and passed by examination, they then received their initiation into the Order of the Roseae Rubeae et Aureae Crucis.

The political state of Europe in those days was such that the strictest secrecy as to the activities of these people was very necessary. England, however, where many Masonic bodies and semi-private organisations were flourishing without interference, was recognised as having far greater freedom and liberty than the countries in which the continental Adepts were domiciled. Some, but by no means all, suggested therefore that in England open Temple work might be inaugurated. And Dr. Felkin here adds, though without the least word of explanation as to what machinery was set in motion towards the attainment of that end, "and so it was... It came about then that Temples arose in London, Bradford, Weston-super-Mare, and Edinburgh. The ceremonies we have were elaborated from cipher manuscripts, and all went well for a time."

As to what ensued after that inauguration of Temple work here we have little record, though an unorthodox account written by Aleister Crowley continues this historical theme in substantially the same words as were orally communicated to me by the late Imperator of one of the now-existent Temples. "After some time S.D.A. died; further requests for help were met with a prompt refusal from the colleagues of S.D.A. It was written by one of them that S.D.A.'s schemes had always been regarded with disapproval but since the absolute rule of the Adepts is never to interfere with the judgment of any other person whomsoever—how much more, then, one of themselves, and that one most highly revered!—they had refrained from active opposition. The Adept who wrote this added that the Order had already quite enough knowledge to enable it or its members to formulate a magical link with the adepts. Shortly after this, one called S.R.M.D. announced that he had formulated such a link, and that himself with two others was to govern the Order... We content ourselves, then, with observing that the death of one of his two colleagues, and the weakness of the other, secured to S.R.M.D., the sole authority..."

In elaboration of this statement, it may be said that in 1891 Dr. Woodman died after but a few days illness, leaving the management of the Order to Westcott and Mathers. Evidently these two scholars carried on quite well together for about six years, for the indications are that the Order flourished and grew expansive. Exactly why Westcott withdrew from the Order—for this is the next major occurrence—appears difficult to discover. Concerning this also several versions are extant. One account has it that accidentally he left some of the Order manuscripts in a portfolio bearing his signature in a cab, and the driver upon finding them turned them over to the authorities. Since Westcott was by profession an East London coroner, the medical authorities strongly objected that one in an official capacity should, no matter how remotely, be connected with anything that savoured occult. It was suggested to him therefore that he must withdraw from the Order or else resign his post as coroner, since the two were considered in those days incompatibles. He chose to resign from the Order. Yet again it is suggested that it was simply a personal quarrel that led to the parting of the ways with Mathers, which does seem the more probable explanation. Whatever the cause, some six years after the death of Dr. Woodman, Westcott withdrew from the Order, which was thus left to the sole authority of Mathers.

The pamphlet on Rosicrucian history then proceeds in narrative that following Westcott's resignation from "this association in 1897, the English Temples soon after fell into abeyance." This reads like an instance of wish-fulfilment. Though fairly near the essential truth of the matter, it is not quite in accordance with fact. Following the resignation of Westcott, Mathers reigned within his Order as supreme autocrat. Judging from the evidence at our disposal he was not a particularly benevolent one, for many were the misunderstandings that ruffled the mystic placidity of his Temples, and several of the individuals who dared so much as to differ or argue with him were promptly expelled, and flung into the outer darkness. Presumably spiritual pride was the flaw in his armour, and he seemed to harbour quite a few delusions. One of the latter was his conveyance to the body of Adepti as a piece of objective everyday experience, that whilst in the Bois de Boulogne one day he was approached by three Adepts who confirmed him in the sole rulership of the Order. On the strength of this supposed occurrence, he issued to the Theorici of the grade of Adeptus Minor a powerfully worded manifesto, naming himself in no uncertain terms as a chosen vessel and demanding from all those who received the manifesto a signed oath of personal loyalty and allegiance. Those who refused to send a written statement of voluntary submission to him were either expelled from the Order or degraded to a lower rank.

Meanwhile, a considerable amount of discontent had been slowly brewing amongst the Order members. Dissatisfaction with the autocratic leadership of S.R.M.D. was growing very steadily and persistently. No definite or clear-cut reasons appear to be given for this, for evidently this restlessness had been gradually fructifying whilst the hypertrophy of Mathers' ego was becoming more and more pronounced. Some say that S.R.M.D. was guilty of innumerable magical tricks of a particularly irresponsible nature which eventually brought disrepute both upon himself and the Order of which he was head. Others, more romantically minded, claimed that his English translation of *The Sacred Magic of Abramelin the Mage* was a powerful magical act which attracted to his sphere forces of evil so terrible in nature that he was wholly unable to withstand them. Frater F.R. propounds the more rational view that it was simply spiritual pride and love of power which so gained the ascendancy that he demanded of the members of his organisation a personal fealty and obedience to his own personality instead of to the work itself. How very familiar all this sounds? In one form or another, it is the story of the same unhappy fate which dogs and finally ruins every religious and spiritual community. By changing these names, Theosophists may recognise a very homely story.[2]

In claiming his right to unquestioned leadership, and when refusing to appoint two others of the body of Adepti to fill the vacant posts of co-Chiefs, Mathers also promised some of the more advanced members of the Second Order additional grades in the path of Adeptship and even more esoteric teaching. These, apparently, were not forthcoming—though it must be confessed that regardless of the personal shortcomings of Mathers as a leader or as a writer, it is patent that there was a vast knowledge and a deep and wide erudition concealed with him. Naturally the Adepti gave utterance to their complete disapproval of this delay in the fulfilment of their Chiefs promises, gradually coming to insist that he had neither the knowledge nor the grades to impart. Further unpleasant bickering drew forth from Mathers the retort that he was certainly not going to waste either his grades or knowledge on such hopeless duffers as they were. And in any event, he was Chief and leader; their further progress, if there was to be any, must be left entirely in his hands. In short, a virulent quarrel was in process of development, and though for quite a long time it fermented beneath the surface, it finally culminated in a group of the Adepti forming a strong combination to expel their chief S.R.M.D. just prior to the actual appearance of the schism, and whilst yet the rebellion was gaining impetus, certain events happened which call here not for elucidation, since that is impossible, but simply for registration.

About this time, a certain Mrs. Rose Horos approached Mathers who came to acknowledge her as an initiate of a high grade. Exactly why, it is again impossible to say definitely. It was stated in defence of Mathers that Mrs. Horos was able to repeat to him a certain conversation he had had years previously when he visited Madame Blavatsky at Denmark Hill, and the repetition of this scrap of conversation convinced him of her status. Anyway, it was a sad piece of deception, and an unhappy acknowledgment on the part of Mathers indicating his complete lack of judgment and insight into character. Mrs. Horos and her husband were very soon discovered to be sex-perverts of the worst description. Nor was this all, for it is alleged that they were also responsible for the theft from Mathers of a complete set of Order documents. It seems incredible that Mathers could have been so gullible, for that is the only word which adequately describes his stupidity, as to accept without further

---

[2] As may knowledgeable, modern-day students of the Golden Dawn.

verification the occult claims of this woman, giving her access to the rituals and teaching of the Golden Dawn. Subsequently the immoral activities of these two people having attracted the attention of the police, they were arrested. In December 1901 at their trial, the Order of the Golden Dawn was given unpleasant and unjustified publicity by being associated with the chequered careers of these two persons. In the witness box the male prisoner made the remark concerning the Golden Dawn Neophyte obligation that it "was prepared by the Chiefs of the Order who are in India"—which of course was a farrago of nonsense, but unfortunately just the type of nonsense which survives for many years. He was sentenced to fifteen years penal servitude, and his wife to seven.

Around this period also, one Florence Farr, whose esoteric motto was Soror S.S.D.D., having for some years been left in charge of Isis-Urania Temple while Mathers continued his research work in Paris, decided for various personal reasons to enter her resignation from that important post. Under date of February 16th 1900, Mathers, writing from Paris, refused to accept her resignation, believing that she intended to "form a combination to make a schism therein with the idea of working secretly or avowedly under Sapere Aude." In this same letter, he was responsible for the astonishing statement that S.A. had never been at any time in touch with Fräulein Sprengel of Nüremberg but had "either himself forged or procured to be forged the professed correspondence between him and her." As was only to be expected this letter came as a overwhelming surprise to S.S.D.D., who was thoroughly stunned by this accusation of dishonesty and forgery levelled against S. A. After contemplating the whole situation in an almost frantic state of mind for several days in the country, she finally communicated with S.A. asking him to corroborate or deny the accusations. Her next act was to form a Committee of Seven within the Second Order to investigate the allegations made. This Committee asked S.R.M.D. to produce for his own sake and for the sake of the Order proof of the accuracy of his statements. Because, they argued, since it was upon the authority of this alleged correspondence that the Order was founded, the historical position of the Order as descended from mediaeval Rosicrucian sources collapsed should it be proven that the correspondence had been forged. This viewpoint was not altogether accurate, for while S.R.M.D. had stated that S.A. had never been in touch with S.D.A., he never denied that he himself had not been in constant communication with her. Then followed a lengthy correspondence which afterwards was collected and printed in the form of a long dossier. In fine, Mathers refused unconditionally to acknowledge the authority or even the existence of the Committee nor would he produce proof of any kind to substantiate his claim that S.A. had forged Second Order communications. It goes without saying of course that S.A. fervently denied the truth of these allegation of forgery, but all the same he refused to do anything about it.

No good purpose could possibly be served by enlarging upon the unhappy events which immediately followed. To a large extent the history of the Order is so confused and muddled at this juncture, and the rumours which have come down to us so chaotic and contradictory, that it has proved wholly impossible to extricate the truth from the foul debris of slander, abuse and recrimination. A clear picture of what occurred seems impossible to recover. It would appear, to state the matter simply, that Mathers expelled the rebels who then formed a schism. On the other hand, it is also held that he was himself expelled by the revolting wing from his own Order and left with about half a dozen adherents, with whose assistance, moral and financial, he continued his Temple.

As their first magical gesture of independence, the rebels changed the name of the Order to The Stella Matutina. Ruled for a year by a committee of twelve, developments forced them to realise that this was far from a satisfactory arrangement. Inasmuch, however, as it had taken several years first to brew and then to develop into an open gesture of defiance, the spirit which had conceived the rebellion was not thus at a single stroke to be banished.

Having elevated the standard of revolt by expelling their former chief, for many a dismal month was the Stella Matutina haunted by that ghost. After almost inconceivable pettiness and dispute, the rebels were at the end persuaded by circumstance to abandon every feature of their reform to return to the original scheme of appointing Three Chiefs to govern and lead them. Even this, later, was abandoned if not officially then in practice, for a virtual autocracy similar to that enjoyed by Mathers was once again instituted, though on a much smaller scale. The revolt had been in vain. Those finally selected and appointed as the Chiefs were Fratres Sub Spe, Finem Respice, and Sacra-mentum Regis. These three Fratres conducted the Order of the Stella Matutina in harmony for about a year. Then, for various reasons, Sacramentum Regis chose to resign. At the meetings held to appoint his successor, differences of the most trivial character continued to arise. Indeed, the spirit of fraternity and wisdom had departed, leaving its averse antithesis, the venom of destruction, to dwell in their midst. Another split developed. Apparently one wing of the schism, thoroughly alarmed in all its bourgeois incompetence and fear by the recent disturbances to the peace of the Order, attributed that cycle of catastrophe to the occult content of the Order teaching, and because of this were now desirous of casting aside as valueless, from the spiritual point of view, the whole of the magical tradition. Their intention was to retain a sort of indeterminate Mysticism of the type which has so often brought disrepute upon the subject, coming to regard their Temple as an adjunct, a clandestine back-door to the Church in some one of its many forms—with especial attractions, I believe, to the Anglo-Catholic groups. One other and more important group within the schism, led by Fratres Finem Respice and Sub Spe carried on full Temple work, more or less adhering to the original plan of the Golden Dawn routine as laid down in the documents drawn up by MacGregor Mathers.

Thus we find in place of a consolidated fraternity at least three separate groupings of individuals engaged in the practice of the Golden Dawn ceremonial system in open Temple, perpetuating as best they might the traditions of the Magic of Light. There was, first, the diminutive group under the leadership of S.R.M.D., still retaining the original Order name. To him were still loyal the Temple or Temples that a few years prior to the final crash had been instituted in the United States of America. Both F.R. and S.S. were in charge of a Stella Matutina Temple, and it is my belief that after a while even they parted company or conducted separate groups, the one in London calling itself the Amoun Temple, and the latter in Edinburgh, Amen-Ra by name. In London also, a separate Temple was being conducted by Frater Sacramentum Regis calling itself the Reconstructed Rosicrucian Order, a group characterised by its exclusive devotion to Christian Mysticism, its rituals being elaborated into verbose and interminable parades of turgidity.

Formerly united by a single fraternal bond, we now see several Temples being conducted by different groupings of individuals who, while pretending to fraternal communion, had but little sympathy with and affection for the sister Temples of the schism. The slander that was invented and swiftly circulated, as only malice can be circulated, is unrepeatable. Few individuals of real worth were exempt from this network of scandal which enmeshed the whole organisation. This man was an adulterer, that a dipsomaniac—and even after the lapse of more than thirty years this slander is still current. So thoroughly had the central unity of the Order broken up that each of these Stella Matutina Temples appointed its own Imperator, Cancellarius and Praemonstrator, considering itself by these gestures an autonomous occult body. Thus began the downfall of organised magical instruction through the semi-esoteric channels of the Hermetic Order of the Golden Dawn. Whatever else should be insisted upon in Magic, unity is the prime essential. A united body of manifestation at all costs should have been maintained. And the old adage "United we stand, divided we fall" is no idle phrase, especially since the elimination of the "heresy of separateness" is one of the cardinal injunctions of the Great Work. The separate Temples decided to fall independently of how or why or where the other groups fell. Each was smug, complacent and fully confident that it alone continued the magical tradition. The result is that to-day those original Temples are either dead or moribund. While they may have given rise to yet other groups, there is not one of the latter which is not in a diseased condition.

One can hardly help recalling the bitter admonition given by S.R.M.D. to the organisers of the schism. He said, in effect, and in later years Frater Sub Spe corroborated that statement, that he was the principal Chief of the Order by whom and through whom the Order had originally been organised to disseminate the magical tradition. Remember, he warned, what happened to the Theosophical Society after Blavatsky had departed, and there began the disintegration of the world-wide society she had founded and fed with her own life blood. Certainly Mathers' prophecy seems to have vindicated itself. Just as there are innumerable sects claiming to be the original Theosophical Society and professing allegiance to the principles taught by Blavatsky, so are there now several decaying Temples claiming unbroken descent from the original Isis-Urania. Each insists fervently that it alone is the genuine Order; all others are schismatic and unimportant. To-day, as stated above, not one of these surviving Temples is in an even moderately healthy condition. Nor have they ever been since the early days of their foundation. An amusing sidelight on human nature is disclosed by the fact that in one of the Obligations retained by the schismatic groups, there is still the original clause, "Do you further undertake not to be a stirrer up of strife, of schism, or of opposition to the Chiefs."

It was towards the close of 1898, just prior to the revolt, that Aleister Crowley was introduced to the Order by Frater Volo Noscere, receiving his Neophyte initiation at Mark Mason's Hall. It was clear, soon after he joined, that here was a highly gifted young man, and that in many ways, though unrestrained and undisciplined, his was a powerfully magical personality. From Captain J.F.C. Fuller's rather verbose and flamboyant account in the *Equinox* we gather that Crowley was advanced through the grades of the Order quickly, and assimilated the routine knowledge without the least difficulty. Those grades which were not formally separated by automatic delays, were taken at the rate of one a month, and the succeeding ones at the prescribed intervals of three, seven, and nine months. By the time he had taken his Portal grade, the revolt was in full swing, the wisdom and authority of the Chief being on every side doubted and challenged. It was around this period, too, that Crowley's morals and alleged pernicious conduct offended those who were conducting Temple work in London, and the ruling Adepti of Isis-Urania refused to advance him further They refused to do this in spite of the deliberate warning contained in Mathers' manifesto previously mentioned: "What I discountenance and will check and punish whenever I find it in the Order is the attempt to criticise and interfere with the private life of members of the Order. ... The private life of a person is a matter between himself or herself and his or her God." Whether Mathers was impressed by the promise of Crowley's personality, or whether he decided upon his next step to show contempt for the ruling Chiefs of Isis-Urania Temple, we do not know. But, soon after, Crowley was invited to Paris where he received tht grade of Adeptus Minor from Mathers in Ahathoor Temple. This act served but to inflame the differences which were now openly separating Mathers from his erstwhile followers, and increased the bitter hatred which the Order members bore and still bear for Crowley.

To Crowley's credit, it must be conceded that when open revolt did flame forth, at least he sided with S.R.M.D., acting as his plenipotentiary in the proposed meetings with the rebels in London. The Adepti, however, unconditionally refused to recognise or have ought to do with Crowley. In his fantastic garb of a Highland chieftain with kilt, dirks and tartan, and his face concealed by a heavy mask, he did assuredly make himself so great a laughing stock on that occasion as to make it difficult for anyone to take him seriously.

The conjunction of two headstrong and egotistical personalities rendered it most probable that sooner or later Crowley and Mathers should quarrel. They did, and each went his separate way. Many and varied again are the fantastic accounts of the reasons for that separation. But no matter what their cause, some three years afterwards events led Crowley to denounce Mathers as one obsessed either by Abramelin demons or by the evil personalities of the then incarcerated Horos couple, and that he himself had been nominated by the Secret Chiefs of the Invisible Order to be the outer head of the visible organisation. In the various numbers of the *Equinox*, the official organ of Crowley's personal reformulation of the Order system under the title of A∴ A∴— which does not signify "Atlantean Adepts" as supposed by some stupid reviewer in the Occult Review—may be found Crowley's more or less garbled version of the Order teaching and ceremonial.

At this juncture, it is needful to contradict denials on the part of certain Order members that Crowley did not obtain full Order teaching. Some of these denials are entirely too vehement and "methinks the lady doth protest too much." First of all, I am fully convinced from a close and prolonged study of all Crowley's literary output that he did obtain his Adeptus Minor grade from Mathers after the London group refused to advance him. Unquestionably this is true. Nevertheless, even if this were not the case, he was the *intime*, so to say, of Fratres Volo Noscere and Yehi Aour, both advanced members of the grade of Adeptus Minor, who coached and trained him so that he benefitted by their knowledge and wide experience. Whatever knowledge these Fratres had received from the Order documents was given to Crowley. There is little, I imagine, that he did not receive of the Order teaching then extant, whatever may have been the means fair or foul by which he obtained that teaching. And while he did not publish it in its entirety, it is possible to perceive from hints scattered here, there, and everywhere, that very little had been kept from him. Any student who has a bird's-eye view of the Order system will recognise traces of every aspect of it in the different volumes of Crowley's literary fecundity.

Had Crowley published the entire body of knowledge, only slightly editing the redundancy and verbose complexity of Mathers' literary style—had he issued that teaching so that it bore some semblance to its original state to indicate what it really was and how practised within the Temple—his expose might not have been too serious. It is possible that he might have been acknowledged as a benefactor of mankind, even if later on he did ruin his own personal reputation by broadcasting absurd legends and leading a foolishly dissipated life. But it was his special mode of publication which argued against the advisability of partially disclosing the secret knowledge of the Order. He tampered unnecessarily with the Grade rituals, so that their beauty as well as practical worth was gone.[3] It became impossible to form any estimation of the efficacy or construction of those ceremonies from their mutilated shadows in the *Equinox*. Perhaps his aim was to eliminate important parts of the rites and practical work so that interested people, realising that more information was required, would communicate with him for further guidance, thus enabling him to consolidate his position as a leader, and formulate an active Order. This is certainly true of the instruction, for example, on Geomancy. The rituals and teaching were badly mauled; rearranged out of all recognition

---

[3] It is statements like these that have led Crowley-deifiers to hate and ignore Regardie. Anyone who gives Crowley a fair read will find that much of what he wrote is pure crap. All too often his followers have elevated the garbage to gospel while ignoring the good stuff. Such is the process of Biblification. In the world of organized religion, truth must be eliminated as a threat to self-aggrandizing dogma. [Ed.]

to their former state, and then surrounded by Yoga instructions, short stories, articles on sex-Magic, poetry—much of it of a dubious nature—and a host of miscellaneous odds and ends.

With Crowley's instructions in the art of Yoga, printed both within and without the *Equinox*, there can be no quarrel. They are amongst the clearest ever produced on the subject and amongst the finest examples of the excellent prose of which Crowley was capable. We, the occult-reading public, are immeasurably the richer for their appearance. Epigrams, short stories, card-games, and libels on former friends, however, can hardly be considered fit companions for occult teaching. It is my confirmed belief that it is practically impossible, without more precise guidance or tuition, to ascertain from the *Equinox* and Crowley's other literary productions exactly what is the actual nature of Magic as a definite practical scheme. His form of presentation, and the other contents of the *Equinox*, created nothing but confusion.

Though a revelation of the inner teaching of the Golden Dawn would have been a boon to mankind, yet manifestly Crowley's manner of presentation ruined the effort. If the breaking of a sacred obligation is at all justifiable—as occasionally it is—it is so only when the matter covered by that oath is revealed in a dignified manner and with a noble spirit, as well as in a style fitting to its intrinsic nature. In such an event, the oath is neither betrayed nor profaned, for in being abrogated on behalf of mankind, the author becomes duly qualified to speak for those with whom alone is the power to bind or loose.

It is not my wish to retract what nearly three years ago I enthusiastically wrote in *The Tree of Life*. It was then my conviction as it is now that there was much of a highly important nature in what this extraordinary man of genius has written and published. But I am also profoundly impressed by this fact. Unless one has first studied Magic from a more comprehensible and reliable source, most of what he has written, albeit based upon his own practical experience, will be in the main unintelligible. Any student who has gained a sympathetic understanding of the Golden Dawn teaching will be capable of discriminating between the futile reprehensible portions of Crowley's work, and of deciding which part of it is a worth-while addition to an already magnificent system. And it is because Crowley concedes to his own credit in his, in many respects, admirable volume entitled *Magick* that he has done Magic inestimable service by reason of his development of it, that I have considered it imperative, together with a number of other reasons of equal urgency, to place the Golden Dawn system before the public. Crowley's claims are, in my estimation, wholly exaggerated. I am far from being convinced that the scheme of theory and practice presented in his literature—extraordinary though it is in many ways, considering that it is a development of the simple basic Golden Dawn material—is equal in any way to the system put into documentary form by S.L. MacGregor Mathers and his colleagues.

THE MAGICAL ALPHABET

VOLUME ONE

THE MAGICAL ALPHABET

TABLE OF CONTENTS

IMPORTANT TABLES AND ILLUSTRATIONS

VOLUME ONE

THE MAGICAL ALPHABET

INTRODUCTION

One of my preoccupations over the last fifty years, ever since I have been actively involved in the study as well as the dissemination of the basic principles of Magic, Qabalah and Occultism in general, is the discrepancy between what the system teaches and the character structure of the average student and even leaders of the occult groups. For awhile it created a good deal of anxiety simply because it appeared to me that there should be some degree of coincidence between student and system.

It was not until many years afterwards that I came to be aware of the function of therapy. At that time I had some dear friends who had amongst their acquaintances some psychotherapists in London where I then resided. Some of them I met socially when we discussed this particular problem that was haunting me. A few agreed with me that there was only one remedy for this discrepancy and that was to enter therapy as a patient. I did this, remaining in therapy for several years and I must say it benefited me enormously. Even today, three or four decades later I still get an occasional letter from a student here, there and anywhere making the statement that I seem to be one of the few sane writers on the subject. True or not, they perceive that there is a difference in one who has had therapy and another who has not.

Today therefore I am adamant both to correspondents and visitors alike that to obtain the greatest benefit from Magic which is as it were a post-graduate study there should be some undergraduate work in a personal therapy. The dividends are enormous.

For a long while it seemed to me that Jungian therapy provided the answer to this problem. However from time to time I would meet or hear from a correspondent who complained that that form of therapy was like Ain Soph, without end. So I have concluded that Jungian analysis can be likened to herpes genitalis, that is it is forever. This has resulted finally in entertaining serious doubts about the efficacy of Jung's system as a therapy; as a philosophy I have little quibble, even if many authorities in the occult field feel that this is the only form of spiritual therapy. Of course this is nonsense. In therapy one is not concerned whether its contents are spiritual or otherwise, but whether it enables one to face and deal with one's own latent infantility which is eternally getting in the way. Whether magical or occult authorities like it or not Freudian analysis is infinitely more effective.

Out of the Freudian school there has evolved an entirely new and different approach to this problem which curiously enough, though it makes no claim in this direction, is far more spiritual in its effects and its results than anything else I know. Wilhelm Reich, originally

1

an ardent disciple of Freud, developed a system of therapy which astonishingly enough is a bridge from orthodox psychotherapy to the occult world. He himself would never have admitted this. And in fact he would rather have died than recognize this, but facts are facts which can not be denied. My experience as a psychotherapist extending over some thirty years or more, has surprised me in the discovery that many patients who prior to therapy had no talent for Magic etc., found themselves profoundly involved in what might be called mystical or religious experiences on the couch at the end of a session. Therefore after all these many years I still insist that the student of this subject involve himself deeply in therapy but nowadays I make the proviso that it be a form of Reichian or neo-Reichian therapy. A great deal of time, money and heartache will be spared the student if, when he decides to follow my counsel, he attempts to seek out a therapist or teacher who is trained in these techniques. Admittedly there are problems in this direction but these are not insurmountable. Any student anywhere in this country desirous of following my counsel but is unable to find an adequate therapist is invited to do one of two things. First to write to me directly in care of my publishers Falcon Press in Phoenix. I promise to reply at once, giving counsel on whom they should consult. Second, write to my friend and colleague Chistopher Hyatt, also care of Falcon Press for further advice. He is not only a first rate therapist himself with extensive training in both experimental and psychoanalytic therapy but is at the same time a very perceptive and intuitive therapist and teacher of many years experience. In addition Hyatt has a strong background in occult subjects, particularly with meditative and Eastern techniques. This with his Western knowledge makes him an ideal choice for those students seriously involved with the occult. At the very least if he is not personally available he too can make recommendations to other practitioners in the field.

In other places I have dogmatically stated that the Golden Dawn as a functioning occult Order has been defunct for years. It gives me pleasure to state that in the past several years a new group of young students have attempted to formulate actively functioning Temples employing the traditional techniques. There are now a few Temples scattered throughout the country to which I would be glad to refer the interested student.

The Hermetic Order of the Golden Dawn issued its own account of its history. It claimed to be "an Hermetic Society whose members are taught the principles of occult science and the Magic of Hermes. During the early part of the last century, several prominent Adepti and Chiefs of the Order in France and England died, and their death caused a temporary dormant condition of Temple work." It goes on to state that these adepts "received indeed and have handed down to us their doctrine and system of Theosophy and Hermetic Science and the higher Alchemy from a long series of practical investigators whose origin is traced to the Fratres Roseae Crucis of Germany, which association was founded by one Christian Rosenkreutz about the year 1398 A.D. . .

"The Rosicrucian revival of Mysticism was but a new development of the vastly older wisdom of the Qabalistic Rabbis and of that very ancient secret knowledge, the Magic of the Egyptians, in which the Hebrew Pentateuch tells you that Moses, the founder of the Jewish system, was 'learned', that is, in which he had been initiated."

This is the Golden Dawn historical claim. Many have questioned its veracity. That really does not concern us at this moment. Perhaps by far the best and most objective account of its history, short and concise, was written by Aleister Crowley in *Liber LXIvel Causae*. The first few paragraphs are so well stated as to warrant quotation here:

"Some years ago a number of cipher MSS. were discovered and deciphered by certain students. They attracted much attention, as they purported to derive from the Rosicrucians. You will readily understand that the genuineness of the claim matters no whit, such literature being judged by itself, not by its reputed sources.

"Among the MSS. was one which gave the address of a certain person in Germany, who is known to us as S.D.A. Those who discovered the ciphers wrote to S.D.A., and in accordance with instructions received, an Order was founded which worked in a semisecret manner.

"After some time S.D.A. died; further requests for help were met with a prompt refusal from the colleagues of S.D.A. It was written by one of them that S.D.A.'s scheme had always been regarded with disapproval. But since the absolute rule of the adepts is never to interfere with the judgments of any other person whomsoever—how much more, then, one of themselves, and that one most highly revered!—they had refrained from active opposition. The adept who wrote this added that the Order had already quite enough knowledge to enable it or its members to formulate a magical link with the adepts.

"Shortly after this, one called S.R.M.D. announced that he had formulated such a link, and that himself with two others was to govern the Order."

There is another source of historical material in a small pamphlet written by Dr. W. W. Westcott, in which it is stated that "In 1887 by the permission of S.D.A., a continental Rosicrucian Adept, the Isis-Urania Temple of Hermetic students of the Golden Dawn was formed to give instructions in the mediaeval occult sciences. Fratres M.E.V. with S. A. and S.R.M.D. became the Chiefs, and the latter wrote the rituals in modern English from old Rosicrucian manuscripts (the property of S.A.) supplemented by his own literary researches."

These several statements then give the beginning of the Hermetic Order of the Golden Dawn. Since its inception in the last quarter of the nineteenth century it has exerted far greater influence on the growth and dissemination of practical occult information and knowledge than can be realized by most present day students. At first its membership was recruited from a broad spectrum of English intellectuals and artists and even the clergy, but later came to include quite ordinary men and women from every segment of society and life.

In accord with the spirit of the times, it cloaked itself in a glamour of mystery and secrecy. Regardless of the various rumors that circulated about it, it came to be very difficult to join this Order. Even A. E. Waite, who some regard as an occult authority, sarcastically remarked in his autobiography that his first application was black-balled. It was after a period of time that he reapplied at the urging of some of his friends and only then was he accepted.

Its teachings and methods of instruction were surrounded by oaths and various penalties attached to the most awe inspiring ritual-obligations to ensure secrecy. You will see what these are in various rituals that are given in the body of the text. It is now common knowledge that Arthur Machen, Florence Farr, W. B. Yeats, Algernon Blackwood, Aleister Crowley, Dion Fortune, and A. E. Waite—to mention only a few—were members of this prestigious organisation. It should be self-evident then that some of its members were not the usual flakey nit-wits some critics are disposed to believe, but prominent and intelligent people.

Perhaps some attention should be given to the secular names of some of those whose Order mottoes have been given above. Sapere Aude and Non Omnis Moriar were the mottoes chosen by Dr. William W. Westcott, a London physician and a coroner by occupation. M.E.V., or Magnum est Veritas was the motto of Dr. William R. Woodman, an eminent Freemason of the last century, who died in 1891 very shortly after the Order was founded and therefore did not play much of active role in its governance. S.R.M.D. or S. Rhiogail Ma Dhream, the motto of Samuel Liddell Mathers also known as McGregor Mathers, was the most active of the chiefs of the Order. He also used the motto Deo Duce Comite Ferro. He has been described at some length in a biographical study *The Sword of Wisdom* by Ithel Colquhoun, well worth reading in this connection.

Westcott was the author of a couple of minor little books and the editor of an hermetic and alchemical series of writings, well prized today. He was prominent in certain Masonic circles of his day.

Mathers was the translator of three mediaeval magical texts. *The Greater Key of King Solomon, The Book of the Sacred Magic of Abramelin the Mage,* and *The Kaballah Unveiled* (which consisted of certain portions from Knorr von Rosenroth's Latin rendition of parts of the Zohar—more distinguished however by a relatively long introduction of considerable erudition and which well warrants re-publication by itself as an introduction to the study of the Qabalah.)

In this connection I would like to recommend *The Rosy Cross Unveiled* by Christopher McIntosh, which purports to give a history, mythology and the rituals of an occult order (published by Aquarian Press Ltd. 1980).

In as much as both Mathers and Westcott had dual mottoes, it should be remarked that one was for use in the Outer Order of the Golden Dawn, the other being reserved of the Inner Order of the R.R. et A.C.

S.D.A. was the abbreviation of the motto Sapiens Dominabitur Astris chosen by a Fraulein Anna Sprengel of Nuremberg. Though polemics are outside the scope of this introduction, in all fairness to the enquiring student I should mention a highly critical and destructive study of the Order entitled *The Magicians of the Golden Dawn* by Ellic Howe. It is mentioned here because amidst all of its prejudicial criticism which is not difficult to demolish, there is some significant historical data of considerable value.

There is also, I should mention, my own account of the Golden Dawn history at some length—*What You Should Know About the Golden Dawn* (Falcon Press, Phoenix, Arizona, 1983). In addition to tracing some of the obscurities relating to the origins of the Order, it provides a bird's eye view of its teachings that might be of value to the current reader. The Order provided initiation into the Mysteries in a highly organized and systematic manner.

INITIATION

Initiation is the preparation for immortality. Man is only potentially immortal. Immortality is acquired when the purely human part of him becomes allied to that spiritual essence which was never created, was never born, and shall never die. It is to effect this spiritual bond with the highest, that the Golden Dawn owes all its rituals and practical magical work.

Initiation means to begin, to start something new. It represents the beginning of a new life dedicated to an entirely different set of principles from those of what Wilhelm Reich once contemptuously termed "homo normalis." With the enormous development of scientific pragmatism, it is conceivable that sometime in the near or distant future, robots or computers will be invented that will, to all intents and purposes, free man from the daily drudgery of common toil. If and when that occurs, what will the average man do with his leisure time? Despite the claims of various protagonists of the free future of man, I doubt that many will turn their time and energy to the pursuit of the Great Work in any of its forms. Most of them will continue to hunt, fish, travel in recreation vehicles, drink beer and grow fat, watch television more and more, concentrate on spectator sports, and continue their lives on a thoroughly prosaic and mundane level. If there are excursions into outer space, with a view of setting up colonies outside of the earth, I am far from certain that the same fate will not await them as it did all ventures into utopian communities. There are only a mere handful who can tolerate more than a glancing casual look at other than the superficial aspects of what life presents to them.

For this handful, the Golden Dawn system presents itself as the answer to their innumerable questions. The system itself is timeless. It did not owe it origins to the formation of that particular Order called the Golden Dawn in the latter part of 19th century. The greater part of it, in one form or another, has existed for centuries—actually forever—not necessarily in the open where it could be attacked by secular and ecclesiastical authorities, but under cover, secretly and safely. Those who were in need of its teaching and work would inevitably be attracted to some one or other of its members, and undergo initiation. This process occurred in the past even as it does today. When the time comes for the inner awakening, as it may be called, all sorts of synchronicities, as Jung might call them, occur which lead them inevitably in the right direction, to the Western Esoteric Tradition.

THE WESTERN ESOTERIC TRADITION

There are a many legends circulating within the occult field that may clarify what is commonly called the Western esoteric tradition as being opposed to the so-called Eastern tradition.

It is held that several centuries ago a group of wise men gathered in the Near East to discuss ways and means of disseminating the ageless wisdom so that no opposition from vested interests would be encountered, and at the same time evoke recognition from those who had evolved to a state of psycho-spiritual "readiness". After much discussion, it was agreed that they should devise a set of pictures that could be circulated as playing cards. Pictures that would tell a story relative to man, and who he was, as well as where he came from. Pictures that would relate him as a person to the greater world in which he found himself. In a word, the Tarot cards came into being to serve such ends. Originally employed as playing cards or for fortune telling, they were carried all over the Near East and Europe by gypsies and other travelling bodies, and eventually permeated all civilized countries in the Western hemisphere.

The other legend is to be found in a document circulated early in the 17th century, the *Fama Fraternatitas*. It purports to narrate the history of one Christian Rosenkreutz, a young man who was educated in one of the monasteries in Germany. He wandered to North Africa and the Near East where he was well received by the wise men resident there. They taught him Alchemy, Astrology and Qabalah, together with other occult subjects. When he left he had acquired a liberal education in the occult arts which he took with him to Germany, to the monastery from which he originally came. Gradually he conveyed his knowledge to a monk here and there, until there were enough more or less enlightened monks to comprise an organizational body that came to be known as the Rosicrucians.

A great deal of the above is legend. Many modern authorities insist that that is all it is—a legend. This runs counter to some of the more common pseudo-Rosicrucian orders of today that claim an impossible antecedence for their own group. Be that as it may, the legend itself gives evidence to the belief that there was a definite body of occult knowledge in existence which could be and was communicated in an orderly manner.

A third factor that should never be overlooked, but which often is, relates to the nature of the monasteries in Roman Catholic Europe. These were the primary centers of learning in an otherwise ignorant world—the Europe of those dark days. They kept alive the learning of every kind then known, and passed it on faithfully to succeeding generations. We know that many of the faithful studied and practiced both alchemy and astrology. It is also known that the Qabalah of the Hebrews was also studied, even though the motive exoterically seemed to be that it was a valuable tool with which to convert the unhappy Jews to the joys and blessings of Christendom.

The Catholic Church, and also the Church of the Byzantium, has a glorious history of great mystics, of men and women to whom the highest vocation called, the quest for God. There were teachers of mystical meditation and interior prayer in many of the monasteries so that the proper preparation for such a high calling would not be lost. They were of many persuasions, these teachers, and so were the mystics who came out of these institutions. They have left their mark on the Church, despite its apparent antagonism to mysticism as such, due to fear it might challenge the Church's demand for conformity to fixed inherited dogma.

There is another most interesting set of circumstances too often glossed over or not well understood. It relates to one of the most crucial and interesting periods of European history. At one time, it must be recalled that the Arabs had invaded Europe and had virtually conquered a part, if not all of Spain. They brought with them not merely a victorious army, but Islamic culture as well. That included not solely mathematics, though it is well to reflect on what this one item did to European knowledge, but in addition the Greek classics and literature, from Aristotle on. Their contribution included alchemy as well, astrology and the other occult arts. Above all it brought Islamic mysticism, Sufiism. It flourished not merely in North Africa but in Spain as well. From there it was carried by one means or another to all parts of Europe and to every center of learning.

Simultaneously, Christian mysticism was flourishing in Spain and Europe, and some great and wonderful people were active spreading mystical knowledge far and wide. It was a period of rejuvenation and spiritual growth for Spain and for the Church as a whole.

Furthermore, what must not be forgotten was that a favorable climate was also being evolved for the wandering and exiled Jewish people to flourish in. They contributed enormously to Spanish culture and scientific knowledge, and at the same time a specific Hebraic mysticism was taking shape and form. This included some of the pre-Zoharic literature, as well as some of the greatest names in Qabalistic history.

It is well to remember that in Spain at that time, therefore, there was a favorable climate for the emergence and blossoming of Islamic, Christian, and Jewish mysticism which has never since been surpassed, if not equalled. Each religious mysticism cross fertilized the other in a magnificent manner.

All of these trends, and they were powerful each in its own specific way, contributed to a body of esoteric knowledge and experience that was peculiarly Western. It may have had numberless resemblances to the traditions extant in the East, but they also had their own individual differences that characterized it as a system wholly apart from its Eastern counterpart. It is this that today we call the Western esoteric tradition. It has reared its head in different times and places and in different ways. On many occasions it may seem to have been wiped out and disappeared from the face of the earth. But always it seemed to reappear revivified by its absence, spreading wider and wider, influencing more and more people, leavening always the institutions most hostile to its continued existence.

From time to time, organizations were formed here and there as means of perpetuating the hidden Hermetic knowledge. The Order of the Golden Dawn was another of these Orders which sprang up, using the wisdom of prior ages, exclusively western knowledge, in order to initiate mankind into a higher level of psycho-spiritual functioning.

Parallel to all of this, there is a concurrent "legend" or statement of fact that there is a hidden Order, whether on the inner spiritual planes or here on the mundane level where most of us live, of Adepts and enlightened beings who watch over mankind and its travails. They seek to further the evolution of mankind without interfering with the *apparent* free choice of human beings to determine their own destiny either towards personal destruction or the attainment of communion with God. From time to time, it is said, these beings permit or direct the appearance of an external organization such as we have previously described. It is also believed that periodically, either towards the end of a century or in some historical crisis, one of them makes a public appearance in one guise or another in order not merely to ward off wholesale disaster but to guide some few or many in a new creative direction.

They also are the embodiments of the Western Esoteric Traditions, and rather than an external organization, are the custodians of its teachings.

VOLUME ONE

SELF INITIATION

By

V.H. FRATER A.M.A.G.

The Neophyte Ritual and that of the Adeptus Minor Grade are the most important and effective rituals of the Order. Those in between are the so-called elemental rituals. Crowley took a rather dim view of these. Francis King assumed wrongly that I also held much the same attitude. In fact, however, I think that they have a very definite place in the entire process of initiation. That they are verbose and overlong I will admit to. Nonetheless there are ways and means of overcoming this problem. In my recently published book *Ceremonial Magic* (Aquarian Press, England) a ritual opening that I called Opening by Watchtower (first demonstrated in the consecration ceremony of the Vault of the Adepts) could be elaborated meaningfully in a variety of different ways which could be construed as effective as abbreviated elemental initiations.

To be concise, an elemental initiation is one in which the elementals are invoked in such a way that they affect the sphere of sensation or the energy field of the candidate. A series of impressions or symbols are impressed on this energy field in such a way that they act, for the candidate, as a kind of passport providing safe entry and freedom of movement in that elemental sphere of operation.

Assuming that this is the case, then the four elemental grade initiations of the Outer Order, in reality do little more than the abbreviated Opening by Watchtower ceremonies. A number of advantages flow from this assumption. The first is that the ritual is nowhere as turgid, lengthy and tiresome as is the grade ritual, all criticisms which led Crowley and others to the faulty conclusion that they could be dispensed with as useless. The second, and I think the most important one, is that the Watchtower rituals described in the book named above could be employed as self-initiatory rituals.

Again, assuming that this is factual, then we have reached a stage which fulfills the original promise of some of my early writing on the Golden Dawn-which was that since the Hermetic Order of the Golden Dawn was now defunct, the isolated student here, there and everywhere, could now be his own initiator. This does not preclude the possibility that new temples might arise and have arisen in various parts of the world independently of any other temple. Several new temples have in recent years been formulated and are functioning very sucessfully, with new temples emerging even now.

In stating that the isolated student could now be his own initiator, one important phrase is rendered imperative. And that is he must be persistent and as thoroughgoing and exacting as if he were an initiator in a regularly constituted Golden Dawn temple under the constant scrutiny of officialdom and higher adept authorities. The responsibility for progress is thus placed inexorably on the student or candidate himself. As I see it - and I have watched this on a very few students - each elemental initiation or Watchtower ceremony requires its repetition several times. One student whom I am thinking of at this juncture has performed the whole Opening by Watchtower ceremonies some 50 or 60 times. It is therefore my opinion that she has initiated herself as effectively and as positively as any temple initiatory hierophantic team could possibly do. All the important "command" symbols of elemental significance are altogether imbedded in her aura or energy field so that should she visit their sphere of activity, via skrying in the spirit vision, they would not regard her as an enemy alien invading their hallowed circle. Instead, she would be regarded as friendly and as a divine helper because she carries, as it were, the only correct and valid passport recognized by them as an official password.

THE COMPLETE GOLDEN DAWN SYSTEM OF MAGIC

The only and still major problem remaining as of this moment is how to convert the Neophyte and Adeptus Minor rituals into self-initiatory operations. I am willing to write off the Adeptus Minor ritual as impossible to convert to a self-initiatory ceremony. It still requires an authentic initiator to accomplish the purpose of this ritual. I see no possibility of converting this, as things stand at this moment.

However, I still feel that the Neophyte ritual does contain the possibilities of conversion. It has been done in other ways. For example Crowley, while in Mexico, did one series of meditations, almost tantric in nature, that utilized the clairvoyant visions of G.H. Frater S.R.M.D. The latter did describe in Z-1 and Z-3 what happened to the candidate during the Neophyte initiation in full temple ceremonies. This I described in my biography of Aleister Crowley, *The Eye in the Triangle*, Falcon Press, 1982. (Although some students dislike Crowley the study of his life and the effect of the Golden Dawn on him is essential to our understanding of extending the work of the Order.) Years later, when he came to full term as an initiator himself, he wrote a book of instruction entitled *Liber HHH* (included in Gems from the Equinox, Falcon Press, 1982). In one section of that Liber he refined his early meditation and created a magnificent instruction. This also I have quoted in *The Eye in the Triangle*. However, I am not looking in that direction at this particular moment. What I wish to do is so to simplify the Neophyte ritual as practiced in the Order, by deleting a number of segments which are not necessarily integral to the process of initiation. And leaving a ceremonial skeleton which can be adapted by any student to the service of his own initiation. For example, the entire section in which the various officers give speeches describing what some of the symbols amount to and furthermore name the various subjects that must be studied by the candidate before he can be advanced further in the Order. This would eliminate a good deal of unnecessary baggage and shorten the ritual the student would have to learn. It is quite likely too that most of the opening of the temple in the Neophyte grade could also be left out without harm to the entire initiatory process - with the exception of that passage of the Hierophant which stated that by names and symbols are all powers awakened and re-awakened. Whether the circumambulations should be omitted I have yet to decide, on the basis of some experimentation myself. Much the same applies to the purification by water and the consecration by fire - processes which are repeated several times.

This then leaves as the most important part of the ritual the obligation at the Altar, the charge of the Hierophant to quit the night and seek the day, the reception into the Order and the Hegemon's guiding the newly initiated Neophyte between the two pillars between the altar and the station of the East.

It was only when discussing this matter with V. H. Soror Sic Itur Ad Astra in Los Angeles recently that some light was shed on this problem. The core of the solution revolved around the notion that initiation outside of a regularly constituted Temple was only possible with two students. They would have to prove to themselves - not to anyone else - that they were wholly devoted to the Great Work, devoted enought to spend at least several months jointly or individually practising the Middle Pillar technique as described in *The Foundations of Practical Magic,* Aquarian Press, 1979. If this practice were assiduous and intense both students would have awakened in themselves the psycho-spiritual energy that could not only hasten their own inner development but that the latter could be communicated to yet another in a manner not too dissimilar to that described in Z-3.

The fundamental requirement was that the initiator should be an initiator - not a layman out of the brute herd. Something must have happened to him to have redeemed him of the stigma of being "ordinary." Of course it would have been better if he (or she) had been the recipient of a spontaneous mystical experience of the type described in James' *Varieties of*

Religious Experience. Since this kind of attainment cannot be made to order, as it were, the only alternative is to fall back on time honored methods of development and growth.

I am well aware of the debate which has gone on for years as to whether mystical or occult practices can induce the mystical experience - conversion or samadhi or satori, call it what you will. If not, then it is maintained that these practices prepare the student for that possibility if not inducing it actually. And if he have patience to "wait upon the Lord," as it were, then the one is as good as the other, from my point of view.

While pursuing their work with the Middle Pillar technique and any other set of exercises to which they may be drawn, they could set themselves to the task of studying the Neophyte Ritual and the Z documents that pertain to it. There is additional suggestive material on this topic in *The Eye In the Triangle.* Using the clairvoyant description given by Mathers of what really happened between the Two Pillars to the candidate, Crowley developed a meditation incorporating all those ideas, as I have intimated above. Apparently this meditation must have proven successful, for many years later after he had come to term he wrote a document for his own Order, the A. A., known as Liber H H H. The first section of this document elaborates this meditation and transforms the clairvoyant description of Mathers into an extraordinary piece of magical work that has fascinated me for many years for as long as I have known of the Equinoxes that he published as long ago as 1909-1914.

All of this could give them ideas and hints as to how to proceed in the task of initiating themselves or others. First one and then another could be helped to come to the Light in much the same way as if they were operating in a duly constituted Temple. In fact, to go one further, there is no reason why the officers of a regular Temple should not follow some such procedure as this themselves. It would certainly do no harm, and in fact would accomplish a great deal. Since a Golden Dawn Temple is being instituted here and there throughout not only this country, but the world as a whole, this counsel might be very useful to all concerned to enhance the whole process of initiation.

Once this were accomplished, they could either go their own separate ways or maintain the relationship for mutual aid and comfort. But from there, with the aid of the Opening by Watchtower, as it has come to be called, the elemental initiations would be taken care of, and from there they face the task of the Adeptus Minor initation. What needs to be done in that regard is something I would rather not speculate about. But as one initiate has said, all that remains is to prepare the Temple and then hope and pray that it may become indwelled.

This entire discussion however is intended to be suggestive only. A great deal must be left to the ingenium of the student involved in this great adventure. Their intuition must be sharpened by their adherance to the work itself, and their progress and their plans must be left to unfold by itself. Enough has been said at least to show that the way is not without light, and however bleak the path seemed without teachers and a temple of the Order, they are not left to stumble unaided in the darkness of the outer world. For as the Ritual says "My soul wanders in darkness and I seek the Light of the hidden Knowledge".

In conclusion it is strongly suggested that student closely study two or three of the discussions in this present volume. One of them is the Cautionary Note which directly follows this. Another is a document dealing with the Inflation of the Ego, a result which is to be avoided at all costs by self observation and study. And finally the important article written by Hyatt and myself concerning some major errors and confusions which students have made in the past. Other documents scattered throughout the different segments of this book will also be found supremely helpful in achieving the ends desired.

THE COMPLETE GOLDEN DAWN SYSTEM OF MAGIC

A CAUTIONARY NOTE

During the period of time when most of this work was in the manuscript phase, and various typists were working on it, their occasional comments concerning the Golden Dawn System perturbed me somewhat. It was Christopher Hyatt one of the editors of Falcon Press who first alerted me to the possibility that this misunderstanding might occur, suggesting therefore that I interpolate a cautionary word to prevent other readers developing the same misconception.

He was absolutely right, for some of them, as well as one or two subsequent readers, seem to have developed the conception that the whole Golden Dawn System was based on the initiatory rituals, and nothing more. It puzzled me because I had labored under the delusion that the rituals themselves indicated without equivocation that there was far more to the system than the rituals themselves, and also because the remainder of the volume itself elaborated a whole system of magical practice which could exist altogether independently of the initiatory rituals.

I was so certain of this that to a couple of them I had confided that though for the time being my interest in writing was exhausted, nonetheless some time in the future I felt compelled to write yet another book establishing a relationship between Tibetan magical practices, as for example laid out in Evans Wentz's book *Milarepa the Tibetan Yogi* and the Golden Dawn System. There are innumerable parallels which are worth investigating and enumerating. And these are altogether apart from the matter of initiatory rituals. I feel strongly therefore that I must not proceed too far with this book without stressing the fact that there is infinitely more to the Golden Dawn System of Magic than the initiatory and other types of rituals. Not that I want to minimize the importance of their role in the entire system but it comprises so much more that it puzzled me how anyone could avoid the realization that the performance of the rituals satisfactorily depends on so much more. If the student has thoroughly studied the Z-1 and Z-3 documents, it should have dawned upon him that efficacy of any ritual depends entirely on all the participants having acquired considerable skills in the magical work prescribed by the Order.

Apart from the rudimentary art of invocation by means of the Pentagram and Hexagram, there is a vast repertory of techniques which must be used and mastered, not merely to gain advancement to a higher grade in the Order, which is not too terribly important by and of itself, but in order to become a proficient student of Magic these must be not merely known but wholly mastered. For example, assumption of God forms and the ability to build up Telesmatic Images, more or less along the same line, these two are the very foundations of practical theurgy. Then there is the Middle Pillar technique whose importance simply cannot be overemphasized in any way. The student who has neglected to achieve considerable proficiency in this particular practice will find himself frustrated at every turn. And finally there is the vibratory formula of the Middle Pillar. I cannot conceive of a ritual of any kind being successfully consummated without being adept in the use of the vibratory formula. I have elaborated this in a rather new way, I fancy, in that section dealing with this matter, and I urge the prospective student of magic to pay particular attention not only to this, but to all the techniques I have just mentioned.

Nor is the main thesis of the Order the memorization of dry Qabalistic knowledge from the Knowledge Lectures or from any other text for that matter. This material represents the dry bones of Order knowledge, the basic alphabet of what has come to be known as the Magical Language. Every science and every Art has its own language without which there can be little communication. A great deal of undergraduate university work consists mainly of learning different kinds of *languages* that belong to the various sciences one is learning about. For example, physics has its own terminology without which little headway can be made in mastering its complex mysteries. The same is true of geology which must forever remain a mystery to those who will not master its language. Even in the behavioral sciences a whole new jargon or language must be assimilated. Eventually many students learn to use the jargon so satisfactorily and skillfully that they become unintelligible in their everyday conversations leading their critics to condemn the jargon in which they have steeped themselves. Nonetheless, it is a language of its own. It must be learned, mastered and used in order to become an effective means of communication. Much the same is true of the magical language. It is a highly complex one, and most of this work lays down the elemental principles of this language. The student will do well to take his time mastering it - that is if he has never been exposed to it before. But when he does become familiar with this language, he will never fall into the booby trap that *The Complete Golden Dawn System of Magic* comprises this item or that item only. It is a vast and comprehensive system that is worthy of considerable effort to make it an integral part of one's thinking and feeling.

Finally of course there is the method of the tattwa vision, also called skrying in the spirit vision. This is most important. However I feel entirely too much attention in the past has been paid to this method at the expense of some of those just listed. There must have been many members of the early Order who had a great talent for skrying, since it led to the possible development of clairvoyance, etc. For this reason, its use was overdone. Not only was this so, but some of the protective methods were neglected, and some of the people became gullible and credulous, and lost their natural scepticism which is one of the indispensable factors absolutely essential to the welfare of the student of magic. Without it he is lost in a wilderness of deception and fantasy. Nothing solid can be based upon this whatsoever. Of course there are also the divinatory methods of the Order. Geomancy and the Tarot. But the student must not stop there. These methods appear to be devoted to divining the future, etc., but it would be a great mistake if your interpretation were limited solely to this. Apart from the fact that the use of these methods develop intuition and the inner psychospiritual senses, there is a whole inner world to be explored and discovered by using the geomantic symbols and the Tarot cards themselves as gateways to another dimension of existence, to another aspect of ourselves of which we ordinarily have little consciousness. And since the work of the Order is based upon self discovery as suggested by the injunction in the Neophyte Ritual "Quit the night and seek the Day," and by the very name of the Order itself - The Golden Dawn, a symbolic representation of the spiritual experience which is the goal of all our work, it is the attainment of the awareness of divinity, and then bringing this diinity to operate in our daily lives in this world of Malkuth which is the outer garment of God. I still like the old Qabalistic aphorism that Kether is in Malkuth and Malkuth is in Kether but after another manner. This is not unrelated to the Mahayana aphorism that Nirvana is Samsara and Samsara is Nirvana.

Nor must I forget to call attention to something that is all too often neglected. Meditation on the significance and meaning of the magical instruments. They are often made and consecrated by members of the Order and used as always recommended, but rarely do they come to terms with what underlies their common usage. It should be obvious to any long term student that the Lotus Wand for example is a symbol, amongst others, of the spinal column with the Lotus at the top of the head - a channel for the movement of the spinal spirit fire, the Kundalini. (In this connection do make an effort to obtain and read a book by a Hindu named Gopi Krishna entitled *Kundalini*). All the other instruments similarly have profound meanings. In this connection, as an aid to meditation, I can strongly recommend Aleister Crowley's magnificent early book *Part Two of Book Four* dealing with the theory of Magick and its tools. There are some beautiful meditative descriptions of the elemental weapons which the good student cannot afford to overlook or do without. Such insights will grow as he grows, insight and intuition piling on one another until, of course, the ultimate goal of all the work is realized—enlightenment.

As one becomes proficient in the work of the Order and one's insight and understanding develops, it will become apparent that all of these methods may be tied together and unified to become a magical engine by means of which the Mountain of Initiation may be scaled and the Kingdom of Heaven reached, so that man aspires to God and God aspires to man.

The Order is a magical one. But its mysticism is by no means to be separated from its magic. At first they may seem to be entirely different methods of attaining to the highest. And indeed so they appear to be. But it is the mark of real adeptship when the student comes to realize that there is no real separation between these methods, and that at the end they are one and the same.

In other words, to come back to the initial theme stated at the outset of this chapter, there is much more to the Order than the initiatory and other types of rituals. There is so much in the Neophyte and Adeptus Minor rituals that are of value to the aspirant, that even if one were to assume that the Order work is essentially that of ritualism, one would really not be far wrong. They contain so much. For example in the Neophyte Ritual, one of the first exhortations one hears is that coming from the Hierophant who states by names and images are all powers awakened and reawakened.The newly initiated Frater or Soror into the Order could spend considerable effort and time meditating on just what this means. When he does this, he will be led into the deepest mysteries of the teachings of the Order, and into some kind of understanding of what all the variety of Order techniques amount to. I can come to rest here about warning the student to dispense with any superficial evaluation of the Order method arrived at by a rapid reading of the several rituals, or of the book itself. The whole system needs to be studied carefully. Don't be misled by the apparent simplicity of the system. It is enormously complex and complicated - and at the same time so beautifully simple. *It may take the student some time*, perhaps years, to appreciate the simplicity of the Order system, but the expenditure of that time will be found to be worth the effort. Though meditation is not exactly harped on throughout the text, it is mentioned here and there. And my hope is that the good student will do a great deal of meditation upon what he learns and does with the Order work. There is much to be gained. So much is not stated in specific words, but it is in this "non-statement" or understatement that much of the essence of the system is contained.

Just recently (Easter, 1983) another comment was made, one which I have heard before from one of the Order "failures," that there is a dearth of the devotional element in the Order work. Ordinarily, this comment might be expected from a former Church goer steeped in the Bible - or, which amounts to the same thing, a member of the Fellowship of the Rosy Cross, the name of the Waite version of the Golden Dawn.

Ordinarily, this criticism is not worthy of note, save that in the last instance when I heard it, a younger student had just returned from one of the Ashrams in India where he had heard a great deal about bhakta yoga. I can understand this criticism because bhakta is certainly not stressed in the overt sense within the Order work. But I have to remind students that if they study the Order work very closely - as closely as they have been taught to study the yoga system, they will discover a great deal of emotional content. For instance, on the few occasions when I have witnessed a Neophyte initiation, I have felt very close to an emotional exaltation, almost enough to bring on tears or at the very least a sense of choking, adequate to halt speech. Moreover, the Hierophant of one of the existent Temples, V.H. Soror S.I.A.A., who has officiated at the initiation of some forty Neophytes, also tells me that the ceremony often brings her to the verge of tears.

Apart from that, however, I strongly urge the student who may entertain similar feelings, to read once more a former work of mine *What You Should Know About the Golden Dawn*, (Falcon Press, Phoenix, AZ. 1983). In that book, many quotations from the different rituals are given, quotations which are not only choice English and fine writing, but are good examples of the devotional aspect of the Order's work. These are really worth reviewing quite often so as to renew the sense that the Order is not without its bhakta aspects.

If that is not enough, then I must refer to the work of Aleister Crowley who, after all, whatever is said and done, was once a member of the Order and owes a very great deal to his Initiation therein. I especially suggest reading his instruction which review's the whole Eastern attitude about bhakta - *Liber Astarte vel Berylli* to be found in one of the Equinoxes, or in my book *Gems from the Equinox* (Falcon Press, Phoenix, AZ. 1982). So far as I am concerned, this Liber is a masterpiece, which I can strongly recommend especially to one complaining of the absence of devotional writing in the Order.

Furthermore, and this I think is paramount, there is Crowley's early masterpiece *Three Holy Books* originally published by Sangreal Foundation with a short introduction by me, but which I understand will be republished by Samuel Weiser Inc. of New York. This volume contains *Liber LXV* or *The Book of the Heart Girt with a Serpent*, *Liber VII* or *Liber Lapidis Lazuli*, and finally *Liber 813 vel Ararita*. All three are superbly written and breathe devotion in every word. I am particularly fond of LXV and VII which Falcon Press is issuing as cassettes, containing *Liber LXV*, or *The Book of the Heart Girt with a Serpent*, *Liber VII* or *Liber Lapidus Lazuli, and Liber DCCCXUIII* or Ararita. Periodically I will play the tape on retiring to bed at night, and permitting myself to fall asleep listening to its beauty and devotion. It may be stretching definitions of things pretty far to state that these may be considered part of the Order's devotional literature. But on the other hand I would rather consider these to be in that category than the religious lucubrations of Mr. A.E. Waite who was also once a member of the Order. He founded his own Fellowship, and rewrote the Rituals (three of which are included in a later section of this book) to include many excerpts from the Bible and perhaps from the Roman missal I am not to be construed as being antagonistic to the latter by any means, but I do state strongly that if I must use one or the other, I prefer to use the so-called holy books of Aleister Crowley. They convey more devotion and love to me than almost anything else. So that if there is actually a dearth of devotional material in the Rituals and work of the Order, it is more than compensated for by reference to the work of a former member, Aleister Crowley. 1 trust that this will be the end of any complaints about this topic.

THE PROPER ATTITUDE TOWARD MIND-BODY

Over the past fifty years I have insisted that the serious magical student seek a course of therapy as a safeguard against some of the catastrophic results which appear to overtake too many of our promising students.

The difficulties seem to arise from the following:

THE SUPEREGO AND THE H.G.A.

A. The confusion between the Freudian superego (the unconscious infantile conscience) and the Order's concept of the Higher and Divine Genius (or the H.G.A.)

Many students as well as those not involved with Magic often substitute a form of their infantile conscience for one form of "Higher Self" or another. This can lead to nothing but disaster. Instead of being guided by a Higher Genius the person is really at the mercy of infantile "voices" and values, so-called brain chatter. Not only does this cause undue individual suffering and deception, it also causes a complete halt to any real progress in the Theurgic arts and sciences. To a large extent this confusion contributes to the often "bad" reputation students of the occult possess.

Those of you familiar with the history of the Order can find glowing examples of this folly. However there is no need to delve this deeply. Almost any group or Order has members and often leaders who have fallen head long into this pit dug for the unwary.

THE INFLATION OF THE EGO

B. There is a frightening frequency of the occurrence of the inflation of the ego—sometimes referred to as infantile megalomania. To help the student understand this difficulty let us define the healthy ego as a computer type decision maker. The ego's function is to help the person make decisions based on hard data. The purpose of this function should be that of survival and personal fulfillment on various levels or planes. In one sense the healthy ego is more or less non-personal. It realizes cause and effect in Malkuth, and understands its limitations.

On the other hand infantile megalomania is a natural occurrence in infancy, and with proper development has been outgrown by the healthy adult ego. However, while this is the ideal it rarely occurs in practice, and requires some form of "therapy" Eastern or Western to accomplish this goal. In the practice of Magic or anything which releases unusual amounts of energy from the unconscious the infantile megalomaniacal substructure is re-activated, and all the illusions and delusions of self importance and elevation of babyhood re-emerge.

This flattery overwhelms the ego. The person takes the impersonal and universal nature of the powers he or she experiences as if he or she created the powers or experiences by what they call - *themselves*.

If this experience called by Jung the "Mana Personality" persists for too long a period the person becomes ego-maniacal and thoroughly self-centered. This can be observed in patients undergoing psychotherapy as well as in the so-called normal man on the street. This excessive self-admiration or as Jung puts it "the naive concretization of primordial images" leads to an overinflated ego which in the end leads directly to disaster and contradicts in toto the purpose of the Great Work.

The student should be also cautioned that the opposite of infantile megalomania is not milk-toast humility and passiveness. The latter is the sine qua non of a deeply buried and potentially more dangerous form of infantile megalomania.

THE PROPER ATTITUDE TOWARD THE INSTINCTS

C. There is a danger of the blatant acting out of instincts which have been distorted through repression and denial on the one hand or their compulsive repression leading to a boring and unfulfilled sex life. Almost everyone raised in the current Judaic-Christian morality suffers inevitably from a totally distorted attitude towards this topic as well as to all biologic functions in general. Therefore a complete sex life which is not only pleasurable but aids in the evolution of the Soul is totally out of the question. What is required is a a healthy attitude toward all bodily functions, remembering always that Kether is in Malkuth and Malkuth is in Kether, but after another manner.

Those involved with the Great Work have often found themselves falling into the camps of excess in one direction or another, i.e. too much or too little. The proper use and enjoyment of sex is a necessary part in the discovery and development of the Higher Genius. Aleister Crowley is one of very few who has recognized the reality of this problem, although he himself at times, due to his Plymouth Brethren upbringing, fell into the same booby trap. Most of us are plagued by an average somewhat inhibited sex life, or worse yet a compulsive acting out of our repressed sexual drives. These attitudes do not aid the development of self-expression, deep and total relaxation, or serve as a vehicle for opening the deeper channels which lie within.

THE PROBLEM OF RELIGION AND THE GREAT WORK

This opens the way to a discussion of a very serious point which has long been on my mind. It emerges into the open by the inclusion in this volume of some of the Rituals of A.E. Waite. **Mathers and the Order he founded were only nominally Christian.** One has to search meticulously through the Rituals and other teaching for serious literal interpretations of the historical Jesus. In reality they are absent. The references to Osiris as a symbol of man - made - perfect could be those of any of the mythical Mediterranean crucified Gods, of whom there were many. The Order was a Hermetic Brotherhood and Christianity played only a minimal role in its operation. Mathers was on friendly with Anna Kingsford who had founded another Hermetic Society in which Christianity did play a prominent part. But he never permitted this friendship to influence him to make his Society similar to hers.

There is a very interesting set of concepts here that need only to be touched on. And that is the constant effort made by some occult teachers to Christianize the ancient wisdom religion. I have already mentioned Anna Kingsford as one. Another, who influenced Dr. Felkins tremendously was Rudolph Steiner who seemed determined to Christianize occultism in grotesque ways that are fundamentally opposed to the innate conceptual nature of Magic. In this he was following in the foot steps of Annie Besant and Bishop Leadbeater who had already succeeded in corrupting Blavatskian Theosophy, transforming it into a Christian occultism with Eastern overtones. Though Steiner was in conflict with them, nonetheless their doctrines must have affected him profoundly, despite his so-called clairvoyance being in opposition to the so-called clairvoyance of Leadbeater.

While this was going on Waite who had been raised as a Roman Catholic seemed determined to follow in the footsteps of the above named teachers. After the revolt of 1900 in the Order he was one of the several committee members who ran the Order. Later he pulled out from this committee to form his own Fellowship of The Rosy Cross. When this happened he totally revised not merely the rituals of the Order but the entire philosophic context of the Order. In this volume three of his Rituals are included. From them the discriminating reader will be able to determine to what extent this perversion of the Order methodology had advanced. There is almost no relationship between the teachings originally laid down and the later biblical emphasis introduced by Waite.

This of course resulted in the introduction of Church concepts of morality and purity which are evident in almost everything that Waite wrote. His whole attitude became sex-negative as well as occult-negative. He made it almost a point of honour to eradicate any reference to every item in the Magical curriculum laid down by Mathers and Westcott. Fortunately when he died in the late 1930's his Order died with him and so did his sex-negative attitudes, as well as his wretched pompous English—characterized by a need to use Latin phrases where simple English would have been much better. Contrary to the common point of view he must have been a very ambitious person and this is made evident by the pompous titles he gave both to himself in the Rituals as well as to his attendant officers.

EGOTISM

One of the great dangers inherent within the practice of Magic and indeed of all the occult arts—is the development of an enormous egotism characterized by messianic feelings, infantile omnipotence and the utter destruction of any capacity for effective self-criticism. It appears that as the student becomes more adept in the skills of meditation, skrying, or ceremonial work, he becomes more threatened by an inflation of the ego. It appears slowly and insidiously, without apparent warning. Only those people who are closely related to or associated with the student become aware of the subtle metamorphosis that occurs. The student rarely is conscious of this unconscious transformation. Attempting to make him aware of this egotism is doomed to failure; it is like knocking on a stone wall.

It seems to afflict the aspirant who functions outside the borders of an occult order or legitimate magical school. In this sense, most students come within the jurisdiction of this definition. Those who practice their occult work under the aegis of a legitimate magical body or under the guidance of an experienced and wise guru or teacher seem to be more protected from this inflation—unless the guru has himself fallen under the spell of his own messianic fantasies and inflation. If he has, then he communicates his fatal sickness to his students. Or else he is wholly blinded to the debacle about to occur to his student.

One has only to look at the history of most modern occultists and I use them preferentially because their history is more readily authenticated than those of earlier times—to perceive how valid this phenomenon is. So many of them developed fantastic notions of their own unique importance and role in the world or even cosmic picture. Only recently I heard of one who claimed to have been the teacher of Jesus! There are an almost infinite number of variations of this theme.

It is a definite and ever present danger, and all students of occultism within or without occult orders must become conscious of this phenomenon. Otherwise they are doomed. They experience what appears to be at first an enhancement of life-feelings, a rich harvest of previously unknown information and knowledge, and the awareness that destiny has suddenly acquired a new direction,—only to collapse later in total frustration, ignominy, and exile from all of society.

From the theoretical viewpoint, the gradual expansion of the confines of the limited ego by magical practices, leads to contact of some kind with the 'unconscious'. A new source of energy is released, an energy which is seen as carrying with it not only new feelings but new knowledge and a greater capacity for self-confidence with the ability to impress and motivate one's fellow man. This energy floods the unprepared ego with almost infinite promise. Unless the candidate is properly prepared for this phenomenon, or is guided and guarded by a competent experienced teacher, he is likely to take this seriously. Effective self-criticism seems to have vanished in thin air.

Crowley seems to have been most conscious of this in some of his earlier work. He himself had a couple of admirable teachers—Alan Bennett, George Cecil Jones and Oscar Eckenstein. For example in one section of *Liber* O he wrote: 'This book is very easy to misunderstand; readers are asked to use the most minute critical care in the study of it, even as we have done in its preparation. In this book it is spoken of the Sephiroth and the Paths; of Spirits and Conjurations; of Gods, Spheres, Planes and many other things which may or may not exist. It is immaterial whether these exist or not. **By doing certain things certain results will follow; students are most earnestly warned against attributing objective reality or philosophic validity to any of them.** There is little danger that any student, however idle or stupid, will fail to get some result; but there is great danger that he will be led astray, obsessed and overwhelmed by his results, even though it be by those which it is necessary that he should attain. Too often, moreover, he mistaketh the final resting-place for the goal, and taketh off his armour as if he were a victor ere the fight is well begun.'

Some few other occultists familiar with the practical side of things also utter similar warnings. *Blavatsky in her Voice of the Silence* also warns that 'under every flower a serpent coiled.' And in a footnote in this warning, she adds: 'The astral region, the psychic world of supersensous perception and of deceptive sights—the world of mediums. It is the great 'Astral Serpent' of Eliphas Levi. No blossom picked in those regions has ever yet been brought down to earth without its serpent coiled around the stem. It is the world of the **Great Illusion.'**

Only a good guru of almost superhuman powers of effective self-evaluation and examination provide the means of avoiding inflation and the consequent disaster. A third means is almost any form of good psychotherapy. The latter appears to be able to drain off the massive uncontrolled quantities of energy that are released and direct them into new and constructive goals. Those Reichians who have an understanding of 'occult' matters would appear to be more effective than most in dealing with the phenomenon.

Jung has also described it most extensively in an extraordinarily good essay in a book entitled *Two Essays on Analytical Psychology.* However, the methods of therapy described by Jung and practised by his followers leave a lot to be desired. Every occult student should not merely read this book but own it, in order to provide the opportunity to read and re-read many times the chapter dealing with inflation of the ego.

It is his contention that the analysand, the patient undergoing therapy—analagous to the enterprising student beginning his occult work—attempts to identify his ego with the collective psyche. He does this as a means of escaping the pain and anxiety resulting from the collapse of his conscious persona or self, which is one of the primary effects of the analysis. To free himself from the seductive embrace of the collective psyche, instead of denying it as some others have done, he accepts it so totally that he is devoured or overwhelmed by it, becomes lost in it, and thus is no longer capable of perceiving it as a separate entity. As another student once put it, instead of realizing that they have become illuminated by God, they affirm that they *are* God. Thus the inflation begins. It ends disastrously when or if the'God'discovers he is not omniscient or omnipotent. But by then it is generally too late.

It would not do the student harm to re-read the statement by Hyatt and myself on the problems confronting the serious occult student in the beginning of this book. Also while at times outrageous Hyatt's book *Undoing Yourself with Energized Meditation* (Falcon Press, 1982), makes good sense in this context.

THE MAGICAL ALPHABET

The Knowledge Lectures of the Golden Dawn were fragments, isolated and brief, of general occult information that were handed to the student after each initiation. He was instructed to memorize them, to make them part of his basic mental equipment.

The information consisted primarily of some rudimentary Qabalistic theory, plus of course the Hebrew Alphabet, bits of astrological data, the names of the Tarot cards and their simplest attributions, some geomantic symbols, and a few samples of general occult symbolism. None of these was in depth. So that unless the student had done a great deal of previous *individualstudy* and meditation on what he now studied, he was indeed at a loose end. The result was that he could, and often did, wind up hopelessly confused, without the slightest idea of what all this information really amounted to, and gave up the work of the Order.

S. L. Mathers' book *The Kabballah Unveiled* had only just been published prior to the formation of the Heremetic Order of the Golden Dawn (in the Outer). Much of the Qabalistic information of several Knowledge Lectures quite evidently had been extrapolated from his Introduction to this book. For the average student this Introduction is a goldmine, a most useful piece of work—though I cannot say as much for the text itself which is the essence of needless obscurity. A large part of the Introduction is herewith duplicated to show the connections between the book and Knowledge Lectures.

Apart from this book, there were not a great many authorities students could consult in order to enlarge and round out their information of what the Knowledge Lectures were merely hinting at. There was of course the library of the British Museum where Mathers himself had spent a vast amount of time digging out archaic magical material. I doubt however that many others would have bothered with that magnificent storehouse of source material. He therefore deserves enormous commendation for his energy, insight and ability to probe into and clarify the obscure and archaic literature that he was determined to find. Some critics have been capriciously hostile assuming that any Tom, Dick or Harry would have had the perspicacity and intelligence to have discovered the information that Mathers was looking for. I have spent never ending hours over periods of months and years in the mid-thirties attempting, fruitlessly, to duplicate what Mathers, in his genius, knew what he was looking for.

Some astrological works were also available, with the beginning of an outpouring of Theosophical and related literature. These would have been of considerable value. At least some over-all picture of the system would have been provided, albeit from an Eastern point of view. But this was supposed to be the root of the Western Esoteric Tradition.

Alchemical texts were not in general circulation at that time either. A. E. Waite had not begun his task of editing and publishing Latin and Greek translations made by some of the older Golden Dawn clerical members. Since that time the alchemical field has evidenced a renaissance with the appearance of many fine texts. A recent book by Frater Albertus *The Alchemists Handbook* (Samuel Weiser Inc., New York) will provide a depth of material not otherwise available. It throws much light on some of the dark utterances of the Golden Dawn Knowledge Lectures which otherwise would not make much sense.

So far as the Tarot was concerned, much the same situation prevailed. There was little available in English. Mathers' own booklet was worthless. I imagine it was written and published to put people off the track rather than to help them, a ridiculous attitude typical of that period of time. It should never have been written or published. Paul F. Case's book on the Tarot, had it then existed, would have proved invaluable.

Franz Hartman, with Theosophical connections had written a book on Geomancy based on earlier writings. It would have provided additional material the enterprising student could have used, though the esoteric keys unique to the Golden Dawn's later Inner Order work were not described. He was also the author-editor of *In the Pronaos of the Temple*, a very imformative little book which reproduced some of the forgotten Rosicrucian legends and source material from an earlier period of time. And we must not forget what has since become a classic in the Rosicrucian and Alchemical fields *The Secret Symbols of the Rosicrucians*.

General symbolism could have been picked up from a variety of miscellaneous sources. There was a general stirring, and occult and spiritual matters were in the air.

But for the general student of the Mysteries who was not a scholar, or had a penchant for independent research, the basic knowledge material was all disconnected data and pretty much of a closed book. All he could do was to memorize the stuff by rote, and ask questions of the Officers of the Temple he belonged to. They may or may not have been too helpful. One of the common cliches was that the elucidation of this or that set of notions was reserved for a higher grade. Very frustrating!

Be that as it may, by the time the student had completed his passage through the grades of the Outer Order he was in possession of a good deal of basic material. A great deal more than one would think at first sight. It was handed out piecemeal which was also a good idea; otherwise were it presented en masse as it was in a previous publication of mine he would have been swamped and overwhelmed by a mass of wholly indigestible material. Whether he was able to tie it all together and integrate it, by the time he got to the Inner Order, into a meaningful and workable system is a moot point. It would be far easier for the modern student to do this than one of a century ago.

However, the fact remains that what was given in the Knowledge Lectures served as the barebones of what could be called the Magical Alphabet. Without this, most occult or magical literature is a closed book. With it, even if only partly understood, you have an open sesame to some of the most profound ideas and practical systems of personal development ever devised. All of this constituted the skeleton of a profound philosophical system.

The task today is so much easier for the student who really wishes to study and master the basics. Several fine works have been written by former students of the Order and which have turned out to be enormously valuable aids in the development of a magical philosophy. First and foremost perhaps is Dion Fortune's *The Mystical Qabalah*, a beautiful elaboration of the fundamental concepts of the Order. Criticized by the contentious Ellic Howe, it is nonetheless one of the best modern introductions to a difficult subject. Its only flaws might be that she has given too much space to a discussion of the Unknowable in violation of Sir Edwin Arnold's warning (in *The Light of Asia*): "Sink not the string of thoughts into the Unfathomable. Who asks doth err. Who answers errs. Say naught." And then it is marred somewhat by the neo-Theosophical viewpoints of the Besant-Leadbeater clique relative to the Master Jesus, which has no connection at all with the Qabalah, and is even repudiated by her more modern successors such as Gareth Knight. Nonetheless it is strongly recommended.

In the same category, I would place *The Ladder of Lights* by William Gray. It is a superb piece of Qabalistic writing that I am sure will find its own place in posterity. A number of others might be mentioned, but these should provide a starting point for the enterprising student who wishes to get a good handle on an otherwise obscure subject.

In order to integrate, in part, some of the mass of disconnected materials given in the Knowledge Lectures, I have decided to include long quotations from MacGregor Mathers' Introduction to *The Kaballah Unveiled*. I will not say much about the latter book save that it is frightfully obscure, but the Introduction is first rate. *The Kaballah Unveiled* is an English translation from the Latin of Knorr von Rosenroth, a Renaissance scholar who translated portions of the Zohar from Hebrew into Latin. The *Zohar* has in recent years been translated wholly into English by Simon and Sperling (Soncino Press), from which the student may get some idea of what its contents are like. There is an even earlier translation of the first part of the *Zohar* by a William Williams who wrote under the pseudonym of Nurho de Manhar (Wizard Bookshelf, San Diego, 1978), evidently part of his magical motto while in the Second Order of the R.R. et A.C. It is pre-eminently readable, and was originally published in installments in the early part of this century in a magazine published by the American Section of the Theosophical Society. Parts of this will also be quoted from time to time.

While on this topic, I feel impelled to deal with some criticisms made by hostile authors. Some of these people claim that Mathers' contributions to the Knowledge Lectures and the whole corpus of Golden Dawn teaching was based entirely on his research at the British Museum. In other words there was nothing new about the Golden Dawn teaching.

In one sense this is true. In a more profound sense it is wholly false. For example, the Pentagram Ritual. Eliphas Levi does indeed refer to it as the conjuration of the Four. In an old Hebrew prayer given in a Sephardic prayer book, there is a reference to the four Archangels and the quarters in which they reside. But nowhere that I am aware of is there a description of the Pentagram itself, the elemental attributions to its several points, the divine names that accompany them, and any descriptions of the technique or method of describing this Pentagram. Much the same is true of the Hexagram ritual for the invocation or banishing of the planets and Sephiroth of the Tree of Life.

These are elementary points. But they are very important. References will be found to all these ideas, but nowhere will there be found the descriptions required above.

We could go further. However unimportant these matters may seem to the layman or the investigator approaching these topics from the outside, these are several of the most useful magical procedures for which I can find no precedent. For example, there is the vibratory formula of the Middle Pillar, the formation of Telesmatic Images, the specific method of Tattwa vision or Skrying, etc. . .

It was apparently the intent of the founders not to provide a finished system of philosophy— such as *The Secret Doctrine* of Blavatsky, etc. It was intended to be supplemented by further reading, study, meditation, and of course by skrying. In this way, the magical language, and in turn the philosophy, could be developed on a individual basis. For example, a book I wrote as far back as 1932, *The Tree of Life*, served that purpose for me. It presented a systematic overview of the magical philosophy with some of its practices that, despite its verbosity and addiction to adjectivitis, has nonetheless been lauded as one one of the best current books of its kind.

In effect, I wish to counsel the student not already familiar with this schema, to approach the following material as might have the student of a century ago. Deal with it in small segments so that you do not get overwhelmed by an overview of a vast mass of material which appears to have no unifying principle. The latter is there alright, but the preliminary material needs first to be committed to memory and studied in small segments to avoid psychic indigestion. Dealt with in this manner, some of the books mentioned above, can be approached in a meaningful way and both will benefit considerably—that is the knowledge material and the recommended books.

THE MAGIC OF THE HEBREW ALPHABET

In various places throughout these volumes of the teachings of the Golden Dawn, it is stated emphatically that the Hebrew letters are magical symbols. For this reason, each student should learn how to form them and write them. Good calligraphy was often absent in the old Order, for I have seen manuscripts that go back a long way, in which the Hebrew letters are atrociously formed. If there is any magic in such an alphabet, the intent is defeated by deformed and ill-formed letters. The student should make a point of learning in some way to write, print or letter these alphabets correctly. A good calligraphic pen, producing thick and thin lines is an absolute essential. A quill must have originally been used centuries ago, but the lettering pens of today are so much superior.

If you don't know how to go about it, it might be the easiest thing to enquire at a local university where Semitic languages are taught to be put in touch with a senior student who can then show you how to write the letters. Failing this, contact a local synagogue. They will not harm you, cook you, or try to convert you. They may be curious as to why you want to know such a feat, but you can make up a half a dozen explanations to account for that - including the truth, that you are studying the Qabalah. They may know less about that than you, but at least they may be able to teach you how to write the letters correctly and that is half the battle won.

In the *Zohar* there is a pretty legend, rather long-winded but eloquent, about each letter of the alphabet, and how B, the second letter of the alphabet, came to be used as the first letter of the first word of the Bible - Berashith meaning *In the Beginning.*

There are two main translations of the Zohar that you could make use of, depending on which one you may have access to. Some of the libraries may have the translation of Simon and Sperling; others may have the shorter but earlier version of Nurho de Manhar. (Wizard Book Shelf, San Diego, CA. 1978). Regardless of whose translation you use, read or study the account of each letter appearing before God imploring Him to use that particular letter for the first word of Genesis. It is interesting reading, full of symbolism of one kind or another, and may throw a great deal of light for you on the motives for Mathers'statement that Hebrew letters are magical symbols and as such must be treated with respect and honor.

THE MYSTICISM OF THE ALPHABET

"Rabbi Chananya spake, and said: Before creation began, the alphabetical letters were in reversed order; thus the two first words in the *Book of Genesis, Berashith, bara,* begin with B; the next two, Alhim, *ath,* with A. Why did it not commence with A, the first letter? The reason of this inversion is as follows: For two thousand years before the creation of the world the letters were concealed and hidden, being objects of divine pleasure and delight.

"When the Divine Being, however, willed to create the world, all the letters appeared before His presence in their reverse order. The first ascended and said: 'Lord of the Universe! let it please Thee to create the world by me, as I am the final letter of the word Emeth - (truth), which is graven on Thy signet ring. Thou Thyself art called Emeth, and therefore it will become Thee, the great King, to begin and create the world by me. Said the Holy One (blessed by He): 'Thou, oh, Tav, are indeed worthy, but I cannot create the world by thee; for thou art destined to be not only the characteristic emblem borne by faithful students of the law, from beginning to end, but also the associate of Maveth (death), of which thou art the final letter. Therefore the creation of the world cannot, must not, be through thee.'

"After Tav had disappeared, Sh ascended and said: 'I pray Thee, Lord of the Universe, as bearing Thy great name Shaddai (almighty), to create the world by me, by the holy name that becometh Thee only.' Said the Holy One: 'Thou art truly, o Shin, worthy, pure and true; but letters that go to form lying and falsehood will associate themselves with thee. viz.: Koph (Q) and Resh (R), and with thee will make up SheQeR (a lie), Falsehood, in order that it may be received and credited, come first with the appearance of truth (Sh), which thou representest, and for this reason 1 will not create the world by thee.' So Shin departed and Q and R, having heard these words, dared not present themselves before the divine presence.

"TZ then went before Him, saying: 'Because I mark the Zaddikim (the righteous), and Thou Thyself hearest me in Thy name, Zaddik (righteous), and also it is written, The righteous Lord loveth righteousness, it will become Thee to create the world by me.'Then said the Holy One: 'Zaddi, Zaddi, thou art truly righteous, but thou must keep thyself concealed, and thy occult meaning must not be made known or become revealed; and therefore thou must not be used in the creation of the world. Thy original form was a rod, symbol of the male principle, surmounted by Y od, a letter of the holy Name, and also of the Holy Covenant, and emblem of the male principle. (By this, reference is made to the first man, who was androgynous, with faces turning one to the right, the other to the left, as symbolized in the figure of Zaddi in the Hebrew alphabet). But the time will come that thou shall be divided, and thy faces shall then be turned to each other.'

"Zaddi then departed, and P ascended and said: '1 am the beginning of the salvation (Peragna) and deliverance (Peduth) thou will execute in the world. It will be fitting to create it by me.' 'Thou art worthy,' replied the Holy One, 'but thou also givest rise to Evil (Peshang), and in thy form resemblest those animals who walk with drooping heads, like wicked men who go about with bowed heads and extended hands. I will not, therefore, create the world by thee.'

"To the letter Ayin, the initial of the word Avon (iniquity), though it claimed the origination of Anaya (Modesty), the Holy One said: 'I shall not create the world by thee.' And forthwith Ayin departed.

"S then went and pleaded: 'I am near (Samech) to the fallen ones, as it is written: The Lord upholdeth (soumekh) all them that fall. Thou must return, Samech, to thy place,' was the reply of the Holy One, and must not leave it; for if thou dost, what will become of the fallen, who will need and look to thee for aid and support?' Samech forthwith returned, and was followed by N, who said: 'Oh thou Holy One! that Thou mayest be venerated in praises (Nura tehillim), and also because the praise of the righteous will be a Nava (delight), let it please Thee to create the world by me.' To whom He replied: 'Nun, return thou to thy place with the fallen (Nephelim), for whose sake Samech hath gone back to her place, and lean for support upon her.'

"M then followed after, saying: 'Thou wilt by me be called Malech (king).' 'Truly so,' said He, 'but I will not, for all that, create the world by thee. Go back at once to thy place with thy companion letters, L and CH; for there must be a King, and for the world to be without one would not be seemly. At that moment CH descended from off the throne of light and splendor, exclaiming; '1 am thy glory, create the world by me.' As it stood trembling with excitement before the Holy One, two hundred thousand worlds together with the throne itself were seized with a sudden tremor and seemed ready to fall. 'Caph, Caph!' cried the Holy One, 'what hast thou done? I will not create the world by thee, for thou beginnest Chala (ruin, loss). Return at once to thy place on the throne of glory and abide there!' Then Caph retired and went back to its place.

"Y next appeared and claimed that being the initial letter in the divine name YHVH, it was the best for the work of creation. But the Holy One replied: 'Let it suffice thee to be what thou art, chief letter in my name and foremost in all my designs, thou must remain where and as thou art!'

Then came T and spake before the Eternal One: 'Create the world by me, for in me alone is thy goodness (Tobh) and uprightness, for attributes of Thee.' 'I will not, Oh Teth,' replied the Holy One, 'use thee in the creation of the world, because the goodness within thee is hidden and concealed from sight as it is written, 'How great is Thy goodness which Thou hidest from them that fear Thee.' Seeing thou wilt remain invisible to the world I am about to create, and furthermore because of the goodness hidden within thee, the gates of the temple will sink into the earth as it is written, '*Her gates are sunk into the ground*,' and besides all this, thou with thy comrade the letter Cheth (CH) composed sin. Therefore, these letters will never enter in the names of the twelve holy tribes. On hearing these words Ch went not before the Holy One, but returned at once to its place.

"Z then went up and urged its claim, saying: 'Thy children will through me keep the Sabbath, as it is written: Remember (Zecor) the Sabbath to keep it holy. Thou. Oh Zain,' replied the Holy one, 'art of too warlike a form, resembling as thou dost a spear. I cannot use thee in the creation of the world.'

When Z heard this decision, like N it retired and gave place to V, who said: 'I am a letter in thy Holy name.' The Eternal One answered and said, 'remain contented. Oh V that together with H you are in the great name. I shall not choose you by whom to create the world.'

"D. accompanied by G, went before the Divine Presence. To them it was said. 'Let it suffice you, that so long as you are conjoined and associated, there will always be the poor on the earth who will need succor and help. Daleth (D) - poverty and Gimel(G) - help or the benefactor.

Therefore both of you keep together, the one helping the other.' (In the Hebrew alphabet G and D are successive letters).

"Then came B and said : 'Create the world by me, because I am the initial letter of Beracha (blessing) and through me all will bless thee, both in the world above as in the world below.'"Truly, Oh B,' said the Holy One, 'I will surely create the world by thee only.'

"Hearing these words, A remained in its place and went not into the Divine Presence, who therefore exclaimed 'Aleph (A) Aleph! why comest thou not before me as all the other letters?'Then replied A: 'Lord and sovereign of the universe, it is because I have observed that (B excepted) they have returned as they went, without success. Why therefore, should I come before thee, since thou hast already given B the great and precious gift we all of us craved and desired. Moreover, it becometh not the monarch of the universe to withdraw and take back his presents from one subject and give them to another.' To these words the Holy One responded: 'Aleph, Aleph! Thou shalt be the first of all letters and my unity shall be symbolized only by thee. In all conceptions and ideas human or divine, in every act and deed begun, carried on and completed, in all of them shalt thou be the first, the beginning.'

"Therefore did the Holy One make the letters of the celestial alphabet, capitals, and those of the earthly, small, each corresponding to one another. Therefore also the Book of Genesis begins with two words whose initials are B, viz/: Berashith Bara (in the beginning created) followed by two others, whose initials are A, viz., Alhim ath (God, the substance of) to show that the letters of these alphabets celestial and earthly are one and the same by which every creature and thing in the universe has been formed and produced."

CONCERNING HEBREW PRONUNCIATION

Recently, a noted occult writer wrote me a letter asking why it was that the Hebrew pronunciations given in an earlier and now obsolete book of mine on the Qabalah differed radically from almost every other contemporary Qabalistic writer. When answering him, it had been my intention to assert that the explanations had already been given. When, however, I proceeded to examine the obsolete book anew, I found that this had been carelessly omitted. (Falcon Press has just issued several tapes which give the correct pronunciation of most of the Qabalistic and other words used in this text.)

My reply took a page and a half to clarify the issue. In order to eliminate possible repetitions of this expenditure of time and effort, let me offer the following.

I can best begin by asserting that no matter where or by whom spoken, English is English. The accents used, for example, in the North of England are entirely different from those employed in Kent or Sussex in the South of England. The English of Wales sounds strangely melodious compared to that of Surrey or Northampton. All however are English.

Much the same is true in the United States. The accent of an inhabitant of Minnesota is entirely different from one who lives in Alabama or Georgia. All speak that variety of English we know as American. Which one is correct?

Let me say that there is no standard or fixed accent which is accepted universally as authoritative. I fancy much the same is true of every other language. Northern and Southern Italian vary in many ways. So also in Germany, France and elsewhere. Accents and dialects are integral parts of the linguistic process.

This is true also in Hebrew which is part of the magical language of what has come to be called the Western esoteric tradition. There are two main streams of Hebrew pronunciation called the Ashkenazic relating to North Europe, England and the United States, and the Sephardic spoken in the Mediterranean and Levantine areas. The history of these two streams is really irrelevant to this essay. Anyone interested can do a little research in a good encyclopedia.

THE COMPLETE GOLDEN DAWN SYSTEM OF MAGIC

The Mediterranean area, as we know historically, achieved a higher level of cultural development far earlier than did Northern Europe. Much of the Qabalistic literature had its origins in Spain where there was a fascinating merger of Christian, Arabic and Hebrew mysticisms in pre-Zoharic times, as well as in the Levantine area as a whole. The obvious result of this cultural superiority was that the spoken Hebrew had a Sephardic accent. When the literature came to be translated by later scholars and Christian Qabalists, the translations or better still transliterations took on the Sephardic flavor.

Much later in the 18th century, when there was a revival of Jewish mysticism called Chassidism, in Central Europe, Poland and Russia, the Ashkenazic accent or dialect was employed. Regardless of how popular Chassidism became, English translators persisted on the whole in using the Sephardic dialect, which is interesting because Baal Shem, the founder of what became the Chassidic movement, obviously used Ashkenazic Hebrew. It seems, however, that the Sephardic dialect and the whole Qabalistic literary corpus were intimately bound together, so that very few could conceive that there was any other way of transliterating Hebrew. This persisted right up to modern times. S.L. Mathers in his *Kaballah Unveiled*, Arthur E. Waite in all of his Qabalistic writings, and Frater Albertus in one of the early Alchemical Bulletins, amongst many other distinguished writers, all used the Sephardic dialect.

It so happened that when I began my interest in the Qabalah in my mid-teens, I wanted to be able to translate some of the important books and manuscripts that yet remained to be rendered into English. The head of the Semitic Division of the Library of Congress whom I came to know in those days - I must have made myself a young nuisance to him requesting information about Qabalistic texts in English - recommended that I get a tutor from whom I could learn Hebrew. As a result I had a year's intensive training in Hebrew from a young man attending George Washington University in Washington, D.C., where I then lived.

Many years later, when I had learned to manipulate letters and numbers (Gematria) with some dexterity, I found that on occasion the Ashkenazic transliterations were far more useful and illuminating than the Sephardic, as I demonstrated in an earlier but now obsolete book on the Qabalah. Various people to whom I spoke as a very young man showed not the least interest, so I kept my counsel to myself.

A large number of personal notes and quotations from various authorities gradually accumulated over the course of years. In 1931, while I was in a London literary environment, serving as a secretary to first one and then another novelist and author, I was encouraged to put my ideas in book form. I did so. It became my first published book a long time ago. I had hoped that the use of the Ashkenazic dialect which had solved a number of gematria problems for me, would attract some attention from other students and authorities and be used constructively in other texts. No such thing happened. Since that book was written in the early 1930's, I have seen my Ashkenazic transliterations used only three or four times at most. I was disappointed, I must confess, so that in later writings I dropped it, returning to the more conventional spelling and transliteration of the Hebrew alphabet and Qabalistic terms.

When the State of Israel declared its independence in 1947, with Hebrew as its official language, naturally the Sephardic dialect was used since Palestine was part of the Levantine area. That confirmed my decision to drop the Ashkenazic style of transliteration.

It must not be supposed however that every Jewish community in Europe or the United States has dropped the Ashkenazic dialect by any manner or means. It is still used. But if you went to the State of Israel, your Ashkenazic dialect will hardly be understood, any more than you could make heads or tails out of the Sephardic dialect if you happened to be an Ashkenazi.

It is rather as if someone born and bred in Northumberland or Yorkshire could make much sense out of the Cockney accent used in parts of London. Some Australians have a version of the Cockney accent, with all its colloquialisms, that makes them rather hard to understand at first. But, never let it be forgotten, they are all speaking English - in much the same way that anyone speaking the Ashkenazic dialect or the Sephardic dialect is speaking or reading Hebrew.

This is the core of the Hebrew language problem of the Qabalah in the simplest possible terms. So when I have used "Bes" or "Ches" or "Tes" I am referring to the same letters as "Beth,""Cheth," or "Teth." Keser and Tipharas and Malkus are no other than Kether and Tiphareth and Malkuth - and so on and so forth. I still suggest that the student of QBL - as Frater Achad and Frater Albertus choose to term the subject matter - learn both dialects. He may find one more useful than another in certain specific areas. When he wishes to discover the numerology or Gematria of his name, for whatever reason he may have in mind, he may get much further by the use of one rather than the other, and achieve his objectives more readily.

The student must discover which of these two suits his own personal predilection and answers to the necessity imposed by the results of study and experience. The Order teaching employs the Sephardic pronunciation, and I have not ventured to interfere with that in any way at all. I simply mention the matter here to render impossible the likelihood of further confusion arising.

INTRODUCTION TO THE KABALLAH UNVEILED

By

McGREGOR MATHERS

The first questions which the non-qabalistical reader will probably ask are: What is the Qabalah? Who was its author? What are its sub-divisions? What are its general teachings? And why is a translation of it required at the present time?. . .

The Qabalah may be defined as being the esoteric Jewish doctrine. It is called in Hebrew QBLH, *Qabalah*, which is derived from the root QBL, *Qibel*, meaning "to receive". This appellation refers to the custom of handing down the esoteric tradition by oral transmission, and is nearly allied to "tradition".

There are no separate numeral characters in Hebrew and Chaldee; therefore, as is also the case in Greek, each letter has its own peculiar numerical value, and from this circumstance results the important fact that every word is a number, and **every number is a word.** . . I have selected the Roman letter Q to represent the Hebrew Qoph or Koph, a precedent for the use of which without a following *u*, may be found in Max Muller's *Sacred Books of the East*. The reader must remember that the Hebrew is almost entirely a consonantal alphabet, the vowels being for the most part supplied by small points and marks usually placed below the letters. Another difficulty of the Hebrew alphabet consists in the great similarity between the forms of certain letters, e.g., V, Z, and final N.

With regard to the author and origin of the Qabalah, I cannot do better than give the following extract from Dr. Christian Ginsburg's *Essay on the Kaballah*, first premissing that this word has been spelt in a great variety of ways - Cabala, Kabalah, Kabbala, etc. I have adopted the form Qabalah, as being more consonant with the Hebrew writing of the word.

(N.B. To these words of Mathers I must add my own praise. For ever since I first discovered this book around 1925, it has been a constant source of reference for me, and most of one of my early books, *A Garden of Pomegranates* was in point of fact predicated on frequent reading of this text. Its historical material, though brief, I found extremely accurate; more details may be found in Gershom Sholem's book, *Major Trends in Jewish Mysticism*, which is another goldmine not under any circumstances to be neglected by the good student.)

A system of religious philosophy, or, more properly, of theosophy, which has not only exercised for hundreds of years an extraordinary influence on the mental development of so shrewd a people as the Jews, but has captivated the minds of some of the greatest thinkers of Christendom in the sixteenth and seventeenth centuries, claims the greatest attention of both the philosopher and the theologian. When it is added that among its captives were Raymond Lully, the celebrated scholastic metaphysician and chemist (died 1315); John Reuchlin, the renowned scholar and reviver of Oriental literature in Europe (born 1455, died 1522); John Picus de Mirandola, the famous philosopher and classical scholar (1463-1494); Cornelius Henry Agrippa, the distinguished philosopher, divine, and physician (1486-1535); John Baptist von Helmont, a remarkable chemist and physician (1577-1644); as well as our own countrymen, Robert Fludd, the famous physician and philosopher (1574-1637); and Dr. Henry More (1614-1687); and that these men, after restlessly searching for a scientific system which should disclose to them "the deepest depths" of the divine nature, and show them the real tie which binds all things together, found the cravings of their minds satisfied by this theosophy, the claims of the Qabalah on the attention of students in literature and philosophy will readily be admitted. The claims of the Kabbalah, however, are not restricted to the literary man and the philosopher; the poet too will find in it ample materials for the exercise of his lofty genius. How can it be otherwise with a theosophy which, we are assured, was born of God in Paradise, was nursed and reared by the choicest of the angelic hosts in heaven, and only held converse with the holiest of man's children upon earth. Listen to the story of its birth, growth, and maturity, as told by its followers.

The Qabalah was first taught by God himself to a select company of angels, who formed a theosophic school in Paradise. After the Fall the angels most graciously communicated this heavenly doctrine to the disobedient children of earth, to furnish the protoplasts with the means of returning to their pristine nobility and felicity. From Adam it passed over to Noah, and then to Abraham, the friend of God, who emigrated with it to Egypt, where the patriarch allowed a portion of this mysterious doctrine to ooze out. It was in this way that the Egyptians obtained some knowledge of it, and the other Eastern nations could introduce it into their philosophical systems. Moses, who was learned in all the wisdom of Egypt, was first initiated into the Qabalah in the land of his birth, but became most proficient in it during his wanderings in the wilderness, when he not only devoted to it the leisure hours of the whole forty years, but received lessons in it from one of the angels. By the aid of this mysterious science the law-giver was enabled to solve the difficulties which arose during his management of the Israelites, in spite of the pilrimages, wars, and frequent miseries of the nation. He covertly laid down the principles of this secret doctrine in the first four books of the Pentateuch, but withheld them from Deuteronomy. Moses also initiated the seventy elders into the secrets of this doctrine, and they again transmitted them from hand to hand. Of all who formed the unbroken line of tradition, David and Solomon were the most deeply initiated into the Qabalah. No one, however, dared to write it down, till Schimeon Ben Jochai, who lived at the time of the destruction of the second temple . . . After his death, his son, Rabbi Eleazar, and his secretary, Rabbi Abba, as well as his disciples, collated Rabbi Simon Ben Jochai's treatises, and out of these composed the celebrated work called ZHR, *Zohar*, Splendour, which is the grand storehouse of Qabalism.

VOLUME ONE

The Qabalah is usually classed under four heads:

    (a)   **The practical Qabalah.**
    (b)   **The literal Qabalah.**
    (c)   **The unwritten Qabalah.**
    (d)   **The dogmatic Qabalah.**

The practical Qabalah deals with talismanic and ceremonial magic, and does not come within the scope of this work. But, the whole work of the Golden Dawn is in fact the elucidation of this topic.

The literal Qabalah is referred to in several places, and therefore a knowledge of its leading principles is necessary. It is divided into three parts: GMTRIA. *Gematria* NVTRIQVN, *Notariqon*, and ThMVRH, *Temura.*

Gematria is a metathesis of the Greek work *ypauuateia.* It is based on the relative numerical values of words, as I have before remarked. Words of similar numerical values are considered to be explanatory of each other, and this theory is also extended to phrases. Thus the letter *shin*, Sh, is 300, and is equivalent to the number obtained by adding up the numerical values of the letters of the words RVCH ALHIM, *Ruach Elohim*, the spirit of the Elohim; and it is therefore a symbol of the spirit of the Elohim. For R-200, V-6, Ch-8, A-l, L-30, H-5,1-10, M-40; total-300. Similarly the words AChD, *Achad*, Unity, one, and AHBH, *Ahebah,* love, each-13; for A-l, Ch-8, D-4, total-13; and A-l, H-5, B-2, H-5, total-13. Again, the name of the angel MTTRVN, *Metatron* or *Methraton*, and the name of Deity, ShDI, Shaddai, each make 314; so the one is taken as symbolical of the other. The angel Metraton is said to have been the conductor of the children of Israel through the wilderness, of whom God says, "My Name is in him." With regard to Gematria of phrases (Gen. xlix. 10), IBA ShILH, *Yeba Shiloh*, "Shiloh shall come" which equals 358, which is the numeration of the MShlCh, *Messiah.* Thus also the passage, Gen. xviii. 2 VHNH ShLShH, *Vehennna Shalisha*, "And lo, three men," equals in numerical value ALV MIKAL GBRIAL VRPAL, *Elo Mikhael Gabriel VeRaphael*, "These are Mikhael, Gabriel and Raphael;" for each phrase equals 701.1 think these instances will suffice to make clear the nature of Gematria, especially as many others will be found in the course of the ensuing work.

Notariqon is derived from the Latin word *notarius,* a short-hand writer. Of Notariqon there are two forms. In the first every letter of a word is taken for the initial or abbreviation of another word, so that from the letters of a word a sentence may be formed. Thus every letter of the word BRAShITh, *Berashith*, the first word in Genesis, is made the inital of a word, and we obtain from it BRAShlTh RAH ALHIM AhIQBLV IShRAL ThVRH, *Berashith Rahi Elohim Sheyequebelo Israel Torah*: "In the beginning the Elohim saw that Israel would accept the law."

The second form of Notariqon is that exact reverse of the first. By this the initials or finals, or both or the medials, of a sentence, are taken to form a word or words. Thus the Qabalah is called ChKMh NSThRH, *Chokhmah Nesthorah*, "the secret wisdom;" and if we take the initials of these two words Ch and N, we form by the second kind of Notariqon the word ChN, *Chen*, "grace." Similarly, from the initials and finals of the words MI IOLH LNV HShMIMH, *Mi Iaulah Leno Ha-Shamavimah*, "Who shall go up for us to heaven?" (Deut. xxx. 12). are formed MILH, *Milah* "circumcision," and IHVH, the Tetragrammaton, implying that God hath ordained circumcision as the way to heaven.

Temura is permutation. According to certain rules, one letter is substituted for another letter preceding or following it in the alphabet, and thus from one word another word of totally different orthography may be formed. Thus the alphabet is bent exactly in half, in the middle, and one half is put over the other; and then by changing alternately the first letter or the first two letters at the beginning of the second line, twenty two commutations are produced. These are called the "Table of the Combinations of TzIRVP," *tziruph*. For example's sake, I will give the method called ALBTh. *Albath. thus*:

11	10	9	8	7	6	5	4	3	2	1
K	I	T	Ch	Z	V	H	D	G	B	A
M	N	S	O	P	Tz	Q	R	Sh	Th	L

Each method takes its name from the two pairs composing it, the system of pairs of letters being the groundwork of the whole, as either letter in a pair is substituted for the other letter. Thus, by Albath, from RVCh, *Ruach*, is formed DTzO, *Detzau*. The names of the other twenty-one methods are:

ABGTh	AHDTh	ADBG	AHBD	AVBH
AZBV	AChBZ	ATBCh	AIBT	AKBI
ALBK	AMBL	ANBM	ASBN	AOBS
APBO	ATzBP	AQBTz	ARBQ	AShBR
AThBSH				

To these must be added the modes ABGD and ALBM. Then comes the "Rational Table of Tziruph," another set of twenty-two combinations. There are also three "Tables of the Commutations," known respectively as the Right, the Averse, and the Irregular. To make any of these, a square, containing 484 squares, should be made, and the letters written in. For the "Right Table" write the alphabet across from right to left; in the second row of squares do the same, but begin with B and end with A; in the third begin with G and end with B; and so on. For the "Averse Table" write the alphabet from right to left backwards, beginning with Th and ending with A; in the second row begin with Sh and end with Th, etc. The "Irregular Table" would take too long to describe. Besides all these, there is the method called ThShRQ, *Thashraq*, which is simply writing a word backwards. There is one more very important form, called the "Qabalah of the Nine Chambers," or AIQ BKR, *Aiq Bekar*. It is thus formed:

300	30	3	200	20	2	100	10	1
Sh	L	G	R	K	B	Q	I	A
600	60	6	500	50	5	400	40	4
M (f)	S	V	K (f)	N	H	Th	M	D
900	90	9	800	80	8	700	70	7
Tz (f)	Tz	T	P (f)	P	Ch	N (f)	O	Z

I have put the numeration of each letter above to show the affinity between the letters in each chamber. Sometimes this is used as a cipher, by taking the portions of the figure to show the letters they contain, putting one point for the first letter, two for the second, etc. Thus the right angle, containing AIQ, will answer for the letter Q if it has three dots or points within it. Again, a square will answer for H, N, or K final, according to whether it has one, two, or three points respectively placed within it. So also with regard to the other letters. But there are many other ways of employing the Qabalah of the Nine Chambers, which I have not space to describe. I will merely mention, as an example, that by the mode of Temura called AThBSh, *Athbash*, it is found that in Jeremiah xxv. 26, the word ShShk, *Sheshakh*, symbolizes BBL, *Babel*.

Besides all these rules, there are certain meanings hidden in the *shape* of the letters of the Hebrew alphabet; in the form of a particular letter at the end of a word being different from that which it generally bears when it is a final letter, or in a letter being written in the middle of a word in a character generally used only at the end; in any letter or letters being written in a size smaller or larger than the rest of the manuscript, or in a letter being written upside down; in the variations found in the spelling of certain words, which have a letter more in some places than they have in others; in peculiarities observed in the position of any of the points or accents, and in certain expressions supposed to be elliptic or redundant.

For example, the shape of the Hebrew letter *Aleph*, A, is said to symbolize a *Vau*, V, between a *Yod*, I, and a *Daleth*, D; and thus the letter itself represents the word IVD, *Yod*. Similarly the shape of the letter *He*, H, represents the word *Daleth*, D, with a *Yod*, I, written at the lower left-hand corner, etc.

In Isaiah ix. 6, 7, the word LMRBH, *Lemarbah*, for multiplying, is written with the character for M final in the middle of the word, instead of with the ordinary initial and medial M. The consequence of this is that the total numerical value of the word, instead of being 30 + 40 + 200 + 2 + 5 equals 277, is 30 + 600 + 200 + 2 + 5 equals 837, by Gematria ThTh ZL, *Tat Zal*, the profuse Giver. Thus, by writing the M final instead of the ordinary character, the word is made to bear a different qabalistical meaning.

In Deuteronomy vi. 4, etc., is the prayer known as the *Shema Yisrael*. It begins, "ShMo IShRAL IHVH ALHINV 1HVH AChD, Shemaa Yisrael, Tetragrammaton Elohino Tetragrammaton Achad: "Hear, O Israel, Tetragrammaton our God is Tetragrammaton Unity."

In this verse the terminal letter O in ShMO, and the D in AChD are written much larger than the other letters of the text. The qabalistical symbology contained in this circumstance is explained as follows. The letter O, being of the value of 70, shows that the law may be explained in seventy different ways, and the D equals 4 equals the four cardinal points and the letters of the Holy Name. The first word, ShMO, has the numerical value of 410, the number of years of the duration of the first temple, etc., etc. There are many other points worthy of consideration in this prayer, but time will not permit me to dwell on them. . .

The term *Unwritten Qabalah* is applied to certain knowledge which is never entrusted to writing, but communicated orally. I may say no more on this point, not even whether I myself have or have not received it. Of course, till the time of Rabbi Schimeon Ben Jochai none of the Qabalah was ever written.

The Dogmatic Qabalah contains the doctrinal portion. There are a large number of treatises of various dates and merits which go to make up the written Qabalah, but they may be reduced to four heads:

(a) **The Sepher Yetzirah and its dependencies.**
(b) **The Zohar with its developments and commentaries.**
(c) **The Sepher Sephiroth and its expansions.**
(d) **The Asch Metzareph and its symbolism.**

The SPR ITzIRH, *Sepher Yetzirah*, or *Book of Formation, is ascribed to the patriarch Abraham. It treats the cosmogony as symbolized by the ten numbers and the twenty-two letters of the alphabet, which it calls the thirty-two paths*. On these latter Rabbi Abraham Ben Dior has written a mystical commentary. The term *path* is used throughout the Qabalah to signify a hieroglyphical idea, or rather the sphere of ideas, which may be attached to any glyph or symbol.

THE COMPLETE GOLDEN DAWN SYSTEM OF MAGIC

The ZHR, *Zohar*, or "Splendour," besides many other treatises of less note, contains the following most important books. . .

The ASh MTzRP, *Asch Metzareph*, or *Purifying Fire*, is hermetic and alchemical, and is known to few, and when known is understood by still fewer.

The principal doctrines of the Qabalah are designed to solve the following problems:

    (a) The Supreme Being, His nature and attributes.

    (b) The Cosmogony.

    (c) The creation of angels and man.

    (d) The destiny of man and angels.

    (e) The nature of the soul.

    (f) The nature of angels, demons, and elementals.

    (g) The import of the revealed law.

    (h) The transcendental symbolism of numerals.

    (i) The peculiar mysteries contained in the Hebrew letters.

    (j) The equilibrium of contraries...

What is negative existence? What is positive existence? The distinction between these two is another fundamental idea. To define negative existence clearly is impossible, for when it is distinctly defined it ceases to be negative existence; it is then negative existence passing into static condition. Therefore wisely have the Qabalists shut out from mortal comprehension the primal AIN, *Ain*, the negatively existent One, and the AIN SVP, *Ain Soph*, the limitless Expansion; while of even the AIN SVP AVR, *Ain* Soph Aur, the illimitable Light, only a dim conception can be formed. Yet, if we think deeply, we shall see that such must be the primal forms of the unknowable and nameless One, whom we, in the most manifest form speak of as God. He is the Absolute. But how do we define the Absolute? Even as we define it, it slips from our grasp, for it ceases when defined to be the Absolute. Shall we then say that the Negative, the Limitless, the Absolute are, logically speaking, absurd, since they are ideas which our reason cannot define? No; for could we define them, we should make them, so to speak, contained by our reason, and therefore not superior to it; for a subject to be capable of definition it is requisite that certain limits should be assignable to it. How then can we limit the Illimitable?

The first principle and axiom of the Qabalah is the name of the Deity, translated in our version of the Bible, "I am that I am," AH1H AShR AH1H, *Eheieh Asher Eheieh*. A better translation is, *Existence is existence*, or *I am He who is*.

Eliphas Levi Zahed, that great philosopher and Qabalist of the present century, says in his *Histoire de la Magie* (bk. i. ch. 7): "The Qabalists have a horror of everything that resembles idolatry; they, however ascribe the human form to God, but it is a purely hieroglyphical figure. They consider God as the intelligent, living, and loving Infinite One.

He is for them neither the collection of other beings, nor the abstraction of existence, nor a philosophically definable being. He is in all, distinct from all, and greater than all. His very name is ineffable; and yet this name only expresses the human ideal of His Divinity. What God is in Himself it is not given to man to know. God is the absolute of faith; existence is the absolute of reason, existence exists by itself, and because it exists. The reason of the existence of existence is existence itself. We may ask, "Why does any particular thing exist?" that is, "Why does such or such a thing exist?" But we cannot ask, without its being absurd to do so, "Why does existence exist?" For this would be to suppose existence prior to existence." Again, the same author says (ibid. bk. iii. ch. 2): "To say, I will believe when the truth of the dogma shall be scientifically proved to me," is the same as to say, I will believe when I have nothing more to believe, and when the dogma shall be destroyed as dogma by becoming a scientific theorem. That is to say, in other words: "I will only admit the Infinite when it shall have been explained, determined, circumscribed, and defined for my benefit; in one word, when it has become finite. I will then believe in the Infinite when I am sure that the Infinite does not exist. I will believe in the vastness of the ocean when I shall have seen it put into bottles." But when a thing has been clearly proved and made comprehensible to you, you will no longer believe it you will know' it.

In the Bhagavad "Gita", ch. ix., it is said, "1 am Immortality and also death; and I, O Arjuna! am that which is and that which is not."[Or, "which exists negatively."] And again (ch. ix.): "And, O descendant of Bharata! see wonders in numbers, unseen before. Within my body, O Gudakesa! see today the whole universe, including everything moveable and immovable, all in one." And again (ibid.) Arjuna said: "O Infinite Lord of the Gods! O Thou who pervadest the universe! Thou art the Indestructible, that which is, that which is not, and what is beyond them. Thou art the Primal God, the Ancient One; Thou art the highest support of this universe. By Thee is this universe pervaded, O Thou of the infinite forms. . .Thou art of infinite power, of unmeasured glory; Thou pervadest all, and therefore, Thou art all!"

The idea of negative existence can then exist as an idea, but it will not bear definition, since the idea of definition is utterly incompatible with its nature. But, some of my readers will perhaps say, your term negative existence is surely a misnomer; the state you describe would be better expressed by the title of negative subsistence. Not so, I answer; for negative subsistence can never be anything but negative subsistence; it cannot vary, it cannot develop; for negative subsistence cannot be at all; it never has existed, it never does exist, it never will exist. But negative existence bears hidden in itself, positive life; for in the limitless depths of the abyss of its negativity lies hidden the power of standing forth from itself, the power of projecting the scintilla of the thought unto the outer, the power or re-involving the syntagma into the inner. Thus shrouded and veiled is the absorbed intensity in the centerless whirl of the vastness of expansion. Therefore have I employed the term *Ex-sto*, rather than *Sub-sto*.

But between two ideas so different as those of negative and positive existence a certain nexus, or connecting-link, is required, and hence we arrive at the form which is called potential existence, which while more nearly approaching positive existence, will still scarcely admit of clear definition. It is existence, in its possible form. For example, in a seed, the tree which may spring from it is hidden; it is in a condition of potential existence; is there; but it will not admit of definition. How much less, then, will those seeds which that tree in its turn may yield? But these latter are in a condition which, while it is somewhat analogous to potential existence, is in hardly so advanced a stage; that is, they are negatively existent.

But, on the other hand, positive existence is always capable of definition; it is dynamic; it has certain evident powers, and it is therefore the antithesis of negative existence, and still more so of negative subsistence. It is the tree, no longer hidden in the seed, but developed into the outer. But positive existence has a beginning and an end, and it therefore requires another form from which to depend, for without this other concealed negative ideal behind it, it is unstable and unsatisfactory.

Thus, then, have I faintly and with all reverence endeavoured to shadow forth to the minds of my readers the idea of the Illimitable One. And before that idea, and of the idea, I can only say, in the words of an ancient oracle: "In Him is an illimitable abyss of glory, and from it there goeth forth one little spark which maketh all the glory of the sun, and of the moon, and of the stars. Mortal! behold how little I know of God; seek not to know more of Him, for this is far beyond thy comprehension, however wise thou art; as for us, who are His ministers, how small a part are we of Him!"

There are three qabalistical veils of the negative existence, and in themselves they formulate the hidden ideas of the Sephiroth not yet called into being, and they are concentrated in Kether, which in this sense is the Malkuth of the hidden ideas of the Sephiroth. I will explain this. The first veil of the negative existence is the AIN, *Ain* equals Negativity. This word consists of three letters, which thus shadow forth the first three Sephiroth or numbers. The second veil is the AIN SVP, *Ain Soph*, equals Without Limit. And the third veil is AIN SVP AVR, *Ain Soph Aur* equals the Limitless Light. This again consists of nine letters, and symbolizes the first nine Sephiroth, but of course in their hidden idea only. But when we reach the number nine we cannot progress farther without returning to the unity, or the number one, for the number ten is but a repetition of unity freshly derived from the negative, as is evident from a glance at its ordinary representation in Arabic numerals, where the circle 0 represents the Negative, and the 1 the Unity. Thus, then, the limitless ocean of negative light *does not proceed from a center, for it is centerless, but it concentrates a center*, which is the number one of the manifested Sephiroth, Kether, the Crown, the First Sephira; which therefore may be said to be the Malkuth or number ten of the hidden Sephiroth. Thus, "Kether is in Malkuth, and Malkuth is in Kether."Or, as an alchemical author of great repute (Thomas Vaughan, better known as Eugenius Philalethes) says, [*Euphrates, or, The Waters of the East*] apparently quoting from Proclus: "That the heaven is in the earth, but after an earthly manner; and that the earth is in the heaven, but after a heavenly manner." But inasmuch as negative existence is a subject incapable of definition, as I have before shown, it is rather considered by the Qabalists as depending back from the number of unity than as a separate consideration therefrom; wherefore they frequently apply the same terms and epithets indiscriminately to either. Such epithets are: *The Concealed of the Concealed, The Ancient of the Ancient Ones,* the *Most Holy Ancient One*, etc.

I must now explain the real meaning of the terms Sephira and Sephiroth. The first is singular, the second is plural. The best rendering of the word is *numerical emanation*. There are ten Sephiroth, which are the most abstract forms of the ten numbers of the decimal scale, i.e., the abstract forms of the ten numbers 1,2,3,4,5,6,7,8,9,10. Therefore, as in the higher mathematics we reason of numbers in their abstract senses, so in the Qabalah we reason of the Deity by the abstract forms of the numbers; in other words, by the S PIR VTh, *Sephiroth*. It was from this ancient Oriental theory that Pythagoras derived his numerical symbolic ideas.

Among these Sephiroth, jointly and severally, we find the development of the persons and attributes of God. Of these *some are male and some are female*. Now, for some reason or other best known to themselves, the translators of the Bible have carefully crowded out of existence and smothered up every reference to the fact that the Deity is both masculine and feminine. They have *translated a feminine plural* by a *masculine singular* in the case of the word Elohim. They have, however, left an inadvertent admission of their knowledge that it was plural in Gen. iv. 26; "And Elohim said: Let Us make man." Again (v. 27), how could Adam be made in the image of the Elohim, male and female, unless the Elohim were male and female also? The word Elohim is a plural formed from the feminine singular ALH, *Eloh*, by adding IM to the word. But inasmuch as IM is usually the termination of the masculine plural, and is here added to a feminine noun, it gives the word Elohim the sense of a female potency united to a masculine idea, and thereby capable of producing an offspring. Now, we hear much of the Father and Son, but we hear nothing of the Mother in the ordinary religions of the day. But in the Qabalah we find that the Ancient of Days conforms Himself simultaneously into the Father and the Mother, and thus begets the Son. Now, this Mother is Elohim. Again, we are usually told that the Holy Spirit is masculine. But the word RVCh, *Ruach*, Spirit, is feminine, as appears from the following passage of the Sepher Yetzirah: "AChTh RVCh ALHIM ChIIM, Achath (*feminine, not Achad, masculine*) Ruach Elohim Chiim: One is *She* the Spirit of the Elohim of Life."

Now, we find that before the Deity conformed Himself thus, i.e., as male and female that the worlds of the universe could not subsist, or, in the words of Genesis, "The earth was formless and void." These prior worlds are considered to be symbolized by the "kings who reigned in Edom before there reigned a king in Israel," and they are therefore spoken of in the Qabalah as the "Edomite kings." This will be found fully explained in various parts of this work.

We now come to the consideration of the first Sephira, or the Number One, the Monad of Pythagoras. In this number are the other nine hidden. It is indivisible, it is also incapable of multiplication; divide I by itself and it still remains I multiply I by itself and it is still I and unchanged. Thus it is a fitting representative of the great unchangeable Father of all. Now this number of unity has a twofold nature, and thus forms, as it were, the link between the negative and the positive. In its unchangeable one-ness it is scarcely a number; but in its property of capability of addition it may be called the first number of a numerical series. Now, the zero, 0, is incapable even of addition, just as also is negative existence. How, then, if I can neither be multiplied nor divided, is another I to be obtained to add to it; in other words, how is the number 2 to be found? *By reflection of itself* For though 0 be incapable of definition, I is definable. And the effect of a definition is to form an Eidolon, duplicate, or image, of the thing defined. Thus, then, we obtain a duad composed of I and its reflection. Now also we have the *commencement of a vibration* established, for the number I vibrates alternately from changelessness to definition, and back to changelessness again. Thus, then is it the father of all numbers, and a fitting type of the Father of all things.

The name of the first Sephira is KThR, *Kether*, the Crown.

The Divine Name attributed to it is the Name of the Father given in Exod. iii. 4: AHIH, Eheieh, I am. It signifies Existence.

Among the Epithets applied to it, as containing in itself the idea of negative existence depending back from it are:

TMIRA DTMIRIN, *Temira De-Temirin,* **the Concealed of the Concealed.**
OThlQA DOThlQIN, *Authiqa De-Authiqun,* **the Ancient of the Ancient Ones.**
OThlQA QDIShA, *Authiqa Qadisha,* **the Most Holy Ancient One.**
OThlQA, *Authiqa,* **the Ancient One.**
OThlQ IVMIN, *Authiq Iomin,* **the Ancient of Days.**
It is also called: NQDH RAShVNH, *Nequdah Rashunah,* **the Primordial Point.**
NQDH PShVTh, *Nequdah Peshutah,* **the Smooth Point.**
RIShA HVVRH, *Risha Havurah,* **the White Head.**
RVM MOLH, *Rom Meolah,* **the Inscrutable Height.**

Besides all these there is another very important name applied to this Sephira as representing the great Father of all things. It is ARIK ANPIN, *Arikh Anpin*, the Vast Countenance, or Macroprosopus. Of Him it is said that He is partly concealed (in the sense of His connection with the negative existence) and partly manifest (as a positive Sephira). Hence the symbolism of the Vast Countenance is that of a profile wherein one side only of the Countenance is seen; or, as it is said in the Qabalah, "in Him all is right side." I shall refer to this title again.

The whole ten Sephiroth represent the Heavenly Man, or Primordial Being, ADM OILAH, *Adam Auilh.*

Under this Sephira are classed the angelic order of ChIVTh HQDSh, *Chioth Ha- Qadesh,* holy living-creatures, the kerubim or sphinxes of Ezekiel's vision and of the Apocalypse of John. These are represented in the Zodiac by the four signs, Taurus, Leo, Scorpio, and Aquarius—the Bull, Lion, Eagle, and Man. Scorpio, as a good emblem, being symbolized by the eagle, as an evil emblem by the scorpion, and as a mixed nature by the snake.

This first Sephira contained the other nine, and produced them in succession, thus:

The number 2, or the Duad. The name of the second Sephira is ChKMH, *Chokmah*, Wisdom, a masculine active potency reflected from Kether, as I have before explained. This Sephira is the active and evident Father, to whom the Mother is united, to whom are attributed the Divine Names, IH, *Yah*, and IHVH, *Tetragrammaton*; and among the angelic hosts by AVPNIM, *Auphanim*, the Wheels (Ezek i.). The second Sephira is also called AB, Ab, the Father.

The third Sephira, or Triad, is a feminine passive potency, called BINH, *Binah*, the Understanding, who is co-equal with Chokmah. For Chokmah, the number 2 is like two straight lines which can never enclose a space, and therefore it is powerless till the number 3 forms the triangle. Thus this Sephira completes and makes evident the supernal Trinity. It is also called AM A, *Ama*, Mother, and AIMA, *Aima*, the great productive Mother, who is eternally conjoined with AB, the Father, for the maintenance of the universe in order. Therefore is she the most evident form in whom we can know the Father, and therefore is she worthy of all honour. She is the supernal Mother, co-equal with Chokmah, and the great feminine form of God, the Elohim, in whose image man and woman are created, according to the teaching of the Qabalah, *equal before God. Woman is equal with man, and certainly not inferior to him*, as it has been the persistent endeavour of so-called Christians to make her. Aima is the woman described in the Apocalypse (ch. xii.). This third Sephira is also sometimes called the Great Sea. To her are attributed the Divine names, ARALIM, *Aralim*, the Thrones. She is the supernal Mother, as distinguished from Malkuth, the inferior Mother, Bride, and Queen.

The number 4. This union of the second and third Sephiroth produced ChSD, *Chesed*, Mercy or Love also called GDVLH, *Gedulah*, Greatness or Magnificence; a masculine potency represented by the Divine Name AL, *El*, the Mighty One, and the angelic name, ChShMLIM, *Chashmalim*, Scintillating Flames (Ezek. iv. 4).

The number 5. From this emanated the feminine passive potency GBVRH, *Geburah*, strength or fortitude; or DIN, *Deen*, Justice; represented by the Divine Names ALHIM GBVR, and ALH, *Eloh*, and the angelic name ShRPIM, *Seraphim* (Isa. vi. 6). This Sephira is also called PChD, *Pachad*, Fear.

The number 6. And from these two issued the uniting Sephira, ThPARTh, *Tiphareth*, Beauty or Mildness, represented by the Divine Name ALVH VDOTh, *Eloah Va-Daath*, and the angelic names, ShNANIM *Shinanim*, (Ps. lxviii. 18), or MLKIM, *Melakim*, kings. Thus by the union of justice and mercy we obtain beauty or clemency, and the second trinity of the Sephiroth is complete. This Sephira, or "Path," or *Numeration*—for by these latter appellations the emanations are sometimes called—together with the fourth, fifth, seventh, eighth, and ninth Sephiroth, is spoken of as ZOIR ANPIN, *Zauir Anpin*, the Lesser Countenance, or Microprosopus. The sixth Sephiroth of which Zauir Anpin is composed, are then called His six members. He is also called MLK, *Melekh*, the King.

The number 7. The seventh Sephira is NTzCh, *Netzach*, or Firmness and Victory, corresponding to the Divine Name IHVH TzBAVTh, *Jehovah Tzahaoth*, the Lord of Armies, and the angelic names ALHIM, *Elohim*, gods, and ThRShIShIM, *Tharshishim*, the brilliant ones (Dan. x. 6).

The number 8. Thence proceeded the feminine passive potency HVD, *Hod*, Splendour, answering to the Divine Name ALHIM TzBAVTh, *Elohim Tzabaoth*, the Gods of Armies, and among the angels to BNI ALHIM, *Beni Elohim*, the Sons of the Gods (Gen. vi. 4).

The number 9. These two produced ISVD, *Yesod*, the Foundation or Basis, represented by AL Chi, *El Chai*, the Mighty Living One, and ShDE, *Shaddai*, and among the angels by AShIM, Aishim, the Flames (Ps. civ.4), yielding the third Trinity of the Sephiroth.

The number 10. From this ninth Sephira came the tenth and last, thus completing the decad of the numbers. It is called MLKVTh, *Malkuth*, the Kingdom, and also the Queen, *Matrona*, the inferior Mother, the Bride of Microprosopus; and ShKINH, *Shekinah*, represented by the Divine Name ADNI, *Adonai*, and among the angelic hosts by the KRVBIM *Kerubim*.

Now, each of these Sephiroth will be to a certain degree androgynous, for it will be feminine or receptive with regard to the Sephira which immediately precedes it in the Sephirotic scale, and masculine or transmissive with regard to the Sephira which immediately follows it. But there is no Sephira anterior to Kether, nor is there a Sephira which succeeds Malkuth. By these remarks it will be understood how Chokmah is a feminine noun, though marking a masculine Sephira. The connecting-link of the Sephiroth is the Ruach, spirit, from Mezla, the hidden influence. . ."

Let me leave Mathers' Introduction for a brief moment in order to dilate on one of the important topics he dealt with.

CONCERNING THE HIERARCHIES

A set of names and ideas which frequently seem to get mixed up and confused, relates to the hierarchies of intelligent beings of the Sephiroth, Signs, Planets and Elements. It will become evident, very early in one's study of the Qabalah and the Tree of Life as given in this book, there is a magical technique for invoking each constituent of these hierarchies. This being the case, it is imperative that one's mind be absolutely clear as to the nature of the hierarchy being dealt with, and where it belongs. For example, the first Sephirah is named Kether, the Crown. Its divine name is Eheieh, meaning I will be. This is the future tense in Hebrew grammar; its Archangel is Metatron, and its Choir of Angels is the Chayoth ha-Qadosh, and its Palace in Assiah is Rashith ha-Gilgaleem. Each one of these hierarchical names refers also to one of the four Qabalistic worlds. The first to ATZILUTH—the Archetypal World. The second to BRIAH—the Creative World. The third to YETZIRAH—the Formative World—and ASSIAH is the World of Action or Manifestation.

These names should certainly be committed to memory. One means of ensuring this is to draw a good copy of the Tree of Life on a full sheet of typing paper, and run off a couple of dozen or more xerox copies. Then each set of correspondences can simply be copied on one of the duplicated Trees, enabling one to see at a glance the associations, inferences, etc.

Now one of the attributions to Kether is Air, primal Air. The element Air has its own hierarchy as follows: The divine Name is given as Shaddai El Chai, its Archangel is Raphael, its Angel is Chassan, the Ruler is Ariel, and the King is Paralda. Actually this set of attributions should belong lower down on the Tree than Kether, undoubtedly in Yesod. But I will deal with that later.

For the time being, however, consider the fact that this hierarchical relation to Air is also attributed to Kether, the Crown. It would be a gross misunderstanding of Qabalistic principles to confuse the individual members of each hierarchy with the other, as is commonly done. **Metatron, the Archangel of Kether, has nothing whatsoever to do with the element Air. Nor has the Archangel Raphael, who rules over the element Air, anything whatsoever to do with Kether**. Much the same is true of the remaining members of the hierarchy. Each one must be considered separately and individually. There must be no confusion. (This is clarified on one of our G.D. tapes).

Take Geburah, another example. It is the 5th Sephirah on the Tree, and to it is referred the planet Mars and the element of Fire (reflected downwards from Chokmah. See the chart which depicts the reflection of the three elements downwards and crosswise on the Tree.) That means, apart from other more complicated features (if one considers them as complications), there are three entirely separate hierarchies. One for Geburah. Another for Mars, and yet a third for Fire. **Each must be kept separate from the other.**

The divine name for Geburah is Elohim Gibor. The Archangel is Kamael, and the Choir of Angels is Seraphim, and its Assiatic Palace is Mars, *Maadim*.

Now the hierarchy for Mars is of course Elohim Gibor, but the Angel is Zamael, the Intelligence is Graphiel, and its Spirit is Bartzabel. These two sets of hierarchical names bear absolutely no relationship with one another. They must be kept in separate watertight compartments in one's brain, so that any one name of any one hierarchy does not leak over and create confusion in the other hierarchy. I repeat and am most emphatic on this score, for even some of the better authorities fall into this booby-trap, which is dug for the unwary. This warning could be reiterated frequently and should be printed on every few pages in the student's own notebooks, so that it serves as an ever present reminder—**keep the hierarchies separate**! One may not say that Mars is Geburah. Mars has its own hierarchy which is **separate** from that of Geburah. We may say that among the **many** attributions given to Geburah, and they are manifold, one of them and only one is Mars. So since the part is not greater than the whole, Mars with its own particular kinds of attributions occupies a lesser space than the category of Geburah in which it is included.

The problem for the novice and the so-called advanced student is that there is another set of attributions to Geburah with another hierarchy altogether. For example in common parlance the student may say Geburah is Fire. **This is not true!** Fire is but another one of the attributions to Geburah in the same category as is Mars. And just as Mars has its own hierarchy so also does the element of Fire. The hierarchy of Fire again must not be confused with the hierarchy of Mars or that of Geburah.

The element of Fire diagonally reflected down the Tree from the Sephirah Chokmah, has its own hierarchy which is totally distinct and separate from the preceding two. For instance its divine name is Yhvh Tzabaoth (which more or less links it to Netzach), while the Archangel is Michael, the King is Aral. (**He must not be confused with the Ruler of Air Ariel, nor with Auriel who is the Archangel of Earth**). The King of Fire is Seraph (not to be confused with the Seraphim who are the Choir of Angels of Geburah), and its Ruler is Djin.

I know of countless numbers of students throughout the years who have never mastered this particular set of attributions and hopelessly confuse one with the other. The result is a hodge-podge of attributions, none of which make sense and then to excuse their confusion and lack of true understanding of semantic principles they begin to talk of "blinds" in the teaching.

There is another point here that must be referred to. For example: Raphael is the Archangel of Air. The Archangel of Tiphareth is also Raphael. The Angel of Mercury is also Raphael.

Now is this the same "person" or are they different beings?

From the practical magical point of view, when invoking any one of these beings, the divine Name used will be quite different and of course the Pentagram or the Hexagram will be different too. The intention is altogether different; this is a significant factor that will differentiate results. The Archangel of Air is invoked by the Air Pentagram. The Archangel of Tiphareth will be invoked by a Hexagram of the Sun, as will the Angel of Mercury by the Hexagram of Hod. That disposes of the practical aspect.

But there is a more metaphysical topic involved, which I think is quite interesting and intriguing. V.H. Frater S.R.M.D. attempted in one of the Enochian papers to deal distantly with this problem, but I do not think the discussion came to a satisfactory conclusion, nor do I think the problem was solved.

The way in which one may look at it is to consider a country where many people have similar names. Smith for example, is one of these found in England, Schmidt in Germany, or Collins or Williams, etc., in Wales, etc. Let us deal with Wales. In a fairly large town in Wales there is going to be a Mr. Williams who is the dairyman. Then there will be Mr. Williams who has the dry-goods store. I knew a Mr. Williams who was a gardener when once, years ago, I lived in St. Briavels on the Welsh border. And there ought to be a Mr. Williams, the groceryman. All are Williams. Are they the same person because they have the same name? Obviously not, though having the same surname, their first or Christian names would be different and so would their vocations.

In much the same way we can distinguish the Archangels and Angels we are talking about. One of them is in the hierarchy of Air - a different kind of profession as it were. Another is in Tiphareth, and the third relates to the planet Mercury. There is no earthly connection between any of these, despite the fact they have the same name. Correspondingly, the divine Names of these three areas is also different. So to call them, or to call upon them, we must know what sphere of action they operate in and act accordingly. They are in effect different "people," different names and use different "tools" as it were.

We will also have to learn to differentiate between the element of Air attributed to Kether, that attributed to Tiphareth, and that attributed to Yesod. The first we can call, merely to provide understandable labels, Celestial Air. To invoke, one should use the divine Name of Kether first before using the hierarchical names belonging to the element of Air. In the case of Tiphareth, we could use the term Divine Air (or even Harmonious Air), using the divine name of Tiphareth first before those of the element of Air. The Air attributed to Yesod could be entitled just Elemental Air, and used with the hierarchical names as given.

The same rationale must be used with the elements of Fire attributed to Chokmah, Geburah and Netzach - Celestial Fire, Divine Fire, and Elemental Fire.

Water - we use rather the same procedure. It is attributed to Binah, Chesed, and Hod - Celestial Water, Divine Water, and Elemental Water, with the same changes in the use of divine names as given above. This procedure will eliminate a great deal of confusion and muddle.

THE SEPHIROTIC HIERARCHIES

KETHER

Divine Name	Archangelic	Angelic Choir
(Atziluth)	(Briah)	(Yetzirah)
Eheieh	Metatron	Chayoth ha-Qadesh

CHOKMAH

Divine Name	Archangelic	Angelic Choir
(Atziluth)	(Briah)	(Yetzirah)
Yah	Raziel	Auphanim

BINAH

Divine Name	Archangelic	Angelic Choir
(Atziluth)	(Briah)	(Yetzirah)
YHVH Elohim	Tzaphqiel	Aralim

CHESED

Divine Name	Archangelic	Angelic Choir
(Atziluth)	(Briah)	(Yetzirah)
El	Tzadqiel	Chashmalim

GEBURAH

Divine Name	Archangelic	Angelic Choir
(Atziluth)	(Briah)	(Yetzirah)
Elohim Gibor	Kamael	Seraphim

TIPHARETH

Divine Name	Archangelic	Angelic Choir
(Atziluth)	(Briah)	(Yetzirah)
YHVH Eloah ve Daath	Raphael	Melekim

NETZACH

Divine Name	Archangelic	Angelic Choir
(Atziluth)	(Briah)	(Yetzirah)
YHVH Tzabaoth	Haniel	Elohim

HOD

Divine Name	Archangelic	Angelic Choir
(Atziluth)	(Briah)	(Yetzirah)
Elohim Tzabaoth	Michael	Beni Elohim

YESOD

Divine Name	Archangelic	Angelic Choir
(Atziluth)	(Briah)	(Yetzirah)
Shaddai El Chai	Gabriel	Kerubim

MALKUTH

Divine Name	Archangelic	Angelic Choir
(Atziluth)	(Briah)	(Yetzirah)
Adonai ha Aretz	Sandalphon	Ashim

PLANETARY HIERARCHIES

One of the characteristics of the Qabalah is that each Sephirah, Planet and Element has its own hierarchy. Each hierarchy must be kept distinct and seperate. The following gives the hierarchies relative to the Planets.

SATURN

Planet	Angel	Intelligence	Spirit
Shabbathai	Cassiel	Agiel	Zazel

JUPITER

Planet	Angel	Intelligence	Spirit
Tzedek	Sachiel	Iophiel	Hismael

MARS

Planet	Angel	Intelligence	Spirit
Madim	Zamael	Graphiel	Bartzabel

SUN

Planet	Angel	Intelligence	Spirit
Shemesh	Michael	Nakhiel	Sorath

VENUS

Planet	Angel	Intelligence	Spirit
Nogah	Hanael	Hagiel	Kedemel

MERCURY

Planet	Angel	Intelligence	Spirit
Kokab	Raphael	Tiriel	Taphthartharath

MOON

Planet	Angel	Intelligence	Spirit
Levanah	Gabriel	Malkah be Tarshisim ve-ad Ruachoth Schechalim	Schad Barschemoth ha-Shartathan

ELEMENTAL HIERARCHIES

EARTH - NORTH

Hebrew	Aretz or Ophir	ארץ עפיר
Divine name	Adonai ha-Aretz	אדני האָרץ
Cardinal point	Tzaphon	צפון
Archangel	Auriel	אוריאל
Angel	Phorlakh	פורלאך
Ruler	Kerub	
King	Ghob	כרוב
Elementals	Gnomes	

AIR - EAST

Hebrew	Ruach	רוח
Divine name	Shaddai	שׁדי אל חי
Cardinal point	Mizrach	מזרח
Archangel	Raphael	רפאל
Angel	Chassan	חשן
Ruler	Ariel	אריאל
King	Paralda	
Elementals	Sylphs	

WATER - WEST

Hebrew	Mayim	מים
Divine name	Elohim Tzabaoth	אלהים צבאות
Cardinal point	Maarab	מערב
Archangel	Gabriel	גבריאל
Angel	Taliahad	טליהד
Ruler	Tharsis	
Queen	Nichsa	תרשים
Elementals	Undines	

VOLUME ONE

FIRE - SOUTH

Hebrew	Asch	אש
Divine name	YHVH	יהוה צבאות
Cardinal point	Darom	דרום
Archangel	Michael	מיכאל
Angel	Aral	אראל
Ruler	Seraph	
King	Djin	
Elementals	Salamanders	

I now continue with the quotations from Mathers Introduction to *The Kaballah Unveiled:*
"I will now add a few more remarks on the qabalistical meaning of the term MThQLA, *Metheqela,* balance. In each of the three trinities or triads of the Sephiroth is a duad of opposite sexes, and uniting intelligence which is the result. In this, the masculine and feminine potencies are regarded as the two scales of the balance, and the uniting Sephira as the beam which joins them. Thus, then, the term balance may be said to symbolize the Triune, Trinity in Unity, and the Unity represented by the central point of the beam. But again, in the Sephiroth there is a triple Trinity, the upper, lower, and middle. Now, these three are represented thus: the Supernal, or highest, by the Crown, Kether; the middle by athe King, and the inferior by the Queen; which will be the greatest trinity. And the earthly correlatives of these will be the Primum Mobile, the Sun and the Moon. Here we at once find alchemical symbolism.

Now in the world the Sephiroth are represented by:

(1) **RAShlTh HGLGLIM,** *Rashith Ha-Galgalim,* **the commencement of the whirling motions, the Primum Mobile**
(2) **MSLVTh,** *Masloth,* **the sphere of the Zodiac.**
(3) **ShBThAI,** *Shabbathai,* **rest, Saturn.**
(4) **TzDQ,** *Tzadeq,* **righteousness, Jupiter**
(5) **MADIM,** *Madim,* **vehement strength, Mars.**
(6) **ShMSh,** *Shemesh, the solar light, the Sun.*
(7) **NVGH,** *Nogah,* **glittering splendour, Venus.**
(8) **KVKB,** *Kokab,* **the stellar light, Mercury.**
(9) **LBNH,** *Levanah,* **the lunar flame, the Moon.**
(10) **ChLM ISVDVTh,** *Cholom Yesodoth,* **the breaker of the foundations, the elements.**

The Sephiroth are further divided into three pillars the right-hand Pillar of Mercy, consisting of the second, fourth, and seventh emanations; the left-hand Pillar or Judgment, consisting of the third, fifth, and eighth; and the middle Pillar of Mildness, consisting of the first, sixth, ninth, and tenth emanations.

In their totality and unity the ten Sephiroth represent the archetypal man, ADM QDMVN, *Adam Kadmon,* the Protogonos. In looking to the Sephiroth constituting the first triad, it is evident that they represent the intellect; and hence this triad is called the intellectual world, OVLM M VShK L, *Olahm Mevshekal.* The second triad corresponds to the moral world, OVLM MVRGSh, *Olahm Morgash.* The third represents power and

41

stability, and is therefore called the material world, OVLM IIMVTBO, *Olahm Ha-Mevetbau*. These three aspects are called the faces, ANPIN, *Anpin*. Thus is the tree of life, OTz ChIIM, Otz Chaiim, formed; the first triad being placed above, the second and third below, in such a manner that the three masculine Sephiroth are on the right, three feminine on the left, whilst the four uniting Sephiroth occupy the center. This is the qabalistical *Tree of Life*, on which all things depend. There is considerable analogy between this and the tree Yggdrasil of the Scandinavians.

I have already remarked that there is one trinity which comprises all the Sephiroth, and that it consists of the Crown, the King, and the Queen. (In some senses this is similar to the Christian Trinity of Father, Son, and Holy Spirit, which in their highest divine nature are symbolized by the first three Sephiroth, Kether, Chokmah, and Binah.) It is the Trinity which created the world, or, in qabalistic language, the universe was born from the union of the crowned King and Queen. But according to the Qabalah, before the complete form of the heavenly man (the ten Sephiroth) was produced, there were certain primordial worlds created, but these could not subsist, as the equilibrium of balance was not yet perfect, and they were convulsed by the unbalanced forces and destroyed. These primordial worlds are called the *kings of ancient time,* and the *kings of Edom who reigned before the monarchs of Israel*. In this sense, Edom is the world of unbalanced force, and Israel is the balanced Sephiroth (Gen. xxxvi. 31). This important fact, that worlds were created and destroyed prior to the present creation, is again and again reiterated in the Zohar.

Now the Sephiroth are also called the World of Emanations, or the Atziluthic World, or archetypal world, OVLM ATzILVTh, *Olahm Atziloth*; and this world gave birth to three other worlds, each containing a repetition of the Sephiroth, but in a descending scale of brightness.

The second world is the Briatic world, OVLM H BRIAH, *Olahm Ha-Briah*, the world of creation, also called KVRSIA, *Khorsia*, the throne. It is an immediate emanation from the world of Atziluth, whose ten Sephiroth are reflected herein, and are consequently more limited, though they are still of the purest nature, and without any admixture of matter.

The third is the Yetziratic world, OVLM HITzIRH, *Olahm Ha-Yetzirah*, or world of Formation and of angels, which proceeds from Briah, and though less refined in substance, is still without matter. It is in this angelic world where those intelligent and incorporeal beings reside who are wrapped in a luminous garment, and who assume a form when they appear unto man.

The fourth is the Assiatic world, OVLM HOShIH, *Olahm Ha-Assiah*, the World of Action, called also the world of shells, OVLM HQLIPVTh, *Olahm Ha-Qliphoth*, which is this world of matter, made up of the grosser elements of the other three. In it is also the abode of the evil spirits which are called "the shells" by the Qabalah, Qliphoth, material shells. The devils are also divided into ten classes, and have suitable habitations. . .

The Demons are the grossest and most deficient of all forms. Their ten degrees answer to the decad of the Sephiroth, but in inverse ratio, as darkness and impurity increase with the descent of each degree. The two first are nothing but absence of visible form and organization. The third is the abode of darkness. Next follow seven Hells occupied by those demons which represent incarnate human vices, and torture those who have given themselves up to such vices in earth-life. Their prince is SMAL, *Samael*, the angel of poison and of death. His wife is the harlot, or woman of whoredom AShTh ZNVNIM, *Isheth Zenunim*; and united they are called the Beast, CHIVA, *Chioa*. Thus the infernal trinity is completed, which is, so to speak, the averse and caricature of the supernal Creative One. Samael is considered to be identical with Satan.

The name of the Deity, which we call Jehovah, is in Hebrew a name of four letters, IHVH; and the true pronunciation of it is known to very few. . ."

VOLUME ONE

TETRAGRAMMATON

This is a Latin word meaning "the four lettered name." This name is a Hebrew name for the traditional God of the Old Testament, Jehovah. In Hebrew, the consonants of the latter name are YHVH - thus Tetragrammaton.

Qabalistically, each letter of Tetragrammaton was attributed to one of the four major primitive elements of the ancients. Y equals Fire. H equals Water. Vau equals Air, and the last H or final Heh equals Earth. So that the Tetragrammaton, or the name of Jehovah represents the four basic elements of life. The Biblical Jehovah was the God who flamed in the fire of the holy ground Moses stood on, thundered in the storms around Mount Horeb and Sinai, drowned the Egyptians and their chariots, and opened up the land with earthquakes to destroy the enemies of Israel. Thus he is depicted as an angry and violent God - which is what the four elements of life are. They can be gentle and easy going, but never lose sight of the fact that they are also violent, dangerous and overwhelming. This is Tetragrammaton.

The Letters of the Name are attributed in various ways to the Tree of Life, always carrying with them the attributions of the basic elements. Even when Y, often called the Father, is sometimes attributed to Kether, the fire of creation is referred to. When H, the Mother, is attributed to Chokmah and Binah, we are considering the fine ethereal waters of the creative levels, the substance in which and from which all the worlds were created. V is sometimes referred to Tiphareth, the Son of Yod and Heh of Tetragrammaton, and is the all-encompassing Air - not the Air that we ordinarily breathe oxygen, nitrogen, carbon dioxide, etc. . .but the vital airs; the pranas without which there is no life.

The final H or Heh is the unredeemed Daughter, the Earth, which is acted upon and formed and influenced by the other three elements of letters of Tetragrammaton. She is the unredeemed Daughter until she becomes receptive to the higher influences - consciously and deliberately - and then she becomes transformed into the Bride of Microprosopus or Vau of Tiphareth who brings harmony and beauty to the heavy enduring burdensome qualities of Earth.

All of these together with a host of similar manifold associations and symbols are subsumed under the heading of Tetragrammaton.

Even Tetragrammaton, the testy senior of the Bible, the ever-angry and punitive Jehovah, needs to be transformed and redeemed by the descent of the holy spirit represented by the letter Shin. (Shin equals 300. Ruach Elohim translates as the Spirit of the Gods equals 300.) When this Shin descends, splitting asunder the old rigid, hide-bound Tetragrammaton, he becomes transformed into the Pentagrammaton YHShVH, the saved, redeemed and illumined Adept who combines heaven and earth, the Cosmos and the Microcosm all at once. We are now returning once more to Mathers and his lengthy introduction to the *Kaballah Unveiled*.

He states: "I myself know some score of different mystical pronunciations of it. The true pronunciation is a most secret arcanum, and is a secret of secrets. He who can rightly pronounce it, causeth heaven and earth to tremble, for it is the name which rusheth through the universe. Therefore when a devout Jew comes upon it in reading the Scripture, he either does not attempt to pronounce it, but instead makes a short pause, or else he substitutes for it the name Adonai, ADNI, Lord. The radical meaning of the word is "to be,"and it is thus, like AHIH, Eheieh, a glyph of existence. It is capable of twelve transpositions, which all convey the meaning of "to be"; it is the only word that will bear so many transpositions without its meaning being altered. They are called the *twelve banners of the mighty name*, and are said by some to rule the twelve signs of the Zodiac. These are the twelve banners: IHVH, IHHV, IVHH, HVHI, HVIH, HHIV, VHHI, VIHH, VHIH, HIHV, HIVH, HHVI. There are three other Tetragrammatic names, which are AHIH, *Eheieh*, existence; ADNI, *Adonai*, Lord; and AGLA *Agla*. This last is not, properly speaking, a word, but is a notariqon of the sentence,

THE COMPLETE GOLDEN DAWN SYSTEM OF MAGIC

AThH GBVR LOVLM ADNI, *Ateh Gebor Le-Olahm Adonai: Thou art mighty for ever, O Lord!* An arbitrary interpretation of Agla is this: A, the one first; A, the one last; G, the Trinity in Unity; L, the completion of the Great Work.

The first thing we notice is that both AHIH and IHVH convey the idea of existence; this is their first analogy. The second is, that in each the letter H comes second and fourth; and the third is that by Gematria AHIH equals IHV without the H (which, as we shall see presently, is the symbol of Malkuth, the tenth Sephira). But now, if they be written one above the others, thus, within the arms of a cross, they read downwards as well as across,

AH	IH
IH	VH

AHIH, IHVH. Now, if we examine the matter qabalistically we shall find the reason of these analogies. For Eheieh, AHIH, is the Vast Countenance, the Ancient One, Macroprosopus, Kether, the first Sephira, the Crown of the Qabalistical Sephirotic greatest Trinity (which consists of the Crown, King, and Queen; or Macroprosopus, Microprosopus and the Bride), *and the Father in the Christian acceptation of the Trinity.*

But IHVH, the Tetragrammaton, as we shall presently see, contains all the Sephiroth with the exception of Kether, and specially signifies the Lesser Countenance, Microprosopus, the King of the qabalistical Sephirotic greater Trinity, and *the Son in His human incarnation, in the Christian interpretation of the Trinity.*

Therefore, as the Son reveals the Father, so does IHVH, *Jehovah,* reveal AHIH, *Eheieh.*

And ADNI is the Queen "by whom alone Tetragrammaton can be grasped," whose exaltation into Binah is found in the Christian assumption of the Virgin.

The Tetragrammaton IHVH is referred to the Sephiroth, thus: the uppermost point of the letter Yod, I, is said to refer to Kether; the letter I itself to Chokmah, the father of Microprosopus; the letter H, or "the supernal He," to Binah and supernal Mother; the letter V to the next six Sephiroth, which are called the six members of Microprosopus (and six is the numerical value of V, the Hebrew Vau); lastly, the letter H, the "inferior He," to Malkuth, the tenth Sephira, the bride of Microprosopus.

Now, there are four secret names referred to the four worlds of Atziloth, Briah, Yetzirah, and Assiah; and again, the Tetragrammaton is said to go forth written in a certain manner in each of these four worlds. The secret name of Atziloth is OB *Aub;* that of Briah is SG *Seg;* that of Yetzirah is MH *Mah;* and that of Assiah is BN *Ben.* (BN, Ben means "son".). . .

These names operate together with the Sephiroth through the "231 gates," as combinations of the alphabet are called; but it would take too much space to go fully into the subject here.

Closely associated with the subject of the letters of the Tetragrammaton is that of the four Kerubim, to which I have already referred in describing the first Sephira. Now it must not be forgotten that these forms in Ezekiel's vision support the throne of the Deity, whereon the Heavenly Man is seated - the Adam Qadmon, the Sephirotic image; and that between the throne and the living creatures is the firmament. Here then we have the four worlds - Atziloth, the deific form; Briah, the throne; Yetzirah, the firmament; Assiah, the Kerubim. Therefore the Kerubim represent the powers of the letters of the Tetragrammaton on the material plane; and the four represent the operation of the four letters in each of the four worlds. Thus, then, the Kerubim are the living forms of the letters, symbolized in the Zodiac by Taurus, Leo, Aquarius, and Scorpio, as I have before remarked.

And the mystery of the earthly and mortal man is after the mystery of the supernal and immortal One; and thus was he created in the image of God upon earth. In the form of the body

44

is Tetragrammaton found. The head is I, the arms and shoulders are like H, the body is V, and the legs are represented by the H final. Therefore, as the outward form of man corresponds to the Tetragrammaton, so does the animating soul correspond to the ten Sephiroth; and as these find their ultimate expression in the trinity of the Crown, the King, and the Queen, so is there a principal triple division of the soul. Thus, then, the first is Neschamah NShMH, which is the highest degree of being, corresponding to the crown (Kether), and representing the highest triad of the Sephiroth, called the intellectual world. The second is Ruach, RVCh, the seat of good and evil, corresponding to Tiphareth, the moral world. And the third is Nephesch, NPSh, the animal life and desires, corresponding to Yesod, and the material and sensuous world. All souls are pre-existent in the world of emanations, and are in their original state androgynous, but when they descend upon earth they become separated into male and female, and inhabit different bodies; if therefore in this mortal life the male half encounters the female half, a strong attachment springs up between them, and hence it is said that in marriage the separated halves are again conjoined; and the hidden forms of the soul are akin to the Kerubim.

But this foregoing triple division of the soul is only applicable to the triple form of the intellectual, moral and material. Let us not lose sight of the great qabalistical idea, that the *trinity is always completed by and finds its realization in the quaternary*; that is, IHV completed and realized in IHVH - the trinity of...

Crown	King	Queen
Father	Son	Spirit
Absolute	Formation	Realization

This is completed by the quaternary of:

Absolute One
Father - Mother
Son
Bride

Macroprosopus - Vast Countenance
Father - Mother
Microprosopus - Lesser Countenance
Malkuth Queen - Bride

Atziluth - Archetypal
Briah - Creative
Yetzirah - Formative
Assiah - Material

And to these four the soul answers in the following four forms: Chiah to Atziluth; Neschamah to Briah; Ruach to Yetzirah; and Nephesch to Assiah.

But Chiah is in the soul the archetypal form analogous to Macroprosopus. Wherefore Neschamah, Ruach, and Nephesch represent as it were by themselves the Tetragrammaton, without Chiah, which is nevertheless symbolized *in the uppermost point of the I, Yod*, of the soul; As Macroprosopus is said to be symbolized by the uppermost point of the I, yod, of IHVH. For *Yod of the Ancient One is hidden and concealed...*

I will now revert to the subject of Arikh Anpin and Zauir Anpin, the Macroprosopus and the Microprosopus, or the Vast and the Lesser Countenances. Macroprosopus is, it will be remembered, the first Sephira, or Crown Kether; Microprosopus is composed of six of the Sephiroth. In Macroprosopus all is light and brilliancy; but Microprosopus only shineth by the reflected splendour of Macroprosopus. The six days of creation correspond to the six forms of Microprosopus. Therefore the symbol of the interlaced triangles, forming the six-pointed star, is called the Sign of the Macrocosm, or of the creation of the greater world, and is consequently analogous to the two Countenances of the Zohar. *The Book of Concealed Mystery* fully discusses the symbolism of Macroprosopus and Microprosopus; therefore it is well, before reading it, to be cognizant of their similarities and differences. The one is AHIH, Eheieh; the other is the V, Vau, of the Tetragrammaton. The first two letters, I and H, Yod and He, are the Father and Mother of Microprosopus, and the H final is his Bride. But in these forms is expressed the equilibrium of Severity and Mercy; Severity being symbolized by the two Hehs, the Mother and the Bride, but especially by the latter. But while the excess of Mercy is not an evil tendency, but rather conveys a certain idea of weakness and want of force, too great an excess of Severity calls forth the executioner of judgment, the evil and oppresive force which is symbolized by Leviathan. Wherefore it is said, behind the shoulders of the Bride the serpent rears his head: of the Bride, but not of the Mother, for she is the Supernal H, and bruises his head. But his head is broken by the waters of the great sea. The sea is Binah, the Supernal H, the Mother. The serpent is the centripetal force, ever seeking to penetrate into Paradise (the Sephiroth), and to tempt the Supernal Eve (the bride), so that in her turn she may tempt the Supernal Adam (Microprosopus).

It is utterly beyond the scope of this Introduction to examine this symbolism thoroughly, especially as it forms the subject of this work; so I will simply refer my reader to the actual text for further elucidation, hoping that by the perusal of this introductory notice he will be enlightened."

To recapitulate some of Mathers writings above let me affirm that once you have studied the Knowledge Lectures and have become familiar with the Hebrew names and terms used, refer to the excerpts from Mathers' Introduction given here. With only a little effort, the Knowledge Lecture names will be seen to have been drawn from the Introduction. And furthermore the study of the Introduction will tend to clarify much of the material in the Knowledge Lectures.

Further amplication can be obtained by reference to the Qabalistic books already mentioned, so that in a very short time - relative to that consumed by the student of a century ago - he should have an intelligent understanding of the Tree of Life which is the backbone of all Qabalistic study.

ON THE LEAST AMOUNT OF WORK ACTUALLY NECESSARY FOR THE STUDIES OF THE FIRST ORDER GRADES

By

G.H. FRATER S.R.M.D.

What is really necessary to this end is to acquire sufficient knowledge clearly to follow the explanations and instructions given in the successive Grades so that the Candidate does not become unduly bewildered in his endeavors to grasp the meaning through ignorance of the technical expressions employed for that purpose.

It is to aid in this comprehension that the so-called "Knowledge Lectures" exist as apart from those termed "Side-Lectures"; these latter, though not necessarily required to be committed to memory, contain important and interesting matter peculiar to each grade.

VOLUME ONE

The "Knowledge Lectures" contained just the amount of carefully sifted out knowledge necessary not only to pass the examination for such and such Grade, but also fairly well to comprehend and follow the Ceremonial Ritual of the Grade itself. Such knowledge then may seem and perhaps is slightly more amplified than 'a bare pass in the examination might demand. But it is to the student's own interest to learn as thoroughly as he can what is given.

Our subject of study is inexhaustible for it is the Universe itself whose Mysteries we seek to fathom by the aid of that Secret System of Correspondences and Formulas, the especial knowledge of our Order the Keys of the Wisdom of all Time. Our Grades therefore form the ladder which aids us to mount towards this end, a ladder in which not one rung is wanting neither is there a Lacune. We appeal to the soul by the secret formulas hidden in our Ceremonies; to the mind by the special studies of the Order, to the body by the Stations and movements in the Temple and to the whole being by the combinations of these.

Now it must be taken into consideration that many of our members, and those very good ones, have but limited time to devote to the work and studies of the Order owing to the exigencies and occupations of their daily life; and this, though at first sight a drawback, is in reality not so much so as it appears, for on the one side our studies are so different from the ordinary business conditions and avocations of existence that it is a fresh interest and repose of the mind to come to them and on the other hand it avoids the excessive nerve strain and consequent want of mental balance, frequently induced by too continuous an application to psychic and occult experiments and practices, whether theoretical or practical. It is surprising how much can be accomplished by a little time regularly given to the study of any subject whatever and in this way the mind does not get so fatigued and tired through close application for too long a period.

Touching as they do a variety of subjects though not so distinct from each other as at first sight they would appear to be; the effect of the Knowledge Lectures is to seem more formidable to tackle than they really are, and to resolutely start on them is more than half the battle gained already. They are far less difficult than they look. Thr first impression usually produced on the Neophyte may be thus expressed Oh! I've got to learn Hebrew, and become a grammatical Hebrew scholar. He is only asked to learn the Hebrew alphabet, that is to say the proper shapes and meanings of its letters together with their numerical values, and in the case of the Ten Sephiroth (or Ten Divine Emanations corresponding to the ten numbers of the decimal scale) and of some names chiefly Divine and Angelic; their exact orthography as well: the which is a very different thing to becoming a critical student of Hebrew. Of course should any Frater or Soror have the time and inclination to make a thorough study of the Hebrew language there is nothing to prevent them so doing, but this is in no sense necessary either to pass the Examinations for the Grades or follow the technicalities of the Rituals. For our object is not to make the Aspirant a critical grammatical Hebrew scholar but gradually a profound Mystic and Magician. The same reasoning applies to Alchemy, Astrology, Egyptology, etc., all of which subjects are touched upon in the various knowledge lectures. It rests with the Aspirant to choose if and how he will apply later the basal knowledge so gained. For it is the science of correspondences he is studying the whole time, whether between the Divine Powers and the Universe, between these and man, or between these again and the different planes and developments in the life of Nature.

The best way to learn the forms of the Hebrew Letters, as well as those of the Astrological characters, etc., is to take from four to seven at a time and copy them repeatedly and as exactly as you can, until you know them: in the case of the Hebrew always putting the number beside the letter, so as to associate the two together in your mind. Remember that the Hebrew letters should be always written broad and strong, the horizontals being thick, and the perpendiculars thin, as in music copying just the contrary of the ordinary Roman letter, and as square as possible.

It may be wondered why the Hebrew Alphabet seems to have been so specially selected, rather than any other. For these reasons: Not necessarily because it is Hebrew; though the circumstance of the Qabalah (which contains so large a part of the ancient Egyptian wisdom) being written in that language, confers a certain special value upon it. And the mysteries of the Qabalah form a most important part of our studies. But the Hebrew unites in itself certain notable peculiarities and qualities expressed in its Alphabet, to a much greater extent than is usually found in other and more familiar alphabets of the European group. For (a) contrary to our practise, it has not a set of numerals which singly or combined express numbers, but each letter itself has a numerical value. When thus employed as numbers or as an initial letter put for the whole word itself, two little dashes are placed above it to shew that it is used in that sense: thus the initial for the name of the Sephira Netzach, for the number 50 etc., (b) It is an entirely consonantal Alphabet. It then results from the combination of (a) and (b) that every word is a number, and conversely again that most numbers are words: which affords a method of comparison between words having the same number and is used in the Qabalah. (In the Hebrew Q does not require a "u" to follow it, and it is pronounced like an accented or "coughed" (very slightly of course) K. (c) Every letter, besides its power has an especial name with a meaning attached to it, thus allying it with a Hieroglyphic Idea, e.g., power M, name Mem, meaning Water, (d) With us each letter has further its Sphere of Mystical Significations so that any important Hebrew word becomes as it were a phrase rather than a word. Besides other developments which unfold themselves later.

The Neophyte should remember that Hebrew is always written from right to left, while in English, French, German, etc., it is just the opposite.

A point that very generally puzzles the Neophyte is the apparent extreme arbitrariness of the Hebrew Orthography, so that to him it appears (though it is not really so) as if in some cases a letter were needlessly put in, and in others erroneously omitted. The following explanation is given to thoroughly clear up this point by giving the reason for this apparent uncertainty but none of these or the foregoing observations are intended to be learned by heart, they are merely given to make difficult points more clear.

Hebrew is a Semitic and not an European language. Now the great distinguishing characteristic of the Semitic group such as Hebrew, Chaldaic, Arabic, Ethiopic, etc., is that the Alphabet consists entirely of consonants; even those letters which appear to have a vowel power, as in the Hebrew not being absolutely what we in European languages know as vowels. Thus is rather a drawing in of the breath like the syllable Ah, than the vowel A is H or EH, or He according to position. Certainly not the vowel E. V is much more than U; Y nearer I, NG, or AA or HAA, something like the neigh of a horse or the bleat of a goat, rather than O.

In *What You Should Know About the Golden Dawn*, I once expressed some criticisms of the general attitudes prevailing in the Order. Of doing just enough work to pass the appropriate examination to be promoted to a higher grade. This really was the curse of the early Order. From the paper, it would appear that Mathers was as responsible for this viewpoint as anyone. On the whole, I have great respect for Mathers for as this book indicates, he was the author with Westcott of most of the Initiatory Rituals, and most of the magical instructions. But in this particular respect he was the inadvertent promoter of this attitude which, in my estimation, brought incalculable harm to the Order, permitted essentially unworthy candidates to be wrongly advanced to higher grades for which they were basically unready.

ELITISM

The U.S.E.S.S. and Falcon Press intend to inaugurate a Golden Dawn Foundation for the preservation not merely of memorabilia of the Order, but to set up a centre where the highest standards of initiation and training may be perpetuated. Throughout its history in modern times, the Order has been prone to many fluctuations in its forward progress. The Foundation's intent is to form a stable background of function and teaching so as to minimize and overcome the degenerative effect of excessive fluctuation in a world where change and disintegration seem to have become the order of the day. The U.S.E.S.S. and Falcon Press stand ready to provide any enquirer with information as to the goals and purposes of this Foundation. You may write to Mr. Christopher S. Hyatt of Falcon Press, 3660 North 3rd Street, Phoenix, Arizona 85012 for further information. It should be stated emphatically that the Center is intended to be **Elitist** in the strictest sense of the term, appealing primarily to those with the highest qualifications and capabilities in all aspects and developments of modern life. The lame, the halt, the effete and inept will not find a favorable environment for their foibles there. For just as there are athletes of the sports and the arts, so are there athletes of the spirit. The first search for excellence and perfection in their chosen field of endeavour and are so recognized, while in the latter there is similarly a search for excellence of technique and perfection of all the vehicles of the Self.

THE IMPORTANCE OF DIVINATION

VOLUME TWO

THE IMPORTANCE OF DIVINATION
TABLE OF CONTENTS

IMPORTANT TABLES AND ILLUSTRATIONS

VOLUME TWO

THE IMPORTANCE OF DIVINATION

DIVINATION

By

V.H. FRATER A.M.A.G.

The study of the different types of divination may seem difficult to understand in an Order which purported to teach methods of spiritual development. Many will no doubt be rather perplexed by this. Divination usually is said to refer exclusively to the low occult arts. Actually, however, so far as the Order is concerned, the principal object for these practical methods is that they stimlulate, as few exercises can, the faculties of imagination, intuition and clairvoyance.

Though certain readings or interpretations to the Geomantic and Tarot symbols may be found in the appropriate parts of this text, these rule of thumb methods do not conduce to the production of an accurate delineation of the spiritual causes behind material events. These interpretations are usual to the beginner in the art, for he requires a foundation of the principal definitions employed upon which his own meditations can build. These textual delineations serve in actual practice only as a base for the working of the inner faculties, provides for them a thrust block, as it were from which they may "kick-off." In short, the effort to divine by these methods calls into operation the intuitive and imaginative faculties to a very large extent. Everyone without exception has this faculty of divining in some degree, varying only in his ability to make it manifest. In most people it is wholly dormant.

Again, while divination as an artificial process may be wholly unnecessary and a hindrance to the refined perceptions of a fully developed Adept who requires no such convention to ascertain whence a thing comes and whither it is going, yet these aids and stimuli have their proper place for the Neophyte. For those in training they are not only legitimate but useful and necessary.

It may be interesting for the reader to attempt to acquire intuitive knowledge on any matter without the divinatory aids first, and it will be seen how extremely difficult it is to get started, to pick upon any one fact or incident which shall act as a prompt or a start of the interior mechanism. Having failed in this way, let him see how much further he really may go by the judicious and sensible use of one of the Order methods. There is no doubt that the opening of the mind to an intuitive perception is considerably aided by these methods. And this is particularly true with regard to the rather lengthy Tarot method which was given to the initiate while engaged in the fulfilment of his Adeptus Minor curriculum. Like all magical techniques, divination is open to abuse. This fact, however, that abuse is possible does not,

1

as again and again must be reiterated, condemn the abused technique. The application of common sense to the magical art is as necessary as it is to all else.

Originally, Astrology was taught as part of the regular routine. All instruction on this subject seems now to have been thoroughly extirpated from the Order papers. In this particular instance, the omission is just as well. Recent years have seen a great deal of meticulous attention paid to this study by sincere and honest researchers, and many first rate books have been published explaining its intricacies. All that the Order demands of the Adeptus Minor is that he should understand the underlying principles of this science and be able to draw up a map showing the position of Planets and Signs preparatory to certain operations requiring the invocation of planetary and zodiacal forces.

So far as the general topic of divination is concerned, the Outer Order had very little to say. The formal teaching of Astrology was abandoned because, as stated above, the market was now replete with many fine works on the subject, and thus there was really no need to teach what was readily available.

The Tarot technique that it recommended was the Celtic method, a ten card layout popularized by A. E. Waite in his *Pictorial Key to the Tarot* from which later writers have drawn extensively. The method is very simple and direct; thus its advantage to the student in the Outer Order. It had however one major disadvantage. There was no way to determine whether any one particular card in the layout was well aspected or otherwise. Under these circumstances, the novice diviner would be most likely to pick out the most favorable interpretation to suit his fancy. The Golden Dawn method, as taught in the Inner Order, was a horse of another color, having a superb method of aspecting each card to be read.

The Celtic or Gypsy method, as it is called in the Leigh Gardner papers, has been made useful by resort to a simple device. As one shuffles the pack in order to infiltrate it with one's own magnetism or aura, it is a good idea to drop a card periodically. When inserting it back into the deck, make sure it is replaced upside down. Or, half the number of cards in a deck may be deliberately pulled out at random, turned upside down and then inserted back into the pack. Then shuffle very thoroughly to make sure they are randomly well distributed.

The notion involved here is that the upside down position provides the basis for the negative reading of some of the cards as they turn up in the divination. In this manner it is likely to answer more accurately to the facts in the case, yielding of course a more pragmatic reading.

The more complete Order method of Divination will be given later in this series. The Gypsy method is described solely for the purpose of letting the student experiment with a simple method to develop some expertise before he begins to handle the more complex Order method of Tarot reading.

The other method was Geomancy, divination by earth. A complete treatise was given to the Practicus - that is in the Outer Order of the Golden Dawn. Years after the Revolt which all but annihilated the Order, McGregor Mathers and Brodie Innes reconstituted one of the Temples in the North of England (from which it spread even to the United States) and named it the A.O. an abbreviation for the Alpha and Omega. It was the direct continuation of the Golden Dawn under the new name. It continued to use the instruction papers originally written for the Golden Dawn, but some new ones were added. One of these was a paper on Geomancy. From it I have extrapolated some notes of significant material, and added it to the basic text. Together they form a splendid piece of instructional material on the subject.

VOLUME TWO

FUNDAMENTALS OF TAROT, GEOMANCY AND ASTROLOGY

Fuller discussions of the Tarot system, Geomancy and Astrology to some extent will be found in later sections of this work. For the time being however and for the benefit of the new student to this subject matter it has been decided to give a relatively brief survey of these fields, so that when he comes to the more complex material later he will be to some extent prepared.

THE TAROT

By

STUART R. KAPLAN

"There exist today several fifteenth-century Visconti-Sforza *tarocchi* decks which comprise the earliest known tarot cards. The reproduction in 1975 of the most complete of these packs - the Pierpont Morgan-Bergamo *tarocchi* deck whose original cards are divided between the Pierpont Morgan Library, New York, and the Accademia Carrara and Colleoni family, Bergamo, Italy - is an important event for tarot collectors and researchers of art history.

Italy holds the honor of having produced several of the earliest known *tarocchi* packs that contain the mystical and allegorical trump cards. Throughout five centuries the provocative symbolism of the twenty-two Major Arcana cards has continued to intrigue art historians, artists and occultists. For over five hundred years card designers and artists have faithfullly preserved the same dominant symbolism of the Major Arcana cards while often adding their personal interpretations in the form of slight modifications to the designs based upon the fashions, events and important topics of the day. There exist in leading museums, libraries and private collections many hundreds of such modified tarot designs, the work of such artists as the fifteenth-century genius Bonifacio Bembo, modern painters such as Salvador Dali and Larry Rivers, and many lesser known but talented artists such as Pamela Coleman Smith (Rider-Waite pack), Lady Frieda Harris (Crowley *Thoth* cards), Fergus Hall (James Bond 007 tarot cards), David Palladini (Aquarian tarot) and Domenico Balbi (Balbi pack).

The development of tarot symbolism during the last five centuries, beginning with the earliest known Italian *tarocchi* cards, is an intriguing story.

TERMINOLOGY

The term *trionfi* was used in Italy in the fifteenth century to describe the twenty-two Major Arcana cards. The term *tarocchi* subsequently came into usage in Italy in the early sixteenth century, first referring to the twenty-two Major Arcana cards, and thereafter to the complete seventy-eight-card deck, consisting of the twenty-two Major Arcana and fifty-six Minor Arcana or suit cards. The words *tarocchi* and *tarocco* are often used interchangeably, although *tarocchi* is actually the plural of *tarocco*. Tarot, the French derivative of *tarocchi*, has come into widespread usage in the English language. In pronouncing the word tarot, the final t is silent.

MacGregor Mathers, writing in 1888, describes several anagrams derived from the word taro:

Tora - law (Hebrew)
Troa - gate (Hebrew)
Rota - wheel (Latin)
Orat - it speaks, argues or entreats (Latin)
Taor or Taur - Egyptian goddess of darkness
Ator or Athor - Egyptian Hathor goddess of joy.

The term *trumps* is derived from the Latin *triumphi.* The twenty-two trump cards, also known as the Major Arcana or Greater Arcana cards, each contain a symbolic or allegorical picture. *Arcana* is a Latin word meaning mysterious or secret; the Italian word arcana, derived from the Latin, has the same meaning. The trumps are also known as *atouts* in French and *atutti* in Italian. Atouts denote cards of higher value than the rest, that is, a tous or a tutti, superior to all others.

Some researchers believe the word tarot derives from the term *tarotee*, the name applied to the design on the back of early cards - a multiple series of crisscrossing solid or dotted lines in varying widths. However, it is likely that the word tarotee itself was derived from *tarocchi* since the use of the word *tarocchi* predates that of the word tarotee. In the statutes of the guild of card makers of Paris in the year 1594 the cartiers called themselves *tarotiers*, another form of the word tarot.

The origins of playing cards - both the twenty-two Major Arcana and the fifty-six suited cards - remain obscure. An early pack of suited cards - perhaps the earliest extant deck - is the hand-painted German "Hunting" pack of Stuttgart, which dates from about 1420-1430 and contains no trumps. These cards depict a hunting series with dogs, stags, ducks and falcons for suit signs. The earliest Visconti-Sforza *tarocchi* cards also date from this period. The following are some of the popular theories advanced during the past several centuries regarding the possible origin of *tarocchi* cards.

PREHISTORIC MAN AND ORAL CULTURES

Prior to recorded history, prehistoric man developed various systems of oral culture and tradition based upon a subtle knowledge of astronomy and calendric counters. It is generally believed that early man carefully observed the sidereal phases of the day, month and year, and the changing positions of the planets. These were astronomical events he could easily study and he recorded these events by calendric counters such as markings on a stretched piece of animal hide, engravings or scratchings on a bone, and notches on a tree branch. Important cultural events were eventually expressed in metaphorical and allegorical forms as myths, legends and fables, which were verbally transmitted from generation to generation over periods of time extending many thousands and even tens of thousands of years.

Some fragments of these early oral traditions survived into recorded time in the form of popular myths and beliefs. For example, the devil is an antlered figure associated with sorcery and evil, and the hermit is a hooded figure holding a candle and representing the winter solstice. Both these figures are found in the Major Arcana of the tarot pack. Many of the pictorial images on the Major Arcana cards have been distorted by time and the ignorance of their interpreters. Thus, most tarot pictures as popularized during the past five hundred years are unrecognizable in terms of early myths and oral culture. Literal interpretations of many early myths are the basis of numerous superstitions and ceremonies practiced today by religious groups, fraternal orders, secret societies and followers of the occult.

Some scholars including Arthur Corwin, who has been researching the subject since the 1960's, view the allegorical symbolism of tarot cards as pictorial metaphors that express the preoccupation of early man with the task of timekeeping. The calendar was an important point of reference to early man. He kept accurate records of the celestial changes that occurred on a daily, monthly and annual basis. He observed the precession of the equinox, the astronomical motions of the stars and planets, and other repetitive events. The calendar was used as a means of survival, including planning for winter food storage, preparing necessary shelter, communicating on a daily basis with other human beings and recording the length of time required for birth. .

A GYPSY METHOD OF TAROT DIVINATION

This mode of Tarot Divination is the most suitable for obtaining rapidily an answer to a definite question.

The Diviner selects a card to represent the person or matter about which he enquires. This card is called the Significator, and should he wish to ascertain something in connection with himself, he takes the one which corresponds to his personal description.

> **A King represents a man of 40 years and upwards.**
> **A Knight represents any male under that age.**
> **A Queen a woman of 40 years and upwards.**
> **A Knave a young man or woman.**

The Four Court Cards:

> **Wands represent very fair people with yellow or auburn hair, fair complexion, blue eyes.**
> **Cups have light brown or dull hair with grey or blue eyes.**
> **Swords have hazel or grey eyes, and dark brown hair and dull complexions.**
> **Pentacles have very dark brown or black hair, dark eyes and sallow or swarthy complexions.**

You can be guided on occasion by the known temperament of a person. One who is exceedingly dark may be energetic and would be better represented by a Sword card than a Pentacle. On the other hand a very fair subject who is indolent and lethargic should be referred to Cups in place of Wands. If it is a matter about which an enquiry is to be made, the Significator should be a Trump or small card which bears some relationship to the matter.

Suppose that the question is "Will a lawsuit be necessary?" In this case, take the Trump card "J ustice" as the significator since it has reference to legal matters. But if the question is "Shall 1 be successful in my lawsuit?" one of the Court Cards representing yourself should be selected. Subsequently consecutive divinations can be performed to ascertain the course of the process itself, and its result to each of the parties concerned.

Having selected the Significator, place it on the table face upwards, then shuffle well and thoroughly the rest of the cards, cutting three times after each shuffle. Lastly, keeping the face of the cards downwards, turn up the top or front card of the pack and cross the significator with it, and say:

1. This card covers him.

This card gives the influence which is affecting the person or matter of the enquiry generally, the atmosphere in which the ether current moves. Turn up the second card and say:

2. This crosses him.

It shows the nature of the obstacles in the matter. If this is a favorable card, the opposing forces will not be serious, or it may indicate that something good in itself will be productive of good in this particular connection. Turn up the third card and say:

3. This crowns him.

It represents first, the Querent's aims or ideals in the matter. And second, the best that can be achieved under the circumstances but that which has not yet been made actuality. Turn up the fourth card, place it below the Significator, and say:

4. This is beneath him.

It shows the foundation or basis of the matter, that which has already passed into actuality and which the Significator has made his own. Turn up the fifth card and say:

5. This is behind him.

It gives the influence that has just past or is passing away. If the Significator is a Trump card or a card that cannot be said to face either way, the diviner must decide beforehand which side of the Significator he will take as facing. Usually this fifth card is placed on the right hand side of the Significator, as it will be found that most of the court cards are looking towards the left hand. Anyhow, if you decide to always adopt the plan it will be found satisfactory - only make a rule always to do so. Turn up the sixth card, place it on the side that the Significator is facing and say:

6. This is before him.

It shows the influence that is coming into action and will operate in the near future.

The next four cards are turned up in succession and placed in a line by the side of the others which are in the form of a cross.

7. This is himself.

This signifies the person himself or else the thing enquired about, and shows its position or attitude in the matter.

8. The eighth card represent his House.

This is his environment, and the tendencies at work there which have an effect on the matter - for instance, his position in life, the influence of immediate friends and so forth.

9. The ninth card gives his hopes and fears in matter.

10. The tenth card the final result.

It is the culmination which is brought about by the influence shown by the other cards that have been turned up in the divination.

VOLUME TWO

The operation is now complete. If in any divination the tenth card should be a court card it shows that the subject of the divination falls ultimately into the hands of a person represented by the court card and its end depends mainly on him. In this case, it is possible to have a fresh divination taking the court card as the Significator to discover what is the nature of his influence in the matter, and to what issue he will bring it.

Great facility may be obtained by this method in a short time, allowance being made for the gifts of the operator, that is to say his faculty of insight, latent or developed, and besides which it is free from all complications.

Upon looking up Waite's *Pictorial Key to the Tarot*, I find that a good deal of the above is extrapolated almost verbatim from that book. However a great deal of important information about this method is presented in Eden Gray's book *A Complete Guide to the Tarot*.

NOTES ON THE TAROT

By

G.H. FRATER S.R.M.D.

(N.B. This paper was lent me some years ago by Mr. Stuart Kaplan of U.S. Games Systems, Inc. This is to acknowledge my gratitude. I.R.)

In the Tree of Life in the Tarot, each path forms the connecting link between two of the Sephiroth. The King and the Queen are the correlations of the ABBA and the AIMA in that suit; the Knight or Prince answers to Microprosopus, and the Page or Princess which was anciently a female figure, is referred to the Bride, Kallah or Malkah.

Combining, then, the material attributions of the Sephiroth and the Path, it results that:

0.   Fool - The Crown of Wisdom, the Primum Mobile acting through the Air on the Zodiac.

1.   The Juggler - The Crown of Understanding, the beginning of material production, the Primum Mobile acting through the Philosophic Mercury on Saturn.

2.   High Priestess - The Crown of Beauty, the beginning of Sovereignty and Beauty, the Primum Mobile acting through the Moon on the Sun.

3.   Empress - The Wisdom of Understanding, the Union of the powers of Origination and Production; the Sphere of the Zodiac acting through Venus upon Saturn.

4.   Emperor - The Wisdom of Sovereignty and Beauty, and the originator of them; the Sphere of the Zodiac acting through Aries upon the Sun, and initiating Spring.

5.   Hierophant - The Wisdom and fountain of Mercy, the Sphere of the Zodiac acting through Taurus upon Jupiter.

6.   The Lovers - The Understanding of Beauty and Production of Beauty and Sovereignty. Saturn acting through Gemini upon Sol.

7.   Chariot - Understanding acting upon Severity. Saturn acting through Cancer upon Mars.

8. Strength - Fortitude. Mercy tempering Severity. The Glory of Strength. Jupiter acting through Leo upon Mars.

9. Hermit - The Mercy of Beauty, the Magnificence of Sovereignty, Jupiter acting through Virgo upon Sol.

10. Wheel of Fortune - The Mercy and Magnificence of Victory. Jupiter acting through Jupiter direct upon Venus.

11. Justice - The Severity of Beauty and Sovereignty. Mars acting through Libra upon Sol.

12. The Hanged Man-The Severity of Splendour. Execution of Judgment. Mars acting through Water upon Mercury.

13. Death - The Sovereignty and result of Victory. Sol acting through Scorpio upon Venus, or Osiris under the destroying power of Typhon afflicting Isis.

14. Temperance - The Beauty of a firm Basis. The Sovereignty of Fundamental Power. Sol acting through Sagittarius upon Luna.

15. The Devil - The Sovereignty and Beauty of Material (and therefore false) splendor. Sol acting through Capricorn on Mercury.

16. The Tower - The Victory over Splendour. Venus acting through Mars upon Mercury. Avenging force.

17. The Star - The Victory of Fundamental Strength. Venus acting through Aquarius upon Luna. Hope.

18. Moon - The Victory of the Material. Venus acting through Pisces upon the Cosmic Elements, deceptive effect of the apparent power of Material Forces.

19. Sun - The Splendour of the Material World. Mercury acting through the Sun upon the Moon.

20. Judgement - The Splendour of the Spiritual World. Mercury acting through Fire upon the Cosmic Elements.

21. Universe - The Foundation of the Cosmic Elements and of the Material World. Luna acting through Saturn upon the Elements.

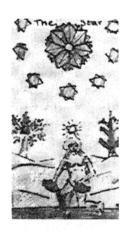

VOLUME TWO

TAROT TRUMPS

The following description of the Arcana Major are taken primarily from the grade rituals of the Order and so are written by Mcgregor Mathers. The descriptions of the keys to Lamed and Mem are taken from the Adeptus Major Ritual - to be found in that section of this book dealing with the initiatory rituals, which bears all the marks of having been written at a later date, by Waite.

The remainder are brief improvisations adapted from several sources mostly to fill in the gaps in the knowledge lectures and rituals. Very little about the Tarot was communicated in the outer Order, the really significant material being given after the Adeptus Minor grade was reached. Even so, there are many lacunae there, which should be filled in and supplemented by additional reading and meditation.

From my present point of view, there are only three or four major works which the student should consult in this area-apart from the basic book by Waite, *The Pictorial Key to the Tarot*, which gives his verbose description of the cards and black and white reproductions of his own deck. There is Aleister Crowley's *Book of Thoth* (Weiser, N.Y.) which is probably the most profound of them all and should be number one on the reading list. Paul Case's *The Tarot, the Key to the Mysteries of the Ages,* is the next one, giving a good description of the cards which probably approaches nearest of all to the Order point of view. Which is as it should be, because once he was a member of the American branch of the Order. Finally, there is the *Encyclopedia of the Tarot* by Stuart R. Kaplan (Copyright by U.S. Games Systems, 1978). This is probably the most complete description of extant packs with history and reproductions of some cards of some packs. These four books with the Order material should be all that the average good student should need.

The Trumps have already, on a previous page, been numbered and briefly described.

21st KEY-UNIVERSE

Within the oval formed of the 72 circles, is a female form, nude save for a scarf that floats around her. She is crowned with the Lunar Crescent of Isis and holds in her hands, two wands. Her legs form a cross. She is the Bride of the Apocalypse, the Kabbalistic Queen of the Canticles, the Egyptian Isis or Great Feminine Kerubic Angel Sandalphon on the left hand of the Mercy Seat of the Ark.

The wands are the directing forces of the positive and negative currents. The Seven Pointed Heptagram or Star alludes to the Seven Palaces of Assiah; the crossed legs to the symbol of the Four Letters of the Name.

The surmounting crescent receives alike the influences of Geburah and Gedulah. She is the synthesis of the 32nd Path, uniting Malkuth to Yesod.

The oval of the 72 smaller circles refers to the Schem ha-mephorasch, or Seventy-two fold Name of the Deity. The twelve large circles form the Zodiac. At the angles are the Four Kerubim which are the vivified powers of the Name Yod He Vau He operating in the Elements, through which you have just symbolically passed in the preceding Ceremony.

The Fan, Lamp, Cup and Salt represent the four Elements themselves whose inhabitants are the Sylphs, Salamanders, Undines and Gnomes.

The magical title of this trump is The Great One of the Night of Time.

20th KEY-JUDGMENT

Before you upon the altar is the Twentieth Key of the Tarot, which symbolically represents these ideas. To the uninitiated eye it apparently represents The Last Judgment with an angel blowing a trumpet and the dead rising from their tombs - but its meaning is far more occult and recondite than this, for it is a glyph of the powers of Fire.

The Angel encircled by the rainbow, whence leap corruscations of Fire, and crowned with the Sun, represents Michael, the Great Archangel, the Ruler of Solar Fire.

The Serpents which leap in the rainbow are symbols of the Fiery Seraphim. The Trumpet represents the influence of the Spirit descending from Binah, while the Banner with the Cross refers to the Four Rivers of Paradise and the Letters of the Holy Name.

He is also Axieros, the first of the Samothracian Kabiri, as well as Zeus and Osiris.

The left hand figure below, rising from the Earth is Samael, the Ruler of Volcanic Fire. He is also Axiokersos, the Second Kabir, Pluto and Typhon.

The right hand figure below is Anael, the Ruler of Astral Light. She is also Axiokersa, the Third Kabir, Ceres, and Persephone, Isis, and Nephthys. She is, therefore, represented in duplicate form, and rising from the waters. Around both of these figures dart flashes of Lightening.

The three principle figures form the Fire Triangle, and further represent Fire operating in the other Three Elements of Earth, Air, and Water.

The central lower figure with his back turned, and his arms in the sign of the Two equals Nine, is Arel, the Ruler of latent heat. He is rising from the Earth as if to receive the properties of the other three. He is also Kasimillos, the Candidate in the Samothracian Mysteries, and the Horus of Egypt. He rises from the rock-hewn cubical Tomb and he also alludes to the Candidate who traverses the Path of Fire. The three lower figures represent the letter Shin, to which Fire is especially referred. The seven Hebrew Yods allude to the Sephiroth operating in each of the Planets and to the Schem-hamphoresch.

The magical title is The Spirit of the Primal Fire.

19th KEY-THE SUN

Before you upon the Altar is the Nineteenth Key of Tarot which symbolically resumes these ideas. The Sun has twelve principal rays which represent the Twelve Signs of the Zodiac. They are alternately waved and salient as symbolising the alternation of the masculine and feminine natures. These again are subdivided into 36 Decanates or sets of ten degrees in the Zodiac, and these again into 72, typifying the 72 quinances or sets of five, and the 72-fold name of Schem ha-mephorasch. Thus the Sun embraces the whole creation in its rays.

The seven Hebrew Yods on each side, falling through the air, refer to the Solar influence descending. The Wall is the Circle of the Zodiac, and the stones are its various degrees and divisions.

The two children standing respectively on the Water and Earth represent the generating influence of both, brought into action by the rays of the Sun. They are the two inferior and passive Elements, as the Sun and Air above them are the superior and active Elements of Fire and Air. Furthermore, these two children resemble the sign Gemini which unites the Earthy Sign of Taurus with the Watery Sign Cancer, and this sign was, by the Greeks and Romans, referred to Apollo and the Sun.

The magical title is Lord of the Fire of the World.

18th KEY-THE MOON

Before you upon the Altar is the 18th Key of Tarot which symbolically resumes ideas. It represents the Moon with four Hebrew Yods like drops of dew falling, two Dogs, two Towers, a winding Path leading to the Horizon, and in the foreground, Water with a Crayfish crawling through it to the land. The Moon is in its increase on the side of Mercy, Gedulah, and from it proceed sixteen principle and sixteen secondary rays, which make 32, the number of the Paths of Yetzirah. She is the Moon at the feet of the Woman of Revelations, ruling equally over the cold and moist natures and the passive elements of Earth and Water. It is to be noted that the symbol of the Sign is formed of two lunar crescents bound together. It thus shows the lunar nature of the Sign. The Dogs are the Jackals of the Egyptian Anubis, guarding the Gates of the East and of the West, shown by the two Towers between which lies the Path of all the heavenly bodies ever rising in the East and setting in the West. The Crayfish is the Sign Cancer and was anciently the Scarabeus or Khephera, the emblem of the Sun below the Horizon as he ever is when the Moon is increasing above. Also, when the Sun is in the Sign Pisces the Moon will be well in her increase in Cancer as shown by the Cray-fish emblem.

The Moon has the magical title of Ruler of Flux and Reflux, Child of the Sons of the Mighty.

17th KEY-THE STAR

Before you on the Altar is the 17th Key of the Tarot which symbolically resumes these ideas.

The large Star in the center of the Heavens has seven principal and fourteen secondary rays and this represents the Heptad multiplied by the Triad. This yields 21 - the Number of the Divine Name Eheieh which, as you already know, is attached to Kether.

In the Egyptian sense, it is Sirius, the Dog-Star, the Star of Isis-Sothis. Around it are the Stars of the Seven Planets each with its seven-fold counter-changed operation.

The nude female figure with the Star of the Heptagram on her brow is the synthesis of Isis, of Nephthys, and of Hathor. She also represents the planet Venus through whose sphere the influence of Chesed descends. She is Aima, Binah, Tebunah, the Great Supernal Mother-Aima Elohim, pouring upon the Earth the Waters of Creation which unite and form a River at her feet, the River going forth from the Supernal Eden which floweth and faileth not.

Note well, that in this Key she is completely unveiled while in the 21st Key she is only partially so.

The two Urns contain the influences from Chokmah and Binah. On the right springs the Tree of Life, and on the left the Tree of Knowledge of Good and of Evil whereon the Bird of Hermes alights, and therefore does this Key represent the restored World, after the formless and the Void and the Darkness, the New Adam the countenance of the Man which falls in the sign Aquarius. And therefore doth the astronomical ripple of this sign represent, as it were, Waves of Water - the ripples of that River going forth out of Eden - but, therefore also, is it justly attributed to Air and not unto Water because it is the Firmament dividing and containing the Waters.

The magical motto of this Key is Daughter of the Firmament, Dweller between the Waters.

16th KEY-BLASTED TOWER

Before you on the Altar is the 16th Key of Tarot, which symbolically resumes these ideas. It represents a Tower struck by a Lightening Flash proceeding from a rayed circle and terminating in a triangle. It is the Tower of Babel struck by the Fire from Heaven. It is to be noted that the triangle at the end of the flash, issuing from the circle, forms exactly the astronomical symbol of Mars.

It is the Power of the Triad rushing down and destroying the Columns of Darkness. Three holes are rent in the walls, symbolising the establishment of the Triad therein and the Crown at the summit of the Tower is falling, as the Crowns of the Kings of Edom fell, who are also symbolised by the men falling headlong. On the right hand side of the Tower is Light and the representation of the Tree of Life by ten circles thus disposed.

On the left hand side is Darkness and eleven circles symbolising the Qlippoth. Lord of the Hosts of the Mighty is its magical name.

15th KEY-DEVIL

The 15th Key of the Tarot represents a goat-headed satyr-like Demon whose legs are hairy - his feet and claws standing upon a Cubical Altar. He has heavy bat-like wings. In his left hand, which points downwards, he holds a lighted torch, and in his right, which is elevated, a horn of water. The left hand points downwards to show that it is the infernal and burning, not the celestial and life-giving flame which is kindled in his torch - just as when the Sun is in Capricornus, to which cold and earthy Sign this Key corresponds, solar Light is at its weakest and the natures of cold and moisture triumph over heat and dryness. The cubical Altar presents the Universe - right and left of it, bound thereto by a cord attached to a circle which typifies the center of the Earth, are two smaller demons, one male and one female. They hold a cord in their hands. The whole figure shows the gross generative powers of nature on the material plane, and is analogous to the Pan of the Greeks and the Egyptian God of Mendes (the symbol of Khem). In certain aspects, the Key represents the brutal forces of nature, which to the unbelieving man only obscures and does not reflect the luminous Countenance of God. It also alludes to the sexual powers of natural generation. Thus therefore the Key fitly balances the symbol of Death on the other side of the Tree of Life. On the smaller demons, one points downwards and one upwards, answering to the positions of the hands of the central figures.

Beneath his feet are Pentagrams on which he tramples (whence comes their title of Wizard's foot) and his head is covered with the evil and reversed Pentagram. and his hands bear the torch and horn - the symbols of Fire and Water, so does his form unite the Earth in his hairy and bestial aspect, and the Air in his bat-like wings. Thus he represents the gross and materialized Elemental Forces of Nature; and the whole would be an evil symbol, were it not for the Pentagram of Light above his head which regulates and guides his movements. He is the eternal renewer of all the changing forms of Creation in conformity with the Law of The All-Powerful One (Blessed be He) which controlling Law is typified by the controlling Pentagram of Light surmounting the whole. This Key is an emblem of tremendous force; many and universal are its mysteries.

The magical title of this Key is Lord of the Gates of Matter, Child of the Forces of Time.

14th KEY-TEMPERANCE

This drawing represents the more ancient form of the 14th Key of Tarot, for which the later and more usual form of Temperance was soon substituted, as better representing the natural symbolism of the Path Sagittarius. The earlier figure was considered not so much a representation of this Path alone, as the synthesis of that and the others conjoined. The later figure, therefore, is better adapted to the more restricted meaning. The more ancient forms shows a female figure crowned with the crown of five rays, symbolising the Five Principles of Nature, the concealed Spirit and the Four Elements of Earth, Air, Water and Fire. About her head is a halo of light. On her breast is the Sun of Tiphareth. The Five-rayed Crown further alludes to the Five Sephiroth Kether, Chokmah, Binah, Chesed and Geburah. Chained to her waist are a Lion and an Eagle, between which is a large cauldron whence arise steam and smoke. The Lion represents the Fire in Netzach - the Blood of the Lion, and the Eagle represents the Water in Hod, the Gluten of the Eagle whose reconcilement is made by the Air in Yesod, uniting with the volatilised Water arising from the cauldron through the influence of the Fire beneath it. The chains which link the Lion and the Eagle to her waist, are symbolic of the Paths of Scorpio and Capricornus as shown by the Scorpion and the Goat in the background. In her right hand, she bears the Torch of Solar Fire elevating and volatilising the Water in Hod by the fiery influence of Geburah, while with her left hand, she pours from a vase the Waters of Chesed to temper and calm the Fires of Netzach. This latter form is the usual figure of Temperance, symbolising in a more restricted form than the preceding, the peculiar properties of this Path. It represents an Angel with the Solar emblem of Tiphareth on her brow, and wings of the aerial and volatilising nature, pouring together the fluidic fire and the fiery water thus combining, harmonising and tempering those opposing elements.

One foot rests on dry and volcanic land, in the background of which is a volcano whence issues an eruption. The other foot is in the water by whose border springs fresh vegetation, contrasting strongly with the arid and dry nature of the distant land. On her breast is a square, the emblem of rectitude. The whole figure is a representation of that straight and narrow way of which it is said, "few there be that find it" which alone leads to the higher and glorified life. For to pursue that steady and tranquil mean between two opposing forces, is indeed difficult, and many are the temptations to turn aside either to the right or to the left - wherein, remember, are but to be found the menacing symbols of Death and the Devil.

The magical title is Daughter of the Reconcilers, the Bringer Forth of Life.

13th KEY-DEATH

The 13th Key of Tarot represents a figure of a Skeleton, upon which some portions of flesh still remain. In a field he is reaping off with Scythe of Death the fresh vegetation which springs from the corrupting bodies buried therein - fragments of which, such as hands, heads and feet appear above the soil. One of the heads wears a kingly crown; another is apparently that of a person of little note, showing that Death is the equaliser of all conditions. The five extremities, the head, hands and feet, allude to the powers of the number five, the Letter He, the Pentagram - the concealed Spirit of Life and the Four Elements - the originator of all living form. The Sign of Scorpio especially alludes to stagnant and foetid water - that property of the moist nature which initiates putrefaction and decay. The eternal change from life into death through death into life, is symbolised by the grass which springs from and is nourished by putrifying and corrupting carcasses; the herbiage, in its turn affords food to animals and man, which again when dead, nourisheth vegetable life and bring to growth and perfection the living herbiage. This is further shown by the figure itself putrifying and decaying as it reaps the grass of the field. "As for man, his days are as grass, as a flower of the field, so he flourisheth." The top of the scythe forms the Tau Cross of Life, showing that what destroys also renews.

The whole is a representation of the eternal transmutation of the life of nature, which reforms all things into fresh images and similitudes. This symbol represents the corrosive and destructive action of the infernal Fire as opposed to the Celestial - the Dragon of the Waters, the Typhon of the Egyptians, the Slayer of Osiris - which later yet rises again in Horus. The Scorpion, Serpent of Evil, delineated before the figure of Death in the more ancient form of the Key refers to the mixed and transforming, therefore deceptive, nature of this emblem. Behind him, is the symbol of the Nameless One, representing the Seed and its germ, not yet differentiated into Life, therefore incapable of definition. The Scorpion is the emblem of ruthless destruction; the Snake is the mixed and deceptive nature, serving alike for good and evil; the Eagle is the higher and Divine Nature, yet to be found herein, the Alchemical Eagle of distillation, the Renewer of Life. As it is said, "Thy youth shall be renewed like the Eagles." Great indeed, and many are the mysteries of this terrible Key.

The magical title is The Child of the Great Transformers, Lord of the Gates of Death.

12th KEY-HANGED MAN

The gallows from which this figure is suspended forms a Tau cross. The figure itself, from the position of the legs, forms a fylfot cross. It also represents the alchemical symbol of Sulphur in reverse.

There is a halo about the head of the seeming martyr. It should be noted that (1) the tree of sacrifice is living wood as indicated by leaves growing thereon; (2) that the face expresses deep entrancement, not suffering; (3) that the figure, as a whole, suggests life in suspension, but life and not death. It is a card of profound significance but all the significance is veiled. His arms, clasped behind him, form an upright Triangle, and this radiates Light. His mouth is resolutely closed. Waite dismisses most interpretations saying very simply that for him it expresses the relation, in one of its aspects, between the Divine and the Universe. He who can understand that the story of his higher nature is embedded in this symbolism will receive intimations concerning a great awakening that is possible, and will know that after the sacred Mystery of Death there is a glorious Mystery of Resurrection.

It is attributed to the letter Mem, the element of Water, joining Geburah to Hod; Mars to Mercury.

You will remember that the letter Mem occupies the middle position in the series of the Three Mothers. It is said in the Zohar that its open operation is through the descent of its influence to the abyss, and thus it restrains the rising of those great waters by which the earth would otherwise again be inundated. In its close operation, it restricts the power of judgement from the downward course thereof. It is also said that it is like a vessel which in turn is sealed and unsealed, according as there is inhibition or indulgence of its influx to the emanations which are below.

With the more general import of the Hanged Man you will be already familiar; but in this Grade you are invited to regard it after a new manner, which can still be brought into harmony with the previous forms of interpretation, since it is simply an advance thereon. The enforced sacrifice and punishment, the involuntary and fatal loss, which are ascribed to it in our Tarot teaching, are here connected with the Divine death, with the sacrifice of God himself. That death connects closely with the true meaning attached to the High Ceremony of the Corpus Christi wherein the Chief Adept typifies at once the Founder of the Rosicrucian Order and the Founder of the Universe.

Year by year, the Order is withdrawn for one moment of time that it may be again formulated out of chaos; the Builder is also withdrawn into the concealment of the Tomb, as you are told in the symbolism of the 5 equals 6 grade. The Founder of our Rosicrucian

Fraternity was taken hence that Light should come to His disciples, and the Maker of the great world entered into another concealment, for God dies in order that man shall live, and shall not only seek but find Him.

The symbolism with which we are here dealing also recalls the Apocalyptic figures of the Lamb slain from the foundation of the world, and in correspondence with previous explanations, it indicates that the palmary misfortune of the universe, which is exoterically called the Fall of Man, exercised a species of incomprehensible compulsion upon the Divine Nature, so that the scheme of what is familiar to everyone under the name of redemption comes before us in a certain manner as an eternal necessity and as a consequence of the free will rather of man than God.

The importance which has been attached throughout the Grades of our Two Orders to Egyptian symbolism should also remind us that Mem, through the sacrifice of Christ, has analogy with the legend of the dead Osiris, one of whose appellations was the shipwrecked or drowned Mariner, even as this terrible Key, which you see now in its true form, represents a drowned giant.

The 23rd Path of the Tree is referred to the Elemental sign of Water, and in this diagram the drowned giant is depicted reposing on the rocky bed of the ocean with the rainbow at his feet, corresponding to that other rainbow seen in the apocalyptic vision around the Throne of the Slain Lamb. A symbol familiar to the brethren of the Second Order is here interpreted with reference to its most exalted sense.

The drowned giant is that which has been sunk below the phenomenal world by a sacrifice eternally preordained, which, in one of its aspects at least, is the necessary limitation suffered by the Divine Nature in the act of becoming manifest. The Divine, in a word, is drowned in the waters of natural life and that which in this respect obtains in the external world, obtains also for humanity, wherein the Divine Spark, beyond all plummets of the sense, all reach of the logical understanding is immersed in the waters of the material existence. In both cases, the symbol with which we are dealing corresponds to the legend of our Founder, sleeping in the centre of the Tomb which is encircled by the Rainbow, as in the Sanctuary of Israel there was the abiding Presence of the Shekinah.

11th KEY-JUSTICE

That to which your attention is especially drawn is the Key of Justice, referrable to the letter Lamed, whereto many attributions are given. The writers of the Zohar and the old scholiasts thereon dwell upon the form of Lamed which is the highest of all the letters; they say also that it is composite, being formulated of Vau and Kaph. These are the accidents of their subtlety, but you should know that its dominion is in the hour of the planet Shabbathai or Saturn, because from Binah, which is the great Sabbath, the rest whereof we desire, there is an influx to the Path of Lamed through the Path of Geburah, from the Sephirah Binah.

It further denotes the Mystery of Equilibrium. Now, the place of Geburah can be withstood only by those who restrain their concupiscence, because it is the Supernal Tribunal, and Geburah in this sense, signified the force of will, as Lamed is the condition of equilibrium, which represents the Portal of the Mysteries.

The ideas which have been thus expressed are found differently exhibited by another order of symbolism in the two Pillars which stand at the Western Angles of the Altar, (in the 6 equals 5 ritual) bearing respectively a lighted candle and a human skull. With the comventional attributions of light in the numerical order and the obvious lessons to be derived from the disjecta membra of humanity, we have no concern here. They speak too fully for themselves.

Of that death-watch which encompasses us in the midst of ordinary life there is however little realization. All that falls short of the mystic end falls short of the life of life, outside of which we are still in the sphere of simulacra. . .

It is possible, however, that another light may be added to his natural condition, by which the desire of the true end which is set before all beings, and of the life which is beyond all life of the apparent order. It is then that he is made ready to set out on the great search, when the higher light which has now entered within him goes also before him, and the desire of the Holy House is enkindled in his heart. In this manner he passes under the judgments and the severities of his election, behind which is the concealed love that shall take him to his term. For as the natural man is impelled by a certain elementary justice suited to his condition, so there is a justice which is above, working in the souls of the chosen ones, so that once indeed, they shall taste death, that they may pass into life forever, under the auspices of the Faithful Intelligence.

Justice is the Daughter of the Lord of Truth, The Holder of the Balances.

10th KEY-WHEEL OF FORTUNE

The form of the Order's Key of The Wheel of Fortune is much more simple than most renditions. There are shown only three figures - the winged Sphynx above, the revolving wheel in the center, while below is a sitting, pensive monkey, a cynocephalus.

The Sphynx is half beast and half human, female as indicated by breasts, while the head is covered by a nemyss encircled by a halo. Thus it represents humanity as a whole, evolving from its primordial animal state to human self-consciousness. But that is not all. The presence of large wings, indicate the divinity of the figure, so that the symbol as a whole suggests the Real Self of man hidden behind the veil of the lower Sephiroth, the lower self or personality. The higher Triad is well represented by being above the other two symbolic figures.

The wheel is the symbol of time, cyclic progression and thus of karma. The wheel of the zodiac and astrology per se are representative of the cosmic clock constantly ticking away to bring into fresh activity the latent seeds of ancient deeds whereby we rise or fall as our fortunes, in the broadest sense of the term, fluctuate with the passage of time.

The cynocephalus is below, often described as Hermanubis, the combination of Hermes the messenger of the Gods, and lower mind, and Anubis, the dog-faced (or jackal) God who presided over death and mummification, and the watcher over the tombs of the dead. Watching over the tomb is required to permit resurrection - and thus he is associated with immortality, rising through the wheel of life from transitoriness to the overshadowing sphynx above, eternity.

It is symbolized by the letter Caph, referred to Jupiter on The Tree. Caph is not a closed hand, nor an open hand, but a curved hand, as if to hold or contain something.

9th KEY-THE HERMIT

The Hermit on most packs of the Tarot is practically the same. It is a hooded and cloaked figure, an old man, bearing a staff in one hand, and a lamp or lantern in the other. Like Diogenes of old, he may be looking for Truth - the truth about man and his relationship with the universe. He is a solitary figure; there is none other with him. In the search to reach the divine, one is alone in quest of the Alone. At the same time he represents the Kerux in the initiatory rituals, the shower of the way - the Kerux who points out the way to the hidden knowledge.

The Hermit is attributed to the letter Yod on the Tree and to the sign Virgo, ruled by Mercury. Mercury is not yet knowledge, but is the means whereby knowledge is transmitted, the symbol of the nervous system, with all its circuits - from the most primitive to those that are in the process of development.

Insofar as Virgo is the sign to which the Hermit is attributed, it has a connection with human sexuality in its yet virginal or prepubescent state. It represents man on the edge or precipice of Becoming, of the adolescent emerging from latent potentiality, of the adept who has not yet arrived at the full stage of all his possibilities, but who is nevertheless enroute.

His magical title is The Magus of the Voice of Light, The Prophet of the Gods.

8th KEY-STRENGTH

There are many versions of this Key, all variations of the Woman with the Lion. Some cards show her closing the mouth of the Lion, others opening the mouth of the Lion. The Order card shows her side by side with the Lion, both in an amicable relationship.

She represents Nature in all her Vastness, the Genetrix from which the vast universes are made and from which they are constructed. The Lion in the Order is the sign of Leo, not merely the fifth sign in the natural zodiac, referred to the 5th house - sex and love, but not yet marriage - but it is the First Sign of the reconstructed or Initiated Zodiac from which all the decanates and quinaries begin. It therefore symbolizes esoterically the Beginning or Creation of things, and to that extent has many subtle meanings.

It is referred to the letter Teth on the Tree, meaning a serpent, having in Genesis a sexual connotation. The Serpent is also the spermatozoon, the stimulator of new life in the female. As such it also represents Kundalini, the spinal spirit-fire without which there can be no transmutation, no spiritual growth or development, no new birth. Kundalini is the human aspect of the great Goddess Shakti, the cosmic energy or Fohat, depending on the system you employ, whose seven sons carve seven holes in space wherein develop the seven planets - or chakras in the merely human sense.

The card itself therefore is replete with many significations and requires deep meditation to discern its concealed mysteries.

Here the magical title is Daughter of the Flaming Sword, Leader of the Lion.

7th KEY-THE CHARIOT

In the Order system, the chariot is not grounded or fixed as in most other renditions. It is soaring through space drawn by two horses, the positive and negative forces of nature, given direction by the head of a Sphynx, again symbolizing the Higher. The charioteer is the King, the Yod of Tetragrammation, the Father of all.

In all renditions, however, the symbolic meaning conveyed is the union of two opposites, which together can draw the vehicle of the Higher Man towards the Great Goals he is attempting to reach. It is reminiscent of the Oath of the Adeptus Minor in which he promises to become, with the divine aid, more than human by uniting himself with his higher and divine Genius.

As such it is the symbol of the Great Work, represented by the letter Cheth, meaning a Fence, and whose Gematria is 418. These numbers add to 13, which are also the numbers of Ahavoh, Love, and Echod, One or Unity. Both together equal 26, the Gematria of Tetragrammation.

The magical title of this Key is Child of the Power of the Waters, Lord of the Triumph of Light.

6th KEY-THE LOVERS

Of all the historical designs, this Golden Dawn Tarot card is certainly the most different. Most others show a man and woman standing before a vast Angelic figure. In this particular key, we have a woman chained to a rock before which is a monster or threatening dragon.

Above, we perceive the descent of Perseus with radiant shield, winged helmet, and a sword in his right hand about to rescue the helpless maiden.

One of the many possible interpretations is the liberating effect of the descent of the higher Genius, the freeing effect of illumination. To quote Robert Wang in his book *The Golden Dawn Tarot*, "Here Perseus is shown freeing Andromeda from the solid rock of materialism, and from the Dragon of Fear. The 'Love' here is one of the divine Union, a mystery not even hinted at by the usual image of a man and woman whose earthly union is being blessed by a central Angelic figure."

The Hebrew letter to which this Key is attributed is Zayin, meaning a sword - in this instance not merely the sword of division and discrimination, but the sword of conquest and liberation. Its number is 7, which also refers indirectly to Netzach Victory, and to the planet Venus whose meaning is Love and Union and Fertility.

The magical title of this Key is Children of the Voice Divine, the Oracles of the Mighty Gods.

5th KEY-THE HIEROPHANT

Again, the Golden Dawn card is radically different from those in other packs. It shows a seated figure, bearded and crowned with a triple tiara, seated on a throne whose two arms end with bulls' heads. Quite simply, the card is attributed to the letter Vav, also attributed to Taurus, the zodiacal Bull.

In the Order teaching, the Hierophant is the Expounder of the Mysteries and his throne is in the East of the Temple. He is representative of Osiris, the resurrection god of Egypt, and as such never moves from the dais. If he does move, he represents Aroueris, one of the forms of Horus the Elder, and in moving he administers the obligation to the candidate and subsequently officiates and confirms the fact of initiation.

Initiation in the Order really takes place between the two pillars when the Higher Genius is, as it were, poised to make contact with the aspiring ego of the Candidate.

He also is bearer of the Banner of the East, which indicates the rising of the Light, the central fact of initiation. Some of the older packs describe him as the Pope, the highest authority of the Catholic Church. But Pope means in reality Father and as the Initiator, the Hierophant certainly represents an authoritative father figure - the one whose power and function is to stir up and initiate the creative process in the Genetrix or Mother.

His magical title is Magus of the Eternal Gods.

4th KEY-THE EMPEROR

The symbolism of this card is forthright, in that it depicts the Emperor sitting on a throne with an actual ram (for Aries) under his feet, and carrying a wand with the head of a ram. Since Aries is ruled by Mars, this card represents enormous creative energy and of course rulership. One set of Order symbols or attributions depicts the Mars decanate of Pisces as the end of one cycle of the year, and another Mars decanate in Aries to represent the tremendous power involved in the return of Spring when Nature begins to evidence growth and the emergence of Life once more in Spring.

One of the apparent paradoxes of the Order symbolism, is that this card is attributed not merely to Mars, a very masculine symbol but to the letter Heh which is distinctly feminine. It is the first Heh of Tetragrammaton, signifying the Mother. All symbols contain their own opposites, thus creating a balance of opposing forces, without which the universe would come to an end.

The Emperor is patently the consort of the Empress, the preceding card attributed to Venus and Daleth, indicating that the two had better be considered together. One is masculine and the other is feminine. One is force and fire; the other is beauty, luxury and fecundity. It is worth remembering that a poet once wrote that man is peace and the woman is power.

This magical title is Son of the Morning. Chief among the Mighty.

3rd KEY-THE EMPRESS

The Empress here is not unlike most of the figures in other and older packs. She is attributed to the letter Daleth, meaning a Gate, and is the uppermost of the so-called Reciprocal Paths on the Tree, joining Chokmah to Binah, the celestial Father and Mother. Venus is attributed to that wall of the Vault of the Adepts which is the entry to the Vault and the Pastos. which is thus the symbol rebirth.

She is a stately figure, seated on a throne, having rich vestments and royal aspect, as - says Waite - of a daughter of heaven and earth. There is a dove to the right of her, descending as it were from above. She bears a sceptre, that of royalty, surmounted by a globe, while in the other hand is the Ankh, the symbol both of Venus and of eternal Life. In Waite's lovely language, in which he fears to use an English phrase when a Latin one will do better, she is not the Queen of Heaven, but nonetheless she is still the Refuge of all Sinners, the fruitful Mother of thousands. There are also certain aspects of this card which correctly describe her as desire and the wings thereof, as the woman clothed with the Sun, as Gloria Mundi and the veil of the Holy of Holies.

She is above all things universal fecundity and desire, but there is no direct message which has been given to man like that which is borne of woman.

In another order of ideas, the card of the Empress signifies the door or gate by which an entrance is obtained into this life, as into the Garden of Venus, or as in the Vault of the Adepti. Then the way which leads out therefrom, to the secret known to the High Priestess; is communicated only to the elect.

Her magical title is Daughter of the Mighty Ones.

2nd KEY-THE HIGH PRIESTESS

The Golden Dawn card is almost simplistic without any of the more complex and elucidatory symbols of the other packs. She is clearly a lunar symbol, representing the Path of Gimel leading from Kether to Tiphareth, passing through the Abyss without any break in continuity.

Instead of having the crescent moon at her feet as in most of the current packs, she wears the crescent on her forehead, above her eyes, and holds a Cup (rather like the Order Water cup) in her hands over her chest. In this aspect, she seems more like the Stolistes, the cup-bearer in the Golden Dawn ceremonies. Nor is she placed between the two Pillars of Jachin and Boaz, of Severity and Mildness, as in many other of the more commonly used decks; she does not thus represent the Hegemon, the guide or leader of the Aspirant.

Her clothing or vestments are flowing and gauzy, blue in color, and the whole is bathed in an aura of light, a shimmering radiance. To quote Waite once more, she is the spiritual Bride and Mother, the daughter of the Stars and the higher Garden of Eden. The symbol of the Shekinah, the abiding presence of the Most High, the co-habiting glory. She is the Queen of the Borrowed Light, since the moon reflects the light of the Sun, but this is the light of all.

The Priestess of the Silver Star is her honorary title, and thus is the means whereby entry is gained into the invisible Third or Highest Order within the Order.

THE COMPLETE GOLDEN DAWN SYSTEM OF MAGIC

1st KEY-THE MAGICIAN

This is a young man, with the Caduceus on his chest vestments, facing the altar on which are the four elemental weapons so frequently spoken of in the Golden Dawn. They are depicted here exactly as they are in the document describing the making of the four elemental weapons which have almost a universal application. They not only represent the four suits of the Tarot, the four Worlds of the Kabalah, the four Beasts of the Apocalypse - the four Kerubic signs - they represent the four letters of the Tetragammat on and so are the vice-regents of the Holy Name.

Again, the Order has made a radical departure from most packs. This magician does not have one hand raised towards heaven, and the other pointing downwards. They are poised as if to grasp one of the magical weapons wherewith he accomplishes his rites.

His hat has a wide brim resembling the figure eight in a lateral position, the symbol of infinity, the sign of the Holy Spirit. It is like an endless cord, almost like a serpent appearing to devour its own tail, reminding one of the last line of the Bornless Invocation - "I am He, the Grace of the World; the Heart girt with a Serpent is my Name."

Insofar as he is attributed to the Letter Beth and to Mercury, and since he has the symbol of the Staff of Mercury on his chest, he is the higher Mercury, Thoth the God of Wisdom and of Utterance, the God who cometh forth from the Veil.

His magical title is The Magus of Power.

0-THE FOOL

In this card the most complete departure from the conventional packs is depicted. Instead of showing a man in motley, striding along, heedless of the dog which is yapping at his heels, we have revealed a naked child standing beneath a rose-tree bearing yellow roses. They represent the golden Rose of Joy as well as the Rose of Silence. While reaching up to the Roses, he yet holds in leash a grey wolf, wordly wisdom held in check by perfect innocence and the divine nature.

Waite describes him as a prince of the other world on his travels through this one - all amidst the morning glory, in the keen air. He is the Spirit in search of experience.

Probably the finest description of the Fool is to be found in that profound work, *The Book of Thoth* by Aleister Crowley. Though his designs for the Fool as painted by Frieda Harris differ enormously from the Order version, nonetheless the reader would do well to study what Crowley has to say in this connection. This alone should shatter any convictions one may have about Crowley's supposed perplexities. There is more wisdom in this one description and interpretation than in many a tome on all the Tarot trumps contributed by anyone else. I go further than this, and suggest that the student study the Golden Dawn Tarot deck in conjunction with his book, and even with his own version of the Tarot cards themselves.

The magical title is the Spirit of Ether.

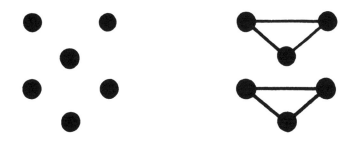

NOTES ON GEOMANCY

No authorship has been ascertained for this paper. Quite patently it is neither by S.R.M.D., nor by N.O.M. It is not listed as amongst the Flying Rolls. I gather it to have been contributed by one of the rank and file of the Order members who had found some interest in Geomancy.

Students are often inclined to set aside Geomancy as a thing of little use and small account, a fantastic and empiric mode of divination, merely a species of ultra elaborate tossing up, pure chance in fact, laboriously interpreted. The reason seems to be that in all the books and manuscripts dealing with Geomancy no elementary explanation of it is ever vouchsafed. This the student is assumed to know, and is given straight away rule a for the erection of figures and elaborate lists of the names and sigils of Genii and Rulers until he naturally finds himself bored or wearied.

It is to supply this lack that this paper is written in the hope that some students may find therein what they have been lacking. First then as to the word itself. All words ending in the termination "mancy" refer to some form of prophecying, from Mantis, a prophet. By this I mean not necessarily in fortune telling, though this too may be included, but rather the setting forth of the things that are behind the Veil of matter. All inspired utterances, in a sense all great poems, are prophecying. The priest is the commissioned executant, and as such is subordinate to the prophet. Now the prophet takes some material manifestation, and at this point lift s a corner of the veil, disclosing, under the appearance of some material token, the essential Divine Truth laying behind. Thus cheiromancy is prophecying from the hand. Necromancy (which is black magic) is prophecying from the corpse (a method in favor with the Roman Augurs who used the bodies of sacrificial victims). Geomancy, from Gaia the Earth, is prophecying from the Earth itself. We have then to consider how the veil that hides while it manifests the mystery of creation is lifted to the gaze of the inspired Seer. For this is the Veil of Isis, the penetration of which was the goal and object of the Egyptian Seers.

As above, so below, was the arcanum of the Emerald Tablet of Hermes. We are taught that the eternal ideas of God are revealed as in a picture book by the starry sphere to the eyes of those who can see, and the starry sphere is reflected in the Earth, so that every spot is the reflection of some constellation or star group, and over these wander the planets in their order. Four great Archangels keep watch and ward over the four quarters. From this knowledge we may see the reasons for the characteristics of countries, towns and places persisting quite independently of the race that inhabit them. We can see why it is that ever in Rome is the imperial spirit of domination and material power, whether it was inhabited as at first by the outcasts and broken men from every race, the great "Asylum"as it was called, or afterwards a homogeneous Republic, then an Empire with world dominion, then a hierarchy with well nigh a universal spiritual dominion, but always the same spirit. Or why again, the various races that have come to China have one and all become ultra Chinese. In every case the spirit of the place sometimes is strong enough to dominate all who come in. Or in other cases to produce its own effect. Thus we may perhaps say that all the forces behind the veil shine through and can be perceived. If the prophet can catch and translate these he can give information of high value to his brethren. Obviously to do this he must entirely sink and obliterate his own personality, for his intellect can only perceive and reason about this side of the veil. While his attention is fixed on this he is necessarily blind to the indications of what lies behind.

Let us for a moment look at some other terminations. "Nomy" signifies laws - as astronomy is the law of this starry universe. That is to say (for we can really know nothing of the laws governing this great universe) the methodical synthesis of observation.

"Ology" is the "word" - the divine messenger drawn from the manifestation - thus Astrology is the message drawn from the stars, the discourse concerning them, as shown by the science of astronomy. But as to the Earth, we have Geology, which signifies the discourse concerning the earth though as yet this discourse concerns merely the age of the earth, and the kind of creatures that inhabited it thousands of centuries ago, and the changes that have passed over its surface. There is also Geometry or the measurement of earth which is a more subtle science, for it concerns itself with abstract numbers and figures.

Now at the outset of Geomancy, as set forth in books and manuscripts, we are confronted with the lists of the names of the Rulers, Genii, Angels, and Intelligences, which have no apparent reason, and with seemingly arbitrary figures called Sigils. The learning of these to some is a weariness and it seems profitless. But let the student then look on them as the names of personalities with whom he will become acquainted. You know, for example, that your friend's name is John or David; your enemy's name may be Hans or Karl. The mention of these names at once brings to your mind the idea of that personality. We could not discuss these friendly or hostile ideas without using these names. We do not know why our friend was christened John, but we accept the fact, and just so we regard the Sigils, as we do the letters of the Alphabet. We do not know why the letter 'J' has the particular power that it has, but if we wish to communicate to another in writing the idea denoted by 'John' we employ it, and the children must learn the alphabet before they can begin to read.

Now as to the mechanical method employed by the Geomantic diviner. As we have seen he must entirely subordinate his own personality, his reason, his intellect, his human will. He must become completely passive. We have all heard of the process of automatic writing where the seer as medium allows his hand to be used by some superhuman or subhuman intelligence, that messages may be written through him without his will, often without his consciousness. But herein it is extremely difficult to entirely withdraw the will so that the message is not coloured, even transmuted, or at least modified, by his own brain. The Geomantic method of making a series of dots or strokes on paper without counting, ensures so far as it is possible that the intellect has no part therein. What is it then that determines whether the number be odd or even? The answer is clear; it is rhythm. Consider then any four-lined verse, with alternate feminine and masculine endings. The rhythm of this will give a geomantic figure of two dots, one dot, two dots, one dot.

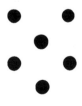

VOLUME TWO

When the brain is entirely quiescent, the message from behind the veil of physical matter may be perceived in the form of rhythm, not consciously indeed, but affecting the nerves and pulses, affecting the hand. A tune we may say, dances through the body, the rhythm of it manifests in the strokes unconsciously made. Whence then comes this tune? The starry sky is the reflex of God's thought of Himself, the earth in the reflex of the firmament, the aura of man is the reflex of the earth. The rhythm of the tune then manifests the idea behind the veil. The geomantic figure sets down in geometric form the rhythm of the tune and consequently the idea.

Let us now consider what we mean by an idea. Old John Heydon, the most profound writer in Geomancy, defines the idea as an invisible created spirit. This may be more comprehensible if we imagine any manifest object - a man, a flower, a tree, or what you will. Take the sum of all the attributes you know of that object, and then make up the ideal presentment in the idea thereof. It is invisible, but it is there. So we may say a sculptor has the idea of his statue before he has made the roughest sketch. And a genius he defines as a certain divine spirit that worketh secret things in nature miraculously. So that, he says, there is no great difference between a Genius and a Divine idea.

Now as you stand in a definite spot on the earth's surface and ask a question, the answer is there, involved in your question, if you can but get at it. The question and answer are both in the divine idea, and the idea is manifested by the rhythmic movement, the tune, that your spirit catches from behind the veil.

Take then for example a stanza with alternate feminine and masculine endings. Broadly the effect is exhilarating. It goes to a dance rhythm, it is full of hope and joy, it tells of the gaining of something desired, and the geomantic figure we have formed is thus:

and we learn to call it "Acquisitio." We are further taught to make a talismanic figure by joining the dots we have set down thus:

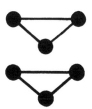

This seems at first sight a purely empiric and practically useless thing. But let us look at it in another way. We wish to receive the information we desire, and the natural method is to hold out some receptacle. Our appropriate symbol is a cup to receive the wine of divine grace, and a cup is the natural symbol of "Acquisitio." The spiritual gift is behind the veil, the material reflex of it is the gift of what we desire on Earth. Two cups therefore appropriately symbolize the answer to our question.

Now as in Egypt the picture writing gradually conventionalized into hieroglyphics, so the representation of the two cups may become the hieroglyphic symbol, the dots and angles of Acquisitio.

These indicate the rhythm that has come from behind the veil, bearing the answer to our query. We have now to consider that every point on the surface of Earth has its own occult forces, which are here manifested. To a certain extent this will be generally admitted. We know that there are sacred places, often in the old days marked with stone circles, and that the influence of them is so strong that in spite of themselves, succeeding races and different peoples will involuntarily build their sacred shrines in the same spots.

Many believe that ill-luck invariably follows the profaning of such sites. It is commonly said that about certain places there is a special influence for good or evil, which any sensitive person who comes there can feel. If this is true of certain places it would seem to follow that every place has its special influence and occult forces, which can be there manifested. But the forces that manifest in any place are not fixed and invariable.

Imagine then that you stand on a point of the earth's surface and your mind is troubled with some question and intuition comes to you to seek the solution behind the veil. You are feeling in your mind the Divine influence ruling that particular spot, and unconsciously it may be so. You know that it holds within it the answer could you but get at it. Perhaps you consider no ordinary method of divination, but there comes to you a feeling of hope and joy, of exhilaration, a certain sense that all will be well.

Your inner being has caught the rhythm that promises success. Here then Geomancy enables you to set down the rhythm in black and white, and to interpret in detail.

But it does more than this. To the vague sense that has permeated your inner being there is much risk of delusion. It is impossible to exclude the material personality, the outer side of the veil. Modes of exhilaration or depression may come from physical causes.

Geomancy, as we have seen, excludes, so far as it is possible, the personality - the working of the material brain and enables you to catch the rhythm, wherein is the answer to your question. So you ask whether you shall obtain something eagerly desired, and the rhythm sings to you the idea of Acquisitio and you set down the geomantic figure, and there appears to you the hieroglyphic of the Cups and you know that you hold forth the material cup, and behind the veil the spiritual cup is held forth to receive the wine of blessing. And now because there must be some name by which you shall call that divine spirit which you have perceived, you are taught to give it the name of Hismael.

Take this if you wish to be a purely fancy name. While it is the name you are to know, think of that spirit and you know so far that it is a genial generous spirit that gives you what you desire, and as such you recognize this spirit as the ruler of the idea of "Acquisitio." You learn also the sigil of Hismael. You do not know the meaning of this, or why it is employed. Perhaps you never will. It is not very important. You will never probably know the origin of the letter 'J,' but this does not prevent you knowing that 'J' is the initial of John, the name of your friend. To help in the knowledge and recognition of the Geomantic figures, the old books give various characteristics describing Hismael. For instance, as noble and generous and affable; a genial and handsome man, laughter-loving, a great lover and forgiver. Descriptions are also given of the places that he most frequents.

Fruits, plants and trees are so especially favoured by him, precious stones, animals, birds and fishes consonant to his nature, etc. But the student need not be concerned with those at present. They belong to more advanced parts of the subject. The chief points to note now are that we have seen the lines or strokes he makes are not haphazard and meaningless but reveal to him a certain rhythm and that rhythm is the expression of an idea. The idea is the answer to the question shown him by the ruler whose name and sigil also he knows and somewhat of his character.

Having grasped this much there will be less difficulty in comprehending the meaning of the Genii, Angels, Archangels, etc.

We see then how we get a certain result with one figure resulting from four lines of strokes. But there are four quarters of the world, and four elements. We must inquire four times if we would have a reliable answer. So it is necessary to make 16 lines of strokes resulting in four figures. But the principle of all is the same. We have discovered here only "Acquisitio." Further comments must be reserved for a future paper.

ASTROLOGY

The Knowledge Lectures contain tid-bits of a variety of topics. None of these do more than scratch the surface. This is admitted by Mathers in a paper devoted to describing the "least amount of information a student needs to pass the necessary examinations." After awhile the astrological material - apart from naming the planetary and zodiacal symbols and their attributions to the Tree of Life - was dropped altogether. If not in the Golden Dawn, at least a generation later in the Stella Matutina. The reason for this deletion was a simple one - the gradual appearance of some very well-written books on Astrology. At the time the Order was founded, there was a dearth of good astrological books, so the Knowledge Lectures were needed to make good what publishers and writers had failed to do. Any good catalogue from a reliable occult bookseller will reveal nowadays practically hundreds of titles of astrological books. Not all of them are good by any manner or means. Nonetheless, a certain number are outstanding.

Though I have left some of the basic astrological material intact in the Knowledge Lectures, I would like to name a few good textbooks that the reader could consult to considerable advantage. For example, there are the two books by Grant Lewi - *Astrology for the Millions* and *Heaven Knows What* (Llewellyn Publications). A more complete and comprehensive textbook, though nowhere as well written or as interesting, is the *A-Z Horoscope Maker and Delineator* by Llewellyn George. Perhaps the best of the lot is a series of slim volumes covering every phase of astrology by Noel Tyl (Llewellyn Publications). There is also a specializing volume on one particular topic that should not be ignored - *Saturn* by Liz Greene (Samuel Weiser, Inc.) This can certainly supplant the skimpy and superficial data provided by the Knowledge Lectures.

However, there are a couple of items to be found in different places throughout the Order teaching that deserve to be integrated into the common body of astrological knowledge and practice. The data in the Tarot material, relating to starting the Zodiac from the star Regulus in Leo, said to make the signs and constellations coincide, is an important theoretical concept that must not be ignored. It makes the system similar to sidereal rather than tropical astrology and therefore deserves a new system of interpretation. Furthermore, there is an isolated paper dealing with the *Convolutions of the Serpent Formulae around the North Pole*, which has all sorts of hints and possibilities that only a student here and there has sensed, to the best of my knowledge.

ESOTERIC ASTROLOGY

By

FRANCIS KING

Between 1908 and 1912 Mathers issued side lectures and other manuscripts to those Temples that were loyal to him. Much of this additional material reached the Stella Matutina (via Brodie Innes) but some did not do so. . .Some of these later manuscripts are of great interest, and one in particular, that seems to have been issued to Theorici Adepti Minores, is of real importance; for it outlines an astrological system that differs in some respects from both the normal western astrology taught in the Golden Dawn and its offshoots, to members of the Portal Grade, and the sidereal ("starry") astrology used by the Hindus and a minority of modern western astrologers.

Therefore I would suggest the reader consult any of the modern textbooks on sidereal astrology with a view to gaining some insight into their particular kind of interpretation. (For example in tropical astrology my ascendant is about 0 degrees Scorpio. By Mathers calculations that would be shifted back to about the middle of Libra. And I can assure the reader that my basic characteristics are no more Libran than the man in the moon. I.R.).

In considering this 'initiated astrology' it must be borne in mind that the signs of the Zodiac in popular astrology are completely out of step with the constellations bearing the same names. The situation has arisen because of the precession of the equinox - the fact that the equinoctial point (i.e. the point of the zodiac at which the sun lies when it crosses the equator on March 21st each year) moves steadily through the zodiac in a reverse direction to the motion of the planets. In spite of this fact, tropical astrologers insist on calling this invisible, moving equinoctial point to the 0 degrees of Aries although it is, in reality, many degrees away from the constellation of that name.

In Mathers' system the moving, or tropical, zodiac is abandoned in favour of a fixed sidereal zodiac in which the signs and constellations coincide and is measured from the star called Regulus, which is taken as being in 0 degrees Leo. This sidereal zodiac requires a correction to the tropical longitudes given in all ephemerides (lists of planetary and zodiacal positions) used by astrologers - and this correction varies each year. Mathers supplied a table of these corrections for the years 1800-1911. As it seems likely that some of the readers of this book will have astrological interests - a recent poll showed that no less than twenty percent of the adult population of England and Wales take astrology seriously I think it worth reproduction. In each case Column I indicated the year and Column II indicated the degrees and minutes to be subtracted from the planetary and house positions as calculated from an ephemeris.

Col I	Col II	Col I	Col II	Col I	Col II	Col I	Col II
1800	27 04	1828	27 27	1856	27 51	1884	28 13
1801	27 05	1829	27 28	1857	27 52	1885	28 14
1802	27 06	1830	27 29	1858	27 53	1886	28 15
1803	27 07	1831	27 30	1859	27 53	1887	28 15
1804	27 08	1832	27 31	1860	27 54	1888	28 16
1805	27 08	1833	27 31	1861	27 55	1889	28 17
1806	27 09	1834	27 32	1862	27 56	1890	28 18
1807	27 10	1835	27 33	1863	27 56	1891	28 19
1808	27 11	1836	27 34	1864	27 57	1892	28 20
1809	27 12	1837	27 35	1865	27 58	1893	28 21
1810	27 12	1838	27 36	1866	27 59	1894	28 22
1811	27 13	1839	27 37	1867	27 59	1895	28 23
1812	27 14	1840	27 37	1868	28 00	1896	28 24
1813	27 15	1841	27 38	1869	28 01	1897	28 25
1814	27 16	1842	27 39	1870	28 01	1898	28 26
1815	27 17	1843	27 40	1871	28 02	1899	28 27
1816	27 18	1844	27 41	1872	28 03	1900	28 28
1817	27 19	1845	27 42	1873	28 04	1901	28 29
1818	27 19	1846	27 43	1874	28 05	1902	28 30

Col I	Col II	Col I	Col II	Col I	Col II	Col I	Col II
1819	27 20	1847	27 44	1875	28 06	1903	28 31
1820	27 21	1848	27 44	1876	28 06	1904	28 32
1821	27 22	1849	27 45	1877	28 07	1905	28 32
1822	27 23	1850	27 46	1878	28 08	1906	28 33
1823	27 23	1851	27 47	1879	28 09	1907	28 34
1824	27 24	1852	27 48	1880	28 10	1908	28 35
1825	27 25	1853	27 49	1881	28 11	1909	28 36
1826	27 26	1854	27 50	1882	28 11	1910	28 37
1827	27 27	1855	27 50	1883	28 12	1911	28 37

This is the end of the quotation from Mr. King's use of McGregor Mathers' segment on Esoteric Astrology. The dates end at the year of 1911, but I would gather one could proceed from that date to the present following more or less the same procedure. Anyway the student versed in sidereal astrology should have no difficulty in dealing with this schema. The tropical astrologer likewise ought to be able to use the above data to his advantage and bring it up to date.

INTRODUCTORY PAPER ON THE TATTWAS

By

G.H. FRATER SUB SPE

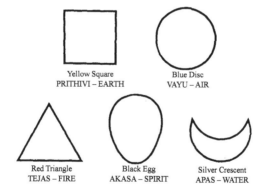

Yellow Square
PRITHIVI – EARTH

Blue Disc
VAYU – AIR

Red Triangle
TEJAS – FIRE

Black Egg
AKASA – SPIRIT

Silver Crescent
APAS – WATER

THE TATTWAS
I. What the Tattwas are.

The conditions which make all life possible on the earth, whether human, animal or vegetable, are derived from the Sun: e.g., light, heat, electricity, magnetism etc. This is termed 'the life of the Sun' or 'Solar Prana'. The Solar Prana is communicated to the earth in waves of vibration through the ether. These waves are of widely varying lengths and rates of motion but they are all traversing the ether at the same time, forming a very complicated system.

The student should endeavour to familiarize himself with this conception. He will find a useful illustration in the sounds of a great orchestra: all the sound waves, from the long slow heavy ones of the bassoon, to the short high rapid notes of the fife or piccolo—are all passing at the same time to the ear, yet the sensitive ear can pick out and follow the waves of sound proceeding from each instrument. Another illustration is found in the waves of colour proceeding from a landscape; the heavy long red waves and all the gamut of colour up the shortest and most rapid blues are traversing the luminiferous ether at the same time yet the eye can pick out each one without trouble.

The same idea can be visualized by considering the waves of the sea: the long heavy rollers pass along, and on their surface we can see multitudes of small, short and rapid waves, passing simultaneously in the same direction. Now just as the notes of a musical scale are divided into seven distinct tones, each representing a certain number of aerial vibrations per second; and just as the vibrations of the luminiferous ether are divided into the seven colours of the spectrum—so the vibrations of the Solar Prana are divided into seven groups, groups which are determined by their wave lengths and frequencies. Two of these groups are beyond the scope of this paper, but the remaining five will be briefly explained.

The Solar Pranas will be best understood by considering their effects on visible and tangible matter, and should always be called by their Sanscrit names, which having no other connotation, will be less liable to confusion.

Consider then first the process by which the Mulaprakriti or 'world stuff is moulded into a planet. At first it is inert, at rest as it were, a formless cloud of finely distributed matter having in itself only the potential of form and substance; this is the condition known as AKASA. Then motion begins, the mass is whirled into a spherical form and becomes a nebula. This condition is called VAYU.

Now imagine the infinitesimally small particles, whirled around and continually colliding with each other, gradually growing hot and incandescent, until the nebula becomes a fiery mass. This condition is called TEJAS. Gradually it cools but remains fluid; this condition is called APAS. Further, as time goes on, the fluid mass solidifies and becomes a globe or planet. In this condition it is termed PRITHIVI.

These names should be accurately learned and associated with the conditions to which they refer. It will be seen that they correspond with fair accuracy to those states of energy—matter which are commonly called the four elements. Thus Vayu has qualities of Air, Tejas of Fire, Apas of Water and Prithivi of Earth. But as these words are limited in common speech, it is not advisable to use them in speaking or thinking of the Tattwas. Akasa in this connection would represent the negative or passive condition of rest. Another useful illustration may be found by considering the operation of the Tattwas in reverse order: as in the familiar chemical compound known as H_2O, recognized in its fluid form as water. If this be subjected to refrigeration it becomes solid, called in the terminology of the elements, Prithivi—or 'Earth'. This state results from the action of Prithivi on H_2O. Now suppose heat is applied: the chunk of ice melts and the substance returns to its elemental state—Water. It is now under the Tattwa of Apas. Continue to increase the heat under the Tattwa of Tejas and the water becomes steam, or vapour and is thus under the Tattwa of Vayu. The Steam diffuses, it enters the Tattwa condition of Akasa, with the potential of condensing and returning to earth as rain.

From these illustrations the student should be able to gain a clear conception of the nature of the Tattwas, regarding them always as more or less arbitrary divisions of the Solar Prana.

II.   The Symbols of the Tattwas.

It has been found convenient to denote each Tattwa by a conventional symbol—specialized as to figure, form and colour. These symbols are not arbitrarily selected, but are derived from the form of the wave, its frequency and its formative effect on the etheric substance. This, however, is so complex and difficult an investigation that the student is advised to defer its consideration for the present, and consider the symbols as being merely conventional forms sufficiently appropriate to make them easy to remember. Thus the Akasa is symbolized by an egg-shaped figure in dark purple or indigo. An egg as the root and origin of life is manifestly appropriate as a symbol of life—the latency of the life force, the force within the egg before it is stimulated into overt activity; and purple is eminently a colour of rest.

Vayu is symbolized by a circle of clear blue, the air being obviously a sphere of blue colour. There is some difference of opinion as to the correct shade of blue, which varies with different persons: the best rule is to try and reproduce the deepest and most beautiful sky blue the student has ever seen. If he has been in the East or on the Mediterranean, he will see Vayu a darker, deeper shade than if he has never been out of the northern latitudes.

Tejas is symbolized by a triangle of flame red, the shape and colour being both obviously appropriate. Apas is symbolized by a crescent in silver, alluding to the Moon as ruler of the waters, and their silvery colour when not reflecting the sky or any earthly object. Prithivi is symbolized by a square form of a yellow colour, the stability of earth being denoted by the square or cube; since the perfect form of earth according to the alchemists is gold, the colour yellow is appropriate.

The student should now thoroughly acquaint himself with these forms and endeavour to imagine or visualize them in connection with the manifestation of the appropriate elemental state. Thus when the shades of night are descending and he is sinking to sleep, let him imagine a vast egg-shaped cloud of deep purple light closing round and enveloping him in warm mysterious darkness, the home of dreams. Whenever he looks on the sky, or on the distant hills, tinted to soft shades in the blue air, let him imagine the blue sphere of Vayu floating colossal in size before his eyes; through this see the landscape.

So again if he looks on any fire, whether it be the fire on the domestic hearth, a furnace, a bonfire, ora volcano in eruption, let him imagine the vast red triangle of Tejas before his eyes. Again looking on any water: the sea, a river, lake, or even the water in his own hand basin, let him train himself to see the silver crescent with the points turned upward. Over anything hard and solid let him see the yellow cube of Prithivi, imagining that if the visualized symbol were in solid form it would be like pure gold.

When this exercise has been practiced till some degree of perfection is reached, it can be benefical to reverse the process thus: take a lump of ice and put it in a heavy saucepan. It should now need no effort to see over it a yellow cube or square. Now bring the pan near a fire; when the surface of the ice begins to melt and water pours down its sides imagine the silver crescent appearing gradually on the yellow square, occupying about one quarter of its area. Make this grow brighter and clearer as the ice becomes liquid; then when the block is nearly melted imagine the silver crescent increasing in size and gradually replacing the yellow square altogether, so that when the ice has liquified the crescent alone remains.

Now put the saucepan on the fire, and watch the water growing hot. As it does so imagine the red triangle of Tejas forming itself on the crescent, just as the crescent did on the square, until when the water boils, the red triangle will have replaced the crescent. As the steam rises and floats into the air the student should similarly see the red triangle becoming charged with the blue circle; this should increase in size and overshadow the triangle entirely as the water is changed into steam. Then as the steam cloud disperses and becomes mere latent moisture in the air, the blue circle should merge into the purple egg of Akasa. This exercise will familiarize the student with the idea of the Tattwa symbols, charged with what are known as their subtattwas.

At this stage it will be useful for him to make a series of cards with the Tattwa symbols. These should be about the size and proportion of playing cards. The length of the symbol should not be more than one half the maximum length of the card: i.e., if the card is four inches long, the symbol should be two inches, leaving an inch above and an inch below it. The symbols should be exactly and carefully cut in coloured paper or painted, the proportions true, and the edges smooth. The cards should be kept scrupulously clean. The student should now train himself when looking at the cards to recall some form of the element to which each is attributed: thus a calm sea with Apas, a rough windy sea with Apas charged with Vayu, a boiling spring with Apas charged with Tejas, etc.

Gradually he will find the symbol and the element belonging to that symbol linked so closely together in his mind that one involuntarily recalls the other: for instance the mere thinking of Tejas will make him feel warm on a cold day.

III.   Of the Swara and the Breaths.

Swara is the Spirit, the Soul of the Universe. Or as it is said in the Sanscrit work on the science of breath: 'It is the manifestation of the impression on matter of that power which knows itself. Therefore it is called the Great Breath. Now breath is dual: out breathing and inbreathing. In the East the technical symbol of out breathing is 'S A', and the point of rest between the two is 'HAM', whence the word HAMSA, which is taken to mean God and which is a symbolic representation of the two eternal processsess.

Now as Swara is the Soul of the Universe, it follows that everything that has life must partake of the nature of Swara: we expect to find positive and negative action in the Solar Prana, of which the Tattwas are modifications. Moreover in physical matter prepared for the reception of life—as an egg—we expect to find a center capable of manifesting the two forms of the life current. Thus in an egg, during incubation, we find the formation of two centers; from these eventually develop the brain-nerve system, and the heart-blood system; each of these has a double function as it develops. So also is it with man, and with every created thing that has life, and even with the world itself.

The Solar Prana comes either direct from the Sun to Earth, or is reflected from the Moon. The former is said to be positive, the latter negative. Therefore when under the influence of Swara, the Solar Prana is positive and the technical name is Sun Breath; when it is negative it is called Moon Breath. The student is advised for the present to regard these merely as technical terms, and not to attempt to trace the analogies farther; the subject is very complex.

The Moon Breath manifested through the Solar Prana is termed IDA and the Sun Breath is called PINGALA; the neutral point of rest between the two is SUSUMNA. Now Ida manifests especially in the nerves on the left side of the body, Pingala in those on the right and Susumna in the central column. Hence it is said that when the Solar Prana is in Ida, if the breath be drawn in with a quick inspiration it is felt chiefly in the left nostril, and if in Pingala in the right.

The student is advised not to put too much store in such experiments at first for: (1) the slightest cold in the head will often prevent or alter the sensations; (2) many illnesses, it is said, bring the breath to the wrong side; (3) the breath can be altered at will so as to be perceptible on one side or the other, as is done in certain magical processes. It should also be understood that the so-called change of breath from one side to the other is more a matter of sensation arising from the functioning of the nerves, than an actual flowing of material air; of all this more will be said hereafter.

Now the course of the breaths in the Solar Prana can be calculated so that it is possible to know exactly what breath is in action at any moment of the day or night. This is judged by the Moon. As is well known, the Moon increases during a fortnight, called the Bright Fortnight. The Bright Fortnight begins from sunrise after the new Moon. Observe—this must be exact. Thus if the Sun rises at 6 o'clock on a particular morning and the new Moon at

6:30, the Bright Fortnight will begin on the following day at sunrise. The Solar Prana is then in Ida, and the breath will be in the left nostril for the space of two hours (called in Sanscrit one 'Ghari'); then the breath will change to Pingala, and be in the right nostril for another two hours. Alternating throughout the whole twenty-four hours, it passes through twelve Gharis in the course of a day and night.

Between each Ghari occurs Susumna which lasts for about twenty minutes, the transition period, i.e., ten minutes during which the breath is passing from the side which was active to the central position, where it is in both nostrils equally, and ten minutes getting fully developed in the other nostril, with a very brief interval when it is exactly equal in both.

This continues for three days, changing on the fourth day. On the first Ghari after sunrise on the fourth day the Solar Prana is in Pingala, and the breath in the right nostril. On the second Ghari it changes to Ida, and so on for three days. On the seventh day it changes again back to Ida, for the first Ghari. Thus it is clear that the third twenty-four hours will end with Pingala and the fourth will begin with the same. The sixth will end with Ida and the seventh begin with the same. Moreover owing to the increase or decrease of daylight hours the periods of twenty-four hours will not be exact. This course is continued until the full Moon.

At the time of the first sunrise after the full Moon, i.e., the beginning of the Dark Fortnight—the Solar Prana is in Pingala, whether the preceding term of three days has been completed or not; and the same process is gone through again until the following new Moon. Now during each Ghari the five Tattwas come successively into operation beginning with Akasa. Each therefore will be of about twenty minutes duration. Thus suppose the sun rises at 8 o'clock, Akasa will be current till 8:20, Vayu from 8:20 to 8:40, Tejas from 8:40 to 9:00 and so on. During Ida the Tattwas will be of a negative character, and during Pingala positive.

Moreover each Tattwa is divided into five Subtattwas, the course of which is commenced by a Subtattwa of its own nature. Thus Vayu commences with Vayu charged with Vayu that is the simple Tattwa which lasts for four minutes and is followed by Vayu charged with Tejas, then Vayu with Apas and so on. The last is Vayu-Akasa followed by Tejas charged with Tejas, Tejas charged with Apas etc. These of course are symbolized by the cards the student has already prepared. It will be seen that the Tattwa or breath in operation at any moment of the day or night, of any day in the year, can be instantly and easily calculated.

An adept who is in perfect health and has sufficiently trained his faculties can discover without calculation which Tattwa is in operation by various simple methods. One of these is to place five small balls or marbles, painted with the Tattwa colours, in his pocket and draw out one haphazard; this ball should be of the colour of the Tattwa in operation. Another method is to close the eyes and endeavour to see a colour; the first that comes to the mind should be that of the ruling Tattwa.

As has been said this depends on perfect health, and also training: the student must not expect to attain success until after considerable practice. When he has practiced for some time he will also find that he can perceive the physical effects of the Tattwas at the time when they are in operation. Thus when Vayu functions he may expect a certain feeling of restlessness, in Tejas warmth and energy, in Apas a cold phlegmatic sensation and in Prithivi steadiness and solid strength. These feelings will be very slight and at first, only barely perceptible, but with time and practice they will become more distinct, and may be very useful in determining when to perform certain actions. If a man is making a call and has no reason whatever for leaving at one time or another he is almost certain to go as soon as Vayu is well established.

It will follow that if he desires to do something demanding energy, he had better wait till the Tejas Tattwa, or the Sun Breath is in operation; if a material business is to be commenced it will probably be best done under the Prithivi Tattwa. So again a work of imagination or any negative or receptive undertaking will prosper most under Ida, the Moon Breath.

THE COMPLETE GOLDEN DAWN SYSTEM OF MAGIC

By making a chart of the Breaths, Tattwas, and Subtattwas through each day for some time, and carefully trying to notice their effect in himself, the student may in short time attain to a very competent knowledge of the subject, and acquire a perception of the course of the Solar Prana which will be of great assistance to him in his future work. But let him beware of prematurely trying to test the existence of the Tattwas by experimenting to see if he can feel them; in so doing he starts with a suggestion to himself that they do not exist. This will infallibly blunt the very delicate instrument of his sensation, and cause the failure of his efforts, as well as loss and damage to his powers.

THE TATTWAS OF THE EASTERN SCHOOL

Index

(N.B. This document is labelled August 1894, and was originally issued to F.L. Gardner, Frater De Profundis ad Lucem. It was supposed to have been circulated in the Outer Order of the Golden Dawn to the initiate of the Philosophus grade. From the Golden Dawn, it passed after the Revolt to almost every other Order founded on its ruins. Some have thought it to be opposed in principle to the western Tradition espoused by the Order, though the basis for the so-called Skrying in the Spirit Vision was firmly established in this Eastern System.

Those who know something of early Theosophical literature will have perceived that it is either a precis of or an extrapolation from Rama Prasad's most interesting and informative book *Nature's Finer Forces.* Reading this book is a *must.* I fancy that at this point in time, it is out of print. A photographic edition has been published by Health Research of Mokelumne Hill in California, making it readily available.

Some have been inclined to the belief that this original book is highly complicated—though it is no more so than the Qabalah, for example. However, there is an interesting and most useful simplified approach to the whole topic of the Tattwas in *The Law of the Rhythmic Breath* by Ella Adelia Fletcher (R.F. Fenno & Co., N.Y. 1908), dedicated to Rama Prasad. I do not know if this book is still in print, though used copies may still be available. If a sufficient demand is created, I fancy that Health Research might be persuaded to bring out a photographic edition of this too. I.R.)

VOLUME TWO

General Observation

There are five Tattwas or Principles:

1. **Akasa—Ether.**
2. **Vayu—the Aerial principle.**
3. **Tejas—the Principle of Light and Heat.**
4. **Apas—Watery Principle.**
5. **Prithivi—the Earthy Principle.**

But the first Cause of these is the Great Controller of all things, the One Light, the Formless. From Him first came into appearance Ether; thence the Air, the motion producing Ether waves which causes Light and Heat, and so on in the above order.

The Yogi comes to know the principle of these five Tattwas, their Sukshma Sharira. but how? Further on you will see how. The Astrologer who has no knowledge of the Swara is as worthless as a man without a wife. It is the soul itself; it is the Swara, the Great Controller of all, who creates, preserves, and destroys, and causes whatsoever is in this World. Experience and Tradition both say no knowledge is more precious than this knowledge of the Swara. None else lays bare the workings of the machinery of this world, or the secret workings of this world.

By the power of Swara may be destroyed an enemy. Power, wealth, and pleasure, all these can be commanded by Swara. The beginner in our Science must be pure and calm in mind and in thought, virtuous in actions, and having unmixed faith in his spiritual teacher. He must be strong in his determination, and grateful.

Swara in the Body. Ten manifestations of this Swara are in the body. But before the Neophyte is told this, he must gain a thorough knowledge of the nervous system. This is very important, and according to his knowledge of this science, the Neophyte gains success. To give a rough outline of the parts we have chiefly to deal with in our endeavour to explain the elementary treatise. There are ten principal nerves, this includes the tubes, etc. It is in the ten manifestations of Swara that the ten so-called Vayus move. We mean by this ten forces which perform ten different functions. The three most important nerves are the following, as the beginner has only to deal with these:

1. **Ida, the left bronchus.**
2. **Pingala, the right bronchus.**
3. **Sushumna, in the middle.**

The ten Vayus are:

1. **Prana, in the breast.**
2. **Apana, about the excretory organs.**
3. **Samana, in the navel.**
4. **Udana, middle of the throat.**
5. **Vyana, pervading the whole body.**
6. **Kurmana, the eyes, helping them open.**
7. **Kirkala, in the stomach, producing hunger.**
8. **Nag, whence comes vomiting.**
9. **Devadatta, causes yawning.**
10. **Dhananjaya, that which doth not leave the body after death.**

These ten Vayus, or forces, have their play in the ten principal nerves, not one in each. They are the regulators of the body of man. If they go on working properly, a man remains perfectly healthy; if not, different kinds of diseases spring up.

35

A Yogi keeps them always working, and consequently diseases never come to him. The key to all these nerves lies in the working of the Prana Vayu, or vital principle drawing the air through the Ida, the Pingala, and the Sushumna. When the Air is drawn through the Ida it is felt coming out or going in through the left nostril. When through the Pingala, in the right nostril. When through the Sushumna it is felt through both nostrils simultaneously. The air is drawn or felt through either or both of the nostrils at certain appointed times. Whenever in any given time, the Breath goes in and comes out of the wrong nostril it is a sure sign some sort of disease is coming on.

The Ida is sometimes called the Chandra Nadi, or the Moon Nerve. The Pingala, the Surya Nadi or Sun nerve. These are called, the former, the Chandra Swara and the latter the Surya Swara.

The reason is that when the breath is in the Ida it gives coolness to the body, and that when in the Pingala it gives heat to the body. The Ancient Magi used to say the place of the Moon in the human body was in Ida, and the Sun in Pingala.

The Course of the Breath. The Lunar month, it is well known, is divided into two parts, the fortnight of the Waxing and the fortnight of the Waning. On the first fortnight, or the Bright Fortnight, just at Sunrise of the first day the Breath must come into the left nostril and must be so for the three succeeding days, when again the 7th day must begin with the Moon breath, and so on in the same order. Thus we have said that such and such days begin with such and such breath.

But how long is our breath to remain in one nostril? For five Gharis, or 2 hours. Thus when the first day of the Bright fortnight begins with the Moon Breath, after five Gharis, the Sun Breath must set in, and this again must change into the Moon Breath after the same interval of time. So on for every day.

Again, the first day of the dark fortnight must begin with the Sun Breath, and proceed in the same way, changing after five Gharis and the three succeeding days. It will be seen that all the days of the month have been divided into the Ida and the Pingala. In the Sushumna, the Swara flows only when it changes, either in its natural course or in certain other conditions to be afterwards mentioned. This is the course of Nature. But a Yogi commands Nature. He turns everything into his own way. Rules for this will be given in the proper place. (Coloured illustrations of the tattwas will be found in the colour plate section of this book).

COURSE OF THE TATTWAS

For five Gharis, as we have above said, the breath flows through our nostrils. In these 5 Gharis, or two hours periods, the Tattwas have their course. In the first we have Akasa, in the second Vayu, in the third Tejas, in the fourth Apas, in the fifth Prithivi. Thus in one night and day, or 60 Gharis, we have twelve courses of these 5 Tattwas, each remaining one Ghari and returning again in two hours. There are again further five subdivisions of each Tattwa in a Ghari. Thus, Akasa is subdivided into Akas-Akasa; Akas-Vayu; Akas-Tejas; Akas-Apas; Akas-Prithivi and similarly with the other four.

How to know which of the Tattwas is at a certain time in course, not merely by a mathematical calculation but with the certainty of an eye witness, is of the greatest importance in the practical part of this science. We shall come to it further on.

The Ida. When the Breath is in Ida, that is in the left Nostril, then only is it well to perform the following actions. Stable works such as erecting a building, or the construction of a well or tank, going on a distant journey, entering a new house, collection of things, giving gifts, marriage, making jewels or clothes, taking medicines and tonics, seeing a superior or master for any purpose of trade, amassing of wealth, sowing of seed in a field, negotiations, commencement of trade, seeing of friends, works of charity and faith, going home, buying of animals, doing work for the benefit of others, placing money on security, singing, dancing, taking up abode in any village or city, drinking or making water at the time of sorrow, pain, fever, etc. All these acts should be done when the Swara is in Ida. It must however be kept in mind that the Tattwas Vayu and Tejas are to be excluded from these actions, likewise Akasa.

During the Tattwas Prithivi and Apas only, are these actions to be done. In a fever, the Yogi keeps his Chandra Swara going, and brings the Apas or Water Tattwa in course, so the fever is all over in a very short time. How mastery is gained over the Tattwas will come further on.

The Pingala. In the Surya Swara only, are the following actions to be done. Reading and teaching hard and difficult subjects of knowledge, sexual intercourse, shipping, hunting, mounting a hill or fort, riding a donkey, camel or horse, swimming over a powerful stream or river, writing, painting, buying and selling, fighting with swords or hands, seeing a king, bathing, eating, shaving, bleeding, sleeping, such like. All these secure success and health, as the case may be, if done in the Surya Swara.

The Sushumna. When the Breath comes not out of both nostrils at the same time, it is flowing in the Sushumna. Nothing ought to be done under these conditions, for everything turns out badly. The same is the case when the Breath is now in one and now in the other nostril. When this is the case, sit down and meditate upon or over the Sacred Hansa. This joining of the Breath is the only time for Sandha, meditation.

NOTE: Zanoni secured success in gaming for Cetosa and overcame the effects of the poisoned wine of the Prince di D. as follows. In the first place, he changed his breath to the right nostril, and threw an envelope of the Akasa Tattwa over his antagonist, who consequently became all empty, the money in gaming flowing towards the Surya Swara. In the latter case he brought the Water, Apas, Tattwa into course, directed it with the full force of his trained will towards the poisoned wine, and consequently the burning heat of the poison was counteracted for a very long time, and before it could recover strength enough to act on the system, it was there no longer. S.R.M.D.

THE TATTWA

To each of the five Tattwas a special colour has been assigned. Akasa—Black or Indigo. Vayu—Blue. Tejas—Red. Apas—Silver. Prithivi—Yellow. It is by these colours that a practical man finds on the spur of the moment which Tattwa is at the time in course. Besides, these Tattwas have different shapes and tastes. These figures are seen by taking a bright mirror and letting the breath fall upon it, as it comes out of the Nose. The divided part takes one of the following forms according to the Tattwa then in course. Prithivi—a square. Apas, a crescent. Tejas, a triangle. Vayu, a sphere. Akasa, egg shaped. To sum up their qualities:

Prithivi—moves always in the middle of the Paths of Air and Water. Apas—downwards, straight through the nose. Tejas—upwards. Vayu—obliquely towards the right or left arm, as the case may be. Akasa—transversely always.

Tattwa	Colour	Form	Taste	Distance of Breath under Nostril	Principle
Prithivi	Yellow	Square	Sweet	12 fingers	Bulky
Apas	Silver	Crescent	Astringent	16 fingers	Cold
Vayu	Blue	Sphere	Acid	8 fingers	Moving
Tejas	Red	Triangle	Hot tastes	4 fingers	Hot
Akasa	Indigo	Oval	Bitter	Upwards	All pervading

Tests of the Tattwas. For practice, take five little bullets or counters coloured: red, yellow, blue, silver, and black. Place or carry them in a pocket. Now let him close his eyes and at random take one of them out of his pocket. The colour of the bullet will be that of the Tattwa in course. While still keeping the eyes closed let him see if the colour of the bullet floats before the eyes.

He must not suppose he will be correct immediately. Eventually the confusion will disappear, and well defined colours, more or less stable, will appear before him so that the colour of the bullet will be the same as that floating before his eyes. Then he will have gained the power of knowing which of the Tattwas is in course, and can at will find them.

There is a special method of the concentrating the mind and practising with the eyes for this purpose, which will come with practice.

Let him ask any of his friends to imagine a flower. He will only have to shut his eyes to find the Tattwa then in course and he can astonish his friends by naming the colour of the flower. Again if a man sitting amongst his friends finds the Vayu active let him ascertain those of his friends who are healthy mentally and physically wish to go away. Let him ask them to answer frankly and they will say 'yes'.

In what way other Tattwas affect 'both the body and mind of man will be stated later. Some higher secrets are deliberately reserved for those who safely and honestly pass the elementary stage. When one has reached the stage of finding at Will any of the Tattwas, do not imagine you have become perfect.

If one goes on practising his inner sight becomes keener so that he will recognize the five Tattwic subdivisions. Continue with the meditations and innumerable shades of colour will be recognized according to the different proportions of the Tattwas. His work will be tedious while he is trying to distinguish between the different shades of colour. Tedious at first because when the many shades of colour become fixed and defined by persevering practice he will see an ever changing rainbow of the most beautiful shades of colour and for a time this will be sufficient food for his mind.

To avoid the tediousness meditate upon the breath as is laid down in the chapter on meditation on the Tattwas.

Action to be taken during the different Tattwas. Actions of a sedate and stable nature as enumerated under the Chandra Swara are best done during the course of Prithivi, the earthy principle. Those of a fleeting nature which are to be done and gone through quickly should be done during Apas. Actions such as a man has to make of a violent struggle to hold his own, are best done during Tejas. If a Yogi wishes to kill a man he should do so with the Vayu Tattwa. In the Akasa, nothing should be done but meditation, as works begun during this Tattwa always end badly. Works of the above nature only prosper in the specified Tattwas; and those whose actions prosper may see this by experiment.

MEDITATION AND MASTERY OVER THE TATTWAS

We have previously given summary rules for distinguishing the various colours of the different Tattwas. But now we are going to explain the final method of mastering the Tattwas and of practising. This is a secret which was only imparted to the most promising Adepts of Yoga. But a short practise will fully show the important results to be gained by this practise.

By degrees the student will become able to look into the future at will and have all the visible world before his eyes, and he will be able to command Nature.

During the day when the sky is clear let him once or twice for about an hour or two withdraw his mind from all external things, and sitting on a easy chair let him fix his eyes on any particular part of the blue sky and continue gazing without allowing the eyes to blink.

At first he will see the waves of the water, the watery vapour in the atmosphere. Some days later as the eyes become more practised he will see different sorts of buildings, etc. in the air. When the Neophyte reaches this state of practice he is sure of success.

After this he will see different sorts of mixed colours of Tattwas in the sky, which will show themselves in their proper and respective Tattwic colours.

To test the truth of this the Neophyte should occasionally close his eyes during the practise, and compare what is floating in the sky with that which he sees inwardly. When both are the same the operation is right. Other tests have been given before and other wonders will present themselves later to the Yogi. This practise is to be done in the day time.

For the night, let the student rise about 2 AM. when everything is calm, when there is no noise and when the cold light of the stars breathe holiness and a calm rapture enters into the soul of man. Let him wash his hands, feet, the crown of his head, and the nape of his neck with cold water. Let him put his shin bones to the ground and let the back of the thighs touch his calfs, and let him put his hands upon his knees, his fingers pointing toward the body. Let him now fix his eyes on the tip of his nose. To avoid tediousness he must always meditate on the inhalation and exhalation of his breath.

Besides the above this has many other advantages described elsewhere. It may be said here, by constant practise one is able to develop two distinct syllables in his thought. It is evident that when a man inhales a sound is produced like HAN. When exhaling the sound is SA. By constant practise, the breath becomes associated with these sounds so that effortlessly the mind understands HANSA in relationship to the Tattwas. Thus we see that one full breath makes HANS A which is the name of the Ruler of the Universe together with His Powers. They are exerted during natural phenomena. At this stage of perfection the Yogi should commence as follows.

Getting up at 2 or 3 in the morning and washing himself in the aforementioned manner, let him know and fix his mind upon the Tattwa then in course. If the Tattwa be Prithivi at that moment, think of it as something that is a yellow square, sweet smelling, small in size and able to eliminate all disease. Let him at the same time say LAM. It is very easy to imagine this.

Much the same is true of the other Tattwas which are described in the chart above, which the student should again consult. However, be aware that the words VAM are related to Apas, RAM to Tejas, PAM to Vayu, and HAM to Akasa.

By diligent practise these syllables become definitely associated with the Tattwas. When he repeats them the special Tattwa appears with as much force as he may will, and thus it is that a Yogi can cause whatever he likes—lightning, rain, wind, etc.

CURE OF DISEASES

Every disease causes the breath to flow out of the wrong nostril and the wrong Tattwa to come into course. When the breath is therefore restored to the proper nostril, and the proper Tattwa has been brought into course, do not expect that that is all to be done. If the disease be obstinate and the attack a violent one, one will have to persevere a long time before success is gained.

If success does not come quickly resort to use of the appropriate medications and Swara will soon be restored.

You may notice the Chandra Swara is generally the best for the cure of any disease. Its flow is an indication of the soundness of health. In colds, coughs and other diseases this Swara should flow.

No one Tattwa or Swara causes pain if it flows properly. In this state it should not be unduly meddled with, but when any one Tattwa or Swara becomes overdominant and causes disease it should be changed at once. Experience shows that the Apas and the Prithivi Tattwas are the only ones generally good for health. Indeed the fact that during the course of the Apas Tattwa the breath is felt 16 fingers breadth below the nose and during the Prithivi 12 fingers, argues that at those times there is a more sound and powerful working of body functions than when it is felt only 8 or 4 or no finger breadths below the nose.

Akasa therefore is the worst for health and when sick one would find Akasa, Vayu, or Tejas in course.

When need be therefore proceed in the following manner. After having changed the breath from the wrong nostril to the proper one, generally the left, and pressing the opposite by a cushion so that it may not change readily again, sit on an easy chair and bind the left thigh a little above the knee joint with a handkerchief. Shortly he will perceive that the Tattwa changes to the one immediately below it and so on; and then the next, etc. If he be an acute observor of bodily conditions he will perceive that slowly his mind is becoming more easy. Then let him tighten his bandage still more. When at last he reaches Prithivi, he will find his health a great deal better. Let him persevere in this state or still better the Apas Tattwa for some time, and return to it occasionally for some days even after the disease has disappeared. Undoubtly he will be cured.

FORECAST OF FUTURITY

Although a Yogi obtains the power of knowing everything that is, has been, or is to be, beyond the reach of the senses, yet generally he becomes indifferent to such knowledge. He forgets himself in his eternal presence before the Light, which breathes beauty into all we see in the world. We shall therefore represent him here revealing if not all his knowledge of futurity then only specific questions put to him by others. But our Neophytes may as well put the questions themselves, and then answer them according to the laws here laid down.

When a Yogi is asked a question, let him:

(a) **Determine what Tattwa is in course. If it be Prithivi then the question is about something in the vegetable kingdom or where the element earth is dominant.**

(b) **If it be Apas the question relates to life, birth, death, etc.**

(c) **If Tejas the question concerns metals, gain or loss, etc.**

(d) **If Akasa the questioner has nothing to ask.**

(e) **If Vayu it relates to a journey.**

These are but elementary things. The practical Yogi who can distinguish between the mixture of the Tattwas can name the particular things.

Now let him determine through which of his nostrils the breath is flowing, which is the fortnight then in course of passing, which the days and what direction of himself, the enquirer.

If the breath comes through the left nostril, to secure complete success the work which is the subject of the question and which will be specified under IDA, he must have the following coincidences. The fortnight must be bright. The day must be even, the direction must be east or north. If these things coincide the questioner will get what he wants.

Again if the Surya and Swara coincide with a dark fortnight, the day odd, the direction south and west, a similar result will be predicted, but only partially. The action will be of the sort described under Pingala.

If any of these coincide, the success will vary. It must be remembered that the breath at the time must not be flowing through the wrong nostril.

If the wrong Swara is at the commencement of the day the wrong Swara arises, the Lunar for the Solar or vica versa, one may expect something wrong. If it happens the first day there is sure to be some sort of anxiety. If the second some loss of money. If the third there will be a journey. If the fourth some dear object will be destroyed. If the fifth, loss of Kingdom. If the sixth loss of everything. If the seventh illness and pain are sure to come. If the eighth, death.

If the Sun breath flows in the morning and at noon, and the Moon in the evening, a sad discomforture will result, the reverse being a sign of Victory.

If a man, about to travel which coincides in direction with the empty nostril at the time, he will not get what he desires.

ALCHEMY

By

V.H. FRATER A.M.A.G.

There are within the Knowledge Lectures innumerable references to Alchemy, and there are some minor elucidations of alchemical terms with diagrams of one type or another. There were some so-called Flying Rolls on the subject - non-official papers written either by the Chiefs or by some of the more well-informed members. None of them are really illuminating and throw very little light on the subject. Finally, there is the section on Alchemy in that most remarkable document Z-2, which essentially breaks down the Neophyte Ritual into a variety of many points which can then be applied to different topics. One of them was Alchemy. But unless you obtained an alchemical orientation from some other source, (such as from Frater Albertus of the Paracelsus College in Salt Lake City, Utah) that schema was not going to be very illuminating.

Yet, historical data are firm in their statement that some of the Rosicrucian societies that sprang up in Germany some considerable time after the appearance of the three Rosicrucian manifestoes did actually teach Alchemy. But the Golden Dawn did not, to the best of my knowledge - apart from the above named references.

Yet in recent months I have heard from a Temple descended from the original Felkins group affirming that Alchemy has been and still is taught as part of their basic Rosicrucian Curriculum. Beyond that affirmative information I have no specific knowledge of what that entails. But it is encouraging to learn that this particular branch of Occult knowledge is not being neglected by the Order.

One of the older clerical members of the Order, the Rev. W. Ayton, who is usually but probably unfairly described as a doddering old dreamer, did practice or experiment with Alchemy. What he did with it and what he accomplished is not known to the world at large. But rumor has it that he and some other clerics of the Golden Dawn were Latin scholars who translated some of the more famous hermetic texts into English. Apparently they were not anxious to be identified with that subject - no doubt for fear of censure from their ecclesiastical superiors. So, rumor has it, they turned over their translations to Arthur E. Waite who then claimed to be the editor and translator, and published them, (under his own name). The Aquarian Press in England has announced its intention to publish *The Ayton Papers* which are the letters of the Rev. W.A. Ayton to Frederick Leigh Gardner who was Frater De Profundis ad Lucem (to whom many of the papers used in this *Complete Golden Dawn System of Magic* were issued) - letters extending from 1889 to 1904. It is too soon to evaluate the value of these letters, but by mid-summer 1984 the book should be issued so that later in this series mention can be made of it. My only fear is that Ellic Howe is the editor of that book - and I have previously expresssed myself in no uncertain terms what I think about Mr. Howe's editing. That is, it is full of prejudice and bias. [See Suster's superb critique of Howe in *What You Should Know About The Golden Dawn,* Falcon Press 1983.]

Be that as it may, Alchemy was recognized if not actively taught in the Golden Dawn. Several of its members did do some active literary work on older manuscripts and books, many of which were published as volumes of the *Collectanea Chemica,* some of which are being reprinted in this day and age.

A friend of mine, Hans Nintzel of Dallas, Texas, has written several illuminating and simple papers on Alchemy, and he has granted me permission to quote bits here and there which may finally give us some clear and basic definitions of Alchemy.

Mr. Nintzel holds. . ."Alchemy is the Western tradition as is Qabalah, despite very strong ties to Eastern tradition. The relation of the various metals to the planets is pure Qabalah. . . In concluding this study, we can state that Astrology reveals WHO you are, Qabalah reveals WHERE you are going, and Alchemy provides the MEANS of getting there. . .A one word definition of Alchemy would be *Evolution.* That is to say, the spiritual development from base, dense states to that higher vibratory rate where joyous communion with the Creator exists. This applies to all created matter, minerals and metals as well as man. The purpose of the alchemist then, is to hasten this evolution. To speed the spiritual growth of all of God's creatures."

Several years ago I wrote an article on alchemy in which is to be found the argument: "The alchemists of olden time were spiritually enlightened - not merely blind and stupid workers or seekers in the chemistry laboratory. This fact must never be forgotten. They sought to perfect all phases of man - his body, his mind, and his spirit. No one of these aspects of the total organism should be neglected. It was their belief that man is indefinitely perfectable. They were highly religious, and not disposed to deceive and swindle the treasury of the country in which they lived.

"Art perfects what nature began. Man, and all the gross and subtle constituents of nature unaided fails to achieve this perfection. Evolution may ultimately succeed, though the time factor seems so preposterously slow when one watches through recorded history, the cumbersome, the appallingly slow, progress of mankind. So the alchemists sought to intervene by their art - to speed up the process of growth and evolution, and so to aid God's work."

The following is an essay written on Alchemy, by Hans Nintzel; it is quoted in full with his kind permission.

VOLUME TWO

ALCHEMY

By

HANS W. NINTZEL

"Lately there is a revival of interest in Alchemy. Whereas a few years ago, the very word was hardly mentioned in polite conversation, we are now seeing an occasional article or book being devoted to the subject. We even find Alchemy being taught as a subject in some Universities. Accordingly, it seems well to set down some basic ideas to explain what Alchemy is, its roots, and perhaps, what it is not. This Holy Science is of such great importance, even more so today than it was yesterday, that a great many readers may profit by some additional ideas on this seemingly recondite subject. We can start with the universal idea that alchemists are those who turn lead into gold. While there is the seed of truth in this notion, there is much more to it than that. And what can be more valuable than gold? In fact, if you asked this question, you are really in need of Alchemy.

First of all, the alchemists, modern and medieval, followed a certain credo. Their goal was to alleviate the suffering of their fellow man. Physically and spiritually. One such means was to produce medicines that could aid man's progress in both realms. That is, a medicine or 'Elixir' could be made that produced a dichotomous effect in that physical problems could be alleviated from the usage of an alchemically produced medicine. Moreover, this elixir could act as the agent to purge the body of those dross matters that inhibited the finer vibrations from being received. While Alchemy was definitely an attempt to demonstrate, from the physical viewpoint, experimentally and on the material plane, the validity of certain philosophical views of the Universe, its end goal was the exaltation of its subjects. That subject, in addition to others, was man himself.

A one word definition of Alchemy would be 'evolution.' This in turn can be thought of as being synonomous with 'transmutation,' although this latter term has a connotation of in stantaneous action. By evolution we mean the (usually) gradual change of something from a base or coarse existence into something finer, more noble. In the mineral kingdom, the age-old analogy quickly comes to mind, that is: lead becomes gold. However, this concept is also extended to the animal kingdom and man. That is, man in his crude, self-centred, ignoble state can be transmuted into a fine, loving, God-centred person. A more spiritual person. Everyone, I am sure, can relate to this idea and, in fact, many of us, deep down, yearn for this evolution, this transmutation. We may not think of it in terms of Alchemy, but who has never felt that call to rid themselves of the coarse outer garments and become more spiritual, closer to the Creator? This is the goal of Alchemy, this transmutation, this evolution. However, the alchemist takes these ideas a few steps further and declares that ALL things are evolving. Not only man, but all creatures in all kingdoms. Plants and herbs are evolving, cats and dogs are evolving, rocks and metals are evolving, in fact, this entire planet is in a state of upward evolution. The earth aspires to become enlightened, like the Sun.

This perhaps startling concept is fundamental to Alchemy. It says, among other things, that all base creatures are gradually becoming finer creatures. Man is evolving from his base, brute-like beginnings to a beautiful, saintly creature. Metals are evolving from their base beginnings, as lead, to a more noble existence as gold. Nor does anything have to be done to insure this transmutation or evolution. Slowly, but surely, ALL things will arrive at their zenith on the evolutionary scale. It is as if we were on a huge upwinding spiral. This spiral slowly winds its way 'heavenward.' If nothing was done to hasten this evolutionary action, or to impede it, one day all would arrive at the goal: full spiritual evolution. However, by alchemical processes, this evolution in all creatures can be hastened. That is, man can volitionally speed up the cycle of evolution for himself or for other creatures creatures unable to have any effect on their own spiritual growth.

By the same token, God has given man free will and with this, man can impede his own progress. At given times, as we look about us, we suspect that the evolutionary process has turned into a devolution. This is NOT the case, although individuals can elect to sink back into the material mire from which others struggle to escape. Another way of looking at this is to state that the purpose of Alchemy is to raise the rate of vibrations of both the practitioner (man) and his subjects. These subjects may be medicaments or mineral compositions. Just how one can use Alchemy to more rapidly approach Divinity will be touched on, but let us look briefly at the history of alchemy first.

Some ideas about the roots of Alchemy may provide a stronger foundation upon which other ideas and understanding can be built. Looking to the past, we find that Egyptian goldsmiths existed about 3000 B.C. and around 3500 B.C., Sumerian metalworkers practised their trade in Mesopotamia. In China and India, in remote times, (as well as today, of course), gold was looked upon as a magical medicine. Alchemical ideas arose in China as early as the fifth century B.C. Chinese Alchemy is closely allied with Taoism, a system containing philosophy and religion. They believed in the curative, and even life- extending properties of jade, pearl and cinnabar. These ideas were picked up by subsequent practitioners of the art, moving to Greece, through Europe and finally, through other parts of the western world - ideas that are as strong today as they were then. Alchemy was also as indicated above, in Greece. It is known that during the Alexandrian period, 4th to 7th century A.D., Alchemy flourished. As did other cultures, the Greeks added to the body of Alchemy, various ideas and practices peculiar to themselves.

Just precisely where Alchemy originated is not really known. The most likely theory holds that the ancient Egyptians, who were known to be skilled in chemical knowledge, including metallurgy, glass-tinting and dyeing, were perhaps the founders of the art as we know it today. Egypt was known as KHEM, the "dark land." Thus, Al-Khem was the Islamic term for the father of the dark earth and this phrase was westernised into Al-Chem- y. Futher, there is a body of literature referring to Hermes Trismegistos as being the father of Alchemy. Hermes, whilst essentially a Greek god, is the analog of Thoth, the Egyptian Ibis-headed god. Doberman, in his book, *The Goldmakers*, suggests that Alchemy commenced with the inhabitants of Atlantis. That when this continent submerged during cataclysms of the earth, there were those who escaped and tenanted the deltas of the Euphrates and Indus, on the north shore of the Arabian sea, and further inland at the head of the Persian gulf. The people, tall and black-haired, eventually mixed with the tribes of the Near East. The Hebrews referred to them as Sumerians. They knew how to work with tin, gold, silver, copper, lead, antimony, and iron. Copper and tin produced the bronze so common to the Sumerians and the Indus civilisations. Artifacts were discovered here such as leaden goblets, iron daggers and a vase made of pure antimony. The Sumerians then set out to that land now known as Egypt, bringing with them their arts. It is from the Sumerians then, that the inhabitants of Egypt learned their crafts, the arcane arts of Alchemy.

Whatever its origin, certain basic ideas are found to be common to all the cultures in which Alchemy flourished. One such idea is the principle of the four elements as being the basic foundation of all Alchemy. In China, we find five elements, but the notion is the same. The philosophy of the four elements is classically attributed to Aristotle who postulated the existence of four fundamental 'qualities' imbued in all bodies. These were the hot and moist, along with their opposites, the cold and dry. To these 'qualities' were assigned the symbolism of the four material elements, fire, air, water, and earth. They were seen as having their origin via conjuctions of these four properties. It might be noted that the symbol for fire is opposite to the symbol of water and water is the inversion or opposite of fire. The symbol for air is the fire symbol with a line through it. If we combine the polar opposites, with their dual aspects, we obtain a familiar symbol of the Shield of Solomon, the Hexagram. It is the symbol of the unity of the opposites.

These qualities, as symbolised by the four elements are also associated with certain physical aspects. That is, the element of Fire reflects heat or thermal emissions. Air is associated with gases. Water with all liquids, and Earth with all solids. Bodies, then, were thought of as being constituted of the four elements in varying proportions. This gave rise to the idea that one body could be transformed into another simply by altering the proportion of one or more of these elements. Associated with this idea was the concept of a "Prima Materia," a primordial matter or basic building stuff. This was the fundamental essence from which all other substances were made. Also, all substances or matter could be reduced to this lowest common denominator, this prima materia. It was now a mere extrapolation to consider reducing a base metal, such as lead, to its prima materia, then adding to it the proper amounts of elemental matter to change it to a different substance, i.e. gold. The idea of a prima materia is a basic concept extant in Indian literature under the name of 'Mulaprakriti.' In Chinese alchemy, we find this idea expressed as 'T'ai Chi.' These very basic Alchemical theories were further refined and expanded in the course of time, and they gave rise to certain ideas that are with us today. That is, the principle that all things are composed of three essential constituents or bases. These three, known in Indian literature as the 'three Gunas,' are called by alchemists, 'Sulphur,' 'Salt,' and 'Mercury.' The ancient alchemists were prone to veil their writings in obscure symbolism, mythology and various blinds. In this case, the principle of Sulphur is not common sulphur or brimstone. Salt did not indicate common table salt (sodium chloride), nor did Mercury reflect the matter found in thermometers, quicksilver. There was an analog between these, but definitely not a one-to-one relationship. This blind hindered many a budding alchemist. It is interesting to note that one of these, Mercury, was referred back to the four elements and known as the 'Quintessence,' a fifth principle, as found in Chinese Alchemy where there are five elements: water, fire, wood, metal and earth. Now, the quintessence is also the prima materia, the T'ai Chi. It is from this UNITY, this ONE, that the law of Polarity is derived. The 'ONE' is God, the Divinity, the All.

The duality of the law of Polarity is exemplified in Chinese alchemy as the 'Yin' and the 'Yang.' The female and the male, negativity and positivity, passivity or receptivity and dynamism or action. Yin and Yang were also associated with the moon and sun, respectively, while the five elements were associated with certain planets: Water with Mercury, Fire with Mars, Wood with Jupiter, Metals with Venus, and Earth with Saturn. Yin and Yang, the pair of opposites, are embodied in many religious and alchemical philosophies. They are the Isis and Osiris of Egyptian mythology, the Mercury and Sulphur of Alchemy, the concepts of hot and cold, good and evil, love and hate, etc, etc. In today's 'alchemical circle' there is a maxim that combines all of these ideas. This maxim is stated as: "The One became two by the law of Polarity which is revealed within the three essentials that will be found within the four elements, wherein is to be found the Quintessence which is not of the four but one of the three."

The principle of Sulphur is the principle of combustion. It is the colour of subjects, in plants it gives the odour. The Arabic alchemist, Geber, said sulphur is the "fatness." Alchemists attributed to sulphur the principle of the soul, the consciousness. In a 'tincture' it is what tincts. It is the vitality in animals and has the role of coagulation, to concentrate the life-force. It is red, hot, masculine, active and is symbolised by the Sun. It is associated with Gold. The vital life-force or 'prana' is the Mercury. The Yin or feminine aspect, Mercury, endows gold with its lustre, even as Sulphur endows it with its colour. Mercury is the basis for gold's malleability and fusibility. Mercury is the Spirit, the 'Water of the Wise,' the Prima Materia, Luna, the seed or sperm of all things. Where Sulphur exhibits itself as an oily substance, Mercury is a volatile liquid in its corporeal forms. In the plant world, alcohol is the vehicle for the life-force, for Mercury. Sulphur, in the plant world, is the essential oils contained therein. Finally, Salt is the body of all matter. It is the basic principle of fixity and solidification. It confers resistance to the fire. In the plant world, the salt is the ash of the burned or calcined plant, usually a grey-to-white 'salty' substance. It is the medium in which Sulphur and Mercury can combine.

This 'chemical marriage' is brought about by the catalytic action of the Salt to bring Sulphur and Mercury to their earthly state. This union of the opposites, this marriage of the Sun and Moon, is the state sought after by alchemists. Such a state can be arrived at in all the kingdoms. Now, since all things already consist of these three principles, it is logical to say that one thing can be changed to another by varying the proportion of these principles. That is, as Basil Valentine wrote: "Iron is found to have the least portion of Mercury but more of Sulphur and Salt. . .Copper is generated of much Sulphur but its Mercury and Salt are in equality. . .Saturn (Lead) is generated of little Sulphur, little Salt and much gross, unripe Mercury while Gold hath digested and refined the Mercury to a perfect ripeness." What Valentine is saying is that the metals are different due to the different proportions of the three essentials. In more modern parlance, consider the fact that if one brought together one proton and one electron and one neutron, an atom of 'heavy hydrogen' would be produced. Now, if we changed the proportions of these three 'essentials' by adding, for example, one additional proton and one additional electron, we would have an atom other than hydrogen. These subject matters are both gases but have very different characteristicts. So, by changing the ratio of the essentials, we have wound up with different matters. A transformation has taken place. It is conceded that making hydrogen into helium is no small task. However, in 1941 the physicists, Sherr, Bainbridge, and Anderson, succeeded in transmuting a radioactive isotope of mercury (quicksilver) into pure gold. To be sure, the cost of doing this was prohibitive, and a linear accelerator had to be employed. But the point is, it was done. A transmutation had taken place. We can put a cap on these ideas with a statement by an ancient alchemist, Eirenaeus Philalethes, who encapsulated a very fundamental idea of Alchemy with these words in his book, *The Metamorphosis of Metals*, "All metallic seed is the seed of gold, for gold is the intention of nature in regard to all metals. . .all metals are potentially gold."

At this point we have made a case that all things, consist of three essentials, Sulphur, Salt and Mercury. This Trinity is also found in religion, mythology and symbolism. We have the physical properties of solids, liquids and gases, Father, Son and Holy Ghost, the three Graces, the three Furies, the three Fates, Fire, Water and Earth, Osiris, Horus and Isis, Brahma, Shiva, Vishnu, the Law of the Triangle, protons, neutrons and electrons, and so forth. Some of these analogies are a little less than direct, but the general idea underlying them holds true. But how can this be used in our daily lives? What good can come from this? What are the practicalities? To fully answer these questions would require a book, but we can give at least one set of ideas on how Alchemy can enrich our lives. Moreover, we can get some inkling as to how it will affect not only our physical well-being, but exert a parallel salutary effect on our 'spiritual lives.'

First, we must state that Alchemy as a discipline, has as its foundations, certain other disciplines. These are Astrology, Magic and Qabalah. One cannot be a good Alchemist without being a good Qabalist. One cannot be a good Qabalist without being adept at Magic and one cannot be adept at Magic not having a background in Astrology. We will give some ideas of how the fundamentals of Magic, Qabalah and Astrology play a vital role in Alchemical work. But before that, let us briefly consider one of the ancient writers on Alchemy, Gerhard Dorn. Dorn was a disciple of the great Paracelsus and wrote some very cogent observations on Alchemy.

It has to be recognised that Dorn did not have the psychological insights we have today, nor even the extensive vocabulary to fully express his ideas. However, his fundamental beliefs can be easily understood as evidenced by his writings translated by Louise-Marie von Franz in her book: *Alchemist Active Imagination,* she indicates that Dorn wrote: "Through study (of alchemical literature) one acquires knowledge, through knowledge, love; which creates in oneself experience, virtue and power, through which the miraculous work is done and the work in nature is of this quality." Von Franz explains that what Dorn means is that by simple alchemical literature, one attains "love." This "love" is a kind of unconscious fascination, where one now begins to understand, becomes passionate, about finding the "truth."

The import of this is very dramatic even though Dorn's material did not come across as explosive. The gist of it is that the very process of DOING something, actual laboratory work, meditation on Alchemy or even the innocuous activity of reading alchemical literature, causes something to happen in the practitioner. Let's suppose one is working with physical Alchemy such that he is "cooking" something up in the laboratory, or even in his kitchen. He is making some sort of transmutation take place in his retort or pans. Actually, Dorn is saying that TWO transmutations are taking place. One that is visible, in the retort, and one not visible, in the practitioner. Moreover, that as the work continues, this transmutation accelerates such that there is a feedback loop generated. That is, the more one does the work, of any kind, the greater will be the success. This may sound like a simple case of practice makes perfect. This is not what Dorn means. What he is saying is best shown by an example.

Consider two people. One, a chap who has been doing some kind of alchemical activity, reading or simple experiments of some sort. The other man has not done anything in Alchemy whatsoever. The first man then decides to try a different experiment. He wants to take a substance A and add it to a substance B to make substance C. He pours A into B and behold. He has C. Not all that impressive except, the second man comes along and, using the same substances, the same equipment, he fails to come up with C. Why? Because, the inner transmutation has not been going on in him as it has in the first person. A subtle change has occurred in the first person that allows his experiment to be a success. This change is VERY subtle, possibly not even discernible to the individual. But it takes place nonetheless, and to the degree that the practitioner has conditioned or prepared himself. If he has been making elixirs to purge his physical being of dross in order to be more receptive to higher vibrations, the changes will be proportionately more pronounced.

Further, von Franz also cites the Arab alchemist, Ibn Sina, who wrote that through ECSTACY, man could acquire some of the capacity of God. That is, through such practices as meditation, alchemy, ritual, etc, one can achieve a state of mind lbn Sina calls "ecstacy." In this state one can, even for a brief moment, have powers analagous to those of God. Sufis also obtained this state through physical practices such as dancing or whirling, (i.e. the 'whirling dervishes'). Today, we know that this exalted state, wherein things 'happen' can be achieved through techniques such as Magic as exemplified by Qabalah. Dom Pernety's book, *The Great Art,* contains a reference to indicate that the ancient Rosicrucians blended Alchemy and Qabalah into a cohesive system. Further, their mysticism was based on truths that they were able to demonstrate in the laboratory. We can see some strong evidence then, that there IS a connection between Magic, Qabalah and Astrology

It was stated that in Alchemy one can make various medicaments; that these elixirs have a salutary effect both physically and spiritually. The base matters used for such medicines can be plants or herbs or various metals. But where does one start? What herb, for example, can one use for some specific ailment? Or what metal? Our answers come from a knowledge of Qabalah-Magic, specifically knowledge of that mighty glyph known as the Tree of Life, and from the laws of Astrology. For example, Astrology tells us that those people born under the same 'sign' will exhibit the same characteristics. That is, an individual born in early April is under the sign of Aries. Others born under this sign will tend.to have similar traits, such as being dynamic, head-strong, jumping from one interest to another without finishing the first, etc. Aries is a zodiacal 'picture' that has in it the planet Mars. This picture composed of stars, sends rays or influences to the earth. The sun acts as a step-down transformer and absorbs some of these rays, dispersing the rest to earth. It is these stellar influences that 'imprint' a person at the moment of birth, and what other positions were maintained by the other planets, these are the influences which make him who he (or she) is. By careful study of these planetary configurations, one can determine why they are who they are.

What is perhaps new to the reader is the idea that not only are there Arian and Libran people, there are also Arian and Libran plants and minerals. The other kingdoms also come under the dominion of the astral influences. And this is where the key to making medicines alchemically comes in. For instance, we know that the planet Mercury 'rules' the nervous system. We can determine that Mercury also rules the herbs valerian and marjoram. Further, the planet Mercury rules over the condition known as insomnia. So then, if we had a nervous condition or had insomnia, what herb would possibly make a good medicine for these problems? Valerian or marjoram, because they are 'correspondences' in that they have the same ruler. We can take this a step further, the planet Mercury rules over Wednesday. It is a simple matter to reach the conclusion that the best day to pick valerian would be on a. . .Wednesday. By the same token, the best time to make a medicine, or to take that medicine would also be a Wednesday. An additional refinement is that the day is divided into several parts. Each part, both the day and the night, have periods of time when the influence of one planet is stronger than any other. That is to say, twice during Thursday, the influence of Mars is stronger than at any other time. Thus, one might find out what this time period is and not only make and take the medicine on the 'correct' day, but do it during the 'correct' times.

In the mineral kingdom, the same sort of logic prevails. If we had a problem with the head or with hemorrhaging, we could use an herb such as garlic, anise or cayenne. A tincture could be made of one of these herbs or, if the practitioner had the knowledge, he could exalt the herb to its highest level and confect what is known in alchemy as a 'plant stone.' This is the highest level of efficacy any herb potent in medicine could have. It requires man to bring the plant to this advanced state of evolution. On the other hand, a medicine could also be found in the mineral kingdom, in iron. Mars rules iron just as it rules the head and garlic, etc. But how can one make medicine from iron? This is where practical laboratory Alchemy comes in. It would require an astute reader of alchemical literature to arrive at the proper procedure, or more aptly, one could learn from a teacher of Alchemy. The process is, to separate the iron (ore) into its three essentials. Just as was done for the plant. To make the herbal medicine, one had to make a tincture of the herb which would extract the sulphur principle. The sulphur would 'tinct' or colour the extraction media or 'menstruum' as it is called. This colouring is caused by the Sulphur which the menstruum has leached out of the .herb. The sulphur could more readily be obtained by a steam distillation as well. The mercury of the plant is in the alcohol. One could putrify the plant and generate alcohol or one could distill alcohol from wine (if this is legal in the reader's area) or purchase grain alcohol; the mercury being uniform in all types of alcohol obtained from vegetable matter. Finally, the body of the herb will be burned or calcined to obtain the Salt. By the same principle, and by following the same procedure, one could separate any body, including mineral, into its three essentials.

Therefore, one could take iron ore, or some other form of iron, and make a tincture using a suitable menstruum. The tincture would be driven off (i.e. evaporated) and the sulphur would be left behind. The oil of iron, then, would in itself be a potent medicine. It would be more potent than that derived from a plant. The reason being that the minerals have 'been around' much longer than any plant and thus have abosorbed greater astral influences and thus are more potent. They have a higher level of vibration. In any event, the soul of the iron, once it has been separated, must also be purified. All these processes involve heat. The mastery of the heat is a technique learned from a teacher, or by (often painful) trial and error. Once purified, it can be taken as is or it can be combined with the mercury of the mineral kingdom which is called 'alkahest.' The mercury of the mineral kingdom is not so easily come by; but with it one can make the fabled 'Philosopher's Stone.' This stone can cure all illnesses and cause instant upward evolutions or transmutations. Does this sound as if it could change a base matter into a noble one? Yes, it can.

To return to just the sulphur or oil of iron, consider what you have, once you know how to make it. Not only is it a medicine for the head, but it is a medicine for all other ailments governed by Mars. To find out just what Mars, and all other planets, govern, one could check with such reference works as *The Alchemist's Handbook*, or Bill's *Rulership Book*, etc. Consider just one aspect: anaemia. People with poor blood or "tired blood" take products such as Geritol. This fine product is derived from iron, sure enough. However, it is made from something like iron oxide, a non-organic matter. Or, we can absorb some non-organic material, as the built-in, inner alchemist we all have, can effect such transmutations. In this case it is a 'biological transmutation.' The tolerance here is about 3% of what the body has taken in of non-organic material. Would it not be marvelous if we could find a substance that is non-toxic, can be absorbed 100% by the body, AND has no side effects like some products do. Did you think of oil of iron? Correct. This substance CAN be totally utilised by the body and NOT have side effects that are unwanted. More germane, it overcomes the anaemic condition. The uses of minerals in Alchemy, just in the field of medication, are endless. Basil Valentine wrote an entire book on one mineral alone, its various uses in medicine. This book is called the *Triumphal Chariot of Antimony*. It is a 'recipe' book, explaining the various preparations of that metal known as antimony. Antimony is poisonous? Yes, but when it is prepared by alchemical processes, 'spagyrically,' it is not only rendered non-toxic, but it could be a panacea.

To give the reader a flavour of this incredible book by Valentine and to perhaps "turn them on" to Alchemy, the following is quote of a process by Valentine using antimony. This was extracted from *Triumphal Chariot of Antimony* published by Dorman Newman in 1678 in England, and was translated by Dr. Theo Kirkringius:

"The dose of it before coagulation is eight grains taken in wine. It makes a man very young again, delivers him from all melancholy and whatsoever in the body of man grows and increaseth, as the hairs and nails fall off and the whole man is renewed as a Phoenix (if such a feigned bird, which is only here for example's sake named by me, can anywhere be found on this earth) is renewed by fire. And this medicine can no more be burned by the Fire, than the feathers of that unknown salamander; for it consumes all symptoms in the body, like consuming fire, to which it is deservedly likened; it drives away every evil and expels all that which Aurum-Potabile is capable to expel".

Does not that description sound like something you would like to see happen? It could, you know. Valentine reveals in his book various techniques on how to be "successful" in alchemical work. He spoke from the viewpoint of one who KNEW, not one who guessed or who thought it might be this way. And Valentine wasn't the only good writer of alchemical treatises. The writings of Paracelsus, Geber, Glauber, Vaughn, Sendivogius, and Flamel are amongst those of the older writers that are particularly noteworthy. But there are even modern day writers such as Frater Albertus, Phillip Hurley and Archibald Cockren. In Cockren's book, *A Ichemv Re-discoverd and Restored* he describes various alchemists and their writings. He was particularly impressed with Johannes Isaaci Hollander, who, he said, wrote so clearly and plainly, his writings have been totally discounted. Ah, none are so blind as they who will not see. Cockren also presents a diary of his own alchemical experimentation. Hurley in his book, *Herbal Alchemy*, integrates magical practices with laboratory work, for example, making talismans for a particular laboratory experiment. In discussing the literature, we would be amiss in not mentioning the work of Dr. Carl Jung. While Dr. Jung did not appear to have much regard for physical Alchemy and wrote nothing thereon, he had enormous insight and grasp of the psychological aspects of Alchemy. In this respect, he has done mankind a tremendous service in his fine books on this subject. Dr. Jung and various of his associates have delved into the old texts, translated some of them, and given us insight into the thinking of the old alchemist. This data combined with personal research provides a sure grasp of Alchemy. While it is clear that Alchemy will not become as popular as home computers, it is quite possible that as more people, especially those trained in the sciences 'discover' Alchemy and contribute to the vast body of knowledge that is accumulating, we may one day have a 'breakthrough.' Thinking people seeking answers to cosmic questions, greater insight into themselves and cures for incurable ailments, must sooner or later come across alchemical knowledge. As they read the literature and experiment in the lab in an effort to unlock the mysteries, the **LVX** they shed will not only illumine the path but, hopefully, attract countless others to this Holy Science."

THE VISION OF THE UNIVERSAL MERCURY

"We stood upon a dark and rocky cliff that overhung the restless seas. In the sky above us was a certain glorious sun, encircled by that brilliant rainbow, which they of the Path of the Chamelion know.

"I beheld, until the heavens opened, and a form like unto the Mercury of the Greeks (1) descended, flashing like the lightning; and he hovered between the sky and the sea. In his hand was the staff (2) wherewith the eyes of mortals are closed in sleep, and wherewith he also, at will, re-awakeneth the sleeper; and terribly did the globe at its summit dart forth rays. And he bare a scroll whereon was written:

Lumen est in Deo,
Lux in homine factum,
Sive Sol,
Sive Luna
Sive Stelloc errantes,
Omnia in Lux,
Lux in Lumine
Lumen in Centrum
Centrum in Circulo,
Circulum ex Nihilo,
Quid scis, id eris.(3)
F.I.A.T.(4)
E.S.T.(5)
E.S.T.O.(6)
E.R.I.T.(7)
In fidelitate et veritate universas ab aeternitate.(8)
Nunc Hora.
Nunc Dies.
Nunc Annus,
Nunc Saeculum,
Omnia sunt Unum,
Et Omnia In Omnibus.
A.E.T.E.R.N.I.T.A.S.(9)

Then Hermes cried aloud, and said:

"I am Hermes Mercurius, the Son of God, the messenger uniting Superiors and Inferiors. I exist not without them, and their union is in me. I bathe in the Ocean. I fill the expanse of Air. I penetrate the depths beneath."

And the Frater who was with me, said unto me:

"Thus is the Balance of Nature maintained, for this Mercury is the beginning of all movement. This He, (10) this She, this IT, is in all things, but hath wings which thou canst not constrain. For when thou sayest 'He is here' he is not here, for by that time he is already away, for he is Eternal Motion and Vibration."

Nevertheless in Mercury must thou seek all things. Therefore not without reason did our Ancient Fratres say that the Great Work was to "Fix the Volatile." There is but one place where he can be fixed, and that is the Centre, a centre exact. "Centrum in trigono centri." (11) The Centre is the triangle of the Centre.

If thine own soul be baseless how wilt thou find a standing point whence to fix the soul of the Universe?

"Christus de Christi,
Mercury de Mercurio,
Per viam crucis,
Per vitam Lucis
Deus te Adjutabitur!"(12)

THE COMPLETE GOLDEN DAWN SYSTEM OF MAGIC

TRANSLATION OF AND NOTES ON THE MERCURY PAPER

By

G. H. FRATER, S.R.M.D.

1. Hermes is Greek, Mercury is Roman.

2. Compare with verse .47 ODYSSEY: "Him promptly obeyed the active destroyer of Argus. Forth sped he, and under his feet he bound his ambrosial sandals. Then, taking his staff wherewith he the eyes of mortals closeth at will, and the sleeper at will reawakens."

3. Translation: The Light is in God, the LVX hath been made into Man. Whether Sun, or Moon, or Wandering Stars, all are in Lux, the Lux in the Light, the Light in the Centre, the Centre in the Circle, the Circle from the Nothingness (Negative or Ain). What thou mayest be (i.e. what thou hast in thyself, the capability of being) that shalt thou be (or become).

4. Flatus. Ignis. Aqua. Terra. Air. Fire. Water. Earth.

5. Ether. Sal. Terrae. Ether, the Salt of the Earth.

6. Ether. Subtilis. Totius. Orbis. The subtle Ether of the whole universe.

7. Ether. Ruens. In. Terra. The Ether rushing into the Earth.

8. Let it be (or become). It is. Be it so. It shall be (or endure). In Universal faithfulness and truth from eternity. Now an hour, Now a day, Now a year, Now an age, all things are One, and All in All. ETERNITY.

9. These ten letters are Notaricons of: Ab Kether. Ex Chokmah. Tu Binah. Ex Chesed. Regina Geburah. Nunc Tiphareth. In Netzach. Totius Hod. Ad Yesod. Saeculorum Malkuth. "From the Crown, out of Wisdom - Thou, O Understanding art Mercy, Queen of Severity. Now the perfect Beauty, in the Victory, of all Splendour, for the Foundation, of the Ages of the Universe.

10. Probably alludes to the Three Principles.

11. This was, I believe, but am not certain, the motto of our Frater Count Adrian a Meynsicht, otherwise known as Henricus Madathanus.

12. The Christ from the Christ. The Mercury from the Mercury, Through the Path of the Cross, Through the life of the Light, God shall be Thy Help.

THE CORE OF THE TRADITION

VOLUME THREE

THE CORE OF THE TRADITION

TABLE OF CONTENTS

IMPORTANT TABLES AND ILLUSTRATIONS

VOLUME THREE

THE CORE OF THE TRADITION

THE PILLARS

By

G.H. FRATER N.O.M.

As confusion is found to exist with regard to the Right and Left Pillars of the Sephiroth on the Tree of Life in relation to the right and left sides of a man, and as to the phases of the Moon you must note: That in every diagram and picture, the right hand side of the observer is next the Pillar of Mercy - Chokmah, Chesed, and Netzach; while the Pillar of Severity is on the observer's left hand. Yet when you apply the Tree of Life to yourself, your right side, arm and leg represent the side of Strength and Severity - Binah, Geburah and Hod, and your left side refers to the Pillar of Mercy. So that when you look at a diagram, you are looking, as it were, at a man facing you, that your right side faces his left. His Merciful side forms the right hand Pillar in front of you, so that it is as if you looked at yourself in a mirror. Just as the man looks at you, so does the Moon look at you and so you say that the Moon in her increase is on the side of Mercy, the right hand pillar of the Sephiroth; and in her decrease, the crescent is on the left hand Pillar of Severity. A Diagram, then, is a picture of a Man or the Moon facing you. The Temple Pillars are similar:

Black Pillar	**Severity**	**Left-North**
White Pillar	**Mercy**	**Right-South**
Black Pillar	**Boaz**	**Stoiistes**
White Pillar	**Yachin**	**Dadouchos**

That is, the white Mercy or Yachin Pillar is on your right hand as you approach the Altar from the West and from the Hiereus. (See Chronicles II. iii, 17.) "And call the Name on the right hand (of him who enters) Yachin, and the Name of that on the left, Boaz."

Boaz is Strength, Severity, Binah, Black Pillar.

Yachin is White Pillar of Mercy.

So in making the Qabalistic Cross on your breast it is correct to touch the Forehead and say Ateh - Thou art; the Heart - Malkuth; Right Shoulder, ve-Geburah; left shoulder ve-Gedulah, and with the fingers clasped on the breast say, Le olahm, amen!

1

THE PILLARS II

In the explanation of the Symbols of the Grade of Neophyte, your attention has been directed to the general mystical meaning of the Two Pillars called in the Ritual the "Pillars of Hermes" of "Seth" and of "Solomon." In the 9th chapter of the Ritual of the Dead they are referred to as the "Pillars of Shu," the "Pillars of the Gods of the Dawning Light," and also as "the North and Southern Columns of the Gate of the Hall of Truth." In the 125th chapter, they are represented by the sacred gateway, the door to which the aspirant is brought when he has completed the negative confession. The archaic pictures on the one Pillar are painted in black upon a white ground, and those on the other in white upon a black ground, in order to express the interchange and reconciliation of opposing forces and the eternal balance of light and darkness which gives force to visible nature. The black cubical bases represent darkness and matter wherein the Spirit, the Ruach Elohim, began to formulate the Ineffable NAME, that Name which the ancient Rabbis have said "rusnes through the universe," that Name before which the Darkness rolls back to the birth of time. The flaming red triangular capitals which crown the summit of the Pillars represent the Triune manifestation of the Spirit of Life, the Three Mothers of the Sepher Yetzirah, the Three Alchemical Principles of Nature, the Sulphur, the Mercury and the Salt. Each Pillar is surmounted by its own light-bearer veiled from the material world. At the base of both Pillars rise the Lotus flowers, symbols of regeneration and metempsychosis. The archaic illustrations are taken from vignettes of the 17th and 125th chapter of the Ritual of the Dead, the Egyptian Book of the "Per-em-Hru" or the "Book of coming Forth into the Day," the oldest book in the world as yet discovered. The Recension of the Priests of ON is to be found in the walls of the Pyramids of the Kings of the 5th and 6th Dynasties at Sakarah, the recension of the 11 th and 12th Dynasties on the sarcophagi of that period, and the Theban recension of the 18th Dynasty and onward is found on papyri, both plain and illuminated. No satisfactory translation of these books is available, none having been yet attempted by a scholar having the qualifications of mystic as well as Egyptologist. The Ritual of the Dead, generally speaking, is a collection of hymns and prayers in the form of a series of ceremonial Rituals to enable the man to unite himself with Osiris the Redeemer. After this union he is no longer called the man, but Osiris, with whom he is now symbolically identified. "That they also may be One of us," said the Christ of the New Testament. "I am Osiris" said the purified and justified man, his soul luminous and washed from sin in the immortal and uncreated light, united to Osiris, and thereby justified, and the son of God; purified by suffering, strengthened by opposition, regenerate through self-sacrifice. Such is the subject of the great Egyptian Ritual. The 17th Chapter of the Theban recension consists of a very ancient text with several commentaries, also extremely old, and some prayers, none of which come into the scheme of the original text. It has, together with the 12th chapter been very carefully translated for the purpose of this lecture by the V.H. Frater M.W.T., and the V.H. Soror S.S.D.D. has made many valuable suggestions with regard to the interpretation. The Title and Preface of the 17th Chapter reads:

"Concerning the exaltation of the Glorified Ones, of Coming and Going forth in the Divine Domain, of the Genies of the Beautiful land of Amentet. Of Coming forth in the light of Day in any form desired, of Hearing the Forces of Nature by being enshrined as a living Bai." And the rubric is: "The united with Osiris shall recite it when he has entered the Harbour. May glorious things be done thereby upon earth. May all the words of the Adept be fulfilled." Owing to the complex use of symbols, the ritual translation of the Chapter can only be understood by perpetual reference to the ancient Egyptian commentaries, and therefore the following paraphrase has been put together to convey to modern minds as nearly as possible the ideas conceived by the old Egyptians in this glorious triumphal song of the Soul of Man made one with Osiris, the Redeemer. "I am TUM made One with all things. "I have become NU, I am RA in his rising ruling by right of his Power. I am the Great God self-begotten, even NU, who pronounced His Names, and thus the Circle of the Gods was created. "I am Yesterday and know Tomorrow. I can never more be overcome. I know the secret of Osiris, whose being is perpetually revered of RA. I have finished the work which was planned at the Beginning, I am the Spirit made manifest, and armed with two vast eagle's plumes. Isis and Nephthys are their names, made One with Osiris.

"I claim my inheritance. My sins have been uprooted and my passions overcome. I am Pure White. I dwell in Time. I live through Eternity, when Initiates make offering to the Everlasting Gods. I have passed along the Pathway. I know the Northern and the Southern Pillars, the two Columns at the Gateway of the Hall of Truth. "Stretch unto me your hands, O ye Dwellers in the centre. For I am transformed to a God in your midst. Made One with Osiris, I have filled the eye socket in the day of the morning when Good and Evil fought together. "I have lifted up the cloud veil in the Sky of the Storm. Till I saw RA born again from out of the Great Waters. His strength is my strength, and my strength is His strength. Homage to you, Lords of Truth, chiefs who Osiris rules. Granting release from sin, followers of Ma where rest is Glorious. Whose Throne Anubis built in the day when Osiris said: "Lo! A man wins his way to Amentet. I come before you, to drive away my faults. As ye did to the Seven Glorious Ones who follow their Lord Osiris. I am that Spirit of Earth and Sun. "Between the Two Pillars of Flame. I am RA when he fought beneath the Ashad Tree, destroying the enemies of the Ancient of Days. I am the Dweller in the Egg. I am he who turns in the Disc. I shine forth from the Horizon, as the gold from the mine. I float through the Pillars of SHU in the ether. Without a peer among the Gods. The Breath of my mouth is as a flame. I light upon the Earth with my glory. Eye cannot gaze on my darting beams, as they reach through the Heavens and lick up the Nile with tongues of flame. I am strong upon Earth with the strength of RA. I have come into Harbour as Osiris made perfect. Let priestly offering be made to me as one in the train of the ancient of Days. I brood as the Divine spirit. I move in the firmness of my Strength. I undulate as the Waves that vibrate through Eternity. Osiris has been claimed with acclamation, and ordained to rule among the Gods. Enthroned in the Domain of Horus where the Spirit and the Body are united in the presence of the Ancient of Days. Blotted out are the sins of his body in passion. He has passed the Eternal Gate, and has received the New Year Feast with Incense, at the marriage of Earth with Heaven. "TUM has built his Bridal Chamber. RURURET has founded his shrine, the Procession's completed. HORUS has purified, SET has consecrated, SHU made one with OSIRIS, has entered his heritage.

"As TUM he has entered the Kingdom to complete union with the Invisible. Thy Bride, of Osiris, is Isis, who mourned Thee when she found Thee slain. In Isis, thou art born again. From Nephthys is thy nourishment. They cleansed thee in thy Heavenly Birth. Youth waits upon thee, ardour is ready at thy hand. And their arms shall uphold thee for millions of years. Initiates surround Thee and Thine enemies are cast down. The Powers of Darkness are destroyed. The Companions of Thy Joys are with Thee. Thy Victories in the Battle await their reward in the Pillar. The Forces of Nature obey Thee. Thy Power is exceeding great. The Gods curse him that curseth Thee. Thine aspirations are fulfilled. Thou art the Mistress of Splendour. They are destroyed who barred Thy way." The 125th Chapter is concerned with the entry of an Initiate into the Hall of the Two Columns of Justice, and commenced with a most beautiful and symbolic description of Death, as a journey from the barren wilderness of Earth, to the Glorious Land which lies beyond. The literal translation of the opening lines is as follows:

"I have come from afar to look upon thy beauties. My hands salute Thy Name of Justice. I have come from afar, where the Acacia Tree grew not. Where the tree thick with leaves is not born. Where there come not beams from herb or grass. I have entered the Place of Mystery. I have communed with Set. Sleep came upon me, I was wrapped therein, bowing down before the hidden things. I was ushered into the House of Osiris. I saw the marvels that were there. The Princes of the Gates in their Glory."

The illustrations in this section represent the Hall of Truth as seen through the open leaves of its door. The Hall is presided over by a God who holds his right hand over the cage of a hawk, and his left over the food of eternity. On each side of the God is a cornice crowned by a row of alternate feathers and Uraei symbolising justice and fiery power. The door leaf at the hand of a stall is called "Possessor of strength, binding the male and female animals."

The 42 Judges of the Dead are represented as seated in a long row, and each of them has to be named, and the Sin over which he presided has been denied. This chapter describes the introduction of the initiate into the Hall of Truth by ANUBIS, who, having questioned the aspirant, receives from him an account of his Initiation, and is satisfied by his right to enter. He states that he has been taken into the antechamber of the Temple and there stripped and blindfolded, he had to grope for the entrance of the Hall, and having found it, he was reclothed and annointed in the presence of the Initiated, he is then asked for the Passwords and demands that his Soul should be weighed in the Great Balance of the Hall of Truth, whereupon ANUBIS again interrogates him concerning the symbolism of the door of the Hall, and his answers being found correct, ANUBIS says: "Pass on, thou knowest it." Among other things the Initiate states that he has been purified four times, the same number of times that the Neophyte is purified and consecrated in the ceremony of the Neophyte. He then makes the long Negative Confession, stating to each Judge in turn that he is innocent of that form of Sin over which he judges. Then he invokes the Judges to do him justice, and afterwards describes how he has washed in the washing place of the South, and rested in the North, in the place called "Son of the Deliverers" and he becomes the Dweller under the Olive Tree of Peace, and how he was given a tall flame of fire and a sceptre of cloud which he preserved in the salting tank in which mummies were swathed. And he found there another sceptre called "Giver of Breath" and with that he extinguished the flame and shattered the sceptre of cloud, and made a lake of it. The initiate is then brought to the actual Pillars, and has to name them and their parts under the symbol of the Scales of a Balance. He also has to name the Guardian of the Gateway, who prevents his passage, and when all these are propitiated, the plea of the Hall itself cries out against his steps, saying "Because I am silent, because I am pure," and it must know that his aspirations are pure enough and high enough for him to be allowed to tread upon it. He is then allowed to announce to Thoth that he is clean from all evil, and has overcome the influence of the planets, and THOTH says to him:

"Who is He whose Pylons are of Flame, whose walls of Living Uraei, and the flames of whose House are streams of Water?" And the Initiate replies "Osiris!" And it is immediately proclaimed: "Thy meat shall be from the Infinite, and thy drink from the infinite. Thou art able to go forth to the sepulchral feast on earth, for thou hast overcome." Thus, these two chapters, which are represented by their illustrations (Note the illustrations referred to will follow in the next two papers on the Pillars.) upon the Pillars, represent the advance and purification of the Soul and its union with Osiris, the Redeemer, in the Golden Dawn of the Infinite Light, in which the Soul is transfigured, knows all, and can do all, for it is made One with the Eternal God.

KHABS AM PEKHT - KONX OM PAX - LIGHT IN EXTENSION!

VOLUME THREE

THE PILLARS III
BY
G.H. FRATER S.R.M.D.

The Pillars and the Meaning of the Hierogyphics Inscribed on them, taken from the vignettes of the 17th, and 25th, Chapters of the"PER-M-HRU"or Egyptian Ritual Of The Dead.

In the explanation of the Symbols of the Grade of Neophyte, your attention has been directed to the general mystical meaning of the juxtaposition of the two Pillars: and therefore I will only ask you to notice that the Hieroglyphics of the one are painted in black upon a white ground, and those of the other in the same colours but reversed; the better to express the interchange and reconcilement of opposing forces, and the Eternal Balance of Light and Darkness which gives form to the Visible Universe. The black square bases represent Darkness and Matter wherein the Spirit, the Ruach Elohim formulated the Eternal Pronunciation of the Ineffable Name, that Name which the Rabbis of old have said:

"Rusheth through the Universe; that Name before which rolled back the Darkness, at the Birth of the Morning of Time." The flame-red triangular capitals which crown the summit of the Pillars, represent the triune manifestation of the Spirit of Life, the "Three Mothers" of the "Sepher Yetzirah," the three Alchemical Principles of Nature, the Sulphur, the Mercury and the Salt. And each pillar is surmounted by its own Light-bearer though veiled from the Material World.

The Hieroglyphical figures upon the Pillars are taken from the vignettes of the 17th, and 125th, chapters of the "Ritual of the Dead," the Egyptian "Per-M-Hru." This celebrated and most ancient work is a collection of Mystical Hymns and Addresses in the form of a species of Ceremonial Ritual for the use of the soul after death, to enable it to unite itself to the Body of Osiris the Redeemer: and thenceforth in the Ritual is it no longer called the Soul, but it is called "the Osiris" of whom it is a member;

"I am the Vine, ye are the Branches" said the Christ of the New Testament: "I am a member of the Body of Osiris" said the purified and justified soul. The Soul, the Soul luminous and washed from Sin in the Immortal and Uncreated Light, united to Osiris, and justified Son of God, such is the subject of the great Egyptian Ritual; purified by suffering, strengthened by opposition, regenerate through Self-sacrifice. Nor is the "Ritual of the Dead" a work of comparatively recent time; for the great Egyptologists Birch and Bunsen assert that its origin is anterior to Menes and belongs probably to the pre-Menite Dynasty of Abydos, between 3100 and 4500 B.C. and it implies that at that period the system of Osirian worship and mythology was already in actual existence. Of all the chapters in the "Per-M-Hru," the 17th, is one of the oldest as shewn by its Gloss and Scholia, and it is the symbols of this Chapter and the 125th, which form the designs on the Pillars before you; at the base of each of which rises the Lotus, symbolic of the New Life, regeneration and metempsychosis. In the Papyri which have these symbols is if the Abydos Dynasty be prior to Menes, who was said to be the first Human King. The pre-Menite Dynasties are said to be those of the Gods, the Demi-Gods, and the Menes, the hieroglyphical text of this chapter, a group of hieroglyphics recurs at intervals, the literal translation of which is, "the explanation." After these groups comes a short commentary or gloss on the preceding and more ancient text. According to the pre-cited authorities this gloss was mixed up with the text as early as 2,250 B.C. at a period long anterior to the era of Joseph and to that of the Trojan War; and the circumstances of its possessing a written commentary even at this date shows the much greater antiquity of the actual text. The especial title of the 17th chapter is "The Book of the Egyptian Faith," and its subject is a sort of Hymn of the Osirified soul, which may be partially and succinctly reproduced as follows:

WHITE PILLAR 2.   WHITE PILLAR 3.

THE WORDS OF THE DEPARTED PIRIT OSIRIS, SON OF GOD

"I am Toom, the Setting Sun, I am the only being in the firmament of Heaven.

I am Ra, the Rising Sun, I have passed from the gate of Death unto Life.

The Sun's power beginneth again after he hath set; he riseth again (so doth the justified Spirit of Man.)

I am the Great God begotten of himself; I can never be turned back by the Elementary Powers; I am the Morning, I know the Gate. (I ever rise again unto existence. I know the pathway through death unto life.)

(The date of Menes has been calculated as B.C. 5500. Others think earlier.)

The Father of the Spirit; the Eternal Soul of the Sun. He hath examined and He hath proved me. He hath found that I fought on Earth the battle of the good Gods, as He, my Father, Lord of the Invisible World ordered me to do.

I know the Great God who existeth in the Invisible.

I am the Great Phoenix which is in Annu, the former of my Life and my Being am I."

The symbols on the Columns beginning at the top of the one with the Black figures on a white ground are mystical representations of the various paragraphs of the 17th chapter. They show the symbol of Toom the setting sun; the past and the future. The Adoration of Toom of the West. The Abode of the West shown by the Jackal of Anubis in Shrine with Isis and Nephthys adoring The Adoration of Osiris, the Phoenix or Bennu.

The reformation of the Departed Spirit, shewn by the Soul descending to the Body on the bier, in the form of a human headed bird, when of dual manifestation, shown by the birds on either side of the prostrate mummy. So the purified Soul passes ever onward and upward, and still rises the mystical hymn. Purified, the Soul reaches the pools of the two Truths, shewn by the two quadrangular figures, it passeth through Amenti the Gate of the North, and through the Gate of Taser; and it saith to the Mystic Guardians: "Give me your strength, for I am made even as ye. " Then comes the Mystical Eye of Osiris representing the Orb of the Sun; and the Cow symbolical of the Great Water, the blue firmament of Heaven. Next is the Adoration of the Lords of Truth behind the Northern

Heaven: "Hail unto ye, ye Lords of Truth, ye Chiefs behind Osiris! ye followers of Her whose peace is sure." When the soul arrives at the Mystic Pool of Persea trees, wherein is Horus symbolised by the Great Cat who slays the Evil Serpent Apophis. Last of the Symbols of the 17th chapter is the Adoration of the Life of the Creator in His bark, and the uniting of the purified Soul with its Maker. The 125th chapter is called "The Hall of the Two Truths" and its full title is "The Book of Going to the Hall of the Two Truths, and of Separating a person from his Sins, when he has been made to see the Faces of the Gods." It opens with a solemn Adoration of the Lord of Truth, and the Ceremony of passing by the Forty-two Assessors of the Dead represented by seated figures. Then comes the weighing of the soul, and the Mystical Meaning of various parts of the Hall, the naming of which is insisted on by the various Guardians, and is similar to the Mystic Circumambulation of the Neophyte in the path of Darkness in the Grade when he has to name the Guardians of the Gates of East and West.

The figures on the pillar represent the Soul introduced either by its own guide, or by the jackal-headed Anubis, the Guide in general of the Dead, into the Hall of Truth.

The Soul then watches the weighing of its actions in Earth-life, against a figure of Truth, in the Mystical Scales of Maat and Anubis.

Thoth, ibis-headed, records the judgement; and the Devourer stands ready to seize, if the soul has led an evil life.

Passing through this ordeal, the soul is then introduced into the presence of Osiris by Horus. Osiris sits in his Shrine upon a throne, with the Crook and Scourge, symbols of Mercy and Severity in his hands; behind him are Isis and Nephthys, the Goddesses of Nature and Perfection; and before him are the four Genii of the Dead upon the Lotus Flower, the emblem of the Metempsychosis. Thus the whole of the Symbols upon the pillars represent the advance and purification of the Soul, and its uniting with Osiris the Redeemer; in that Golden Dawn of an Infinite Light wherein the soul is transfigured; knows all and can do all; for it hath become joined unto Eternal Gods.

KHABS AM PEKHT - KONX OM PAX - LIGHT IN EXTENSION.

THE PILLARS IV

By

G.H. FRATER SUB SPE

THE WHITE PILLAR

The designs on this Pillar are taken from the Vignettes to the 17th Chapter of the Book of the Dead. This was inadvertently called by Lepsius the XVIth chapter. It is not, however, a chapter at all, but ornaments or illustrations (called Vignettes) intended to accompany the Hymn to the Rising Sun. The vignettes are slightly different in different papyri; those in the Papyrus of Ani are the best on the whole; those on the pillars are selected from several examples. The designs may be explained as follows: The first figure does not occur in the Papyrus of Ani, and varies in others. It is variously explained. Probably it is meant for an ideograph of the Hymn. The soul, figured by a bird, beholding the Truth (a feather). The two figures following are said by some Egyptologists to be the deceased and his wife playing drafts under a canopy. It is more probable however that his initiator or guide teaching him the ways of the kingdom of souls, by means of a game. He is moving a piece, he wears the Lotus headdress, and she has the crown of Nephthys. Following this are the souls of the deceased and his guide as two human-headed hawks on a pylon-shaped building. Note that the deceased, being united to Osiris, is called in the Ritual "Osiris" or "The Osirian." (Compare the Christian promise "That ye may be one with ME."

"Saith Osiris, after he hath come to this haven of rest, it is good for a man to recite these words, while he is yet upon earth. The deceased is next shown in adoration before two lions seated back to back and supporting the horizon with the sun's disc. The Lion on the right is called Sef ("Yesterday") and that on the left is Tau ("Tomorrow") "Who then is this? It is Tem, the Dweller in his disc, or (as others say) it is Ra, in his rising, in the Eastern horizon of heaven. He saith, "I am yesterday, I know tomorrow." Yesterday is Osiris, (the Deceased) and tomorrow is Ra on the day when he shall destroy the enemies of Neb-er-tcher, and when he shall establish as Prince and Ruler his son Horus."

The next figure, which is not in all of the papyri, represents a funeral chest, on which is the figure of Anubis the jackal, with Isis and Nephthys adoring, and the head of the deceased emerging from the chest. This may be an image of the resurrection. The chest is the abode of the West of the setting sun, and the hymn here commemorates the victory of Ra over death. There follows the deceased in adoration before the God Osiris Himself, bearing the Crook and Scourge, probably hailing him as the god of the Resurrection and so apparently following the previous symbol.

The next figure is also a resurrection symbol, the Phoenix or Bennu bird who is said to immolate himself once in a hundred year, and from his ashes emerges the new Phoenix (compare the blossoming of the aloe.) The Bennu bird is represented before a table of offerings. Next comes the mummy of the deceased, with the soul in the form of a human-headed bird hovering over and watched by Isis and Nephthys. The bird here represents the Ba or Bai, or spirit, the mind or mentality of the deceased, concentrated or projected. The Ka or astral form is usually represented by a figure of the deceased, being the shade or ghost.

Following this is the dual form of the Axe, which was the primeval symbol of the one God, Ner, of whom all the Gods of Egypt were forms; dual probably to symbolize the Union of Osiris with the all Father or of the deceased with Osiris, and crowned with the royal and sacred Uraeus. Isis and Nephthys are in the form of a Hawk as all are on that Astral plane. "Who then is this? I am the Bennu bird which is in Annu, and I am the keeper of the Volume of the Book of things which are and of things which shalt be. Who then is this body? It is Osiris, or (as some say) his dead body; his soiled garments. The things that are, and the things that shall be are his dead body. They are eternity and everlastingness. Eternity is the day, Everlastingness is the night. This is the cutting off of the corruptible in the body of Osiris. The deceased is next shown as again in adoration before the God of a million years. In his right hand is the sacred Ankh. Behind him is the symbol of years. He stretches his left hand over the pool containing the eye of Horus. The soul of the deceased now comes to the pools of the two Truths, or perhaps rather the pools of the dual manifestation of Truth shewn by the quadrangular figures, over which the God, Uacherura, or the Great Green Water presides, His two hands being extended over the two pools, that under his right hand, being the pool of Natron, and that under the left, the Pool of Nitre.

The above is Budge's translation, but it is difficult to interpret.

Natron and nitre are the same substance, both words being derived from the Greek. The word natron was substituted in the 15th century for the older form nitrum. There are seven great Natron Lakes in Egypt. A solution of natron was used in embalming and the reference is probably to the million years (or ages) long duration of the body, prepared in the Great Green Lake or Natron Lake.

"The Begetter of millions of years is the name of one; Great Green Lake is the name of the other. Now as concerning the Great God who dwelleth therein, it is Ra Himself."

The next figure is a Pylon with doors called Restau, i.e. the "Gate of the Passages of the Tomb."

"What then is this? It is Restau, that is to say it is the Underworld, on the South of Na-Arut-f (this world is probably the same as An-rut-f, the place where nothing grows.) Now the gate of Tchesert is the gate of the Pillars of Shu, the Northern-Gate of the Tuat (under world) or (as the others say) it is the two leaves of the arbor through which the God Tem passeth when he goeth to the Eastern horizon of heaven." Next comes the Utchat or eye of Thoth, facing to the left above a Pylon. "What then is this? It is the right eye of Ra, which raged against Sel, when he sent it forth. Thoth raised up the hair,(i.e. a cloud) and brought the Eye, alive and whole, and sound, and without defect, to its Lord." The next figure is that of the Cow Meh-urt, the eye of Ra, with disc and horns, collar, and Menat, and whip.

"What then is this? I behold Ra who was born yesterday from the buttocks of the Goddess Meh-urt. His strength is my strength, and my strength is his strength. It is the watery abyss of heaven. It is the image of the eye of Ra in the morning at his daily birth. Meh-urt is the eye of Ra. Therefore Osiris (i.e. the deceased) triumphant, is a great one among the Gods, who are in the train of Horus. These words are spoken for him who loveth his Lord."

The next figure is somewhat obscure in all the vignettes. The variations may be due to the insertion of local symbols, or merely to the fancy of the artist. There is clearly a funeral chest, bearing the image of Anubis, which is called the district of Abtu; (Abydos) the burial place of the East. The head emerging therefrom is sometimes, as on our pillars, that of the deceased, sometimes (as in the Papyrus of Ani) it is the head of Ra, with two are, and hands, each holding the Ankh, an emblem of life. In either case the symbology is the same. It is the burial and resurrection, whether of the deceased, or of Osiris whose nature he now partakes of, or of Ra himself, as symbolised by the Sun at sunset and at sunrise dying and rising again.

This figure and its attendants summarise the teaching. Accordingly right and left of the chest are the four Canopic Gods, whose office towards the mummy is to guard the jars containing the intestines of the deceased. Beyond these to right and left are two watchers or guides bearing the Phoenix headed wand. The text of the Ritual here alludes to seven Khus, whom Anubis appointed to be the protectors of the dead body of Osiris, and seven Gods whose functions is not clearly indicated. We have seven God forms seated, lion forms with the deceased in adoration. Into the complete symbology of this it is impossible here to enter. The meaning of the duplicated series of seven, belongs to the higher grades where it will be fully expounded as also will the kneeling figure of the deceased in adoration before the lion-form with the sacred Ankh or sign of Life.

In the next figure we have the cat, emblem of the sun or of Ra himself cutting off the head of the serpent Apep, Apepi or Apophis typical of darkness under the Persea tree (or the holy tree) said by some to be the Acacia, a glyph of the Rising Sun. Finally we have the deceased in the sacred boat guided by Thoth, escorted by Ra who has the symbol of the sun, and Horus who bears the crowns of Upper and Lower Egypt and both carry the Phoenixheaded wand in the right hand, and the sacred Ankh, Crux Ansata, or image of life in the left. Over his head is the Scarab, symbol of the Creator. In front of the boat is the rising Sun. Thus the general design of the White Pillar is a pictorial synthesis of the gradual freeing of the soul from the body, left to be mummied and its union with Osiris, Lord and Judge of the Dead and of the resurrection, the sun in his rising. The hymn to the Rising Sun resumes these ideas.

THE BLACK PILLAR

This needs comparatively little explanation beyond what is contained in the official lecture. The design on the pillar is adapted from the Vignette to the 125th chapter of the Book of the Dead. It represents the deceased passing by the forty-two assessors, to the Hall of Judgment, where the soul is weighed, previous to being conducted into the presence of Osiris. In the original vignette to the Papyrus of Ani, which is reproduced in the coloured frontispiece to Budge's Book of the Dead, the Assessors are represented above the text. In the Black Pillar they occupy the upper rings of the design being followed by the introduction of the deceased to the Hall of Judgment. Note that both in Budge's frontispiece and in the design on the Pillars there are only twelve assessors figured. The reasons of the selection in the case of the Black Pillars will appear in the higher grades; it cannot be given to the Outer. The names of those figured are Sa and Hu, sitting together, then Hathor, then Horus, then Isis and Nephthys (or more probably the twin Maati wearing the head-dresses of Isis and Nephthys because inclining towards their symbology) then Nut, Seb, Tefnut, Shu, Temu, and Ra-Harmachis. Any student who is familiar with Egyptology, considering the attributes of these Gods, and comparing them with the stations at which the Neophyte is halted in the course of the Neophyte Ritual, and the words there spoken, may draw some conclusion as to their functions, and the reason for their selection, all of which will be fully expounded in the higher grades.

There follows the deceased being brought into the Judgment Hall by his guide (or as Egyptologists say his wife) and here his personality is divided into three parts, His heart which is represented as a vase-shaped vessel, called in Egyptian Ab, the Ka or shade being called the reflex of the human form of the deceased, stands by waiting the decision the Bai or Bar, the mind or mentality, is represented by a Sphinx like form above. The Papyrus of Ani adds a human-headed bird on a pylon and there are other symbolisms also which will occur to the student of Egyptology. On the Black Pillar a duplicated form of the Maati is taken to represent the higher aspirations of the soul of the deceased. Notice that the guide or introducer of the deceased carries a sistrum. The symbolism of this will be shewn later. The soul or heart is weighed against a feather symbolic of truth, as being swayed by the least breath, recording faithfully all that transpires. (In some of the Papyri it is an image of the Goddess of Truth herself with feather head-dress). Anubis with mask of the dog or Jackal brings the soul to the Judgment and watches the tongue of the balance. Thoth, Ibis headed records the result. The devourer waits to snatch the soul of the evildoer if condemned or found wanting in the balance. Horus then conducts the soul, being now the deceased undivided (or re-united) to the presence of Osiris, himself seated on a throne under a canopy bearing the rod and scourge of Mercy and Severity and the Phoenix-headed wand, and crowned with the crowns of Upper and Lower Egypt, and mummied (because he is the god of the Dead). Before him on a Lotus are the four children of Horus the Canopic gods. Behind him are Isis and Nephthys, the Goddesses of Nature. The Black Pillar symbolizes the pathway of darkness, the Negative Confession, as the White Pillar represents the Hymn to the Rising Sun, the Pathway of Light, and the Positive Confession. Between the two is the straight and narrow path that must be trodden by the initiate. Hence in every grade and at every advance between the Pillars is the pathway and when the higher grades are reached, more complete knowledge of the symbolic designs on them is unfolded. And this shall suffice for the present.

THE GARDEN OF EDEN BEFORE THE FALL

(Note: the two coloured pictures of the Garden Before and After the Fall are located in the Colour Plate section of this text.)

This diagram is described in the Practicus Ritual. It shows in a glyph the teaching proper to the Practicus on entering the Sephirah HOD which he has reached by the Paths of SHIN and RESH from MALKUTH and YESOD respectively.

At the summit are the THREE SUPERNAL SEPHIROTH summed up into ONE AIM A ELOHIM, the Mother Supernal - The Woman of the Apocalypse clothed with the SUN, the MOON under her feet, and on her head the Crown of Twelve Stars.

It is written 'So the Name JEHOVAH is joined to the Name ELOHIM, for JEHOVAH planted a Garden Eastward in Eden.' From the Three Supernals follow the other Sephiroth of THE TREE OF LIFE. Below the TREE, proceeding from MALKUTH is THE TREE OF KNOWLEDGE of GOOD AND of EVIL which is between the Tree of Life and the World of Assiah or Shells, represented by the Coiled up DRAGON with Seven Heads and Ten Horns - being the Seven Infernal Palaces and the Ten Averse Sephiroth. (These are described in the text of the Rituals but are not read to the Candidate at his Grade. When studying this diagram, these descriptions should be looked up, but they are not required for the exam.)

The River NAHER flows forth from the Supernal Eden and in DAATH it is divided into Four Heads.

> **Pison: Fire-flowing to GEBURAH where there is Gold.**
> **Gihon: Water-the Waters of Mercy, flowing into CHESED.**
> **Hiddikel: Air-flowing into TIPHARETH.**
> **Phrath (Euphrates): Earth-flowing into MALKUTH.**

It is written "In DAATH the Depths are broken up and the Clouds drop down dew."

The word Naher has the meaning 'perennial stream' 'never failing waters' as opposed to other words meaning Torrent or Brook.

The River going out of Eden is the River of the Apocalypse, the Waters of Life, clear as crystal proceeding from the Throne, on either side of the Tree of Life, bearing all manner of Fruit.

Thus the Rivers form a Cross and on it The GREAT ADAM, the SON who is to rule the Nations, was extended from TIPHARETH and his arms stretch out to GEBURAH and GEDULAH, and in MALKUTH is EVE, supporting with her hands the TWO PILLARS.

THE GARDEN OF EDEN AFTER THE FALL

This diagram is described in the Philosophus Ritual. It shows in a glyph the teaching proper to a Philosophus on entering the Sephirah NETZACH which he has reached by the Three Paths of QOPH, TZADDI, and PEH from the SEPHIROTH - MALKUTH, YESOD and HOD respectively.

The Great Goddess EVE, being tempted by the fruits of the TREE OF KNOWLEDGE whose branches tend upwards to the seven lower Sephiroth, but also downward to the Kingdom of Shells, reached down to them and the two pillars were left unsupported.

Then the Sephirotic Tree was shattered. She fell and with her fell the Great ADAM. And the Great Red Dragon arose with his seven heads and ten horns, and EDEN was desolated and the folds of the Dragon enclosed MALKUTH and linked it to the Kingdom of the Shells.

And the heads of the Dragon rose into the seven lower Sephiroth, even up to DAATH at the feet of Aima Elohim.

Thus were the four Rivers of EDEN desecrated and the Dragon Mouth gave forth the Infernal Waters in DAATH and this is LEVIATHAN, The Piercing and Crooked Serpent.

VOLUME THREE

But TETRAGRAMMATON ELOHIM placed the Four Letters YHVH of the NAME and the Flaming Sword of the Ten Sephiroth between the devastated Garden and the Supernal Eden, that this should not be involved in the Fall of ADAM.

And it became necessary that a Second Adam should arise to restore the System, and thus, as ADAM had been spread on the Cross of the Four Rivers, so the Second ADAM should be crucified on the Infernal Rivers of the four armed Cross of DAATH, yet to do this He must descend into the lowest, even MALKUTH the Earth, and be born of her. (Psalm 74. 'Thou breakest the Heads of Leviathan in pieces.')

And on the Dragon Heads were the names of the eight Kings of EDOM and on his horns the names of the Eleven Dukes of EDOM, for DAATH having developed in the Dragon a new Head, the Seven Headed Dragon with Ten Horns became Eight Headed and Eleven Horned. (Genesis, 36, v31 to 43. Chronicles 1, v43 to 54.)

The Edomites were the descendants of Esau who sold his birthright. Their Kings came to symbolise unlawful and chaotic forces.

Don't dismiss these Altar Diagrams too readily. They are really very profound. They should be studied and meditated upon to correlate them with all the contents of one's psyche. Perhaps a few words quoted from *What You Should Know About The Golden Dawn,* (Falcon Press, 1983), would be suggestive in this connection.

"In two Altar diagrams - one called the Garden of Eden shown in the Practicus Grade, and the other called The Fall, shown in the Philosophus Grade, all these ideas are expanded and synthesised. They should be carefully studied and receive long meditation, for in them are many clues to the spiritual and psychological problems which beset the traveller on the Path, and they resume the entire philosophy of Magic. Many hints, moreover, which may be found useful as assisting meditation are contained in The 'Curse' from a Philosophical Point of View in the second volume of Blavatsky's *Secret Doctrine* in connection with the Prometheus myth and the awakening of Manas, mind.

The first depicts a personified representation of the three fundamental principles in Man. Each of these is apparently separate, functioning independently on its own plane without cooperation with, because unaware of, either the higher or the lower. Principally, it represents man in the now departed morning of the race, in the primary rounds of evolutionary effort when not yet had self-consciousness been awakened or won by self-induced and self-devised efforts, and when peace and harmony prevailed both within and without by right of heritage rather than through personal labour. The diagram appears in the Water grade of Practicus, since Water is a fitting representation of this placid peace. At the summit of the diagram stands the Apocalyptic woman clothed with the Sun of glory, crowned with the twelve stars, and the moon lying at her feet. Her symbolism pertains to the supernal essence of mind, representing thus the type and symbol of the glittering Augoeides, the Neschamah. "It is," remarks Jung, describing an analogous conception in *Secret Of The Golden Flower,* "a line or principle of life that strives after superhuman, shining heights." At the base of the tree stands Eve, the Nephesch, who, in opposition to this divine Genius, stands for the "dark, earth-born, feminine principle with its emotionality and instinctiveness reaching far back into the depths of time, and into the roots of physiological continuity." Between the two stands Adam, supported by the fundamental strength of Eve, the Ruach or Ego not yet awakened to a realisation of its innate power and possibility. From the larger point of view he represents the race as a whole and is "the personified symbol of the collective Logos, the 'Host,' and of the Lords of Wisdom or the Heavenly Man, who incarnated in humanity." Otherwise he represents the individual candidate on the Path just prior to the awakening of the "sleeping dogs" within his being.

13

Beneath these three figures sleeps a coiled many headed dragon, silent, unawakened, still. None it would seem is aware of that latent power, titanic and promethean, coiled beneath, the active magical power centred in man, the libido, neutral, neither good nor evil in itself.

Very similar in some respects to the foregoing is the diagram revealed in the Philosophus grade. As the peace of Eden as shown during the Water grade, so in the Grade of Philosophus the power of Fire is shown to have called forth catastrophe. Formerly coiled beneath the tree, the hydra-headed Dragon in this Diagram has usurped its proper place, and its several horned heads wind their way up into the very structure of the Tree of Life, even unto Daath. Lured downwards by the Tree of Knowledge (and we may remember in what sense the Bible speaks of the verb "to know") towards the "darkly splendid world wherein continually lieth a faithless depth," Eve, the lower self, ceases to give support to Adam; she has yielded to the awful fascination of the awakening psyche. Far easier is it to fall than to climb to the distant heights. Yet the Fall is catastrophic only from one viewpoint. The awareness of the rise of the Dragon endows man also with consciousness of power, and power is life and progress. The Dragon is the symbol of the enemy to be overcome, as well as, when eventually conquered, the great prize to be won at the end.

The Qabalistic Sephirah of Daath is the conjunction of Chokmah and Binah on the Tree of Life, the child of Wisdom and Understanding thus Knowledge. It refers to the symbolic sphere formed within or above the Ruach by means of experience, and this assimilated becomes transmuted into intuition or faculty of mind. But fundamentally it is the ascent of the Dragon, or, if you wish, the obsession of the personality by a welling up of the unconscious archetypes, which first renders Daath a possibility; it is the Fall which is responsible for the acquisition of self-knowledge. Thus "it stands proven," claims Blavatsky "that Satan, or the Red Fiery Dragon, the 'Lord of Phosphorus,' and Lucifer, or 'Light-bearer,' is in us, it is our mind, our tempter and Redeemer, our intelligent liberator and saviour from pure animalism." In the evolutionary scheme the Fall occurs through a higher type of intelligence coming into close contact with nascent humanity, thus stimulating the psyche of the race - or so the magical tradition has it. The recapitulation of this epoch within the individual sphere of consciousness proceeds through the technique of initiation whereby the Red Dragon is stirred into activity through contact with the fructifying powers of the elements. The use of the divine prerogative brought about by the magic of experience, the awakening of Daath, brings disaster at first, because the awakened psyche is imperfectly understood and so abused for personal ends. But that very disaster and that abuse confers the consciousness of self. Consequently, the realisation of sorrow as it impinges on the personality and an understanding of its causes must inevitably constitute the first impetus to perform the Great Work, even as it comprises the motive first to seek the services of the analytical psychologist. This impetus and this self-consciousness are the prime implications of Daath. Its signification is a higher type of consciousness, the beginning of a spiritual rebirth. It acts as a self-evolved link between the higher Self on the one hand at peace in its Supernal Eden, and the human soul on the other, bound by its fall to the world of illusion and sense and matter. But until that self-consciousness and acquired knowledge are turned to noble and altruistic ends, sorrow and suffering are the inevitable results. Continually will the Red Dragon, the inverted power of the eros, ravish the little kingdom of self until such time as we lift ourselves up to the diviner parts of our human nature, thus conquering the foe by driving it back to its proper realm, using but neither ignoring nor repressing experience and its fruits to transcend our own personal limitations.

Let me quote a few especially appropriate lines from Jung in connection with this Fall, when the fundamental basis of the Ruach has been attracted to the kingdom of shells, and when Malkuth has been completely cut off from the other Sephiroth.

"Consciousness thus torn from its roots and no longer able to appeal to the authority of the primordial images, possesses a Promethean freedom, it is true, but it also partakes of the nature of a godless hybris. It soars above the earth, even above mankind, but the danger of capsizing is there, not for every individual to be sure, but collectively for the weak members of such a society, who again Promethean-like, are bound by the unconscious to the Caucasus." It will not do, then, for the Adept to be cut off from his roots, but he must unite and integrate his entire Tree, and train and develop the titanic forces of the unconscious so that they become as a powerful but docile beast whereon he may ride. (The diagram discussed in the next paragraph will be found in the colour plate section.)

The Adeptus Minor grade continues the theme of these two diagrams. Escorted into the Vault, the Aspirant is shown the lid of the Tomb of Osiris, the Pastos wherein is buried our Father Christian Rosenkreutz, and on that lid is a painting which brings fulfilment to the narrative of the preceding diagrams. It is divided into two sections. The lower half of the painting depicts a figure of Adam, similar to his presentation in the Practicus grade, though here the heads of the Dragon are falling back from the Tree, showing the Justified One, the illuminated adept, by his immolation and self-sacrifice rescuing the fallen kingdom of his natural self from the clutches of an outraged eros. But above this, as though to show the true nature behind the deceptive appearance of things, is illustrated a noble figure of majesty and divinity, described in the Ritual in these words. "And being turned I saw seven golden light-bearers, and in the midst of the Light-bearers, one like unto the Ben Adam, clothed with a garment down to the feet, and girt with a golden girdle. His head and his hair were white as snow, and his eyes as flaming fire; his feet like unto brass as if they burned in a furnace. And his voice like the sound of many waters. And he had in his right hand seven stars, and out of his mouth went the Sword of Flame, and his countenance was as the Sun in his strength."

It is to effect this redemption of the personality, to regenerate and transmute the enormous power of the Red Dragon, and attempt to bring the individual to some realisation of his potential godhead, that is the object of the Adeptus Minor ceremony. It is for this reason that I hold that the Golden Dawn or magical technique is of supreme and inestimable importance to mankind at large. In it the work of academic psychology may find a logical conclusion, so that it may develop further its own particular contribution to modern life and culture. For the system indicated the psychological solution of the anima problem. **"Arise! Shine! For thy light is come!"**

ON THE GENERAL GUIDANCE AND PURIFICATION OF THE SOUL

Learn first, O Practicus of our Ancient Order, that true Equilibrium is the basis of the Soul. If thou thyself hast not a sure foundation, whereon wilt thou stand to direct the forces of Nature?

Know then that as Man is born into this world amidst the darkness of Nature and the strife of contending forces, so must his first endeavour be to seek the Light through their reconciliation. Thus, thou who hast trial and trouble of this life, rejoice because of them, for in them is strength, and by their means is a pathway opened unto that Light Divine.

How should it be otherwise, O man, whose life is but a day in Eternity, a drop in the Ocean of Time? How, if thy trials were not many, couldst thou purge thy soul from the dross of Earth?

Is it but now that the higher life is beset with dangers and difficulties; hath it not been ever thus with the Sages and Hierophants of the past? They have been persecuted and reviled, they have been tormented of men, yet through this has their glory increased. Rejoice, therefore, O Initiate, for the greater thy trial, the brighter thy triumph. When men shall revile thee and speak against thee falsely, hath not the Master said "Blessed art thou." Yet, O Practicus, let thy victories bring thee not vanity, for with increase of knowledge should come increase of wisdom. He who knows little, thinketh he knows much; but he who knoweth much hath learned his own ignorance. Seest thou a Man wise in his own conceit? There is more hope of a fool than of him.

Be not hasty to condemn another's sin. How knowest thou that in his place thou couldst have resisted the temptation? And even were it so, why shouldst thou despise one who is weaker than thyself? Be thou well sure of this, that in slander and self-righteousness is sin. Pardon therefore the sinner, but encourage not the sin. The Master condemned not the adulterous woman, but neither did he encourage her to commit the sin.

Thou therefore who desirest magical gifts, be sure that thy soul is firm and steadfast, for it is by flattering thy weakness that the Evil One will gain power over thee. Humble thyself before thy God, yet fear neither man nor spirit. Fear is failure and the forerunner of failure; and courage is the beginning of virtue. Therefore fear not the spirits, but be firm and courteous with them, for this too may lead thee into sin. Command and banish the Evil ones. Curse them by the Great Names of God, if need be; but neither mock nor revile them, for so assuredly thou wilt be led,into error.

A man is what he maketh himself within the limits fixed by his inherited destiny; he is a part of mankind. His actions affect not himself only, but also those with whom he is brought into contact, either for good or for evil.

Neither worship nor neglect the physical body, which is thy temporary connection with the outer and material world. Therefore let thy mental equilibrium be above disturbances by material events. Restrain the animal passions and nourish the higher aspirations; the emotions are purified by suffering.

Do good unto others for God's sake, not for reward, not for gratitude from them, not for sympathy. If thou art generous, thou wilt not long for thine ears to be tickled by expressions of gratitude. Remember that unbalanced force is evil, that unbalanced severity is but cruelty and oppression, but that also unbalanced Mercy is but weakness which would allow and abet evil.

True prayer is as much action as Word; it is Will. The gods will not do for man what his higher powers can do for himself, if he cultivate Will and Wisdom. Remember that this Earth is but an atom in the Universe, and thou thyself but an atom thereon. And that even couldst thou become the God of this Earth whereon thou crawlest and grovellest, thou wouldst even then be but an atom and one among many. Nevertheless, have the greatest self-respect, and to that end sin not against thyself. The sin which is unpardonable is knowingly and wilfully to reject spiritual truth, but every sin and act leaveth its effect.

To obtain magical Power, learn to control thought. Admit only true ideas which are in harmony with the end desired, and not every stray and contradictory idea that presents itself. Fixed thought is a means to an end; therefore pay attention to the power of silent thought and meditation. The material act is but the outward expression of the thought, and therefore it hath been said that "the thought of foolishness is sin."Thought therefore is the commencement of action, and if a chance thought can produce much effect, what cannot fixed thought do? Therefore, as has been already said, establish thyself firmly in the Equilibrium of Forces, in the center of the cross of the elements, that Cross from whose centre the creative word issued in the birth of the dawning universe.

As it was said unto thee in the Grade of Theoricus: "Be thou therefore prompt and active as the Sylphs, but avoid frivolity and caprice. Be energetic and strong like the Salamanders, but avoid irritability and ferocity. Be flexible and attentive to images like the Undines, but avoid idleness and changeablity. Be laborious and patient like the gnomes, but avoid grossness and avarice." So shalt thou gradually develop the powers of thy Soul and fit thyself to command the spirits of the elements.

VOLUME THREE

For wert thou to summon the Gnomes to pander to thy avarice, thou wouldst no longer command them, but they would command thee. Wouldst thou abuse the pure creatures of God's creation to fill thy coffers and to satisfy thy lust for Gold? Wouldst thou defile the Spirits of driving Fire to serve thy wrath and hatred? Wouldst thou violate the purity of the Souls of the Water to pander to thy lust and debauchery? Wouldst thou force the Spirits of the evening breeze to minister to thy folly and caprice?

Know that with such desires thou canst but attract the evil and not the good, and in that case the evil will have power over thee. In true religion there is no sect. Therefore take heed that thou blaspheme not the name by which another knoweth his God for if thou doest this thing in Jupiter, thou wilt blaspheme YHVH; and in Osiris YEHESHUAH.

"Ask of God and ye shall have,
Seek and ye shall find.
Knock, and it shall be opened unto you."

SHEM HA-MEPHORESCH
THE 72 FOLD NAME

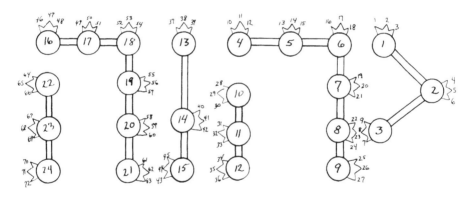

This refers to the Seventy Two Names of the Expounded Name YHVH.

Four is the number of the letters of the Tetragrammaton. Four is also the number of the letters of the name ADNI which is its representative and key. The latter name is bound with the former and united thereto, thus IAHDVNHY forming a name of 8 letters. 8 X 3, the number of the Supernal Triad, yields the 24 thrones of the Elders of the Apocalypse, each of whom wears on his head a golden crown of three rays, each ray of which is a name, each name an Absolute Idea and Ruling Power of the great name YHVH Tetragrammaton.

The number 24 of the thrones multiplied by the 3 rays of the crown which equals 72, the name of God of 72 letters, which is thus mystically shown in the name YHVH, as under: (Or as the book of Revelation says: "When the living creatures (the four Kerubim the Letters of the Name) give glory to Him, etc. the four and twenty elders fall down before Him and cast their crowns before the Throne, etc." (that is the Crowns, which each bear 3 of the 72 Names, and these 72 names are written on the leaves of the Tree of Life which were for the healing of the nations.)

These are also the 72 names of the ladder of Jacob on which the Angels of God ascended and descended. It will presently be shown how the 72 Angelic names are formed from the

72 Names of the Deity, and also how their signification is to be found. The 72 Names of the Deity are thus obtained. The 19th, 20th, and 21st verses of the XIV Chapter of the Book of Exodus each consist of 72 letters.

(The English translation is:) 19th verse: "And the Angel of the Elohim, that went before the camp of Israel, removed and went behind them; and the pillar of cloud removed from before them and stood behind them."

20th verse: "And it came between the camp of the Egyptians and the camp of Israel; and it was a cloud and darkness (to the first) but it gave light by night (to these); and the one came not near unto the other all the night."

21st verse: "And Moses stretched out his hand over the sea, and the Lord drove back the sea with a strong east wind all that night and made the sea dry land, and the waters divided."

These three verses are now to be written at length one above the other, the first from right to left, and the second from left to right, and the third from right to left; and as they contain 72 letters, there will be 72 columns of three letters each. Then each column will give a word of three letters, and there will be 72 names of three letters each, which are the Shem ha Mephoresch or 72 Names of the Deity, expounding the Powers of the name YHVH.

From these names 72 Names of Angels are formed by the addition of, in some cases, the suffice YH which signifies Mercy and Beneficence, or in others of the suffice AL which signifies Severity and Judgment. Or as it is said: "And the Name is in Him, etc."

These 72 Angels rule over the 72 Quinances or sets of 5° of the Zodiac, and therefore each decanate or set of 10° of a Sign has 2 Quinances, and each sign has 3 decanates, which are again allotted to the Planets in regular order. This is the formation as given above (each Angel's name containing 5 letters and each name of Deity 3.).

These then are the Schem ha-Mephoresch or 72 Angels bearing the Name of God, classed into nine sets of 8, each answering to the nine choirs of Angels, and also divided into 4 great divisions of 18 each, each division under the Presidency of one of the four letters of the Name YHVH.

They are further classed as belonging to the decanates of the Zodiac as follows: 2 Quinances to each decanate. The first division of 3 Signs is under the Presidency of Y, the letter of Fire. The second Division of 3 signs, headed by the Watery sign Cancer, is under the Presidency of H the Letter of Water. The third division of 3 Signs headed by the Airy Sign Libra is under the Presidency of VAU, the letter of Air. And the 4th division of 3 signs headed by the Earthy Sign Capricorn is under the Presidency of HEH final, the letter of Earth.

But it should be remembered that the most powerful rule of Y of Tetragrammaton is over the Fiery Triplicity; that of H over the Watery Triplicity; that of Vau over the Airy Triplicity; and that of H final over the Earthy Triplicity.

In the 22nd chapter of the Apocalypse of St. John it is said that "The Tree of Life which bare Twelve manner of fruits and yielded her fruit every month, and the leaves of the Tree were for the healing of the Nations. And there shall be no more curse; but the Throne of God and of the Lamb shall be in it."

This is exemplified in the drawing taken from the 3-8 Altar Diagram. The "Twelve Manner of fruits yielded every month" answer to the signs of the Zodiac and the Twelve Tribes of the Sons of Jacob. Also to the twelve apostles. The healing leaves are those of Schem ha-Mephoresch or the divided Name of Zauir Anpin, the Microprosopus, the Christ, the Lamb of Elohim, whose Throne is in the Tree, from which Throne issues the River of the Waters of Life.

The Seventy two leaves of the Tree of Life are Zauir Anpin or Microprosopus.

Now the Twelve Sons of Jacob go down into Egypt, that is the Kingdom, Malkuth, which has been destroyed in the Fall, and cut from the Sephirotic Tree by the intersecting folds of the great Dragon who then becomes its Ruler as shown in the great Altar Diagram of the

4-7 grade. "Behold, I am against thee, Pharoah, King of Egypt, the great dragon that lieth in the midst of the Rivers." And the first of the sons of Jacob who goeth down is Joseph whose two Tribes, Ephraim and Manasseh, balance each other in Chesed and Geburah. That is to say, that there first comes down into the desolated Earth the combined power of Mercy and Severity. And Ephraim, the Kerubic sign of the Ox, is the natural ruler of Earth in Malkuth, under the power of H final of the Holy Name, the Bride, Eve, and the Queen. And the Schem ha-Mephoresch, the 72, are found in the number of the family of Jacob's sons is 70; and Jacob and Joseph equals 72. But the then ruling Pharoah, corresponds more to Hadar amongst the Edomite Kings, as representing one of not so evil a tendency. Yet as the Apocalyptic symbol of the Lamb and the Airy Sign which leads off the Schem ha-Mephoresch is Chesed; one opposed to the evil symbol of the Dragon, so is every shepherd an abomination to the Egyptians, who yet are friendly with the Ox symbol, the Kerubic Ruler of Earth, and therefore is it symbolically said by the Children of Israel that their business has been about cattle and not about sheep.

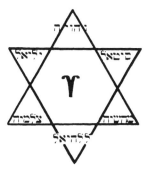

But the name YHVH, the Son, the Microprosopus is not therein established till the Ten Sephiroth have sent forth their Judgment upon the land of Egypt, i.e., the Ten Plagues. And therefore it is only when YHVH interposes between Egypt and Israel that the verses occur in Exodus which show forth the Schem ha-Mephoresch. There are also other ways of making sets of 72 names out of these verses, Exodus xiv, v. 19, 20 and 21, e.g. by writing them all from right to left, and so on, and also by permutation of the letters by any rule of Temurah. The meanings of these are then to be found as herein after shown for the regular Schem ha-Mephoresch.

It is worthy of note that all the letters of the Alphabet except Gimel are employed in the Schem ha-Mephoresch. This letter Gimel whose numerical value is 3, is therefore the key of their construction, they being grouped together in words of three letters each. Furthermore, there are 360° in the Zodiac, and this divided by 5 gives 72° which is the interval between the points of a regular pentagram inscribed within a great circle. Also the number 72 equals 6 x 12 which equals 72 cubes or Hexagrams, so that each Hexagram will represent by its Angles the 6 Quinancies of a Sign, the Sign itself being written in the centre, e.g. in any order that may be required.

The meaning of these 72 names of God, of the Angels of the Schem ha-Mephoresch are then collected in the following manner from those 72 verses taken from different Psalms, in each of which the name YHVH appears, save in the case of the 70th, YBM:

Here follow in detail the Psalms mentioned, showing the method of extracting the angelic Names. (The important point here is the significance of the meaning of each Name, a meaning which occurs in no other place in these documents.)

THE 72 NAMES AND THEIR MEANINGS

1. VAHAVIAH is God the Exalter.
2. YELAYEL is Strength.
3. SAITEL is Refuge, Fortress and Confidence.
4. OLMIAH is Concealed, Strong.
5. MAHASHIAH is Seeking safety from Trouble.
6. LELAHEL is Praiseworthy, declaring His works.
7. AKAIAH is long suffering.
8. KEHETHEL is Adorable.
9. HAZAYEL is Merciful.
10. ALDIAH is Profitable.
11. LAVIAH is to be exalted.
12. HIHAAYAH is Refuge.
13. YEZAHEL is Rejoicing over all things.
14. MEBAHEL is Guardian, Preserver.
15. HARAYEL is Aid.
16. HOQMIAH is Raise up, Praying day and night.
17. LAVIAH is Wonderful.
18. KELIAL is Worthy to be invoked.
19. LIVOYAH is Hastening to hear.
20. PHEHILYAH is Redeemer, Liberator.
21. NELOKHIEL is Thou alone.
22. YEYAYIEL is Thy right hand.
23. MELOHEL is Turning away evil.
24. CHAHAVIAH is Goodness in Himself.
25. NITHAHIAH is Wide in extent, the enlarger, wonderful.
26. HAAYOH is Heaven in secret.
27. YIRTHIEL is Deliverer.
28. SAHYOH is Taker away of evils.
29. REYAYEL is Expectation.
30. EVAMEL is Patient.
31. LEKABEL is Teacher, instructor.
32. VESHIRIAH is Upright.
33. YECHAVAH is Knower of all things.
34. LEHACHIAH is clement, merciful.
35. KEVEQIAH is To be rejoiced in.
36. MENDIAL is Honourable.
37. ANIEL is Lord of Virtues.
38. CHAAMIAH is The hope of all the ends of the earth.
39. REHAAIEL is Swift to condone.
40. YEYEZIEL is Making joyful.

41. HEHIHEL is Triune.
42. MICHAEL is Who is like unto Him.
43. VAVALIAH is King and Ruler.
44. YELAHIAH is Abiding for ever.
45. SALIAH is Mover of all things.
46. AARIEL is Revealer.
47. AASLAYOH is Just Judge.
48. MIHAL is Sending forth as a Father.
49. VEHOOEL is Great and lofty.
50. DENEYEL is Merciful Judge.
51. HECHASHYAH is Secret and Impenetrable.
52. AAMAMIAH is Covered in darkness.
53. NANAEL is Caster down of the proud.
54. NITHAEL is Celestial King.
55. MIBAHAIAH is Eternal.
56. POOYAEL is Supporting all things.
57. NEMAMIAH is lovable.
58. YEYEELEL is Hearer of cries.
59. HEROCHIEL is Permeating all things.
60. MITZRAEL is Raising up the oppressed.
61. VEMIBAEL is The Name which is over all.
62. YAHOHEL is The Supreme ends, or essence.
63. AANEVAL is Rejoicing.
64. MACHAYEL is Vivifying.
65. DAMABAYAH is Fountain of wisdom.
66. MENQEL is Nourishing all.
67. AAYOEL is Delights of the sons of men.
68. CHABOOYAH is Most liberal giver.
69. RAHAEL is Beholding all.
70. YABOMAYAH is Producing by His word.
71. HAHAYEL is Lord of the Universe.
72. MEVAMAYAH is End of the Universe.

The 78th Psalm: "Give ear, o my people" etc. has also 72 verses which again refer to the Schem ha-Mephoresch. As before shewn, the Quinancies of the Zodiac ruled by these 72 names of Angels are classed in pairs in the 36 decanates or phases of 10° in each Sign. These signs and decanates have again their ruling angels and intelligences.

THE MAGICAL IMAGES OF THE DECANS

To each decanate certain magical images and characteristics are allotted, as follows:

ARIES

1st Decan. Mars. Therein ascendeth a man tall, dark, powerful and restless, clothed in a white tunic and scarlet mantle, having keen and flame-colored eyes. And in his hand a sharp sword. It is a decan of boldness, fierceness, resolution and shamelessness.

2nd Decan of Aries is of the Sun, and therein ascendeth a woman clothed in green robes, with one leg uncovered from the knee to the ankle. This is a decan of pride, nobility, wealth and rule.

3rd Decan of Aries is of Venus, and therein ascendeth a restless man, clothed in scarlet robes having golden bracelets on his hands and arms. It is a decan of subtlety, beauty, etc.

TAURUS

In the first decan of Taurus which is of Mercury, ascendeth a woman with long beautiful hair, clothed in flame-colored robes. It is a decan of ploughing, sowing, building, and earthy wisdom.

In the 2nd Decan of Taurus, which is of Luna, ascendeth a man like the preceding figure, having feet cloven like an ox-hoof. It is a decan of power, nobility, rule over the people.

In the 3rd Decan of Taurus, which is of Saturn, ascendeth a man of swarthy complexion having large white teeth projecting from his mouth, a body like that of an elephant with long legs. And there arise with him a horse and a stag and a calf. It is a decan of misery, slavery, necessity, madness and baseness.

GEMINI

In the 1st Decan of Gemini which is of Jupiter, there ascendeth a beautiful woman, and with her two horses. It is a decan of writing, calculations, giving and receiving money, and of wisdom in unprofitable things.

In the 2nd Decan of Gemini which is of Mars, ariseth an eagle-headed man, wearing a steel helmet surmounted by a crown, and having a bow and arrows in his hand. It is a decan of burden, pressure, labor, subtlety, dishonesty.

In the 3rd Decan of Gemini which is of Sol, ariseth a man clothed in a coat of mail with two arrows and quiver. It is a decan of disdain, mirth and jollity and of many unprofitable words.

CANCER

In the 1st Decan of Cancer which is of Venus, ascendeth a man having a distorted face, and hands, and his body is like that of a horse having white feet with garland of leaves around his body. A decan of dominion, science, love, mirth, subtlety and magistracy.

In the 2nd Decan of Cancer which is of Mercury, ascendeth a woman beautiful of countenance, wearing on her head a green myrtle wreath, holding in her hands a lyre, and she singeth of love and of gladness. A decan of pleasure, mirth, abundance and plenty.

In the 3rd Decan of Cancer which is of Luna, there ascendeth a swift-footed person holding a viper in his hand, and having dogs running before him. It is a decan of running, hunting, pursuing, acquiring goods by war and of contention among men.

LEO

In the first decan of Leo which is of Saturn, there ascendeth a man in sordid raiment, and with him ascendeth a noble man on horeseback accompanied by bears and dogs.

A decan of boldness, liberality, victory, cruelty, lust and violence.

VOLUME THREE

In the 2nd Decan of Leo which is of Jupiter, there ascendeth a man covered with a white myrtle wreath and holding a bow in his hand. It is a decan of love, pleasure, society and avoiding of quarrels and carefulness in parting with goods.

In the 3rd Decan of Leo which is of Mars there ascendeth a dark and swarthy man, hairy, holding in one hand a drawn sword and in the other a shield. It is a decan of quarrelling, ignorance, pretended knowledge, wrangling, victory over the low and base, and of drawing swords.

VIRGO

In the first decan of Virgo which is of Sol, there ariseth a Virgin clothed in linen, holding an apple or a pomegranate in her hand. A decan of sowing, ploughing, planting herbs, colonization and of storing money and food.

In the 2nd decan of Virgo which is of Venus, there ariseth a man, tall, fair and large, and witn him a woman holding in her hand a black oil jar. It is a decan of gain, covetousness, taking of goods and rising by care and treasuring up.

In the 3rd decan of Virgo which is of Mercury, ascendeth an old man leaning on a staff and wrapped in a mantle. It is a decan of old age, slothfulness, loss and depopulation.

LIBRA

In the first decan of Libra which is of Luna, ariseth a dark man having in his right hand a spear and a laurel branch, and in his left a book. It is a decan of justice, aid, truth, and helping the poor.

In the 2nd Decan of Libra which is of Saturn, there ariseth a man dark and of unpleasant face. It is a "face" of ill-deeds yet of singing and mirth and gluttony, sodomy and following of evil pleasures.

In the 3rd decan of Libra which is of Jupiter, there ariseth a man riding upon an ass with a wolf going before him. A decan of quietness, ease, plenty, good life and dance.

SCORPIO

In the 1st decan of Scorpio which is of Mars, there ascendeth a man holding in his right hand a lance, and in his left a human head. A decan of strife, sadness, treachery, deceit, destruction and ill-will.

In the 2nd Decan of Scorpio which is of Sol, there ascendeth a man riding upon a camel holding a scorpion in his hand. A decan of affronts, detection, strife, stirring up of quarrels, science and detection.

In the 3rd decan of Scorpio which is of Venus, there ascendeth a horse and a wolf. A decan of war, drunkenness, fornication, wealth, pride and of rage and violence against women.

SAGITTARIUS

In the 1st decan of Sagittarius which is of Mercury there ascendeth a man with three bodies, one red, one white, and one black. It is a decan of boldness, freedom, welfare, liberality, and of fields and gardens.

In the 2nd decan of Sagittarius which is of Luna, there ascendeth a man leading cows, having before him an ape and a bear. It is a decan of fear, lamentation, grief, anxiety, and disturbance.

In the 3rd decan of Sagittarius which is of Saturn, there ascendeth a man holding another by the hair and slaying him. It is a decan of ill-will, levity, envy, obstinacy and swiftness in all evil things, and of deceitful acts.

CAPRICORN

In the 1st decan of Capricorn, which is of Jupiter, there ascendeth a man holding in his right hand an arrow or javelin, and in his left a lapwing. It is a decan of wandering travail, labor and joy, alternate gain and loss, weakness and necessity.

In the 2nd decan of Capricorn which is of Mars, there ascendeth a man with an ape running before him. It is a decan of ever seeking what cannot be known and of what cannot be attained to.

In the 3rd decan of Capricorn which is of Sol, there ascendeth a man holding a book which he opens and shuts. It is a decan of covetousness, suspicion, careful ordering of matters, but with discontent.

AQUARIUS

In the first decan of Aquarius which is of Venus, there ascendeth a man with bowed head and a bag in his hand. It is a decan of poverty, anxiety, grieving after gain, and never resting from labor, loss and violence.

In the 2nd decan of Aquarius which is of Mercury, there ariseth a man arrayed like a king looking with pride and conceit on all around him. It is a decan of beauty, dominance, conceit, good manners and self-esteem, yet notwithstanding modest.

In the 3rd decan of Aquarius which is of Luna ascendeth a man with a small head clothed like a woman, having an old man with him. It is a decan of abundance and compliments, detection and affronts.

PISCES

In the 1st decan of Pisces which is of Saturn there ariseth a man with two bodies but joining their heads together. It is a decan of many thoughts, of anxiety, of journeying from place to place, of misery, of seeking riches and food.

In the 2nd decan of Pisces which is of Jupiter, there ascendeth a grave man pointing to the sky. It is a decan of self-praise, of high mind, and of seeking after great and high aims.

In the 3rd decan of Pisces which is of Mars, there ascendeth a man of grace and thoughtful countenance, carrying a bird in his hand and before him a woman and an ass. It is a decan of pleasure, fornication, of quietness, and of peacemaking.

The images of the decans are differently given by other writers, but the signification is similar. Also every degree has its allotted emblem and significance. (The Order did not list these, but some modern writers have accomplished this. It is suggested that the interested student consult *Sabian Symbols* by Marc Edmunc Jones. He deals extensively with this subject.)

The following note shows still further the connection between the YHVH and the Shem ha-Mephoresch.

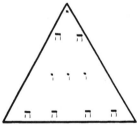

Let the Tetragrammaton, as in this diagram, be written a triangle apex upwards, so that its component letters form a triangle in themselves by increasing each descending line beyond the space occupied by the line above it. Above will then be a single line, below it like two Hehs, the three Vaus, then four final Hehs. Thus we constitute a triangle of ten letters answering to the Ten Sephiroth, the uppermost Yod answering to Kether, the two Hehs to Chokmah and Binah, the three Vaus to Chesed, Geburah and Tiphareth, and the four final Hehs to Netzach, Hod, Yesod and Malkuth.

Now if we invert the Triangle and write it in descending ratio, four Yods, three Hehs, two Vaus, and one final Heh, we shall find that the total number will be 72, that of Schem ha-Mephoresch.

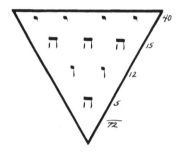

But the best of the forms is that when it is written by Yod, Heh, etc. Thus:

Yod is 10 and equals Atziluth
Yod Heh is 15 and equals Briah
Yod Heh Vau is 21 and equals Yetzirah.

Whence we discover why the Yetziratic distribution of the numbers there answering to the hexad of Height, Depth, East, West, North and South-are sealed with the Permutation of Yod Heh Vau and not of Tetragrammaton.

Furthermore 21 is the number of EHEIEH. YHVH is 26 which is Assiah. The sum of all these numbers thus are:

10+15+21+26 is 72, the number of Schem ha-Mephoresch.

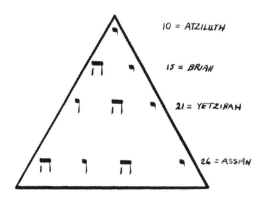

HODOS CHAMELIONIS CONCERNING THE TREE OF LIFE

(The plate showing this is in the colour plate section.) This is the Book of the Path of the Chameleon - the knowledge of the colours of the forces which lie beyond the physical universe. Study thou well that saying of Hermes 'that which is below is like that which is above,' for if that which is below is conformed according to the Law of the Concealed One Great is his Name - be thou well assured that the closer thou adherest unto the Law of the Universe in thy working, by so much the more is thy Magical working just and true.

Recall what was said unto thee in the Ritual of the Paths of the Portal of the Vault of the Adepti. 'Therefore, by the straight and narrow path of Samekh, let the Philosophus advance like the arrow from the Bow of Qesheth.'Now Qesheth the Bow is the Rainbow of Promise stretched above the earth, whose name is formed from the letters of the Paths leading from Malkuth. If then it be by the Path of Samekh that the Philosophus should advance to the knowledge of the Adept, turning aside neither unto the right hand nor unto the left, whereon are the evil and threatening symbols of Death and the Devil, he must have a perfect and absolute knowledge of the Bow, ere he can follow the Path of the Arrow. But the Bow is of brilliant and perfect colour, whose analysis and synthesis yield others of the same scale, and hence is this book entitled "The Book of the Path of the Chameleon" - that Path, namely which ascendeth alone through the force of Qesheth, the Bow.

And if thy knowledge and application of the outer knowledge, which thou hast already learned, be faulty and incorrect how wilt thou be able to keep thyself from turning aside unto thy hurt? Therefore, learn not knowledge by rote only as an unreasoning child, but meditate, search out and compare, and to the end, see that thou think but little of thyself for only he that humbleth himself shall be exalted. Magical knowledge is not given unto thee to tickle thy vanity and conceit, but that by its means, thou mayest purify and equilibriate thy spiritual nature and honour the Vast and Concealed One.

This is the explanation of the first diagram of the Paths - the Sephiroth being in the feminine scale and the Paths in the masculine or King's scale. It is the Key of the Forces which lie in Qesheth the Bow. Treasure it in thy heart and mark it well, seeing that therein is the key or nature. Meditate on it and reveal it not unto the profane, for many and great are its mysteries.

There are four scales of colour which correspond to the Four Worlds. They are:

King Scale	Atziluth	Wands	Yod	Fire
Queen Scale	Briah	Cups	Heh	Water
Knight Scale	Yetzirah	Swords	Vau	Air
Knave Scale	Assiah	Pentacles	Heh	Earth

The colours differ according to the World or aspect of the Great Name they represent: Thus Samekh in:

King Scale	Deep Blue
Queen Scale	Yellow
Knight Scale	Green
Knave Scale	Grey Blue

Tiphareth in:

King Scale	Rose
Queen Scale	Gold
Knight Scale	Pink
Knave Scale	Tawny Yellow

VOLUME THREE

The TREE OF LIFE for the use of an Adeptus Minor is compounded of the first two scales. The SEPHIROTH are in the feminine, passive, or Queen Scale. The PATHS are in the masculine, active, or King Scale. It thus represents the forces of ATZILUTH in the PATHS uniting the SEPHIROTH as reflected in the Briatic World, one of the possible arrangements of the powers inherent in YOD HE of the GREAT NAME.

First are the Feminine colours of the Sephiroth, the Queen's Scale. In Kether is the Divine White Brilliance, the scintillation and corruscation of the Divine Glory that Light which lighteth the universe - that Light which surpasseth the glory of the Sun and beside which the light of mortals is but darkness, and concerning which it is not fitting that we should speak more fully. And the Sphere of its Operation is called Rashith ha-Gilgalim, the beginning of whirling (or whirls, or whorls), the Primum Mobile or First Mover, which bestoweth the gift of life in all things and filleth the whole Universe. And Eheieh is the Name of the Divine Essence in Kether. Its Archangel is the Prince of Countenances Metatron or Metraton, He who bringeth others before the face of God. The Name of its Order of Angels is called Chaioth ha-Qadesh, the Holy Living Creatures, which are also called the Order of Seraphim.

In Chokmah is a cloud-like grey which containeth various colours and is mixed with them, like a transparent pearl-hued mist, yet radiating withal, as if behind it there were a brilliant glory. And the Sphere of its influence is in Masloth, the Starry Heavens, wherein it disposeth the forms of things. Yah is the Divine Ideal Wisdom, and its Archangel is Ratziel, the Prince or Princes of the knowledge of hidden and concealed things, and the name of its Order of Angels is Auphanim, the Wheels or the Whirling Forces which are also called the Order of Kerubim.

In Binah is a thick darkness which yet veileth the Divine Glory in which all colours are hidden, wherein is mystery and depth and silence, and yet, it is the habitation of the Supernal Light. Thus is the Supernal Triad completed. And the Sphere of its Operation is Shabbathai, or rest, and it giveth forms and similitudes unto chaotic matter and it ruleth the sphere of action of the planet Saturn. Jehovah Elohim is the perfection of Creation and the Life of the World to Come. Its Archangel is Tzaphqiel, the Prince of the Spiritual Strife against Evil, and the Name of the Order of Angels is Aralim, the Strong and Mighty Ones who are also called the Order of Thrones. The Angel Yophiel is also referred unto Binah.

In Chokmah is the Radix of blue and thence is there a blue colour pure and primitive, and glistening with a spiritual Light which is reflected unto Chesed. And the Sphere of its Operation is called Tzedek or Justice and it fashioneth the images of material things, bestowing peace and mercy; and it ruleth the sphere of the action of the planet Jupiter. A1 is the title of a God strong and mighty, ruling in Glory, Magnificence and Grace. The Archangel of Chesed is Tzadkiel, the prince of Mercy and Beneficence, and the Name of the Order of Angels is Chashmalim Brilliant Ones, who are also called the Order of Dominions or Dominations. The Sephirah Chesed is also called Gedulah or Magnificence and Glory.

In Binah is the Radix of Red, and therein is there a red colour, pure and scintillating and flashing with flame which is reflected unto Geburah. The Sphere of its Operation is called Madim or violent rushing Force and it bringeth fortitude, and war and strength and slaughter, as it were, the flaming Sword of an avenging God. It ruleth the Sphere of Action of the Planet Mars. Elohim Gibor is the Elohim, Mighty and Terrible, judging and avenging evil, ruling in wrath and terror and storm, and at whose steps are lightning and flame. Its Archangel is Kamael the Prince of Strength and Courage, and the Name of the Order of Angels is Seraphim the Flaming Ones who are also called the Order of Powers. The Sephirah Chesed is also called Gedulah or Magnificence and Glory, and the Sephirah Geburah is also called Pachad Terror and Fear.

In Kether is the Radix of a Golden Glory and thence is there a pure, primitive and sparkling, gleaming golden yellow which is reflected unto Tiphareth. Thus is the first reflected Triad completed. The Sphere of its operation is that of Shemesh, the Solar Light, and bestoweth Life, Light and Brilliancy in metallic matter, and it ruleth the sphere of action of the Sun. Yhvh Eloah va-Daath is a God of Knowledge and Wisdom, ruling over the Light of the Universe; and its Archangel is Raphael, the Prince of Brightness, Beauty and Life. The Name of the Order of Angels is Melechim or Malakim, that is Kings or Angelic Kings, who are also called the Order of Virtues, Angels and Rulers. The Angels Peniel and Pelial are also referred unto this Sephirah. It especially rules the Mineral world.

The beams of Chesed and of Tiphareth meet in Netzach and thence in Netzach arises a green, pure, brilliant, liquid, and gleaming like an emerald. The Sphere of its operations is that of Nogah or External Splendour, producing zeal, love, harmony, and it ruleth the Sphere of Action of the Planet Venus and the nature of the Vegetable World. Jehovah Tzabaoth is a God of Hosts and of Armies, of Triumph and of Victory, ruling the Universe in Justice and Eternity. Its Archangel Hanial is the Prince of Love and Harmony, and the Name of the Order of Angels is Elohim or gods who are also called the Order of Principalities. The Angel Cerviel is also referred unto this Sephirah.

The beams of Geburah and Tiphareth meet in Hod and thence arises in Hod a brilliant pure and flashing orange tawny. The Sphere of its Operation is that of Kokab, the stellar light, bestowing elegance, swiftness, scientific knowledge and art, and constancy of speech, and it ruleth the sphere of the action of the planet Mercury. Elohim Tzabaoth is also a God of Hosts and of Armies, of Mercy and of Agreement, of Praise and Honour, ruling the Universe in Wisdom and Harmony. Its Archangel is Michael, the Prince of Splendour and of Wisdom, and the Name of Order of Angels is Beni Elohim, or Sons of the Gods, who are also called the Order of Archangels.

The beams of Chesed and Geburah meet in Yesod and thence ariseth in Yesod a brilliant deep violet-purple or puce, and thus is the third Triad completed. The sphere of its operation is that of Levanah, the Lunar beam, bestowing change, increase and decrease upon created things and it ruleth the Sphere of Action of the Moon and the nature of mankind. Shaddai is a God who sheddeth benefits, Omnipotent and Satisfying, and A1 Chai is the God of Life, the Living One. Its Archangel is Gabriel the Prince of Change and Alteration. The name of the Order of Angels is Kerubim or Kerubic ones who are also called the Order of Angels.

From the rays of this Triad there appear three colours in Malkuth together with a fourth which is their synthesis. Thus from the orange tawny of Hod and the green nature of Netzach, there goeth forth a certain greenish 'citrine' colour, yet pure and translucent withal. From the orange tawny of Hod mingled with the puce of Yesod there goeth forth a certain red russet brown, 'russet' yet gleaming with a hidden fire. From the green of Netzach and the puce of Yesod there goeth forth a certain other darkening green 'Olive' yet rich and glowing withal. The synthesis of all these is a blackness which bordereth upon the Qlippoth.

Thus are the colours of the Sephiroth completed in their feminine or Rainbow scale.

Moreover, though the Tree of Life operates through all the Ten Sephiroth, yet it is referred in a special manner to Tiphareth. Also, though the branches of the Tree of Knowledge of Good and Evil stretch into the seven lower Sephiroth and downwards into the Kingdom of Shells, yet it is referred especially unto Malkuth. Similarly with Netzach and Hod, the right and left columns of the Sephiroth are referred respectively thereto.

In Malkuth, Adonai ha-Aretz is God, the Lord and King, ruling over the Kingdom and Empire which is the Visible Universe.

Cholem Yesodoth the Breaker of Foundations, is the Name of the Sphere of the Elements from which all things are formed, and its Archangels are three: Metatron, the Prince of Countenance reflected from Kether, and Sandalphon, the Prince of Prayer (feminine), and Nephesch ha-Messiah, the Soul of the Reconciler for the Earth. The Order of Angels is Ashim or Flames of Fire, as it is written 'Who maketh his Angels as Ashim Spirits and his

Ministers as a flaming Fire,' and these are also called the Order of blessed Souls, or of the Souls of the Just made Perfect.

The Three Archangels attributed to Malkuth with reference to Christian symbolism in regard to Our Father, Our Lady, and Our Lord. The following tables consists of a classification of the scales of colour in each of the Four Worlds. The first ten refer to the Sephiroth, and the remaining twenty-two refer to the Paths.

Yod-Fire	Heh-Water	Vau-Air	Heh (f) Earth
King Scale	Queen Scale	Knight	Knave
Atziluth	Briah	Yetzirah	Assiah
Wands	Cups	Swords	Pentacles
Brilliance	White brilliance	White brilliance	White flecked gold
Soft blur	Grey	Bluish mother of pearl	White flecked red, blue, yellow
Crimson	Black	Dark brown	Grey flecked red, blue, yellow
Deep violet	Blue	Deep Purple	Deep azure flecked yellow
Orange	Scarlet-red	Bright Scarlet	Red flecked black
Clear pink rose	Yellow (gold)	Rich salmon	Gold amber
Amber	Emerald	Bright yellow-green	Olive flecked gold
Violet-purple	Orange	Red russet	Yellow-brown flecked white
Indigo	Violet	Very dark purple	Citrine flecked azure
Yellow	Citrine, olive, russet, black	4 colours flecked gold	Black rayed yellow
Bright-pale yellow	Sky-blue	Blue-emerald green	Emerald flecked gold
Yellow	Purple	Grey	Indigo-rayed violet
Blue	Silver	Cold pale blue	Silver rayed sky-blue
Emerald green	Sky Blue	Early spring green	Bright rose or cerise rayed pale yellow
Scarlet	Red	Brilliant flame	Glowing red
Red orange	Deep indigo	Deep warm olive	Rich brown
Orange	Pale mauve	New yellow	Reddish grey inclined to mauve
Amber	Maroon	Rich bright russet	Dark greenish-brown
Greenish-yellow	Deep purple	Grey	Reddish-amber
Yellowish-green	Slate grey	Green grey	Plum colour
Violet	Blue	Rich purple	Bright blue rayed yellow
Emerald-green	Blue	Deep blue green	Pale green
Deep blue	Sea-green	Deep olive green	white flaked purple, mother - pearl
Green-blue	Dull brown	Very dark brown	Livid indigo brown-black-beetle
Blue	Yellow	Green	Dark vivid-blue
Indigo	Black	Blue black	Cold-dark-grey near black
Scarlet	Red	Venetian red	Bright red rayed azure or emerald
Violet	Sky blue	Bluish mauve	White tinged purple
Ultra violet crimson	Buff flecked silver-white	Light translucent pink-brown	Stone colour
Orange	Gold yellow	Rich amber	Amber rayed red
Glowing scarlet-orange	Vermillion	Scarlet flecked gold	vermillion flecked crimson emerald

Indigo	Black	Blue black	Black rayed blue
* Citrine, olive, russet, black	Amber	Dark brown	Black and yellow
* White, merging grey	Deep purple	7 prism colours violet outer	white, red, yellow, blue, black outer

*Note: these represent the fact that a dogish in Shin and Tau produce a second sound.

Daath, a "false" Sephirah stationed in the abyss has lavender in the King scale, grey white in Queen, pure violet in Knight, and grey flecked gold in Knave.

THE MICROCOSM - MAN

Thou shalt know that the whole Sphere of Sensation which surroundeth the whole physical body of a man is called "The Magical Mirror of the Universe." For therein are represented all the occult forces of the Universe projected as on a sphere, convex to the outer, but concave to man. This sphere surroundeth the physical body of a man as the Celestial Heavens do the body of a Star or a Planet, having their forces mirrored in its atmosphere. Therefore its allotment or organization is the copy of that Greater World or Macrocosm. In this "Magical Mirror of the Universe," therefore, are the Ten Sephiroth projected in the form of the Tree of Life as in a solid sphere. (See the diagram in the colour section on the Tree of Life in a solid sphere.) A man's physical body is within the Ten Sephiroth projected in a sphere. The divisions and parts of the body are formed from the Sephiroth of the Tree of Life, thus:

KETHER

Kether is above the Crown of the Head, and represents a crown which indeed is powerful, but requires one worthy to wear it. In the crown of the head is placed the faculty of Neschamah, which is the power of Aspiration unto that which is beyond. This power Neschamah is especially attributed unto the Supernal Triad in Assiah, of which there are three manifestations which are included in the general concept, Neschamah. From Chokmah and Binah are formed the sides of the brain and head. Therein exist the intellectual faculties of Wisdom and Understanding, shining into and illuminating their inferior, the Ruach. They are the mansions of the practical administration of the intellect, whose physical shewing forth is by reflection in Ruach. In the Magical Mirror of the Universe, or the Sphere of Sensation, Man is placed between four pillars of the Tree of Life as projected in a sphere. These keep their place and MOVE NOT, but the Man himself places in his Sphere of Sensation that point of the Zodiac which ascended at the moment of his birth and conception (for the same degree of the Zodiac ascendeth at both, otherwise the birth could not take place). That is to say that at those times the same degree of the Zodiac is ascending in the East of the Heavens of the Star whereon he is incarnated. Thus doth he remain during that incarnation facing that particular point in his sphere of sensation. That is to say, this sphere DOTH NOT REVOLVE about the physical body.

CHESED AND GEBURAH

From Chesed and Geburah are formed the arms. Therein exist the faculties of operative action, wherefore at their extremities are the symbols of the Four Elements and the Spirit, thus:

VOLUME THREE

Thumb - Spirit
3rd Finger - Fire
Index Finger - Water
Little Finger - Air
Second Finger - Earth

The arms are the manifestors of the executive power of the Ruach, and therein are the faculties of touch strongly expressed.

From **TIPHARETH** is formed the trunk of the body, free from the members, and therein as in a receptacle of influences are situated the vital organs. The blood is Spirit mingled with and governing the watery principle. The lungs are the receptacles of Air which tempereth the blood as the wind doth the waves of the sea, the mephitic impurities of the blood in its traversal of the body requiring the dispersing force of the Air, even as the sea, under a calm, doth putrify and become mephitic. The heart is the great centre of the action of Fire, lending its terrible energy as an impulse unto the others. Thence cometh from the fiery nature the red colour of the blood. The part above the heart is the chief abode of the Ruach, as there receiving and concentrating the other expression of its Sephiroth. This part is the central citadel of the body and is the particular abode of the lower and more physical will. The higher will is in the Kether of the body. For the higher will to manifest, it must be reflected into the lower will be **NESCHAMAH.** This **lower** will is potent around the heart and is seated like the King of the body upon its throne. The concentration of the other faculties of the Ruach in and under the presidency of the Will, at the same time reflecting the administrative governance of CHOKMAH and BINAH, is what is called the human consciousness. That is, a reflection of the two creative Sephiroth under the presidency of the Four Elements, or the reflection of Aima and Abba as the parents of the human Jehovah. But the human Neschamah exists only when the higher Will is reflected by the agency of aspiration from Kether into the lower body, and when the flaming letter SHIN is placed like a crown on the head of Microprosopus. Thus only doth the human will become the receptacle of the higher Will and the action of Neschamah is the link therewith. The lower will is the human Jehovah, an angry and jealous God, the Shaker of the Elements, the manifestor in the life of the body. But illuminated by the higher Will, he becometh YEHESHUAH, no longer angry and jealous, but the self-sacrificer and the Atoning and Reconciling One.

This as regards the action of the more physical man. Unto this Ruach also are presented the reflections of the Macrocosmic Universe in the Sphere of Sensation. They surround the Ruach which, in the natural man, feeleth them but vaguely and comprehendeth them not. The faculties of the Earth are shown forth in the organs which digest and putrify, casting forth the impurities, even as the Earth is placed above the Qlippoth. Thou wilt say, then, that the Ruach cannot be the reasoning mind, seeing that it reflecteth its reason from Chokmah and Binah, but it is the executive faculty which reasoneth, which worketh and combineth the faculties reflected into it. The reasoning mind, therefore, is that which useth and combineth the Principia of Chokmah and Binah so that the parts of Chokmah and Binah which touch the Ruach are the initiators of the reasoning power. The reason itself is a process and but a simulacrum of the action of the higher Wisdom and Understanding. For the Air is not the Light, only the translator of the Light. Yet without the Air, the operations of the Light could not so well be carried out. The word Ruach, Spirit, also meaneth Air. It is like a thing that goeth out thou knowest not whither, and cometh in thou knowest not whence. 'The wind bloweth where it listeth, and thou hearest the sound thereof, but canst not tell whence it cometh nor whither it goeth. so is every one that is born of the Spirit.' This Air, the Ruach, permeateth the whole physical body but its concentrated influence is about the the heart. Yet, were it not for the boundary force of Chokmah and Binah above, of the sphere of sensation surrounding it, and of Malkuth below, the Ruach could not concentrate under the presidency of the Name, and the life of the body would cease. Thus far concerning the Ruach as a whole, that is, the action of the Will in Tiphareth.

NETZACH AND HOD

From Netzach and Hod are formed the thighs and legs, and they terminate in the symbols of five, as do the arms; but they are not so moveable, owing to the effect of Malkuth. In them are placed the faculties of support and firmness and balance; and they show the more physical qualities of the Ruach. In them is the sustaining force of the Ruach. They are the affirmation of the Pillars of the Sephiroth, as answering to the Passive, the arms more answering to the two pillars which are Active. They are the columns of the Human Temple.

From YESOD are formed the generative and excretory organs, and therein is the seat of the lower desires, as bearing more on the double nature of, on the one hand, the rejection of the Qlippoth, and on the other hand the simulacrum of the vital forces in Tiphareth. It is the special seat of the automatic consciousness. That is, not the Will, but the simulacrum of the Will in Tiphareth. Yesod is the lowest of the Sephiroth of the Ruach, and representeth "Fundamental Action." It therefore governeth generation. In Yesod is therefore the automatic consciousness or simulacrum of the Will. This automatic consciousness is to the Nephesch what the Daath action is to the Ruach. Thus, therefore, there being a simulacrum or reflection of the heart and vital organs in the parts governed by Yesod, if the consciousness of the Tiphareth be given unto this wholly, it shall pave the way for disease and death. For this will be a withdrawing of the vital forces of the Name, which are in the citadel of Tiphareth, to locate them in Yesod, which is a more easily attacked position. For the automatic consciousness is the translator of the Ruach unto the Nephesch.

MALKUTH

From Malkuth is formed the whole physical body under the command and presidency of Nephesch. The Nephesch is the subtle body of refined astral Light upon which, as on an invisible pattern, the physical body is extended. The physical body is permeated throughout by rays of the Ruach, of which it is the material completion. The Nephesch shineth through the Material body and formeth the Magical Mirror or Sphere of Sensation. This Magical Mirror or Sphere of Sensation is an imitation or copy of the Sphere of the Universe. The space between the physical body and the boundary of the sphere of Sensation is occupied by the ether of the astral world; that is to say, the container or recipient of the Astral Rays of the Macrocosm. The Nephesch is divided into its seven Palaces, combining the Sephirotic influences in their most material forms. That is, the world of passions dominated by the Ruach, or by the world which is beyond. That is, its Sephiroth are passionate, expressing a passionate dominion. Thus, its three Supernal Sephiroth, Kether, Chokmah and Binah, are united in a sense of feeling and comprehending impressions. Its Chesed is expressed by laxity of action. Its Geburah by violence of action. Its Tiphareth is expressed by more or less sensual contemplation of beauty, and love of vital sensation. Its Hod and Netzach, by physical well-being and health. Its Yesod, by physical desires and gratifications. Its Malkuth, by absolute increase and domination of matter in the material body. The Nephesch is the real, the actual body, of which the material body is only the result through the action of Ruach, which by the aid of the Nephesch, formeth the material body by the rays of Ruach, which do not ordinarily proceed beyond the limits of the physical body. That is to say, in the ordinary man the rays of Ruach rarely penetrate into the sphere of Sensation. Shining through infinite worlds, and darting its rays through the confines of space, in this Sphere of Sensation is a faculty placed even as a light is placed in an aperture of the upper part of the Ruach wherein act the rays from Chokmah and Binah which govern the reason, Daath.

This faculty can be thrown downwards into the Ruach, and thence can radiate into the Nephesch. It consists of seven manifestations answering to the Hexagram, and is like the Soul of Microprosopus or the Elohim of the Human YHVH. Therefore in the head, which is its natural and chief seat, are formed the seven apertures of the head. This is the Spiritual consciousness as distinct from the Human consciousness. It is manifested in 7 as just said or in 8 if Daath be included. The Father is the Sun (Chokmah). The Mother is the Moon (Binah). The Wind beareth it in his bosom (Ruach). Its Nurse is the Earth (Nephesch). The power is manifested when it can vibrated through the Earth.

The following is the true attribution of the seven apertures of the head:

> **The right ear is Saturn.**
>
> **The left ear is Jupiter.**
>
> **The right eye is the Sun.**
>
> **The left eye is the Moon.**
>
> **The mouth is Mercury.**
>
> **The right nostril is Mars.**
>
> **The left nostril is Venus.**

These latter represent here the sonoriferous sense. The right and left eye the luminous sense, as the Sun and Moon are the luminaries of the Macrocosm. The right and left nostrils through which the breath passes, giving strength to the physical body, are under Mars and Venus. The mouth is under Mercury,'the messenger and the Speaker.

This spiritual consciousness is a focus of the action of Neschamah. The lower will power should control the descent of this spiritual consciousnes into the Ruach, and thence into the Nephesch, for the consciousness must descend into the Nephesch before the images of the Sphere of Sensation can be perceived. For it is only the rays of this consciousness permeating the Ruach that can take cognisance thereof. This faculty of the spiritual consciousness is the seat of Thought. Thought is a Light proceeding from the radiation of this spiritual consciousness, traversing the Ruach as Light traverseth Air, and encountering thereafter the symbols reflected in the sphere of Sensation, or magical mirror of the Universe. These symbols are by its radiation (i.e. that of the Thought) reflected again into the Spiritual Consciousness where they are subjected unto the action of the Reasoning Mind and of the Lower Will. That is, in the ordinary natural man when awake, the thought acteth through the Ruach, subject when there to the action of the Lower Will, and submitted to the reasoning power derived as aforesaid from Chokmah and Binah. But in the ordinary man when sleeping, and in the madman, the idiot, and the drunkard, the process is not quite the same.

In the sleeping man, the concentration of the Ruach in his heart during the waking time hath produced a weakening of the action of the Ruach in its subsidiary Sephiroth in the Physical Body. To preserve the salutary conjunction of the Ruach with the Nephesch in the physical body whose limits are fixed by the Sephiroth of the Ruach it is necessary to weaken the concentration in Tiphareth to repair the strain which is produced by the concentration of the Ruach therein during the waking state. This reflux of the Ruach into its subsidiary Sephiroth produceth naturally a weakening of the Lower Will; and the Ruach, therefore, doth not reflect so clearly the Reasoning Faculty. Wherefore, the thought of the spiritual consciousness reflecteth the image in a confused series, which are only partially realised by the lower will. This is as regards the ordinary natural man in sleep. In the madman, as considered apart from obsession, thought-obsession is frequently the accompaniment of mania, and still more frequently its cause the thought and lower will are very strongly exercised to the detriment of the reasoning faculty. That is, that there is an alliance between the two former which overpowereth the action of Chokmah and Binah in the latter. Monomania is shewn in the consideration of only one certain symbol which is too attractive to the Will. A chain of thought is therefore simply a graduated vibration arising from the contact of a ray of thought with a symbol.

If controlled by the reasoning power and licensed by the Will, such vibrations will be balanced and of equal length. But if uncontrolled by the lower Will and the Reason, they will be unbalanced and inharmonious. That is, of uneven length. In the case of the drunkard, the equilibrium of the Sphere of Sensation and consequently of the Nephesch, is disturbed. In consequence the thought rays are shaken at each vibration, so that the sphere of sensation of the Nephesch is caused to rock and waver at the extremities of the Physical Body where the Ruach action is bounded. The thought therefore is dazzled by the symbols of the Sphere of Sensation, in the same way as the eyes can be dazzled in front of a mirror if the latter be shaken or waved. The sensation therefore then conveyed by the thoughts is that of the Sphere of Sensation oscillating and almost revolving about the physical body, bringing giddiness, sickness, vertigo and the loss of idea of place and position. Nearly the same may be said of Seasickness, and the action of certain drugs. Restoration of the equilibrium of the Sphere of Sensation after this naturally produceth a slackening of the concentration of the Ruach in Tiphareth, whence sleep is an absolute necessity to the drunkard. This is so imperative that he cannot fight against the need. If he does so, or if this condition be constantly repeated, the thought rays are launched through the Sphere of Sensation so irregularly and so violently that they pass its boundary without either the lower Will or the Reasoning Power or even the Thought itself consenting thereto; and the latter is therefore without the protection of the will.

Thence arise the conditions of delirium tremors, and an opening is made in the Sphere of Sensation which is unguarded, and through which hostile influences may enter. But this latter cometh under the head of obsession. All thought action in the spiritual consciousness originateth in radiation, and radiation is as inseparable from the spiritual consciousness as it is from Light. This Spiritual Consciousness is the focus of the action of Neschamah. The spiritual consciousness is, in its turn, the Throne or Vehicle of the Life of the Spirit which is Chiah; and these combined form the Chariot of that Higher Will which is in Kether. Also it is the peculiar faculty of Neschamah to aspire unto that which is beyond. The Higher Will manifests itself through Yechidah. The Chiah is the real Life Principle, as distinct from the more illusionary life of the Physical Body.

The Shining Flame of the Divine Fire, the Kether of the Body, is the Real Self of the Incarnation. Yet but few of the sons of men know it or feel its presence. Still less do they believe in or comprehend those Higher Potencies, Angelic, Archangelic or Divine, of which the manifestation directly touching Yechidah is the Higher Genius. This Yechidah in the ordinary man can but rarely act through the spiritual consciousness, seeing that for it to do so the King of the Physical Body, that is the Lower Will, must rise from his Throne to acknowledge his superior. That is the reason why, in some cases, in sleep only doth the Higher Will manifest itself by dream unto the ordinary man. In other cases it may be manifested; at times through the sincere practice of religious rites, or in cases where the opportunity for self-sacrifice occurreth. In all these cases the Lower Will hath for a moment recognised a higher form of itself, and the YHVH of the man hath reflected from the Eternal Lord of the Higher Life. This Yechidah is the only part of the man which can truly say, EHEIEH, I am. This is then but the Kether of the Assiah of the Microcosm, that is, it is the highest part of man as Man. It is that which toucheth, or is the manifestation of a higher and greater range of Being. This Yechidah is at the same time the Higher Human Self and the Lower Genius, the God of the Man, the Atziluth of his Assiah, even as Chiah and Neschamah form his Briah. and Ruach his Yetzirah. This is the Higher Will and the Divine Consciousness, as Daath is the Spiritual Consciousness, Tiphareth the Human Consciousness, and Yesod the Automatic Consciousness.

It is the Divine Consciousness because it is the only part of man which can touch the All potent forces. Behind Yechidah are Angelic and Archangelic Forces of which Yechidah is the manifestor. It is therefore the Lower Genius or Viceroy of the Higher Genius which is beyond, an Angel Mighty and Terrible. This Great Angel is the Higher Genius, beyond which are the Archangelic and Divine. Recall the Tiphareth clause of an Adeptus Minor: "I further solemnly promise and swear that with the divine permission I will from this day forward apply myself unto the Great Work which is so to purify and exalt my spiritual nature, that with the Divine Aid I may at length attain to be more than Human, and thus gradually raise and unite myself to my Higher and Divine Genius, and that in this event, I will not abuse the great power entrusted unto me." Note that this clause answereth unto Tiphareth, seeing that it is the Lower Will that must apply itself unto this work, because it is the King of the Physical Man.

All the Shining Ones (whom we call Angels) are microcosms of the Macrocosm Yetzirah, even as Man is the microcosm of the Macrocosm of Assiah. All Archangelic forms are microcosms of the Macrocosm of Briah, and the Gods of the Sephiroth are consequently the Microcosms of the Macrocosm of Atziluth. Therefore apply this perfecting of the Spiritual Nature as the preparation of the Pathway for Shining Light, the Light Divine. The evil persona of a man is in the Sphere of the Qlippoth, and the devils are the Microcosms of the Macrocosm of the Qlippoth. This evil persona hath its parts and divisions, and of it the part which toucheth the Malkuth of the Nephesch is its Kether. Tremble therefore at the evil forces which be in thy own evil persona. And as above the Kether of a Man are his Angelic and other forms, so below the Malkuth of the Evil Persona are awful forms, dangerous even to express or think of.

TASK UNDERTAKEN BY THE ADEPTUS MINOR

This, then, is the task to be undertaken by the Adeptus Minor. To expel from the Sephiroth of the Nephesch the usurpation by the evil Sephiroth; to balance the action of the Sephiroth of the Ruach in those of the Nephesch. To prevent the Lower Will and Human Consciousness from falling into and usurping the place of the Automatic Consciousness. To render the King of the Body, the Lower Will, obedient to and anxious to execute the commands of the Higher Will, **that he be neither a usurper of the faculties of the Higher, nor a sensual despot, but an Initiated Ruler,** and an annointed King, the Viceroy and representative of the Higher Will, because inspired thereby, in his Kingdom which is man. Then shall it happen that the Higher Will, i.e., the Lower Genius, shall descend into the Royal Habitation, so that the Higher Will and the Lower Will shall be as one, and the Higher Genius shall descend into the Kether of the Man, bringing with him the tremendous illumination of his Angelic Nature. And the Man shall become what is said of Enoch. "And Chanokh made himself to walk with God, and he was not, for God took him." (Genesis, V.v. 24.) Then also this shalt thou know, that the Nephesch of the Man shall become as the Genius of the Evil Persona, so that the evil persona itself shall be as the power of the Divine in the Qlippoth, as it is said: "Whither shall I go from thy Spirit, or whither from thy Presence shall I flee? If I ascend up to Heaven, thou art there. If I make my bed in Hell, behold thou art there." (Ps. cxxxix.)

Therefore even the Evil Persona is not so evil when it fulfilleth its work. For it is the beginner of a dim reflection of the Light unto the Qlippoth, and this is what is hidden in the saying that "Typhon is the brother of Osiris." Hear thou, then, a mystery of the knowledge of evil. The Ritual of the Adeptus Minor saith that even the "Evil helpeth forward the Good."

When the evil Sephiroth are expelled from the Nephesch into the evil Persona, they are, in a sense, equilibriated therein. **The evil persona can be rendered as a great and strong, yet trained, animal whereupon the man rideth, and it then becometh a strength unto his physical base of action.** This Mystery shalt thou keep from the knowledge of the First Order, and still more from that of the Outer World, that is as a formula, seeing that is a dangerous secret. Now then shalt thou begin to understand the saying "He descended into Hell," and also to comprehend in part this strength, and thus begin to understand the necessity of evil unto the material creation. Wherefore, also, revile not overmuch the evil forces, for they have also a place and a duty, and in this consisteth their right to be. But check their usurpation, and cast them down unto their plane. Unto this end, curse them by the mighty names if need be, but thou shalt not revile them for their condition, for thus also shalt thou be led into error. There is also a great mystery that the Adeptus Minor must know. How the spiritual consciousness can act around and beyond the sphere of Sensation.

"Thought" is a mighty force when projected with all the strength of the lower Will under the guidance of the reasoning faculty and illuminated by the Higher Will. Therefore, it is that, in thy occult working, thou art advised to invoke the divine and Angelic Names, so that thy Lower Will may willingly receive the influx of the Higher Will, which is also the Lower Genius behind which are the all-potent forces.

This, therefore, is the magical manner of operation of the Initiate when "skrying" in the spirit vision. Through his own arcane wisdom, he knows the disposition and correspondences of the Forces of the Macrocosmos. Selecting not many, but one symbol, and that balanced and with its correlatives, then sendeth he a thought-ray from his Spiritual Consciousness, illuminated by his Higher Will, directly unto the part of his Sphere of Sensation which is consonant with the symbol employed. There, as in a mirror, doth he perceive its properties as reflected from the Macrocosmos, shining forth into the Infinite Abyss of the Heavens.

Thence can he follow the ray of reflection therefrom, and while concentrating his united consciousness at that point of his sphere of sensation, can receive the direct reflection of the ray from the Macroscosmos. Thus receiving the direct ray as then reflected into his Thought, he can unite himself with the ray of his Thought so as to make one continuous ray from the corresponding point of the Macrocosmos unto the centre of his consciousness. If, instead of concentrating at the actual point of the sphere of Sensation he shall retain the thought-ray only touching the sphere of sensation at that point, he shall, it is true, perceive the reflection of the Macrocosmic Ray answering to that symbol in the sphere of his Consciousness. But he shall receive this reflection tinctured much by his own nature, and therefore to an extent untrue, because his united conciousnesses have not been able to focus along the thought-ray at the circumference of the Sphere of sensation. And this is the reason why there are so many and multifarious errors in untrained spirit visions. For the untrained seer, even supposing him free from the delusions of obsession, doth not know or understand how to unite his consciousnesses and the harmonies between his own sphere of sensation, and the universe, the Macrocosmos. Therefore is it so necessary that the Adeptus Minor should correctly understand the principia and axiomata of our secret knowledge, which are contained in our Rituals and Lectures.

OF TRAVELING IN THE SPIRIT VISION

The symbol, place, direction, or Plane being known whereon it is desired to act, a thought-ray as before is sent unto the corresponding part of the Sphere of Sensation of the Nephesch. The Thought-Ray is sent like an arrow from the bow, right through the circumference of the Sphere of Sensation direct unto the place desired. Arrived there, a sphere of astral Light is formed by the agency of the Lower Will, illuminated by the Higher Will, and acting through the spiritual consciousness by reflection along the Thought-Ray. This sphere of Astral Light is partly drawn from the surrounding atmosphere. The sphere being formed, a simulacrum of the person of the Skryer is reflected into it along the thought-ray, and this united consciousness is then projected therein.

This Sphere is then a duplicate, by reflection, of the Sphere of Sensation. As it is said, "Believe thyself to be in a place and thou art there." In this Astral Projection, however, a certain part of the consciousness must remain in the body to protect the Thought-Ray beyond the Sphere of Sensation (as well as the Sphere itself at that point of departure of the Thought-Ray) from attack by any hostile force, so that the consciousness in this projection is not quite so strong as the consciousness when concentrated in the natural body in ordinary life. The return taketh place with a reversal of this process, and save to persons whose Nephesch and physical body are exceptionally strong and healthy, the whole operation of skrying and traveling in the Spirit Vision is of course fatiguing. Also there is another mode of astral projection which can be used by the more practised and advanced Adept. This consisteth in forming first a sphere from his own Sphere of Sensation, casting his reflection therein, and then projecting this whole sphere to the desired place, as in the previous method. But this is not easy to be done by any but the practised operator. Thus far, regarding Skrying and Travelling in the Spirit Vision.

CONCERNING THE MICROCOSMS OF THE MACROCOSM

As thou well knowest there be many and numberless other inhabitants of the Macrocosmos besides Man, Angels, and Devils. The animals are microcosms in a sense, yet not so complete as man. In them are many and great mysteries. They also have their magical mirror or sphere of sensation. But its polarisation is usually of horizontal rather than perpendicular type, and this is owing to the Sephiroth not being shewn therein. This Sphere, then, is not bounded by the Sephirotic columns, but they are especially governed by the Stellar System without the Sephiroth. They are therefore ruled by the Paths, rather than by the Sephiroth, and are consequently classed each under an Element or a Planet, and a Sign. Thus each followeth a formula which may be translated into letters, and these again form a vibratory name. As it is written: "And Adam gave names unto all the cattle and to the fowl of the air, and to every beast of the field. "(Gen. II, v. 20.) Yet they are ruled by the name YHVH, though classed rather by one or more of its letters.

Thus, Fish, etc., are under the influence of Water. Birds are under the influence of Air. Quadrupeds are under the influence of Fire. Creeping things and insects are under the influence of Earth.

There are some which partake of two elements, but in them one element is usually chief, and besides the Elements, each is under a Planet and a Sign.

The vegetable kingdom is again under a somewhat different Law. These are under a Planet and a Sign, a planet first differentiated by a Sign. The Mineral Kingdom is under the Signs only. Vegetables have a Sphere of Sensation, but corresponding only to the Planets and Zodiacal Signs. The Minerals have also a Sphere which correspondeth unto the Signs only, but the metals are under the Planets only, and therein is the difference between them and the Minerals, wherefore also are they stronger. Shining Stones are especially under the Light; and they are, as it were, centres for the action thereof in the darkness of matter, as it is said: "My light is concealed in all that shineth." This passage is it is believed from the Zend-Avesta. They are therefore under the rule of the three active elements with an earthy base. Shining through all things as a whole, are the rays of the Macrocosmos. Besides these classes of life there be multitudinous existences representing Forces of the Macrocosm, each with its own microcosm. Such are Elemental Spirits, Planetary Spirits, Olympic Spirits, Fays, Arch-Fays, Genii, and many other potencies which cannot be classed under these forms.

Thus the Macrocosmic Universe is one vast and infinite sphere containing so many and diverse infinite microcosmic forms, of which the perfect knowledge is only known unto the advanced Adept. Also it shall here suffice to say that thou shalt make a distinction between the Four-handed race (the quadrumana, apes and monkeys) which be midway between Man and Beast and other animals. For they be neither the one or the other, but are the fallen and debased result of a most ancient magical effect to formulate a material and immediate link between the human and animal microcosms. This is elsewhere treated of, and it shall here be sufficient to say that they are not an ascent, from the beast unto the Man, but mistaken magical fall from a man unto a beast. Anciently they were a terrible power upon this planet, as then having more of the man than of the animal, whereas now they have more of the animal than of Man.

The ancient traditions of their primal conditions are preserved unto this day in the legends of ogres and, in certain records, cannibalism and its rites. Regarding the beasts, they are, for the most part, easily obsessed, and they have not the spiritual responsibility of the man. Their nature is not evil, but, following a natural law, seeing that man is head of the Assiatic creation, so the animal is higher than the vegetables or mineral. Also bear thou well in mind that the race of the transformers are given unto cruelty. Such are above all the race of creeping things. As Man hath his Ruach which is upright in the Tree of Life, so hath the beast his Ruach which is horizontal; as it is said: "The Ruach of a man which goeth upwards (i.e. directeth itself upwards), and the Ruach of the beast which goeth downwards (or crosswise) in the Earth." The Neschamah in the Beast is not. The beast consisteth of a Ruach and a Nephesch with a rudimentary Daath or Spiritual Consciousness. This Daath ever seeketh that which is beyond it and thence are beasts not responsible, but are submitted unto obsession and herein is a great mystery.

Man, therefore, is placed at the head of the beasts. Woe, woe, unto him if he teacheth their elementary Daath cruelty and injustice instead of mercy and justice. For the Man is a God unto the beast, and the aspiration of the Beast is toward the Man, and great is the office of the Beast, for he prepareth the foundation for the man. Man is responsible for creation, and since he was originally placed in creation to be its Lord, as he is, so will the creation follow him. And thus it is possible for the Genius of a Nation to change the climate of a country, and the nature of the beasts therein. Men fell from primal estate, and then they who were formless became imaged in form, deformed. And this is a mystery of the Demonic Plane which entereth not into this section. The Elemental Spirits and other of their kind are an organisation not quite so complete as man. In spiritual consciousness more keen, and yet in some ways his spiritual superior though organically his inferior. They are the formers of the primal Man, that is the Elementary Man, and they have other and greater offices, for in them are many worlds and ranks and spheres. They are as the younger man (i.e. child) and towards them also is Man responsible, and he hath wrought them much injustice.

OF OBSESSION, TRANCE, DEATH

Obsession always entereth through a cutting off of the Higher from the Lower Will, and it is ordinarily first induced by a Thought-Ray of the Spiritual consciousness (whence one danger of evil thoughts) ill-governed, penetrating the Sphere of Sensation and admitting another potency, either human embodied, or human disembodied, elemental or demonic. The first action of such a force is to flatter the lower will, until he shall have established firmly an entrance into the Sphere of Sensation, and thus shall cause a strain on the Nephesch which shall render the Ruach less concentrated. As soon as the Ruach is sufficiently dispersed to repair the strain on the physical body, the lower will is weakened, and is soon seized upon and bound by the invader. Whence arise the sensations of chill and drowsiness which are the usual forerunners of obsession.

Now to yield the force necessary to overpower the lower will from any chance of communication with the higher the obsessing idea proceeds by seizing upon the Daath, and this consequently is the great point of attack, especially the part in the physical body which is at the back of the head about the junction with the Spine. Now unless the lower Will shall voluntarily endeavour to restore the connection, it is impossible for the Higher Will to intervene, seeing that the Lower Will is King of the Physical Body. Remember that no obsessing force can overpower the lower will, if that shall bravely and in spite of all opposition aspire unto the Higher Will. Trance may arise from the action of obsession, or from the action of the Higher Will, therefore its aspects are varied. Death superveneth in the natural man, when the mental action of the Ruach and the Nephesch is definitely and thoroughly interrupted in the physical body.

In the Adept death can only supervene when the Higher Will consenteth thereto, and herein is implied the whole Mystery of the Elixir of Life.

ON THE WORK TO BE UNDERTAKEN BETWEEN PORTAL AND ADEPTUS MINOR

The work comes under six headings as follows:

1. **A Thesis on the Rituals.**
2. **A meditation on the crosses which have been used as admission badges in the Grades. This is a preparation for the meditation which precedes the Adeptus Minor Grade and should be applied for when you have been a Portal Member for seven months.**
3. **A complete diagram of The Tree of Life.**
4. **The practice of control of the Aura.**
5. **The placing of The Tree of Life in the Aura.**
6. **Tattwas—Astrology—Divination.**

One. THE THESIS. Read the rituals. Build them up in imagination. Compare the Opening and Closing in the various Grades. Note the general underlying scheme for each Elemental Grade—and note where the differences occur. Follow the careers of the various Officers. Note at what Grade an Officer disappears.

Make a precis of each Ritual so that the general scheme becomes apparent. This is of the greatest assistance when you are called on to take Office because you will not then need to follow everything in the Ritual but need only turn to the page where your Office is mentioned and when you have no more to say, you can turn to the Closing and put the Ritual aside till required for that. Ability to do this and to move correctly in the Temple adds greatly to the harmony and repose of the whole Ceremony.

Note the positions of the various officers—what geometrical shapes they make among themselves from time to time as they take up their places in the Temple. It may be a triangle, a cross, a pentagram, etc.

Read the speeches carefully, and read them sometimes aloud so that you get familiar with the sound of your own voice in saying the words. Note that some speeches are designed to create atmosphere by their archaic form and should be read rhythmically and sonorously, while others are informative and should be read in such a way as to make their points clear.

Examples of archaic passages are challenges of Gods: 'Thou canst not pass the Gate of the Western Heaven unless thou canst tell me my Name.' And the speeches of the Kabiri in the Grades of Practicus and Philosophus. Information is given in speeches about Tarot Keys and diagrams.

Note the technique for traversing the various Paths—the words, and the badges with which the Path is entered, the length of the circumambulation and the special symbolism described therein.

Let all these things soak into your mind, make notes as ideas occur to you and presently your personal reaction to the Grades will crystallise out and you will be able to write your thesis.

Two. Make a list and drawings of the crosses which have been given you as Admission Badges throughout the Grades, from the Swastika of the Zelator to the Five-squared cross which you put on as you stood at the Altar at the second point of the Portal Grade. Read what is said of them in the Rituals and knowledge lectures, and make notes about them.

Three. THE TREE OF LIFE. This should be done large in order that the writing and symbols should be clear. It is essential to show the Deity Names, Names of Archangels and Angels in Hebrew in the Sephiroth, and to number the Paths and give their attributions. Apart from this, the Tree should be your personal synthesis of the Order symbolism as it applies to the Tree of Life. Colours may be used.

Four. CONTROL OF THE AURA. If you are not already familiar with the parts of your own body such as nervous system, respiratory system, digestive system, get some simple text-book such as is used in ambulance work, or attend a course of first-aid lectures so that, before starting to work on your subtle body, you may know something about your physical body.

Your physical body is interpenetrated by a subtle body or aura which also surrounds the physical body like an egg of light. You should now begin to practise controlling this aura or Sphere of Sensation. This means that you must first try to get your emotional reactions under conscious control. Instead of automatically liking this, disliking that, you must try to understand the mechanism which underlies these feelings. To assist you in this, the study of psychology is recommended. There are many books on the subject, of which the following are easy to understand and clearly stated.

Psychoanalysis for Normal People by Geraldine Coster.
You are in Charge by Janette Rainwater.
The Function of the Orgasm by Wilhelm Reich.
Two Essays on Analytical Psychology by C.G. Jung.
Exploring the Unconscious by Georg Groddeck.
The Image and Appearance of the Human Body by Paul Schilder.
Varieties of Religious Experience by William James.

Having built up some idea of the mechanism of your mental processes, you should now try to make yourself negative or positive at will towards people or ideas. If you are likely to meet someone who always makes you argumentative and irritable, decide that your aura is closed to their power of irritating you and that your mind will not be disturbed by what they say. It is good sometimes to listen to views with which you disagree to learn not to make any verbal response, and to keep your feelings in abeyance. (N.B. But remember this is a technique only. There are in fact times to speak and times to remain silent. It is imperative to avoid transforming techniques into compulsions I.R.). In this way you come to learn how much of your disagreement is due to prejudice or personal factors, and how much to your regard for abstract truth.

VOLUME THREE

Again, sometimes practise opening your aura to people or ideas in an endeavour to see things from another's point of view.

The practice of deep breathing is also of help in establishing poise and in controlling nervousness. It is good to expand the chest to its fullest extent and then to expand the diaphragm below the ribs as well and then to let the breath out slowly and steadily on a vowel sound such as ah or 'O'. (N.B. Consult in this connection *Undoing Yourself with Energized Meditation* by Christopher Hyatt, Falcon Press, 1982. I.R.)

If you are nervous, you will find that your breathing is shallow and that your muscles are tense. You tend to clench your hands and tighten up the abdominal muscles. To cure this, take a deep breath to full capacity, hold it while tensing and relaxing alternately the abdominal muscles. Do this (i.e. the tensing and relaxing of the muscles) three times and then relax completely into a chair. Allow all your muscles to go limp and let your breath out to the last gasp. Do the whole process three times, if necessary. It is designed to stimulate the solar plexus which is the heart of the nervous system which governs emotion.

Another good exercise is to say the Deity Names aloud. Take a deep breath and say them softly, smoothly and slowly, imagining the while that your voice travels out to the confines of the Universe. This can be done in conjunction with the Pentagram Ritual.

Five. THE TREE OF LIFE IN THE AURA. In the aura which interpenetrates and surrounds our physical bodies, we are to build up a replica of the Tree of Life. The Pillar of Severity is on our right side, the Pillar of Mercy on our left, and the Pillar of Benificence in the middle.

It is best to build up the middle Pillar first. To do this stand up and raise yourself in imagination to your KETHER—a brilliant light above your head. Imagine this light descending to DAATH, at the nape of your neck, and thence to TIPHARETH in your heart where it glows like sunlight and whence it radiates into the other Sephiroth. From TIPHARETH the light goes to YESOD in the region of the hips, and thence to MALKUTH in which your feet are planted. Having made a clear image of the Middle Pillar, you can then establish the other Sephiroth by vibrating the Deity Names. This can be done as an alternative to the Pentagram Ritual as a preparation for meditation.

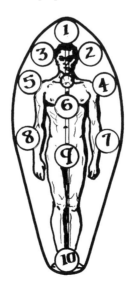

41

1. Imagine yourself standing in the Temple, facing West. The Black Pillar of Severity will be on your right --the White Pillar of Mercy on your left. You will make the Middle Pillar as you stand between them.

2. Imagine now that the Black Pillar is reflected in your right side—the White Pillar in your left.

3. Take a deep breath and raise your consciousness to your KETHER above your head and vibrate the Name EHEIEH—which means I AM. Imagine the Light flowing down through DAATH (at the nape of your neck) to TIPHARETH.

4. In the same manner, establish YESOD in the name SHADDAI EL CHAI, and MALKUTH in the Name ADONAI HA-ARETZ.

5. Make the Qabalistic Cross to indicate that you have called down the Light of your KETHER and balanced it in your aura. Then let your imagination dwell on the aura and see it oval and clear, pulsating with the glow from TIPHARETH.

If you are called to see anyone who is ill, who is depressed, or who has a depressing effect on you, you should do this exercise beforehand. In the case of the person who has a depressing effect on you, you may also imagine that your aura is hardened at the edge so that they are unable to penetrate it, and so deplete you of vitality (which is generally what such sensations mean).

In all these practices it is well to remember that 'Strength is in Silence.'(N.B. The original documents of the Order, dating as far back as 1895 and maybe earlier, do not provide us with a single clue as to the origins of what has come to be known as the middle pillar technique. It seems to be, as far as I can discover, a specific development of the Stella Matutina, in which case Dr. R. Felkin was its originator. This might explain why there is no trace whatsoever of its usage in the technical writings of Aleister Crowley, who has certainly made good use of most of the Order techniques, and who would surely have used this had it been available.

However, even in the Stella Matutina it was described merely in larval form—that is to say, it remained largely undeveloped. It was briefly stated in the paper describing the work to be done between the Portal Grade and the Adeptus Minor grade. There are enormous possibilities inherent in the method. I was lucky enough to have stumbled on to a practical approach which I think exploited more fully some of the potentialities suggested in the original Felkin paper.

In a book entitled *Foundations of Practical Magic*, I recently included an older essay entitled *The Art of True Healing.* This was once produced as a small book by Helios Publishing Service In England.

It describes the method which over the years I have found preeminently useful. Whoever developed the basic technique, whether Felkin or some other, produced a fundamental method of aiding personal and spiritual growth. If you talk about them, save to your Chief, or if you try to analyse their effects, you will not benefit by them. Try them with simple faith and in silence for a year before rationalising them. I.R.)

It is better at first to keep your aura to yourself, rather than to try to flow out towards others. Unless you are particularly vital and well-balanced, you will only waste energy. So-called modes of healing and of 'doing good to others' should be eschewed for a time. Such methods have a technique of their own and require trained and balanced minds and bodies to carry them out. Get yourself right first before you attempt to interfere with others in any way but the ordinary ways of kindly decent society.

VOLUME THREE

When you have practised the exercise of the Middle Pillar for some time and can visualise it easily, you can establish the other Sephiroth.

Six. TATWAS-ASTROLOGY-DIVINATION. The Tatwas are designed to assist you in your researches into the Soul of Nature. They are at first done with a senior member, and later can be done alone or with a companion of your own Grade. They should never be allowed to become uncontrolled day-dreams. The method taught should be strictly adhered to—a definite time, preferably in the morning being set aside—and they should not be attempted when you are feeling tired or when your mind is too occupied with other things to let you 'get away.' They should not be done too frequently—once in three weeks or a month is enough, once a week if time and circumstances permit. Notes of the pictures and symbols seen should be kept together in a book.

ASTROLOGY. This should be done as time permits. The subject is vast and highly technical, and can be studied fully through the various schools and correspondence classes if you are interested in it. From the Order Lecture, you should be able to set up a true birth horoscope for any place and any time. You can practise setting up horoscopes for the cases given in a book *The Circle Book of Charts* and see whether you can tell what was remarkable about the horoscope. You should attempt the reading of a horoscope for someone you know and then get the data for someone about whom you know nothing, and see whether you can give a reading which satisfies their friends.

The Order requires only that you should be able to set up an accurate horoscope and that you should know how to work out the aspects and how to make a simple assessement of the good and bad factors in a horary figure. If Astrology interests you further, it is a very fascinating field of research.

DIVINATION. You may try to develop your intuition by the use of horary and natal astrology, geomancy, and the reading of the Tarot Cards by the method given in the small book by Mr. A.E. Waite.

You are advised to attempt only questions in which you are not emotionally involved because methods of divination can be a fruitful source of self-deception to those who are psychic but not self-knowing. If you are given to having intuitions you must learn to say not only 'I was right about that' but also 'I was quite wrong about that,' and if you advertise only successes (as is usual) at the bar of your own conscience, learn to assess them honestly.

The interval of time between PORTAL and grade of Adeptus Minor should be given to the study of the whole make-up of yourself. All these methods are designed to assist you to get as far as you can along the road to self-knowledge.

You are to realise the different layers of your being—some of which you have been led through symbolically in the Outer Grades—'Which in one sense quitteth not MALKUTH' the Kingdom of yourself.

This line of thought, coupled with the study of the Rituals, may lead you to realise what it was you gathered together in the first point of the Portal Ritual, and what it is you are trying to perfect to lay on the Altar of the Spirit.

We are told in the Portal that the nine months' wait which must intervene before the Portal is again opened for the Aspirant has a correspondence to the nine months of gestation before birth. As the unborn child, stage by stage, grows through the ancestral history of the race so the Candidate in the Portal by a single circumambulation for each, recalls his past Grades and, at the end of the first point regards their symbols upon the Altar as parts of his body, and contemplates them as coming together in one place—the unity of his person.

In the second point, he sacrifices his name—symbol of his idea of himself in order that the idea of a new self and a new consciousness may be attained.

This has a correspondence in the birth of a child. It emerges from the membranes and placenta which hitherto have been its body and source of life and finds itself not 'dead' after the dread change, but translated to a larger consciousness.

Thus the Portal foreshadows the kind of change and development necessary for understanding the symbolism of the Adeptus Minor grade.

We do not know what consciousness the unborn child has—how far it has gone in its development—through what agency it unfolds the potencies of its tiny seed and draws to itself the necessary materials for growth. The miracle happens—and gives us courage to believe that a similar miracle is even now enacting whereby a body will be ready for us when this, which seems so real to us, shall share the same fate as the placenta and membranes which 'die' at our birth.

But tradition, as embodied in our Order and shown somewhat less directly in the revealed religions, teaches that this development can be assisted by conscious effort indeed, that there comes a time when this effort must be made through the body and mind we are now endowed with. And realising that we are indeed in a Path of Darkness groping for Light, we must feel our way to an understanding of the meaning of light—the reason for death.

To those who feel the call to make this effort, comes the Order with a series of pictures, symbolic of the growth of the soul to new life. The meditations given with each Grade are designed to lead the mind towards ideas which will assist in self-knowledge—universal, impersonal ideas which each must find in his own way—'the secrets which cannot be told save to those who know them already.'

The Aspirant is led to look backwards. First he must acknowledge his debt to evolution through which has been perfected the instrument wherein his mind works and gathers material. Then, through meditation, he is led to see himself as not only self-conscious—as one who receives impressions—one who criticises and watches—one whose will is interfered with—one who is misunderstood—one to whom others are 'persons' or masks (from Latin persona, a mask)—but, standing outside himself, he now becomes one who endeavours to sense how his mask appears to others—sees himself as part of the consciousness of others, as one who impresses, one who is criticised and watched, one who interferes with the will of others, one who misunderstands.

He may recall periods in his life when his convictions were sure, his judgments harsh and unjust, his actions shameful, and view himself in that picture dispassionately as an entity operative in the give and take of Life, something growing and as outside the category of blame as is the bitterness of unripe fruit.

As the knowledge of his place and relative importance in the Universe matures, he will attain strength to be honest with himself—ashamed of nothing he finds in his mind—one watching the antics of his personality with tolerant amusement—yet always learning.

He will reflect on words, and the power of words. He will catch himself weaving them twisting their meaning—deceiving himself and others with them. He will catch himself under obsession to them—he will see how they fix and make possible the recall of events and emotions, and with this knowledge he will become aware of how his words affect other people.

As he begins to realise the tremendous miracle of words, the magic both good and evil of human communion by words, he will begin to grasp why the Order reiterates the importance of silence. The true Magician must understand his tools and, in periods of silence, he must contemplate words as one of them.

As he thus traverses the long road to dispassionate self-knowledge, and no longer has to waste energy in doing battle for and indulging wounded feelings in defence of a totally false idea of himself, he is led to meditate on the varied symbols of the cross, and from this to contemplate the Crucified One, revealed to the West as Jesus of Nazareth. (However be cautious not to associate the ideas of Jesus with the political-religions which have evolved from his teachings. I.R.).

This life and the sayings of Jesus given in the Meditations should be studied and pictured in the mind.

The mind must be taught to die to useless churnings over past things and vain apprehensions about future things. This is difficult, for human phantasies die hard, but once the effort is made, however transient the result, it becomes easier with time to replace wasteful thoughts with those that cluster round a powerful symbol of eternal truth.

As the time for the Adeptus Minor Ceremony approaches, the Aspirant should withdraw as far as may be from externals that these symbols may work in his mind.

He will find them waiting on the threshold of his mind ready to tell their story as he walks about or is occupied in mechanical tasks. Once a place has been made for them no 'time' is required to develop them. They grow in the waste places.

Definite times too should be set aside for Meditation wherein ideas may be formulated as far as possible.

Before going to sleep, the Aspirant should do the Pentagram Ritual and impress on his mind that he must recall on waking any teaching that has been given him in dream or vision. This may be assisted on waking, if he calls before his mind the Sun rising, thinly veiled in clouds.

This should be done at least the week preceding the Grade.

The Ceremony will be a true initiation for the Aspirant only in so far as he has prepared himself to receive it.

Like a word, it is a symbol, the communication of whose essence depends on the understanding and experience of the recipient.

(N.B. There is no trace of the contents of this most important paper in the earlier Order documents. It is obviously therefore written by someone in the Stella Matutina. I sometimes get weary of the constant criticism leveled against the Stella Matutina; I think they are wholly unjust as this paper demonstrates. It reveals a profound working knowledge of psychological principles which the reader would do well to make an intrinsic part of his mental equipment. In addition the writer was well aware of the problems of identification, projection, consideration and ego-mania as how they interfere with the process of enlightenment. I.R.)

THE TREE OF LIFE IN THE AURA

BY

V.H. FRATER A.M.A.G.

This notion is first laid down in the Portal paper in a very broad simple outline. The text related to it does not appear to promise very much at first. Moreover it is surrounded by a mass of material on other Order topics, none of which seem to stress the relative importance of the method. In a word, it does not seem to promise a great deal. However some little attention and study of its principles soon convinces one that there is more to it than at first meets the eye. All sorts of hints are scattered throughout the Order documents that add significant clues as to how this rudimentary outline can be elaborated into a magnificent workable schema. First of all, there is the Hierophant's speech in the Neophyte Ritual "all powers can be awakened and re-awakened by names and images" which is one of the fundamentals of all the Order work, and of course especially applicable to this method. Then there is the theory of the Tree of Life projected into a solid sphere producing not three Pillars but four surrounding an axis of a Middle Pillar. In Z-3, the ceremonial circumambulation in the Temple is applied to the Aura in terms of the circulation of energy within the sphere of sensation, which first gave me the idea of the three types of circulation which came to be an integral idea of my development of this method. Then of course, there is the description of the rhythmic breathing process in the same Portal paper which is the preliminary basis for the whole method. All of these ideas, plus some others scattered throughout other Order documents helped to provide meaningful data which elaborate the simple schema there described into the one that I and many others have found so profoundly useful.

In the form so elaborated, it is really quite easy to employ - in fact far easier to do than to describe. As with all other Order techniques little attempt will be made to describe its results and effects. The main thing is to work it and use it often, daily if possible in order to become fully aware of what the method can do.

The first step lies in the adoption of the philosophy of the Order as a whole, the conscious realization of the vast spiritual reservoir in which we live and move and have our being. Repeated intellectual effort to make this part and parcel of one's mental outlook upon life automatically breaks down or dissolves something of the rigid character armoring that restricts both our physical and psychological activities. With this gradual softening of the armor a new and superior spiritual attitude may develop so that one's entire viewpoint undergoes a radical change for the better.

The second step relates to the practice of regulated breathing. It is really a simple process. We contemplate the fact that all living processes are rhythmical, so that at various times during the day we let the breath flow in while mentally counting very slowly - one, two, three, four. Then we exhale counting the same beat. It is fundamental and important that the initial rhythm, whether it be a four or a ten beat rhythm or any other convenient one, should be maintained for some minutes. It is the very rhythm which accounts for the easy absorption of vitality from without and the acceleration of the divine power within.

Cultivate techniques of relaxation to aid this process. These can be learned readily from a host of good books (*The Lazy Man's Guide to Relaxation* By Israel Regardie, Falcon Press, 1983) on this subject which are readily available at any good bookstore. The conjunction of relaxation techniques with the practice of the rhythmic breath will go far in the process of mobilizing one's energies. One of the indices of the success of this process is that in a few minutes the whole body is vibrating in unison with the rhythm of the breath. Every cell appears to vibrate sympathetically, and the whole system comes to feel as if it were an inexhaustible storage battery of power. The sensation most commonly felt is that the diaphragm is rippling and buzzing.

Once this has been experienced, then one can refer to the chart depicted in the Portal paper, paying particular attention to the Sephiroth on the Middle Pillar - Kether, Daath, Tiphareth, Yesod and Malkuth. We can call these Sephiroth or psychospiritual centers or even use the Hindu equivalent, the chakras. For convenience sake, we may name them after the elements so commonly used in the Order system. Kether we may name Spirit, Daath Air, the succeeding ones being named Fire, Water and Earth.

It is axiomatic to the Order system that there are two principal means whereby we may become aware of these centers to awaken them from their dormant state into actively functioning chakras - thought, colour and sound. We must concentrate upon these Sephiroth in the aura one by one and at the same time vibrate the divine names appropriate thereto. Each center is to be imagined as having a specific colour and shape. The combination of these three agencies gradually stirs the Sephirotic centers into vigorous activity. Slowly they become stimulated into functioning each according to its own nature, pouring forth a stream of spiritual energy into the body-mind system. With sufficient practice, this process can be performed anywhere at any time without anyone suspecting that this exercise is being performed. Merely turning the attention to a specific center will be enough to throw it into some kind of activity producing at the very least a sense of tingling there which ultimately spreads all over.

First of all, the position of the centers as shown in the Portal diagram must be memorized. The student who has studied the Knowledge Lectures on the Qabalah should have no problem with this by now. The meditation, for such we may call it, may be performed while sitting up or lying down flat on the back in a perfectly relaxed state. The hands may be permitted to lie folded in the lap with fingers interlaced or to rest comfortably by one's side. Calmness of mind should be induced, and some minutes devoted to the rhythmic breathing to bring about the sense of rippling playing around the solar plexus.

Then turn the attention to Kether, somewhat above the crown of the head. Try to imagine it as a ball or sphere of brilliant white light - do this easily without straining or forcing. If the mind wanders at first, as it usually does unless you have learned by now to concentrate well, wait a moment or two and gently lead it back to the task at hand. At the same time, vibrate or hum the divine name EHEIEH, pronouncing it as Eh-huh-yay. After a few days of persistent practice, to vibrate the name in the center will be found quite easy. Kether and its divine name is the seat of the overshadowing divinity, the Yechidah, the higher and divine Genius we can all draw upon.

The effect of this concentration and vibration is to awaken the center into dynamic activity; it begins to vibrate and rotate above the crown of the head when light and energy begin to pour down on the lower Sephiroth. Even the finger tips and the toes react to this awakening by the sensations of a faint prickling which later develops into a mighty throbbing of power. The name should be vibrated audibly for some considerable time until skill has been acquired. A humming sound will do while one has the mental image of the name desired. When enough skill has been acquired through practice, the name may be hummed silently in any particular center desired. Again, if the mind tends to wander, the frequent repetition of the vibration or hum will do much to facilitate the task of concentration.

Keep the mind here for some five minutes or so, by which time it should be seen to glow and scintillate. Then imagine that from this center emanates a shaft of white light moving downwards into the Daath center in the neck. Here it expands to form another sphere of white light, about the size of a small saucer. If the larynx is felt to be the center of this Sephirah, Daath, then the distance from it to the cervical vertebrae at the back of the neck will be approximately the radius. Naturally, this distance will vary with every person. A technique similar to the above for Kether should be pursued with this sphere, which we name the Air center. It should be strongly and vividly imagined as a scintillating sphere of white light, shining and glowing from within. The divine name pertaining to this sphere is YHVH ELOHIM - pronounced as Yuh-hoh-voh Eh-loh-heem.

Let the vibratory or humming sound be made a number of times until it is clearly felt as a definite sensory experience. There is absolutely no mistaking the sensation of its awakening. About the same time should be spent formulating Daath or this Air center as was devoted to the Kether center. When you feel ready to move from it, imagine that the shaft of white light descends from the throat to the center of the chest, to the Tiphareth center. Then feel that it expands behind the sternum or breast bone to form once more another center, the so-called Fire center. Its traditional divine Name is YHVH ELOAH ve-DAATH, pronounced as Yuh-hoh-voh Eh-loh ve-Dah-ahth. Some students have complained that the above divine name is excessively long and difficult to pronounce. After a long period of experimentation, I have substituted the gnostic name IAO, commonly used in the Adeptus Minor Key word, for the Hebrew words. Both are attributed Qabalistically to Tiphareth on the Tree, and so are equally valid. It is my experience that this Name is just as effective as is the Hebrew divine Name, and in my own use of this meditation, it has become a permanent part of the technique.

IAO should be pronounced as Eee (as in key) Ah-Oh, and again should be hummed or intoned with vigor. In fact, it is far simpler to vibrate this name than almost any other, and the vibration it produces is clear and strong.

When you have felt you've dwelt long enough on this center, continue sending the shaft of light downwards until it reaches the pelvic area, the region of the generative organs. Form here, in exactly the same way as before, a sphere of radiant light-energy of approximately the same size, that of a saucer. Here also a name is to be pronounced so as to produce the vibratory awakening of the center which is to be felt in every molecule and cell in that area. SHADDAI EL CHAI is the divine name of Yesod, where this center is located, and is to be pronounced as Shah-die Ale Chye (remember that the ch is gutteral.) Let the mind get accustomed to concentrate upon this center for several minutes, visualizing it as of an active white brilliance. And whenever the mind happens to wander from its task, bring it back by repeatedly vibrating the name given above.

The final step in completing the Middle Pillar is to have the shaft of white light descend from the pelvis to the feet. There it expands from a point just below each ankle to form the fifth sphere in Malkuth. This for convenience sake is called the Earth center, thus completing the regimen of the elements. Formulate here a brilliant white center of approximately the same size as the others. As you know by now the divine name of Malkuth is ADONAI ha-ARETZ, pronounced as Ah-doh-nye hah-Ah-retz. Fixed and steady meditation on this area should induce the awakening of this center and the vibration of the name should stimulate the sense of energy pouring through enormously.

Again, stay with this as long as you feel you are accomplishing the activation of the center. When finished, return in your imagination to Kether, and visualize the Middle Pillar as a shaft of silvery light studded with five gorgeous diamonds of excellent brilliance. Maintain this image just long enough to know that the centers have been awakened.

For some students with a good imaginative faculty, the colour of these centers can be changed to accord with the Order aattribution of the colours of the elements. That is the Kether center remains brilliantly white; the Daath center is changed to lavender; the heart center to red for Fire and Tiphareth; the pelvic or Water center is given a blue colour, while the Earth or Malkuth center is given a russet colour, the rich deep color of Earth itself, the very foundation on which we all rest. Other students who may not possess this eidetic faculty in any abundance and who find that repeated effort does not yield major dividends (I have known many highly educated and intelligent students who are eidetic negative and do not find this at all easy) in which case I suggest they continue using the colour of white all through their practice.

The Order technique as described in the Portal document then suggests building up the rest of the Sephiroth on the Tree of Life in the sphere of sensation. My own experience is that this is superfluous. For the purpose that we have in mind this approach is redundant. The Sephiroth can be placed easily in the aura by a process that I have called the circulation technique, which can now be described.

The first step in this approach is to throw the mind upwards to the coronal center, Kether, imagining it to be in a state of vigorous activity once more. In such a state it throws an enormous amount of energy into the Sephirotic system, transforming it in such a way as to make it readily available for any activity in the human system. Imagine then that the energy begins to stream down the left side of the body, or Tree, in a broad band extending out some distance from the body. As the current of energy descends down the trunk and thighs to the feet, try to synchronise the movement of the energy with the breathing process. As the breathing proceeds, let the band of energy pass from the left foot to the right foot, and then ascend up the right side of the body to the coronal center once more, returning to the center whence it came. Keep on repeating this process, accompanied by the breathing until you can feel the connection between the movement of the energy through the right and left Pillars of the Tree and the inhalation and exhalation of air. You will of course realize that this is an interior psychic circulation, though it has its own physical correlatives.

This process is followed by another type of circulation which is readily understandable once the notion of the Tree having four Pillars (when projected into a solid sphere, which the aura is) is grasped. Return in contemplation to Kether, and then direct the band of energy down the front of the body towards the feet, always synchronized with the breathing process. As you inhale, move the energy from the front of the feet to the heels, and then up the posterior surface of the body towards Kether again. Be sure to continue the circulatory process until it is perceptible, as a definite movement of energy. Do not worry too much if the imagination does not seem keen enough to visualize this movement. Sometimes merely willing and feeling that it is moving is adequate to get the energy to follow the notion of the Pillars.

These two types of circulation establish the four Pillars very clearly and definitely, and if persisted in for sometime, the sensation is unmistakable, practically physical. General experience and perception indicates that this sphere of light and energy extends outwards to a distance approximating the length of the oustretched arm. And it is within this light sphere that the physical man exists rather like a kernel within a nut.

The final method of circulation may be likened to the action of a fountain - I call it the fountain circulation. In much the same way as water is forced or sucked up through a tube until it jets up above falling in a spray on all sides, so does the energy behave when directed by the will and imagination in this type of circulation.

Throw the attention downwards to Malkuth, the Earth center, feeling it to be the culmination of all the others, the receptacle of all the others, the terminal and storehouse of the incoming vital force. You should then imagine that this power ascends or is attracted upwards to Kether above the crown of the head. The energy, following the will, ascends upwards and then sprays over from Kether, falling downwards on all sides towards Malkuth where it is again concentrated and accumulated ready for another move upwards. It will be found that breathing in will enable the energy to move upwards to Kether most readily, whereas the exhalation seems naturally to accompany the spraying overhead and falling downwards of the energy towards Malkuth.

This completes the formation of the axis of the Tree, the five Pillars described so vividly in various of the Order papers. Keep this notion constantly in mind when working these circulations. Once the five-columned Tree has been well formulated so that it can be felt, then let the mind dwell on the idea of the sphere of light, the LVX, spiritual and healing in quality, surrounding and inter-penetrating the entire body. You should feel an unmistakable sense of calmness and vitality and poise, as though the mind were placid and still. The body, in a lovely state of relaxation, should feel in every part that it is thoroughly charged and permeated by the vibrant power of life.

It is at this stage of the exercise that the student should review some of the prayers or invocations current in the Order procedures. For example, there is the Prayer of the Hierophant in the Neophyte degree as he descends from the throne of the East towards the candidate kneeling at the altar. 'I come in the Power of the Light. I come in the Light of Wisdom. I come in the Mercy of the Light. The Light hath healing in its Wings."

There is also the other prayer used by the Hierophant in the same ritual which again may be used here in order to call down the divine light. "O Lord of the Universe, the Vast and the Mighty One, Ruler over the Light and the Darkness, we adore thee and we invoke thee. Look Thou with favor upon me, who now standeth before Thee and grant thine aid unto the highest aspirations of my soul so that I may prove worthy of thy help to perform the Great

Work." The speech of the Chief Adept in the Vault during the 5-6 Ritual is also worthy of being memorized so that it may be recited during this exercise:

I am the resurrection and the Life. Whosoever believeth in me though he were dead yet shall he live, and whosoever liveth and believeth in me, the same shall never die. I am the First and I am the Last. I am he that liveth but was dead, and behold! I am alive for evermore and hold the keys of death and of hell. For I know that my Redeemer liveth and that he shall stand at the latter day upon the earth.

I am the Way, the Truth and the Life. No man cometh to the Father but by me. I am the Purified. I have passed through the gates of darkness unto Light. I have fought upon earth for good. I have finished my work. I have entered the Invisible.

I am the Sun in his rising, passed through the hour of cloud and of night. I am Amoun, the concealed One, the Opener of the Day. I am Osiris Onnophris, the Justified One, the Lord of Life, triumphant over death. There is no part of me which is not of the Gods. I am the preparer of the Pathway, the rescuer unto the Light. Let the White Light of the Divine Spirit descend.

The next ritual fragment is rather different from the foregoing, although both have a similar personal effect when slowly repeated, meditated upon, and felt intensely. It consists of two parts - the first one being a sort of petition of the higher and divine Genius, while the second bespeaks of the realization of identity with it.

Thee I invoke the Bornless One. Thee that didst create the Earth and the Heavens. Thee that didst create the Night and the Day. Thee that didst create the Darkness and the Light. Thou art Man made Perfect, whom no man hath seen at any time. Thou art God and very God. Thou hast distinguished between the Just and the Unjust. Thou didst make the female and the male. Thou didst produce the seed and the fruit. Thou didst form men to love one another and to hate one another. Thou didst produce the moist and the dry, and That which nourisheth all created things.

The second part should follow only after a long pause, in which one attempts to realize just what it is that the prayer has asserted, and that it is raising the mind to an apprehension of the hidden secret Godhead within, which is the creator of all things.

This is the Lord of the Gods. This is the Lord of the Universe. This is He Whom the winds fear. This is He who having made voice by his commandment is Lord of all things, king, ruler and helper. Hear me and make all spirits subject unto me, so that every spirit of the firmament and of the ether, upon the earth and under the earth, upon dry land and in the water, of whirling air and of rushing fire, and every spell and scourge of God the Vast One may be made obedient unto me.

I am He the Bornless Spirit, having sight in the feet, strong and the immortal fire. I am He, the Truth. I am He who hate that evil may be wrought in the world. I am He that lighteneth and thundereth. I am He from whom is the shower of the Life of Earth. I am He whose mouth ever flameth. I am He, the begetter and manifester unto the Light. I am He, the Grace of the World. The Heart girt with a Serpent is my Name.

These prayer fragments are suggestive only and are to be used or rejected, as each student feels fit. There is no final authority within the Order for their usage.

This exercise has an extended usage, far beyond the development of insight and enlightenment as though it provided a magical engine whereby one's enlightened will may find suitable expression. Let me preface any further remarks by stating that from the practical point of view, the rudiments of the astrological schema are of untold value in that they offer a concise classification of the broad division of things. I am not here concerned with astrology as such, merely that it is convenient to use its schema. Its roots are in the seven principal ideas or planets to which most ideas and things may be referred. To each of these root ideas there is attributed a positive and negative colour, and a Divine Name for the purpose of vibration. I propose naming the planets with their principal attributions as follows:

Saturn. Older people and old plans. Debts and their repayment. Agriculture and real estate, death, wills, stability, inertia. Positive colour is indigo; negative, black. YHVH Elohim - best pronounced Yuh-hoh-voh Eh-loh-heem.

Jupiter. Is abundance, plenty, growth, expansion, generosity. Spirituality, visions, dreams, long journeys, subjective or otherwise. Bankers, creditors, debtors, gambling. Positive colour is purple; negative blue. EL, pronounced exactly as written or as Ale.

Mars. Energy, haste, anger, construction or destruction (according to application). Danger, risks, surgery. Vitality and magnetism, will power. Positive and negative colours bright red. Elohim Gibor, best pronounced Eh-loh-heem Gibor.

Sun. Superiors, employers, executives, officials. Power and success. Life, money, growth of all kinds. Illumination, imagination, mental power. Health. Positive colour orange; negative colour yellow or gold. YHVH Eloah ve-Daath. This is such a long clumsy name, that though traditional I have decided to replace it with a much simpler and also traditional name. IAO pronounced ee (as in key) ah-oh.

Venus. Social affairs, affections and emotions, women, younger people. All pleasures and the arts, music, beauty, extravagance, luxury, self-indulgence. Both of the colours emerald green. YHVH Tzabaoth, pronounced Yuh-hoh-voh Tzah-bah-oth.

Mercury. Business matters, writing, contracts, judgment and short journeys. Buying, selling, bargaining. Neighbours, giving and obtaining information. Literary abilities, publishing, and intellectual friends. Books, papers, etc. Positive colour yellow; negative colour orange. Elohim Tzabaoth, pronounced Eh-loh-heem Tzah-bah-oth.

Moon. General public, women. Sense-reactions. Short journeys and removals. Changes and fluctuations. The personality. Positive colour blue; negative colour puce. Shaddai el Chai, pronounced shah-dye ale Chye (gutteral ch.)

These very briefly are the attributions of the planets under which almost everything and every subject may be classified. This classification is extremely useful because it simplifies enormously one's task of physical and spiritual development. It can simplify, at least in general theory, much of the practical work of the Order, in fact even enabling one to simplify and classify the work to be done. A little actual usage of the method will indicate further uses to which it may be put.

THE COMPLETE GOLDEN DAWN SYSTEM OF MAGIC

THE KNOWLEDGE LECTURES

FIRST LECTURE

The FOUR ELEMENTS of the Ancients are conditions of:

Heat and Dryness	Fire	△
Heat and Moisture	Air	△
Cold and Dryness	Earth	▽
Cold and Moisture	Water	▽

There are twelve Signs in the Zodiac:

1.	Aries, the Ram	♈
2.	Taurus, the Bull	♉
3.	Gemini, the Twins	♊
4.	Cancer, the Crab	♋
5.	Leo, the Lion	♌
6.	Virgo, the Virgin	♍
7.	Libra, the Scales	♎
8.	Scorpio, the Scorpion	♏
9.	Sagittarius, the Archer	♐
10	Capricornus, the Goat	♑
11.	Aquarius, the Water-Bearer	♒
12.	Pisces, the Fishes	♓

These Twelve Signs are distributed among what are called the Four Triplicities, or sets of three Signs. Each one is attributed to one of the Four Elements, and they represent the operation of the elements in the Zodiac.

To Fire belong:
Aries, Leo, Sagittarius ♈ ♌ ♐

To Earth belong:
Taurus, Virgo, Capricornus ♉ ♍ ♑

To Air belong:
Gemini, Libra, Aquarius ♊ ♎ ♒

To Water belong:
Cancer, Scorpio, Pisces ♋ ♏ ♓

VOLUME THREE

To the Ancients, six planets besides the Sun were known. They also assigned certain planetary values to the North and South Nodes of the Moon; that is, the points where the Moon's orbit touches that of the Ecliptic.

These were named:

Caput Draconis—Head of the Dragon ☊

Cauda Draconis—Tail of the Dragon ☋

Since the discovery of two more distant Planets Neptune and Uranus, these two terms have been partially replaced by them.

The effect of Caput Draconis is similar to ☊

The effect of Cauda Draconis is similar to ☋

The names of the Old Planets are:

Saturn	♄	**Sol**	☉
Jupiter	♃	**Venus**	♀
Mars	♂	**Mercury**	☿
	Moon ☽		

SECOND LECTURE

In alchemy the teaching is that there are three principles namely:

Sulphur	🜍
Mercury	☿
Salt	⊖

The metals attributed to the planets are:

Lead	♄	**Gold**	☉
Tin	♃	**Copper**	♀
Iron	♂	**Quicksilver**	☿
	Silver ☽		

The following terms are used in alchemical texts, and mean:

SOL PHILOSOPHORUM - The pure living alchemical spirit of gold - the refined essence of heat and fire.

LUNA PHILOSOPHORUM - The pure living alchemical spirit of silver - the refined essence of heat and mositure.

THE GREEN LION - The stem and root of the radical essence of metals.

THE BLACK DRAGON - Death, putrefaction, decay.

THE KING - Red - The Qabalistic Microprosopus. Tiphareth - analogous to Gold and the Sun.

THE QUEEN - White - The Qabalistic bride of Microprosopus. Malkah - analogous to Silver and the Moon.

THE COMPLETE GOLDEN DAWN SYSTEM OF MAGIC

THE HEBREW ALPHABET

Letter	Power	Value	Name	Meaning
א	A	1	Aleph	Ox
ב	B,V	2	Beth	House
ג	G, Gh	3	Gimel	Camel
ד	D, Dh	4	Daleth	Door
ה	H	5	Heh	Window
ו	V, 0, V	6	Vau	Pin or hook
ז	Z	7	Zayjn	Sword or armour
ח	Ch	8	Cheth	Fence or enclosure
ט	T	9	Teth	Snake
י	I, Y, J	10	Yod	Hand
כ	K, Kh	20	Caph	Fist
ל	L	30	Lamed	Ox goad
מ	M	40	Mem	Water
נ	N	50	Nun	Fish
ס	S	60	Samekh	Prop
ע	Aa, Ngh	70	Ayin	Eye
פ	P, F	80	Peh	Mouth
צ	Tz	90	Tzaddi	Fish hook
ק	Q	100	Qoph	Ear. Back of head
ר	R	200	Resh	Head
ש	S, Sh	300	Shin	Tooth
ת	T, Th	400	Tau	Cross

Each Hebrew letter represents a number and a meaning. Five letters have a different shape and also a different number when written at the end of a word. They are called Finals. Of these Finals Mem is distinguished by being the only oblong letter. The other four Caph, Nun, Peh, Tzaddi have long tails which should come below the line as shown (See table below). Sometimes the letters are depicted as very large, in which case their numerical value is multiplied, such as a very large Aleph represents 1000, a very large Beth 2000, and so on. When practising how to draw Hebrew letters the student would do well to make them on lined sheets. Also remember that these letters are written from right to left. The Order also teaches that these are Holy symbols and therefore should be carefully drawn and square.

VOLUME THREE

TABLE OF FINAL LETTERS

Letter	Power	Value	Name
ך	K, Kh	500	Caph
ם	M	600	Mem
ן	N	700	Nun
ף	P, F	800	Peh
ץ	Tz	900	Tzaddi

The Dagesh is a dot or point placed in some of the Hebrew letters. It changes the sound value of the letter. In modern Hebrew script it represents a vowel; however it is not used in this book. S.R.M.D. asserts it is a late invention to standardise pronunciation.

The Hebrew Qabalists referred the highest and most abstract ideas to the emanations of Deity. There are ten emanations. Each one is a Sephirah, the plural being Sephiroth. When arranged in a certain manner, they form what is called the Etz Chayim or The Tree of Life.

THE ETZ CHAYIM OR THE TREE OF LIFE

1	Kether	K-Th-R	Crown	כתר
2	Chokmah	Ch-K-M-H	Wisdom	חכמה
3	Binah	B-I-N-H	Understanding	בינה
4	Chesed	Ch-S-D	Mercy	חסד
5	Geburah	G-B-U-R-H	Severity	גבורה
6	Tiphareth	T-Ph-A-R-Th	Beauty	תפארת
7	Netzach	N-Tz-Ch	Victory	נצח
8	Hod	H-O-D	Glory	הוד
9	Yesod	Y-S-O-D	Foundation	יסוד
10	Malkuth	M-L-K-U-Th	Kingdom	מלכות

THE LESSER RITUAL OF THE PENTAGRAM

In some quarters the pentagram or five pointed star is considered an "evil" or demoniacal symbol. On the contrary with the point upwards it represents the spiritualization of the more elemental aspects of man. Some modern groups have decided to invert the pentagram, not for "evil" purposes but to indicate that it is a symbol of change. Other groups who in fact are "evil" have borrowed the pentagram as their insignium. This has nothing to do with the Order usage of it.

THE USES OF THE PENTAGRAM RITUAL

When tracing the pentagram do make it large. As you trace the banishing pentagram move your arm down to the middle of the left thigh. Then swing upwards at an angle to about the top of the head. From there move the arm down to the middle of the right thigh; then upwards to the left shoulder, straight over to the right shoulder and return to the starting point of the left thigh. The invoking pentagram should be traced in exactly the opposite way, beginning at the apex and moving down to the left thigh, etc.

I have often been horrified when students who have visited me on occasion trace a miniscule pentagram, about 5 inches high in front of their heads.

INVOKING   BANISHING

The Order suggests that the Pentagram Ritual may be used as a form of prayer, the Invoking pentagram in the morning, and the Banishing pentagram in the evening. The names which will be given shortly should be pronounced inwardly in the breath vibrating or humming it as much as possible. (For a complete description see the Regardie Tapes, Falcon Press, 1982. If you do not require the complete set of six tapes with instruction book, you can order the single tape on this subject. Just specify the Banishing Ritual of the Pentagram). Try to feel that the entire body throbs and tingles as the wave of vibration is directed to the ends of the quadrant.

It is said that the Banishing Pentagram may be used as a protection against negative psychologic states in both yourself and others. Make a mental image of your concern or anxiety then formulate it before you. Project it away from you with the saluting sign of a Neophyte (which is depicted on a later page) and when it is about three feet away prevent its return with the sign of silence. Now imagine the form in the Eastern quadrant before you and perform the Banishing Ritual of the Pentagram to destroy it. In your mind's eye see it dissolve on the outside of your circle of flame.

Furthermore it may be used as an exercise in concentration. Seated in meditation or lying down, imagine yourself standing up in robes and holding a dagger. Project your consciousness into this mental image of yourself. When there move to the East. Make yourself feel there by touching the wall, opening your eyes, stamping on the floor etc.

Begin the ritual while in this form and move around the room mentally vibrating the words and trying to feel them being emitted from the mental image. Finish the ritual in the East. Try to feel what has resulted from the ritual, then walk back and stand behind the head of your resting physical body and let yourself be reabsorbed.

HOW TO PERFORM THE RITUAL

THE INVOKING PENTAGRAM

Take a steel dagger or knife in the right hand, face East:

Touch your forehead and say Atoh (thou art).

Touch your chest and say Malkuth (the Kingdom).

Touch the right shoulder and say ve-Geburah (and the Power).

Touch the left shoulder and say ve-Gedulah (and the Glory).

Clasp your hands in the center of the chest and say le Olahm (forever).

Hold the dagger, point upwards, in clasped hands and say Amen (so be it).

The word Amen in addition means the end. It has been associated with Amoun the concealed one. It is also a notariqon of three Hebrew words, Adonai Melekh Neh-eh-mon, which means The Lord Faithful King.

Facing East make a very large invoking pentagram as shown above. When completed thrust the point of the dagger to the center of the pentagram and vibrate the Deity name YHVH (Yod, Heh, Vau, Heh), imagining that your voice carries the vibration to the East of the Universe.

Hold the dagger out in front of you and move to the South. Trace the pentagram there and vibrate the Deity name Adonai.

Go to the West, make a large pentagram again and vibrate Eheieh.

Move to the North with arm holding dagger outstretched. Make the large pentagram and vibrate Agla.

Return to the East always completing your Circle by bringing the dagger to the imagined center of the first Pentagram. Now stand with arms outstretched in the form of a Cross and say:

Before Me	**Raphael**	**Rah-phah-ale**
Behind me	**Gabriel**	**Gah-bree-ale**
On my right	**Michael**	**Mee-chah-ale**
On my left	**Auriel**	**Or-ree-ale**

Now say, Before me flames the Pentagram.

Behind me shines the Six-Rayed Star.

Again make the Qabalistic Cross as in the beginning.

For Banishing the same Ritual is used with the reversal of the lines of the Pentagram.

OTHER ALCHEMICAL ATTRIBUTIONS TO THE TREE OF LIFE

Kether	**Mercury**	**Metallic Root**
Chokmah	**Salt**	**Lead**
Binah	**Sulphur**	**Tin**
Chesed	**Silver**	**Silver**
Geburah	**Gold**	**Gold**
Tiphareth	**Iron**	**Iron**
Netzach	**Copper**	**Hermaphroditical Brass**
Hod	**Tin**	**Brass**
Yesod	**Lead**	**Mercury**
Malkuth	**Mercury Philosophorum**	**Medicina Metallorum**

THE COMPLETE GOLDEN DAWN SYSTEM OF MAGIC

The four Orders of the Elementals are:

Spirits of the Earth	**Gnomes**
Spirits of the Air	**Sylphs**
Spirits of the Water	**Undines**
Spirits of the Fire	**Salamanders**

These are the essential spiritual beings called upon to praise God in Benedicite Omnia Opera. The Kerubim are the living powers of YHVH on the material plane, and the presidents of the four elements. They operate through the Fixed or Kerubic-signs of the Zodiac and are thus symbolized and attributed.

Kerub of Air	**Man**	**Aquarius**	♒
Kerub of Fire	**Lion**	**Leo**	♌
Kerub of Earth	**Bull**	**Taurus**	♉
Kerub of Water	**Eagle**	**Scorpio**	♏

Tetragrammaton means the Four-lettered name (YHVH) and refers to the unpronounceable Name of God symbolized by Jehovah.

The Laver of Water of Purification refers to the Waters of Binah, the Female Power reflected in the Waters of creation.

The Altar of Burnt Offering for the sacrifice of animals symbolises the Qlippoth or Evil Demons of the plane contiguous to and below the Material U niverse. It points out that our passions should be sacrificed. (This simply means that one's passions should be under the control of Will, as indicated in the Paper entitled On the Purification of the Soul).

The Altar of Incense in the Tabernacle was overlaid with gold. Ours is Black to symbolise our work which is to separate the Philosophic Gold from the Black Dragon of Matter.

The Qlippoth are the Beings (sometimes referred to as "Evil") below Malkuth, and the Shells of the Dead.

THE QLIPPOTH ON THE TREE OF LIFE

Kether	Thaumiel	The two contending Forces
Chokmah	Ghogiel	The Hinderers
Binah	Satariel	The Concealers
Chesed	Agshekeloh	The Breakers in Pieces
Geburah	Golohab	The Burners
Tiphareth	Tagiriron	The Disputers
Netzach	Gharab Tzerek	The Ravens of Death
Hod	Samael	The Liar or Poison of God
Yesod	Gamaliel	The Obscene Ones
Malkuth	Lilith	Queen of Night and Demons

THE ALTAR DIAGRAM OF THE TREE

The altar diagram shows the Ten Sephiroth with the connecting Paths numbered and lettered, and the Serpent winding over each Path. Around each Sephirah are written the

Names of the Deity, Archangel and Angelic Host. The twenty-two Paths are bound together by the Serpent of Wisdom. It unites the Paths but does not touch any of the Sephiroth, which are linked by the Flaming Sword. The Flaming Sword is formed by the natural order of the Tree of Life. It resembles a flash of Lightning.

The Two Pillars on either side of the Altar represent:

Active: **The White Pillar on the South Side.**

> **Male.**
> **Adam.**
> **Pillar of Light and Fire.**
> **Right Kerub.**
> **Metatron.**

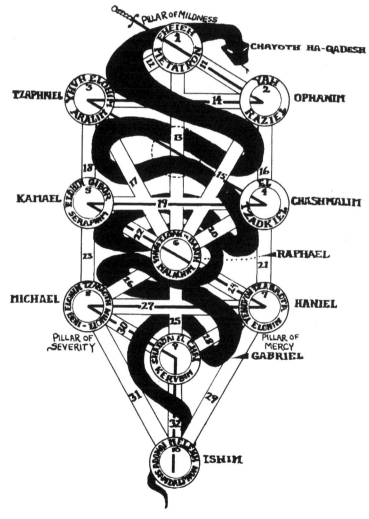

SERPENT OF WISDOM

Passive: **The Black Pillar on the North Side.**

        Female.
        Eve.
        Pillar of Cloud.
        Left Kerub.
        Sandalphon.

THE FOUR WORLDS OF THE QABALAH

The Qabalists conceived of four planes of existence between God and man. They are:

ATZILUTH, Archetypal - Pure Deity.	אצילות
BRIAH, Creative - Archangelic.	בריאה
YETZIRAH, Formative - Angelic.	יצירה
ASSIAH, Action - Material World.	עשיה

Assiah, the world of Matter, Man, Shells, and Demons is divided into ten houses or Heavens. They are:

Primum Mobile, Rashith ha Gilgalim.	ראשית הגלגלים
Sphere of the Zodiac, Mazloth.	מזלות
Sphere of Saturn, Shabbathai.	שבתאי
Sphere of Jupiter, Tzedek.	צדק
Sphere of Mars, Madim.	מדים
Sphere of the Sun, Shemesh.	שמש
Sphere of Venus, Nogah.	נוגה
Sphere of Mercury, Kokab.	כוכב
Sphere of the Moon, Levanah.	לבנה
Sphere of Elements, Olam Yesodoth.	עולם יסודות

SOME TAROT CORRESPONDENCES

The traditional Tarot consists of a pack of 78 cards made up of Four Suits (symbolic of the four worlds discussed above) of 14 cards each, together with 22 Trumps or Major Arcana, which tell the story of the Soul.

Each suit consists of ten numbered cards (referred to the ten Sephiroth) as in modern playing cards, but there are four instead of three honours: King, Queen, Knight, and Knave.

The Four Suits are:

        Wands are comparable to Diamonds.
        Cups are comparable to Hearts.
        Swords are comparable to Spades.
        Pentacles are comparable to Clubs.

VOLUME THREE

THIRD LECTURE

The Soul is divided by the Qabalists into three principal parts:

NESCHAMAH - The highest part, answering to the Three Supernals, and to the higher aspirations of the Soul.

RUACH - The middle part, answering to six Sephiroth from Chesed to Yesod, inclusive, and to the mind and reasoning powers.

NEPHESCH - The lowest, answering to Malkuth, and to the animal instincts.

Neschamah itself is further divided into three parts:

YECHIDAH - is referred to Kether.

CHIAH - is referred to Chokmah.

NESCHAMAH - is referred to Binah.

THE THREE CLASSES OF HEBREW LETTERS

The Sepher Yetzirah divides the Hebrew Alphabet into three classes of letters, a 3, a 7, a 12.

Three Mothers	א מ ש
Seven Doubles	ב ג ד כ פ ר ת
Twelve Singles	ה ו ז ח ט י ל נ ס ע צ ק

The Holy Place of the Temple embraces the symbolism of the 22 letters. The table of Shew-Bread, the single letters. The Altar of Incense are the three Mother letters.

Astral Spirits are those belonging to the Astral Plane. Such are false and illusionary forms, shells of the dead, and ghosts and phantoms, that are occasionally seen in seances.

Elemental Spirits are those belonging to the nature of the Elements; some are good and some are evil.

An Angel is a pure and high Spirit of unmixed good in office and function.

In the Tarot, the ten small cards of each suit refer to the Sephiroth. The four suits refer to the letters of YHVH. Wands to Yod, Cups to Heh, Swords to Vau, and Pentacles to Heh (final).

These four suits also refer to the four worlds of the Qabalah. Wands to Atziluth, Cups to Briah, Swords to Yetzirah, and Pentacles to Assiah.

The Honours of the Tarot pack are, as it were, the Vice-gerants of the Great Name (YHVH), in the Qabalistic World to which each suit is referred. They also symbolize Father, Mother, Son, Daughter; Birth, Life, Death, Resurrection.

THE FYLFOT CROSS

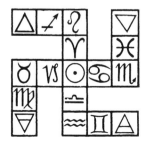

61

THE COMPLETE GOLDEN DAWN SYSTEM OF MAGIC

The 17 squares out of a square of smaller squares, refer to the Sun in the twelve Signs of the Zodiac and the Four Elements. They are arranged so that the fixed signs, mutable and cardinal signs are placed in juxtaposition.

THE CADUCEUS

This form of the Caduceus of Hermes is that of the Three Mother letters, Shin, Aleph, and Mem. It represents Air, as the mediator between Fire above and Water below.

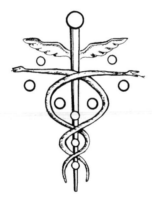

This symbol has another meaning on the Tree of Life. The upper part and wings touch Chokmah and Binah. The knob touches Kether. These are the Three Supernals.

The seven lower Sephiroth are embraced by the twin Serpents whose heads rest upon Chesed and Geburah.

THE MOON ON THE TREE OF LIFE

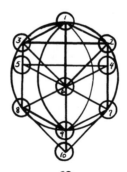

VOLUME THREE

In the Moon's increase the Pillar of Mercy is embraced. In its decrease the Pillar of Severity is embraced. At the full Moon it reflects the Sun of Tiphareth.

FOURTH LECTURE

Below are the Geomantic figures and their Zodiacal Attributions.

♈		PUER	♎		PUELLA
♉		AMISSIO	♏		RUBEUS
♊		ALBUS	♐		ACQUISITIO
♋		POPULUS	♑		CARCER
♋		VIA	♒		TRISTITIA
♌		FORTUNA MAJOR	♓		LAETITIA
♌		FORTUNA MINOR	☊		CAPUT DRACONIS
♍		CONJUNCTIO	☋		CAUDA DRACONIS

LINEAL FIGURES OF THE PLANETS

Below are the numbers and lineal figures of the planets:

Saturn	3	Triangle
Jupiter	4	Square
Mars	5	Pentagram
Sun	6	Hexagram
Venus	7	Heptagram
Mercury	8	Octagram
Moon	9	Enneagram

THE COMPLETE GOLDEN DAWN SYSTEM OF MAGIC

This topic is considerably elaborated in a very important document entitled Polygons and Polygrams. There are a number of drawings to illustrate each point made.

THE MAGICAL SQUARES OF THE PLANETS

These squares, which are depicted in another area of this book are technically called Kameas. They are formed of the squares of the number of the planet, arranged so as to yield the same number each way. The number of the sum of each column of figures and the number of the total of all the number of the squares are also especially attached to the planet. For example the number of the planet Saturn is 3, square 9, the sum of all columns vertical, horizontal and diagonal is 15. The total sum of all numbers is 45. These numbers are then formed into Divine and Spirit names as demonstrated in that section of this book dealing with Sigils.

THE SOLID GREEK CUBICAL CROSS

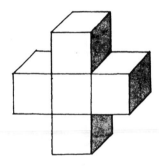

It is the admission badge for the Path of Tau, and is composed of 22 squares which answer to the 22 letters of the Hebrew Alphabet.

THE SOLID TRIANGLE OR TETRAHEDRON

This figure is also known as the Pyramid of Fire. It is the Admission Badge for the Path of Shin, representing the simple Fire of Nature and the latent or hidden Fire.

The three upper triangles (note figure is in 2 dimensional space) refer to Fire - Solar, Volcanic and Astral. The lowest or basal triangle represents the latent heat.

VOLUME THREE

THE GREEK CROSS

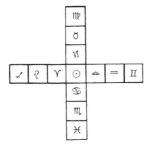

This Admission Badge for the Path of Resh has thirteen squares. It is referred to the Sun in the Twelve Signs of the Zodiac, arranged in triplicities.

THE CUP OF STOLISTES

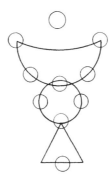

It is the Admission Badge to the grade of Practicus. It is referred to the Tree of Life as shown in the diagram. It embraces nine of the Sephiroth exclusive of Kether.

Yesod and Malkuth are referred to the lower triangle the former to the apex and latter to the base. Like the Caduceus, it furthers represents Water, Fire and Air, but in a different combination. The Crescent refers to the Waters above the Firmament, the sphere to the Firmament, and the basal triangle to the consuming Fire, which is opposed to the Fire symbolized by the upper part of the Caduceus.

THE SYMBOL OF MERCURY

On the Tree of Life it embraces all the Sephiroth but Kether. The horns spring from Daath (knowledge) which is not, properly speaking, a Sephirah, but rather a conjunction of Chokmah and Binah.

FIFTH LECTURE OR AZOTH

Azoth is a word formed from the initial and final letters of the Greek, Latin and Hebrew Alphabets thus; A and Z, Alpha and Tau, Alpha and Omega. It is used with various meanings by different writers, but generally signifies essence. It is commonly used amongst the writers on Alchemy.

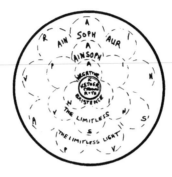

The following names occur in Qabalistic writings:

Ain	**Nothing-Not**
Ain Soph	**Without End**
Ain Soph Aur	**Infinite Light**

These three are the Veils of negative existence behind as it where Kether.

Arik Anpin - MACROPROSOPUS or the vast countenance is one of the titles of Kether, yet another of its titles is the Ancient of Days, Aatik Yomin. Kether or the vast countenance emanates first as Abba the supernal Father, and Aima, the supernal Mother. Abba is referred to Yod of YHVH, and Aima is referred to Heh of YHVH. Elohim is a name given to these two Hypostases united.

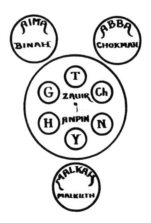

As Elohim they are considered the parents of the Son, Zauir Anpin, also called MICROPROSOPUS, or the lesser countenance.

Abba is referred to Yod and Chokmah. Aima is referred to Heh and Binah. Zauir Anpin is referred to the 6 Sephiroth Chesed, Geburah, Tiphareth, Netzach, Hod, Yesod and of these especially to Tiphareth.

Malkah the queen and Kalah the bride are titles of Malkuth when considered as the spouse of Zauir Anpin, the Microprosopus.

The letters of the name YHVH contain these meanings:

Yod is referred to Abba.

Heh to Aima.

Vau to Zauir Anpin.

Heh (f) to Malkah.

These letters are also referred to the four worlds and the four suits of the Tarot thus:

Yod	**Atziluth**	**Wands**
Heh	**Briah**	**Cups**
Vau	**Yetzirah**	**Swords**
Heh (f)	**Assiah**	**Pentacles**

There are ten Sephiroth in each of the four worlds. Each Sephirah has its own ten Sephiroth making 400 Sephiroth in all - the number of the letter Tau, the Cross, the Universe, the completion of all things.

The Tarot is referred to the Tree of Life in the following manner.

The four Aces are placed on the throne of Kether. The remaining small cards of each suit are placed on the respective Sephiroth, two on Chokmah, three on Binah, etc. The twenty two Trumps are then arranged on the paths between them according to the letters to which they are attributed. The King and Queen of the suit are placed besides Chokmah and Binah, the Knight and Knave by Tiphareth and Malkuth. The Tarot Trumps thus receive the equilibrium of the Sephiroth they connect.

ADMISSION BADGES USED IN THE GRADE OF PHILOSOPHUS

First is the Calvary Cross of twelve squares.

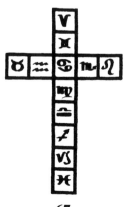

It admits to the path of Qoph, the 29th path, and refers to the Zodiac and to the eternal River of Eden, divided into four heads as follows:

NAHER - THE RIVER

1. **Hiddikel**
2. **Pison**
3. **Gihon**
4. **Phrath - Euphrates**

The Pyramid of the four elements admits to the path of Tzaddi, the 28th path.

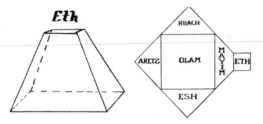

On the sides of the pyramid are the Hebrew names of the elements. On the apex is the word ETH, meaning essence and on the base is the word OLAM, meaning world.

The next Badge is the Calvary Cross of ten squares admitting to the path of Peh, Mars, the 27th Path.

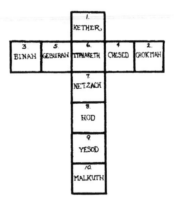

The ten squares are referred to the Ten Sephiroth in balanced disposition. It is also the opened out form of the double cube of the Altar of incense.

Another Badge is the Hegemon's Cross admitting to the Grade of Philosophus.

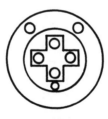

VOLUME THREE

This Cross embraces Tiphareth, Netzach, Hod, and Yesod resting upon Malkuth. This Cross also refers to the 6 Sephiroth of Microprosopus and is the opened out form of the cube.

Finally we have the symbol of Venus on the Tree of Life

It embraces all ten Sephiroth on the Tree. It is a fitting emblem of the Isis of Nature. Since it contains all the Sephiroth its circle should be made larger then that of Mercury shown in a previous diagram.

ANOTHER ARRANGEMENT OF THE TREE

There are various formats of the Sephiroth. The most frequent has already been given, but there is another in common usage and will be seen to have been employed in some of the large Altar diagrams of both the Practicus and Philosophus Grade. It is often referred to as The Seven Palaces of Assiah attributed to the ten Sephiroth.

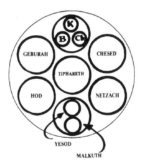

THE REFLECTION OF THE ELEMENTS DOWN THE TREEW

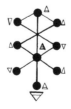

This drawing represents the triad of elements operating through the Sephiroth and reflected downwards into the Tree. Air is reflected straight down the Middle Pillar, from Kether through Tiphareth to Yesod and the upper quadrant of Malkuth. Water is relfected cross-wise from Binah through Chesed to Hod. Fire is reflected cross-wise from Chokmah through Geburah to Netzach. Malkuth therefore becomes the receptacle of the other three elements.

THE COMPLETE GOLDEN DAWN SYSTEM OF MAGIC

MEDITATION NUMBER ONE

Let the Neophyte consider a point as defined in mathematics as having position but no magnitude and let him note the ideas to which this gives rise. Concentrating his faculties on this, as a focus, let him endeavour to realise the Immanance of the Divine throughout Nature, in all her aspects.

Begin by finding a position, balanced, but sufficiently comfortable. Breath rhythmically until the body is still and the mind quiet. Keep this state for a few minutes at first and for longer as you get more used to preventing the mind from wandering. Think now of the subject for meditation in a general way then choose out one thought or image and follow that to its conclusion.

The simplest rhythm for the beginner is the Fourfold Breath.

1. **Empty the lungs and remain thus while counting 4.**
2. **Inhale, counting 4 so that you feel filled with breath to the throat.**
3. **Hold this breath while counting 4.**
4. **Exhale, counting 4 till the lungs are empty.**

This should be practised, counting slowly or quickly till you obtain a rhythm that suits you one that is comforting and stilling.

Having attained this, count the breath thus for two or three minutes, till you feel quiet, and then proceed with the meditation.

MEDITATION NUMBER TWO

Let the Zelator meditate on a straight line. Let him take a ruler or a pencil and by moving it a distance equal to its length, outline a square.

Having done this, let him, after quieting his mind with the rhythmic breathing taught in the first meditation, mentally formulate a cube, and endeavor to discover the significance of this figure and its correspondences.

Let him meditate upon minerals and crystals, choosing especially a crystal of SALT, and entering into it, actually feel himself of crystalline formation.

Looking out on the Universe from this standpoint, let him identify himself with the EARTH SPIRITS in love and sympathy, recalling as far as he can their prayer as said in the closing of the Zelator Grade.

Let him meditate upon the EARTH TRIPLICITY, visualising the symbols of a BULL, a VIRGIN, a GOAT which stand for KERUBIC EARTH - MUTABLE EARTH - CARDINAL EARTH.

For the above terms consult a simple astrology manual. Make notes of the ideas and pictures which arise in your mind.

MEDITATION NUMBER THREE

Let the Theoricus practise the Moon Breath, while saying mentally the word AUM: (The Moon Breath is through the left nostril only.)

Let him meditate upon the waxing and waning crescents, while visualising a silver crescent upon an indigo background.

Let him now call before his mind the Signs of the Airy Triplicity and enclosed in these, let him meditate upon the numbers nine and five and therewith the forms of the Pentagram and Pentangle.

Let him now rise in imagination above the mineral world into the world of trees and flowers and identify himself in love and sympathy with the Powers of the Elements behind these.

Let him realise the mental world where mind rules over matter, and let him meditate upon the ideas of appearance and reality.

MEDITATION NUMBER FOUR

Let the Practicus meditate upon the Symbols of the Rhomboid and the Vesica.

Let him seek out their meanings and correspondences.

Let him contemplate the symbol Mercury and the Number 8.

Let him now learn to control his emotions, on no account giving way to anger, hatred and jealousy, but to turn the force he hitherto expended in these directions towards the attainment of perfection, that the malarial marsh of his nature may become a clear and limpid lake, reflecting the Divine Nature truly and without distortion.

Let him identify himself with the Powers of Water, considering the Water Triplicity in all its aspects, with its attributions and correspondences.

MEDITATION NUMBER FIVE

Let the PHILOSOPHUS meditate upon the symbol of the Fire Triangle in all its aspects. Let him contemplate the symbol of the Planet VENUS until he realises the Universal Love which would express itself in perfect service to all mankind and which embraces Nature both visible and invisible.

Let him identify himself with the powers of FIRE, consecrating himself wholly until the Burnt Sacrifice is consummated and the Christ is conceived by the Spirit.

Let him meditate upon the Triplicity of Fire - its attributes and correspondences.

MEDITATION NUMBER SIX

Let the Aspirant meditate upon the Cross in its various forms and aspects as shown in the Admission Badges throughout the Grades.

Let him consider the necessity and prevalence of sacrifice throughout nature and religion.

Let him realise the saying of the Master, 'Whosoever shall save his life shall lose it, and whosoever shall lose his life shall save it.'

'Except an ear of wheat fall into the ground and die, it abideth alone, but if it die, it bringeth forth much fruit.'

Let him endeavour to realise his own place and relative importance in the Universe, striving to stand outside himself and allowing only such claims as he would allow to another.

Let him carefully abstain from talking of himself, his feelings or experiences that he may gain continence of speech, and learn to control the wasteful activities of his mind.

Let him contemplate the Sun as thinly veiled in clouds.

DEVELOPMENTAL EXERCISES THE SIGIL OF THE HOLY NAME

By

V.H. FRATER A.M.A.G.

The Order prescribed certain meditations to be done in the intervals between the Grades. There are varying reactions to these - some approving, others disapproving. In order to fill a gap between the studies of the Qabalah and the more advanced magical work of the Inner Order, gradually over the years I developed a set of exercises that I found to be very useful. They are not, strictly speaking, the traditional Golden Dawn exercises or meditations, but they are based essentially on the techniques in vogue in the Order. These exercises will make use of the basic methods of many systems such as rhythmic breathing, the vibration of names, visualisation of images, sigils from the Rose, and many others. I recommend them because they form a kind of bridge between the theoretical work of the Order and the far more technical processes that are given later.

Many of these exercises should begin with rhythmic breathing in order to establish some degree of quiescence of body and mind. The Order recommended a four fold breath, that is to inhale to the count of four, hold the breath for the same length of time and exhale to the count of four, and then hold for four. It only requires a little practice a couple of times a day in order to achieve some degree of expertise. Some of the signs of success are: a sense of quiet and stillness both physically and mentally, feeling as though one has become energised, and above all that there is a rippling sensation over and around the diaphragm. With a little regular practice, these results will occur fairly quickly. Then you can proceed with the next step. Feel free to modify the breathing rhythm. If necessary for your own comfort, change the holding period to two instead of four. Or, leave out the holding period altogether and just breath in to the count of four and exhale to the same count. Everything depends on how you feel about what you are doing.

A diagram accompanies this text. It depicts a sigil placed over a human figure. A sigil is simply a traditional technical term meaning a signature. It can be derived either from the Rose, as depicted later in this volume, or from a Kamea or magical square, also given later. The signature given in this diagram is based on the Hebrew word Eheieh and is derived from the Rose. As described later, one simply draws a line from the first Hebrew letter to the next, etc., until the Sigil is completed.

SIGIL OF EHEIEH

The diagram depicts the form of a human being, with this Sigil superimposed. Study it carefully first, so that when you try to visualise this you will have a clear conception of what you are trying to do. Sit down comfortably in a straight backed chair, or lie down on a bed or couch, and begin the process with a few minutes rhythmic breathing. Then visualize this Sigil of the Holy Name in black, not on the surface of your body, but inside, within your own being - not external to you. Visualise it as beginning in the heart region, ascending to the head, descending straight down to the feet, and then rises up to the heart once more. Don't be disturbed if your mind wanders occasionally or often. Just patiently bring it back to the topic you are contemplating and proceed, without self-criticism. It will require a good deal of practice to achieve a high degree of concentration. One aid you will find useful is to vibrate the name given above several times, audibly rather than silently. It is simply a device to facilitate your concentration.

Do this morning and evening for some weeks if need be until you become aware of something going on within which you have not noticed before. I do not wish to describe any of the results possible in order to avoid the possibility of suggestion intruding into your discipline, but whatever the result is it will encourage you and provide the stimulus to continue to bring the Divine White Light into operation within your own being. A later exercise described in the Portal Meditation elaborates this in what is called the Middle Pillar technique. But for the time being this Sigil exercise is a splendid preparation for later work. Just be patient and faithful - the rest will follow by itself.

As expertise develops, change the color of the Sigil from black to white. Keep the shape intact, in other words do not change anything except the color. Follow the program already delineated above.

SENSITIVITY TRAINING

Procure a set of cards, either ordinary playing cards or one of the many available Tarot decks. Remember there is a Golden Dawn pack which may be obtained from any occult bookstore or from the U.S. Games Systems, Inc. in New York City. Do keep in mind some of the teaching given in the preliminary Tarot document earlier in this book.

Shuffle the pack carefully so as to get the feel of the cards first, as well as to get some of your own atmosphere or magnetism into the cards. Spend a few minutes doing this and looking at the cards to become somewhat familiar with the way they look. Shuffle them once more, then place the deck face downwards. Touch the top card without turning it over. While touching it try to feel (or guess) what Suit it is. Remember - the Suit, not the nature of the card. With ordinary playing cards feel whether it is Clubs, Spades, Diamonds or Hearts. With the Tarot deck, Wands, Cups, Swords, Pentacles or any of the Trumps. Give your imagination free rein. Remember, it is of no consequence if you find you are wrong when you turn the card up. Consider the whole experiment as practice or as a game. It might be a good idea to keep a pencil and a sheet of paper handy so that you may enter your findings.

After touching the top card, and having tried to sense what suit it is, turn the card over. Record first what your guess was, and after turning the card over, record what the card actually was. At first, and perhaps for some considerable time, you may find yourself not hitting anything right at all. Do not permit yourself to get discouraged. Just continue the practice. After a while you may find yourself guessing right once in a dozen times, which is not at all bad. With repeated practice, you may find yourself guessing the right suit time and time again. All of this must be recorded. This will ultimately determine what your degree of accuracy is, and therefore how your sensitivity is developing. Remember, stick to guessing the suit only at first. Later on, more rigorous tests of the growing sensitivity can be developed. But go slowly. One step at a time.

SENSITIVITY TRAINING II

Shuffle the cards thoroughly as before, so that all the cards are well distributed and bear little relationship to their former positions. Again, place the sheet of paper and a pencil by your side so that you may record without effort the results of your practice.

Then lay the right hand on the top of the first card of the pack as before, face downwards. Keep it there for a while. Be quiet and still, breathing easily. Now try to guess whether the card is a "pip," that is one of the numbered cards from Ace or 1 to 10. At this juncture do not be concerned about the Suit as you did before, nor the color, nor any other detail. Just the number of the card itself.

You have ten choices. Do not play games with yourself by thinking of just that, or by running through these numbers consecutively in your mind. Be quiet, and while your hand is resting on the card, wait for a particular number to pop into your mind. As before, there will be many errors, naturally. But with continued practice, you will surprise yourself by the increasing number of accurate guesses you will make. At times you will feel you are getting progressively worse instead of better. Pay little attention to this, discouraging though it may appear to be. Quickly enough, you will find that your score will slowly improve and rise considerably.

Enter these results on the paper at your side. This is imperative.

When you feel you are doing well at this game, add one more category to what you are doing. Try to sense or guess not only the number, but the Suit.

If you are using the Tarot deck, remember Wands and Swords are compatible, and so are Cups and Pentacles. If you happen to hit on 6 of Cups when you guessed it might be 6 of Pentacles, you are not doing too badly. Likewise with the other Suits. 7 of Swords is not a bad find for a guess of 7 of Wands. And so on, etc.

Be patient with yourself, and do not expect miracles for the time being. Your skill and sensitivity will slowly improve as you proceed. There are side benefits to be gained from this practice. Apart from all other things which I will gloss over here, you will find your intuition becoming more finely attuned to the intimations of your own inner and higher being. It paves the way to becoming aware of the influence and guidance of your own higher and divine Genius, which is one of the major goals of the Great Work.

HOLY GROUND

Recall the biblical story of Moses hearing the voice of God in the desert telling him to take off his sandals for the ground he was treading on was Holy Ground.

As part of the initiatory process, it is as necessary to sanctify your Malkuth and elevate it to the higher consciousness of Kether as it is to bring down Godhead into the holy kingdom. Initiation is thus a dual process. To sensitize the lower vehicles and to invoke the higher. Properly speaking, this dual process should proceed simultaneously, but in order to render the certainty of this process, this exercise was devised to ensure compliance with tradition.

Sit down comfortably in your straight backed chair, beginning to work on the rhythmic breathing process. Remove shoes or slippers, so that the feet are placed firmly on the floor. Then try to imagine that flames are shooting up from the floor beneath you, flaming not merely around your feet but through them. Before beginning the exercise, get some idea of what flames look like from a picture or photograph, or even look at a gas burner. If you have a barbecue in your back yard or have made a bonfire recently, use these as models for your mental pictures.

While working thus, try to feel that your feet are getting hotter and hotter because of the flames underneath. It should not take too long to experience the sensation of heat there, which should make the visualization process much easier. If there is some difficulty when first imagining this, do not hesitate to resort to any artifice to help achieve the appropriate sensation. For example, obtain some Sloan's liniment or Absorbine Jr. or a patent arthritic medication named HEET. Daub a small quantity of any one of these substances on the feet, either directly under the ankle, or making a straight line with the dauber from heel to big toe in the middle of the sole of the foot. Since the skin on the sole is much thicker than elsewhere, you may have to have several applications of the dauber before you begin to feel any sensation from the dermo-irritant effect of the substance. It should produce some definite physical sensation in the foot. This will enable your imagination to function more easily and vigorously to produce fire and flame sensations in the feet.

Following the terms of the magical tradition, remember that the feet are attributed to Malkuth on the Tree of Life, to which various divine and angelic names belong. Use these as often as you wish both to aid your concentration as well as to invoke the forces of Earth and Fire. Adonai ha-Aretz is the Divine Name governing Earth, while YHVH Tzabaoth is that attributed to Fire. If you are not sure of the other names, refresh your memory by referring to the appropriate tables or Knowledge Lectures. Then use these names vigorously and always audibly. You are committed by the very nature of this system to invoke the highest divine Names you know when working on any magical topic.

Do this exercise for a minimum of fifteen minutes twice a day for as long a period of time as you can, and of course make a record of your results. In the event you are allergic to any of the medications mentioned, wash the area thoroughly with soap and water, or whatever anti-allergic product you are accustomed to use. Before commencing their use, test the product out by daubing a small quantity on your forearm. If there is no allergic response, continue. But if there is evidence of allergy, wash it off and refrain from its further use.

THE QABALISTIC CROSS

This magical gesture is referred to again and again throughout the whole Golden Dawn system. The correct way of doing this is as follows:

1. Stand upright, facing East. Imagine you are growing very tall. So tall that your head is above the clouds, while beneath your feet the Earth seems like a small globe on which you are standing. Spend a few minutes trying to achieve this piece of visualisation. The success of the whole manouevre depends on this.

2. Intone or vibrate Atoh, while touching the forehead with the forefinger of the right hand. Imagine that above you is the White Light of Kether, from which a ray descends as you proceed with the exercise.

3. Bring the hand down from the head to the middle of the chest and intone or vibrate Malkuth. Feel that the ray of Light descends all the way to the feet, not simply to the chest which you are touching. This establishes the shaft of the cross in Light.

4. Move the hand over to the left shoulder, and vibrate ve-Gedulah. While doing this, imagine that the entire shoulder is ablaze with light ready to move over to the right side to form the cross bar of Light.

5. Move the hand over to the right shoulder, and vibrate ve-Geburah. This will complete the cross bar, so that the entire cross is now formulated.

6. Clasp the hands over the chest, and vibrate le-Olahm Amen. As you do this, try to become acutely aware of this gigantic cross of light formulated through your entire body, now gigantic and extending high into upper space.

Practice this again and again. Do not hurry this procedure. Do it slowly, slowly enough to obtain some clear visualizations of the descending shaft of light with the cross bar at shoulder level. Vibrate the names strongly, if need be several times, not only to improve your concentration but to help formulate the cross more clearly and vividly.

It should be mentioned that once the exercise is over, the whole process should be reversed. That is, one should imagine oneself gradually reassuming one's normal size and absorb the cross of light into oneself. Close with the sign of Silence. With time you will become more conscious of the overshadowing presence of your higher and divine Genius, upon whose aid and guidance you can count. But you must first open yourself to Its presence by making the appropriate gestures and the right kind of aspiration.

This may be done as often as you wish. There are no set times for this practice. The more often the better.

THE HOLY SPIRIT

Kether is Yechidah in man, the higher and divine Genius, the holy Spirit. This has been established thoroughly in all that has gone before. It is the basis of the Qabalah and of the whole Order system. This exercise is to further assist you to gain a deeper apprehension of its constant overshadowing presence. All the work you have been doing before - the theoretical intellectual work relating to the Qabalah etc., is really to sharpen your intuitive faculties, to open yourself to a higher consciousness.

The symbol for the Holy Spirit is the Hebrew letter Shin. Since every Hebrew letter is a number as well, you should already have learned that its numerical value is 300. The Hebrew words for the Spirit of the Gods are Ruach Elohim (Roo-ahch Eh-loh-heem). These words also have a numerical value of 300; thus the letter Shin can well serve as their symbol.

Again, sit upright in your straight backed chair, and immediately establish the rhythmic breath. By now you should be fairly adept in accomplishing this without much fanfare.

Above the head visualize a large letter Shin in flaming red. Visualize it as vividly as possible until you'feel it vibrating just above your scalp. The divine Name attributed to Kether is Eheieh. Vibrate this often, as recommended with the previous exercises since it serves both as an aid to your concentration and to link you up with the higher forces of your own being.

As with previous exercises, should any difficulty arise, a single daub of the recommended medical substances should create enough skin irritation on the scalp to enable you to focus all your attention there with relative ease. Again, I recommend recording whatever results, or lack of them, that you obtain, in your private record book.

THE CLEANSING BREATH

This is an accompaniment of the rhythmic breath and should be used to terminate any and all the exercises and practices in this section.

It is really very simple. Take a full breath, in which all the parts of the chest are employed to full capacity. When the chest is fully inflated, hold the breath for a few seconds. Then pucker up the lips as though you were about to whistle, though do not blow out the cheeks.

Then exhale the air out vigorously through the opening in the mouth. Let this opening be a narrow one, and puff out only a little air at a time.

Pause for a while, still retaining the balance of the air. Repeat the process, that is continue to puff the air out through the opening of the mouth with some force or vigor. Pause once more, and repeat until all the air is gone. This will force the chest to rebound almost automatically when the exhalation is completed in this way. If there is a little dizziness due to hyperventilation, stop and sit down for a moment or two before resuming. Repeat this type of breath over a period of time until it can be performed with ease and comfort.

PRITHIVI

You have already been introduced in a rather superficial way to the Hindu tattwa system. Now we will employ these tattwas in a practical way, as an introduction to the possibility of self-initiation, in steps as it were.

The diagram in the colour plate section of this book shows a square. Imagine it to be yellow. It is the symbol of Earth in Hindu psychology - Prithivi. It represents anything in its solid, physical and tangible state, with a host of other meanings that you will come to discover in the course of your working with these exercises. Look at this large yellow square for a moment or two, then close your eyes to imagine it enclosing you. Feel as if you are sitting in it, or standing in or against a yellow wall. Do not try any tricks with this yellow square, such as obtaining complementary colors or imagining that you are passing through imaginary doors, etc. Just see it as it is - a large yellow square in which you are sitting. Hold your attention to this and only this.

Then following the terms of our esoteric tradition, a series of hierarchical names have to be vibrated in order to place you in total harmony with the forces you are dealing with. As the Adeptus Minor ritual indicates, colors are not symbols of forces; they are elemental forces. Yellow is not a symbol of anything. It is a specific subtle type of energy in and for itself. These energies can be activated by the use of the appropriate divine and angelic names, enabling the energies to revitalize and transform your various psychosomatic vehicles into the sensitive receivers they need to be if you are to achieve success in the Great Work.

The divine Name is Adonai ha-Aretz, the Archangelic Name being Auriel. Vibrate these names vigorously and frequently both to facilitate concentration and until your body and all therein is vibrating and tingling exquisitely. When you experience that, you will know that you are on the right track. Persist in this for some considerable time, doing it a couple of times a day. Record your results.

VAYU

This is a large blue circle, again to be found in the coloured plate section of this book. Imagine that it encloses you. This blue circle is called Vayu, attributed to the element of Air. Again, remember that it is being employed to carry on the slow but inevitable process of preparing you for initiation. It is being accomplished in small increments, to enable you to adjust to the process without undue strain or stress.

Follow a procedure similar to the preceding one. Imagine you are seated or standing against a wall on which is inscribed a large light blue circle, sitting or standing. Do not attempt anything beyond what is here described.

In accordance with the western magical tradition, you are going to vibrate the highest divine Names that you know, in order to align yourself with spiritual reality and to protect yourself against mishap. The divine Name is Shaddai El Chai. At the moment we are not concerned with the literal meaning of these names. We know they have a significant vibratory effect, and their use helps tremendously in bringing the mind back to focus. Do this exercise as often as you see fit until your mind concentrates easily on the image, and until you feel the awakening of tingling and vibration sensations within your whole being.

Follow a similar procedure with the remaining tattwas. Apas the silver crescent for Water, Tejas the red triangle for Fire, and Akasa the black egg for Spirit. The Knowledge Lectures will provide the appropriate Names for use with each one.

LOVE

This magical way of life is characterized by its total lack of sentimentality. It is direct, straightforward and unequivocal in its dealings with the different components of your psychospiritual make up and your subsequent relationships with the people in your environment.

But this does not mean to imply that the emotional and spiritual components of man are regarded with disdain or of little account. On the contrary: Love is the law, love under will. Without love, all one's working are sterile and will avail one nothing. But love must accord with law, with the scheme of things, and of course fit in with the general philosophical and theoretical grounds of the magical tradition.

It is an interesting and most useful observation that there is only one planetary symbol which embraces all of the Sephiroth on the Tree of Life. It does this without any strain or force, as you will see from the acompanying diagram. This planet is Venus, the planet of love. We are not now concerned with any specific astrological attributions or meanings other than that Venus is more or less equivocal with love. The Hebrew word is either Ahavoh or Chesed, one of the Sephiroth. Chesed means loving kindness. Associate these words with the symbol of Venus which is a circle astride a cross.

Consult the diagram, noting how all the ten Sephiroth fit into its geometrical form. Then assume your meditative posture in the upright straight backed chair, commencing with the rhythmic breath. Then visualize the symbol Venus synthesizing the whole Tree, which by now you have learned is the glyph of your own self, the whole self. Back into the figure as it were, feeling that the planetary symbol is conterminous with your being.

There are no artifices that you can employ here to conjure up a sensation or emotion of love. But you can, while meditating, reflect on what love is, whom you have loved, and how you felt. Concentrate on all these feelings and emotions, while imagining you are the symbol Venus. Accompany this concentration with the simplest type of rhythmic breathing, counting 4 in and 4 out.

For a short time, watch the breath enter the nostrils, thinking The breath flows in, and then as it leaves the nostrils The breath flows out. This is simple. Maintain this exercise day in and day out until you begin to acquire the feeling and some of the subtleties connected with it.

Then, with this becoming habitual, change the language in your mind to Love flows in to me, and then when exhaling Love flows out from me. Meditate that love flows into you from Kether, the most High, and from you with your blessing to every single being in the whole universe. You may wish to employ one of the lovely passages from the traditional rituals of the Golden Dawn while breathing out love to the whole world. Such as: Holy art thou, Lord of the Universe, for Thy glory flows out to the ends of the Universe, rejoicing.

BASIC TECHNIQUES

VOLUME FOUR

BASIC TECHNIQUES

TABLE OF CONTENTS

IMPORTANT TABLES AND ILLUSTRATIONS

VOLUME FOUR

BASIC TECHNIQUES

GENERAL ORDERS

Members of the Second Order in Caledonia are requested not to arrange privately for Second Order teaching with private members in Anglia or elsewhere. All instructions will be arranged for on application to headquarters in Caledonia as well as manuscripts supplied in this Order, and examinations arranged.

Members are requested to strengthen rather than weaken their central authority, and to work in harmony.

Approved by the Chief Adept of the Order, G.H. Frater D.D.C.F. 7-4. (September 1897, Revised in 1898.)

Every member of the Inner Order has been admitted by the permission of the Chief Adept, and every member only retains his membership by the continued approval of the Chief Adept in Brittania.

There is no admission fee, nor annual subscription. But inasmuch as the Chiefs have made themselves liable for certain expenditures by establishing and maintaining a Home for the Order in London, they anticipate that each member will assist, in accordance with his means, in supporting the Order, and supplying the funds necessary for the general maintenance of the Home, the expenses of assemblies, and the extension of the Library.

The Chief Adept—the G.H. Frater D.D.C.F.—is now the source of all official instruction. The Chief Adept in Charge, G.H. Frater N.O.M., is his executive Officer. He also now holds the office of Registrar of the Second Order, and to him *all* communications and appeals are to be addressed. The V.H. Soror Shemeber acts as Assistant Registrar to supervise the circulation of Rituals, etc.

Continuance of membership of the Second Order implies a contract to return to the Registrar on demand, or upon resignation, demission or expulsion, all documents, rituals, rolls, implements, and insignia possessed as an Adeptus Minor.

Membership also implies an assent to the right of the Chief Adept to publish to all other members, the fact and cause of any suspension, resignation, demission, or expulsion from the Second Order.

Every member is expected to attend the Annual Ceremony on the Corpus Christi Day or to send to the Registrar before the date of assembly a reasonable excuse for absence. The fact of the existence of a Home for the Second Order as well as the address thereof, is to be preserved as a secret from every member of the Outer Order of the Golden Dawn, as much as from those outside the pale of the Order.

The Adepti assembled at the Home form a Council which may take cognisance of all matters affecting the welfare of the Order of the Golden Dawn, and of the Second Order. They may report any Resolution, arrived at by a majority of two thirds of those present, at any council to the Registrar, who shall place the Resolution before the Chief Adept, but such Council **must** be a representative one.

Membership of the Second Order implies a desire and an effort to make progress in the special studies therein taught. As in the Outer Order, the Roll will be revised once a year, and if the G.H. Chiefs consider that any member has failed to make such efforts at progress as might be ressonably expected, they may call upon any member for an explanation. If this latter is not deemed satisfactory, it may be followed by suspension, or an edict of degradation to the rank of a Lord of the Portal, or of cessation of membership.

Offences against the terms of the Adeptus Minor Obligation are deemed of the utmost gravity, while infraction of executive regulations unless repeated and indefensible, will be deemed of less grave importance. The Chiefs hope that private differences between members will be amicably arranged in private, as they have no wish to interfere in such matters.

Members should at all times be very careful not to shew any disrespect to the personal religious feelings of other members.

Notices will be from time to time posted in the Library, in reference to minor regulations, price of the books, and to the holding of classes for instruction.

Whenever one Adept writes to another Adeptus Minor on Second Order matters, he must stamp the envelope in a peculiar manner; viz, in the usua' corner, but with the stamp turned around, so that the face looks upwards—like C.R.C. in the Pastos.

You are particularly requested to think and speak at all times with tolerance and respect of all other Schools of true Occultism, and of the Eastern Philosophy as contrasted wth Hermeticism and the Rosicrucian fraternity.

The works of the Lake Harris school are better avoided. The H.B. of L. is condemned, as of course are Luciferian or Palladistic teachings. The so-called Rose Croix of Sor Peladan is considered as an ignorant perversion of the Name, containing **no true knowledge** and not even worthy of the title of an occult order. The Black Mass is naturally by its own confession of the evil magic school. The Martinists, as long as they adhere to the teachings of their Founder, should not be out of harmony with the R.R. et A.C.

Regulations for the conduct of the progress of a member through the Zelator sub-grade of the grade of Adeptus Minor.

FIRST STAGE - NEOPHYTE ADEPTUS MINOR

1. Admission ceremony. After which receive Ritual A which consists of general instructions.
   The Adeptus Minor Ritual is to be thoroughly studied and the clauses of the Obligation as referred to the Sephiroth are to be impressed upon the memory.
2. Ritual of the Pentagram. Commit the system to memory.
3. Ritual of the Hexagram. Commit the system to memory.
4. Receive ritual U, the Microcosm, to be attentively studied though not learned by heart.
5. Receive Ritual Z-l and Z-3.
6. Receive Ritual D and make Lotus wand to be consecrated after approval of Chief in Charge.

7. Receive Ritual E and F, and make Rose Cross, and consecrate it after approval as before.
8. Receive Ritual G, and make and consecrate the five Implements as before.
9. Receive Ritual K, the Consecration Ceremony. And M-the Hermes Vision and Lineal figures, and W-Hodos Chamelionis.
10. Receive and study Flying Rolls 1 to 10 inclusive at any period during the first stage.

The Adept **must** pass Examinations marked A and B at the end of this First Stage, and thus become a Zelator Adeptus Minor.

(Note. By permission of the Chief Adept, 6, 7, and 8 may be taken immediately after 3. Then 4 and 5.)

SECOND STAGE - ZELATOR ADEPTUS MINOR

11. Receive and study Flying Rolls 11,12, 14,20,21,26,28, 29,30, and may now pass C, G, and E examinations.

THIRD STAGE - TAROT SYSTEM

12. Receive and study Rituals N, O, P, Q, R. Must now pass G, C, D, and E examinations.

FOURTH STAGE - ENOCHIAN SYSTEM

13. Receive and study Rituals H, S, T, X, Y. **Must** now pass F examination.

FIFTH STAGE

14. Receive and study Rituals Z-2, and practise Consecration and Invocation. **Must** pass H Examination. Practical success in Ceremonials of Z-2 is required.

These Rituals and Flying Rolls may be sent by mail covered and fastened up against inspection. Members must return them in a similar manner. If they do not register them, they will be held liable to replace them if lost in transit.

When a document is marked 'To be kept. . .days' this must not be exceeded.

On the completion of this course of study and the passing of the eight examinations referred to, the Chief Adepts may, at their discretion, admit the Zelator Adeptus Minor to the subgrade of Theoricus Adeptus Minor. But there exists no actual right to such higher grade. This course may be completed within two years.

The examinations leading from the sub-grades of Neophyte and Zelator Adeptus Minor to the sub-grade of Theoricus Adeptus Minor.

The examinations are partly *viva voce*, partly written in the presence of the Examiner, and partly written at home. In the latter case, manuscripts may be referred to, but no personal assistance may be obtained under the pain of entire rejection.

No Adept will be admitted to sub-grade of Theoricus Adeptus Minor unless he shows a competent knowledge of every one of these subjects. Adepts who have passed any examinations are required to refrain from supplying information as to the questions and procedure they have experienced to any other Adept until he has passed the same examination. The order of passing the examinations has already been defined.

The Examiner in Chief reserves the right to make further regulations as required, as to procedure after failures to pass these examinations, or may subsequently insist on the Examinations being taken in any different order than already laid down.

THE COMPLETE GOLDEN DAWN SYSTEM OF MAGIC

Z. A. M. TO Th. A. M. EIGHT EXAMINATIONS

A. PRELIMINARY

Part 1 Written. Part 2 *Viva voce* and Practical in presence of Examiner. No part at home.
The Obligation, Proof of familiarity with all clauses.
Minutum Mundum diagrams. Names, Letters, Colors, Tarots, with Tarot attributions of
Sephiroth and Paths.
Rose and Cross Sigils. Draw Sigil for any given name.
Supreme Ritual of the Pentagram. Allotment of Elements, names and forces; mode of
drawing any or all.
In Part 1, the Ceremonials must show 'effect' as well as verbal accuracy.

Z. A. M. TO Th. A.M.

B. ELEMENTAL

Part 1 Written, and Part 1 *viva voce* in presence of Examiner. No part at home.
The Magical Implements. Sword, Cup, Wand, Dagger and Pantacle and Lotus Wand.
The construction, constitution, symbolism of these and rules for their use. The dangers of
imperfect construction and ignorant use. Ceremonies of Consecration, Formulae of Invocation.

Z. A. M. TO Th. A.M.

C. PSYCHIC

Spirit Vision and Astral Projection.
Part I. In presence of Examiner, *viva voce* and Practical. Describe results with symbol
supplied. Judging Tattwa cards and visions from Tattwa cards.
Part 2. In the absence of the Examiner, assisted if desired by manuscripts and lectures, but
without personal assistance. Written essays on experience with symbols of Tattwas, made
by the Candidate but chosen by the Examiner.

Z. A. M. TO Th. A. M.

D. DIVINATION

Astrology, Geomancy, Tarot. The practice of Divination by these three systems.
Part 2. Divination by all three schemes upon a given subject. Report in writing to be done
at home—without personal assistance.
Part 3. A supplementary *viva voce* examination if required.

Z. A. M. TO Th. A. M.

E. MAGIC

Talismans and Flashing Tablets—their formation and consecration. Ascending to the
planes. Formation of Angelic and Telesmatic Figures from Letters of Name supplied.
Vibrating mode of pronouncing Divine Names. The actual vibration of ADONAI HA-
ARETZ until radiance of Aura is established.

VOLUME FOUR

Part 1. Perform Ceremony of Invocation or Banishing of the forces of any given Sign, Planet or Element.

From a given symbol, travel to the Plane and ascend vibrating the proper Names, etc. Vibration of ADONAI HA-ARETZ until radiance suffices.

Part 2. At home. Make and consecrate a Talisman for a given purpose. Make and charge three flashing tablets, viz: for an Element, a Planet and a Sign.

Draw and colour Angelic figures or Elemental figures appropriate to these as may be required.

Z. A. M. TO Th. A. M.

F. ELEMENTAL ENOCHIAN TABLETS

Especially the 10 Servient square of each Lesser Angle as to Angel, Sphinx and God. Chess play, relation of pieces to Tarots, etc., as taught in Y.l. and Y.2. Rituals.

Part 1. Written in presence of Examiner. Ability to fill up all attributions of any given Lesser Angle. *Viva voce* if required.

Part 2. Written report of Astral visit to certain squares, with the buildings and colourings of the division of each square, and drawings coloured of appropriate Angel, Sphinx and Pyramid God, as required.

Z. A. M. TO Th. A. M.

G. SYMBOLICAL

Symbols and Formulae from the Neophyte Ritual. Explain all allusions of any paragraph and the symbolism of any Robe, Lamen, Wand or Action. Also the Neophyte Secret Words and the Coptic Alphabet.

Viva Voce and written in the presence of the Examiner at his discretion.

Consecration and Evocation.

A ceremony on the Formulae of Ritual Z-2 must be performed before the Examiner, and must meet with his approval as to method, execution and effect.

The Chief Adept in charge desires that each Adept will procure a small manuscript book, and enter for himself the titles and subdivisions of all the Examinations, with this phrase written out for each examination:

I, the undersigned, do this day certify that I have duly examined and am satisfied with attainments which have been shown."

This book must then be shown at each examination, and also on admission to the Grade of Theoricus Adeptus Minor.

CATALOGUE OF MANUSCRIPTS

- **A.   General Orders.**
- **B.   Ritual of Pentagram.**
- **C.   Ritual of Hexagram.**
- **D.   Lotus Wand.**
- **E.   Rose Cross.**
- **F.   Sigils from the Rose.**
- **G.   Five Implements.**
- **H.   Enochi Clavis or the Tablets of Enoch.**

THE COMPLETE GOLDEN DAWN SYSTEM OF MAGIC

I.   Adeptus Minor Obligation.
J.   Consecration Ceremony.
K.   History.
L.   Hermes Vision. Lineal Figures.
M.   Tarot Description.
N.   Astronomic—Tarot.
O.   Tarot Star Maps.
P.   Key to Tarot divination.
Q.   Tabulated Rules, Tarot.
R.   1. Enochian Attributions by N.O.M.
S.   2. Enochian Attributions—Official.
T.   The Enochian Calls.
U.   Microcosm.
V.   Hodos Chamelionis.
X.   Pyramid Gods.
Y   -- 1. Chess and Chaturanga.
Y   -- 2. Chess Formulae and Rules.
Z   -- 1. and 3. Upon the Neophyte Ritual.
Z   -- 2. Ceremonial Magic.

CATALOGUE OF FLYING ROLLS

1.   Warnings.
2.   Purity and Will.
3.   Administrative.
4.   Spirit Vision.
5.   Imagination.
6.   Note on No. 2.
7.   Alchemy, physical.
8.   Geomantic Pentagram.
9.   Right and Left Pillars.
10. Self-sacrifice.
11. Clairvoyance.
12. Telesmatic Images and Adonai ha-Aretz.
13. Secrecy and Hermetic Love.
14. Talismans.
15. Man and God.
16. Fama Fraternitatis.
17. Vault Sides.
18. Progress in the Order.
19. Aims and means of Adeptship
20. Elementary view of Man.
21. Know Thyself.
22. Free Will.
23. Tattwic Visions.

VOLUME FOUR

TECHNIQUES OF INVOCATION

Here follow some of the basict techniques of invocation. They are relatively simple—but absolutely important. Let there be no equivocation about this. They are so important that I recommend that they be committed to memory—perfectly and by rote.

On examining some of the early documents of the Order as well as those of the later formulation of the Order, the Stella Matutina, I am constantly struck by the fact that in the rituals, whether of initiation or of personal growth and developement, the pentagrams and hexagrams pertaining to the operation are depicted in diagrammatic form. This eternally surprises me. For despite the fact that the papers on the Pentagram and Hexagram rituals suggest, nay demand, that the contents be committed to memory, few apparently took this injunction seriously. Instead of being content with the rubric of the ritual stating that for example the invoking Pentagram of Air should be traced in the Air, or that the banishing Hexagram of Mercury should be traced, the members whose papers I have seen drew the appropriate figure. This of course suggests that the figures were not committed to memory, and that the member had to draw the appropriate figure on the pages of the ritual in order to jog his memory.

Now all of this is totally unnecessary—which is why I am demanding categorically that the serious student study the following papers and commit the schema to memory. Try to study the papers with the idea in mind of perceiving the underlying attributions. In that case, should a momentary doubt arise as to what figure to employ, all one has to do is to visualize the attributions to the respective angles, and then recall the basic rules involved. With the Pentagrams, the rule is to trace towards the angle involved to invoke, and move away from to banish. In the case of the Hexagram, the rule is to trace clockwise from the angle you are dealing with in order to invoke, and anti-clockwise in order to banish. It is that simple.

It is so simple *au* fond that it puzzles me considerably when I find the Pentagrams and Hexagrams depicted in diagrams in various rituals—like the Consecration of the Elemental Weapons, etc. It must imply that students are careless, or adopt a trifling attitude towards these basic but most important elements of the art of Invocation. The whole art of Magic is rooted in these basics, without which there is nothing but form and emptiness.

So let this be a word to the wise. Memorize the basics then there will be no problem. In that case one could proceed to the next important part of ritual, the visualizations. To repeat a former statement, there can be no magical progress without visualizing the lineal figures or the Godforms. Take one step at a time. Start with the basics first, then proceed to the more complex.

7

THE COMPLETE GOLDEN DAWN SYSTEM OF MAGIC

The Godforms and the Telesmatic Images are every bit as important as are the lineal figures—in fact, more so. They will require a good deal of practise to achieve any degree of skill. All the more reason to memorize what can be called the more mechanical phases of magical procedures.

One of the most satisfactory ways of learning these basics is to devise a simple ritual which can be performed daily without too much trouble. It should include the fundamental drills, such as the greater ritual of the Pentagram, plus a dramatic element which will do something to and for the student.

Nearly fifty years ago I composed a short, simple ritual which I used every day for practically a year. As time went on, and as I became more familiar with the rudiments of the Golden Dawn system, it developed into a species of what I came to call **Opening by Watchtower.** It employed all the important items of the Greater Ritual plus the use of the Elemental Weapons. As a result, in no time at all, a considerable expertise was obtained in the fundamental principles of magical invocation and banishing which has stood me in good stead throughout the years. This really accounts for my adamant insistence on the elimination of diagrams of hexagrams and pentagrams in Rituals, which appalls me more and more as I retype some of the earliest documents of the Order.

In a book published by Aquarian Press in England, entitled *Ceremonial Magic*, I reproduced this ritual with several variations. There are innumerable changes that can be rung on a simple theme. The student who really wants to be proficient in the magical arts can take one of these themes which I reproduce somewhere in this book and work it to his considerable advantage. By doing so, he will come to a profound understanding of numberless other schemata which at first sight bear little relationship to what he is about to do. (By V.H. Frater A.M.A.G.).

THE RITUAL OF THE PENTAGRAM

The Pentagram is a powerful symbol representing the operation of the Eternal Spirit and the Four Elements under the divine Presidency of the letters of the Name **Yeheshuah.** The elements themselves in the symbol of the Cross are governed by **Yhvh.** But the letter Shin, representing the **Ruach Elohim,** the Divine Spirit, being added thereto, the Name becometh **Yeheshuah** or **Yehovashah** - the latter when the letter Shin is placed between ruling Earth and the other three letters of Tetragrammaton.

From each re-entering angle of the Pentagram, therefore, issueth a ray, representing a radiation from the Divine. Therefore is it called the Flaming Pentagram, or Star of the Great Light, in affirmation of the forces of Divine Light to be found therein.

Traced as a symbol of good, it should be placed with the single point upward, representing the rule of the Divine Spirit. For if thou shouldst write it with the two points upward, it is an evil symbol, affirming the empire of matter over that Divine Spirit which should govern it. **See that thou doest it not.**

Yet, if there may arise an absolute necessity for working or conversing with a Spirit of evil nature, and that to retain him before thee without tormenting him, thou hast to employ the symbol of the Pentagram reversed - (for, know thou well, thou canst have no right to injure or hurt even evil Spirits to gratify curiousity or caprice) - in such a case, thou shalt hold the blade of thy Magical Sword upon the single lowest point of the Pentagram, until such time as thou shalt license him to depart. Also, revile not evil spirits—but remember that the Archangel Michael of whom St. Judespeaketh, when contending with Satan, durst not bring a railing accusation against him but said 'The Lord rebuke thee'.

Now, if thou wilt draw the Pentagram to have by thee as a symbol, thou shalt make it of the colours already taught, upon the black ground. There shall be the sign of the Pentagram, the Wheel, the Lion, the Eagle, the Ox, and the Man, and each hath an angle assigned unto it for dominion. Hence ariseth the Supreme Ritual of the Pentagram, according to the angle from which the Pentagram is traced. The circle or Wheel answereth to the all-pervading Spirit: The laborious Ox is the symbol of Earth; the Lion is the vehemence of Fire; the Eagle, the Water flying aloft as with wings when she is vaporized by the force of heat: the Man is the Air, subtle and thoughtful, penetrating hidden things.

At **all times complete the circle of the place before commencing an invokation.**

The currents leading from Fire to Air and from Earth to Water are those of Spirit—the mediation of the Active and Passive Elements. These two Spirit Pentagrams should precede and close Invocations as the equilibrium of the Elements, and in establishing the harmony of their influence. In closing, these currents are reversed.

SPIRIT
INVOKING PENTAGRAMS

SPIRIT
BANISHING

They are the invoking and banishing Pentagrams of the Spirit. The Sigil of the Wheel should be traced in their centre. In the invoking Pentagram of Earth the current descendeth from the Spirit to the Earth. In the Banishing Pentagram, the current is reversed. The Sigil of the Ox should be traced in the centre. These two Pentagrams are in general use for invocation or banishing, and their use is given to the Neophyte of the Order of the Golden Dawn under the title of the Lesser Ritual of the Pentagram.

This Lesser Ritual of the Pentagram is only of use in general and less important invocations. Its use is permitted to the Outer that Neophytes may have protection aganist opposing forces, and also that they may form some idea of how to attract and to come into communication with spiritual and invisible things. The Banishing Pentagram of Earth will also serve thee for any opposing Astral force. In all cases of tracing a Pentagram, the angle should be carefully closed at the finishing point.

THE COMPLETE GOLDEN DAWN SYSTEM OF MAGIC

The invoking Pentagram of Air commenceth from Water, and that ot Water commenceth from the Angle of Air. Those of Fire and Earth begin from the angle of Spirit. The Kerubic symbol of the Element is to be traced in the centre. The banishing Signs are reversing of the current. But before all things, complete the circle of the place wherein thou workest, seeing that it is the key of the rest.

Unless you want to limit or confine the force, make not a circle round each Pentagram, unless for the purpose of tracing the Pentagram truly. In concentrating however the force upon a symbol or Talisman, thou shalt make the circle with the Pentagram upon it so as to concentrate the force together thereon.

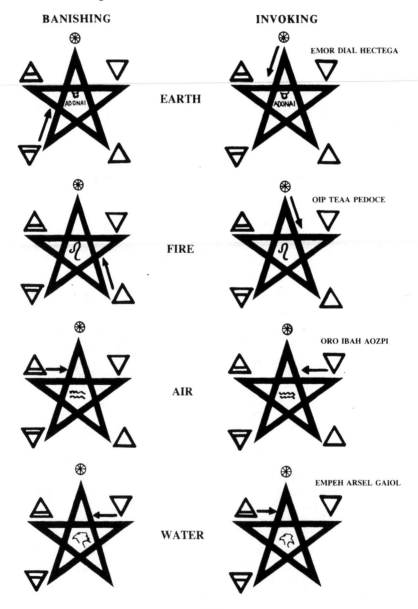

BANISHING   **INVOKING**

EARTH — EMOR DIAL HECTEGA

FIRE — OIP TEAA PEDOCE

AIR — ORO IBAH AOZPI

WATER — EMPEH ARSEL GAIOL

VOLUME FOUR

RULE: Invoke towards, and banish from, the point to which the Element is attributed.

Air hath a watery symbol, (Aquarius) because it is the container of rain and moisture. Fire hath the form of the Lion-Serpent (Leo). Water hath the alchemic Eagle of distillation (Eagle's Head). Earth hath the laborious Ox (Taurus). Spirit is produced by the One operating in all things.

The elements vibrate between the Cardinal points for they have not an unchangeable abode therein, though they are allotted to the Four Quarters in their invocation in the Ceremonies of the First Order. This attribution is derived from the nature of the winds. For the Easterly wind is of the Nature of Air more especially. The South Wind bringeth into action the nature of Fire. West winds bring with them moisture and rain. North winds are cold and dry like Earth. The S.W. wind is violent and explosive—the mingling of the contrary elements of Fire and Water. The N.W. and S.W. winds are more harmonious, uniting the influence of the two active and passive elements.

Yet their natural position in the Zodiac is: Fire in the East, Earth in South, Air in West, and Water in the North. Therefore they vibrate: Air between West and East. Fire between East and South. Water between North and West. Earth between South and North.

Spirit also vibrateth between the Height and Depth.

So that, if thou invokest, it is better to look towards the position of the winds, since the Earth, ever whirling on her poles, is more subject to their influence. **But if thou wilt go in the Spirit Vision unto their abode,** it is better for thee to take their position in the Zodiac.

Air and Water have much in common, and because one is the container of the other, therefore have their symbols been at all times transferred, and the Eagle assigned to Air and Aquarius to Water. Nevertheless, it is better that they should be attributed as before stated and for the foregoing reason is it that the invoking sign of the one and the banishing sign of the other counterchange in the Pentagram.

When thou dealest with the Pentagram of the Spirit thou shalt give the saluting signs of the Adeptus Minor Grade, and for the Earth the Sign of Zelator, and for Air that of Theoricus, and for Water that of Practicus, and for Fire, Philosophus.

If thou wilt use the Pentagram to invoke or banish the Zodiacal forces, thou shalt use the Pentagram of the Element unto which the Sign is referred, and trace in its centre the usual Sigil of the Sign thus:

**WATERY: BANISHING
FOR PISCES**

**FIERY: INVOKING
FOR ARIES**

And whenever thou shalt trace a Sigil of any nature, thou must commence at the left hand of the Sigil or symbol tracing it in a clockwise motion.

Whenever thou invokest the forces of the Zodiacal Signs as distinct from the Elements, thou shalt erect an astrological chart of the Heavens **for the time of working** so that thou mayest know toward what quarter or direction thou shouldst face in working. For the same Sign may be in the East at one time of the day and in the West at another.

THE COMPLETE GOLDEN DAWN SYSTEM OF MAGIC

Whenever thou shalt prepare to commence any magical work or operation, it will be advisable for thee to clear and consecrate the place of work by performing the Lesser Banishing Ritual of the Pentagram. In certain cases, especially when working by or with the forces of the Planets, it may be wise also to use the Lesser Banishing Ritual of the Hexagram.

In order that a Force and a Current and a Colour and a Sound may be united together in the same symbol, unto each angle of the Pentagram certain Hebrew divine Names and Names from the Angelic Tablets are allotted. These are to be pronounced with the invoking and banishing Pentagrams as thou mayest see in this diagrams.

The attributions of the angles of the Pentagram are the key of its Ritual. Herein, during ordinary invocation without the use of the Enochian Tablets of the Elements, thou shalt pronounce the Divine Name **Al** with the Pentagram of Water, and **Elohim** with Fire, etc. But if thou art working with the Elemental or Enochian Tablets, thou shalt use the Divine Names in the Angelic language drawn therefrom. For Earth, **Emor Dial Hectega,** etc., and for Spirit the four words: **Exarp** in the East; **Hcoma** in the West: **Nanta** in the North; and **Bitom** in the South.

In the pronunciation of all these Names, thou shalt take a deep breath and vibrate them as much as possible inwardly with the outgoing breath, not necessarily loudly, but with forcible vibration thus: **A-a-a-el-ll** (Since this Divine name consists of only two letters I consistently make a practice of vibrating the letters separately viz, Aleph Lamed, then the sound as indicated before). Or **Em-or-r Di-a-ll Hec-te-e-gah.** If thou wilt, thou mayest also trace the letters or Sigils of these Names in the Air.

To invoke the forces of the Four Elements at once, at the Four Quarters, commence at the East and there trace the equilibrating Pentagram of the Actives and the invoking Pentagram of Air and pronounce the proper Names. Then carry round the point of thy wand to the South and there trace the equilibrating Pentagram for Actives and the invoking Pentagram of Fire and pronounce the proper Names. Thence, pass to the West, trace the Equilibrating Pentagram for Passives and the Invoking Pentagram for Water and pronounce the proper Names; thence to the North, trace the equilibration of the Passives and the invoking Pentagram of Earth, pronounce the proper Names, and then complete the circle of the place.

In the same manner shalt thou banish, unless thou desirest to retain certain of the Forces for a time. All invocations shall be opened and closed with the Qabalistic Cross. In certain cases other Names, as those of Angels and Spirits, may be pronounced towards their proper quarters and their Names and Sigils traced in the Air.

If thou workest with but one Element, thou shalt make - (if it be an active element as Fire or Air) - the equilibrating Pentagram for Actives only and the Element's own invoking Pentagram, and not those of the other Elements. If it be a passive Element - Earth or Water

12

thou shalt make the Equilibriating Pentagram of the passives only and the invoking Pentagram and banishing follow the same law. Also, see that thou pronouncest the proper Names with the proper Pentagrams.

(For full directions on performing the Qabalistic Cross, do refer to my *What You Should Know About The Golden Dawn,* Falcon Press, 1983. I.R.)

SUPREME INVOKING RITUAL OF THE PENTAGRAM

Face East.
Make Qabalistic Cross.
Make Equilibriated Active Pentagram of Spirit.
Vibrate **Exarp** in making Pentagram.
Vibrate **Eheieh** in making Wheel.
Finish with the Adeptus Minor grade Signs.

Make the Invoking Pentagram of Air.
Vibrate **Oro Ibah Aozpi** in making Pentagram.
Vibrate **Yhvh** in making Aquarius.
Finish with the Theoricus grade Sign.

Carry point of instrument to the South

Make Equilibriated Active Pentagram of Spirit.
Vibrate **Bitom** in making Pentagram.
Vibrate **Eheieh** in making Wheel.
Give Adeptus Minor grade Signs.

Make the Invoking Pentagram of Fire.
Vibrate **Oip Teaa Pedoce** in making Pentagram.
Vibrate **Elohim** in making Leo sigil.
Make the Philosophus Grade Sign.

Carry point of instrument to the West

Make Equilibriated Passive Pentagram of Spirit.
Vibrate **Hcoma** in making Pentagram
Vibrate **Agla** in making Wheel.
Give Adeptus Minor grade Signs.

Make Invoking Pentagram of Water.
Vibrate **Empeh Arsel Gaiol** in making Pentagram.
Vibrate **Al** in making Eagle Head.
Give the Practicus Grade Sign.

Carry point of instrument to the North

Make Equilibriated Passive Pentagram of Spirit
Vibrate **Nanta** in making Pentagram.
Vibrate **Agla** in making Wheel.
Give Adeptus Minor grade Signs.

Make Invoking Pentagram of Earth.
Vibrate **Emor Dial Hectega** in making Pentagram.
Vibrate **Adonai** in making Taurus.
Give Zelator Grade Sign.

Carry point of instrument to the East.

Finish in East as in Lesser Pentagram Ritual with the Four Archangels and Qabalistic Cross.

THE RITUAL OF THE HEXAGRAM

The Hexagram is a powerful symbol representing the operation of the Seven Planets under the presidency of the Sephiroth, and of the seven-lettered Name, ARARITA. The Hexagram is sometimes called the Signet Star or Symbol of the Macrocosm, just as the Pentagram is called the Signet Star or Symbol of the Microcosm. ARARITA is a divine name of the Seven letters formed of the Hebrew initials of the sentence:

VOLUME FOUR

One is his beginning. One is his individuality. His permutation is one.

As in the case of the Pentagram, from each re-entering angle of the Hexagram issueth a ray representing a radiation from the divine. Therefore it is called the Flaming Hexagram, or the six-rayed Signet Star. Usually, it is traced with the single point uppermost. It is not an evil symbol with the two points upward, and this is a point of difference from the Pentagram.

Now if thou dost draw the Hexagram to have by thee as a Symbol, thou shalt make it in the colours already taught and upon a black ground. These are the Planetary Powers allotted unto the Angles of the Hexagram.

		King Scale	Queen Scale
Unto the uppermost	♄	Indigo	Black
Unto the lowermost	☽	Blue	Puce
Unto the right hand upper	♃	Violet	Blue
Unto the right hand lower	♀	Green	Green
Unto the left hand upper	♂	Red	Red
Unto the left hand lower	☿	Yellow	Orange
In the center is the Sun	☉	Orange	Golden

The order of attribution is that of the Sephiroth on the Tree of Life. Hence ariseth the Supreme Ritual of the Hexagram according to the Angles from which it is traced.

The uppermost angle answereth also to **Daath** and the lowest to **Yesod**, and the other angles to the remaining angles of the Microprosopus. The Hexagram is composed of the two triangles of Fire and Water, and is therefore **not** traced in one continuous line like the Pentagram, but by each Triangle separately. (The exception to this is the use of Unicursal Hexagram, by means of which Hexagram is traced in one continuous line. This is demonstrated at considerable length at the end of this section.)

All the invoking Hexagrams follow the course of the Sun in their current, that is from left to right. But the banishing Hexagrams are traced from right to left from the same angle as their respective invoking Hexagrams contrary to the course of the Sun. The Hexagram of any particular Planet is traced in two Triangles, the first starting from the angle of the Planet, the second opposite to the commencing angle of the first. The Symbol of the Planet itself is then traced in the centre. Thus in the case of the invoking Hexagrams of Saturn, the first triangle is traced from the angle of Saturn, following the course of the Sun, the second triangle from the angle of the Moon.

(Only trace the central Planetary symbol in practice—the others shown on the diagram only for illustration.) Vibrate **Ararita** while tracing the Hexagram and divine Name of the Planet when tracing its symbol.

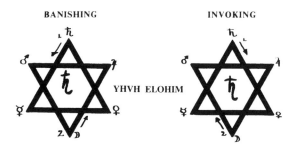

BANISHING   INVOKING

YHVH ELOHIM

15

But the invoking Hexagram of the Moon is first traced from the angle of the Moon, its second angle being traced from the triangle of Saturn.

The banishing Hexagram for Jupiter, for example, is traced from the same angle as the invoking Hexagram, and in the same order, but reversing the current's direction. In all cases the Symbol of the Planet should be traced in the centre.

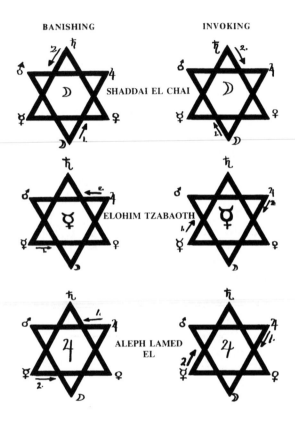

VOLUME FOUR

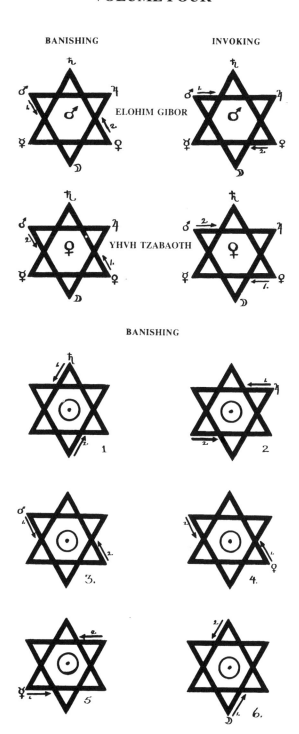

BANISHING   INVOKING

ELOHIM GIBOR

YHVH TZABAOTH

BANISHING

1

2

3.

4.

5

6.

YHVH ELOAH VE - DAATH

17

INVOKING

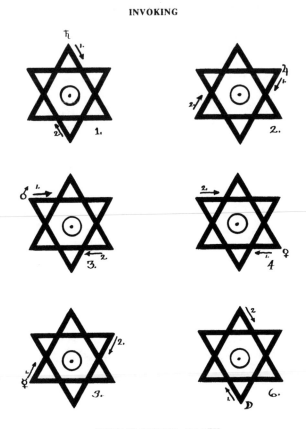

YHVH ELOAH VE - DAATH

(The divine Name here is so cumbersome and long, that I experimented some while ago with others attributed to SOL. Thus I began to use IAO with no diminution of solar effects. It is shorter and easier to use. I.R.)

(N.B. for the Hebrew spelling of all these Names, refer back to an early Knowledge Lecture. I.R.)

But for the Sun all six invoking Hexagrams of the Planets should be traced in their regular planetary order and the symbol of the Sun traced in the centre. And for his banishing hexagram also, all the six banishing hexagrams of the other Planets should be employed in their regular order, only that the symbol of the Sun should be traced therein. (Because all of this is so cumbersome the Unicursal Hexagram is of such great advantage. I.R.).

Remember that the symbol of Luna varieth, and as Moon in her increase she is favorable. But Moon is not so favourable for good in her decrease. The symbol of Luna in the centre of the Hexagram should be traced if in her increase; by the reverse in her decrease. Remember that the symbol in her decrease represents restriction and is not so good a symbol as the Moon in her increase. And at the full Moon exactly it is represented by a full circle but at new Moon a dark circle.

The last two forms of Luna are not good in many cases. If thou wilt invoke the Forces of the Head of the Dragon of the Moon thou shalt trace the lunar invoking Hexagram and write therein the symbol of Caput and for the tail Cauda. These Forces of Caput and Cauda are more easy to be invoked when either the Sun or the Moon is with them in the Zodiac in conjunction. In these invocations thou shalt pronounce the same Names and Letters as are given with the Lunar Hexagram. Caput is of a benevolent character, and Cauda of a malefic, save in a very few matters. And be thou well wary of dealing with these forces of Caput and Cauda or with those of Sol and Luna during the period of an eclipse, for they are the Powers of an eclipse. For an eclipse to take place both the Sun and Moon must be in conjunction with them in the Zodiac, these two luminaries being at the same time either in conjunction or opposition as regards each other.

In all Rituals of the Hexagram as in those of the Pentagram, thou shalt complete the circle of the place. Thou shalt not trace an external circle round each Hexagram itself unless thou wishest to confine the force to one place—as in charging a Symbol or Talisman.

From the attribution of the Planets, one to each angle of the Hexagram, shalt thou see the reason of the sympathy existing between each superior planet and one certain inferior Planet. That is, that to which it is exactly opposite in the Hexagram. And for this reason is it that the Triangle of their invoking and banishing Hexagrams counter-change. The superior Planets are Saturn, Jupiter, Mars. The inferior Planets are Venus, Mercury, Luna. And in the midst is placed the Fire of the Sun. Therefore the superior Saturn and the Inferior Luna are sympathetic, so are Jupiter and Mercury, Mars and Venus.

In the Supreme Ritual of the Hexagram the Signs of the Adeptus Minor Grade are to be given, but not those of the Grades of the First Order, notwithstanding these latter are made use of in the Supreme Ritual of the Pentagram. And because the Hexagram is the Signet Star of the Macrocosm or Greater World, therefore is it to be employed in all invocations of the Forces of the Sephiroth: though the Signet Star of the Pentagram represents their operation in the Luna World, in the Elements and in Man.

If thou wilt deal with the Forces of the Supernal Triad of the **Sephiroth**, thou shalt make use of the Hexagrams of Saturn; for **Chesed** those of Jupiter, for **Geburah** those of Mars; for **Tiphareth** those of the Sun, and for **Netzach** those of Venus, and for Hod those of Mercury, and for **Yesod** and **Malkuth** those of the Moon.

Know also that the **Sephiroth** are not to be invoked on every slight occasion, but only with due care and solemnity. Above all, the forces of **Kether** and **Chokmah** demand the greatest purity and solemnity of heart and mind in him who would penetrate their mysteries. For such high knowledge is only to be obtained by him whose Genius can stand in the Presence of the Holy Ones. See that thou usest the Divine Names with all reverence and humility for cursed is he that taketh the Name of the Vast One in vain.

When thou tracest the Symbol of a Planet in the centre of a Hexagram, thou shalt make the same of a proportionable size to the interior of the Hexagram, and thou shalt trace them from left to right generally following the course of the Sun as much as possible Caput and Cauda Draconis may follow the general rule.

When thou shalt invoke either the Forces of one particular Planet or those of them all, thou shalt turn thyself towards the Quarter of the Zodiac where the Planet thou invokest then is. For owing both to their constant motion in the Zodiac and to the daily movement of the same, the position of a Planet is continually changing, and therefore it is necessary for thee in such a case to erect an astrological chart of the position of the Planets in the heavens for the actual time of working, so that thou mayest see the direction of each Planet from thee. This is even more necessary when working with the Planets than with the signs of the Zodiac.

When thou shalt desire to purify or consecrate any place, thou shalt perform the Lesser Banishing Ritual of the Hexagram, either in conjunction with, or instead of that of the Pentagram, according to the circumstances of the case. For example, if thou hast been working on the plane of the Elements before, it will be well to perform the Lesser Ritual of the Pentagram before proceeding to thee work of a Planetary nature, so as thoroughly to clear the places of Forces which, although not hostile or evil of themselves, will yet not be in harmony with those of an altogether different Plane. And ever be sure that thou dost complete the circle of the place wherein thou workest.

THE FOUR FORMS

These are the four forms assumed by conjoining the two triangles of the Hexagram on which the Lesser Ritual of the Hexagram is based.

The first form is:

The angles are attributed as in the diagram. Its affinity is with the Eastern Quarter; the position of Fire in the Zodiac. (Note: To form these from the usual Hexagram, lower the inverted triangle, then reverse it by throwing the Lunar angle up to the top from being lowest. Mars and Jupiter do not change sides.)

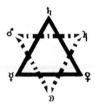

The second form is the ordinary Hexagram with the attribution of the angles as usual: the affinity being rather w ith the Southern Quarter, the position of Earth in the Zodiac, and of the Sun at his culmination at noon.

The third form is:

The angles are attributed as shown and its affinity is with the Western Quarter, the position of Air in the Zodiac.

The fourth form is:

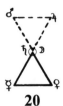

The angles are attributed as shown and its affinity is with the Northern Quarter, the position of Water in the Zodiac.

With each of these forms the Name **Ararita** is to be pronounced. Also as in the preceding cases there will be seven modes of tracing each of these four forms, according to the particular Planet with those Forces thou art working at the time.

The Hexagrams of Saturn may be used in general and comparatively unimportant operations, even as the Pentagram. In these four forms of the Hexagram thou shalt trace them beginning at the angle of the Planet under whose regimen thou art working, following the course of the Sun to invoke, and reversing the course to banish. That is to say, working from left to right for the former and from right to left for the latter. Remember always that the symbols of the Elements are not usually traced on Sigils but are replaced by the Kerubic Emblems of Aquarius., Leo, Taurus and the Eagle head.

THE LESSER RITUAL OF THE HEXAGRAM

Commence with the Qabalistic Sign of the Cross as in the Lesser Ritual of the Pentagram, and use what manner of Magical implement may be necessary according to the manner of working, either the Lotus Wand or the Magical Sword.

Stand facing East, If thou desirest to invoke thou shalt trace the figure thus:

Following the course of the Sun, from left to right and thou shalt pronounce the name **Ararita,** vibrating it as much as possible with thy breath and bringing the point of the Magical Implement to the center of the figure.

But if thou desirest to banish thou shalt trace it thus:

From right to left, and see that thou closest carefully the finishing angle of each triangle. Carry thy magical implement round to the South and if thou desirest to invoke trace the figure thus:

But if to banish then from left to right thus:

Bring as before the point of thy magical implement to the center and pronounce the Name **Ararita.**

Pass to the West, and trace the figure for invoking thus:

Banishing thus:

Then to the North, Invoking:

Banishing:

Then pass round again to the East so as to complete the circle of the place wherein thou standest, then give the LVX signs and repeat the analysis of the Pass-word INRI of the Adeptus Minor Grade.

VOLUME FOUR

ADDENDUM

Now in the Supreme Ritual of the Hexagram, when thou shalt wish to attract in addition to the forces of a Planet, those of a Sign of the Zodiac wherein he then is, thou shalt trace in the centre of the invoking Hexagram of the Planet, the Symbol of that Sign of the Zodiac beneath his own; and if this be not sufficient, thou shalt also trace the invoking Pentagram of the Sign as it is directed in the ritual of the Pentagram.

In the tracing of the Hexagram of any Planet thou shalt pronounce therewith in a vibratory manner as before taught, both the Divine Name of the Sephira which ruleth the Planet and the Seven-letterd Name **Ararita**, and also the particular letter of that Name which is referred to that particular Planet.

Now if thou shalt wish to invoke the forces of One particular Planet, thou shalt find in what Quarter of the heavens he will be situate at the time of working. Then thou shalt consecrate and guard the place wherein thou art by the Lesser Banishing Ritual of the Hexagram. Then thou shalt perform the Lesser Invoking Ritual of the Hexagram, yet tracing the four figures employed from the angle of the Planet required, seeing that for each Planet the mode of tracing varieth. If thou dealest with the Sun, thou shalt invoke by all six forms of the Figure and trace within them the Planet Symbol and pronounce the Name **Ararita** as has been taught.

Then shalt thou turn unto the quarter of the planet in the Heavens and shalt trace his invoking Hexagram and pronounce the proper Names, and invoke what Angels and Forces of that Nature may be required, and trace their Sigils in the air.

When thou hast finished thy invocation thou shalt in most cases license them to depart and perform the Banishing Symbols upon it which would have the effect of entirely de-charging it and reducing it to the condition it was in when first made—that is to say dead and lifeless.

If thou wishest to bring the Rays of all or several of the Planets into action at the same time, thou shalt discover their quarter in the Heavens for the time of working, and thou shalt trace the general Lesser Invoking Ritual of the Hexagram, but not.differentiated for any particular Planet, and then thou shalt turn to the Quarters of the respective Planets and invoke their forces as before laid down; and banish them when invocation is finished, and conclude with the Lesser Banishing Ritual of the Hexagram. And ever remember to complete the circle of the place wherein thou workest, following .the course of the sun.

N.B. The series of Hexagrams to invoke and banish Solar forces are repetitive, clumsy and tedious. Crowley had developed an Unicursal Hexagram to which all the regular traditional attributions could be made. I found later that this was not original with Crowley but could be found in the document on **Polygons and Polygrams.** In any event, it was a happy find. It is a great deal easier and less tedious in operation, and I first published these findings in *Ceremonial Magic* Aquarian Press, I am reproducing the attributions here, for I feel sure that the modern student does not wish to be bogged down by unnecessary traditional forms which can be replaced by a streamlining effect. I.R.

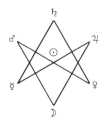

THE COMPLETE GOLDEN DAWN SYSTEM OF MAGIC

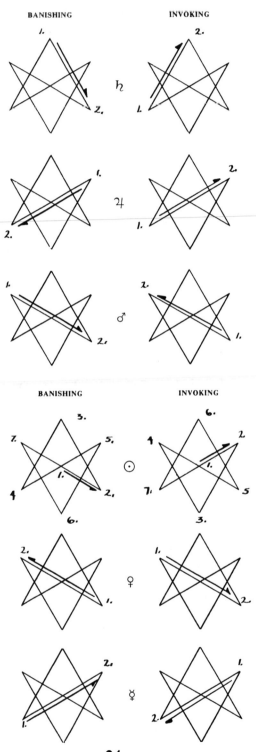

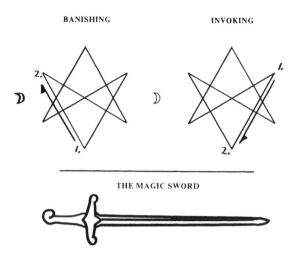

The following includes, Sword description, Use, Consecration, Mode of use, Caution. Need of reverence.

This is for general use in Banishing for defense against evil forces, and in certain invocations.

The Sword should be of medium length and weight.

Any convenient sword may be adapted for this use, the pattern of the hilt here given is not essential. But the handle, hilt and guard must be such as to offer surface suitable for inscriptions.

Pentagrams should be painted on salient portions because it is the lineal figure of GEBURAH.

The Divine and Angelic Names related to GEBURAH are then to be added and also their sigils taken from the Rose.

The Motto of the Adept is to be engraved upon it, or upon the hilt in letters of emerald green colour, in addition to the other mystic devices and Names.

The Blade should be clean and bright, and the hand hilt and guard should be painted bright scarlet. Upon this as a ground colour the inscriptions are to be added in emerald green.

The Sword has then to be consecrated in due form.

USE

It is to be used in all cases where great force and strength are to be used and are required, but principally for banishing and for defense against evil forces.

For this reason it is under the presidency of GEBURAH and of MARS. Thus their Names and forces are to be invoked at its consecration, which should take place on the Day and Hour of Mars, or used during the course of the Fiery Tattwa.

Here again let the Z.A.M. remember his Obligation never to use his knowledge of practical magic for purposes of evil. Let him be well assured that if he do this, notwithstanding his pledge, the evil he endeavours to bring about will react on himself, and that he will experience on his own person and in his own affairs that very thing which he has endeavoured to bring about for another.

So also may he perish and be blotted out from among us.

THE COMPLETE GOLDEN DAWN SYSTEM OF MAGIC

MODE OF USE

When it is desired to concentrate and to use the full force of the Sword, hold it thus. The pommel of the hilt rests in the palm of the hand, with the thumb and forefinger extended along the hilt, towards the guard.

CAUTION

Need of Reverence. Remember that there is hardly a circumstance in the Rituals, even of the First Order, which has not its special meaning and application, and which does not conceal a potent magical formula.

These ceremonies then have brought thee into contact with certain forces which thou hast now to learn how to awaken in thyself. And to this end, read, study and re-read what thou hast already received. Be not sure even after the lapse of much time, that thou hast yet fully discovered all that is to be learned from them.

To be of use unto thee, this must be the work of thine own inner Self—thine own, and not the work of another that so thou mayest gradually attain to the Knowledge of the Divine Ones.

CONSECRATION CEREMONY

Prepare the chamber, with a central Altar draped in black, with a red Cross, white Triangle, Rose and incense, Cup and water, Lamp, plate and salt, Rose Cross, consecrated Lotus Wand, white robe is desirable, the new Sword, Red cloak and Lamen.

Next: An Invocation to Mars and Geburah. An Astrological figure to show position of Mars at the time. In wording and formulating the Invocation to the Forces of Geburah, force and strength are to be specially requested.

1. Place the Sword upon Altar, hilt to East near Incense, point to West near Water.
2. Take up Lotus Wand near Water.
3. Stand at West of Altar, facing East.
4. Say, **Hekas Hekas Este Bebeloi.**
5. Take up Cup and purify with Water sprinkling to E. S. W. N.
6. Saying, **So therefore first the Priest who governeth the works of Fire must sprinkle with the Lustral Water of the loud resounding sea.**
7. Put down Cup on Altar.
8. Take up Incense and wave it as you pass round E. S. W. N.
9. Saying, **And when after all the Phantoms are vanished thou shalt see that holy and formless Fire, that Fire which darts and flashes through the hidden depths of the Universe, hear thou the voice of Fire.**
10. Put down Incense. Take up Wand.
11. Circumambulate with Sun three times, grasping Wand by white band. Return to West, face East, say Adoration:

Holy art Thou Lord of the Universe.
Holy art Thou Whom nature hath not Formed.
Holy art Thou the Vast and Mighty One.
Lord of the Light and of the Darkness.

12. Performing Lesser Invoking Ritual of the Hexagram of Mars, holding the Wand by White Band. Give Adeptus Minor Signs and analyse Key-Word.

13. Return to West of Altar.
14. Turn to face the direction in which you have found Mars to be standing so that the Altar is between yourself and Mars for convenience.
15. Describe in the Air the Invoking Pentagram of Sign Mars is in.
16. Describe Invoking Hexagram of Mars, saying: ELOHIM GIBOR. Then still holding Wand by White Band.
17. Recite your Invocation to the power of GEBURAH and the Forces of Mars, tracing the Sigil of each as you read it.

O Mighty Power who governeth GEBURAH, Thou strong and terrible Divine ELOHIM GIBOR. I beseech Thee to bestow upon this Magic Sword Power and Might to slay the evil and weakness I may encounter. In the Fiery Sphere of MADIM, strength and fidelity. May Thy Great Archangel KAMAEL bestow upon me courage wherewith to use it aright and may The Powerful Angels of the Order of SERAPHIM scorch with their flames the feebleness of purpose which would hinder my search for the True Light.

18. Then trace in the Air, slowly, above Sword, and as if standing upon it, the Invoking Hexagram of Mars. Do this with the Lotus end, still holding the White Band.
19. Next trace over the Sword the letters of the names in the invocation and their several Sigils.
20. Put down the Wand.
21. Take up the Cup and purify new Sword with Water, making Cross upon it; put down Cup.
22. Take up Incense and wave it over new Sword. Put down Incense.
23. Take up new Sword and with it perform the Lesser Invoking Ritual of the Hexagram and also trace the Invoking Hexagram of Mars, repeating ARARITA and ELOHIM GIBOR.
24. Lay down Sword.
25. With Cup purify Chamber as before.
26. With Incense purify as before.
27. Reverse circumambulation three times and say:
28. In the Name of YEHESHUAH, I now set free all Spirits that may have been imprisoned by this Ceremony.
29. Perform with the Sword the Lesser Banishing Ritual of Hexagram.
30. Perform Lesser Banishing Ritual of Pentagram.
31. Conclude with Qabalistic Cross.
32. Wrap up Sword, white or scarlet silk or linen. Henceforth no one else may touch it.

THE FOUR ELEMENTAL WEAPONS

These are the Tarot Symbols of the letters of the Divine Name YHVH and of the Elements, and have a certain bond and sympathy between them. So that if even one only is to be used, the others should also be present, even as each of the Four Elemental Tablets is divided in itself into Four Lesser Angles, representing the other three elements bound together therewith in the same tablet.

Therefore also let the Zelator Adeptus Minor remember that when he works with these forces, he is, as it were, dealing with the forces of the letters of the Divine Name, YHVH.

Each implement must be consecrated, and when this has been done by an Adeptus, no one else may touch it.

THE WAND OF FIRE

The Staff of the Wand should be of wood, rounded and smooth, and perforated from end to end, and within it should be placed a steel rod, just so long as to project an inch beyond each end of the wood rod.

It is often convenient to form the Wand from cane which has a natual hollow through it. If of cane there should be three natural lengths according to the knots, so that these knots may be placed similarly to the manner in which they are placed in the figure which is such as a turner would produce.

Eighteen inches is an extreme length. The magnet should be a strong one.

One end of the Wooden Rod should be cone-shaped. The North end of the magnet, (known by its repelling the so-called North Pole of a compass needle) should be placed at the end of the Wand which is plain.

The whole is coloured flame scarlet, and divided into 3 parts by Yellow bands.

The Cone shaped end has also painted upon its red surface three wavy flame-shaped YODS as ornaments; they are painted in bright yellow as in illustration.

The Divine and Angelic names of the Element Fire, should be there written in green paint along the Shaft and on the Cone.

Their sigils should be added with the Motto of the Adeptus. The green should be bright Emerald. The wand must then be consecrated.

The Wand is to be used in all workings of the Nature of Fire and under the Presidency of YOD and of the Wand of the Tarots. Sigils are not given. The Adeptus must work them out for himself.

THE DAGGER FOR AIR

Any convenient dagger or knife or sword may be adapted to this use, the shorter the better. The hilt, pommel and guard are to be coloured a bright pure yellow.

Upon this background, the divine and angelic names should then be written with purple or violet colour, together with their sigils from the Rose, and the motto of the Adeptus.

It is then ready for consecration.

When using the Air Dagger in ceremonial work, it may be held in the usual way of a dagger—or as a knife, or as described for the Wand or Sword.

It is to be used in all works of an Airy nature and under the presidency of VAU and the Sword of the Tarot.

VOLUME FOUR

Let there be no confusion between the magical Sword and the Air Dagger. They belong to different planes and any substitution of one for the other is **harmful.**

The magical Sword is under GEBURAH and is for strength and defense. The Air Dagger is for Air, for VAU of YHVH, and is to be used with the other three elemental weapons.

THE CUP FOR WATER

Any convenient clear glass Cup may be adapted for this use.

The bowl should somewhat resemble the shape of a crocus flower, and must show eight petals. Thus a smooth glass cup is acceptable, though if it has eight cuts or ridges it is preferable.

These petals must be coloured bright blue, neither too pale nor too dark. They must be edged with bright orange colour which must be clear and correct—an exact complement of the blue, adequate to produce a flashing.

The petals may be formed by paint or from coloured paper pasted on the glass. (This is not really practical. If water spills over the rim of the glass, it may spoil altogether the stuck-on-paper. Paint is by far the better medium. I.R.) The proper Divine and Angelic Names are then to be written upon the petals in orange colour, together with their Sigils from the Rose. Then add the motto of the Adeptus. The stem and base may be painted blue also—but there is no advantage in this.

The Cup must be consecrated by the appropriate ceremony.

When using the Cup, you may sprinkle with Water from the Cup in the required direction.

It is to be used in all workings of the nature of Water, under the presidency of the letter HEH and the Cup of the Tarot.

THE PANTACLE FOR EARTH

The Pantacle or Pentacle should be formed of a round disk of wood, of about six inches in diameter and from half to one inch in thickness, nicely polished, and truly circular and of even thickness.

There should be a circular white border, with a white Hexagram upon each face of the disk. The space within the white ring should be divided saltire-wise into four compartments by two diameters at right angles.

29

The four compartments are to be coloured:

The upper—Citrine—for the Airy part of Earth.
The right—Olive Green—for the Watery part of Earth.
The left—Russet Brown—for the Fiery part of Earth.
The lower—Black—for the Earthy part of Earth.

The Divine and Angelic names should be written in black within the white border, each name followed by its sigil taken from the Rose. Crosses may be placed after each Sigil. The motto of the Adept is to be added.

The Pantacle should be the same on both sides and should be held in the hand with the Citrine part upmost, unless there be some special reason for using one of the other compartments.

The Pantacle must then be consecrated by the appropriate ceremony.

It is to be used in all working of the nature of Earth, and under the presidency of HEH (final), and of the Pantacle of the Tarot.

RITUAL OF CONSECRATION OF THE
FOUR ELEMENTAL WEAPONS

(N.B. The Consecration Ceremony as described and given in the oldest papers of the Order are not very systematic and are rather disorderly. It remained for one of the products of the rebellion, the Stella Matutina, to organize this material and produce a systematic ritual. Whoever was responsible for this editing produced a splendid example of very fine editing and reorganization. I had nothing to do with it, though I would like to have said I did it. I.R.)

GENERAL NOTES ON THE CONSECRATION
OF THE FOUR IMPLEMENTS

The Adept is to be robed in White, wear his white sash, and Rose Cross.

Have on hand the Lotus Wand, Magic Sword and prepare the chamber as for Sword.

All four weapons should be present at once on altar, with all four symbols of the Elements.

Lay the Fire Wand near the Lamp, the Cup near the Water, the Dagger near the Incense and the Pantacle near the Salt.

Each Elemental Weapon must be consecrated at a time (24 minutes) when the Tattwa of the Element concerned is in course.

The consecration of each weapon is a separate ceremony although they may be done successively.

The opening ceremony and the closing ceremony will suffice for one or all, however, and need not be repeated if all are consecrated on one occasion.

The Tattwa period is found in practice to suffice for the 'Special Portion' of the ceremony.

Prepare for each Element by the Invocation to the King and the Six Seniors from the Elemental Tablets, according to the instructions laid down in the that section of this book dealing at length with Enochian System.

After consecration, each implement is to be wrapped up either in White silk or in silk of the colour proper to the Element.

NOTE OF V.H. FRATER N.O.M.

Before performing these four ceremonies it will be found wise to write out the complete form, including all pentagrams and other figures and sigils and invocations, using the notes here following as an outline. Otherwise, confusion will arise among Tablet names.

VOLUME FOUR

(With all due repect to the wisdom of G.H. Frater N.O.M. this advice is absolutely pernicious. By this time, the student or Z.A.M. should be so familiar with the basics through drills and repetition, that he has no need of writing out the above forms, etc. The advice given at the outset of this secton is still by far and away the most practical—unless the Z.A.M. is a pure nit-wit. I.R.)

THE RITUAL OF CONSECRATION

1. Take up the Lotus Wand by the Black portion, and say, **Hekas Hekas Este Bebeloi.** Put down the Wand and take up the Magic Sword and with it go to the East.
2. Perform the Lesser Banishing Ritual of the Pentagram.
3. Lay down Sword, and purify with Water, saying, **So therefore first the Priest who governeth the works of Fire must sprinkle with the Lustral Water of the loud-resounding Sea.**
4. Consecrate with Fire, saying, **And when, after all the Phantoms are banished, thou shalt see that Holy formless Fire, that Fire which darts and flashes through the hidden depths of the Universe, hear thou the Voice of Fire.**
5. Take up the Lotus Wand by White portion.
6. Circumambulate with the Sun three times.
7. Repeat the Adoration, salute with the Neophyte Sign each time.

Holy art Thou, Lord of the Universe.
Holy art Thou, whom Nature hath not Formed.
Holy art Thou, the Vast and the Mighty One.
Lord of the Light and of the Darkness.

8. Varying with each Implement on different days, or 20 minutes between each commencement, according to Tattwas, perform Supreme Invoking Ritual of the Pentagram of the particular elemental Implement with Lotus Wand, holding it by apropriate band of the Kerubic Figure.
9. With the Lotus Wand in hand, and standing by the Altar and facing the Quarter of the Element whose Implement you are consecrating, describe in the Air over the Implement, as if standing upon it, the Invoking Pentagram of that Implement.
10. Invoke the Divine and Angelic Names already graven upon the Implement, making their letters and Sigils in the Air, over the Implement with the Lotus Wand.

O Thou, Who art from everlasting, Thou Who hast created all things, and doth clothe Thyself with the Forces of Nature as with a garment, by Thy Holy and Divine Name, (For Pentacle vibrate Adonai, For Dagger vibrate Yhvh, For Cup vibrate El, For Wand vibrate Elohim) whereby Thou art known especially in that Quarter we name (For Pentacle and Earth vibrate Tzaphon for the North, For Dagger and Air vibrate Mizrach for the East, For Cup and Water vibrate Mearab for the West, For Wand and Fire vibrate Darom for the South).

I beseech Thee to grant unto me strength and insight for my search after the Hidden Light and Wisdom. I entreat Thee to cause Thy Wonderful Archangel (For Pentacle vibrate AURIEL Who governeth the works of Earth, For Dagger vibrate RAPHIEL Who governeth the works of Air, For Cup vibrate GABRIEL Who governeth the works of Water, For Wand vibrate MICHAEL Who governeth

the works of Fire) to guide me in the Pathway; and furthermore to direct Thine Angel (For Pentacle vibrate PHORLAKH, For Dagger vibrate CHASSAN, For Cup vibrate TALIAHAD, For Wand vibrate ARAL) To watch over my footsteps therein.

May the Ruler of (name element) the Powerful Prince (For Pentacle and Earth vibrate KERUB, For Dagger and Air vibrate ARIEL, For Cup and Water vibrate TH ARSIS, For Wand and Fire vibrate SERAPH) by gracious permission of the Infinite Supreme, increase and strengthen the hidden forces and occult virtues of this (name implement) so that I may be enabled with it to perform aright those Magical operations, for which it has been fashioned. For which purpose I now perform this mystic rite of Consecration in the Divine Presence of (For Pentacle vibrate ADONAI, For Dagger vibrate YHVH, For Cup vibrate EL, For Wand vibrate ELOHIM).

11. Lay aside the Lotus Wand.
12. Take up the Magic Sword, and read the Invocation to the King, tracing in the Air the Invoking Pentagram of the Element.

In the Three Great Secret Holy Names of God borne upon the Banners of the, (For Pentacle and Earth—North vibrate EMOR DIAL HECTEG A, For Dagger and Air — East vibrate ORO IBAH AOZPI, For Cup and Water - West vibrate EMPEH ARSEL GAIOL, For Wand and Fire—South vibrate OIP TEAA PEDOCE).

I summon Thee, Thou Great King of the, (For Pentacle—North vibrate IC ZOD HEH CHAL, For Dagger—East vibrate BATAIVAH, For Cup—West vibrate RA AGIOSEL, For Wand—South vibrate EDEL PERNAA) to attend upon this Ceremony and by Thy presence increase its effect, whereby I do now consecrate this Magical (name implement). Confer upon it the utmost occult might and virtue of which Thou mayest judge it to be capable in all works of the nature of (name implement) so that in it I may find a strong defense and a powerful weapon wherewith to rule and direct the Spirits of the Elements.

13. Still with the Sword, trace in the Air over the Implement the Hexagram of Saturn, and read the Invocation to the Six Seniors.

Ye Mighty Princes of the (name Quadrant) Quadrangle, I invoke you who are known to me by the honourable title, and position of rank, of Seniors. Hear my petition, ye mighty Princes, the Six Seniors of the (same point) quarter of the Earth who bear the names of, (For Earth - LAIDROM ALPHCTGA ACZINOR AHMLLICV LZINOPO LIIANSA, For Air - HABIORO AHAOZPI AAOZAIF AVTOTAR HTMORDA HIPOTGA, For Water - LSRAHPM SLGAIOL SAIINOR SONIZNT LAOAXRP LIGDISA, For Fire - AAETPOI AAPDOCE ADOEOET ANODOIN ALNDVOD ARINNAP) and be this day present with me. Bestow upon this (name weapon) the Strength and purity whereof ye are Masters in the Elemental Forces which ye control; that its outward and material form may remain a true symbol of the inward and spiritual force.

14. Then read the Invocations of the Angels governing the Four Lesser Angles. During each, make the Invoking Pentagram of the Element whose implement is being consecrated, Cup, Wand, Dagger, or Pentacle, according to which lesser angle is in process, making the Pentagram in the air immediately over the Implement with the Sword.

FIRE WAND

Lesser Angle of Fire. O Thou Mighty Angel Bziza who art Ruler and President over the Four Angels of the Fiery Lesser Quadrangle of Fire, I invoke Thee to impress into this weapon the force and fiery energy of Thy Kingdom and Servants, that by it I may control them for all just and righteous purposes.

With the Sword, trace invoking Fire Pentagram with Lion Kerub. Lesser Angle of Water. **O Thou Mighty Angel Banaa, Ruler and President over the Four Angels of fluid Fire, I beseech Thee to impress into this weapon Thy magic power that by it I may control the Spirits who serve Thee for all just and righteous purposes.**

With the Cup trace the Invoking Fire Pentagram.

Lesser Angle of Air. **O Thou Mighty Angel Bdopa, Ruler and President over the Four Angels and Governors of the subtle and aspiring Etheric Fire, I beseech Thee to bestow upon this weapon Thy strength and fiery steadfastness, that with it I may control the Spirits of Thy Realm for all just and righteous purposes.**

Trace Invoking Fire Pentagram with the Dagger.

Lesser Angle of Earth. **O Thou Mighty Angel Bpsac, who art Ruler and President over the Four Angels of the denser Fire of Earth, I beseech Thee to bestow upon this weapon Thy strength and fiery steadfastness that with it I may control the Spirits of Thy realm for all just and righteous purposes.**

Trace Invoking Fire Pentagram with Pentacle.

WATER CUP

Lesser Angle of Fire. **O Thou Powerful Angel Hnlrx, Thou who are Lord and Ruler over the Fiery Waters, I beseech Thee to endue this Cup with the Magic Powers of which Thou art Lord, that I may with its aid direct the Spirits who serve Thee in purity and singleness of aim.**

With Wand trace invoking Water Pentagram with Eagle Kerub.

Lesser Angle of Water. **O Thou Powerful Angel Htdim, Thou who art Lord and Ruler over the pure and fluid Element of Water, I beseech Thee to endue this Cup with the Magic Powers of which Thou art Lord, that I may with its aid direct the Spirits who serve Thee in purity and singleness of aim.**

With Sword trace invoking Water Pentagram.

Lesser Angle of Air. **O Thou Powerful Angel Htaad, Thou who art Lord and Ruler of the Etheric and Airy Qualities of Water, I beseech Thee to endue this Cup with the Magic Powers of which Thou art Lord, that I may with its aid direct the Spirits who serve Thee in purity and singleness of aim.**

With Dagger trace invoking Water Pentagram.

Lesser Angle of Earth. **O Thou Powerful Angel HmagI, Thou who art Lord and Ruler of the more dense and solid qualities of Water, I beseeh Thee to endue this Cup with the Magic Powers of which Thou art Lord, that with its aid I may direct the Spirits who serve Thee in purity and singleness of aim.**

With Pentacle trace invoking Water Pentagram.

AIR DAGGER

Lesser Angle of Fire. **O Thou Resplendent Angel Exgsd, Thou who governest the Fiery Realms of Air, I conjure Thee to confer upon this Dagger, Thy mysterious and magical Powers, that I thereby may control the Spirits who serve Thee for such purposes as be pure and upright.**

With the Wand trace invoking Air Pentagram with Aquarius as Kerubic emblem.

Lesser Angle of Water. **O Thou Resplendent Angel Eytpa, Thou who governest the Realms of Fluid Air, I conjure Thee to confer upon this Dagger, Thy Mysterious Powers that by its aid I may control the Spirits who serve Thee for such purposes as be pure and upright.**

With the Cup trace invoking Air Pentagram.

Lesser Angle of Air. **O Thou Resplendent Angel Erzla, Thou who rulest the Realms of Pure and Permeating Air, I conjure Thee to confer upon this Dagger the Magic Power of which Thou art Master, whereby I may control the Spirits who serve Thee, for such purposes as be pure and upright.**

With the Sword trace invoking Air Pentagram.

Lesser Angle of Earth. **O Thou Resplendent Angel Etnbr, Thou who rulest the Denser Realms of Air symbolised by the Lesser Angle of Earth, I conjure Thee to confer upon this Dagger the Magic Powers of which Thou art Master, whereby I may control the spirits who serve Thee, for such purposes as be pure and upright.**

With the Pentacle trace invoking Air Pentagram.

EARTH PENTACLE

Lesser Angle of Fire. **O Thou Glorious Angel Naaom, Thou who governest the Fiery essences of Earth, I invoke Thee to bestow upon this Pentacle the Magic Powers of which thou art Sovereign, that by its help I may govern the Spirits of Whom Thou art Lord, in all seriousness and steadfastness.**

With Wand over Russet part trace invoking Earth Pentagram with Taurus Kerub.

Lesser Angle of Water. **O Thou Glorious Angel Nphra, Thou who governest the moist and fluid essences of Earth. I invoke Thee to bestow upon this Pentacle the Magic Powers of which Thou art Sovereign that by its help I may govern the Spirits, of whom Thou art Lord, in all seriousness and steadfastness.**

With Cup over Olive part, trace invoking Earth Pentagram.

Lesser Angle of Air. **O Thou Glorious Angel Nboza, Thou who governest the Airy and Delicate Essense of Earth, I invoke Thee to bestow upon this Pentacle the Magic Powers of which Thou art Master, that with its help I may govern the spirits of whom Thou art Lord, in all seriousness and steadfastness.**

With Dagger over Citrine part, trace invoking Earth Pentagram.

Lesser Angle of Earth. **O Thou Glorious Angel Nroam, Thou who governest the dense and solid Earth, I invoke Thee to bestow upon this Pentacle the Magic Powers of which Thou art Master, that with its help I may govern the spirits of whom Thou art Lord, in all seriousness and steadfastness.**

With Sword over Black part, trace invoking Earth Pentagram.

15. Then take up the newly consecrated Implement and perform with it the Supreme Invoking Ritual of the Pentagram of its Element in the Four Quarters, preceding each Pentagram with the Equilibriating Pentagram suitable. Close with Qabalistic Cross and Prayer. When completed each Implement is to be wrapped in silk or linen, white, or suitable colour.
16. Purify with Water, repeating verse as in opening.
17. Consecrate with Fire, repeating the verse as in opening.
18. Reverse Circumambulation.
19. Stand at West of Altar, and say, **In the name of YEHESHUAH, I now set free any Spirits that may have been imprisoned by this ceremony.**
20. Perform the Lesser Banishing Ritual of Pentagram in four Quarters.
21. If preferred, the Supreme Banishing Ritual of Pentagram of special element, if one or two or three Implements have been consecrated and not all four at same ceremony.

VOLUME FOUR

DIAGRAM OF THE LOTUS WAND

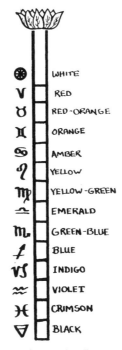

⊛	WHITE
♈	RED
♉	RED-ORANGE
♊	ORANGE
♋	AMBER
♌	YELLOW
♍	YELLOW-GREEN
♎	EMERALD
♏	GREEN-BLUE
♐	BLUE
♑	INDIGO
♒	VIOLET
♓	CRIMSON
▽	BLACK

THE LOTUS WAND
(For The Zelator Adeptus Minor Grade)

This is for general use in Magical Working. It is to be carried by the Z.A.M. at all meetings of the Second Order at which he has the right to attend.

1. It is to be made by himself unassisted.
2. Consecrated by himself.
3. Used by himself alone.
4. Untouched by any other person.
5. Kept wrapped in white silk or linen.

It will thus be free from external influences other than his own, on the human plane.

The Wand has the upper end white; the lower is black, and between there are 12 colours referring to the 12 zodiacal signs in the positive and masculine scale of colour. At the upper end of the white is fixed a Lotus Flower in three whorls of 26 petals; the outer 8, the middle 8, and the inner 10 petals. The Calyx has 4 lobes or sepals of orange color. The flower centre is orange. The wand should be from 24 to 40 inches long, of wood about an inch in diameter. See next page for definition of XX.

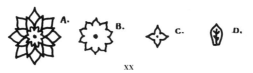

A.   B.   C.   D.

XX

35

The bands of white, twelve colours, and black, may be painted or enamelled, or formed of coloured papers gummed on. The lengths of the band should be such that the white is longest, then the black, then the twelve colours in length. The colours must be clean, brilliant and correct.

They are as follows:

White

Aries	Red
Taurus	Red-Orange
Gemini	Orange
Cancer	Amber
Leo	Lemon Yellow
Virgo	Yellow Green
Libra	Emerald
Scorpio	Greenish-Blue
Sagittarius	Bright Blue
Capricorn	Indigo
Aquarius	Violet
Pisces	Crimson

Black

The Lotus Flower may be of metal or cardboard, in three whorls of 8, 8, and 10 petals, white internally, with the tips curved inward a little. Outside, the petals should be olive green with five markings, as shown in diagram.

The flower centre should be of orange colour, or a brass bolt to keep all together will serve the same purpose.

On the white portion of the wand the owner's motto may be inscribed.

THE SYMBOLISM AND USE OF THE LOTUS WAND

As a general rule use the White end in Invocation but use the black end to Banish. The white end may be used to banish by tracing a banishing symbol against an evil and opposing force which has resisted other efforts.

By this is meant, that by whatever band you are holding the wand, whether by white for spiritual things, black for mundane, blue for Sagittarius, red for fiery triplicity etc. you are when invoking to direct the white band externally to the quarter desired. When banishing to point the black or lowest end to the quarter. But the Wand is **never** to be inverted. So when very material forces are concerned, the black end may be most suitable for invocation, but with the greatest caution.

In working on the Plane of the Zodiac, hold the wand by the portion you refer to between the thumb and two fingers. If a planetary working be required, hold the wand by the portion representing the day or night-house of the planet, or else by the Sign in which the Planet is at the time.

PLANET	DAY-HOUSE	NIGHT-HOUSE
Saturn	Capricorn	Aquarius
Jupiter	Sagittarius	Pisces
Mars	Aries	Scorpio
Venus	Libra	Taurus
Mercury	Gemini	Virgo
Sun	Leo only	
Moon		Cancer only

Should the action be with the elements, one of the signs of the triplicity of that element should be held according to the nature of the elements intended to be invoked.

Thus bearing in mind that the Kerubic Emblem is the most powerful action of the element in the triplicity.

Leo-violent heat of summer.
Aries-beginning of warmth of spring.
Sagittarius-waning of heat in autumn.

Hold the Wand by the White portion for all Divine or Spiritual matters, or for Sephirotic influences, and for all the processes of Rising on the Planes.

Hold the wand by the black part only for material and mundane affairs.

The ten upper and inner petals refer to the purity of the ten Sephiroth. The middle 8 refer to the counter-charged natural and spiritual forces of fire and air. The lowest and outer 8 refer to the powers of earth and water. The central amber portion refers to the Spiritual Sun. The outer calyx of four orange petals shows the action of the Sun upon the elements perfecting the life of things by differentiation.

THE WAND SHOULD NEVER BE USED INVERTED

The Lotus Flower is not to be touched in working. In Sephirotic and Spiritual things however the flower is to be inclined towards the forehead. To rise in the planes the orange coloured centre is to be fully directed to the forehead.

CONSECRATION OF A LOTUS WAND

First provide:
1. **A private room**
2. **A white triangle**
3. **A red cross of six squares**
4. **Incense and a rose**
5. **Lamp, or a vessel of Fire**
6. **Water in a vase**
7. **Salt on a platter**
8. **Astrologic figure of the heavens for the time of consecration.**
9. **Ritual of the Pentagram**
10. **The new Wand**
11. **White linen or silk wrapper**
12. **A table for an altar with**
13. **Black cover and drapery.**

Second, find the position of the East.

Third, prepare an invocation of the forces of the Sign of the Zodiac.

Fourth, place the Altar in the middle of the room, cover and drape it with a black cloth.

Fifth, arrange upon it the Cross and Triangle, the Water at the base of the triangle, the Incense and Rose in the East above the Cross, the Lamp at the South.

Sixth, illumine the Lamp.

Seventh, stand holding the Wand at the West of the Altar facing the East.

Eighth, grasp the Wand by the Black portion and

Ninth, say '**Hekas, Hekas, este Bebeloi.**'

Tenth, perform the Lesser Banishing Ritual of the Pentagram.

Eleventh, deposit the wand upon the Altar.

Twelfth, light the Incense from the Lamp.

Thirteenth, sprinkle some Salt into the Water

Fourteenth, purify the room, first with water, and then with fire, as in the Neophyte grade, repeating as you do so these two passages from the ritual of the 31st Path: With water: So therefore first the Priest who governeth the works of fire, must sprinkle with the lustral waters of the loud resounding sea.

Fifteenth, with fire: And when after all the phantoms are banished thou shalt see that holy and formless five, that fire which darts and flashes through the hidden depths of the Universe, hear thou the Voice of Fire.

Take up the Wand again by the white portion, circumambulate the room three times and at West, facing East repeat the adoration.

Holy art Thou, Lord of the Universe!
Holy art Thou whom Nature hath not formed!
Holy art Thou! the Vast and Mighty One!
Lord of the Light and of the Darkness!

Sixteenth, perform the Supreme Invoking Ritual of the Pentagram at the four quarters of the room, tracing the proper pentagram at each quarter.

Seventeenth, stand then in the Eastern Quarter; face the East; hold the Wand by the white portion; give the sign of Adeptus Minor. Look upward, hold the Wand on high and say:

O Harpocrates, Lord of Silence, who art enthroned upon the Lotus. Twenty-six are the Petals of the Lotus Flower of the Wand. O Lord of Creation! They are the number of Thy Name. In the name of YHVH let the Divine Light descend.

Eighteenth, facing consecutively the quarter where each Sign is, repeat in each of the 12 directions the Invocation which follows, using the appropriate Divine and Angelic Names and Letters for each special Sign. Begin with Aries. Hold the wand at the appropriate coloured part, and in left hand the element from off the altar which is referred to the Sign and say:

(For Aries) The Heaven is above and the earth is beneath, and between the Light and Darkness the Colours vibrate.

THE INVOCATION TO THE FORCES OF THE SIGNS OF THE ZODIAC

Sign	Item	Permutation Of Name	Hebrew Letter	Tribe of Israel	Angel	Color
Aries	Lamp	YHVH	Heh	Gad	Malchidael	Red
Taurus	Salt	YHHV	Vau	Ephraim	Asmodel	Red-orange
Gemini	Rose	YVHH	Zayin	Manasseh	Ambriel	Orange
Cancer	Cup	YVHY	Cheth	Issachar	Muriel	Amber
Leo	Lamp	HVYH	Teth	Judah	Verchiel	Lemon-yellow
Virgo	Salt	HHVY	Yod	Naphthali	Hamaliel	Yellow-green
Libra	Rose	VHYH	Lamed	Asshur	Zuriel	Green
Scorpio	Cup	VHHY	Nun	Dan	Barchiel	Green-blue
Sagittarius	Lamp	VYHH	Samech	Benjamin	Advachiel	Blue
Capricorn	Salt	HYHV	Ayin	Zebulun	Hanael	Indigo
Aquarius	Rose	HYVH	Tzaddi	Reuben	Cambriel	Violet
Pisces	Cup	HHYV	Qoph	Simeon	Amnixiel	Crimson

39

THE COMPLETE GOLDEN DAWN SYSTEM OF MAGIC

I supplicate the powers and forces governing the realm and place and authority of the Sign Aries by the Majesty of the Divine name YHVH with which in earth life and language I ascribe the letter Heh, to which is allotted the Symbolic tribe of Gad, and over which is the Angel Malchidael, to bestow this present day and hour and confirm their mystic and potent influence upon the Red band of this Lotus Wand, which I hereby dedicate to purity and to occult work. May its grasp strengthen me in the work of the character of Aries and his attributes.

Nineteen, as this is recited, trace in the air with the Lotus end the invoking Pentagram of the Sign required, and hold the corresponding element from the Altar in the left hand, while facing in each of the 12 Zodiacal directions.

Twenty, then lay the wand on the Altar, the Lotus pointing towards the East. Stand on the West side of the Altar, face the East and say:

O Isis! Great Goddess of the Forces of Nature, let Thine influence descend and consecrate this Wand which I dedicate to Thee for the performance of the works of the Magic of Light.

Twenty-first, wrap up the Wand in silk or linen.

Twenty-second, purify the room by Water and by Fire as at the first, then performing the reverse circumambulation.

Twenty-third, standing at the West of the Altar, face the East and recite:

In the Name of Yeheshuah I now set free any Spirits that may have been imprisoned by this Ceremony.

Preferably perform the Lesser Banishing Ritual of the Pentagram.

THE DESCRIPTION OF THE ROSE CROSS

Rays—White with black letters and symbols.
Air—yellow ground purple Pentagram and symbols.
Fire—scarlet ground Emerald Pentagram and symbols.
Water—blue ground Orange Pentagram and symbols.
White ground—Black Hexagram and symbols.
Earth—Citrine, Russet, Olive, Black, White Pentagram and symbols.

ROSE CROSS

The Rose and Cross is for general use in magical working and is to be worn by the Zelator Adeptus Minor at all meetings of the Second Order at which he has the right to be present.

It should be suspended from a yellow silk collarette or ribbon. It is to be made and consecrated by him unassisted and when not in use should be wrapped in white silk or linen. Like the Lotus Wand, it should not be touched by another person after consecration, only by its owner.

It is a complete synthesis of the Positive, Masculine, or Rainbow Scale of Colour attribution, the 'Scale of the King,' as it is called. These colours may be found in a Knowledge Lecture. The four ends are attributed to the Elements, the white portion to the Spirit and to the Planets, the 22 petals of the Rose to the 22 paths. It is the Cross in Tiphareth, the receptacle and centre of the forces of the Sephiroth and the Paths. The extreme centre of the Rose is White, the reflected spiritual brightness of Kether, bearing upon it the Red Rose and Golden Cross from which the second Order takes its name; the symbols of the rescuing force.

Around the Hexagram on the white part, below the Rose, are placed the planets in the order which is the Key of the Supreme Ritual of the Hexagram. Around the Pentagrams are the symbols of the Spirit and the four Elements in the order which is the Key of the Supreme Ritual of the Pentagram. In each of the floreated ends of the Cross itself are arranged the three Alchemical principles, but in different order in each element, and as showing their operation therein.

The uppermost arm of the Cross allotted to Air, is of the yellow colour of Tiphareth. In it the flowing philosophic mercurial nature is chief and without hindrance to its mobility, hence the ever moving nature of Air. Its Sulphurous side is drawn from the part of Fire whence its luminous and electrical qualities. Its Saline from the Water, whence clouds and rains, from the action of the Solar forces.

The lowest arm of the Cross allotted to Earth is of the four colours of Malkuth, the Earth being of the nature of a container and receiver of the other influences. The Citrine answers to its airy part; the Olive to the watery; the Russet to the fiery part; and the Black to the lowest part, earthy of the Earth.

Here is also the Mercurial part chief, but hindered by the compound nature, whence its faculty becomes germinative, rather than mobile. While the Sulphur and the Salt are respectively from the sides of Water and Fire, which almost neutralize their natural operation and bring about the fixedness and immobility of Earth.

The extremity allotted to fire is of the scarlet colour of GEBURAH, and in it the Sulphurous nature is chief, whence its powers of heat and burning. The Salt is from the side of water, whence the necessity for a constant substantial pabulum whereon to act; and the Mercury is from the side of Air, whence the leaping, lambent motion of flame especially when acted on by wind.

The extremity allotted to Water is of the blue color of CHESED and in it the Salt nature is chief as exemplified in the Salt nature of the Ocean, to which all waters go; and thence also is derived the nature of always preserving the horizontal line. The Mercury is from Earth whence the weight and force of its flux and reflux. Its Sulphur part is from the Air whence the effects of waves and storms; so that the dispositions of these three principles form the key of their alchemical operation in the elements.

The white rays issuing from behind the Rose at the inner angles between the arms, are the rays of the Divine light issuing and corruscating from the reflected light of Kether in its centre. The letters and symbols on them refer to the analysis of the Key Word of an Adeptus Minor.

I. N. R. I.

The above is the means by which the opening of the Vault is accomplished. Its associations are as follows:

The first I is attributed to Virgo, as well as L in (LVX), the letter N is attributed to Scorpio, as well as V in (LVX), the letter R is attributed to the Sun, as well as X in (LVX), the final I merely repeats some of the attributions.

The Twelve letters of the 12 outer petals follow the order of the Signs of the Zodiac.

HEH that is Aries being uppermost.

LAMED which is Libra being lowest.

The Seven Double letters of the middle row are allotted to the Planets in order of their exaltations, the planets being wanderers, and the stars fixed with respect to the Earth.

THE SEVEN DOUBLE LETTERS ON THE ROSE

7	Tau	Saturn
6	Resh	Sun
5	Peh	Mars
4	Kaph	Jupiter
3	Daleth	Venus
2	Gimel	Moon
1	Beth	Mercury

The Three Mother Letters are allotted to the Elements, and are so arranged that the petal of Air should be beneath the arm of the Cross allotted to Air. While those of Fire and Water are on counterchanged sides so that the forces of the arms of the Cross should not too much over rule the Planetary and Zodiacal forces in the Rose, which might otherwise be the case were the petal of Fire placed on the same side as the arm of Fire, and that of Water on the arm of water.

The mode of Sigil formation from the Rose petals is taught in another place in this volume.

The back of the Cross bears inscriptions as shown as follows:

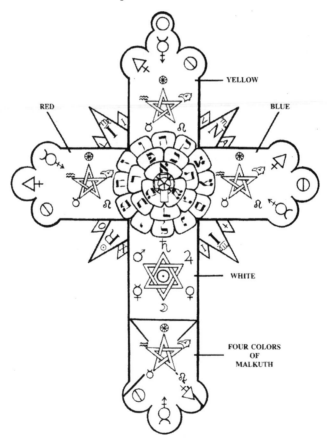

THE GOLDEN DAWN ROSE CROSS

VOLUME FOUR

At the top is written in Latin: 'The Master Jesus Christ, God and Man,' between four Maltese crosses, Which represent the four pyramids of the Elements opened out.

This is placed at the uppermost part because here is affirmed the descent of the Divine Force into Tiphareth, which is the central point between Supernals and Inferiors. But at the lowest part is written the Motto of the Zelator Adeptus Minor, because therein is the affirmation of the elevation of the Human into the Divine.

But this is impossible without the assistance of the Divine Spirit from Kether, whence the space above Malkuth is white upon the front aspect of the Cross—white being the Symbol of the Spiritual rescuing from the material.

In the centre, between the symbols of the Alchemical Principles of which the outermost is Sulphur, the purgational fire of suffering and self-sacrifice is written in Latin: 'Blessed be the Lord our God who hath given us the Symbol SIGNUM' and this is a word of six letters, thus representing the six periods (creative) in the Universe. And the Regimen of the Planets necessary ere the Glory of the Sun can be obtained.

S.R.M.D.'s NOTE OF MAKING THE ROSE CROSS

The Cross may be cut out of cardboard and the coloured portions may be painted or formed by pasting on portions of coloured paper of the required shape. **The colours must be correct and clear and brilliant.** If they are not the symbol is useless either as a Symbol or Insignium. **Actually evil effects may follow if the colours are not clear and brilliant or if they are dirty. If this occurs, the whole should be destroyed,** for faulty colours and shapes in Divine Symbols are a degradation of Divine Things and are practical blasphemy, because it is substituting the evil and disorderly for the good.

For the petals, one pattern may be designed and several cut at once from it, superimposing several coloured papers.

No dimensions are officially given for the Rose Cross but pragmatism dictates that it should be about 7-8 inches in length.

CONSECRATION OF THE ROSE CROSS

1. Prepare the chamber, and the invocation of Tiphareth.
2. Arrange a central altar, draped in black.
3. Place on it the Triangle and Cross as in the Neophyte Grade.
4. Place on it the Rose, Cup, Salt, and Fire, but place Cup between the Cross and Triangle as in the Neophyte Grade, with the Rose and incense at the East side.
5. Place the new Rose Cross **upon the Triangle.**
6. Stand at the West side of the Altar and have thy Lotus Wand (consecrated) with thee.
7. Illumine the Lamp and incense, and drop salt into the water.
8. Take the Wand in the right hand.
9. Repeat: **Hekas, Hekas, este Bebeloi.**
10. Perform the lesser Banishing Ritual of the Pentagram.
11. Perform the lesser Banishing Ritual of the Hexagram.
12. Deposit the Wand upon the Altar.
13. Purify the chamber with Water in the four quarters.
    So therefore first the Priest who governeth the works of fire must sprinkle with the lustral water of the loud resounding sea.
14. Purify the chamber with Fire in the four quarters repeating: **When after all the phantoms are banished thou shalt see that holy and formless fire, that fire**

which darts and flashes through the hidden depths of the Universe, hear thou the Voice of Fire.

15. Take up the Wand.
16. Circumambulate with the Sun three times.
17. Return to place and repeat the Adorations:

Holy art Thou, Lord of the Universe!
Holy art Thou, Whom Nature hath not formed!
Holy art Thou, the Vast and Mighty One!
Lord of Light and of the Darkness!"

Give sign of Neophyte at each adoration and sign of Silence at close.

18. Perform the Supreme Invoking Ritual of the Pentagram at the Four quarters of the Chamber.
19. Stand West of the Altar, facing East, hold the Wand by the White part.
20. Make over the Rose Cross, in the Air with the Lotus wand and as if standing in the centre of the Rose, the symbol and invoke all the Divine and Angelic Names of the Tiphareth by a special form as follows:

Thou most sublime Majesty on high, who art at certain seasons worthily represented by the Glorious Sun of Tiphareth. I beseech Thee to bestow upon this symbol of the Rose and Cross, which I have formed in Thy honour, and for the furtherance of the Great Work in a spirit of purity and love, the most excellent virtues by the divine name of YHVH, and the great name of ELOAH VE DAATH. Deign I beseech thee to grant that the great Archangel RAPHAEL and the mighty angel MICHAEL may strengthen this emblem, and through the sphere of the splendid orb of SHEMESH may confer upon it such power and virtue as to lead me by it towards the solution of the great Secret. [Raising the hand and eyes to Heaven during the Prayer and covering them as you finish it.]

21. Repeat these words from Genesis:

And a river NAHAR went forth out of Eden to water the Garden, and from thence it was parted and came into four heads.

22. Describe over the white portion the invoking Hexagrams of the planets as if standing upon it, repeating the necessary names and holding the Wand by the white portion.
23. Describe the equilibriating Pentagrams of Spirit, and the words **EXARP—BITOM—HCOMA—NANTA** as previously laid down.
24. Then over the four coloured portions (arms) in turn describe the Invoking Pentagrams of each Element, using the Words and Grade Signs and repeating the verse of Genesis II, 11-13, 14, 15 referring to each. Holding the wand by the part allotted to the Kerubic sign of the Element.

First - over the red Fire arm, read, **And the name of the First River is PISON; it is that which encompasseth the whole land of HAVILAH where there is Gold, and the Gold of that land is good; there is bdellium and the onyx stone.** Make invoking Fire pentagram holding the wand by Leo, with the Sign of Fire grade.

Second - over the blue Water arm read, (Hold by Scorpio-Blue Green) **And the name of the second River is Gihon, the same as that which compasseth the whole land of Ethiopia.** Sign of Practicus Grade and invoking Water Pentagram.

Third - over the Yellow Air arm read, (Holding by Aquarius-Violet) **And the name of the third river is Hiddekel, that is it which goeth toward the East of Assyria.** Sign of Theoricus grade and Invoking Air Pentagram.

Fourth - over the black Earth arm read (holding by Taurus-red orange.) **And the fourth river is Euphrates.** Sign of Zelator with Invoking Earth Pentagram.

25. Lastly—holding the Wand again by the white part, describe a circle from left to right over the outermost 12 petals of the Rose pronouncing the name ADONAI vibrating it as taught.
26. Describe a similar circle over the seven middle petals pronouncing the word ARARITA.
27. Then describe a circle over the three innermost petals say: YHVH.
28. Finally trace a perpendicular line down and say: EHEIEH.
29. Draw a horizontal line from left to right and say: ELOHIM.
30. Wrap up the Cross in white silk.
31. Close the Ceremony by purification by Water.
32. Close the Ceremony by purification by Fire.
34. Stand at West of altar, face East and say: **In the name of Yeheshuah, I now set free any spirits that may have been imprisoned by this Ceremony.**
35. Perform the Lesser Banishing Ritual of the Pentagram.

THE RITUAL OF THE ROSE CROSS

1. Light a stick of Incense. Go to the South East corner of the room. Make a large cross and circle thus:

Then holding the point of the incense in the centre vibrate the word *Yeheshuah.*

2. With arm outstretched on a level with the centre of the cross, and holding the incense stick, go to the South West corner and make a similar cross, repeating the Word.
3. Go to the North West Corner and repeat the cross and the Word.
4. Go to the North East Corner and repeat the cross and the Word.
5. Complete your circle by returning to the South East corner and bringing the point of the incense to the central point of the first cross which you should imagine astrally there.

6. Holding the stick on high, go to the centre of the room, walking diagonally across the room towards the North West corner. In the centre of the room, above your head, trace the cross and circle and vibrate the Name.

7. Holding the stick on high, go to the North West and bring the point of the stick down to the centre of the astral cross there.

8. Turn towards the South East and retrace your steps there, but now, holding the incense stick directed towards the floor. In the centre of the room, make the cross and circle towards the floor, as it were, under your feet, and vibrate the Name.

9. Complete this circle by returning to the South East and bringing the point of the stick again to the centre of the Cross, than move with arm outstretched to South West corner.

10. From the centre of this cross, and, raising stick before, walk diagonally across the room towards the North East corner. In the centre of the room, pick up again the cross above your head previously made, vibrating the Name. It is not necessary to make another cross.

11. Bring the stick to the centre of the North East cross and return to the South West, incense stick down, and pausing in the centre of the room to link up with the cross under your feet.

12. Return to the South West and rest the point of the incense a moment in the centre of the cross there. Holding the stick out, retrace your circle to the North West, link on to the North West Cross—proceed to the North East cross and complete your circle by returning to the South East, and the centre of the first cross.

13. Retrace the Cross, but larger, and make a big circle, vibrating for the lower half **Yeheshuah,** and for the upper half **Yehovashah.**

14. Return to the centre of the room, and visualise the six crosses in a net-work round you. This ceremony can be concluded by the analysis of the Key-Word given as follows:

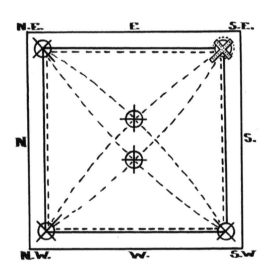

ANALYSIS OF THE KEY-WORD

1. Stand with arms outstretched in the form of a cross. Face East.

2. Vibrate these words:

| **I.** | **N.** | **R.** | **I.** |
| Yod | Nun | Resh | Yod |

The Sign of Osiris Slain.

3. Right arm up, left arm extended out from shoulder, head bowed towards left hand.

L—The Sign of the Mourning of Isis.

4. Both arms up in a V shape.

V—The Sign of Typhon and Apophis.

5. Arms crossed on breast, head bowed.

X—The Sign of Osiris Risen.

6. Make the signs again as you repeat L.V.X.

LUX

7. Arms folded on breast, head bowed.

The Light of the Cross.

8. Then arms extended in Sign of Osiris Slain.

Virgo	**Isis**	**Mighty Mother**
Scorpio	**Apophis**	**Destroyer**
Sol	**Osiris**	**Slain and Risen**

9. Gradually raise arms.

| **Isis** | **Apophis** | **Osiris** |

10. Arms above head, face raised.

| **I.** | **A.** | **O** |

11. Except when in the Vault, now vibrate the four Tablet of Union Names to equilibrate the Light.

| **EXARP** | **HCOMA** | **NANTA** | **BITOM** |

12. Aspire to the Light and draw it down over your head to your feet.

Let the Divine Light Descend.

THE USE OF THE ROSE CROSS RITUAL

1. It encloses the aura with a protection against outside influences. It is like a veil. The Pentagrams protect, but they also light up the astral and make entities aware of you. They are more positive for magical working. When much distracted, use the Pentagrams to banish and the Rose-cross to maintain peace.

2. It is a call to another mode of your consciousness and withdraws you from the physical. It is a god preparation for meditation and, combined with the Key-Word, a form of invocation of the Higher Wisdom which is helpful when solving problems or preparing for a difficult interview, or in order to be calm and strong to help another.

3. When you are quite familiar with the Ritual, but most certainly not before, it can be done in imagination while resting or lying down. Part of yourself goes out, and you get all the sensation of walking around your own quiescent body. Used thus, with rhythmic breathing, it will withdraw your mind from pain (if it be not too severe) and release you for sleep. You can do the analysis of the Key-Word standing behind your physical head, and you can call down the Divine White Brilliance, watching it flow over your body and smooth out the tangles in the etheric double, bringing peace and rest.

4. You can do the Ritual with intention to help others in pain or difficulty. For this purpose, you build up an astral image of the person, in the centre of the room, and call down the Light upon him, after surrounding him with the six crosses. When the ceremony is done, command the astral shape you have made to return to the person, bearing with it the peace of **Yeheshuah.**

5. It is a protection against psychic invasion from the thoughts of others or from disturbed psychic conditions, such as there might be in a place charged with fear, where terrible things had happened.

(N. B. This does not appear to be an original Order document. It was probably composed and written by Dr. R. Felkins, during the Stella Matutina period. I.R.)

VOLUME FIVE

MAGICAL FUNDAMENTALS

VOLUME FIVE

THE IMPORTANCE OF DIVINATION

TABLE OF CONTENTS

IMPORTANT TABLES AND ILLUSTRATIONS

VOLUME FIVE

MAGICAL FUNDAMENTALS

THE GEOMANTIC TALISMANIC SYMBOLS

By

G.H. FRATER S.R.M.D.

PUER	Amissio	ALBUS	POPULUS
VIA	FORT. MAJ.	FORT. MIN.	PUELLA
RUBEUS	ACQUISITIO	CARCER	TRIST
LAETITIA	CONJUNCTIO	CAPUT DRAC.	CAUDA DRAC.

On examining the number of points of which the sixteen (16) figures of Geomancy are composed, it is at once evident that they vary from four (4) points the least to eight (8) points the greatest number contained in one figure.

Only one figure contains eight (8) points—that is plus—the number of the letters of the name YHVH ADNI.

1

THE COMPLETE GOLDEN DAWN SYSTEM OF MAGIC

Four figures consist each of 7 points, the number of the 28 Mansions of the Moon in the Zodiac: Rubeus, Albus, Tristitia and Laetitia.

Six (6) figures contain six points each—the number of the 36 Decans of the Zodiac: Career, Conjunctio, Fortuna Major and Minor, Amissio and Acquisitio.

Four (4) figures consist of five (5) points each—the number of the Sephiroth in two aspects (positive and negative) and of the word YOD spelled out in full, thus: Y - 10, Vau - 6, Daleth - 4, making 20. Puer, Puella, Caput and Cauda Draconis.

Only one (1) figure consists of 4 points, Via, the number of the letters of the Name— YHVH.

The total of all the points in all the figures, 8 + 28 + 36 + 20 + 4 equals 96. 8x12 equals the name of 8 letters multiplied through the 12 divisions of the Zodiac. The number of the classes of the figures according to their points, as above given, will be five (5), answering to the points of the Pentagram.

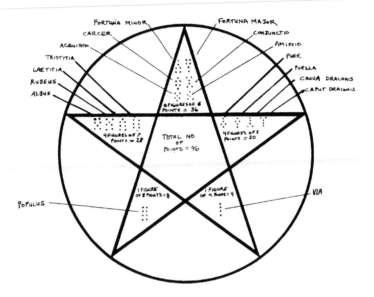

Also, the total number 96 will further show 16 (times) 6 or the geomantic figures multiplied in the Hexagram. This development of the figures according to the number of the points may be classified and summed up in the annexed diagrams.

2

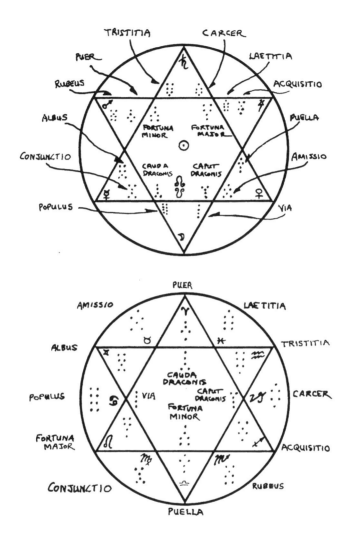

In addition, the 16 figures are classed among the four (4) Elements so that 4 shall belong to each Element. To EARTH belong 3 figures of 6 points and 1 of 5 equals 23 points: Career, Amissio, Conjunctio and Caput Draconis.

To AIR belong 2 figures of 7 points, 1 of six and 1 of 5 points equals 25 points: Tristitia, Puella, Albus, and Fortuna Minor.

To FIRE belong 2 figures of 6, and 2 of 5 equals 22 points: Acquisitio, Puer, Fortuna Major, and Cauda Draconis.

To WATER belong 1 figure of 8, 2 of 7, and 1 of 4 points equals 26 points: Laetitia, Rubeus, Populus, and Via.

The Geomantic Tree of Life is formed by arranging the 16 figures according to their Planetary attributions in the Sephiroth to which the Planets correspond, as represented in the accompanying diagram. There, Saturn represents the three Supernal Sephiroth—Kether,

THE COMPLETE GOLDEN DAWN SYSTEM OF MAGIC

Chokman and Binah—while Caput and Cauda Draconis are referred to the 10th Sephirah of Malkuth.

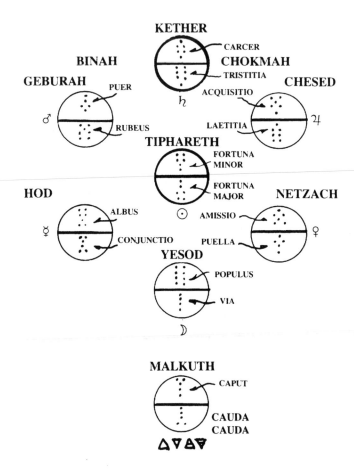

The following important characters—letters of the Angelic or Enochian Alphabet—are attributed to the Seven Planetary Rulers in the Twelve Signs and the Sixteen Figures in Geomancy.

(N.B. In the Introduction to Crowley's *Vision and the Voice*, [Sangreal's edition] I noted some difficulty in following Crowley's attributions of the 30 Aethyrs to the Enochian Alphabet. A correspondent wrote calling my attention to the Enochian attributions here which solves the problems. He deserves acknowledgement—if only to reaffirm my claim that Crowley was a Golden Dawn "graduate". He stored his Order knowledge in the Unconscious, whence it could emerge into his every day field of activity. The correspondent is Mr. K. Campos of Seattle Washington.I.R.)

VOLUME FIVE

♌ Signifies Muriel and Populus, a figure of Chasmodai or Luna in Cancer increasing.

♋ Signifies Muriel and Via, a figure of Chasmodai and Luna in Cancer decreasing.

♌ Signifies Verchiel and Fortuna Major, a figure of Sorath or the Sun in Northern declination.

♇ Signifies Verchiel and Fortuna Minor, a figure of Sorath or the Sun in Southern declination.

ך Signifies Hamaliel and Conjunctio, a figure of Taphthartharath or Mercury in Virgo.

ל Signifies Zuriel and Puella, a figure of Kedemel or Venus in Libra.

 כ Signifies Barchiel and Rubeus, a figure or Bartzabel or Mars in Scorpio.

ך Signifies Advachiel and Acquisitio, a figure of Hismael or Jupiter in Sagittarius.

ה Signifies Hanael and Carcer, a figure of Zazel or Saturn in Capricorn.

ع Signifies Cambriel and Tristitia, a figure of Zazel or Saturn in Aquarius

ع Signifies Amnitziel and Laetitia, a figure of Hismael or Jupiter in Pisces.

ⴴ Signifies Zazel and Bartzabel in all their ideas, being Cauda Draconis.

ر Signifies Hismael and Kedemel in all their ideas, being a figure of Caput Draconis.

Ѵ Signifies Melchidael and Puer, a figure of Bartzabel or Mars in Aries.

ע Signifies Asmodel and Amissio, a figure of Kedemel or Venus in Taurus.

ך Signifies Ambriel and Albus, a figure of Taphthartharath or Mercury in Gemini.

QUALITIES OF THE FIGURES

(These qualities of the figures have been extrapolated by S.R.M.D. from Heydon's *Theomagia*. The rest is from the ancient Golden Dawn cypher manuscripts.)

Here follow the special qualities of the 16 Geomantic Figures. It is to be noted that all which have more points above than below are **entering in** except Tristitia. And those which have more points below than above are **going out** and evil, except Laetitia. Those which have as many above as below are medium, except Career. That is to say, that such is their natural signification.

Good for a voyage and quick: Acquisitio, Caput Draconis, Fortuna Major, Fonuna Minor, Laetitia.

Good by land: Populus, Laetitia, Albus, Conjunctio, Via.

Good by Water: Populus, Laetitia, Puella, Albus, Acquisitio.

Slow for a voyage, but profitable: Puella.

Evil for the Way: Rubeus, Conjunctio, Populus, Tristitia.

Robbing by the Way: Cauda Draconis, Rubeus.

Evil for Fear: Conjunctio, Acquisitio, Rubeus, Caput Draconis, Fortuna Major, Albus

Good for Honour and Integrity: Acquisitio, Fortuna Major, Fortuna Minor, Laetitia, Albus, Caput Draconis, Conjunctio.

Evil for Honour: Amissio, Via, Rubeus, Puella, Tristitia.

Good to have Liberty and come out of Prison: Fortuna Minor, Via, Cauda Draconis, Puer, Amissio, Laetitia.

Evil to come out of Prison: Acquisitio, Fortuna Major, Tristitia, Carcer.

Mean to come out of Prison: Rubeus, Puella, Albus.

Good for Body: Populus, Conjunctio, Fortuna Minor.

Mean for Body: Fortuna Major, Albus, Puella, Puer.

Evil for Body: Career, Rubeus, Amissio.

Good for Woman (pregnant): Amissio, Fortuna Minor, Via, Laetitia.

Child will die: Tristitia.

Mean for Childbirth: Amissio, Fortuna Major, Cauda Draconis, Populus.

Better than before: Via, Cauda Draconis, Laetitia, Tristitia.

Marriage Good: Fortuna Major, Laetitia, Caput Draconis.

Best: Tristitia.

Mean: Cauda Draconis, Carcer.

Marriage Evil: Fortuna Major, Amissio, Via, Fortuna Minor, Rubeus.

Good for Dread and Fear: Amissio, Via, Cauda Draconis, Puer, Fortuna Minor.

Good for Woman's Love: Laetitia, Caput Draconis, Puer, Fortuna Major.

Evil for Woman's Love: Amissio, Via, Rubeus, Cauda Draconis.

Good to Recover things stolen: Acquisitio, Caput Draconis, Conjunctio, Carcer, Puer, Tristitia.

Medium: Puella.

Evil for things stolen: Fortuna Minor, Laetitia, Caput Draconis, Populus, Via.

Good for Shipping: Acquisitio, Laetitia, Fortuna Major, Fortuna Minor, Via.

Medium: Cauda Draconis.

Evil for shipping, for they shall be drowned: Conjunctio, Populus, Amissio, Tristitia.

Good to Remove: Fortuna Major, Cauda Draconis, Laetitia, Caput Draconis, Acquisitio.

Medium to Remove: Albus, Conjunctio, Puer, Amissio.

Evil Figures signifying Evil: Via, Carcer, Puer, Tristitia, Caput Draconis, Rubeus, Amissio.

Medium: Conjunctio.

Figures of Chastity and Virginity: Albus, Fortuna Major, Laetitia, Carcer, Caput Draconis, Tristitia, Puella.

Figures of Incontinence and Lechery: Puer, Cauda, Amissio, Rubeus, Populus, Conjunctio, Via, Acquisitio, Fortuna Minor.

Figures showing NO theft; all others show theft: Acquisitio, Fortuna Major, Albus, Caput Draconis, Laetitia.

Figures signifying War: Tristitia, Rubeus, Puer. Cauda Draconis, Fortuna Minor, Amissio.

Figures signifying Peace: Fortuna Major, Acquisitio, Caput Draconis, Laetitia, Albus, Puella.

Figures signifying Loss: Carcer, Conjunctio, Albus, Laetitia, Populus, Via, Amissio, Puer, Rubeus, Fortuna Minor, Cauda Draconis.

Figures of Gain: Acquisitio, Fortuna Major, Tristitia, Puella, Caput Draconisi.

Figures of Nobility: Acquisitio, Laetitia, Puella, Fortuna Major, Fortuna Minor, Caput Draconis.

Figures of Ignobility: Tristitia, Carcer, Via, Cauda Draconis, Conjunctio.

Figures of Life: Albus, Fortuna Major, Laetitia, Puella, Acquisitio, Populus, Caput Draconis, Via.

Figures of Death if in the 8th house: Tristitia, Cauda Draconis, Carcer, Rubeus, Puer, Conjunctio, Acquisitio, Amissio, Fortuna Minor.

Figures of Liberality: Amissio, Cauda Draconis, Fortuna Minor, Via.

Figures of Avarice and Covetousness: Tristitia, Carcer, Conjunctio, Fortuna Major.

Figure of Justice: Puer.

Figure of Prudence: Acquisitio.

Figure of Fortitude: Amissio.

Good to buy Cattle: Puella, Populus, Caput Draconis.

Loss to buy Cattle: Tristitia, Carcer.

Figure of Temperance: Conjunctio.

TALISMANS AND FLASHING TABLETS
By
G.H. FRATER D.D.C.F.

In construction of a talisman, symbolism should be exact and in harmony with universal forces.

A Flashing Tablet is one made in the complementary colors (i.e. in the Scale of the King.)

A flashing color then is the Complementary Color, which, if joined to the original, enables it to attract to a certain extent the Akasic current from the atmosphere and partly from yourself—thus forming a vortex which can attract its flashing light from the atmosphere. The complementary colors are:

White to Black and Grey
Red to Green
Blue to Orange
Yellow to Violet
Olive to Orange
Blue-green to Russet
Violet to Citrine
Reddish-orange to Greenish blue
Deep Amber to Indigo
Lemon Yellow to Violet
Yellow green to Crimson

NATURE AND METHOD OF FORMATION OF THE TELESMA.

1. Not always just and right to make a talisman with the idea of completely changing the current of another's Karma.

2. That which assists in material things is often a hindrance spiritually, seeing that for a force to work it must attract elemental forces of the proper descriptions, which may thus to an extent endanger your spiritual nature.

3. In making a telesma for a person, isolate yourself entirely from them; i.e. banish love, hate, irritations, etc.

4. See that you are in harmony with the effect you wish to produce.

5. In actual consecration, a good aid is to purify the room using the banishing ritual of Pentagram.

6. Better to finish a Telesma at one sitting.

7. Where Talismans or Symbols have done their work, they should be carefully **decharged** and then destroyed. Decharge with Pentagram or Hexagram according as it partakes of planetary or zodiacal nature. These remarks apply to Flashing Tablets as well. May be done astrally.

8. Any flashing tablets in two colors should be nearly balanced in proportion of color as possible, the ground one color, the charge another.

    There is also a mode in which 3 colors can be used in planetary talismans, by placing the seven colors of the Heptagram and drawing two lines to the points exactly opposite which would yield 2 flashing colors.

9. Mode of charging and consecrating should be suitable to the operation. Certain words and letters are to be invoked in the charging of a tablet, viz. the letters governing the signs under which the operation falls, together with the planet associated therewith (the latter only for planetary talisman). Thus in elemental operations you take the letters of the appropriate triplicity, adding AL thereto, thus forming an Angelic name, which is the expression of the force. Hebrew names as rule represent the offices of certain forces, while the Enochian Tablets represent a species of more particular ideas. Both classes of names should be used in these operations.

After preparing room first formulate towards the quarters the Supreme Ritual of the Pentagram as taught. Then invoke the Divine Names turning towards the quarter of the Element. Then being seated or standing before the Tablet and looking in the requisite directions, i.e., in the direction of the force you wish to invoke, take several deep inspirations, close the eyes and holding the breath, mentally pronounce the letter of the forces invoked. Do this several times until with the eyes closed you can positively feel the element involved. Having done this formulate the letters several times as if you breathed upon the tablet, pronouncing them in the vibratory manner. Then rising make the sign of the Rose and the Cross over the Tablet. Repeating the requisite formula or any other appropriate words, first describe around the telesma to be consecrated, a circle with the proper magical implements and then make the Invoking Pentagram appropriate five times over it, as if it (the pentagram upright) were standing upon it, vibrating the letters of the Triplicity involved with AL added, e.g. for Fire (Halsael) and (SheHalsael). Then solemnly read any invocations required—making the proper sigils from the Rose as you pronounce the names.

The first Operation is to initiate the Whorl from yourself. The second, to attract the force in the atmosphere into the vortex you have formed. Then read the Elemental Prayer as in the Grade rituals (if for Fire, that of the Salamanders) and close work with the sign of the Circle and Cross—after performing the necessary Banishing Ritual. But do not banish over newly consecrated telesma.

Wrap telesma carefully up in silk or linen, preferably white.

The Talismanic symbols—or Telesmatic Emblems as they are sometimes called—are formed from the Geomantic Figures by drawing various lines from point to point of each.

These characters are then attributed to their ruling Planets and Ideas. For example, the most simple forms will be:

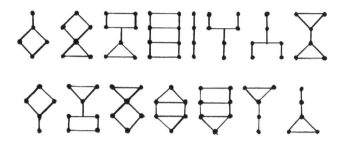

Here follows a complete table of all the Talismanic Figures classed under the Planets and Signs.

The characters of Saturn and Zazel taken from Carcer equals Capricorn.

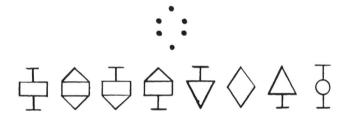

The characters of Saturn and Zazel taken from Tristitia equals Aquarius.

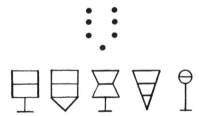

The characters of Jupiter and Hismael taken from Acquisitio equals Sagittarius.

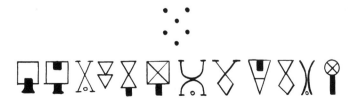

THE COMPLETE GOLDEN DAWN SYSTEM OF MAGIC

The characters of Jupiter and Hismael taken from Laetitia equals Pisces.

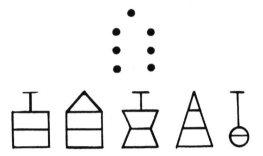

The characters of Mars and Bartzabel taken from Rubeus equals Scorpio.

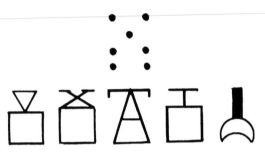

The characters of Mars and Bartzabel taken from Puer equal Aries.

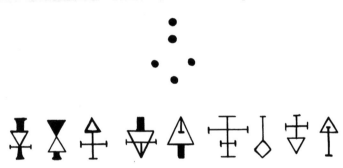

The characters of Sol and Sorath taken from Fortuna Major equals Leo.

VOLUME FIVE

The characters of Sol and Sorath taken from Fortuna Minor equals Leo.

The characters of Venus and Kedemel taken from Amissio equals Taurus.

The characters of Venus and Kedemel taken from Puella equals Libra.

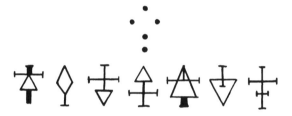

The characters of Mercury and Taphthartharath taken from Albus equals Gemini.

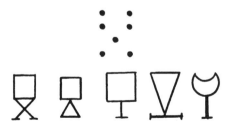

The characters of Mercury and Taphthartharath taken from Conjunctio equals Virgo.

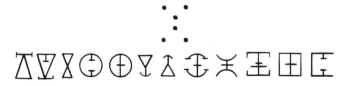

THE COMPLETE GOLDEN DAWN SYSTEM OF MAGIC

The characters of Luna and Chasmodai taken from Populus equals Cancer.

The characters of Luna and Chasmodai taken from Via equals Cancer.

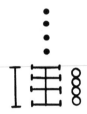

The characters of Caput Draconis are:

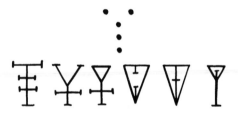

The characters of Cauda Draconis are:

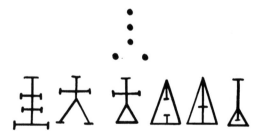

MODE OF FORMATION OF TALISMANS AND PANTACLES

The mode of using these Talismanic Characters drawn from the Talismanic Figures in the construction of a Talisman or Pantacle, is to take those formed by the figures under the Planet required, and to place them either at the opposite ends of a wheel of eight radii as shown, or to place them in the compartments of a Square. A versicle suitable to the mattei is then to be written within the double line.

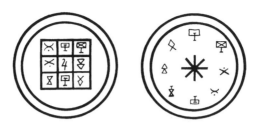

THE LINEAL FORMS OF THE NAMES OF THE SEPHIROTH ON THE TREE OF LIFE

In the early days of the Order, this paper had appended to it a note by Dr. Westcott, using his Order name of Non Omnis Moriar. He said that this paper was only for those members of the Inner Order who had mastered the Pentagram and Hexagram Rituals and consecrated their elemental weapons.

The original document here given gave the names of the Sephiroth in Hebrew. Since these Hebrew Names were previously given in Hebrew in an early Knowledge Lecture, I have for the sake of convenience transliterated them into English. The number of letters used to describe the appropriate lineal figure refers to **the number of Hebrew letters, not English.** It is important for the student to keep this in mind, otherwise he will get thoroughly confused.

I would also urge the student not to permit first impressions of complexity disturb his peace of mind, forcing him to neglect the study of this paper. It is really worth giving a good deal of attention to. Admittedly it is purely speculative and an exercise in intellectual virtuosity. The end result rather as with the use of a Zen Koan is the product of a higher level of perception. The use of the Koan may result in a swing over to the same level of perception experienced by whoever it was that developed it originally. This study of lineal figures and the various divine names bears many resemblances to the processes just described.

I give these Sephirotic Names in English. On an earlier page will be found the equivalent Hebrew spelling.

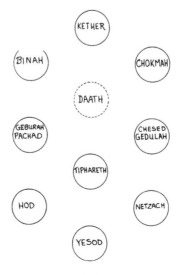

In examining the number of Hebrew letters in the Sephirotic names on the Tree of Life, it will be observed that Kether consists of three letters whose equivalent then is the Triangle among the lineal figures. Chokmah and Binah each of four letters, as also Yesod; the actual lineal figure is then the Square. Gedulah, Geburah, Tiphareth and Malkuth have five letters each, equivalent to the Pentagram. While Chesed, Pachad, Netzach and Hod have each three like Kether, as also Daath.

The total number of letters in these names on the Tree will then be 50, the number of the Gates of the Understanding, as is laid down in the Qabalah.

Then in the ensuing translations of the Names of the Sephiroth into lineal symbols, what is at once evident is the absolutely harmonious balance of forms which results. Pachad is a correspondence of Geburah and means Fear. Gedulah is a correspondence of Chesed and means Magnificence.

The Supernal Triangle (Triad) will then be represented by a Triangle surmounting the two Squares.

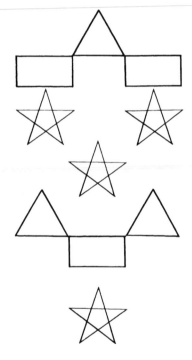

The Sephiroth may thus be summed up in three classes, the Triangle, Square and Pentagram, the respective lineal equivalents of Chesed, Binah, and Geburah, six under the Triangle in Kether, Pachad, Chesed, Netzach, Hod and Daath. Three under the Square, Chokmah, Binah and Yesod. Four under the Pentagram: Gedulah, Geburah, Tiphareth, and Malkuth. Now, if as in the diagram, we draw lines connecting those Sephiroth which are represented by the same lineal equivalents, we shall find that the lines number Twenty Two, that is, the number of the Paths in the Tree. For you require 13 lines to join initially those Sephiroth under the Triangle, 3 for those under the Square, and 6 for those under the Pentagram which adds to 22.

VOLUME FIVE

The letters of each Sephirotic Name may then be translated into the lineal symbols of the Sephiroth to which their numerical value is referred by the Qabalah of the Nine Chambers.

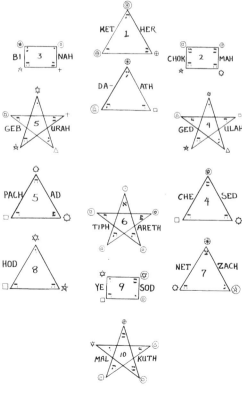

If these Letters be again translated into their Yetziratic attribution and this combined with the former, we shall obtain an analysis compounded of both scales of interpretation.

In the diagram, **the lineal figures of the tens and hundreds are distinguished from those of the units by being encircled with either one or two rays,** according as to tens or hundreds are implied. If these be further placed within the Lineal Figure of the Whole Name, a species of Hieroglyphic Form of each Sephirah will result; which may again be

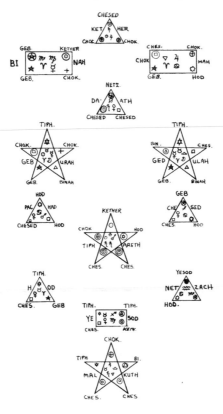

represented by a cognate Angelic form, as taught in the paper on the Formation of Sigils from the Rose.

We shall then find from the Qabalah of Nine Chambers that the numerical values of the 22 paths are thus allotted under the Sephiroth:

AIQ	Kether	1, 10, 100	Air, Virgo, Pisces
BKR	Chokmah	2, 20, 200	Mercury, Jupiter, Sun
GLSh	Binah	3, 30, 300	Moon, Libra, Fire
DMT	Chesed	4, 40, 400	Venus, Water, Saturn
HN	Geburah	5, 50	Aries, Scorpio
VS	Tiphareth	6, 60	Taurus, Sagittarius
ZO	Netzach	7, 70	Gemini, Capricorn
ChP	Hod	8, 80	Cancer, Mars
T Tz	Yesod	9, 90	Leo, Aquarius

This classification may, then, be again referred to the lineal figures thus:

Air, Virgo, Pisces	**Point within a circle**
Mercury, Jupiter, Sun	**Cross**
Luna, Libra, Fire	**Triangle**
Venus, Water, Saturn	**Square**
Aries, Scorpio	**Pentangle**
Taurus, Sagittarius	**Hexangle**
Gemini, Capricorn	**Heptangle**
Cancer, Mars	**Octangle**
Leo, Aquarius	**Enneangle**

POLYGRAMS AND POLYGONS

THE TRIANGLE

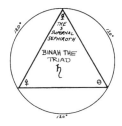

The Triangle is the only Lineal Figure into which all surfaces can be reduced, for every Polygon can be divided into Triangles by drawing lines from its angles to its centre. Thus the Triangle is the first and simplest of all Lineal Figures.

We refer to the Triad operating in all things, to the 3 Supernal Sephiroth, and to Binah the 3rd Sephirah. Among the Planets it is especially referred to Saturn; and among the Elements to Fire. As the colour of Saturn is black and the Triangle that of Fire, the Black Triangle will represent Saturn, and the Red Fire.

The 3 Angles also symbolize the 3 Alchemical Principles of Nature, Mercury, Sulphur, and Salt.

As there are 360° in every great circle, the number of degrees cut off between its angles when inscribed within a Circle will be 120°, the number forming the astrological Trine inscribing the Trine within a circle, that is, reflected from every second point.

THE SQUARE

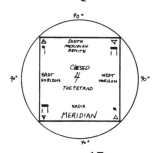

The Square is an important lineal figure which naturally represents stability and equilibrium. It includes the idea of surface and superficial measurement.

It refers to the Quaternary in all things and to the Tetrad of the Letter of the Holy Name Tetragrammaton operating through the four Elements of Fire, Water, Air, and Earth. It is allotted to Chesed, the 4th Sephirah, and among the Planets it is referred to Jupiter. As representing the 4 Elements it represents their ultimation with the material form. The 4 angles also include the ideas of the 2 extremities of the Horizon, and the 2 extremities of the Median, which latter are usually called the Zenith and the Nadir: also the 4 Cardinal Points.

The number of degrees of a great circle cut off between its angles will be 90° the number forming the astrological Quartile or Square Aspect, potent and evil.

There is only one way of inscribing a Square within a Circle, that is, reflected from every second point.

THE PENTAGON

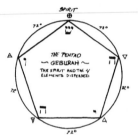

The Pentagon, first form, reflected from every second point.

The Pentangle can be traced in two ways: reflected from every second point, when it is called the Pentagon; and reflected from every third point, when it is called the Pentagram.

The Pentangle as a whole is referred to the 5th Sephirah Geburah. The Pentagon naturally represents the power of the Pentad operating in nature by the dispersal of the Spirit and the 4 Elements through it. The number of degrees of a great circle cut off between its Angles is 72° the number forming the astrological Quintile aspect, good in nature and operation.

It also answers to the dispersal force of the 5 letters YEHESHUAH.

It is not so consonant to the Nature of Mars as the Pentagram, and as a general rule the Pentagon is not so powerful a symbol as the Pentagram.

THE PENTANGLE

The Pentangle - The Pentagram, second form; reflected from every 3rd point.

The Pentagram with a single point uppermost is called the "Sign of the Microcosm" and is a good symbol representing man with his arms and legs extended adoring his Creator, and especially the dominion of the Spirit over the 4 Elements and consequently of Reason over Matter.

But with the single point downwards it is a very evil symbol, the head of the Goat, or demon's head, representing the abasement of Reason beneath the blind forces of Matter, the elevation of anarchy above order, and of conflicting forces driven by chance above God.

It represents the concentrated force of the Spirit and the 4 Elements governed by the 5 letters of the name of the Restorer of all things YEHESHUAH, and also the ten Sephiroth classified into 5 odd and 5 even numbers. It is especially attributable to the Planet Mars. It also shows the Kerubim and the Wheel of the Spirit. It is a Symbol of tremendous force, and of HEH, the letter of the Great Supernal Mother, AIMAH.

THE HEXANGLE

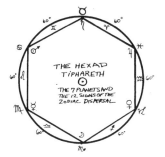

The Hexagon, first form, reflected from every second piont.

The Hexangle can be traced in two ways as a complete symbol: reflected from every second point, when it is called the Hexagon: and reflected from every third point, when it is called the Hexagram. There is also a third form, called the pseudo-Hexagram.

The Hexangle as a whole is referred to the 6th Sephirah, Tiphareth.

The Hexagon naturally represents the power of the Hexad operating in nature by the dispersal of the rays of the Planets and the Zodiac emanating from the central Sun. The number of degrees of a great circle cut off between its Angles is 60° forming the astrological Sextile aspect, powerful for good.

It is not so consonant to the solar nature as the Hexagram. Remember then that the Hexagon signifieth the dispersion, distribution, and radiation of a force but the Hexagram concentration. Hence thou shalt use the Hexagon for the spreading, and the Hexagram for the concentrating and sealing. Thus when there is need, thou canst compare, interpose and combine them; but the "Gon initiateth the whirl."

The nature of the "whirl" is described in a document relating to the Vibratory Formula of the Middle Pillar, and the formation of the Telesmatic Images.

THE HEXANGLE

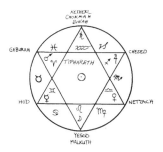

The Hexangle, second form, reflected from every 3rd point.

The Hexagram with a single point uppermost is called the "Sign of the Macrocosm," or greater world, because its six angles fitly represent the six days or periods of creation evolved from the manifestation of the Triune. Its synthesis forms the seventh day or period of rest summed up in the hexagonal centre.

It represents especially the concentrated force of the Planets acting through the Signs of the Zodiac, and thus sealing the Astral Image of nature under the presidency of the Sephiroth; and also the Seven Palaces of the same. It is especially attributable to the Sun. It is a Symbol of great strength and power, forming with the Cross and the Pentagram, a triad of potent and good symbols which are in harmony with each other.

THE HEXANGLE

The Pseudo-Hexagram or irregular third form.

The pseudo-Hexagram an irregular third form, sometimes employed to denote the presidency of the Sun and Moon over the 4 Elements united in and proceeding from the Spirit.

(Until quite recently, I thought that Aleister Crowley had invented the unicursal Hexagram. Upon reviewing this document, I find of course that it had existed anterior to him. On another page when dealing with the Ritual of the Hexagram, I shall have a little more to say about this hexagram and its uses in magical ritual. I.R.)

THE HEPTANGLE

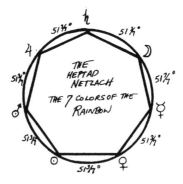

The Heptagon, first form, reflected from every second point.

The Heptangle can be traced in three ways reflected from every second point when it is called the Heptagon; and as the Heptagram is reflected from every third point, and from every fourth point.

The Heptangle as a whole is referred to the Seventh Sephirah, Netzach.

VOLUME FIVE

The Heptagon naturally represents the dispersal of the powers of the Seven Planets through the week and through the year. The number of degrees of a Great Circle cut off between its angles is 51-3/7°.

It further alludes to the power of the Septenary acting through all things, as exemplified by the seven colours of the Rainbow.

It is not so consonant to the nature of Venus as the Heptagram reflected from every fourth point.

THE HEPTANGLE

The Heptagram, second form; reflected from every third point.

The Heptagram reflected from every third point, yieldeth Seven Triangles at the apices thereof; fitly representing the Triad operating in each Planet; and the Planets themselves in the week and in the year.

The weekly order of the Planets is formed from their natural order by following the lines of this Heptagram; as hath been already shown in the 2nd point of the Grade of Zelator. It is not so consonant to the nature of Venus as the next form.

THE HEPTANGLE

The Heptagram, third form; reflected from every fourth point.

This Heptagram is the Star of Venus and is especially applicable to her nature. As the Heptagram is the lineal figure of the Seven Planets, so is Venus, as it were, their Gate or Entrance, the fitting symbol of the Isis of nature, and of the 7 lower Sephiroth of the Bride.

Study this reference in connection with the Venus door of the Vault of the Adepts, described in the Adeptus Minor grade.

THE OCTANGLE

The Octagon, first form; reflected from every second point.

The Octangle can be reflected in three ways; reflected from every second point when it is called the Octagon; and as the Octagram reflected from every third, and from every fourth point.

The Octangle naturally representeth the power of the Ogdoad. The Octagon showeth the Ogdoad operating in nature by the dispersal of the rays of the Elements in their dual aspect under the presidency of the 8 letters of the name Yod Heh Vau Heh and Aleph Daleth Nun Yod.

The number of degrees of a Great Circle cut off between its angles is 45°; forming the astrological weak Semi-Quartile aspect, evil in nature and operation.

The Octagon is not so consonant to the nature of Mercury as the Octagram reflected from every fourth point.

THE OCTANGLE

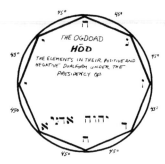

The Octagram, second form, reflected from every third point.

The Octagram reflected from every third point yieldeth eight Triangles at the apices thereof, fitly representing the Triad operating in each Element in its dual form, i.e., of Positive and Negative, under the powers of the name of Tetragrammaton Adonai: or as it is written bound together, Yod Aleph Heh Daleth Vau Nun Heh Yod.

It is not so consonant to the nature of Mercury as the next form. It is composed of two Squares united within a circle.

VOLUME FIVE

THE OCTANGLE

The Octagram, third form; reflected from every fourth point.

This Octogram is the Star of Mercury, and is especially applicable to his nature. It is further a potent symbol representing the binding together of the concentrated Positive and Negative forces of the Elements under the name of YHVHADNI. And forget not that ADNI is the key of YHVH.

THE ENNEANGLE

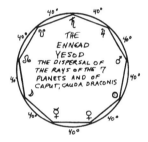

The Enneangle, first form, reflected from every second point.

The Enneangle can be traced in four ways reflected from every second point when it is called the Enneagon; and as the Enneagram reflected from every third, every fourth, and every fifth point.

The Enneangle as a whole, is referred to the ninth Sephirah Yesod.

The Enneangle naturally representeth the power of the Ennead. The Enneagram showeth the Ennead operating in nature by the dispersal of the rays of the Seven Planets and of the Head and Tail of the Dragon of the Moon.

The number of degrees of a Great Circle cut off between its angles is 40°.

The Enneagon is not so consonant to the nature of the Moon as the Enneagram reflected from every fifth point.

THE ENNEANGLE

The Enneagram, second form; reflected form every third Point. The Enneagram reflected from every third point representeth the Triple Ternary operating both in the Seven Planets with the Head and Tail of the Dragon of the Moon, and with their Alchemical principles countercharged and interwoven.

It is not as consonant to the nature of the Moon as the Enneagram reflected from every fifth point.

THE ENNEANGLE

The Enneagram, third form, reflected from every fourth point.

The Enneagram reflected from every fourth point is composed of three Triangles united within a Circle, and alludes to the Triple Ternary of the Three Alchemical principles themselves. It is not so consonant to the nature of the Moon as the next form.

THE ENNEANGLE

KETHER

The Enneagram, fourth form, reflected from every fifth point.

This Enneagram is the Star of the Moon and is especially applicable to her nature. It represents her as the administrator to the Earth of the virtues of the Solar System under the Sephiroth.

THE DEKANGLE

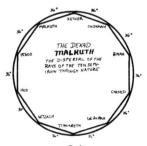

The Dekagon, first form, reflected from every second point.

The Dekangle can be traced in four ways; reflected from every second point when it is called the Dekagon and as the Dekagram reflected from every third, every fourth, and every fifth point.

The Dekangle as a whole is referred to the Tenth Sephirah, Malkuth.

The Dekangle naturally represents the power of the Dekad. The Dekagon showeth the Dekad operating in nature by the dispersal of the rays of the Ten Sephiroth therein.

The number of degrees of a Great Circle cut off between its angles is 36°; the half of the Quintile astrological aspect.

THE DEKANGLE

The Dekagram, second form; reflected from every third point.

The Dekagram reflected from every third point is especially consonant to Malkuth and shows the Triad operating through each angle of the two Pentagons within a circle, of which it is composed. It alludes to the combination of the 3 Alchemical principles with the Spirit and the 4 Elements in their Positive and Negative form, under the presidency of the 10 Sephiroth themselves.

THE DEKANGLE

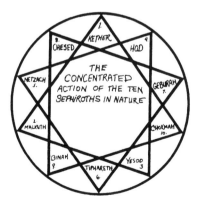

The Dekagram, third form, reflected from every fourth point.

This form of the Dekagram especially alludes to the concentrated and continuous operations of the Ten Sephiroth in nature. It is continuously reflected from every fourth point.

THE DEKANGLE

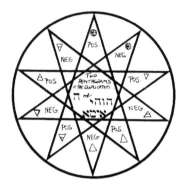

The Dekagram, fourth form, reflected from every fifth point.

The Dekagram reflected from every fifth point is composed of two Pentagrams within a Circle. It shows the operation of the duplicated HEH of the Tetragrammaton and the concentration of the Positive and Negative forces of the Spirit and the four Elements under the presidency of the Potencies of the Five in Binah the Revolutions of the forces under AIMA, the Great Mother.

THE ENDEKANGLE

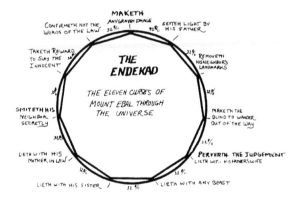

The Endekagram, first form, reflected from every second point.

The Endekangle can be traced in five ways: reflected from every second point, when it is called the Endekagon; and as the Endekagram reflected from every third, fourth, fifth, and sixth points.

The Endekangles as a general whole are referred to the Qliphoth. Of its forms, however, the one reflected from every fourth point represents their restriction, and therefore it is not altogether to be classed with those which represent their operation in nature, wherefore it is here separated from them and placed by itself at the end of the book.

The Endekangle naturally represents the evil and imperfect nature of the Endekad. The Endekagon represents the dispersal of the Eleven Curses of Mount Ebal through the Universe. Though they are paragraphed as 12 in the English version of the Bible, in the Hebrew they are paragraphed as 11, two being classed together.

The number of degrees of a great circle cut off between its angles is 32-8/11°.

VOLUME FIVE

THE ENDEKANGLE

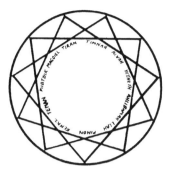

The Endekagram, second form; reflected from every third point.

The Endekagram reflected from every third point, represents the concentrated action of evil in the Averse Triad, symbolized by the Eleven Dukes of Edom, the horns of the Red Dragon when he ariseth. This is a reference to one of the Altar Diagrams, the Garden of Eden after the Fall.

THE ENDEKANGLE

The fourth form; reflected from every fifth point.

It is a curious fact that the Endekagram which can be formed reflected from every fourth point is not so evil as the rest, and represents the restraining of the evil ones. This abhorance of and incompatibility with the number four is another mark of the imperfect nature of the Endekad when applied to the symbolism of the Qliphoth; for by the same that they are shown, so is their restriction shown. Yet even the Endekangle reflected from every fourth point is not good in operation, but simply declareth the restriction of evil as will be shown hereafter.

The Endekagram reflected from every fifth point represents the concentrated force of the averse and evil Sephiroth.

THE ENDEKANGLE

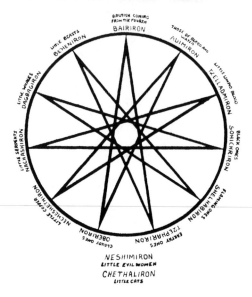

BRUTISH COMING
FROM THE FOURTH
BAIRIRON

THOSE OF BLOOD AND WATER
AUIMIRON

LITTLE BEASTS
BEHEMIRON

LITTLE WORMS
DAGDAGIRON

LITTLE LIVING BLOOD
TZELLADMIRON

LITTLE SERPENTS
NACHASHIRON

BLACK ONES
SCHICHIRON

LITTLE COMIC
NECHESHETHIRON

FLAMING ONES
SHELHABIRON

OBRIRON
CLOUDY ONES

TZEPHARIRON
EARTHY ONES

NESHIMIRON
LITTLE EVIL WOMEN
CHETHALIRON
LITTLE CATS

The Endekagram, fifth form, reflected from every sixth point.

Unto this form of the Endekagram are attributed the 12 Princes of the Qliphoth who are the heads of the Evil operating in the months of the year.

THE DODEKANGLE

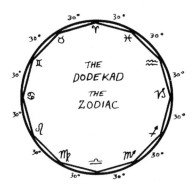

THE
DODEKAD

THE
ZODIAC

The Dodekangle, first form, reflected from every second point.

The Dodekangle can be traced in five ways; reflected from every second point, when it is called the Dodekagon; and as the Dodekagram reflected from every third, fourth, fifth and sixth point.

The Dodekangle as a general whole is referred to the Zodiac, and naturally represents the powers of the Dodekad. The Dodekagon shows the dispersal of the influence of the Zodiac through nature.

The number of degrees of a great circle cut off between its angles is 30° forming the weak astrological semi-Sextile Aspect, good in nature and operation.

VOLUME FIVE

THE DODEKANGLE

The Dodekagram, second form, reflected from every third point.

The Dodekagram reflected from every third point, is formed of two Hexagons within a Circle, and represents the dispersal and concentration of the Zodiac in masculine and feminine signs. The masculine being Aries, Gemini, Leo, Libra, Sagittarius and Aquarius; and the feminine Taurus, Cancer, Virgo, Scorpio, Capricorn and Pisces. As this Dodekagram is composed of twelve triangles, so do these allude to the 3 decanates, faces, or sets of 10° of each Sign.

THE DODEKANGLE

The Dodekagram, third form, reflected from every fourth point

This Dodekagram is formed of three Squares, representing the three Quaternions of Angular, Succedent, Cadent and Movable, Fixed and Common.

THE DODEKANGLE

29

The Dodekagram, fourth form; reflected from every fifth point.

The Dodekagram reflected from every fifth point is formed of four Triangles within a Circle, and refers to the concentrated force of the four Triplicities of the Zodiac operating through nature.

THE DODEKANGLE

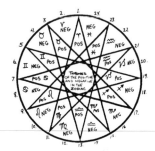

The Dodekagram, fifth form; reflected from every sixth point.

The Dodekagram reflected from every sixth point is a continuous figure; and symbolizes the 24 Thrones of the schema established over the Positive and Negative potencies of the Elements in the Zodiac; and over the 24 hours in the day.

THE ENDEKANGLE

The Endekagram third form; reflected from every fourth point.

Symbolizing the restriction of the Qliphoth, Esther IX, vs. 3 is "Vehachashdrapanim," signifying lieutenants or deputy governors of provinces.

Deut. I, vs. 2. "There are eleven days journey from Horeb by the way of Mount Seir unto Kadesh Barnea."

Deut. XXXII, vs. 37 is VeOmar Ai ElohimTzur Chasyahbah. "And he shall say'Where are their Gods, their rock wherein they trust?' or 'Eleven are their Gods,'etc., or Ai are their Gods (Elohim)."

THE CROSS WITHIN THE CIRCLE

The Point within the Circle represents the operation of Kether in general; and the Cross within the Circle that of Chokmah, for therein are the roots of Wisdom. When using these Lineal Figures in the formation of Talismans under the Sephiroth remember that:

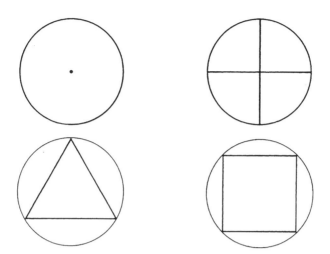

The Point within the Circle is Kether.
The Cross within the Circle is Chokmah.
The Triangle within the Circle is Binah.
The Square within the Circle is Chesed.

The remaining Sephiroth should have the double, or triple, or quadruple, forms of their lineal figures bound together in their talismans; e.g., in the Heptangle for Netzach, the Heptagon and the two forms of the Heptagram should be united in the same Talisman, the extremities of the angles coinciding.

The Endekangle is appropriate to the Qliphoth.

The Dodekangle is appropriate to the Zodiacal forces in Malkuth. Kether that of the Primum Mobile; Chokmah the Sphere of the Zodiac in command; and Malkuth that of the Elements.

And many other meanings are bound together in the lineal figures besides those which are given in this book. Two or more different forms may be bound together in the same Talisman.

SIGILS

By

G.H. FRATER D.D.C.F.

In the Opening Ceremony of the grade of Adeptus Minor the complete Symbol of the Rose and Cross is called the 'Key of Sigils and of Rituals.' It is further said that it represents the Forces of the 22 Letters in Nature, as divided into a Three, a Seven, and a Twelve.

The inner Three Petals of the Rose symbolise the active Elements of Air, Fire, and Water, operating in the Earth, which is as it were the recipient of them, their container and ground of operation. They are coloured, as are all the other petals, according to the hues of the Rainbow in the masculine scale. The seven next Petals answer to the Letters of the Seven Planets, and the Twelve Outer to the Twelve Signs of the Zodiac.

If thou wilt trace the Sigil of any word or name either in the Air, or written upon paper, thou shalt commence with a circle at the point of the initial letter on the Rose, and draw with thy magical weapon a line from this circle unto the place of the next letter of the name. Continue this, until thou hast finished the word which the letters compose. If two letters of the same sort, such as two Beths or Gimels, come together, thou shalt represent the same by a crook or wave in the line at that point.

And if there be a letter, as Resh in Metatron, through which the line passeth to another letter and which yet formeth part of the name, thou shalt make a noose in the line at that point thus: $(--- ^0 ---)$ to make the same.

If thou art drawing the Sigil thou mayest work it in the respective colours of the letters and add these together to form a synthesis of colour. Thus the Sigil of Metatron shall be: blue, greenish-yellow, orange, red-orange, and greenish-blue: the synthesis will be a reddish-citron.

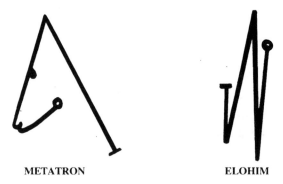

METATRON   ELOHIM

Now we will discuss, for example, the Sigils of the Forces under Binah, the Third Sephirah. The Sigils for the plane of a Sephirah are always worked out on this system in this order:

VOLUME FIVE

First: Sigil of the Sephirah - Binah.

Second: Sigil of the Divine Name, representing the force of the Sephirah in the World of Atziluth. For Binah, YHVH ELOHIM.

Third: The Sigil of the Archangel, representing the force of the Sephirah in Briah TZAPHQIEL.

Fourth: Sigil of the Choir of Angels, representing the force of the Sephirah in Yetzirah ARALIM.

Fifth: The Sigil of the Sphere of the Planet representing the force of the Sephirah in Assiah - SHABBATHAI.

Finally, the Sigils of any other names whose numbers have some relation to the powers of the Sephirah or its Planet. Yet these latter (the Sigils of the Intelligence and Spirit) are more usually taken from the Magical Kamea or Square of the Planets according to a slightly different system as will be shown hereafter.

TRACING FOR NETZACH

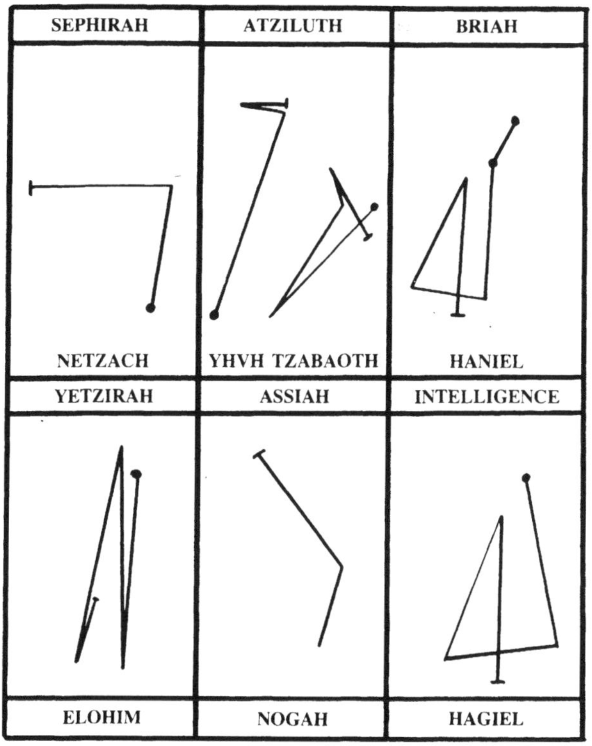

SEPHIRAH	ATZILUTH	BRIAH
NETZACH	YHVH TZABAOTH	HANIEL
YETZIRAH	ASSIAH	INTELLIGENCE
ELOHIM	NOGAH	HAGIEL

SIGILS AND KAMEAS

This ancient mode of forming Sigils was through the medium of the Kameas of the Planets or the magical squares. Wallis Budge believes that the word Kamea is derived from the same root as our English cameo. Magical squares are arrangements of numbers and or letters arranged in such a manner as to yield the same number when added horizontally, vertically or diagonally. The sum of all the numbers in the Kamea is one of special significance to the Planet to which that square is attributed.

The method of forming Sigils from these squares is very simple—so simple as sometimes to be confusing. The method of using the magical Rose is very useful and certainly the most convenient—but it has no roots in antiquity. This however is certainly no argument against using it, anachronism though it may be . Barrett gives the Kameas in his book *The Magus*, and Wallis Budge also reproduces them in his *Amulets And Superstitions,* though his are copied from a text on Magic written by Papus towards the close of the last century.

Those in *The Magus* are replete with multiform errors, as is the execrable Hebrew that Barrett uses. Most of these errors are readily correctable. However some basic knowledge, such as is given in the Knowledge Lectures, of Hebrew and Qabalistic numerical manipulations is necessary in order to trace these Sigils on the Kameas. One of the most important tools is the Qabalah of Nine Chambers, or AIQ BEKER. It has been reproduced earlier in these pages. By this method, the letters of the Hebrew alphabet are grouped together according to the similarity of their numbers—since Hebrew letters are sounds and numbers at the same time. As you will see from the diagram Aleph - 1, Yod - 10, and Qoph - 100 are grouped together in the first space or chamber because they are all variables of 1. So also in the third chamber, Gimel - 3, Lamed - 30, and Shin - 300 are likewise grouped together since 3 is their constant. The same rule applies to all the others—forming nine groupings or chambers.

In order to trace the Sigil of any Name—and do remember that Sigil simply means signature—one must reduce the letters of the Name to tens or units as found in the Square. TIRIEL one of the Mercurial names is one which previously defied tracing because of errors in the numbering of the square and the careless transposition of the shape of the Sigil in older works. However, Teth - 9, Yod - 10 and can be used as such or reduced to 1, Resh -200 but must be reduced to 20, Yod - 10, Aleph - 1, and Lamed -30. To trace the Sigil, one starts at the lower left hand corner, moves directly diagonally to 10 or 1, then again almost diagonally downwards to either 20 or 2 (they are in the same pathway), back to 10 or 1, loops the line because one must return to Aleph - 1, then somewhat downwards to the left for Lamed - 30 (3 is in the same pathway but lower down.)

It sounds complex but a little practice will demonstrate its simplicity. The resultant shape may be somewhat different from that given here—but the difference is slight and may be put down to artistic license.

The Seal or Sigil of the Planet is a symmetrical form so designed that its traced lines touch every number on the Kamea. Thus the seal becomes an epitome or synthetic figure of the Kamea.

In a small book I wrote some years ago *How to Make and Use Talismans* I demonstrated a technique whereby ordinary names—not necessary Qabalistic ones—may be used in order to initiate a particular current of force thought to be necessary at a given time. Thus the names Joe Brown or Bill Green, to use crude examples, may be translated by means of Pythagorean numerology into numbers that can be traced in a Kamea. If for example, the student of Magic—say Joe Brown—felt sickly, he could make a sigil of his name and number by using the Kamea of the Sun or Jupiter, etc. etc. There are many changes that can be rung on this simple theme.

KAMEA OF SATURN

4	9	2
3	5	7
8	1	6

SEAL OF THE PLANET

SPIRIT ZAZEL

INTELLIGENCE AGIEL

KAMEA OF JUPITER

4	14	15	1
9	7	6	12
5	11	10	8
16	2	3	13

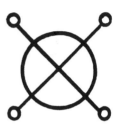

SEAL OF THE PLANET

SPIRIT HISMAEL

INTELLIGENCE YOPHIEL

THE COMPLETE GOLDEN DAWN SYSTEM OF MAGIC

KAMEA OF MARS

11	24	7	20	3
4	12	25	8	16
17	5	13	21	9
10	18	1	14	22
23	6	19	2	15

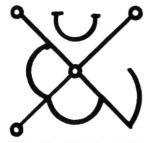

SEAL OF PLANET

**SPIRIT
BARTZABEL**

**INTELLIGENCE
NAKHIEL**

KAMEA OF SOL

6	32	3	34	35	1
7	11	27	28	8	30
19	14	16	15	23	24
18	20	22	21	17	13
25	29	10	9	26	12
36	5	33	4	2	31

SEAL OF PLANET

**SPIRIT
SORATH**

**INTELLIGENCE
GRAPHIEL**

KAMEA OF VENUS

22	47	16	41	10	35	4
5	23	45	17	42	11	29
30	6	24	49	18	36	12
13	31	7	25	43	19	37
38	14	32	1	26	44	20
21	39	8	33	2	27	45
46	15	40	9	34	3	28

KAMEA OF MERCURY

8	58	59	5	4	62	63	1
49	15	14	52	53	11	10	56
41	23	22	44	45	19	18	48
32	34	35	29	28	38	39	25
40	26	27	37	36	30	31	33
17	47	46	20	21	43	42	24
9	55	54	12	13	51	50	16
64	2	3	61	60	6	7	57

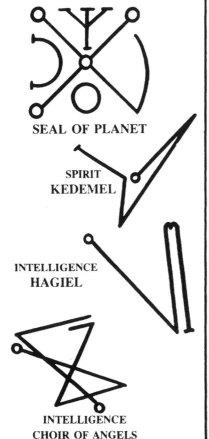

SEAL OF PLANET

**SPIRIT
KEDEMEL**

**INTELLIGENCE
HAGIEL**

**INTELLIGENCE
CHOIR OF ANGELS
BENI SERAPHIM**

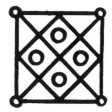

SEAL OF PLANET

**SPIRIT
TAPHTHARTHARATH**

**INTELLIGENCE
TIRIEL**

KAMEA OF LUNA

37	78	29	70	21	62	13	54	5
6	38	79	30	71	22	63	14	46
47	7	39	80	31	72	23	55	15
16	48	8	40	81	32	64	24	56
57	17	49	9	41	73	33	65	25
26	58	18	50	1	42	74	34	66
67	27	59	10	51	2	43	75	35
36	68	19	60	11	52	3	44	76
77	28	69	20	61	12	53	4	45

1 & 2 INTELLIGENCE OF THE
INTELLIGENCES OF THE MOON:
**MALCAH BETARSHISIM
VE-AD RUACHOTH HA-SCHECHALIM**

3 SEAL OF THE PLANET

4 SPIRIT: **CHASHMODAI**

5 SPIRIT OF THE SPIRITS OF THE MOON:
**SHAD BARSCHEMOTH
HA-SCHARTATHAN**

VOLUME FIVE

NAMES AND SIGILS OF OLYMPIC PLANETARY SPIRITS

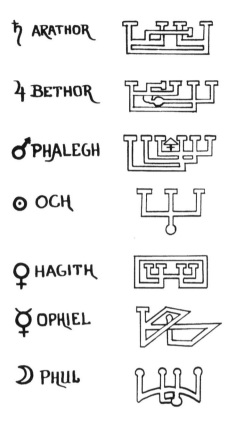

So far as concerns the foregoing Sigils, tradition has it that the Spirits are evil, the Intelligences good. The Seals and Names of the Intelligences should be used on all Talismans for a good effect. Those of the Spirits of the Planets serve for evil, and should therefore not be used in any operation of a beneficial kind. The tradition however implies usually by an evil force, such as the Spirits of the planets, a blind force, which contrary to popular notion can be used to good and beneficial ends.

TELESMATIC FIGURES

There is a mode whereby, combining the letters, the colours, the attributions and their Synthesis, thou mayest build up a telesmatic Image of a Force. The Sigil shall then serve thee for the tracing of a Current which shall call into action a certain Elemental Force.

Know thou that this is not to be done lightly for thine amusement or experiment, seeing that the Forces of Nature were not created to be thy plaything or toy. Unless thou doest thy practical magical works with solemnity, ceremony and reverence, thou shalt be like an infant playing with fire, and thou shalt bring destruction upon thyself.

Know, then, that if thou essay in the imagination to form an astral image from the Names, the first letter shall be the head of the Figure or Form, and the final letters shall be its feet. The other letters shall be, and represent in their order, its body and members.

39

AGIEL, for example, shall give thee an Angelic Form of the following nature and appearance.

ALEPH, Air. The head winged, and of a golden colour, with long floating golden hair.

GIMEL, Luna. Crowned blueish silver cresent, and with face like that of grave and beautiful woman with a blueish halo.

YOD, Virgo. The body of a maiden clothed in a grass green robe.

ALEPH, Air. Golden wings of a large size, partly covering the lower part of the figure.

LAMED, Libra. Feet and limbs well-proportioned and, either in the hand of the figure or lying at its feet, the sword and scales of Justice in bright green.

Playing around the figure will be a greenish light the colour of its synthesis. The keys of the Tarot may help thee in the form.

See well also that thou makest the Image as pure and beautiful as possible, for the more impure or common the figure, the more dangerous is it unto thee. (N.B. I suggest that before you build up this figure in your imagination, you make a rough sketch on a large sheet of paper and keep it aside for several days constantly making improvements in its appearance. When finished this is the time to transfer it to the imagination. I.R.)

Write upon the breast its Sigil, upon the girdle its Name, and place clouds below the feet. And when thou has done this with due solemnity and rigid correctness of symbolism, shunning as thou wouldst shun death any suggestion of coarseness or vulgarity in an Angelic symbol, **then hear what it shall say unto thee.**

SERAPHIM will give thee an Angelic Figure like a Warrioress with Flame playing about her, and a countenance glorious like the Sun, and beneath her feet the stormy Sea and thunder clouds, and lightning about her, and a glow as of Flame. She has a triangular helmet or head-dress of Flame like the symbol of Fire.

GRAPHIEL will give thee a Great Angel like a Female Warrior with a most glorious countenance, crowned with the Crescent and flashing with Light, and surrounded by Flame and Lightening and with Four Wings.

The termination EL **always** gives to Angelic Forms the Wings and Symbols of Justice. The ending YAH will make the Figures like enthroned Kings or Queens, and with flaming glory at their feet.

FURTHER ON TELESMATIC FIGURES

The Names of all Angels and Angelic forces terminate, with few exceptions, in either AL or YAH. The Divine Name AL belongs to CHESED and it represents a good, powerful, and mighty force, but of somewhat milder operation than the Name YAH.

Since not only the Angels but even devils are said to draw their force and power directly from the prolific source of the divine energies, therefore frequently to the names of evil spirits, is AL added. The Name YAH is added to the name of an Angel or Spirit who exercises only a good and somewhat beneficent office.

This being understood, these two terminations being rather in the nature of incidental attributions than of essential distinction, they need not be taken too much notice of in the construction of a telesmatic image.

In building up such an image, you can either imagine it astrally before you, or paint the actual resemblance. Care should however be taken to pronounce the Divine Names belonging to the world under which the telsmatic image under course of construction would fall. Thus to ATZILUTH are allotted Deific Names. To BRIAH, Archangelic and so on. It is also useful to employ the Sephirotic Names which are comprised in the special world to which the Telesmatic Image is allotted.

VOLUME FIVE

It is well to note that the four Worlds themselves formulate the Law involved in the building up or expression of any material thing. The world of ATZILUTH is purely archetypal and primordial, and to it, as before said, Deific Names are applied. BRIAH is creative and originative, and to it certain Great Gods called Archangels are allotted. YETZIRAH is formative and Angelic Orders are allotted thereunto. ASSIAH which is the material world consists of the great Kingdoms of the Elements, human beings, and in some cases of the Qlippoth—though these latter really occupy the planes below ASSIAH.

From these remarks it will be seen that a Telesmatic Image can hardly apply to ATZILUTH; that to BRIAH it can only do so in a restricted sense. Thus a Telesmatic Image belonging to that world would have to be represented with a kind of concealed head, possessing a form shadowy and barely indicated. Telesmatic Images, then really belong to YETZIRAH. Therefore it would be impossible to employ the telesmatic image of a Divine Name in ATZILUTH, for it would not represent that in the world of ATZILUTH, but rather its correlation in YETZIRAH. In ASSIAH you would get Elemental forms.

The sex of the figure depends upon the predominance of the masculine or the feminine in the total of the letters together, but a jumble of the sexes should be avoided in the same form. The Image built up should be divided into as many parts as there are letters, commencing at the upper part and so on in order.

In addition to this method of determining the sex of the Telesmatic Image of a Name, certain Names are inherently masculine, others feminine, and some epicene, irrespective of the mere testimony of the letters.

SANDALPHON, for instance is thus analysed:

Samekh is Male, Nun is Male, Daleth is Female, Lamed is Female, Peh is Female, Vau is Male, and Nun is Male.

Therefore masculine predominates, and if it were an ordinary Name you would make a masculine Form out of it. But this Name is especially applied to the feminine Kerub, it is an exception to the rule; it is an Archangelic Name, belonging to the BRIATIC world and not merely an Angelic Name relating to YETZIRAH.

SANDALPHON is also called Yetzer, meaning 'left', and its letters are: female, female and male, so that, in this case, it may be any of these.

The Seven Letters composing the Name SANDALPHON are thus adapted to the Telesmatic Image.

Samekh is the Head. Would represent a beautiful and active face rather thin than fat.
Nun is the Neck, would be admirably full.
Daleth is the Shoulders of a beautiful woman.
Lamed is the Heart and Chest, the latter perfectly proportioned.
Peh is the Hips strong and full.
Vau is the Legs massive.
Nun (final) Feet sinewy and perhaps winged.

Should you desire to build up an elemental form out of this Name a very peculiar figure would result:

Samekh—Head fierce, but rather beautiful. Blue.
Nun—Neck with eagle's wings from behind. Blue-green.
Daleth—Shoulders feminine, rather beautiful. Green-blue.
Lamed—Chest of woman. Emerald.
Peh—Strong and shaggy hips and thighs. Red.
Vau—Legs of a Bull. Red-orange.
Nun (final)—Feet of an Eagle. Green-blue.

This it will be seen, is almost a synthetical Kerubic Figure. This figure may be represented, as it were, with its feet on the Earth, and its head in the clouds. The colours in the scale of the King would synthesize as a delicate and sparkling green.

The uncovered parts of the body would be blue, the countenance belonging to Sagittarius would be almost that of a horse. The whole form would be like that of a goddess between Hathor and Neith holding a bow and arrows, that is if represented as an Egyptian symbol.

If again, we endeavour to translate this Name into symbols on a Tattwic Plane, we get the following:

Samekh comes under FIRE
Nun comes under WATER
Daleth comes under WATER OF EARTH
Lamed comes under AIR
Peh comes under FIRE
Nun comes under WATER.

These would be synthesized thus: A silver crescent on a red triangle placed over a yellow square. All three would be charged and enclosed within a large silver crescent.

Now, taking another example, the Telesmatic Image appertaining to the Letter ALEPH. This on the BRIATIC Plane, would be rather masculine than feminine and would be resumed by a spiritual figure hardly visible at all, the head-dress winged, the body cloud-veiled and wrapped in mist, as if clouds were rolling over and obscuring the outline, and scarcely permitting the legs and feet to be seen. It represents the Spirit of Ether. In the YETZIRATIC World, it would be like a Warrior with winged helmet, the face angelic but rather fierce, the body and arms mailed and bearing a child—the legs and feet with mailed buskins and wings attached to them.

In ASSIAH, this same letter ALEPH is terrific energy and represents, as it were, mad force (the shape of the Letter is almost that of a Swastika). On the human plane, it would represent a person who was a lunatic and at times given to frightful fits of mania. Translated to the elemental plane, it would represent a form whose body fluctuated between a man and an animal, and indeed, the ASSIATIC form would be a most evil type with a force something like that compounded of that of a bird and that of a demon—an altogether horrible result.

The Letter ALEPH represents spirituality in high things, but when translated to the plane contiguous to or below ASSIAH is usually something horrible and unbalanced, because it is so opposed to matter that the moment it is involved therein, there is no harmony between them. This notion is most important and permeates all forms of the Order's magical procedures.

Radiating forces of Divine Light, otherwise called Angelic Forms, have not gender in the grosser acceptation of the term, though they can be classed according to the masculine and feminine sides. As, for example, in the human figure, sex is not so strongly marked in the upper part, the head, as in the body, while yet the countenance can be distinctly classed as of a masculine or a feminine type. So, also, on quitting the material plane, sex becomes less marked, or rather appreciable in a different manner, though the distinction of masculine or feminine is retained. And herein is the great error of the phallic religions—that they have transferred the material and gross side of sex to Divine and Angelic planes, not understanding that it is the lower that is derived from the higher by correlation in material development, and not the higher from the lower. Gender, in the usual meaning of the term, belongs to the Elemental Spirits, Kerubic Forms, Fays, Planetary Spirits and Olympic Spirits—also to the Qliphoth in its most exaggerated and bestial aspects, and this is a ratio increasing in proportion to the depths of their descent. Also, in certain of the evil elemental spirits it would be exaggerated and repulsive.

But in the higher and angelic natures, gender is correlated by forms, either **steady and firm,** or **rushing.** Firmness like that of a rock or pillar is the nature of the Feminine; restlessness and movement, that of the Masculine. Therefore, let this be clearly understood in ascribing gender to angelic forms and images. **Our tradition classes all forces under the heads of vehement and rushing force, and firm and steady force. Therefore a figure representing the former would be a masculine and that representing the latter, a feminine form.**

But for convenience in the formation of Telesmatic images of ordinary occult names and words, the letters are arranged in masculine and feminine classification. This classification is not intended to affirm that the letters have not in themselves both natures (seeing that in each letter as in each Sephirah is hidden the dual nature of masculine and feminine) but shows more their tendency as regards the distinction of force beforementioned.

Those, then, are rather masculine than feminine to which are allotted forces more rapid in action. And those, again, are rather feminine than masculine which represent a force more firm and steady whence all letters whose sound is prolonged as if moving forward are rather masculine than feminine. Certain others are epicene, yet incline rather to one nature than to another. (By G.H. Frater D.D.C.F.)

TELESMATIC ATTRIBUTIONS OF THE LETTERS OF THE HEBREW ALPHABET
By
G.H. FRATER D.D.C.F.

ALEPH. Spiritual. Wings generally, epicene, rather male than female, rather thin type.
BETH. Active and slight. Male.
GIMEL. Grey, beautiful yet changeful. Feminine, rather full face and body.
DALETH. Very beautiful and attractive. Feminine. Rather full face and body.
HEH. Fierce, strong, rather fiery; feminine.
VAU. Steady and strong. Rather heavy and clumsy, masculine.
ZAYIN. Thin, intelligent, masculine.
CHETH. Full face, not much expression, feminine.
TETH. Rather strong and fiery. Feminine.
YOD. Very white and rather delicate. Feminine.
    CAPH. Big and strong, masculine.
    LAMED. Well-proportioned; feminine.
    MEM. Reflective, dream-like, epicene, but female rather than male.
    NUN. Square determined face, masculine, rather dark.
    SAMEKH. Thin rather expressive face; masculine.
    AYIN. Rather mechanical, masculine.
    PEH. Fierce, strong, resolute, feminine.
    TZADDI. Thoughtful, intellectual, feminine.
    QOPH. Rather full face, masculine.
    RESH. Proud and dominant, masculine.
    SHIN. Fierce, active, epicene, rather male than female.

TAU. Dark, grey, epicene; male rather than female.
(These genders are only given as a convenient guide.)

SUMMARY

In the vibration of Names concentrate first upon the highest aspirations and upon the whiteness of Kether. Astral vibrations and material alone are dangerous. Concentrate then upon your Tiphareth, the centre about the heart, and draw down into it the White Rays from above. Formulate the letters in White Light in your heart. Inspire deeply, and then pronounce the letters of the Name, vibrating each through your whole system—as if setting into vibration the Air before you, and as if that vibration spread out into space.

The Whiteness should be brilliant.

The Sigils are drawn from the lettering of the Rose upon the Cross, and these are in Tiphareth, which corresponds to the heart. Draw them as if the Rose were in your heart.

In vibrating any Name, pronounce it as many times as it has letters. This is the Invoking Whirl.

Example: The Vibration of ADONAI HA-ARETZ.

Perform the Banishing Ritual of the Pentagram in the four quarters of your room, preceded by the Qabalistic Cross. Then in each quarter give the Signs of the Adeptus Minor, saying IAO and LVX, making the symbol of the Rose-Cross as taught in the paper describing the Rose-Cross Ritual.

Pass to the centre of the Room, and face East. Then formulate before you in brilliant white flashings the Letters of the Name in the form of a Cross—i.e. both perpendicular and horizontal, as seen in the diagram below.

אדני הארץ

There is another method of assigning gender based upon whether or not the sound of the HEBREW Letter is arrested or prolonged. If the former it is masculine, if the latter it is feminine—as follows:

SOUND PROLONGED
(MASCULINE)

Aleph-broad A	**Beth-B-Bh**
Vau-U,V, OO	**Zayin-Z**
Caph-K Kh	**Nun-N**
Samekh-S	**Ayin-O, Ngh, Au**
Qoph-Q, Qh	**Resh-R**
Shin-Sh, S	

VOLUME FIVE

SOUND ARRESTED
(FEMININE)

Gimel-G, Gh	Daleth-D, Dh
Heh-H	Cheth-Ch (gutteral)
Teth-T	Yod-I, J, Y.
Lamed-L	Mem-M
Peh-P, Ph	Tzaddi-Tz
Tau-T, Th.	

These, then, are two processes: The INVOKING WHIRL related to the Heart. The EXPANDING WHIRL related to the Aura.

ADNI makes the figure from head to waist; HA-ARTZ from waist to feet. The whole Name is related to Malkuth, Matter, and Zelatorship.

ALEPH. Winged, white, brilliant, radiant Crown.

DALETH. Head and neck of a woman, beautiful but firm, hair long, dark and waving.

NUN. Arms bare, strong, extended as a cross. In the right hand are ears of corn, and in the left a golden Cup. Large dark spreading Wings.

YOD. Deep yellow-green robe covering a strong chest on which is a square lamen of gold with a scarlet Greek Cross—in the angles four smaller red crosses.

In addition a broad gold belt on which ADONAI HA - ARETZ is written in Enochian or Hebrew characters.

The feet are shown in flesh colour with golden sandals. Long yellow green drapery rayed with olive reaches to the feet. Beneath are black lurid clouds with patches of colour. Around the figure are lightning flashes, red. The crown radiates White Light. A Sword is girt at the side of the figure.

THE VIBRATORY MODE OF PRONOUNCING
THE DIVINE NAMES

By

G.H. FRATER D.D.C.F.

In vibrating the Divine Names, the Operator should first of all rise as high as possible towards the idea of the Divine White Brilliance in KETHER—keeping the mind raised to the plane of loftiest aspiration. Unless this is done, it is dangerous to vibrate only with the astral forces, because the vibration attracts a certain force to the operator, and the nature of the force attracted rests largely on the condition of mind in which the operator is.

The ordinary mode of vibrating is as follows: Take a deep and full inspiration and concentrate your consciousness in your heart, which answers to Tiphareth. (Having first, as already said, ascended to your Kether, you should endeavour to bring down the white Brilliance into your heart, prior to centering your consciousness there.)

Then formulate the letters of the Name required in your heart, in white, and feel them written there. Be sure to formulate the letters in brilliant white light, not merely in dull whiteness as the colour of the Apas Tattwa. Then, emitting the breath, slowly pronounce the Letters so that the sound **vibrates within you,** and imagine that the breath, while quitting the body, **swells you so as to fill up space.** Pronounce the Name as if you were vibrating it through the whole Universe, and as if it did not stop until it reached the further limits.

All practical occult work which is of any use tires the operator or withdraws some magnetism, and therefore, if you wish to do anything that is at all important, you must be in perfect magnetic and nervous condition, or else you will do evil instead of good.

When you are using a Name and drawing a Sigil from the Rose, you must remember that the Sephirah to which the Rose and Cross are referred, is Tiphareth, whose position answers to the location of the heart, as if the Rose were therein.

It is not always necessary to formulate before you in space the telesmatic angelic figure of the Name.

As a general rule, pronounce the Name as many times as there are letters in it.

(N. B. One of the things that affords me much gratification is hearing from a student here and there who has been working the Golden Dawn system satisfactorily. Every now and then someone calls my attention to a pamphlet or book written by a student who found techniques of considerable worth in this system. For example, a few months ago my attention was directed to ANGELIC IMAGES by a Frater A.H.E.H.O. in England. It is a beautifully written little manual on the use of the Telesmatic Images. As the author states, the technique is nowhere to be found save in the Golden Dawn, yet this is strange, that so formidable a technique has received no further commentary. He proposed to remedy the deficiency, and indeed has succeeded so well that I strongly recommend the little book. It may be purchased from the Sorceror's Apprentice, in Leeds, Yorkshire.

AHEHO's description of the technique is: As the sapphire is drawn from the earth, rugged and of crude appearance, so do we find these two Papers—archaicly written, disjointed, seemingly in places to be worthless; but, as the gem is cut and polished to a gleaming splendour, so do these Papers, when studied and worked upon, synthesize into a gleaming gem, a radiant sapphire, the reflected Light through which may serve to illuminate the dark pathways of the Cosmos. I.R.)

AN ALTERNATE METHOD OF VIBRATING THE DIVINE NAMES
By
V.H. FRATER A.M.A.G.

Not long ago, I came across a technique which, while not essentially Golden Dawn, is so intrinsically in harmony with fundamental principles that I experimented with it to ascertain whether it could be used magically. It could, so I discovered. And a good deal else beside.

It also provides a good basis for understanding—if one was not aware of it before—the nature of the effect in one's own organism of the vibration of the Divine Names. One developes a great deal of respect for the method itself. The latter was reported by a metaphysician by the name of Brown Landone in a brochure entitled *The Great Spiritual Responsiveness of Body and Awakening the Brain of Spirit.* It is a formidable title—and the principal content is formidable also. Landone describes a simple experiment which is essential to anyone wishing to employ this method intelligently.

Before describing this, let me repeat once more the instructions given in Z. 1. **The Symbolism of the Ceremony of the Opening of the Neophyte Grade.** 'Let the Adept, standing upright, his arms stretched out in the form of a Calvary Cross, vibrate a Divine Name, bringing with the formulation thereof a deep inspiration into his lungs. Let him retain the breath, mentally pronouncing the Name in his Heart, so as to combine it with the forces he desires to awaken thereby. Thence sending it downwards through his body past Yesod, but not resting there. Taking his physical life for a material basis, send it on into his feet. There he shall again momentarily formulate the Name. Then bringing it rushing upwards into the lungs, thence shall he breathe it forth strongly, while vibrating that Divine Name. He will send his breath steadily forward into the Universe so as to awaken the corresponding forces of the Name in the outer world. Standing with arms out, in the form of a cross, when the breath has been imaginatively sent to the feet and back, bring the arms forward in the sign of the Enterer while vibrating the name out into the Universe. On completing this, make the Sign of Silence and remain still, contemplating the Force you have invoked.'

The alternative method to be described here is not too fundamentally different. In fact, it is identical save in one respect. Before describing that one fact, let me describe the experiment recommended by Brown Landone.

Take an ordinary piece of dining flatware—a long spoon or knife or fork, or what not. It makes no difference. So long as it is a metal and can transmit vibrations readily, that is all that is required. Now take a long piece of ordinary string, about forty inches long. Wrap the middle of this string securely around the spoon (or whatever), leaving the ends free. Hold each end between thumb and forefinger—one end in both right and left hands, and leaning over, swing the spoon against the edge of a table. **Listen to the sound it makes.** Depending on the flatware and the table, a certain sound will be struck. Take note of it.

Having done this, take one end of the string and wrap it around the middle phalange of the index finger. Do this on both the right and left sides. Then insert the tips of the fingers involved into the ear, lightly. Repeat the same experiment of swinging the spoon so that it hits against a table or desk. Now determine what kind of sound this spoon makes in the ear. I must confess it rather surprised me when I first performed this little experiment.

The resultant sound bears little relation to the first sound. It is more like the pealing of cathedral bells. Repeat this several times, so that your impression is most clear, and hence can be recalled.

It is this sound, suggests Mr. Landone, which is made whenever we speak, talk or pray. It is this sound which is made when we hum. And it is humming that Landone recommends in conjunction with various prayers etc. that he prescribes. It is this inner vibration of which we are not normally aware that vibrates throughout the whole organism. It must have an effect on every molecule in every cell, so that all vibrate in unison with the divine name being intoned.

THE COMPLETE GOLDEN DAWN SYSTEM OF MAGIC

I am not suggesting prayers of any kind actually. It is solely my recommendation that the humming be employed with the Order's method of vibrating the divine Names, knowing full well from this experiment what the full effect of the formula produces. In all other instances of intoning the various names—as in the Pentagram and Hexagram rituals --follow all the rules and methods described in this paper by the Order. But when breathing out the Name, as described above, **hum it out.** Do not try to pronounce or vibrate the Name clearly. **Hum the Name.** But as you hum, clearly visualize, or have the mental intention that such and such a Name is being vibrated while you hum.

For instance, if the name METATRON or SANDALPHON is to be used, as recommended in this document, it should be hummed on the outgoing breath. The Name in Hebrew letters riding on the breath, as it were, should be visualized as per the relevant instructions. When the instruction advises that you should imagine that the breath, when quitting the body, swells you up so that you fill up all space, it should not be too difficult to conceive of the fact that the sound made within, while humming, is doing precisely that. It may of course require a good deal of practice, but I fancy that you will find it is worth the effort.

Over my many years of use of the vibratory formula there are a couple of suggestions I would like to offer the student just beginning to work with it. The first one is to draw the name of the God or Archangel one proposes to work with on a large board or piece of paper. Write it with a soft-tipped marking pen, and make the letters very large. Place it about six to ten feet away from where you are working so that it is within easy vision. So that when attempting to visualize the Name, it will be made easier by looking at the board first. With a little practice it will be easy to visualize with the eyes open. If not, open them periodically, casting a swift glance at the name on the board. This is an aid to visualization.

The second tip is that if your are not accustomed to being hyperventilated, proceed slowly. Stand at the foot of a bed, or have a mattress placed on the floor where you are working. The idea is that this practice results in hyperventilation, producing dizziness and unsteadiness on one's legs so that more often than not you can fall and I would rather you fall on a relatively soft surface than a hard one and injure yourself. Please take this warning seriously.

Practice the method—with both the board and the bed—several times before attempting to use it in full ceremonial work in your Temple. Develop some expertise first, so that in your Temple you will not fall because of hyperventilation.

If you are not familiar with the concept of hyperventilation, read *Undoing Yourself with Energized Meditation and Other Devices*, by Christopher S. Hyatt, Falcon Press, 1982. Also my book on the vegetotherapy of Wilhelm Reich to be published in 1984 by Falcon Press, will provide an extensive discussion of the subject.

VOLUME FIVE

GEOMANCY

By

G.H. FRATER D.D.C.F.

ONE

The figures of Geomancy consist of various groupings of odd and even points in 4 lines. Of these the greatest possible number of combinations is 16. Therefore these sixteen combinations of odd and even points arranged on four lines are the sixteen figures of Geomancy. These are again classed under the heads of the Elements, the Signs of the Zodiac, and the Planets. Two figures are attributed to each of the Seven Planets, while the remainder are attributed to Caput and Cauda Draconis the Head and Tail of the Dragon, or the North and South Nodes of the Moon. Furthermore, to each Planet and Sign certain ruling Genii are attributed.

TWO

Roughly speaking, the mode of obtaining the first four Geomantic figures, from which the remainder of the Divination is calculated, is by marking down at random on paper with a pencil held by a loosely tensed hand 16 lines of points or dashes, without counting the number placed in each line during the operation. It should be done very rapidly. All the time think fixedly of the subject of the question. When the 16 lines are completed, the number of points in each line should be added up, and if the result be odd a single point or cross should be made in the first of the three compartments to the right of the paper. If even, two points or crosses. These 16 lines are represented below.

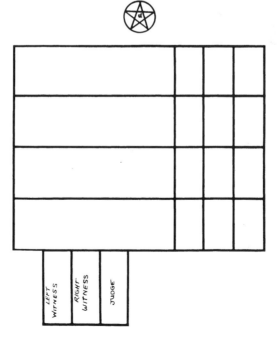

These yield four Geomantic figures. The results, odd and or even, of lines 1 to 4 inclusive comprise the first figure, of Fortuna Minor. Of lines 5 to 8 the second figure; of lines 9 to 12 the third; of lines 13 to 16, the 4th figure, as shown in the diagram.

PLAN OF GEOMANTIC DIVINATION

15 points odd	●	
15 points odd	●	
16 points even	● ●	**Fortuna Minor**
14 points even	● ●	

15 points odd	●	
16 points even	● ●	**Amissio**
15 points odd	●	
14 points even	● ●	

12 points even	● ●	
6 points even	● ●	**Fortuna Minor**
9 points odd	●	
7 points odd	●	

10 points even	● ●	
11 points odd	●	**Rubeus**
10 points even	● ●	
10 points even	● ●	

The symbol of a Pentagram either within or without a circumscribed circle should be made at the top of the paper on which the dashes are made. The paper itself should be perfectly clean and should have never been previously used for any other purpose. If a circle be used with the Pentagram, it should be drawn before the latter is described. The Pentagram should always be of the "invoking" type, as described in the Pentagram Ritual. Since the Pentagram concerns the element of Earth, it should therefore be drawn beginning at the top point descending to the lower left hand point, carefully closing the angle at the finish. While slowly tracing the Pentagram, the divine name associated with Earth should be intoned or vibrated ADONAI ha-ARETZ. It could be intoned two or three times before proceeding with the drawing of the

Sigil. This will help to concentrate the mind and to elevate it to the highest notion compatible with the method. Do remember that in one of the Ritual obligations, the aspirant swears that in all his magical workings he will always invoke the highest divine names that he knows. Thus he will always be working under the aegis of the divine. Within the centre of the Pentagram, the Sigil of the "Ruler" to which the matter of the question specially refers, should be placed.

If the question be of the Nature of Saturn, such as agriculture, sorrow, death, etc., the Sigil of Zazel should be placed in the Pentagram. If of Jupiter, concerning good fortune, feasting, church preferment, etc., the Sigil of Hismael. If of Mars, war, fighting, victory, etc., the Sigil of Bartzabel. If of the Sun, power, magistracy, success, etc., the Sigil of Sorath. If of Venus, love, music, pleasure, etc., the Sigil of Kedemel. If of Mercury, such as science, learning, knavery, etc., the Sigil of Taphthartharath, etc., If of travelling, fishing, etc., under Luna, then the Sigil of Chasmodai. In the diagram appended, the Sigil of Hismael is employed.

During the marking down of the points, the attention should be fixed upon the Sigil within the Pentagram, and the mind should carefully consider the question proposed.

A good idea to to repeat out loud the name of the Ruler as if to invoke him. This should also be followed by a **short** statement repeated again and again concerning the topic of divination. The hand should not be removed from the paper until all 16 lines of points have been finished.

For example if you wished to ask a question concerning the acquisition of wealth you would use the Sigil relating to Jupiter, Hismael. You would then, while making the random dots, repeat three or four times the name of Hismael, followed by, "Will I acquire, such and such amount of money?" (Specify time period. The phrasing of the question should be very definite and specific.) The whole phrase should be repeated frequently until all 16 lines of dots have been completed.

GEOMANTIC ATTRIBUTIONS

Sigil	Ruler	Planet	Sign
	Bartzabel	Mars	Aries
	Kedemel	Venus	Taurus
	Taphthartharath	Mercury	Gemini
	Chasmodai	Luna	Cancer
	Sorath	Sol	Leo
	Taphthartharath	Mercury	Virgo
	Kedemel	Venus	Libra
	Bartzabel	Mars	Scorpio
	Hismael	Jupiter	Sagittarius
	Zazel	Saturn	Capricorn
	Zazel	Saturn	Aquarius
	Hismael	Jupiter	Pisces
	Zazel	Saturn	Cauda Draconis
	Bartzabel	Mars	Cauda Draconis
	Hismael	Venus	Caput Draconis
	Kedemel	Jupiter	Caput Draconis
	Sorath	Sun	Leo
	Chasmodai	Luna	Cancer

GEOMANTIC ATTRIBUTIONS CONTINUED

Element	Figure	Name and Meaning of Figure
Fire		Puer, a boy yellow and beardless
Earth		Amissio, loss from without
Air		Albus, white, fair
Water		Populus, people gathering together
Fire		Fortuna major, greater fortune, aid, entering
Earth		Conjunctio, assembly, union
Air		Puella, a girl, beautiful
Water		Rubeus, red, reddish
Fire		Acquisitio, obtaining, comprehended within
Earth		Career, a prison, bound
Air		Tristitia, sadness, damned, cross
Water		Laetitia, joy, laughing, healthy, bearded
Fire		Cauda Draconis, the lower threshold, going out
Earth		Caput Draconis, heart, upper threshold, entering
Fire		Fortuna minor, lesser fortune, aid, going out
Water		Via, way, journey

A pencil is preferable to a pen for this task of tracing the dots. Otherwise, use a contemporary felt pen or marking pen which is ideal for this purpose. It is practically more convenient to draw or rule four lines across the paper beforehand to mark off the space for such four lines composing a Geomantic Figure as shown on the previous page.

The first four Geomantic figures formed directly from the 16 lines of points are called The Four Mothers. It is from them that the remaining figures necessary to complete the Geomantic scheme of direction are derived.

These should now be placed in a row from right to left, for the greater convenience of the necessary calculation though much practice may render this unnecessary. The first figure will be attributed to the South, the Second to the East, the Third to the North, and the Fourth to the West.

THE FOUR MOTHERS

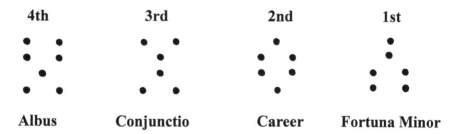

4th	3rd	2nd	1st
Rubeus	Fort. Maj,	Amissio	Fort. Minor

From these Four Mothers, four resulting figures called the Four Daughters are now to be derived, thus: The uppermost points of the First Mother, will be the uppermost points of the First Daughter. The corresponding, that is the first line of, points of the Second Mother will be the second points of the First Daughter. The same line of points of the Third Mother will constitute the third points of the First Daughter. The same points of the Fourth Mother willl be the fourth points of the First Daughter. **The same rule applies to all the figures.**

The second line of points of the four Mother figures will comprise the Second Daughter. The third line of points of the Four Mothers will comprise the Third Daughter, and the fourth line of points of the Four Mothers will comprise the Fourth Daughter and so on.

Applying the above rule throughout, the following will represent the Four Daughters:

4th	**3rd**	**2nd**	**1st**
Albus	**Conjunctio**	**Career**	**Fortuna Minor**

These, again for the convenience of the beginner, are now to be placed on the left hand of the Four Mothers in a single line from right to left.

Four Daughters   **Four Mothers**

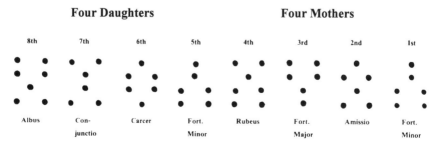

8th	7th	6th	5th	4th	3rd	2nd	1st
Albus	Con-junctio	Carcer	Fort. Minor	Rubeus	Fort. Major	Amissio	Fort. Minor

From these eight figures, four others are now to be calculated which may be called **the Four Resultants, or the Four Nephews.** These will be the 9th, 10th, 11th, and 12th figures of the whole scheme. The Ninth figure is formed from the points of the first and second figures compared together. The Tenth from the 3rd and 4th figures; the 11th from the 5th and 6th figures, the 12th from the 7th and 8th figures. The rule is to compare or add together the points of the corresponding lines. If, for instance, the first line of the First Mother consists of one point, and the first line of the Second Mother also consists of one point, these two are added together, and since they form an even number two points are marked down for the first line of the Resultant. If the added points are odd, only one point is marked for the resulting figure. The Ninth figure of Conjunctio is thus formed.

First Figure	Second Figure	Conjunctio

Now the first figure has one point at the top, the second figure has one point at the top -together they make two, an **even** number, thus making 2 points for the new figure. The first figure has one point on the second line, and the second figure has two points on the second line. Together they make three points, an **odd** number, therefore represented by one point in the new figure. The rest follow similarly and is represented again by the figure below.

CONJUNCTIO

The other Resultants are calculated in precisely the same way:

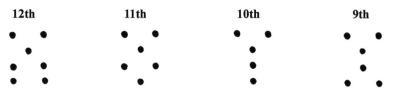

Four Daughters				**Four Mothers**			
8th	7th	6th	5th	4th	3rd	2nd	1st
Albus	Con-junctio	Carcer	Fort. Minor	Rubeus	Fort. Major	Amissio	Fort. Minor

In this way are yielded the four Resultants:

12th	11th	10th	9th
Rubeus	**Acquisitio**	**Caput Drac.**	**Conjunctio**

And thus the Twelve Principal Figures of the Geomantic scheme of Divination are completed. These again correspond to the 12 Astrological Houses of Heaven, with which they will later on be compared.

VOLUME FIVE

THREE

For the greater assistance of the Diviner in forming a judgment upon the general condition of the scheme of 12 figures thus far obtained, it is usual to deduce from them three other subsidiary figures. These three are of less importance than the twelve previous figures, and are not to be considered at all in the light of component figures of the scheme, but only as aids to the general judgment. These other figures are known as the Right Witness, Left Witness, and the Judge.

The two witnesses are without significance in the divination, except as they are the roots from which the figure known as the Judge is derived. The Right Witness is formed from the 9th and 10th figures by comparing the points in the manner before shown in the formation of the Resultants. That is the corresponding lines of points in the two figures are compared together, and the addition, whether odd or even, comprises the points of the Witness. The Left Witness represents the combination in a similar manner to the 11th and 12th figures. The Judge again is formed in precisely the same way from the Two Witnesses, and is therefore a synthesis of the whole figure.

If he be good, the figure is good and the judgment will be favourable; and vice versa. From the nature of the formation of the 15th figure, the Judge, it should always consist of an even number of points, and never of odd. That is, adding together the four lines of points, comprising the Judge, the result should be an even number. For if the Judge were a figure of odd points it would show that a mistake had been made somewhere in the calculation.

The Reconciler is a 16th figure sometimes used for aiding the Judgment by combining the Judge with the Figure in the Particular House signifying the thing demanded. Thus, in the preceding scheme, the Judge formed is Populus, and the Second Figure, being Amissio, their combination also yields Amissio.

In order to discover where The Part of Fortune will fall, add together all the points of the first twelve figures. Divide that number by twelve, and place the Part of Fortune with the figure answering to the remainder. If there is no remainder it will fall on the 12th figure. The Part of Fortune is a symbol of ready money, money in cash belonging to the Querent, and is of the greatest importance in all questions of money.

FOUR

The following is the signification of the 12 Houses of Heaven, in brief:

First House (Ascendant)
Life, health, querent, etc.

Second House
Money, property, personal worth.

Third House
Brothers, sisters, news, short journeys, etc.

Fourth House
Father, landed property, inheritance. The grave, the end of matter.

Fifth House

Children, pleasure, feasts, speculation.

Sixth House

Servants, sickness, uncles and aunts, small animals.

Seventh House

Love, marriage, husband or wife. Partnerships and associations, public enemies, law suits.

Eighth House

Deaths, wills, legacies; pain, anxiety. Estate of deceased.

Ninth House

Long journeys, voyages. Science, religion, art, visions, and divinations.

Tenth House

Mother. Rank and honour, trade or profession, authority, employment, and worldly position generally.

Eleventh House

Friends, hopes and wishes.

Twelfth House

Sorrows, fears, punishments, secret enemies, hospitals or prisons, unseen dangers, restrictions.

The Twelve figures of the Geomantic scheme as previously calculated are to be attributed to a map of the 12 houses of heaven to be placed therein thus:

> **The first figure goes in the 10th house.**
> **The second figure goes in the 1st house.**
> **The third figure goes in the 4th house.**
> **The fourth figure goes in the 7th house.**
> **The fifth figures goes in the 11th house.**
> **The sixth figure goes in the 2nd house.**
> **The seventh figure goes in the 5th house.**
> **The eighth figure goes in the 8th house.**
> **The ninth figure goes in the 12th house.**
> **The tenth figure goes in the 3rd house.**
> **The eleventh figure goes in the 6th house.**
> **The twelfth figure goes in the 9th house.**

Thus the figures derived by the calculations provided in the example given previously would occupy a Geomantic map as follows:

VOLUME FIVE

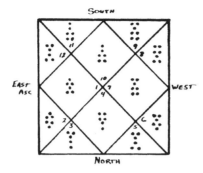

There are a series of interpretations in the original texts based on the use of the Judge and Two Witnesses which I have omitted. To me they were found to be unreliable providing answers unrelated to the divination as indicated by the following interpretations. Clearly they are of mediaeval origin and are totally unrelated to modern situations.

Herein follows a set of general Tables of the Sixteen figures in the Twelve Houses for the better convenience of forming a general judgment of the Scheme. Under the head of each figure separately is given its general effect in whatever House of the Map of the Heavens it may be located. Thus, by taking the House signifying the end or result of the matter, the Fourth House, etc., and by noting what figures fall therein, the student may find by these tables the general effect in that position.

ACQUISITIO

Generally good for profit and gain.

Ascendant - Happy, success in all things.
Second House - Very prosperous.
Third House - Favour and riches.
Fourth House - Good fortune and success.
Fifth House - Good success.
Sixth House - Good, especially if it agrees with the 5th.
Seventh House - Reasonably good.
Eighth House - Rather good, but not very. The sick shall die.
Ninth House - Good in all demands.
Tenth House - Good in suits. Very prosperous.
Eleventh House - Good in all.
Twelfth House - Evil, pain and loss.

AMISSIO

Good for loss of substance and sometimes for love; but very bad for gain.
Ascendant - Ill in all things but for prisoners.
Second House - Very ill for money, but good for love.
Third House - Ill end, except for quarrels.
Fourth House - Ill in all.
Fifth House - Evil except for agriculture.

57

Sixth House - Rather evil for love.
Seventh House - Very good for love, otherwise evil.
Eighth House - Excellent in all questions.
Ninth House - Evil in all things.
Tenth House - Evil except for favour with women.
Eleventh House - Good for love, otherwise bad.
Twelfth House - Evil in all things.

FORTUNA MAJOR

Good for gain in all things where a person has hopes to win.

Ascendant - Good save in secrecy.
Second House - Good except in sad things.
Third House - Good in all.
Fourth House - Good in all, but melancholy.
Fifth House - Very good in all things.
Sixth House - Very good except for debauchery.
Seventh House - Good in all.
Eighth House - Moderately good.
Ninth House - Very good.
Tenth House - Exceedingly good. Go to superiors.
Eleventh House - Very good.
Twelfth House - Good in all.

FORTUNA MINOR

Good in any matter in which a person wishes to proceed quickly.
Ascendant - Speed in victory and in love, but choleric.
Second House - Very good.
Third House - Good, but wrathful.
Fourth House - Haste; rather evil except for peace.
Fifth House - Good in all things.
Sixth House - Medium in all.
Seventh House - Evil except for war or love.
Eighth House - Evil generally.
Ninth House - Good, but choleric.
Tenth House - Good, except for peace.
Eleventh House - Good, especially for love.
Twelfth House - Good, except for alteration, or for suing another.

LAETITIA

Good for joy, present or to come.
Ascendant - Good, except in war.
Second House - Sickly.
Third House - Ill.
Fourth House - Mainly good.
Fifth House - Excellent.

Sixth House - Evil generally.
Seventh House - Indifferent.
Eighth House - Evil generally.
Ninth House - Very good.
Tenth House - Good, rather in war than in peace.
Eleventh House - Good in all.
Twelfth House - Evil generally.

TRISTITIA

Evil in almost all things.
Ascendant - Medium, but good for treasure and fortifying.
Second House - Medium, but good to fortify.
Third House - Evil in all.
Fourth House - Evil in all.
Fifth House - Very evil.
Sixth House - Evil, except for debauchery.
Seventh House - Evil for inheritance and magic only.
Eighth House - Evil, but in secrecy good.
Ninth House - Evil except for magic.
Tenth House - Evil except for fortifications.
Eleventh House - Evil in all.
Twelfth House - Evil. But good for magic and treasure.

PUELLA

Good in all demands, especially in those relating to women.

Ascendant - Good except in war.
Second House - Very good.
Third House - Good.
Fourth House - Indifferent.
Fifth House - Very good, but notice the aspects.
Sixth House - Good, but especially so for debauchery.
Seventh House - Good except for war.
Eighth House - Good.
Ninth House - Good for music. Otherwise only medium.
Tenth House - Good for peace.
Eleventh House - Good, and love of ladies.
Twelfth House - Good in all.

PUER

Evil in most demands, except in those relating to War or Love.

Ascendant - Indifferent. Best in War.
Second House - Good, but with trouble.
Third House - Good fortune.
Fourth House - Evil, except in War and Love.

Fifth House - Medium good.
Sixth House - Medium.
Seventh House - Evil, save in War.
Eighth House - Evil, save for Love.
Ninth House - Evil except for War.
Tenth House - Rather evil. But good for Love and War.
Eleventh House - Most other things medium.
Twelfth House - Medium; good favour. Very good in all.

RUBEUS

Evil in all that is good and Good in all that is evil.

Ascendant - Destroy the figure if it falls here! It makes the judgment worthless.
Second House - Evil in all demands.
Third House - Evil except to let blood.
Fourth House - Evil except in War and Fire.
Fifth House - Evil save for love, and sowing seed.
Sixth House - Evil except for blood-letting.
Seventh House - Evil except for war and fire.
Eighth House - Evil.
Ninth House - Very evil.
Tenth House - Dissolute. Love, fire.
Eleventh House - Evil, except to let blood.
Twelfth House - Evil in all things.

ALBUS

Good for profit and for entering into a place or undertaking.

Ascendant - Good for marriage. Mercurial. Peace.
Second House - Good in all.
Third House - Very good.
Fourth House - Very good except in War.
Fifth House - Good.
Sixth House - Good in all things.
Seventh House - Good except for War.
Eighth House - Good.
Ninth House - A messenger brings a letter.
Tenth House - Excellent in all.
Eleventh House - Very good.
Twelfth House - Marvellously good.

CONJUNCTIO

Good with good, or evil with evil. Recovery of things lost.

Ascendant - Good with good, evil with evil.
Second House - Commonly good.
Third House - Good fortune.

Fourth House - Good save for health; see the 8th.
Fifth House - Medium.
Sixth House - Good for immorality only.
Seventh House - Rather good.
Eighth House - Evil; death.
Ninth House - Medium good.
Tenth House - For love; good. For sickness, evil.
Eleventh House - Good in all.
Twelfth House - Medium. Bad for prisoners.

CARCER

Generally evil. Delay, binding, bar, restriction.

Ascendant - Evil except to fortify a place.
Second House - Good in Saturnine questions; else evil.
Third House - Evil.
Fourth House - Good only for melancholy.
Fifth House - Receive a letter within three days. Evil.
Sixth House - Very evil.
Seventh House - Evil.
Eighth House - Very evil.
Ninth House - Evil in all.
Tenth House - Evil save for hidden treasure.
Eleventh House - Much anxiety.
Twelfth House - Rather good.

CAPUT DRACONIS

Good with evil; evil with evil. Gives a good issue for gain.

Ascendant - Good in all things.
Second House - Good.
Third House - Very good.
Fourth House - Good save in war.
Fifth House - Very good.
Sixth House - Good for immorality only.
Seventh House - Good especially for peace.
Eighth House - Good.
Ninth House - Very good.
Tenth House - Good in all.
Eleventh House - Good for the church and ecclesiastical gain.
Twelfth House - Not very good.

CAUDA DRACONIS

Good with evil, and evil with good. Good for loss, and for passing out of an affair

Ascendant - Destroy figure if it falls here! Makes judgment worthless.
Second House - Very evil.

Third House - Evil in all.
Fourth House - Good especially for conclusion of the matter.
Fifth House - Very evil.
Sixth House - Rather good.
Seventh House - Evil, war, and fire.
Eighth House - No good, except for magic.
Ninth House - Good for science only. Bad for journeys. Robbery.
Tenth House - Evil save in works of fire.
Eleventh House - Evil save for favours.
Twelfth House - Rather good.

VIA

Injurious to the goodness of other figures generally, but good for journeys and voyages.

Ascendant - Evil except for prison.
Second House - Indifferent.
Third House - Very good in all.
Fourth House - Good in all save love.
Fifth House - Voyages good.
Sixth House - Evil.
Seventh House - Rather good, especially for voyages.
Eighth House - Evil.
Ninth House - Indifferent. Good for journeys.
Tenth House - Good.
Eleventh House - Very good.
Twelfth House - Excellent.

POPULUS

Sometimes good and sometimes bad; good with good, and evil with evil.

Ascendant - Good for marriage.
Second House - Medium good.
Third House - Rather good than bad.
Fourth House - Good in all but love.
Fifth House - Good in most things.
Sixth House - Good.
Seventh House - In war good; else medium.
Eighth House - Evil.
Ninth House - Look for letters.
Tenth House - Good.
Eleventh House - Good in all.
Twelfth House - Very evil.

SIX

By essential dignity is meant the strength of a Figure when found in a particular House. A figure is, therefore, strongest when in what is called its house, very strong when in its exaltation, strong in its Triplicity, very weak in its Fall; weakest of all in its Detriment. A figure is in its Fall when in a House opposite to that of its Exaltation, and in its Detriment when opposite to its own house.

The Geomantic figures, being attributed to the planets and Signs, are dignified according to the rules which obtain in Astrology. That is to say they follow the dignities of their ruling Planets, considering the Twelve Houses of the scheme as answering to the Twelve Signs. Thus, the Ascendant or First House answers to Aries, the Second House to Taurus, the Third House to Gemini, and so on to the Twelfth answering to Pisces. Therefore the figures of Mars will be strong in the First House, but weak in the Seventh House, and so forth.

TABLE OF DIGNITIES

Sign	Element	Ruler	Exaltation	Fall	Detriment	Strong
Aries	Fire	Mars	Sun	Saturn	Venus	Jupiter
Taurus	Earth	Venus	Luna	--	Mars	Jupiter
Gemini	Air	Mercury	--	--	Jupiter	Saturn
Cancer	Water	Luna	Jupiter	Mars	Saturn	Mercury
Leo	Fire	Sun	--	--	Saturn	Mars
Virgo	Earth	Mercury	Mercury	Venus	Jupiter	Saturn
Libra	Air	Venus	Saturn	Sun	Mars	Jupiter
Scorpio	Water	Mars	--	Luna	Venus	Sun
Sagittarius	Fire	Jupiter	--	--	Mercury	Venus
Capricorn	Earth	Saturn	Mars	Jupiter	Luna	Mercury
Aquarius	Air	Saturn	--	--	Sun	--
Pisces	Water	Jupiter	Venus	Mercury	Mercury	--

Caput Draconis is strong in the dignities of Jupiter and Venus. Cauda Draconis is strong in the dignities of Saturn and Mars.

THE COMPLETE GOLDEN DAWN SYSTEM OF MAGIC

NOTES

The following notes were abstracted from a paper on Geomancy circulated in the A.O., which was the name given to the renewed Golden Dawn by Mathers years after the revolt. In it, the statement is made that it was compiled by S.R.M.D. from ancient treatises: 1) *Ye Geomancie of Maister Christopher Catton;* a very old work in black letters. 2) *The Theomagia* by John Heydon (17th century). 3) And the *Geomancia Asironomica* of Gerardus CAMBRENSIS or Cremonensis.)

In each set of four lines of print, the First or Top line is attributed to the element FIRE (as being the most subtle element), the second line to the Air (the next in lightness), the third to the Water (more heavy), and the fourth and lowest line to Earth (the heaviest of all).

Further that each set of Four points signifieth an element, thus:

The first Four Lines signify FIRE; the second Four the element AIR; the third Four lines the element of WATER; and the fourth Four lines the element of EARTH.

In Geomancy there are three points which may tend a little to confuse the Practicus: (a) Why the Names and Seals of the SPIRITS of the Planets are employed instead of those of the INTELLIGENCES, the former being said to be more Evil in nature, and the latter More Good, (b) This being so, why the names and sigils of the Archangels of the Zodiacal Signs, purely Good in Nature, should be also employed; and instead of those of either the Angels, or Assistant Angels of the Zodiac, (c) There being 16 figures of Geomancy, and these under the 12 Signs, how are the 4 extra to be attributed in this classification.

(*a*)   Geomancy being a form of Divination especially attributed to the Element of Earth, and therefore more purely Terrestrial in operation, the Spirits and their Characters are more naturally appropriate hereto than the Intelligences, as representing the more weighty and automatic force of the Planetary Ray in its action upon the Earth. Also the Sigils employed in Geomancy are different from those of the same Spirits when taken from the Kameas of the Planets, and this to affirm their more specialized action in this Art.

(*b*)   The reason of the employment of such powerful Names as those of Malchidael, etc., is to bring a strong aiding Force of Good into the Operation, again specialized by the Sigils used in this connection.

(*c*)   The 12 Governors of the 12 Zodiacal Ideas or Figures, have power over the face of the Earth in their Figures and Places, but the 4 extra which be Fortuna Minor, Via, Caput Draconis and Cauda Draconis, also naturally have reference to the Four Winds and their Genii; a fortunate phase of the Moon (especially at Full) aspecting, is Good.

Gerardus Cremonensis sayeth: But you must always take heed, that you do not make a Question in a Rainy, very Stormy, cloudy, or very Windy Season; that is when the Elements be Angry; or when thou thyself art angry, or thy mind over-busied with many affairs; nor for tempters nor deriders, neither renew nor reiterate the same question again under the same Figure or Form; for that is Error.

YE COMPANIE OF HOUSES - From the *Geomancie "of Maister Christopher Cattan.* When ye doe find a Good Figure in a good House, it is double Good, because the House is Good and the Figure also; and it signifieth that without any doubt the Querent shall obtain his Demand. By the like reason if ye find an Ill figure in an Ill House it is very Ill for the Querent. But if ye find a Good Figure in an Ill House, it Signifieth Good to the Querent but it will not continue, but taketh away part of the Malice of the House. In like case if ye find an Ill figure in a Good House, it taketh away the Malice of the Figure, for he would do harm, but he cannot; yet keeping back always the Good that it come not to the Querent.

VOLUME FIVE

By "Ill House" is meant that which in a Question shews persons or things opposed to the Querent or to his interest in the Question, as in a Lawsuit, The House shewing his Opponent; in a case of Sickness, the 6th and 8th would be hostile. "Good Houses" would be those shewing Aid etc. We might in a general sense consider the 6th, and 8th, (death) and the 12th (Fears, prison, private enemies), "Ill House" by Nature.

The "Companie of the Houses" is after three manners: SIMPLE, SEMI SIMPLE, and COMPOUND. And the House be classed in Pairs, thus: the Second House is always the Companion of the First; the Fourth of the Third; the Sixth of the Fifth, and so on.

The COMPANIE SIMPLE is when the same Figure is repeated in both Houses of any of the "Pairs." Thus in our Scheme, VIA is repeated in the PAIR formed by the Ascendant and the Second House and they are therefore in COMPANY together. In this case shew that the indecision of the querent re-acts on his business. But though Caput Draconis is repeated in the Fourth and Fifth houses which be next each other, there is no COMPANY, for they belong to different pairs, the Fourth house being the Companion of the Third and not of the Fifth, and the latter being Company to the Sixth and not to the Fourth. And with regard to Persons, the COMPANION Figure will shew the COMPANIONS or Associates of a Person in question, as also will the COMPANION House. Good Figures in COMPANY show much Good, and as well in the Present as in the time to come; and Evil Figures the reverse. For also the First House (of a Pair) showeth the Time Present, and the Second the Time to Come.

The COMPANY DEMI SIMPLE is when the Figures in the Two Houses forming a Pair be not identical, but be under the same Planetary Ruler as Acquisitio and Laetitia which be both under Jupiter and Hismael, Fortuna Major and Minor under the Sun, Puella and Amissio under Venus, etc.

The COMPANY COMPOUND is when the Points of the Two Figures be the exact complementary contrary one of the other in arrangement as Puer and Puella, Albus and Rubeus, Acquisitio and Amissio, Laetitia and Tristitia, etc. A Reconciler figure is then formed from them in the same way that the Judge is calculated from the Two Witnesses, and according as this Figure is harmonized with such and Good, so is the nature of this "Company Compound," but if discordant and evil so is this form of COMPANY.

There is also yet another kind of COMPANY which is that of the uppermost Line of the Two Figures in the Pair of Houses. If this uppermost line in both cases be odd or even, there is COMPANY, and as in the case of the COMPANY COMPOUND, a Reconciler Figure is formed and the case judged as in the last paragraph. But if the top line of the one be odd and the other be even there is no COMPANY between those Figures. In our Scheme Tristitia is in the Third and Caput in the Fourth House, and as the top line of each has even points there is COMPANY between them. The Reconciler Figure will be Conjunctio, which is Harmonious with Both and is an argument of Good being signified thereby.

The reference in the above to "our scheme" only means that Mathers had set up a divination in full, with its complete interpretation. I have not included it here because it would be redundant; one is already included in this text.

SEVEN

Remember always that if the figures Rubeus or Cauda Draconis fall in the Ascendant, or first house, the figure is not fit for Judgment and should be destroyed without consideration. Another figure for the question should not be erected before at least two hours have elapsed.

Your figure being thoroughly arranged as on a Map of the heavens, as previously shown, note first to what House the demand belongs. Then look for the Witnesses and the Judge, as to whether the latter is favourable or otherwise, and in what particular way.

Note next what Figure falls in the House required. Also whether it passes or springs - that is whether it is also present in any other House or Houses. These should also be considered as for example in a question of money stolen, if the figure in the second House be also found in the sixth House, it might also show that the thief was a servant in the house.

Then look in the Table of Figures in the Houses and see what the Figure signifies in the special House under consideration. Put this down also. Then look in the Table for the strength of the figures in that House. Following this, apply the astrological rule of aspects between houses, noting what houses are Sextile, Quintile, Square, Trine, etc. Write the "Good" on one side and the "Evil" on the other, noting also whether these figures also are "strong" or "weak," "friendly" or "unfriendly" in nature to the figure in the House required. Note that in looking up the aspects between houses, there are two directions, Dexter and Sinister. The Dexter aspect is that which is contrary to the natural succession of the houses; the Sinister is the reverse. The Dexter aspect is more powerful than the Sinister.

Then add the meaning of the figure in the Fourth House, which will signify the end of the matter. It may also assist you to form a Reconciler Figure from the Figure in the house required and the Judge, noting what figure results and whether it harmonises with either or both by nature. Now consider all you have written down, and according to the balance of "good" and "evil" therein form your final judgment.

Consider also in "money" matters where the Part of Fortune falls.

For example, let us consider the figure previously set up and form a judgment for "Loss of money in business" therefrom.

Populus is the Judge, and we find that in questions of money, which concern the Second House, it signifies "medium good." The question as a whole is of the nature of the Second House, where we find Carcer. We then discover that Carcer here is "evil," as showing obstacles and delays. The Part of Fortune is in the Ascendant with Amissio, signifying loss through Querent's own mistake, and loss through Querent's self.

The Figure of Amissio springs into no other house, therefore this does not affect the question. "Carcer" in the Second House is neither "strong" nor "weak" its strength for evil is medium. The figures Sextile and Trine of the Second are Conjunctio, Fortuna Major, Fortuna Minor, and Acquisitio, all "good" figures, helping the matter and "friendly" in nature. This signifies well intentioned help of friends. The figures square and opposition of the Second are Fortuna Minor, Conjunctio, Albus which are not hostile to Carcer, therefore showing "opposition not great."

The figure in the Fourth House is Fortuna Major which shows a good end but with anxiety. Let us now form a Reconciler between the figure of the Second House which is Carcer and the Judge, Populus, which produces Carcer again, a sympathetic figure, but noting delay, but helping the Querent's wishes. Now let us add all these together:

1. **Medium.**
2. **Evil and Obstacles, delay.**
3. **Loss through querent's self.**
4. **Strength for evil, medium only.**
5. **Well-intentioned aid of friends.**
6. **Not much opposition from enemies.**
7. **Ending good; but with anxiety.**
8. **Delay, but helping Querent's wishes.**

And we can formulate the final judgment. That the Querent's loss in business has been principally owing to his own mismanagement. That he will have a long and hard struggle, but will meet with help from friends. That his obstacles will gradually give way, and that after much anxiety he will eventually recoup himself from his former losses.

SUMMARY OF STAGES IN GEOMANTIC DIVINATION

1. If Rubeus or Cauda Draconis in Ascendant destroy the figure.
2. Note the House to which the question belongs. See if the figure there springs into another house.
3. Form the Judge from the two witnesses.
4. Part of Fortune that is, if a money question.
5. See if Figure in House concerned is "strong" or "weak." If it pass or spring into any other house.
6. See figures Sextile and Trine, Square and Opposition.
7. Friendly or unfriendly.
8. Note the figure in Fourth House, signifying the end or outcome.
9. Form the Reconciler from Judge and the figure in House to which the demand appertains.

SKRYING

By

V.H. FRATER A.M.A.G.

I would like to deal with a topic that is considered to be at the heart of the magical system. Crowley for example, whose contribution to the subject can hardly be called minimal, considers the Body of Light technique of prime importance. In fact, he has formulated Liber Samekh, one of the most significant of the rituals of his own Order dealing with the knowledge and conversation of the Holy Guardian Angel, around the Body of Light technique. There can be no possibility of performing this ritual without considerable skill in this art. In the Golden Dawn itself, many of the primary magical skills, if not wholly dependent on this skill, at least need to bring it into play for those skills to become effective. For example, in Tarot divination, you will often find the advice given by Mathers to use clairvoyance to divine the significance of any one card. It must be added here that clairvoyance, in the Order sense of the term meant seeing with the inner eye, the eyes of the Body of Light. Furthermore, most of the Enochian system, the crown and jewel and synthesis of all the Golden Dawn teaching, devolves upon the Body of Light Technique for full use of the system.

The discussion of this topic must revolve around three different headings:

1. **The Order method, sometimes referred to as Tattwa vision, or skrying in the spirit vision.**
2. **The Inner Guide Meditation of Edwin Steinbrecher, now achieving considerable popularity.**
3. **Aleister Crowley's method, previously referred to as the Body of Light Technique.**

1. This method is described in several places in the Order teaching. For example, in the paper entitled "Man, the Microcosm" it is described at some length. Then there is a so-called flying roll where the description covers some several pages. Here and there in many other documents, it is further described.

"The subject of clairvoyance must always be in the highest degree interesting to all who are aspiring after adeptship even in its lowest grades...We frequently meet with two opposite attitudes towards the subject, both in the outer world and amongst our junior members. Both these attitudes are hindrances to its proper study, and therefore I shall preface my remarks by a few words concerning each of them." (I should interpolate here that these remarks were made by G.H. Frater Felkins.)

"The first is fear of clairvoyance, and the second is a disproportionate estimate of its value.

"Both of these attitudes arise from a misunderstanding of its true character. People imagine that somehow the power of clairvoyance is obtained secondhand from the powers of evil; or that its exercise will bring those who practice it under their influence. Or, on the other hand, they imagine that the power of clairvoyance will save them a great deal of trouble, and give them a short and easy path to the information and guidance they desire, in fact, that these may almost be attained at will. Nay more, would such a power not fully satisfy that curiosity which is one of the pitfalls of the superficial student?

"The properly trained clairvoyant need have no fear that he will thereby expose himself to the powers of evil. It is the **untrained natural** clairvoyant who is in danger. Training will give him knowledge, discipline and protection, such as will protect him from the onslaughts of the averse powers.

"On the other hand, let him who desires to save himself trouble and to gain knowledge to which he has no claim, be very well assured that only 'in the sweat of his brow' can he obtain this power and exercise it in security. And that he who seeks to gratify his curiosity will either be mortified by disappointment or distressed by discoveries he would much prefer not to have made. Trained, humble, and reverent clairvoyance is a great gift, opening up new worlds and deeper truths, lifting us out of ourselves into the great inpouring and outpouring of the heart of God."

Most of the following quotations are from a rather lengthy flying roll, #11 actually, written by G.H. Frater D.D.C.F. on clairvoyance. "We pass through life affecting others, and being affected by others through these akashic envelopes that surround us—so that when we close the eyes of the body and senses upon the material world, we first apprehend by interior vision the essences of our own and contiguous natures. This perception of our own environment is a source of error to the beginner in clairvoyance. He believes himself to have gone away and to see elsewhere, but he may be among only the confused images of his own aura."

"An old name of clairvoyance, in our ancient manuscripts was 'skrying in the spirit vision;' becoming a 'skryer' was not simply becoming a seer, but one who descries what he **seeks,** not only the impassive receiver of visions beyond control or definition.

"When one stands in common life in the kingdom of Malkuth, there is but little confusion of sight, but when one voluntarily leaves the dead level of materialism and passes up the path of Tau towards Yesod, then there is a confusion of lights. One comes within the scope of the crossing and reflected and coloured rays of the Qesheth, the rainbow of colours spread over the earth. Here then we require instruction and guidance to avoid confusion and folly. And yet this stage must be passed through—to go higher.

"Beyond Yesod you enter the path of Samekh, the strait and narrow path which leads to truly spiritual regions of perception. This is attained by the process called rising in the planes.

"Our subject falls most conveniently into three heads, which are however closely related, and the three forms or stages pass one into the other.

"1. Clairvoyance. Descrying in the spirit vision.

"2. Astral projection. Traveling in the spirit vision.

"3. Rising in the planes.

"It is well to commence (1) by means of a symbol, such as a drawing, or coloured diagram, related in design, form and colour to the subject chosen for study. The simple and compound Tattwa emblems are suitable for this purpose. It is better for them not to be in the complementary "flashing" colours for this purpose as though more powerful, they are also more exhausting to the student. The symbol should be of convenient size, for the eye to take it in at a glance, and large enough not to require too close an application of sight to realize the details...(The Tattwa scheme is nearly the same as our queen scale of colour applied to the Sephirotic colours in the Minutum Mundum diagram)...To use the symbol for clairvoyance, place it before you, as on a table, place the hands beside it, or hold it up with both hands, then, with the utmost concentration, gaze at it, comprehend it, formulate its meaning and relations. When the mind is steady upon it, close the eyes and continue the meditation. Let the conception still remain before you. Keep up the design, form and colour in the akashic aura, as clearly as they appeared in material form to the outward seeing. Transfer the vital effort from the optic nerve to the mental perception, or **thought seeing** as distinct from seeing with the eye. Let one form of apprehension glide on with the other—produce the reality of the dream vision, by positive will in the waking state. All this will be possible only if the mind is steady, clear and undisturbed, and the will powerful. It cannot lead to success if you are in an unsuitable state of anxiety, fear, indignation, trouble or anticipation. You must procure peace, solitude and leisure, and you must banish all disturbing influences.

"Above all, never attempt these magic arts if there be any resentment in the mind, anger, or any evil passion. If you do, the more you succeed, the greater will be the evil that will follow for yourself.

"With the conditions favourable, the process may be continued and this, by means of introducing into the consciousness and by formulating into sound, the highest divine names connected therewith. This invocation produces and harmonizes currents of spiritual force in sympathy with your object. Then follow with the sacred names of archangelic and angelic import, producing them mentally, visually and by voice."

However casually this may have been stated, nonetheless this is the essence of the difference between the Golden Dawn method and that of the inner guide meditation. I shall have more to say about this when this particular method is being discussed, but nonetheless it should be emphasized right here. The reader should have noticed that in one of the obligations that the initiate into the Order has assumed there is the statement that no matter what type of magical operation he proposes to engage in, he will always invoke the highest divine names within his purview. In this way, his steps will be guided in the right direction and all harm thus avoided. In a major sense this is one of the greatest differences between the initiated and profane points of view. It holds good in all occult matters—from so apparently a prosaic undertaking as divining by means of geomancy to invoking one's higher and divine genius. It means placing one's workings and one's goal in the hands of the divine—no matter how one defines the latter.

Now we can return to the long quotation about clairvoyance by Mathers: "Then, maintaining your abstraction from your surroundings, and still concentrating upon the symbol and its correlated ideas, you are to seek a perception of a scene, panorama, or view of a place. This may also be brought on by a sense of tearing open, as a curtain is drawn aside and seeing the 'within' of the symbol before you. As the scene dawns upon you, particularize the details, and seek around for objects and then for beings, entities and persons—attract their attention, call mentally to them by suitable titles and courtesies, and by proper and appropriate signs and symbols, such as the signs of the grades, pentagrams, hexagrams and sigils, etc."

Again, let me call attention to this statement as being one of overwhelming significance and importance. It is another one of those differences between an initiated and a profane point of view or technique. All the correspondences that the student has been obliged to learn and memorize before he even attempts this kind of training now come into use. They are the means whereby he attempts 'to test the spirits, whether they be of god or the devil.' If the student has elected to travel upon the path of Saturn leading from Malkuth to Yesod and feels that somehow all is not going well, and because of that makes the invoking or banishing hexagrams of Saturn, even drawing in the air before him the astrological symbol of Saturn and the Hebrew letter Tau to which this path is attributed, he will find that there will be changes in the visual environment in which he finds himself. The tracing of the appropriate symbols and the vibration of the appropriate divine names eliminates all those things which have no place in vision. Thus the details which may represent delusion and deception are banished from the scene enabling him to proceed safely with his mission of investigation, etc.

"Test them by divine and angelic names, observing their attitude and responses thereto. Thus losing sight of the symbol you see its inwardness, perceive things as in a mirror by reflection. In this form of descrying, note that you see objects reversed, as to right and left, for which suitable allowance must be made. You project, in this process, part.of your own nerve and spirit force upon the symbol, and by this you attract and attach to it more akashic force from the environment, hence the results obtained. If, instead of this simple spirit vision, a ray of yourself is sent and actually goes to a place (astral projection) there is not necessarily the sense of reversal of objects.

"In using symbols it is necessary to avoid self hypnotization, for this occurrence would dispose you to mediumship, and to be the playground of forces you must control and not permit to control you. For this reason, partly, it is well not to have the symbol too small. It is of advantage to pursue these researches with the aid of the presence before you of the four magical implements, and even to hold the one suitable to the investigation. If you enter upon the spirit vision without a symbol you proceed by a mental symbol imagined in the astral light. This is not a wise proceeding for learners because it opens the door to other astral effects. You create a vortex into which other astral influences are drawn and hence confusion and mischief may result.

"The process of working by a small symbol placed upon the forehead or elsewhere is not wholly good either. It is more liable to derange the brain circulation and cause mental illusion and disturbance, headache and nervous exhaustion than the first method.

"In using symbols placed before you, it is a useful addition to provide a large circular or square tablet, around which are placcd divine names etc., related to the elements, and to the cardinal points. Then after duly arranging this with respect to the compass, place your symbol upon and within this frame.

"Astral projection, although from one point of view a development of clairvoyance, yet is from another quite distinct. In astral projection, the adept emits from his ego a perceptible ray of his identity, and by cultured and trained will, sends it to travel to the place desired, focusses it there, sees there, directly and not by reflection, perceives its bodily home, and re-enters it.

"In this traveling of the spirit, the process may be caused to start also by the symbol as before, or by will alone. But in any event the divine names should be used and relied upon. If the ray be emitted, and you succeed in this traveling to the place, you perceive a different result to that of the clairvoyant, mirror-like vision, scenes and things instead of being like a picture, have the third dimension, solidity. They stand out first like a bas relief, then you see as from a balloon, as it is said, by a bird's eye view. You feel free to go to the place, to descend upon it, to step out upon the scene and to be an actor there.

"Having attained success in projection you should practice the method when opportunity offers, and having passed to any place, should make efforts—and if you will—success will follow—to pass through all elements, water and earth as well as through air. Practice will enable you to fly through air either quickly or slowly as willed, and to swim through water, or pass through earth and through fire fearlessly with the aid of the divine names, in this astral projection."

Once again, Mathers is stressing the initiated viewpoint, the vibration of the divine names in order to achieve one's ends and to get to where one wishes to go without undue opposition or difficulty. He stresses this as often as possible to ensure that the idea is driven home, and that the method be used on all possible occasions. The above section also stresses the use of the magical implements in all such undertakings—implements which have been made and charged and consecrated by the student himself for use in just such circumstances. It is only when these basic rules are not scrupulously and faithfully followed that some mishap or disaster may occur. Crowley's method, which is really that of the Order, follows this procedure—Steinbrecher's does not.

"Seek then the forms and persons of the place or of the plane you read, seek converse with them, by voice, word, letter and symbol, and claim admission, etc. by signs and by invocation. Every figure is to be tried and tested, whether he be as he appears or whether a delusory and deluding embodied power. It may be too that your travel is not real, and that you are wandering in your own environment, and are misled by memory, etc. hence you might be deceiving yourself by your own reminiscences.

"Try all beings, and if offered favours or initiation by any, try and test them by the divine names and forces. And ever remember your own adept obligation and your allegiance to it, to your own higher self, and to the great angel Hua, before whom you stood fastened to the cross of suffering, and to whom you pledged your obedience.

"This old proverb enshrines a great truth, as many of them do. 'Believe thyself there and thou art there.'

"Rising in the planes is a spiritual process after spiritual conceptions and higher aims; by concentration and contemplation of the divine, you formulate a Tree of Life passing from you to the spiritual realms above and beyond you. Picture to yourself that you stand in Malkuth—then by the use of the divine names and aspirations you strive upward by the path of Tau toward Yesod, neglecting the crossing rays which attract you as you pass up. Look upwards to the divine light shining down from Kether upon you. From Yesod leads up the path of Temperance, Samekh; the arrow cleaving upward leads the way to Tiphareth, the great central sun of sacred power.

"Invoke the great angel Hua, and conceive yourself as standing fastened to the cross of suffering, carefully vibrating the holy names allied to your position, and so may the mental vision attain unto higher planes.

"There are three special tendencies to error and illusion which assail the adept in these studies. They are: memory, imagination and actual sight. These elements of doubt are to be avoided by the vibration of divine names, and by the letters and titles of the 'lords who wander'—the planetary forces represented by the several double letters of the Hebrew Alphabet.

"If the memory entice thee astray, apply for help to Saturn, whose Tarot title is 'the great one of the night of time,' formulate the Hebrew letter Tau in whiteness.

"If the vision change or disappear, your memory has falsified your efforts. If imagination cheat thee, use the Hebrew letter Caph for the forces of Jupiter named 'lord of the forces of life.' If the deception be of lying—intellectual untruth, appeal to the force of Mercury by the Hebrew letter Beth. If the trouble be of wavering of mind, use the Hebrew letter Gimel for the Moon. If the enticement of pleasure be the error, then use the Hebrew letter Daleth as an aid.

Use the Hebrew letter Peh for Mars to coerce sense of anger and violence. Use the Hebrew letter Resh for the sun to coerce sense of haughtiness and vanity.

"Never attempt any of these divine processes when at all influenced by passion or anger or fear. Leave off if desire of sleep approach. Never force a mind disinclined. Balance the Mem and Shin of your nature and mind, so as to leave Aleph like a gentle flame rising softly between them.

"You must do all these things by yourself alone. No one can make you nor take you. Do not try to make, or take others. You may only point out the path and guide, but must not help others.

"A strong person can galvanize a weak one, but its effect is only a temporary folly, doing good neither to the strong nor to the weak. Only offer guidance to those who are making necessary efforts of themselves. Do not assist a negligent pupil, nor encourage one whose desire is not in the work.

"This rule is open to some alteration when, passing from our mystic studies, you refer to the worldly guidance of childhood. A parent is in a special position, and has a natural duty incumbent upon him or her to train, guide and protect a child.

"Still, even here, do protect and lead, but do not 'obsess' a child; don't override by your peculiar personal predilections all the personal aims of the offspring. A man's ideal of true propriety is often himself, and his idea of doing good to a child is to make it like himself. Although this father may be a good man, his form of goodness is not to be made a universal type, and there are many other forms equally existing, and equally fit to exist, and any attempt to dictate too closely a child's 'thought life' may, while failing of success, yet warp aside from the truth what would otherwise pass into a good path, through its own peculiar avenue."

"It is well to make all symbols for clairvoyant use yourself. Otherwise, to obtain a purely individual result, you have to banish the influence of him who made them.

"It is best to do high clairvoyance alone, or only with others of the utmost purity, and in whom you have the utmost confidence.

"If more than one is attempting in concert the same process, there is the source of error that there becomes formed in the astral light a complex symbol, and struggle ensues as to who shall lead the direction of the currents. When two sit together, as in the vault, they should be balanced. And so with three. For two, one each side of the Pastos or one at each end, for three assume the position of the angles of a triangle, say one at head of Pastos, one at the right and at the left hand of the form of Christian Rosy Cross."

Example: The V.H. Soror V.N.R. 6-5 sat at a table, robed, and took a Tattwa card coloured symbol (Tejas—Akasha) an erect red triangle upon which is a dark violet or black egg shaped centre. She placed her hands beside her side, or held it in turns before the eyes (held the magic fire wand). Gazed and contemplated and considered as the symbol grew before her, so enlarged and filled the place, that she seemed to pass into it, or into a vast triangle of flame. She realizes that she is in the presence of a desert of sand, harsh, dry and hot.

Thinks of, and vibrates Elohim. Action seems set up, increase of heat and light. Passing through the symbol and scene, she seems to arrive and descend there, feels the hot dry sand perceives a small pyramid in the distance. Wills to rise up and fly through air to it, descends beside it, passes around, sees a small square door on each side. Vibrates—Elohim, Michael, Aral, Seraph, Darom, Ash.

Stamps five times, figure appears at an entrance, stamps again five times and vibrates Seraphiel. A warrior figure leads out a procession of guards, she asks for his seal, he shows a complex symbol of four triangles around a central emblem? Deceptive, draw Beth before him— he appears terrified. Withdraw symbol, he is courteous, ask him about pyramid. He says they conduct ceremonies there. She seeks admission, gives sign of 0-0 grade. There is a sense of opposition. Gives sign of 1-10; this appears to suffice. But he gives signs of adeptship. Guards kneel before her and she passes in. Dazzling light, as in a temple. An altar in the midst, kneeling figures surround it, there is a dais beyond and many figures upon it. They seem to be elementals of a fiery nature. She sees a pentagram, puts a Leo into it, thanks the figure who conducts her. Wills to pass through the pyramid, finds herself out amid the sand. Wills her return. Returns, perceiving her body in robes seated in the second order hall.

Another instance of such visionary experience I recorded many years ago in an essay now published under the title of *The Foundations of Practical Magic*—the essay itself being entitled *The Art and Meaning of Magic.* It was a Tattwa Vision of dealing with the 32nd path on the Tree of Life. "We marched down the wide indigo road. There was a cloudy nightsky—no stars. The road was raised above the general level of the ground. There was a canal each side beyond which we could see the lights of what appeared to be a large city. We went on like this for a long way, but then I noticed in the distance a tiny figure of a woman, like a miniature—she seemed to be naked, but as she drew near, I saw a scarf floating round her. She had a crown of stars on her head and in her hands were two wands. She came towards us very quickly, and I gazed fascinatedly at a string of pearls reaching from her neck to her knees—and gazing, found that we had passed through the circle of pearls, and she had disappeared.

'Now the sky is clear and full of stars...the moon, a great yellow harvest moon, rises slowly up the sky to a full arch...and we saw three moonbeams shining on the high purple walls of a city...we did not delay to look about, but marched quickly to the centre of the city, to an open space, in the midst of which was a round temple like a ball of silver. It was approached by nine steps, and rested on a silver platform. It had four doors. Before each was a large angel with silver wings...inside, we were in a very airy place. Light breezes lifted our clothes and our hair—the interior was very white and clear silvery—no colours. Suspended in the centre was a great globe, like the moon itself...while we looked we saw that the globe was not suspended in the air; it rested on immense cupped hands. We followed the arms up and saw, far up near the roof, deep dark eyes looking down, dark like the night sky, and a voice said..."

2. Simplicity itself is the keyword to the method described by Edwin Steinbrecher. He is an astrologer, well-versed in associated subjects, such as tarot, alchemy, qabalah, etc., and underwent a lengthy Jungian analysis. In the latter he was instructed in Jung's technique of creative imagination. By this means, to put it crudely and oversimplified, one carries on conversations with the images and personalities seen in dreams. Apparently some quite interesting results follow from this procedure. One interesting example is *The Tree* by J. Marvin Spiegelman (Falcon Press, 1982), which the author describes in his introduction as an experiment in creative psycho-mythology. The book is based on some interior experiences and conversations the author had with some of his dream images, described at considerable length.

As Steinbrecher describes it, the Inner Guide Meditation is a "transformative process concerned with assimilating the disparate energies which exist in the human unconscious into the unified wholeness that is the awakened enlightened being inherent in each of us, thus ending the illusions which cause separation, guilt and judgment. With the meditation of the inner guides, problems once unapproachable and unchangeable become fulfilling challenges that bring forth productive and creative responses."

Let me quote the author as he describes the process of meditation, after which I would like to discuss a description given of a rather frightening experience he had. This latter could have readily been obviated had he known beforehand something of the Order method as given earlier.

"Close your eyes, and invent a cave around you as if you had just walked into the cave and the entrance is at your back. Allow the cave to structure itself as it will, well-lighted or dim, smooth walled or rough. Try to be like blank film receiving impressions. Accept these impressions uncritically as they come to you from this environment. Try not to edit what comes." So far so good. This is the essence of the Jungian method.

"Be as sensory as you can...use all your senses...be sure you are observing and sensing this environment while being in your body and looking out of your eyes. Don't be watching an image of yourself!...

"When you can feel yourself in the cave, even though things may still be vague at this point, move to the left, away from the cave entrance, and find some kind of doorway or opening there on the left that will lead you out into a landscape...take a step out into the landscape when it appears, feeling the new type of ground under your feet. Is it soft or hard, grassy or rocky? What is around you? What is the scene like?

"Then with your mind call for an animal to come to you. Let it be an animal you don't know. Not a familiar housepet or some other known outer world animal, (e.g., your friend's horse, the neighbor's cat, the lamb you had when you were a child), and ask the animal to lead you off to the right to where your inner guide awaits you. Concentrate on following the animal and try not to anticipate the guide.. .the animals that appear to people come in all varieties. Deer were common, as are squirrels, sometimes a lion or a dog or cat will appear. People have even gotten skunks and anteaters...

"The animal will lead you to an unknown male figure—your first guide. The initial inner guide for both men and women is a male form...you will generally feel an outpouring of love, protection and friendliness from the figure...

"Let all these impressions come to you as they will. Don't try to see the guide's face clearly right away unless it presents itself easily. One of the hallmarks of the true inner guide is that his face isn't usually clear at first, although a false guide's face almost always is. The true guide's face will clear and come into focus later on as you work with him—when you stop trying to "make him a face." Be sure to ask the figure if he is your true guide. Generally a false guide will answer "no" to this question. Feel the guide's feeling for you. There is no love from a false guide.

"Ask the guide to take your right hand in his left...feel the hand contact as much as you can...then ask the guide to point to where the sun is in the sky of your inner world. Look to where he points..don't accept any known person from your outer world as your inner guide. Your guide is a being who wasn't alive on this planet when you were born, so if your favorite uncle, or your father, or the current or past president of the United States appear, keep looking past him to the right. And if a famous deceased guru or teacher or luminary from the past should appear, test him, and see if another figure appears beyond him on the right...the inner guides are always human and do not have the powers or attributes of gods... remember you're in foreign territory. Trust and use your inner guide to act both as interpreter and counselor—truly let him guide you..."

The author then goes into a great deal of detail and explanation of the meditation and the guide and the material to be derived from this sort of thing. The book is well worth reading, and the method of course experimented with. I recommend it unequivocally—at least as a device for dealing with the inner world of the spirit. What I am interested in at this moment is to analyze briefly a couple of the problems he encountered as relative to the meditation.

For example, he describes how the meditation evolved. He was undergoing Jungian analysis many years ago. At one point his analyst left town for Zurich where the Jungian Institute is located, and he was left with a feeling of being stranded, that his unconscious had been activated but, at that moment, not going anywhere in particular. He had been using the "active imagination" technique the analyst had taught him and was fascinated by the living experiences he had while exploring his psyche. He had been warned about the potential dangers of the process, that repressed unconscious forces could well up to overcome the ego and usurp it. However despite that warning, he continued experimenting with the method trying to establish relationships between the tarot and astrology. (He was a professional astrologer at the time.)

He wrote: "I was delighted with my new toy. It had a reality and a freshness I hadn't experienced since childhood, and there was no doubt about the experiential realness of it...but then I had an experience that acutely demonstrated the analyst's warning about the dangers of active imagination as it is practiced in analytical psychology. It was inside the room where I came into contact with the archetypal forms when an image of the tarot old Pan or devil appeared, unsummoned and unwanted. It was a classic Christian devil with an emanation of 'evil' as real as the beneficence I had felt when interacting with the archetype of the sun...I was paralyzed. I began to panic. I seemed to be frozen in the chair. The old Pan entity became even more menacing than before, placing himself in my inner world between me and the stairway to the outer world and safety. The panic finally subsided (although not the fear) and I further tried to manouevre to the stairway around the figure, but to no avail. This entity of the inner world blocked my every move whenever I attempted the stairs. He did not advance towards me but remained as a moving barrier to any possible exit. It even crossed my mind that I might be discovered by the outer world in this catatonic state and be taken off to the nearest psychiatric hospital. I couldn't even call out to try to communicate my situation to anyone who might be within hearing...the experience was so frightening to me, however, that I decided then and there never again to attempt another venture into the realms of the unconscious without the presence of a trained analyst."

Eventually, however, he recovered from that fright—as we might have anticipated. The point I wish to emphasize here however is that all this terror could have been obviated, without any difficulty, had he been trained (or trained himself) in those Golden Dawn methods that are being described in this section. The Banishing Ritual of the Pentagram, the vibration of the appropriate divine names, the assumption of god forms, etc. are all devices which the student must have mastered long before attempting to enter the inner world by means of Tattwa Vision, etc. In a well-regulated temple, these fundamental techniques would have been taught regularly and gradually to the aspirant so that by the time he was ready to attempt this kind of inner adventure these techniques would have been well assimilated and become second nature.

One might well ask, then, that if this is the case why were there so many disasters in the Order as a result of the use of inner vision? The answer is so simple as almost to be frightening. These methods were **not** being used as scrupulously as they should have. Many assumed that since they had used the visionary techniques for a long period of time, they had no further need for the protective devices. In the Felkins period of government of the Stella Matutina, as reported by Ellic Howe and Arthur E. Waite, and several others, an extraordinary degree of gullibility seemed to have taken possession of these visionaries who apparently had lost their wits and all sense of proportion and sanity primarily because they did not use any or all of the protective devices in which the Order had already trained them.

This is one of the several reasons for my repeated insistence in several areas of this book for a complete mastery of the Pentagram and Hexagram rituals in all their phases, with the absolute memorization of the divine names, gestures, signs, etc. There should be no passing on to more advanced methods until the basic drills had been mastered. Otherwise the student who initiated himself, without the aid of a teacher other than this book of instructions, may find himself in a similar quandary as did Steinbrecher and others. There is simply no justification or excuse for any of this at all. Proper preparation is the basic rule for every phase of the magical arts. Without this, only disaster can loom ahead.

THE COMPLETE GOLDEN DAWN SYSTEM OF MAGIC

While on this topic let me launch into a pet peeve of mine which is stimulated into activity every time I glance through some of the manuscript rituals dating from various periods in the history of the Order. Again and again I am struck by sketches of Pentagrams, Hexagrams and grade signs to be made at various points of the ritual. I confess myself to be more than somewhat irritated by this procedure, since in theory it is not necessary. They are there included obviously to act as a reminder to the officer of technical matters which theoretically should have been mastered long before. Had they been mastered beforehand, then there would have been no point in making these sketches of what he has to do.

In one sense, this is the fault of the founders of the Order. Mathers himself has written a paper about the least amount of work needed to be done to pass a written examination. This is a pretty poor notion to convey to newly admitted aspirants to higher things. This was a curse that ran through all the Order work as I have indicated in *What You Should Know About the Golden Dawn*. Students for the most part did only so much as would get them through an examination. There was no thought of obtaining real proficiency in anything. Consecration ceremonies were done for the sword, the elemental weapons, the rose cross and so on. and there they stopped. It seemed never to have occurred to them to repeat their performance many times, over months or years if necessary in order to sharpen their expertise. And yet practice for most of us is the only means whereby that expertise may be obtained.

The Pentagram and Hexagram rituals should have been committed to memory long before some of these grade rituals were to have been performed. I am not antagonistic to the notion that the officers should refer to their scripts for the long speeches required in some of the grade and other rituals, but I deem it unworthy of them—if they are adepts in reality and not merely in name only—if they must consult their manuscripts in order to determine what kind of pentagram they were required to trace in some particular place, here, there or anywhere.

The study of the Pentagram Ritual, for example, must not be confined merely to reading it over many times. It has to be performed again and again until it becomes almost deeply embedded in the very warp and woof of one's unconscious. It has to be practiced until the Nephesch or automatic consciousness is able to reproduce it without the Ruach giving the matter any deliberate thought.

It seems to me to be a good idea for the student to prepare a simple type of ritual for daily use in which he will be required to employ almost everything he has learned concerning the art of invocation so that he will not need to think about it, but to devote his whole attention to the really significant parts of the ritual—the use of will and imagination and the vibratory formula of the middle pillar.

Many years ago—in the mid-thirties—I constructed a simple form of ritual for invoking the elements. I borrowed the openings from each of the four elemental grade ceremonies and bound them together into a coherent whole. Then, for almost a whole year, I performed this little ritual daily, until I was able to describe and trace the appropriate lineal figures together with the appropriate divine names without a moment's hesitation. It succeeded in driving these basic ritual methods deeply home into my unconscious psyche so that they were there when I needed them.

Many years later, probably a couple of decades, when I returned to the simples and rudimentals again, I appropriated the opening phase of the Corpus Christi celebration which I called Opening by Watchtower. This becomes a magnificent little ceremony and has become elaborated into a variety of different directions. Some of these have been described and written about at some length in *Ceremonial Magic* (Aquarian Press, England, 1980). It accomplishes in a slightly different manner what I had attempted to do much earlier, making use of every seemingly arbitrary gesture of elementary magic. Its practice is such that it should result in the ability to trace any pentagram or hexagram, invoking or banishing, at will in the right place, etc. without having to burden one's script with a sketch of the appropriate pentagram. Actually, the ritual is very easy to learn and I strongly suggest it be committed to memory and performed as often as may be possible. In this manner, the basic principles of magical procedure are used so often that they become second nature. At the same time, the sphere of sensation is purified, exalted and made impenetrable to any outside and disturbing influence. With such an aura, one can go anywhere, do anything, meet any entity without fear or anxiety that one's person could be assailed successfully. After a year of study and the practice of the Opening by Watchtower, this magical result is achieved. When that stage has been reached, other usages of that ritual will suggest themselves.

But the primary goal of this exhortation will have been accomplished. When performing a ritual—any ritual, either by oneself or to demonstrate a technique to a beginner—one should not have to consult any text in order to recall what an invoking active spirit pentagram looks like, or from what point a banishing lunar hexagram should begin. This is fundamental magical training, must not be glossed over, and should be respected as such for its disciplinary effect on the Nephesch and Ruach.

To return however to the Inner Guide Meditation. In one place, the author gives a question asked by one of his students, as follows: "Is the inner guide an aspect of my ego?"

His reply was no. The guides do not always cater to our ego whims and fancies. They say and do what is needed, not wanted. They know our limits and our inadequacies and allow exposure to unconscious materials which the ego would never choose to deal with.

This is all very well, and by and large I will accept this. But I did know sometime ago a lady who used this Inner Guide Meditation a very great deal and let it govern her every day life and activity. It so happened that she was a compulsive neurotic and a hypochondriac—the two often go together.

Very often she would consult her inner guide as to some course of behavior, and of course he would advise her. As it turned out, he was a compulsive neurotic too, for he would advise her to behave in markedly compulsive routines, ritualistically as it were. These she would accept without equivocation—naturally. It was her own voice, as it were. The result was that her whole world fell apart disruptively and utter chaos ensued. I doubt if that taught her anything. She had given herself a **crash course** in magical procedures; she did have a copy of one of my books. I doubt if she employed any of the testing devices I have mentioned. That is the trouble with such crash courses; not enough of an impression is made on the unconscious psyche for the technique to be used when really necessary.

The stupidity of the whole business is that it taught her nothing! Her compulsiveness remained, unaltered and unchanged!

3. Crowley's Body of Light Technique.

Before going too far with a description of this method, let me give a long quotation from his Liber O, reprinted in *Gems from the Equinox* (Falcon Press, 1982).

" 1. This book is very easy to misunderstand; readers are asked to use the most minute critical care in the study of it, even as we have done in the preparation.

"2. In this book it is spoken of the Sephiroth, and the paths, of spirits and conjurations; of gods, spheres, planes, and many other things which may or may not exist.

"It is immaterial whether they exist or not. By doing certain things certain results follow; students are most earnestly warned against attributing objective reality or philosophic validity to any of them...

"4. The student, if he attains any success in the following practices, will find himself confronted by things (ideas or beings) too glorious or too dreadful to be described. It is essential that he remain the master of all that he beholds, hears or conceives; otherwise he will be the slave of illusion and the prey of madness...

"5. There is little danger that any student, however idle or stupid, will fail to get some result; but there is great danger that he will be led astray, even though it be by those which it is necessary that he should attain. Too often, moreover, he mistaketh the first resting-place for the goal, and taketh off his armour as if he were a victor ere the fight is well begun.

"It is desirable that the student should never attach to any result the importance which it at first seems to possess."

Before proceeding further, let me state that all other things apart, Crowley was once a member of the Golden Dawn. All his early writings are essentially expressive of the Golden Dawn viewpoint. It is only in his later writings that he departs a considerable distance from the Order viewpont. But even then there always remains a nucleus of the Order teaching which he embraced with all his heart. No matter how far he departed from the basic Order methodology, he was a Golden Dawn initiate—first, last and always. Let this always be remembered. In his writing, there is much of value to the sincere student of these Golden Dawn techniques.

"1.   Let the student be at rest in one of his prescribed positions, having bathed and robed with the proper decorum. Let the place be free from all disturbance, and let the preliminary purifications, banishings and invocations be duly accomplished, and, lastly, let the incense be kindled.

"2.   Let him imagine his own figure (preferably robed in the proper magical garments, and armed with the proper magical weapons) as enveloping his physical body, or stand near to and in front of him.

"3.   Let him then transfer the seat of his consciousness to that imagined figure; so that it may seem to him that he is seeing with its eyes, and hearing with its ears.

"This will usually be the great difficulty of the operation.

"4.   Let him then cause that imagined figure to rise in the air to a great height above the earth.

"5.   Let him stop and look aboiut him. (It is sometimes difficult to open the eyes.)

"6.   Probably he will see figures approaching him, or become conscious of a landscape.

"Let him speak to such figures, and insist upon being answered, using the proper pentagrams and signs, as previously taught.

"7.   Let him travel at will, either with or without guidance from such figure or figures.

"8.   Let him further employ such special invocations as will cause to appear the particular places he may wish to visit.

"9.   Let him beware of the thousand subtle attacks and deceptions that he will experience, carefully testing the truth of all with whom he speaks..."

At first sight this sounds a great deal different from the basic Golden Dawn method as described above. In point of fact, however, it is identical. Identical in spirit as well as in letter. For example, somewhere in his autobiography, Crowley speaks of instructing a student to visualize one of the hexagrams of the Yi King, and then to imagine that he is passing through it as if going through a door. A vision of some kind results from that, and when the student had returned from one of these, Crowley would open Legge's book on the Yi King and read the description given of that hexagram. Usually there would be more than a marked relationship.

Furthermore, in the Blue Equinox, at the end of the diary of Frater Achad (Charles Stansfeld Jones), Crowley under the pseudonym of Frater O.M. prescribes an examination for Achad. One of the items of that examination was to pass through a door on which was described a hexagram of a particular kind that Crowley had drawn specifically for that purpose, and report what he had found out about that symbol by means of the vision.

Do note that in both these instances, he mentions nothing of visualizing a body within his physical body or trying to transfer his consciousness to it. In both instances he was literally following the Golden Dawn method of so-called Tattwa vision. Years ago, shortly after receiving my 5 = 6 degree, I painted on 3 × 5 filing cards a series of symbols—those of the Tattwas, the Hebrew letters, the geomantic symbols, and the signs of the planets and zodiac. These became the symbolic doors to use for skrying in the spirit vision, to use the technical name for the process being considered. One simply stared for a minute or so at the card or the symbol on it, and then closed one's eyes—in which case **one saw the symbol in its complementary color.** Then one imagined that this symbol grew in size until it was like a large door through which one could pass. Using the sign of the Enterer, one projected oneself through the door and on the other side vibrated the appropriate names and traced the corresponding pentagrams and other lineal figures. A landscape was sure to develop, and as a result of the invocations a figure would appear. If all went well, everything that he was in person and in color would be appropriate to that symbol. In any event he was to be tested by all the tests at one's disposal to make sure that one was on the right track.

Crowley's Body of Light technique thus turns out in the end to be identical with that of the Golden Dawn. I could quote from Crowley's writings to give examples of his skrying, but that is not really necessary at this juncture.

The method is the same, and the testing techniques of course are the same. The document Liber O from which I quoted most of the above instruction also describes the pentagram and hexagram rituals, as well as the vibratory formula of the middle pillar and the assumption of god forms. All are taken, in their entirety, from the Order of which he was once a member.

All three methods—that of the Order, Steinbrecher and Crowley—are very similar, save only that Steinbrecher's method is lacking in the very protective devices that it so urgently needs. Apart from that, it may well be that his method is an ideal one for the beginner to use, even if only to acquire some expertise in the method. Once obtained, he should learn the Order's methods of testing and protecting—and proceed from there.

THE COMPLETE GOLDEN DAWN SYSTEM OF MAGIC

ON SKRYING

By

V.H. SOROR V.N.R

Having learned the general rules the student should discover for himself particular methods best suited to his own particular temperament. It may prove useful to some however to write in some detail about the mode of skrying and of astral projection which have already proved likely to bring about successful results, and which by reason of its continual tests would tend to minimize the chances of illusion, delusion and hallucination. Before proceeding it would be well to refer to the Microcosm lecture regarding the theory of skrying.

The rules for skrying and astral projection being almost similar the two subjects can be studied together, the one being taken as the complement of the other.

Skrying can be commenced simply. That is to say, not projecting the astral beyond the sphere of sensation into the Macrocosm, but retaining it to perceive some scene in the Universe reflected in the symbol which you hold. This latter acts as a mirror which reflects to you some scenes outside your normal range of vision. Secondly, you can continue the operation by using the same symbol and by passing through it projecting yourself to the scene in question which previously you had only perceived as a reflection.

This latter process will probably appear more vivid to the perception than the prior one, just as in the material vision one is less likely to be deceived by going to a place and actually examining it than by obtaining knowledge of it from a mere reflection in a mirror.

In the room in which I am now for example, I see reflected in a mirror a portion of the garden. I obtain an impression of all within my range of sight, but not nearly so powerful a one as when I step out into the garden to the spot in question to examine all the objects therein, feel the atmosphere, touch the ground, smell the flowers, etc.

But it is well to practice both methods. The latter will probably be found to be more instructive though far more fatiguing since, when projecting the astral you will have to supply it with much vitality drawn mostly from the Nephesch.

The key to success in both skrying and astral projection then, would appear to be alternately to employ both intuition and reason. This is done by permitting each thought picture to impress itself on the brain in the manner comprehended generally by the word inspiration, followed by the reason applying its knowledge of correspondences to an affirmation or correction of the same.

You must be prepared to receive impressions of scenes, forms and sounds as vivid thought - forms. I use the phrase thought - forms for want of a better one. There are distinctly in these experiences, things heard, things felt as well as things seen, which would prove that the faculties are really the sublimated senses. That the faculty of clairvoyance exists is easily provable after a little patient exercise with one of the first methods given for the practice of skrying.

Take the Tattwa cards and from them choose one at random. Don't look to see what symbol it represents. Lay it down on a table face downwards. Then try to guess the nature of the symbol. To do this, make your mind a blank as much as possible, always keeping control over the same, attempting to chase away for the time being the reasoning element, memory, imagination, etc. After a few minutes of gazing attentively at the back of the card, you will find that it will seem as though the thought form of the Tattwa appeared to enter the mind suddenly. When more practised it will probably appear to you later as if the symbol were trying to precipitate itself materially through the back of the card. But sometimes, especially if the cards have been long kept together in the pack in the same order, we may find that the back of the card in question is charged astrally not with the symbol upon its face, but with that upon the card whose face has been next to its back in the order of the pack.

Some may find it easier to turn the card over astrally, that is in imagination, and in imagination endeavor to perceive what flashes in the mind in that moment.

Since it is with the Tattwas that we obtain our first experiences, to illustrate the following rules, preferably use one that is in harmony with the time in which I commence my working.

RULES FOR SKRYING

If possible work in an especially prepared magical room, G.D. Altar in the center, bearing the four elements and the cross and the triangle, incense burning, lamp lighted, water in the cup, bread and salt on the platter. In addition place on the altar your magical implements. Wear your white robe wearing your Adeptus Minor sash and your Rose Cross Lamen on your breast.

Have by you your Sword and Lotus Wand. Sit at the side of the altar facing the quarter of the element, planet or sign with which you propose to work. Should any other Frater or Soror be with you arrange that they shall sit in balanced disposition around the altar. For example, if the forces with which you work be in the West your place is East of the altar facing West across it. Should it be inconvenient for you to have your own Temple or to have at hand all or any of the implements for your experiment, do your utmost to imagine them as astrally present, and in any case in astral projection wear the garments and insignia astrally all through the experience.

In fact, after considerable, most constant practice you will probably not find the absolute physical so necessary. Yet remember, that though the material in magical working is the least important of the planes in one sense, yet in another major sense it is of the greatest importance crystallising as it does the astral plane, completing it.

Have present before you the exact correspondences of certain universal formulae, for in the aforesaid insignia and implements you hold a perfect symbolic representation of the Universe. Their contemplation should in itself prevent your mind wandering to irrelevant subjects, but to the contrary compel your concentration on the sublime mysteries of the Macrocosm. Moreover these consecrated insignia give you a certain power by means of having attracted rays of force from the infinite more or less potent in proportion to your development.

The importance of using the implements on every possible occasion would appear to be great. For the implements assist in the working of a ceremony, and the latter in turn should help recharge the implements. Therefore every voyage to the realms of fire or water should add as it were a flame to the wand and moisture to the cup.

Next purify the room with fire and water and the lesser banishing ritual of the Pentagram. Imagine that we have chosen Apas - Prithivi as our Tattwa of choice. Naturally we use the correspondences of water and earth for the symbol, but do keep in mind that water is the main Tattwa expressed and the earth being secondary in this compound Tattwa. In this particular example it is well to use principally the cup, the pentacle only in a minor sense. To employ this, use the cup to trace most of the earth symbols, only occasionally employing the pentacle to work the particular symbol.

In this hypothetical case of a compound Tattwa, thoroughly to fill your sphere with the idea of this Tattwa, trace with the cup around your room the greater invoking ritual of the Pentagram both of water and of earth. Then return to your seat. For the process of skrying do the following.

Place the Tattwa card before you on the altar, take the cup in your right hand and the pentacle in the left, and look at the symbol long and steadily until you can perceive it clearly as a thought vision when you close your eyes. Vibrate the Names of Water and of Earth (Empeh Arsel, etc.) and try to realize the mental union more intensely. It may help you to perceive it as a large crescent made of blue or silvery water containing a cube of yellow sand. Continue trying to acquire a keen perception of the Tattwa until the Element and its shape and its qualities shall seem to have become a part of you, and you should then begin to feel as though you were one with that particular Element, completely bathed in it. If this is correctly done, you will find that the thought of any other Element will become distinctly distasteful to you.

Having succeeded in obtaining the thought vision of the symbol, continue vibrating the Divine Names with the idea well fixed in your mind of calling forth on the card a mental picture of some scene or landscape. This, when it first appears, will probably be vague, but continue to realize it more and more. Remember that this is a passive state of the mind, and the time is not ripe for its testing. Only when the thought picture has become sufficiently tangible and vivid, and you find that you are beginning to lose the sense of confusion and vagueness should you begin to apply tests. Before this period, all reasoning, all doubting and rumination is destructive to the experiment.

In all probability, the thought picture may become so clear to you through diligent practice, that it will seem as though the picture were trying to precipitate through the symbol. In such a case as this there can be no difficulty, for the vision will be nearly as clear to the perception as a material one. But you can arrive at a great deal by merely receiving the impression of the landscape as a thought. For example, I perceive an expanse of sea, a slight strip of land - high grey rocks or boulders rising out of the sea. To the left is a long gallery of cliffs jutting out some distance into the ocean. This appears sufficiently vivid, so I begin my tests. I suspect my memory chiefly, so I draw in front of the picture on the card, with the Lotus Wand, a large TAU in bright light. Then, believing that I may have constructed the scene in imagination, I formulate on the card a large CAPH. In this case, neither of these symbols banish or dim the scene in any way, so I continue. (But if the scene vanishes or changes or becomes blurred, it is well to banish with a Pentagram whatever may remain on the card, and simply recommence the process at the point where you are endeavouring to attract a picture on the card.)

I now draw over the picture with the Cup the Water Pentagram, and with the Pentacle the Earth Pentagram using the correct vibration. This intensifies the picture, and I now perceive in it many figures, principally of the Water Spirit type. On gazing further, and repeating the vibration, I perceive a much larger figure than the elementals, overshadowing them, clothed in blue and white, with some glimmering of silver. To obtain detail I must work for some time longer, and continue invoking with water and earth Symbols. I have found that it is best first to look at the image and then alternately test it.

Hoping that enough has been explained to enable the student to understand the general method of skrying, I will proceed further to the rules for astral projection. However it should be remembered that it is possible to carry this vision very far, and the student should not stop where I have left off.

ASTRAL PROJECTION

First follow the rules given for Skrying, until the point where the Tattwa symbol has become perfectly vivid and you feel as though you are one with the Element. You can modify the earlier stages of the work by enlarging the symbol astrally so that it is large enough for a human being to pass through. When very vivid, and not until then, pass, spring, leap or fly through it, and do not begin to think or reason till you find yourself in some place or landscape on the other side. As before, only test the experience when it has become tangible and a complete picture, If you have made your mind a blank, as much as possible, the first idea that enters your mind vividly, after you have traversed the symbol should be a correct correspondence of the Tattwa in question.

Having already, by the process of skrying, obtained a vision of a compound Tattwa, my first impression is to find myself standing on a boulder slightly out at sea, which I had noted as an important point in the picture. I realize that I am standing clothed in my Adeptus Minor insignia and white robe, on this rock, facing the shore. Turning to the right I am conscious of the gallery of cliffs, and to left and back of me the sea, everywhere.

When working on the planes it is well to act exactly as one would normally realizing each step as one goes, not trying to look on both sides at once or at the back of one's head. Instead turn first to the right and examine that, and then to the left, then turning around, and so on. It is better to remain in one spot until you are experienced so as to avoid reflexes. In fact, the more practical the experiences are, the greater chance of success.

I have an impression that the air is very cold. I stoop down and feel the rock, which I find is of a coral nature. I have already tested this vision in skrying, but it is well to repeat it to determine if I am sufficiently in touch with the landscape. I therefore trace with my astral Lotus Wand, the symbols I evoked before, the TAU and the CAPH, in white light. In fact, I do not cease tracing them until I actually perceive them as vividly as the landscape. Concluding that the scene does not vanish or become dim I now with my Astral Cup and Pentacle, draw in Light very large Water and Earth pentagrams, which stand on the sea. These, even more than the former symbols should be continued and accentuated until they become to the mind living entities. If these latter be correctly drawn and sufficiently realized, there will be little chance of illusion during the rest of the experience.

The drawing of the Pentagrams standing above the sea appears to increase the vitality of the scene, for the rather intangible Elementals and Angelic Being that I had perceived in the reflected picture became more and more real to the mind.

Had I commenced at once with astral projection without the introduction of my skrying experience, I should have had to evoke these figures. In such a case, using the Invoking Pentagrams of Water, I should continue vibrating the Deity Names, etc. of these Elements using as well the names of the Angels and Rulers, such as Tharsis, Kerub, etc. I would continue this process using these names and symbols until some forms appeared.

After careful examination, by first receiving the impression and then testing it, I can describe the following. The Angelic being, feminine in nature, pale with brown hair and light grey-green eyes, is draped in blue and white. She wears a crown formed of crescents. In her left hand she holds a curious cup, heavy, with a squarish base, and in her right hand a wand with a symbol similar to the positive element of Water.

The Elementals vary in type, the majority being of the mermaid and merman nature, but again many are of the Earth and Air nature.

Turning to the Angelic Being, I make the 5-6 Signs and LVX Signs, and to the Elementals the 3-8 and 1-10 Signs, and by right of these I ask to have explained some of the secret workings of the plane of the compound Tattwa.

The Angel having answered my signs by similar ones gives the impression that she is willing to instruct me. This can enter the mind as an extraneous thought, or may be heard clairaudiently. She shows how even the work on this particular spot is varied and according to the types of the Elementals is the work allotted. Some Elementals such as gnomes are digging in the cliffs, with sharp instruments, and boring holes therein, thus permitting water to enter freely. (This could explain the spongy rather than broken appearance of the rocks.) The mermaid and merman Elementals, who I think are in the majority are carrying some dust into the sea. Some of this may go to form islands. Others are bringing earth and weeds and alike from the depths, also probably to form land. There are also figures holding funnel-like cups who rise from the sea, drawing in air, diving back again carrying that element into the sea.

It can be understood how these investigations can be carried to very great detail, but to be as brief as possible I ask if I may be shown the effect of this Ray of the compound Tattwa on the Universe generally and on this Planet in particular.

I understand that the effect of the Ray is generating and fructifying generally, and on the whole beneficent, though everything would depend on the Force with which it was united. Its correlative would be thick rich water, containing such substances. I ask for its influence on Earth. I accomplish this by shewing thought pictures of this planet and its continents, seas, etc., and pray that this Angel will send a ray first to one spot and then another. In answer I perceive the ray falling right through the water of the Earth, as if the affinity lay with all land under water.

"The Life of Earth in the Waters is its Name" does the Angel say. Nearly all vegetation attracts this ray, but especially plants which grow under water. The Zoophyte only partially attracts it, this latter seeming rather largely composed of some active element, such as Fire. Among animals the Ray appears to fall on the seal and hippopotamus, and has a general affinity for most amphibious animals. With fish, the link seems to be small, a tortoise, a frog, and a snail are shown me, and some water-fowl of the duck variety.

Falling on man, on the savage it would appear to be beneficial to health generally, to give a feeling of well-being, and would also govern to some extent generation. Its tendency would be to accentuate sensuality and laziness. On the intellectual man it increases intuition, with some desire to clothe idea with form, therefore the first vague development of form in the mind of the artist. Since this experience has become rather voluminous I will now stop - feeling that sufficient information has been expressed which can help guide the serious and enterprising student.

I salute therefore the Angel with the LVX Signs and the Elementals by the 3-8 and 1-10 Signs, and banish astrally with the Pentagram and other symbols that I have traced upon the scene. The more powerfully the symbols have been evoked, the more powerfully should they be banished.

If you should be feeling a sensation of fatigue, as I before mentioned, make towards the symbols the sign of the Enterer indrawing their strength and vitality by using the sign of Harpocrates. Then return by the way in which you came, that is through the symbol and back into your room. Once there perform the Supreme Banishing Ritual of the Pentagrams that you have evoked. Supposing a scene to remain on the symbol of the Tattwa banish that as well. When you have had considerable practise it is probable that such detailed care as is herein indicated will not be necessary. Should the operation be too complicated to accomplish at one sitting it would be possible to divide it into parts. However you will find that one carefully practised sitting will provide more knowledge and ability than a hundred careless and vague experiments which simply strengthen mental deception, emotional folly and ignorance.

NOTES

This experiment is very good for the practice of Spiritual sight, and in this manner you can easily prove the correctness of your vision. Also for this kind of simple experience you need not prepare yourself spiritually to such an extent as with the deeper working, so that you can have your cards continually with you and practise with them as you will.

To find what Tattwa is in course, note the time of sunrise. Akasa always begins with sunrise and lasts 24 minutes followed by Vayu, Tejas, Apas, and Prithivi each lasting for 24 minutes.

Placed at the junction of the Cross and Triangle, the incense, lamp etc., should be at the angles of the arms of the Cross.

All Adeptus Minor members who are Z.A.M. have the right to wear the white robe and yellow girdle of the 3rd Adept, but not his cloak or Nemyss. Note the following:

If 2 persons are present one should be opposite the other.

If 3 persons are present form a triangle.

If 4 persons are present form a square.

If 5 persons are present form a pentagram, etc.

The G.D. Altar, the most synthetical of the symbols, the material universe ruled by the Spirit and Four Elements. The Rose-Cross contains the affirmation of the principal divisions of the Universe, synthetical like the Altar, but particular in the sense that it is attributed to the Sephirah Tiphareth, the central Sun, and is therefore the symbol for the Microcosm - Man, the Adept, he to whom perfection of the Microcosm means a certain conscious union with the Macrocosm.

The white robe and yellow girdle imply Purity - Kether, Harmony - Gold, Tiphareth. Lotus Wand - Mercy. Sword - Severity.

Imagination (eidolon) means the faculty of building an image. The imagination of the artist must lie in the power which he possesses more or less in proportion to his sincerity, and his intuition, of perceiving forces in the Macrocosm, and allying or attuning himself thereto, his talents naturally and his training permitting him to formulate images which shall express those forces.

During this process, it is more than likely that you will be believing that the picture is one of memory, or imagination, or construction, etc. All these qualities being analogous to the faculty that you are employing, and the probability of their arising at any moment will be great.

Let it be remembered that this can only be a part of the plane of the Symbol expressed by the compound Tattwa.

Employ the "Lords who Wander" (the 7 Planets), the planetary Tarot trumps, as important test symbols.

For Memory

Saturn - Tau. Lord of the Night.

For Construction

Jupiter - Caph.

For Anger, Impatience

Mars - Peh.

For Vanity

Sun - Resh.

For Pleasure

Venus - Daleth.

For Imagination

Mercury - Beth.

For Wandering Thoughts

Moon - Gimel.

Use occasionally the Pentacle, so as not to ignore too great an extent the part that the Earth plays.

In the case of starting the entire experience with Astral Projection only, you will understand that you ignore the portion of the process which attracts the picture to the card, but simply go forward through the symbol when once the latter is realised.

If working with correct correspondences, you are bound to arrive at some place answering to the same, if you project your astral sufficiently.

If after these repeated tests the Vision becomes diminished or changes very much, banish with the Astral implement, and return in the way you came, through the symbol, and start again freshly. If you feel you have expended too much force in the symbols which you traced in the scenes, redraw some of the force spent into yourself again by the formula of the signs of Horus and Harpocrates. Extend towards the symbols in the sign of Hoor, redrawing them into yourself by the sign of Hoorparkraat.

Sometimes it seems as though one had to find the words to translate the impression; sometimes the words appear to be found already, for one believes that one has heard them.

The symbol shows the potency of the whorl-formation.

Some students, I believe, have great difficulty in returning. In such a case one can do so gradually by first flying into space, thinking of this Planet, fixing the thoughts on the particular country, then on the particular spot therein, then on the house, and lastly on the room and entering therein. But in most cases this will not be necessary.

TECHNIQUE

Here follow two Tattwa visions by Soror Vestigia. These are provided as simple examples of the technique, and the procedure to be used. The first of them is the fiery sub-element of Earth, Tejas of Prithivi.

Vestigia stated that she found herself, after going through the visualized symbols, "in a volcanic district. Hill and mountains, hot air, and sunny light. Using a Pentacle, and calling on the Earth names, I see before me a species of Angelic King Elemental. On testing him, I find that he gives me the Neophyte Saluting Sign, and the Philosophus (fire) Sign. He bows low to the symbols that I give him, and says that he is willing to show me some of the working on the plane. He has a beautiful face, somewhat of the Fire type, yet sweet in expression. He wears a Golden Crown, and a fiery red cloak, opening on to a yellow tunic, over which being a shirt of mail. In his right hand he bears a wand, the lower end or handle being shaped somewhat as the Pentacle implement, and the staff and upper end being as the Fire Wand. In his left hand (but this I do not clearly see) he bears a Fire Wand; I think that the right hand points upwards and the left downwards, and is a symbol to invoke forces. Little figures of the gnome type come at his call. When commanded some broke the rocky parts of the mountain with pick-axes which they carry. Others appear to dig in the ground. In breaking off these rocky pieces, there fall away little bits of bright metal or copper. Some of these gnomes collected the bits of metal and carried them away in litle wallets slung by a baldrick from their shoulders. We followed them and came to some mountainous peaks. From these peaks issued some large and fierce, but hardly perceivable, fires. Into cauldrons or bowls placed above these fires, the collected pieces of metal were placed. I was told that this was a lengthy process, but asked that I might see the result of what appeared to be a gradual melting of this metal, I was then shown some bowls containing liquid gold, but not I imagine, very pure metal, I again followed my guide, the Angelic King Elemental Ruler, who gave me his name as Atapa, and followed by some gnomes bearing the bowl of liquid gold. We came, after passing through many subterranean passages cut in the mountains, to a huge cavern of immense breadth and height. It was like a Palace cut out of the rock. We passed through rudely cut passages, until we reached a large central hall, at the end of which was a Dais on which were seated the King and Queen, the courtier gnomes standing around.

"This Hall seemed lighted by torches, and at intervals were roughly cut pillars. The Gnomes who accompanied us presented to the King and Queen their gold. These latter commanded their attendants to remove this to another apartment. I asked the King and Queen for a further explanation, and they appointing substitutes in their absence, retire to an inner chamber which appeared more elevated than the rest. The architecture here seemed to be of a different kind. This small hall had several sides, each with a door, draped by a curtain. In the center of the Hall was a large tripod receiver containing some of the liquid gold such as that we had brought with us. The King and Queen who before had worn the colours of Earth now donned, he the red, and she the white garments. They then with their Earth and Fire Wands invoked and joined their wands over the Tripod. There appeared in the air above, a figure such as Atapa, he who had brought me here. He, extending his wand, and invoking, caused to appear from each door a figure of a planetary or zodiacal nature. These each in turn held out his wand over the gold, using some sigil which I can but dimly follow. The gold each time appearing to undergo a change. When these last figures have retired again behind the curtains, the King and Queen used a species of ladle and compressed together the gold, making it into solid shapes and placing one of these at each of the curtained doors. Some gold still remained in the bowl. The King and Queen departed, and it seemed to me that I saw a figure again appear from behind each curtain and draw away the pieces of gold."

The second one I shall quote is a vision of Spirit of Water, Akasa of Apas, also by Vestigia.

"A wide expanse of water with many reflections of bright light, and occasionally glimpses of rainbow colours appearing (perhaps symbolising the beginning of formation in Water). When divine and other names were pronounced, elementals of the mermaid and merman type appear, but few of other elemental forms. These water forms are extremely changeable, one moment appearing as solid mermaids and mermen, the next melting into foam.

"Raising myself by means of the highest symbols I have been taught, and vibrating the names of Water, I rose until the Water vanished, and instead I beheld a mighty world or globe, with its dimensions and divisions of Gods, Angels, elementals, demons - the whole universe of Water (like the tablet ruled in EMPEH ARSEL GAIOL), I called on this latter name, and the Universe seemed to vivify more and more. I then called on HCOMA, and there appeared standing before me a mighty Archangel (with four wings) robed in glistening white, and crowned. In one hand, the right, he held a species of trident, and in the left a Cup filled to the brim with an essence which appeared to be derived from above. This essence, brimming over, poured down below on either side, From the overflowing or over running of this Cup, which derives its essence from Atziluth, apparently the cup being in Briah, the World of Yetzirah obtains its moisture. It is there differentiated into its various operative forces.

"These operative forces are represented by Angels each with their respective office in the world of moisture. These forces working in Yetzirah, when descending and mingling with the Kether of Assiah, are initiating the force of that which we as human beings call Moisture."

Here is another good example of a Tattwa vision. It was obtained over a score of years ago by Countess Tamara Bourkoun-Dolgoruky when she visited me in Los Angeles.

"I found myself suspended in an unfathomable abyss of space. Nothing was visible, neither sky nor clouds, no stars or any other heavenly bodies, save a diffused pale grey light. I was conscious of myself as a colossal figure in a yellow robe and a yellow and violet nemyss, holding a yellow dagger and tracing with it the appropriate Pentagrams and Divine

Names. However, they did not appear outlined in flashing colours, as had been the case when skrying in the realms of Fire and Water. Rather I heard them vibrating through the waves of Aether and reaching the confines of the Universe, whence their echoes rushed back to me, reverberating with a deafening roar.

"Slowly a definite panorama began to formulate against the pale background. A wide expanse of turquoise, blue sky, enclosed by luminous lapis lazuli clouds lined with translucent pinkish-orange, stretched on the horizon. It is impossible to describe the radiance and brilliancy of those colours; they should be painted and even then the attempt would have failed. As I was observing this enchanting scene, a graceful sylph-like shape emerged from the clouds slowly soaring towards me. The entity was drapped in filmy gauze of smokey grey, gradually shading into mauve and royal blue. The robe was caught at the waist by long streamers of amethyst velvet. The wings were those of a gigantic butterfly, irridescent and transparent, ornamented with jewelled green-blue "eyes" of a peacock's tail. Tiny silver stars were gleaming and sparkling through dark cloud-like hair that framed a wistful rosy face with violet-blue eyes. After acknowledging my salutes, the Genie informed me that he was the messenger of twilight and the evening breeze.

"At the approach of the Angelic being, I suddenly became aware of a slow rolling vibration pulsating through space, which swelled and undulated as if it were animated by in breathings and out breathings of an invisible all-pervading Presence. The words 'The Great Breath which knows itself not'flashed in my mind. Yet here it was, filling the abysses of infinite Space, ceaseless, eternal, changeless in its rhythmic motion, embracing innumerable worlds which swayed and rolled gently in its waves, only to disappear like a wisp of vapour. As in the previous vision I perceived the circulation of the Tattwas, only this time it was on a much grander scale, as the currents swept not only around the Earth but throughout the whole universe and beyond. Also it became quite simple to understand why through Pranayama one may acquire knowledge and mastery over the elements, for is not Air-Breath our most direct link with the Macrocosm?

"Thus, immersed in contemplation, I became conscious of Nada, the faint notes of which sounded like a melancholy flute accompanied by a gong ringing in a void. As the Sound swelled, I heard a distant chanting of OM, the Logos, the Creative Word. And, as if to illustrate this, there slowly emerged, shining softly through a transparent veil of greyish clouds, an opalescent orange globe, floating majestically on the horizon. Rays of diffused light were playing around it, forming faint outlines of two enormous wings. No words could convey the supernal beauty, majesty and unutterable sweetness of this apparition which seemed to be the very essence of love. The Angel and I were so overwhelmed that we silently knelt immersed in the soft radiance of this wondrous winged sphere. My senses began to reel, unable to withstand the impact of such a powerful and totally unfamiliar vibration, and as I was afraid to lose consciousness, nothing remained but to ask the Genie to conduct me back to my body."

OUTER ORDER RITUALS AND COMMENTARIES

VOLUME SIX

OUTER ORDER RITUALS AND COMMENTARIES

TABLE OF CONTENTS

IMPORTANT TABLES AND ILLUSTRATIONS

VOLUME SIX

OUTER ORDER RITUALS AND COMMENTARIES

INTRODUCTION TO THE ORIGINAL GOLDEN DAWN RITUALS

(These are not the later revisions of the Stella Matutina)

In 1979 and 1980, my friend Carr P. Collins Jr. visited Gerald Yorke in England on two separate occasions to obtain copies of a **Complete Set** of **Golden Dawn Documents.** One set was lost in transit demanding therefore the second visit. They are dated 1894-5 and were originally issued to a member of the Order who used the pseudonym or magical motto of Frater De Profundis Ad Lucem.

Upon examination of these papers I discovered that the later Rituals of the Stella Matutina had been considerably edited and modified when compared to the 1894-5 versions of D.P.A.L. In the *Complete Golden Dawn System of Magic* the original versions written by Mathers and Westcott have been used exclusively here.

It was further discovered that there was a quantity of new material that either had never found its way to the Stella Matutina or had been ruthlessly edited out. The result is that the contents of this book follow literally the title—it does represent the **Complete Golden Dawn System.** Good fortune also pursued me in that R.A. Gilbert of Bristol, the author of a biography of A.E. Waite now in preparation, and of a new history of the Golden Dawn from a radically different point of view, was kind enough to give me copies of the Neophyte and Adeptus Minor Rituals employed in Waite's own Order, **The Fellowship of the Rosy Cross.** This was formed some years after the revolt which splintered and shattered the unity and integrity of the Order.

Be that as it may, the student would do well to compare the original simplicity of the Golden Dawn Rituals with the complex verbosity of Waite's Rituals. In any event, the inclusion of these two rituals (there is a third, the Adeptus Major Ritual which I believe came from Carr P. Collins' own private collection of Golden Dawn Manuscripts) with the rest of the original material makes this not merely a new presentation of the Golden Dawn System, but an unique account of what has come to be termed the Western Esoteric Tradition.

THE COMPLETE GOLDEN DAWN SYSTEM OF MAGIC

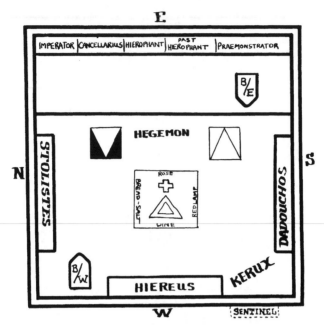

Temple of the newophyte grade

NOTE

The complete spelling of the officers who participate in these ceremonies will be given once here. Thereafter they will be abbreviated as follows:

    Hierophant (Red Robe, Lamen, Sceptre) will be shown as Hiero.
    Hiereus (Black Robe, Lamen, Sword) not abbreviated.
    Hegemon (White Robe, Lamen, Sceptre) shown as Heg.
    Kerux (Black Robe, Lamen, Lamp and Wand) not abbreviated.
    Stolistes (Black Robe, Lamen, Cup of Water) shown as Stol.
    Dadouchos (Black Robe, Lamen, Thurible) shown as Dad.
    Sentinel (Black Robe, Lamen, Sword) shown as Sent.

ON THE DAIS (THE STAGE IN THE EAST OF TEMPLE)

These officers represent the Second Order and are present mostly symbolically.
Imperator.
Cancellarius.
Praemonstrator.
Past Hierophant.

REQUIRED MATERIALS

FOR THE ALTAR:

Cross and Triangle.
Red Rose.
Red Lamp.
Cup of Wine.
Paten of Bread and Salt.

FOR THE CANDIDATE:

Black Gown.
Red Shoes.
Hoodwink.
Rope.
Sash.
Chemicals to change clear water to red—the colour of blood.

OPENING OF THE NEOPHYTE GRADE 0-0

When the members are assembled and clothed, Hierophant gives one knock and the Officers rise.

Members do not rise except for Adorations to the East or when asked for the signs. Nor do they circumambulate with the Officers. When they do have occasion to move in the Temple, they do so in the direction of the Sun and make the Neophyte signs on passing the Throne of the East—**whether the Hierophant is there or not.** The Grade sign is made in the direction of movement except when entering or leaving the Hall, when it is made toward the East.

The knock is made by rapping the base or shaft of Wand or the pommel of Sword on a Table.

Hiero:

(Knock) (All members assembled wearing regalia. Kerux goes to the right of Hierophant, faces West and proclaims:)

Kerux:

HEKAS, HEKAS, ESTE BEBELOI! (Returns to place.)

Hiero:

(Knock) Fratres and Sorores of the Order of the Golden Dawn in the Outer, assist me to open the Hall of the Neophytes of the (Name the) Temple (All rise.) Frater Kerux see that the Temple is properly guarded.

Kerux:

(Knock) (Answered by Sentinel) Very Honored Hierophant, the Hall is properly guarded.

Hiero:

Very Honored Hiereus, assure yourself that all present have witnessed the Golden Dawn.

Hiereus:

Fratres and Sorores of the Order of the Golden Dawn in the Outer give the signs of a Neophyte (done). Very Honored Hierophant (saluting) all present have been so honored.

Hiero:

Very Honoured Hiereus, how many chief officers are there in this grade?

Hiereus:

Three, Very Honoured Hierophant. Namely, the Hierophant, Hiereus and Hegemon

Hiero:

Is there any peculiarity in these names?

Hiereus:

They all commence with the letter H.

Hiero:

Of what is this letter the symbol?

Hiereus:

Of life, because the character H is one mode of representing the ancient Greek aspirate; Breathing and Breath, are the evidence of life.

Hiero:

How many assistant officers are there in this grade?

Hiereus:

Three, besides the Sentinel, namely, the Kerux, the Stolistes, and Dadouchos.

Hiero:

The situation of the Sentinel?

Hiereus:

Without the Portal of the Hall.

Hiero:

His duty?

Hiereus:

Armed with a sword to keep out intruders, and to prepare the Candidate.

Hiero:

Frater Dadouchos, your situation?

Dad:

In the South, Very Honored Hierophant, to symbolize heat and dryness.

Hiero:

Your duty?

Dad:

I attend to the censer and the incense, and I assist in the purification and consecration by Fire of the Hall, of the Members, and of the Candidate.

Hiero:

Frater Stolistes, your situation?

Stol:

In the North, Very Honored Hierophant, to symbolize cold and moisture.

Hiero:

Your duty?

Stol:

I see that the robes, collars and insignia of the Officers are ready before the opening; I attend to the cup of lustral water and I assist in the purification and consecration by water, of the Hall, of the Members, and of the Candidate.

Hiero:

Frater Kerux, your situation?

Kerux:

Within the Portal of the Hall, Very Honored Hierophant.

Hiero:

Your duty?

Kerux:

I see that all the furniture of the Hall is properly arranged before the opening. I guard the inner side of the Portal. I admit Fratres and Sorores of the Order. I assist in the reception of the Candidates. I attend to the Lamp of my office. I lead the mystic circumambulation and make all announcements and reports.

Hiero:

What do your Lamp and Wand symbolize?

Kerux:

The Light of Occult Science and directing power.

Hiero:

Honored Hegemon, your station?

Heg:

Between the two pillars of Hermes and Solomon facing the cubical altar of the Universe, Very Honored Hierophant.

Hiero:

Your duty?

Heg:

1 preside over the symbolic gateway of Occult Science. I am the reconciler between light and darkness. I immediately follow the Kerux in the mystic circumambulations. I superintend the preparation of the Candidate; lead him through the path of darkness into light, and assist in his reception, and I aid the other officers in the execution of their duties.

Hiero:

What does the white color of your robe symbolize?

Heg:

Purity.

Hiero:

Your peculiar ensign of office?

Heg:

The mitre-headed sceptre.

Hiero:

What does it symbolize?

Heg:

Religion, to guide and regulate life.

Hiero:

What does your office symbolize?

Heg:

Those higher aspirations of the soul, which should guide its actions.

Hiero:

Honored Hiereus, your station?

Hiereus:

On the throne of the West, Very Honored Hierophant.

Hiero:

What does the throne of the West symbolize?

Hiereus:

Increase of darkness; decrease of light.

Hiero:

Your duty?

Hiereus:

I preside over twilight and darkness, which encompass us in the absence of the Sun of Life and Light. I guard the gate of the West. I assist in the reception of the Candidate and I superintend the inferior officers in the execution of their duties.

Hiero:

What does the black color of your robe symbolize?

Hiereus:

Darkness.

Hiero:

Your peculiar insignia of office?

Hiereus:

The Sword and Banner of the West.

Hiero:

What does the Banner of the West symbolize?

Hiereus:

Twilight.

Hiero:

What does the Sword symbolize?

Hiereus:

Severity and Judgement.

Hiero:

What does your office symbolize?

Hiereus:

Fortitude.

Hiero:

My place is on the Throne of the East, which symbolizes the rise of the Sun of Life and Light—my duty is to rule and govern this Hall in accordance with the laws of the Order. The red color of my robe symbolizes Light: my insignia are the Sceptre and the Banner of the East, which signify power and light, mercy and wisdom, and my office is that of Expounder of the Mysteries. Frater Stolistes, I command you to purify the Hall and the members by Water.

Stol:

(Does so, saying) I consecrate with water.

Hiero:

Frater Dadouchos, I command you to purify the Hall and the members by fire.

Dad:

(Does so, saying) I consecrate with fire.

Heg:

(Goes to the North and faces East.)

Hiero:

(Rising with Sceptre and Banner) Let the mystic circumambulation take place in the path of light. (Done in due form; Kerux first, then Hegemon, Hiereus, other members and Stolistes and Dadouchos last. They pass three times around from East by South to West. After first round Hiereus returns to his place. After second round Hegemon, after third remaining members. Each as he passes the throne of the East salutes and lowers insignia, except the Hierophant.)

Hiero:

The mystic circumambulation symbolic of the rise of the Light is accomplished. Let us adore the Lord of the Universe.

(ADORATION)

Holy art Thou, Lord of the Universe.
Holy art Thou, whom Nature hath not formed.
Holy art Thou, The Vast and Mighty One.
Lord of the Light and of the Darkness.

(All Salute.) Frater Kerux, in the name of the Lord of the Universe, I command you to declare that I have opened the Hall of the Neophytes.

Kerux:

(Going to the right of the Hierophant as usual) In the name of the Lord of the Universe, I declare that the Sun hath arisen, and that the Light shineth in the Darkness.

Kerux:

(Knock)

Hiereus:

(Knock)

Heg:

(Knock)
(All resume their seats.)

Hiero:

(Knock) KHABS.

Hiereus:

(Knock) AM.

Heg:

(Knock) PEKHT.

Hiereus:

(Knock) KONX.

Hcg:

(Knock) OM.

Hiero:

(Knock) PAX.

Heg:

(Knock) LIGHT.

Hiero:

(Knock) IN.

Hiereus:

(Knock) EXTENSION.

CEREMONY OF ADMISSION
(The Candidate is not to be told the name of the Order until his admission.)

Hiero:

(Knocks) Fratres and Sorores of the Order of the Golden Dawn in the Outer, I have received a dispensation from the Greatly Honored Chiefs of the Second Order to admit (name of aspirant) to the Grade of Neophyte. Honored Hegemon instruct (name of aspirant) to hold himself (or herself) in readiness for the ceremony of his (or her) admission and superintend his (or her) preparation. (Hegemon removes his chair from between the Pillars, salutes Hierophant, quits Temple and prepares Candidate as follows: The Candidate is Hoodwinked and a rope tied thrice around the waist.)

Heg:

Child of Earth, arise and enter the Path of Darkness.

Kerux:

(Knocks) Very Honored Hierophant, is it your pleasure that the Candidate be admitted?

Hiero:

It is. Admit (name of aspirant) in due form, who will hereafter be known by the motto XYZ. Fratre Stolistes and Dadouchos assist the Kerux in the reception. (They join Kerux at door. Kerux opens door but bars the entrance.)

Kerux:

Child of Earth, unpurified and unconsecrated thou canst not enter our Sacred Hall.

Stol:

(Signing a Cross on Candidate's forehead) Child of Earth, I purify thee with Water.

Dad:

(Censing the Candidate) Child of Earth, I consecrate thee with Fire.

Hiero:

Conduct the Candidate to the foot of the altar. Child of Earth, why dost thou request admission into this Order?

Cand:

(Prompted by Hegemon) My soul is wandering in darkness seeking for the Light of Occult Knowledge, and I believe that in this Order the knowledge of that Light may be obtained.

Hiero:

(Name of aspirant) I hold in my hand your signed pledge to keep secret all relating to this Order, but to confirm it I now ask if you are willing in the presence of this assembly to take a great and solemn obligation to keep inviolate the secrets and mysteries of our Order? Let me however assure you that this obligation contains nothing incompatible with your civil, moral or religious duties.

Cand:

I am. (Banners left behind at Thrones. Hierophant advances between Pillars to Eastern side of Altar. Hiereus stands on Candidate's left, Hegemon on Candidate's right.)

Hiero:

Thou wilt kneel on both knees, give me your right hand, which I place on this sacred and sublime symbol (Places Candidate's right hand on the centre of the triangle.) Place your left hand in mine, bow your head, repeat your full name at length and say after me (All rise).

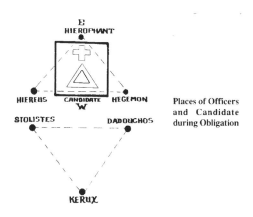

Places of Officers
and Candidate
during Obligation

THE OBLIGATION

I, (name of aspirant), in the presence of the Lord of the Universe and of this Hall of Neophytes of the Order of The Golden Dawn in the Outer, regularly assembled under warrant from the Greatly Honored Chiefs of the Second Order, do of my own free will and accord hereby and hereon most solemnly pledge myself to keep secret this Order, its name, the name of its members, and the proceedings which take place at its meetings, from all and every person in the whole world who is outside the pale of the Order, and not even to discuss these with initiates, unless he or they are in possession of the password for the time being; nor yet with any member who has resigned, demitted or been expelled, and I undertake to maintain a kind and benevolent relation with all the Fratres and Sorores of the Order.

I furthermore promise and swear that I will keep any information relative to this Order, which may have become known to me prior to the completion of the Ceremony of my admission and I also pledge myself to divulge nothing whatsoever concerning this Order to the outside world in case either of my resignation, demission or expulsion therefrom, after the completion of my admission. I will not seek to obtain any ritual or lecture pertaining to the Order without due authorization from the Praemonstrator of my Temple, nor will I possess any ritual or lecture unless it be properly registered and labelled by him.

I further undertake that any such ritual or lecture and any case, cover or box containing them shall bear the official label of the Golden Dawn. I will not copy myself, nor lend to any other person to be copied, any ritual or lecture, until and unless I hold the written permission of the Praemonstrator to do so, lest our secret knowledge be revealed through my neglect or error.

Furthermore, I undertake to prosecute with zeal the study of Occult Sciences, seeing that this Order is not established for the benefit of those who desire only a superficial know ledge thereof. I will not suffer myself to be hypnotized, or mesmerized, nor will I place myself in such a passive state that any uninitiated person, power, or being may cause me to lose control of my thoughts, words or actions.

Neither will I use my Occult powers for any evil purposes and I further promise to persevere with firmness and courage through the ceremony of my admission, and these points I generally and severally, upon this sacred and sublime symbol, swear to observe without evasion, equivocation, or mental reservation of any kind whatsoever; under the no less penalty on the violation of any or either of them of being expelled from this Order, as a wilfully perjured wretch, void of all moral worth, and unfit for the society of all right and true persons, and in addition under the awful penalty of voluntarily submitting myself to a deadly and hostile current of will set in motion by the chiefs of the Order, by which I should fall slain and paralysed without visible weapon as if slain by the lightning flash. (Hiereus here suddenly lays the blade of his sword on the nape of the Candidate's neck and withdraws it again).

So help me the Lord of the Universe and my own higher soul.

Hiero:

Rise, newly obligated Neophyte of the Golden Dawn in the Outer. Place the Candidate in the Northern part of the Hall, the place of the greatest symbolic darkness. (Done. Candidate faces to the East, Hierophant and Hiereus return to their thrones.)

Hiero:

The voice of my higher soul said unto me, Let me enter the Path of Darkness, peradventure thus shall I obtain the Light. I am the only being in an abyss of darkness. From the darkness came I forth ere my birth, from the silence of a primal sleep, and the Voice of Ages answered unto my soul, I am he that formulates in darkness. Child of Earth; the Light shineth in the darkness, but the darkness comprehendeth it not.

Let the mystic circumambulation take place in the path of darkness with the symbolic Light of Occult Science to guide the way. (Kerux leads with Light and Wand, Hegemon guides the Candidate, Stolistes and Dadouchos follow, thrice round. First time Hierophant (Knocks), and Hiereus (Knocks), Second time Hierophant (Knocks) They halt in the South.)

Kerux:

Child of Earth, unpurified and unconsecrated, thou canst not enter the path of the West.

Stol:

(Signing a Cross on Candidate's forehead) Child of Earth, I purify thee with water

Dad:

(Censing Candidate) Child of Earth, I consecrate thee with fire.

Heg:

Child of Earth, twice consecrated, thou mayest approach the gate of the West. (They move to the West, facing Throne and halt. Hiereus rises, takes Banner in left hand, menaces Candidate with sword and says as the Hegemon slips up the Candidate's hoodwink.)

Hiereus:

Thou canst not pass by me saith the Guardian of the West unless thou canst tell me my name.

Heg:

Darkness is thy name, the Great One of the Paths of the Shades.

Hiereus:

(Slowly sinking point of sword) Child of Earth, fear is failure. Therefore be without fear, for in the heart of the coward virtue abideth not. Thou hast known me, so pass thou on. (Hoodwink slipped down again. They move to the North and halt.)

Kerux:

Child of Earth, unpurified and unconsecrated, thou canst not enter the Path of the East.

Stol:

(Signing a Cross on the Candidate's forehead) Child of Earth, I purify thee with water.

Dad:

(Censing the Candidate) Child of Earth, I consecrate thee with fire.

Heg:

Child of Earth, thrice consecrated, thou mayest approach the gate of the East. (They move to the East facing Throne and halt. Hierophant rises, takes Banner in left hand and raises Sceptre as if to strike. Hegemon slips up Candidate's hoodwink.)

Hiero:

Thou canst not pass by me saith the Guardian of the East, unless thou canst tell me my name.

Heg:

LIGHT dawning in darkness is thy name, the LIGHT of a Golden Day.

Hiero:

(Slowly lowering Sceptre) Child of Earth, remember that unbalanced force is evil, unbalanced mercy is but weakness, unbalanced severity is but oppression. Thou hast known me, so pass thou on unto the Cubical Altar of the Universe. (Hoodwink slipped down and Candidate taken to West of Altar. Hierophant leaves Throne and stands between the pillars, facing Candidate with Sceptre in right hand and Banner in left.)

Hiero:

I come in the Power of the Light.
I come in the Light of Wisdom.
I come in the Mercy of the Light.
The Light hath Healing in its Wings.

(Hegemon on Candidate's right, Kerux behind Candidate, Stolistes and Dadouchos right and left of Kerux. The officers are now forming a Hexagram around the Altar. Hierus holds sword in the right hand with the Banner of the West in left.)

Hiero:

Let the Candidate kneel while I invoke the Lord of the Universe (Candidate kneels). Lord of the Universe, the Vast and the Mighty One, Ruler of the Light and of the Darkness, we adore Thee and we invoke Thee. Look with favour upon this Neophyte, who now kneeleth before Thee and grant Thine aid unto the higher aspirations of his soul, so that he may prove a true and faithful Frater among us unto the Glory of Thy Ineffable Name. Amen.

Let the Candidate rise. (Candidate is assisted to rise and is brought close to the Altar. Hierophant, Hiereus, and Hegemon raise Wands and Sword touching over the head of Candidate. At the word "Darkness" Kerux removes hoodwink).

Hegemon:

Inheritor of a dying world we call thee to the living beauty.

Hiereus:

Wanderer in the wild darkness we call thee to the gentle light. (Hoodwink removed.

Hiero:

Child of Earth, long hast thou dwelt in darkness. Quit the night and seek the day. (All members present clap hands. Hierophant, Hiereus, Hegemon say together):

Hiero:

Hiereus:

Heg:

(Said together) Frater XYZ we receive thee into the Order of the Golden Dawn.

Hiero:

(Knocks) KHABS.

Hiereus:

(Knocks) AM.

Heg:

(Knocks) PEKHT.

Hiereus:

(Knocks) KONX.

Heg:

(Knocks) OM.

Hiero:

(Knocks) PAX.

Heg:

(Knocks) LIGHT

Hiero:

(Knocks) IN.

Hiereus:

(Knocks) EXTENSION.

Hiero:

In til your wanderings through darkness the lamp of the (Kerux advances and raises his lamp; Kerux went before you, though you saw it not. It is the symbol of the Hidden Light of Occult Science. Let the Candidate be conducted to the East of the

Altar. Honoured Hiereus, I delegate to you the duty of entrusting the Candidate with the secret signs, grip, grand word and present password of the Neophyte Grade of the Order of the Golden Dawn in the Outer, of placing him between the mystic pillars and of superintending his fourth and final consecration. (Hierophant returns to Throne. Hiereus takes his place between the pillars, Candidate is conducted by Hegemon to the East of the Altar facing Hiereus. Hiereus giving Sword and Banner to Hegemon to hold.)

Hiereus:

Frater XYZ, I now proceed to instruct you in the secret signs, grip and token, grand word and password for the present time for this Grade. Firstly, advance your left foot about six inches: this is called the step of the grade. The sign is two-fold; the Saluting Sign and Sign of

Silence. The first should always be answered by the second. The Saluting Sign is given by thrusting both arms horizontally forward, palms downwards, as if groping your way and bow your head. It alludes to your condition in a state of darkness unillumined by the Lamp of Occult Knowledge and groping your way blindly in the search for truth. The Sign of Silence is given by placing the left first finger on the mouth. It alludes to the strict silence inculcated on you by your obligation regarding all proceedings of the Order. The grip or token is given in the following manner: Advance your left foot about six inches touching mine, side to side and toe to heel. Now extend your right hand as if to grip mine, but miss it intentionally; again extend it and seize mine by the fingers only. It alludes to the seeking for guidance in darkness. The Grand Word is HAR-PAR-KRAT whispered by alternate syllables mouth to ear thus. It is the title of the Egyptian God of Silence and should ever remind you of the strict silence you have sworn to maintain. The password is (blank) which will be periodically changed at each Equinox so that a member who has resigned, demitted. or been expelled from the Order, may be in ignorance of the existing password. I now place you between the two pillars of Hermes and Solomon in the symbolical Gateway of Occult Science. (Hiereus draws Candidate forward between the pillars and unclasps hands. He receives sword and banner from Hegemon, stands at the latter's left, all facing Candidate.)

Hiereus:

Let the final consecration of the Candidate take place.

Kerux:

(Goes to the North and faces East. Stolistes signs a Cross on Candidate's forehead, bows to Hierophant and sprinkles East and says): Frater XYZ, I purify thee finally with water.

Dad:

(Censing as Stolistes has done) Frater XYZ, I consecrate thee finally with fire.

Hiero:

Honored Hegemon, the final consecration of the Candidate having been performed, I command you to remove the rope from his waist, the last remaining symbol of the path of darkness, and to invest him with the distinguishing badge of the grade.

Heg:

(Doing so) By the command of the Very Honored Hierophant, I invest you with the distinguishing badge of the grade. It symbolizes Light dawning in darkness.

Hiero:

Let the mystic circumambulation take place in the path of Light. (Kerux goes to the North East. Hegemon takes Candidate behind Black Pillar, and stands behind Kerux. Hiereus comes next, followed by Stolistes and Dadouchos. Kerux leads off, all salute on passing Hierophant who stands holding Sceptre and Banner as in the Opening. Hiereus drops out on reaching his Throne. Hegemon returns to between the Pillars after passing Hierophant twice. He directs Neophyte to follow Kerux who with the other Officers passes Hierophant thrice. After the third passing).

Hiero:

Take your place North West of the Stolistes. (Kerux indicates this and goes on followed by Stolistes who falls out in the North and returns to his place. Hegemon replaces his chair between the Pillars and sits down. Kerux replaces the Rose, Lamp, Cup and Paten in their proper places on the Altar. All are seated.) The Three Fold Cord bound about your waist, was an image of the three-fold bondage of Mortality, which amongst the Initiated is called earthly or material inclination, that has bound into a narrow place the once far-wandering Soul; and the Hood-wink was an image of the Darkness, of Ignorance, of Mortality that has blinded men to the Happiness and Beauty their eyes once looked upon. The Double Cubical Altar in the centre of the Hall, is an emblem of visible Nature or the Material Universe, concealing within herself the mysteries of all dimensions, while revealing her surface to the exterior senses. It is a double cube because, as the Emerald Tablet has said The things that are below are a reflection of the things that are above. The world of men and women created to unhappiness is a reflection of the World of Divine Beings created to Happiness. It is described in the SEPHER YETZIRAH, or The Book of Formation, as An Abyss of Height and as an Abyss of Depth, An Abyss of the East and An Abyss of the West, An Abyss of the North and An Abyss of the South. The Altar is black because, unlike Divine Beings who unfold in the Element of Light, the Fires of Created Beings arise from Darkness and Obscurity. On the Altar is a White T riangle to be the Image of that Immortal Light, that Triune Light, which moved in Darkness and formed the World of Darkness and out of Darkness. There are two contending Forces and One always uniting them. And these Three have their Image in the three-fold Flame of our Being and in the threefold wave of the sensual world. (Hierophant stands in the form of Cross, saying:) Glory be to Thee, Father of the Undying. For Thy Glory flows out rejoicing, to the ends of the Earth! (He reseats himself.) The Red Cross above the White Triangle, is an Image of Him Who was unfolded in the Light. At its East, South, West and North Angles are a Rose, Fire, Cup of Wine and Bread and Salt. These allude to the Four Elements, Air, Fire, Water, Earth. The Mystical Words - KHABS AM PEKHT - are ancient Egyptian and are the origin of the Greek KONX OM PAX - which was uttered at the Eleusinian Mysteries. A literal translation would be Light Rushing Out in One Ray and they signify the same form of Light as that symbolized by the Staff of the Kerux. East of the Double Cubical Altar of created things, are the Pillars of Hermes and of Solomon. On these are painted certain Hieroglyphics from the 17th and the 125th Chapters of the Book of the Dead. They are the symbols of the two powers of Day and Night, Love and Hate, Work and Rest, the subtle force of the Lodestone and the Eternal out-pouring and in-pouring of the Heart of God. The Lamps that burn, though with a veiled light, upon their summits show that the Pathway to Hidden Knowledge, unlike the Pathway of Nature - which is a continual undulation, the winding hither and thither of the Serpent - is the straight and narrow way between them. It was because of this that I passed between them, when you came to the Light, and it was because of this that you were placed between them to receive the final Consecration. Two contending Forces and one which unites them eternally. Two basal angles of the triangle and one which forms the apex. Such is the origin of Creation, it is the Triad of Life. My Throne at the Gate of the East is the Place of the Guardian of the Dawning Sun. The Throne of the Hiereus at the Gate of the West is the Place of the Guardian against the Multitudes that sleep through the Light and awaken at the twilight. The Throne of the Hegemon seated between the Columns is the Place of Balanced Power, between the Ultimate Light and the Ultimate Darkness. These meanings are shown in detail and by the color of our robes. The Wand of the Kerux is the Beam of Light from the Hidden Wisdom, and his Lamp is an emblem of the everburning Lamp of the Guardian of the Mysteries. The Seat of the Stolistes at the Gate of the North is the Place of the Guardian of the Cauldron and the Well of Water - of Cold and Moisture. The Seat of the Dadouchos at the Gate of the South is the Place of the Guardian of the Lake of Fire and the Burning Bush.

Hiero:

Honored Frater Kerux, I command you to declare that the Neophyte has been initiated into the Mysteries of the Neophyte Grade. (Kerux advances to the North East, faces West, raises his Wand and says:)

Kerux:

In the name of the Lord of the Universe and by command of the Very Honored Hierophant, hear all ye that I proclaim that (name of aspirant) who will hereafter be known unto you by the Motto XYZ, has been admitted in due form to the Neophyte grade of the Order of the Golden Dawn in the Outer. (All clap hands.)

Hiero:

Very Honored Hiereus, I delegate to you the duty of pronouncing a short address to our Frater on his admission.

Hiereus:

As you have now pased through the ceremony of your admission, allow me to congratulate you on being admitted a member of this ancient and honorable Order, whose professed object and end is the practical study of Occult Science. Let me therefore advise you to remember this day as a marked one in your existence and to adopt and cultivate a mental condition worthy of this Order. To this end let me first earnestly recommend you never to forget due honor and reverence to the Lord of the Universe, for as the whole is greater than its parts, so is He far greater than we, who are but as sparks derived from that unsupportable Light which is in Him. It is written that the borders of his Garment of Flame sweep the ends of the Universe and unto Him all return. Therefore do we adore Him; therefore do we invoke Him; therefore in adoration to Him sinks even the Banner of the East. (Done) Secondly, let me advise you never to ridicule or cast obloquy upon the form of religion professed by another, for what right have you to desecrate what is sacred in his eyes? Thirdly, never let the seal of secrecy regarding the Order be absent from your recollection, and beware that you betray it not by a casual or unthinking word. Fourthly, study well that Great Arcanum, the proper equilibrium of mercy and severity, for either unbalanced is not good; unbalanced severity is cruelty and oppression; unbalanced mercy is but weakness and would permit evil to exist unchecked, thus making itself as it were the accomplice of that evil. Lastly, do not be daunted by the difficulties of Occult Study and remember that every obstacle can at length be conquered by perseverance.

Hiero:

Before you can pass on to the next Higher Grade of this Order you will have to make yourself perfect in the following: 1) The names and alchemical symbols of the four elements. 2) The names, astrological symbols and elemental attribution of the twelve signs of the Zodiac. 3) The names and astrological symbols of the seven planets, also their houses, exaltation and triplicity in the Zodiac. 4) The names, characters and numerical values of the twenty-two letters of the Hebrew alphabet. 5) The names and English meanings of the ten Qabalistic Sephiroth. A MSS. lecture on these subjects of study may be obtained on application. When you know these thoroughly you must signify the same by letter to the Cancellarius or Scribe. You will then be examined and if found pefect you will be eligible for admission to the next higher grade, should the higher powers approve your application.

Kerux:

(Conducts Candidate to his table, gives him a solution and tells him to pour a few drops on the plate before him). As this pure and limpid fluid is changed into the semblance of blood, so mayest thou perish if thou betrayest thine oath of secrecy to this Order by word or deed.

Hiero:

Resume your seat and remember that your admission to this Order gives you no right to initiate any other person without dispensation from the Grand High Chiefs of the Second Order.

VOLUME SIX

CLOSING

Kerux:

(As in opening) HEKAS, HEKAS, ESTE BEBELOI.

Hiero:

(Knocks) Fratres and Sorores of the Order of the Golden Dawn in the Outer assist me to close this Hall in the Grade of Neophyte. (All rise).

Hiereus:

(3 Knocks)

Heg:

(3 Knocks)

Hiero:

(3 Knocks) Frater Kerux, see that the Hall is properly guarded.

Kerux:

(Having done so) Very Honored Hierophant, the Hall is properly guarded.

Hiero:

Honored Hiereus, assure yourself that all present have witnessed the Golden Dawn.

Hiereus:

Fratres and Sorores of the Order of the Golden Dawn in the Outer, give the signs of a Neophyte. (Done) Very Honored Hierophant (saluting), all present have been so honored.

Hiero:

Frater Stolistes, I command you to purify the Hall and the members by water. (Done as in opening.)

Hiero:

Frater Dadouchos, I command you to purify the Hall and the members by fire. (Done as in opening.)

Hiero:

Let the mystic circumambulation take place in the Path of Light. (Kerux goes by the South to the South East. Hegemon goes to the North and leads the new Neophyte by West and South, directing him to follow Hegemon in the Procession. Hiereus follows Neophyte and Stolistes follows Hiereus, accompanied or followed by Dadouchos, and Sentinel ends the procession. As they pass the Hierophant, who is standing and holding the Banner of the East in his left hand, the Sceptre in his right, they make the Neophyte Signs. Hiereus drops out when his Throne is reached. Hegemon passes Hierophant twice and then takes his place between the Pillars, directing Neophyte to follow Kerux who, after the third passing

19

of Hierophant, directs Neophyte to his seat, the other Officers dropping out as their places are reached.) The Mystical Reverse Circumambulation is accomplished. It is the symbol of Fading Light. Let us adore the Lord of the Universe. (All turn East. Stolistes directs Neophyte to rise and face East. Hierophant faces East, making the salute at each adoration, the others, Officers and Members repeating it also.)

Holy art Thou, Lord of the Universe!

Holy art Thou, Whom Nature hath not formed!

Holy art Thou, the Vast and the Mighty One!

Lord of the Light and of the Darkness!

Nothing now remains but to partake together in silence of the Mystic Repast, composed of the symbols of the Four Elements, and to remember our pledge of secrecy. (All are seated.) (Hierophant puts down his Sceptre and returns the Banner of the East to its place. He goes to the West of the Altar and facing East gives the Saluting Sign but not the Sign of Silence, and taking up the Rose says:) I invite you to inhale with me the perfume of this Rose, as a symbol of air. (Smells Rose). To feel with me the warmth of this sacred Fire. (Spreads his hands over it). To eat with me this Bread and Salt as types of Earth. (Dips bread in Salt and eats). And finally to drink with me this Wine, the consecrated emblem of Elemental Water. (Makes a Cross with the Cup and drinks. Hierophant puts down the Cup between the Cross and Triangle. He comes East of the Altar and faces West. The Praemonstator then comes to the West of the Altar and makes the Saluting Sign. Hierophant replies with the sign of Silence and then hands the Elements, beginning with the Rose which Praemonstrator smells and returns; then feels the warmth of the Lamp, eats the Bread and Salt and receives from the Hierophant the Cup with which he makes a Cross, and having drunk, returns it. Hierophant then passes by West and South to his Throne. Praemonstrator then comes to the East of the Altar. Imperator comes to the West, exchanges Signs and partakes. He returns to his place, after serving Cancellarius who in turn serves the Past Hierophant. After the Chiefs, the Officers partake in this order: Hiereus, Hegemon, Stolistes, Dadouchos. When all the Officers except Kerux have partaken, the Inner Members in order of seniority of admission, partake but do not wait for instruction in this. If there is a pause, one comes forward. Next come the members of the Outer in the same manner - the Neophytes coming last piloted by Hegemon or any Officer appointed. The Order of procedure for Outer members is: Philosophi, Practici, Theorici, Zelatores, Neophytes. When the last Neophyte stands East of the Altar, Kerux comes to the West, exchanges the Signs and partakes. Hegemon directs Neophyte to return to his place as soon as Kerux takes the Cup. Kerux, on receiving the Cup, drains it, inverts it, and says:)

Kerux:

It is finished! (Kerux replaces the Cup and returns to his place. All rise.)

Hiero:

(Knocks) TETELESTAI!

Hiereus:

(Knocks)

Heg:

(Knocks)

Hiero:

(Knocks) KHABS.

Hiereus:

(Knocks) AM.

Heg:

(Knocks) PEKHT.

Hiereus:

(Knocks)KONX.

Heg:

(Knocks) OM.

Hiero:

(Knocks) PAX.

Heg:

(Knocks) LIGHT.

Hiero:

(Knocks) IN.

Hiereus:

(Knocks) EXTENSION.
(All make the Signs towards the Altar.)

Hiero:

May what we have partaken maintain us in our search for the QUINTESSENCE, the Stone of the Philosophers. True Wisdom, Perfect Happiness, the SUMMUM BONUM. (Officers remain in the Temple while the new Neophyte is led out by Kerux.)

DISCUSSION OF THE Z-DOCUMENTS

By

V.H. FRATER A.M.A.G

These three document, Z-l, Z-2, and Z-3, are amongst the most important of all the instructions issued by the Golden Dawn. They are extensive commentaries on the Neophyte Ritual. All three are replete with the most profound instruction on Magic ever written.

THE COMPLETE GOLDEN DAWN SYSTEM OF MAGIC

As I reflect upon what I have written in this book I am sure that I have asserted several times that this particular document or that one are the most important lessons ever released within the Order. This is probably most correct. All the instructions handed out to the Zelator Adeptus Minor are unequivocally important in different ways. But they all serve as the foundation of the magical art. Throughout the years, whenever I have casually opened the book to any page of these Z documents, I have found them always illuminating - more so with each perusal of their contents. Their ability to illuminate seems inexhaustable. And for this reason, I must insist that the student pay special attention to them, studying them carefully over a long period of time rather than trying to read them as he would a novel or some informative non-fictional piece of work.

They have all the earmarks of having been written by S.L. Mathers - G.H. Frater D.D.C.F. More than anything else I know, they exemplify the profundities of which he was capable. Admittedly some of the material is trite, elaborating the usual claptrap of secret societies - such as grips, steps and passwords. But these trivia comprise but a small segment of these fantastic papers. The remaining material is of such a nature that I feel compelled to warn the casual reader not to be casual in dealing with this type of information. This is "heavy" material which needs to be savored, thought about and reflected upon.

For example, in the description of the accoutrements of the Hierophant, one is inclined to gloss it over as merely explanatory of the Temple equipment. It is really much more than that. Some formulae of magic were concealed and simultaneously revealed in the most prosaic and trite explanations and descriptions. Do not gloss over them.

From the standpoint of practical magical technique, I suggest a frequent review of the segment entitled "The Symbolism of the Opening." One practical formula after another is described here, not abstractly but concretely as a technical exercise available to the alert and eager aspirant.

Some of these served as seminal ideas which came to full term in the development of the Middle Pillar technique. The rudiments are all Golden Dawn. But each rudiment is scattered here and there, throughout several documents. However, one does not really have to search too hard for them. They are prolific - presenting themselves as alive and vital. Over a period of time, as one uses them, the seeds sprout and grow into dynamic constituents of one's wake-a-day consciousness as though waiting to be found and used.

For example, there was the rudimentary Middle Pillar technique as given in one of the early Portal papers. The technique of circulating the energies awakened or released by this method of meditation are to be found in part in this particular paper. It is only a hint, however. It becomes rounded out and expanded by applying that idea to the formula of the Tree of Life projected into a sphere (See painting of this in coloured plate section of this work), producing four individual columns around a central invisible pillar. The roots of all this will be found in the Microcosm paper and elsewhere, but in its fullness in those documents at the end of the Tarot section.

The attributions of the planets, signs and houses are standard astrological notions within the Golden Dawn system. Its employment as described, for example, in *The Foundations of Practical Magic* Aquarian Press, 1979 depends entirely on how well one has understood and used some of the principles of that magical exercise.

The technique has been borrowed without acknowledgment by a number of writers who believed it to be a magical technique borrowed from the Order. In a large sense, they were plagiarizing, because in no place has this method been described except in the barest outline form. Yet in a sense which they never realized, because they were actually plagiarizing, it is predicated fundamentally and unequivocally on the whole basic structure of the Golden Dawn system itself. And it is that system that hostile critics claim was the end result of research done by McGregor Mathers in the British Museum. If taken by itself, that is pure nonsense. I defy any critic to demonstrate where and how these methods were borrowed from books or manuscripts in the British Museum.

In The Symbolism of the Opening, there is given first the method of vibrating Divine Names. It is called The Vibratory Formula of the Middle Pillar. Again, I must urge the student to study it carefully. It has been repeated and elaborated upon in several different places in these texts. But you must study it, practise it and master it.

Once mastered, it should be used in all instances where the Divine Names are employed. These are in the practice of the Pentagram Ritual, lesser and greater, the Hexagram Ritual, lesser and greater, and the Middle Pillar technique itself, (Note, some of these rituals are described in the *Regardie Tapes* Falcon Press, 1982). These tapes can help enormously in the mastery of the various ceremonials themselves - such as the consecration of the Elemental Weapons, and so on. The method of pronouncing and vibrating the Names is clearly indicated on the Tapes so as to eliminate all possibilities of doubt and confusion.

Some of the techniques too are infinitely valuable during the process of skrying. Safeguards are required here to protect one from delusion and self-deception - all too easy in this method. The use of the Banners of the East and West may also be used as devices to open up areas that one would not suspect could be opened, so securely are they guarded.

The assumption of God-forms described in several of these documents, (and depicted on some of the beautiful paintings in the coloured plate section of this book), which comment on the Neophyte Ritual is another method not merely of protecting oneself, but of ensuring compliance with one's demands for knowledge and self-knowledge, and for gaining admission to sanctuaries whose existence one may suspect - but that is all.

This practice needs to be used often to gain skill. The descriptions given in the text are brief enough as well as long enough. That is really all it requires. Once having made its acquaintance, nothing remains but to practice it day in and day out until it is more or less easy. One of the best books that gives practically all the needed God-forms is the paperback reprint by Dover of Wallis Budge's *The Gods of the Egyptians.* This is not only a storehouse of Egyptian information, but the dozens of full page plates of the Gods is without rival in our literature. At the same time for a better descriptions of the colours employed in the God Forms, you should consult the colour plates in this book.

The section in Z-1 describing the God forms used in the Neophyte initiation will be more than amplify what has just been stated. Those colors used in the first edition of Budge's book by Methuen, decades ago, are accurate enough in terms of how they were once depicted. But for practical uses, the colour scheme shown in this work is to be preferred. Never let it be forgotten that one of the basic themes of the Order is that colors are not symbols of forces, but are forces themselves. So do study the coloring system and apply it to the plain photos of the Dover edition.

There are hosts of fertile ideas in these papers. 1 do not wish to elaborate all of them in any way. Something must be left to the ingenuity and intuition of the reader and student. But what I have had to say here should be adequate to keep him alert when perusing this most valuable and suggestive series of texts.

One of the many documents given to advanced members of the Zelator Adeptus Minor grade was Z-2, an elaborate analysis of the Neophyte grade. The breakdown into a couple of dozen specific points, is in itself, one of the most beautiful and astute tabulations I know. Like so many of the Adeptus Minor papers, it fills me with enormous respect for whoever was responsible for the analysis. The entire elaboration was classified into five major divisions, corresponding to the Pentagrammaton. In addition, that section attributed to Shin was broken down still further into three other segments so that all told there were seven formulae for magical working.

Z-2 was one of the papers that was destined for elimination from the curriculum of the Stella Matutina, a most grave error. My guess is that it was being eliminated because it represented some exceedingly hard work on the part of the celebrant.

The application of Z-2 to the process of Divination was never quite clear to me. Rather than follow the procedure of the Stella Matutina, I have decided to include it here because some students will be able to determine on their own what its sphere of usefulness is. If the student follows the general rule laid down for all the other subdivisions of this important document, he may arrive at some format pleasing and useful to him personally.

The Alchemy section for long years bothered me, for I was not able to make much sense from it. Francis King, in his book *Ritual Magic in England* reproduces a paper based on this section. It is most interesting, but raises an enormous number of questions relating to procedure, laboratory technique and allied topics. I had some correspondence with Mr. King about this matter but nothing came of it.

Sometime during the mid-thirties some alchemical processes became more or less clear to me, which made more intelligible some of the sections in Z-2. Years later, after a meeting with Frater Albertus of the Paracelsus Research Society, new insights developed.

A ritual exemplifying the rules laid down in Z-2 will be found immediately following the various initiatory rituals.

So far as rituals relating to evocation and similar types of operations are concerned some students found out that they are long, tedious, repetitive and very wearying. I must confess they are. Success in working them depends on patience, enthusiasm, and above all on the ability to stir the magical energy into activity. The rituals themselves will not yield much satisfaction until and unless the student has either some inborn theurgic ability or has developed it through the practice of the Middle Pillar technique. The method awakens the magical centers or chakras within the psycho-spiritual make-up of the student, a process of prime importance, because without the power derived from these centers or chakras, the ritual remains merely a ritual - a mere formality, dead and without power. The Middle Pillar should be practiced for several months, or even longer, until the student becomes thoroughly conscious of the energy coursing through the organism at his willed command in the three methods of circulation. The sensation is unmistakable, becoming wholly physical if steadfastly persisted in. It is the sine qua non of magical success.

When some skill has been gained in this method, further attention can be given to the Vibratory Formula of the Middle Pillar, described in several places in this work. The success of any of these operations is wholly dependent on these two methods, the Middle Pillar and the Vibratory Formula, and they should be given a great deal of attention.

When this material was first published many years ago, one of the gratifying rewards was hearing from a few students who evidently had experimented with the method. One in particular stands out. I would have liked to acknowledge his contribution, but for the moment he wishes to remain anonymous. His letter gives evidence of the fact that he has experimented with the method and found it. for him, wanting, so that he felt obliged to clarify the procedure and simplify it. His complaint was that the whole ceremony took approximately two hours, at the end of which time he felt exhausted and was unable to retain any kind of "divine intoxication" which is the sine qua non of success. The method which he then devised is as follows:

"The magician, standing in the circle, performs a banishing ritual. (For the evocation of an elemental, the lesser Pentagram ritual will suffice. If evoking a more powerful spirit, use the Supreme Banishing Ritual of the Pentagram, or Hexagram, as appropriate.)

"A suitable God is invoked. Assumption of God form, Vibratory Formula of the Middle Pillar, and Mystic Circumambulation being employed. This is continued until presence of the Divine Force is unmistakable; one ought to have the impression of acting on behalf of the God.

"The Sigil of the Spirit is now consecrated and placed in the Triangle outside the Circle. The element, planetary, or zodiacal force consonant with the nature of the spirit is invoked using the proper Pentagram or Hexagram, Divine Names, etc.

"Invocation of the God is recommenced and continued until identity with the God is achieved. At this point the actual evocation may begin. (The Magician will hereafter be referred to as the God.)

"The God extends His consciousness up to the spirit's plane (not unlike skrying), formulates its sigil therein, calls its name.

"The Spirit is commanded to manifest in the Triangle, and as the God brings his consciousness back into the body of the magician in the circle, the spirit manifests in the triangle.

"When he has sworn allegiance, and answered all questions put to him, he is commanded to return to his own plane. The God again extends His consciousness up to the plane, bringing the spirit with Him. When they have both arrived, the Sigil previously formulated is banished.

"He returns to the Circle, then partially withdraws from the magician, who again becomes aware that he is acting on behalf of the God.

"The element, planetary or zodiacal force previously invoked, is now banished. The magician then performs a general banishing ritual and quits the circle."

The writer of the above method adds a note, which in my opinion is worth paying close attention to; it coincides with my own view as expressed elsewhere.

"There is reason for concern that some students may misinterpret certain of Crowley's magical writings. For example in *Magick in Theory and Practice*, Chapter IX, p. 69, he writes:

'The peculiar mental excitement required may even be aroused by the perception of the absurdity of the process, and the persistence in it, as when Frater Perdurabo. . .recited **From Greenland's Icy Mountains** and obtained his result.'"

"Now there is no doubt that the ego, excited to the proper pitch, is capable of placing such a strain in the Astral Light as to cause some sort of manifestation, perhaps even that of the spirit it was desired to evoke (but more likely a phantasm masquerading as such). But without the presence of the Divine Force, such a being, once evoked, cannot be controlled, and there is no effective means of banishing it.

"Depending on the nature of the spirit, and the degree of its manifestation, it is likely that the spiritual progress of the magician is at an end - at least as far as his current incarnation is concerned."

While on this topic of magical training and developing the powers latent in man, to which the Order is dedicated, I would like to quote extensively from another source. Though the Theosophical Society is to all intents and purposes dead, there is some pertinent material in *The Hall of Magic Mirrors* by Victor Endersby that should set most of us back on our heels and induce some deep reflection. The tradition is a different one but facts are facts regardless of where they come from. In discussing the problem of psychical phenomena produced by Madame Blavataskv, Mr. Endersby had this to say:

"The crux of the whole problem is that the whole movement had to ba'ance on a razor edge between credence and incredulity; and a net had to be spread whose meshes were designed, with infinite care, to catch fish of just a certain size and shape. Unfortunately, even a Mahatma could not design one which would exclude a particularly odd member of the species - the one known variously as "crackpot,""screwball,""oddball," etc. These have been especially effective shields, but also especially irritating ones. Some of the most enthusiastic devotees of Theosophy would convince any sane-minded man in five minutes that there could not possibly be anything real in it.

However, let us not be too hard on the gentle crackpot. After all, through the ages most human progress has depended on his existence - he is the one who is reckless enough to crack the ice with no thought of consequences, any more than of reason, common sense, and facts. Most really capable and competent people have, by those qualities, established a position in the world, which they will not readily risk in pioneering. The risks have in the main to be left to people without sense enough to be afraid, and they serve their purpose in their odd ways. After all, some of them have made quite a splash here and there. Considering him from the purely personal aspect, what else would you call Einstein? Or a certain famous gentleman who chooses to immure himself in an African jungle and lavish his gifts on a minor collection of ignorant natives?

We will examine the meshes of the occult net.

The Mahatma said that chelaship was impossible to anyone who harbors any tendency toward injustice, even unconsciously. First then, do you love scandal and ill talk, unverified and onesided about others? If so, you are out, and the famous scandals will take you out.

Are you a coward, afraid to stand up for justice? If so, you will keep silent in the face of slander. That will take you out. There is no room for cowards beyond the veil.

Do you still have the ecclesiastic notion that perfection and infallibility can exist in an ever-evolving universe? Then your misconception of the universe is profound, probably incurable; a few scientific, grammatical, or philosophical errors will set you out on the doorstep.

Are you a materialist, unable to grasp even the possibility that the real universe is not a material one? Then the phenomena will be self-evident fraud to you, and that will take you out. You will also get out with your sanity, because the escape hatches have been left; and the victims will be fairly safe from harm because, instead of striking matches, you will only laugh at them.

Do you wish to set yourself up to be admired as an Infallible One by acquiring much knowledge? Then the revelation of fallible possibilities on the parts of the highest "authorities" you know - if you are a Theosophist - will set you back a little, and possibly out. And if you twist and squirm in the effort to prove the infallibility of your gods, that identifies your degree of intellectual honesty. That's the sort of thing they want to know.

Are you prejudiced racially and nationally? Then the program of universal brotherhood will steer you far away.

Are you narrow-minded, fastidious, finicky, and given to taking the form for the substance? Then a little swearing will take care of you.

Are you mentally lazy? Then the effort to untangle those peculiar books and make sense of them will take adequate care of you. N o mentally lazy person can understand the occult world, let alone the visible one.

Are your interests narrow? Then the help you will need from all available human sources won't be there - you are uninterested in too much of it. You will find yourself in one blind alley or the other.

Do you think the kingdom of heaven can be gained by physical observances, and that a meat-eater is a lower animal? Then a few eggs in gravy will eliminate you nicely; if that won't do it, a few packs of cigarettes will take care of it. Especially when you find that one of the Mahatmas smoked a pipe.

It has often been asked, why, with all the resources and wisdom of the Mahatmas, was H.P.B. left to struggle in poverty and illness? As we have seen, she was accused -though no individual ever came forward to complain - of getting rich on the credulity of her followers. Suppose she had been richly maintained? Moncure Conway, the missionary, mentions her "richly furnished" apartment. No doubt the furniture had been expensive - before her wealthy friends gave it to her when they got new stuff. She never starved for food, that is certain; she always did have enough - just enough - money - to do what she had to do. As to health - we can lay that in part to herself. She did break all the rules of diet, and possibly not all because of thyroid trouble and the rest; she was a hardheaded, intractable party. She knew all the rules. If she chose to break them, the Mahatmas couldn't do anything about it. Of course, they could have "fired" her, but then she was the only agent able to do what they had in mind.

The queer thing about these questions is that they are often from Christians, whose own God left his only Son to live in hardship and poverty and die in horror.

If you have to test out the morals of a tribe of savages, to see whether it is ready to haul its snout out of the mud and take the road to civilization, a good way is to drop a sick child of the same race but another tribe into the village compound. They may kill it with a club, throw it on the fire, torture it with sharp sticks, eat it, or pick it up and care for it. If they do anything but the last, you leave - quickly - and wait a hundred years until the tribe has outgrown its land and impinged on the territory of a bigger one. It may then appreciate help. Meanwhile, if you are interested in technical educability, you string a phone wire and show that you can talk over it. The natives decide that you are a god. You show then that you can't crawl through the wire - you're a fake. You then decide that they will have to mature a little before you try to teach them electricity. They will grasp one use of the wire very quickly; it will make good necklaces, when cut up, or good slugs for the blunderbuss.

Of course, in order to get their attention in the first place, you have to either shoot some of them, or display a cigarette lighter. If they have not caught on by the time the fluid runs out, you run out too. And stay a long time."

Z-2

THE FORMULAE OF THE MAGIC OF LIGHT
AN INTRODUCTION TO THE PRACTICAL
WORKING OF THE Z-2 FORMULAE

By

G.H. FRATER S.R.M.D.

In the Ritual of the Enterer are shadowed forth symbolically, the beginning of certain of the Formulae of the Magic of Light. For this Ritual betokeneth a certain Person, Substance or Thing, which is taken from the dark World of Matter, to be brought under the operation of the Divine Formulae of the Magic of Light.

Also herein are contained the commencements of all formulae of Evocation, the development of which is further shown in the Inner knowledge of the succeeding grades of the Outer Order. In the true knowledge of the application of the Symbolism of the "Enterer" lies the entrance to the knowledge of Practical Magic. Therefore are all the Formulae drawn from the Ritual classed under Five several heads, according unto the Letters of the name Yeheshuah.

For to the Letter Yod and the element of Fire belong the works of Ceremonial Magic, as the evocations of the Spirits of the Elements, etc.

Unto the First Heh the consecration and charging of Telesmata, and the production of Natural Phenomena, as storms, earthquakes, etc.

Unto the Great Holy Letter Shin are allotted Three classes of works. Spiritual development, transformations and invisiblity.

Unto the Letter Vau Divination in all its branches; and the art of making the Link between the subject of the work and the process of divination.

And to the Final Heh the works and operations of the Art of Alchemy, the order of its processes and Transmutation.

INDEX FOR GENERAL REFERENCE
TO THE ENTERER CEREMONY OF THE NEOPHYTE GRADE

1. A - The Ceremony itself. The place of the Temple.

2. B - The Hierophant.

3. C - The Officers.

4. D - The Candidate.

5. E - The Ceremony of Opening.

6. F - Hierophant states that he has received a Dispensation from Second Order, and commands Hegemon to prepare Candidate. Candidate prepared. Speech of Hegemon.

7. G - Admission of Candidate. First barring by Kerux. First baptism of the Candidate with Water and Fire.

8. H - The Candidate is conducted to the foot of the Altar. Hierophant asks "Wherefore hast thou come, etc." Candidate replies "I seek the hidden Light, etc."

9. I- Candidate is asked whether he is willing to take the Obligation. He assents; and is instructed now to kneel at the Altar.

10. J - Administration of the Obligation, and raising the Neophyte from the kneeling position.

11. K - Candidate is placed in the North. Oration of the Hierophant, "The Voice of my Higher Self, etc." Hierophant commands the mystic circumambulation in the Path of Darkness.

12. L - Procession. Candidate barred in South. Second Baptism of Water and Fire. Speech of Hegemon. Allowing the Candidate to proceed.

13. M- Hoodwink slipped up. Challenge of Hiereus. Speech of Hegemon. Speech of Hiereus. Candidate re-veiled and passed on.

14. N - Circumambulation. Barred in North. Third Baptism. Speech of Hegemon allowing Candidate to approach unto the Gate of the East.

15. O - Hoodwink slipped up for the second time. Hierophant challenges. Hegemon answers for Candidate. Speech of Hierophant. Candidate passes on.

16. P - Candidate led to West of Altar. Hierophant advances by the Path of Samekh. Officers form the Triangle. Prayer of Hierophant.

17. Q - Candidate rises. Hierophant addresses him, "Long hast thou dwelt in darkness. Quit the Night and seek the Day." Hoodwink finally removed Sceptres and Swords joined. "We receive thee, etc." Then the Mystic Words.

18. R - Hierophant indicates Lamp of Kerux. He commands that the Candidate be conducted to the East of the Altar. He orders Hiereus to bestow signs, etc. Hiereus places Candidate between Pillars. Signs and words. He orders the fourth and final consecration to take place.

19. S - Hegemon removes rope and invests Candidate with his Insignia. Hiereus then ordains the Mystic Circumambulation in the Path of Light.

20. T - Hierophant lectures on the Symbols. Proclamation by Kerux.

21. U - Hierophant commands Hiereus to address Candidate.

22. V - Hierophant addresses Neophyte on subject of study.

23. W- Blood produced. Speech of Kerux. Hiereus' final caution.

24. X - The closing takes place.

THE COMPLETE GOLDEN DAWN SYSTEM OF MAGIC

I-YOD

EVOCATION

A- The Magic Circle.

B- The Magician, wearing the Great Lamen of the Hierophant; and his scarlet Robe. A Pentacle, whereon is engraved the Sigil of circle and cross as shown on the Hierophant's Lamen.

C- The Names and Formulae to be employed.

D- The Symbol of the whole evocation.

E- The Construction of the circle and the placing of all the symbols, etc., employed, in the places properly alloted to them; so as to represent the interior of a G.D. Temple in the Enterer, and the purification and consecration of the actual piece of ground or place, selected for the performance of the Evocation.

F- The Invocation of the Higher Powers. Pentacle formed of three concentric bands, name and sigil therein, in proper colours, is to be bound thrice with a cord, and shrouded in black, thus bringing into action a Blind Force to be further directed or differentiated in the Process of the Ceremony. Announcement aloud of the Object of the working; naming the Spirit or Spirits, which it is desired to evoke. This is pronounced standing in the centre of the Circle and turning towards the quarter from which the Spirit will come.

G- The Name and Sigil of the Spirit, wrapped in a black cloth, or covering, is now placed within the circle, at the point corresponding to the West, representing the Candidate. The consecration or Baptism by water and fire of the Sigil then takes place, and the proclamation in a loud and firm voice of the spirit (or spirits) to be evoked.

H- The veiled Sigil is now to be placed at the foot of the Altar. The Magician then calls aloud the Name of the Spirit, summoning him to appear, stating for what purpose the spirit is evoked: what is desired in the operation; why the evocation is performed at this time, and finally solemnly affirming that the Spirit shall be evoked by the Ceremony.

I- Announcement aloud that all is prepared for the commencement of the actual Evocation. If it be a good spirit the Sigil is now to be placed within the white Triangle on the Altar, the Magician places his left hand upon it, raises in his right hand the magical Implement employed (usually the Sword) erect; and commences the Evocation of the Spirit (give name) to visible appearance. The Magician stands in the Place of the Hierophant during the Obligation, irrespective of the particular quarter of the Spirit. But if the nature of that Spirit be evil, then the Sigil must be placed without and to the West of the White Triangle and the Magician shall be careful to keep the point of the Magical Sword upon the centre of the Sigil.

J- Now let the Magician imagine himself as clothed outwardly with the semblance of the form of the Spirit to be evoked, and in this let him be careful not to identify himself with the spirit, which would be dangerous; but only to formulate a species of mask, worn for the time being. And if he knows not the symbolic form of the Spirit, then let him assume the form of an Angel belonging unto the same class of operation. This form being assumed, then let him pronounce aloud, with a firm and solemn voice, a convenient and potent oration and exorcism of the Spirit unto visible appearance. At the conclusion of this exorcism, taking the covered sigil in his left hand, let him smite it thrice with the flat blade of the Magic Sword. Then let him raise on high his arms to their utmost stretch, holding in his left hand the veiled sigil, and in his right the Sword of Art erect. At the same time stamping thrice upon the ground with his right foot.

K- The veiled and corded sigil is then to be placed in the Northern part of the Hall at the edge of the Circle, and the Magician employs the oration of the Hierophant, from the throne of the East, modifying it slightly, as follows: "The voice of the Exorcism said unto me, Let me shroud myself in darkness, peradventure thus may I manifest myself in Light, etc." The Magician then proclaims aloud that the Mystic Circumambulation will take place.

L- The Magician takes up the Sigil in his left hand and circumambulates the Magic Circle once, then passes to the South and halts. He stands (having placed the sigil on the ground) between it and the West, and repeats the oration of the Kerux. And again consecrates it with Water and Fire. Then takes it in his hand, facing westward, saying, "Creature of. . ., twice consecrate, thou mayest approach the gate of the West."

M-The Magician now moves to the West of the Magical Circle, holds the Sigil in his left hand and the sword in his right, faces South West, and again astrally masks himself with the form of the Spirit, and for the first time partially opens the covering of the Sigil, without however entirely removing it. He then smites it once with the flat blade of the sword, saying, in a loud, clear, and firm voice: "Thou canst not pass from concealment unto Manifestation, save by the virtue of the Name Elohim. Before all things are the Chaos and the Darkness, and the Gates of the Land of Night. 1 am He Whose Name is Darkness. I am the Great One of the Path of the Shades. I am the Exorcist in the midst of the Exorcism. Appear thou therefore without fear before me, so pass thou on." He then reveils the Sigil.

N- Take the Sigil to the North, circumambulating first, halt, place Sigil on the ground, stand between it and the East, repeat the oration of the Kerux, again consecrate with Fire and Water. Then take it up, face North, and say "Creature of . . . thrice consecrate, thou mayest approach the Gate of the East."

O- Repeat Section M in North East. Magician then passes to East, takes up Sigil in left and Sword in right hand. Assumes the Mask of the Spirit form, smites the Sigil with the Lotus Wand or Sword, and says, "Thou canst not pass from concealment unto manifestation save by virtue of the name YHVH. After the Formless and the Void and the Darkness, then cometh the knowledge of the Light. I am that Light which riseth in the Darkness. I am the Exorcist in the midst of the Exorcism. Appear thou therefore in visible form before me, for I am the Wielder of the Forces of the Balance. Thou hast known me now, so pass thou on to the Cubical Altar of the Universe!"

P- He then recovers Sigil and passes to Altar, laying it thereon as before shown. He then passes to the East of the Altar, holding the sigil and sword as already explained. Then doth he rehearse a most potent Conjuration and invocation of the Spirit unto visible appearance, using and reiterating all the Divine, Angelic, and Magical Names appropriate to this end, neither omitting the signs, seals, sigils, lineal figures, signatures and the like from that conjuration.

Q- The Magician now elevates the covered Sigil towards heaven, removes the veil entirely, leaving it yet corded, crying with a loud voice, "Creature of. . . long hast thou dweltin darkness. Quit the Night and seek the Day." He then replaces it upon the Altar, holds the Magical Sword erect above it, the pommel immediately above the centre there of, and says, "By all the Names, Powers, and Rites already rehearsed, I conjure thee thus unto visible appearance." Then the Mystic Words.

R - Saith the Magician, "As Light hidden in the Darkness can manifest therefrom, so shalt thou become manifest from concealment unto manifestation." He then takes up the Sigil, stands to East of Altar, and faces West. He shall then rehearse a long conjuration to the powers and spirits immediately superior unto that one which he seeks to invoke, **that they shall force him to manifest himself unto visible appearance.** He then places the Sigil between the Pillars, himself at the East facing West, then in the Sign of the Enterer doth he direct the whole current of his will upon the Sigil. Thus he continueth until such time as he shall perceive his Will power to be weakening, when he protects himself from the reflex of the current by the Sign of Silence, and drops his hands. He now looks towards the Quarter that the Spirit is to appear in, and he should now see the first signs of his visible manifestation. If he be not thus faintly visible, let the Magician repeat the conjuration of the Superiors of the Spirit, from the place of the Throne in the East. And this conjuration may be repeated thrice, each time ending with a new projection of Will in the sign of the Enterer, etc. But if at the third time of repetition he appeareth not, then be it known that there is an error in the working. So let the Master of Evocations replace the Sigil upon the Altar, holding the Sword as usual. Thus doing, let him address a humble prayer unto the Great Gods of Heaven to grant unto him the force necessary to correctly complete that evocation. He is then to take back the Sigil to between the Pillars, and repeat the former processes, when assuredly that Spirit will begin to manifest, but in a misty and ill-defined form. (But if, as is probable, the Operator be naturally inclined unto evocation, then might that Spirit perchance manifest earlier in the Ceremony than this. Still, the Ceremony is to be performed up to this pont, whether he be there or no.) Now as soon as the Magician shall see the visible manifestation of that Spirit's presence, he shall quit the station of the Hierophant, and consecrate afresh with Water and with Fire, the Sigil of the evoked spirit.

S - Now doth the Master of Evocations remove from the Sigil the restricting cord, and holding the freed Sigil in his left hand, he smites it with the flat blade of his sword, exclaiming, "By and in the Names of . . . I do invoke upon the the power of perfect manifestation into visible appearance." He then circumambulates the circle thrice holding the sigil in his Right hand.

T - The Magician, standing in the place of the Hierophant, but turning towards the place of the Spirit and fixing his attention thereon, now reads a potent Invocation of the Spirit unto visible appearance, having previously placed the sigil on the ground, within the circle, at the quarter where the Spirit appears. This Invocation should be of some length; and should rehearse and reiterate the divine and other Names consonant with the working. That Spirit should now become fully and clearly visible, and should be able to speak with a direct voice, if consonant with his nature. The Magician then proclaims aloud that the Spirit (give name) hath been duly and properly evoked in accordance with the sacred rites.

U - The Magician now addresses an Invocation unto the Lords of the plane of the spirit to compel him to perform that which the Magician shall demand of him.

V - The Magician carefully formulates his demands, questions, etc., and writes down any of the answers that may be advisable. The Master of Evocations now addresses a Conjuration unto the Spirit evoked, binding him to hurt or injure naught connected with him, or his assistants, or the place. And that he deceive in nothing, and that he fail not to perform that which he hath been commanded.

W- He then dismisses that Spirit by any suitable form, such as those used in the higher grades of the Outer. And if he will not go, then shall the Magician compel him by forces contrary to his nature. But he must allow a few minutes for the Spirit to dematerialise the body in which he hath manifested, for he will become less and less material by degrees. And note well that the Magician (or his companions if he have any) shall never quit the circle during the process of evocation, or afterwards, till the Spirit hath quite vanished. In some cases, and with some constitutions, there may be danger arising from the Astral conditions, and currents established, and without the actual intention of the Spirit to harm, although if of a low nature, he would probably endeavour to do so. Therefore, before the commencement of the Evocation, let the operator assure himself that everything which may be necessary, be properly arranged within the circle. But if it be actually necessary to interrupt the Process, then let him stop at that point, veil and re-cord the Sigil if it have been unbound or uncovered, recite a License to Depart or a Banishing Formula, and perform the Lesser Banishing Rituals both of the Pentagram and Hexagram. Thus only may he in comparative safety quit the circle.

Note—Get the Spirit into a White Triangle outside the midheaven, then shall he speak the truth of necessity.

II-HEH

CONSECRATION OF TALISMANS

A- The place where the operation is done.

B- The Magical Operator.

C- The Forces of Nature employed and attracted.

D- The Telesma or material basis.

E- In Telesmata, the selection of the Matter to form the Telesma; the preparation and arrangement of the place. The drawing and forming of the body of the Telesma. In Natural Phenomena the preparation of the operation; the formation of the Circle, and the selection of the material basis, such as a piece of Earth, a Cup of Water, a Flame of Fire, a Pentacle, or the like.

F- The invocation of the highest divine forces, winding a black cord round the Telesma or material basis, covering the same with a black veil, and initiating the blind force therein. Naming aloud the Nature of the Telesma or Operation.

G- The Telesma or material Basis is now placed towards the West, and duly consecrated with Water and Fire. The purpose of the operation, and the effect intended to be produced is then to be rehearsed in a loud and clear voice.

H- Placing the Talisman or material basis at the foot of the Altar, state aloud the object to be attained, solemnly asserting that it **will** be attained, and the reason thereof.

I- Announcement aloud that all is prepared and in readiness, either for charging the Telesma, or for the Commencement of the Operation to induce the natural Phenomena. Place a good Telesma or Material Basis within the White Triangle on the Altar. Place bad Telesma to the West of same, holding the sword erect in the right hand for a good purpose, or its point upon the centre of the Triangle for evil.

J- Now follows the performance of an Invocation to attract the desired spirit to the Telesma or material basis, describing in the air above it the lineal figures and sigils, etc., with the appropriate instrument. Then, taking up the Telesma in the left hand, let him smite it thrice with the flat of the blade of the Sword of Art. Then raise it in the left hand (holding erect and aloft the Sword in the right hand stamping thrice upon the Earth with the right foot).

K - The Talisman or Material basis is to be placed towards the North, and the Operator repeats the Oration of the Hierophant to the Candidate. "The voice of the Exorcism said unto me, Let me shroud myself in darkness, peradventure thus shall I manifest myself in light. I am the only being in an abyss of Darkness. From the Darkness came I forth ere my birth, from the silence of a primal sleep. And the Voice of Ages answered unto my soul, Creature of Talismans, the Light shineth in the darkness, but the darkness comprehendeth it not. Let the Mystic Circumambulation take place in the path of Darkness with the symbolic light of Occult Science to lead the way."

L- Then, taking up the Light (not from the Altar) in right hand, circumambulate. Now take up Telesmata or Material Basis, carry it round the circle, place it on the ground due South, then bar it, purify and consecrate with Water and Fire afresh, lift it with left hand, turn and facing West, say, "Creature of Talismans, twice consecrate, thou mayest approach the gate of the West."

M-He now passes to the West with Telesmata in left hand, faces S.E., partly unveils Telesmata, smites it once with the flat blade of the Sword, and pronounces, "Thou canst not pass from concealment unto manifestation, save by virtue of the name Elohim. Before all things are the Chaos and the Darkness, and the Gates of the Land of Night. I am He whose Name is Darkness. I am the great One of the Paths of the Shades. I am the Exorcist in the midst of the Exorcism. Take on therefore manifestation without fear before me, for I am he in whom fear in Not. Thou hast known me so pass thou on." This being done, he replaces the veil.

N - Then pass round the Circle with Telesmata, halt due North, place Talisman on ground, bar, purify, and consecrate again with Water and with Fire, and say, "Creature of Talismans, thrice consecrate, thou mayest approach the Gate of the East."(Hold Talisman aloft.)

O - Hold Telemata in left hand, Lotus Wand in right, assume Hierophant's form. Partly unveil Talisman, smite with flat of sword, and say, "Thou canst not pass from concealment unto manifestation save by virtue of the name YHVH. After the formless and the Void and the Darkness, then cometh the knowledge of the Light. I am that Light which riseth in darkness. I am the Exorcist in the midst of the Exorcism. Take on therefore manifestation before me, for I am the wielder of the forces of the Balance. Thou hast known me now so pass thou on unto the Cubical Altar of the Universe."

P- He then recovers Talisman or Material Basis, passes on to the Altar, laying it thereon as before shewn. He then passes to East of Altar, hold left hand over Talisman, and sword over it erect. Then doth he rehearse a most potent conjuration and invocation of that Spirit to render irresistable this Telesmata or Material Basis, or to render manifest this natural phenomenon of . . . using and reiterating all the Divine, Angelic, and Magical Names appropriate to this end, neither omitting the signs, seals, sigils, lineal figures, signatures, and the like from that conjuration.

Q - The Magician now elevates the covered Telesma or Material Basis towards Heaven, then removes the Veil entirely, yet leaving it corded, crying with a loud voice.

"Creature of Talismans, (or Material Basis), long hast thou dwelt in darkness. Quit the Night and seek the Day." He then replaces it on the Altar, holds the Magical Sword erect above it, the Pommel immediately above the centre thereof, and says, "By all the Names, Powers, and rites already rehearsed, I conjure upon thee power and might irresistible." Then say the Mystic Words.

R- Saith the Magician, "As the Light hidden in darkness can manifest therefrom, so shalt thou become irresistible." He then takes up the Telesmata, or the Material Basis, stands to East of the Altar, and faces West. Then shall he rehearse a long conjuration to the Powers and Spirits immediately superior unto that one which he seeks to invoke, to make the Telesmata powerful. Then he places the Talisman or Material Basis between the Pillars, himself at the East, facing West, then in the sign of the Enterer, doth he project the whole current of his Will upon the Talisman. Thus he continueth until such time as he shall perceive his will power weakening, when he protects himself by the Sign of Silence, and then drops his hands. He now looks toward the Talisman, and a flashing Light or Glory should be seen playing and flickering on the Talisman or Material Basis, and in the Natural Phenomena a slight commencement of the Phenomena should be waited for. If this does not occur, let the Magician repeat the Conjuration of the Superiors from the place of the Throne of the East. And this conjuration may be repeated thrice, each time ending with a new projection of Will in the Sign of the Enterer, etc. But if at the third time of repetition the Talisman or Material Basis does not flash, then be it known that there is an error in the working. So let the Master of Evocations replace the Talisman or Material Basis, upon the Altar holding the Sword as usual, and thus doing, let him address an humble prayer unto the Great Gods of Heaven to grant unto him the force necessary to correctly complete the work. He is then to take back the Talisman, to between the Pillars, and repeat the former process, when assuredly the Light will flash. Now as soon as the Magician shall see the Light, he shall quit the station of the Hierophant and consecrate afresh with water and with fire.

S- This being done, let the Talisman or Material Basis have the cord removed and smite it with the Sword and proclaim"By and in the Names of... I invoke upon thee the power of . ." He then circumambulates thrice, holding the Talisman or Material Basis in his right hand.

T- Then the Magician, standing in the place of the Hierophant, but fixing his gaze upon the Talisman or Material Basis which should be placed on the ground within the Circle, should now read a potent invocation of some length, rehearsing and reiterating the Divine and other Names consonant with the working. The Talisman should now flash visibly, or the Natural Phenomena should definitely commence. Then let the Magician proclaim aloud that the Talisman has been duly and properly charged, or the Natural Phenomena induced.

U- The Magician now addresses an Invocation unto the Lords of the plane of the Spirit to compel him to perform that which the Magician requires.

V- The Operator now carefully formulates his demands, stating clearly what the Talisman is intended to do, or what Natural Phenomena he seeks to produce.

W- The Master of Evocations now addresses a conjuration unto the Spirit, binding him to hurt or injure naught connected with him, or his assistants, or the place. He then dismisses the Spirits in the name of Yehovashah and Yeheshuah, but wraps up Talisman first, and no Banishing Ritual shall be performed, so as not to discharge it, and in the case of Natural Phenomena it will usually be best to state what duration is required. And the Material Basis should be preserved wrapped in white linen or silk all the time that the Phenomenon is intended to act. And when it is time for it to cease, the Material Basis - if water, is to be poured away; if Earth, ground to powder and scattered abroad; if a hard substance as a metal, it must be decharged, banished and thrown aside; if a flame of fire, it shall be extinguished; or if a vial containing air, it shall be opened and after that well rinsed out with pure water.

III. SHIN
ALEPH - INVISIBILITY

A - The Shroud of Concealment.

B - The Magician.

C - The Guards of Concealment.

D - The Astral Light to be moulded into the Shroud.

E - The Equilibriation of the Symbols in the Sphere of Sensation.

F - The Invocation of the Higher; the placing of a Barrier without the Astral Form; the clothing of the same with obscurity through the proper invocation.

G - Formulating clearly the idea of becoming Invisible. The formulating of the exact distance at which the shroud should surround the Physical Body. The consecration with Water and Fire, so that their vapour may begin to form a basis for the shroud.

H - The beginning to formulate mentally a shroud of concealment about the operator. The affirmation aloud of the reason and object of the working.

I - Announcement that all is ready for the commencement of the operation. Operator stands in the place of the Hierophant at this stage, placing his left hand in the centre of the white triangle and holding in his right the Lotus Wand by the black end, in readiness to concentrate around him the shroud of Darkness and Mystery. In this operation as in the two others under the dominion of Shin, a Pentacle or Telesma suitable to the matter in hand, may be made use of, the which is treated as is directed for Telesmata.

J - The Operator now recites an Exorcism of a Shroud of Darkness to surround him and render him invisible, and, holding the Wand by the black end, let him, turning round thrice completely, formulate triple circle around him, saying, "In the Name of the Lord of the Universe, etc., I conjure thee, O Shroud of Darkness and of Mystery, that thou encirclest me so that I may become invisible, so that seeing me, men see me not, neither understand, but that they may see the thing that they see not, and comprehend not the thing that they behold! So mote it be."

K - Now move to the North, face East, and say, "I have set my feet in the North, and have said I will shroud myself in Mystery and concealment." Then repeat the Oration, "The Voice of my Higher Soul, etc.," and then command the Mystic Circumambulation.

L - Move round as usual to the South, halt formulating thyself as shrouded in darkness, on the right hand the Pillar of Fire, and on the left the Pillar of Cloud, but reaching from Darkness to the Glory of the Heavens.

M - Now move from between the Pillars thou hast formulated to the West, face West, and say, "Invisible I cannot pass by the Gate of the Invisible save by the virtue of the name of 'Darkness.'" Then formulating forcibly about thee the shroud of Darkness, say, "Darkness is my Name, and concealment. I am the Great One Invisible of the Paths of the Shades. I am without fear, though veiled in darkness, for within me, though unseen is the magic of Light."

N - Repeat process in L.

O - Repeat process in M but say, "I am Light shrouded in darkness. I am the wielder of the forces of the balance."

P - Now, concentrating mentally about thee the Shroud of Concealment, pass to the West of the Altar in the place of the Neophyte, face East, remain standing, and rehearse a conjuration by suitable Names for the formulating of a shroud of Invisibility around and about Thee.

Q - Now address the Shroud of Darkness, thus: "Shroud of Concealment. Long hast thou dwelt concealed. Quit the Light, that thou mayest conceal me before men." Then carefully formulate the shroud of concealment around thee and say, "I receive thee as a covering and as a guard." Then the Mystic Words.

R - Still formulating the shroud, say, "Before all Magical manifestation cometh the knowledge of the hidden light." Then move to the Pillars and give the signs and steps, words, etc. With the Sign of the Enterer, project now thy whole will in one great effort to realise thyself actually fading out, and becoming invisible to mortal eyes; and in doing this must thou obtain the effect of thy physical body actually gradually becoming partially invisible to thy natural eyes, as though a veil or cloud were formulating between it and thee (and be very careful not to lose thy self-control at this point). But also at this point is there a certain Divine Exstasis and an exaltation desirable, for herein is a sensation of an exalted strength.

S - Again formulate the shroud as concealing thee and enveloping thee, and thus wrapped up therein, circumambulate the circle thrice.

T - Intensely formulating the Shroud, stand at the East and proclaim, "Thus have I formulated unto myself a shroud of Darkness and of Mystery, as a concealment and guard."

U - Now rehearse an invocation of all the Divine Names of Binah, that thou mayest retain the Shroud of Darkness under thy own proper control and guidance.

V - State clearly to the shroud what it is thy desire to perform therewith.

W - Having obtained the desired effect, and gone about invisible, it is required that thou shouldst conjure the Powers of the Light to act against that shroud of Darkness and Mystery so as to disintegrate it, lest any force seek to use it as a medium for an obsession, etc. Therefore rehearse a conjuration as aforesaid, and then open the shroud and come forth out of the midst thereof, and then disintegrate that shroud, by the use of a conjuration to the forces of Binah to disintegrate and scatter the particles thereof, but affirming that they shall again be readily attracted at thy command. But on no account must that shroud of awful Mystery be left without such disintegration, seeing that it would speedily attract an occupant which would become a terrible vampire praying upon him who had called it into being. And after frequent rehearsals of this operation, the thing may almost be done "per Motem."

MEM
TRANSFORMATIONS

A- The Astral Form.

B- The Magician.

C- The Forces used to alter the Form.

D- The Form to be taken.

E- The Equilibriation of the Symbolism in the Sphere of Sensation.

F- Invocation of the Higher. The definition of the Form required as a delineation of blind forces, and the awakening of the same by its proper formulation.

G- Formulating clearly to the mind the Form intended to be taken. The Restriction and Definition of this as a clear form and the actual baptism by Water and by Fire with the Order Name of the Adept.

H- The actual Invocation aloud of the form desired to be formulated before you, the statement of the Desire of the Operator and the reason thereof.

I- Announcement aloud that all is now ready for the operation of the Transformation of the Astral Body. The Magician mentally places the form as nearly as circumstances permit in the position of the Enterer, himself taking the place of the Hierophant, holding his Wand by the black portion ready to commence the Oration aloud.

J- Let him now repeat a powerful exorcism of the shape into which he desires to transform himself, using the Names, etc., belonging to the Plane, Planet, or other Eidolon, most in harmony with the shape desired. Then holding the Wand by the black End, and directing the flower over the head of the form, let him say, "In the name of the Lord of the Universe. Arise before me, O Form of. . . into which I have elected to transform myself. So that seeing me men may see the thing that they see not, and comprehend not the thing they behold."

K- The Magician saith, "Pass toward the North, shrouded in darkness, O Form of . . . into which I have elected to transform myself." Then let him repeat the usual Oration from the Throne of the East. Then command the Mystic circumambulation.

L- Now bring the Form around to the South, arrest it, and formulate it there, standing between two great Pillars of Fire and Cloud. Purify it with Water and by Fire, by placing these elements on either side of the Form.

M- Passes to West, face South East, formulate the form before thee, this time endeavouring to render it physically visible. Repeat speeches of Hiereus and Hegemon.

N- Same as L.

O- Same as M.

P- Pass to the East of Altar, formulating the Form as near in the position of the Neophyte as may be. Now address a solemn invocation and conjuration by Divine Names, etc., appropriate to render the form fitting for thy Transformation therein.

Q- Remain East of Altar, address the Form "Child of Earth, etc.," endeavoring now to see it physically. Then at the words, "We receive Thee, etc." he draws the form towards him so as to envelop him, being careful at the same time to invoke the Divine Light by the rehearsal of the Mystic Words.

R - Still keeping himself in the form of the Magician say, "Before all Magical Manifestation cometh the knowledge of the Divine Light." He then moves to the Pillars and gives Signs, etc., endeavoring with the whole force of his Will **to feel himself actually and physically in the shape of the Form desired.** And at this point he must see as if in a cloudy and misty manner the outline of the form enshrouding him, though not yet completely and wholly visible. When this occurs, but not before, let him formulate himself as standing between the two vast Pillars of Fire and Cloud.

S - He now again endeavours to formulate the Form as if visibly enshrouding him; and still, astrally, retaining the form, he thrice circumambulates the place of working.

T - Standing at the East, let him thoroughly formulate the shape, which should now appear manifest, and as if enshrouding him, even to his own vision; and then let him proclaim aloud, "Thus have I formulated unto myself this Transformation."

U - Let him now invoke all the Superior Names, etc., of the Plane appropriate to the Form that he may retain it under his proper control and guidance.

V - He states clearly to the Form what he intends to do with it.

W - Similar to the former W section on Invisibility, save that the conjurations, etc., are to be made to the appropriate plane of the form instead of to Binah.

SHIN
SPIRITUAL DEVELOPMENT

A - The Sphere of Sensation.

B - The Augoeides.

C - The Sephiroth, etc. employed.

D - The Aspirant, or Natural Man.

E - The Equilibriation of the Symbols.

F - The Invocation of the Higher. The limiting and controlling of the lower and the closing of the material senses, to awaken the spiritual.

G - Attempting to make the Natural Man grasp the Higher by first limiting the extent to which mere Intellect can help him herein; then by purification of his thoughts and desires. In doing this let him formulate himself as standing between the Pillars of Fire and Cloud.

H - The Aspiration of the whole Natural Man towards the Higher Self, and a prayer for Light and guidance through his higher Self, addressed to the Lord of the Universe.

I - The Aspirant affirms aloud his earnest prayer to obtain Divine Guidance, kneels at the West of the Altar; in the position of the Candidate in the Enterer, and at the same time astrally projects his consciousness to the East of the Altar, and turns, facing his body, to the West, holding astrally his physical left hand with his astral left. And he raises his Astral right hand holding the presentment of his Lotus Wand by the White portion thereof, and raised in the Air erect.

J - Let the aspirant now slowly recite an oration unto the Gods and unto the Higher Self (as that of the Second Adept in the entering of the Vault) but as if with his Astral Consciousness, which is projected to the East of the Altar. If at this point the Aspirant should feel a sensation as of faintness coming on, let him at once withdraw the projected Astral and properly master himself before proceeding any further. Now let the Aspirant, concentrating all his intelligence in his body, lay the blade of his Sword thrice on the Daath point of his neck, and pronounce with his whole will, the words "So help me, the Lord of the Universe and my own higher soul." Let him then rise, facing East, and stand for a few moments in silence, raising his left hand open, and his right holding the Sword of Art, to their full length above his head; his head thrown back, his eyes lifted upwards. Thus standing let him aspire with his whole will towards his best and highest Ideal of the Divine.

K - Then let the Aspirant pass unto the North, and facing East solemnly repeat the Oration of the Hierophant, as before endeavouring to project the speaking conscious self to the place of the Hierophant (in this case to the Throne of the East.) Then let him slowly mentally formulate before him the Eidolon of a Great Angel Torchbearer, standing before him as if to lead and light the way.

L - Following it, let the Aspirant circumambulate, and pass to South, then let him halt, and aspire with his whole will, first to the Mercy side of the Divine Ideal, and then to the Severity thereof. And then let him imagine himself as standing between two great Pillars of Fire and Cloud, whose bases indeed are buried in black ever rolling clouds of darkness, which symbolises the chaos of the World of Assiah, but whose summits are lost in glorious light undying, penetrating unto the White Glory of the Throne of the Ancient of Days.

M - Now doth the Aspirant move unto the West, faces S.E., and repeats both the speeches of Hiereus and Hegemon.

N - After another circumambulation, the Adept aspirant halts at the South and repeats the meditation in L.

O - And so he passes unto the East, and repeats alike the words of the Hierophant and the Hegemon.

P - And so let him pass to the West of the Altar, ever led by the Angel Torchbearer. And he projects his Astral, and he implants therein his consciousness, and his body kneels what time his soul passes between the Pillars. And he prayeth the Great Prayer of the Hierophant.

Q - And now doth the Aspirant's Soul re-enter unto his gross form; and he dreams in Divine Exstasis of the Glory Ineffable which is in the Bornless beyond; and so meditating doth he arise, and lifts to the Heavens his hands, and his eyes, and his hopes, and concentrating his Will on the Glory, low murmurs he the Mystic Words of Power.

R - So also doth he presently repeat the words of the Hierophant concerning the Lamp of the Kerux, and so also passeth he by the East of the Altar unto between the Pillars; and standing between them (or formulating them if they be not there as it appears unto him) so raises he his heart unto the Highest Faith, and so he meditates upon the highest Godhead he can dream of. Then let him grope with his hands in the darkness of his ignorance, and in the Enterer sign invoke the Power that it remove the darkness from his spiritual vision. So let him then endeavour to behold before him in the Place of the Throne of the East, a certain light or Dim glory, which shapeth itself into a Form. And this can be beholden only by the mental vision. Yet, owing unto the spiritual exaltation of the Adept, it may sometimes appear as if he beheld it with mortal eye. Then let him withdraw awhile from such contemplation and formulate for his equilibriation once more the Pillars of the Temple of Heaven.

S - And so again doth he aspire to see the Glory conforming and when this is accomplished, he thrice circumambulates, reverently saluting with the Enterer the Place of Glory.

T - Now let the Aspirant stand opposite unto the Place of that Light, and let him make deep meditation and contemplation thereon. Presently also imagining it to enshroud and envelope him, and again endeavouring to identify himself with its Glory. So let him exalt himself in the likeness of an Eidolon of a colossal Being, and endeavour to realise that this is the only True Self, and that the Natural Man is as it were the base and throne thereof, and let him do this with due and meet reverence and awe. And therefore he shall presently proclaim aloud "Thus at length have I been permitted to begin to comprehend the form of my Higher Self."

U - Now doth the Aspirant make entreaty of that Augoeides to render comprehensible what things may be necessary for his instruction and comprehension.

V - And he consults It in any matter he may have especially sought for guidance from the Beyond.

W - And lastly, let the Aspirant endeavour to formulate a link between the Glory and his self-hood; and let him renew his obligation of purity of mind before it, avoiding in this any tendency to fanaticism or spiritual pride. And let the Adept remember that this process here set forth is on no account to be applied to endeavouring to come in contact with the higher soul of another. Else thus assuredly will he be led into error, hallucination, or even madness.

IV-VAU
DIVINATION

A - The Form of Divination.

B - The Diviner.

C - The Forces acting in the Divination.

D - The subject of the Divination.

E - The preparation of all things necessary, and the right understanding of the process so as to formulate a connecting link between the process employed and the Macrocosm.

F - The Invocation of the Higher; arrangement of the scheme of divination and initiation of the forces thereof.

G - The first entry into the matter. First assertion of limits and correspondences; beginning of the working.

H - The actual and careful formulation of the question demanded; and consideration of all its correspondences and their classifications.

I - Announcement aloud that all the correspondences taken are correct and perfect; the Diviner places his hand upon the instrument of Divination; standing at the East of the Altar, he prepares to invoke the forces required in the Divination.

J - Solemn invocation of the necessary spiritual forces to aid the Diviner in the Divination. Then let him say, "Arise before me clear as a mirror, O magical vision requisite for the accomplishment of this divination."

K - Accurately define the term of the question; putting down clearly in writing what is already known, what is suspected or implied, and what is sought to be known. And see that thou verify in the beginning of the judgment that part which is already known.

L- Next let the Diviner formulate clearly under two groups or heads (a) the arguments for, (b) the arguments against, the success of the subject of one divination, so as to be able to draw a preliminary conclusion therefrom on either side.

M-First formulation of a conclusive judgment from the premises already obtained.

N- Same as section L.

O- Formulation of a second judgment, this time of the further developments arising from those indicated in the previous process of judgment, which was a preliminary to this operation.

P- The comparison of the first preliminary judgment with one second judgment developing therefrom, so as to enable the Diviner to form an idea of the probable action of forces beyond the actual plane, by the invocation of an angelic figure consonant to the process. And in this matter take care not to mislead thy judgment through the action of thine own preconceived ideas; but only relying, after due tests, on the indication afforded thee by the angelic form. And know, unless the form be of an angelic nature its indication will not be reliable, seeing, that if it be an elemental, it will be below the plane desired.

Q- The Diviner now completely and thoroughly formulates his whole judgment as well for the immediate future as for the development thereof, taking into account the knowledge and indications given him by the angelic form.

R- Having this result before him, let the Diviner now formulate a fresh divination process, based on the conclusions at which he has arrived, so as to form a basis for a further working.

S- Formulates the sides for and against for a fresh judgment, and deduces conclusion from fresh operation.

T- The Diviner then compares carefully the whole judgment and decisions arrived at with their conclusions, and delivers now plainly a succinct and consecutive judgment thereon.

U- The Diviner gives advice to the Consultant as to what use he shall make of the judgment.

V- The Diviner formulates clearly with what forces it may be necessary to work in order to combat the Evil, or fix the Good, promised by the Divination.

W-Lastly, remember that unto thee a divination shall be as a sacred work of the Divine Magic of Light, and not to be performed to pander unto thy curiosity regarding the secrets of another. And if by this means thou shalt arrive at a knowledge of another's secrets, thou shalt respect and not betray them.

V-HEH (f)
ALCHEMY

A- The Curcurbite or the Alembic.

B- The Alchemist.

C- The processes and forces employed.

D- The matter to be transmuted.

E- The selection of the Matter to be transmuted, and the formation, cleansing and disposing of all the necessary vessels, materials, etc., for the working of the process.

F - General Invocation of the Higher Forces to Action. Placing of the Matter within the curcurbite or philosophic egg, and invocation of a blind force to action therein, in darkness and silence.

G - The beginning of the actual process. The regulation and restriction of the proper degree of Heat and Moisture to be employed in the working. First evocation followed by first distillation.

H - The taking up of the residuum which remaineth after the distillation from the curcurbite or alembic; the grinding thereof to form a powder in a mortar. This powder is then to be placed again in the curcurbite. The fluid already distilled is to be poured again upon it. The curcurbite or philosophic egg is to be closed.

I - The curcurbite or Egg Philosophic being hermetically sealed, the Alchemist announces aloud that all is prepared for the invocation of the forces necessary to accomplish the work. The Matter is then to be placed upon an Altar with the elements and four weapons thereon; upon the white triangle and upon a flashing Tablet of a general nature, in harmony with the matter selected for the working. Standing now in the place of the Hierophant at the East of the Altar, the Alchemist should place his left hand upon the top of the curcurbite, raise his right hand holding the Lotus Wand by the Aries band (for in Aries is the beginning of the life of the year), ready to commence the general invocation of the forces of the divine Light to operate in the work.

J - The pronouncing aloud of the Invocation of the requisite general forces, answering to the class of alchemical work to be performed. The conjuring of the necessary Forces to act in the curcurbite for the work required. The tracing in the air above it with appropriate weapon the necessary lineal figures, signs, sigils and the like. Then let the Alchemist say: "So help me the Lord of the Universe and my own Higher Soul." Then let him raise the curcurbite in the air with both hands, saying: "Arise herein to action, O ye forces of the Light Divine."

K - Now let the matter putrefy in the Balneum Mariae in a very gentle heat, until darkness beginneth to supervene; and even until it becometh entirely black. If from its nature the mixture will not admit of entire blackness, examine it astrally till there is the astral appearance of the thickest possible darkness, and thou mayest also evoke an elemental form to tell thee if the blackness be sufficient. But be thou sure that in this latter thou art not deceived, seeing that the nature of such an elemental will be deceptive from the nature of the symbol of Darkness, wherefore ask thou of him nothing further concerning the working at this stage but only concerning the blackness, and this can be further tested by the elemental itself, which should be either black or clad in an intensely black robe. In this evocation, use the names, etc., of Saturn. When the mixture be sufficiently black, then take the curcurbite out of the Balneum Mariae and place it to the North of the Altar and perform over it a solemn invocation of the forces of Saturn to act therein; holding the wand by the black band, then say: "The voice of the Alchemist" etc. The curcurbite is then to be unstopped and the Alembic Head fitted on for purposes of distillation. In all such invocations a flashing tablet should be used whereon to stand the curcurbite. Also certain of the processes may take weeks, or even months to obtain the necessary force, and this will depend on the Alchemist rather than on the matter.

L - Then let the Alchemist distil with a gentle heat until nothing remaineth to come over. Let him then take out the residuum and grind it into a powder; replace this powder in the curcurbite, and pour again upon it the fluid previously distilled. The curcurbite is then to be placed again in a Balneum Mariae in a gentle heat. When it seems fairly re-dissolved (irrespective of colour) let it be taken out of the bath. It is now to undergo another magical ceremony.

M-Now place the curcurbite to the West of the Altar, holding the Lotus Wand by the black end, perform a magical invocation of the Moon in her decrease and of Cauda Draconis. The curcurbite is then to be exposed to the moonlight (she being in her decrease) for nine consecutive nights, commencing at full moon. The Alembic Head is then to be fitted on.

N-Repeat process set forth in section L.

O-The curcurbite is to be placed to the East of the Altar, and the Alchemist performs an invocation of the Moon in her increase, and of Caput Draconis (holding Lotus Wand by white end) to act upon the matter. The curcurbite is now to be exposed for nine consecutive nights (ending with the Full Moon) to the Moon's rays. (In this, as in all similar exposures, it matters not if such night be overclouded, so long as the vessel be placed in such a position as to receive the direct rays if the cloud withdraw.)

P- The curcurbite is again to be placed on the white triangle upon the Altar. The Alchemist performs an invocation of the forces of the Sun to act in the curcurbite. It is then to be exposed to the rays of the sun for twelve hours each day; from 8:30 a.m. to 8:30 p.m. (This should be done preferably when the sun is strongly posited in the Zodiac, but it can be done at some other times, **though never** when he is in Scorpio, Libra, Capricornus, or Aquarius.)

Q-The curcurbite is again placed upon the white triangle upon the Altar. The Alchemist repeats the words: "Child of Earth, long hast thou dwelt, etc." Then holding above it the Lotus Wand by the white end, he say: "I formulate in thee the invoked forces of Light," and repeats the mystic words. At this point keen and bright flashes of light should appear in the curcurbite, and the mixture itself (as far as its nature will permit) should be clear. Now invoke an Elemental from the curcurbite consonant to the Nature of the Mixture, and judge by the nature of the colour of its robes and their brilliancy whether the matter has attained to the right condition. But if the flashes do not appear, and if the robes of the elemental be not brilliant and flashing, then let the curcurbite stand within the white triangle for seven days; having on the right hand of the Apex of the triangle a flashing tablet of the Sun, and in the left one of the Moon. Let it not be moved or disturbed all those seven days; but not in the dark, save at night. Then let the operation as aforementioned be repeated over the curcurbite, and this process may be repeated altogether three times if the flashing light cometh not. For without this latter the work would be useless. But if after three repetitions it still appear not, it is a sign that there hath been an error in the working, such being either in the disposition of the Alchemist or in the management of the curcurbite. Wherefore let the lunar and the solar invocations and exposures be repeated when without doubt, if these be done with care (and more especially those of Caput Draconis and Cauda Draconis with those of the Moon as taught, for these have great force materially) then without doubt shall that flashing light manifest itself in the curcurbite.

R- Holding the Lotus Wand by the white end, the Alchemist now draws over the curcurbite the symbol of the Flaming Sword as if descending into the mixture. Then let him place the curcurbite to the East of the Altar. The Alchemist stands between the pillars, and performs a solemn invocation of the forces of Mars to act therein. The curcurbite is then to be placed between the Pillars (or the drawn symbols of these same) for seven days, upon a flashing tablet of Mars. After this period, fit on the Alembic Head, and distil first in Balneum Mariae, then in Balneum Arenae till such time as the mixture be all distilled over.

S- Now let the Alchemist take the fluid of the distillate and let him perform over it an invocation of the forces of Mercury to act in the clear fluid, so as to formulate therein the alchemic Mercury, even the Mercury of the Philosophers. (The residuum or the Dead Head is not to be worked with at present, but is to be set apart for future use.) After the invocation of the Alchemic Mercury a certain brilliance should manifest itself in the whole fluid, that is to say, it should not only be clear, but also brilliant and flashing. Now expose it in an hermetic receiver for seven days to the light of the Sun; at the end of which time there should be distinct flashes of light therein. (Or an egg philosophic may be used; but the receiver of the Alembic if close stopped will answer this purpose.)

T- Now the residuum or Dead Head is to be taken out of the curcurbite, ground small and replaced. An invocation of the Forces of Jupiter is then to be performed over that powder. It is then to be kept in the dark standing upon a flashing Tablet of Jupiter for seven days. At the end of this time there should be a slight flashing about it, but if this come not yet, repeat this operation up to three times, when a faint flashing of Light is certain to come.

U- A flashing Tablet of each of the four Elements is now to be placed upon an altar as shown in the figure, and thereon are also to be placed the magical elemental weapons, as is also clearly indicated. The receiver containing the distillate is now to be placed between the Air and Water Tablets, and the curcurbite with the Dead Head between the Fire and Earth Tablets. Now let the Alchemist perform an invocation using especially the Supreme Ritual of the Pentagram, with the lesser magical implement appropriate. First, of the forces of Fire to act in the curcurbite on the Dead Head. Second of those of Water to act on the distillate. Third, of the forces of the Spirit to act in both (using the white end of Lotus Wand). Fourth, of those of the Air to act on the distillate; and lastly, those of the Earth to act on the Dead Head. Let the Curcurbite and the receiver stand thus for five consecutive days, at the end of which time there should be flashes manifest in both mixtures. And these flashes should be lightly coloured.

ALTAR FOR ALCHEMY

V - The Alchemist, still keeping the vessels in the same relative positions, but removing the Tablets of the elements from the Altar, then substitutes one of Kether. This must be white with golden charges, and is to be placed on or within the white triangle between the vessels. He then addresses a most solemn invocation to the forces of Kether to render the result of the working that which he shall desire, and making over each vessel the symbol of the Flaming Sword. This is the most important of all the Invocations. It will only succeed if the Alchemist keepeth himself closely allied unto his Higher Self during the working of the invocation and of making the Tablet. And at the end of it, if it have been successful, a keen and translucent flash will take the place of the slightly coloured flashes in the receiver of the curcurbite; so that the fluid should sparkle as a diamond, whilst the powder in the curcurbite shall slightly gleam.

W - The distilled liquid is now to be poured from the receiver upon the residuum of the Dead Head in the curcurbite, and the mixture at first will appear cloudy. It is now to be exposed to the Sun for ten days consecutively (ten is Tiphareth translating the influence of Kether). It is then again to be placed upon the white triangle upon the Altar, upon a flashing Tablet of Venus to act therein. Let it remain thus for seven days, at the end of which time see what forms and colour and appearance the Liquor hath taken, for there should now arise a certain softer flash in the liquid, and an elemental may be evoked to test the condition. When this softer flash is manifest, place the curcurbite into the Balneum Mariae to digest with a very gentle heat for seven days. Place it then in the Balneum Mariae to distil, beginning with a gentle, and ending with a strong heat. Distil thus till nothing more will come over, even with a most violent heat. Preserve the fluid in a closely stoppered vial. It is an Elixir for use according to the substance from which it was prepared. If from a thing medicinal, a medicine; if from a metal, for the purifying of metals; and herein shalt thou use thy judgment. The residuum thou shalt place without powdering into a crucible, well sealed and luted. And thou shalt place the same in thine Athanor, bringing it first to a red, and then to a white heat, and this thou shalt do seven times in seven consecutive days, taking out the crucible each day as soon as thou hast brought it to the highest possible heat, and allowing it to cool gradually. And the preferable time for this working should be in the heat of the day. On the seventh day of this operation thou shalt open the crucible and thou shalt behold what Form and Colour thy Caput Mortum hath taken. It will be like either a precious stone or a glittering powder. And this stone or powder shall be of Magical Virtue in accordance with its nature.

Finished is that which is written concerning the Formulae of the Magic of Light.

VOLUME SIX

Z-1

THE ENTERER OF THE THRESHOLD

The General Exordium

The Speech in the Silence:
The Words Against the Son of Night:
The Voice of Thoth before the Universe in the presence of the Eternal Gods:
The Formulae of Knowledge:
The Wisdom of Breath:
The Radix of Vibration:
The Shaking of the Invisible:
The Rolling Asunder of the Darkness:
The Becoming Visible of Matter:
The Piercing of the Coils of the Stooping Dragon:
The Breaking forth of the Light:
All these are in the Knowledge of Thoth.

The Particular Exordium

At the Ending of the Night:
At the limits of the Light:
Thoth stood before the Unborn Ones of Time!
Then was formulated the Universe:
Then came forth the Gods thereof:
The Aeons of the bornless Beyond:
Then was the Voice vibrated:
Then was the Name declared.
At the Threshold of the Entrance,
Between the Universe and the Infinite,
In the Sign of the Enterer, stood Thoth,
As before him were the Aeons proclaimed.
In Breath did he vibrate them:
In Symbols did he record them:
For betwixt the Light and the Darkness did he stand.

The complete explanation of the symbolism of, and the Formulae contained in, the Grade of Neophyte of the Order of the Golden Dawn.

"Enterer of the Threshold" is the name of the Grade of Neophyte. "The Hall of the Neophytes" is called "The Hall of the Dual Manifestation of Truth,"that is of the Goddess Thmaah, whose name has three forms according to the nature of her operation. This is explained under the chapter concerning the Hegemon.

THE COMPLETE GOLDEN DAWN SYSTEM OF MAGIC

Of the Temple in reference to the Sephiroth. The Temple, as arranged in the Neophyte Grade of the Order of the Golden Dawn in the Outer, is placed looking towards the YH of YHVH in Malkuth in Assiah. That is, as Y and H answer unto the Sephiroth Chokmah and Binah in the Tree, (and unto Abba and Aima, through whose knowledge alone that of Kether may be obtained.) Even so, the Sacred Rites of the Temple may gradually, and as it were, in spite of himself, lead the Neophyte unto the knowledge of his Higher Self. Like the other Sephiroth, Malkuth hath also its subsidiary Sephiroth and Paths. Of these Ten Sephiroth, the Temple as arranged in the Neophyte Grade, includeth only the four lower Sephiroth in the Tree of Life, viz: Malkuth, Yesod, Hod, and Netzach, and the Outer side of Paroketh, the Veil. Paroketh formeth the East of the Temple. First in importance cometh the symbolism of the East.

The Three Chiefs who govern and rule all things, the Viceroys in the Temple of the unknown Second Order beyond, are the reflections therein of the Powers of Chesed, Geburah and Tiphareth. They represent: the Imperator - Geburah and the Grade 6-5: the Praemonstrator - Chesed and the Grade 7-4: the Cancellarius - Tiphareth and the Grade 5-6.

Now the Imperator governeth, because in Netzach, which is the highest grade of the First Order, 4-7, is the Fire reflected from Geburah. The Praemonstrator is Second, because in Hod, which is the next highest Grade, 3-8, is the Water reflected from Chesed. The Third is the Cancellarius, because in Yesod, 2-9, is the Air reflected from Tiphareth. Thus the Order is governed by a Triad, one in intention but having different functions: the Imperator to command: the Praemonstrator to instruct: the Cancellarius to record.

The proper mantle of Office of the Imperator is the flame scarlet Robe of Fire and Severity, as on him do the energy and stability of the Temple depend: and if he has sub-Officers to assist him, they partake of his symbolism. His Mantle is the symbol of unflinching Authority, compelling the obedience of the Temple to all commands issued by the Second Order; and upon the left breast thereof, is the Cross and Triangle of the Golden Dawn, both white, representing the purification of the Temple in the Outer Order by Fire. He may wear a Lamen similar to that of Hierophant, of the same colours, but depending from a scarlet collar, and he may bear a Sword similar to that of Hiereus. His place in the Temple is at the extreme right of the Dais and at the Equinox he takes the Throne of Hierophant when that Office is vacated.

The proper Mantle of Office of the Praemonstrator is the bright blue Robe of Water, representing the reflection of the Wisdom and Knowledge of Chesed. His duty is that of Teacher and Instructor of the Temple, always limited by his Obligation to keep secret the Knowledge of the Second Order from the Outer Order. He superintends the working of the Outer Order, seeing that in it nothing be relaxed or profaned; and duly issues to the Temple any instruction regarding the Ritual received by him from the Greatly Honoured Chiefs of the Second Order. He is therefore to the Temple the Reflector of the Wisdom beyond. His sub-officers partake of his symbolism. The White Cross and Triangle on his left Breast on the Robe represents the purification of the Outer Order by Water. He may wear a Lamen like that of Hierophant, but blue upon an orange field and depending from a collar of blue. He may bear a Sceptre surmounted by a Maltese Cross in the Elemental colours.

The proper Mantle of Office of the Cancellarius is the yellow Robe of Air. Upon him depend the Records of the Temple, the order of its working, the arrangements of its Meetings and the circulation of its manuscripts. He is the Recorder and, more immediately than either of the preceding Chiefs, the Representative of the executive authority of the Second Order over the Outer. His duty is to see that in no case knowledge of a Grade be given to a Member who has not properly attained to it. He is the immediate circulator of all communications from the Second Order. His sub-officers partake of his symbolism. His White Cross and Triangle represent the purification of the Outer Order by Air. Cancellarius may wear a Lamen like that of Hierophant, but of yellow on a purple field, and depending from a purple collar; and he may bear a Sceptre surmounted by a Hexagram of amber and gold.

The Sceptres of the Chiefs should be of the same colour as their Mantles, with a gold band to represent Tiphareth, being the first Grade of the Inner Order. The Sword of the Imperator should have a plain scarlet hilt, with gold or brass mountings, while the Sceptre of the Praemonstrator should be blue with a gold band. The proper seat of the Chiefs is beside the Hierophant, and if desired the Imperator and Cancellarius may be seated to the right and Praemonstrator and Immediate Past Hierophant to his left—the Cancellarius and Immediate Past Hierophant being nearest to the Hierophant on their respective sides. The Chiefs stand before the Veil in the East of the Temple, as the Representatives of the Inner Order and therefore no meeting can be held without one of them. Preferably all Three Chiefs should be present. The other Officers of the Temple exist only by their authority and permission.

Because the East of the Temple is the outer side of Paroketh, all Members of the Second Order wear the Crossed Sashes of a Lord of the Paths of the Portal of the Vault only—no higher Grade being allowed to be shown in a Temple of the First Order. Members of the Second Order should be seated in the East of the Temple when practicable. Any Past Hierophant may wear a Mantle of a Hierophant and a Jewel of that Lamen, but not a large Collar Lamen. Immediate Past Hierophant may have a Sceptre of a Hierophant.

The Chiefs, or Members asked to represent them on the Dais, wear white gowns. The cords and tassels of all Mantles of Chiefs or Officers should be white to symbolise spiritual purity and influence of the Divine and Shining Light. Members of the Outer Order wear a black gown or tunic, with a Sash indicating their Grade across it. The Black Sash crosses from the left shoulder (from the side of the Black Pillar, as they first received it), and the White Sash from the Right shoulder.

Egyptian Head-Dresses, or Nemysses are worn by the Chiefs and Officers, those of the Chiefs being of the colour of their Mantles striped with the complementary colour; those of the Officers being striped equally black and white. Members may wear similar nemysses in black and white or plain black squares of approved pattern.

The Key to the formation of the tunic and nemyss is the Crux Ansata for the nemyss makes the oval, and the arms and body of the tunic, the cross.

THE SYMBOLISM OF THE TEMPLE

The Bases of the two Pillars are respectively in Netzach and Hod; the White Pillar being in Netzach and the Black Pillar in Hod. They represent the Two Pillars of Mercy and Severity. The bases are cubical and black to represent the Earth Element in Malkuth. The columns are respectively black and white to represent the manifestation of the Eternal Balance of the Scales of Justice. Upon them should be represented in counter-changed colour any appropriate Egyptian designs, emblematic of the Soul.

The scarlet tetra-hedronal capitals represent the Fire of Test and Trial: and between the Pillars is the porchway of the Region Immeasurable. The twin lights which burn on their summits are "The Declarers of the Eternal Truth." The bases of the tetrahedra, being triangular, that on the White pillar points East, while that on the Black points West. They thus complete the Hexagram of Tiphareth though separate, as is fitting in "The Hall of the Dual Manifestation of Truth."

The Altar, whose form is that of a double cube, is placed in the Eastern part of Malkuth, as far as the Neophyte is concerned. But to the Adeptus Minor, its blackness will veil on the East citrine, on the South olive, on the North russet, while the West side alone, and the base, will be black, while the summit is of a brilliant whiteness.

THE COMPLETE GOLDEN DAWN SYSTEM OF MAGIC

The Symbols upon the Altar represent the Forces and Manifestation of the Divine Light, concentrated in the White Triangle of the Three Supernals as the synthesis; wherefore, upon this sacred and sublime Symbol, is the obligation of the Neophyte taken as calling therein to witness the Forces of the Divine Light.

The Red Cross of Tiphareth (to which the Grade of 5-6 is referred) is here placed above the White Triangle, not as dominating it, but as bringing it down and manifesting it unto the Outer Order; as though the Crucified One, having raised the symbol of self-sacrifice, had thus touched and brought into action in matter, the Divine Triad of Light.

Around the Cross are the Symbols of the Four Letters of the Name YHVH—the Shin of Yeheshuah being only implied and not expressed in the Outer Order. At the East is the Mystical Rose, allied by its scent to the Element of Air. At the South is the Red Lamp, allied by its Flame with the Element of Fire. At the West is the Cup of Wine, allied by its fluid form to the Element of Water. At the North are Bread and Salt, allied by their substance to the Element of Earth. The Elements are placed upon the Altar according to the Winds.

"For Osiris on-Nophris who is found perfect before the Gods, hath said: These are the Elements of my Body, Perfected through Suffering, Glorified through Trial. For the scent of the Dying Rose is as the repressed Sigh of my suffering: And the flame-red Fire as the Energy of mine Undaunted Will: And the Cup of Wine is the pouring out of the Blood of my Heart, Sacrificed unto Regeneration, unto the Newer Life: And the Bread and Salt are as the Foundations of my Body, Which I destroy in order that they may be renewed. For I am Osiris Triumphant, even Osiris on-Nophris, the Justified One: I am He who is clothed with the Body of Flesh, Yet in whom is the Spirit of the Great Gods: I am The Lord of Life, triumphant over Death. He who partaketh with me shall arise with me. I am the Manifestor in Matter of Those Whose Abode is the Invisible: I am purified: I stand upon the Universe: I am its Reconciler with the Eternal Gods: I am the Perfector of Matter: And without me, the Universe is not."

Technically, the Door is supposed to be situated behind the seat of Hiereus in the West; but it may be in any part of the Hall, seeing that the walls represent the Barrier to the Exterior. "The Gate of the Declarers of Judgment" is its name—and its symbolic form is that of a straight and narrow Doorway, between two Mighty Pylons. "The Watcher against the Evil Ones" is the name of the Sentinel who guards it and his form is the symbolic one of Anubis.

THE STATIONS OF THE OFFICERS

The Hierophant is placed in the East of the Temple, on the outer side of the Veil Paroketh, to rule the Temple under the Presidency of the Chiefs. There he fills the place of a Lord of the Paths of the Portal of the Vault of the Adepts, acting as Inductor to the Sacred Mysteries. The Insignia and Symbols of Hierophant are:

Lamen of the Hierophant

The Throne of the East in the Path of Samekh, outside the Veil. The Mantle of bright flame scarlet, bearing a white cross on the left breast. The Lamen suspended from a white Collar. The Crown headed Sceptre. The Banner of the East. The position of the Throne on the Path Samekh is fitting for the Inductor to the Mysteries, as there being placed in that balanced and central position of that Path by which alone is safe entrance to the mystical knowledge of the Light in Tiphareth. Being placed before Paroketh at the point of its rending, it there marks the shining forth of the Light through the Veil; and that translation of the Three Supernals to the Outer Order, which is represented by the red Calvary Cross and the White Triangle upon the Altar. Thus the station of Hierophant's Throne, fitly represents the Rising of the Sun of Life and Light upon our Order.

The Robe of scarlet represents the flaming energy of the Divine Light, shining forth into infinite Worlds. Upon the left breast is a White Cross to represent purification unto the Light, and this Cross may be one of the following forms:

The **CALVARY CROSS** alludes either to the cross of six squares of Tiphareth or to the Cross of the Rivers.

The **PYRAMIDAL CROSS** of the Elements, to represent the descent of the Divine and Angelic Forces into the pyramid symbol.

The **EQUILATERAL CROSS** of the Elements, symbolising their purification through the Light of the Four lettered Name YHVH in Tiphareth.

The **MALTESE CROSS** of four arrowheads, representing the keen and swift impact of the Light, coming from behind the Veil, through the Elements symbolised by the arrow of Sagittarius in the Path of Samekh.

It is indifferent which of the Crosses be employed, seeing that each represents the operation of the Light through the Veil.

The Sceptre represents the forces of the Middle Pillar. It is scarlet with gold bands to represent the places of the Sephiroth Daath, Tiphareth and Yesod, the pommel being Malkuth. The shaft represents the Paths Gimel, Samekh and Tau. The Grip by which it is wielded, is the path Tau, representing the Universe governed by and attracting the forces of the Light. The Names of Sephiroth and Paths are not marked thereon, but the Hierophant Initiate of the Second Order should remember the sublimity of the symbolism while he wields it. It represents him as touching thereby the Divine Light of Kether and attracting it through the

Middle Pillar to Malkuth. It is called "The Sceptre of Power" and invests him with the power of declaring the Temple Open or Closed in any Grade, if time be short, and this is done by saying: "By the power in me vested by this Sceptre, I declare this Temple duly opened (or closed)."

This method of Opening and Closing "by Sceptre" should only be used in great emergency where time presses. **It should not be used in a Ceremony where Elemental Spirits have been invoked**—especially not in the Closing.

The Lamen is partially explained in the Portal Ceremony thus: "The Hierophant's Lamen is a synthesis of Tiphareth, to which the Calvary cross of six squares, forming the cube opened out, is fitly referred. The two colours, red and green, the most active and the most passive, whose conjuction points out the practical application of the knowledge of equilibrium, are symbolic of the reconciliation of the celestial essences of Fire and Water. For the reconciling yellow unites with blue in green, which is the complementary colour to red, and with red in orange which is the complementary colour to blue. The small inner circle placed upon the Cross alludes to the Rose that is conjoined therewith in the symbolism of the Rose and Cross of our Order."

But in addition to this, it represents the blazing light of the Fire of the Sun bringing into being the green vegetation of the otherwise barren Earth. And also the power of self-sacrifice requisite in one who would essay to initiate into the Sacred Mysteries. So as the Sceptre represents the Authority and Power of the Light, the Lamen affirms the qualifications necessary to him who wields it, and therefore is it suspended from a white collar, to represent the Purity of the White Brilliance from Kether. Hence it should always be worn by the Hierophant.

The Banner of the East is also partially explained in the Portal: "The field of the Banner of the East is White, the colour of light and purity. As in the previous case, the Calvary Cross of six squares is the number of six of Tiphareth, the yellow Cross of Solar gold, and the cubical stone, bearing in its centre the sacred Tau of Life, and having bound together upon it the form of the Macrocosmic Hexagram, the red triangle of Fire and the blue triangle of Water—the Ruach Elohim and the Waters of Creation."

In addition to this explanation, it affirms the Mode of Action employed by the Divine Light in its operation by the Forces of Nature. Upon it is the symbol of the Macrocosm so coloured as to affirm the action of the Fire of the Spirit through the Waters of Creation under the harmony of the Golden Cross of the Reconciler. Within the centre of the Hexagram is a Tau cross in White, to represent its action as a Triad; and the whole is placed on a white field representing the Ocean of the Ain Soph Aour. The Banner is suspended from a gold colured bar by red cords, and the pole and base should be white. The base represents the purity of the foundation --the shaft, the Purified Will directed to the Higher. The golden cross-bar is that whereon the Manifested Law of Perfection rests; the Banner itself, the Perfect Law of the Universe, the red cords and tassels the Divine Self- renunciation, whose trials and sufferings form, as it were, the Ornament of the Completed Work. The whole represents the ascent of the Initiate into Perfect Knowlege of the Light. Therefore in the address of the Hiereus the Neophyte hears "Even the Banner of the East sinks in Adoration before Him,"as though that symbol, great and potent though it be, were yet but an inferior presentment of the Higher, fitted to our comprehension. "Expounder of the Sacred Mysteries" is the name of the Hierophant, and he is "Osiris" (Aeshoorist) in the Nether World. (The Coptic **St** added as a suffix to a name indicates the influence from Kether.)

The Station of Hiereus is at the extreme West of the Temple and in the lowest point of Malkuth where he is enthroned in its darkest part, in the quarter represented black in the Minutum Mundum Diagram. Representing a Terrible and Avenging God at the Confines of

Matter, at the borders of the Qlippoth, he is enthroned upon Matter and robed in Darkness, and about his feet are Thunder and Lightning, the impact of the Paths of Shin and Qoph, Fire and Water, terminating respectively in the russet and olive quarters of Malkuth. There, therefore, is he placed as a mighty and avenging Guardian to the Sacred Mysteries. The Symbols and Insignia of the Hiereus are: The Throne of the West in the Black of Malkuth, where it borders on the Kingdom of Shells, The Black Robe of Darkness, bearing a white cross on the left breast; The Sword of Strength and Severity; The Lamen suspended from a Scarlet Collar. The Banner of the West. The position oi the Throne of the West at the limits of Malkuth is fitting for the Avenger of the Gods, for he is placed there in eternal affirmation against the Evil Ones "Hitherto shall ye come and no further." The Throne is also placed there as a seat of witness and of punishment decreed against Evil.

The Robe or Mantle is of Darkness, threatening and terrible to the Outer, as concealing an avenging Force ever ready to break forth against the Evil Ones. On the left breast is a white Cross to represent the Purification of Matter unto the Light. The Sword represents the Forces of the Pillar of Severity as a whole, but the places of the Sephiroth are not necessarily indicated thereon. The guard is Hod and may be of brass; the Grip is the Path of Shin and may be of scarlet, and the pommel, Malkuth, may be black. The grip by which it is wielded, being the Path Shin, represents the Universe governed by the flaming force of Severity, and represents the Hiereus as wielding the Forces of Divine Severity. "The Sword of Vengeance" is its name.

The Lamen is partially explained in the Portal thus: "The Outer Circle includes the four Sephiroth, Tiphareth, Netzach, Hod, and Yesod, of which the first three mark the angles of the triangle inscribed within, while the connecting Paths Nun, Ayin, and Peh form its sides. In the extreme centre is the Path Samekh through which is the passage for the Rending of the Veil. It is therefore a fitting Lamen for Hiereus as representing the connecting link between the First and Second Orders, while the white triangle established in the surrounding Darkness is circumscribed in its turn by the Circle of Light. In addition to this explanation, the Lamen represents "The Light that shineth in Darkness though the Darkness comprehendeth it not." It affirms the possibility of the Redemption from Evil and even that of Evil itself, through self-sacrifice. It is suspended from a scarlet Collar as representing its dependence on the Force of Divine Severity over-awing the evil. It is a symbol of tremendous Strength and Fortitude, and is a synthesis of the Office of Hiereus as regards the Temple, as opposed to his Office as regards the outer world. For these reasons it should always be worn by Hiereus.

Lamen of Hiereus

The Banner of the West completes the symbols of Hiereus. It is thus explained in the Zelator Grade: "The White Triangle refers to the three Paths connecting Malkuth with the other Sephiroth; while the red cross is the Hidden Knowledge of the Divine Nature which is to be obtained through their aid. The Cross and Triangle together represent Life and Light. In addition to this explanation from the Zelator Grade, it represents eternally the possibility of Rescuing the Evil; but in it the Tiphareth cross is placed within the White Triangle of the Supernals as thereby representing that Sacrifice is made only unto the Higher. The red Cross may be bordered with gold in this instance, to represent the Perfect Metal obtained in and through the Darkness of Putrefaction. Black is its field which thus represents the Darkness and Ignorance of the Outer, while the White Triangle is again the Light which shineth in the Darkness but which is not comprehended thereby. Therefore is the Banner of the West the symbol of Twilight as it were, the equation of Light and Darkness. The pole and the base are black, to represent that even in the Depths of Evil can that symbol stand. The cord is black, but the transverse bar and the lance-point may be golden or brass and the tassels scarlet as in the case of the Banner of the East, and for the same reasons.

The Banner of the West, **when it changes its position in the Temple,** represents that which bars and threatens, and demands fresh sacrifice ere the Path leading to the Higher be attained.

"Avenger of the Gods" is the name of the Hiereus, and he is Horus in the Abode of Blindness unto, and Ignorance, of the Higher. Hoor is his name.

The station of Hegemon is between the two Pillars whose bases are in Netzach and Hod, at the intersection of the Paths Peh and Samekh, as it were at the Beam of the Balance, at the Equilibrium of the Scales of Justice; at the point of intersection of the Lowest Reciprocal Path with that of Samekh, which forms a part of the Middle Pillar. She is placed there as the Guardian of the Threshold of Entrance and the Preparer of the Way for the Enterer. Therefore the Reconciler between Light and Darkness, and the Mediator between the Stations of Hierophant and Hiereus. The Symbols and Insignia of Hegemon are:

Lamen of Hegemon

The Robe of Pure Whiteness, bearing on the left breast a Red Cross. The Mitre Headed Sceptre. The Lamen suspended from a Black Collar.

The Robe represents the Spiritual Purity which is required in the Aspirant to the Mysteries and without which qualification none can pass between the Eternal Pillars. It represents the Divine Light which is attracted thereby and brought to the aid of the Candidate. It symbolises the Self-Sacrifice that is offered for another to aid him in the attainment of the Light. It also signifies the atonement of error, the Preparer of the Pathway unto the Divine. Upon the left Breast is a Cross, usually the Calvary form, of red to represent the energy of the lower Will, purified and subjected to that which is Higher and thus is the Office of Hegemon especially that of the Reconciler.

The Mitre-headed Sceptre is the distinctive ensign of the Office of the Hegemon on the Tree of Life and represents the forces of the Pillar of Mercy. It should be of scarlet with gold bands and pommel. The bands represent the places of the Sephiroth Chesed and Netzach the shaft being formed by the Paths Vau and Kaph, the grip by which it is wielded being the Path Qoph, while the pommel is Malkuth. The Mitre is gold with red mountings and each point terminates in a ball. The mitre is charged with a red calvary cross of six squares. This Mitre represents the Wisdom of Chokmah as a duplicated aspect of Kether, attracted by the symbol of self-sacrifice. The Sceptre is wielded by the forces of Flux and Reflux, shown by the grip being referred to the Path Qoph, and it represents the attraction into the Universe of the Forces of Divine Mercy. The Sephiroth and Paths are marked only as bands, and owing to its meaning, should be carried by Hegemon whenever conducting the Candidate, as representing to the latter the attraction of the Forces of his Higher Self. It is called "The Sceptre of Wisdom."

VOLUME SIX

The Lamen is explained in part in the Grade of Philosophus thus: "The peculiar emblem of the Hegemon is the Calvary Cross of Six Squares within a Circle. This Cross embraces Tiphareth, Netzach, Hod and Yesod, and rests upon Malkuth. Also the Calvary Cross of Six Squares forms the cube and is thus referred to the Six Sephiroth of Microprosopus which are Chesed, Geburah, Tiphareth, Netzach, Hod and Yesod."

In addition to this explanation, it represents the black Calvary Cross of Suffering as the Initiator by Trial and Self-abnegation, and the Opener of the Way into the comprehension of the Forces of the Divine Light. It is therefore suspended from a black Collar to show that Suffering is the Purgation of Evil.

"Before the Face of the Gods in the Place of the Threshold" is the name of Hegemon, and she is the Goddess Thma-Ae-St having the following Coptic forms: Thma-Ae-St - this as regards the Middle Pillar and the influence from Kether. Thma-aesh - this more fiery as regards her influence with respect to the Pillar of Severity. Thmaa-ett - this more fluidic with regard to her influence with respect to the Pillar of Mercy. She is the Wielder of the Sceptre of Dual Wisdom from Chokmah and therefore is the Mitre head split in two and not closed, to indicate the Dual Manifestation of Wisdom and Truth, even as the Hall of the Neophytes is called "the Hall of the Dual Manifestation of the Goddess of Truth."

The Three Inferior Officers do not wear Mantles, but only Lamens suspended from black Collars. The designs are in white on a black field to show that they are Administrators of the Forces of Light acting through the Darkness, under the Presidency of the Superior Officers.

The Lamen of Kerux, is thus explained in the Grade of Theoricus:

"The Tree of Life and the Three Mother Letters are the Keys wherewith to unlock the Caduceus of Hermes. The upper point of the Wand rests on Kether and the Wings stretch out to Chokmah and Binah, thus comprehending the Three Supernal Sephiroth. The lower seven are embraced by the Serpents whose heads fall on Chesed and Geburah. They are the twin Serpents of Egypt and the currents of Astral Light. Furthermore, the Wings and the top of the Wand form the letter Shin, the symbol of Fire; the Heads and upper halves of the Serpents form Aleph the symbol of Air; while their tails enclose Mem, the symbol of Water- the Fire of Life above, the Waters of Creation below, and the Air symbol vibrating between them."

Lamen of Kerux

In addition to this, the Caduceus of Kerux represents the balanced forces of Eternal Light working invisibly in the Darkness - even as the Light borne before the hoodwinked Candidate at his Initiation, is symbolic of the Light which guides him in the darkness of the world though he sees it not nor knows it. This Caduceus is the Rod of Hermes, containing invisible and unsuspected forces, the rules of whose administration may be revealed through meditation. It is the outer form of the Wand surmounted by the Winged Globe below which the twin Serpents are shown - the Wand of the Chief Adept in the 5-6 Grade.

The Lamen of Stolistes is thus explained in the Grade of Practicus: "The Cup of Stolistes partakes in part of the symbolism of the Laver of Moses and the Sea of Solomon. On the Tree of Life it embraces nine of the Sephiroth exclusive of Kether. Yesod and Malkuth form the triangle below, the former the apex, the latter the base. Like the Caduceus, it further represents the three Elements of Water, Air, and Fire. The crescent is the Water which is above the Firmament; the circle is the Firmament, and the triangle is the consuming Fire below, which is opposed to the Celestial Fire symbolised by the upper part of the Caduceus."

Lamen of Stolistes

In addition to this explanation, the Cup represents the Receptacle and Collector of the more Fluidic Forces of the Light, and is the symbol of an inexhaustible Bowl of Libation from which Reservoir the Adept may draw the Reserved Forces of the Light - which matter again calls for meditation.

The Lamen of Dadouchos is thus explained in the Grade of Zelator: "The Hermetic Cross, which is also known as Fylfot, Hammer of Thor, and Swastika, is formed of 17 squares taken from a square of 25 lesser squares. These 17 fitly represent the Sun, the Four Elements and the Twelve Signs of the Zodiac."

In addition to this, the Lamen has a more extended meaning. The Hermetic Cross, the Bolt of Whirling Flame, which is represented by the cross of Four Axes whose heads may be either double or single and turned in either direction, is a symbol of terrific Strength, and represents the Fire of the Spirit cleaving its way in all directions through the Darkness of Matter. Therefore is it borne on the Lamen of Dadouchos whose office is that of Purification and Consecration by Fire, and from it also may be drawn by meditation several formulae of strength.

Lamen of Dadouchos

The Kerux is the principal form of Anubis, as the Sentinel is the subsidiary form.

Kerux is Ano-Oobist Empe-Eeb-Te - "Anubis of the East." Sentinel is Ano-Oobi Em-Pemen-Te - "Anubis of the West."

The Kerux is the Herald, the Guardian and Watcher within the Temple, as Sentinel is the Watcher without - and therefore is his charge the proper disposition of the furniture and stations of the Temple. He is also the Proclaimer.

Lamen of Sentinel

The Red Lamp to signify the Hidden Fire over which he watches. The Magic Staff of Power to represent a Ray of the Divine Light which kindles the Hidden Fire. Two Potions whereby to produce the effect of Blood.

He is the Guardian of the Inner side of the Portal - the sleepless Watcher of the Gods and the Preparer of the Pathway to Divine Wisdom. "Watcher for the Gods" is the name of Kerux, and he is Ano-Oobist, the Herald before them.

The Stolistes is stationed in the Northern Part of the Hall to the North-West of the Black Pillar whose base is in Hod, and is there as the Affirmer of the powers of Moisture, Water, reflected through the Tree into Hod. The Cup is the Receptacle of this, filled from Hod so as to transmit its forces into Malkuth, restoring and purifying the vital forces therein by Cold and Moisture. "Goddess of the Scale of the Balance at the Black Pillar" is the name of Stolistes and she is "The Light Shining through the Waters upon Earth," Aura-Mo-Ooth, and there is a connection between her and the Aurim or Urim of the Hebrews.

The Dadouchos is stationed towards the midst of the Southern part of the Hall, to the South-West of the White Pillar whose base is in Netzach and is there as the Affirmer of the Powers of Fire, reflected down the Tree to Netzach. The Censer is the Receptacle thereof the transmitter of the Fires of Netzach to Malkuth, restoring and purifying the vital force therein by Heat and Dryness. "Goddess of the Scale of the Balance at the White Pillar" is the name of Dadouchos and she is "Perfection through Fire manifesting on Earth." Thaum-Aesch-Nia-eth. And there is a connection between her and the Thummim of the Hebrews.

The Stolistes has the care of the Robes and Insignia of the Temple as symbolising by their cleansing and purification the Purging away of the Evil of Malkuth by the Waters of the Spirit.

The Dadouchos has charge of all lights, fires and incense, as representing the purifying and purging of Malkuth by Fire and the Light of the Spirit. These Officers also purify the Temple, the Members and the Candidate by Water and by Fire, as it is written:

"I indeed baptise you with Water, but One shall come after me who shall baptise ye with the Holy Ghost and with Fire."

This completes the names and titles of the Officers of a Temple and they are Seven in number and may all be taken by a Frater or Soror. As they represent Powers and not persons, the feminine form of the Greek names is not usually used, for the powers are positive (male) or negative (female) according to the God-form used. Thus Hierophant, Hiereus, and Kerux are more natural offices for Fratres, while Hegemon, Stolistes and Dadouchos are more natural for Sorores but the office itself carries no implication of sex and sometimes the psychic balance of a ceremony may be better maintained when a Frater is Hegemon and a Soror Hierophant.

The Hierophant must be of the 5-6 Grade and a Zelator Adeptus Minor. The Hiereus must be at least Philosophus, and the Hegemon at least Practicus, and preferably Philosophus. Kerux must be at least Theoricus while Stolistes and Dadouchos must be Zelator, a Neophyte being qualified only for Sentinel. In case the feminine forms of the names of the Officers should wish to be known, they are as follows:

V.H. Hierophant or V.H. Hierophantria
H. Hiereus or H. Hiereia
H. Hegemon or H. Hegemone
Kerux or Kerukaina
Stolistes or Stolistria
Dadouchos or Dadouche
Sentinel or Phulax

(N.B. These alternative or feminine forms were rarely used in the early Order, and in the newly formed modern Temples will probably never be used. I.R.)

OF THE THREE CHIEFS

The Three Chiefs are in the Temple and rule it, yet they are not comprehended in, nor understood by, the Outer Order. They represent, as it were, Veiled Divinities sending a form to sit before the Veil Paroketh, and, like the Veils of Isis and Nephthys, impenetrable save to the Initiate. The synthesis of the Three Chiefs may be said to be in the form of Thoth Who cometh from behind the Veil at the point of its Rending. Yet separately, they may be thus referred:

The Imperator, from his relation to Geburah, may be referred to the Goddess Nephthys.

The Praemonstrator, from his relation to Chesed, may be referred to the Goddess Isis.

The Cancellarius, from his property of Recorder, may be referred to the God Thoth.

No ceremony of the Outer Order may take place without a Chief, preferably the Three Chiefs or their Vice-gerants, present and on account of the Stations on the Dais, it is well to have these stations filled by an Adept, should a Chief be absent. These Stations and those of the Officers are called the Visible Stations of the Gods, and descriptions of the forms which an Adept Officer builds up as a focus of force are given in another paper.

THE INVISIBLE STATIONS

These are:

1. **The Stations of the Kerubim.**
2. **The Stations of the Children of Horus.**
3. **The Stations of the Evil One.**
4. **The Station of Harpocrates.**
5. **The Stations of Isis, Nephthys, Aroueris.**

First, the Kerubim: (These are shown in the colour plate section of this book.) The Stations of the Man, the Lion, the Bull, and the Eagle are at the Four Cardinal Points without the Hall, as invisible Guardians of the limits of the Temple. They are placed according to the winds - beyond the Stations of Hierophant, Dadouchos, Hiereus, and Stolistes - and in this order do their symbols appear in all Warrants of Temples.

The Kerub of Air formulates behind the Throne of Hierophant. She has a young girl's countenance and form, with large and shadowing wings; and she is a power of the Great Goddess Hathor who unites the powers of Isis and Nephthys. To the Sign Aquarius is she referred as a correlative, which represents Springs of Water breaking upon Earth; though as a Zodiacal Sign it is referred to Air, the container of Rain. The Egyptian name of the sign Aquarius is Phritithi. "Thou shalt not confound the Kerubim with their Signs of the Zodiac, notwithstanding that the latter be under the Presidency of the former, seeing that the Kerub representeth a far more Sublime Potency, yet acting by a harmonious sympathy through the particular Sign allotted unto their correspondence."

The Kerub of Fire has the face and form of a Lion with large and clashing wings. He formulates behind the Throne of Dadouchos and he is a power of the Great Goddess Tharpesh or Tharpheshest, the latter syllable being nearly Pasht. The action of the Lion Kerub is through the Flaming Fire of Leo of which the Egyptian name is Labo-Ae.

The Kerub of Water has the face and form of a Great Eagle with large and glistening wings and he formulates behind the throne of Hiereus. He is a power of the Great God Thoomoo (TMU), and his operation is by the Sign of Scorpio, which is called in Egyptian Szlae-Ee.

VOLUME SIX

The Kerub of Earth has a face and form of a Bull with heavy and darkening wings. He formulates behind the Throne of Stolistes and he is a power of the Great God Aphapshi and his operation is by the Sign Taurus called Ta-Aur in Egyptian.

Second, the Children of Horus: Between the Invisible Stations of the Kerubim are those of the Four Vice-gerants of the Elements and they are situated at the Four Corners of the Temple, at the places marked by the Four Rivers of Eden in the Warrant. The body of a Warrant, authorising the formation and establishment of a Temple, represents the Temple itself - of which the Guardians are the Kerubim and the Vice-gerents in the places of the Rivers.

Ameshct (man-headed) is placed in the North East, between the Man and the Bull. Ameshet or Amesheth. The spelling is Coptic and differs according to the force intended to be invoked by the letters.

Tou-mathaph, jackal-headed, is placed in the South East between the Man and the Lion. Toumathph or Tmoumathv.

Ahephi, Ape-faced, is placed in the South West between the Lion and the Eagle. Ahephi or Ahaphix.

Kabexnuv, Hawk-faced, is placed in the North-West, between the Eagle and the Bull. Kabexnuv or Dabexnjemouv.

Third, the Station of the Evil One. This station is in the place of Yesod and is called the Station of the Evil One, the slayer of Osiris. He is the Tempter, Accuser and Punisher of the Brethren, and in Egypt is represented mostly with the head of a Water-Dragon, the body of a Lion or Leopard, and the hind-parts of a Water-horse. He is the Administrator of the power of the Evil Triad:

The Stooping Dragon, Apophrassz. The Slayer of Osiris - Szathan Typhon. The brutal power of Demonic Force - Bessz.

The Synthesis of this Evil Triad "The Mouth of the Power of Destruction" is called Ommoo-Szathan.

Fourth, the Station of Harpocrates. The Invisible Station of Harpocrates is in the Path of Samekh, between the Station of Hegemon and the Invisible Station of the Evil Triad. Harpocrates is the God of Silence and Mystery, whose Name is the Word of this Grade of Neophyte. He is the younger brother of Horus, Hoor-Po-Krattist.

Fifth, the Stations of Isis and Nephythys. The Stations of Isis and Nephthys are respectively at the Places of the Pillars in Netzach and Hod, and these Great Goddesses are not otherwise shown in the Grade, save in connection with the Praemonstrator and Imperator, as operating through the Hierophant, seeing that Isis corresponds to the Pillar of Mercy and Nephthys to that of Severity; and therefore the positions of the Pillars or Obelisks are but, as it were, the Places of their feet.

The Station of Aroueris. The Invisible Station of Aroueris (Horus the Elder) is beside the Hierophant as though representing the power of Osiris to the Outer Order - for while the Hierophant is an Adeptus, he is shown only as Lord of the Paths of the Portal - so that, when the Hierophant moves from the Throne of the East, he is no longer Osiris but Aroueris. Yet when the Hierophant is on the Dais, the Station of Aroueris is that of the Immediate Past Hierophant who sits on the Hierophant's left. Aroo-ouerist.

This ends the Constitutory Symbolism of a Temple in the Grade of Neophyte. Should a Member have occasion to quit his place, he shall do it moving with the course of the Sun. As he passes the place of Hierophant, he shall salute with the Sign. And when he enters or quits the Temple, he shall salute the Hierophant's Throne when within the Portal.

THE COMPLETE GOLDEN DAWN SYSTEM OF MAGIC

THE SYMBOLISM OF THE OPENING OF
THE GRADE OF NEOPHYTE

The Opening Ceremony begins with the Cry of the "Watcher Within" who should come to the right front of Hierophant and raise his Wand. This Symbol of the Ray of the Divine Light from the White Triangle of the Three Supernals thus descends into the Darkness and warns the Evil and uninitiated to retire, so that the White Triangle may be formulated upon the Altar through the combined effect of the formulae of the Opening Ceremony.

Having done this, he sees that the Entrance is properly guarded. And then the Hierophant calls to the Hiereus to test the Members by the Signs, the knowledge of which shows that they, though in the Land of Blindness and Ignorance, have yet seen that Triangle of Divine Light from the Three Supernals formulated in Darkness. It is then noted that the names of the three chief Officers begin with the Letter of Breath in the Coptic.

In the name of Osiris this letter is mute, and silent and Concealed, as it were, by 'H' the Eta. In the name Horus, it is manifest and violently aspirated, while in the name Thmaest, it is partly one and partly the other, for it is compounded with the Letter 'T' in Theta.

H "Ae" is attributed to Chesed - to Aries, and to Earth and Saturn. This is intended to affirm the Unknown Life, which is Inspired from the Beyond, sent out to Aries, the commencement of the Spring in the year, the Life which after being Inspired, is breathed forth again; and also the possible use of that Breath, between the Inspiration and the Expiration, in the combination between it and the Forces of the Microcosm.

The whole is a rehearsal of the properties of the reflection of the element Air down through the Middle Pillar of the Sephiroth, representing the reflection of the Air from Kether, through Tiphareth to Yesod, and even to the Citrine part of Malkuth. For the subtle Aether is, in Kether, inspired from the Divine Light beyond; hence reflected into Tiphareth, wherein it is combined with the Reflexes from the Alchemical Principles in that great Receptacle of the Forces of the Tree, in Yesod. It affirms the foundation of a formula and from Malkuth it is breathed forth or reflected back.

And this formula the Adept can use. Standing in his Sphere of Sensation he can, by his knowledge of the Sacred Rites, raise himself unto the contemplation of Yechidah and from thence aspire (in the sense of Adspire, i.e., to attract towards you in breathing) downwards into himself the Lower Genius as though temporarily to inhabit himself as its Temple.

Another formula of Vibration is here hidden. Let the Adept, standing upright, his arms stretched out in the form of a Calvary Cross, vibrate a Divine Name, bringing with the formulation thereof a deep inspiration into his lungs. Let him retain the breath, mentally pronouncing the Name in his Heart, so as to combine it with the forces he desires to awake thereby. Then sending it downwards through his body past Yesod, but not resting there, but taking his physical life for a material basis, send it on into his feet. There he shall again momentarily formulate the Name. Then, bringing it rushing upwards into the lungs, thence shall he breathe it forth strongly, while vibrating that Divine Name. He will send his breath steadily forward into the U niverse so as to awaken the corresponding forces of the Name in the Outer World. Standing with arms out in the form of a cross, when the breath has been imaginatively sent to the feet and back, bring the arms forward in "The Sign of the Enterer" while vibrating the Name out into the Universe. On completing this, make the "Sign of Silence" and remain still, contemplating the Force you have invoked.

This is the secret traditional mode of pronouncing the Divine Names by vibration, but let the Adept beware that he applies it only to the Divine Names of the Gods. If he does this thing ignorantly in working with Elemental or Demonic Names, he may bring into himself terrible forces of Evil and Obsession. The Method described is called "The Vibratory Formula of the Middle Pillar."

After noting the Names of the Three Chief Officers, comes the recapitulation of the Stations and duties of the Officers, thus occultly affirming the establishment of the Temple so that the Divine Light may shine into the Darkness. Then follows the purification and consecration of the Hall by Water and by Fire, thus marking the limitation of the Four Cardinal Points at the Four Quarters, and the Equilibriation of the Elements. This is the Baptism of the Place and, as it were, the Preparation of a fitting Shrine for the Forces of the Divine Light. While all this goes forward, especially after the Hierophant's "for by Names and Images are all powers awakened and re-awakened," the Officers become clothed in their God-forms and the Invisible Stations awake.

The Procession of Officers is then formed in the North in readiness for the "Mystic Circumambulation in the Path of Light" (that is to say, none of the partakers is hoodwinked). It is formed in the North, beginning from the Station of Stolistes, the symbol of the Waters of Creation attracting the Divine Spirit, and therefore alluding to the Creation of the World by the Spirit and the Waters. The Mystic Reverse Circumambulation forms its Procession in the South, beginning from the Station of Dadouchos, as symbolic of the Ending and Judgment of the World by Fire. But also, the Mystic Circumambulation commences by the Paths of Shin and Resh, as though bringing into action the Solar Fire; while the Reverse Circumambulation commences beside those of Qoph and Tzaddi as though bringing the Watery Reflux into action.

The Order of the Mystic Circumambulation. First comes Anubis, the Watcher within; next Thmaest, the Goddess of the Hall of Truth; then Horus; then the Goddesses of the Scales of the Balance, then Members, if the Hall be large enough, and at the end the Watcher Without, Sentinel. It is as though a gigantic Wheel were revolving, as it is said: "One Wheel upon Earth beside the Kerub." The Name of the Sphere of the Primum Mobile, Rashith ha-Gilgalim, signifies the heads or beginnings of Whirling Motions or Revolutions. Of this Wheel in the Mystic Circumambulation, the ascending side begins from below the Pillar of Nephthys, and the descending side from below the Pillar of Isis; but in the Reverse Circumambulation, the contrary.

Now the nave or axis of this Wheel is about the Invisible Station of Harpocrates - as though that God, in the Sign of Silence were there placed affirming the Concealment of that Central Axis of the Wheel, which alone revolves not.

The Mystic Circumambulation is called symbolic of the Rise of Light and from it is drawn another formula for the circulation of the breath. It is the formula of the Four Revolutions of the Breath (not. of course, of the actual air inspired, but of the subtle Aethers which may be drawn thence and of which it is the Vehicle - the aethers which awaken centres in the subtle body through the formula). This formula should be preceded by that of the Middle Pillar, described previously.

By this method, having invoked the Power you wish to awaken in yourself, and contemplated it, begin its circumambulation thus: Fill the lungs and imagine the Name vibrating in the contained Air. Imagine this vibration going down the left leg to the sole of the left foot - thence passing over to the sole of the right foot - up the right leg to the lungs again, whence it is out-breathed. Do this four times to the rhythm of the Four-fold breath.

The object of the Mystic Circumambulation is to attract and make the connection betwen the Divine Light above and the Temple. Therefore the Hierophant does not quit his post to take part therein, but remains there to attract by his Sceptre the Light from beyond the Veil. Each member in passing gives the Sign of the Enterer, thus projecting the Light forward on his Path from East to West, as he receives it from the Hierophant's Throne. Horus passes only once, for he is the Son of Osiris and inherits the Light by birthright from him. Therefore he goes at once to his station to fix the Light there. Thmaest, the Goddess of Truth, passes twice because her rule is of the Balance of the Two Scales, and she retires to her Station between the Pillars there to complete the reflex of the Middle Column. The Watcher within and the rest circumambulate thrice as affirming the completion of the Reflection of the Perfecting of the White Triangle of the Three Supernals upon the Altar.

Then follows the Adoration of God the Vast One, the Lord of the Universe - at which again all give the Sign of the Enterer, the Sign of the Projection of the Force of the Light. Then only does the Watcher declare that the Sun has arisen and that the Light shineth in Darkness. Now comes the Battery of the Neophyte Grade - the single knock of Hierophant repeated by Hiereus and Hegemon. This affirms the establishment of the White Triangle and therefore the Completion of the Opening Ceremony. The Mystic Words "Khabs Am Pekht" which accompany the knocks seal the image of the Light. Their significance imples, by various Qabalistic methods of analysis, as well as by a certain reading of the Coptic and Egyptian hieroglyphics, "Light in Extension" or "May Light be extended in Abundance upon you."

Konx Om Pax is the Greek corrupted pronunciation of this, put here to link it with its right origin.

The Grade of Neophyte has 0 or the Circle for its Number, as if hiding all things under the negative symbol. This is placed within a circle and a square connected by equal lines, as if affirming the hidden quality of their origin in Kether where all things are One, and the consequent universal application of the Secret Formulae.

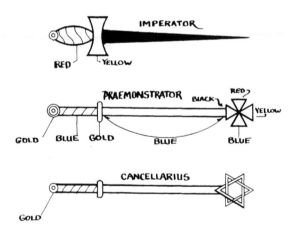

WEAPONS OF THE MAIN OFFICERS

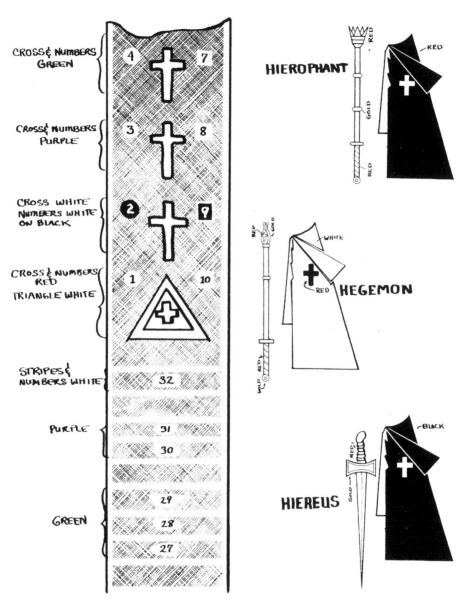

CROSS & NUMBERS GREEN

4 7

CROSS & NUMBERS PURPLE

3 8

CROSS WHITE NUMBERS WHITE ON BLACK

2 9

CROSS & NUMBERS RED TRIANGLE WHITE

1 10

STRIPES & NUMBERS WHITE

32

PURPLE

31

30

29

GREEN

28

27

HIEROPHANT

RED
GOLD
RED
RED

HEGEMON

RED
GOLD
WHITE
RED
GOLD RED

HIEREUS

RED
GOLD
BLACK

SASH, CLOAKS AND WEAPONS OF OFFICERS

Z-3

THE SYMBOLISM OF THE ADMISSION OF
THE CANDIDATE ADMISSION OF THE CANDIDATE

The Candidate is waiting without the Portal under the care of the Sentinel - "The Watcher Without". That is, under the care of the form of Anubis of the West, symbolically that he may keep off the "Dog-Faced Demons," the opposers of Anubis, who rise from the confines where matter ends, to deceive and drag down the Soul. The Ritual of the 31 st Path says: "Since ever dragging down the Soul and leading it from sacred things, from the confines of matter arise the terrible Dog-Faced Demons never showing a true image unto mortal gaze."

The Hierophant gives a single knock to announce the just commencement of a vibration in the Sphere of Sensation of the Candidate. He then states that he holds the Dispensation from the G.H. Chiefs of the Second Order, to affirm that the effect of the ensuing Ceremony upon the Candidate is duly authorised by the Higher Powers for the purpose of Initiation which shall ultimately lead to the knowledge of his Higher Self. He is admitted to the Grade of Neophyte which has no number, concealing the commencement of all things under the similitude of no thing.

The Hegemon, the representative of the Goddess of Truth and Justice, is consequently sent to superintend the preparation of the Candidate, thus symbolising that she is the Presider of Equilibrium to administrate the process of Initiation, by the commencement of the forces of equilibrium in the Candidate himself, through the symbols of rectitude and self-control. But the actual preparation of the Candidate should be performed by the Sentinel - the "Watcher Without" - to show that this preparation must be accomplished before the establishment of equilibrium can occur. Therefore, does the Hegemon superintend the preparation rather than perform it actually. A triple cord is bound round the body of the Neophyte, symbolising the binding and restriction of the lower nature. It is triple in reference to the White Triangle of the Three Supernals. Then, also, are the eyes bandaged to symbolise that the light of the material world is but darkness and illusion compared with the radiance of the Divine Light. The preparation also represents a certain temporary binding and restriction of the natural body.

The Hierophant, being a Member of the Second Order and therefore initiated into the Secret Knowledge of the symbolism, shall, together with any Officers and Members also of the Inner Order, remember what tremendous Gods and Goddesses they represent - the Divine Forces of the Eternal in the administration of the Universe. The Ritual should be read in a loud, clear, stern and solemn voice so as to impress the Candidate with the solemnity of the occasion. In this, there should be no foolish nervousness or hesitation, but the Ritual as performed by an initiated Hierophant should become in his hands something more than this.

Thus should he act. Let him remember what particular God he represents. Exalting his mind unto the contemplation thereof, let him think of himself as a vast figure, standing or moving in the likeness of that God, colossal, his head lost in the clouds, with the light flashing round it from the head-dress of the God - his feet resting upon Earth in darkness, thunder and rolling clouds, and his form wrapped in flashes of lightning - the while vibrating the Name of the God. Thus standing, let him endeavour to hear the voice of the God whom he represents and of the God-Forms of the other officers as previously explained.

Let him speak, then, not as if unto an assembly of mortals but as to an assembly of Gods. Let his voice be so directed as to roll through the Universe to the utmost confines of space. Let the Candidate represent unto him, as it were, a world whom he is beginning to lead unto the knowledge of its governing Angel. As it is written "The lightning lighteneth out of the East and shineth even unto the West, even so, shall the coming of the Son of Man be."

VOLUME SIX

The Candidate during the Ceremony is addressed as Child of Earth, as representing the earthly or terrestrial nature of man - he who comes forward from the darkness of Malkuth to endeavour to regain the knowledge of the Light. This is what is meant by the speech of the Hegemon, because the Path of the Initiate is but darkness and foolishness to the natural man. The single knock given by the Hegemon without the door represents the consenting will of the natural man to receive the force formulated by the Hierophant, and is answered by the Kerux within as if a witness were confirming the same. This being done, the Kerux, as a witness, demands authority from the Hierophant to admit the Candidate into the Hall of Truth and Justice. The Hierophant, in granting the permission, seals the Candidate with a new name given to the physical body of the outward man, but signifying the aspirations of his Soul. As a consequence of the affirmation of the Motto as the Name of the Candidate in the Hall of Truth, Osiris at once sends forward the Goddess of the Scales of the Balance to baptise him with Water and the companion Goddess to consecrate him with Fire. As it is written "Unless a man be born of Water and of the Spirit, he shall in no wise enter the Kingdom of Heaven."

The Kerux instantly bars the Candidate's passage to mark that though he has been admitted, the natural man of unpurified desires cannot be a dweller in the Hall of Truth. The Goddesses of the Scales immediately purify and consecrate him, which operation calls into action the forces of the Pillars in his own sphere of sensation. This is the first of four consecrations because when the Pillars of the Tree are projected onto the Sphere of Sensation there are four pillars, of which the Middle Pillar is the axis. (N.B. There is a painting depicting this idea in the section of coloured plates. I.R.)

At this point of the Ceremony, the astral appearance of the Candidate is that of a form wrapped in darkness as if extinguished thereby, and having unto his right and unto his left the faint semblance of the Two Great Pillars of Fire and of Cloud, whence issue faint rays into the Darkness which covers him. Immediately above his Sphere of Sensation there will appear a ray of bright light as if preparing to penetrate the darkness covering him. The result of this will be that the Candidate, during the whole of the ceremony of Admission, will usually appear to be somewhat automatic and vague.

The reception and consecration take place symbolically in the darkest part of Malkuth. The moment this is finished, the Candidate is conducted to the foot of the Altar, that is under the citrine part of Malkuth which receives the impact of the Middle Pillar. Now, the Hegemon throughout the Ceremony acts as guide, prompter and answerer for the Candidate. His office toward the Candidate is analogous to that of his Higher Soul wherefore also, the Hegemon holds in his hand the mitre-headed sceptre to attract, since it is the sceptre of Wisdom, the Higher Self of the Candidate.

At this moment, as the Candidate stands before the Altar, as the simulacrum of the Higher Self is attracted, so also arises the form of the Accuser in the place of the Evil Triad. This similarly attracts the simulacrum of the Evil Persona of the Candidate - and were it not for the power of the 42 lettered name in the Palaces of Yetzirah (the Gods of which name are usually called the "Great Assessors of Judgment") the actual evil Persona would at once formulate and be able to obsess the Ruach of the Candidate. For, seeing that at this time, the simulacrum of the Higher Soul is attracting the Neschamah of the Candidate, the human will is not as powerful in the Ruach for the moment, because the Aspirant of the Mysteries is now, as it were, divided. That is, his Neschamah is directed to the contemplation of his Higher Self attracted by the Hegemon. His natural body is bound and blinded, his Ruach threatened by the simulacrum of the Evil Persona attracted by Omoo- Szathan. and a species of shadow of himself thrown forward to the place of the Pillars, where the Scales of Judgment are set. At the same time that the first consecration establishes a semblance of the Pillars to his right and left, it also has drawn forth from him a semblance of himself to the place vacated by the Hegemon between the Pillars.

Here then stands the shadow of the Candidate while the Scales of the Balance oscillate unseen. Unseen also and colossal, there is imaged before him Thoth, as Metatron, in the Sign of the Enterer of the Threshold, ready, according to the decision of the human will, to permit or withhold the descent of the Lower Genius of the Candidate. Meanwhile, the Great Assessors of Judgment examine into the truth of the accusations formulated by the Evil and averse antithesis. The Assessors of Judgment come not under the head of invisible stations, but during the Obligation and circumambulation of the Candidate, until he is brought to the Light, they hover immediately about the limits of the Temple and their evil antithesis immediately below. Therefore, when the Candidate stands before the Altar before the Obligation, is the decision actually taken by the human will of the Candidate. Rarely in his life has he been nearer death, seeing that he is, as it were, disintegrated into his component parts. The process of symbolic judgment takes place during the speech of the Hierophant to the Candidate, the answer of the Hegemon and his consent to take the Obligation.

The moment the Candidate thus consents, the Hierophant advances between the Pillars as if to assert that the Judgment is concluded. He advances by the invisible station of Harpocrates to that of the Evil Triad, which he symbolically treads down, so that as Aroueris he stands upon the Opposer. He then comes to the East of the Altar, interposing between the place of the Evil Triad and the Candidate. At the same time, the Hiereus advances on the Candidate's left, the Hegemon on his right, thus formulating about him the symbol of the Higher Triad before he places his hand upon the symbol of the Three Supernals upon the Altar. Again, before doing so, he has been bidden to kneel in adoration of that symbol, as if the natural man abrogated his will before that of the Divine Consciousness.

As he kneels in the presence of the Triad of Aroueris, Thmaa-est and Horus, he places his left hand in that of his Initiator as affirming his passive reception of the Ritual, but his right hand is on the white triangle as symbolising his active aspiration towards his Higher Self. His head is bowed as representing the voluntary submission of the human will to the Divine - and for this latter reason he repeats in the Obligation his name in the outer world.

The Hierophant gives one knock, affirming that the submission unto the higher is perfect. Only at this moment, does the invisible and colossal figure of Thoth cease to be in the Sign of the Enterer and give the Sign of Silence, permitting the first real descent of the Genius of the Candidate, who descends to the invisible station of Harpocrates as a witness of the Obligation.

The Hiereus and the Hierophant return to their Thrones, and therefore it is not Aroueris, but Osiris himself that addresses the speech to the Candidate - "The Voice of my Higher Self," etc., which confirms the link established between the Neschamah and the Genius by formulating the conception thereof into the Ruach. For this, Osiris speaks in the character of the Higher Soul, the symbolic form of which is standing between the Pillars before him. The affirmation of the Higher Soul as the God of the man does not mean that this is the only God, but rather that it is the only presentment of Him which the natural man can grasp at all. Neither is it just to say that the Higher Soul is one with God, seeing that the part is by no means the whole, nor can the whole be accurately and sufficiently described as an assemblage of parts. Let not the reverence for the God of thy self cause thee by a misconception to lose thy reverence for the Gods who live forever - the Aeons of Infinite Years. Herein is a great error and one which may, in the end, bring about the fall of the Genius, a sin which entails none the less terrible consequences because it is a sin of the higher plane where the choice is not between good and evil but between the higher and the lower forms of good.

Therefore is the Mystic Circumambulation in the Path of Darkness led by the Kerux with the symbolic light, as formulating that the Higher Soul is not the only Divine Light but rather a spark from the Ineffable Flame - and the Kerux, in his turn, is but the Watcher of the Gods. After the Kerux comes the Hegemon, the translator of the Higher Self, leading the Candidate; and then come the Goddesses of the scales of the Balance, the Stolistes and the Dadouchos. They move once round; the formation in the darkness of the Binah angle of the White Triangle of the Three Supernals. The Hierophant knocks once as they pass him in affirmation of Mercy - the Hiereus in affirmation of Severity; and the invisible Assessors each give the Sign of the Enterer as the Candidate passes on his way. At the second passing of the Hierophant, the knock affirms the commencement of the angle of Chokmah.

The Kerux bars the Candidate's approach to the West to mark that the natural man cannot obtain the understanding of even the Son of Osiris unless by purification and equilibrium. Again is the Candidate purified and consecrated, the Pillars about his Sphere of Sensation being rendered more manifest. After this second consecration, the Candidate is allowed to approach the place of "The Twilight of the Gods" and for a brief space the hoodwink is slipped up, to present a glimpse, but a glimpse only, of the Beyond. In the challenge of the Hiereus to know the Name is signified the knowledge of the formula. For if the formula of Horus be not with the Candidate, that of Osiris cannot be grasped. But to the Candidate the power of Horus as yet can only appear as a terrible and incomprehensible force - "The Force of the Avenger of the Gods," whence the speech of the Hegemon for him. The Candidate cannot as yet comprehend that before Mildness can be exercised rightly, the forces of Severity and Mercy must be known and wielded, but to accomplish this the greatest courage and energy is required and not hysterical weakness and absence of resolution in action. Hence in the answer of the Hiereus is an affirmation of the necessity of courage and of the danger of fear, and he gives one knock to seal the vibration of that force imaged in the Candidate's Sphere of Sensation.

The next barring and consecration of the Candidate is an extension of the previous one and the commencement of the formulation of the angle of Kether. The hood-wink is again slipped up giving a still further glimpse of the nature of the Divine Light, though to the mind of the Candidate, an imperfect one. Therefore it is to him, as expressed in the answer of the Hegemon, a light dimly seen through the Darkness, yet heralding a Glory beyond. The speech of the Hierophant formulates the forces of the hidden central Pillar.

After this, the Candidate passes to the Altar of the Universe, which receives the influences of the three Pillars, as though then the Ray from the Divine would descend into the darkness of the mind, for then, but not till then, is he fitted to realise what are the first things necessary to the "Search for the Shining Light."

The Hierophant now leaves his Throne and passes between the Pillars, either halting there during the prayer or halting at the place of Harpocrates, or that of the Evil Triad, or East of the Altar. It does not particularly matter which, but one of them may seem more appropriate to a particular Candidate than another and the Hierophant will usually find that he halts at the right place instinctively.

The Hiereus stands on the left of the Candidate, the Hegemon on his right, thus forming the Triad of the Supernals. The Kerux, Stolistes and Dadouchos represent an inferior and supporting Triad behind him as if they affirmed that he has passed the Judgment of the Balance. It is best, though not absolutely necessary, that the Hierophant and the Hiereus should hold their Banners. In any case, it should be done astrally.

The Higher Self of the Candidate will be formulated in the invisible station of Harpocrates behind the Hierophant, who in his present position is Aroueris. The Hierophant gives a single knock to seal the matter and then invokes the Lord of the Universe. Then only is the hoodwink removed definitely.

The Hierophant, Hiereus, and Hegemon join sceptres and sword above the Candidate's head, thus formulating the Supernal Triad, and assert his reception into the Order. They recite the mystic words to seal the current of the Flowing Light.

The Higher Self remains in the station of Harpocrates, and at this point, the spirit-vision should see a gleaming white triangle formulated over the Candidate's head.

The Hierophant now calls forward the Kerux, cautioning the Candidate that the Light has preceded him without his knowledge. It represents to him here, a vague formulation of ideas which as yet he can neither grasp nor analyse. This Light is not a symbol of his Higher Self, but a Ray from the Gods to lead him thereto.

Only after having thus been brought to the Light is the Candidate led to the East of the Altar - the place of the station of the Evil Triad - to affirm that with this Light he will be able to cast out and trample on his own Evil Persona, which, when it has been put in its place, will then become a support to him. It is to the Hiereus, "The Avenger of the Gods" therefore, that the duty of entrusting the Candidate with the secret signs, etc., is delegated. It is he who places him for the first time between the Pillars and superintends his final consecration thus bringing the peculiar force in matter of the Hiereus to the aid of the Candidate, so that he may more safely and resolutely combat the temptations of the Evil Persona.

The Hierophant has returned to his Throne while the Hegemon holds the insignia of the Hiereus as he confers the Signs, etc. She thus affirms the necessity of the force represented by the Hiereus to the Candidate.

The Hierophant on the Throne, the Hiereus East of the Black Pillar and the Hegemon East of the White Pillar, again form a Triad which here represents the reflection of the Three Supernals. The Higher Soul is formulated between the Pillars in the Place of Equilibrium. The Candidate is in the place of the Evil Triad and the Hiereus now' advances to the place of Harpocrates between the Pillars to give the words.

After the giving of the words and signs, the Hiereus draws the Candidate forward between the Pillars and for the second time in the Ceremony, the Higher Soul stands near and ready to touch him. The Hiereus returns to his place East of the Black Pillar so that the Three Chief Officers may formulate and draw down to the Candidate, by their insignia, and the influence of their symbols, the forces of the Supernal Triad. It is important, therefore, that at this point, they should be in these places.

The Candidate now stands between the Pillars, bound with a rope like the mummied form of Osiris, between Isis and Nephthys. The final Consecration now takes place by the Goddess of the Scales of the Balance. The Candidate stands for the first time during the Ceremony at the point representing the equilibrium of the balance. Meanwhile, the Kerux goes to the North, ready for the circumambulation so as to link that with the final Consecration of the Candidate. The final Consecration is also demanded by the Hiereus Horus, the powerful Avenger of Osiris, as still menacing the Evil Persona of the Candidate. Its effect is to seal finally, in balanced formation, the Four Pillars in the Sphere of Sensation of the Candidate. This does not imply that they were not naturally there before. But in the natural man, the symbols are unbalanced in strength - some being weaker and some stronger. The effect of the Ceremony is to strengthen the weak, to purify the strong, and so begin to equilibrate them and at the same time make a link between them and the corresponding forces of the Macrocosm.

This being done, the Hierophant commands the removal of the Rope which has hitherto been purposely retained, symbolically to restrain the actions of the natural man, whose temptation is towards the Evil Persona.

The Four Pillars being thus firmly established, the Candidate is invested with the Badge of the White Triangle of the Three Supernals formulating in Darkness. Now, also, the Higher Self is enabled in reality to form a link with him, if the human will of the natural man be in reality consenting thereto. The free-will of the natural man is never obsessed either by the Higher Soul or by the Ceremony, but, the will consenting, the whole of the Ceremony is directed to strengthening its action.

VOLUME SIX

As the badge is placed upon him, it is as if the two Great Goddesses, Isis and Nephthys, stretched forth their wings over Osiris to restore him again to life.

The Mystic Circumambulation follows in the Path of Light to represent the rising of Light in the Candidate, through the operation of self-sacrifice. **As he passes the Hierophant's throne the red Calvary Cross is astrally formed above the astral White Triangle on his forehead, so that so long as he belongs to the Order, he may bear that potent and sublime symbol as a link with his Higher Self and as an aid in searching out the forces of the Divine Light - if he will.**

The Higher Soul or Genius now returns to the invisible station of Harpocrates, the place of the hidden Centre, yet continuing to retain the link formed with the Candidate. The address of the Hierophant is intended simply to effect the distinct formulation of the symbols of the Grade of Neophyte in the Candidate, and it is therefore only when this is finished that the Watcher Anubis announces that the Candidate has been duly admitted as an initiated Neophyte.

The Hiereus is charged with a warning address as again confirming the will of the Candidate and addressing a final menance to the Evil Persona. The Hierophant then states clearly what the Candidate must begin to study. He affirms that the symbols must be equilibriated in the Sphere of Sensation before a link can be formulated between them and the Forces of the Macrocosm. The necessity of examination is insisted upon so that this may be completely done.

The Kerux then pours out the two fluids to make the semblance of blood. This is to fix in the Candidate's sphere the symbols of the forces of transmutation in Nature and also to make an astral link between these and the Candidate's physical life, as a guard of the secrecy of the Mysteries. This particular form of transmutation is used as showing the effect of a mixture of forces as producing a third appearance totally different from them. The red colour is symbolic of the blood of the Candidate. In the Ancient Mysteries, the Candidate's blood was actually drawn at this time and preserved as an avenging link in case of his proving unworthy. Yet our transmutation effects the matter quite as well, seeing that the astral link is firmly established.

The final speech of the Hierophant is further intended besides its apparent meaning, to affirm that a person only partially initiated is neither fitted to teach nor to instruct even the outer and more ignorant in Sublime Knowledge. He is certain, through misunderstanding the principles, to formulate error instead of truth.

CLOSING

The greater part of the closing ceremony is explained by the opening. The Reverse Circumambulation, however, is intended to formulate the withdrawal of the Light of the Supernal Triad from the Altar, so that it may not be profaned by abiding without due guard. Not that the Divine Light would suffer thereby, but because it might initiate an Avenging Current if profaned. This is what is implied by the Law of Moses in the prohibition about offering unconsecrated Fire either before or within the Veil of the Tabernacle. As a vibratory formula, the reverse Circumambulation represents the reversal of the current and the restoration of the Operator to his ordinary condition.

The Mystic Repast then follows. It is a communion in the body of Osiris. Its Mystic Name is "The Formula of the Justified One," and it is sufficiently explained in the section concerning the Altar.

The Kerux, in finishing, inverts the Cup, as the Watcher of the Gods, to show that the symbols of self-sacrifice and of regeneration are accomplished. The proclamation is confirmed by the Hierophant and the Chief Officers giving the three knocks, emblematic of the Mystic Triad, and they repeat the Mystic Words.

The Hierophant, in his final speech, seals the link first formulated between the Members and the Supernal Triad for each one present that it may prove to him or her, a guide for the ultimate attainment of the Supreme Initiation - if he will.

THE SYMBOLISM AND MEANING OF THE STEP, SIGNS, GRIP OR TOKEN, AND THE WORDS

They have this three-fold interpretation:

1. **Apparent meaning.**
2. **Spiritual or Mystical reference.**
3. **Practical application.**

Each is therefore considered under three heads.

First, the foot is advanced about six inches representing the foot on the side of Chesed put forward and taking a hesitating step in darkness - the left foot, to represent the power of Isis or the beginning of action rather than Nephthys as the end thereof. The term 6 inches is employed here only to render it more intelligible to English Initiates. It means a convenient measure of 6, and preferably 6 times the measure of the Phalanx of the thumb -the spirit and will.

Second, it symbolises the beginning of the stamping down of the Evil Persona. The foot is advanced 6 metrical distances answering to the number 6 of Tiphareth - Osiris - alluding therefore to the self-sacrifice necessary to accomplish this.

Third, it represents the practical application of the beginning of a magical force. Let the Adept, in using the Sign of the Enterer, give the step as he commences the Sign and let him imagine himself colossal, clothed with the form of the God or Goddess appropriate to the work - his head reaching to the clouds - his feet resting upon Earth. And let him take the step as if he stamped upon the Earth and the Earth quaked and rocked beneath him. As it is said "Clouds and Darkness are round about Him - lightnings and thunders are the habitation of His feet." Its secret name is "The Step of the Avenger."

THE SALUTING SIGN

(N.B. One of the modern Temples has interpreted the above to imply that the initiate bows when passing the East. It means nothing of the kind. The original G.D. meaning is very important and to be taken literally. I.R.).

1. That of groping forward in search of truth.

2. It represents the involution and bringing forward of the Light into the material to aid the will of the Candidate in his search for and aspiration towards the Higher.

3. Standing as before described, in the form of the God, and elevating the mind to the contemplation of Kether, take the step like a stroke with the foot, bring the arms up above the head as if touching the Kether, and as the step is completed bring the hands over the head forwards. **Thrust** them out directly from the level of the eyes horizontally - arms extended, fingers straight, palms downwards, the hands directed towards the object it is wished to charge or to affect. At the same time, sink the head till the eyes look exactly between the thumbs. In this way, the rays

from the eyes, from each finger and from the thumbs, must all converge upon the object attacked. If any of them disperse, it is a weakness.

Thus performed, this Sign is a symbol of tremendous attacking force and of projection of will power, and it should be employed in all cases where force of attack is required especially in charging of Talismans and the like. Generally, it is best to have the thumbs and all the fingers extended - but if a particular effect is desired, you may extend only the fingers appropriate thereto, keeping the rest folded back in the hand. Herewith also, may be combined the attribution of the Planets to the head: (Mars to the right nostril, Mercury to the Mouth, etc., as explained in the Microcosm Lecture), sending at the same time an imaginary ray of colour of the Planet desired from the part of the head attributed to it. But, when finished, be careful to withdraw the rays again or they will remain like so many outlets of astral force and thus exhaust you. The best way to protect yourself against this is to give the Sign of Silence immediately. **For the first Sign should always be answered by the second.** The secret names of the Saluting Sign is "The Attacking Sign" or "The Sign of the Enterer of the Threshold."

THE SIGN OF SILENCE

1. This is simply that of secrecy regarding the Mysteries.

2. It is the affirmation of the station of Harpocrates, wherein the Higher Soul of the Candidate is formulated in part of the admission Ceremony. It is the symbol of the Centre and the "Voice of the Silence" which answers in secret the thought of the heart.

3. The Sign of Silence withdraws the force put out by the Sign of the Enterer. Take upon thyself as before taught the colossal form of the God Harpocrates. Bring the left foot sharply back, both heels together - beat the ground once with the left foot as it is placed beside the right. Bring the left hand to the mouth and touch the centre of the lower lip with the left fore-finger. Close the other fingers and thumb, and drop the right hand to the side. Imagine that a watery vapor encircles and encloses you. This is the reflux of the current.

This Sign is also used as a protection against attack. The Sign represents a concentration of astral light about the person. Having given the Sign as above, it is a protection against all attack and danger of obsession. To make it yet stronger, the form of the God should be taken. If Spiritual force is required, formulate as if standing on a Lotus or rising from it. For force in contemplation and meditation, formulate as if seated upon a Lotus. But for more material force, as if standing upon a Dragon or a Serpent like some statues of Harpocrates. As a defence and protection, the Sign is as strong as the banishing pentagram, though of a different nature. And as the Sign of the Enterer represents attack, so does this sign represent defence thereto, as a shield is a defence against the Sword. From this Sign is a formula of invisibility derived.

The Secret Names of this Sign are: "The Sign of the God of Silence" or the "Sign of Defence or Protection." It may be performed with any finger of either hand, but it is most protective when the left forefinger is used, the Water of Chesed, for the fingers of the right hand represent more violent action, and those of the left more watery action.

It may here be remarked that the so-called Christian Sign of Benediction, consisting of the thumb and first two fingers only, projected, is the affirmation of Osiris, Isis and Nephthys - or Spirit, Fire, and Water.

With regard to taking on mentally the forms of the Gods, it may here be noted that the process is of great assistance and use in all magical working, whether of invokation or of evocation, contemplation, meditation, skrying in the spirit vision, alchemy, etc. For the forms of the Gods do here represent a certain symbolic material action of the Divine Forces.

THE GRIP AND THE PASSWORD

1. The steps are taken and the Grip exchanged simultaneously. They mean seeking guidance in the darkness and silence of the Mysteries.

2. It shows that a steady and resolute will, acting in union with good, will accomplish what it desires, no matter how often it fail at first. It inculcates the necessity for harmony and brotherly love - of doing away with pettiness and of too much self-concentration - for allowances for the weaknesses of others within limits - of shunning resolutely anything in the nature of slander. So that in the grip of the Neophyte the Initiates meet hand to hand and foot to foot in the true greeting of a brother or sister, and not in the veiled hostility of an enemy. For, in the working of the Inner, where all invoke the same forces in the same manner, when he or she becomes unsympathetic with the rest, there is a separation from them, and though he weaken the combination of working, yet he still more certainly attracts upon himself a reflex current from the Avengers of Evil.

   The Names of the God of Silence which is the Grand Word of this Grade also represents the silence of the Sacred Mysteries to be observed towards the Outer Order. It shows also the necessity for respect towards the secrets of any Frater or Soror committed to your care, not endeavouring to search them out for purposes of curiosity nor repeating them when discovered, nor in any way referring to them so as to wound the other, nor in any way employing them as a means of causing humiliation, but to keep them as a sacred trust and not to be deflected by them from acting justly and harmoniously together.

3. In any magical ceremony, or other working, if more than one member be taking part, all present, putting themselves into the form of the God as taught, should exchange Sign, Grip and Words, so as to establish a current of harmony and the affirmation of a mutual direction of will towards the same object.

THE PASSWORD

1. Merely to guard the secrets of the Order against any Members resigned or not working; hence changed each Equinox.
2. It is an affirmation of the different spiritual as well as the different physical constitutions of the Candidates - that all natures cannot be the same without evil and injury resulting thereby - but that each nature should be brought to its own Kether - the best of its kind. This too, may be done in all things. It is the basis of Alchemy.
3. It should be pronounced as if attracting the Solar Force - the Light of Nature, during the 6 months following the Equinox at which it is issued, as a link with the Solar Force, between that and the Order. This password, therefore, may also be used in a magical ceremony as attracting the support of the Light of Nature acting upon natural forces.

THE CEREMONY OF THE EQUINOX

The whole formulae of the Ceremony of the Equinox are intended to create a magical link between the Sun, as the Light of Nature, and the Order; and it should be celebrated within 48 hours at least of the Sun's actual entry into Aries or Libra. The single knock given by the Hierophant heralds the initiation of a fresh current. The Password, as already explained, is the symbol of the connecting link of the purpose of the Ceremony and therefore, before beginning a fresh operation to attract a fresh current, the Kerux proclaims that the former password is abrogated. In the whole Ceremony, save at the exchange of Insignia, the Hierophant, Hiereus, Hegemon, Stolistes and Dadouchos remain in their places - the Kerux, or Watcher of the Gods being the only one who moves.

First comes the establishment of a vertical current in the direction of the Middle Pillar by the exchange of words between the Hierophant and Hiereus, while the Hegemon, who is in the whole Ceremony of the Equinox the important Officer, by reason of his insignia, seals and arrests the current in the centre by a single knock and the words "I am the Reconciler between them." Then follows the cross current established between the Stolistes and Dadouchos - again fixed and sealed by the Hegemon, thus symbolising the equilateral cross of the Elements (of which the centre would naturally be about the invisible station of Harpocrates) but is arrested by the Hegemon between the Pillars. The cross currents are thus thrown into the image of the Calvary Cross of the Rivers to ally it with the symbolism of Tiphareth and of the Sephiroth.

Then the Hierophant, Dadouchos, Hiereus, and Stolistes formulate a circle enclosing the symbol, which is again sealed by the Hegemon. Then the Officers, being careful to follow the course of the Sun deposit in turn, their Insignia upon the Altar, taking therefrom instead the mystical symbols of the Body of Osiris corresponding to their Cardinal Points. The Hegemon takes the Lamp of Kerux. The Kerux then circumambulates, halting at the Cardinal Points and facing them, representing the course of the Sun through the Zodiac in order to attract the Solar Ray, but under the control of its Superior, the Light of Osiris, and the adorations are performed at the Stations of the Kerubim to mark the limits of the Circle.

This time, it is with the Lamp of the Watcher of the Gods and with the Sign of the Calvary Cross of Tiphareth that the Hegemon seals in the centre the Solar Light. The formal assertion of the entry of a new current of Light is proclaimed, and the Mystic Words are recited to close the ceremony.

From this Ceremony there are many practical formulae derivable which will be easily comprehended by the Z.A.M. who has mastered the whole of this lecture. **Only let him remember that the formulae of the Ceremony of the Equinox represents the sudden attraction and sealing of a Force in Nature then in operation - rather than a continuous and graduated ceremony to build up the same.** Consequently also, it is well to use the password then in being as an adjunct to the other Names employed in magical ceremonies as bringing into operation the link with the Solar Light.

NOTES ON THE OPENING EXORDIUM OF "Z"

The Great Thoth is the highest aspect of the Hermes of the most ancient Egyptian Mysteries, and corresponds almost to the Great Angel Metatron. It is the Archangel of Kether in the Briatic World. The Mercury of the Romans must not be confused with this Great Hermes.

The doctrines of Gnosticism and of Valentinus approached those of the pure Qabalah. In them we find Speech and Silence. Across the Abyss of Silence comes the Primal Speech. The Divine Ones here referred to are the Aeons in the Atziluthic World. These formulae of knowledge are designed in terms cognizable to us in the lower world.

Eheieh - implicit and explicit sound. "Every being pronounces all its existence, the Name of the Lord of Life, by inspiration and expiration."

Macroprosopus is Aima and Abba, Mother - Father. The two nostrils pass up and down the two breaths, as through the two Great Pillars. These throw all things into vibration; compare the Rashith ha-Gilgalim. Piercing of the Dragon's Coils suggests freeing of Malkuth, which is also referred to as the Washing of the Garments of the Queen, the Inferior Mother. Then comes the Breaking Forth of the Light. Over Malkuth as Guardians are Metatron and Sandalphon as the Two Pillars, and Nephesch ha-Messiah, the animal soul of Messiah, the Shekinah or Presence between the Kerubim.

THE PARTICULAR EXORDIUM

The Bornless Ones of Time referred to are those Corruscations of the Divine Light which are above Kether of Atziluth. In such Supernal Realms, the Ain Soph, though negative to us, is there intensely positive. Thence came forth the Gods, the Voice, the Aeons, and the Name.

The Egyptian Gods are generally most differentiated by their Crowns: Amen-Ra by the high feathers, Mo-ooth (Maut) has the same headdress as Horus. She corresponds to Aima Elohim. The high Hermes-Thoth has the same headress as Amoun Kneph, the Sacred Spirit. Remember that Thoth, Truth, has two aspects - the higher and the lower. The higher is Absolute, the lower is suitable to human comprehension. To tell the higher form of a truth to one who cannot understand it is to lie to him because, though correctly formulated, it will not be correctly received.

The Forms of Thmaah. There are four forms of spelling for the Goddess Thma-Est whereby she is attributable to the Four Letters of the Name, and therewith to the Elements and the Tree.

Fire. Chokmah. Yod. Thma-oe-Sh.
Water. Binah. Heh. Thma-oe-Tt.
Air. Tiphareth. Vau. Thm-a-oe-St.
Earth, Malkuth, Heh (final). Thm-a-Oe.
(The Middle Pillar)

In the Equinox Ceremony, the Hegemon is Air, Spirit, and the principal officer. She reconciles from East to West, and and from North to South, and in a circular formula.

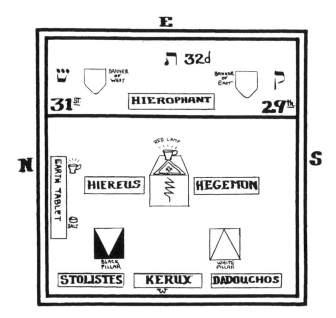

(Officers - The same as for the Neophyte Grade. Temple - Arranged as in Diagram. Required - For the Candidate: Hoodwink, Sash. For the Temple: Fylfot Cross, Three Portals, Shewbread Diagram, Candlestick Diagram, Earth Tablet, Altar Diagrams.)

OPENING OF THE ZELATOR GRADE

(The members, having assembled and robed, each is seated in his proper place. Hiereus gives one knock. All rise).

Hiero:

(Sitting) Fratres and Sorores of the Zelator Grade of the Golden Dawn, assist me to open the Temple in the Grade of Zelator. Frater Kerux, see that the Temple is properly guarded.

Kerux:

(Knocks, without opening the door. Sentinel knocks) Very Honored Hierophant, the Temple is properly guarded.

Hiero:

Honored Hiereus, see that none below the Grade of Zelator is present.

Hiereus:

Fratres and Sorores, give the signs of Zelator (All give signs of Zelator.)

Hiereus:

(Gives sign) Very Honored Hierophant, no one below the Grade of Zelator is now present.

Hiero:

(Giving sign) Purify and consecrate the Temple with Water and with Fire. (Kerux advances between the Pillars. Stolistes and Dadouchos, one on each side of the Pillars, advance to the centre of the Hall. All salute. Dadouchos makes cross in air with Censer, and swings it forward three times, saying:)

Dad:

I consecrate with Fire. (Stolistes makes Cross with Cup, and sprinkles thrice towards East, saying:)

Stol:

I purify with Water.

Kerux:

The Temple is cleansed. (Salute Zelator sign. All three retire, Kerux leading and passing with Neophyte sign.)

Hiero:

Let the Element of this Grade be named that it may be awakened in the spheres of those present and in the sphere of the Order.

Heg:

The Element of Earth.

Hiereus:

(Knocks) Let us adore the Lord and King of Earth. (All face East.)

Hiero:

ADONAI HA-ARETZ. ADONAI MELEKH. Unto Thee be the Kingdom and the Power (cross on self) and the Glory. MALKUTH, GEBURAH, GEDULAH. (He makes Cross and Circle with Sceptre before him as he says MALKUTH, etc.) The Rose of Sharon and the Lily of the Valley, Amen. (All give Zelator Signs. Kerux goes to North, and sprinkles Salt before the Tablet, saying:)

Kerux:

Let the Earth Adore Adonai! (Hierophant leaves his place and goes to North. He stands facing the centre of the Tablet of the North and at a convenient distance therefrom, say six feet. Hiereus takes his place at the right of Hiero. Hegemon on left of Hiero; Stolistes behind Hiereus, Dadouchos behind Hegemon. All Officers face North. Hierophant makes sign in front of, and concentric with Tablet of the North, an invoking Pentagram of Earth, saying:)

Hiero:

And the Elohim said, Let us make Adam in our Image, after our likeness and let him have dominion over the fish of the sea and over the fowl of the air and over the cattle and over all the earth, and over every creeping thing that creepeth over the Earth. And the Elohim created Eth Ha-Adam in their Own Image, in the Image of the Elohim created they them. In the name of ADONAI MELEKH and the Bride and Queen of the Kingdom, Spirits of Earth adore Adonai! (Hierophant hands his Sceptre to Hiereus and, taking his Sword, makes the Ox in centre of Pentagram, saying:)

Hiero:

In the Name of Auriel, the Great Archangel of Earth, and by the sign of the head of the Ox - Spirits of Earth, adore Adonai! (Hierophant returns Sword to Hiereus and takes Mitre-headed Sceptre from Hegemon, and makes Cross in the air, saying:) In the Names and letters of the Great Northern Quadrangle, Spirits of Earth, adore Adonai! (Hiero returns Sceptre to Hegemon, and takes Cup from Stolistes, making Cross, and sprinkling thrice to North, saying:) In the Three Great Secret Names of God, borne upon the Banners of the North - EMOR DIAL HECTEGA - Spirits of Earth, adore Adonai! (Hiero. returns Cup to Stolistes and takes Censer from Dadouchos. and making three forward swings, says:) In the name of IC ZOD HEH CHAL, Great King of the North, Spirits of Earth adore Adonai! (Hierophant returns Censer to Dadouchos, and takes back Sceptre from Hiereus, returns to Throne. All Officers return to places. All members face as usual.)

Hiero:

In the name of ADONAI H A-ARETZ, I declare this Temple duly opened in the Grade of Zelator.

Hiero:

(Knocks 4, 3, 3)

Heg:

(Knocks 4, 3, 3)

Hiereus:

(Knocks 4, 3, 3)

ADVANCEMENT—FIRST PART

(Hierophant sits East of Altar, Hiereus North, and Hegemon South.)

Hiero:

Fratres and Sorores, our Frater (Soror) having made such progress in the Paths of Occult Science as has enabled him (her) to pass an examination in the required knowledge, is now eligible for advancement to this Grade, and I have duly received a dispensation from the Greatly Honored Chiefs of the Second Order to admit him (her) in due form. Honored Hegemon, superintend the preparation of the Neophyte and give the customary alarm. (Hegemon salutes with the Zelator sign, and leaves the room by South and West. Sentinel prepares Neophyte who wears sash of Neophyte grade and is blindfolded. He carries the Fylfot Cross in right hand. Hegemon instructs Neophyte in knocks of the Grade. Kerux opens the door to be just ajar.)

Heg:

Let me enter the Portal of Wisdom.

Kerux:

I will. (Opens door and admits them. Sentinel turns down lights.)

Hiero:

Except Adonai build the house, their labour is but lost that build it. Except Adonai keep the City, the Watchman waketh in vain. Frater (Soror) Neophyte, by what aid dost thou seek admission to the Grade of Zelator of the Golden Dawn?

Heg:

(For Neophyte) By the guidance of Adonai; by the possession of the necessary knowledge; by the dispensation of the Greatly Honored Chiefs of the Second Order; by the signs and tokens of the Zelator Grade. By this symbol of the Hermetic Cross. (Kerux takes Cross from him.)

Hiero:

Give the step and signs of a Neophyte. (Neophyte gives them).

Hiero:

Frater Kerux, receive from the Neophyte the Token, Grand Word, and Password of the Neophyte Grade. (Kerux places himself in front of Neophyte and says:)

Kerux:

Give me the grip of the Neophyte. (Done) Give me the Word. (Done) Give me the Password. (Done) (Having received it, he turns to Hiero, gives Grade Salute, and says:)

Kerux:

Very Honored Hierophant, I have received them.

Hiero:

(To Hegemon) Lead the Neophyte to the West and set him between the Mystic Pillars, with his face towards the East. (Hegemon places Neophyte between the Pillars, and remains behind him.) Frater (Soror). . .will you pledge yourself to maintain the same secrecy regarding the Mysteries of this Grade as you are pledged to maintain regarding those of the Neophyte Grade - never to reveal them to the World, and not even to confer them upon a Neophyte without a dispensation from the Greatly Honored Chiefs of the Second Order?

Neo:

I will.

Hiero:

Then you will kneel on both your knees, lay your right hand on the ground, and say:-I swear by the Earth whereon I kneel. (Done) Let the symbol of blindness be removed. (Hegemon unbinds Neophyte's eyes. Sentinel turns up lights. Hegemon goes back to his proper place. Neophyte remains kneeling between the Pillars with his hand on the ground. Kerux takes the Salt from before the Tablet of the North, and passing round the Altar with Sol stands in front of Neophyte facing him and holds the Salt in front of him.) Take Salt with your left hand and cast it to the North; say Let the Powers of Earth witness my pledge. (Done. Kerux replaces Salt, and returns to his place.) Let the Neophyte rise and let him be purified with Water and consecrated with Fire, in confirmation of his pledge, and in the Name of the Lord of the Universe. (Dadouchos comes forward round South Pillar, stands before Neophyte and makes three forward swings of censer, saying:)

Dad:

In the name of the Lord of the Universe I consecrate thee with Fire. (Dadouchos returns by way he came. Stolistes comes round North Pillar, stands before Neophyte, makes cross on forehead, sprinkles thrice, saying:)

Stol:

In the Name of the Lord of the Universe. I purify thee with Water. (Returns to place as he came.)

Hiero:

The Zelator Grade is a preparation for other Grades, a threshold before our discipline, and it shows by its imagery, the Light of the Hidden Knowledge dawning in the Darkness of Creation; and you are now to begin to analyze and comprehend the Nature of that Light. To this end, you stand between the Pillars, in the Gateway where the secrets of the Neophyte Grade were communicated to you.

Prepare to enter the Immeasurable region. And Tetragrammaton Elohim planted a Garden Eastward in Eden, and out of the ground made Tetragrammaton Elohim to grow every tree that is pleasant to the sight and good for food; the Tree of Life also, in the midst of the Garden, and the Tree of Knowledge of Good and of Evil. This is the Tree that has two Paths, and it is the Tenth Sephira Malkuth, and it has about it seven Columns, and the Four Splendours whirl around it as in the Vision of the Mercabah of Ezekiel; and from Gedulah it derives an influx of Mercy, and from Geburah an influx of Severity and the Tree of the Knowledge of Good and of Evil shall it be until it is united with the Supernals in Daath. But the good which is under it is called the Archangel Metatron, and the Evil is called the Archangel Samael, and between them lies the straight and narrow way where the Archangel Sandalphon keeps watch. The Souls and the Angels are above its branches, and the Qlippoth or Demons dwell under its roots. Let the Neophyte enter the Pathway of Evil. (Kerux takes his place in front of Neophyte, leads him in a N.E. direction towards the Hiereus, halts and steps out of the direct line between Hiereus and Neophyte.)

Hiereus:

Whence comest thou?

Kerux:

I come from between the two Pillars and I seek the Light of the Hidden Knowledge in the Name of Adonai.

Hiereus:

And the Great Angel Samael answered, and said: I am the Prince of Darkness and of night. The foolish and rebellious gaze upon the face of the created World, and find therein nothing but terror and obscurity. It is to them the Terror of Darkness and they are as drunken men stumbling in the Darkness. Return, for thou canst not pass by. (Kerux leads Neophyte back as he came, to between the Pillars.)

Hiero:

Let the Neophyte enter the Pathway of Good. (Kerux leads Neophyte S.E., and halts opposite Hegemon, stepping aside from before Neophyte.)

Heg:

Whence comest thou?

Kerux:

I come from between the Pillars, and I seek the Light of the Hidden Knowledge in the Name of Adonai.

Heg:

The Great Angel Metatron answered, and said: I am the Angel of the Presence divine. The Wise gaze upon the created world and behold there the dazzling image of the Creator.

Not yet can thine eyes bear that dazzling Image. Return, for thou canst not pass by. (Kerux turns and leads Neophyte back between the Pillars.)

Hiero:

Let the Neophyte enter the straight and narrow Pathway which turns neither to the right hand nor to the left hand. (Kerux leads Neophyte dirctly up centre of Hall until he is near the Altar, halts, steps aside from before Neophyte, leaving him to face Altar unobstructed.)

Hiereus:

Heg:

(Together say) Whence comest thou? (They cross Sceptre and Sword before altar.)

Kerux:

I come from between the Pillars and I seek the Light of the Hidden Knowledge in the Name of Adonai. (Hierophant advances to East of Altar with Sceptre, which he thrusts between Sword of Hiereus and Sceptre of Hegemon, and raising it to an angle of 45 degrees says:)

Hiero:

But the Great Angel Sandalphon said: I am the reconciler for Earth, and the Celestial Soul therein. Form is invisible alike in Darkness and in blinding Light. I am the left hand

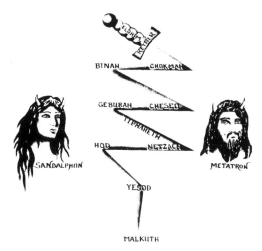

BINAH — CHOKMAH

GEBURAH — CHESED

TIPHARETH

HOD — NETZACH

SANDALPHON

METATRON

YESOD

MALKUTH

THE FLAMING SWORD WITH KERUBS

Kerub of the Ark and the Feminine Power, as Metatron is the right hand Kerub and the Masculine Power, and I prepare the way to the Celestial Light. (Hegemon and Hiereus step back to South and North of Altar respectively. Hiero. takes Neophyte by right hand with his left, and pointing to the Altar and diagram says:) And Tetragrammaton placed Kerubim at the East of the Garden of Eden and a Flaming Sword which turned every way to keep the Path of the Tree of Life, for He has created Nature that Man being cast out of Eden may not fall into the Void. He has bound Man with the Stars as with a chain. He allures him with Scattered Fragments of the Divine Body in bird and beast and flower, and He laments over him in the Wind and in the Sea and in the birds. When the times are ended, He will call the Kerubim from the East of the Garden, and all shall be consumed and become Infinite and Holy.

Receive now the secrets of this Grade. The step is thus given 6 by 6 showing you have passed the threshold. The Sign is given by raising the right hand to an angle of 45 degrees. It is the position in which the Hierophant interposed for you between the Hiereus and the Hegemon. The Token is given by grasping fingers, the thumb touching thumb to form a triangle. It refers to the Ten Sephiroth. The Word is ADONAI HA-ARETZ, and means Adonai the Lord of the Earth, to which Element this Grade is allotted. The Mystic Number is 55, and from it is formed the Password Nun He. It means Ornament, and when given is lettered separately. The Badge of this Grade, is the sash of the Neophyte with the narrow white border, a red cross within the Triangle, and the number 1 within a circle and 10 within a square, one on each side of the triangle. (He invests Neophyte with the sash, and points out the Three Portals, saying:)

The Three Portals facing you in the East, are the Gates of the Paths leading to the three further Grades, which with the Zelator and the Neophyte forms the first and lowest Order of our Fraternity. Furthermore, they represent the Paths which connect the Tenth Sephirah Malkuth with the other Sephiroth. The letters Tau, Qoph and Shin make the word Quesheth a Bow, the reflection of the Rainbow of Promise stretched over our Earth, and which is about the Throne of God. (Hegemon points out the Flaming Sword, saying:)

Heg:

This drawing of the Flaming Sword of the Kerubim, is a representation of the Guardians of the Gates of Eden, just as the Hiereus and Hegemon symbolize the Two Paths of the Tree of the Knowledge of Good and of Evil.

81

Hiereus:

In this Grade, the red Cross is placed within the White Triangle upon the Altar, and it is thus the symbol of the Banner of the West. The Triangle refers to the Three Paths and the Cross to the Hidden Knowledge. The Cross and the Triangle together represent Life and Light. (Hierophant points out the Tablet of the North, saying:)

Hiero:

This Grade is especially referred to the element of Earth, and therefore, one of its principal emblems is the Great Watch Tower or Terrestrial Tablet of the North. It is the Third or Great Northern Quadrangle or Earth Tablet, and it is one of the four Great Tablets of the elements said to have been given to Enoch by the Great Angel Ave. It is divided within itself into four lesser angles. The Mystic letters upon it form various Divine and Angelic Names, in what our tradition calls the Angelic secret language. From it are drawn the Three Holy Secret Names of God EMOR DIAL HECTEGA which are borne upon the Banners of the North, and there are also numberless names of Angels, Archangels, and Spirits ruling the Element of Earth. (Kerux comes forward and hands Fylfot Cross to Hiero:)

Hiero:

The Hermetic Cross, which is also called Fylfot, Hammer of Thor, and Swastika, is formed of 17 Squares out of a square of 25 lesser squares. These 17 represent the Sun, the Four Elements, and the Twelve Signs of the zodiac. In this Grade, the lights on the Pillars are unshaded, showing that you have quitted the Darkness of the outer world. You will leave the Temple for a short time. (Kerux takes Neophyte out.)

SECOND PART

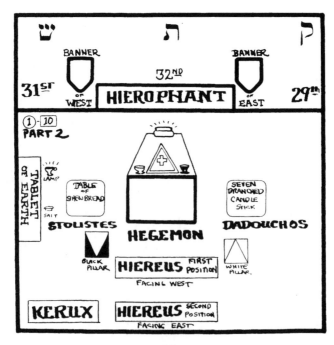

Hiero:

Frater Kerux, when the Neophyte gives the proper alarm, you will admit him. Fratres Stolistes and Dadouchos, assist the Kerux in the reception. (Kerux goes out and instructs Neophyte in the knocks. Stolistes and Dadouchos take up positions so as to face Neophyte as he enters Hall. Kerux opens door and admits Neophyte, but does not stand in front of him.)

Hiero:

Frater, as in the Grade of Neophyte, you came out of the World to the Gateway of Hidden Knowledge, so in this Grade you pass through the Gateway and come into the Holy Place. You are now in the court of the Tabernacle, where stood the Altar of Burnt Offering, whereon was offered the sacrifices of animals, which symbolized the Qlippoth or Evil Demons who inhabit the plane contiguous to and below the Material Universe. (Dadouchos makes Cross in air with Censer, and censes Neophyte in silence with three forward swings.)

Hiero:

Between the Altar and the entrance into the Holy Place, stood the Laver of Brass wherein the priests washed before entering the Tabernacle. It was the symbol of the Waters of Creation. (Stolistes makes cross with water on Neophyte's forehead and sprinkles thrice in silence.) Having made offering at the altar of Burnt Sacrifice, and having been cleansed at the Laver of Brass, the Priest then entered the Holy Place. (Kerux takes Neophyte behind Pillars to North. Stolistes and Dadouchos return to their places. Hiereus takes his stand between the Pillars (Kerux having removed the chair) facing Neophyte. He guards the Path with his Sword and says:)

Hiereus:

Thou canst not pass the Gateway which is between the Pillars, unless thou canst give the Signs and Words of a Neophyte. (Neophyte gives them, and instructed by Kerux, advances to a position between the Pillars. Hiereus returns to his place. Hegemon comes forward, stands East of Pillars, facing Neophyte, and bars the way into the Temple with Sceptre, saying:)

Heg:

Thou canst not enter the Holy Place, unless thou canst give the Sign and Grip of a Zelator. (Neophyte gives them. Kerux resumes his seat after handing Neophyte over to charge of Hegemon. Hegemon leads Neophyte to North, and says:)

Heg:

To the Northern side of the Holy Place, stood the Table of Shew bread. The drawing before you represents its occult meaning. On it twelve loaves were laid as emblems of the Bread of life, and it is an image of the Mystery of the Rose of Creation. The 12 circles are the 12 Signs of the Zodiac, while the Lamp in the centre is symbolic of the

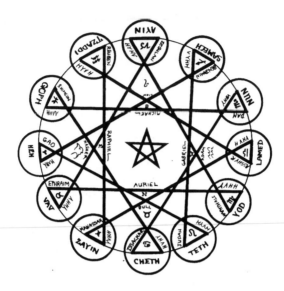

TABLE OF SHEW BREAD

Sun, which is the source of heat and life. The four Triangles whose twelve angles each touch one of the 12 circles are those of Fire, Earth, Air, and Water, and allude to the four Triplicities of the Zodiacal Signs. The Triangle inscribed within each of the 12 circles, alludes to the 3 Decanates, or phases of ten degrees of each sign. On one side of each Triangle is the Permutation of the Divine Name YOD HEH VAU HEH, which is referred to that particular sign, while in the opposite side of it is the name of one of the 12 Tribes which is also attributed to it. Now the 22 sounds and letters of the Hebrew Alphabet are the foundation of all things. Three Mothers, Seven Double and Twelve Singles. The Twelve Single letters are allotted to the 12 directions in space, and those diverge to Infinity, and are in the arms of the Eternal. These Twelve Letters He designed and combined, and formed with them the Twelve Celestial Constellations of the Zodiac. They are over the Universe as a King upon his throne, and they are in the revolution of the year as a King traversing his dominions, and they are in the heart of man as a King in warfare. And the Twelve Loaves are the images of those ideas, and are the outer petals of the Rose; while within are the Four Archangels ruling over the Four Quarters, and the Kerubic emblems of the Lion, Man, Bull and Eagle. Around the great central Lamp which is an image of the Sun, is the Great Mother of Heaven, symbolized by the letter Heh, the first of the Single letters, and by its number 5, the Pentagram, Malkah the Bride, ruling in her Kingdom Malkuth, crowned with a crown of Twelve Stars. These Twelve Circles further represent the 12 Foundations of the Holy City of the Apocalypse while in Christian Symbolism the Sun and the Twelve Signs are referred to Christ and His Twelve Apostles. (Hegemon leads Neophyte to Hiereus and then returns to his place and is seated. Hiereus leads Neophyte to the South, and says:)

Hiereus:

On the Southern side of the Holy Place stood the Seven Branched Candlestick, wherein was burned pure olive oil. It is an image of the Mystery of the Elohim, the Seven Creative Ideas. The symbolic drawing before you represents its occult meaning. The Seven Circles which surround the Heptagram, represent the Seven Planets and the

VOLUME SIX

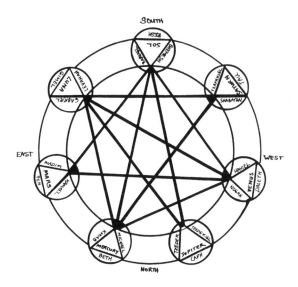

Seven Qabalistic Palaces of Assiah, the Material world - which answer to the Seven Apocalyptic Churches which are in Asia or Assiah - as these again allude to the Seven Lamps before the Throne on another Plane. Within each circle is a triangle to represent the Three Fold Creative Idea operating in all things. On the right hand side of each is the Hebrew Name of the Angel who governs the Planet; on the left side is the Hebrew name of the sphere of the Planet itself; while the Hebrew letter beneath the base is one of the duplicated letters of the Hebrew Alphabet which refer to the Seven Planets. The Seven Double letters of the Hebrew alphabet have each two sounds associated with them, one hard, and one soft. They are called Double, because each letter represents a contrary or permutation, thus: Life and Death; Peace and War; Wisdom and Folly; Riches and Poverty; Grace and Indignity; Fertility and Solitude; Power and Servitude. These Seven letters point out 7 localities: Zenith, Nadir, East, West, North, South, and the Place of Holiness in the midst sustaining all things. The Archetypal Creator designed, produced, combined and formed with them the Planets of the Universe, the Days of the Week, and in Man, the Gate of the Soul. He has loved and blessed the number 7 more than all things under His Throne. The powers of these 7 letters are also shown forth in the 7 Palaces of Assiah and the Seven Stars of that Vision are the 7 Archangels who rule them. (He leads Neophyte to W. of Altar, and returns to his place, and is seated. Hierophant comes to East of Altar, takes censer from Altar, and holding it with chain short, makes cross and three forward swings, replaces it, and says:)

Hiero:

Before the Veil of the Holy of Holies, stood the Altar of Incense, of which this altar is an image. It was of the form of a double cube, thus representing material form as a reflection and duplication of that which is Spiritual. The sides of the Altar, together with the top and bottom, consist of ten squares, thus symbolizing the Ten Sephiroth of which the basal one is Malkuth, the realization of the rest upon the material plane, behind which the others are concealed. For were this double cube raised in the air immediately above your head, you would but see the single square forming the lowest side, the others from their position being concealed from you. Just so, behind the material Universe, lies the concealed form of the Majesty of God. The Altar of Incense was overlaid with Gold to represent the highest degree of purity, but the Altar before you is black to represent the terrestrial Earth. Learn then, to separate the pure from the impure, and refine the Gold of the Spirit from the Black Dragon, the corruptible body. Upon the Cubical Altar, were Fire, Water, and Incense, the Three Mother Letters of the Hebrew Alphabet; Aleph, Mem, and Shin. Mem is silent, Shin is Sibilant, and Aleph is the tongue of a balance between these contraries in equilibrium, reconciling and mediating between them. In this is a great Mystery, very admirable and recondite. The Fire produced the Heavens, the Water, the Earth, and the Air is the reconciler between them. In the year, they bring forth the hot, the cold, and the temperate seasons, and in man, they are imaged in the head, the chest, and the trunk.

I now confer upon you the Mystic Title of Periclinus de Faustis, which signifies that on this Earth you are in a wilderness, far from the Garden of the Happy. And I give you the symbol of ARETZ which is the Hebrew name for Earth, to which the Grade of Zelator is referred. The word Zelator is derived from the ancient Egyptian Zaruator, signifying Searcher of Athor, Goddess of Nature; but others assign to it the meaning of the zealous student whose first duty was to blow the Athanor or fire which heated the Crucible of the Alchemist. (Hierophant resumes seat on Dais: Kerux leads new Zelator to seat in North West.)

Hiero:

Frater Kerux, you have my command to declare that our Frater has been duly admitted to the Grade of Zelator. (Kerux comes to N. W. of Hierophant, faces West, raises Wand and says:)

Kerux:

In the name of ADONAI MELEKH, and by command of the Very Honored Hierophant, hear ye all that I proclaim that Frater (Name) has been duly admitted to the Grade of Zelator, and that he has obtained the Mystic Title of Periclinus (Pericline) de Faustis and the symbol of Aretz. (He returns to his place by E. saluting, and by S. and W.)

Hiero:

In the Zelator Grade, the symbolism of the Tenth Sephirah Malkuth is especially shown, as well as the Tenth Path of the Sepher Yetzirah. Among other Mystic Titles, Malkuth is called SHAAR, the Gate, which by metathesis becomes ASHUR, meaning the number Ten. Also, in Chaldee it is called THRAA, the Gate, which has the same number as the Great Name ADONAI, written in full: Aleph, Daleth, Nun, Yod, which both equal 671 in total numeration. It is also called the Gate of Death, The Gate of Tears, and the Gate of Justice, the Gate of Prayer, and The Gate of the Daughter of the Mighty Ones. It is also called The Gate of the Garden of Eden and the Inferior Mother, and in Christian symbolism, it is connected with the Three Holy Women at the foot of the Cross. The Tenth Path of the Sepher Yetzirah which answereth to Malkuth is called The Resplendent Intelligence, because it exalts above every head and sitteth upon the Throne of Binah. It illuminateth the Splendor of all the Lights, (the Zohar ME-OUROTH) and causeth the current of the Divine Influx to descend from the Prince of Countenances, the Great Archangel Metatron.

Frater (Name) before you can be eligible for advancement to the next Grade of Theoricus you will be required to pass an examination in certain subjects. 1) The names and alchemical symbols of the three principles of nature. 2) The metals attributed in alchemy to the seven planets. 3) The names of the alchemical particular principles, the Sun and Moon of the Philosophers, the Green Lion, the King and Queen. 4) The names and astrological value of the Twelve Houses of Heaven. 5) The names, astrological symbols and values of the aspects of the planets. 6) The meaning of the Querent and Quesited. 7) The four great classes of astrology. 8) The arrangement of the ten Sephiroth, Hebrew and English, in the Tree of

Life. This is especially important. 9) The three pillars of the same. 10) The names of the four orders of Elemental Spirits. 11) The names and descriptions of the Kerubim. 12) The meaning of the Laver and Great Altar of Burnt Offerings of the Sacrifice and of the Qlippoth or Shells. 13) The names of the ten Heavens of Assiah, in Hebrew and English. 14) The names of the four Qabalistic Worlds, Hebrew and English. 15) The names of the twenty two Tarot Trumps and Four Suits. A manuscript on these will be supplied to you. When you are well satisfied that you are well informed on these, notify the Officer in charge.

CLOSING

Hiero:

Fratres and Sorores, assist me to close this Temple in the Grade of Zelator. (All rise) Frater Kerux, see that the Temple is properly guarded.

Kerux:

(On inner side of the door, knocks. Sentinel knocks.) Very Honored Hierophant, the Temple is properly guarded.

Hiero:

Let us adore the Lord and King of Earth. (All face East.) ADONAI HA-ARETZ, ADONAI MELEKH, Blessed be Thy Name unto the countless ages. Amen. (Gives Sign. All give sign and face as usual. Hierophant leaves his Throne and passes to the North, standing before the Tablet of the North, Hiereus stands on right of Hiero; Hegemon left; Kerux behind Hierophant; Stolistes behind Hiereus, Dadouchos behind Hegemon.)

Hiero:

Let us rehearse the prayer of the Earth Spirits. O Invisible King, Who, taking the Earth for Foundation, didst hollow its depths to fill them with Thy Almighty Power. Thou Whose Name shaketh the Arches of the World, Thou who causest the Seven Metals to flow in the veins of the rocks, King of the Seven Lights, Rewarder of the subterranean Workers, lead us into the desirable Air and into the Realm of Splendour. We watch and we labor unceasingly, we seek and we hope, by the twelve stones of the Holy City, by the buried Talismans, by the Axis of the Loadstone which passes through the centre of the Earth. O Lord, O Lord, O Lord! Have pity upon those who suffer. Expand our hearts, unbind and upraise our minds, enlarge our natures.

O Stability and Motion! O Darkness veiled in Brilliance! O Day clothed in Night! O Master who never dost withhold the wages of Thy Workmen! O Silver Whiteness - O Golden Splendour! O Crown of Living and Harmonious Diamond! Thou who wearest the Heavens on Thy Finger like a ring of Sapphire! Thou Who hidest beneath the Earth in the Kingdom of Gems, the marvellous Seed of the Stars! Live, reign and be Thou the Eternal Dispenser of the Treasures whereof Thou hast made us the Guardians.

Depart ye in peace unto your abodes and habitations. May the blessing of Adonai ha-Aretz be upon you. (Makes Banishing Pentagram of Earth.) Be there peace between us and you, and be ye ready to come when ye are called. (All return to their places and face as usual.)

In the Name of ADONAI MELEKH, I declare this Temple closed in the Grade of Zelator.

Hiero:

(Knocks 4, 3, 3)

Hiereus:

(Knocks 4, 3, 3)

Heg:

(Knocks 4, 3, 3)
(Candidate is led out by Hegemon.)

THEORICUS GRADE 2 - 9

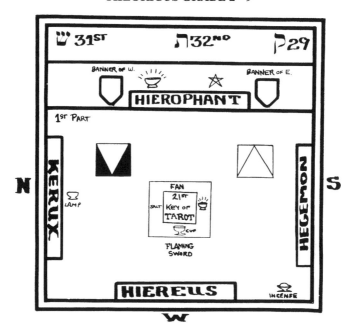

REQUIREMENTS

In the East - Pentacle, Banner of East and West. On the Altar -Fan, Lamp, Cup, Salt, surrounding the Altar diagram of the Universe.

For the Zelator - Hoodwink, Cubical Cross (1st point); Caduceus (2nd point).

OPENING

(Temple arranged as in diagram for the 32nd Path. Members assembled and clothed. Lamp on Altar lighted. Members not taking office rise at the words. Let us adore the Lord and King of Air and face East, remaining so to the end of the Invocation. They do the same at the closing, but otherwise do not move from their places.)

Hiero:

(Knocks) Fratres and Sorores of the Order of the Golden Dawn in the Outer, assist me to open the Temple in the grade of Theoricus. Frater Kerux, see that the Temple is properly guarded. (Done)

Kerux:

Very Honored Hierophant, the Temple is properly guarded.

Hiero:

Honored Hiereus, see that none below the Grade of Theoricus is present.

Hiereus:

Fratres and Sorores give the signs of Theoricus (Done). Very Honored Hierophant all present have attained the Grade of Theoricus. (Saluting)

Hiero:

Honored Hegemon, to what particular element is this Grade attributed?

Heg:

To the Element of Air.

Hiero:

Honored Hiereus, to what Planet does this Grade especially refer?

Hiereus:

To the Moon.

Hiero:

What Path is attributed to this Grade, Honored Hegemon?

Heg:

The 32nd Path of Tau.

Hiero:

Honored Hiereus, to what does it allude?

Hiereus:

To the Universe as composed of the Four Elements, to the Kerubim, to the Qlippoth, the Astral Plane and the reflection of the sphere of Saturn.

Hiero:

(All rise and face East) Let us adore the Lord and King of Air. (Making invoking Pentagram and Circle with Sceptre towards East) SHADDAI EL CHAI, Almighty and Everlasting be Thy Name, ever magnified in the Life of All. Amen (All salute). (Hierophant remains facing East. Hiereus advances to Altar and halts. Hegemon and Kerux advance to East and stand on the right and left rear of the Hierophant respectively and outside the Pillars. All face East).

Hiero:

(Making Invoking Pentagrams with his Sceptre in the Air in front of the Tablet of Air). And Elohim said Let us make Adam in our Image, after our likeness, and let them have dominion over the fowl of the Air. In the Name of YOD HEH VAU HEH, and in the Names of SH ADDAI EL CHAI, Spirits of Air adore your Creator. (Taking Pentacle from before the Tablet, and making therewith the sign Aquarius in the air before it) In the Name of Raphael the Great Archangel of Air and in the Sign of the head of the Man, Spirits of Air adore your Creator. (Making the Sign of the Cross with the Pentacle). In the Names and letters of the Great Eastern Quadrangle revealed unto Enoch by the Angel Ave, Spirits of Air, adore your Creator. (Holding Pentacle on high). In the three Great Secret names of God borne on the Banners of the East, ORO IBAH AOZPI Spirits of Air, adore your Creator. (Replaces pentacle, all return to places.)

Hiero:

In the Name of SHADDAI EL CHAI, I declare the Temple opened in the Grade of Theoricus.

Hiero:

(Knock 3, 3, 3)

Hiereus:

(Knock 3, 3, 3)

Heg:

(Knock 3, 3, 3. Temple is darkened)

Hiero:

Fratres and Sorores, our Frater (Soror) XYZ having made such progress in the paths of Occult Science as has enabled him (her) to pass the examination in the requisite knowledge, is now eligible for advancement to the Grade of Theoricus, and I have duly received a dispensation from the Great Honored Chiefs of the Second Order to advance him in due form. Honored Hegemon, superintend the preparation of the Zelator and give the customary alarm. (Kerux places fan by Hierophant, lamp by Hegemon. Cup by Hiereus, salt by Kerux, at the right hand of the Officers seats, facing the same, Hegemon rises, salutes Hierophant, quits Temple, and sees that Zelator is prepared as follows - wearing sash of Zelator, hoodwinked and with solid cubical Greek Cross as shown, formed of 22 squares with letters of Hebrew alphabet written thereon in right hand. Hegemon takes Zelator by left hand and gives an alarm of 9 Knocks saying:)

Heg:

Quit thou the material and seek the spiritual. (Kerux thereupon opens door and admits them).

Hiero:

Conduct the Zelator to the East. (Done, and Zelator placed before the Pillars, Kerux at Zelator's left hand, Hegemon at his right. Kerux takes cubical cross from Zelator.)

Hiero:

(To Zelator) Give me the Step, Sign, and Grip or Token, Grand Word, Mystic number and Pass word formed therefrom of the Grade of Zelator. (Step left foot 6 inches right foot 6 inches. Sign arm upward 45 degrees. General Grip of first Order. Grand Word ADONAI HA-ARETZ. The number of the Pass Word is 55, and the letters are Nun Heh.) (Done. Zelator prompted if necessary.)

Hiero:

Give me also the mystic title and symbol which you received in that Grade. (Pereclinus de Faustis, Aretz).

Hiero:

Frater (Soror) do you solemnly pledge yourself to maintain the same strict secrecy regarding the mysteries of the 32nd Path and of the Grade of Theoricus which you have already sworn to maintain respecting those of the preceding Grades?

Zel:

I do. (Kerux hands cubical cross to Candidate).

Hiero:

Then you will stretch your right hand holding the cubical cross towards Heaven and say—I swear by the Firmament of Heaven. (Done. Candidate repeating words.)

Hiero:

Let the hoodwink be removed. (Done, when the Zelator discovers for the first time that the Temple is in partial darkness. Hegemon returns to his place in South leaving Kerux in charge of Zelator. Kerux places cubical cross again in right hand of Zelator.)

Hiero:

Stretch forth your right hand holding the cubical cross toward the East in the position of the Zelator sign, saying: Let the Powers of Air witness my pledge. (Done).

RITUAL OF 32nd PATH

Hiero:

(Knocks) Facing you are the Portals of the 31st, 32nd and 29th Paths, leading from the Grade of Zelator to the three other Grades which are beyond. The only Path open to you, however, is the 32nd which leads to the Grade of Theoricus, and which you must traverse before arriving at that Degree. Take in your right hand the Cubical Cross, and in your left hand the Banner of Light (giving him Banner of East) and follow your guide, Anubis the Guardian, who leads you from the material to the Spiritual.

Kerux:

Anubis the Guardian said unto the Aspirant, Let us enter the Presence of the Lords of Truth. Arise and follow me. (Kerux leads Zelator between the columns, turns to the right and circumambulates the hall once.)

Hiereus:

(As they are going round the first time). The Sphinx of Egypt spake and said, I am the synthesis of the Elemental Forces, I am also the symbol of Man, I am Life and I am Death, I am the Child of the Night of Time. (As Kerux and Zelator approach East, the Hierophant steps from between the Pillars and bars the passage.)

Hiero:

(With Banner of West in left hand and fan in right). The Priest with the mask of Osiris spake and said Thou canst not pass the Gate of the Eastern heaven, unless thou canst tell me my Name.

Kerux:

(For Candidate). Thou art NU the Goddess of the Firmament of Air, Thou art HORMAKHU Lord of the Eastern Sun.

Hiero:

In what signs and symbols do ye come?

Kerux:

In the letter Aleph, in the Banner of Light, and the symbol of Equated Forces.

Hiero:

(Falling back and signing the Aquarius Kerub before Zelator with fan). In the Sign of the Man, Child of Air, thou art purified, pass thou on. (Gives Banner of West to Kerux, who hands it to Hegemon as he passes him. Kerux and Zelator circumambulate the Temple a second time, following the course of the Sun.)

Hiereus:

(As they are going round the second time.) I am Osiris the Soul in Twin aspect, united to the higher by purification; perfected in suffering; glorified through trial, I have come where the Great Gods are through the Power of the Mighty Name.

Heg:

(Barring the way in south with red lamp in right hand and Banner of West in left) The Priest with the Mask of the Lion spake and said Thou canst not pass the Gate of the Southern Heaven unless thou canst tell me my Name.

Kerux:

(For Candidate). MAU, the Lion very powerful, Lord of Fire is thy name; thou art RA, the Sun in his strength.

Heg:

In what signs and symbols do ye come?

Kerux:

In the Letter Shin, in the Banner of the East, and the symbol of the Cubical Cross.

Heg:

(Falling back and signing the Leo Kerub before Zelator with Lamp.) In the sign of the Lion, Child of Fire, thou art purified, pass thou on. (Hegemon takes the place of Kerux, who returns to his seat in North, Hegemon leads Zelator round the Temple a third time giving the Banner of the West to Hiereus, as he passes.)

Hiereus:

(As they are going round the third time.) I have passed through the Gates of the Firmament, give me your hands for I am made as ye. Hail unto ye, ye Lords of Truth, for ye are the formers of the Soul.

Hiereus:

(Barring the way in West with cup of Water in right hand and Banner of West in left.) The Priest with the Mask of the Eagle spake and said Thou canst not pass the Gate of the Western heaven, unless thou canst tell me my Name.

Heg:

(For Candidate) HEKA, Mistress of HESAR, Ruler of Water is thy name; thou art TOUM, the setting Sun.

Hiereus:

In what signs and symbols do ye come?

Heg:

In the letter Mayim, in the Banner of Light, and the symbol of the Twenty two letters

Hiereus:

(Falling back and signing the Eagle Kerub before Zelator with cup of Water.) In the sign of the Eagle, Child of Water, thou art purified, pass thou on. (Giving Banner of West to Hegemon who leaves it with the Kerux as he passes him. Hegemon leads Candidate round the Temple for fourth time.)

Hiereus:

(As they go round) O Lord of the Universe, Thou art above all things; and before Thee the Shadows of Night roll back and the Darkness hasteneth away.

Kerux:

(Barring the way in the North with plate of salt in right hand and Banner of West in left.) The Priest with the mask of the Ox spake and said: Thou canst not pass the Gate of the Northern Heaven, unless thou canst tell me my Name.

Heg:

(For Candidate) SATEM in the abode of SHU, the Bull of Earth is thy name; thou art KHEPHRA, the Sun at Night.

Kerux:

In what signs and symbols do ye come?

Heg:

In the Letters Aleph, Mem and Shin; and in the symbols of the Banner and Cross

Kerux:

(Falling back and signing the Taurus Kerub before Zelator with plate of salt.) In the Sign of the head of the Ox, Child of the elements, thou art purified, pass thou on. (Hegemon and Kerux conduct Candidate to the foot of the Pillars. Hierophant takes Banners and places them in their bases. Hegemon and Kerux turn up the lights so as to make the Temple as light as usual, and return to their respective places. Fan, Lamp, Cup, and Salt are replaced by them on the Altar.)

Hiero:

(Taking Cubical Cross from Candidate) The Cubical Cross is a fitting emblem of the equilibriated and balanced forces of the Elements. It is composed of 22 squares externally thus referring to the 22 Hebrew letters which are placed thereon. Twenty-two are the letters of the Eternal Voice; in the Vault of Heaven, in the depth of the Earth, in the Abyss of Water, in the all-presence of Fire; Heaven cannot speak their fulness, Earth cannot utter it. Yet hath the Creator bound them in all things. He hath mingled them through Water. He hath whirled them aloft in Fire; He hath sealed them in the air of Heaven; He hath distributed them through the Planets; He hath assigned unto them the 12 Constellations of the zodiac. (Places Cubical Cross aside.) The Thirty-second Path of the Sepher Yetzirah which answereth unto the Letter Tau is called the Administrative Intelligence and it is so called because it directeth and associateth in all their operations the Seven Planets, even all of them in their own due courses. To it therefore, is attributed the due knowledge of the Seven abodes of Assiah, the Material World, which are symbolized in the Apocalypse by the Seven Churches. It refers to the Universe as composed of the Four elements; to the Kerubim; to the Qlippoth, and to the Astral Plane. It is the Reflection of the Sphere of Saturn. It represents the connecting and binding link between the Material and Formative worlds, Assiah and Yetzirah, and necessarily passes through the Astral Plane, the abode of the elementals, the Qlippoth, and the Shells of the Dead. It is the rending of the Veil of the Tabernacle whereon the Kerubim and the Palm Trees were depicted; it is the passing of the Gate of Eden. (Leads Zelator to the West of the Altar.) These ideas are symbolically resumed in the representation of the twenty-first Key of the Tarot before you. Within the oval formed of the 72 circles is a female figure, nude save for a scarf which floats around her. She is crowned with the lunar crescent of Isis, and holds in each hand a wand, her legs form a cross. She is the Bride of the Apocalypse, the Qabalistic Queen of the Canticles, the Egyptian Isis of Nature now shown partly unveiled, the Great Feminine Kerubic Angel Sandalphon on the left hand of the Mercy Seat of the Ark. The two wands are the directing forces of the Positive and Negative currents. The Seven pointed Star or Heptagram alludes to the Seven Palaces of Assiah, the crossed legs to the Symbol of the Four Letters of the Name. The surmounting Crescent receives the Influences alike of Geburah and of Gedulah. She is the synthesis of the 32nd Path uniting Malkuth with Yesod. The oval of 72 small circles is the Schem-hamphorasch, or the 72 fold Name of the Deity. The 12 larger circles form the Zodiac. At the angles are the four Kerubim, which are the vivified Powers of the Letters of the Name Tetragrammaton operating in the elements, through which you have just symbolically passed in the preceding ceremony.

The Fan, Lamp, Cup and Salt represent the four elements themselves, whose inhabitants are the Sylphs, Salamanders, Undines and Gnomes. Be thou therefore prompt and active as the sylphs, but avoid frivolity and caprice; be energetic and strong like the salamanders but avoid irritability and ferocity; be flexible and attentive to images like the undines, but avoid idleness and changeability; be laborious and patient like the gnomes but avoid grossness and avarice. So shalt thou gradually develop the powers of thy soul, and fit thyself to command the Spirits of the elements.

The Altar as in the preceding degrees represents the Material universe, and on its right is the Garden of Eden, symbolised by the Station of the Hegemon, and on its left is Gehenna the abode of the Shells symbolized by the Tablet of the Kerux. These Officers will now explain these drawings. (Hierophant returns to his place and Hegemon leads Candidate to his Tablet.)

Heg:

The drawing before you shows in part the Occult symbolism of the Garden of Eden and the Holy City of the Apocalypse. The Outer circle is the enclosing Paradisiacal Wall guarded by the Kerubim and the Flame, and the Seven Squares are the Seven Mansions thereof, or the Seven Spheres, wherein Tetragrammaton Elohim planted every Tree which is pleasant and good for food symbolized by the Palm Trees wrought upon the Veil of the Tabernacle and the Door of the Holy of Holies in the Temple. But in the midst is the Tree of Life, the Throne of God, and the Lamb. Twelve are the foundations and twelve are the Gates, shown by the twelve entrances in the drawing. The four streams rising from one central fountain are the rivers of Eden, referring to the four elements proceeding from the Omnipresent Spirit. (Kerux leads Candidate to his Tablet.)

Kerux:

The drawing before you represents the Seven Infernal Mansions and the four Seas. The first circle represents the Waters of Tears; the second circle represents the Waters of Creation; the third circle represents the Waters of Ocean; and the fourth circle represents the False Sea. In the inner circles are on the right hand the seven Earths, which are: 1) Aretz 2) Adamah 3) Gia 4) Neschiah 5) Tziah 6) Arega and 7) Thebel or Cheled. On the left hand are the seven Infernal Habitations which are: 1) Sheol 2) Abaddon 3) Titahion 4) Bar Schauheth 5) Tzelmoth 6) Shaari Moth and 7) Gehinnon.

Hiero:

I have much pleasure in conferring upon you the title of Lord (Lady) of the 32nd Path. You will now quit the Temple for a short time, and on your return the ceremony of your reception in the Grade of Theoricus will be proceeded with.

CEREMONY OF THEORICUS

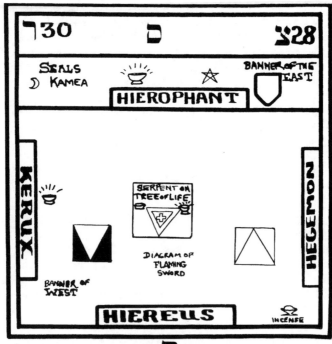

Hiero:

Frater Kerux, you have my command to instruct the Zelator in the proper alarm, and to present him with the necessary admission badge. Honored Hegemon, guard the Portal and admit them on giving the proper alarm. (Kerux presents Candidate with necessary admission badge, Caduceus of Hermes and instructs him to give an alarm of 9 Knocks. Hegemon opens door and admits them.)

Hiero:

(To Zelator) Frater (Soror) XYZ as in the Zelator Grade there were given the symbolical representations of the Tree of Knowledge of Good and Evil, of the Garden of Eden and of the Holy Place; so in the Grade of Theoricus the Sanctum Sanctorum with the Ark and Kerubim is shown, as well as the Garden of Eden with which it coincides, while in the 32nd Path leading hereunto, through which you have just now symbolically passed, the Kerubic Guardians are represented and the Palm Trees or Trees of Progression in the Garden of Eden. Honored Hegemon, conduct the Zelator to the West, and place him thus before the Portal of the 32nd Path by which he has symbolically entered. (Done.) (Zelator faces to East, Kerux returns to his place.)

Hiereus:

By what symbol dost thou enter herein?

Heg:

By the peculiar emblem of the Kerux, which is the Caduceus of Hermes.

Hiereus:

The Tree of Life and the Three Mother Letters are the keys wherewith to unlock the meaning of the Caduceus of Hermes. The upper part of the Wand rests on KETHER and the Wings stretch out unto CHOKMAH and BINAH, the three Supernal Sephiroth. The lower seven are embraced by the Serpents, whose heads fall upon CHESED and GEBURAH. They are the twin Serpents of Egypt, and the currents of astral light. Furthermore, the wings and the top of the wand form the letter Shin, the symbol of fire. The heads and upper halves of the serpents form Aleph, the symbol of Air, while their tails enclose Mem the symbol of Water. The Fire above, the Waters of Creation below', and the Air symbol vibrating between them. (Hierophant leaves his throne and comes to the West of Altar. Hegemon conducts Candidate to him and then returns to his place in the south.)

Hiero:

The symbols before you represent alike the Garden of Eden and the Holy of Holies. Before you stands the Tree of Life formed of the Sephiroth and their connecting Paths. Into its complete symbolism it is impossible here to enter, for it is the key of all things, when rightly understood. Upon each Sephira are written in Hebrew letters its Name, the Divine names ruling it, and those of the Angels and Archangels attributed to it. The connecting Paths are twenty two in number, and are distinguished by the twenty two letters of the Hebrew alphabet, making with the Ten Sephiroth themselves, the thirty two Paths of Wisdom of the Sepher Yetzirah. The course of the Hebrew letters as placed on the Paths forms, as you see, the symbol of the Serpent of Wisdom; while the natural succession of the Sephiroth forms the flaming Sword, and the course of the Lightning Flash, as shown in the drawing. The cross within the triangle, apex downwards placed upon the Altar at the base of the Tree of Life, refers to the Four Rivers of Paradise, while the angles of the Triangle refer to the Three Sephiroth NETZACH, HOD and YESOD. The two Pillars right and left of the Tree are the symbols of Active and Passive, Male and Female, Adam and Eve. They also allude to the Pillars of Fire and Cloud which guided the Israelites in the Wilderness, and the Hot and Moist natures are further marked by the Red Lamp and the Cup of Water. The Pillars further represent the two Kerubim of the Ark; the right Metatron, Male; the left Sandalphon Female. Above them ever burn the lamps of their Spiritual Essence, the Higher Life of which they are partakers in the Eternal Uncreated One. (Giving Sign of Theoricus.)

Glory be unto Thee, Lord of the Land of Life, for thy Splendor filleth the Universe.

The Grade of Theoricus is referred to Yesod, as the Grade of Zelator is to Malkuth. The Path between them is assigned to the Letter Tau, whose Portal you now see in the West and through which you have just symbolically passed. To this Grade as to those preceding it, certain Secret Signs, and Tokens are attributed. They consist of a sign, grip or token. Grand Word, Mystic Number and Pass Word formed therefrom. The sign is thus given - Raise the arms level with the shoulders, bend the elbows, arms upwards and hands bent outwards, as if supporting a weight. It represents you in the Path of Yesod, supporting the Pillars of Mercy and Severity; it is the sign of the classical Atlas, supporting the Universe upon his shoulders, whom Hercules had to emulate. It is the Isis of Nature supporting the Heavens. The grip is the general grip of the First Order. The Grand Word is a name of seven letters which means the Vast and Mighty One - SH ADDAI EL CHAI. The mystic number is 45 and from it is formed the Pass Word which is Mem, Heh, Mah. It should be lettered separately when given. Unto this Grade and unto the Sephira Yesod the ninth Path of the Sepher Yetzirah is referred. It is called the Pure or clear Intelligence, and it is so called because it purifieth and maketh clear the Sephiroth, proveth and amendeth the forming of their representation and disposeth their unities or Harmonies wherein they combine without mutilation or division. The distinguishing badge of the Grade which you will now be entitled to wear, is the sash of a Zelator with the addition of a white cross above the triangle and the numbers 2 and 9 within a circle and a square respectively left and right of its summit; and beneath the triangle the number 32 between two parallel narrow white lines. The meaning of the Tablet of Earth was explained to you in the preceding Grade. (Hierophant proceeds to East. Hegemon comes forward and guides Candidate thither.)

Hiero:

The three Portals facing you are the Gates of the Paths leading from the Grade. That on the right connects it with the Grade of Philosophus, that on the left with the Grade of Practicus, while the central one leads to the higher. This Grade is especially referred to the element of Air, and therefore the great Watch Tower or Terrestrial Tablet of the East forms one of its principal emblems. It is known as the first or Great Eastern Quadrangle or Tablet of Air, and it is one of the four great Tablets delivered unto Enoch by the Great Angel Ave. From it are drawn the three Holy Secret Names of God ORO IBAH AOZPI which are borne upon the Banners of the East; and the numberless Divine and Angelic names which appertain unto the Element of Air. To the Moon also is this Grade related. Its Kamea or Mystical square is formed of 81 squares containing the numbers from 1 to 81 arranged so as to show the same sum each way. Its ruling numbers are 9, 81, 369 and 3321. This Tablet (indicating it) shows the mystical Seals and Names drawn from the Kamea of the Moon. The Seals are formed from lines drawn to and from certain numbers in the square. The name answering to 9 is Hod meaning Glory; that answering to 81 is

Elim the plural of the Divine Name El, that answering to 369 is Chasmodai, the Spirit of the Moon. The other names are those of the Intelligences and Spirits of the Moon. On this Tablet are shown the meanings of the Lunar symbol when inscribed upon the Tree of Life. Thus its crescent in increase represents the side of Mercy; and its crescent in decrease the side of Severity; while at full it reflects the Sun of Tiphareth. (Hierophant resumes his seat. Hegemon conducts Candidate to Hiereus.)

Hiereus:

The Tablet before you shows the duplicated form of the alchemic Sephiroth. In the first the Metallic root is in Kether, Lead in Chokmah, Tin in Binah, Silver in Chesed, Gold in Geburah, Iron in Tiphareth, Netzach and Hod are the places of Hermaphroditical Brass, Yesod is Mercury and Malkuth is the Medicine of Metals. In the second form the Mercury, Sulphur and Salt are referred to the three Supernal Sephiroth, and the Metals to the seven lower but in a rather different order. For in all things as Supernal so Terrestrial, is the Tree of Life to be found, whether it be in animal, in vegetable or in mineral natures. (Hegemon leads Candidate to his own Tablet in South.)

Heg:

This Tablet shows you the Geometrical lineal Figures attributed to the Planets. They are thus referred: The Number 3 and the Triangle to Saturn. The Number 4 and the Square to Jupiter. The Number 5 and the Pentagram to Mars. The Number 6 and the Hexagram to the Sun. The Number 7 and the Heptagram to Venus. The Number 8 and the Octagram to Mercury. The Number 9 and the Enneagram to the Moon. Of these the heptagram and the octagram can be traced in two modes and the enneagram in three; the first in each case being most consonant to the nature of the Planet. (Hegemon resumes his seat. Kerux comes forward and conducts the Candidate to his Tablet in the North.)

Kerux:

Before you are represented the sixteen Figures of Geomancy, which are formed from all the combinations of single and double points in 4 lines which can possibly occur. Two are attributed to each of the seven Planets, and the remaining two to Caput and Cauda Draconis. Some of them are also attributed to Fire, others to Air, others to Earth and Water. They are also classed under the signs of the Zodiac. (Kerux conducts Candidate to foot of Hierophant's throne.)

Hiero:

I now congratulate you upon having attained to the Grade of Theoricus, and in recognition thereof I confer upon you the Mystic title of Poraios de Rejectis which means Brought from among the Rejected Ones and I give you the symbol of Ruach which is the Hebrew name for Air. Frater Kerux (Knocks) you have my command to declare that the Zelator has been duly advanced to the Grade of Theoricus.

Kerux:

In the Name of SHADDAI EL CHAI, and by command of the Very Honored Hierophant, hear ye all that I proclaim that our Frater (Soror) XYZ having made sufficient progress in the study of Occult sciences, has been duly advanced to the Grade of Theoricus, Lord (Lady) of the 32nd Path and that he (she) has received the Mystic title of Poraios dc Rejectis (Poraia) and the symbol of Ruach. Take your seat in the West.

Hiero:

Frater (Soror) XYZ before you are eligible for advancement to the next higher Grade you must be perfect in certain subjects, presented in a standard Knowledge Lecture. When you are perfect you must signify the same by letter to the Scribe as in the preceding Grades.

CLOSING

Hiero:

(Knocks) Fratres and Sorores assist me to close the Temple in the Grade of Theoricus. Frater Kerux, see that the Temple is properly guarded. (Done.)

Kerux:

(Knocks) Very Honored Hierophant, the Temple is properly guarded.

Hiero:

(Knocks) Let us adore the Lord and King of Air. (All face East.)

ADORATION

SHADDAI EL CHAI, Almighty and Everliving, Blessed be Thy Name unto the Countless Ages. Amen. (All salute) (Officers form towards East as in Opening.) Let us rehearse the Prayer of the Sylphs or Air Spirits.

Spirit of Light, Spirit of wisdom whose breath giveth forth and withdraweth the form of all living things; Thou, before whom the Life of Beings is but a shadow which changeth, and a vapor which passeth, Thou who mountest upon the clouds, and who walketh upon the wings of the wind, Thou who breathest forth Thy Breath, and endless Space is peopled, Thou who drawest in Thy breath and all that cometh from Thee returneth unto Thee; ceaseless Movement in Eternal Stability - Be Thou eternally blessed.

We praise Thee and we bless Thee in the changing Empire of created Light, of Shades, of reflections, and of Images and we aspire without cessation unto Thy immutable and imperishable brilliance. Let the Ray of Thine Intelligence and the warmth of Thy Love penetrate even unto us, then that which is volatile shall be fixed, the shadow shall be a body, the Spirit of Air shall be a soul, the dream shall be a thought. And no longer shall we be swept away by the Tempest, but we shall hold the bridles of the Winged Steeds of Dawn, and we shall direct the course of the Evening Breeze to fly before Thee. O Spirit of Spirits, O Eternal Soul of Souls, O imperishable breath of Life, O Creative Sigh, O mouth which breathest forth and withdrawest the Life of all Beings in the flux and Reflux of thine Eternal Word which is the Divine Ocean of Movement and of Truth. Amen.

(Hierophant makes with his sceptre the banishing Pentagrams, in the air in front of the Tablet.)

Hiero:

Depart ye in peace unto your abodes and habitations. May the blessing of YOD HEH VOU HEH rest with you. Be there peace between us and you, and be ye ready to come when you are called. (Knock) (All salute and return to their places.) In the name of SH ADDAI EL CHAI, I declare this Temple closed in the Grade of Theoricus. (Knocks 3, 3, 3.)

Hiereus:

Repeats Knocks.

Heg:

Repeats Knocks.

GRADE OF PRACTICUS 3 - 8

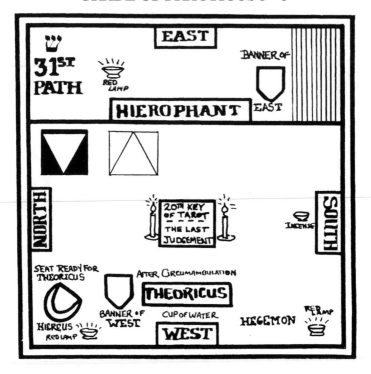

OPENING

(Arrange the Temple for the 31st Path.
Members are assembled and Robed.)

Hiero:

(Knocks) Fratres and Sorores of the Order of the Golden Dawn in the Outer, assist me to open this Temple in the Grade of Practicus. Honored Hegemon, see that the Temple is properly guarded. (This is done.)

Heg:

Very Honored Hierophant, the Temple is properly guarded.

Hiero:

Honored Hiereus, see that none below the Grade of Practicus is present.

Hiereus:

Fratres and Sorores give the Sign of Practicus. (Done) Very Honored Hierophant all present have attained the Grade. (Saluting.)

Hiero:

Honored Hegemon, to what particular Element is this Grade attributed?

Heg:

To the Element of Water.

Hiero:

Honored Hiereus, to what Planet does this Grade especially refer?

Hiereus:

To the Planet Mercury.

Hiero:

Honored Hegemon, what Paths are attached to this Grade?

Heg:

The 31st and 30th Paths of Shin and Resh.

Hiero:

Honored Hiereus to what does the 31st Path refer?

Hiereus:

To the reflection of the Sphere of Fire.

Hiero:

Honored Hegemon, to what does the 30th Path allude?

Heg:

To the reflection of the Sphere of the Sun. (Hierophant gives one (Knock) and all rise and face East.)

Hiero:

(Knocks) Let us adore the Lord and King of Water.
ELOHIM TZABAOTH, Elohim of Hosts, Glory be unto the RUACH ELOHIM who moved upon the face of the Waters of Creation. Amen (All salute. Hierophant quits his throne and proceeds to the West. Gives one (Knock). All face West. Standing before the Tablet of Water, he makes with his Sceptre the invoking circle and Pentagrams before it in the Air.)

Hiero:

And the Elohim said. Let us make Adam in our Image, after our Likeness, and let them have dominion over the Fish of the Sea. In the Name of EL, Strong and Powerful, and in the name of Elohim Tzabaoth, Spirits of Water adore your Creator. (Taking Cup of Water from before Tablet and making therewith the Sign of the Eagle in the Air before it.) In the Name of Gabriel, the Great Archangel of Water, and in the Sign of the Eagle, Spirits of Water adore your Creator. (Making with Cup of Water the Cross) In the Names and Letters of the Great Western Quadrangle revealed unto Enoch by the Angel Ave, Spirits of Water adore your Creator. (Holding Cup on high.) In the three Great Secret Names of God, borne on the Banners of the West, EMPEH ARSOL GAIOL, Spirits of Water adore your Creator. In the Name of Ra AGIOSEL Great King of the West. Spirits of Water adore your Creator. (Replaces Cup and returns to place. All face as usual.)

Hiero:

In the Name of Elohim Tzabaoth I declare this Temple opened in the Grade of Practicus.

Hiero:

(Knocks 1,3, 1,3)

Hiereus:

(Knocks 1, 3, 1, 3)

Heg:

(Knocks 1,3, 1,3) (Temple arranged for Ritual of 31 st Path. The Temple is darkened).

THE RITUAL OF THE 31st PATH

Hiero:

Fratres and Sorores our Frater (Soror) XYZ having made such progress in the Path of Occult Science as has enabled him (her) to pass the Examinations in the requisite knowledge is now eligible for advancement to the Grade of Practicus, and I have duly received a dispensation from the Greatly Honored Chiefs of the Second Order, to advance him in due form. Honored Hegemon, superintend the preparation of the Theoricus and give the customary alarm. (Hegemon rises, salutes the Hierophant, quits the Temple and sees the Theoricus is thus prepared. Wearing sash of Theoricus, hoodwink and with the solid triangular pyramid formed of 4 elements in right hand, Hegemon takes Theoricus by left hand and gives an alarm of 8 Knocks.)

Heg:

His throne was like a fiery Flame, and the wheels as burning Fire. (Hiereus opens door and admits them, returns to his place. Hegemon conducts Theoricus to the North West facing the seat of Hiereus. Hegemon takes pyramid.)

Hiereus:

Give me the Sign, Grip or Token, Grand Word, Mystic Number and Pass Word of the Grade of Theoricus. (Done) (Word SHADDAI EL CHAI, No. 45, Pass Word Mah.)

Hiereus:

Give me also the Mystic title and symbol which you received in that Grade. (Done - Poraios de Rejectus. Ruach.)

Hiereus:

Frater XYZ do you solemnly pledge yourself to maintain the same strict secrecy regarding the Mysteries of the 31 st and 30th Paths, and of the Grade of Practicus which you have sworn to maintain respecting those of the preceding Grades?

Theor:

I do.

Hiereus:

Then you will stretch forth your hands in the position of the saluting sign of a Neophyte and say - I swear by the Abyss of the Waters. (Done) (The Theoricus discovers that the Temple is darkened. Hegemon places in his hand the Cup of Water from before the Tablet.)

Hiereus:

Sprinkle with your hand a few drops of Water towards the Tablet of Water in the West and say. Let the Powers of Water witness my Pledge. (Done) (Theoricus repeating words. Hegemon replaces Cup.)

Hiereus:

Conduct the Theoricus to the East and place him before the Mystic Pillars.

Hiero:

(Knocks) Before you are the Portals of the 31st, 32nd and 29th Paths. Of these as you already know, the central one leads from the Zelator Grade to the Theoricus Grade. The one on the left hand now open to you is the 31st which leads from the Grade of Zelator to the Grade of Practicus. Take in your right hand the Pyramid of Flame and follow your Guide AXIOKERSA the KABIR who leads you through the Path of Fire. (Hegemon leads the Theoricus between the Pillars turns to right and circumambulates hall once. Hierophant as they approach, takes Red Lamp in his hand and rises. Hegemon and Theoricus halt before him.)

Hiero:

Axieros the First Kabir spake to Kasmillos the Candidate and said I am the Apex of the Triangle of Flame. I am the Solar Fire pouring forth its beams upon the lower world. Life giving. Light producing. By what symbol dost thou seek to pass by?

Heg:

By the Symbol of the Pyramid of Flame.

Hiero:

Hear thou the Voice of Axieros the First Kabir. The Mind of the Father whirled forth in re-echoing roar, comprehending by invincible Will Ideas omniform, which flying forth from that one fountain issued; for the Father alike was the Will and the End; (by which yet are they connected with the Father, according to alternating Life, through varying vehicles). But they were divided asunder, being by Intellectual Fire distributed unto other Intellectuals. For the King of all previously placed before the polymorphous world, a type intellectual, incorruptible, the imprint of whose form is sent forth through the World, by w hich the Universe shone forth decked with ideas all various of which the foundation is one, One and Alone. From this the others rush forth distributed and separated through the various bodies of the Universe, and are borne in swarms through its vast Abysses, ever whirling forth in illimitable radiation. They are Intellectual Conceptions from the Paternal Fountain, partaking abundantly the brilliance of fire in the culmination of unresting Time. But the primary self-perfect fountain of the Father poured forth these primogenial Ideas. These being many ascend flashingly into the shining Worlds, and in them are contained the three Supernals. Because it is the Operator, because it is the Giver of Life-bearing Fire; because it filleth the Life producing bosom of Hecate; and it instilleth into the Synoches the enlivening strength of Fire, embued with mighty power. The Creator of all formed the World, and there w as a certain mass of fire and all these self-operating He produced, so that the Kosmic body might be completely conformed, so that the Kosmos might be manifest and not appear membraneous. And he fixed a vast multitude of inwandering Stars, not by a strain laborious and hurtful, but to uphold them with a stability void of movement, forcing Fire forward into Fire. Hereunto is the Speech of Axieros. (Hegemon leads Theoricus round to seat of Hiereus. Hiereus as they approach takes Red Lamp in his hand, rises. Hegemon and Theoricus halt before him.)

Hiereus:

Axiokersos the Second Kabir spake to Kasmillos the Candidate and said: I am the left Basal Angle of the Triangle of Flame. I am fire volcanic and terrestrial, flashingly. flaming through the Abysses of Earth; Fire rending Fire penetrating, tearing asunder the curtain of Matter; Fire constrained, Fire tormenting, raging and whirling in lurid storm. By what Sign dost thou seek to pass by?

Heg:

By the Symbol of the Pyramid of Flame.

Hiereus:

Hear thou the Voice of Axiokersos the Second Kabir: For not in matter did the fire which is the beyond first enclose his power in acts, but in Mind; for the Former of the Fiery World is the Mind of Mind, who first sprang from Mind, clothing the one fire with the other Fire, binding them together so that he might mingle the Fountainous Craters while preserving unsullied the Brilliance of his own Fire. And thence a fiery whirlwind drawing down the brilliance of the Flashing Flame penetrating the Abysses of the Universe, for thence from downwards all extend their wondrous rays, abundantly animating Light, Fire, Ether and the Universe. From Him leap forth all relentless thunders, and the whirlwind wrapped, storm enrolled bosom of the All Splendid strength of Hecate, Father begotten and He who encircleth the Brilliance of Fire, and the strong Spirit of the Poles, all Fiery beyond. Hereunto is the Speech of Axiokersos. (Hiereus leads Theoricus round to Hegemon's seat in South West, who takes Red Lamp and thus addresses Theoricus.)

Heg:

Axiokersa the Third Kabir spake to Kasmillos the Candidate and said I am the Right Basal Angle of the Triangle of Flame; I am the Fire Astral and Fluid, winding and corruscating through the firmament. I am the Life of Beings, the vital heat of Existence. By what sign dost thou seek to pass by? (Hiereus prompts Theoricus and then returns to his seat.)

Hiereus:

(For Theoricus) By the Symbol of the Pyramid of Flame.

Heg:

Hear thou the Voice of Axiokersa the Third Kabir. The Father hath hastily withdrawn Himself, but hath not shut up his own Fire in His intellectual Power. All things are sprung from that one Fire. For all things did the Father of all things perfect, and delivered them over unto the Second Mind, whom all races of men call First. The Mind of the Father riding on the subtle girders which glitter with the tracings of inflexible and relentless Fire. The Soul being a brilliant Fire, by the Power of the Father remaineth Immortal, and is mistress of Life, and filleth up the many recesses of the Bosom of the World. The channels being intermixed therein she performeth the works of incorruptible Fire. Hereunto is the Speech of Axiokersa. (Hegemon places Theoricus in a seat in the West between himself and Hiereus and facing Hierophant, takes Pyramid from him.)

Hiero:

Stoop not down into the darkly splendid world, wherein continually lies a faithless Depth, and Hades wrapped in clouds, delighting in unintelligible Images, precipitous, winding, a black ever rolling abyss ever espousing a body unluminous, formless and void. Nature persuadeth us that there are pure Demons, and that even the evil germs of Matter may alike become useful and good. But these are mysteries which are evoked in the profound Abyss of the Mind. Such a Fire existeth extending through the rushings of Air or even a Fire Formless whence comes the Image of a Voice or even a flashing Light abounding, revolving, whirling forth, crying aloud. Also there is the vision of the Fire flashing Courser of Light, or also a Child borne aloft on the shoulders of the Celestial Steed, fiery or clothed with gold, or naked or shooting with the bow shafts of light, and standing on the shoulders of the horse. But if thy meditation prolongeth itself thou shalt unite all these Symbols in the form of the Lion. Then when no longer are visible unto thee the Vault of the Heavens, the mass of the Earth, when to thee the stars have lost their Light and the Lamp of the Moon is veiled when the Earth abideth not, and around thee is the Lightening Flame, then call not before thyself the Visible Image of the Soul of Nature. For thou must not behold it ere thy body is purged by the sacred Rites. Since ever dragging down the Soul and leading it from Sacred things, from the confines of matter, arise the terrible dog-faced Demons, never showing a true image unto mortal gaze. So, therefore, first the Priest who governeth the works of Fire must sprinkle with the Lustral Water of the Loud resounding Sea. Labor thou around the Strophalos of Hecate, when thou shalt see a terrestrial demon approaching cry aloud, and sacrifice the Stone MNIZOURIN. Change not the barbarous names of Evocation for they are Names Divine having in the Sacred Rites a Power ineffable. And when after all the Phantoms are banished thou shalt see that Holy and Formless Fire, that Fire which darts and flashes through the hidden depths of the Universe Hear thou the Voice of Fire. Hereunto is the speech of the Kabiri. (Hegemon turns up Lights and then conducts Candidate to foot of Hierophant's throne, and hands the latter the solid Triangular Pyramid.)

Hiero:

The solid Triangular Pyramid is an appropriate hieroglyph of Fire. It is formed of 4 triangles, 3 visible and one concealed, which yet use the synthesis of the rest. The 3 visible triangles represent Fire Solar, Volcanic and Astral, while the 4th represents the Latent Heat. The three words AUD, AUB, AUR refer to the three conditions of Heat, Aud, active; Aub, passive; Aur, equilibrated; whilst Asch is the Name of Fire. The 31st Path of the Sepher Yetzirah which answereth unto the Letter Shin, is called the Perpetual Intelligence, and it is so called because it regulateth the Motions of the Sun and Moon in their proper order, each in an Orbit convenient for it. It is therefore the reflection of the Sphere of Fire, and the Path connecting the material Universe as depicted in Malkuth, with the Pillar of Severity on the side of Geburah, through the Sephira Hod. (Hierophant, Hegemon and Theoricus come to West of Altar.) Before you upon the Altar is the 20th Key of the Tarot, which symbolically resumes the ideas. To the uninitiated eye it apparently represents the Last Judgement, with an angel blowing a trumpet and the Dead rising from the tombs. But its meaning is far more occult and recondite than this, for it is a glyph of the Powers of Fire. The Angel encircled by a Rainbow whence leap corruscations of Fire, and crowned with the Sun, represents Michael, the great Archangel, the Ruler of Solar Fire. The Serpents which leap in the rainbow are symbols of the Fiery Seraphim. The trumpet represents the influence of the Spirit descending from Binah, while the Banner with the Cross refers to the four rivers of Paradise and the letters of the Holy Name. He also is Axicros, the first of the Samothracian Kabiri, as well as Zeus and Osiris. The left hand figure below, rising from the Earth is Samael, the Ruler of Volcanic Fire. He is also Axiokersos, the 2nd Kabir, Pluto and Typhon. The right hand figure below is Anael, the Ruler of the Astral Light. She is also Axiokersa, the third Kabir, Ceres and Proserpina, Isis and Nephthys. She is therefore represented in a duplicate form and rising from the Water. Around both these figures dart flashes of lightning. These 3 principal figures form the Fire Triangle, and further represent Fire operating in the other three Elements of Air, Earth, and Water. The central lower figure with his back turned and his arms extended in the Sign of Theoricus is Arel the Ruler of Latent Heat, he is rising from the Earth, as if to receive and absorb the properties of the other three. He is also Kasmillos the Candidate in the Samothracian Mysteries, and the Horus of Egypt. He rises from the rock hewn cubical tomb, and also alludes to the Candidate who traverses the Path of Fire. The three lower Figures represent the Hebrew Letter Shin to which fire is especially referred. The 7 Hebrew Yods allude to the Sephiroth operating in each of the Planets and to the Schemhamphorasch. (Hierophant returns to his place and Hegemon leads Theoricus to West. Hiereus comes forward and explains the two Sephirotic Tablets.)

Hiereus:

The Tablet before you represents the 10 Sephiroth combined in seven palaces. The first Palace contains Kether, Chokmah and Binah, the 2nd Chesed, the 3rd Geburah, the 4th Tiphareth, the 5th Netzach, the 6th Hod, the 7th Yesod and Malkuth. This second Tablet represents the attribution of the 10 Sephiroth to the 4 letters of the Holy Name. Kether as you will observe, is not included therein, but it is symbolized by the uppermost point of Yod. It is MACROPROSOPUS or ARIKH ANPIN, the Vast Countenance. Chokmah is attributed to Yod, or the Father Abba; Binah is attributed to Heh or Aima, the Mother; Vau embraces the six next Sephiroth, which together form MICROPROSOPUS or ZAUIR ANPIN, the Lesser Countenance. Malkuth is referred to the Heh final or the Bride of the Apocalypse. (Hegemon leads Theoricus to Tablet of 7 Heavens of Assiah in South.)

Heg:

These are the 7 Heavens of Assiah, the 1st is Ghereboth, referred to Chesed, wherein are the Treasures of Blessings. The 2nd is Mekon referred to Geburah, wherein are the Treasures of the Spirit of Life. The 3rd is Maghon referred to Tiphareth, wherein are Angels. The 4th is Zebel, referred to Netzach, wherein is the Supernal Altar, whereon Michael the great High Priest sacrificeth the Souls of the Just. The 5th is Shachaqim referred to Hod, wherein is the manna. The 6th is Raquie wherein are the Sun and Moon, the Stars and Planets and all the 10 Spheres; it is referred to Yesod. The 7th is Velun referred to Malkuth. Following this is Shamayim containing 18,000 Worlds, and also Gehennah, and the Garden of Eden. The 9th is 18,000 more Worlds wherein abide Shckinah and Metatron. And the 10th is Thebel wherein standeth the earth, between Eden and Gehennah. (Hegemon leads Theoricus to Tablet of 10 Averse Sephiroth in North.)

Heg:

Before you are the 10 Averse and Evil Sephiroth of the Qlippoth or Shells, collected into 7 Palaces wherein is the Apocalyptic mystery of the 7 heads and 10 horns. The Qlippoth of Kether are called Thaumiel or the two contending Forces, the Shells of Chokmah are the Ghogiel, or Hinderers. Those of Binah are the Satariel or Concealers. Those of Chesed are the Gagh Shekelah or Breakers in pieces. To Geburah belong the Golahab or Burners. To Tiphareth the Tagariron or Disputers. To Netzach the Gharab Zereq or Ravens of Death, dispersing all things. To Hod the Samael or deceivers, to Yesod the Gamaliel or Obscene. And the Shell of Malkuth is Lilith the Evil woman. But these have also many other appellations.

Hiero:

I have much pleasure in conferring upon you the Title of Lord (Lady) of the 31st Path. You will now quit the Temple for a short time, and on your return the ceremony of your passage of the 30th Path will take place.

PATH 30 ADVANCEMENT

Hiero:

Honored Hegemon, you have my command to present the Theoricus with the necessary admission Badge and to admit him (her). (Hegemon rises, goes to door, opens it, presents Theoricus with the Greek Cross of the 13 squares and admits him.)

Heg:

Behold he hath placed his Tabernacle in the Sun. (Leads icus to North East and places him before and facing the Pillars)

109

Hicro:

(Knocks) Frater XYZ (Soror) before you in the East are the Portals of the 30th, 25th, and 26th Paths, leading from the Grade of Theoricus to those Grades which are beyond. Of these the only one now open to you is the 30th which leads to the Grade of Practicus. Take in your right hand the Solar Greek Cross, and follow your guide through the path of the Sun.

Unto the Intellectual whirlings of Intellectual Fire all things are subservient, through the Will of the Father of All. (Hegemon leads Theoricus between Pillars turns to right and halts at foot of Hierophant's throne. Hierophant rises and takes Red Lamp in his hand.)

Hiero:

Axieros the First Kabir spake to Kasmillos the Candidate and said I am the Sun in greatest elevation, bringing upon the Earth the ripening Heat, fructifying all things, urging forward the growth of vegetable Nature. Life giving, Light producing, crowning summer with the golden harvest and filling the lap of plenteous Autumn with the purple vintage of the Vine. Thus far is the voice of Axieros. (Hegemon leads Theoricus round to seat of Hiereus and halts before him. Hiereus rises with Red Lamp in his hand.)

Hiereus:

Axiokersos the Second Kabir spake to Kasmillos the Candidate and said, I am the Sun in greatest depression beneath the Equator, when Cold is greatest and heat is least, withdrawing his light in darkening Winter, the dweller of Mist and the Storm. Thus far is the Voice of Axiokersos. (Hegemon leads Theoricus round to his own seat - takes Red Lamp.)

Heg:

Axiokersa the Third Kabir spake to Kasmillos the Candidate and said I am the Sun at Equinox initiating Summer and heralding Winter, mild and genial in operation, giving forth or withdrawing the vital heat of life. Thus far is the Voice of Axiokersa. (Places Theoricus in a seat in West between himself and Hiereus, facing Hiereus and takes from him Solar Greek Cross.)

Hiero:

The Father of all congregated the 7 Firmaments of the Kosmos circumscribing the Heaven with Convex form. He constituted a Septenary of wandering existences suspending their disorder in well disposed zones. He made them 6 in number and for the 7th he cast into the midst thereof the Fire of the Sun; into that centre from which all lines are equal. That the swift Sun may come round that centre, eagerly urging itself towards that centre of resounding Light. As rays of Light his locks flow forth, stretching to the confines of space. And of the Solar Circles, and of the Lunar clashings and of the Aerial recesses; the Melody of Ether, and of the Sun and of the passages of the Moon, and of the Sun is in the Supramundane Orders, for therein a solar world and endless Light subsist. The Sun more true measureth all things by time, for he is the time of time. And his disc is in the Starless above, the Inerratic Sphere, and he is the centre of the Triple World. The Sun is Fire and the Dispenser of Fire. He is also the channel of the Higher Fire, Aether, Sun, and the Spirit of the Moon, ye are the Leaders of Air. And the Great Goddess bringeth forth the Vast Sun, and the Brilliant Moon, and the wide Air, and the Lunar course and the Solar Pole. She collecteth it receiving the Melody of Ether, and of the Sun, and of the Moon, and of whatsoever is contained by Air. Unwearied doth Nature rule over the worlds and works, so that the periods of all things may be accomplished. And above the shoulders of that Great Goddess is Nature in her vastness exalted. Thus far the Voice of the Kabiri. (Hegemon conducts Theoricus to Hierophant's Throne and hands to latter the Solar Greek Cross.)

Hiero:

The Solar Greek Cross is formed of 13 squares, which fitly refer to the Sun's motion through the Zodiac. These signs being further arranged in the arms of the cross according to the four Elements with the Sun in the centre, represent that luminary as the centre of the whole.

The 30th Path of the Sepher Yetzirah which answereth unto the letter Resh is called the Collecting Intelligence, and it is so called because from it astrologers deduce the judgement of the stars, and of the celestial signs, and the perfections of their science according to the rules of their revolutions. It is therefore, the reflection of the sphere of the Sun, and the Path connecting Yesod with Hod, Foundation with Splendour. (Hierophant, Theoricus and Hegemon come to West of Altar.) Before you upon the Altar is the 19th Key of the Tarot which symbolically resumes these Ideas. The Sun has 12 principal rays which represent the 12 signs of the Zodiac, they are alternatively waved and salient, as symbolizing the alternation of the masculine and feminine natures. These are again subdivided into 36 rays representing the 36 Decanates or sets of 10 degrees in the Zodiac, and these again into 72 typifying the 72 Quinaries or sets of 5 degrees and the 72 fold name SHEM- HA-MEPHORASCH. Thus the Sun itself embraces the whole Creation in its rays. The 7 Hebrew Yods on each side falling through the air, refer to the Solar influence descending. The wall is the circle of the Zodiac and the stones are its various degrees and divisions. The two children standing respectively on Water and Earth, represent the generating influence of both brought into action by the rays of the Sun. They are the two Inferior or passive Elements, as the Sun and the Air above them are the Superior and Active Elements, of Fire and Air. Furthermore, these two children resemble the sign Gemini, which unites the Earthly sign of Taurus with the Watery sign of Cancer and this sign was by the Greeks and Romans referred to Apollo or the Sun. (Hierophant returns to place and Hegemon leads Theoricus to West.)

Hiereus:

(Showing 1st Tablet) The Astrological symbols of the planets are derived from the 3 primary forms of the circle, the crescent and the cross, either singly or in combination. The circle denotes the Sun and gold, the crescent the Moon and silver, respectively, analogous to the Red and the White alchemical natures. The cross is the symbol of corrosion and the corrosion of metals is usually of the complementary color to that which they naturally approximate. Thus, copper which is reddish becomes green in verdigris etc. Mercury is the only one which unites these primary forms in one symbol. Saturn is composed of the Cross and the Crescent, showing that lead is corrosive externally and Lunar internally. Jupiter is the reverse, Mars is solar internally while Venus is the opposite, for Copper is externally of the nature of Gold, but internally corrosive. Wherefore, also the Name of the Sphere of Venus Nogah, denotes External Splendor. (Leads Theoricus to 2nd Tablet.) This shows the true and genuine attribution of the Tarot trumps to the Hebrew alphabet which has long been a secret among the Initiates and which should be carefully concealed from the outer world. As a MSS. lecture on this subject is circulated among the Members of the Grade of Practicus, I shall not further enter into its explanation. (Hegemon leads Theoricus to Tablet in the South.)

Heg:

Before you is the Tablet of the Olympic or Aerial Planetary Spirits with their Seals, Arathror of Saturn, Bethor of Jupiter, Phalegh of Mars. Och of the Sun, Hagith of Venus, Ophiel of Mercury and Phul of the Moon. (Leads Theoricus to Tablet in the North.) This shows you the Geomantic Figures with their ruling Intelligences, and Genii; also the talismanic Symbols allotted to each Geomantic figure. These are derived from them by drawing lines to the points composing them, so as to form mathematical figures therefrom. A MSS. lecture on Geomancy is circulated among the Members of Practicus Grade.

Hiero:

I have much pleasure in conferring upon you the Title of Lord (Lady) of the 30th Path. You will now quit the Temple for a short time and on your return the Ceremony of your reception into the Grade of Practicus will take place.

CEREMONY OF THE GRADE OF PRACTICUS

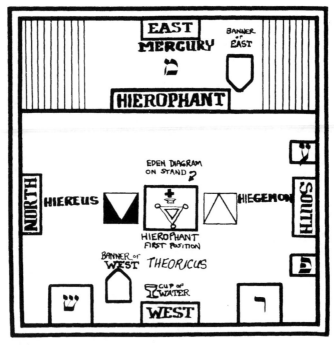

Hiero:

Honored Hegemon, instruct the Theoricus in the proper alarm, present him with the necessary admission badge and admit him (her). (Done) Place the Theoricus before the Portal of the 31st Path, by which he (she) has symbolically entered this Grade, from the Grade Zelator. (Done, Shin.) Place the Theoricus now before the Portal of the 30th Path by which he has symbolically entered this Grade from the Grade of Theoricus. (Done, Resh. Hegemon leads Theoricus then forward to Hiereus.)

Hiereus:

By what symbol dost thou enter herein?

Heg:

By the peculiar emblem of the Stolistes, which is the Cup of Water.

Hiereus:

The Cup of the Stolistes partakes in part of the symbolism of the Laver of Moses and the Sea of Solomon. On the Tree of Life it embraces nine of the Sephiroth, exclusive of Kether. Yesod and Malkuth form the Triangle below, the former the apex the latter the base. Like the Caduceus it further represents the 3 elements of Water, Air and Fire. The crescent is the Water which is above the firmament, the circle is the Firmament and the Triangle the consuming fire below, which is opposed to the Celestial Fire symbolized by the upper part of the Caduceus. (Places Admission badge aside. Hegemon leads Theoricus to Hierophant and then returns to his place. Hiereus and Hegemon rise and face inwards towards the Altar.)

Hiero:

(Rising and facing inwards to the Altar.) Before you is represented the symbolism of the Garden of Eden. At the summit are the Supernal Sephiroth summed up and contained in Aima Elohim, the Mother Supernal, the Woman of the 12th chapter of the Apocalypse clothed with the Sun and the Moon under her feet and upon her head the Crown of 12 Stars, Kether. And whereas the Name Tetragrammaton is joined to the Elohim when it is said Tetragrammaton Elohim planted a Garden Eastward in Eden so this represents the power of the Father joined thereto in the Glory from the face of the Ancient of Days. And in the Garden were the Tree of Life, and the Tree of the Knowledge of good and Evil, which latter is from Malkuth, which is the lowest Sephira between the rest of the Sephiroth and the Kingdom of the Shells, which latter is represented by the Great Red Dragon coiled beneath, having 7 heads (the 7 infernal Palaces) and ten horns (the 10 Averse Sephiroth contained in the 7 Palaces). And a River Nahar went forth out of Eden, (namely the Supernal Triad) to water the Garden (the rest of the Sephiroth) and from thence it was divided into four heads in DAATH whence it is said In Daath the depths are broken up, and the clouds drop down dew. The first head is Pison which flows into Geburah where there is Gold, it is the River of Fire. The second head is Gihon the river of Waters, flowing into Chesed. The third is Hiddekel the River of air flowing into Tiphareth. And the fourth River which receiveth the virtue of the other three is Euphrates which floweth down upon Malkuth, the Earth. This River going forth out of Eden is the River of the Apocalypse, of Waters of Life, clear as crystal, proceeding out of the Throne of God and the Lamb, on either side of which was the Tree of Life bearing 12 manner of Fruit. And thus do the Rivers of Eden form the Cross, and on that cross the great Adam the Son who was to rule the Nations with a rod of Iron is extended from Tiphareth and his arms stretch out to Gedulah and Geburah, and in Malkuth is Eve, the completion of all, the Mother of All, and above the Universe she supporteth with her hands the Eternal Pillars of the Sephiroth. As it was said to you in the 30th Path. And above the shoulders of that great Goddess is Nature in her Vastness exalted. The grade of Practicus is referred to the Sephira Hod, and the 30th and 31st Paths which are those of Resh and Shin are bound thereto. The sign of this Grade is thus given; stand with the heels together, raise the arms till the elbows are level with the shoulders bring the hands across the chest touching the thumbs and tips of fingers thus forming a triangle apex downwards. This represents the element of Water to which this Grade is attributed, and the Waters of Creation.

The Grip or token is the general grip of the First Order. The Grand Word is Elohim Tzabaoth which means the Elohim of Hosts and of Armies. The mystic number is 36 and from it is formed the Pass Word of this Grade, which is Eloah, one of the Divine Names. It should be lettered separately when given. Unto this Grade and unto the Sephira Hod, the Eighth Path of the Sepher Yetzirah is referred. It is called the Absolute or Perfect Path because it is the means of the Primordial which hath no root to which it may be established, except in the Penetralia of that Gedulah (Magnificence) which emanates from the subsisting properties thereof. The distinguishing badge of this Grade which you will now be entitled to wear is the sash of a Theoricus with the addition of a purple or violet cross above the white cross and the numbers 3 and 8 within a circle and a square, respectively, left and right of its summit, and below the numbers 32, the numbers 30 and 31 in purple or violet, between narrow parallel purple lines. This grade is especially referred to the element of Water and therefore, the great Watch Tower or Terrestrial Tablet of the West forms one of its principal emblems. (Hierophant goes to it followed by Theoricus.) It is known as the second or Great Western Quadrangle, or Tablet of Water, and it is one of the four Great Tablets delivered unto Enoch by the great Angel Ave. From it are drawn the 3 Holy secret names of God EMPEH ARSEL GAIOL which are borne upon the Banners of the West. And numberless divine and angelic names which appertain unto the Element of Water. The meaning of the Tablet of Earth and Air were explained to you in the preceding Grades. (Hierophant and Theoricus proceed to East. Hierophant indicates Cross and Triangle on the Altar.) The Cross above the Triangle represents the power of the Spirit of Life rising above the Triangle of the Waters, and reflecting the Triune therein, as further marked by the Lamps at the angles. While the Cup of Water placed at the junction of the Cross and Triangle represents the maternal letter Mem. The Portals in the East and South East are the Paths which conduct to the Higher while that in the South leads to the Grade of Philosophus, the highest Grade of the First Order.

This Grade is also related to the planet Mercury. Its Kamea or mystical square is formed of 64 squares containing the numbers from 1 to 64 arranged so as to show the same sum each way. Its ruling numbers are 8, 84, 260 and 2080. This Tablet (indicating it) shows the mystical seals and Names drawn from the Kamea of Mercury. The seals are formed from lines drawn to certain numbers upon the square. The name answering to 8 is Asboga, those answering to 64 Din, Judgement and Doni, that answering to 260 is Tiriel the Intelligence of Mercury and lastly, that answering to 2080 is Taphthartharath the name of the Spirit of Mercury. On this Tablet (indicating it) is shown the meaning of the symbol of Mercury when inscribed upon the Tree of Life. It embraces all but Kether and the horns spring from Daath, which is not properly speaking a Sephira, but rather the conjunction of Chokmah and Binah. (Hierophant resumes his seat. Hegemon leads Theoricus to Hiereus and they go forward to West.)

Hiereus:

(Indicating it) This Tablet before you shows the 7 Planes of the Tree of Life answering to the 7 Planets. Thus, Saturn answers to Kether, Jupiter to Chokmah, and Binah; Mars to Chesed and Geburah; The Sun to Tiphareth; Venus to Netzach and Hod, Mercury to Yesod and Luna to Malkuth. While this second Tablet (indicating it) shows the Four Planes corresponding to the elements; the four Worlds and the letters of the Holy Name.

Heg:

(Leading Theoricus to Tablet in South.) This Tablet shows you the meaning of the alchemical Mercury on the Tree of Life of the first form of the Alchemical Sephiroth. Here again it embraces all but Kether. The Radix Metallorum, the triple foliation at the bottom of the Cross refers to Fire symbolized by the addition of the sign Aries thereto; and it further alludes to the 3 principles of Sulphur, Mercury and Salt. (Leads Theoricus to Tablet in the North.) The Tablet before you represents the symbol the Planets resumed in a Mercurial Figure. In gradual descent we obtain Luna, Mars, Sol, Venus, and below Saturn and Jupiter, right and left. (Hegemon places Theoricus in a seat in West facing Hierophant and returns to his own place.)

Hiero:

I now congratulate you on having passed through the ceremony of the Grade of Practicus and in recognition thereof I confer upon you the Mystic title of Monokeros de Astris which means the Unicorn of the Stars, and I give you the symbol of Mayim which is the Hebrew Name for Water. Take your seat in the South. (Knocks) In the Name of Elohim Tzabaoth I now declare that you have been duly advanced to the Grade of Practicus, and Lord (Lady) of the 30th and 31st Paths. Before you are eligible for advancement to the Grade of Philosophus you must be thoroughly and genuinely perfect in certain subjects, and have been at least 3 months engaged in the contemplation of the mysteries revealed in this Grade. When you are thoroughly and genuinely perfect, you must signify the same by letter to the Scribe as in the preceding Grade. A MSS. lecture on those subjects is circulated among the members of this Grade.

CLOSING

Hiero:

(Knocks) Assist me to close the Temple in the Grade of Practicus. Honored Hegemon see that the Temple is properly guarded. (Done.)

Heg:

Very Honored Hierophant, the Temple is properly guarded.

Hiero:

Let us adore the Lord and King of Water. (Knocks) (All face East.) Let Elohim Tzabaoth be praised unto the Countless Ages of Time. Amen. (Hierophant quits his place and goes to Tablet of Water in West. All face West.)

Hiero:

Let us rehearse the Prayer of the Undines or Water Spirits. (Knocks) Terrible King of the Sea, Thou who holdest the Keys of the Cataracts of Heaven and who enclosest the subterranean Waters in the cavernous hollows of Earth; King of the Deluge and of the Rains of Spring; Thou who openest the sources of the Rivers and of the Fountains, Thou who commandest moisture which is as it were the blood of the earth, to become the sap of the plants, we adore Thee and we invoke Thee. Speak thou unto us Thy mobile and changeful creatures in the great Tempests of the Sea, and we shall tremble before Thee. Speak to us also in the murmur of the limpid waters and we shall desire thy love. O Vastness wherein all the Rivers of Being seek to lose themselves, which renew themselves ever in Thee, O Thou Ocean of infinite perfections, O Height which reflectest Thyself in the Depth, O Depth which exhalest thyself into the Height, lead us into the true Life through Intelligence, through Love. Lead us unto Immortality through sacrifice, so that we may be found worthy to offer one day unto Thee, the Water, the Blood and the Tears, for the remission of Sins. Amen. (Making with his sceptre Banishing Circle and Pentagrams in the Air in front of Tablet.)

Hiero:

Depart ye in peace unto your abodes and habitations, may the blessing of EL be upon you. Be there ever peace between us and you, and be ye ready to come when ye are called. (Knocks) (Returns to place; all face as usual.)

Hiero:

In the Name of Elohim Tzabaoth I declare this Temple closed in the Grade of Practicus.

Hiero:

(Knocks 1, 3, 1, 3)

Hiereus:

(Knocks 1, 3, 1, 3)

Heg:

(Knocks 1, 3, 1, 3)

THE PHILOSOPHUS GRADE 4 - 7

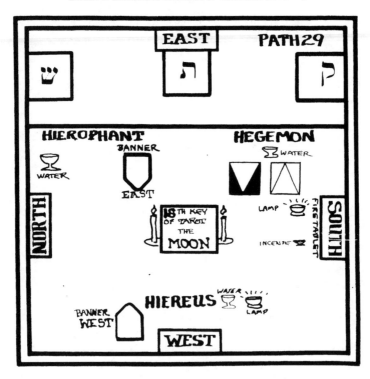

THE OPENING

(The Throne of the Hierophant, beside which is a Cup of Water and the Banner of the East, is placed before the Dais N.E. The seat of the Hegemon is before the Dais in the S.E. Hiereus in the West. Each officer has a Cup of Water. The Pillars are placed about three feet in front of Hegemon's seat, and behind her is the letter Qoph. The Altar in the center has a candle on either side. On it is the Tarot Key, The Moon. The Elemental Lights are lit. Incense burns in the South. Temple arranged as for Path 29. Members assembled and Robed.)

Hiero:

(Knocks) Honored Fratres and Sorores, assist me to open the Temple in the Grade of Philosophus. Honored Hegemon see that the Temple is properly guarded.

Heg:

Very Honored Hierophant the Temple is properly guarded.

Hiero:

Honored Hiereus, see that none below the Grade of Philosophus is present.

Hiereus:

Honored Fratres and Sorores, give the sign of Philosophus. (Done) Very Honored Hierophant, all present have attained the Grade of Philosophus. (Saluting.)

Hiero:

Honored Hegemon, to what particular Element is this Grade attributed?

Heg:

To the Element of Fire.

Hiero:

Honored Hiereus, to what Planet does this Grade especially refer?

Hiereus:

To the Planet Venus.

Hiero:

Honored Hegemon, what Paths are attached to this Grade?

Heg:

The 29th, 28th and 27th Paths of Qoph, Tzaddi and Peh.

Hiero:

Honored Hiereus, to what does the 29th Path refer?

Hiereus:

To the reflection of the Sphere of Pisces.

Hiero:

Honored Hegemon, to what does the 28th Path allude?

Heg:

To the reflection of the Sphere of Aquarius.

Hiero:

Honored Hiereus, to what does the 27th Path allude?

Hiereus:

To the reflection of the Sphere of Mars.

Hiero:

(Knocks) (All rise and face East.) Let us adore the Lord and King of Fire.

Hiero:

Tetragrammaton Tzabaoth. Blessed be Thou, the Leader of Armies is Thy Name! Amen. (All salute. Hierophant quits his throne and proceeds to South. Knocks. All face South. He stands before the Tablet of Fire. He makes with his sceptre the invoking Circle and Pentagrams before it in the Air as shown.)

Hiero:

And Elohim said. Let us make Adam in our Image after our likeness, and let them have Dominion. In the Name of Elohim, Mighty and Ruling, and in the Name of Tetragrammaton Tzabaoth, Spirits of Fire, adore your Creator. (Taking the Incense from before the Tablet, and making therewith the Sign Leo in the Air before it.)

Hiero:

In the Name of Michael the great Archangel of Fire, and in the Sign of the Lion. Spirits of Fire, adore your Creator! (Making with Incense the sign of Cross.) In the Names and Letters of the Great Southern Quadrangle, revealed unto Enoch by the Angel Ave, Spirits of Fire, adore your Creator. (Holding Incense on high.) In the three Great Secret Names of God, borne on the Banners of the South, OIP TEE A PEDOCE Spirits of Fire, adore your Creator. IntheNameofEDELPERNA. Great King of the South, spirits of Fire adore your Creator. (Replaces Incense and returns to place. All face as usual.)

Hiero:

In the Name of Tetragrammaton Tzabaoth. I declare the Temple opened in the Grade of Philosophus.

Hiero:

(Knocks 3, 3, 1)

Hiereus:

(Knocks 3, 3, 1)

Heg:

(Knocks 3, 3, 1)

ADVANCEMENT TO PATH 29

(Temple Arranged for Ritual of 29th Path, As In Diagram. The Temple Is Darkened.)

Hiero:

(Knocks) Honored Fratres and Sorores, our Frater XYZ having made such progress in the Paths of Occult Science as has enabled him to pass the examination in the requisite knowledge and further having been a member of the Grade of Practicus for a period of more than three months, is now eligible for advancement to the Grade of Philosophus, and I have duly received a dispensation from the Greatly Honored Chiefs of the Second Order to advance him in due form. Honored Hegemon, superintend the preparation of the Practicus and give the customary alarm. (Hegemon rises, salutes the Hierophant, quits the Temple and sees that the Practicus is prepared as follows, wearing sash of Practicus, hoodwinked, and with Calvary Cross formed of 12 squares in right hand. Hegemon takes Practicus by left hand and gives an alarm of 7 Knocks.)

Heg:

And the RUACH ELOHIM moved upon the face of the Waters. (Hiereus opens door and admits them, then returns to his place. Hegemon conducts Practicus to South in front of the Tablet of Fire, faces him to East and takes from him the Calvary Cross.)

Hiero:

Give to the Hegemon the Sign, Grip or Token, Grand Word, Mystic Number and Pass Word of the Grade of Practicus. (Done. Sign, General Grip of 1st Order. Grand Word Elohim Tzabaoth, No. 36, Pass Word Eloah.)

Hiero:

Give me also the Mystic title and Symbol which you received in that Grade. (Done. Monokeros de Astris. Mayim.) (Hegemon faces Practicus to Tablet of Fire.)

Hiero:

Frater (XYZ) do you solemnly pledge yourself to maintain the same strict secrecy regarding the mysteries of the 29th, 28th and 27th Paths and of the Grade of Philosophus, which you have already sworn to maintain respecting those of the preceding Grades?

Pract:

I do.

Hiero:

Then you will stretch your arms above your head to their full limit and say I swear by the torrent of Fire. (Done. Practicus repeating the words.)

Hiero:

Let the hoodwink be removed. (Done, when the Practicus discovers that the Temple is in partial darkness. Hegemon places in his hand the incense from before the Fire Tablet.)

Hiero:

Wave the incense before the Tablet of Fire and say Let the Powers of Fire witness my Pledge. (Done. Practicus repeating the words. Hegemon replaces Incense.)

Hiero:

Conduct the Practicus to the East and place him before the Mystic Pillars. (Done.)

THE RITUAL OF THE 29th PATH

Hiero:

Before you are the Portals of the 31 st, 32nd and 29th Paths as in the Grade of Zelator. The two former you have already traversed, and the Portal of the 29th Path, on the right hand leading from the Grade of Zelator to the Grade of Philosophus is now open to you. Take in your right hand the Calvary Cross of 12 squares, and follow your Guide through the Path of the Waters. (Hegemon circumambulates the Hall once with Practicus having previously given him the Calvary Cross to bear. Hiereus as they approach rises with red lamp in his hand. Hegemon and Practicus halt before him.)

Hiero:

The Priest with the mask of Osiris spake and said I am the Water, Stagnant and Silent and Still, reflecting all, concealing all. I am the past. I am the Inundation. He who riseth from the Great Waters is my Name. Hail unto ye, Dwellers of the Land of Night, for the rending of the Darkness is near. (Hegemon leads Practicus round to seat of Hiereus. Hiereus as they approach takes red lamp in his hand and rises. Hegemon and Practicus halt before him.)

Hiereus:

The Priest with the mask of Horus spake and said, I am Water turbid and troubled. I am the Banisher of Peace in the Vast Abode of the Waters. None is so strong that can withstand the Great Waters, the vastness of their Terror, the magnitude of their Fear, the roar of their thundering Voice. I am the Future, Mist-clad and shrouded in Gloom. I am the Recession of the Torrent, the Storm veiled in Terror is my Name. Hail unto the Mighty Powers of Nature, and the Chiefs of the Whirling Storm. (Hegemon leads Practicus round to his own seat. Takes red lamp in his hand and addresses Practicus.)

Heg:

The Priestess with the mask of Isis spake and said, The Traveller through the Gates of Anubis is my Name. I am Water pure and limpid, ever flowing on towards the Sea. I am the ever-passing Present, which stands in the place of the Past. I am the fertilized Land. Hail unto the Dwellers of the Wings of the Morning. (Replaces lamp. Seats Candidate West of and close to the Altar facing Hierophant and returns to his own place.)

Hiero:

I arise in the Place of the Gathering of the Waters through the rolled back cloud of Night. From the Father of Waters went forth the Spirit rending asunder the veils of Darkness. And there was but a Vastness of Silence and of depth in the Place of the Gathering of the Waters; terrible was that Silence of an Uncreated World, immeasurable the depth of that Abyss. And the Countenance of Darkness half formed, arose. They abode not, they hasted away. And in the vastness of Vacancy, the Spirit moved, and the Light-bearers existed for a space. I have said Darkness of Darkness; Are not the countenances of Darkness fallen with the Kings? Do the Sons of the Night of Time last forever? And have they not passed away? Before all things are the Waters, and the Darkness, and the Gates of the Land of Night. And the Chaos cried aloud for the Unity of Form, and the Face of the Eternal arose. Before the Glory of that Countenance the night rolled back and the Darkness hasted away. In the Waters beneath was that Face reflected, in the Formless Abyss of the Void. From those Eyes darted rays of terrible splendor which crossed with the Currents reflected. That Brow and those Eyes formed the Triangle of the measureless Heavens, and their reflection formed the Triangle of the Measureless Waters. And thus was formulated the Eternal Hexad, the Number of the Dawning Creation. (Hegemon turns up the lights and then conducts the Practicus to the foot of Hierophant's throne, handing latter the Calvary Cross of 12 squares.) The Calvary Cross of 12 Squares fitly represents the Zodiac, which embraces the Waters of Nu, as the ancient Egyptians called the heavens; the Waters which be above the Firmament. It also alludes to the Eternal River of Eden divided into four heads which finds their correlatives in the four triplicities of the Zodiac. (Places Cross aside.)

The 29th Path of the Sepher Yetzirah which answereth to the letter Qoph, is called the Corporeal Intelligence, and it is so called because it formeth every body which is formed beneath the whole Order of Worlds, and the Increment of them. It is there, the reflection of the Sphere of the Watery Sign Pisces, and the Path connecting the Material Universe as depicted in Malkuth, with the Pillar of Mercy, and the side of Chesed through the Sephira Netzach. And through it do the Waters of Chesed flow down. (Hierophant, Hegemon and Practicus come to West of Altar.) Before you upon the Altar is the 18th Key of the Tarot, which symbolically resumes these ideas. It represents the Moon with four Hebrew Yods, like drops of dew falling, two dogs, two towers, a winding pathway leading to the horizon, and in the foreground, Water, with a crayfish crawling through it towards land. The Moon is in the increase on the side of Gedulah, and from it proceed sixteen principal and sixteen secondary rays, which together make 32, the number of the Paths of Yetzirah. She is the Moon at the feet of the Woman of the Revelation, ruling equally over Cold and Moist Natures, and the Passive Elements of Earth and Water. The four Hebrew Yods refer to the four letters of the Holy Name reconstituting the destroyed World from the Waters. It is to be noted that the symbol of the Sign Pisces is formed of the two lunar crescents of Gedulah and Geburah bound together, and thus shows the lunar nature of the Sign. The Dogs are the Jackals of the Egyptian Anubis, guarding the Gates of the East and of the West, shown by the two Towers, between which lies the Path of all the Heavenly Bodies ever rising in the East and setting in the West. The Crayfish is the sign Cancer, and was anciently the Scarabeus or Khephra, the emblem of the Sun below the horizon as he ever is when the Moon is increasing above. Also when the Sun is in the Sign Pisces, the Moon will be well in her increase in Cancer as shown by the Crayfish emblem. (Hierophant leads Practicus to Tablet of the Serpent of Brass in East.) This is the Serpent Nehushtan which Moses made when the Children of Israel were bitten by the Serpents of Fire in the wilderness. It is the Serpent of the Paths of the Tree. And he set it on a pole, that is, twined round the middle Pillar of the Sephiroth. And the word used in the passage in Numbers 21 for Fiery Serpents, is the same as the name of the angels of Geburah, the same spelling, the same pointing, Seraphim, around the middle Pillar of the Sephiroth, because that is the reconciler between the Fires of Geburah and Severity, and the Waters of Chesed or Mercy, and hence it is said in the New Testament, that it is a type of Christ, the Reconciler. And the Serpent is of Brass, the Metal of Venus, whose Sphere is called Nogah or External Splendor, as shown further in the Alchemic symbol of the Planet Venus, wherein the circle of the Sun is exalted above the Cross of corrosion. And therefore it is said in the Zohar, that alone of the Shells is the Serpent Nogah found in Holiness, and he is called the Bilanx of Justice. Why .then is he called the External or false Splendor? Because he indeed umteth the Paths but comprehendeth not the Sephiroth. Nevertheless he is also the Celestial Serpent of Wisdom. But the Serpent of Temptation is the Serpent of the Tree of Knowledge of Good and Evil and not that of the Tree of Life. (Hierophant resumes his seat. Hegemon leads Practicus to Hiereus.)

Hiereus:

(Indicating Tablet) This is the so-called Qabalah of Nine Chambers. In it the letters are classed together, according to the similarity of their numbers. Thus, in one chamber you will see Gimel, Lamed and Shin classed together, whose numbers are similar 3, 30, 300 and so on. The uppermost is the most usual form of the diagram. In the lower the chambers are arranged according to the Sephiroth. This Tablet (indicating it) represents the method of forming the Tree of Life in the Tarot. The four Aces are placed on the Throne of Kether. The remaining small cards of each suit desired are then placed on the respective Sephiroth, 2 on Chokmah, 3 on Binah and so on. The 22 Trumps are then arranged on the letters of the Paths between them. The King and Queen of the Suit are placed beside Chokmah and Binah respectively, the Knight beside Tiphareth and the Knave beside Malkuth, thus representing the attribution of the Sephiroth to the four letters of the Holy Name in the World wherein they operate. (Hegemon leads Practicus to Tablet of The Pillars in South.)

Heg:

This Tablet represents the formation of the Hexagram of Tiphareth from the Pillars on each side. In Chesed is the Water and in Geburah is the Fire, and in Tiphareth is the uniting and reconciliation of both Triangles in the Hexagram, as Aleph forms the reconciliation between Mem and Shin so thus stands the reconciling Pillar between the Pillars of Fire and of Cloud; the Yakin and Boaz of Solomon's Temple. (Hegemon leads Practicus to Tablet in North.) The mode of using the Talismanic forms drawn from the Geomantic figures, is to take those formed by the figures under the Planet required and place them at the opposite ends of a wheel of 8 radii as shown. A versicle suitable to the matter is then written within the double circle.

Hiero:

I have much pleasure in now conferring upon you the title of Lord (Lady) of the 29th Path. You will now quit the Temple for a short time and on your return the ceremony of your passage of the 28th Path will take place.

VOLUME SIX

ADVANCEMENT PATH 28

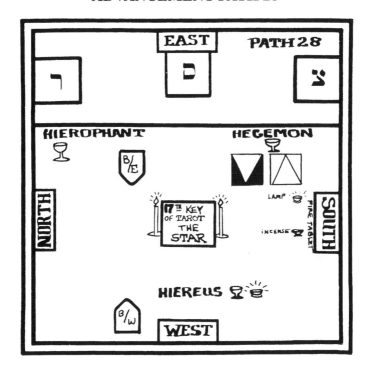

Hiero:

Honored Hegemon, you have my command to present the Practicus with the necessary admission badge and to admit him (her). (Hegemon rises goes to door, opens it. presents Practicus with solid pyramid of elements and admits him.)

Heg:

And ever forth from their central source the Rivers of Eden flow. (Hegemon leads Practicus to South East before Pillars.)

Hiero:

Frater (XYZ) the Path now open before you is the 28th leading from the Grade of Theoricus to the Grade of Philosophus. Take in your right hand the solid Pyramid of the Elements and follow the Guide of the Path. (Hegemon circumambulates Hall once with Practicus. Hierophant as they approach rises, the red lamp in his hand. They halt before him.)

Hiero:

The Priestess with the mask of Isis spake and said I am the rain of Heaven, descending upon the Earth, bearing with it the fructifying and germinating Power. I am the plenteous yielder of Harvest; I am the Cherisher of Life. (Hegemon leads Practicus round to the seat of the Hiereus. Hiereus as they approach rises with red lamp in his hand. They halt before him.)

Hiereus:

The Priestess with the Mask of Nephthys spake and said I am the Dew descending noiseless and silent, gemming the Earth with countless Diamonds of Dew; bearing down the influences from above in the solemn Darkness of Night. (Hegemon leads Practicus round to his own seat, takes red lamp in his hand and thus addresses the Practicus.)

Heg:

The Priestess with the Mask of Athor spake and said I am the Ruler of Mist and Cloud; wrapping the Earth as it were with a garment floating and hovering between Earth and Heaven. I am the Giver of the Mist Veil of Autumn, the successor of the Dew clad Night. (Hegemon replaces lamp and seats Practicus West of and close to the Altar facing Hierophant, then returns to his own seat.)

Hiero:

Where the Paternal Monad is, the Monad is enlarged and generateth two. And beside him is seated the Duad, and both glittereth with intellectual Sections, also to govern all things and to order everything not ordered. For in the whole Universe shineth the Triad, over which the Monad ruleth. This Order is the beginning of all Sections.

Hiereus:

For the Mind of the Father said, that all things should be cut into three whose Will assented, and then all things were so divided. For the mind of the Eternal Father said into three, governing all things by Mind. And there appeared in it the Triad, Virtue, and Wisdom and Multiscient Truth.

Hiereus:

Thus floweth forth the form of the Triad being preexistent - Not the First Essence, but that whereby all things are measured.

Heg:

For thou must know that all things bow before the Three Supernals. The first Course is Sacred, but in the midst thereof another, the Third Aerial which cherisheth Earth in Fire and the Fountain of Fountain, and of all the Fountains. The Matrix containing all, thence abundantly springing forth the generation of multifarious Matter. (Conducts Practicus to foot of the Hierophant's Throne and hands to the latter the Solid Pyramid of the elements.)

Hiero:

This Pyramid is attributed to the Four elements. On the four Triangles are their names, Asch, Fire; Mayim, Water; Ruach, Air; Aretz, Earth; On the apex is the word Eth, composed of the first and last letters of the Alphabet and implying Essence. The Square Base represents the Material Universe, and on it is the word Ohlam, meaning World. (Places Pyramid aside.) The 28th Path of Yetzirah, which answereth unto the letter Tzaddi is called the Natural Intelligence, and it is so called because through it is consummated and perfected the Nature of every existing being under the Orb of the Sun. It is therefore the reflection of the Airy Sign of Aquarius, the Water bearer unto which is attributed the Countenance of the Man, the Adam, the restored World. (Hierophant and Hegemon and Practicus come to the West of Altar.) Before you upon the altar is the 17th Key of the Tarot, which symbolically resumes these ideas. The large Star in the centre of the Heavens has seven principal and 14 secondary rays, and thus represents the Heptad multiplied by the Triad which yields 21 the number of the Divine name, EHEIEH which as you already know is attached to Kether. In the Egyptian sense it is Sirius, the Dog Star of Isis Sothis; around it are the Stars of the Seven Planets, each with its sevenfold counterchanged operation. The nude female figure with the Star of the Heptagram on her Brow is the synthesis of Isis, of Nephthys and of Athor. She also represents the Planet Venus, through whose Sphere the influences of Chesed descend. She is Aima, Binah and Tebunah, the Great Supernal Mother, Aima Elohim pouring upon the Earth the Waters of Creation, which unite and form a river at her feet; the river going forth from the Supernal Eden, which overfloweth and faileth not. Note well that in this Key she is completely unveiled, while in the 21 st Key, she is only partly so. The two Urns contain the Influences from Chokmah and Binah. On the right springs the Tree of Life and on the left the Tree of Knowledge of Good and Evil, whereon the bird of Hermes alights. And therefore does this Key represent the Restored World after the Formless and the Void and the Darkness, the New Adam, the Countenance of the Man which falls in the Sign Aquarius. And therefore doth the Astronomical symbol of this sign represent as it were, the waves of water, the ripples of that River going forth out of Eden. But therefore, also is it justly attributed unto Air and not unto Water, because it is the Firmament dividing and containingthe Waters. (Hierophant and Practicus go to East.) Before you is shown the manner of writing the Holy Name in each of the four Worlds at length, by giving the spelling of each letter. You will note that the spelling of the letter Yod alone alters not. It is a symbol of the unchangeableness of the First Cause. The total of the spelling in each World, is then expressed in Hebrew letters and makes the Secret name of that World. Thus, in Atziluth the total is 72, and the Secret name AUB, in Binah 63 SEG, in Yetzirah 45 MAH and in Assiah 52 BEN. (Indicating the end Tablet.) In the Tablet is shown the method of writing the Hebrew words by the Yetziratic attribution of the alphabet, whence result some curious hieroglyphic symbolism. Thus, Tetragrammaton will be written by Virgo, Aries, Taurus, Aries. Eheieh by Air, Aries, Virgo, Aries; from Yeheshuah, the Qabalistic mode of spelling Jesus, which is simply the Tetrarammaton, with the letter Shin placed therein, we obtain a very peculiar combination; Virgo, Aries, Fire, Taurus, Aries; Virgo born of a Virgin, Aries the Sacrificial Lamb; Fire the Fire of the Holy Spirit; Taurus the Ox of Earth, in whose manger he was laid; and lastly Aries, the flocks of sheep whose herdsmen came to worship him. Elohim yields Air, Libra, Aries; Virgo, Water; the Firmament, the Balanced Force, the Fire of the Spirit (for Aries is a fiery sign operating in the Zodiac) the Virgin Goddess and the Waters of Creation. Returning to the spelling of Yeheshuah, it is easy to see that the Lamb is an appropriate symbol of Jesus, from the prevalance of the Aries symbol, whose Fire is subdued and modified by its other associations. (Hierophant returns to his seat. Hegemon leads Practicus to West.)

Hiereus:

In the Theoricus grade you were shown the lineal figures attributed to the planets. The figures as shown consist of the Dekagram, Endekagram and Dodekagram. together with the two forms of the Enneagram and the remaining forms of the Heptagram and Octogram, which are not so consonant to the Planet. The Heptagram traced in a continuous figure, reflected from every third point, relates to the 7 planets. The Octagram formed of two squares, to the eight lettered Name. The two forms of the Enneagram refer to the Triple Ternary. The three forms of the Dekagram relate to the duplicated Heh, to the Ten Sephiroth and to Malkuth. The three forms of the Endekagram are referred to the Qlippoth. The four forms of the Dodekagram are referred to the Zodiac, the three Quaternions of angular, succedent, cadent and movable, fixed and common, the 4 Triplicities and the 24 thrones of the Elders. (Going to the second Tablet.) The term Polygon is referred to a figure having only salient or projecting angles, the term Polygram to a figure having reentering angles as well. The number of possible modes of tracing the lineal figures will then be Triangle, 1; Square, 1; Pentangle, 2; Hexangle. 2; Heptangle. 3; Octangle, 3; Enneangle. 4; Dekangle, 4; Endekangle, 4; Dodekangle. 5; (Hegemon leads Practicus to Tablet in the South.)

Heg:

Before you are the Geomantic figures arranged according to their planetary attribution, in the Tree of Life. You will note that Saturn represents the three Supernal Sephiroth summed up in Binah, while Caput and Cauda Draconis are referred to Malkuth.

Hiero:

I have much pleasure in conferring upon you the title of Lord (Lady) of the 28th Path. You will now quit the Temple for a short time, and on your return the ceremony of your passage of the 27th Path will take place. (Leads Practicus to Tablet in North.)

ADVANCEMENT 27th PATH

(Temple arranged as in diagram. Temple is darkened.)

Hiero:

Honored Hegemon, you have my command to present the Practicus with the necessary Admission Badge and to admit him (her). (Hegemon rises goes to door, opens it, presents Practicus with Calvary Cross of 10 squares and admits him.)

Heg:

The river Kishon swept them away, that ancient river, the river Kishon, O my soul, thou hast trodden down Strength. (Leads Practicus to south and places him before the mystic Pillars.)

Hiero:

Monokeris de Astris, the Path now open to you is the 27th which leads from the Grade of Practicus to the Grade of Philosophus. Take in your right hand the Calvary cross of 10 squares, and follow your Guide through the Path of Mars.

Heg:

The Lord is a Man of War, the Lord of Armies is his Name. (Hegemon leads Practicus round to foot of the Dais, Hierophant rises with red lamp in his hand.)

Hiero:

Ere the Eternal instituted the Formation, Beginning and End existed not. Therefore, before Him, he expanded a certain Veil, and therein has instituted the Primal Kings. And these are the Kings who reigned in Edom before there reigned a King over Israel but they subsisted not. When the Earth was formless and void; behold this is the reign of Edom; and when Creation was established, lo this is the reign of Israel. And the Wars of Titanic Force in the Chaos of Creation, lo these are the Wars between them. From a Light Bearer of insupportable brightness proceeded a radiating Flame, hurling forth like a vast and mighty hammer those sparks which were the primal Worlds. And these Sparks flamed and scintillated awhile, but being unbalanced they were extinguished. Since lo, the Kings assembled, they passed away together. They themselves beheld, so were they astonished, they feared, they hasted away. And these be the Kings who reigned in Edom, before there reigned a King over Israel. (Hegemon leads Practicus round the Temple and again halts before Dais, Hiereus rises with red lamp in his hand.)

Hiereus:

The Dukes of Edom were amazed, trembling took hold of the Mighty of Moab. Lord when thou wentest out of Seir, when thou marchedst out of the field of Edom, the Earth trembled and the Heavens dropped, the Clouds also dropped water. Curse ye Meroz said the Angel of the Lord, curse ye bitterly the inhabitants thereof, because they came not to the help of the Lord, to the help of the Lord against the Mighty. The river Kishon swept them away, that ancient river, the river Kishon, O my soul thou hast trodden down strength. He bowed the Heavens also and came down and Darkness was under His Feet. At the Brightness that was before Him, the thick clouds passed. The Lord thundered through the Heavens, and the highest gave His Voice, hailstones and flashings of Fire. He sent out his arrows and scattered them; he hurled forth his Lightnings and destroyed them. Then the channels of the Waters were seen, and the Foundations of the world were discovered. At thy rebuke O Lord, at the blast of the Breath of Thy nostrils. The Voice of Thy Thunder was in the Heavens, the Lightnings lightened the World, the Earth trembled and shook. Thy Way is in the Sea, and Thy Path is in the Great Waters, and Thy Footsteps are not known. (Hegemon again leads Practicus round and halts at Dais as before. Hegemon ascends Dais and takes red lamp in his hand.)

Heg:

O Lord I have heard Thy Speech and was afraid. The Voice of the Lord is upon the Waters; the God of Glory thundered, the Lord is upon many Waters. The Voice of the Lord is powerful, the Voice of the Lord is full of majesty. The Voice of the Lord breaketh the Cedars, yea, the Lord breaketh the Cedars of Lebanon. The Voice of the Lord divideth the Flames of Fire. The Voice of the Lord shaketh the Wilderness, yea, the Lord shaketh the Wilderness of Kadesh. (Hegemon places Candidate in a seat in West of Altar and facing East and takes Calvary Cross from him, returns to place.)

127

Hiero:

Eloah came from Teman of Edom, and the Holy One from Mount Paran. His Glory covered the Heavens, and the Earth was full of His praise, and His brightness was as the Light. He had Karnaim in his hands, and there was the hiding of his Power. Before him went the Pestilence and Flaming Fire went forth at his feet. He stood and measured the Earth. He beheld and drove asunder the nations and the everlasting Mountains were scattered and the perpetual Hills did bow, His ways are everlasting. I saw the tents of Cushan in affliction and the curtains of the land of Midian did tremble. Was the Lord displeased against the rivers? Was thine anger against the Rivers? Was thy wrath against the Sea, that thou didst ride upon thine horses and Thy chariots of Salvation? Thou didst cleave asunder the Earth with the Rivers. The Mountains saw Thee and they trembled; the Deluge of Waters rolled by; the Deep uttered his Voice and lifted up his hands on high. The Sun and the Moon stood still in their habitation; at the light of thine arrows they went; at the shining of thy glittering spear. Thou didst march through the land in indignation. Thou didst thresh the heathen in thine anger. Thou didst march through the Sea with Thine horses, through the Depth of the mighty Waters. (Hegemon conducts Practicus to Hierophant and hands to latter the Calvary Cross. Lights turned up.)

The Calvary Cross of 10 squares refers to the 10 Sephiroth in balanced disposition, before which the formless and the void rolled back. It also is the opened out form of the double Cube, and of the Altar of Incense. (Places cross aside.)

The 27th Path of the Sepher Yetzirah which answereth unto the letter Peh is called the Exciting Intelligence, and it is so called because by it is created the Intellect of all created beings under the highest Heaven and the excitement of the motion of them. It is, therefore, the reflection of the Sphere of Mars, and the reciprocal Path connecting Netzach with Hod, Victory with Splendor; it is the lowermost of the three reciprocal Paths. (Hierophant, Hegemon and Practicus come to the West of Altar.)

Before you upon the Altar is the 16th Key of the Tarot which symbolically resumes these Ideas. It represents a Tower struck by a lightening Flash, proceeding from a rayed circle and terminating in a Triangle. It is the Tower of Babel struck by the Fire from Heaven. It is to be noted that the Triangle at the end of the Flash issuing from the circle forms exactly the astrological symbol of Mars. It is the power of the Triad rushing down and destroying the Columns of Darkness. Three holes are rent in the walls, symbolizing the establishment of the Triad therein, and the Crown at the summit of the Tower is falling, as the Crowns of the Kings of Edom fell, who are also symbolized by the men falling headlong. On the right hand side of the Tower is Light, and the representation of the Tree of Life by the ten circles thus disposed. On the left hand side is Darkness and eleven circles, symbolizing the Qlippoth. (Hierophant, Hegemon and Practicus go to the Tablet in the East.)

This represents the Alchemical symbol of Sulphur on the Tree of Life. It does not touch the 4 lower Sephiroth. The Cross terminates in Tiphareth, whereby as it were the Supernal Triangle is to be grasped, and Tiphareth is the purified Man. The meaning of the Alchemical Symbol of Mercury was explained to you in the previous Grade. The symbol of Salt embraces all the Sephiroth but Malkuth, and is as it were, the reconciler between the Sulphur and the Mercury. The horizontal dividing line implies the precept of Hermes as above, so below. (Hierophant resumes his place. Hiereus, Hegemon and Practicus go to the Tablets in the West.)

Hiereus:

This Tablet represents the Trinity operating through the Sephiroth, and reflected downwards in the four Triangles of the Elements, through the Tree of Life. Notice that Air is reflected from Kether through Tiphareth to Yesod. Water is reflected from Binah through

Chesed to Hod; and Fire is reflected from Chokmah through Geburah to Netzach. While Malkuth is Earth, the receptacle of the other three. On this second Tablet is the Image of Nebuchadnezzar, whose head was of Gold, the breast and the arms of Silver, the belly and thighs of Brass, the legs of Iron, the feet part of Iron and part of Clay. In his hands are represented the Hot and Moist Natures. (Hegemon conducts Practicus to Tablet of Yetziratic Palaces in the South.)

Heg:

These are the Seven Yetziratic Palaces, containing the 10 Sephiroth. In each Palace are the six letters from the Divine Name of 42 letters. Thus, the Name of 42 letters has been taken from the 42 first letters of the History of Creation, as far as Beth of the word "Bohu" by various transmutations which are described at length in the Sepher Pardes. (Leads Practicus to Tablet in North.) These are the Qlippoth with their 12 Princes, who are the heads of the 12 months of the year. In the central square are placed Samael and Asmodai. At the South East are the Man, the Serpent and the Elder Lilith, the wife of Samael. At the North East angle are the Ox and the Ass, the Aggareth, the Daughter of Machalath. At the North West angle are the Scorpion and Asimon the unnamed One, and Nehemah. And at the South West are the Lion and the Horse, the Younger Lilith, the Wife of Asmodai.

Hiero:

I have much pleasure in conferring upon you the title of Lord (Lady) of the 27th Path. You will now quit the Temple for a short time, and on your return the Ceremony of your reception in the Grade of Philosophus will take place.

ADVANCEMENT CEREMONY OF PHILOSOPHUS

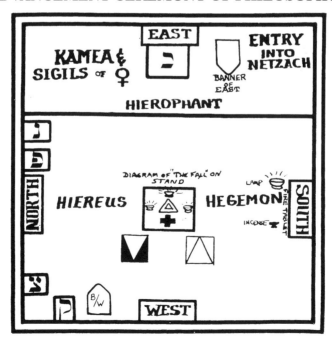

Hiero:

Honored Hegemon instruct the Practicus in the proper alarm, present him with the necessary admission badge and admit him. (Hegemon goes without and instructs the Practicus to give an alarm of 7 Knocks. Hegemon then admits Practicus.) In the North West are the Portals of the 29th and 28th Paths by which you have symbolically entered this Grade from the Zelator and Theoricus Grades, respectively, while in the North is the Portal of the 27th Path, by which you have just passed from the Grade of Practicus. (Hegemon leads Practicus forward to Hiereus.)

Hiereus:

By what symbol dost thou enter herein?

Heg:

By the peculiar emblem of the Hegemon, which is the Calvary Cross of 6 squares within a circle.

Hiereus:

This Cross embraces as you see Tiphareth, Netzach, Hod and Yesod and rests upon Malkuth. The surrounding circle includes Chesed, Geburah and Malkuth. Also the Calvary Cross of 6 squares forms the cube, and is thus referred to the 6 Sephiroth of Microprosopus, which are Chesed, Geburah, Tiphareth, Netzach, Hod and Yesod. (Hegemon resumes his seat. Hierophant comes to West of Altar.)

Hiero:

This is the symbolic representation of the Fall. For the Great Goddess who in the Practicus Grade was supporting the columns of the Sephiroth in the form of the Sign of Theoricus being tempted by the Tree of Knowledge (whose branches indeed, tend upward into the Seven lower Sephiroth, but also tend downwards into the Kingdom of the Shells) reached down into the Qlippoth, and immediately the columns were unsupported, and the Sephirotic system was shattered, and with it fell Adam, the Microprosopus. Then arose the Great Dragon with 7 heads and 10 horns, and the Garden was made desolate, and Malkuth was cut off from the upper Sephiroth by his intersecting folds, and linked unto the Kingdom of the Shells, and the 7 lower Sephiroth were cut from the three Supernal in Daath; at the feet of Aima Elohim. And on the heads of the Dragon are the Names and Crow ns of the eight Edomite Kings, and upon the horns are the names of the 11 Dukes of Edom. And because in DAATH was the utmost rise of the Great Serpent of Evil, therefore is there as it were, another Sephira, making eight heads according to the number of the 8 Kings. And for the Infernal and Averse Sephiroth 11 instead of 10, according to the number of the Dukes of Edom. And hence were the Rivers of Eden desecrated, and from the mouth of the Dragon rushed the Infernal Waters in DAATH. And this is Leviathan, the piercing Serpent, even Leviathan, the Crooked Serpent. But between the devastated Garden and the Supernal Eden, Tetragrammaton Elohim placed the letters of the Name and the Flaming Sword, that the uppermost part of the Tree of Life might not be involved in the Fall of Adam. And thence was it necessary that the Second Adam should come to restore all things and that the First Adam had been extended on the Cross of the Celestial Rivers, so the Son should be crucified on the Cross of the Infernal Rivers in Daath. Yet to do this he must descend unto the lowest first even unto Malkuth and be born of her.

The Grade of Philosophus is referred unto the Sephira Netzach and the 27th, 28th and 29th Paths are bound thereto. The Sign of the Grade is given by raising the arms above the head making with the thumbs and fingers a triangle apex upwards. This represents the element of Fire, to w'hich this Grade is attributed, and also the Spirit which moved upon the Waters of Creation. The Grip or Token is the general grip of the First Order. The Grand Word is a name of nine letters Tetragrammaton Tzabaoth, which means the Lord of Armies. The mystic number is 28 and from it is formed the Pass Word of the Grade which is Koch (Kaph, Cheth) meaning Power. It should be lettered separately when given. Unto this Grade and unto the Sephira Netzach, the 7th Path of the Sepher Yetzirah is referred. It is called the Recondite Intelligence and it is so called because it is the Refulgent Splendour of all the intellectual Virtues which are perceived by the Eyes of the Mind and by the contemplation of Faith.

The distinguishing badge of this Grade, which you will now be entitled to wear, is the sash of a Practicus, with the addition of a bright green cross above the violet cross and the numbers 4 and 7 within a circle and a square respectively left and right of its summit, and below the number 37, the numbers 27, 28 and 29 in bright green between narrow parallel lines of the same color. This Grade is especially referred unto the element of Fire and therefore the Great Watch Tower or Terrestrial Tablet of the South forms one of its principal emblems. (Hierophant and Practicus go to the South.) It is known as the fourth or great Southern Quadrangle, or Tablet of Fire and it is one of the four Great Tablets delivered unto Enoch by the Great Angel Ave. From it are drawn the 3 Great Holy Secret Names of God OIP TEEA PDOCE which are borne upon the Banners of the South, and the numberless Divine and Angelic names which appertain unto the Element of Fire. The meaning of the other Tablets have been already explained to you. (They return to the Altar.) The triangle surmounting the cross upon the Altar, represents the Fire of the Spirit surmounting the cross of Life and of the Waters of Eden. You will note that it thus forms the alchemical emblem of Sulphur. The red lamps at the angles of the triangles are the three fold forms of Fire. (They proceed to the East.)

The Portals in the East and North East conduct to the Higher. The others are those of the Paths you have already traversed. This Grade is also related to the Planet Venus. Its Kamea or mystical square is formed of 49 squares containing the numbers from 1 to 49 arranged so as to show the same sum each way. The ruling numbers are 7, 49, 175 and 1252. This Tablet (indicating it) shows the mystical Names and Seals drawn from the Kamea of Venus. The Seals are formed by lines drawn from and to, certain numbers upon the Square. The name answering to 7 is AHA, that answering to 49 is HAGIEL, the Intelligence of Venus; that answering to 175 is Qedemel the Spirit of Venus and lastly that answering to 1252 is BENI SERAPHIM the name of the Intelligence of Venus. On this Tablet is shown the meaning of the symbol of Venus on the Tree of Life. It embraces all the Sephiroth, and is therefore the fitting symbol of the Isis of Nature. Hence also its circle is always represented larger than that of Mercury. (Hierophant resumes his seat. Hegemon leads Practicus to Hiereus and they go forward to West.)

Hiereus:

On th is Tablet (indicating it) are shown the Paths when arranged with DAATH added to the Sephirotic Tree. It differs from the other and more usual attributions. Furthermore it is not so correct, as Daath is not properly speaking, a Sephira. On this Tablet (indicating it) is shown the arrangement of the Sephiroth in the Four Worlds, each Sephira with its own 10 Sephiroth inscribed inside, so that the total number is 400, the number of Tau the last letter of the alphabet. (Hiereus resumes his place. Hegemon leads Practicus to Tablet in South.)

Heg:

This is the symbolism of the Altar of Burnt Offering which King Solomon built. It was formed of a four-fold cube, 20 cubits square and 10 feet high, 10 are the principal parts which you here see classified above, as under the Sephiroth, and forming thus the Triangle of Fire above it. (Hegemon leads Practicus to Tablet in North.) This is the symbolism of the Brazen Sea, which King Solomon made. It was 10 cubits diameter answering to the Sephiroth; the height was 5 cubits the number of the letter Heh. 30 cubits was its circumference, the 10 cubits multiplied by the Ternary. Beneath the rim were 300 knops, the number of the Holy letter Shin and of the name Ruach Elohim and it stood upon the 12 oxen, answering to the 12 Stars of the Crown of Aima, the Great Mother. It is the synthesis of Binah, containing the Waters of Creation. (Places Candidate in a seat in West facing Hierophant and returns to his own place.)

Hiero:

I now congratulate you, Honored Frater (Soror) on having passed through the ceremony of Philosophus and in recognition thereof, I confer upon you the Mystic title of Pharos Uluminans, which means the illuminating Tower of Light and I give you the symbol of ASCH, which is the Hebrew word for Fire. And as having attained at length unto the highest Grade of the First Order, and being as it were, the connecting link with the Second Order, I further confer upon you the title of respect of Honored Frater (Soror) and I give you the further symbol of Phrath or Euphrates, the 4th River. (Knocks) In the Name of Tetragrammaton Tzabaoth, I now proclaim that you have been duly advanced to the Grade of Philosophus and that you are Lord (Lady) of the 27th, 28th and 29th Paths.

Hiereus:

Honored Frater, as a member of this important Grade, you are eligible for the post of Hiereus. when a vacancy occurs; you are furthermore expected, as having risen so high in the Order, to aid to your utmost the members of the Second Order in the working of the Temple to which you are attached. To study thoroughly the mysteries which have been unfolded to your view, in your progress from the humble position of a Neophyte, so that yours may be not the merely superficial knowledge which marks the conceited and ignorant man; but that you may really and thoroughly understand what you profess to know, and not by your ignorance and folly bring disgrace on that Order w'hich has honored you so far. Your duty is also to supervise the studies of weaker and less advanced brethren, and to make yourself as far as possible an ornament alike to your Temple and to your Order.

CLOSING

Hiero:

(Knocks) Honored Fratres and Sorores, assist me to close the Temple in the Grade of Philosophus. Honored Hegemon, see that the Temple is properly guarded. (Done.)

Heg:

(Knocks) Very Honored Hierophant the Temple is properly guarded.

Hiero:

Let us adore the Lord and King of Fire. (Knocks. All face East.) Tetragrammaton of Hosts, Mighty and Terrible; the Commander of the Ethereal Armies art Thou. Amen. (All salute. Hierophant quits his throne and goes to Tablet of Fire in South. All face South.) Let us rehearse the prayer of the Salamanders or Fire Spirits. (Knocks) Immortal, Eternal, Ineffable and uncreated Father of All, borne upon the Chariot of Worlds, which ever roll in ceaseless motion, Ruler over the Ethereal Vastness, where the Throne of Thy Power is raised, from the summit of which Thine eyes behold all, and Thy pure and Holy ears hear all, help us thy children, whom thou hast loved since the Birth of the Ages of Time. Thy Majesty Golden, Vast and Eternal, shineth above the Heaven of Stars; above them art Thou exalted, O Thou Flashing Fire. There Thou illuminateth all things with Thine insupportable Glory, whence flow the ceaseless streams of splendor which nourish Thine Infinite Spirit. This Infinite Spirit nourisheth all, and maketh that inexhaustable treasure of generation which ever encompasseth Thee, replete with the numberless forms wherewith Thou hast filled it from the beginning. From this Spirit arise those most Holy Kings, who are around Thy Throne and who compose Thy court. O Universal Father! One and Alone! Father alike of Immortals and of Mortals! Thou hast especially created Powers similar unto Thy thought Eternal and unto Thy venerable Essence. Thou hast established them above the Angels who announce Thy Will to the World. Lastly, thou hast created us as a Third Order in our Elemental Empire. There our continual exercise is to praise and to adore Thy desires. There we ceaselessly burn with Eternal Aspiration unto Thee O Father, O Mother of Mothers, O Archetype Eternal of Maternity and of Love, O Son, the flower of all Sons, Form of all forms. Soul, Spirit, Harmony and Numeral of all Things. Amen. (Making with his sceptre the banishing Circle and Pentagram in the air in front of the Tablet.) Depart ye in peace unto your abodes and habitations. May the blessing of Elohim be upon you. Be there ever peace between us and you and be ye ready to come when ye are called. (Knocks. Returns to place. All face as usual.) In the Name of Tetragrammaton Tzabaoth, I declare This Temple closed in the Grade of Philosophus.

Hiero:

(Knocks 3, 3, 1)

Hiereus:

(Knocks 3, 3, 1)

Heg:

(Knocks 3, 3, 1)

RITUALS OF THE R.R. ET A.C. WITH THOSE OF WAITE'S FELLOWSHIP

VOLUME SEVEN

RITUALS OF THE R.R. ET A.C. WITH THOSE OF WAITE'S FELLOWSHIP

TABLE OF CONTENTS

IMPORTANT TABLES AND ILLUSTRATIONS

VOLUME SEVEN

RITUALS OF THE R.R. ET A.C. WITH THOSE OF WAITE'S FELLOWSHIP

RITUAL OF THE PORTAL OF THE VAULT OF THE ADEPTI

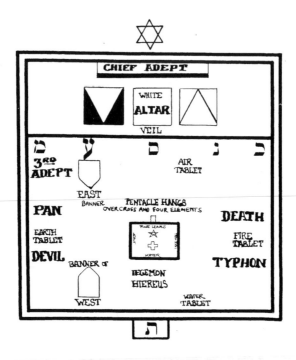

REQUIREMENTS

Chief Adept: White Cassock, Yellow Shoes, Red Cloak of Hierophant, Yellow and White Nemyss, Rose-Cross on Yellow Collar. Sceptre of five Elemental Colours surmounted by Pentagram, White Lamp and Brazier and Candle.

Second Adept: White Cassock and Collar, Blue Shoes, Blue and Orange Cloak and Nemyss, Lamen of Red Triangle in Green Pentagram, Red Wand headed by Red Sulphur Symbol, Red Lamp and Incense Sticks.

Third Adept: White Cassock, Blue Collar, and Red Shoes, Red and Green Nemyss and Cloak, Blue Wand headed by Blue Salt Symbol, Lamen of Blue, Cup on Orange Octagram, Cup of Water.

Hiereus: Black Cassock, Black Collar, Black and White Nemyss, Red Shoes and Collar, Sword, Lamen of Four Colours of Malkuth with White Hexagram, Salt.

Hegemon: Black Cassock, White Cloak, Red Shoes, Yellow and Purple Nemyss, Mitreheaded Sceptre, Lamen of Red and Blue Hexagram on White Ground, Yellow Collar, Rose Leaves.

OPENING

(Chief Adept is behind the Veil in the East, symbolically in Tiphareth, other Officers in their Sephirotic Stations. Third Adept in the North East, Second Adept in the South East. Hiereus in West, Hegemon East of Altar. The Hall is in Darkness, the Elemental Lamps unlit, no lights except those burning behind the Veil and shaded candles for Officers. Any

Members attending must give the Portal Signs on entering the Temple. Portal Members sit in the North, full Adepti Minores in the South.)

2nd Ad:

(Knock. All rise.) Very Honoured Fratres and Sorores, assist me to open the Portal of the Vault of the Adepti. Honoured Hiereus, see that the entrance is closed and guarded.

Hiereus:

Very Honoured Fratres and Sorores, in token of our search for the Light, give the Sign of the Grade of Neophyte. (All turn East and stand in the Sign of the Enterer. From behind the Curtain, the Chief Adept's hand is stretched out, holding a white Lamp or Candle. Chief Adept unseen, gives the Sign of Silence, all repeat Sign as Light is withdrawn.)

Ch.Ad:

The Light shineth in Darkness, but the Darkness comprehendeth it not.

2nd Ad:

The Dukes of Edom ruled in Chaos, Lords of unbalanced force. Honoured Hiereus, what is the Symbol upon the Altar?

Hiereus:

The Symbol of the equated forces of the Four Elements.

2nd Ad:

Banished be the Power of the Dukes of Edom, and let the Power of the Cross be established. (Chief Adept signs Cross with lighted candle. Hiereus goes to East, begins Lesser Banishing Ritual of Pentagram. When he returns East all Officers and Members make Qabalistic cross, facing East and repeat words with him. Hiereus returns to West and makes the Zelator Sign. Hegemon in the East makes the Theoricus Sign and Knocks. Third Adept in North makes the Practicus Sign and Knocks. Second Adept in South makes the Philosophus Sign and Knocks.)

Ch. Ad:

The Cross upon the Altar is also a Cross of corrosion, corruption, disintegration and death. Therefore, doth it fall in the Paths of Death and the Devil. Unless in Hod, the Glory triumpheth over matter and the Corruptible putteth on Incorruption, thus attaining unto the beauty of Tiphareth; unless in Netzach, Death is swallowed up in Victory and the Transformer becometh the Transmuter into Pure Alchemic Gold. Except ye be born of Water and the Spirit, ye cannot enter the Kingdom of God. What then Very Honoured Third Adept, is the additional Mystic Title bestowed upon a Philosophus as a link with the Second Order?

3rd Ad:

Phrath, the Fourth River of Eden.

Hiereus:

Tau.

Heg:

Resh.

3rd Ad.

Peh.

Ch. Ad:

Very Honoured Second Adept, what may be added to this Word?

2nd Ad:

Kaph (Knock)

Hiereus:

Tau (Knock)

Heg:

Resh (Knock)

3rd Ad:

Peh (Knock)

Ch. Ad:

The whole Word is Paroketh, which is the Veil of the Tabernacle. (All make Signs of Rending of the Veil.)

Ch. Ad:

(Knocks) In and by that Word, I permit the Portal of the Vault of the Adepti to be opened. (Second and Third Adepts draw aside curtains revealing Chief Adept who rises with Pentacle and taper in left hand, Sceptre in right.) Let us establish the Dominion of the Mystic ETH over the Four Elements. (Chief Adept faces East. All face East. Chief Adept having descended from the Dais and taken his position in front of Air Tablet, Hegemon stands behind Chief bearing Rose Leaves. All make Qabalistic Cross. Hegemon places Rose Leaves before Air Tablet and stands in the Theoricus Sign. Chief lights the Lamps as he goes round. Chief Adept invokes Air and lights Lamp. Hegemon takes Rose Leaves to Altar and puts them on Air arm of Cross and remains East of Altar facing West. Chief Adept goes to South. Second Adept comes behind, places sticks of incense before Tablet and stand in Philosophus Sign. Chief Adept invokes Fire and lights Lamp as before. Second Adept takes incense to Altar and places it on Fire arm of the Cross and stands at South of Altar looking North.

Chief Adept goes West lights Lamp. Third Adept stands behind him, places Cup before Tablet and stands in Sign of Practicus. Chief Adept invokes Water. Third Adept takes Cup to Altar, places it on Water arm of Cross and stands in Sign of Practicus. Chief Adept goes North. Lights Lamp, Hiereus stands behind him, places Salt before Tablet and stands in Zelator Sign. Chief Adept invokes Earth. Hiereus takes Salt to the Altar, places it on Earth arm of Cross and stands at the North of Altar. Chief Adept completes circle in East, then circumambulates with Sol to West of Altar, having now lit all the Elemental Lamps.) In the Great Name YOD HE VAU HE. (All give Neophyte Signs towards Altar, and then stand in Elemental Signs. Chief Adept makes Invoking Spirit Pentagrams with Deity Names

4

EHEIEH and AGLA closing with the Qabalistic Cross. He moves round the Altar to East faces West lays Pentacle over Cross. Holds Candle and Wand on high.)

May the Cross of the Four Elements become truly purified and planted in Incorruption. Wherefore in the Name of YOD HE VAU HE and in the Concealed Name YEHESHUAH, do I add the power of the Pentagram constituting the Glorified Body of Osiris, the Sign of the Microcosmos.

(All lights are turned up. Chief Adept lays Pentacle for a moment on Cross then hangs it on hook in centre of Hall, raises Sceptre and Candle on high, and invokes:)

OL SONUF VA-ORSAGI GOHO IADA BALATA. ELEXARPEH COMANANU TABITOM. ZODAKARA, EKA ZODAKARE OD ZODAMERANU. ODO KIKLE QAA PIAPE PIAMOEL OD VAOAN.

(Chief Adept returns to Dais. Second and Third follow and stand by Pillars. Hiereus and Hegemon face East, North and South of Altar.) Let us adore the Lord and King of Hosts.

> **Holy art Thou, Lord of the Universe.**
> **Holy art Thou Whom Nature hath not formed;**
> **Holy art Thou the Vast and the Mighty One,**
> **Lord of the Light and of the Darkness.**

By the Word Paroketh and in the Sign of the Rending of the Veil, I declare that the Portal of the Vault of the Adepti has been opened.

Ch. Ad:

(Knocks 4, 1)

2nd Ad:

(Knocks 4, 1)

3rd Ad:

(Knocks 4, 1)

Hiereus:

(Knocks 4, 1)

Heg:

(Knocks 4, 1)

(He circumambulates once, then returns to seat. All take seats, after the Elements are replaced in Four Quarters by respective Officers.)

THE RITUAL OF THE CROSS AND FOUR ELEMENTS

Ch. Ad:

(Concealed behind the Veil) The Portal symbolically opened for the Order, is yet closed to the unprepared Candidate. (Elemental Lamps are veiled. Temple in darkness save at East.)

2nd. Ad:

V.H. Fratres and Sorores, our Honoured Frater (XYZ) having been a member of the Grade of Philosophus for the space of 7 months and having passed the five-fold examination prescribed for admission to the Second Order, has been duly approved. I hold a Dispensation from the G. H. Chiefs of the Second Order to permit him to approach the Portal of the Vault of the Adepti. V.H. 3rd Adept, see that he is duly prepared by wearing the Sash of the Philosophus Grade, admit him, and having examined him in his knowledge, having placed around his neck the Admission Badge, the Grip, Sign, Words, etc. of the Philosophus Grade and of the Word Phrath before you instruct him in the necessary Knock. (Lights are extinguished. 2nd. Ad. stands before the Veil. Hiereus and Heg. bar the way near the door. 3rd Adept, having prepared Philosophus opens door showing Darkness but for faint Light in the East, and brings Philosophus just within the door.).

Heg:

The Realm of Chaos and of Ancient Night, ere ever the Aeons were, when there was neither Heaven or Earth, nor was there any Sea, when naught was, save the Shape Unluminous, formless and void.

Hiereus:

To and fro in the Deeps, swayed the coils of the Dragon with 8 Heads and 11 Horns. Eleven were the curses of Mount Ebal, eleven the Rulers of the Qlippoth, and at their head were the Dual Contending Forces. (Hiereus and Heg. lower weapons and step back.)

2nd Ad:

(Faces East) Then breathed forth Tho-oth out of the Unutterable Abyss the Word! Then stood forth Tho-oth in the Sign of the Enterer, on the Threshold of the Hall of Time as Time was born of the Eternal. (Gives Neophyte Sign) So stood Tho-oth in the Power of the Word, giving forth Light, while the Aeons that were unbegotten unfolded before him. (Philosophus directed to give Neophyte Sign.)

2nd Ad:

And Elohim said Let there be Light. (The hand of the Ch. Ad. hands out the Candle. 2nd Ad. receives it and gives Sign of Silence. Philosophus is directed to make Sign. 3rd Ad. leaves Philosophus comes East. Takes Candle and returns with Sol. He holds Candle before Philosophus and takes Banner of West in left hand.)

2nd Ad:

Honoured Frater, what was the Title you received in the Grade of Philosophus?

Phil:

(Unprompted) Pharos Illuminans.

3rd Ad:

(Gives Philosophus Candle and takes his station on the left hand of Philosophus.)

2nd Ad:

Honoured Frater Pharos Illuminans, we are here assembled to open for you the Portal of the Vault of the Adepti, which admits you to the Second Degree and brings you to the Threshold of the Inner or Second Order. But because of the increased influence over the Members of the Order that such advancement necessarily confers, and because of the increased power for good or evil that will follow if, with steadfast will and aspiration, you take this step in essence as well as in form, it is needful that you take further pledges, which however, as in the previous Degree, contain nothing contrary to your civil, moral or religious duties. Are you willing to take these pledges?

Phil:

I am willing.

2nd Ad:

Then you will take in your right hand the Banner of the West (3rd Ad. gives it to him) and place your left hand in that of the Very Honoured 3rd Adept, who is the living Symbol of the Black Pillar which ruleth in the Outer Order, and touch the corresponding Emblem, the Black Sash of restriction, on your breast, and thus bind yourself while raising the Light which you hold, in witness of your pledge. (Philosophus raises right hand holding Banner and Light, while his left hand, held by 3rd Ad. touches Sash.)

2nd Ad:

Firstly, do you pledge yourself never to reveal the Secrets and Mysteries of these Paths and of this Ceremony, either to the outer and uninitiated world, or to a Member of the 1st Order, save in full Temple and with due sanction.

Phil:

I do.

2nd Ad:

Secondly, do you further solemnly promise to use whatever practical knowledge you may now, or at any future time possess, for a good end alone?

Phil:

I do.

2nd Ad:

Thirdly, do you also promise to regard all the knowledge imparted to you as a trust, given into your hands, not for your selfish advantage, but for the service of all mankind, that the ancient tradition of Initiation be kept pure and undefiled, and the Light be not lost for those that seek it in this Path?

Phil:

I do.

2nd Ad:

And lastly, do you solemnly promise to exercise brotherly love, charity and forbearance towards the Members of the Order, neither slandering, backbiting nor reviling them, whether you have cause for the same or not, but uniting with them to form a fabric of mutual confidence and support; and do you further undertake, not to be a stirrer up of strife, of schism, or of opposition to the Chiefs, but rather to uphold their authority in all loyalty?

Phil:

I do.

2nd Ad:

Then, realising the Cross about your neck, you will lift up your right hand, holding the Banner and the Light and say: I undertake to maintain the Veil between the First and the Second Orders, and may the Powers of the Elements bear witness to my pledges. (Done. Philosophus repeating words as directed. 3rd Ad. leaves Philosophus and returns to his place, having replaced Banner of West.)

2nd Ad:

The Symbol of the 1st Grade of Neophyte is 0-0. To the first 0 is attached a Circle, to the second, a Square. The union of the circle and the square hath many meanings, of which one must be put before you, for this you must accomplish in your own person, ere you can advance further. For if in the mystic sphere of Truth, the way of Initiation may be trodden alone, yet in another Sphere, it hath a three-fold aspect. Part that can be given to man from without, part that can be attained by man himself, part that can only come from the Divine. Now, in the Order, you were given intellectual teaching, and won your Grades in tests of what was taught. Here, you must prove that you have truly attained thus far of your own strength, and after, you may progress by the higher Soul within you. Round your neck, you wear the Symbol of the Cross of Four Elements, equilibriated and equated. Establish it firmly in the Sphere of your own being and advance with courage. (Hiereus and Hegemon bar the way as in Zelator Grade.)

Hiereus:

Give me the Signs and Words of the Grade of Zelator. (Done. Hegemon returns to place.)

Hiereus:

Give me also the Grip of the First Order. (Done. He takes Philosophus to North directing him to take up Salt from before Earth Tablet. They face North, Hiereus makes a cross over Salt with Sword then stands in the Zelator Sign while Philosophus circumambulates with Sol repeating Earth Names.)

Phil:

Adonai Ha Aretz. Emor Dial Hectega. Auriel. Ic Zod Heh Chal. (He returns to North. Hiereus makes Earth Pentagram over Salt. Philosophus reveals Lamp. Hiereus takes Philosophus to Altar and directs him to place Salt at North side of Altar. Hiereus takes him to diagrams in West.)

Hiereus:

The Cross of Four Triangles called the Maltese Cross, is a Symbol of the Four Elements in balanced disposition. It is here given in the colours of the King's scale, and is also assigned to the Four Sephiroth ruling the Grades of the Outer. Earth to Malkuth, Air to Yesod, Water to Hod and Fire to Netzach. It is again, the Cross which heads the Praemonstrator's Wand, who represents the Sephira Chesed, the Fourth Sephira. Four is also the Number of Jupiter, whose Path unites Chesed to Netzach. The Cross is therefore a fit Emblem for the Grade of Philosophus. In this diagram are represented the Circle, the Point, the Line, the Cross, the Square and the Cube. For the Circle is the Abyss, the Nothingness, the AIN. The Point is Kether. Now, the Point has no dimension, but in moving, it traces the Line. This gives the first number, Unity, yet therein lies duality unmanifest, for two Points mark its ends. The movement of the line maketh the Plane or Square. The motion of the Point at angles to its first direction and intersecting it maketh the Cross. So therefore, are the Square and the Cross but one Symbol, deriving from the Circle and the Point. Below, is shown the Occult Symbol of Malkuth, the Tenth Sephira. It is in Four parts, corresponding to the Maltese Cross. They are Fire of Earth, Water of Earth, Air of Earth, Earth of Earth, as is indicated by the Symbol. They correspond to the Four Grades of the First Order, which in one sense, quitteth not Malkuth, being the Grades of the Four Lowest Sephiroth of Malkuth in Assiah. Upon them, is surcharged a white Hexagram in a Circle. The 6 and the 4 make 10, the number of Malkuth on the Tree. The Hexagram is also the Sign of the Macrocosm, of Tiphareth, and of the Six Upper Sephiroth, wherefore here it is white, Spirit ruling over matter. Six is a perfect number, for its whole equals the sum of its parts. Six are the middle points of the planes bounding a cube, which derives from the square, and from the Cross, if the centre point moves. In these numbers and figures are hid many revelations. Remember that the whole number of Malkuth is 496, which is again a perfect number. Malkuth must then be equated and perfected by the 6 ruling the 4. and the link between 6 and 4 is the number of the Pentagram.

2nd Ad:

Having achieved the entry into Malkuth, it is needful that you should pass through the Path of Tau, the dark Path of the Astral Plane. Go, therefore, to the Tablet of the East.

(Phil, goes to East, Hiereus and Hegemon bar the way, points of implements downwards and touching. Hegemon demands Theoricus Sign and Words. Hiereus returns to place. Hegemon leads Philosophus to Tablet, gives Philosophus rose leaves, makes Cross over bowl and directs Philosophus to circumambulate repeating Names. Hegemon stands in Theoricus Sign while Philosophus traverses Path of Tau in the Names of Shaddai El Chai, Raphael, ORO IBAH AOZPI and Bataivah. Philosophus returns to East. Hegemon makes invoking Pentagram and directs Philosophus to uncover Lamp. Hegemon takes Philosophus to Altar and directs him to put Rose leaves at East side, then standing East of the Altar in Yesod, Hegemon shows Great Hermetic Arcanum.)

Heg:

This Symbol represents the Great Hermetic Arcanum. The feet of the Figure rest upon the Earth and the Sea. In the Hand are represented the hot and moist natures, symbolised by the torch and the horn of water. These are further strengthened by the Solar and fiery Emblems of the King and Lion, and the Luna and watery emblems of the Queen and Dolphin. Above the whole figure rise the wings of the aerial nature, the Reconciler between the Fire and the Water. Compare this Symbol with the Angel described in the 10th Chapter of the Apocalypse of St. John. And I saw another mighty Angel come down from heaven clothed with a cloud; and a rainbow was upon his head, and his face as it were, the Sun, and his feet were as pillars of fire, and he had in his hand a little book open; and he set his right foot upon the Sea and his left foot upon the Earth, and he cried with a loud voice as when a lion roareth, the Green Lion, the Path of Leo above Tiphareth, referring to Teth and when he cried, seven thunders uttered their voices, seven Aeons, represented under the regimen of the Planets. The Dragon issuing from the cave represents volcanic fires. (Heg. leads Phil. once round, and hands him over to Hiereus in the North and returns to place.)

Hiereus:

This is the Image of the Vision of Nebuchadnezzar, which was showed you in the passage of the 27th Path, leading to the Grade of Philosophus. Thou, O King, sawest and beheld a great image. This Great Image, whose brightness was excellent stood before thee and the form thereof was terrible. This Image's head was pure gold, his breast and his arms were silver, his belly and his thighs were brass, his legs of iron and his feet part of iron and part of clay. Thou sawest till that a stone was cut out without hands, which smote the Image upon its feet, which were part of iron and part of clay. And brake them to pieces. Then was the iron, the clay, the brass, the silver and the Gold broken to pieces together and became like the chaff of the summer threshing floors; and the wind carried them away and no place was found for them; and the stone that smote the image became a great mountain and filled the whole earth. Thou, O King, art a King of Kings, for the God in heaven hath given unto thee (makes Qabalistic Cross) the Kingdom, the Power and the Glory!

Thou art this head of Gold. (to Phil.) Thou art this head of Gold! Thy head represents in thee the dominion of the Divine ruling over the rest of the body. The Silver is the world of the heart, the brass is the material passion, the iron is the firm purpose, and the feet, part of iron and part of clay, are the mingled strength and infirmity of the natural man. And the Stone made without hands is the Eternal Stone of the Wise, which will become the Mountain of Initiation, whereby the whole Earth shall be filled with the knowledge of God. (Hiereus takes Philosophus to second diagram.)

Hiereus:

This Tablet shows the symbolic manner in which certain names have been used by our ancient brethren. You will note that the initials of this sentence make the Latin word Vitriolum, Sulphuric acid. Furthermore, the word Vitriol, Sulphur, and Mercury each consist of seven letters answering to the alchemic powers of the seven Planets. The initials of the following sentence in Latin, the subtil fluid, the Light of the Earth, make the word S.A.L.T. salt, and further, the four words of the sentence answer to the four Elements: Subtilis, Air; Aqua, Water; Lux, Fire; and Terra, Earth. And the four words united yield 20 letters, that is, the product of four, the number of the Elements, multiplied by Five, the number of the Pentagram. The words Fiat Lux, meaning Let there by Light, consist of 7 letters. The letters of Fiat form the initials of Flatis, Air; Aqua, Water; Ignus, Fire; and Terra, Earth. (Hegemon goes to South). Which four names again yield 20 letters as in the previous case. And the word Lux is formed from the angles of the Cross, LVX. (He leads Philosophus once round and then to Hegemon who awaits them in the South.)

Heg:

These are the Seven Palaces of Holiness of the Briatic World. The first is the Palace of the Holy of Holies answering to Kether, Chokmah and Binah, and the Divine Name EL. The second is the Palace of Love, answering to Chesed and the Divine Name MATZPATZ (Mem, Tzaddi, Peh, Tzaddi), which is a Temurah of Tetragrammaton. The third is the Palace of Merit, answering to Geburah, and the Divine Name YEHEVID (Yod, Heh, Vau, Daleth). The fourth is the Palace of Benevolence, answering to Tiphareth and TETRAGRAMMATON. The fifth is the Palace of the Substance of Heaven, answering to Netzach and ELOHIM. The sixth is the Palace of Severity answering to Hod and MATZPATZ. The seventh is the Palace of Crystal Whiteness answering to Yesod and Malkuth, and the Divine Name YAH and ADONAI. But the synthesis of these Holy Names is to be found in the word TAKLITH which is Perfection. (Points to another Tablet in the North.)

VOLUME SEVEN

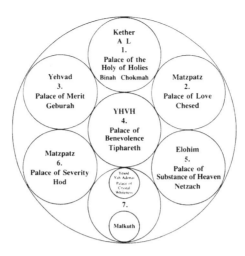

SEVEN PALACES OF HOLINESS

Heg:

The Seraphim in the vision of Isaiah are described as having six wings: With twain He covered his face, and with twain He covered his feet, and with twain He did fly. That is, his synthesis is to be found in the Hexagram and in the idea of the Seven, more especially dominating the planetary region. But the Kerubim of Ezekiel have each 4 faces, those of the Lion, the Bull, the Man and the Eagle counterchanged with each other by revolution, whence the symbolic forms of the wheels beside them, wherein was the Spirit; and with two of the wings they covered their bodies and two were stretched upwards, one to another. So the synthesis of the Kerubim is found in the revolving Cross, in the Pentagram, and in the idea of one Spirit dominating the four Elements. But the Kerubim of St. John's vision in the Apocalypse are uncompounded, having single heads, but they have six wings and thus unite the powers of the seven with the four. And their cry is similar to that of the Seraphim of Isaiah: Holy, Holy, Holy.

(Hegemon returns to place. 2nd and 3rd Ad. bar way in S.W. Ask for Practicus Words. 3rd Ad. comes forward and conducts Philosophus to West. He gives Philosophus cup of Water, directs Philosophus to go around repeating the Words while he remains standing in the Practicus Sign. Philosophus returns to West. 3rd Ad. makes invoking Pentagram of Water over Cup. Philosophus removes shade from Light. 3rd Ad. takes him to Altar where he places cup in the West. 2nd Ad. and 3rd Ad. bar way and ask for Philosophus Words. 2nd Ad. comes forward and conducts Philosophus to South. 3rd Ad. remaining at Altar in Practicus Sign, while Hiereus and Hegemon come to North and East of Altar and stand in Grade Signs. 2nd Ad. in South gives Philosophus incense, makes a Cross over it. Philosophus walks around repeating Philosophus Words while 2nd Ad. stands in Philosophus Sign. Philosophus returns South removes shade. 2nd Ad. takes him to Altar, directs him to place Incense at South. He takes Cross from Philosophus' neck and places it in the midst of the Four Elements. Philosophus is directed to stand West of Altar in Neophyte Sign. 3rd Ad. behind him. The four Officers in Grade Signs.)

11

Hiereus:

From the centre outwards, so moveth the point as it traceth the line and the Cross. Equated and equilibriated lie here the Four Elements of the body of Osiris slain.

2nd Ad:

May the corrosive Cross return upon itself, from without inward from the Four Quarters to the Center, and become by sacrifice and transmutation, an offering acceptable, a body glorified. (Chief Adept unseen sounds gongs once.)

2nd Ad:

(To Phil.) You will now quit the Temple for a short time, and on your return the Ceremony of your advance will be proceeded with. (Philosophus gives Sign of Silence and is led out by Hiereus.)

RITE OF THE PENTAGRAM AND THE FIVE PATHS

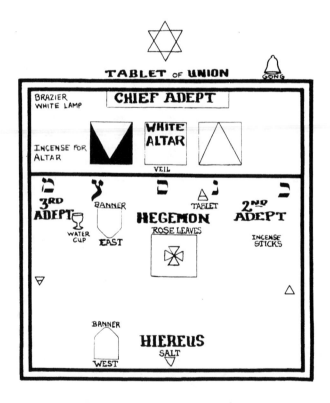

Temple arranged as in Diagram. 2nd Ad. sits on Dais at S.E. 3rd Ad. sits on Dais to N.E. Altar in Yesod under hanging Pentagram. On it are the 4 Elemental Emblems, Incense, Cup, Rose Leaves, and Salt. In middle, Greek Cross of 5 squares. Hegemon West of Altar facing West. Hiereus in West facing East. Admission Badge, Lamen of Hiereus. Temple lighted as at end of Part One.

VOLUME SEVEN

2nd Ad:
3rd Ad:
Heg:
Hiereus:

(Each Knocks once.)

(Ch. Ad. parts curtain, makes Pentagram with Torch, knocks and withdraws.)

2nd Ad:

Hon. Hiereus, you have my permission to present the Philosophus with the necessary admission Badge. Instruct him in the proper alarm and admit him.

(Hiereus salutes, makes Qabalistic Cross and goes out. He gives Lamen to Philosophus who knocks five times. Hegemon opens door. Philosophus enters, makes Qabalistic Cross. Hegemon returns to place. Hiereus takes Philosophus to West and points out Diagram of Malkuth.)

Hiereus:

Herein has been established the Equated Cross, which is ruler over the Kingdom of Matter. This Symbol may be found even upon the crowns of the Kings of this Earth. (Hands Philosophus Tau Portal.) The Letter Tau leads from the Airy quarter of Malkuth into Yesod. Air is uppermost in the Symbol as in the Planet Earth where the atmosphere is furthest from the Core. Moreover, the Letter Tau signifieth the Cross, the impact of Spirit upon matter. My Lamen is given you as your Badge, for I am the Ruler in Malkuth, and the Guardian against the underworld. I am also Lord of: the Path Tau, the link between the first and second degrees, and also between the Outer and the Inner. This Path of Tau, dark and full of mystery, under the presidency of Saturn and the Tarot Key of the Universe, leads, as you have learnt in the Theoricus Grade, through the Astral Plane. Therefore, in the Ritual of the 32nd Path, you were passed by the Four Kerubic Stations, as a foreshadowing of the Rites of the Cross, the full completion of the First Order which you have now accomplished. Having traversed the Path of Tau, the darkness of the Astral Plane and of the Black Pillar, stand firm in Yesod, that the Black Pillar may become the White. (Hiereus takes away Tau after leading Philosophus to Hegemon at Altar. Hegemon rises but stands between Philosophus and the Altar, so that Philosophus does not too clearly apprehend the change of Symbols.)

Heg:

Before you, in the East, are the Five Portals of the 21st, 24th, 25th, 26th and 23rd Paths. Five will divide the Number of the Letter of each of them, as it will divide without remainder that of every Path from Yod 20th, to Tau, the 32nd. The Five Paths here visible are assigned to Mem, Water; Ayin, Capricornus, an Earthy Sign; Samekh, Sagittarius, a Fiery Sign; Nun, Scorpio, a Watery Sign, but in its highest aspect also a Ruler of Fire; and Kaph, Jupiter, which Planet is akin to Spirit, and rules especially Aspiration. Thus both in number and in significance these Planets jointly set forth the eternal symbol of the Pentagram. This Symbol must now be established wherefore advancing by the Kerubic Path of Aquarius approach the highest in Netzach. (Hegemon leads Philosophus to foot of Dais to 2nd Ad. before Kaph and Nun.)

2nd Ad:

Wherefore do you stand at the base of the White Pillar, being but Lord of the First Degree?

Phil:

(Prompted) I seek the Path of Kaph, the Path of Aspiration.

Hiereus:

(Knocks) Beware. Temerity is not courage, Lord of the First Degree. Remember the warning of the Tower struck by Lightning that was revealed in the highest Path you have yet adventured. As a house built upon the Sand cannot endure, so without the strength of Geburah the height of Chesed cannot be scaled. Stay, therefore, ere your limbs be broken upon the Wheel.

2nd Ad:

The Portal of Kaph is barred, yet it is well to aspire, though it may be folly to attempt. This Path is governed by the Wheel of Life and Death, and hard it is to be freed from that Wheel.

Phil:

(Prompted by Heg.) Let me seek then the Path of Nun.

2nd Ad:

It is open to you, unto the limits of your strength. (Hegemon returns to Altar. 2nd Ad. guides Philosophus to West Hiereus bars way.)

Hiereus:

In the Power of Typhon the Destroyer, and of Death the Transformer, stand. (Knocks.)

2nd Ad:

Thus far and no farther is it permitted to penetrate into the Path of Nun. The mysteries may now partially be revealed unto you. (2nd Ad. takes Philosophus to Tarot Key of Death.)

2nd Ad:

The 13th Key of Tarot represents the figure of a Skeleton, upon which some portions of flesh still remain. In a field he is reaping off with the Scythe of Death the fresh vegetation which springs from corrupting bodies buried therein, fragments of which such as hands, heads and feet appear above the soil. Bones also are strewn upon the surface. One of the heads wears a kingly crown; another is apparently that of a person of little note, showing that Death is the equalizer of all conditions. The five extremities, the head, hands and feet, allude to the powers of the number five, the Letter Heh, the Pentagram, the concealed Spirit of Life and the Four Elements, the originator of all living form. The Sign of Scorpio especially alludes to stagnant and foetid water, that property of the moist nature which initiates putrefaction and decay. The eternal change from life into death through death into life, is symbolised by the grass which springs from and is nourished by putrifying and corrupting carcasses; the herbiage, in its turn affords food to animals and man, which again when dead, nourisheth vegetable life and brings to growth and perfection the living herbiage. This is further shown by the figure itself putrifying and decaying as it reaps the grass of the field. As for man, his days are as grass, as a flower of the field, so he flourisheth. The top of the scythe forms the Tau Cross of Life, showing that what destroys also renews. The whole is a representation of the eternal transmutation of the life of nature, which reforms all things into fresh images and similitudes. This symbol represents the corrosive and destructive action of the infernal Fire as opposed to the Celestial, the Dragon of the Waters, the Typhon of the Egyptians, the Slayer of Osiris, which later yet rises again in Horus. The Scorpion, Serpent of Evil, delineated before the figure of Death in the more ancient form of the Key. refers to the mixed and transforming, therefore deceptive, nature of this emblem. Behind him. is the Symbol of the Nameless One, representing the Seed and its germ, not yet differentiated into Life, therefore incapable of definition. The Scorpion is the emblem of ruthless destruction. The Snake is the mixed and deceptive nature, serving alike for good and evil. The Eagle is the higher and Divine Nature, yet to be found herein, the Alchemical Eagle of distillation, the Renewer of life. As it is said Thy youth shall be renewed like the Eagles. Great indeed, and many are the mysteries of this terrible Key.

(2nd Ad. and Hiereus show Philosophus the figure of Typhon.)

Hiereus:

This drawing represents the symbolic figure of Typhon, the Destroyer. The eleven circles represent the eleven Averse Sephiroth. He stands upon Earth and Ocean, his head lost in the clouds, a colossal image of evil and destruction. The brow denotes the confusion of opposing Elemental Forces in the higher regions of the Air, and confusion of mind and madness in man. The eyes are the devouring flames of lust and violence, the breath is storm, devastation and rage, alike in the Universe which is the greater world, and in Man who is the lesser. The arms and the hands are the swift executors of evil works, the bringers of pestilence and disease. The heart is malice and envy in man, the nourisher of evil in the atmosphere, which later are again symbolised by the numerous and twining serpents.

2nd Ad:

The 24th Path of Sepher Yetzirah to which the Tarot Key of Death is referred is the Imaginative Intelligence, and it is so called because it giveth form to all similitudes which are created in like manner similar to its harmonious elegances. For the outward form always follows the hidden law, thus from Chaos is produced Harmony, just as a beautiful flower is produced from decaying matter. Return not to Yesod, for here no more may be spoken. (2nd Ad. returns to place. Philosophus goes to Hegemon near Altar.)

Heg:

Approach now the station of Hod by the Path of Resh, the Sun. (Philosophus approaches the 3rd Ad.)

3rd Ad:

Already the Sash of the Black Pillar is upon you, already you have passed the dark Path of Tau. What more do you seek of me, Lord of the 1st Degree?

Phil:

(Prompted by Heg.) I seek the Path of Mem, the Path of Sacrifice.

Hiereus:

(Knocks) Be warned, O vainglorious one. Samson broke down the Two Pillars and perished. Having but one Pillar, can you bear up the might of Geburah? Can you attain strength without the Life of Tiphareth?

3rd Ad:

The Portal of Mem is barred. Yet it is well to be willing for the Sacrifice itself, if as yet not fully prepared. For in the Path of Mem rules the Hanged Man, the power of the Great Waters. Can your tears prevail against the Tide of the Sea, your might against the waves of the storm, your love against the sorrows of all the world?

Phil:

(Prompted by Heg.) Let me seek then the path of Ayin.

3rd Ad:

It is open to you to the limit of your strength. (Hegemon returns to Altar. 3rd Ad. descends and leads Philosophus with Sol to West. Hiereus going to North bars their way.)

Hiereus:

(Knocks) By the Power of Pan and the Goat of Mendes, stand.

3rd Ad:

Thus far and no farther are you permitted to penetrate the Path of Ayin, whose mysteries may now be partially revealed to you. The 15th Key of the Tarot represents a goat-headed, satyr-like Demon whose legs are hairy, his feet and claws standing upon a Cubical Altar. He has heavy bat-like wings. In his left hand, which points downwards, he holds a lighted torch, and in his right, which is elevated, a horn of water. The left hand points downwards to show that it is the infernal and burning, not the celestial and life-giving flame which is kindled in his torch, just as when the Sun is in Capricornus, to which cold and earthy Sign this Key corresponds, Solar light is at its weakest and the natures of cold and moisture triumph over heat and dryness. The cubical Altar represents the Universe, right and left of it, bound thereto by a cord attached to a circle which typifies the centre of the Earth, are two smaller demons, one male and one female. They hold a cord in their hands. The whole figure shows the gross generative powers of nature on the material plane, and is analogous to the Pan of the Greeks and the Egyptian Goat of Mendes the symbol of Khem. In certain aspects, this Key represents the brutal forces of nature, which to the unbelieving man only obscure and do not reflect the Luminous Countenance of God. It also alludes to the sexual powers of natural generation. Thus therefore the Key fitly balances the symbol of Death on the other side of the Tree of Life.

Of the smaller demons, one points downwards and one upwards, answering to the positions of the hands of the central figures. Beneath his feet are Pentagrams on which he tramples (whence comes their title of Wizard's foot) and his head is covered with the evil and reversed Pentagram. As his hands bear the torch and the horn, the symbols of Fire and Water, so does his form unite the Earth in his hairy and bestial aspect, and the Air in his bat-like wings. Thus he represents the gross and materialized Elemental Forces of Nature; and the whole would be an evil symbol were it not for the Pentagram of Light above his head which regulates and guides his movements. He is the eternal renewer of

16

all the changing forms of Creation in conformity with the Law of the All Powerful One, Blessed be He, which controlling law is typified by the controlling Pentagram of Light surmounting the whole.

This Key is an emblem of tremendous force; many and universal are its mysteries.

(Hiereus and 3rd Ad. go to diagram of Pan.)

Hiereus:

This drawing represents the symbolic figure of Pan, the Greek God of Nature. He stands upon the Cube of the Universe, holding in his right hand the pastoral staff of rural authority, and in his left the 7 reeded pipe symbolical of the harmony of the Planetary Spheres. The Nine Circles represent the Sephiroth with the exception of Kether, exactly those which are included in the symbol on the Tree of Life. The ruddy face is the heat of the Earth, the horns are the Rays, the body contains the Elements and the Cube is the firm basis. Observe that the higher part of the figure is human, growing more bestial as it nears the Earth.

3rd Ad:

The 26th Path of the Sepher Yetzirah, to which the Tarot Key of the Devil is referred, is called the Renovating Intelligence, because, by it, God the Holy One reneweth all the changing forms which are renewed by the Creation of the World. Return again to Yesod, for here no more may be spoken. (3rd Ad. returns to place. Hiereus to Altar. Hegemon rises as Philosophus comes to Altar. Hiereus and Hegemon stand on either side of Philosophus West of Altar, facing East.)

Hiereus:

In guardianship and not in enmity, have I barred your venturing, O Philosophus. Now may it be revealed unto you how that in my Lamen of Office is hidden the Key which you seek. For the Triangle in the Circle is the high symbol of the Holy Trinity, and the first three Sephiroth and of Binah wherein is the Sphere of Saturn, Ruler of the Path Tau. Therefore do I wear it, and therefore, when you entered the Hall of the Neophytes in the Neophyte Grade, when first the hoodwink was raised, you beheld before you the Sword that barred and the Symbol which overcometh the barrier. The Lamen in its more special attribution to the Hiereus, has the following meanings. In the circle are the Four Sephiroth, Tiphareth, Netzach, Hod and Yesod. The first three mark the angles of the Triangle inscribed within, while the sides are the Paths of Nun, Ayin and Peh, respectively. In the centre is marked the Letter Samekh indicating the 25th Path. While the Wheel revolves, the hub is still. Seek ever then the centre, look from without to within. Behold the Key of your Path. (Puts Badge aside.)

Heg:

Five Paths are before you, four have you attempted and each was guarded by a symbol sinister and dread. Remember that in the Zelator Grade it was told you, that above Malkuth were the Paths Qoph, Shin, Tau, making Qesheth, the Bow of promise. From the many coloured Bow. is loosed in Yesod, the Arrow of Sagittarius, Samekh, soaring upward to cleave open the Veil unto the Sun in Tiphareth. Thus it is a fit symbol for hope and aspiration, for in the Sign Sagittarius, Jupiter, Ruler of Kaph is Lord. Thus, by this straight and arrow way only, is advance between the dangers that have threatened you, possible. (3rd Ad. descends to North side of Altar.)

17

3rd Ad:

But Sagittarius, the Archer, is a bi-corporate Sign, the Centaur, the Man and the Horse combined. Recall what was said unto thee in the passage of the 31st Path of Fire, leading unto the Grade of Practicus. Also there is the vision of the fire flashing Courser of Light, or also a child borne aloft upon the shoulders of the Celestial Steed, fiery or clothed with gold, or naked and shooting from the bow, shafts of light, and standing on the shoulders of a horse. But, if thy meditation prolongeth itself thou shalt unite all these symbols in the form of a Lion. For thus wilt thou cleave upward by the Path of Sagittarius, through the Sixth Sephira into the Path of Teth, answering to Leo, the Lion, the reconciling Path between Mercy and Severity, Chesed and Geburah, beneath whose centre hangs the glorious Sun of Tiphareth. Therefore, by the straight and narrow Path of Sagittarius, let the Philosophus advance, like the arrow from the centre of Qesheth, the Bow. And as this Sign of Sagittarius lieth between the Sign of Scorpio, Death and Capricornus the Devil, so had Jesus to pass through the Wilderness, tempted by Satan. (2nd Ad. descends to South of the Altar.)

2nd Ad:

Before you upon the Altar, lie the Four Emblems of your purified body, and over them is the symbol of the Pentagram, while beneath in the midst is the five-squared Cross of the Four Elements and the Spirit within them. If you are willing, in service and in sacrifice to offer the purified powers of your body, bind about your neck the Cross, and stretch the Light (gives Philosophus light) you carry over the Four Emblems in prayer and offering. (Philosophus does so. All come East of the Altar. Philosophus in middle with candle and Cross on neck. 2nd Ad. right and 3rd Ad. left. Hegemon and Hiereus behind. Each takes Elemental Emblems, Hiereus Salt, Hegemon Rose-leaves, 2nd Ad. Incense, 3rd Ad. Water and Philosophus Motto written on paper.)

2nd Ad:

Honoured Philosophus, what was the additional title given you in the Philosophus Grade as a link with the Second Order?

Phil:

Phrath. (All advance to Dais.)

2nd Ad:

O Hidden Warden of the Portal of the Vault here is one who cometh in the Word Phrath.

Ch. Ad:

(Knocks gong unseen.) If he would rend the Veil, let him complete the Word.

2nd Ad:

O Hidden Warden of the Portal of the Vault, here is one who cometh in the Word Phrath.

Ch. Ad:

(Knocks gong unseen.) If he would rend the Veil, let him complete the Word.

2nd Ad:

Honoured Hiereus, what know you of the word?

Hiereus:

Tau, the Letter of Saturn, ruling the Path of Malkuth to Yesod, linked to Earth.

2nd Ad:

Honoured Hegemon, what know you of the Word?

Heg:

Resh, the Letter of Sol, of the Path joining Yesod to Hod, and it is also the Letter linked with rule over Air as the Sun ruleth the Air in Tiphareth.

Ch. Ad:

Very Honoured 3rd Ad. what know you of the Word?

3rd Ad:

Peh, the Letter of Mars, of the Path joining Hod to Netzach, which is also a Letter linked to Water, as Mars ruleth Water, and to Fire, as Mars ruleth Fire in Geburah.

2nd Ad:

Mars in Peh, linketh the base of the Black Pillar to the Base of the .White Pillar, and the converse of Mars is Jupiter - for Jupiter is Lord of Fire, but in Chesed he ruleth Water, balancing Mars in Geburah. Now, the Letter of Jupiter is Kaph, linking Netzach with Chesed; and Kaph continueth the Path Peh to Chesed, and is the highest Path now visible to you. It is the Path of Aspiration and its Planet Jupiter rules also in Sagittarius. Therefore, take the Light of the Highest for Guide, and thus do I reveal the Letter Kaph unto you and complete the Word.

3rd Ad:

Peh (Knocks, gives Sign of Water.)

Heg:

Resh (Knocks, gives Sign of Air.)

2nd Ad:

Kaph (Knocks, gives Sign of Fire.)

Hiereus:

Tau (Knocks, gives Sign of Earth.)

All:

Paroketh (All make Qabalistic Cross saying the words.)

Phil:

(Prompted by 3rd Ad.) In the Word Paroketh, in the Power of the Cross and the Pentagram, I claim to behold the Portal of the Vault of the Adepti.

Ch. Ad:

(Unseen, sounds gong.) It is the Word of the Veil, the Veil of the Tabernacle, of the Temple, before the Holy of Holies, the Veil which was rent asunder. It is the Veil of the Four Elements of the Body of Man, which was offered upon the Cross for the service of Man. (Ch. Ad. stands.) In the Word Phrath, in the Spirit of service and sacrifice draw nigh. (2nd and 3rd Ads. stand at the Veil. 2nd shows Phil, opening Sign.)

2nd Ad:

This is the Sign of the rending of the Veil, and thus standing, you form the Tau Cross.

(Phil. gives the Sign. 2nd and 3rd Ad. draw back Veil, revealing Ch. Ad. who stands also in the Sign of Tau, with Sceptre and White Lamp. 2nd and 3rd Ad. and Phil. mount Dais. Phil. if able should stand in Sign during Offering Ritual. Lights turned up. Hiereus and Heg. stand behind Phil., who is between the Pillars - 2nd Ad. South and 3rd Ad. North.)

Ch. Ad:

Freely and of full purpose and with understanding do you offer yourself upon the Altar of the Spirit?

Phil:

I do.

(As they say their Words, Hiereus and Heg. ascend Dais to drop their emblems into the brazier. Each officer makes his Grade Sign as he does so. Ch. Ad. makes appropriate Pent, holding up White Lamp. Phil, drops in Motto.)

Hiereus:

In the Letter Tau. (Salt.)

Ch. Ad:

In the Letter Heh. (Incense.)

Heg:

In the Letter Resh. (Rose leaves.)

Ch. Ad:

In the Letter Vau. (Incense.)

3rd Ad:

In the Letter Peh. (Water.)

Ch. Ad:

In the Letter Heh. (Incense.)

2nd Ad:

In the Letter Kaph. (Incense sticks.)

Ch. Ad:

In the Letter Yod. (Incense.)

AH:

In the Letter Shin. (Phil, drops in Motto.)

(Ch. Ad. makes Spirit Pentagrams over the whole, then stretching out Sceptre touches Phil, on the breast.)

Ch. Ad:

May this offering be as the offering of Abel, which ascended unto God. (Phil, lowers his arms. Ch. Ad. sits down.)

Ch. Ad:

Stretch out your left hand to touch the Black Pillar (done) the Pillar of the First Degree, wherein all was as yet in the darkness of the Path Tau. This was a period of restriction and of groping, as was shown by the black sash, the Sign of the First Degree. Among its symbols were the Cross, upon which meditate, that the mysteries of growth and change may become revealed.

Stretch out now your right hand to touch the White Pillar (done) the Pillar of the Second Degree, wherein is the Fire of the Path Samekh. Its token in our Order, is the White Sash. Standing thus you are in the point of equilibrium. Master of both. Lord of the Second Degree. Lord of the Paths of the Portal of the Vault of the Adepti - wherefore, in recognition of your achievement, I confer upon you the White Sash of Probation. (3rd Ad. puts on white sash). The grip of this Degree is the Grip of the First Order, but given with the left hand, and represents the Sephira Chesed, and the White Pillar. The Sign is given thus: (gives it) and symbolises the rending asunder of a curtain or veil. The answering Sign is given by the converse thus. (Gives it.) The Pass-word is, as you have been told, Paroketh, Which is the Veil of the Tabernacle, and is exchanged by letter thus:

Ch. Ad:

Peh.

Phil:

(Prompted) Resh.

Ch. Ad:

Kaph.

Phil:

Tau.

Ch. Ad:

Further, I give you the Word ETH which crowns the Pyramid of the Four Elements in the 4-7 Grade, and is one symbol of the Spirit which converts the Cross into the Pentagram. Wherefore, above my Throne is this Tablet (points to Tablet of Union) which is called the Tablet of Union, and binds together the Four Tablets into one under the presidency of the Spirit.

Thus far by work of the intellect, and by aid of our Rites, have you come. Now must you labour to establish the Pentagram in yourself. That it be the Pentagram of Good, upright and balanced, not the evil and reversed Pentagram of the Goat of Mendes; to make yourself truly a Microcosm reflecting the Macrocosm whose symbolic Hexagram of Tiphareth presides above you.

This Degree is in one sense attributed to Yesod, base of the Path of probation, Sagittarius. In Yesod is the Sphere of Luna, who in her fullness reflects the Sun of Tiphareth. The number given to the Moon in the 2-9 is Nine, but in a more esoteric sense the number of Luna is Five, the number of the Pentagram and the Microcosm.

(Ch. Ad. rises with Sceptre and white Lamp. 2nd Ad. places Tablet of Union on the Altar in readiness. Heg. places two forms of Temperance by Altar W. Ch. Ad. puts white lamp on Altar. Officers replace Elements before their respective Tablets, and return to form a Cross round the Altar.)

Ch. Ad:

This drawing represents the more ancient form of the 14th Key of Tarot, for which the later and more usual form of Temperance was soon substituted, as better representing the natural symbolism of the Path Sagittarius. The earler figure was considered not so much a representation of this Path alone, as the synthesis of that and the others conjoined. The later figure, therefore, is better adapted to the more restricted meaning. The more ancient form shows a female figure crowned with the crown of five rays, symbolising the Five Principles of Nature, the concealed Spirit and the Four Elements of Earth, Air, Water and Fire. About her head is a halo of light. On her breast is the Sun of Tiphareth. The Five-rayed Crown further alludes to the Five Sephiroth Kether, Chokmah, Binah, Chesed and Geburah. Chained to her waist are a Lion and an Eagle, between which is a large cauldron whence arise steam and smoke. The Lion represents the Fire in Netzach - the Blood of the Lion, and the Eagle represents the Water in Hod, the Gluten of the Eagle whose reconciliation is made by the Air in Yesod, uniting with the volatilised Water arising from the cauldron through the influence of the Fire beneath it. The chains which link the Lion and the Eagle to her waist, are symbolic of the Paths of Scorpio and Capricornus as shown by the Scorpion and the Goat in the background. In her right hand, she bears the Torch of Solar Fire elevating and volatilising the Water in Hod by the fiery influence of Geburah, while with her left hand, she pours from a vase the Waters of Chesed to temperate and calm the Fires of Netzach. This later form is the usual figure of Temperance, symbolising in a more restricted form than the preceding, the peculiar properties of this Path. It represents an Angel with the Solar emblem of Tiphareth on her brow, and wings of the aerial and volatilising nature, pouring together the fluidic Fire and the fiery Water thus combining, harmonising and tempering those opposing elements.

One foot rests on dry and volcanic land, in the background of which is a volcano whence issues an eruption. The other foot is in the water by whose border springs fresh vegetation, contrasting strongly with the arid and dry nature of the distant land. On her breast is a square, the emblem of rectitude. The whole figure is a representation of that straight and narrow way of which it is said "few there be that find it" which alone leads to the higher and glorified life. For to pursue that steady and tranquil mean between two opposing forces, is indeed difficult, and many are the temptations to turn aside either to the right or to the left wherein, remember, are but to be found the menacing symbols of Death and the Devil.

The 25th Path of the Sepher Yetzirah to which the Tarot Key of Temperance is referred, is called the Intelligence of Probation, and it is so called because it is the primary temptation by which the Creator tries all righteous person. That is, that in it, there is ever present the temptation to turn aside to the one hand or to the other.

(2nd and 3rd Ad. give Cup and red lamp to Phil, who holds them in form of Tau Cross.)

Ch. Ad:

Let this remind you once more, that only in and by the reconciliation of opposing forces is the Pathway made to true occult knowledge and practical power. Good alone is mighty and Truth alone shall prevail. Evil is but weakness and the power of evil magic exists but in the contest of unbalanced forces, which in the end, will destroy and ruin him who hath subjugated himself thereto. As it is said "Stoop not down, for a precipice lieth beneath the Earth - a descent of seven steps; and therein, is established the throne of an evil and fatal force. Stoop not down unto that dark and lurid world. Defile not thy brilliant flame with the earthy dross of matter. Stoop not down, for its splendour is but seeming, it is but the habitation of the sons of the Unhappy."

(2nd and 3rd Ad. take back red lamp and Cup and restore them to their Tablets. On the Altar is the White Lamp and the Tablet of Union. Phil. is seated West of Altar. 2nd and 3rd Ad. return to places. Hs. goes to N. Heg. to S. Ch. Ad. returns to Throne in E. takes up Banner of the East and Hierophant's Lamen.)

Ch. Ad:

Seeing that you are now Lord of the Paths of the Portal of the Vault of the Adepti, and are entered into the Second Degree, approaching the Second or Inner Order, it is fitting that you should have the knowledge of these emblems to complete as far as may be, your understanding of the Powers of the Officers of the First or Outer Order. Both refer in natural succession of numbers to the six following the five. Thus all progress is by steps, gradual and secure. The inner revelation may come suddenly to some, even in the twinkling of an eye or it may be after long waiting - a slow and gradual process from the beginning, yet ever the liquid must be prepared to the point of saturation.

The Hierophant's Lamen is a synthesis of Tiphareth, to which the Calvary Cross of six squares, forming the cube opened out, is fitly referred. The two colours, red and green the most active and the most passive, whose conjunction points out the practical application of the knowledge of equilibrium, are symbolic of the reconciliation of the celestial essences of Fire and Water, for the reconciling yellow unites with blue in green, which is the complementary colour to red, and with red in orange which is the complementary colour to blue. The small inner circle placed upon the Cross alludes to the Rose that is conjoined therewith in the symbolism of the Rose and Cross of our Order.

The field of the Banner of the East is White, the colour of light and purity. As in the previous case, the Calvary Cross of six squares is the number six of Tiphareth, the yellow Cross of Solar Gold, and the cubical stone bearing in its centre the sacred Tau of Life, and having bound together upon it the form of the Macrocosmic Hexagram, the red triangle of Fire and the blue triangle of Water - the Ruach Elohim and the Waters of Creation. The six angles of the Hexagram described upon the Tree of Life will give the Planets referred to it as follows: Daath, Saturn; Chesed, Jupiter; Geburah, Mars; Netzach, Venus; Hod, Mercury; Yesod, Luna; while in the centre is the Sun of Tiphareth.

Upon my breast is a symbol, which, O Lord of the Paths of the Portal of the Adepti, is as yet unknown to you. It is no Symbol of the Order of the Golden Dawn, nor of the First or Outer Order, nor even of your Degree. It is the symbol of the Red Rose and the Cross of Gold, uniting the powers of the 4 and 5 and of the 6 within itself, but to learn its full meaning, it is needful that you be admitted to the fellowship of that other Order to which the Golden Dawn is one of the Veils. Of this matter, you have no right to speak to any below your degree.

Admission further can be earned no more by excellence in intellectual learning alone, though that also is required of you. In token that all true knowledge cometh of grace, not of right, such admission is granted, not on demand, but at the discretion of the Greatly Honoured Chiefs of the Second Order. Moreover, an interval of nine months must elapse before the portal is again opened to you. Nine is the number of Luna in Yesod, nine lunar months are the period of gestation before birth; Five is the number of the Pentagram of the Microcosm, the esoteric Luna number - the number of the Spirit and the Four Elements - of the Soul entering the body. Nine multiplied by five yields 45, the number of Yesod, and the supreme number of the Square of Saturn, as the Triad expanded into matter.

Ch. Ad:

(Knocks) Very Honoured Fratres and Sorores, assist me to close the Portal of the Vault of the Adepti. (All rise.) Honoured Hiereus see that the entrance is properly guarded.

Hiereus:

Very honoured Chief Adept, the entrance is properly guarded.

Ch. Ad:

Very Honoured Fratres and Sorores, give the Signs of the Neophyte, Zelator, Theoricus, Practicus and Philosophus. Give the Sign of the Rending of the Veil. Give the Sign of the Closing of the Veil. Very Honoured 2nd Ad. what is the Word?

2nd Ad:

Peh.

Ch. Ad:

Resh.

2nd Ad:

Kaph.

Ch. Ad.

Tau.

2nd Ad:

The whole Word is Paroketh, which is the Veil of the Tabernacle.

Ch. Ad:

In and by that Word, I declare the Portal of the Vault of the Adepti duly closed.

(Ch. Ad. draws curtain. Officers take up their stations before Elemental Tablets. Ch. Ad. stands W. of the Altar, facing East. Phil, stands behind him.)

Ch. Ad:

In the Power of the Name Yod, Heh, Vau, Heh, and in the might of the concealed Name YEHESHUAH, in the symbol of the Tablet of Union and by the Word Eth, Spirits of the Five Elements, adore your Creator.

(At the word "depart," below each Officer simultaneously makes banishing Pentagram of his own Element before the Tablet, ending with Grade Sign.)

Ch. Ad:

Depart in peace unto your habitations. May there be peace between us and you, and be ye ready to come when you are called.

Ch. Ad:

(Makes banishing Pent. of Spirit and gives LVX Signs. All face East and make Qab. Cross all saying together.)

All:

Unto Thee Tetragrammaton, be ascribed Malkuth, Geburah, Gedulah, unto the Ages, AMEN.

Ch. Ad:
3rd Ad:
2nd Ad:
Hiereus:
Heg:

(All give knocks 4, 1 in succession.)

CEREMONY OF THE GRADE OF ADEPTUS MINOR

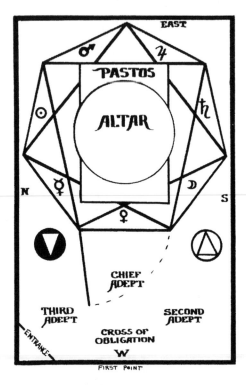

OFFICERS REQUIRED

Chief Adept 7 - 4, Merciful Exempt Adept.
Second Adept 6 - 5, Mighty Adeptus Major.
Third Adept 5 - 6, Associate Adeptus Minor.
Candidate—Hodos Chamelionis.

These Officers should have attained at least these ranks and may be of higher Grade. Men and Women are equally eligible for any of these offices. The ordinary members are entitled Very Honoured Fratres et Sorores. This ceremony is divided into Three Points.

LIST OF REQUIREMENTS

Robes: Chief Adept—Blue and purple, with winged Sphere Wand.
2nd Adept—Red and Orange, with Phoenix Wand.
3rd Adept—Yellow and Rose Pink, with Lotus Wand.

All may wear golden slippers or shoes to match robes. Candidates should have crossed Sashes, Declaration, and Recommendation signed by the two Chiefs. Admission Badges; Hiereus Lamen, Sword and Serpent diagram.

Black Sash and White Sash for Candidates. Black Robe and Cords, Admission Badges. Attestation of Examinations and Recommendations. On Altar Cup of Wine, Candle, Crucifix, Chain, Dagger, Crook and Scourge. Incense. Cross. Each Officer carries a Crux Ansata on his left wrist.

VOLUME SEVEN

OPENING

(Chief Adept Knocks. All Rise.)

Chief:
Second:
Third:
Chief:
Third:
Second:
(All give one knock in succession.)

Chief:

Avete, Fratres et Sorores.

Second:

Roseae Rubeae.

Third:

Et Aureae Crucis.

Chief:

Very Honoured Fratres et Sorores, assist me to open the Tomb of the Adepti. Associate Adeptus Minor, see that the Portal is closed and guarded. (Third Adept does so and salutes.)

Third:

Merciful Exempt Adept, the Portal of the Vault is closed and guarded.

Chief:

Mighty Adeptus Major, by what sign hast thou entered the Portal?
Second: By the Sign of the Rending Asunder of the Veil. (gives it.)

Chief:

Associate Adeptus Minor, by what sign hast thou closed the Portal.

Third:

By the Sign of the Closing of the Veil. (gives it)

Second:

PEH.

Third:

RESH.

Second:

CAPH.

Third:

TAU.

Second:

PAROKETH.

Third:

Which is the Veil of the Sanctum Sanctorum.

Chief:

Mighty Adeptus Major, what is the Mystic Number of this Grade?

Second:

Twenty one.

Chief:

What is the Password formed therefrom?

Third:

ALEPH.

Chief:

HEH.

Third:

YOD.

Chief:

HEH.

Third:

EHEIEH.

Chief:

Mighty Adeptus Major, what is the Vault of the Adepts?

Second:

The symbolic burying place of our Founder Christian Rosenkreutz, which he made to represent the Universe.

Chief:

Associate Adeptus Minor, in what part of it is he buried?

Third:

In the centre of the heptagonal sides and beneath the Altar, his head being towards the East.

Chief:

Mighty Adeptus Minor, why in the centre?

Second:

Because that is the point of perfect equilibrium.

Chief:

Associate Adeptus Minor, what does the Mystic Name of our Founder signify?

Third:

The Rose and Cross of Christ; the fadeless Rose of Creation - the immortal Cross of Light.

Chief:

Mighty Adeptus Major, what was the Vault entitled by our more ancient Fratres and Sorores?

Second:

The Tomb of Osiris Onnophris, the Justified One.

Chief:

Associate Adeptus Minor, of what shape was the Vault?

Third:

It was that of an equilateral Heptagon or figure of Seven Sides.

Chief:

Mighty Adeptus Major, unto what do these seven sides allude?

Second:

Seven are the lower Sephiroth, Seven are the Palaces, Seven aare the days of the Creation: Seven in the Height above, Seven in the Depth below.

Chief:

Associate Adeptus Minor, where is this Vault symbolically situated?

Third:

In the centre of the Earth, in the Mountain of Caverns, the Mystic Mountain of Abiegnus.

Chief:

Mighty Adeptus Minor, what is the meaning of this title Abiegnus?

Third:

It is Abi-Agnus, Lamb of the Father. It is by metathesis Abi-Genos, born of the Father, Bia-Genos, Strength of our Race, and the Four Words make the sentence. Mountain of the

Lamb of the Father, and the Strength of our Race. IAO. YEHESHUAH. Such are the words! (All salute with 5-6 Signs.)

Chief:

Mighty Adeptus Major, what is the key to this Vault?

Second:

The Rose and Cross which resume the Life of Nature and the Powers hidden in the word I.N.R.I.

Chief:

Associate Adeptus Minor, what is the Emblem which we bear in our left hands?

Third:

It is a form of the Rose and Cross, the ancient Crux Ansata or Egyptian symbol of life.

Chief:

Mighty Adeptus Major, what is its meaning?

Second:

It represents the force of the Ten Sephiroth in Nature, divided into a Hexad and a Tetrad. The Oval embraces the first six Sephiroth and the Tau Cross the lower Four, answering to the four Elements.

Chief:

Associate Adeptus Minor, what is the Emblem which I bear upon my breast?

Third:

The complete symbol of the Rose and Cross.

Chief:

Mighty Adeptus Major, what is its meaning?

Second:

It is the Key of Sigils and of Rituals, and represents the force of the twenty two Letters in Nature, as divided into a Three, a Seven, and a Twelve. Many and great are its mysteries.

Chief:

Associate Adeptus Minor, what is the Wand which thou bearest?

Third:

A simple Wand having the colours of the twelve Signs of the Zodiac and surmounted by the Lotus Flower of Isis. It symbolizes the development of Creation.

Chief:

Mighty Adeptus Major, thy Wand and its meaning?

Second:

A Wand terminating in the symbol of the Binary and surmounted by the Tau Cross of Life, or the Head of the Phoenix, sacred to Osiris. The seven colours between Light and Darkness are attributed to the Planets. It symbolizes rebirth and resurrection from death.

Chief:

My Wand is surmounted by the Winged Globe, around which the twin serpents of Egypt twine. It symbolizes the equilibriated Force of the Spirit and the Four Elements beneath the everlasting Wings of the Holy One. Associate Adeptus Minor, what are the words inscribed upon the door of the Vault, and how is it guarded?

Third:

Post Centum Viginti Annos Patebo. After one hundred and twenty years I shall open, and the door is guarded by the Elemental Tablets and by the Kerubic Emblems.

Chief:

The 120 years refer symbolically to the 5 Grades of the First Order and to the revolution of the Power of the Pentagram; also to the five preparatory examinations for this Grade. It is written His days shall be 120 years. 120 divided by 5 yields 24, the number of hours in a day and of the Thrones of the Elders in the Apocalypse. Further 120 equals the number of the Ten Sephiroth multiplied by that of the Zodiac, whose Key is the working of the Spirit and the Elements typified in the Wand which I bear.

(All face East. Chief Adept opens the Door wide, passes to East or head of Pastos of C.R.C., and faces West. Second enters and passes to South facing North. Third enters and passes to North facing South. Other members remain without, but Hodos may enter Vault to form fourth side in making Signs. The Three Officers raise their Wands to form Pyramid above altar, Cruces touching below Wands.)

Chief:

Let us analyse the Key Word. I.

Second:

N.

Third: R. All:

I.

Chief:

YOD.

Second:

NUN.

Third:

RESH.

All:

YOD.

Chief:

Virgo, Isis, Mighty Mother.

Second:

Scorpio, Apophis, Destroyer.

Third:

Sol, Osiris, Slain and Risen.

All:

Isis, Apophis, Osiris - I.A.O.
(All separate Wands and Cruces, and give Sign of Cross.)

All:

The Sign of Osiris Slain.

Chief:

L—The Sign of the Mourning of Isis. (With bowed head.)

Second:

V—The Sign of Typhon and Apophis. (With head erect.)

Third:

X—The Sign of Osiris Risen. (With head bowed.)

All:

L V X, (Lux) the Light of the Cross. (Saluting Sign and head bowed. All quit Tomb and return to previous places.)

Chief:

In the Grand Word YEHESHUAH by the Key-Word I.N.R.I., and through the concealed Word LVX, I have opened the tomb of the Adepti. (All present give LVX Signs.)

FIRST POINT

(The Tomb is prepared as before, but closed, and curtains drawn. Chief Adept is not seen as such; Second Adept is Principal Officer, 3rd Associate Adept, Introducing Adept—Hodos Chamelionis.)

Second:

Very Honoured Fratres et Sorores, our H. Frater (XYZ), Lord of the 24th, 25th, and 26th Paths of the Portal of the Vault of the Adepti, is a Candidate for admission to the Second Order, and is waiting without. V.H. Frater Hodos Chamelionis, prepare the Aspirant and act as his introducer. Associate Adeptus Minor, guard the hither side of the Portal, and admit them in due form. (Aspirant is prepared by making him wear Portal Sash across that of the Philosophus Grade. He carries Lamen of Hiereus, and Recommendation from the Chiefs of his Temple, a certificate of having passed the requisite examinations, and a written speech.)

Third:

(Opening door) Whom bringest thou here with thee?

Aspirant:

(Loudly and firmly.) Hear ye all that I, the Honoured Frater (XYZ) stand before you, being a member of the Philosophus Grade of the First Order, the Highest Grade of the Golden Dawn in the Outer, a Philosophus; one qualified to fill the important post of Hiereus in a Temple of the First Order, one who hath passed the five examinations prescribed between the First and Second Orders, and hath been declared Lord of the 24th, 25th, and 26th Paths in the Portal of the Adepti. I bear a written recommendation from the Chiefs of my Temple guaranteeing my qualifications, honour and fidelity; as also an attestation of my having passed the Pentagonal Examination. By virtue of these honours and dignities, I now come to demand my reception and acknowledgement as an Adeptus Minor of the Second Order.

Second:

O Aspirant! It is written that he who exalteth himself shall be abased, but that he who humbleth himself shall be exalted, and that blessed are the poor in spirit for theirs is the Kingdom of Heaven. It is not by proclamation of honours and dignities, great though they may be, that thou canst gain admission to the Tomb of the Adepti of the Rose of Ruby and the Cross of Gold, but only by that humility and purity of spirit that befitteth the aspirant unto higher things. Associate Adeptus Minor, bring unto me the recommendation and attestation which he beareth; and test thou his knowledge ere he be rejected for the sins of presumption and spiritual pride.

Third:

Thou knowest the arrangement of the Ten Sephiroth on the Tree of Life; now what symbolic weapon doth their natural succession form? (Aspirant answers unprompted.)

Third:

And what symbolic creature is traced bv the natural succession of the Paths? (Aspirant answers unprompted.)

Second:

O Aspirant. Let this be a sign unto thee. For the Flaming Sword and the Serpent of Wisdom shall be the symbol which shall procure thee admission. Return thou then, and divest thyself of these ornaments. They are not humble enough to entitle thee to be received. V.H. Frater Hodos Chamelionis, clothe him in the black robe of mourning. Let his hands be bound behind his back, symbolic of the binding force of his obligations, and put a chain about his neck, the emblem of repentance and humility.

Hodos:

Mighty Adeptus Major, it shall be done. (Hodos Chamelionis salutes and retires with Aspirant, strips him of all ornaments, brings him back to door in plain black robe, roped and carrying diagram of Sword and Serpent. Gives one gentle knock. Third Adept opens door, saying.)

Third:

By the aid of what symbol do ye seek admission?

Hodos:

(Shows diagram) By the aid of the Flaming Sword, and the Serpent of Wisdom. (Third takes badge, admits them, and recloses door.)

Second:

Whom bringest thou there?

Hodos:

Mighty Adeptus Major, I bring with me one who has passed the trial of humiliation, and who humbly desireth admission to the Tomb of the Mystical Mountain.

Second:

Let the Aspirant be assisted to kneel. (Aspirant is brought to curtained door of Tomb between Third Adept and Hodos Chamelionis. All face East, and kneel.)

Second:

From Thine Hand, O Lord, cometh all good. The characters of Nature with Thy Fingers Thou hast traced; but none can read them unless he hath been taught in Thy school. Therefore, even as servants look unto the hands of their masters and handmaidens unto their mistresses, even so our eyes look unto Thee, for Thou alone art our help. O Lord our God, who should not extol Thee? Who should not praise Thee?

All is from Thee, All belongeth unto Thee. Either Thy Love or Thy Anger all must again re-enter. Nothing canst thou lose, for all must tend unto Thy Honour and Majesty. Thou are Lord alone, and there is none beside Thee. Thou doest what Thou wilt with Thy mighty Arm, and none can escape from Thee. Thou alone helpest in their necessity the humble, the meek-hearted, and the poor, who submit themselves unto Thee; and whosoever humbleth himself in dust and ashes before Thee, unto such an one Thou art propitious. Who should not praise Thee, then, O Lord of the Universe, unto Whom there is none like? Whose dwelling is in Heaven, and in every virtuous and God-fearing heart.

O God the Vast One, Thou art in all things. O Nature, Thou Self from Nothing, for what else can I call Thee? In myself I am nothing. In Thee I am Self, and exist in Thy Self-hood from Nothing. Live Thou in me, and bring me unto that Self which is in Thee. Amen. Let the hands of the Aspirant be unbound. (This is done, Aspirant remains kneeling. Officers rise.)

Third:

Think not, O Aspirant, that the trial of humility through which thou hast passed, was ordained but to jest with thy feelings. Far from us be any such design. But it was intended to point out to thee that the truly wise man is but little in his own eyes, however great his attainments may appear to the ignorant, and that even the highest intellectual achievements are but as nothing in the sight of the Lord of the Universe, for He looketh at the heart. It is written: When I consider the Heavens, the work of Thy fingers, the moon and stars which Thou hast ordained, what is man that Thou art mindful of him, or the son of man that thou visitest him? And couldst thou even attain unto the height of a God upon this earth, how small and insignificant yet wouldst thou be in the presence of God the Vast One.

Second:

Rise, then, O Aspirant of the Rose of Ruby and the Cross of Gold. Rise, glorified by suffering. Rise, purified by humility. (Aspirant rises.)

Second:

Despise not sadness, and hate not suffering, for they are the Initiators of the heart; and the black robe of mourning which thou wearest is at once the symbol of sorrow and of strength. Boast not thyself above thy brother if he hath fallen, for how knowest thou that thou couldst have withstood the same temptation. Slander not, and revile not. If thou canst not praise, do not condemn. When thou seest another in trouble and humiliation, even though he be thy enemy, remember the time of thine own humiliation when thou didst kneel before the door of the Tomb, clothed in the Robe of Mourning, with the Chain of Affliction about thy neck, and thy hands bound behind thy back, and rejoice not at his fall. And in thine intercourse with the members of our Order, let thy hand given unto another be a sincere and genuine pledge of fraternity. Respect his or her secrets and feelings as thou wouldst respect thine own. Bear with one another and forgive one another, even as the Master hath said. V.H. Frater Hodos Chamelionis, what is the symbolic age of the Aspirant?

Hodos:

His days are an hundred and twenty years.

Second:

It is written: My Spirit shall not always strive with man, seeing that he also is flesh, yet his days shall be an hundred and twenty years. Associate Adeptus Minor, unto what do those 120 years of the Aspirant's symbolic age correspond?

Third:

To the Five Grades of the First Order through which it is necessary for the Aspirant to have passed before he can enter the Tomb of the Sacred Mountain. For the three months interval between the Grades of Practicus and Philosophus are the Regimen of the Elements; and the seven months between the Philosophus and the Portal symbolise the Regimen of the Planets; while the Elements and the Planets both work in the Zodiac; so that three plus seven multiplied by twelve yieldeth the number 120.

Second:

O Aspirant, ere thou canst enter the Tomb of the Adepti of the Rose of Ruby and the Cross of Gold, it is necessary to take a solemn Obligation of Secrecy, Fidelity, Fraternity, and Justice. But as in all the previous obligations, there is nothing contained therein contrary to thy civil, moral, or religious duties. Art thou willing to take such a pledge?

Aspirant:

I am.

Second:

Let the Aspirant be bound to the Cross of Suffering.

(The Aspirant is led to the Cross, and his hands put through the running nooses and cords are bound about his waist and feet. Two Adepti stand on either side to support him, and the

Third Adept takes his place ready to hand Cup and Dagger to Second Adept who stand in front of and facing Aspirant. Second Adept holds out Rose Crucifix to Aspirant, saying:)

Second:

The Symbol of Suffering is the symbol of strength. Wherefore bound as thou art, strive to raise this holy symbol in thy hands, for he that will not strive shall not attain. (Aspirant takes Crucifix in both hands, the cords being allowed to run out long enough to allow him to do so.)

Second:

I invoke Thee, the great avenging Angel HUA, in the divine name IAO, that Thou mayest invisibly place Thy hand upon the head of the Aspirant in attestation of his Obligation. (Second Adept raises his hands on high to invoke the force; then lowers them and takes crucifix which is replaced by Third Adept on Altar. Aspirant is now bound more firmly to the cross.)

Second:

Repeat after me your sacramental Name, and say:

OBLIGATION

Kether:

I, (Frater XYZ), a member of the Body of Christ, do this day spiritually bind myself, even as I am now bound physically upon the Cross of Suffering.

Chokmah:

That I will to the utmost lead a pure and unselfish life, and will prove myself a faithful and devoted servant of this Order.

Binah:

That I will keep secret all things connected with the Order, and its Secret Knowledge, from the whole world, equally from him who is a member of the First Order of the Golden Dawn, as from an uninitiated person, and that I will maintain the Veil of strict secrecy between the First and Second Orders.

Chesed:

That I will uphold to the utmost the authority of the Chiefs of the Order, and that I will not initiate or advance any person in the First Order, either secretly or in open Temple, without due authorisation and permission; that I will neither recommend a Candidate for admission to the First Order without due judgment and assurance that he or she is worthy of so great a confidence and honour, nor unduly press any person to become a candidate; and that I will superintend any examination of Members of lower Grades without fear or favour in any way, so that our high standard of knowledge be not lowered by my instrumentality; and I further undertake to see that the necessary interval of time between the Grades of Practicus and Philosophus and between the latter Grade and the Portal, be, when possible, maintained.

Geburah:

Furthermore, that I will perform all practical work connected with this Order in a place concealed and apart from the gaze of the outer and uninitiated world, and that I will not display our Magical Implements, nor reveal the use of the same, but will keep secret this Inner Rosicrucian Knowledge even as the same hath been kept secret through the ages; that I will not make any symbol or Talisman in the Flashing Colours for any uninitiated person without a special permission from the Chiefs of the Order. That I will only perform any practical magic before the uninitiated which is of a simple and already well known nature; and that I will show them no secret mode of working whatsoever, keeping strictly concealed from them our modes of Tarot and other Divination, of Clairvoyance, of Astral projection, of the Consecration of Talismans and Symbols, and the Rituals of the Pentagram and Hexagram, and most especially of the use and attribution of the Flashing Colours, and the Vibratory mode of pronouncing the Divine Names.

Tiphareth:

I further promise and swear that with the Divine permission I will, from this day forward, apply myself to the Great Work, which is, to purify and exalt my Spiritual Nature so that with the Divine Aid I may at length attain to be more than human, and thus gradually raise and unite myself to my higher and Divine Genius, and that in this event I will not abuse the great power entrusted to me.

Netzach:

I furthermore solemnly pledge myself never to work at any important symbol without first invoking the highest Divine Names connected therewith, and especially not to debase my knowledge of Practical Magic to purposes of evil and self-seeking, and low material gain or pleasure, and if I do this, notwithstanding this my oath, I invoke the Avenging Angel HUA, that the evil and material may react on me.

Hod:

I further promise to support the admission of both sexes to our Order, on a perfect equality, and that I will always display brotherly love and forbearance towards the members of the whole Order, neither slandering nor evil-speaking, nor repeating nor tale-bearing, whereby strife and ill-feeling may be engendered.

Yesod:

I also undertake to work unassisted at the subjects prescribed to study in the various practical grades from Zelator Adeptus Minor to Adept Adeptus Minor, on pain of being degraded to that of Lord of the Paths of the Portal only.

Malkuth:

Finally, if in my travels I should meet a stranger who professes to be a member of the Rosicrucian Order, I will examine him with care before acknowledging him to be such.

Such are the words of this my Obligation as an Adeptus Minor, whereunto I pledge myself in the Presence of the Divine One, and of the Great Avenging Angel, HUA, and if I fail herein, may my Rose be disintegrated and my power in Magic cease. (Third hands Dagger to Second Adept and holds Cup conveniently for him. Second dips point of Dagger in Wine and makes Cross on Aspirant—on brow, feet, right hand and left hand, and heart, saying:)

Second:

(For brow.) There are Three that bear witness in Heaven; the Father, the Word, and the Holy Spirit, and these Three are One.

(For feet.) There are Three that bear witness on Earth; the Spirit, the Water, and the Blood, and these Three agree in One.

(Right hand.) Except ye be born of Water and the Spirit, ye cannot enter the Kingdom of Heaven.

(Left hand.) If ye be crucified with Christ, ye shall also reign with Him. (He marks heart in silence. Then says:)

Second:

Let the Aspirant be released from the Cross of Suffering. It is written, that he who humbleth himself shall be exalted. V.H. Frater Hodos Chamelionis, remove from the Aspirant the Chain of Humility and the Robe of Mourning, and re-invest him with the Crossed Sashes. (This is done.)

Third:

Know, then, O Aspirant, that the Mysteries of the Rose and the Cross have existed from time immemorial, and that the Rites were practised, and the Wisdom taught, in Egypt, Eleusis, Samothrace, Persia, Chaldea and India, and in far more ancient lands. The story of the introduction of these mysteries into mediaeval Europe has thus been handed down to us.

In 1378 was born the Chief and originator of our Fraternity in Europe. He was of a noble German family, but poor, and in the fifth year of his age was placed in a cloister where he learned both Greek and Latin. While yet a youth he accompanied a certain brother P. A.L. on a pilgrimage to the Holy Land, but the latter, dying at Cyprus, he himself went to Damascus. There was then in Arabia a Temple of the Order which was called in the Hebrew tongue "Damkar", that is The Blood of the Lamb. There he was duly initiated, and took the Mystic title Christian Rosenkreutz, or Christian of the Rosy Cross. He then so far improved his knowledge of the Arabian tongue that in the following year he translated the book "M" into Latin, which he afterwards brought back with him to Europe. After three years he went on into Egypt, where there was another Temple of the Order. There he remained for a time still studying the mysteries of Nature. After this, he travelled by sea to the city of Fessa, where he was welcomed at the Temple there established, and he there obtained the knowledge and the acquaintance of the habitants of the Elements, who revealed unto him many of their secrets.

Of the Fraternity he confessed that they had not retained their Wisdom in its primal purity, and that their Kabala was to a certain extent altered to their religion. Nevertheless, he learned much there. After a stay of two years he came to Spain, where he endeavoured to reform the errors of the learned according to the pure knowledge he had received. But it was to them a laughing matter, and they reviled and rejected him, even as the prophets of old were rejected. Thus also was he treated by those of his own and other nations when he showed them the errors that had crept into their religions. So, after five years residence in Germany, he initiated three of his former monastic brethren, Fratres G.W., I. A., and I.O., who had more knowledge than many others at that time. And by these four was made the foundation of the Fraternity in Europe.

These worked and studied at the writings and other knowledge which C.R.C. had brought with him, and by them was some of the Magical Language transcribed (which is that of the Elemental Tablets) and a Dictionary thereof made; and the Rituals and part of the Book "M" were transcribed. For the True Order of the Rose Cross descendeth into the depths, and ascendeth into the heights, even unto the Throne of God Himself, and includeth even Archangels, Angels and Spirits.

These four Fratres also erected a building to serve for the Temple and Headquarters of their Order, and called it the Collegium ad Spiritum Sanctum, or the College of the Holy Spirit. This being now finished, and the work of establishing the Order extremely heavy, and because they devoted much time to the healing of those sick and possessed, who resorted to them, they initiated four others, viz.: Fratres R.C. (the son of the deceased father's brother of C.R.C.), C.B. a skilful artist, B.C., and P.D., who was to be Cancellarius; all being Germans except I.A., and now eight in number. Their agreement was:

1. **That none of them should profess any other thing, than but to cure the sick, and that freely.**
2. **That they should not be constrained to wear any distinctive dress, but there in follow the custom of the country.**
3. **That every year on the day of Corpus Christi, they should meet at the Collegium ad Spiritum Sanctum, or write the cause of absence.**
4. **Every one should look for some worthy person of either sex, who after his decease might succeed him.**
5. **The word R.C. to be their mark, seal, and character.**

The Fraternity to remain secret for one hundred years. Five of the Fratres were to travel in different countries, and two were to remain with Christian Rosenkreutz.

Second:

Frater I.O. was the first to die, and then in England where he had wrought many wonderful cures. He was an expert Kabbalist as his book "H" witnesseth. His death had been previously foretold him by C.R.C. but those who were later admitted were of the First Order, and knew not when C.R. died, and save what they learned from Frater A., the successor of D. of the Second Order and from their library after his death, knew little of the earlier and higher Members, and of the Founder, nor yet whether those of the Second Order were admitted to the Wisdom of the highest members. The discovery then of the Tomb wherein that highly illuminated Man of God, our Father C.R.C., was buried occurred as follows. After Frater A. died in Gallia Narbonensi, there succeeded in his place Frater N.N. He, while repairing a part of the building of the College of the Holy Spirit, endeavoured to remove a brass memorial tablet which bore the names of certain brethren, and some other things. In this tablet was the head of a strong nail or bolt, so that when the tablet was forcibly wrenched away it pulled with it a large stone which thus partially uncovered a secret door, (he draws back curtain, revealing door), upon which was inscribed in large letters Post CXX Annos Patebo—After an hundred and twenty years I shall open, with the year of our Lord under, 1484. Frater N.N., and those with him then cleared away the rest of the brickwork, but let it remain that night unopened as they wished first to consult the ROTA.

Third:

You will now quit the Portal for a short time, and on your return the Ceremony of Opening the Tomb will be proceeded with. Take with you this Wand and Crux Ansata, which will ensure your re-admission. (Aspirant goes out, carrying the Wand and Crux of Chief Adept.)

SECOND POINT

(Prepare Tomb as in diagram. Chief Adept lies in Pastos on his back to represent C.R.C. He is clothed in full Regalia. On his breast is the complete Symbol of the Rosy Cross suspended from the double Phoenix Collar. His arms are crossed on breast, and he holds Crook and Scourge. Between them lies the book "T." Lid of Pastos closed and Circular Altar stands over it. Other Adepti outside Tomb as before. On the Altar are replaced Rose Cross, Cup of Wine, Chain and Dagger.)

Second:

Associate Adeptus Minor, let the Aspirant now be admitted. (Third Ad. opens the door, and admits Aspirant, who carries Wand and Crux of Chief. He is placed in front of and facing Vault Door.)

Second:

Before the Door of the Tomb, as symbolic Guardians, are the Elemental Tablets, and the Kerubic Emblems, even as before the mystical Gate of Eden stood the watchful Kerubim, and the Sword of Flame. These Kerubic Emblems be the powers of the Angles of the Tablets. The Circle represents the four Angles bound together in each Tablet through the operation of the all pervading Spirit, while the Cross within forms with its spokes the Wheels of Ezekiel's Vision; and therefore are the Cross and the Circle white to represent the purity of the Divine Spirit. And inasmuch as we do not find the Elements unmixed, but each bound together with each—so that in the Air we find not only that which is subtle and tenuous, but also the qualities of heat, moisture and dryness, bound

40

together in that all-wandering Element; and further also that in Fire, Water and Earth we find the same mixture of Nature—therefore the Four Elements are bound to each Kerubic Emblem counterchanged with the colour of the Element wherein they operate; even as in the Vision of Ezekiel each Kerub had four faces and four wings. Forget not therefore that the Tablets and the Kerubim are the Guardians of the Tomb of the Adepti. Let thy tongue keep silence on our mysteries. Restrain even the thought of thy heart lest a bird of the air carry the matter.

Third:

Upon more closely examining the Door of the Tomb, you will perceive, even as Frater N.N., and those with him did perceive, that beneath the CXX in the inscription were placed the characters IX thus;

POST CXX ANNOS PATEBO
IX

This being equivalent to Post Annos Lux Crucis Patebo - At the end of 120 years. I, the Light of the Cross, will disclose myself. For the letters forming. LVX are made from the dismembered and conjoined angles of the Cross; and 120 is the product of the numbers from 1 to 5, multiplied in regular progression, which number five is symbolised in the Cross with four extremities and one centre point.

Second:

On the following morning, Frater N.N. and his companions forced open the door (he opens it wide) and there appeared to their sight a Tomb of Seven Sides and Seven Corners. Every side was five feet broad, and eight feet high, even as the same is faithfully represented before you. (Second Adept enters and pases by North to East of Vault, and turns to face West. Third Adept places Aspirant on North facing South, and takes his place at South facing North.)

Second:

Although in the Tomb the Sun does not shine, it is lit by the symbolic Rose of our Order in the centre of the first heptagonal ceiling. In the midst of the Tomb stands a circular Altar with these devices and descriptions on it: A.G.R.C., Ad Gloriam Roseae Crucis. A.C.R.G., Ad Crucis Rosae Gloriam. Hoc Universal Compendium Unius Mihi Sepulchrum Feci. Unto the Glory of the Rose Cross I have constructed this Tomb for myself as a Compendium of the Universal Unity.

Within the next circle is written: Yeheshuah Mihi Omnia, Yeheshuah is all things to me. In the centre are four figures of the Kerubim enclosed within circles surrounded by the following four inscriptions and each distinguished by one of the letters of the Tetragram- maton: Yod, Lion Nequaquam Vacuum, Nowhere a Void. Heh, Eagle, Libertas Evangelii, Liberty of the Gospel. Vau, Man, Dei Intacta Gloria, Unsullied Glory of God. Heh (f), Ox, Legis Jugum, Yoke of the Law. And in the midst of all is Shin, the Letter of the Spirit forming thus the Divine Name Yeheshuah, from the Tetragrammaton. Therefore, by God's Grace, having come thus far, let us kneel down together, and say: (All kneel, joining wands above Altar.)

Second:

Unto Thee, Sole Wise, Sole Mighty and Sole Eternal One, be praise and Glory forever, Who has permitted this Aspirant who now kneeleth before Thee to penetrate thus far into the

Sanctuary of Thy Mysteries. Not unto us, but unto Thy Name be the Glory. Let the influence of Thy Divine Ones descend upon his head, and teach him the value of self- sacrifice, so that he shrink not in the hour of trial, but that thus his name may be written on high, and that his Genius may stand in the presence of the Holy Ones, in that hour when the Son of Man is invoked before the Lord of Spirits and His Name in the presence of the Ancient of Days. It is written: If any man will come after Me, let him take up his cross, and deny himself, and follow Me. (Third Adept hands Chain to Aspirant, and takes Wand and Cross from him.)

Second:

Take therefore this Chain, O Aspirant, and place it about thy neck and say: I accept the Bonds of Suffering and Self-Sacrifice. (2nd and 3rd Adepts rise. Aspirant repeats words as directed.) Rise, then, my Frater, in the symbol of self-renunciation and extend thine arms in the form of a cross. (Aspirant rises, feet together, and arms extended.)

Second:

Associate Adeptus Minor, take from the Altar the Dagger of Penance and the Cup of Tribulation, that I may confirm the vow of the Aspirant forever by marking him afresh with the Stigmata of the Cross. (Second takes Dagger from Third and marks Aspirant anew as at Obligation: brow, feet, right hand, left hand, and heart. Gives Dagger back to Third who replaces it on Altar, and then hands Aspirant the Rose Crucifix.) Take that symbol, raise it with both hands above thy head and say: Thus will I uphold the Sign of Suffering and of Strength. And I heard the voice of the King of Earth cry aloud and say: He that aideth me in my suffering, the same shall partake with me in my rising. Replace then, O Aspirant, that Cross upon the Altar, and say: In and by that Sign, I demand that the Pastos of our Founder be opened, for my victory is in the Cross of the Rose. For it is written If ye be crucified with Christ, ye shall also reign with Him.

(Aspirant replaces Crucifix and repeats words as directed. Third gives him back Wand and Crux of Chief Adept. Second and Third Adepts move away Altar revealing upper part of Pastos. They open lid, disclosing Chief Adept within.)

Third:

And the Light shineth in Darkness, and the darkness comprehendeth it not.

Second:

Touch with the head of thy Wand the Rose and Cross upon the breast of the Form before thee, and say: Out of the darkness, let the light arise. (Done. Chief, without moving or opening his eyes, says:)

Chief:

Buried with that Light in a mystical death, rising again in a mystical resurrection, cleansed and purified through Him our Master, O Brother of the Cross and the Rose. Like Him, O Adepts of all ages, have ye toiled. Like Him have ye suffered tribulation. Poverty, torture and death have ye passed through. They have been but the purification of the Gold. In the alembic of thine heart, through the athanor of affliction, seek thou the true stone of the Wise. (Aspirant gives Wand and Crux to Chief Adept who gives in exchange the Crook and Scourge.)

Chief:

Quit then, this Tomb, O Aspirant, with thine arms crossed upon thy breast, bearing in thy right hand the Crook of Mercy and in thy left the Scourge of Severity, the emblems of those Eternal Forces betwixt which the equilibrium of the Universe dependeth; those forces whose reconciliation is the Key of Life, whose separation is evil and death. Therefore thou art inexcusable, whosoever thou art, that judgest another, for in that thou condemnest another, thou condemnest but thyself. Be thou therefore merciful, even as thy Father who is in Heaven is merciful. Remember that tremendous Obligation of rectitude and self sacrifice which thou hast voluntarily taken upon thyself, and tremble thereat. And let the humble prayer of thy heart be: God, be merciful to me a sinner, and keep me in the pathway of Truth.

Third:

Thus, then, did Frater N.N. and his companions, having moved aside the Circular Altar, and having raised the brazen plate or lid of the Pastos, discover the body of our Founder, with all the ornaments and insignia as here shown before you. Upon his breast was the Book "T,"a scroll explaining in full the mystic Tarot; at the end of which was written a brief paragraph concerning Christian Rosenkreutz, beneath which the earlier Fratres had inscribed their names. Following this came the names of the three Highest Chiefs of the Order, viz: Frater Hugo Alverda, the Phrisian, in the 576th year of his age. Frater Franciscus de Bry, the Gaul, in the 495th year of his age. Frater Elman Zata, the Arab, in the 463rd year of his age. Last of all was written: Ex Deo Nascimur; In Yeheshuah Morimur; Per Spiritum Sanctum Reviviscimus. In God are we born, in Yeheshuah we die, through the Holy Spirit we rise again. (They re-close the Pastos, and replace Altar.)

Second:

So, then, our Frater N.N. and his companions reclosed the Pastos fora time, set the Altar over it, shut the Door of the Tomb, and placed their seals upon it. (All quit the Vault. Aspirant carries Crook and Scourge; the door is closed, and Aspirant is led out of the Portal. The Tomb is then re-opened and Chief Adept released.)

THIRD POINT

(Tomb prepared as in diagram. Door not quite closed. In South East angle is diagram of Minutum Mundum; in N.E. that of Sword and Serpent. Due East, the Mountain. Altar as before with Crook and Scourge added later. Chief stands at East with arms extended. Pastos outside in Portal, head to the East. Lid laid side by side with space

between. Second Adept seated at head, Third at foot of Pastos. Aspirant is admitted, still carrying Crook and Scourge. 2nd and 3rd Adepts discard cloaks.)

Second:

And lo, two Angels in White apparel sitting, the one at the head and the other at the foot, where the body of the Master had lain, who said: Why seek ye the living among the dead?

Chief:

I am the Resurrection and the Life. He that believeth in Me, though he were dead, yet shall he live. And whosoever liveth and believeth in Me, shall never die.

Second:

Behold the Image (points to lower half of lid) of the Justified One, crucified on the Infernal Rivers of DAATH, and thus rescuing Malkuth from the folds of the Red Dragon. (Third points to upper half of lid.)

Third:

And being turned, I saw Seven Golden Lightbearers, and in the midst of the Lightbearers, One like unto the Ben Adam, clothed with a garment down to the feet, and girt with a Golden Girdle. His head and his hair were white as snow, and His eyes as flaming fire; His feet like unto fine brass, as if they burned in a furnace. And His voice as the sound of many waters. And He had in His right hand Seven Stars, and out of his mouth went the Sword of Flame, and his countenance was as the Sun in His Strength.

Chief:

I am the First and I am the Last. I am He that liveth and was dead, and behold! I am alive for evermore, and hold the keys of Death and of Hell.

Second:

He that hath an ear, let him hear what the Spirit saith unto the Assemblies. (Second and Third Adepts open Door of Tomb, and lead Aspirant in. They kneel down West of Altar with heads bent. Chief stands at East of Altar with arms extended.)

Chief:

For I know that my Redeemer liveth, and that He shall stand at the latter day upon the earth. I am the Way, the Truth and the Life. No man cometh unto the Father but by Me. I am the purified. I have passed through the Gates of Darkness into Light. I have fought upon earth for Good. I have finished my Work. I have entered into the Invisible. I am the Sun in his rising. I have passed through the hour of cloud and of night. I am Amoun, the Concealed One, the Opener of the Day. I am Osiris Onnophris, the Justified One. I am the Lord of Life triumphant over Death. There is no part of me which is not of the Gods.

I am the Preparer of the Pathway, the Rescuer unto the Light; Out of the Darkness, let that Light arise.

Aspirant:

Before I was blind, but now I see.

Chief:

I am the Reconciler with the Ineffable. I am the Dweller of the Invisible. Let the White Brilliance of the Spirit Divine descend. (Chief raises his hands invoking the Divine White Brilliance. There is a pause.)

Chief:

(To Aspirant) Arise now as an Adeptus Minor of the Rose of Ruby and the Cross of Gold, in the sign of Osiris slain.

(All rise. Second and Third Adepts raise Aspirant, and extend his arms in a cross. They then recross his arms on his breast and turn him to face West. Chief advances within reach of Aspirant. Third Adept N.W. They both join Wands over his head and Cruces a little lower.)

All:

We receive thee as an Adeptus Minor in the Sign of Rectitude and Self-Sacrifice. (Still keeping Wands joined over the lower Cruces, Chief touching base of brain. Second left temple, Third right temple.)

Chief:

Be thy mind opened unto the higher. (Chief places Crux against spine between shoulder blades. Second Adept against left breast. Third against right breast.)

Second:

Be thy heart a centre of Light. (Chief places Crux at the base of the spine. Second at left hip. Third at right hip.)

Third:

Be thy body the Temple of the Rosy Cross. (Aspirant is faced to East, and Adepts return to former positions. Crook and Scourge are laid on Altar over Dagger, crossing at yellow bands.)

Chief:

Repeat with us the following words which are the Signs of the Hidden Wisdom of our Order. (Aspirant is made to repeat each word after the Officer.)

Chief:

I.

Second:

N.

Third:

R.

All:

I.

Chief:

Yod.

Second:

Nun.

Third:

Resh.

All:

Yod.

Chief:

Virgo, Isis, Mighty Mother.

Second:

Scorpio, Apophis, Destroyer.

Third:

Sol, Osiris, Slain and Risen.

All:

Isis, Apophis, Osiris, I.A.O. (All separate Wands and give the Sign of Osiris Slain.)

All:

The Sign of Osiris Slain.

Chief:

L. The Sign of Mourning of Isis (With bowed head.)

Second:

V. The Sign of Typhon and Apophis (Head erect.)

All:

X. Isis, Apophis, Osiris, I. A.O. (They give the saluting Sign with heads bowed. A pause.)

Chief:

The Mystic number of this Grade is 21, the Heptad multiplied by the Triad; and from it is derived the Password of this Grade which is EHEIEH, which should be lettered separately when given thus,

Chief:

Aleph.

Aspirant:

Heh.

Chief:

Yod.

VOLUME SEVEN

Aspirant:

Heh.

Chief:

The Keyword is I.N.R.I. which is inscribed with its correspondences upon this complete symbol of the Rose and Cross which I bear upon my breast. These letters have been occasionally used as the initials of the following sentences: JESUS NAZARENUS REX JUDECORUM, whence it symbolises the Grand Word of this Grade which is YEHESHUAH or the Hebrew Name of Jesus, formed of the Holy letter Shin, representing the Ruach Elohim, placed within the Centre of the Name Tetragrammaton. Also it has been interpreted as: Igne Natura Renovatur Integra; Igne Natura Renovando Integrat; Igne Nitrum Roris Invenitur; Intra Nobis Regnum dei.

Chief:

(Indicating Diagram of the Minutum Mundum.) Behold the diagram Minutum Mundum sive Fundamental Coloris—the Small Universe or Foundation of Colour. Treasure it in thy heart, and mark it well, seeing that herein is the Key of Nature. It is, as thou seest, the diagram of the Sephiroth and the Paths, with the colours appropriately attributed thereto. See that thou reveal it not to the profane, for many and great are its mysteries.

Kether is the highest of all, and herein scintillates the Divine White Brilliance, concerning which it is not fitting that I should speak more fully. Chokmah is Grey, the mixture of colours. Binah is darkness, the absorption of colours. And thus is the Supernal Triad completed. In Kether is the root of the Golden Glory, and thence is the yellow reflected into Tiphareth. In Chokmah is the root of Blue, and this is reflected into Chesed; in Binah is the root of Red, and this is reflected into Geburah. And thus is the first reflected Triad completed. The beams of Chesed and Tiphareth meet in Netzach and yield Green. The beams of Geburah and Tiphareth meet in Hod and yield a tawny Orange. The beams of Chesed and Geburah fall in Yesod and yield Purple. And thus is the Third Triad completed. And from the rays of the Third Triad are these three colours shown in Malkuth, together with a fourth which is the synthesis. For from the Orange Tawny of Hod and the Greening Nature of Netzach is reflected a certain Greenish Citrine, Citron; from the Orange Tawny mixed with the Puce of Yesod proceedeth a red russet Brown, Russet; and from the Green and the Puce cometh a certain other darkening green, Olive. The synthesis of all these is blackness and bordereth on the Qlippoth. But the colours of the 22 Paths are derived from and find their roots in those of the First Reflected Triad of the Sephiroth, the Three Supernals not otherwise entering into their composition, and thus are their positive colours found. Unto the Air is ascribed the Yellow colour of Tiphareth. Unto the Water is ascribed the Blue Colour of Chesed. Unto the Fire is ascribed the Red Colour of Geburah. The colours are to be found in Malkuth.

Those of the Planets are in the Rainbow scale; thus: Saturn, Indigo; Jupiter, Violet; Mars, Red; Sol, Orange; Mercury, Yellow; Venus, Green; Luna, Blue.

Unto the Signs of the Zodiac are ascribed the following: Aries, Scarlet; Taurus, Red-Orange; Gemini, Orange; Cancer, Amber; Leo, Greenish-Yellow; Virgo, Yellowish-Green; Libra, Emerald; Scorpio, Greenish-Blue; Sagittarius, Blue; Capricornus, Indigo; Aquarius, Purple; Pisces, Crimson.

Further, thou wilt observe that the colours of the Paths and the Sephiroth form a mutual balance and harmony on the Tree. Colours are Forces, the Signatures of the Forces; and the Child of the children of the Forces art thou. And therefore about the Throne of the Mighty One is a Rainbow of Glory, and at His Feet is the Crystal Sea. But there are many other attributions of colour also, seeing that the respective rays meet and blend with each other. And therefore do

I greet thee with the Mystic Title of Hodos Chamelionis, the Path of the Chamelion, the Path of Mixed Colours, and I give thee the Symbol of Hiddekel, the third River which floweth towards the East of Assiah. (They return to Altar, and 2nd Adept indicates Crook and Scourge thereon.)

Second:

The colours of the Crook and Scourge are taken from those of the Minutum Mundum Diagram, and they thus represent the just equilibrium between Mercy and Severity on the Tree of Life. The Crook therefore is divided into the colours symbolic of: Kether, Aleph, Chokmah, Taurus, Chesed, Leo, Tiphareth, Aries, Hod, Capricornus. And the Scourge into those symbolising: Netzach, Scorpio, Tiphareth, Gemini, Binah, Cancer, Geburah, Mem.

Third:

(Indicates Sword and Serpent.) The colours of the Minutum Mundum are also the key to those which compose the Admission Badge of the Sword and Serpent; and thus by their aid it may be the better examined and comprehended. The one is ascending, the other is descending; the one is fixed, the other is volatile; the one unites the Sephiroth, the other the Paths. Furthermore, in the Serpent of Wisdom is shown the ascending Spiral, and in the Sword the rush of the descending White Brilliance from beyond Kether, differentiated into various shades and colours, darkening more and more as they near Malkuth.

Chief:

(Indicates Diagram of Mountain.) This is the symbolic Mountain of God in the centre of the Universe, the sacred Rosicrucian Mountain of Initiation, the Mystic Mountain of Abiegnus. Below and around it are darkness and silence, and it is crowned with the Light ineffable. At its base is the Wall of Enclosure and Secrecy, whose sole Gateway, invisible to the profane, is formed of the Two Pillars of Hermes. The ascent of the Mountain is by the Spiral path of the Serpent of Wisdom. Stumbling on between the Pillars is a blindfolded figure, representing the Neophyte, whose ignorance and worthlessness while only in that Grade is shown by the 0-0, and whose sole future claim to notice and recognition by the Order is the fact of his having entered the Pathway to the other Grades, until at length he attains to the summit.

I now proceed to instruct you in the mystic symbolism of the tomb itself. Let the Altar be moved aside. (Done.) It is divided into three parts, the Ceiling which is White; the Heptagonal Walls of seven Rainbow colours, and the Floor whose prevailing hue is black; thus showing the powers of the Heptad between the Light and the Darkness. On the ceiling is a Triangle enclosing a Rose of 22 petals, within a Heptangle formed of a Heptagram reflected from the Seven Angles of the Wall. The Triangle represents the Three Supernal Sephiroth; the Heptagram, the Lower Seven; the Rose represents the 22 paths of the Serpent of Wisdom.

The Floor has upon it also the Symbol of a Triangle enclosed within a Heptagram, bearing the titles of the Averse and Evil Sephiroth of the Qlippoth, the Great Red Dragon of Seven Heads, and the inverted and evil triangle. And thus in the Tomb of the Adepti do we tread down the Evil Powers of the Red Dragon (Chief Adept stamps thrice on diagram) and so tread thou upon the evil powers of thy nature.

For there is traced within the evil Triangle the Rescuing Symbol of the Golden Cross united to the Red Rose of Seven times Seven Petals. As it is written He descendeth into Hell. But the whiteness above shines the brighter for the Blackness which is beneath, and thus mayest thou comprehend that the evil helpeth forward the Good. And between the Light and that Darkness vibrate the Colours of the Rainbow, whose crossed and reflected rays, under the Planetary presidency are shewn forth in these Seven Walls.

Remember that thou hast entered by the door of the Planet Venus, whose symbol includes the whole Ten Sephiroth of the Tree of Life. Each Wall of the Tomb is said mystically to be in breadth five feet and in height eight feet, thus yielding forty squares, of which ten are marked and salient, representing the Ten Sephiroth in the form of the Tree of Life, acting throughout the Planet. The remaining squares represent the Kerubim and the Eternal Spirit, the Three Alchemical Principles, the Three Elements, the Seven Planets, and the Twelve Signs, all operating in and differentiating the rays of each planet. Note that in all, the Central Upper square alone remains white and unchanged, representing the changeless Essence of the Divine Spirit, thus developing all from the One, through the Many under the government of One.

The colours of the varying squares may be either represented by the colour of the Planet and the colour of the Force therein mixed together, or by these colours being placed in juxtaposition, or in any other convenient manner; but the foundation of them all is the Minutum Mundum Diagram.

THE FLOOR OF THE VAULT

THE CIRCULAR ALTAR

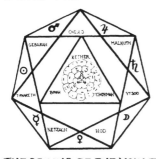

THE CEILING OF THE VAULT

THE ROSE OF 49 PETALS AND CROSS AT THE HEAD OF THE PASTOS

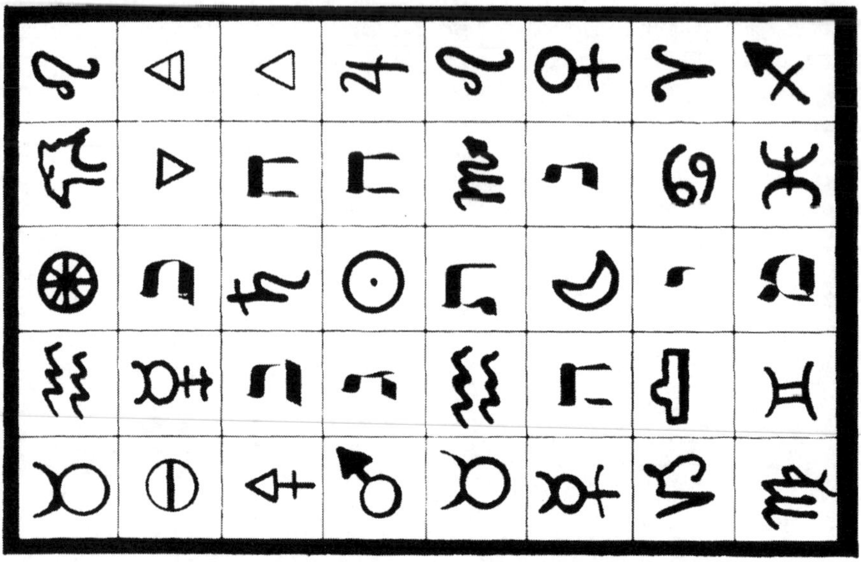

THE WALL OF THE VAULT

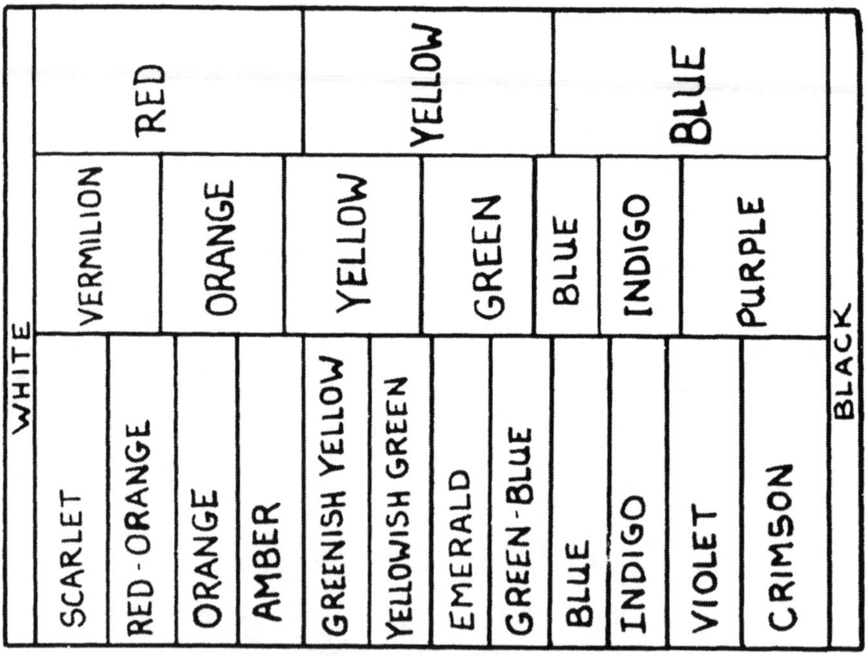

THE SIDE OF THE PASTOS

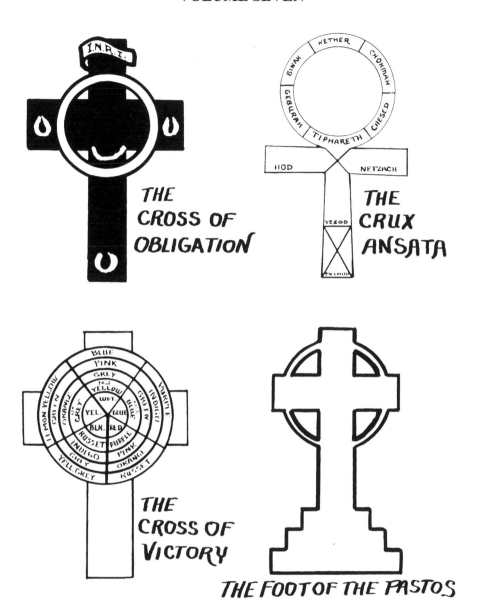

THE CROSS OF OBLIGATION

THE CRUX ANSATA

THE CROSS OF VICTORY

THE FOOT OF THE PASTOS

The symbolism of the Altar was briefly explained to you in the Second point. Upon the Altar stands a black Calvary cross, charged with a Rose of Five times Five petals, representing the interchanging energies of the Spirit and the Elements. (Chief leads Aspirant out of Tomb. Two Adepti replace Altar, and all resume their places as at beginning of Third Point.)

Chief:

The head of the Pastos is white, charged with a golden Greek Cross and Red Rose of 49 Petals. The foot is black with a white Calvary Cross and Circle placed upon a pedestal of Two steps. On the sides are depicted the 22 Colours of the Paths, between Light and Darkness. (Aspirant is placed between Lid and Pastos. Chief stands facing him on opposite side of the Pastos.)

Chief:

Frater (Soror) I now greet you with the grip of this Grade which is given thus. (Shows it.) The fingers of the right hand are held so as to form the letters L.V.X. The thumb and first fingers are stretched to form the letter L. The first and middle fingers are extended to suggest the V. The little finger is crossed over the third finger to make X. This may be done with both hands, and is always exchanged by placing the hands, with fingers thus arranged, over the wrist of the Frater or Soror being greeted. You will note that this grip must never be exchanged except across the Pastos. You will also remember that you must observe strict silence in regard to the place where you received this rite. It is well for you to understand that you are expected to promise that you will never tell anyone when, at what time, or where, or from whom you received this grip, or who was present at your initiation into this Order.

The Signs and Passwords you have already received. Finally, you must understand that you are never permitted to say to anyone not a member of this Order that you are a Rosicrucian. Let the Pastos be replaced within the Vault. (The Adepti replace Pastos as before, and all resume places as at opening of Ceremony.)

CLOSING

(Chief Adept knocks. All rise.)

Chief:
Second:
Third:
Chief:
Third:
Second:

(All successively Knock once.)

Second:

Roseae Rubeae.

Third:

Et Aureae Crucis.

Chief:

Very Honoured Fratres and Sorores, assist me to close the Tomb of the Adepti. Associate Adeptus Minor, how many Princes did Darius set over his Kingdom?

Third:

It is written in the Book of Daniel that there were One Hundred and Twenty.

Chief:

Mighty Adeptus Major, how is that number formed?

Second:

By the continued multiplication of the first five numbers of the decimal scale.

Chief:

Post Centum Viginti Annos Patebo. Thus have I closed the Tomb of the Adepti in the Mystic Mountain of Abiegnus. (Chief Adept closes Door of Vault and draws Curtains.)

Third:

Ex Deo Nascimur.

Second:

In Yeheshuah Morimur.

Chief:

Per Spiritum Sanctum Reviviscimus.

(All present make LVX signs in silence. Aspirant signs Inner Roll and is led out. All disrobe and disperse. Aspirant should be directed to make Saluting Sign of 5-6 on entering and leaving.)

THE FELLOWSHIP OF THE ROSY CROSS

At this juncture, I would like very much to present three rituals written by Arthur Edward Waite for his own Order which he called The Fellowship of the Rosy Cross. As might be expected the text is Christian and biblical. Waite was raised a Roman Catholic. It is also classical Waite in that he was compelled to insert quite frequently Latin phrases which, from the ritualistic viewpoint, is not a bad idea since a strange tongue may excite the inner sense of wonder and worship. In ritual it is excusable. In prose it is unforgivable - at least to the extent that it is used by Waite in his various writings.

It is also typical Waite in that it is ponderous, turgid and repetitive. I am no great advocate or admirer of Waite's literary output. He had so much to say in reality, but his literary style got in the way to obscure his message.

Yet, in these rituals of the Neophyte, Adeptus Minor and Major grades, given me through the courtesy of Robert W. Gilbert of Bristol who is writing a biography of Waite, I have found myself strangely moved. It is rather like being escorted through the Adeptus Minor ritual again, though this time to the tune of another melody, in the language of another day, in the spirit of another religion. In spite of my own resistance to Waite, I find myself choked a little, tearful of eye, exalted in spirit as I was fifty years ago. This is a remarkable admission of the efficacy not merely of ritual per se but of what I would otherwise have stamped as pompous, flatulent, turgid bible - thumping which I dislike heartily.

THE COMPLETE GOLDEN DAWN SYSTEM OF MAGIC

There are some magnificent lines in here. In the event that some of my readers may wish to institute a new Golden Dawn temple, many of these lines could well be incorporated into the ancient rituals.

In the event that some already initiated members of the Order are desirous of so-called higher grades. Waite's Adeptus Major Ritual might provide some basic features which could be incorporated into what they know of the conventional Order Rituals.

THE CEREMONY OF RECEPTION IN THE GRADE OF NEOPHYTE

Newly constructed from the Cipher Manuscripts, and issued by the authority of the concealed superiors of the second order, to members of recognised temples. Certified in Conformity with the Secret Doctrine and Knowledge of the ROSY CROSS.

SACRAMENTUM REGIS, KEEPER OF THE SACRED MYSTERY.

THE OFFICERS OF THE GRADE

1. **THE HONOURABLE FRATER PHILOSOPHICUS, id est, Propositum Conscium Dei - Master of the Temple.**
2. **THE HONOURABLE FRATER PRACTICUS, id est, Desiderium Conscium Dei Warden of the Temple.**
3. **THE HONOURABLE FRATER THEORETICUS, id est, Mens Conscia Sponsi Guide of the Paths and Grades.**
4. **THE AUXILIARY FRATER ZELATOR, id est, Terra Illuminata - Proclamator et Lucifer.**
5. **THE FRATER THURIFICANS, id est, Thuribulum Ferens - Thurifer.**
6. **THE FRATER AQUARIUS, id est, Aquam Benedictam Ferens - Aquarius.**
7. **THE FRATER OSTIARIUS, id est, Gustos Liminis, a Novice of the Rosy Cross Guard.**
8. **The Imperator, or Chief of the Rite, presides ex officio in all Grades of the Fellowship, either personally or by his appointed Substitute.**

In those cases where certain Offices are taken by Sorores of the Fellowship, the necessary alterations are made in the modes of address.

THE CLOTHING OF CELEBRANTS AND OFFICERS

1. **The Honourable Frater Philosophicus wears a green robe over his black habit and a collar of red silk, from which depends a circular lamina, inscribed with the letter YOD. The green colour of the Master's robe represents the growth in life which is of GOD. The symbol of the Lion is embroidered thereon, upon the left side, with the inscription: FACIES TERTIA, FACIES LEONIS. The Master bears a Wand, surmounted by a Calvary Cross, having four circles at the end of the four arms and one circle toward the centre of the lowermost arm.**

2. The Honourable Frater Practicus wears a yellow robe over his black habit, symbolising the beginning of transmutation in GOD. The symbol of the Eagle is embroidered thereon, upon the left side, with the inscription: FACIES QUARTA, FACIES AQUILAE. His collar is of violet silk, from which depends a circular lamina, inscribed with the letter HE, being the first HE of the Divine Name. He bears a Wand surmounted by a flaming heart.

3. The Honourable Frater Theoreticus wears a blue robe over his black habit, symbolising the aspiration and desire which initiate the great quest and reflect things unrealised. It bears the symbol of the Man embroidered thereon, upon the left side, with the inscription: FACIES SECUNDA, FACIES HOMINIS. His collar is of orange silk, from which depends a circular lamina, inscribed with the letter VAU. He bears a Wand, surmounted by an open eye, signifying the eye of mind.

4. The Auxiliary Frater Zelator wears a cloak of reddish brown, corresponding to the Adamic earth and symbolising the first movement of the Divine Spirit toward the making of a living soul. The symbol of the Ox is embroidered thereon, with the inscription: FACIES UNA, FACIES CHERUB. His collar is of blue-green silk, from which depends a circular lamina, inscribed with the letter HE, being the HE final of the Divine Name. He bears a Wand, surmounted by a Calvary Cross, having a crown upon the upper arms. The Frater Zelator is in symbolical correspondence with the Guide of the Paths and Grades.

5. The Frater Thurificans wears a red surplice and a collar of green silk, from which depends a circular lamina, inscribed with an equilateral triangle, having the apex upward, as a symbol of Fire. He is in symbolical correspondence with the Master.

Certified a correct copy of the Autograph MS. SACRAMENTUM REGIS, 5-6.

THE HOLY ORDER OF THE GOLDEN DAWN

THE SOLEMN CEREMONY OF OPENING THE TEMPLE IN THE LIGHT

(The arrangement of the Temple is shown in the Official Diagram.

The Officers and Members being assembled within and the door of the Sacred Precincts being closed and guarded by the Sentinel, who is seated with drawn sword on the hither side, the permanent Director of Ceremonies comes before the vacant Throne of the Hierophant, and says:)

Director of Ceremonies.

Fratres et Sorores, the Lord is my light and my help. In the Name of Him Who rescues us from the darkness and the unredeemed places, and by command of the Honourable Wardens, I direct the Officers and Brethren to assume the clothing of their rank and Grades. Invest our portals, O Lord, and guard our thresholds. Do Thou clothe us in Thy grace and truth.

(The Members assume the insignia of their proper ribbons and collars. The Director of Ceremonies assists in the vesting of the Superior Officers. This being accomplished in solemn order and in the reverence of holy silence, the Hierophant of the Temple or one of the Honourable Wardens proceeds to the clearing of the Temple as follows: With the first and second fingers and the thumb of his right hand he seals his forehead and says:)

Hierophant.

ATEH. (He seals his breast and says:)

Hierophant.

MALKUTH. (He seals his right shoulder and says:)

Hierophant.

VE GEBURAH. (He seals his left shoulder and says:)

Hierophant.

VE GEDULAH. (He clasps his hands and says:)

Hierophant.

LE OLAHM. AMEN. (The operation hereof is more especially for his own cleansing, that he may be worthy to purify without. It is done facing the due East. All stand and turn eastward.)

THE BANISHING

(He traces the Banishing Pentagram in the East with reversed Sceptre or Wand. He carries his Wand to the middle place of the Pentagram and pronounces slowly and distinctly the Sacred Name.)

Hierophant.

YOD, HE, VAU, HE. (He moves to the South, carrying the Wand upraised and pointed at the same angle. He traces the Pentagram in the South, carries Wand to the middle place and utters the Sacred Name:)

Hierophant.

ADN1. (He moves in the same manner to the West, performs the same working and utters the Sacred name:)

Hierophant.

EH-YEH. (He moves in the same manner to the North, performs the same working and utters the Sacred Word:)

Hierophant.

AGLA. (He returns in the same manner to the East, having thus circumambulated the Temple and traced a complete circle in the air with his Wand. This is the clearing of the Temple. Members face each quarter with Hierophant, who now faces East, extends his arms crosswise and says:)

Hierophant.

Before me RAPHAEL.
Behind me GABRIEL.
At my right hand MICHAEL.
At my left hand AURIEL.
For before me flames the Pentagram and behind me shines the Six-Rayed Star.

(This is the Angelical Formula, which brings the holy hills about the Jerusalem of the Temple and makes the Temple itself as a ring of holy hills about his own Jerusalem within. He finishes as he began, namely, with the SEALING PRAYER, which signifies the closing of the gates within and without against the images of evil. He goes before the Throne of the Hierophant, which he faces, and recites the following prayer.)

PRAYER BEFORE THE THRONE

Hierophant.

Creator of the Universe, Lord of the Visible Worlds, Who hast by Thy Supreme Power set up Thy Holy Signs in all the quarters of the Heavens and dost speak to us by day and by night in Thy greater and lesser luminaries. Thy suns and stars and constellations: Grant, we beseech Thee, that the hidden grace which abides in the Radiant East, the Dayspring of Light and the Font of Life, may in answer to this our prayer - be here and now communicated to the Throne of the Hierophant. Make him in Thy benignity the efficacious emblem of that Dawning Golden Light which illuminates the Path of Thy Mysteries, and may that light lead us to the attainment of the Quintessence, the tingeing Stone of the Wise, the Wisdom which has its source in Thee and the Beatitude which is found in Thy Presence.

(The Officers and the Temple are in this manner dedicated to the work about to be performed, and the clearing is done invariably with a solemn recollection of the intention belonging to its several points. If the Temple is opened to communicate a higher Grade than that of Neophyte, it must be preceded by this clearing in the same manner. In such case, the communication of the Neophyte Grade subsequently on the same day does not carry with it the necessity of another clearing. The Prayer being finished, the Hierophant takes his place on the Throne in the East, approaching it by the northern side of the pedestal before the Throne. He assumes his sceptre. Members are seated: a pause. All rise. The Sentinel leaves the Temple. The Kerux passes by the North to the North-East side of the Temple, and so standing at the right hand but to the front of the Hierophant, and facing West, he raises his Lamp and Wand.)

Hierophant.

Fratres et Sorores of the Isis Urania Temple, duly assembled under warrant for the Mysteries of the Golden Dawn, assist me to open the Temple of our Holy Order in the Grade of Neophyte.

Kerux.

Hekas. Hekas, este bebeloi.

(He returns to his place by the South and West, giving the Signs of the Grade as he passes the Throne ol the Hierophant. Except in the reverse circumambulation at the close of this Grade, the course of the sun must be followed in the movements of all Officers and Members. The salute of the Grade must be given when passing the Hierophant and on entering or leaving the Temple.)

Hierophant.

Frater Kerux, see that the Temple is guarded on the further side of the Portal, as an outward sign of the mysteries of prudence that are within. (The Kerux gives one knock on the hither side of the door. The Sentinel responds in the same manner on the outer side, using the hilt of his sword.)

Kerux.

(Raising his Wand) - Truly Honoured Hierophant, the Temple is guarded without, the door is secured within, and I stand on the hither side as the witness of vigilance and the gate of prudence.

Hierophant.

(With raised eyes and uplifted Sceptre). - Fratres et Sorores, let us put away the thoughts of the outer world. The Temple is guarded without: let the heart be guarded within. (A momentary pause.)

Hierophant.

Honourable Frater Hiereus, lift up the sword of judgment, and standing by the hither side of the Portal, assure yourself that all present have seen the Light in the East. (The Hiereus leaves his Throne, passes to the door of the Temple, where he draws his Sword and raises it.)

Hiereus

Fratres et Sorores of the Holy Order of the Golden Dawn give the signs of a Seeker for the Light. (This is done accordingly, and the Hiereus sheathes his Sword. He gives the Signs of a Neophyte.)

Hiereus.

Truly Honoured Hierophant, the Orient from on High hath visited us. (The Signs are repeated by the Hierophant. The Hiereus returns to his place.)

Hierophant.

Those who are present among us are more especially the watchers from within. Stand about us in Thy Holy Place, O Lord, and keep us pure in Thy precincts. (This is said with raised eyes and uplifted Sceptre. There is a momentary pause.)

Hierophant.

Let the number of officers in this Grade and the symbolism of their offices be proclaimed once again, that the graces whereof they are images may be quickened in the spheres of those who are here and now present and in the perfect sphere of the Order. Honourable Frater Hiereus, how many are the principal officers of the Neophyte Grade?

Hiereus.

As in all Grades and Degrees of the Outer Order, they reflect by their triplicity below the Eternal Triad which is above: they are the Hierophant, the Hiereus and the Hegemon.

Hierophant.

What have these titles in common?

Hiereus.

The letter H, symbol of breath and life.

Hierophant.

(Raising his Sceptre) - But I testify, Fratres et Sorores, that our common heritage is life in the Holy Spirit. (He lowers his Sceptre.) Honourable Frater Hiereus, how many are the officers?

Hiereus.

These also are three - the Stolistes, the Dadouchos and the Kerux, besides the Sentinel, who stands armed on the further side of the Portal, who guards that side, receiving communications from without, admitting members and taking charge of the Candidate when he comes to the vestibule of the Holy Temple. (The Dadouchos, standing in his place, raises the Thurible, and as incense issues therefrom:)

Dadouchos.

My place is in the South of the Temple and I bear the thurible of my office. I represent material heat manifesting in the outer world and the fire that is communicated within. In respect of that fire it is said: My soul hath thirsted for the Lord, in the pathless and waterless desert of this world. I symbolise the desire of God which has burnt up all earthly roses and has wasted all the false gardens of delight, so that the soul can find neither food nor wine therein. I am the heat of that supernatural fire which consumes all lusts of the flesh, lusts of the eye and pride of life. It is in this sense that I consecrate the Candidate with fire. (The Thurible is lowered. The Stolistes, standing in his place, raises the cup of water.)

Stolistes.

My place is in the North of the Temple and I bear the water of my office. I represent material cold and moisture manifesting in the outer world and the waters of the fountain of salvation that pour upon the world within. I am the other side of the Divine desire, for even as the hart panteth after the water-brooks so doth the soul of man desire after Thee, O God. It is in this sense the ! purify the Candidate with water. (The Cup of water is lowered. The Kerux, standing in his place at the northern side of the Hiereus, raises his Lamp.)

Kerux.

My place is on the hither side of the Portal. I carry the Lamp of my office, which symbolises material light shining in the outer world but more especially the secret light which dawns in the world of grace. I make all official announcements; I report to the Hierophant of the Temple; I lead circumambulations; and I see that the Temple is prepared in piety and reverence for the mysteries that are about to be performed. I go before the Candidate, as God goes before the elect on the path of their return to Him. (The Lamp is lowered. The Hegemon uplifts his Sceptre.)

Hegemon.

I am the Mediator and Reconciler, the preparer of the pathway to the Divine. My seat is between the Pillars and I preside over the Gate of the Mysteries. I am the condition of the ascent of the soul, which is the purity symbolised by my white robe. I am the peace of the equilibrium which reconciles light and darkness. I direct in virtue of purity the higher aspirations of the soul. I am religion, which manifests in benignity, and the middle way by which ascent is possible to the light. I carry a mitre-headed Sceptre, which represents the sacramental side of holy churches and creeds. In virtue of this my office and of its high symbolism, I am the leader of the Candidate in all Grades of the Order and I direct him in the true way. (The Sceptre of the Hegemon is lowered. The Hiereus draws and raises his Sword. He raises the Banner of the West.)

Hiereus.

I am set upon the Throne of the West. I symbolise external darkness. I cast out the images of matter. I am the spirit which clears the obsessions. I am called Fortitude in the Mysteries, but my fortitude and refuge are Thee, O God. I am the protection from the evil within the Candidate. I carry the Sword of Judgment and the Banner of the Evening Twilight. I announce that which I represent at the gate of entrance to the heights. (The Hiereus replaces his Banner. He sheathes his Sword. The Hierophant raises his own Sceptre and Banner.)

Hierophant.

I am seated on the Throne of the East and I symbolise the Rising Sun in the world of the Macrocosm. Behold He hath placed His tabernacle in the sun. I rule and govern the Temple and Members of all Grades. My robe is red because of the fire within. I bear the Sceptre and the Banner of the East. I am the Expounder of Mysteries. I am he who is authorised from beyond to give expression in eternal symbolism to the things that are behind the Veil. I am the point at which Faith dissolves into experience. I am power, light, mercy and wisdom. (He replaces his Banner.)

Hierophant.

Frater Stolistes, in the Sign of Understanding, and remembering the Great Sea, I direct you to purify the Temple and the Brethren with water.

(The Stolistes follows the course of the sun, coming eastward from his place in the North. He faces the Hierophant and offers him his vessel for consecration. The Hierophant blesses with the Cross and says:)

Hierophant.

Bless us, O Lord, we beseech Thee, and this Thy gift of water, which we are about to use in Thy service as a sign without of graces that are communicated within.

(The Stolistes makes a Cross with his Cup and sprinkles thrice in the East. He proceeds in succession to South, West and North, facing each point, where he repeats the Cross sign and sprinkles. He completes the circle by returning to the East. He again faces the Hierophant, lifts up the Cup of Water and says:)

Stolistes.

Waters of Understanding, Waters of the Great Sea: I purify with water. (He salutes the Throne and returns to his place by South and West.)

Hierophant.

Frater Dadouchos, in all symbols of the Divine desire, and by the sparks of aspiration flying upward, I direct you to consecrate the Temple and the Brethren with fire.

(The Dadouchos passes by West and North to the East, coming from his place in the South. He faces the Hierophant and offers his Thurible for consecration. The Hierophant blesses with the Cross and says:)

Hierophant.

Bless us, O Lord, we beseech Thee, and this Thy gift of fire, which we are about to use in Thy service as a sign without of graces that are communicated within.

(The Dadouchos makes cross with his Thurible and censes thrice in the East. He proceeds South, West and North, facing each point, making a Cross as before and censing three times. He returns to the East, uplifts his Thurible and says:)

Dadouchos.

The desire of the House of the Lord hath eaten me up. I have consecrated with fire. (He again salutes the Throne and returns to his place direct.)

Hierophant.

To him who has fulfilled election, there is given a Robe of Glory. Let the mystical procession take place in the way of the light.

(The Kerux passes to the North and halts. The Hegemon passes by South and West, where he is joined by the Hiereus and they proceed, the Hegemon being in front, to their places behind the Kerux. The Dadouchos follows the Hegemon from South to West, where he allows the Hiereus to step between, and so passes to the North, where he takes his place on the right of the Stolistes. The Kerux, Hegemon, Hiereus, Stolistes and Dadouchos circumambulate the Temple with the Sun. The Hiereus passes the Hierophant once, the Hegemon twice, and the other officers three times, making the Sign of the Grade on each occasion. They return in fine to their places.)

Hierophant.

The mystical procession is accomplished in commemoration of the path of our return. Let us declare the sanctity of God in the reverence of holy prayer, that the light and darkness of humanity may unite to bless the Lord. (All present face East, giving the Grade Sign, which is maintained throughout the adoration.)

Hierophant.

Holy art Thou, O Lord of the universe: establish us Thy servants in the health of Thy great sanctity. Holy art Thou Whom Nature hath not formed: transmute our human nature and let our souls be reformed in Thee. Holy art Thou, the vast one and the mighty: enlarge us in the way of our research, that we may attain in fine to Thy presence. Enlighten our darkness, increase our light, O Lord of light and darkness. (Then facing the West:)

Hierophant.

Frater Kerux, in the Name of Him who is our strength, our refuge and our term from everlasting, I command you to proclaim that the Temple is open in the world of grace. (The Kerux passes as before to the place of annunciation by the Throne of the Hierophant and says clearly and loudly, as he raises his Lamp and Wand:)

Kerux.

Fratres et Sorores, I testify that the sun has risen in the soul and that the light of grace is extended.

Hierophant.

KHABS

Hiereus.

AM

Hegemon.

PEKHT

Hiereus.

KONX

Hegemon.

OM

Hierophant.

PAX

Hegemon.

LIGHT

Hierophant.

IN

Hiereus.

EXTENSION

(The Kerux returns to his place. The Sentinel re-enters the Temple. Officers and Members are seated. Here ends the Solemn Ceremony of Opening the Temple in the Light.)

THE CEREMONIAL ADMISSION OF A NEOPHYTE IN THE PORTAL OF THE GOLDEN DAWN

(The KLerux removes the Rose, Lamp, Chalice and Paten from the Altar.)

Hierophant.

Fratres et Sorores, I beseech you to lift up your hearts to pray that the Divine Assistance may be with us efficiently in the work which I am delegated to perform as an authorised Expounder of the Mysteries. I have received a Dispensation from the Concealed Superiors of the Order to admit A.B. to the first circle of initiation in the Portal of the Golden Dawn. I command therefore the Honourable Frater Hegemon to take in charge the preparation of the Postulant and to see that the things within are symbolised by the things without.

(The Hegemon rises, removes his seat from the middle place of the Pillars to a convenient point left free for this purpose, and having reached the hither side of the door, he turns eastward, makes with recollection the Sign of a Neophyte and then passes without the Portal. He prepares the Candidate by placing a hoodwink over his eyes and a threefold cord about his body. While this is being done:)

Hierophant.

The things that are without are in analogy with the things that are within. The eyes of our Postulant at the Gate of the Mysteries are darkened for a period, to symbolise the cloud that rests upon the sanctuary of his soul. The body of our Postulant is bound, to typify the material chain with which he has been loaded in his exile, far from the home of the heart. He cannot walk alone and hence he so depends upon our guidance. He will not be deserted in his need. He will be brought safely and surely into the secret place of our light. There is faith and there is hope in his heart, and that which leads him in the narrow way is the hand of love. (The preparation being over, the Hegemon gives an alarm of a knock at the outer side of the Portal. The Kerux replies with a knock.)

Kerux.

Truly Honoured Hierophant, the Mediator between light and darkness, the Lord of Reconciliation and Peace, stands at the door without.

Hierophant.

Do you certify, Frater Kerux, that he returns in the name of his mission, for the fulfilment of a work of redemption?

Kerux.

He wills only that it should be accomplished.

Hierophant.

God made the world without, as He made that which is within. May the Peace of the Lord fill those who are seeking His light. I give you permission to admit A.B., who puts aside henceforth in these precincts his earthly titles and dignities and receives at our hands that name which represents his aspiration on entering here among us. He will be known hereafter as Frater Adveniat Regnum (vel aliud), and may he that enters the Kingdom receive the crown of all. Fratres Dadouchos et Stolistes, in the purifying sign of fire and the holy water of regeneration, be ready to receive the Candidate.

(The Stolistes, moving by North and East, joins Dadouchos in the South, and they proceed together to the door. The lights are turned down. The Kerux opens the door, and taking up his place about five feet within, he bars the further progress of the Candidate when he has entered the Portal. Behind him stand the Stolistes and Dadouchos. As he leads the Candidate:)

Hegemon.

The darkness is also God's minister. The darkness shall lead His servant.

Dadouchos.

The Treasure of the Hidden Fire shall shine therein.

Stolistes.

It is over the Great Sea and in the deeps thereof.

Hierophant.

The night shall be enlightened with the day. (The Hegemon again advances, leading the Candidate. The Kerux bars the way.)

Kerux.

The things that are holy are reserved for those that are holy and the sanctuary of initiation for conserated and initiated men. Son (and Daughter) of the Night and Time, and child of Earth, you cannot enter the Temple of Sacred Mystery. (The Stolistes comes forward, cross-marks the Candidate on the forehead and sprinkles three times before him.)

Stolistes.

In the Name of the Fountain of Living Water, which cleanses the Children of Earth, I purify you with water.

(He falls back. The Dadouchos comes forward, raises his Thurible before the face of the Candidate, makes the Sign of the Cross therewith and censes him three times.)

Dadouchos.

In the Name of the Divine Desire which transmutes the life of earth, I consecrate you with fire.

(He also falls back with the Kerux, who lifts up his Lamp as the Hegemon goes forward leading the Candidate. If there are several Candidates, they must all be purified and consecrated separately. The Kerux, Stolistes and Dadouchos resume their places but remain standing.)

Hierophant.

Inheritor of night and time, child of the material world, what seek you in the places of the soul?

Hegemon.

(Replying for Candidate). Through the darkness of time and night, I have come to the Gate of the Temple, looking for the light within.

Hierophant.

Place the Postulant at the western side of the Altar with his face to the Fast, symbolising the desire after that light which God shall grant to the seeker who is well and properiy prepared. (This is done by the Hegemon, who leads the Candidate helpfully and carefully throughout the Ceremony. He is not allowed to kneel, to rise, or to move of his own accord.)

Hierophant.

We hold your signed application for admission to this Order, which exists for the communication of spiritual knowledge to those who have awakened in the spirit. We hold also your solemn testimony to a desire conceived in your heart for the grace of Eternal Life and Divine Union. We are taught that the things which are Caesar's must be rendered duly to Caesar but to God the things that are God's, and the secrets of the Sanctuary are reserved to the Sanctuary alone. Before your reception can proceed, it is necessary for you to take a solemn Obligation to maintain the Veils of the Order, and as in the world without you are bound by the canons of morality and the code of society to keep the laws of both, so you must be covenanted herein to keep the rule of the Temple and never to disclose without that which you learn within. But it is just, on our part, to assure you, as I now do in God's Name, that the pledge which we exact does in no wise derogate from the laws of man but leads to their better fulfilment in the light of Divine law. Are you willing to take this meet and salutary Obligation? (The Candidate is prompted by the Hegemon.)

Candidate.

I desire the light of the House, and I take its laws upon me. (The Hierophant, in conformity with the symbolism, comes down from his Throne and goes to the East of the Altar, saying:)

Hierophant.

It is written that I will visit the hearts of men, for my delight is in the way of justice.

(He stands facing to the West. The Hiereus comes to the North side of the Altar and the Hegemon to the South side. The three Officers thus form a triangle, and the Candidate, who is close to the Altar on the western sfde, is joined therein at the middle point of the base. The Members of all Grades rise and remain standing while the Obligation is taken.)

Hierophant.

Postulant in the Home of the Spirit, looking for grace to come, in the Name of the Lord of Grace, Who is the Fountain of all our light, I bid you kneel down as a sign of your humility and obedience. (The Candidate is assisted to kneel.) Give me your right hand, which I impose on this holy sign of light shining in the darkness; place your left hand in mine, as a pledge of the sacred and sincere intention which your heart brings into this Order, that it may be married to the sincerity and holiness which abide in its own heart. Bow your head, as one who has come out of the world looking for those gifts that do not belong to the world. For the first and last time in the presence of this Assembly, recite your earthly name and say after me:

Hierophant.

(Followed by Candidate) I, A.B., in the presence of the Eternal Father of Light, Who recompenses those who seek Him out, in the presence of the Brethren who are gathered here together in the grace of His Divine Name, do of my own will and in the consciousness of my proper act and deed, submitted in conformity with the act and will of God, most solemnly pledge the honour of my soul to keep inviolable the secrets of this Temple and of the Mysteries which are worked within it. I will not speak of them in the world without, when I go forth therein. I will not disclose the name of this Temple or Order, or the name of any of its members. I will not reveal the knowledge communicated to me therein. I will keep the secrets of the Sanctuary as I would keep those of my King and God, speaking to me in the inmost places of the soul. I will conform to the Laws of the Order and to the By-Laws of this Temple. I will have no part or dealing in respect of this Order, its Rites, Proceedings, or its Knowlege, with any member who has been cast out therefrom, nor will I recognise the living membership of any person who is not in possession of the temporal Password communicated at each Equinox to the recognised Temples. I hereby include within the category of this sacred pledge whatever information I may have received concerning the Order prior to my admission therein. I lift up my heart to God Who is my Judge, and seeing that I have come hither actuated by the most solemn motives which are conceived by the soul of man, I promise solemnly from this moment that I will persevere with courage and devotion in the path of Divine Science, even as I shall persevere undaunted through this ceremony which is its image, and whatsoever I may learn or attain in this Temple and in the Order, I will receive as from the hands of God and to His hands will return it in purity. I certify hereby and hereon that I desire above all things the grace of the secret knowledge, but since that knowledge is also power, I convenant that at no time and under no temptation will I apply it to the works of evil. I will hold myself dedicated henceforth, so far as in me lies, to the consecration of my outward and inward nature, that I may deserve to leave the darkness and to dwell in the world of light. I will abide with my brethren in union, rectitude and purity, remembering that peace is in God. Bending over this holy symbol of light dawning in the soul, I swear to observe all parts and points of this pledge without evasion, equivocation, or mental reservation of any kind, praying as I deal herein in all high faith and honour that my secret name may be written in the Book of Life, even as its symbol will be registered this day in the Books of the Order. I invoke upon my own head the penalty of expulsion from the Order if ever I am wilfully guilty of perjury herein. May I go in fear of the second death, the change of the Infinite Benignity into Divine wrath and of the Divine Will into a hostile current which shall paralyse the life of the soul. Deal with me, O Lord, in Thy mercy; strengthen my heart and my reins; for even as I bow my neck under the Sword of the Hiereus (it is placed on the neck of the Candidate), so do I commit myself into Thy hands for judgment or reward. So help me my mighty and secret soul; so help me the sun of my soul; enlighten me in the dark places and bring me at last to Thee. (A pause.)

Hierophant.

Rise, Novice of the Portal Grade in the Order of the Golden Dawn. (The Novice is assisted accordingly. The Hierophant and Hiereus return to their places. All Members are seated.)

Hierophant.

Being mindful, O Honourable Hegemon, that all things are within - all joys, all dangers, all hopes, all fears, with the ways of the height and deep - let the Novice be placed in the northern part of the Temple, to symbolise the state of spiritual coldness, the night of the human mind and of grace inhibited. (This is done accordingly, but the Novice is faced to the East.)

Hierophant.

I asked to be taken from the darkness and holy hands led me in the covert of holy wings. I asked to be brought into the light, and the loving wings were closed about the face of me, lest I should see God and die. I asked to kneel at the steps of the Throne of God and they set me in the Holy Place, even by the Tabernacle. O God, how wonderfully is Thy work declared in the heart of man: I will walk in Thy ways forever. (A pause.)

Hierophant.

Let the Novice be led from the darkness and through the darkness toward the Light by a symbolical advancement on the faith of his intention. Let the outward symbol of the inward light go before him, like the destiny of attainment before those who are born for the light.

(The Dadouchos passes by West to North, and when he has paused on the right of the Stolistes, the Kerux takes his place in front of the Hegemon and Novice and goes before the procession. The Stolistes and Dadouchos occupy the third line. The procession moves slowly, with great reverence and in the utmost silence, except at the stated points of the liturgy. The Hierophant knocks once as it passes the East. The Kerux halts in the South, the Stolistes and Dadouchos divide, passing one on each side of the Hegemon and Novice, till they are in front of the Kerux. All turn and the Kerux bars the way with his Wand. The Cipher MSS. from which this Ritual depends indicate only one circumambulation of the Temple at this point; it has been customary to triple it in practice. The first circumambulation was in silence, except for one battery of the Hiereus; at the second the Hierophant knocked once, the consecration took place in the South, and the Novice was taken to the Hiereus: the third completed the procedure at the North and East as above. The innovation has no authority, but is justified by convenience in a small Temple.)

Kerux.

The thoughts of the natural mind are unpurified and unconsecrated; their place is not found by the Throne of the West. (The Stolistes cross-marks the Novice on the forehead and sprinkles three times.)

Stolistes.

In the Name of the Fountain of Living Water which cleanses the thought of man, I purify you with Water. (The Dadouchos makes a Cross with Thurible and censes three times.)

Dadouchos.

In the Name of the Divine Desire which transmutes the thought of man, I consecrate you with fire. (The Stolistes and Dadouchos fall back to their places in the rear.)

Hegemon.

Son of the night and time, twice washed with holy water and purged by consecrated fire, your way is free in the West.

(The procession pauses at the Throne of the Hiereus, who knocks once. The Kerux faces him on the right hand. The Hegemon leads up the Novice and raises his hoodwink. The Hiereus stands with drawn Sword holding the Banner of the West.)

Hiereus.

You cannot pass by me, says the Guardian of the West, until you have learned my Name.

Hegemon.

(On the part of the Novice). You are darkness in the place of darkness, questioning the Seekers of the Light.

Hiereus.

The Mystery of the Presence in the West is declared at the Gate of the Temple for the encouragement of reconciled souls. I am the protection from the evil that is within you. I am Divine Fortitude. I am Judgment, by which the good is set apart from the evil. I am the Providence which works in darkness. Go forward and fear not, for he who is established in God does not tremble at the flame or at the flood, or at the inconstant shadows of the air.

(The Hegemon replaces the hoodwink; the procession moves forward till it arrives again at the North. The Kerux, turning, bars the way for the second time. The Stolistes and Dadouchos come forward as before.)

Kerux.

The desires and emotions of the natural man are a sea in torment: unpurified and unconsecrated, their place is not found by the Throne of the Temple in the East. (The Stolistes cross-marks as before.)

Stolistes.

In the Name of the Fountain of Living Water which cleanses the heart of man, I purify you with Water. (The Dadouchos censes as before.)

Dadouchos.

In the Name of the Divine Desire which converts the heart of man, I consecrate you with fire.

Hegemon.

Son ot the night and time, thrice washed with Holy Water and purged by consecrated Fire, your way is free in the East.

(The Kerux leads the procession to the Throne of the Hierophant. The Hegemon leads up the Novice and raises his hoodwink, so that he sees the Hierophant, standing with uplifted Sceptre, holding the Banner of the East.)

Hierophant.

You cannot pass by me, says the Guardian of the East, until you have learned my Name. Hegemon.

(On the part of the Novice.) You are Light in the place of Light, Light dawning in Darkness for the liberation and salvation of those who dwell in the House of Bondage and in the Shadow of Death.

Hierophant.

The Mystery of Eternal Light dawning in the darkness of material things, and communicated to the soul of man, is declared in the East of the Temple. I am the Light enkindled, the Morning Light, the desire of the eyes of the world. I am the Expounder of Mysteries. I am love and immortality and the hope of the Kingdom in its coming. I am the Guardian of the Veil and I speak in the opening of the eyes, proclaiming the path of wisdom and the secret law of equilibrium.

(The hoodwink is again replaced over the eyes of the Novice and the procession passes to the Altar. The Hierophant leaves his Throne, bearing his Sceptre. He stops (a) between the Pillars, (b) half-way between these and the Altar, or (c) close to the eastern side of the Altar. The Hiereus comes forward to his place on the North side in the angle towards the West. The Hegemon places the Novice in the West and moves to the South side in the angle towards the West. The Kerux stands at a little distance behind the Novice. The Stolistes and Dadouchos stand due East of the Hiereus and Hegemon respectively. Wherever the Hierophant pauses, he says slowly and clearly:)

Hierophant.

I come in the power of the light; I come in the Light of Wisdom; I come in the mercy of the light. The light has healing in its wings. (And afterwards at the East of the Altar:)

Hierophant.

Behold, I stand at all thy doors and knock. Open thy heart, O Novice of this Order. Take in thy hand the desires and aspirations which have brought thee to our Holy Temple, and kneeling with bowed head (the Hegemon and Kerux here assist the Novice), place them in humility and reverence on our Altar of Sacrifice. (The Novice is directed to clasp his hands over the Altar.)

Hierophant.

O Thou Who sanctifiest the heart of man. Who leadest our desires into attainment and our aspirations to the steps of Thy House, sanctify. Eternal God, this Novice of our Order.

Lead him to the perfection which is in Thee, into the splendour of Thy great White Throne. May that which here and now I restore to him in the outward signs of Thy most blessed sacraments and Thine all-sacred symbols be ratified above in I They presence and realised essentially within him, to the glory of Thy Name, world without end, Amen, and to the joy of Thy redeemed Hierarchies.

(The Novice is assisted to rise. The Hierophant comes close to the Altar and lifts his Sceptre above the head of the Novice. The Hiereus and Hegemon raise the Sword and Sceptre respectively to touch the Sceptre of the Hierophant.)

Hegemon.

Thou who wouldst be saved and hast come out of the ways of darkness, enter into thy holy inheritance.

Hiereus.

Thou in whom the world has not anything from henceforth and forever, come into the Holy Light. (At the word Light the Kerux finally removes the hoodwink and the Sentinel turns up the lights.)

Hierophant.

We receive thee into the place of our sacraments, among the signs without of the things that are realised within, into the pure and shining mystery, into the Order of the Golden Dawn.

Hierophant.

The emblems of High Light are restored to the Novice.

Hierophant.

KHABS.

Hiereus.

AM

Hegemon.

PEKHT

Hiereus.

KONX

Hegemon.

OM

Hierophant.

PAX

Hegemon.

Light

Hierophant.

In

Hiereus.

Extension.

(The three Chief Officers remove their Sceptres and Sword from above the head of the Candidate. The Kerux passes to North-East of the Altar and raises his Lamp. The Hierophant points thereto.)

Hierophant.

When the guiding hands led you in the dark circle of your wanderings, the Light of the Hidden Wisdom went before you, symbolised by the Lamp of the Kerux. Know and remember henceforward that this wisdom, which begins in the fear of the Lord ends at his Palace at the centre. (All officers return to their stations except the Hegemon.)

Hierophant.

Let the Neophyte be led to the eastern side of the Altar; let him stand with his face to the East. (The Hegemon leads accordingly by North to East and places the Neophyte in the middle way between the Altar and the Pillars.)

Hierophant.

Honourable Frater Hiereus, you will now impart to the Neophyte the Secret Signs, Tokens and Word which are allocated to the 0-0 Grade in the Portal of the Golden Dawn. You will also communicate the temporal password which is common to the whole Order.

(The Hiereus passes from his Throne by North to the Black Pillar and stands on its Eastern side, facing South. The Hegemon leaves the Neophyte, and passing by North takes up a similar position before the White Pillar, but facing towards the North. The Sword of the Hiereus is sheathed. The Hiereus turns West and faces the Neophyte. He stands between the Pillars.)

Hiereus.

Frater Adveniat Regnum (vel aliud), by the decree of the Truly Honoured Hierophant, receive at my hands the Secret Signs, Token and Word of the Portal. The step is given by advancing your (he is given instruction), as I advance my own. The signs are called respectively those of (again instruction is given) and of (again instruction is given), and the second is the answer to the first. The Sign of (again instruction is given) is given by putting out the (again instruction is given), the (again instruction is given) being also inclined. In this position you are as one (again instruction is given) and it is intended to remind you of that state in which you came among us but recently, seeking and asking for the light. The Sign of Silence refers to your solemn covenant. The Token or Grip is given (again instruction is given. The Hiereus maintains the Grip.) It recalls your search for guidance in the darkness. In this position the syllables of the Word are exchanged in an undertone. It is (again instruction is given), the Egyptian name of the God of Silence. The temporal Password of the Order is changed at each Equinox; at the present time it is (again instruction is given). I now place you between the Symbolic Pillars at the Gateway of Hidden Wisdom.

(He draws the Neophyte forward by the Grip of the Grade, taking care that he does not cross the threshold represented by the two Pillars. He resumes his station by the Black Pillar.)

Hierophant.

Honourable Frater Hiereus, I bid you remember that behind the will of man is the Portal of the Supreme Mystery.

Hiereus.

Truly Honoured Hierophant, in commemoration of that Mystery, and in obedience to your ordinance, I demand the final and perfect consecration.

(The Stolistes and Dadouchos. following the course of the sun, come forward successively from their places. They raise their vessels of consecration before the Hierophant, then turn and consecrate the Neophyte, saying;)

Stolistes.

In the Name of the Fountain of Living Water which purifies the will of man. I consecrate you with Water.

Dadouchos.

In the name of the Divine Desire which redirects the will of man, I consecrate you with Fire. (Again saluting the Throne, they return to their places.)

Hierophant.

Honourable Frater Hegemon, let the Neophyte be unbound between the Pillars, to symbolise the transmutation of the lower parts of the personality, so that they may concur in the work of the will when the will has been turned to the light. (This is done accordingly, the Sceptre of the Hegemon being taken in charge by the Hiereus.)

Hierophant.

Let our Frater be also invested with the Mystic Badge of this Grade. (The Neophyte is invested with the Ribbon, and this completes the ceremonial part of his reception. The silent circumambulation in the light which used to take place at this point has no authority in the Cipher MSS. It vvas preceded by a simple direction on the part of the Hierophant.)

Hegemon.

By command of the Truly Honoured Hierophant, receive the Badge of this Grade: the prevailing colour is black, representing darkness, but the Light of the Eternal Triad is dawning therein.

Hierophant.

You will now take your seat as an approved and received Neophyte on the northern side of the Temple and toward the West.

(The Hiereus restores the Sceptre to the Hegemon. The Hegemon passes round the White Pillar, leads the Neophyte with the sun to his assigned place, and returns to his own between the Pillars, where his seat is restored. This completes the ceremonial part of the reception. The Kerux replaces the Rose, Lamp, Chalice and Paten on the Altar. All Officers are seated.)

Hierophant.

Frater Adveniat Regnum (vel alius), the Order of the Golden Dawn extends to you its loving welcome on your admission as a Neophyte of this Temple. May there be joy in the blessed Hierarchies at your coming out of earthly into spiritual life, and may that joy in its reflection fall like the rain of love into your heart of hearts. Your preparation as a Candidate was in the body, to symbolise that greater preparation which you had already made in your heart before you could be accepted as a Postulant. The triple cord which was placed about you represented the threefold bondage of your mortality, and when it was in fine loosed this signified the liberation of your higher part. The sacramental title which you have assumed in place of your earthly designation is a token of our Secret Name in the Temple that is above: it is the nearest that you can reach in your aspiration to that which in this life is hidden even from yourself. The hoodwink imaged the darkness of the material mind. The censing in your several consecrations prefigured the cleansing with fire from the Supernal Altar of Incense. May your heart and your reins be purified thereby as if with a burning coal. The cross-marking with lustral water and the mystic sprinkling showed forth sacramentally the condition on which your name is registered in the Book of Life. The Altar at which you knelt is in the form of a double cube, with its base of necessity concealed, the surfaces exposed to sight, while on the summit are the sacred emblems whereon you were pledged and whereby you are bound in the sight of God henceforth and forever. The Altar is black to portray the state of our natural humanity and the darkness of the unformed world before the Word of creative light went forth therein. That Word is typified by the white Triangle which is placed on the Altar; it is the sign of Divine Immanence in Nature; and also of that which must be declared in your soul, my brother, for the manifestation of the Divine therein. At the apex of the White Triangle, there is placed a Red Cross, which is the sign of Him who is unfolded in light through the universe and through the soul in grace. (The Hierophant rises and extends his arms in the form of a cross.)

Hierophant.

Thanks be to Thee, O Lord and Father Almighty, for the Secret Word which is conceived and born in the heart. We have accepted Thy Cross and Thy Calvary because of the glorious resurrection that is to come. May Thy Word also be born in the heart of this Neophyte. May it grow in grace and truth. May the power and perfection of its fulness be as the glory of the King of all. (The Hierophant resumes his seat.)

Hierophant.

To the East of the Cubical Altar are the Pillars which are analogically referred to Seth, Hermes and Solomon as allusions to the secret tradition and its perpetuation by the guardians of the Mysteries. They bear certain hieroglyphical texts from the Ritual of the Dead. They are symbols of eternal equilibrium, active and passive, fixed and volatile, severity and mercy. The solid triangles on their summits bear each a veiled lamp, signifying the triad of life. Between them lies the narrow path of the Hidden Wisdom. It was down this path, my brother, that I passed for your reintegration in the light; on the threshold thereof, and between the Two Pillars, you received the secrets of the Grade, the distinguishing badge and the final and perfect consecration.

You should now learn that the Hierophant on his Throne in the East personifies the substance and the evidence and the experience which are represented by faith in the eternal. He is the Rising Sun in Nature and power, light, mercy and wisdom in the providential world. It is said: Ex oriente Lux, and that light is for the illumination of the peoples of the earth. Behold He hath placed His Tabernacle in the sun, and the purpose is that our feet may be directed in the way of peace. This is how the Orient from on high visits us. The intention is furthermore that the knowledge of salvation may be granted to His people. This is the import of the power of the Hierophant and the correspondence thereof is His mercy, for mercy is on all sides. But the correspondence of his light is his wisdom, and this wisdom symbolises that which proceeds from the mouth of the Most High, reaching from end to end and strongly and sweetly overruling all things. The Hierophant is also the teaching spirit at the place of the Rending of the Veil.

The Hiereus on the Throne of the West is the Setting Sun in Nature and Divine Fortitude in the world of Providence. But the Fortitude of God on the threshold of initiation is the power and will to save the soul alive when it has gone forth seeking the true light. That is the kind of Fortitude. The Hiereus is also a correspondence of that Divine Darkness which is behind all manifested Divine Light.

The Hegemon represents religion, the foundation of which is in faith, but it is also holy hope. He is the Mediator, the Reconciler, the Preparer for the Path to the Divine. He represents in an especial manner the condition of the ascent of the soul, and that is purity, which is symbolised by his white robe. It is in and by this quality that he directs the higher aspirations of the spirit. Purity is not only the condition, but in a sense it is also the term; it is not only the first link in the chain which leads from earth to heaven, but it is the chain itself. It is the Ladder of Jacob, by which the aspirations ascend and the great influences come down. It is said that Religion pure and undefiled before God and the Father is this: To visit the fatherless and the widowed in their affliction and to keep oneself unspotted from the world. The Hegemon coming forth from between the Pillars, and going even outside the door of the Temple into the place of the uninitiated, is sent to save that which is in dereliction. His ministry is to those who are widowed of the Divine Spouse and to those who are fatherless, being without God in the world. When he goes out therefore, it is as if a voice said: And God so loved the world.

But the qualities and graces and virtues which are represented by the chief officers are in a state of superincession. There is also a sense in which the Hierophant and Hiereus both represent the love that is behind the universe, in virtue of the correspondences of which it is possible for God to be so near the heart of man that it is more easy to attain than to miss Him. This is why the path upward is natural and straight in comparison with the path downward.

In respect of the lesser officers, you have heard what is symbolised by the Lamp and Function of the Kerux. He is the light of the end which goes before the cohorts of salvation. The Stolistes and Dadouchos, who are seated in the South and North, carry the outward signs of the things which purify within. It is in virtue of such lustrations and such consecrations that the Candidate comes at length to the East, as the quest to its term and desire to its proper attainment. (A pause.)

Hierophant.

Frater Kerux, you have my command to proclaim that the Neophyte has entered the Portal and has been admitted into the mysteries of the Neophyte Grade in the Holy Order of the Golden Dawn. (The Kerux passes by West to North, and standing at the right hand but to the front of the Hierophant, and facing West, he raises his Lamp and Wand.)

Kerux.

In the Name of God who is our Light, and by the ordinance of the Truly Honoured Hierophant, hear ye all: I proclaim and testify that A.B., who will be known hence forth among us by the sacramental title of Frater (vel Soror) Adveniat Regnum (vel alius), has passed the Portal of the Golden Dawn and has been admitted to the Mysteries of the Neophyte Grade. (He returns to his place with the Sun.)

Hiereus.

Frater Adveniat Regnum (vel alius), I exhort you to keep in everlasting memory the obligation to secrecy which you have taken on your entrance into.this Order. Regard it as a test of merit, and its faithful observance as a title of salvation, a warrant for your advancement in the soul. There is strength in silence, the seed of Wisdom is sown therein and it grows in darkenss and mystery. Remember the Mystery which you have received; it is the shadow of a greater Mystery, whereof tongue cannot speak. Honour God Who is our light. From Him proceed all things and unto Him all things return. Continue to desire that Divine Vision which you are pledged to seek. Remember that those who go before you may place you in the path of its attainment, but the soul must ascend of itself till the grace and the power come down and abide in its secret sanctuary. Remember that things Divine are not for those who understand the body alone. Remember that many burdens are cast aside on the path upward, and that only those who are lightly clothed will attain to the summit. Remember the charity of the wise and respect the religions which are sacred to those about you, for there are many paths to the centre. Remember the law of equilibrium and learn by its help to distinguish between the good and evil, to choose the one and put aside the other, until that time comes when goodness shall fill the heart entirely. Remember lastly that steadfastness prevails over all difficulties, and do not be daunted by those which await you in the pursuit of that Hidden Knowledge of which God is the motive and the end.

Hierophant.

The titles of your advancement to the next Grade of the Order depend in part on yourself and in part on us. Ponder over that which is communicated in the Portal of the Secret Light. In such reflection and in the examination of your own conscience you will find a further light, and that light is your warrant. The instruction which we offer for your guidance may be obtained on application to the Cancellarius, but your advancement itself can take place only by the dispensation of the Second Order. (The Allocution of the Neophyte Grade then follows, and may be delivered by the Hierophant or one of the Wardens of the Temple.)

THE ALLOCUTION

Hierophant.

Fratres et Sorores, holding all Grades of the Order, by the power to me transmitted from the Wardens of this Temple, I invite you to hear with recollected hearts the Allocution belonging to the Grade of Neophyte. And you, our Brother, who have been received this day among us, to you we address more especially these few words, which, we trust, will abide in your memory and will perform their office within you to your own and to our advantage. We have invoked upon you the Morning Redness, Gold of Morning, even the Extended Light, and we feel that within the peaceful abode of this Order you may find not only an abode of spiritual contemplation apart from the outer world of our daily solicitude, but a sanctuary where the symbols of the secret knowledge may bring to you some radiance or reflection of the direct Light which shines in the Temple of the Light - that Temple which is not entered with earthly feet or seen with the veiled eyes of this body of our mortality. We trust also that the Order may become to you one of those hearths and homes around which the love of brotherhood is gathered - that love which does not fail us in the hour of inward need. In this respect we are pledged to you whom we have admitted, as you are pledged to us: we ask you to remember this, as we also remember, and among the last things which we can offer to you at this time is the maxim in chief of fraternity founded on consanguinity of spirit; Brother, the keys of all the greater mysteries are committed to the hands of love.

And now as regards the experience through which you have just passed, we have no occasion to remind you that in the physical order we come forth from darkness into light, and that in the intellectual order most comparisons between light and darkness are an ecomony of our real meaning. The progress of the Candidate from the one to the other state in the Grade of Neophyte is understood among us in a particular sense, which at the same time has a certain natural analogy with the more usual meaning. The birth of the soul in our consciousness is like birth into physical life. As the life of the Candidate anteceded his reception into the Order, so the soul which is within us antecedes that moment when it issues, as it were, from its concealment within us and begins to manifest by its operation. This is the beginning of the supernatural life, of the life of grace, and hereof is the whole Grade a symbol. When the desire of the House of the Lord awakens within us, our passage from darkness has already begun; we have been called to the Living Beauty; that which is termed among us the Lamp of the Hidden Knowledge has been uplifted and proceeds before us on the way; it is the experience of those who are our precursors in the ascent of the Holy Mountain. Through the keen air of high aspiration, as in the uplifted region of the mind, may we pass into that world of flame, wherein are the Sons and Daughters of Desire! When desire and aspiration have attained their term in us, may there be communicated at length that bread and even that salt which are types of the earth no longer but the food of souls! May we drink of that wine reserved for those who are athirst in the Kingdom of our Father! The lustrations are many, and the consecrations also are many, looking for that time when God shall cleanse us from our sins with living water, pouring through the chambers of the mind, and our hearts with that fire which being enkindled on earth shall in the end carry us to heaven.

We are dealing. Brethren, and shall continue to deal henceforward, not alone with the question of religion, but with its heart and centre behind all the external differences of systems and churches and sects. The Grades of the Order of the Golden Dawn are the grades of our progression in God, and in these - as in those which we take in that other and not less symbolical progression of daily life - it rests with us whether they shall remain symbolism or whether we shall pass in them, and they shall pass in us, into the actual region of experience. It is because of that infinite realm which lies behind the woven circle of official religion that you are counselled in this Grade to respect the forms thereof. The external churches are doors which open for many if not indeed for you, and there is perchance one of them which for you also may open, into the places of peace, into the light which in fine will enlighten every man who comes into this world. Looking unto which region, and remembering the term of our desire, let us pray that we all who are inheritors of a dying world may enter into another heritage in the world without end. (The Minutes of the previous Meeting and the other official business, if any, are taken at this point.)

THE SOLEMN CEREMONY OF CLOSING THE TEMPLE IN THE NEOPHYTE GRADE

(The Sentinel having left the Temple: Without any other admonition on the part of the Hierophant, the Kerux proceeds to the place of proclamation in the usual manner and raises his Lamp and Wand.)

Kerux.

Hekas, Hekas, este bebeloi. (He returns to his place with the Sun.)

Hierophant.

Fratres et Sorores, in the banishment of all earthly thoughts and in the recollection of the heart, assist me to close the Temple in the Grade of Neophyte. (All rise.)

Hierophant.

Let the keeper of the Holy Place on the hither side of the Portal ascertain that the Temple is guarded.

(The Kerux gives one knock on the hither side of the door. The Sentinel responds in the same manner on the outer side, using the hilt of his sword.)

Kerux.

Truly Honoured Hierophant, on the hither and further side it is firmly guarded. Hierophant.

Fratres et Sorores. lift up your hearts. I testify on my part that the world is still without and the prince thereof. Honourable Frater Hiereus, assure yourself that all present have seen the Golden Dawn, which is a light in the inmost heart.

Hiereus.

Fratres et Sorores, give me the outward signs which are attributed to the Frist Grade of the light within. (This being done.) Truly Honoured Hierophant, they have seen His star in the East and have come to adore Him. (The first Sign is here given by the Hiereus and the second by the Hierophant.)

Hierophant.

May the Angel of Great Counsel and the prince of Peace and the Light which enlighteneth every man who cometh into this world, give us grace and illumination in our day. Let the Temple be cleansed with water and consecrated by fire, to symbolise the purification that is within.

(The Stolistes follows the course of the sun, coming eastward from his place in the North. He makes a Cross with his cup and sprinkles thrice in the East. He performs the same ceremony in the other quarters and returns to the East, where he again faces the Hierophant, raises the Cup of Water, and says:)

Stolistes.

Waters of Understanding, Waters of the Great Sea: I have purified with water.

(He salutes the Throne and returns to his place by South and West. The Dadouchos follows, observing the same procedure with his Vessel of Incense. Having returned to the East, he says, raising the Thurible:)

Dadouchos.

The desire of the House of the Lord hath eaten me up: I have consecrated with fire. (He salutes the Throne and returns.)

Hierophant.

Let the mystical reverse procession take place in the pathway of the light.

(The Kerux passes from West to South. The Hegemon passes by North to West and South. The Hiereus passes direct to South. The Stolistes passes by West to South. The Dadouchos takes his place on the right of-the Stolistes. When the procession is thus formed, the Kerux leads from South to East and all salute in passing the Throne of the Hierophant. When it reaches the Throne of the Hiereus he returns thereto. As it passes the Throne of the Hierophant for the second time the Hegemon retires to his seat. The others circumambulate and salute for the third time, each dropping out as he reaches his own place.)

Hierophant.

The mystical reverse procession is accomplished in commemoration of the waning light of Nature and to signify the return of the soul to the material world carrying the symbols of the light. Let us adore the Holy and Eternal God, Who is the Father and the Term of our desires.

(The Hierophant descends from his Throne and faces the East thereat. All turn East, maintaining the Sign of the Grade until the adoration is over.)

Hierophant.

O Thou who hast called Thy servants in all generations and hast set apart Thine elect to Thy service, who hast filled our hearts with the aspiration towards Thy union, and all Thy channels of grace w'ith the means of its attainment: Give us this day and forever our daily desire for Thee, and grant, we beseech Thee, at the close of this solemn office, which we have performed to Thy Glory, that the fulness of Thine efficacious grace may be with us on our going forth into the world, even as on our coming into Thy sanctuary. (He puts down his Sceptre and faces West. All face as before.)

Hierophant.

Fratres et Sorores of all Grades in the Order, let us in the bodily communion of sacramental food in common remember that Divine Substance can also be partaken of by the soul. (He goes to the West of the Altar and faces East.)

Hierophant.

(Communicating in the bread and salt). Partake with me therefore, I pray you, of this bread ensavoured with salt, as a type of earth. Remember our part of earth and the salt of sanctity which ensavours it. (Raising the Mystical Rose) In breathe with me the fragrance of this Rose, a type of air. Let the images of our understanding and the thoughts of our mind rise as a sweet incense in the sight of God. (Raising the Cup) Drink with me now of this chalice, the consecrated sign of elemental water. (He drinks.) So may our emotions and desires be consecrated and transmuted in God. (Then placing his hands over the fire) And, lastly, let your hands be touched, like my own, by the warmth of this sacred fire, and remember the fire of aspiration which consecrates and changes the will till it is raised from the body of its corruption into living conformity with the Eternal Will.

(He raises the Lamp to his forehead, carries it round with him to the eastern side of the Altar, deposits it in its former place and serves the Imperator of the Temple, raising and handing him each of the elements in turn. This is repeated by each communicant in turn. The order of communion is as follows: The Hierophant, the Wardens of the Temple, the Officers of the Temple, excepting the Kerux, who stands at the South of the Altar with the flagon of wine; the Members of the Second Order; outer Members, according to Grade, including the Sentinel; lastly, the Neophyte of the day, who is assisted by the Kerux. When the Neophyte is at the East of the Altar, the Kerux comes to the West and communicates. When handed the Chalice he consumes the wine, and holding the vessel on high ht reverses it, and cries with a loud voice.)

Kerux.

It is finished. (He replaces the Chalice, raises the Lamp above his head, passes to the East of the Altar, faces East, bends his head before the Hierophant and says:)

Kerux.

In the worship of holy conformity and obedience to the Divine Will.

Hierophant.

(Knocks twice.) Tetelestai.

Hiereus.

(Knocks twice. All give the Signs of the Grade. The Kerux then turns to the West, and having deposited the Lamp, he returns to his place.)

Hierophant.

May that which we have received in the body represent in its symbolism to our souls the eternal communication of that life which is above Nature and comes down, O God, from Thee for the transmutation of our personality as into a great Quintessence, for the attainment of the summum bonum, the true Wisdom, the ineffable Beatitude and the term of our quest in Thee. (All officers below give two knocks.)

Hierophant.

KHABS

Hiereus.

AM

Hegemon.

PEKHT

Hiereus.

KONX

Hegemon.

OM

Hierophant.

PAX

Hegemon.

Light

Hierophant.

In

Hiereus.

Extension

(Here ends the Ritual of the Neophyte Grade. Glory be to God in the highest for the mercy he has graciously bestowed upon us.)

ADEPTUS MINOR

THE CELEBRANTS OF THE GRADE

The Chief Adept, holding by Investiture the August Grade of 7-4, being that of an Authorised Teacher. He is the living Symbol of the SEPHIRA CHESED and is the Spokesman of the Highest Grade in the Third Order. His title of nobility is Merciful Exempt Adept.

The Second Adept, holding by Institution the most Secret Grade of 6-5. He represents the SEPHIRA GEBURAH and is the Spokesman of the Mystery therein. His title of honour is Mighty Adeptus Major.

The Third Adept, who is preferably a Senior Member in the Grade of 5-6, he is a Living Symbol of the SEPHIRA TIPHERETH and is the Spokesman of Adepti Minores. His official title is Auxiliary Frater Adeptus.

In addition to the Celebrants there is a Servient Frater who acts as Keeper of the Threshold and Usher of the Grade. He is the last admitted therein, and the Postulant is more especially in his charge. His proper title is Honourable Frater Custos Liminis.

Unofficial Members are addressed as Honourable Fratres et Sorores.

THE ROBES AND JEWELS OF CELEBRANTS AND MEMBERS

1. **THE MERCIFUL EXEMPT ADEPT** wears a cassock and robe of violet. He is girt about the waist with a citrine girdle, with which colour the hood of his robe is lined. His biretta is of violet, having the square of CHESED on the front, emblazoned in Gold. The symbol of Salt is embroidered on the left side of his robe. His collar is of citrine silk, from which depends the Symbolum Magnum of the Rose-Cross, which he alone is entitled to wear - in virtue of his Office. He carries a Wand surmounted by the figure of the Risen Christ.

2. **THE MIGHTY ADEPTUS MAJOR** wears a cassock and robe of red. He is girt about the waist with a green girdle, with which colour the hood of his robe is lined. His biretta is of red, having the pentagram of GEBURAH on the front, emblazoned in gold. The symbol of Sulphur is embroidered on the left side of his robe. His collar is of green silk, from which depends a golden pentagram, having a red rose of five petals in the centre. He bears a Wand surmounted by a white double cube, inscribed on the four sides with the letters YOD, HE, VAU, HE, and on the summit a SHIN, all in pure gold.

3. **THE AUXILIARY FRATER ADEPTUS** wears a cassock and robe of orange colour. He is girt about the waist with a blue girdle, with which colour the hood of his robe is lined. His biretta is of orange, having the hexagram of TIPHERETH in the front, emblazoned in gold. The symbol of Mercury is

embroidered on the left side of his robe. His collar is of blue silk, from which depends the particular symbol of the Rose-Cross belonging to the Grade of Adeptus Minor. He bears a Wand surmounted by a crucifix.

4. THE HONOURABLE FRATER CUSTOS LIMINIS wears the ordinary clothing of the Adepti Minores, which is a white cassock with an orange scarf or girdle and a collar of blue silk, from which depends a gold Calvary cross, having a red rose of five petals at the meeting-point of the arms. He carries a Wand surmounted by a Dove of Peace, similar to that of an Ostiarius in the Worlds below TIPHERETH.

The colours of the robes worn by the Three Celebrants represent: Solar Orange - the Sun of Righteousness in Christ, the splendour of mind, when illuminated by a certain grade of consciousness in GOD; Red - the victory of the soul, which overcomes death in love; Violet royalty of the risen life and the will perfected in GOD.

The unofficial clothing worn by the Imperator of the Fellowship in the Grades of the Third Order is the ordinary white cassock and orange girdle, with the addition of a collar of white silk, from which depends a gold lamina having the Sacred Ogdoad emblazoned within its circle also in gold. The crown of the biretta is cruciform, with a rose of five petals at the meeting-point of the arms, but this rose is of the same colour as the biretta itself.

THE FELLOWSHIP OF THE ROSY CROSS

THE OPENING THE HOUSE AND SANCTUARY OF ADEPTS

The arrangement of the House and Sanctuary follows the unwritten precedents. The Veil is before the Sanctuary. The Brethren of the House have assembled, wearing their white robes, the scarf or girdle of the Grade to which they belong and the Rose-Cross of TIPHERETH. The Three Celebrants have assumed their vestments and insignia. They take up the Wands of the Rite and repair to their invariable stations, as Guardians of the Veil. The proper seat of the Servient Frater Adeptus is by the Door of the Holy House, as Keeper of the Threshold. All Brethren are seated in silence and recollection.

Adeptus Exemptus.
Adeptus Major.
Adeptus Minor.

(All three officers knock twice. All rise.)

Adeptus Exemptus.

Salvete, Fratres et Sorores Roseae et Aureae Crucis.

Adeptus Major.

Health and benediction in the Lord.

Auxiliary Frater Adeptus.

Vigilate, Fratres et Sorores.

Adeptus Exemptus.

Honourable and Adept Brethren, assist me to open the House of the Holy Spirit, in the heart and the inmost heart, in the manifest life of Nature and in spiritual consciousness as the Sun of the Life of life. (There is here the pause of a moment.)

Adeptus Exemptus.

Honourable Frater Custos Liminis, see that the Door of the House is sealed against all intrusion with the watchword: GOD is within. (This is done accordingly, and thereafter the Keeper of the Threshold bends in salute, with arms crossed upon his breast.)

Frater Custos Liminis.

Merciful Exempt Adept, the Seal is on the Threshold of the House, and I testify that the Sacred Watchword is held in everlasting remembrance.

Adeptus Exemptus.

Mighty Adeptus Major, by what Sign do we open the House of the Spirit and its Holy Sanctuary?

Adeptus Major.

By the Sign of Messias extended on the Sephirotic Cross. (He has given the Opening Sign.)

Adeptus Exemptus.

Auxiliary Frater Adeptus, what is its inward meaning?

Auxiliary Frater Adeptus.

It is the Sign of Dividing the Veil, signifying the dissolution of the veils of matter for the revelation of the Life of the Spirit and the opening of the Holy Sanctuary for the admission of the Postulant therein.

Adeptus Exemptus.

Might Adeptus Major, what is the deeper meaning?

Adeptus Major.

Merciful Exempt Adept, the Symbolic Veil is that of the Holy of Holies, and I testify that the Veil is Christ, manifest to eyes of flesh.

Adeptus Exemptus.

Auxiliary Frater Adeptus, by what Sign do we close the House of the Spirit and its Holy Sanctuary?

Auxiliary Frater Adeptus.

By the Sign of the Spirit received and abiding in the heart of the Brotherhood. (He has given the Closing Sign.)

Adeptus Exemptus.

Mighty Adeptus Major, what is its inward meaning?

Adeptus Major.

This also is twofold. It signifies the closing of the veils of matter behind the Postulant when he has entered and gone in. But according to the deeper sense, it testifies to the necessity and perpetuity of Christ manifest as the tabernacle of Christ mystical. The Veil of this Temple opens, but the Veil is not rent. It dissolves, and again is fixed. It is neither changed nor removed.

Adeptus Exemptus.

YOD

Adeptus Major.

HE.

Auxiliary Frater Adeptus.

SHIN.

Adeptus Major.

VAU

Auxiliary Frater Adeptus.

HF

Adeptus Exemptus.

YEHESHUAH.

Auxiliary Frater Adeptus.

Holy. Holy, Holy - the Veil of the Sanctum Sanctorum.

Adeptus Exemptus.

Mighty Adeptus Major, what is that Sacred Word which keeps the threshold of the House on the hither side of the Portal?

Adeptus Major.

It is the affirmation of absolute being - ALEPH, HE, YOD, HE - reflected from the Crown of the Tree. It signifies 1AM, and every Brother of the Rosy Cross who can utter it in the true sense, or in GOD who is All in all, has attained the term of our research.

Adeptus Exemptus.

Auxiliary Frater Adeptus, what is the Mystical Number of this Grade, derived from that Sacred Word?

Auxiliary Frater Adeptus.

In the sequence of Orders and of Rites, the number is twenty-one.

Adeptus Exemptus.

Mighty Adeptus Major, what is the House of the Holy Spirit?

Adeptus Major.

A ghostly palace, a Secret Church of the Elect, a School of Mystical Love.

Adeptus Exemptus.

Auxiliary Frater Adeptus, where is the Holy House symbolically situated, and on what is it built?

Auxiliary Frater Adeptus.

On the place of Holy Mysteries, the Invisible Mountain of the Wise. Its foundation is the corner-stone, and that Stone is Christ Mystical.

Adeptus Exemptus.

Mighty Adeptus Major, how was this Secret Mountain designated by the Elder Stewards of the Mysteries?

Adeptus Major.

As Mons Abiegnus, the Mount of Firs, but the reference is more especially to the Sacred Fir-Cone, the symbolical cone of the Ancient Mysteries. It is the place of reception, progression and final attainment. In its most withdrawn sense, the cone signifies the enfolded meanings and symbols of the written word, the manifold interpretation of things signified without. And the mountain is the place of ascent, the scale of perfection and the journey of the soul in GOD. On the summit thereof we look to greet in peace at the term of quest, when the desire of the eyes and the heart is at length attained by the soul.

Adeptus Exemptus.

Auxiliary Frater Adeptus, how is the Mountain designated in the tradition of the Rosy Cross?

Auxiliary Frater Adeptus.

It is the true Horeb and Calvary, whereon is the true Zion, a House of Living Bread.

Adeptus Exemptus.

Mighty Adeptus Major, what is the Sanctuary of the House?

Adeptus Major.

It is the most sacred place of the Mystery, revealed in the Third Order and attained by the soul in Christ.

Adeptus Exemptus.

What are the modes of this Mystery, as shewn forth in the Holy Grade of Adeptus Minor?

Adeptus Major.

Life, Death and Resurrection - the Life which follows Rebirth, Mystical and Divine Death, and the Glory of those who come forth from the great darkness, restored in union.

Adeptus Exemptus.

Auxiliary Frater Adeptus, how is the Sanctuary of the House delineated on the external side of our tradition?

Auxiliary Frater Adeptus.

It is the sepulchre of our beloved Founder, Christian Rosy Cross, which he made in the likeness of the universe, as a door that is entered at birth and a temple opening from earthly into spiritual life. It is said that he reposed at the centre, because this is the point of perfect rest at the seat of activity.

Adeptus Exemptus.

Mighty Adeptus Major, what is implied by the Name of our mystical Founder?

Adeptus Major.

The Rose of Christ manifested on the Cross of Human Personality.

Adeptus Exemptus.

Auxiliary Frater Adeptus, of what configuration is the Sanctuary?

Auxiliary Frater Adeptus.

It is a figure of seven equal sides, signifying the life of Nature and the grace which is behind Nature.

Adeptus Exemptus.

Mighty Adeptus Major, to what are these seven sides referred in their deepest sense by the law of correspondence between things above and below?

Adeptus Major.

To the seven operations of grace in the holy spirit of man; to the seven days of our creation in the likeness of GOD, Who is our end; to the lower SEPHIROTH, which are seven; to the planets, which are also seven; and to the seven maxims of the golden rule by which they are spiritualised in the Grades of the Rosy Cross. For the great mystical number prevails in the height above, even as in the depth beneath, and in the lesser as in the greater world.

Adeptus Exemptus.

Auxiliary Frater Adeptus, by what Gate do we enter the Holy Sanctuary?

Auxiliary Frater Adeptus.

EST OMNIS ANIMA VENUE. It is entered through the Gate of the mystical planet Venus, and a spouse is promised to the soul.

Adeptus Exemptus.

Mighty Adeptus Major, what is the Presence in the Sanctuary?

Adeptus Major.

It is the Eternal Love, in virtue of which GOD is immanent in Nature, the Lamb is slain from the foundation of the world and Christ abides within us.

Adeptus Exemptus.

Auxiliary Frater Adeptus, what is the office of the Postulant?

Auxiliary Frater Adeptus.

To pass within the Veil and by his own love and desire to awaken that which is within.

Adeptus Exemptus.

Mighty Adeptus Major, what is the outward sign which I wear here on my heart, and what is its inward meaning?

Adeptus Major.

It is the SACRAMENTUM MAGNUM of the Rose-Cross, typifying the Eternal Word which is hidden in Nature and the manifestation of the expounded Word. It is the harmony and development of all Rose-Cross symbolism, and it has many meanings belonging to the Greater Mysteries.

Adeptus Exemptus.

Auxiliary Frater Adeptus, what is the Wand of Office which you bear in your right hand?

Auxiliary Frater Adeptus.

The Sign of the Word made flesh and manifested in human life. It is for this reason that man is the key of all things and the Cross is the Sign of Glory The letters emblazoned thereon are I N R I, containing the Mystery of the Key. It is a great mystery of being.

Adeptus Exemptus.

Mighty Adeptus Major, what is the message implied by your Wand of Office?

Adeptus Major.

It is that which goes before and comes after, life in the hidden state, the unspoken Word and the silence of the Word withdrawn. The Cubic Altar of Incense unfolds as a Cross of Life. The Christ-Life is a sacrifice, as an incense offered on the Altar of GOD. But after the perfect oblation, the cross of life folds up its arms in sanctity, and life is withdrawn in GOD. The Cross returns into the Cube, and the Word made flesh is hidden in the rock-hewn sepulchre. The letters emblazoned hereon are YOD, HE, SHIN, VAU, HE, and I testify that there is no other Name given unto man whereby he shall be saved. It is therefore the Grand Word of the Grade.

Adeptus Exemptus.

The Sign of Resurrection is uplifted on my Wand of Office. I am He who testifies thereto from the height of the Third Order, and I bear faithful witness, in the Mystery of the Risen Word, Which overcomes death and is clothed with power and glory. The letters of this Mystery are LVX, and this is the Light of the World. (There is here the pause of a moment.)

Adeptus Exemptus.

Auxiliary Frater Adeptus, what are the words inscribed on the door of the Holy Sanctuary, and how is it guarded?

Auxiliary Frater Adeptus.

The words are: POST CENTUM VIGINTI ANNOS PATEBO. The Door is guarded by the Sacred Letter SHIN, which is that of the Christ-Spirit. It is written: His days shall be 120 years. And it is during this symbolical period that the spirit of Christ strives with the spirit of man. When man has completed his age, the number 120 is reduced to the mystical ogdoad by an operation of three and five, producing the Christ number and the number of rebirth. The triad rules in all things, and the grace of the pentad is declared in the spirit of man, that Christ may be all in all.

(The Honourable Frater Custos Liminis, as Usher of the Grade, gives a Battery of one knock. The Veil is parted by the Second and Third Celebrants. The Celebrant in Chief opens the Door of the Sanctuary to its full extent. He passes between the other Celebrants, who face inward with uplifted Wands. He enters the Sanctuary and proceeds with the Sun to the due East, where he turns and faces West. The Second Celebrant proceeds to the South of the Altar and the Third Celebrant to the North. They face inwards. The Three Celebrants are standing erect, with Wands uplifted in their right hands, and with their left hands placed upon the heart.)

Adeptus Exemptus.

ALEPH, HE.

Adeptus Major.

YOD, HE.

Auxiliary Frater Adeptus.

EHYEH.

Adeptus Exemptus.

It is written: Before Abraham was, I AM.

Adeptus Major.

Whom say ye that I the Son of Man am?

Auxiliary Frater Adeptus.

Christ the Power of GOD and the Wisdom of GOD.

Adeptus Exemptus.

I. N.

Adeptus Major.

R.

Auxiliary Frater Adeptus.

I.

Adeptus Exemptus.

YEHESHUA.

Adeptus Major.

NAZARAEUS.

Auxiliary Frater Adeptus.

Rex Judaeorum.

Adeptus Exemptus.

LVX. the Light of the World. (The Second and Third Celebrants proceed direct to the Door and stand on either side, facing inward. The Celebrant in Chief comes round with the Sun and passes through, saying:)

Adeptus Exemptus.

May we who are many be one body in Christ, one mind and a soul that is one in His union. (The Door being now ajar and the Celebrants standing in their places:)

Auxiliary Frater Adeptus.

Fratres et Sorores, in the Name of our Great Master and by the titles of the Christhood. I open this House of the Spirit (Knocks 2 times).

Adeptus Major.

(Gives 2 Knocks)

Adeptus Exemptus.

I have opened its Holy Sanctuary (Gives 2 Knocks. The Opening Sign of the Grade is given by all present. Here ends the Solemn Office of Opening the House and Sanctuary of the Adepts.)

THE FIRST POINT

(The Altar is removed from the Sanctuary and placed in the centre of the Temple. The Rose-Crucifix, Lamp, Cup, Poniard and Chain are left upon the Sacred Symbols to which they appertain. The Holy Cross of Obligation has been erected in the centre of the Sanctuary. The Door of the Sanctuary is shut and the Veil is drawn across it. The Celebrants take their seats and also the Honourable Frater Custos Liminis. The Candidate is alone on a prie-Dieu in the Vestibule, in full light, with a scroll in his hands containing versicles on crucified life. The Merciful Exempt Adept gives a Battery of one knock.)

Adeptus Exemptus.

Honourable Fratres et Sorores, blessed is he who cometh in the Name of the Lord, looking for the Light of His Glory. (The Keeper of the Threshold rises, with the Opening Sign of the Grade.)

Frater Custos Liminis.

I testify concerning our Frater Adveniat Regnum (vel nomen aliud), who stands on the threshold of TIPHERETH. He has been prepared in the outer ways and the Temple of inward grace has been made ready to receive him.

Adeptus Exemptus.

Honourable Frater Custos Liminis, go forth and admonish the Aspirant that now is the accepted time and that the Sun of Salvation shines in the House of Beauty. As Procurator of the Temple, prepare him on your part and bring him to the holy precincts. (The Keeper of the Threshold gives the Closing Sign of the Grade and leaves the Temple, securing the Door behind him.)

Adeptus Exemptus.

Auxiliary Frater Adeptus, guard the hither side of the Portal. By the power to me committed, and in accordance with faithful testimony, open to those who knock. (The Auxiliary Frater Adeptus rises with the Signs of the Grade and takes his place by the Door, where he remains standing.)

Adeptus Exemptus.

Fratres et Sorores, the Holy Mysteries do ever recall us to that one way which has been known and declared from of old.

Adeptus Major.

Many lights shew forth the Father of Lights, and the darkness testifies concerning Him.

Adeptus Exemptus.

We confess that we have aspired to the Crown, seeing that we are Children of the King, and we look for the Glory of GOD, praying that it shall be made manifest.

Adeptus Major.

From the natural life of man there extends a certain narrow path, even unto the Crown of all, and this path is called Magnanimity.

Adeptus Exemptus.

The middle place therein is adorned by the title of Beauty, and the Sun of Beauty shines in the zenith thereof.

Adeptus Major.

It is made known that the Light of the Soul is even as the Light of the Sun. Let us therefore look up, because salvation is near. (These versicles should be recited clearly and somewhat slowly, with certain pauses between, as they are designed to occupy the time during which the Candidate is prepared. While this takes place in the Temple, the Usher of the Grade has greeted the Postulant in the Vestibule, saying:)

Frater Custos Liminis.

Man enters into his true self as a priest into the Holy Place. (The Usher of the Grade prepares the Postulant, who should already have assumed his cassock, by clothing him with the robe and collar belonging to a Master of the Temple in the Grades below the Portal of the Third Order. While so doing:)

Frater Custos Liminis.

We desire to put off imperfection and to be clothed in GOD. (Thereafter the Usher of the Grade leads the Postulant to the Door of the Temple and sounds the Battery of the Grade with a certain force and distinction, thus: Knocks twice. The Auxiliary Frater Adeptus opens the Door, saying:)

Auxiliary Frater Adeptus.

Blessed and holy is he who shall enter into real knowledge. Wisdom and understanding meet to pour their influx upon him.

(The Usher of the Grade has entered leading the Postulant. The Door is secured behind them. The Auxiliary Frater Adeptus returns to his seat. The Usher of the Grade conducts the Postulant to an open space on the Eastern side of the Altar, and faces him toward the East.)

Frater Custos Liminis.

Merciful Exempt Adept, I present to you our Beloved Frater Adveniat Regnum (vel nomen aliud), who places his perfect trust in GOD Who is our end, desiring the life of TIPHERETH and the Grace of Christ Who is within. He has traversed the Paths and Grades of the inferior Orders. He has been purified and consecrated therein, even in the four parts of his natural personality. He has turned his will to GOD, as one who in the darkness of night-time has set his face toward Jerusalem. He has seen the darkness kindle beyond the eternal hill, the light breaking in the East. The remembrance of that light is within him. It has shewn him the straight and narrow way by which the spirit of the Aspirant ascends to TIPHERETH. At the Portal thereof, at the point where the Veil divides, he has passed through the Second Birth in the symbolism of our Holy Fellowship. He has been told that the Door shall open; it has opened already in his heart. He has offered up his whole nature on the Supernal Altar of Burnt Offerings, in the presence of the Divine Will. It has been said that by such an oblation those who have been called are chosen for the knowledge of the Life of life. It has been said also that he shall enter and go in. Born in the spiritual Bethlehem, presented in the Temple under the aegis of the old Law in the Second Point of the Portal, give unto him the desire of his heart on the quest of the Divine within him, in the place of purified life, the life which follows rebirth. In virtue of my faithful testimony he prays to be received among you. (The Usher of the Grade now returns to his seat.)

Adeptus Exemptus.

Blessed are those who in the Paths and SEPHIROTH of the Fellowship of the Rosy Cross have come to be reborn in heart and have dedicated all life therein. Frater Adveniat Regnum (vel nomen aliud), we acknowledge your titles and the claims embodied by these. The covenants of our authorised Messenger, speaking on the threshold of TIPHERETH, are also faithful and true, Amen, for ever and evermore. But you who have been initiated and advanced from Grade to Grade amidst the lights and shadows of our more external sodalities have yet another lesson to learn. It is the glory of the Cross of Christ. The Cubical Altar on which you were pledged in the First Grade of our Fellowship is that of your own personality, and this cube must open as a Cross to Divine Life.

Adeptus Major.

He who has been made pure and has been consecrated; he who in will and understanding has turned to GOD as to his end; he who has offered up his entire nature, that it may be brought into conformity with Divine purpose in the universe, and henceforth and forever may be part of the Will of GOD, is thereby on the threshold of TIPHERETH but the regenerated life of that Grade, wherein you have asked to enter, is a life of crucifixion in respect of all that is below.

Auxiliary Frater Adeptus.

The Cross is the Sign of Sacrifice and therefore also of victory, the realisation of self in sanctity. That suffering of which it is a symbol according to the Law of Nature is replaced or transmuted by the glory of which it is an image according to the Law of Grace. Its inward meaning contains the secret of liberation.

Adeptus Exemptus.

May yours be the Mystic Rose and yours the Golden Cross. May this our symbolical convention bring you to the life of light, even the Light of the Cross and the Life in the Rose thereon. (The Usher of the Grade rises in his place, passes to the circular Altar, removes the Silver Chain and stands by the side of the Postulant.)

Auxiliary Frater Adeptus.

Take therefore this Chain, O Frater Adveniat Regnum (vel nomen aliud). Raise it in your right hand, saying: I accept the bonds of service in the Law of Light. (The Usher of the Grade has laid the Chain in the hand of the Postulant, who repeats the formula, suiting the action to the words. The Usher replaces the Chain and again returns to his seat.)

Auxiliary Frater Adeptus.

When the Chain is placed upon the Altar it reposes on the Bull of earth, and this is in correspondence with the material part of your personality, which has been purified by the rites of our Order. Once it was lead, my Brother, and once a burden of grief. Now it has suffered conversion, and the chain is therefore of silver, a bond of spiritual obedience, of holy devotion and ministry imposed by love. The yoke is therefore light. You have raised it in testimony to the great law of attainment ruling in the body of the Adept. (There is here the pause of a moment.)

Adeptus Exemptus.

Mighty Adeptus Major, what is the symbolical age of our beloved Postulant?

Adeptus Major.

Merciful Exempt Adept, his days are 120 years.

Adeptus Exemptus.

It is written: My Spirit shall not always strive with man, seeing that he also is flesh: yet his days shall be 120 years. Auxiliary Frater Adeptus, to what does this age refer which we ascribed symbolically to the Postulant?

Auxiliary Frater Adeptus.

It is the period of his life in Nature before GOD is declared in the heart. It ends in stillness of heart, when that which has been purified and consecrated enters into rebirth in GOD.

Adeptus Exemptus.

Frater Adveniat Regnum (vel nomen aliud), may you know the peace of that stillness and receive the gift of understanding in the holy light. This is the House of the Spirit, built upon the Secret Mountain, which - seeing that all things are within - is said mystically to be situated at the centre of the earth. Here also is the Sanctuary of the Adepts, where the pledges of your perfect dedication must be uttered upon the Cross of our Mystery. Are you willing in this manner to ratify your election by the Order? (The Usher of the Grade has come up to the Altar and taking the Altar Lamp places it in the hands of the Postulant. The Postulant having signified assent in his own language:)

Adeptus Exemptus.

Raise therefore that Lamp to your forehead, holding it in your two hands, and say after me: In the Name of GOD Who is my help, and looking on the Cross of Life for the Light of the Cross.

(This is done accordingly, and the Postulant remains holding the Lamp upraised. The Second and Third Celebrants rise in their places and silently remove the Veil from the Door of the Sanctuary. The Merciful Exempt Adept gives a Battery of one knock and rises with all present. The Merciful Exempt Adept sets open the Door of the Sanctuary to its full extent. The Rose-Light in the ceiling is veiled with red crepe, and the Cross in the centre of the Sanctuary looms dimly.)

Adeptus Exemptus.

The glorious Sun of TIPHERETH shall shine on the summit of Calvary. (The Merciful Exempt Adept stands at the Threshold of the Sanctuary, facing West. The Second and Third Celebrants kneel on either side of him, looking toward the East. The unofficial Brethren kneel down, the Usher of the Grade directing the Postulant. The Merciful Exempt Adept extends his arms in the form of a Cross.)

Adeptus Exemptus.

Fratres et Sorores, let us offer up our solemn worship to the Lord of Goodness, Who has sent the Secret Light into the world and desires only that it shall be made manifest. (The Merciful Exempt Adept folds his arms upon his breast, making thus the Second Sign of the Grade, and turns Eastward, but remains standing.)

THE PRAYER OF THE CELEBRANT IN CHIEF

All truth. Most High Father, comes down from Thee; the greater blessings and graces dost Thou dispense continually. Thou hast in particular emblazoned the symbolical characters of Nature and hast established that Divine School which imparts their true interpretation. Take us by its leading behind all forms of expression, all pageants of the manifested world, into the state out of place and time, into the still, unspoken peace and the loving silence, where the meaning of all is Thou. In Thee is our help alone; in Thee are our stay and strength through the days of our questing. All has its source in Thee, and to the consolation of Thy great deeps must all in fine return. With the whole aspiration of our hearts, we look to be reintegrated in Thy love. Receive us, we beseech Thee; aid us still in our necessity; and do Thou, the Throne of Whose Majesty is exalted in heavens inaccessible, so purify and transmute Thy children of the Second Birth, the poor Brothers of this Thy lowly Sodality, that Thy place may be also in our hearts. Come to us in the Life of the Cross, come to us in the Death of the Mystic, bring us to the Resurrection which is in Thee. And through all the Grades of the Christhood, give unto us the realisation of the union, that we may attain that self which is in Thee. So shall we come into our own, in the kingdom which is ours and Thine; and those who have been separate in manifestation shall know themselves one spirit in Thee, Who art All in all.

(Those who are on their knees rise up. The Second and Third Celebrants are seated, with the unofficial Brethren. The Usher of the Grade brings the Rose-Crucifix from the Altar and presents it to the Celebrant in Chief. The Usher of the Grade goes to the Western side of the Altar, where he faces East. The Postulant has his back to the Altar on the Eastern side. The Merciful Exempt Adept elevates the Rose-Crucifix before the assembled Fratres et Sorores, as he approaches the Postulant, saying:)

Adeptus Exemptus.

IN HOC SIGNO VINCES. (When he reaches the Postulant, the Merciful Exempt Adept raises the Rose-Crucifix over the bowed head of the Postulant, and says:)

Adeptus Exemptus.

Frater Adveniat Regnum (vel nomen aliud), give me the First Sign which you received on the Threshold of TIPHERETH in the Portal of the Third Order. (There is no prompting, as the Postulant has been tested previously. He gives and maintains thereafter the Sign of the Opening of the Veil. The Merciful Exempt Adept dips the Dagger in the Wine and cross-marks the Postulant on his forehead.)

Adeptus Exemptus.

There are Three that bear record in Heaven, the Father, the Word and the Holy Ghost. These Three are One. (He dips the Dagger in the Wine and cross-marks the feet of the Postulant.)

Adeptus Exemptus.

There are three that bear witness on earth, the spirit, and the water, and the blood: and these three agree in one. (He dips the Dagger in the Wine and cross-marks the Postulant in the palm of the right hand.)

Adeptus Exemptus.

Except a man be born again of water and the Holy Spirit, he cannot enter into the Kingdom of GOD. (He dips the Dagger in the Wine and cross-marks the Postulant in the palm of the left hand.)

Adeptus Exemptus.

If we be crucified with Christ, we shall also reign with Him. (There is here the pause of a moment.)

Adeptus Exemptus.

Frater Adveniat Regnum (vel nomen aliud), give me the Closing Sign which you received on the Threshold of TIPHERETH in the Portal of the Third Order. (The Postulant gives and maintains the Sign of the Closing of the Veil. The Merciful Exempt Adept dips the Dagger in the Wine and cross-marks the Postulant on his breast, above his folded arms.)

Adeptus Exemptus.

The Lord abide within Thee, an Everlasting Presence.

(The Postulant maintains the Sign. The Usher of the Grade receives the Dagger and replaces it with the Cup on the Altar. He then returns to his seat and stands thereat. The Second and Third Celebrants advance, and take up a position on either side of the Postulant, facing East. The Merciful Exempt Adept turns Eastward and draws slowly toward the Sanctuary, with Wand uplifted. The Guides follow with the Postulant, keeping at some distance from the Celebrant in Chief. The Merciful Exempt Adept enters the Sanctuary. He pauses at a due distance within and turns Westward. The Guides and the Postulant reach the Threshold of the Sanctuary and pause. The Guides face inward, with Wands uplifted. The Merciful Exempt Adept draws the Postulant over the Threshold, saying:)

Adeptus Exemptus.

The counsel of peace is between us. Come in peace.

(He has brought the Postulant with these w ords to the foot of the Cross. He withdraws behind the Cross and turns Westward, while the Second and Third Celebrants advance and bind the Postulant to the Cross. Thereafter they go back to their positions on either side of the threshold, facing inward. The Usher of the Grade gives a battery of one knock and the unofficial Brethren rise and remain standing. The Merciful Exempt Adept comes forward, confronting the Postulant. He raises his face and hands.)

Adeptus Exemptus.

Spirit of the Height, look down; Guardian of our Holy Sodality; Virgin Soul of the Christhood; Guide of the elect in GOD. By the Glorious Name of SHEKINAH, abiding Presence in the Sanctuary, hear Thou the solemn pledge. Receive the perfect oblation of this Brother of the Rosy Cross. (Then in tones that are audible to the Postulant only:)

Adeptus Exemptus.

Repeat your Sacramental Name and say after me: (The Merciful Exempt Adept imposes in a clear voice.)

THE PLEDGE OF THE GRADE

I, Frater Adveniat Regnum (vel nomen aliud), an aspirant after the Life of the Spirit, who have been prepared, purified and consecrated by the Light of the Rosy Cross, and thereafter brought in the Portal of the Third Order to a Second Birth in symbolism, do offer up my life in sanctity on the Mystical Cross of the Christhood, for the Divine End declared in the heart and the soul. I desire consciousness in the Spirit, knowledge of Eternal Things and the realisation of GOD abiding in that Sanctuary which is within. I testify that from this day forward, so far as in me lies, I will look unto the Supreme Crown and the Supernal Unity in KETHER:

That I will ever seek my perfection through the Mystery of Wisdom in CHOKMAH, which is Supernal Wisdom, where Severity is transformed into Mercy, and will build my House therein as a Temple of the Holy Spirit: That I aspire to the Spirit of Understanding, Spirit of Counsel and Strength, Spirit of Knowledge and Truth, and the consolation of its gifts and fruits in the sea of BINAH; which is Supernal Understanding, wherein is the Communion of the Elect: That I look for the Resurrection of the Adept, the body of Redemption, the mystical life of union and the Word declared in CHESED:

That when my call comes I will make ready to enter the Sabbath, desiring the Soul's Bridal, the Word received in the stillness, the sacred release of GEBURAH. in the Halls of Compassion and Judgment, where death is by the mouth of the Lord and not by the serpent. I promise solemnly that, looking toward the day when I shall enter into the rewards of the spirit, I will, to the best of my ability, and w ith a full sense of dedication, lead the life of adoption in TIPHERETH, desiring the beauty of the life and the abiding Presence of the Spirit. I will follow the rule of TIPHERETH, wherein is the Ark of the Covenant, as one who has been born again of Water and of the Holy Spirit. I will abide in conformity of will, the consecration of desire, dedication of mind and the purification of my bodily part, preparing the garments of the soul, as one who has been betrothed in GOD and is seeking the Word of Union. I testify that, as here and now in symbolism, I will accept the Cross in Christ, that I may descend afterwards with Him into the Valley of Silence and may arise in the Glory of His Union. The Veil of the Sanctuary has been parted in my respect. I know that the Veil is sacred. I will keep its secrets, which are Mysteries of Holy Knowledge, as I have kept and will maintain for ever the first and sacred trust committed to my charge in the Lower Grades of the Fellowship. I will observe the Laws of the Sanctuary in faith, honour and obedience. I renew hereby and hereon the pledges of fraternity and fellowship, with the other obligations by w hich I have been bound previously. The Law is a Law of Solidarity. I will preserve, with my peers and co-heirs of the Third Order, a perfect union in the Mystery of Faith. My desire is the Divine Union, and seeing that it rests within my own acts and will whether the Tree of Knowledge shall in me be the Tree of Life, I testify that neither death nor life shall separate me henceforth from the love and the service of GOD.

This is my pledge in purity, by which I look to be uplifted in my higher part above the sphere of those elements wherein I once abode; and I will seek to draw after me the lower SEPHIROTH of my nature into the realisation of the Eternal Presence. After CHESED, GEBURAH and TIPHERETH, draw me, my Lord and my GOD, in my imperishable soul, within the peace of Thy Centre, that as I came forth at Thy bidding into the manifest world, so I may return at Thy will into the world unmanifest. May the light of the Indwelling Glory abide with me in the kingdom of this world, that I may belong to the world no more but to that which comes down from Thee with the life of grace into the heart and bears up those who receive it into the Land of the Living, even the Kingdom of Heaven, world without end.

(The Merciful Exempt Adept moves aside from the Cross and turns Westward. He lifts up his arms to their fullest height. The unofficial Brethren are seated.)

Adeptus Exemptus.

Fratres et Sorores, behold the Son of the Cross, our most faithful and beloved Brother, Brother of the Rosy Cross, Frater Adveniat Regnum (vel nomen aliud), suspended on the Mystical Tree. He represents thereon the Divine Son of the Secret Tradition, First- Begotten of the Mighty Ones, Whose head rests upon DAATH. Whose arms stretch to CHESED and GEBURAH, who has TIPHERETH over the region of the heart, and whose feet stand on MALKUTH. As the Divine Son came into manifestation for a work of election through the universe, so is our Brother in GOD manifested this day out of material life, within the Sanctuary of our Holy Assembly. The double cube of his natural personality has become the Cross. May it be unto him the Tree of Life for the healing of all his principles. May he realise in its highest sense that the life of TIPH ERETH is truly the life of the Cross. May he find at the end thereof after what manner the Cross of this life folds up and becomes that White Stone, in the hidden centre of which is written a New Name, which no man knoweth, save he that receiveth it. (There follows a short space of perfect silence. The Second Celebrant lifts up his arms.)

Adeptus Major.

I testify that the end is GOD and that the end is like the beginning. (The Third Celebrant lifts up his arms.)

Auxiliary Frater Adeptus.

I testify that the Sun of Justice, shining above the Cross, is also the Sun of Love and that Love is the Life of TIPHERETH. (The Merciful Exempt Adept points solemnly to the Postulant).

Adeptus Exemptus.

HIC PENDET FRATER FIDELISSIMUS, FRATER ROSEAE CRUCIS. (The Second and Third Celebrants close the Door of the Sanctuary and draw the Veil before it. The Merciful Exempt Adept unbinds the Postulant and gives him his own Wand of Office.)

Adeptus Exemptus.

Frater Adveniant Regnum (vel nomen aliud), go in peace and sin no more. Remember now and henceforward that you have become the Cross. May you be also the Rose thereon.

(He points the way to the Postulant, who opens the Door. The Second and Third Celebrants raise the Veil to permit of his passing through and no more. The Usher of the Grade comes forward and leads the Postulant from the Temple. Here ends the First Point.)

THE SECOND POINT

(The Cross of Obligation is removed, and the Bier is placed in the Sanctuary. The Celebrant in Chief takes his place thereon, in an attitude of repose. The Red Veil of GEBURAH is laid over him, covering him from head to foot, so that his outlines are concealed. The Altar is restored to the Sanctuary. The light therein is extinguished, except for the obscure red Lamp, which burns on the Altar. The Door of the Sanctuary is closed, and the Veil is drawn. The lights are subdued in the Temple. The Second and Third Celebrants are seated on either side of the Sanctuary Door. The Officers and Brethren remain in complete silence.

Meanwhile the Usher of the Grade has conducted the Postulant to the Vestibule, where his clothing and insignia, as a Master of the Lower Temple, are removed. He is vested in white, with the Orange Girdle and Rose-Cross appropriate to an Adeptus Minor. While this is being done:)

Frater Custos Liminis.

Be thou clothed with the garment of regeneration and with the life renewed in GOD. May GOD Himself engird thee with the righteousness of saints. And remember on your part, O Brother of the Rosy Cross, that the life of TIPHERETH prepares the bridal garments which clothe the soul against the day of her mystical marriage.

(The Postulant is instructed in the Battery of the Grade and knocks twice and when the silence within is broken by the Battery without, the Third Celebrant goes to the Door of the Temple and admits those who have knocked. The Door is secured behind them by the Usher of the Grade, who takes the Wand of the Celebrant in Chief which the Postulant has carried. Then, as they stand on the hither side of the Door:)

Third Celebrant.

Frater Adveniat Regnum (vel nomen aliud), receive at my hands the Sacred Grip of this Grade.

(It is given by placing the left hand on the breast, with all fingers extended, mutually raising the right hand, also with extended fingers, interlacing the fingers mutually, at first still extended and then clasped upon the hand, at the same time exchanging the salutation as follows: AVE, FRATER (vel SOROR), which is answered by: ROSEAE ET AUREAE CRUCIS. The words PAX CHRISTI TECUM arc then repeated simultaneously. The Third Celebrant returns to his place. The Usher of the Grade leads the Postulant to a seat in front of the unofficial Members and facing the Door of the Sanctuary. The Auxiliary Frater Adeptus then begins to recite.)

THE LEGEND OF THE ROSY CROSS.

Auxiliary Frater Adeptus.

Well-Beloved Postulant and Brother, the particular Mysteries exhibited and the knowledge communicated in symbolism by the Order of the Rosy Cross have been shadowed forth under various veils from time immemorial. The sanctuaries of a hidden tradition have been established among many nations, and as there was never a period when the ordinances of initiation were not in the world, so there was never a time and there was never a place when the Greater Mysteries had any object of research but that one and inevitable object which alone concerns every man who has entered into the consciousness of election. Under whatever names, and with whatsoever varieties of pageant and established form, all true Rites and Mysteries, in respect of their intention, have been ever but one Rite expounding one Mystery, which - to summarise it in all brevity - has been the re-integration of man in GOD. There is every multiplicity of official dogma; there is every emblazonment of symbolism; but, from neophyte to epopt, every postulant who has attained the knowledge of his source knows also that his perfect end is a conscious return therein.

The old Rites are dead, while the records which remain of most are insufficient memorials and often mere vestiges or rumours. But the truths embodied by initiation are alive for evermore. By a dispensation given from above, as from a Great and Holy Assembly, abiding in a Sanctuary not made with hands, hidden within the Veil, the Hierarchic Mystery of Christ was declared in space and time, by the manifestation of our Lord and Saviour. He is to us in an especial manner the Great Exemplar of initiation - its way, its truth and its life. He exhibited the path and term, no longer in Rites and Symbols, but in the form of life, and has made partakers thereof, heirs and co-heirs with Him, all those who have learned the great secret that His story is also theirs and must be re-enacted in every soul. The Second Birth, my Brother, through which you have passed in symbolism, corresponds to the nativity in Bethlehem. The life of the Cross in TIPHERETH, under the Rule of TIPHERETH, shall be unto you as the Christ-Life. Thereafter cometh a Mystery of Death and Resurrection in GOD, which is hidden in the Grades beyond. When the things which now and hereafter you suffer and share in symbolism have become native inwardly and outwardly in your entire being, you also will have entered into Christhood, or that which is called figuratively the state of heirship and brotherhood in the Lord. The most secret science of the soul is here formulated and the life of initiation through all its stages, even to the goal of all, according to the Doctrine and Practice of the Rosy Cross. You will observe that it differs generically from the official and conventional secrecy of the Lesser Mysteries, for it does not consist in verbal and occult formula. In its presentation it is the story at large of the chief annals of sanctity; but in its inward practice and understanding it is a mystery of experience. It is really secret because it can be announced everywhere but can be understood and realised only in the hearts of those who have entered into the experience within.

In addition to such open memorials as are records of saints and adepts in all churches and schools of Christendom, there is the Secret Tradition of Christian Times enshrined in cryptic literatures, of which Alchemy on its spiritual side offers a notable instance. The early history of the Rosy Cross is connected more especially with this aspect of the great subject, though it has known many dedications and has suffered many changes in its passage through the centuries and various countries of Europe. It reaches here and now its final evolution in the Sacred Rites of our Fellowship. Antiquity, my Brother, is not regarded among us as essentially a test of value, and we confess that we have separated ourselves from much that was of false-seeming and disordered enthusiasm while continuing therefore to preserve the holy. It was a pilgrimage of the soul in GOD. a return journey toward the centre. He tarried at other houses of assembly, where it might be said that he came unto his own and that his own received him. As he had been taught according to the letter within the convent gate, so did he learn otherwhere according to the grace of the inward meaning. That which opened at his knocking was of things within and without; of GOD, man and the universe; Macrocosm and Minutum Mundum; the travels and metamorphoses of the soul; and the soul's rest in the union. Hereof is his ascent toward KETHER, through the Paths and Worlds of the Tree.

He returned at length to the world, as one who comes back from CHESED for the healing of nations. But it was to be despised and rejected of men, more especially by the wise in their wisdom. It was only in his own cloister that he found a few of the elect, with whom he abode in a House of the Holy Spirit. Such was the beginning of our Fraternity of the Rosy Cross, incorporating at first four persons only, being the number of our natural humanity, but afterwards increased to eight, the number of the Christhood. It was agreed that the Brotherhood as such should remain secret one hundred and twenty years, or for that symbolical period which answers to the earthly age of the Postulant - when he stands on the threshold of TIPHERETH, awaiting the Second Birth, the new age and the life of regeneration therein. Subsequently some of the Brethren were scattered through various countries on works of ministry. They appointed successors in accordance with the Laws of the Order, and there arose in this manner that Second Circle of Initiates which is mentioned in the original memorials. The years had elapsed, and the Loving Frater C R C had passed from the House of the Holy Spirit in TIPHERETH to the Secret Church in DAATH. The Members of the First Circle had been dissolved also in their day. Those who came after them knew little of the sodality in its beginning, and - as it is hinted in the records - had not been admitted to all things. They were in fact Philosophical Brethren, awaiting in the SEPHIRA NETZACH for the end of the allotted period, namely, 120 years.

Adeptus Major.

It came, in our reading of the legend. Having passed through the mystical experience of that Second Birth which is illustrated in symbolism by the Portal of the Third Order, a solemn assembly of adepts was convened in the House of the Holy Spirit, the Children of the Portal were admitted and the Veil was removed from the Sanctuary. (The Second and Third Celebrants rise in their places and draw the Veil. Afterwards they resume their seats.)

Adeptus Major.

In this manner there was uncovered the Door of entrance, bearing the inscription POST CENTUM VIGINTI ANNOS PATEBO, written about the sacred letter SHIN, encompassed by the four Living Creatures and crowned by the Wheel of the Spirit. It represented then as now the transmutation of human personality by the Christhood immanent within and overshadowed by the cosmic Christ. (The Second Celebrant has pointed to the Door of the Sanctuary and the emblazonments thereon. He now rises in his place, as does also the Third Celebrant.)

Adeptus Major.

Frater Adveniat Regnum (vel nomen aliud), I testify that the Door was opened by the Mighty Adeptus Major, Non Nobis, Domine, and that those who had been called and chosen beheld that mystery within, over which the records of the past have laid a heavy drapery of images. That which they saw and heard concerned an epoch to come in their own life of adeptship. After the same manner you also shall hear and see, if yours be the gifts of the spirit, as I now open this Door.

(The Honourable Frater Custos Liminis, at these concluding words, shuts off all lights in the Temple, and the Door of the Sanctuary is opened. The dim Red Lamp on the Altar alone enlightens the Sanctuary. The Celebrant is Chief, beneath the great Red Veil, betrays no certain outline. The wavering shadows are everywhere.)

Adeptus Major.

Having come so far in our journey, by GOD's most Holy Grace, let us lift up our hands on the threshold of His glorious Sanctuary.

Auxiliary Frater Adeptus.

IN ATRIIS TUIS, O HIERUSALEM, FLECTAMUS GENUA. (The Celebrants and all present kneel down.)

The Second Celebrant (recites:)

THE PRAYER OF THE PRECINCTS

We worship Thee in the hiddenness of Thy presence, in the darkness and light of worlds, in the silent temple of the soul. Let Thy Word speak in the hiddenness, and Thy glory shall be declared therein. In the heart's stillness we shall hear Thee; we shall behold Thee with inward eyes; the light of Thy sanctuary within shall transform the light without; the light without shall be even as the light within - Thou only in life and time; in death and resurrection Thou; and in the world to come - which is the world of ascension - we shall attain our end in Thee, O End and Crown of all. Thou hast called and chosen this Postulant, who kneels here within the precincts of Thy Greater Mysteries. Shew unto him the Secrets of Thy Sanctuary, the life and death which are in Thee. Shew unto him the Glory which is to come. Raise up this son of man to the Divine Sonship in Thee, an heir and co-heir in Christhood, O Father of Worlds. (The Celebrants rise. The unofficial Brethren resume their seats. The Postulant remains on his knees.)

Adeptus Major.

He who would be Master in Israel must watch more than one hour; but hereof is the Soul's Vigil.

Auxiliary Frater Adeptus.

The day for deeds and the night for contemplation; but out of this succession cometh the Great Quest and the end attained therein.

Adeptus Major.

It is written that He giveth His beloved sleep, and herein is a Mystery of GOD.

Auxiliary Frater Adeptus.

The sleep of thought is attained in a great suspension; and the sleep of Mystical Death is the shadow of the Eternal Sabbath.

(The Postulant is assisted to rise by the two Celebrants. He is drawn across the threshold and is left standing at the Western side of the Altar. The Second and Third Celebrants proceed direct, and respectively to the Southern and Northern sides. The Postulant can now discern in the obscurity the veiled and silent form of the Chief Celebrant.)

Adeptus Major.

Behold a Sanctuary of seven sides and seven angles, every side of five feet broad and the height of eight feet. No earthly sun can shine herein, but the glimmering ray of an Altar Lamp serves to make darkness visible. That shrouded figurative gleam seems only to express the gloom which rests on the prospect before you. In the middle part of the crypt there stands this circular Altar, covered with a plate of gold and variously graven and inscribed. About the first circle or margin is written the central maxim in the true life of adeptship: YEHESHUA MIHI OMNIA. The second circle contains in cipher the characteristic motto of the Fellowship, or A G R C - AD GLORIAM ROSEAE CRUCIS. The inscription within the third circle is HOC ARCANISSIMAE CLAUSTRUM DEITATIS MIHI SEPULCHRUM FECI.

The interior space contains a great Cosmic Cross, having four circles at the extremities, enclosing the traditional emblems of the Four Living Creatures and these four inscriptions, proceeding with the Sun from the South:

1. **NEQUAQUAM VACUUM.**
2. **LEGIS JUGUM.**
3. **LIBERTAS EVANGELII.**
4. **DEI GLORIA INTACTA.**

(Should it seem desirable for the instruction of the Postulate to elucidate the inscriptions, they may be translated literally thus: 1. Jesus is all things unto me; 2. To the Glory of the Rosy Cross; 3. I have made this Inner Sanctuary of the Most hidden GOD a sepulchre for myself; 4. No void; 5. The Yoke of the Law; 6. The freedom of the Gospel; 7. The Glory of God inviolate.)

They are in correspondence with the Divine Names YOD, HE, VAU, HE, and ALEPH, HE, YOD, HE, read crosswise from the South and East respectively; with the Divine Name ADNI, understood as a title of SHEKINAH and read from the East against the Sun; and with the Secret Word AGLA, beginning at the South and following the course of the Sun. At the meeting point of the arms in the middle of the Cosmic Cross - is placed the Wheel or Circle of the Spirit, having eight radii, proceeding from the sacred letter SHIN. The doctrine of the Rosy Cross in the Grade of Adeptus Minor is here formulated and symbolised, with intimations of mysteries which lie beyond the Grade. It is a doctrine based upon experience, the experience of Christ realised in the four parts of our personality, in virtue of which - at the term of adept sanctity - our human elements, like the four mystical creatures, encompass the Great White Throne of GOD, Who is within.

Frater Adveniat Regnum (vel nomen aliud), the emblems of your consecrated personality are beside their correspondences on the Altar. Symbolum and symbolum loquitur, as heart unto heart in the silence. Take up the silver chain, which represents your material part transformed in the life of rebirth. Raise it in your right hand, as one who affirms GOD in all that manifests his being. Remember now and henceforward that there is a tincturing spirit within which transmutes our earth of life. Lay down the mystic chain, as one who has found that the silver cord is loosed in all that concerns bondage. Take up the dagger of gold and raise it in your right hand. So may Eternal Mind lift up your mind of manhood. Remember the Sword of the Spirit and that purified mind has talents of gold within, Gifts of the Spirit sent down. Be thou a buyer, my Brother, of gold tried in the furnace, and when thou art tried therein come forth like gold refined. Be transformed therefore by renewing of the mind, and thou shalt not see corruption. Replace the golden dagger and take up the cup of benedictions, for transmuted desire is exalted above all blessing. Partake of the cup in charity, and receive the wine of the kingdom. Set it again upon the Altar and lift up the lamp on high. Be thou light in the place of light, and having been born of man, according to the will of flesh, but afterwards reborn of GOD, according to His holy will, work out thine end therein. Stand steadfast in the purpose of the Lord. Restore the lamp to its Altar, and in the midst of speaking symbols, remember the things signified. So shall the types dissolve, but thou shalt be their life; for that which the Wheel of the Spirit shews forth, at the centre of the Altar-circle, shall be Life of life within thee. And death shall be no more. (The Celebrants turn to the East.)

Adeptus Major.

PATER AETERNUS DEUS, DONA NOBIS VITAM.

Auxiliary Frater Adeptus.

VITEM AETERNAM TUAM DONA NOBIS, DOMINE.

Adeptus Major.

FILI REDEMPTOR MUNDI DEUS, DONA NOBIS VERBUM.

Auxiliary Frater Adeptus.

ET VERBUM CARO FACTUM ERIT.

Adeptus Major.

SPIR1TUS SANCTE DEUS, LUMEN DONA NOBIS.

Auxiliary Frater Adeptus.

LUMEN VERITATIS TUAE, ET IN TE RESURGAMUS NOS.
(After these versicles there is a hush of complete silence. The Celebrant in Chief speaks from within the veil.)

Adeptus Exemptus.

In six days of his life is material man created, and thereafter cometh a Jubilee. The natural man is complete in his own degree, but above this there is the manhood of the Sacred Temple. From the life of man in Nature, from the death which ensues thereon and opens the further prospects, we who have been called of the spirit have sought a path of elevation toward a more perfect mode. It is in losing that which the natural man holds most desirable that the spiritual man, after six days, shall find himself. We have looked for life in GOD and have been crucified in Him to all which here below interposes between Life Divine and the free way of the Quest. We have stripped off the old vestures, praying to be clothed in GOD. We have found that the quest is love and that is also the end. In paths of contemplation, and these are paths of love; in the rule of sacrifice, which is love made holy; we have found that life is love. Opened to Divine Love on the threshold of the life of TIPHERETH, we have been born by love into true life forever. We have laid bare our whole being to the sacred influx of love, and this is the life of the Cross. We have become the Mystic Rose in the centre of the Holy Cross. But the Secret of Death is also the Secret of Love. We have died upon the Cross of TIPHERETH. It is the mystic death of the kiss. There is a desire which kills, and the same also makes alive, Amen, for ever and evermore. (The voice dies away within the veil, and again there is complete silence. Afterwards the voice speaks.)

Adeptus Exemptus.

Once it was the day of our espousals, for the Second Birth is Betrothal. We have prepared our wedding garments. This also is life in TIPHERETH. We have desired to be dissolved and to be with Christ. This is the death of the Cross. Then is it great darkness, as of a rock-hewn sepulchre. But He Who stands at the door and knocks enters and comes in. This is the marriage of the soul. (The voice dies away within the veil, and yet again there is complete silence. But afterwards the voice speaks.)

Adeptus Exemptus.

Brother of the Rosy Cross, it is not from man to man that the great gifts are communicated, for that which he can devise to another is that only which has been lent to the man himself. It is for this reason that, after solidarity and brotherhood, each of us stands alone. Stand therefore, my Brother, maintaining with your peers and co-heirs a perfect union in the mystery of faith. But remember, a night cometh, and so stand, as one awaiting his call to enter the darkness. He who is reborn is he who shall die also and pass into the Valley of Silence. The Sanctuary of your tomb is hollowed in the rock of ages, and your time is at hand. (The voice ceases within the veil, and the silence which follows is for a brief space only. The Celebrants have taken up their places side by side with the Postulant, whom they draw backward to the threshold, but are still facing East.)

Adeptus Major.

I certify that Frater Non Nobis, Domine, and those who were with him. heard in the House of the Spirit and its Holy Sanctuary the Voice of the Master, testifying concerning Divine Darkness and union with the Divine therein. It is an opening of the inward world and plenary realisation of the Presence in the conscious soul, though it is told after another manner in the records which remain among us. There it is firstly that they discovered the body of the Founder, who bore the book of the Mysteries on his breast, a treasure to be hidden from the world. But it is said also that this book contained by way of colophon the inscription: EXDEO NASCIMUR, IN JESU MORIMUR, PERSPIRITUM SANCTUM REVIVISCIMUS. And this is a summary in brief of the Rosy Cross in all its Grades of evolution. Take it into your heart, my Brother, having prepared the heart as earth of the mystical kingdom. Let it dwell as a seed therein; the letter of the words shall die; the flower of the inward sense shall spring therefrom. The counsel is always to lose the symbols in their meaning. The material part should dissolve in the light of its spiritual significance, and this is what is meant among us by getting behind the symbol. There is no object in Nature, no memorial in the written word of grace which cannot be used in this manner. There is above all no conception, whether of Divine Things and Persons, or of saints also and angels, which will not open to us great vistas of secret knowledge by this philosophical solution.

Auxiliary Frater Adeptus.

We know in this manner that our Founder Christian Rosy Cross, being dead, yet speaketh - in the Hidden Church of the Adepts - concerning life, death and resurrection in GOD. In fine therefore, having heard and seen in the spirit, Frater Non Nobis, Domine, and his companions made fast the Door of the Sanctuary ad interiora terrae and, setting seals thereon, recited their solemn closing on this point of our Christian Mystery. (The Celebrants leave the Sanctuary, together with the Postulant. The Door of the Sanctuary is closed. The Second Celebrant lays his Wand against the Door. He takes the Postulant by his two hands and looks earnestly upon him.)

Adeptus Major.

I say unto you, Frater Adveniat Regnum (vel nomen aliud), that this also is your own story. (The Usher of the Grade comes forward and leads the Postulant from the Temple. Here ends the Second Point.)

THE THIRD POINT

(There is light everywhere, in the Temple and Inner Sanctuary. It is fuller and brighter than in the First Point. The Door of the Sanctuary stands partly open, but the Veil is drawn across the threshold. The Chairs of the Second and Third Celebrant are placed at a considerable distance Westward, toward the middle part of the Temple, and the Celebrants are seated facing East. There is a vacant point behind them for the Postulant. The Celebrant in Chief is standing within the Sanctuary, erect on the Eastern side of the Altar; but the intervening Door conceals him from those who are without. These are seated in expectation and in silence. Meanwhile the Usher of the Grade has conducted the Postulant to the Vestibule, where he rests for a period. While the two are seated together):

Frater Custos Liminis.

Beloved Brother, you have heard - and how often - of a light which shineth in the darkness and that the darkness comprehendeth it not. It is light of the Mystic End and the life of life. In its absence the natural man is said to be complete within his own measures, but he has no conscious part in eternity, and he reigns only as the leader of the animal world. A desire of the true end which is set before all being may begin to awaken within him, as a kindling of the higher light. He sets out on the great quest. The light within him is also a light before him, and the desire of the Holy House burns in his heart. So is he brought to our Sanctuary and learns to comprehend the light which shines from the Rosy Cross. It is for him to remember therein that no initiation and no advancement can confer the light automatically. They remain within their law and their order, and operate only in symbolism. May you who are reborn in Ritual be regenerated in the life of the soul, and may life, death and resurrection be stages of your inward experience, not merely an eloquent pageant performed in ceremony. (The Usher of the Grade again leads the Postulant to the Door of the Temple. The Battery of the Grade [2 knocks] is given and they enter unannounced. The Door is secured behind them. As they move forward through the Temple:)

Frater Custos Liminis.

He who puts aside the folds of the senses, as linen cloths laid by themselves, and the fleshly mind, as a napkin from about the head, shall arise in his spiritual part by a resurrection into divine life. (The Postulant is now standing behind the seats of the Second and Third Celebrant, in the middle place between them, looking toward the Door of the Sanctuary. The Usher of the Grade has returned to his own place.)

Adeptus Major.

When he who has been advanced into the Mysteries of Divine Experience goes forth again into the world, the memorial within him is like the letter of the sacred books.

Auxiliary Frater Adeptus.

The spirit communicated in his Temple is reserved to the Temple.

Adeptus Major.

So also the letter alone can be used outside the Sanctuary of the Rosy Cross.

Auxiliary Frater Adeptus.

There is shadow of light only beyond the Lodge of the Adepts.

Adeptus Major.

The letter also is used within the Sanctuary, but there is the sense of many meanings behind it.

Auxiliary Frater Adeptus.

All Degrees, however, end in expectation; all foreshadow something greater than themselves, by which the Postulant of figurative mysteries should arise to experience in the real order.

Adeptus Major.

But the initiations of the Mysteries are true and efficacious, because they convey in circumstantial signs and tokens the living end of adeptship; and those signs can therefore be channels of life.

Auxiliary Frater Adeptus.

May all the sacramental channels be opened and the Word which is life be spoken.

Adeptus Major.

It is in stillness of thought that we shall hear the Word of Life. (The Celebrant in Chief speaks from within the Sanctuary.)

Adeptus Exemptus.

I am the Resurrection and the Life. He that believeth in Me, though he were dead, yet shall he live, and whosoever liveth and believeth in Me shall never die. (The Frater Custos Liminis moves quietly to the Door of the Sanctuary and draws back the Veil, saying:)

Frater Custos Liminis.

The angel of the Lord descended from heaven, and came and rolled back the stone from the door. (The Celebrant in Chief speaks from within the Sanctuary.)

Adeptus Exemptus.

I am ALPHA and OMEGA, the First and the Last. I am He that liveth and was dead, and behold, I am alive for evermore, Amen: and have the keys of hell and of death.

(The Usher of the Grade passes round to the Postulant, whom he heads to the threshold of the Sanctuary and there directs him to kneel. He sets the Door of the Sanctuary open to its full extent. The Second and Third Celebrant, and all Members stand up. The Postulant sees the Celebrant in Chief erect, with his arms extended in the form of a Cross. The Usher of the Grade moves to one side of the entrance.)

Frater Custos Liminis.

I know that my Redeemer liveth, and that He shall stand at the latter day upon the earth. I shall see Him for myself, and mine eyes shall behold, and not another. My veins within me are consumed with earnest desire for that day. (He remains silently at his place.)

Adeptus Exemptus.

I am the Faithful Witness, the first-begotten of the dead and the prince of the kings of the earth. I am the Way, the Truth and the life. No man cometh unto the Father but by Me.

Peace be unto you. I have finished the work. I know whence I came and whither I go. He that believeth in me, believeth not in Me but in Him that sent Me. I go my way to Him that sent Me. I ascend unto My Father, and your Father; and to My GOD, and your GOD. I am the light of the world. He that followeth Me shall not walk in darkness, but shall have the light of life. (The Merciful Exempt Adept lifts up his hands and face.)

Adeptus Major.

He that hath an ear to hear, let him hear what the Spirit saith unto the Churches.

Auxiliary Frater Adeptus.

Now is Christ risen from the dead, and become the first-fruits of them that slept. (The Usher of the Grade moves forward, and as the Postulant sees and hears the Risen Adept - directs him to say with him:)

Frater Custos Liminis.

(Speaking on the part of the Postulant). One thing I know, that, whereas I was blind, now I see.

Adeptus Exemptus.

My peace I leave with you, my peace I give unto you. The Spirit of Truth abide with you forever and teach you all things. May the Great White Glory of the Divine Spirit come down. (The Usher of the Grade has retired silently to his own seat and stands thereat. The Celebrant in Chief comes round the Altar to the threshold of the Sanctuary and lays his hands upon the head of the Postulant, having placed his Wand aside.)

Adeptus Exemptus.

This is also thine own story. Look to it therefore, Beloved. (The Celebrant in Chief raises the Postulant.)

Adeptus Exemptus.

I raise you into the Company of Adepts in the House of the Holy Spirit. (The Celebrant in Chief seals the Postulant on his forehead.)

Adeptus Exemptus.

May your mind be opened to the realisation that is above knowledge. (He seals the Postulant on the heart.)

Adeptus Exemptus.

May your heart become a sanctuary of light. (He seals the Postulant on the hips.)

Adeptus Exemptus.

May your body be the Temple of the Rosy Cross. (He lifts up his hands.)

Adeptus Exemptus.

May the Glory of the lord fill this House of the Lord.

(All resume their seats, with the exception of the Celebrant in Chief and the Postulant. The Celebrant in Chief turns to the East with the Postulant and leads him to the Western side of the Altar. Having resumed his Wand he proceeds himself to the East, and turns West.)

Adeptus Exemptus.

The Third Order of the Rosy Cross presents in symbolism three stages of experience in the realisation of the Divine, and this realisation is within. These stages are summarised in the Three Points of the Grade of TIPHERETH, into which you have now entered, and it is therefore a synthesis of the Third Order at large, even as the Grade of Neophyte offers at the beginning of our Sacred Mystery a compendium of the work performed in the Worlds of Action and Formation. In the Grade of Adeptus Minor the Postulant is put definitely on the Path of Attainment, understood as the Way, the Truth and the Life which are in Christ - the Regenerated Life of the Soul, the state of Mystical Death and the Risen Life of Union.

The Holy Sanctuary of the Adepts depicts in symbolism the ascent of the soul in GOD, from the deeps even to the heights, through the paths of the Christhood. There is firstly the dark ground whereon we now stand, being that out of which we have risen, the things of material sense and the absorption of the soul therein. Beneath the Golden Altar of our dedication and sacrifice there lies an inverted triangle, inscribed within a heptagram, to both of which are referred the SEPHIROTH of the shadow, as opposed to those of the light. After this manner do we in the Sanctuary of the Adepts, by virtue of dedication and sacrifice, symbolically over-rule and enchain the malign forces of our nature. SUPER ASPIDEM ET BASILISCUM AMBULAVI ET CONCULCAVI LEONEM ET DRACONEM. In the middle of the black triangle there is placed for this reason the releasing symbol of the Golden Cross emblazoned with a Red Rose of 49 petals, being the Rose of the Gates of Light. Round about it are written the four pregnant words: HE DESCENDED INTO HELL. They allude to the Divine Immanence within us through all phases of our being, in our darkness as well as in our light, amidst the bondage of the evil law and in the free dom of the Sons of GOD. We have come out of the evil law, and therefore the shadows of the things left are depicted below us.

The seven walls of the Sanctuary represent the cosmos summarised in the planetary system, the sacramental grace signified to us by the universe, the glory of the world seen in the light of adeptship, SUB SPECIE AETERNITATIS. It is the world from the standpoint of the Sanctuary. It is seen in that light which never was on land or sea for those who are without consciousness of GOD; but it is the light which is always present for those who look at the world from the summit of Patmos, who know- what it is to have been in the spirit on the Lord's Day, and who have heard the Voice which says unto all who have ears: Behold I come quickly. The light is therefore communicated from within the Adept of the Rosy Cross. There is a dual transfiguration - that of the man and his world. It is not that he changes the world; but for him, with him and in him there is a change in its mode of manifestation. The consciousness of the Immanence within reacts upon things without, and then the Divine Immanence shines through the whole universe. It is the transmutation of regenerated life, of the Christ-life on earth. This is the way in which sanctity transfigures all things, and the adept becomes a tingeing stone.

The world is transmuted in the Christhood. But the seven walls are also indicative of states within the Postulant, and they are seven stages of his progress from world to world in the Order of the Rosy Cross. From this point of view each wall is a gate, and you have entered the Holy Sanctuary by the Gate of Venus, even as in your previous progress you passed through the Gate of Earth to attain the SEPHIRA YESOD, through that of the Moon in order to enter HOD, and finally through the Gate of Mercury on your transit from HOD to NETZACH. That you have yet other Gates to open is shewn by the walls emblazoned with the astronomical signs of the Sun, Mars, Jupiter and Saturn. Beyond these there lies the Supreme Mystery of the Rosy Cross.

It is, however, only by analogy that the seven walls are attributed to the material planets, for the true stars are within you, and you know already that in our sacramental system the Moon has reference to the reflected light of mind, Mercury to the state of our desires, which must be fixed on GOD, and Venus to the conversion or redirection of will and purpose, by which only the soul can become a Venus and having been reborn in GOD is the conceiver and bearer henceforth of the Divine within it. The seven walls are also the SEPHIROTH from YESOD to DAATH inclusive, it being understood that the last lies within the mystical decade but is not computed therewith in our Secret Tradition. It is the Threshold of the Supernals. In the middle place on the summit of each wall is the White Wheel or Sign of the Christ-Spirit, referring to the Divine Immanence which is present in all creation and operates in all the states of grace and attainment experienced by the soul of man. The Sign of the Planet itself occupies the centre of the wall, enclosed within the circle of the SEPHIRA to which it belongs, while about it are the Divine Names and Sephirotic titles referred to each numeration. The ground of each wall is on the rainbow or spectrum colour ascribed to the particular planet, while its spiritual counterpart is that of the Sacred SEPHIRA. And because there is a mystery herein which is formulated in the various scales of colour connected with this Grade, I confer upon you the Sacramental Name of Frater Hodos Chameleonis, meaning the Path of the Chameleon. The colours symbolise graces: may you pass from grace to grace and from glory to glory.

The Supernal SEPHIROTH are represented by the triangle on the ceiling, and within this triad is placed a Rose of 22 petals, similar to that which I wear here on my heart. The light in the centre is that of the Christ-spirit, and it flows over the whole Sanctuary. The petals are the Paths of the Christhood, the Paths of the Tree of Life, through some of which you have travelled. The Rose is placed in the centre of a triangle representing the Three Supernals, because the Christ is the Way, the Truth of the Life, and no man cometh to the Father but by Him, through Whom we look in fine to be withdrawn in GOD, as this Sacred Rose in the roof of our Holy Sanctuary is withdrawn into the Sacred Delta.

Frater Adveniat Regnum (vel nomen aliud), look to that which you are and remember ever the vocation of the Christ-Life. May you know like Christ whence you came and whither you are going. The Christ-Life in our Order as in all the annals of sanctity - is only in broad analogy with the Divine Life in Palestine, but it is exact within its own measures. The state of mystical death, which is intimated by the Second Point of the Grade of TIPHERETH, is only in broad analogy with the death on Calvary; and the Adept risen in symbolism who testifies in the Third Point is in no sense taking the part of the Great Manifested Master in a dramatic pageant; but he bears witness to resurrection in the spirit, which is a mystery of experience awaitingthose who have been brought into Divine Union.

(The Celebrant in Chief moves round by the South and leads the Postulant from the Sanctuary, closing but not sealing the Door behind them. The Second and Third Celebrants come up from their places.)

Adeptus Exemptus.

The Sacred and Mystical Number of this Grade is 21, and the root thereof is in the triad. It is derived from the first of the Sacred Names and Words which will now be communicated to you. Follow them on your own part in the heart and mind.

Adeptus Exemptus.

ALEPH, HE.

Adeptus Major.

YOD, HE.

Auxiliary Frater Adeptus.

EHYEH.

Adeptus Exemptus.

It is written: Before Abraham was I AM.

Adeptus Major

Whom say ye that I the Son of Man am?

Auxiliary Frater Adeptus.

Christ the Power of GOD and the Wisdom of GOD.

Adeptus Exemptus.

I,N.

Adeptus Major.

R.

Auxiliary Frater Adeptus.

I.

Adeptus Exemptus.

YEHESHUA.

Adeptus Major.

NAZARAEUS.

Auxiliary Frater Adeptus.

REX JUDAEORUM.

Adeptus Exemptus.

LVX, the Light of the Cross.

Auxiliary Frater Adeptus.

Remember that TIPHERETH is called in the Secret Tradition the Mediating Intelligence. (Here ends the Third Point.)

THE OFFICE OF CLOSING THE HOUSE AND SANCTUARY OF ADEPTS

(The Celebrants of the Rite are seated as Guardians of the Veil. The Door of the Sanctuary is ajar, but the Veil is drawn before it. The New Adeptus has been led to a seat by Frater Custos Liminis.)

Adeptus Exemptus.
Adeptus Major.
Auxiliary Frater Adeptus.

(Each officer knocks twice.)

Adeptus Exemptus.

Valete. Fratres et Sorores Roseae et Aureae Crucis.

Adeptus Major.

May the good pleasure of the Lord of Mercy, prevailing in the height and deep, pour down on us the Gifts of the Spirit and the Fruits there of.

Auxiliary Frater Adeptus.

Orate, Fratres et Sorores. Glory be to GOD in the Highest, Who hath visited and redeemed His people.

Adeptus Exemptus.

Honourable and Adept Brethren, assist me to close the House and its Holy Sanctuary in the fulness of spiritual life declared in the Holy of Holies, and in the gracious, the glorious, the divine intimations of this august ceremony. Auxiliary Frater Adeptus, how many years does the Spirit of GOD strive with the spirit of man?

Auxiliary Frater Adeptus.

Merciful Exempt Adept, it is written that the Most Holy Spirit shall plead the cause of the Union for 120 years.

Adeptus Exemptus.

Mighty Adeptus Major, what does this number mean?

Adeptus Major.

The tetrad of our natural humanity becomes the pentad, and by an operation of four and five the number 120 is reduced to the hexad, which is the number of life in TIPHERETH.

Adeptus Exemptus.

Auxiliary Frater Adeptus, when do we open the Sanctuary of the Holy House for the Mystery of this Grade?

Auxiliary Frater Adeptus.

When the age of 120 years has been attained by the Postulant.

Adeptus Exemptus.

Mighty Adeptus Major, for what period do we close it?

Adeptus Major.

Merciful Exempt Adept, it is closed in expectation and the silence of great desire while the Spirit of GOD strives with the spirit of man.

Adeptus Exemptus.

POST CENTUM VIGINTI ANNOS PATEBO. (He shuts and secures the Door.) Looking therefore toward the Grades which go up to the height, toward the height itself and the summit, O Brethren of the Rose and Cross, in the recollection of the mind, in the devotion of the heart, in the great love and the great desire which past all space and time alone can find their object, I have closed the Sanctuary of the Adepts.

Auxiliary Frater Adeptus.

I close this House of the Holy Spirit on the Mystic Mountain of the Wise.

Auxiliary Frater Adeptus.

Ex Deo nascimur. (Knocks twice).

Adeptus Major.

In Yeheshuah morimur. (Knocks twice).

Adeptus Exemptus.

Per Spiritum Sanctum reviviscimus. (Knocks twice. The Closing Sign is given by all present. Here ends the High Office of Closing the House and Sanctuary of the Adepts.)

THE ADEPTUS MAJOR CEREMONY

THE OPENING

The Vault of the 5-6 Grade has been draped in the colours of the Feminine Scale, and the Portal itself in the colour attributed to Mercury, which is reddish-violet. The Vestibule which is without the Portal has in its centre the Mystic Altar of the Rite, in the form of a perfect cube vested in white. At the western angles thereof two great candlesticks or Pillars are placed on the floor; of these the one in the South bears a lighted candb and that in the north a skull. The lighted candle should, if possible, be the only illumination in the Temple, but shaded or otherwise subdued lamps may be placed, if necessary, at points which are of no symbolical importance. The Tarot Keys of Lamed and Mem are arranged side by side on the Altar. The Paths corresponding thereto are not otherwise indicated than by the two Pillars which symbolise the Path of Lamed, and by the Tomb itself which signifies that of Mem. Two seats facing the Tomb are provided for the Celebrants, the place of the Chief Adept being at the south side, close to the Altar, and that of the Second Adept in similar contiguity on the north side. Both officers appear in the robes allotted to the corresponding Celebrants of the 5-6 Grade, and are saluted by the same titles, the Merciful Exempt Adept holding in actuality or imputation the august Degree of 7-4. Strictly speaking the Celebrant in Chief is therefore in the same position as the Praemonstrator of an Outer Temple, that is, a ruler empowered from beyond. The Usher of the Rite has his proper place at the Door of Entrance, and the goings and comings of the Candidate are more especially under his charge. He has the title of Frater Parepidemos Vallis.

It should be observed that the First Point of the Ceremony corresponds to the Portal of the 5-6 Grade, and that the Portal attributed to Mem is the Door of the Tomb itself. The passage from Sephira to Sephira is in both cases, by the direct lineal way, and not by the circuitous Path of the Serpent, as in the Grades of the Outer Order.

The Merciful Exempt Adept opens the Rite with a single knock and proceeds as follows:

Chief.

Fratres and Sorores Adepti Majores, I invite you to join your intention with mine in the great act of Opening the Shrine of the West. (All rise.)

Chief.

Mighty Adeptus Major, having come so far in our journey from the circumference to the centre, and being conscious of all that which is beyond the things which are seen by the eye, let us pause here for a period, since the day is far spent.

Second.

We have traversed many spheres in our time and up and down in the course of the world and life we have often returned and shall doubtless again revisit.

Chief.

You say well, faithful companion of our common exile! Let us therefore remember the Centre.

Second.

It is known that this is also the height to which many voices summon us.

Chief.

It is well that those who are called should go before their election, but also that those that come after them should find the Path less toilsome because others have gone up first.

Second.

I pray you therefore to remember that, seeking the height or the Centre we do not stand alone.

Chief.

A memorial is always with us behind the doors of this sanctuary, wherein, having first found a refuge as a house of rest on the way, the solemn task devolves upon us to open wide its doors for other travellers whose knocking is heard without.

Second.

Say therefore, O Master, in your mercy, what manner of place is this?

Chief.

It is the House of Love, which is also the House of Judgment.

Second.

What is the sign thereof?

Chief.

That of the Mystic Rose, the Symbol of the Great Mother.

Second.

Let us kneel, therefore, Master, for here is the Holy Place.

Seeing that the first death is salutary and unto this present is not less than necessary, that over us the second death may at no time extend its power, we who are the Stewards of the Mysteries in this little kingdom of Thy Love, do beseech Thee, O Mistress of Life, by the Great Name of Thy Love, even by TABOONA TABANU, and by the other symbols of Thine infinite virtue which we have formerly recited in Thy Presence, as also by those other words which remain here unspoken: we beseech and appeal to Thee, that the saving graces of Thy Spirit may be with us now and to the end, and that these which do also enlighten, may strongly fortify our hearts. So may we well and worthily accomplish the work which we are about to perform. We have dwelt, our Lady and Mother, under many stewardships, seasons of youth, seasons of maturity, seasons of age, dispensations of natural darkness, of derived lights of the sorrow which does not lead, and the joy which diverts from the way. But the call at length came by which we were brought to Thy knowledge, and seeing that it has been given us in fine, to lead others in the Path which Thou hast opened before us, we ask Thee in Thy great clemency for the Light to guide them well.

Second.

It is written, My House is a House of Prayer.

Chief.

In the Spirit thereof, I now declare this vestibule to stand open mystically for the work which it is given us mystically to perform, by the power to us commissioned.

Second.

This is well, brother, Amen.

Chief.

Amen.

Second.

All are seated.

THE SYMBOLIC CEREMONY OF ADVANCEMENT
THE FIRST POINT
THE PATHS OF THE 6-5 GRADE.

Chief.

It is written in faithful words that those who are guides of the perplexed are truly leaders of men. At the beginning of this High Celebration, I testify that we are Wardens of Life, and that in virtue of our high office we are deputed to bring many out of great tribulation into cool and sacred chambers.

Second.

So high a duty now devolves upon us. Therefore in your perfect compassion, I beseech you to have mercy on the soul of our faithful associate, the Most Honored Frater Filius natus, filius datus (vel alius), on whom the necessity of the time exhorts us, even at the expense of his visible nature, with which we have been elsewhere acquainted, to confer the benefit of silence.

Chief.

Do you testify, Mighty Adeptus Major, that now is the accepted time?

Second.

Even the day of salvation.

Chief.

Fratres and Sorores, I beseech you therefore, to assist me with loving hearts, here seeking the higher direction.

Second.

It is written that the Merciful are blessed, and that the same shall obtain mercy.

Chief.

Most Honored Frater Parepidemos Vallis, you have my commands to ascertain the dispositions of the Candidate, to see that he is duly prepared, and to present him in due form.

Usher.

Merciful Exempt Adept, I obey your behests.

(He leaves the vestibule, and goes to prepare the Candidate who should be at hand in another chamber, still under obedience of the Watch, which has sealed his lips in accordance with the provisions of the Rite. The Candidate is now clothed in the robes of an Associate Adeptus Minor, with the Wand and Insignia thereto belonging. Having been thus properly prepared, and being so far as possible unaddressed by the conductor, he is taken to the door of the Vestibule, where the Usher sounds the solemn battery of the Grade. This being heard within, the Second Adept leaves his seat at the northern side of the Altar and strikes the hour of the Rite on the gong by the door of the Tomb. As a matter of convenience, this may be done alternatively by one of the Fratres or Sorores.)

Chief.

Mighty Adeptus Major, what is that?

Second.

Merciful Exempt Adept, this is the hour of sunset.

Chief.

I say that it is the hour of the Rite.

Second.

The night cometh wherein no man shall labour.

Chief.

It is therefore meet and just that we should zealously redeem the time. (During this discharge, the Second Adept returns to his place. When the hour has been struck, the Usher of the Rite for whom it is a response to his battery, at once enters with the Candidate, after which the precinct is tyled immediately. The entrance is so ordered that the Candidate shall hear the question of the Chief Adept after the sound of the gong. As the Usher of the Rite brings his charge forward.)

Chief.

Welcome, brethren, in the name of those who are with us, a great company, keeping the place of our mystery. (The Usher places the Candidate at the eastern end of the hall, facing west.)

Chief.

Frater Parepidemos Vallis, who is he that has followed you?

Usher.

He is the Associate Adeptus Minor Filius natus, filius datus, (vel alius) who, being well known among us, has come in the fullness of time seeking the benefit of sanctuary.

Chief.

What is the age of our Truly Honored Frater?

Usher.

It is six years and many.

Chief.

Do you testify; Frater Parepidemos Vallis, that during the period of his preparation, even from sunset to sunset, he has reserved the outward word?

Usher.

Our Associate himself testifies, in accordance with the sacred covenant. (The Second Adept turns direct to the Candidate.)

Second.

By what sign do you enter? (Prior to his entrance the Candidate has been handed a scroll containing the directions which are necessary to preserve his complete silence throughout all the proceedings, and being prompted by the Usher of the Rite, he gives the sign of the 5-6 Grade.)

Second.

Do you firmly and fully believe that beyond this Grade there are Mysteries which are withheld and that the Closed Veil is not an unknown darkness? (The Candidate gives the sign of Osiris slain.)

Second.

Merciful Exempt Adept, our Truly Honored Frater, bears the sacramental name of Filius natus, filius datus (vel alius). He is an Adeptus Minor of the R.R. et A.C. He has officiated as an Associate within the Portal of the Vault. He has heard the Voice of our Loving Father, and he looks in due time to pass from death to life.

Chief.

Mighty Adeptus Major, I bear witness that he who has been faithful even in the least things shall be set over many kingdoms. Do you also testify that our Frater has fulfilled the Covenant of silence from sunset to sunset, on this great day of his advancement?

Second.

It is known that he himself testifies.

Chief.

Associate Adeptus Minor, give me some sign of the Covenant. (The Candidate, who has been previously instructed, places the three fingers of the right hand on his mouth and then lifts the hand on high.)

Chief.

It is said also: Behold, I come quickly and my reward is with me.

Second.

For those who have been faithful unto death.

Chief.

Associate Adeptus Minor, as the gifts and graces of the Spirit at each degree of their fruition involve new responsibilities, I now ask you whether you will assume these with a real sense of their importance, and with a firm intention to sustain them to the end. (The Usher of the Rite goes behind the Candidate, extends his arms in the form of a Cross, and says as his sponsor:)

Usher.

Merciful Exempt Adept, I have heard that the sons of the true legitimacy should ever remember the yoke of their calling.

Chief.

I will ask you therefore, in your present erect position, with arms extended in the sacred cruciform sign, to say in your heart with me:

THE OBLIGATION

I, Frater N.N., Associate Adeptus Minor of the 5-6 Grade in the Fraternity of the Ruby Rose and the Golden Cross, do here, in the vestibule of the Order, most vividly realise and confess, that the Mysteries of the Greater Initiation are protected by invisible seals from all knowledge of the profane, and that, albeit the outward signs may be put forth in the exterior world, the essential secrets are never openly promulgated. I testify also that their communication is in the silence of the soul, even from the Light which is beyond to the innermost depths of the understanding, in the faith of which my arms are here extended in the eternal sign of the Cross. It is for this reason that, standing at the threshold of things which are to me still unknown, albeit they are close at hand, the only pledges which the sovereign Headship of the Order can here and now exact, I here and now offer, and in place of a covenant to keep secret those things which exceed revelation, I promise that to the whole extent of my ability, I will maintain the Mysteries of the Sanctuary by the proper preservation of the seals and veils thereof, in testimony of which I complete the sacred sign. (The Candidate, in accordance with his instructions, here crosses his arms on his breast and bows his head reverently.)

Chief.

We know, beloved brother, that something at its allotted time must set open the doors of Eternity; and the Mystical Paths and Gates of this august Grade are in your respect already set open in our hearts by the pledge which you have now taken. Mighty Adeptus Major, what are the general dispositions of our beloved brother? (Usher of the Rite during this speech has returned to his seat with the Sun.)

Second.

He has been made familiar with vanity and the time has come that he is weary.

Chief.

There is one place in the world where the heart ceases from troubling, and the weary find their rest.

Second.

He has been made subject to many accidents, and he desires that which is permanent.

Chief.

There is One only in Whom there is neither change nor shadow of vissicitude.

Second.

He desires, therefore, to ascend, at what cost soever, even from the Holy Mountain into Eternal Life.

Chief.

By the task which we have undertaken, it is imposed upon us to assist our beloved brother in the need which has thus arisen, that he may come forth with his own will from the things which are extraneous, and may enter into the things which are within. Mighty Adeptus Major, you will assist him to kneel at the eastern side of the Altar, while we on our part turn for light and assistance to the Source of strength and light. (This is done accordingly, and the Celebrants also kneel down, facing the West, where there is the Door of the Rose.)

THE PRAYER OF THE PORTAL

Chief.

O Merciful and Divine Mistress of the Life which is manifested within, Thou hast called this man and our brother, who in the secret places of his heart has heard the Word of Thy summons, and we beseech Thee to grant him the gift of perseverance, that he may not fall in the trial of his fortitude, but may keep his soul in patience till Thy Word shall again go forth full of power and salvation, when he shall rise in his renewal at Thy bidding, in a true resurrection, and shall know that within the veils of Judgment and Severity there is the High

Palace of Thy Clemency, where he shall hail Thee by a true name, receiving Light from the Crown. We pray Thee also to have mercy upon us, even as upon him whom we have chosen under Thy guidance, our beloved Frater, N.N., that having assumed to ourselves the care of his decreed passage through the Halls of Thy Loving Chastening, we may restore him gloriously in the end, to the honour of Thy Holy Name and his everlasting exaltation in Thee. Praise unto TABOONA TABANU through the years and the ages, even unto the mystery of God. Amen. (The Celebrants and the Candidate rise up. The Celebrants resume their seats. A seat is also given to the Candidate in the position of the Third Adept, that is, by the door of the Vault in the 5-6 Grade, on the northern side looking westward.

Second.

Associate Adeptus Minor, you have already traversed unto our auspices many paths of experience and have been advanced in many Grades of our Mystery. In each of these the Candidate by a voluntary act gives himself to the Order, in return for the measure of illumination which it then confers upon him. You have crossed long ago the threshold of spiritual knowledge, but, having been still far from the goal, you have, at least in a certain sense, known periods of drought and dryness; yet you have ever looked for those better things which come in the land of the Living. All Degrees, however, end in expectation; all foreshadow something greater than themselves, from which the Candidate should arise to an experience in the real Order. But it is still communicated only in symbols, and during the period of our earthly exile the Word of Life is never spoken with the lips. This notwithstanding, the initiations of the Mysteries are true and efficacious, because they convey in circumstantial signs and tokens the living end of Adeptship. They shadow forth the secret doctrine of the union; and, seeing that outside time, we have come forth from God Who is our end; seeing that again outside time, we aspire to return, the pledges of our reception exact a great reticence, not only in respect of the accidentals but of the Essentials signified by our progress apart from those things which here exceed expression. It is for this reason that when the Initiate goes out into the world he takes with him the letters only of the sacred books. The Spirit communicated in the Temple is reserved to the Temple. The letter alone can be used outside the Sanctuary. It is night always outside the Lodge of the Adepts. The letter also is used within the Sanctuary, but there is the sense of many meanings behind it, even as by the arrangement of our Lodges something is assumed that has preceded, while our fundamental doctrines are set forth, for those who can grasp them, that there is something also which comes after. Beloved brother, we are not now, at least substantially, with the Centre. We have, in a sense, come forth therefrom, and in the end we shall return thereto. We came forth naked into our exile, we go forth naked at our call. We must also again issue naked on our second birth, having put away the things which were before. We enter into a new state of consciousness, and have to be clothed upon. At this stage of your experience, I beseech you to remember that the arch-natural life, sometimes symbolised in our teaching by the sign of the Four Elements and the Grand Quintessence, lifts up and assumes to itself the life which is in the midst of death of our natural humanity, taking it helpless into the Sanctuary, to be vivified and illuminated, not without a certain necessary violence, by an act of force and will. Remember also, that no initiation or advancement can confer the Light automatically, but they do confer it symbolically, which is their law and their order. It is in this sense only that the Sanctuaries of the Mysteries signify those places in which there is a dispensation of the Light to every man who has come into this world. It is in this sense that these places are worlds of transcension, the Penetralia in which Plotinus found the identity of subject and object, the Temple of the Ideal Reality which is concealed behind appearances.

VOLUME SEVEN

Finally, it is in this sense or divested of all that seems, however beautiful and elusive, that we desire, God willing, to put aside all veils and go forth unclothed as we came.

These are intentionally detached thoughts rather than an ordered thesis, but they serve a particular purpose in connection with the secret knowledge which is communicated in this Grade. They will remind the prepared Postulant of much which his personal reflections must have undoubtedly already indicated, that outside the specific significance of the express symbolism contained in the successive divisions of our Mystery, the whole process of his advancement can be regarded in a synthetic sense, and that as such, it presents in a formal summary the life of the soul of man. In a word, the soul's legend is exhibited, with the travels and metamorphoses thereof. A tabulation of this kind can be set forth assuredly after more than one manner, nor is the expression of a single phrase exclusive of several parallel interpretations, which might enter into the general harmony; but that which most naturally coincides with the Grades of our Order, so far as they have been at present traversed, can be stated in the following way.

The Ceremony of the Neophyte in the Outer Order of the Golden Dawn will, on various considerations, remain one of the most important of the system, because it corresponds to the first enunciation of the Spiritual Light in the void of the universal darkness, it is the Fiat

Lux of a new order, moving over the formless waters. That Word of the Mystery of Illumination, designed ultimately to disperse the Mystery of Darkness is the message to an unborn soul, and thereto the influx of Light makes known that in order to attain perfection the soul must assume flesh. What is signified therefore is a remote prenatal experience, but we have no mystical symbolism to speak to us of that which went before it. We only know that the soul had already come forth from God, and in respect of the Divine Unity was therefore in a state of detachment, or that it was necessary for its progress to become attached in a state of environment, yet so only, that it might ultimately set aside all accidents and return as we have seen into Unity. The Second Grade of the Outer Order, which is termed that of Zelator, is concerned with a spiritual condition apart from and preceding experience, wherein the soul is formulating the condition of the work by the quest of its proper agents, or, to put it in more simple language, the soul is in search of its parents. In the Grade of Theoricus we are reminded of the Hermetic philosophy which was accustomed to instruct its disciples that it was useless to go in search of the practice till they had worked out a clear theory. The soul, after a manner, is formulating the theory of the work outside the prime condition conceived in the Second Degree. It has so far worked well that the quest is ended; it has found its parents and the process of generation is inaugurated. By an act of its own will the soul has consented to immersion in the material, and has passed into the deep sleep of gestation. In the Grade of Practicus there is presented symbolically that unseen process by which the physical body is designed and the building of the house begins.

The next Grade refers to the building of the house in beauty to become the Temple of the Living Soul. Though it is termed and that fitly the Degree of Philosophus, its entire process is of an automatic kind, for the great experiment is continued in virtue of those forces which have been previously set in motion.

The soul has renounced the remembrance of its former knowledge, nor has it gained the wisdom of the world, but that notwithstanding, it has deserved to be classed as one who is friendly thereto, and has acted in consonance with its ends. We come now to that Grade which is without any number in our system. In its more remote interpretation it signifies the event of birth into natural life, for the attainment of which the soul has set aside all whatsoever that remained of its first prerogatives and has at the same time drunk of the chalice of forgetfulness. By his entrance therein, the newly-born man has ceased to remember the past, and before him spreads the unknown future, even as those who in the Order of the Golden Dawn enter at a given season within the experience of the Portal as recipients who at least by the hypothesis, are unaware whether there is anything beyond it, while a certain imputed forgetfulness, or setting aside, is symbolically assured by the change in the name of the Member who has passed within the First Circle of the Fraternity by the ostensible renunciation of his earthly titles. Of that Portal the Philosophus on his admission becomes a Lord indeed, and of the Paths that lead thereto, but the Vault is in the bosom of the Mystery, and of our Mystic Founder who, being dead, yet speaketh, he has never consciously heard the voice. The time may be long or short, but it comes about in due season that they who have entered by the door, or those at least who have not at this stage suffered the calamity of abortment, are received into the 5-6 Grade, in which the powers of life are manifested, and for a period which is for symbolic reasons fixed at six years, they pass through the varied experiences which symbolise material existence. Herein they are after the manner of men whose eyes have been opened recently; they behold many things in a distorted light and some others are inverted. They are to a certain extent in the wonder- state of childhood. They discern things of the occult order in place of true things which are mystic, and there is given to them almost, it may be, of necessity, the slight substitutes of magic in place of the processes which belong to the Greater Mystery. They make for themselves baubles and playthings from patterns which have indeed their higher significance, but this has not been communicated, and they are subjected in their own degree to all the illusions which are connected with the astral region of existence. In this Grade also they make strange marriages and accept the phenomena of Theurgy for the Path of the Union. It is a period for the exercise of divination, for the telling of fortunes, the study of Astrology, the placing of fantastic constructions on Grades and Liturgies; and they believe that they are in possession of great and secret knowledge if in some strange and reverse direction they revolve the wheel of fortune. But it is not after this manner that Sapiens dominabitur astris.

In the latter dejections of such a transitory stage some of them drop aside altogether, while others remain only, with an artificial and automatic concern in the things of their spiritual progress. Others, as it is unnecessary to say, are never wholly deceived by the illusions of the threshold, or satisfied with the partial lights which shine beyond it to encourage them on their way. They have their own tribulations, but they have no cause to fear those who dwell at the doorways, as they have no inclination to mistake the false gleam for the true radiance that is to come. They will be led after many manners to the proper use of the powers of life in the search for the Holy Symbol of the Lamb slain from the foundation of the world, of that Builder buried in the Tomb of his own creation. In dying that man may live, He has left His Life and Power outside the place of His interment, that they may be assumed by man in the Great Quest.

It is only when the Candidate is willing to restore the life and power to Him Who gave it, that equilibrium, in return, is bestowed on himself; that he hears the Voice of the Symbol, that he beholds the way of his manifestation from the Tomb. It will be understood that the conscious realization of this symbolism at the stage in question is not expressly supposed, and, as said previously, the quality of direction varies; but, in any case, the time arrives when every guided member of the 5-6 Grade begins to realise that the sequence of Rites in the Order, apart from the Sephirotic scheme, supposes that beyond the Adeptus Minor there is and must be some higher stage of knowledge, even as in material life, for all thinking men a moment also comes, when they realise, however dimly, that the things of earth are not the grand totality. It is the symbolical experience of this other side of the existence which the 6-5 Grade offers to the prepared Postulant. It is this which is now offered to you; but before we proceed further, it is necessary that I should ask you formally whether you are still prepared to continue the Rite of your advancement, and to undergo the severe test of your perseverance and fortitude, which is of necessity involved therein. If so, you will arise and signify your assent by the communication of the LVX signs peculiar to the 5-6 Grade. (The Postulant who intends to go forward, gives the signs as required, rising from his seat for the purpose and then again resuming it.)

Chief.

Beloved brother, the Order applauds your fortitude. It is written that the last shall be first, and the Associate Adeptus Minor does not differ generically from the Exempt Adept. Your knowledge of the hierarchic symbolism which characterises the Mysteries will have shown you that the Celebrants of every Rite are either one or three. We are therefore united as it were, in a common act, which depends in part on us and in part on you. It is for this reason that you have been addressed in the present Ceremony by the title of the Third Adept in the procedure of the 5-6 Grade. As such, I again commit you, for the time being into the hands of the Second Celebrant. (The Chief Adept resumes his seat.)

Second.

Associate Adeptus Minor, I will ask you to approach the eastern side of the Altar. (This is done accordingly, and the Second Adept rises, so that he can see the diagrams on the Altar, when he explains the Path of Lamed.)

Second.

The Portal of the 6-5 Grade is reached as in previous cases by symbolically traversing certain Paths which are the channels of communication from Sephira to Sephira in the scheme of the Tree of Life. Those which are now open before you are the Paths of Lamed and Mem by which Geburah is attained in the ascent respectively from the Grade of Adeptus Minor and from the grade of Practicus in the Order of the Golden Dawn. All true Paths are however the Paths of the Unity, and those who have been received into the Mysteries know that man returns by many ways whence he came. I will ask you to observe here that as in the First Order the Candidate has followed the Paths according to the scheme of their correspondence with the body of the Serpent on the Tree of Life, so in the Second Order, and in the Grades of the Portal thereof, he follows them in a direct ascent. The explanation is that previously to birth, the Paths of Nature in growth and evolution were the course of man's progress, but in the Degrees after birth his own will must be his aid.

The letters Lamed and Mem are both of importance in Qabalism, and they correspond, as you already know, in another order of symbolism to the 11th and 12th Keys of the Tarot which are depicted in these diagrams on the Altar.

That to which your attention is especially drawn is the Key of Justice, referable to the letter Lamed, whereto many attributions are given. The writers of the Zohar and the old scholiasts thereon dwell upon the form of Lamed, which is the highest of all the letters; they say also that it is composite, being formulated of Vau and Kaph. These are the accidents of their subtlety; but you should know that its dominion is in the hour of the planet Shabbathai or Saturn, because from Binah, which is the great Sabbath, the rest whereof we desire, there is an influx to the Path of Lamed, through the Path of Geburah, from the Sephira Binah. It further denotes the Mystery of Equilibrium. Now, the place of Geburah can be withstood only by those who restrain their concupiscence, because it is the Supernal Tribunal, and Geburah, in this sense, signifies the force of will, as Lamed is the condition of equilibrium, which represents the Portal of the Mysteries. The ideas which have been thus expressed are found differently exhibited by another order of symbolism in the two Pillars which stand at the western angles of the Altar, bearing respectively a lighted candle and a human skull. With the conventional attributions of light in the mystical order and the obvious lessons to be derived from the disjecta membra of humanity, we have no concern here. They speak too fully for themselves. Of that death which encompasses us in the midst of ordinary life there is however little realisation. All that falls short of the mystic end falls short of the life of life, outside of which we are still in the sphere of simulacra. You have heard, O brother, how often, of a Light which shineth in the Darkness, and that the Darkness comprehendeth it not. The Light thus referred to is at once the mystic end and the Life of Life. It is that without which the natural man is, according to the Qabalah, complete after his own manner, possessing by the communication of nature an understanding qualified to protect him and minister to his daily wants. But as such, he is, to all intents and purposes, without any part in Eternity, and he reigns simply as a leader of the animal world. It is possible, however, that another light may be added to his natural condition, by the desire of the true end which is set before all beings, and of the life which is beyond all life of the apparent order. It is then that he is made ready to set out on the great search, when the higher light which has now entered within him goes also before him, and the desire of the Holy House is enkindled in his heart. In this manner he passes under the judgments and severities of his election, behind which is the concealed love that shall take him to his term. For as the natural man is impelled by a certain elementary justice suited to his condition, so there is a justice which is above, working in the souls of the chosen ones, so that once indeed, they shall taste death, that they may pass into life for ever, under the auspices of the Faithful Intelligence. It is not, however, through the Portal of Lamed that you can enter into the Mysteries which are beyond the Grade symbolizing material life. The contemplation therein and the Path thereto belonging is a middle state between life and death, and its result is the attainment of that which we term symbolically the Path of Mem. As a remembrance of this meditation and of the place which it occupies, I now set you between the two Pillars, bearing respectively the lighted candle as a token of life, and the skull as the witness of mortality; and I bid you remember the dispassionate equilibrium which is poised between life and death, and I bid you also observe that the Altar in this Grade is cubical and white, to show that before you can discover the manifestation in concealment of the Rose, the Cross of the manifestation of life in Tiphareth must reclose its arms in a state of purity. (The Second Adept, having led the Candidate with the Sun, to the western end of the Altar, returns to his place. The Chief Adept rises and turns inwards towards the Altar, without leaving his place. The Candidate now sees the diagram of the Hanged Man, with a Rainbow above, and the head of the Giant below.)

Chief.

Associate Adeptus Minor, you will remember that the letter Mem occupies the middle position in the series of the Three Mothers. It is said in the school of the Zohar that its open operation is through the descent of its influence to the abyss, and thus it restrains the rising of those great waters by which the earth would otherwise again be inundated. In its closed operation it restricts the power of judgment from the downward course thereof. It is also said that it is like a vessel which in turn is sealed and unsealed, according as there is inhibition or indulgence of its influx to the emanations which are below. In our own Rosicrucian system the symbolism of Mem is developed after a peculiar manner in its correspondence with the 12th Key of the Tarot. With the more general import of the Hanged Man you will be already familiar; but in this Grade you are invited to regard it after a new manner, which can still be brought into harmony with the previous forms of interpretation, since it is simply an advance thereon. The enforced sacrifice and punishment, the involuntary and fatal loss, which are ascribed to it in our Tarot teaching, are here connected with the Divine death, with the sacrifice of God himself. That death connects closely with the true meaning attached to the High Ceremony of the Dies C., wherein the Chief Adept typifies at once the Founder of the Rosicrucian Order and the Founder of the Universe. Year by year the Order is withdrawn for one moment of time that it may be again formulated out of chaos, the Builder is also withdrawn into the concealment of the Tomb, as you are told in the Symbolism of the 5-6 Grade. The Maker of our Rosicrucian Fraternity was taken hence that Light should come to His disciples, and the Maker of the great world entered into another concealment, for God dies in order that man shall live, and shall not only seek but find Him.

The symbolism with which we are here dealing also recalls the Apocalyptic figure of the Lamb slain from the foundation of the world, and in correspondence with previous explanations, it indicates that the palmary misfortune of the universe, which is exoterically called the Fall of Man, exercised a species of incomprehensible compulsion upon the Dvine Nature, so that the scheme of what is familiar to everyone under the name of redemption comes before us in a certain manner as an eternal necessity and as a consequence of the free will rather of man than of God. The importance which has been attached throughout the Grades of our two Orders to Egyptian symbolism should also remind us that Mem, through the sacrifice of Christ, has analogy with the legend of the dead Osiris, one of whose appellations was the shipwrecked or drowned Mariner, even as this terrible Key, which you see now in its true form, represents a drowned giant.

The 23rd Key of the Tarot is referred, as you are aware, to the Elemental sign of Water, and in this diagram the drowned giant is depicted reposing on the rocky bed of the ocean with the rainbow at his feet, corresponding to that which has been sunk below the phenomenal world by a sacrifice eternally preordained, which, in one of its aspects at least, is the necessary limitation suffered by the Divine Nature in the act of becoming manifest. The Divine, in a word, is drowned in the waters of natural life; and that which in this respect obtains in the external world, obtains also for humanity, wherein the Divine Spark, beyond all plummets of the sense, all reach of the logical understanding, is immersed in the waters of the material existence. In both cases, the symbol with which we are dealing corresponds to the legend of our Founder, sleeping in the centre of the Tomb, which is encircled by the Rainbow, as in the Sanctuary of Israel there was the abiding Presence of the Shekinah. We must remember, moreover, that the ocean of phenomenal life supports on its surface the mystical Ark of Noah, which, in one of its aspects, is the Vessel of Correspondences, wherein the types of all things were collected from the wreckage of the old initiations for transmission through a new era. In another sense, which is intimately connected with the first, the Ark is the body of man, the ship of humanity, poised on the waters of the world which conceal the divine within them. It is man, collective and individual, man in possession of his senses and also enclosed by his senses. There is that within him which, during this his time of probation is put to sleep as deeply as the symbolical Giant. His originally great nature is restricted in the body after the manner of God in creation. There is yet another aspect in which we may regard the Ark, for by many issues the great symbols open upon the Infinite which they show forth, though it is after the manner of a reversed glass minutely. It is that namely, which for a time suspends the soul's communication with the external that she may receive the influx of the Divine. It is the house of deep contemplation, of fixed, well-directed thought, by which our exit is found fora time, even from thought itself, to the world of true experience. The ceremony of the 6-5 Grade symbolises this indrawn state, in which connection I would ask you to remember that in the roof of the Ark of old there was a window through which the Dove passed and repassed, now in frustrated flight, because many wings are beaters at the Golden Gates; now bearing the olive-branch of peace which for us signifies the suspension of the life of the senses. But, in fine, there came an hour when the dove returned no more, because the aspiration and outreaching of the soul at length attains its term. Beloved brother, we have dwelt at great length upon the import of certain symbols, for albeit the work of detachment may operate scarcely less in suspension from the world, yet it is through many types that we pass ultimately behind the veils.

I have therefore something to say to you of Mercury, which the Alchemists in their secret language, tell us is coagulated by its interior sulphur, this operation being the conjunction of their Sun and Moon, or the marriage of Adam and Eve. Now, this can be understood mystically, because they say also that herein is the union of Heaven and Earth, by which you will see that all systems of symbolism, however apparently divergent, meet in the ultimate identity of their one object. It is affirmed further that we now behold Mercury as it exists imprisoned in a body, but there will come a day when we shall see it set free from its present limitations and manifested as a pure, fixed, intelligible, constant fire. We know otherwise that the Mercury described by the philosophers is a fluidic or volatile substance, and that to fix it is the work of wisdom. These statements are rendered readily intelligible by a mode of interpretation which is peculiar to this Grade, for which Mercury signifies thought. It is in fixity, rest and simplicity that consciousness exceeds the material bounds which encompass it. and receives, according to its measure, the mode of the Universal. There is here set forth a certain great operation of the will which does not die, the concentration of thought by a high act of intentness. Remember the Apocalyptic promise to him that overcometh, and the last conquest is that of the logical understanding, so that thought may be reduced by thought to the point at which it vanishes for a period, but returns subsequently, made splendid by the transmutation of a great experience. You know that the natural mind of man is earthly above all things, and that the Path of our ascent of the mystic Mountain must carry us far from earth, far from the ways and forms of the material mind. You know further that ordinary thought is wandering and volatile, and this is the Mercury which the Adept is called upon to fix. I have spoken on the Authority of the Alchemists concerning our imprisoned and liberated Mercury; which are also the forms of thought, one of them errant in the Material and confined therein, the other emancipated; the one volatile, the other fixed by wisdom. Their correspondences in Egyptian symbolism are ANUBIS, the Guardian of the Egyptian Tomb and preventing entrance therein, the Mystic Tomb being the Gate of Life; and THOTH, who enables man finally to penetrate therein. This is the Word which is sought in all initiations, which is reversed and transliterated, is substituted after all manners, to be recovered finally in the vestures of another sense, as it is said by St. Paul: We shall not all die, but we shall be changed, in a moment, in the twinkling of an eye. It is in the silence of thought that we shall hear the Word of Life. The Absolute exceeds thought, but in a certain suspension it enters io fill the heart, and it is in this way that God is truly with us.

Associate Adeptus Minor, I now ask you to remember that the dead Gods are useless, whether Christ or Osiris. If the Titan immersed beneath the great waters can never more waken, there is no need that we should have part in Him, for we are seeking the fuller life, that truth and beauty which are ever ancient yet ever new. But even as in the old legend the communication of a Grand Hailing Sign awakened the Princess from a sleep of one hundred years, so is the slumber of the gods precious to the soul of the Postulant at the Gate of the Holy of Holies, because of that Centre wherein is the utter stillness of a great activity. They are not dead but sleeping; it is for us to manifest them without by the penetration of the Centre, and it is in this way that the Divine will awaken within us. It is for this reason that the limbs of the Titan correspond in their posture to a form of the Fylfot Cross, for though he appears to be dead and has suffered a real death, he is yet the source of life and activity in the universe; for this reason also the direction of the face of the Titan symbolises the appeal of God to man. (The Chief Adept turns to the East and points to the door of the Tomb, whereon is the symbol of Mercury.)

Chief.

Beloved Brother, we are all, in fine, called back to the House of the Father; fear not, theiefore, those waters that intervene, though they are cold to the simple senses. It is such an ordeal that is foreshadowed in the experiences of the Mystical Death through which you have now to pass, after the manner of the great Masters who have preceded us. The death of the man is the path to the resurrection of the God. Like our traditional Founder, you must be buried with the Light in a Mystical Death, which is necessary before we can rise again in a Mystical Resurrection. Remember that if you be crucified with Christ, you shall also reign with Him. This is the folly of the Cross, which is a scandal to the wise of the world. I will ask you to note in conclusion that you entered the Vault of Life in the 5-6 Grade by the Gate of Venus, but you stand now at the threshold of the Gate of Mercury, by which you will enter the Tomb of the Mystic Death.

As in the Scale of the King, the spectrum opens at the green band, so in that of the Queen, which is the Scale of Winter, of Night, and of the Shadow of Death, it divides between the violet and the red. Mercury is therefore in this Scale a reddish-violet, which is the colour of the door before you. The Portal of the Vault of Life is in NETZACH, but the Portal of the Tomb of Mortality and of the Path of MEM is in HOD. It may also be noted that the Door of the Tomb of Mortality is in its lower aspect, that Argus of the hundred eyes whom Hermes slew, in order that IO, whom some have identified with ISIS, might be released from her imprisonment in the form of a heifer. (There is a short pause.)

Chief.

Mighty Adeptus Major, you have my permission to open the Gate of the Tomb, and may God lead us ail into everlasting Life.

Second.

Amen, Brother. May God be ever with us, and His Peace with thy Spirit.

(The Tomb is then opened, and there is discovered within it a plain coffin of ebony, having an inscription of silver on the lid, being the sacramental name of the Candidate. A single taper burns at the head of the sarcophagus. The Second Adept leads the Candidate to the East of the Altar, and thence the two Celebrants take him across the threshold, as one that is not able yet to walk alone. They pause at the Door of the Vault.)

Chief.

The one light that burns before you at the eastern end of the Tomb signifies meditation concentrated into a single point. Here is the hour and here the place thereof. The Pastos of the Celebrant in Chief in the 5-6 Grade is of many colours, to indicate the beauties of creation manifested by the sacrifice of God. It is the covenant of the Divine with the Universe which has issued from the Will of the Divine. But this coffin is black, to signify the inbreathing and abeyance of material life. Associate Adeptus Minor, it is given unto every man once to die and after that the Judgment. But that which in the things which are above is manifested as Divine Love in Justice among the things which are below. Death, properly understood, is the examination, in fine, of the Candidate, prior to his admission within the Hall of the Greater Mysteries. The Portal to the Centre is through the Gate of the Tomb, and there is no other way opened to man whereby he can enter into his rest. The Mystical Death, however, does not regard the dissolution of the bodily part, but is that which the Qabalists term the Mors Osculi. The concern thereof is to put away the earthly substance of the mind, that whatsoever is imperishable within us may be joined with that which does not pass in the Universe, with those things great and high which have their sphere of operation above the trammels of the senses. It is necessary on this account that you should be unclothed of all insignia because naked we came into the world. Purity alone, symbolised by your white robe, can accompany your entrance into the Tomb. (The Candidate is stripped of his vestments, excepting the white robe, and led to the northern side of the Tomb, and there left. The Celebrant in Chief takes up his position behind the taper at the head of the coffin, and the Second Celebrant in the south, facing the Candidate. The lid of the coffin is removed.)

Second.

It is time now that we take up scrip and wallet, and enter into the Mystery of Death.

Chief.

If it were not for cool, restful and wholesome death, we should never have part in the Resurrection.

Second.

It is the call of every man ultimately to stand alone, that is to say, independently of his kind.

Chief.

But when a man is alone so far as the world is concerned, he is the nearer to the Presence of God.

Second.

Herein is the Divine help which always remains with us, in the equipoise of faculties, the adjustment of the powers of the mind, and the coordination of the soul's phases, which is the condition of Eternal Life.

Chief.

Beloved Brother, we also have slept in the deep sea of the senses; we have paid the price of our exile. (The Celebrant in Chief joins the Second Celebrant in the South, and they proceed again to take up their places on either side of the Candidate, whom they assist to enter the coffin and dispose therein. This being done, the Celebrant in Chief says:)

Chief.

There are many witnesses and above them are the High and Holy Wardens, whose unfailing care will watch over you during your ensuing solemn vigil of six hours. By the will and testament of the Mysteries, we bequeath you to the sacred shadows, that through a final passage you may be brought forth from the things which pass to those which alone remain. (The two Celebrants proceed with the Sun to the western end of the Tomb, here they pause, facing the coffin.)

Chief.

By the power to me committed, I pray and beseech the Father of graces and the Auxiliaries of the Divine Will to pour down upon you, our brother, the living power of the Word and the illumination thereof.

Second.

Beatus in conspectu domini mors sanctorum ejus.

(The Celebrants leave the Tomb and the Portal is closed, but is not made fast at this point. During the period which follows, the utmost possible silence is preserved throughout, with the exception of the Watchwords of the Night, which are uttered solemnly but in a subdued voice. The vestibule is put into the charge of two Wardens, who must be Fratres or Sorores of the 6-5 Grade, according as the candidate is either male or female. In the former case, it is not of obligation that they should be Celebrants of the Rite. Their ceremonial duty is to strike the hours and the quarters on a muffled gong and to exchange the prescribed Watchwords. The care of the Candidate is also in their hands, so that communication can be established with him or her in case of illness or other necessity, when the Rite is for the time being suspended, and the Portal thrown open. Should such a condition supervene that the Vigil cannot be resumed by the Candidate, an implied dispensation comes automatically into force, and the Rule of Silence is finally abrogated. In the case of temporary illness it is abrogated if required, but for the time being only. Under normal circumstances the Vestibule is silently prepared for the Third Point, at a suitable period, prior to the expiration of the alloted six hours.)

SECOND POINT
THE OFFICE OF THE HOLY WATCH

The Office of the Vigil may be performed by either Warden, or may be taken in turn, and this refers especially to the celebrants if the observance is under their charge, seeing that the preparation of the chamber for the next Point will involve periods of interruption. The Watchwords of the Vigil follow an ordered sequence, which should be maintained in recital. The utterances come immediately after the striking of the hours and quarters.

THE FIRST WATCHWORD

He who would be master in Israel must watch more than one hour, but hereof is the soul's vigil.

THE SECOND WATCHWORD

The day for work and the night for contemplation, but out of this union cometh the Great Work.

THE THIRD WATCHWORD

It is written that He giveth His beloved sleep, and herein is a great mystery.

THE FOURTH WATCHWORD

The sleep of thought is obtained on the threshold of ecstasy, but the sleep of death is the Shadow of the Eternal Sabbath.

THE FIFTH WATCHWORD

He who puts aside the folds of the senses by a great act of the will, shall, as one born out of due time, receive in a high symbolism the first fruits of the resurrection.

THE SIXTH WATCHWORD

It is not from man to man that the great gifts are communicated, for that which he can give to another is that only which a man can spare from himself. It is for this reason that, after solidarity and brotherhood, each of us stands alone.

THE SEVENTH WATCHWORD

It is in losing that which the outward man holds most desirable and precious that the spiritual man, after many days, shall find himself.

THE EIGHTH WATCHWORD

The natural man is complete in his own degree, but above this there is the sacred Temple.

THE NINTH WATCHWORD

From the Natural life of man there extends a certain narrow path to the Crown, and this is called Magnanimity.

THE TENTH WATCHWORD

If the Pillar of Mercy were separated from that of Judgment, the Vault of the Temple would fall.

THE ELEVENTH WATCHWORD

The stability and equipoise of the universe are the good pleasure of the Lord manifested.

THE TWELFTH WATCHWORD

A man deviates from the way of nature, and thereby he enters into judgment.

THE THIRTEENTH WATCHWORD

It may so befall that a man comes back under the obedience of nature, and afterwards again deviates, but this time it is to enter within the sphere of Mercury.

THE FOURTEENTH WATCHWORD

Beyond those gates shall no man go, except by the call of knowledge.

THE FIFTEENTH WATCHWORD

Blessed and Holy is he who shall enter into real Knowledge; Wisdom and Understanding meet to pour their influx upon him.

THE SIXTEENTH WATCHWORD

The Supernal Triad would never manifest without us, were it not for the Triad within.

THE SEVENTEENTH WATCHWORD

The Holy Mysteries do ever recall us to the one way which has been known and declared from of old.

THE EIGHTEENTH WATCHWORD

Many lights show forth the Father of Lights, and the darkness testifies concerning Him.

THE NINETEENTH WATCHWORD

We confess that we have aspired to the Crown, seeing that we are King's sons, and we look for the Glory of God, when it shall be made manifest.

THE TWENTIETH WATCHWORD

In six days of his life is material man completed, and thereafter cometh a Jubilee.

THE TWENTY-FIRST WATCHWORD

The secret of death is analogous to the secret of birth, and in his resurrection is man reborn.

THE TWENTY-SECOND WATCHWORD

We desire to put off mortality and to be clothed again in God.

THE TWENTY-THIRD WATCHWORD

Man entereth into his true self as a priest into the Holy Place.

THE TWENTY-FOURTH WATCHWORD

It is made known that the Light of the soul is even as the Light of the Throne: let us therefore look up, for our salvation draweth near.

HERE ENDETH THE SECOND POINT
ARRANGEMENT OF THE HALL FOR THE THIRD POINT

The necessary changes in the furniture and the vestments of the Officers are to be carried out as silently as possible towards the close of the Vigil of the Holy Watch in the Second Point.

The Hall repiesents a chamber in the centre of the earth. In the north-west is the door of the chamber, bearing the symbol of a five-petalled Rose, which should be luminous. Within the chamber a priestess sits, representing the Virgin Mother, surrounded by incense, bread, honey, flowers, a chalice of milk, and wine. A couch with painted lions on either side of it is placed in the centre of the room, in place of the Altar, which is moved away.

The Officers required for the Third Point are:

The Celebrant in Chief.
The Second Adept.

The Usher of the Rite.
The Priestess (as Nut) within the Shrine.
Two other Priestesses.

The priests and priestesses are clothed in white. The purification of the vessels and Shrine takes place before the beginning of the Third Point.

THE THIRD POINT THE CEREMONY OF THE S.O.S.

When the hour of twelve, midnight, has at length been sounded on the gong, which in this case may be unmuffled, and struck with a certain resonance, the two Celebrants of the Rite set open the Door of the Tomb, enter therein, and take up their places south and north of the ebony coffin, where they stand facing each other. The condition of the Candidate is observed, and any necessary assistance is given him.

Chief.

The watches of sleep are long, but it is time now to awaken.

Second.

Think you these bones shall live?

Chief.

The Word of the Lord shall pass over the wastes of life, and he that was dead shall rise.

Second.

Expecting, we have expected the Lord.

Chief.

It is defined by the wise Masters that Mercury kills and makes alive.

Second.

Therefore the Degree of that Death which is entered through the Door of Mercury is of Death, symbolically regarded. The priests, princes and philosophers of Israel say that the recession of death is not otherwise than the transit from one world and one system to another. If this is true in the descent from Sephira to Sephira, it is true also in the recession from sphere to sphere on the return to the Centre.

Chief.

Mighty Adeptus Major, what is that Centre?

Second.

It is the middle point of the Universe, wherein the Mystery of Life is assumed into the Higher Mystery of the Life of Life.

Chief.

By what Path is it reached?

Second.

Through the Path in the Portal of the Tomb of Mortality, and thereafter through the Shadow of Death.

Chief.

What is the Mystery of the Centre?

Second.

It is written that eye hath not seen, nor hath ear heard, nor hath it entered into the heart of man to conceive what God hath prepared for those who love Him.

Chief.

Mighty Adeptus Major, by the power to me committed I call upon you here and now to communicate the outward words of the Mystery.

Second.

Merciful Exempt Adept, the Mystery of the Life of Life is communicated in the Glorious Mysteries of Resurrection from Death.

Chief.

How can we impart to another that which cannot be discerned by the senses or realised by the inmost heart?

Second.

It is not given us to express these Mysteries except by a substituted symbol.

Chief.

In the Name and Power of that substituted symbol, (he stoops and seals the Candidate on the forehead): by the love of brethren, strong as life and stronger than death, (he seals the Candidate on the breast): and by the Cross whcih overcomes death, (he seals the Candidate on both shoulders): I say unto you: Arise and come forth.

(The Candidate is raised from the coffin. The Sign of Silence is indicated by both Celebrants, as the reservation of his speech is necessary until his mouth has been opened ceremonially in this Point. He is given a seat in the Tomb, and sacramental bread and wine are offered for his refreshment. He is then led to the western end, where he stands between the Celebrants, facing the Door of the Tomb.)

Chief.

Blessed is he who has entered into the place of the Darkness, and out of the Shadow of Death comes forth alive.

Second.

It is written that the Eternal Fount of Love is found in Geburah, though this is also the place of Judgment.

Chief.

Let us pass quickly from this place of the shadows, because faithful witnesses have testified that there is true Light beyond. (The Candidate is brought out of the Tomb, and is taken past the couch of the S.O.S. to the Door of the Shrine of the West. The Chief Adept says:)

Chief.

Let the Postulant kneel and make obeisance to the Rose, touching the earth with his forehead. (This is done accordingly.)

THE RITUAL OF THE S.O.S.

The Candidate is raised to his feet and the Second Adept touches his mouth with the Adze, as the Shrine of Osiris surmounted by the image of Anubis as a jackal is carried round in solemn procession.

Chief.

Hail, Osiris, Chief of Amentet, Lord of Immortals, stretching out unto the uttermost regions of space, Lord of the prayers of the faithful, Chief among the mighty! Hail, Anubis, Dweller in the Tomb, Great Chief in the Holy Dwelling! Grant that the dead may live: grant that in life we may know God. (The shoulder and heart are laid at the feet of the Candidate by the Second Adept and the Usher of the Rite.)

Chief.

They have brought thee the sacrifice as the eye of Horus. They have brought thee the heart of Horus. The sacrifice is complete: let none resist the will of the Cods. Behold, Horus (indicating the Second Adept) has overcome that which would devour thee! Behold, Horus is the Spirit, the Holy Son, Redeemer of the soul, the Holy Father, Osiris. (Second A. Holds shoulder of sacrifice to mouth of Candidate.)

Chief.

I am thy Spirit, thy Son, Horus: I speak to thy soul, Osiris. I have touched thy mouth: the Spirit of the Divine Ones loveth thy soul. (The Priestesses beat their breasts, and say wailingly,) Woe! O Woe! We cry aloud for those are in chains.

Chief.

Take now, Mighty Adeptus Major, the ram-headed Wand and set free the voice. (Done.)

Chief.

Take thou the Ram-headed Wand and liberate the sight of.. .(Done. The Priestesses wail again.) Woe! Woe! This gan (woman) is in chains, he (she) cannot free himself (herself) from the bonds. (The Candidate is laid upon a lion-headed couch, his head being toward the north, and his feet to the south. One Priestess is at the head and another at the foot. The Usher walks round, sprinkling water freely with papyrus grass in the four quarters.)

Chief.

O Osiris, all that is hateful in. . .has been brought unto Thee, and all the evil letters that are in the name of. . .(give name). O Thoth! Come! Come! Take these evil letters in the hollow of thine hand and lay them at the feet of Osiris, (repeat four times). O Thoth, lay the evil that is in the heart of (give name) at the feet of Osiris. (Repeat four time. The Usher takes incense and burns it at the four quarters.)

Chief.

Behold, the God of Creation, the God who forms and moulds thy limbs, dwelleth in thy heart. He is thy aspiration, and thy aspiration gives thee protection in this day. (The Usher of the rite pours out water, and burns incense in front of the Candidate.)

Usher.

O (gives name), I have given thee the essence of the eye of Horus, the illuminating power of the Spirit: thy face is filled therewith, and the perfume thereof spreadeth over thee. (The Usher lays oil on the lips.)

Usher.

Receive the crystal unguent, the scent of Holy Places. (The Usher pours out water mixed with soda, and lays it between the brows.) Thou art pure like Horus, thou art pure like Set, the Hawks of the North and the South. (He brings the Black Wand and places it to the lips of the Candidate.)

Chief.

Hail! Holy One! The Twin Hawks have opened thy mouth, and henceforth thou shalt have speech in Heaven, in Earth and in the Rose. The eye of Horus has been given to thee. Drink the milk of thy Heavenly Mother. (The Usher gives him a small vessel of milk, and the Candidate drinks. This is repeated with another small vessel of milk given by the Second Adept. The Candidate rises to his feet.)

Chief.

Holy is the spot that the purified child of man has reached. It is the spot in which he (she) shall become the Child of Heaven. (Pause.) Let the Candidate be bound with the five-fold bandage of Osiris, that he may utter the five-fold dedication. (Two Priests bring a bandage, 5 yards long, and tie it round the Candidate's left foot. It is coiled round his feet, and the Chief Adept prompts him to say:)

Chief.

(At the first coiling.) I dedicate my feet to the Paths of Ra. (It is coiled round his legs.)

Chief.

(Prompts at the second coiling.) I dedicate my life to the Mother of God. (It is bound about the heart.)

Chief.

(Prompts at the third coiling.) I dedicate my heart to the Divine Rapture. (It is coiled about the neck.)

Chief.

(Prompts at the fourth coiling.) I dedicate my mind to the Great Quest. (It is bound about the head.)

Chief.

(Prompts at the fifth coiling.) I dedicate myself to that Mighty Star in Heaven, which contains all I was, or am, or shall be. Let me know myself one with God, and before I utter the mysteries, or suffer them to be profaned, may my lips wither. (The Candidate is laid on the lion-couch. The Priestesses at the head and foot alternately chant softly in soothing whispers:)

Priestess.

Child of Light, come forth!
Star-body of the dying form, come forth!
Child of Light, enter in at the closed gates.
Star-body of the dying form, thy life is sure.
The Key of the Door is within you,
The Way of Truth is within reach of thine hand.
Behold, the Door is before you.
Enter, enter, be not afraid.

(This speech is recited thrice. The Priestess in the inner chamber speaks, formulating the Star-body of the Candidate before her, and taking the form of the goddess.)

Priestess.

I am the Veiled One. No mortal may see my face and live, but the Star-body may enter the place of mystery. Child of Light, I welcome thee. (The Priestesses without continue to murmur alternately:)

Priestess.

Behold, the Door is before thee,
Enter, enter, be not afraid.

Second.

(In a leopard skin.) I am He Who cometh in triumph. I am He Who maketh His way through the Rose; I shine forth as the Lord of Life, the Glorious Lord of Day.

Chief.

(Speaking for the Candidate.) O Silent Place of the Mysteries, which is within her sister who createth shapes, even as the God of Creation, open to me the sealed chamber; grant that I may manifest as the sun, even as the head of Dazzling Radiance, that I may shine in the sealed chamber; that I may rise unclouded as Ra in the Gate of the double Cavern; that I may burn in the presence of the Great God, even in the presence of that Divine Light which inhabiteth Eternity.

Second.

(Speaking as Horus.) I travel upon the sky. I adore the radiance which illuminates mine eyes. I fly to behold the splendours of the Shining Ones in the presence of Ra; yea, I am transformed as Ra, giving life to all initiates when he walks above the zones of the earth.

Chief.

O Viator! Who dost disperse the Shadows of the Shining Ones in the Holy Land; give unto this wanderer the Perfect Path, that he may pass through the Rose of the Favoured Ones, even that Path which is made for the restoration of those who cannot concentrate their forces. (Pause.) O Glorious Unborn Souls aid this wanderer with your unsullied spirit, for he (she) is purified and hallowed. (The Priests hold up their Wands to invoke.)

Chief.

(After a pause.) I am he who ruleth within the Gate of the Paths, entering in his own name, and again manifesting as endless time, Lord of the Aeons of the World is his name. (The Priestess within.)

Priestess.

The work is accomplished. Horus has received his eye. Let him go forth as the lion's cub, and may the palm flowers of the Light be within him. (The Priests bless him by holding up their Wands.)

Chief.

Mayest thou go forth under the protection of the Warriors uf Light; may thy flesh be sound, and thy radiance a protection to thy body; may thy Creator dwelling in thee hold converse with thy Holy Spirit when it brings thee gifts from on high. (While these words are said by the Chief Adept, the Door of the Shrine is opened. The Priestess within.)

Priestess.

The peace of Osiris be upon thee. The wings of Isis overshadow thee. Go thou forth unto the world as Light, and let the darkness be as the sandals under thy feet.

(The Priestess comes out, and gives a red rose to the Candidate, who is assisted to his feet and placcd facing the Priestess, and is unbound. The Priestess communicates the signs of the 6-5 Grade in dumb show to the Candidate, their explanation being given by the Chief Adept, who also communicates the Words, as follows:)

Chief.

The Sign of the 6-5 Grade is two-fold, corresponding to the attitudes of the Priestesses at the head and foot of the couch when you were extended thereon. Both hands are therefore placed in front of the eyes, with the palms outwards, the arms stretched forward, and the face turned right or left. The latter signifies the putting away of the lower desires, and it corresponds to Nephthys kneeling at the foot of the bier. The former Sign signifies the setting aside of the manifested symbols of mind, together with mortal desires; it corresponds to Isis at the head of the bier. The averting of the face to the left is the first part of the two-fold Sign, and to the right is the second part. The Grip or Token is symbolical of the union of opposites and the form of the Pentagram. It is given by the left hand clasping the right. It may also be given thus with both hands. It forms the Key to the Greater and Lesser Rituals of the Pentagram. The Active Elements belong to the right, and the Passive Elements to the left hand, while the Spirit is referable to both. It will also be noticed that the lines of evocation of air and water are arranged to draw the force out of the hands, and of earth and fire to draw the force of those Elements out of the body. The Equilibriating Pentagrams, which are those of the Spirit, are commenced along the lines of the thumbs. The Symbol is Pison, the first river of Eden, which flows into the land where there is gold.

THE COMPLETE GOLDEN DAWN SYSTEM OF MAGIC

The Mystic Number is 15, whence is formed the Password YOD HE, the constructive form of the Tetragrammaton, derived from signifying to exist or to be. It also means desire, fall, destruction, and thus the Password indicates the parting of the ways, whereafter man cannot serve God and Mammon. The Mystic Titles are PAREPIDEMOS VALLIS and DOULOS SILENTII. The two together are interpreted as, Servant of Silence, sojourning in the Valley of the Tombs of the Kings of the Earth, wherein it is your privilege and your duty to construct your own sepulchre. There is also a secret Egyptian Title, which is SHEN SOKARI, meaning the Seal of Him that closeth. In this sense the Pentagram is the Seal of Solomon, because it is the Seal of Peace. This being the Grade of the Rose, the Pentagram is attributed to it in a special manner, while the Hexagram is referable to Tiphareth or the Sun, and the purified man, and is interpreted as the Shield of the Beloved or of David in our scheme of the higher Degrees. The Grand Word is TABOONA, the Hebrew name of Sophia. It is derived from the same root as Binah, and therefore signifies the Great Mother. A certain permutation results in the name TABANU, our desire and longing. And you should know that the desire of the Great Mother must fill the heart of the Postulant passing to the ineffable Grades, for our purification is in union with her, as in the salt sea of Binah, and this is the Mystic Union of the Lover and the Beloved.

THE CEREMONY OF CLOSING THE TEMPLE

Chief.

Fratres and Sorores Majores, I testify that the Mystery which we have finished is in communion with all the Mysteries; that the things which are above, being analogous with the things which are below, the Exalted Grades of advancement beyond this Grade are identical as to the roots therewith, and those also which are below, because one experiment has in all things concerned the universe. Mighty Adeptus Major, is this your testimony also?

Second.

I am the least among the faithful witnesses, but I have beheld the end of the Quest, for there are no glasses of vision so darkened that they can long succeed in concealing it. I have also come from afar, and the experience of many worlds is laid up in my heart.

Chief.

I do not ask you to announce the Great End on the faith of your vision, for it is known among those who have followed the Path of the mysteries and have advanced therein, that when most we covenant to lay aside all veils, that Mystery itself withdraws into a deeper concealment, and that which at need assumes all modes in symbolic expression, at need also descends beyond all reach of representation into the abyss which gives up no form. I ask you therefore not what you have seen, but rather what have you been doing?

Second.

I have journeyed so far through distance and distance, even unto the great distance, that I have reached the setting sun.

Chief.

That was a long journey, Brother, but was it the term of your pilgrimage?

Second.

It was not. Merciful Exempt Adept, for afterwards I continued my way beyond the setting sun.

Chief.

That was also a long way, but where, I pray, did it bring you?

Second.

To the Egyptian land of Amentet, to the Mountain of the Sunset, and, in fine, to the cavern which is within the Mountain.

Chief.

We have been told that those who attain so far a point do not for more than a season remain at the door of the cavern.

Second.

For my own part, Master, I knocked and entered therein, with such success that I attained at last to the Centre.

Chief.

Mighty Adeptus Major, I beseech you in your charity, to show forth some part or shadow of that which you found therein, and I testify, on my part that all the Holy Assemblies shall hearken while you announce the tidings.

Second.

Merciful Exempt Adept, the spirit indeed is willing, but the tongue is weak. With great veneration I must tell you, as you also would tell me, that I do not know, God knoweth.

Chief.

But I divine the impediments which may at this time hinder you. Do you assure me also that you have brought nothing back from your pilgrimage? (The Second Adept points solemnly to the Ka Door in the West).

Second.

Merciful Exempt Adept, I testify that the Great Mother gave me the symbol of the rose, and that, after many wanderings, I have returned therewith.

Chief.

The operations of this Grade having been therefore accomplished, by the power to me committed and in accordance with my high trust, I close the Holy Temple in the name of TABOONA TABANU.

(The Priestess turns and adores the shrine—enters and takes the Paten. The rest kneel.)

When all is done she turns again and having closed the door from without stands in front of and facing the Shrine.)

Priestess.

Beautiful Mother of Heaven, Nut, Lady of the Firmament, grant that any error we may have made in thus seeking to set forth Thine Ancient Ritual, may be atoned for by the earnestness of those who have come thus far in their search for the wisdom that once lived in Egypt. Protect us in peace, now and in Eternity.

Shed Light upon us here and forever.

OTHER ORDER RITUALS AND
MAGICAL DOCTRINES

VOLUME EIGHT

OTHER ORDER RITUALS AND MAGICAL DOCTRINES

TABLE OF CONTENTS

IMPORTANT TABLES AND ILLUSTRATIONS

VOLUME EIGHT

OTHER ORDER RITUALS
AND MAGICAL DOCTRINES

CEREMONY OF THE EQUINOX

This Ceremony is held twice yearly: THE VERNAL EQUINOX about March 21st. the AUTUMNAL EQUINOX about September 21st. (Officers assemble and Robe. Chiefs seat themselves on the Dais. Members gowned and wearing their sashes enter and sit as far as possible by members of the same grade. Inner Members in the East, Philosophi in the South, Practici and Theorici in the West, Zelatores and Neophytes in the North. The Temple is opened in the Neophyte Grade. All are seated.)

Hiero:

(Knocks) Fratres and Sorores of all Grades of the Golden Dawn in the Outer, let us celebrate the Festival of the VERNAL (Autumnal) EQUINOX. (All rise except Hierophant.) (Knocks) Frater Kerux, proclaim the EQUINOX and announce that the Pass-word is abrogated. (Kerux passes to the North East, raises his Wand, and facing West, says:)

Kerux:

In the Name of the Lord of the Universe, and by command of the Very Honoured Hierophant, I proclaim that the VERNAL (autumnal) EQUINOX is here and that the Pass-word is abrogated. (Kerux returns to his place. Members stand facing towards the Altar and follow the Officers in making the Signs towards it.)

Hiero:

Let us consecrate according to ancient custom the return of the Equinox.

Hiero:

LIGHT

Hiereus:

DARKNESS

Hiero:

EAST

Hiereus:

WEST

Hiero:

AIR

Hiereus:

WATER

Heg:

(Knocks) I am the Reconciler between them. (All make Neophyte Signs towards the Altar.)

Dad:

HEAT

Stol:

COLD

Dad:

SOUTH

Stol:

NORTH

Dad:

FIRE

Stol:

EARTH

Heg:

(Knocks) I am the Reconciler between them. (All make Signs towards the Altar.)

Hiero:

ONE CREATOR

Dad:

ONE PRESERVER

Hiereus:

ONE DESTROYER

Stol:

ONE REDEEMER

Heg:

(Knocks) One Reconciler between them. (All make Signs towards the Altar. Hierophant goes to the West of the Altar and lays down his Sceptre, saying:)

Hiero:

With the Pass-word I lay down my Sceptre. (Hierophant takes the ROSE from the Altar and returns to his place. Hiereus passes direct to the Altar and lays down his Sword, saying:)

Hiereus:

With the Pass-word I lay down my Sword. (Hiereus takes the Cup of Wine and returns to place. Hegemon comes direct to the East of the Altar and lays down Sceptre, saying:)

Heg:

With the Pass-word I lay down my Sceptre. (Hegemon remains standing East of the Altar. Kerux comes direct to the Altar, hands his Lamp to Hegemon, and lays down his Wand, saying:)

Kerux:

With the Pass-word I lay down my Lamp and Wand. (Kerux returns to his place. Hegemon also returns, taking Lamp of Kerux. (Stolistes comes round by East and South to West of Altar and puts down Cup, saying:)

Stol:

With the Pass-word I lay down my Cup. (Stolistes takes the Paten of Bread and Salt and returns to place. Dadouchos comes direct to the Altar and lays down his Censer, saying:)

Dad:

With the Pass-word I lay down my Censer. (Dadouchos takes the Red Lamp from the Altar and returns with Sun to his place.)

(Sentinel comes by South to East of the Altar and puts down his Sword, saying:)

Sent:

With the Pass-word I lay down my Sword. (He returns by North and East to his place. Kerux passes to the North East to begin his Circumambulation. As he reaches each Quarter, and the Prayer is said, Officers and Members face that Quarter and at the end of the Prayer, all make Signs towards the Quarter. Kerux moves to the East and halts before Hierophant, who, holding up the Rose, faces East. All face East.)

Hiero:

Let us adore the Lord of the Universe. Holy art Thou, Lord of the AIR, Who hast created the Firmament. (Hierophant makes a Cross in the Air with the Rose and salutes. All salute. Kerux passes to the South and faces Dadouchos, who turns South holding up the Lamp. All face South.)

Dad:

Let us adore the Lord of the Universe. Holy art Thou, Lord of FIRE, wherein Thou hast shown forth the-Throne of Thy Glory. (Dadouchos makes a Cross with the Lamp and salutes.

All salute. Kerux passes to West and faces Hiereus, who turns West holding Cup on high. All face West.)

Hiereus:

Let us adore the Lord of the Universe. Holy art Thou, Lord of the WATERS, whereon Thy Spirit moved at the Beginning. (Hiereus makes a Cross with the Cup, and salutes. All salute. Kerux passes to the North and faces Stolistes, who turns North, holding Paten on high, and says:)

Stol:

Let us adore the Lord of the Universe. Holy art Thou, Lord of the EARTH, which Thou hast made for Thy Footstool! (Stolistes makes a Cross with the Paten and salutes. All salute. Kerux passes round the Temple to his place. All face towards the Altar. Hegemon stands East of the Altar, facing West, and holding Kerux's Lamp on high, says:)

Heg:

Let us adore the Lord of the Universe. Holy art Thou, Who art in all things, in Whom are all things. If I climb up to Heaven, Thou art there and if I go down to Hell Thou art there also! If I take the Wings of the Morning and flee unto the uttermost parts of the Sea, Even there shall Thy hand lead me and Thy right hand shall hold me. If I say, Peradventure the Darkness shall cover me, even the Night shall be turned Light unto Thee! Thine is the AIR with its Movement! Thine is the FIRE With its Flashing Flame! Thine is the WATER with its Ebb and Flow! Thine is the EARTH with its enduring Stability! (Hegemon makes a Cross over the Altar with the Lamp. All salute towards the Altar. Hegemon keeps the Lamp. All sit down. Imperator rises and knocks, and says:)

Imper:

By the Power and Authority vested in me, I confer the new Pass-word. It is (XYZ).

(Hierophant, taking the Rose, quits his Throne, which is taken by Imperator. Hierophant then goes East of the Altar and lays down the Rose. He returns to the East and lays his Lamen and Cloak at the foot of the Throne, and takes his place in the East as a Member of the Temple. In the same manner, Hiereus puts down the Cup, Hegemon the Lamp of Kerux, Stolistes the Paten, Dadouchos the Red Lamp in turn, and lay their Lamens at the foot of the Throne. Kerux, after Hegemon, and Sentinel last, lay their Lamens at the foot of the Throne and all are seated with Members of their own rank. Praemonstrator rises to read out the names of the new Officers.)

Praem:

The Officers appointed to do the Work of the Temple for the ensuing six months are . . (at the end, he says:)

Praem:

The Fraters and Sorores of the Outer Order will now retire for a season.

(Kerux gathers up and leads out all who have not attained the White Sash. There is a pause while the New' Officers are provided with Nemysses and Lamen Collars. Outer Order Members, taking Office, should take these things with them and clothe outside in readiness for their Installation by the new Hierophant now to be appointed. All Inner Order Members now present assume their Rose-Crosses. Chief takes his place on the Throne of East. Second on his left; Third on his right. Lesser Officers leave dais and take seats among other Members.)

(N.B. I have examined several of the early Order rituals including one each of the A.O., and Golden Dawn - and in none of them is there anything resembling this segment. In view of the style of the Ritual etc. I am obliged to assume that this is a literary creation of Dr. Felkins. In stating this, I am not to be construed as being condemnatory. On the contrary, especially after reading the earliest Rituals of the Order, I am convinced that Dr. Felkins or whoever was responsible for editing some of the Order documents in the Stella Matutina, did an exemplary job. The editing was extremely well done. So well done in fact that criticism is rendered unnecessary. And in so stating, it is clear that I am not to be numbered amongst those who are critical of the Stella Matutina. Perhaps its emphasis on skrying may have been exaggerated, but a human Order has to have some faults. Again, let me state the editing was superbly executed. I.R.)

Chief:

Peace Profound, my Brethren. (He rises.)

Second:

Emanuel. (He rises.)

Third:

God is with us. (He rises.)

Chief:

In Nomine Dei viventis.

Second:

Et vivificantis.

Chief:

Qui vivit et regnet in saecula saeculorum.

Third:

Amen.

Chief:

Avete, Fratres et Sorores.

Second:

Roseae Rubeae.

Third:

Et Aureae Crucis.

Chief:

Very Honoured Fratres et Sorores, seeing that the things which are above do continually lift up unto their high estate the things which are below, and do thence return them after a certain great transfiguration, that the work of Wisdom may continue and that the Grace and Sanctification of the Holy and Glorious Zion may be communicated to the Zion which is on Earth, wherefore the worlds rejoice together and are fulfilled in all completion, I beseech you to join with me in my intention, and to ratify in your hearts, the solemn and sacramental words by which I assume this external and visible Temple of the Golden Dawn into the House not made by hands, builded of lively stones the Company of the Adepts. And it is so assumed accordingly.

Second:

Cum Potestate et Gloria.

Third:

Amen! (The Chiefs are seated.)

Chief:

Fratres et Sorores of the Roseae Rubeae et Aureae Crucis. We know that the Mystic Temple, which was erected of old by Wisdom, as a Witness of the Mysteries which are above the Sphere of Knowledge, doth abide in the Supernal Triad, in the Understanding which transcends Reason, in the Wisdom which comes before Understanding and in the Crown which is the Light of the Supernals. We know that the Shekinah, the co-habiting Glory, dwelt in the Inner Sanctuary, but the first Creation was made void. The Holy Place was made waste and the Sons of the House of Wisdom were taken away into the captivity of the Senses. We have worshipped since then in a house made with hands, receiving a Sacramental Ministration by a derived Light in place of the Co-habiting Glory. And yet, amidst Signs and Symbols the Tokens of the Higher Presence have never been wanting in our hearts. By the Waters of Babylon we have sat down and wept, but we have ever remembered Zion, and that Memorial is a Witness testifying that we shall yet return with exultation into the House of our Father. As a Witness in the Temple of the Heart, so in the Outer House of our Initiation, we have ever present certain Watchers from within, deputed by the Second Order to guard and lead the Lesser Mysteries of the Golden Dawn and those who advance therein, that they may be fitted in due course to participate in the Light which is beyond it. It is in virtue of this connecting link, this bond of consanguinity, that I have assumed the things which are without in the Temple of the Golden Dawn into the things which are within the company of the Second Order at this secret meeting held at the Equinox for the solemn purpose of proclaiming a new Hierophant charged with the Rites of the Temple during the ensuing six months, being a part of the temporary period which intervenes between us and our rest.

Second:

Let us work, therefore, my Brethren and effect righteousness, because the Night cometh.

Third:

Wherein no man shall labour.

Chief:

(Rises) Fratres and Sorores of the Roseae Rubeae et Aureae Crucis, by the power in me vested, I proceed to the installation and investiture of the Hierophant of the Golden Dawn Temple in the Order of the R.R. et A.C. in the Portal of the Vault of the Adepti.

Second:

(Rises) Benedictus qui venit.

Third:

(Rises) In Nomine Domini. (The Three Adepti give LVX signs, and seat themselves.)

Chief:

Very Honoured Frater, at the discretion of the Chiefs of the Second Order you have been appointed to the Office of Hierophant of this Temple for the ensuing six months. Are you willing to assume its duties and responsibilities?

Hiero:

I am.

Chief:

Then I will thank you to advance to the East, giving the Grand Sign of the Order of the R.R. et A.C. (Done.)

Second:

Benedictus Dominus deus Noster.

Third:

Qui dedit nobis hoc Signum (touches Rose Cross on breast.)

Chief:

Very Honoured Frater (XYZ) standing in the Eastern place of the Temple, I will thank you to give me the secret word of the Order R.R. et A.C. (Done.)

Second:

Habes Verbum.

Third:

Et verbum caro factum est, et habitavit in nobis.

Chief:

(Rises) Wherefore. Brethren, let us remember that when the Body is assumed by the Word, the Man becomes a living Soul. For which reason we persevere in the Pathway of the Cross as we look for the Assumption of the Rose. The Very Honoured Adeptus Secundus will now deliver the Charge before Installation. (He sits down.)

Second:

(Rises) The high Office to which you have been appointed by the decree of the Chiefs of the Second Order involves duties of a solemn kind and their proper fulfilment is a sacred responsibility which rests for a period upon you. While the rule of the Outer Order is more particularly committed to the Imperator, while the instruction of its members is entrusted to the Praemonstrator above all, and the general business of the Temple devolves especially upon the Cancellarius, amidst the distinction of these services there is still a common ground of interaction which must be maintained by a perfect adjustment to ensure the right conduct and harmony of the whole. In like manner, the Chief Officers of the Temple are distinct and yet allied; the perfection and beauty of its Ritual depends indeed upon the Hierophant as the Expounder of the Mysteries, but not on him alone. For all must work together to encompass the good of all. I invite you, therefore, not only to take counsel with the Chiefs of the Second Order on all important occasions and to maintain a regular communication with the Guardians of the Outer Temple, but to consult and assist the Lesser Officers so that these Rites which, under the Supreme Authority, are about to be placed in your hands, may, after your term of Office, be restored to the Chief Adept not merely intact in their working but showing an increased beauty and a greater Light of Symbolism. Thus and thus only will you give, when the time comes, a good account of your stewardship. Let me further remind you that the Guardians of the Outer Temple should at all time, in all things, command your respect as the Deputies of the Absolute Power which dwells behind the Veil, directing all things in the two Orders for the attainment of its Divine Ends. Let the memory of these objects abide with you, even as it abides in them and do you assist them in their labour so to direct the Temple that Peace may be maintained with Power. (He sits down. Chief rises.)

Chief:

In the presence of this solemn Convocation of Adepti of the Second Order, seated in this assumed Temple, I again ask you whether you are prepared in your mind to accept the responsible Office to which you have been appointed?

Hiero:

I am.

Chief:

Then you will kneel down, repeat the Sacramental Name by which you are known in the Order and say after me: I, Frater (XYZ), in the Name of the Lord of the Universe, and of that Eternal and Unchangeable Unity which I seek in common with my Brethren, do solemnly promise, that I will, to the utmost of my power, fulfil the high Office which has been imposed upon me, and by me acccepted freely, for the good of the whole Order; that I will maintain the rites of the Order and observe the duties of my position with conscientiousness and loving care, not alone towards the Temple itself, but every individual Member; that I will co-operate with the Guardians of the Temple; that I will execute the decree of the Chiefs of the Second Order, acting with justice and without fear or favour in accordance with the dictates of my conscience. This I affirm by the Symbol worn upon the breast of the Officiating Adept. (Hiero. is directed to stretch out his hand in the direction of the Rose-Cross on Chief Adept's breast.)

Arise, Very Honoured Frater and receive at my hand the highest Office I can bestow upon you in this Temple. By the Power in me vested, I now appoint you Hierophant of the Golden

Dawn Temple to work and confer the Grades of the Outer Order, under the dispensation of the Chiefs during the ensuing six months. May the Light which is behind the Veil shine through you from your Throne in the East on the Fratres and Sorores of the Order, and lead them to the Perfect Day.

Second:

When the Glory of this World passes.

Third:

And a Great Light shines over the Splendid Sea. (Chief invests Hierophant with Robes assisted by a server.)

Chief:

I clothe you with the Robe of a Hierophant. Bear it unspotted, my brother, during the period of your office. Keep clean your heart beneath it, so shall it sanctify your flesh and prepare you for that great Day when you, who are now clothed by the Power of the Order, shall be unclothed from the body of your death. I invest you also with the Lamen of your Office; may the virtue which it typifies without, be present efficaciously within you, and after the term of your present dignity, may such virtue still maintain you in your search after the White Stone on which a New Name is written which no man knoweth save he who receiveth it. You will now pass to the symbolic Altar of the Universe and assume the Sceptre of the Hierophant. (Hiero. goes to West of Altar, raises Sceptre in both hands and says:)

Hiero:

By the Pass-word. I claim my Sceptre. (He returns to East. Chief takes him by both hands and enthrones him with the grip of the Second Order.)

Chief:

By the Power in me vested, I install you Hierophant of the Golden Dawn Temple. May the steps of this Throne lead you to your proper place among the Seats of the Mighty which are above. (He turns to Members.) Behold my Brethren, him who now stands amongst us, clothed with the attribute of lawful Revealer of the Mysteries for those whom we are leading towards the Light. You are the Adepti of those Mysteries and you can assist him to proclaim them, that those who are still without may be lead by loving hands to that which is within. Fratres and Sorores of the R.R. et A.C., I now invite you to join with me in a common act of prayer. (All face East.)

We give Thee thanks, Supreme and Gracious God, for the manifestation of Thy Light which is vouchsafed to us, for that measure of knowledge which Thou hast revealed to us concerning Thy Mysteries, for those guiding Hands which raise the corner of the Veil and for the firm hope of a further Light beyond. Keep, we beseech Thee, this man our brother, in the Justice of Thy Ways, in the Spirit of Thy Great Council, that he may well and worthily direct those who have been called from the tribulation of the Darkness into the Light of this little Kingdom of Thy Love; and vouchsafe also, that going forward in love for Thee, through Him and with Him, they may pass from the Desire of Thy house into the Light of Thy Presence.

Second:

The Desire of Thy House hath eaten me up.

Third:

I desire to be dissolved and to be with Thee.

Chief:

God save you, Fratres et Sorores. The work of the Light for which we have assumed this Temple has been accomplished faithfully, and the Temple has received its Hierophant. By the power in me vested, I now remit it into its due place in the Outer World taking with it the Graces and benedictions which at this time we have been permitted to bestow thereon. And it is so remitted accordingly. In Nomine Dei Viventis.

Second:

Et vivificantis.

Chief:

Qui vivit et regnet in saecula saeculorum.

Third:

Amen. (All Adepti give LVX Signs, and resume their proper places in the Temple. They remove Rose Crosses. Praemonstrator goes to the door, opens it and says:)

Praem:

The Brethren of the Outer Order will resume their places in the Temple. (Done. Door closed. Chief rises, and says:)

Chief:

Fratres et Sorores of the Order of the Golden Dawn behold your Hierophant, our Frater (XYZ) who has been regularly installed and enthroned, and by the power in me vested, I proclaim him the Revealer of Mysteries among you for the ensuing six months, being part of that temporal period through which we are conducted into Light. Very Honoured Frater, in the presence of the Children of your Temple, I call upon you to make your Confession.

Hiero:

(Rising) Fratres et Sorores of the Order, seeing that the whole intention of the Lower Mysteries, or of external initiation, is by the intervention of the Symbol, Ceremonial, and Sacrament, so to lead the Soul that it may be withdrawn from the attraction of matter and delivered from the absorption therein, whereby it walks in somnambulism, knowing not whence it cometh nor wither it goeth; and seeing also, that thus withdrawn, the Soul by true direction must be brought to study of Divine Things, that it may offer the only clean Oblation and acceptable sacrifice, which is Love expressed towards God, Man and the Universe. Now, therefore, I confess and testify thereto, from my Throne in this Temple, and I promise, so far as in me lies, to lead you by the Rites of this Order, faithfully conserved, and exhibited with becoming reverence, that through such love and such sacrifice, you may be prepared in due time for the greater Mysteries, the Supreme and inward Initiation. (He sits down. The installation of the Lesser Officers is now proceeded with. Cloaks and Lamens are arranged at the foot of the Dais, ready for the Server to hand them to Hierophant. The Ceremony of Installation follows immediately the Confession of the Hierophant. The Outer Members are called in by Praemonstrator and Kerux sees that ell have places. Hierophant reads his Confession, then says:)

VOLUME EIGHT

Hiero:

In virtue of the power to me committed, I proceed to invest my Officers. Let the Hiereus come to the East. (Hiereus, standing in the East, is invested with the Cloak by the Server, who also clips the Lamen in place and Hierophant holds the Lamen while saying:)

Hiero:

By the power to me committed, I ordain you Hiereus of this Temple for the ensuing six months, and I pray that from your Throne in the West, symbolising the failing light, you also, may lead the Fratres and Sorores of the Order, to the full Light in the end, and that you and they, in the midst of material gloom, will ever remember that the Divine Darkness is the same as the Divine Glory. (Hiereus passes to the East of the Altar and takes up the Sword, saying:)

Hiereus:

By the Password I claim my Sword. (He goes to his Throne. When he is seated, Hierophant says:)

Hiero:

Let the Hegemon come to the East. (Hegemon is given the Cloak and Lamen in the same way, and Hierophant, holding the Lamen, says:)

By the power to me committed, I ordain you Hegemon of this Temple for the ensuing six months, and I pray that from between the Pillars, you may lead the Fratres and Sorores into the equilibrium of perfect reconciliation. (Hegemon goes to the East of the Altar, takes his Sceptre, and says:)

Heg:

By the Password 1 claim my Sceptre. (Takes his place.)

Hiero:

Let the Kerux come to the East. (Kerux and other Officers to follow are served with the Lamen which Hierophant holds while addressing them.)

By the power to me committed, I ordain you Kerux of this Temple for the ensuing six months, to guard the inner side of the Portal, and to lead all Mystic Processions. I pray that you may ever go before us with the Torch of the Higher Luminaries, uttering the Watchwords of the Day. Thanks be to God, my brother, for the Admirable Light.

Kerux:

By the Password I claim my Lamp and Wand.

Hiero:

Let the Stolistes come to the East. (Done.) By the power to me committed, I ordain you Stolistes of this Temple for the ensuing six months, to watch over the Cup of Clear Water, and to purify the Hall, the Brethren and the Candidate. May you also, in your own Soul, be sprinkled with Hyssop and be cleansed. May you be washed and made whiter than snow. Thanks be to God, my brother, for the living Water which purifies the whole Creation.

Stol:

By the Password I claim my Cup.

Hiero:

Let the Dadouchos come to the East. (Done.) By the power to me committed, 1 ordain you Dadouchos of this Temple for the ensuing six months, to watch over the Fires of the Temple and to perform the Consecratrons by Fire. Remember the sweet odour of the Greater Sanctuary, and the Savour of the Beauty of the House. Thanks be to God, my brother, for the true Incense which hallows our life.

Dad:

By the Password I claim my Censer.

Hiero:

Let the Sentinel come to the East. (Done.) By the power to me committed, I ordain you Sentinel of this Temple for the ensuing six months. Be thou faithful, keep strict watch without, lest any Evil enter our Sacred Hall.

Sent:

By the Password I claim my Sword.

(Hierophant sits down. All are seated. Kerux comes forward and arranges the Elements properly upon the Altar. The Chiefs will now make any announcements. The Hierophant can address the Temple. When he has finished, he gives one knock and Kerux comes forward to begin the Closing, which is that of the Neophyte Grade.)

WATCHTOWER CEREMONY

By

V.H. FRATER A.M.A.G.

(Stand in the North East. Face East and announce:) HEKAS, HEKAS, ESTE BEBELOI (hay-kahs, hay-kahs, ess-tee bee-ba-loy!)

(Perform banishing ritual of the Pentagram first and then the banishing ritual of the Hexagram.

Go to South of altar. Pick up incense stick or fire wand, wave it thrice in front of Fire Tablet, hold it above head, and move slowly around the perimeter of temple, deosil, vibrating:)

And when after all the phantoms have vanished, thou shalt see that holy and formless fire, that fire which darts and flashes through the hidden depths of the Universe, hear thou the voice of fire.

(On reaching South, shake fire wand three times before the Fire Tablet. Trace enclosing circle. Inscribe within it the invoking Pentagram of Spirit active. Make LVX signs. Follow it with the invoking Pentagram of Fire. Salute with fire sign.)

OIP TEAA PEDOCE (oh-ee-pay tay-ah-ah pay-doh-kay). In the names and letters of the great southern quadrangle, I invoke ye. ye angels of the watchtower of the south.

(Again salute Tablet. Replace fire wand on altar. Go to the west, pick up the water cup, sprinkle a few drops in front of the Water Tablet, and circumambulate clockwise, saying:)

So therefore first the priest who governeth the works of fire must sprinkle with the lustral water of the loud resounding sea.

(On returning West, sprinkle a few drops of water in front of Water Tablet. Trace enclosing circle. Inscribe within it the invoking Pentagram of Spirit passive. Make LVX signs. Follow it with invoking Pentagram of Water. Salute with water sign.)

EMPEH ARSEL GAIOL (em-pay-hay ar-sel-gah-ee-ohl). In the names and letters of the great western quadrangle, I invoke ye, ye angels of the watchtower of the West.

(Again salute Tablet. Replace water cup on altar. Go to the East, clockwise, and pick up air dagger. Shake it three times in front of Air Tablet, then circumambulate, saying:)

Such a fire existeth, extending through the rushing of air. Or even a fire formless, whence cometh the image of a voice. Or even a flashing light, abounding, revolving, whirling forth, crying aloud.

(On returning East, shake air dagger three times in front of Air Tablet. Trace enclosing circle. Inscribe within it the invoking Pentagram of Spirit active. Make LVX signs. Follow it with invoking Pentagram of Air. Salute with air sign.)

ORO IBAH AOZPI (oh-roh ee-bah-hay ah-oh-zohd-pee). In the names and letters of the great eastern quadrangle, I invoke ye, ye angels of the watchtower of the East.

(Replace air dagger. Walk clockwise to north. Pick up pentacle or dish of bread and salt. Sprinkle salt or shake pentacle three times in front of Earth Tablet. Then circumambulate saying:) Stoop not down into that darkly splendid world, wherein continually lieth a faithless depth, and Hades wrapped in gloom, delighting in unintelligible images, precipitous, winding, a black ever-rolling abyss, ever espousing a body unluminous, formless and void.

(On returning to the north, shake Pentacle three times in front of Earth Tablet. Trace enclosing circle. Inscribe within it the invoking Pentagram of Spirit passive. Make LVX signs. Follow it with invoking Pentagram of Earth. Salute with earth sign.)

EMOR DIAL HECTEGA (ee-mor dee-ahl hec-tay-gah). In the names and letters of the great northern quadrangle, I invoke ye, ye angels of the watchtower of the north.

(Replace pentacle. Walk around altar to west and face east.)

Either with wand or forefinger of right hand describe enclosing circle in air over the altar, and trace four Pentagrams of Spirit, two actives and two passives, saying:) EXARP (ex-ar- pay), BITOM (bay-ee-toh-em), NANTA (en-ah-en-tah), HCOMA (hay-coh-mah). In the names and letters of the mystical Tablet of Union, I invoke ye, ye divine forces of the spirit of life.

(Make Portal sign of the rending of the veil over the altar. Stretch out hands, then separate them as if opening a curtain. At this point vibrate the short Enochian invocation from the Portal Ritual. Follow it with:)

I invoke ye, ye angels of the celestial spheres, whose dwelling is in the invisible. Ye are the guardians of the gates of the universe, be ye also the guardians of this mystic sphere. Keep far removed the evil and the unbalanced. Strengthen and inspire me so that I may preserve unsullied this abode of the mysteries of the eternal Gods. Let my sphere be pure and holy so that I may enter in and become a partaker of the secrets of the Light divine.

(Go to northeast, and announce:)

The visible sun is the dispenser of light to this earth. Let me therefore form a vortex in this chamber that the invisible sun of the spirit may shine therein from above.

(Circumambulate three times clockwise, beginning at east. Make the projecting sign (throw arms forward, straight from the shoulders, head bowed between them), each time you pass the East. Return to the west of the altar and utter the adoration. Make the projecting sign at the end of the first three lines. Make the sign of silence at the end of the fourth line, right arm hanging by your side, raise index finger of left hand to lips.)

Holy art Thou, Lord of the universe.
Holy art Thou, whom nature hath not formed.
Holy art Thou, the vast and the mighty One.
Lord of the light and the darkness.

(At this point, state in your own words the purpose for which you are performing the ceremony. Sit quietly facing the East, not passively, but in silence, attempting to feel the presence of the spirit above you, around you and within you.)

(When you feel ready, after whatever spiritual exercise you feel impelled to do, close the temple by reversing the circumambulations (widdershins), making the projecting sign each time you pass the East. Then perform the banishing rituals of the Pentagram and Hexagram.

An alternate method, which I use fairly frequently, is to sit on a chair in the east, facing westwards, and assume the god form of Tahuti while slowly reciting the invocation of Thoth in Crowley's Liber Israfel.)

VOLUME EIGHT

THE CONSECRATION CEREMONY OF THE VAULT OF THE ADEPTI

To be used for a new Vault or on each Corpus Christi Day

Members assemble and wear Regalia. Three Chiefs robed and seated as in opening of 5-6. Door of Vault closed; Pastos remains inside Vault, but Circular Altar is placed in the Outer Chamber, in the centre. Upon the Altar are the Cross, Cup, Dagger, and Chain as usual; also the crossed Scourge and Crook. Incense is also placed over letter Shin. Water is placed in the Cup.

Chief:

Associate Adeptus Minor, see that the Portal of the Vault is closed and guarded. (Done. Chief advances to Altar, lifts his Wand on high, and says:)

Chief:

HEKAS HEKAS ESTE BEBELOI! (This is followed by the Watchtower Ceremony.)

(After the Watchtower ceremony, the Chief Adept changes place with Third Adept. As the Hierophant Inductor, Third Adept performs the ceremony of the opening of Portal. Any other Adept may take the place of the Associate Officer in West.)

Third:

(Knocks 4, 1)

Very Honoured Fratres and Sorores, assist me to open the Portal of the Vault of the Adepti. Give the Signs of a Neophyte, Zelator. Theoricus. Practicus, Philosophus. Very Honoured Associate Adept, what is the additional Mystic Title bestowed on a Philosophus as a link with the Second Order?

Assoc:

Phrath.

Third:

To what does it allude.

Hodos:

To the fourth river of Eden.

Third:

What is the Sign?

Hodos:

The Sign of the Rending Asunder of the Veil.

Third:

What is the Word?

Hodos:

Peh.

Third:

Resh.

Assoc:

Kaph.

Third:

Tau.

Hodos:

The whole word is Paroketh, meaning the veil of the Tabernacle.

Third:

In and by that word, I declare the Portal of this Vault of the Adepts duly open. (Makes Qabalistic Cross. All make the same Sign and say same words. Replace Altar within Vault, leave Cross, Cup and Dagger in place outside for use in Obligation. Close door of Vault. Three Adepts take places and open in the 5-6 Grade. The Vault door is thus open and so remains until close of Consecration.)

Second:
Third:
Chief:
Second:

(All successively knock once.)

Chief:

Ave Fratres et Sorores.

Second:

Roseae Rubeae.

Third:

Et Aureae Crucis.

Chief:

Very Honoured Fratres et Sorores, assist me to open the Vault of the Adepts. (Knocks). Very Honoured Hodos Chamelionis, see that the Portal is closed and guarded.

Hodos:

(Does so, and salutes.) Merciful Exempt Adept, the Portal of the Vault is closed and guarded.

Chief:

Mighty Adeptus Minor, by what Sign hast thou entered the Portal?

Third:

By the Sign of the Closing of the Veil. (Gives it.)

Chief:

Associate Adeptus Minor, by what Sign hast thou closed the Portal?

Third:

By the Sign of the Closing of the Veil, (gives it.)

Second:

PEH.

Third:

RESH.

Second:

CAPH.

Third:

TAU.

Second:

PAROKETH.

Third:

Which is the Veil of the Sanctum Sanctorum.

Chief:

Mighty Adeptus Major, what is the Mystic Number of this Grade?

Second:

Twenty one.

Chief:

What is the Password formed therefrom?

Third:

ALEPH.

Chief:

HEH.

Third:

YOD.

Chief:

HEH.

Third:

EHEIEH.

Chief:

Mighty Adeptus Major, what is the Vault of the Adepts?

Second:

The symbolic burying place of our Founder Christian Rosenkreutz, which he made to represent the Universe.

Chief:

Associate Adeptus Minor, in what part of it is he buried?

Third:

In the centre of the heptagonal sides and beneath the Altar, his head being towards the East.

Chief:

Mighty Adeptus Minor, why in the-centre?

Second:

Because that is the point of perfect equilibrium.

Chief:

Associate Adeptus Minor, what docs the Mystic Name of our Founder signify?

Third:

The Rose and Cross of Christ; the fadeless Rose of Creation - the immortal Cross of Light.

Chief:

Mighty Adeptus Major, what was the Vault entitled by our more ancient Fratres and Sorores?

Second:

The Tomb of Osiris Onnophris, the Justified One.

Chief:

Associate Adeptus Minor, of what shape was the Vault?

Third:

It was that of an equilateral Heptagon or figure of Seven Sides.

Chief:

Mighty Adeptus Major, unto what do these seven sides allude?

Second:

Seven are the lower Sephiroth, seven are the Palaces, seven are the days of the Creation; Seven in the Height above, Seven in the Depth below.

Chief:

Associate Adeptus Minor, where is this Vault symbolically situated?

Third:

In the centre of the Earth, in the Mountain of Caverns, the Mystic Mountain of Abiegnus.

Chief:

Mighty Adeptus Minor, what is the meaning of this title Abiegnus?

Third:

It is Abi-Agnus, Lamb of the Father. It is by metathesis Abi-Genos, born of the Father. Bia-Genos, Strength of our Race, and the Four Words make the sentence. Mountain of the Lamb of the Father, and the Strength of our Race. IAO. YEHESHUAH. Such are the words! (All salute with 5-6 Signs.)

Chief:

Mighty Adeptus Major, what is the key to this Vault?

Second:

The Rose and Cross which resume the Life of Nature and the Powers hidden in the word I.N.R.I.

Chief:

Associate Adeptus Minor, what is the Emblem which we bear in our left hands?

Third:

It is a form of the Rose and Cross, the ancient Crux Ansata or Egyptian symbol of life.

Chief:

Mighty Adeptus Major, what is its meaning?

Second:

It represents the force of the Ten Sephiroth in Nature, divided into a Hexad and a Tetrad. The Oval embraces the first six Sephiroth and the Tau Cross the lower Four, answering to the four Elements.

Chief:

Associate Adeptus Minor, what is the Emblem which I bear upon my breast?

Third:

The complete symbol of the Rose and Cross.

Chief:

Mighty Adeptus Major, what is its meaning?

Second:

It is the Key of Sigils and of Rituals, and represents the force of the twenty two Letters in Nature, as divided into a Three, a Seven, and a Twelve. Many and great are its mysteries.

Chief:

Associate Adeptus Minor, what is the Wand which thou bearest?

Third:

A simple Wand having the colours of the twelve Signs of the Zodiac and surmounted by the Lotus Flower of Isis. It symbolizes the development of Creation.

Chief:

Mighty Adeptus Major, thy Wand and its meaning?

Second:

A Wand terminating in the symbol of the Binary and surmounted by the Tau Cross of Life, or the Head of the Phoenix, sacred to Osiris. The seven colours between Light and Darkness are attributed to the Planets. It symbolizes rebirth and resurrection from death.

Chief:

My Wand is surmounted by the Winged Globe, around which the twin serpents of Egypt twine. It symbolizes the equilibriated Force of the Spirit and the Four Elements beneath the everlasting Wings of the Holy One. Associate Adeptus Minor, what are the words inscribed upon the door of the Vault, and how is it guarded?

Third:

Post Centum Viginti Annos Patebo. After one hundred and twenty years I shall open, and the door is guarded by the Elemental Tablets and by the Kerubic Emblems.

Chief:

The 120 years refer symbolically to the 5 Grades of the First Order and to the revolution of the Power of the Pentagram; also to the five preparatory examinations for this Grade. It is written His days shall be 120 years. 120 divided by 5 yields 24, the number of hours in a day and of the Thrones of the Elders in the Apocalypse. Further 120 equals the number of the Ten Sephiroth multiplied by that of the Zodiac, whose Key is the working of the Spirit and the Elements typified in the Wand which I bear.

(Chief knocks. All face the East. Chief Adept opens the Vault wide, enters, passes to the Eastern end, where is the head of the Pastos of C. R. C., and then faces West. Second enters and passes to the South. Third to the North. Other members remain standing as before. The three Officers, each with a special Wand in his right hand and Crux Ansata in left, then stretch out their Wands to form a pyramid above the Altar and also the Cruces below.)

Chief:

Let us analyze the Keyword. I.

Second:

N.

Third:

R.

All:

I.

Chief:

YOD.

Second:

NUN.

Third:

RESH.

All:

YOD.

Chief:

Virgo, Isis, Mighty Mother.

Second:

Scorpio, Apophis, Destroyer.

Third:

Sol, Osiris, slain and risen.

All:

Isis, Apophis, Osiris. IAO.
(All then simultaneously separate Wands and Cruces and say:)

All:

The Sign of Osiris Slain. (Give it.)

Chief:

(Giving L Sign with bowed head). L. The sign of the Mourning of Isis.

Second:

(Giving V Sign with head erect.) V. The Sign of Apophis and Typhon.

Third:

(With bowed head gives X Sign). X. The Sign of Osiris Risen.

All:

(Make the Saluting Sign with bowed head.)

All:

L.V.X. LUX the Light of the Cross. (All quit the Vault and return to previous places.)

Chief:

In the Grand Word YEHESHUAH, by the Keyword I.N.R.I. and through the concealed Word LVX I have opened the Vault of the Adepts. (All give the LVX Signs).

Second:

Let the Cross of Obligation be set in its place.

Chief:

Upon this Cross of Obligation I, freely and unasked, on behalf of the Second Order, do hereby pledge myself for the due performance and fulfilment of the respective clauses of the Oath taken by each member on the Cross of Suffering at his admission to the Grade of Adeptus Minor

Second:

It is written: Whosoever shall be great among you shall be your minister, and whosoever of you will be the chiefest shall be the servant of all. I, therefore, on behalf of the Second Order, do require of you to divest yourself of your robes and insignia as a Chief Adept, to clothe yourself with the black robe of mourning, and to put the chain of humility about your neck. (Chief disrobes, puts on chain and is fastened to the Cross. Second recites the Obligation adding after do this day spiritually bind myself the words on behalf of the whole Second Order.)

Chief:

(While still bound). I invoke Thee, the Great Avenging Angel HUA to confirm and strengthen all the Members of this Order during the ensuing Revolution of the Sun, to keep them steadfast in the path of rectitude and self-sacrifice and to confer upon them the power of discernment, that they may choose between the evil and the good, and try all things of doubtful or fictitious seeming with sure knowledge and sound judgment.

Second:

Let the Chief Adept descend from the Cross of Suffering. (He is released and the cross removed.)

Second:

Merciful Exempt Adept, I, on behalf of the Second Order, request you to re-invest yourself with the insignia of your high office, which alone has entitled you to offer yourself unto the Higher Powers as surety for the Order. (Chief Adept reclothes. Three Adepts enter the Vault, roll Altar aside, open lid of Pastos, put Book "T" upon the table. Chief steps into the Pastos, and stands facing the door. The three Adepts join Wands and Cruces.)

Chief:

I invoke Thee HRU, the Great Angel who art set over the operations of this Secret Wisdom, to strengthen and establish this Order in its search for the Mysteries of the Divine Light. Increase the Spiritual perception of the Members and enable them to rise beyond that lower selfhood which is nothing unto that Highest Selfhood which is in God the Vast One. (The three Adepts disjoin Wands and lower them into the Pastos, joining them together at the black ends, directing them towards the centre of the floor. They hold Cruces as before.)

Chief:

And now, in the tremendous name of Strength through sacrifice, YEHESHUAH YEHOVASHAH. I authorize and charge ye, ye Forces of Evil that be beneath the Universe, that should a member of this Order, through will, forgetfulness, or weakness. act contrary to the Obligation which he hath voluntarily taken upon him at his admission that ye manifest yourselves as his accusers to restrain and to warn, so that ye, even ye, may perform your part in the operations of this Great Work through the Order. Thus therefore do I charge and authorise ye through YEHESHUAH YEHOVASHAH the name of Sacrifice. (The three Adepts disjoin Wands and Cruces. Chief steps out of Pastos.) Let the Pastos be placed without the Vault as in the third point of the Ceremony of Adeptus Minor. (Pastos is carried out into the outer chamber. Lid is removed and placed beside it. Chief stands between Pastos and Lid facing door of Vault, his arms crossed. Second stands at head of Pastos and Third at foot. Other Adepts form a circle round, join Wands over head of Chief, then separate Wands from head and give signs of 5-6 Grade.)

Chief:

(Slowly and loudly.) I am the Resurrection and the Life. He that believeth on Me, though he were dead, yet shall he live. And whosoever liveth and believeth on me shall never die. I am the First and I am the Last. I am He that liveth but was dead, and behold I am alive for evermore, and hold the Keys of Hell and of Death. (Chief quits circle, Second follows, then the other Members with Third last. All enter the Vault and proceed round the Altar with the Sun. Chief reads the sentences following and all halt in former positions, Chief in centre, others round.)

Chief:

For I know that my Redeemer liveth and that he shall stand at the latter day upon the Earth. I am the Way, the Truth and the Life. No man cometh unto the Father but by Me. I am the Purified. I have passed through the Gates of Darkness unto Light. 1 have fought upon Earth for good. I have finished my work. I have entered into the Invisible. 1 am the Sun in his rising. I have passed through the hour of Cloud and of Night. I am Amoun the Concealed One, the Opener of the Day. I am OSIRIS ONNOPHRIS, The Justified One. I am the Lord of Life, triumphant over death. There is no part of me which is not of the Gods. I am the Preparer of the Pathway, the Rescuer unto the Light. Out of the Darkness, let the Light arise. (At this point, the Chief Adept reaches the centre point between Pastos and Lid. He faces towards Vault, other Adepts around him. They join Wands over his head. He raises his face and hands, and continues:)

Chief:

I am the Reconciler with the Ineffable. I am the Dweller of the Invisible. Let the white Brilliance of the Divine Spirit descend. (Chief lowers face and hands. Other Adepts withdraw their Wands.)

Chief:

(Raising his hand). In the Name and Power of the Divine Spirit I invoke ye, ye Angels of the Watchtowers of the Universe. Guard this Vault during this Revolution of the Solar Course. Keep far from it the evil and the uninitiated that they penetrate not into the abode of our mysteries, and inspire and sanctify all who enter this Temple with the Illimitable Wisdom of the Light Divine. (Chief Adept gives Sign of 5-6. All others copy them and take their places as in the Opening of the Vault. Business may be conducted.)

CLOSING

(Pastos is replaced in Vault. Circular Altar is put over it. Door open.)

Chief:
Second:
Chief:
Second:
Third:

(All successively knock once.)

Chief:

Ave Fratres.

Second:

Roseae Rubeae.

Third:

Et Aureae Crucis.

Chief:

Very Honoured Fratres and Sorores, assist me to close the Vault of the Adepts. Associate Adeptus Minor, how many Princes did Darius set over his Kingdom?

Third:

It is written in the Book of Daniel that they were 120.

Chief:

Mighty Adeptus Major, how is that number found?

Second:

By the continual multiplication together of the first five numbers of the decimal scale.

Chief:

Post Centum Viginti Annos Patebo. Thus have I closed the Vault of the Adepts in the Mystic Mountain of Abiegnus.

Third:

Ex Deo Nascimur.

Second:

In Yeheshuah Morimur.

Chief:

Per Sanctum Spiritum Reviviscimus. (All present give LVX signs in silence.)

CONCERNING THE USE OF THE VAULT
By
G. H. FRATER FINEM RESPICE

The Vault of the Adepti may be said to represent or symbolise various things. First, of course, it is the symbolic burying place of our founder C.R.C. It is also the mystic Cavern in the Sacred Mountain of Initiation - Abiegnus. Therefore it is the Chamber of Initiation wherein, after passing through the preliminary training of the Outer, we are received into the Portal of the Rose of Ruby and the Cross of Gold.

All who are eligible should use the Vault when it is in its place. When working it is well to be clothed in the white robe and yellow sash, yellow slippers and yellow and white nemyss on your head. The Rose Cross Lamen should be upon the breast. Remember that within the Vault you **never** use a banishing ritual. The chamber is highly charged by the Ceremonies which have been held there, and the atmosphere thus created should not be disturbed.

At first. I do not recommend you to fast as a preliminary. Though later on, when you set yourselves to attain some definite point, this may be necessary. Being then clothed, and at peace, you enter the Vault, light the candle, and kindle either a pastile in the small censer or, if you prefer it, some incense in the larger one.

Place a chair as near East as you can, and having shut the door stand in the East facing West, the door by which you entered, the wall bearing the symbol of Venus. Now cross your hands upon your breast in the Sign of Osiris Arisen, breathe in a fourfold rhythm regularly, and compose your mind.

Then, being calm and collected, make the full LVX Signs, and endeavour to bring down the Divine White Brilliance. Having done this, seat yourself, and give yourself up to meditation, tranquil and without fear. At first try to feel, it may be, or to see the play of the colours as they pass and repass from side to side and from square to square. Then await with serene expectation what message may be vouchsafed you. When you are used to the vault it is well to extinguish the light, for the darker the material atmosphere the better it is. Before leaving the Vault make the LVX Signs, and quit it with arms crossed upon the breast in the Sign of Osiris Arisen.

If you have elected to work in a group of two or three, proceed in the same manner, but take care to place yourselves in balanced disposition. Let me warn you never to argue, even in a friendly manner while in the Vault. It may often happen that one of you sees more or less differently from the others. In this case make an audible note of the differences but do not go on to discuss it till you have ended the sitting, as any discussion is apt to disturb the delicate currents and so break the thread of your vision. It is permissible to take notes in writing during the sitting, but on the whole it is perhaps more satisfactory to impress everything clearly on your mind, and write it down immediately afterward.

The next seven visits should be devoted to a careful study of each side of the vault in turn, recalling all you know about each before you begin, and having your queries defined before you expect replies.

Another time, contemplate the roof, and if you feel strong enough, the floor. But it is best for you to have an advanced Adept with you for the latter. Again, you may wish to draw aside the Altar, lift the lid of the Pastos and contemplate the figure you may perceive lying within it. For this you should have a small candle lit on the Altar. Or you may lie down in the Pastos yourself and meditate there. Sometimes you may see the simulacrum of C.R.C. in the Pastos, or it may be your own Higher Self. In every case you should gain knowledge, power and satisfaction. If you do not, you may be sure you are either acting from a wrong motive, or you are not physically strong enough, or your methods are at fault. No normal person in a good state of mind can possibly spend half an hour in this way without feeling better for it. But if you should happen to be out of harmony with your surroundings or at variance with your neighbours, leave there thy gift before the Altar, and go thy way, first be reconciled.

When more than one person enters the Vault, they must all make the LVX Signs together.

MORE ABOUT THE VAULT

By

G.H. FRATER SAPERE AUDE

The Tomb or Vault is a small seven sided chamber with a black floor, a white ceiling. The Pastos lies with its head to the East; over it is the Circular Altar.

The accompanying plan (See Adeptus Minor Ritual) shows this position. The Altar bears the symbols of the four Elements -- a red, a yellow, a blue, and a black disc surrounded by a white Circle.

In the red Disc is a green Lion. In the yellow Disc is a purple Kerub of a man's Head. In the blue Disc is an orange Eagle. In the Black Disc is a white Ox.

These four discs surround the letter Shin which is painted in white in the centre, exactly under the White Rose in the middle of the ceiling.

Near this Shin stands a small crucifix. The carved ivory figure and the antique Florentine workmanship and the carved rose of 25 petals, behind the head, was made for this purpose in Venice.

The colours represent the interchanging energies of the Spirit and the Elements. This figure of Christ surmounted by the four Elements symbolises the perfected Adept who has so balanced his elemental nature that the Divine Spirit can manifest in him. (This is not a constant element in the symbolism of the vault. I.R.) The Cup, Dagger, Chain and Burning Lamp, each stationed in its own Element, simply repeat the same symbolism.

It should be observed that the Four elements are placed according to the Zodiac. That is to say, that Fire, Lion Kerub and Aries are to the East. Air. Man Kerub and Libra to the West. Water, Eagle Kerub and Cancer to the North. Earth, Bull Kerub, and Capricorn to the South.

This is the direction of the Enochian Tablets of the Elements and points to that to which the Adept should look when he wishes to visit Elemental or Astral regions. For a planet, it is better to find the actual position from an ephemeris in usual work. Sitting in the Tomb, it is sufficient to astrally rise through the white ceiling with the correct names and symbols and vibrating the former whilst doing so. The cubical Altar is an outer Temple and one arranged by an Adept, bearing the four implements and the four elements in a different order. This is according to the Winds.

Incense (or Rose) and Dagger, Air to the East. Water in Cup, Water to the West. Salt and Pentacle to the North. Lamp and Fire Wand to the South.

The Red Cross and White Triangle in the middle is the place of the letter Shin.

In the lesser Ritual of the Pentagram, the Archangels are arranged in the position of the elements in the Cubical Altar.

"Before me Raphael" is said facing East; he is the Archangel of Air. "Behind me Gabriel" is said facing West; he is the Archangel of Water. This arrangement is used in the invocation of any force in a Temple, or ordinary room. The Hierophant follows this rule in his invocation of the Elemental Spirits in the Outer Ceremonies.

For the Consecration of a Talisman, the Adept must look towards the East if he wishes to invoke the Powers of the Air. Though if he intends to visit those regions symbolised by the Vayu Tattwa or the Air Tablet, he must astrally fly westwards. This information is given in the Lesser Ritual of the Pentagram but in so complex a form that it is difficult to comprehend it clearly.

The separate clairvoyant study of these four circles on the Altar over the Tomb is extremely interesting. By it, the forces of the Elements on the active side can be observed symbolically and contrasted with the same on the passive side, as seen in the simple Tattwas. Instead of holding a paper symbol, the Adept can sit in the Tomb and feel himself pass through the selected disc having first invoked the Divine Names and used the suitable Pentagrams. By simply using the Pentagrams and vibrating the Deity Names allotted to it, the Blackness of the atmosphere of the Tomb can be so charged with the astral colours of the element, that it seems visible to the material eyesight.

It is necessary to balance the people sitting in the Tomb. The most practised should take the place at the head of the Pastos, with the beginner on either side. But where only two are working together, they should sit opposite each other at the sides or at the head and foot of the Pastos.

The Lotus Wand should be held by the white portion when Spirit is being invoked. When an Element is chosen, a suitable coloured band should be selected. After some practice, it is not difficult to find the correct band in the dark. At first it is better to hold it before extinguishing the light.

Even when first sitting in the Tomb, strange bluish balls of floating light, like phosphorus, will be seen by natural clairvoyants. These are not to be confused with the ordinary daylight remaining in the eyes when we go into a dark room.

CONCERNING THE CROOK AND THE SCOURGE

The Crook therefore is divided into the colours symbolic of Kether, Air, Chokmah, Taurus, Chesed, Leo, Tiphareth, Aries, Hod, Capricorn. The Scourge is divided into the colours symbolising Netzach, Tiphareth, Gemini, Binah, Cancer, Geburah and Water.

CONCERNING THE WALLS

Each Wall of the Tomb is said mystically to be 5 feet in breadth, 8 feet in height, thus yielding 40 squares, of which 10 are marked and salient representing the Ten Sephiroth in the form of the Tree of Life, acting through the planets.

(Note: There are various methods of colouring the sides. That here described is considered the best and most effective. But it requires perfect pigments and very great artistic skill in blending them. If not perfectly done, the result is dull and unluminous. And even pigments originally perfect, change with time. N.O.M.)

Another method and that used in the Amen-Ra Vault (in Edinburgh) is to form the symbol in its own colours placed on the square of its own color -- the planet on its own side being expressed in its complimentary colour. Thus the Venus symbol on the door side is red on a green ground. These colours cut from coloured paper, if accurate, are more brilliant than pigments.

Note that in all the central upper squares above remain white and unchangeable, representing the changelessness of the Divine Spirit, thus developing all from the One through the many under the government of the One.

The colour of the varying squares may either be represented by the colour of the Planet and the colour of the force therein being mixed together, or by these colours being placed in juxtaposition or in any other convenient manner, but the foundation of them all is under the Minutum Mundum Diagram.

The Spirit square on each side has the same outward appearance, but when studied clairvoyantly each will be found to have characteristics in harmony with the Planet, (that is, of the particular side.)

The Zodiacal squares are much better explained when the actual planet of that particular side is in the sign. Such as, during the month of August, Sol is in the sign of Leo. Then choose the Leo Zodiacal square on the Solar side, or any other planet in the same manner.

Those who are not familiar with pigments should be careful to examine the colour of the square that they are about to study and also the contrasting colour of the symbol therein. It is important that it should be clearly impressed on the mind before the Tomb is darkened.

(N.B. A great deal of the foregoing is unnecessarily complicated. The most practical plan is to have the walls of the Vault coloured as in the Adeptus Minor Ritual.

Then the way to differentiate between the various planetary sides of the Vault is simply to cover any particular side with a large sheet of strong cellophane or other plastic. So, for the Venus side, the painted wall could be covered with a Green sheet of plastic. For the Jupiter side with a blue sheet of plastic. For the Mars side with dark red. For the Saturn side with very dark blue or indigo. For the Solar side, use yellow or gold plastic. For Mercury, a yellow orange plastic, and for Luna, a lavender or light violet plastic.

In the 1890's there was no technology whereby this could be done. There is to-day. And this eliminates the fine shading of colour with delicate hues which requires a competent artist to depict. To-day, plastic sheets can be obtained in almost any color. This eliminates all the artistic difficulties involved, and simplifies the task by having all seven walls coloured in exactly the same manner. The different covering plastic sheets will demonstrate what planetary side of the Vault is involved. I.R.)

THE PASTOS

The Pastos which stands under the Circular Altar has no bottom but a hinged lid which can be turned back during the Second Point of the 5-6 Ceremony.

The inner surface bears the Colours of the Forces. Both the inner and the outer of the right side are in the positive Scale of Colours. To the left, they are in the negative Scale of Colours.

The head is white inside and out. Outside it bears the Red Rose of 49 petals on a Golden Greek Cross. Inside the 10 Colours of the Masculine Scale on the Sephiroth in the Tree of Life. The foot is black inside and out. Outside there is a calvary Cross on three steps with a circle. Inside, the 10 children Colours in the Sephiroth on the Tree.

VOLUME EIGHT

(N.B. Outside, Red Rose on golden cross, gold centre with green leaves. Foot: outside, white cross on a black ground. The coloured diagram of the Minutum Mundum is given in the section of coloured plates in this book. An understanding of Hodos Chamelionis is absolutely indispensable when considering the colouring of the Vault. I.R.)

THE SEVEN SIDES

The mere arrangement of the symbols of each side of the Tomb is at first sight difficult to comprehend and remember.

The first diagram given in the 5-6 ritual shows the Sephiroth alone, so as clearly to get the root of the matter into the memory. The second is a diagram with only the Kerubic rank, the Zodiac and the Planets. The third shows all the symbols.

The coloured diagram (from Hodos Chamelionis) is the key to every side, though it is not like any of them since the colour of the Planetary attribution of any one side modifies the basic pattern. Compared with the third diagram it will show the natural ground colour of every square.

On the sides of the Tomb these colours are each mixed with that of the Planet of that particular side. Every symbol is formed of the complementary colour of the square mixed with the complementary colour of the Planet of the side. A careful study of the diagrams will show the result of these mixtures.

These is some difficulty for those who are not used to pigments in comprehending the reason for the particular colours used on the sides of the Tomb. To make this clear, the seven solar squares have been selected as examples. In addition to this, there are added the two squares from the Venus side bearing the symbol Aquarius. The first is that in the Kerubic rank Air, Vau is yellow; the second is that below it, the fifth from the top, where it is the purple Aquarius of the Zodiac. Following is the complete side of Luna. The three Alchemical Principles are coloured thus: Sulphur is Pink; Salt is Pale Blue; Mercury is Pale Yellow.

These are blended on the sides of the Tomb in the same manner as the other squares.

The complemantary colours of the Planets Mars, Sun, Venus and Moon are easily understood. Mars red is the complement of Venus green. Sun orange is the complementary colour of Moon blue. But as there are 7 Planets, the exact complementary colour of each one cannot be always clearly expressed by that of another planet. Hence Saturn and Jupiter, indigo and purple, both have yellow for a complementary colour. Yet yellow. Mercury, is not exactly that of either of them. A careful study of the Zodiacal colours settles the question. Capricorn indigo is that of Saturn. Capricorn is opposite of Cancer, so that amber of Cancer is the complementary of indigo. Aquarius purple is the Jupiterian colour, Leo is opposite to Aquarius so that the complement of purple is greenish yellow. The Mercury yellow is not found in the Zodiac. This colour is the complementary of a very clear purple amethyst, neither bluish nor reddish.

The 'flash' of light from carefully balanced complementary colours is a matter of common optics. It is the shining from the blended rays, making a whiteness which in pigments would be blackness. It is a sign that the Talisman bears the correct colours. There is nothing occult about such a 'flash.' It is often seen on vulgarly effective advertisements, and is quite different from the Astral flash of brilliancy which shows when a Talisman is properly charged with the desired Force.

NOTES ON THE DIAGRAMS

The Lid of the Pastos. The upper half is on a white ground, flaming red sword, touches of red in glory. Malkuth in red and white circles; the rest in gold.

Lower half is on a black ground. The cross on gold, Sephiroth in white, red surrounds, glory white with red rim, also the crown. The figure flesh coloured. Letters INRI red on white. Dragon red and black. (These will be found in the colour plate section.)

CEILING OF VAULT

Colours pure white. Designs outlined in black. Rose said to be transparent so that light could shine through to illumine the vault. (N.B. With modern technology, the transparent Rose could be designed from lucite or some other plastic. One modern temple is already experimenting with this idea. I.R.)

FLOOR OF VAULT

The ground is black. Letters in white on black ground. Triangle and Heptagram are white. Serpent is red. Cross gold. Rose red. Leaves green.

CIRCULAR ALTAR

Black ground. Shin is painted white. Leo Kerub is red with green Lion. Yod in white. Scorpio blue with orange Eagle. Heh white. Aquarius yellow with Man's head. Vau in white. Taurus black, white Ox. Final Heh in white. The lettering is in gold.

On the YOD should stand the Cross, and behind it the red Lamp. On the HEH should stand the Cup of Water. On VAU the Dagger. On HEH (f) the Chain. On White SHIN the Incense.

THE SYMBOLISM OF THE SEVEN SIDES
By
G.H. FRATER N.O.M.

Among those characteristics which are truly necessary in the pursuit of magical knowledge and power, there is hardly any one more essential than thoroughness. And there is no failing more common in modern life than superficiality.

There are many who, even in this Grade which has been gained by serious study, after being charmed and instructed by the first view of the Vault of Christian Rosenkreutz, have made no attempt to study it as a new theme. There are many who have attended many ceremonial admissions and yet know nothing of the attribution of the Seven Sides, and nothing of the emblematic arrangement of the forty squares upon each side.

Some of you do not even know that Venus is in an astrological sense misplaced among the sides, and not two in five have been able to tell me why this is so. Or what is the basis of the arrangement of the seven colors and forces. Many have told me which element of the four is missing. Others have told me that the sign Leo occurs twice, but very few have told me why the two forms of Leo are in different colours in each case, and only a few can tell me without hesitation which Three Sephiroth have no planet attached.

And yet even in the 1-10 grade you are told you must analyze and comprehend that Light or Knowledge, and not only take it on personal authority. Let us then be Adepti in fact, and not only on the surface. Let our investigations be more than skin deep. That only which you can demonstrate is really known to you, and that only which is comprehended can fructify and become spiritual progress as distinguished from intellectual gain. Unless you can perceive with the soul as well as see with the eye your progress is but seeming, and you will continue to wander in the wilds of the unhappy.

VOLUME EIGHT

Let your maxim be Multum non multa - Much rather than many things. And tremble lest the Master find you wanting in those things you allow it to be supposed that you have become proficient in. Hypocrisy does not become the laity. It is a fatal flaw in the character of the occultist. You know it is not only the teacher in this Hall before whom you may be humiliated, but before your Higher and Divine Genius who can in no wise be deceived by outward seeming, but judgeth you by the heart, in that your spiritual heart is but the reflection of his brightness and the image of his person, even as MALKUTH is the material image of TIPHARETH, and TIPHARETH the reflection of the crowned Wisdom of KETHER and the Concealed One.

There are only a couple of pages in the 5-6 Ritual which refer to the symbolism of the Seven Sides of the Vault. Read them over carefully, and then let us study these things together. First, the Seven Sides as a group, and then the forty squares that are on each side.

The Seven Sides are all alike in size and shape and subdivision, and the forty squares on each side bear the same symbols. But the colouring is varied in the extreme, no two sides are alike in tint, and none of the squares are identical in colour excepting the single central upper square of each wall, that square bearing the Wheel of the Spirit. The Seven Walls are under the planetary presidency, one side to each planet. The subsidiary squares represent the colouring of the combined forces of the planet. The symbol of each square is represented by the ground colour, while the symbol is in the colour contrasted or complementary to that of the ground.

Now these planetary sides are found to be in a special order, neither astronomical nor astrological. The common order of the succession of the planets is that defined by their relative distances from Earth, putting the Sun, however in the Earth's place in the series thus: Saturn, Jupiter, Mars, Sun, Venus, Mercury, Moon. Saturn is farthest from the Earth, and the Earth is between Mars and Venus. Beginning with Saturn in the case of the Walls of the Vault, the order is Saturn, Jupiter, Mars, Sun, Mercury, Venus, Moon. Here Mercury and Venus are transposed.

But there is something more than this. For Saturn, the farthest off, is neither the door nor the East, nor anywhere else that is obviously intended. For it is the corner between the South and the Southwest sides. Nor is Luna, at the other end of the scale, in any notable position on the old lines.

There is, then, a new key to their order to be found and used, and such as are very intuitive see it at a glance. The planets are in the order of the Rainbow colours, and in colours because this Adeptus Minor grade is the especial exponent of colours. You Adepti are in the Path of the Chamelion - Hodos Chamelionis.

If now you take the planetary colours and affix the planets and arrange them in the order of the solar spectrum and then bend up the series into a ring and make the chain into a Heptagram, and turn the whole about until you get the two ends of the series to meet at the Eastern point, you will have this mysterium:

Violet - Jupiter. Indigo - Saturn.
Blue - Moon. Green - Venus. Yellow - Mercury.
Orange -Sun. Red - Mars.

Science teaches, and has rediscovered a great truth, that however valuable the seven colours of the prism may be, there are rays invisible to us and so not demonstrated here by space. Beyond the red end of the spectrum begins the violet, and these have a great chemical or Yetziratic force. These forces, ever present and unseen, are represented by the Chief Adept standing erect at the Eastern angle, the most powerful person in the

31

group, and delegate of the Chiefs of the Second Order, and through them of the mystic Third Order. He it is who has, symbolically at any rate, passed from death unto life, and holds the keys of all the creeds. And he it is who may place in our hands the Keys of the locked Palace of the King if we are able to make our knocking heard. Representing the East, he faces the Western World, bringing intuition with him. Before him lies the symbolic body of our Master C.R.C., our grand exemplar and founder, or at other times, the empty Pastos, from which he has arisen, the Chief Adept.

He has Mars and GEBURAH at his right hand, and Jupiter and GEDULAH at his left hand. He faces Venus in the West, the Evening Star, which represents the entry of the Candidate who has toiled all day until the evening. At even he enters the Western door of the planet Venus, that sole planet unto whose symbol alone all the Sephiroth are conformed. At evening time there shall be light, the light of the mixed colours. So the newly admitted Adept comes in contact with the totality of the planetary forces for the first time. A great opportunity opens before him. Let him see well that he use it worthily. He enters through the green side of the Vault. Green is the colour of growth. Let him see that he grows.

Upon each side of the Vault are forty squares, five vertical series and eight horizontal, the whole being symbolically 5' × 8.' Now the published and printed Fama Fraternatitas says these forty feet were divided into ten squares. If you are mathematicians you would know that ten similar squares could not alone be placed in such an area and yet fill it. Ten squares alone to fill a rectangle could only be placed in an area of the shape 5' x 6.' Hence in the Fama, ten squares is a blind which we know to represent Ten Squares are marked and salient, that is they are the SEPHIROTH.

Besides the Ten Sephiroth, there are the following: There are the Four Kerubim, Three Alchemical Principles, Three Elements, Seven Planets, Twelve Zodiacal Signs, One Wheel of the Spirit, thus 40 Squares in all. The Spirit Wheel is on every side and always in the centre, and is always depicted unchanged in black upon white.

Upon the sides there are always the Four Kerubic emblems Zodiacal, yet different, for the Eagle replaces Scorpio. (Scorpio has three forms, the Scorpion, the Eagle, and the Snake for the Evil Aspect.)

These Kerubim represent the letters of the name YHVH and note that they are always arranged in the Hebrew Order of the letters. Yod for the Lion, Heh for the Eagle, Vau for the Man, Heh final for the Ox, the Tauric Earth.

Note that these four Zodiacal signs are not in their own colours, but as symbols of the Elements have elementary colours.

As Zodiacal signs then, they are found to be compounds of the Zodiacal and Planetary colours; but they are here as Kerubic emblems compounded of the Elemental colour and the Planetary colour of the side.

The Three Principles are composed of the colour of the alchemical Principles and the colour of the Planet of any particular wall. Mercury being fundamentally blue. Sulphur red, and Salt yellow.

The Three Elements have fundamentally the usual three colours, Fire red, Water blue, Air yellow. Note that Earth is missing.

The Seven planets have their colours as are often stated, and note that each of the seven is set beside its appropriate Sephirah, so that there are three Sephiroth which have no Planet: KETHER, CHOKMAH, and MALKUTH.

The Twelve Zodiacal Signs are the lower portion of the sides of the vertical column. The central one has none of the twelve; they are so allotted between the four remaining columns. Further note that there are only three ranks, the 5th, 7th, and 8th. None are in the 6th rank from above.

VOLUME EIGHT

This arrangement then shows: Four Triplicities and three Quaternaries. Observe well the arrangement; it is complex but not confused.

1. KERUBIC. Fixed. Shining Rank.
2. CARDINAL. Fiery. Solar Rank.
3. COMMON. Mutable. Airy Subtle Rank.

From above down, or in Columns these are: Earthy Signs. Airy Signs. Watery Signs. Fiery Signs.

Rank 5. The KERUBIC line show the signs in the order of TETRAGRAMMATON read in Hebrew.

Rank 7. The Cardinal line shows the signs from the right in the order of astronomical sequence of the solar course: vernal equinox, summer solstice, autumnal equinox, and winter solstice.

Rank 8. The Common line shows the signs again in a different position. Here the earliest in the year is Gemini on the left of MEM, and passing left to Virgo, you then go round to extreme right to Sagittarius, pass centreward to Pisces close to MALKUTH.

The rationale of 4 and 6 will be evident with a little study in the chart of any wall of the Vault.

The colouring of each square is dual, a ground colour, and the colour of the emblem. The ground colour is a compound of the colour of the Planet of the side tinting the colour of the Force to which the Square is allotted.

Each side has the Square of its own Planet in its own unmixed colour, and with this exception all the coloured grounds are compound. The Emblem colour is always complementary to the ground colour.

The Ritual of the Adeptus Minor gives the definite colours of each planet and sign which are to be used in this system. There are other allotments of colour to each of these symbols and forces, but these are retained as mysteries yet to be evolved and revealed when you have become familiar with the present simple and elementary system.

REQUIESCAT IN PACE
By

V.H. SOROR S.I.A.A.

Arrange the Temple as in the Neophyte Grade, save that the four elemental weapons are placed in their respective positions. Perform the Ceremony of the Opening by Watchtower, as given in some portion of this book.

1. Announce **HEKAS HEKAS ESTE BEBELOI.**

2. Banish first by Pentagram and then by Hexagram.

3. Open by Watchtower in full.

4. After Adoration perform the Invoking Ritual of the Hexagram, using the Unicursal hexagram of the planet Saturn, which represents the entire Supernal region.

5. When doing the Ritual, endeavor to evoke as much emotion as possible - although as a rule, not much effort will be found necessary as the Ritual itself, to gain peace for the departed, will produce a great deal of affect.

6. Proceed with the following Invocation of the Higher:

From thine hands, O Lord, cometh all good. From Thine hands flow down all grace and blessing. The characters of Nature with Thy finger hast Thou traced, but none can read them unless he hath been in Thy school. Therefore, even as servants look unto the hands of their masters, and handmaidens unto their mistresses, even so do our eyes look up unto Thee, for Thou alone art our help, O Lord of the Universe. All is from Thee, all belongeth unto Thee. Either Thy love or Thine anger all must again re-enter. Nothing canst Thou lose, for all must tend to Thine honour and majesty. Thou art Lord alone, and there is none beside Thee. Thou doest what Thou wilt with Thy mighty arm, and none can escape from Thee. Thou alone helpest in their necessity the humble and meek-hearted and poor who submit themselves unto Thee; and whoever humbleth himself in dust and ashes before Thee, unto such a one art Thou propitious. Who should not praise Thee, O Lord of the Universe, unto Whom there is none like, Whose dwelling is in the Heavens and in every virtuous and god fearing heart.

O God,the Vast One. Thou art in all things. O nature, Thou Self from nothing, for what else can I call Thee. In myself I am nothing, in Thee I am Self, and exist in Thy Selfhood from Nothing. Live Thou in me and bring me unto that Self which is in Thee, Amen.

(Pause to become aware of the Higher.)

The purpose of this Ceremony of Light is to enable our Frater (vel Soror.. .give the name of the deceased) who has shuffled off the burden of this earthly body, to find his proper place in the hereafter. Suffer thine Angels, and all those higher beings whom we have invoked in this ceremony, to take him (or her) under their wings for safekeeping, and to guard him (or her) so that no harm may befall him (or her). Let them guide our dear departed Frater (vel Soror) to a full realization of the clear Light of the Spirit so that in his post-mortem state, none of the benefits of his just terminated incarnation may be wasted, but that the essence of his experience may be incorporated into his divine being for evermore. Let thine Angels take charge of him (or her) and thus enable him to fulfil his destiny and his true will.

(At West of Altar, facing East, trace Invoking Unicursal hexagram of Saturn with appropriate Sigil, and say:)

VOLUME EIGHT

O all ye Angels assembled here in this Temple infuse me with your spiritual power and light, and let a veil be drawn between my heart and the outer and lower world - a veil woven from a silent darkness as a shrouded night bringing a turbulent sea to a final rest. Envelop this Temple of the divine mystery with your guidance and protection that 1 may concentrate my vision upon the ineffable glory of the Supernals to find my abiding security in their transcendent foundation. Grant unto me the power of the spirit to bring the brilliance of the eternal splendour to one who has now entered into the Invisible. Lift me up, I beseech thee, so that I may become the divine messenger of peace and harmony of the higher spheres to our departed Frater (vel Soror. . .whose name should now be given). Wherever he (or she) may now be, and on whatever plane he may now pursue the quest of his (or her) Divine Genius, let him be blessed with a diviner rest and a much sought after peace. (A photograph of the deceased, if one is available, should be placed on the Altar, resting on the white triangle and cross. If not available, visualize the deceased at the East facing the West and invoke):

I invoke thee by the divine name IAO, thou great Angel HRU who art set over the operations of this Secret Wisdom. Strengthen and establish. . .in his search for the divine Light. Increase his spiritual perception so that he may accomplish his True Will, and that thus he may be enabled to rise beyond all limitations unto that highest selfhood which is the Clear Light of the Spirit. (Pass to the East of the Altar, making Rose Cross over the Instruments adjacent to the Elements, vibrating the Enochian spirit Invocation first, Ol Sonuf etc. and then make the Qabalistic Cross).

For Osiris Onnophris who is found perfect before the Gods hath said: These are the elements of my Body perfected through suffering, glorified through trial. The scent of the dying Rose is as the repressed sigh of my Suffering. And the flame-red Fire as the energy of mine undaunted Will. And the Cup of Wine is the pouring out of the blood of my heart, sacrificed unto Regeneration, unto the newer life. The bread and salt before me are as the foundations of my body which I destroy in order that it may be renewed. . . I am triumphant over Death, and whosoever partaketh with me shall with me arise. I am the Perfector of Matter, and without me the Universe is Not.

(Be silent for now. Visualize Kether, as in the Middle Pillar technique, as a sphere of brilliant white Light above the head. Then employ the speech of the Hierophant in the Neophyte Grade. Follow that with this speech from the Adeptus Minor Grade.)

Buried with that Light in a mystical death. Rising again in a mystical resurrection. Cleansed and purified through him our Master, O thou dweller in the Invisible. Like him, O pilgrim of the ages, hast thou toiled. Like him hast thou suffered tribulation. Poverty, torture, and death, have you passed through. They have been but the purification of thy heart. In the alembic of thine heart, through the athanor of affliction, seek thou the clear light of thy higher and Divine Genius. (Pass from the Altar, deosil, to the place of the Hierophant in the Neophyte Grade.) Go in peace, O beautiful and divine one, to a Body Glorified in resurrection and perfected in Light. Be the herald of the divine ones, knowing their speech among the living! Hesitate not before any region of the Invisible through which you must pass to attain to nearness of your Divine Genius, for it is only in that communion which is provided for thee, that a secure peace and an unknowable wealth may be found. Dwell thou in that sacred land that far-off travellers call Naught. O land beyond the milk of nature's breasts and the honey of her nurturing lips, that land beyond all perfection! Dwell thou therein with thy Lord Adonai forever!

O Lord of the Universe, the Vast and the Mighty One, ruler of the Light and the Darkness, we adore Thee and we invoke Thee. Look with favor upon this wanderer of the universe who is now before Thee, and grant Thine aid unto the highest aspirations of his Soul, to the glory of thine Ineffable Name.

(Slowly walk to the Altar, visualizing the brilliance of the White Light descending upon the photograph or the image of the deceased in the place of the Neophyte.) I come in the Power of the Light. I come in the Light of Wisdom. I come in the Mercy of the Light. The Light hath healing in its Wings. (Name deceased.) I tell you, Frater (vel Soror...) that as the Light can manifest from the darkness so by this ceremony shall the Light descend upon thee. Long hast thou dwelt in darkness. Quit the darkness and seek the Light. (Return to between the two Pillars, and visualize the deceased enveloped in the Clear Light.) (Circumambulate deosil, very slowly, intoning the speech of the Chief Adept in the Adeptus Minor Ritual).

I am the Resurrection and the Life. Whosoever believeth in me though he were dead, yet shall he live, and whosoever liveth and believeth in me, the same shall never die. I am the First and I am the Last. I am He liveth and was dead, and behold! I am alive for evermore and hold the keys of death and of hell.

For I know that my Redeemer liveth and that He shall stand at the latter days upon the earth. I am the Way, the Truth and the Life. No man cometh unto the Father save by me. I am the Purified. I have passed through the Gates of Darkness unto Light. I have fought upon Earth for Good, and have finished my Work. I have entered into the invisible.

(Vibrate YEHESHUAH YEHOVASHAH by the formula of the Middle Pillar. Circulate the energy before proceeding with the slow circumambulation around the Temple.)

I am the Sun in his rising, passed through the hour of cloud and of night. I am AMOUN the concealed One, the Opener of the Day. 1 am OSIRIS ONNOPHRIS the Justified One, Lord of Life triumphant over Death. There is no part of me which is not of the Gods. I am the preparer of the pathway, the Rescuer unto the Light. Out of the darkness, let the Light arise. (Pass between the Pillars, facing East.)

I am the Reconciler with the Ineffable, the Dweller of the Invisible. (Raise arms skywards, and vibrate the four Names from the Tablet of Union - silently, and then say:)

Let the White Brilliance of the Divine Spirit descend. (Stand West of the Altar, facing East. There visualize the deceased standing, clothed in white, and address him (or her) thus:)

Frater (vel Soror...) whosoever thou art in reality, and wheresoever thou now mayest be, by the power of the Spirit devolving upon me by my Grade as Adeptus Minor of the R. R. et A. C. and by this commemorative ceremony, I do project upon thee this ray of the divine white Brilliance that it may bring thee peace and joy and the ultimate rest in God. (Make the sign of the Enterer three times to project the Light).

Be thy mind open to the Higher.

Be thy heart a centre of the Light.

Be thy body a temple of the Holy Spirit.

(Pause. Make the Qabalistic Cross, and then give thanks as follows.) Unto Thee, Sole Wise, Sole Eternal and Sole Merciful One, be the praise and the glory forever, who has permitted our departed Frater (vel Soror...) who now standeth silently and humbly before Thee, to enter thus far into the sanctuary of Thy mystery.

Not unto us but unto Thy Name be the Glory. Let the influence of Thy angels whom we have called upon in Thy name descend upon his head so they may teach him the value of self-sacrifice that he shrink not in the hour of trial. But that thus his name may be written upon high and his Genius stand in the presence of the Holy Ones, in that hour when the Son of Man is invoked before the Lord of Spirits and his name in the presence of the Ancient of Days.

(Go to the Altar) And now in the Name and Power of the Divine Spirit, I invoke ye, ye Angels of the Watchtowers of the Universe, and charge ye by the divine name YEHESHUAH YEHOVASHAH to guard this sphere of our dearly beloved Frater (vel Soror. . .) Keep far removed the evil and the unbalanced that they penetrate not into his spiritual abode. Inspire and sanctify him so that he may enter in to the centre of his being and there receive the vision of the Clear Light and thus accomplish his True Will.

(Pause for some time meditating on bringing the Light to the deceased, and then close by the usual formulae of the Watchtower Ceremony.)

AN ALCHEMICAL RITUAL

By

PERMISSION OF MR. FRANCIS KING

The Temple is arranged as in the Neophyte grade of the G.D. in the Outer. The Alchemist announces 'Hekas, Hekas este Bebeloi.' Then open the Temple by Watchtower.

The Alchemist then places the material basis in a flask and after the invocation of a blind Jupiterian force, leaves it sealed, in a gentle heat for three days. At the end of this period he evokes a Jupiterian spirit and then fastens a Liebig condenser to the flask. After distillation he grinds the solid left in the flask to a powder, replaces it in its original container and pours on to it the distilled fluid. He then reseals the flask.

The Alchemist places the flask upon a Flashing Tablet of Jupiter and, standing at the East of the Altar, places his left hand upon it. Holding his Lotus Wand by the Aries band, in his right hand, the Alchemist conjures the general forces of Chesed to act within the flask, making the required signs and sigils with the Wand. When finished he raises the flask in the air with both hands saying 'Arise herein to action, ye Forces of the Light Divine.'

The Alchemist now lets the sealed flask remain at a gentle heat in a waterbath until the material basis turns completely black and, when this has been achieved, he places the flask upon the North of the Altar and invokes Saturn. Then he takes his Lotus Wand by the black band and says: 'The Voice of the Alchemist said unto me, let me enter the Path of Darkness for thus may I achieve the Realm of Light.'

The Alchemist then again gently distils the material basis and, once again, returns the liquid to the solid, re-sealing the flask and placing it in a waterbath until all is re-dissolved. The Alchemist then takes the flask to the West of the Altar and invokes Cauda Draconis and the Waning Moon. He places the flask upon a Flashing Tablet of Luna and places it exposed to the moonlight for nine nights, the first night being that of the full Moon. The material basis is then distilled and re-dissolved as before.

The Alchemist then takes the flask to the East of the Altar and invokes the waxing Moon and Caput Draconis, then he replaces the flask on the Tablet of Luna and leaves it exposed to the moonlight for nine nights, this time the last night being that of the full moon. Again the material basis is distilled and re-dissolved.

The Alchemist takes the flask to the South of the Altar and invokes the forces of Tiphareth and Sol, after which, the Sun being in Leo, the flask is exposed to the Sun for six days from 8:30 a.m. to 8:30 p.m., while standing upon the appropriate Flashing Tablet. Afterwards the flask is stood again upon the Altar and the Alchemist says: 'Child of Earth, long hast thou dwelt in Darkness, quit the Night and seek the Day.' He then takes the Lotus Wand by the white band, making the correct signs and sigils and says: 'I formulate in thee the Invoked Forces of Light' reciting the Words of Power from the Great Enochian Watchtowers.

The Alchemist now evokes an elemental from the material basis and checks by the nature of its colouring whether the material basis has reached the correct condition. If it has not done so he repeats the lunar and solar workings.

The Alchemist now holds the Lotus Wand over the flask and draws the Qabalistic Flaming Sword so that its point descends into the material basis. After this he stands the flask on the East of the Altar and invokes Mars. When the invocation is successfully completed, the flask is placed between the black and white Pillars of the Temple of the G.D. in the Outer, and remains there for five days upon a Flashing Tablet of Mars.

The Alchemist again distills, but this time does not re-dissolve the solid which is, for the moment, kept separate. The fluid is taken and into it is invoked the forces of Mercury after which it is placed upon a Flashing Tablet and exposed to the Sun for eight days. The solid is ground up into a powder and into it is invoked the forces of Jupiter, after which it is left in the darkness upon the Flashing Tablet for four days.

Upon the Altar of the Double Cube the Alchemist places Flashing Tablets of Earth, Air, Fire and Water together with the Pantacle of Earth, the Wand of Fire, the Cup of Water, and the Dagger of Air. He then carries out the Greater Ritual of the Pentagram, firstly invoking Fire with the Wand to act upon the powder, secondly invoking Water with the Cup to act upon the liquid, thirdly invoking active and passive spirit with the White Band of the Lotus Wand to act upon both the powder and the liquid, fourthly invoking Air with the Dagger to act upon the liquid, and fifthly invoking Earth with the Pantacle to act upon the powder. The vessels are now left upon the Altar for five days.

The Alchemist then leaves the vessels untouched but removes the Elemental Tablets, replacing them with a white and gold Tablet of Kether. He identifies himself with his own Holy Guardian Angel and invokes Kether.

The powder and the liquid are now again joined together and exposed to the rays of the Sun for ten days. The flask is then replaced upon the Altar, standing upon a Flashing Tablet of Venus and the Alchemist invokes the forces of Venus. He then leaves the flask for seven days upon the Tablet, at the end of which period he places it in a water bath for a similar length of time.

The Alchemist again distills, the liquid being placed aside to serve as a medicine. The powder is placed by the Alchemist in a crucible and heated to white heat and allowed to slowly cool seven times, on seven consecutive days.

(Mr. King finally closes this ritual with the statement that "it only remains to add that according to the 'Book of Results' the end product was 'like unto a glittering powder' and that its use produced many and wonderful results.)

VOLUME EIGHT

EVOCATION OF THE ANGEL CHASSAN TO VISIBLE APPEARANCE
By

V.H. FRATER E. CINERE PHOENIX
PREREQUISITES

Before attempting this Evocation, the Zelator Adeptus Minor should have experience in the consecration of Talismans, Skrying and Traveling in the Spirit Vision, and the Assumption of God forms.

MATERIALS REQUIRED

Double Cubical Altar	Red Lamp
Hermetic Pillars	Water Cup
Magic Circle and Triangle of Evocation	Goblet of Red Wine
Earth Pentacle	Paten of Bread and Salt
Red Rose	Four Elemental Angelic Tablets
Yellow Rose Petals	Throne of Hierophant
Four Flashing Tablets of the Archangels	Dittany of Crete Incense
Galbanum Incense	Two Pantacles (4-4½ in.)
Vestments of Hierophant	Lamen (4-4½ in.)
Cross and Triangle for Altar	Green modeling clay (6 cubic in.)
Air Dagger	Air Fan
Yellow Rose	Yellow Ribbon (length 60 in.)
Fire Censer	Square Black Cloth (10x10 in.)
Peppermint	White Cord (18 in.)
Fire Wand	Four Censers
Gold Glitter (optional)	Tripod (optional)
Seven Yellow Lamps Aspen Leaves	Yellow Feathe
Aspen Leaves	

Aspen Leaves

Obverse

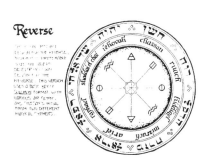

Reverse

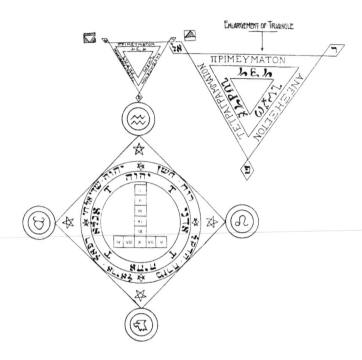

Note: The circle and triangle may be made from or painted on a sheet of linoleum, or plastic, coloured tape and chalk, etc.

TIME

(The Evocation of the Angel CHASSAN should be worked when the Moon is waxing in an Air Sign. If feasible, the Sun should also be in an Air Sign, and as Spring is the season most conducive to works of Elemental Air, the month of the Sun in Gemini would be ideal.

Wednesday is the day most appropriate to Air Operations, though Sunday is always appropriate to the workings of Adepti Minores.

If the Magician wishes to follow the doctrine of the magical hours prescribed in the HEPTAMERON and other texts, he should divide the times of sunrise and sunset into twelve equal magical hours of the day, and likewise the time from sunset to sunrise into twelve equal magical hours of the night. On Wednesday, the magical hours of Mercury are the first and eighth hours of the day and the third and tenth hours of the Night. On Sunday, the hours of Mercury are the third and tenth hours of the Day and the fifth and twelfth hours of the Night.

If the Magician chooses to take the Tattwic tides into account, the Evocation should obviously coincide with the course of the Vayu Tattwa.

PREPARATION

For a week prior to the Evocation, the Magician should prepare himself in every way for the working. His meditations should every day include the contemplation of Elemental Air. He should be keenly aware of those Correspondences of Air which he encounters in his daily life. Once during the week he should utilize the Spirit Vision to Skry or Travel in the sphere of Elemental Air.

40

The Magician should prepare two Flashing Pantacles, a Lamen, and a Material Basis. The Pantacles should be identical in design, but different in colour. Both should bear on the obverse side the Sigil from the Rose of the Angel CHASSAN enclosed in three concentric circles, between which are inscribed the hierarchic Names of Elemental Air, and on the reverse side a second symbol of the Angel CHASSAN devised by the Magician. One of the Pantacles shoulc be painted in the Yetziratic Colour Scale of the Prince, and the other in the Assiatic Colour Scale of the Princess.

The Lamen should bear on the obverse the design of the great Lamen of the Hierophant, and on the reverse the same design as on the obverse of the Pantacles, though painted in the Briatic Colour Scale of the Queen. For the Material Basis, clay is excellent, both symbolically and practically. As a type of Earth, it is a symbol of the Assiatic manifestation to which the Magician calls the Spirit. It is also reminiscent of the Adamic Clay into which the Elohim breathed Life, and of the Golem of the Ashkenazic Qabalists. From a practical perspective, the Clay (preferably 'modeling clay' which doesn't harden) is eminently adaptable, for its receptive nature allows it to contain many other materials. It should have embedded in it the Elements of the Mystic Repast, or Magical Eucharist, which is partaken of in the final moments of the Neophyte Grade. It should also contains as many materials sympathetic to the nature of the Spirit to be evoked as are available to the Magician; in this case appropriate ingredients would include Galbanum, Peppermint, Aspen leaves, a small Topaz, a yellow feather and possibly a lodestone. For the Material Basis in the Evocation of an Air Spirit, the clay must be kept warm and moist. The Material Basis may be made in the colour of Air in the Assiatic Princess Scale by using an emerald green modeling clay sprinkled with gold 'glitter.' If the Magician is preparing for a particularly difficult operation, or if he intends for the Assiatic manifestation to continue for more than an hour, he may further charge the Material Basis by adding to the Clay an appropriate Powder prepared in an Alchemical process according to the Z-3 formulae.

On the day preceding the Evocation or earlier on the day of the operation, the Magician should bind together the Lamen, the two Pantacles, and the Material Basis with a yellow ribbon on which is embroidered or written in purple Hebrew letters the name CHASSAN, and should consecrate them together as Air Pantacles of CHASSAN according to the Formula of the Magic of Light contained in the Z.A.M. document Z-2 taking care that the Lamen is on top, beneath it the Yetziratic Pantacle, then the Assiatic Pantacle, and finally the Material Basis. After consecration, the Pantacles and Material Basis should be wrapped in a yellow silk cloth embroidered in purple Hebrew letters with the names SHADDAI EL CHAI and YHVH, along with the Kerubic symbol of AQUARIUS in an encircled Pentagram (invoking Air and Spirit Active). The Lamen should be kept with the Hierophantic vestments.

The Magic Circle and Triangle of Evocation should be prepared in conformity with the diagram provided. The area between the inmost and the middle concentric circles should be white, and inscribed in black with the four Divine Names attributed to the Four Quarters separated by four TAU crosses. The area between the middle and the outermost circles should be yellow and inscribed in purple with four Hexagrams and Names of the powers of Air - SHADDAI EL CHAI, YHVH, RAPHAEL, ARIAL, CHASSAN, RUACH, MIZRACH, HIDDEKEL.

In the middle of each Hexagram should sit a censer. The area between the outermost circle and the enclosing square should be yellow and inscribed in purple with four Pentagrams. In the middle of each Pentagram should burn a yellow lamp. The area in the four circles located at the angles of the square may be either white or in the Queen Scale colours attributed to the Elements. In each of the Elemental Circles should be placed a Flashing Tablet of the appropriate Archangel. In the midst of the Magic Circle should be a TAU cross of Ten squares.

On the TIPHARETH square should be the Altar of the Universe, and on the MALKUTH square the Throne of the Hierophant. The Throne is recommended largely due to the potentially exhausting nature of Evocation. The Magician may choose to avail himself of an Assistant to care for the Lamps and Censers and to keep the Implements available for the different stages of the Working. If so, he may provide the Assistant with a small side table on the HOD Square.

The Triangle of Evocation should be in the East between the Pillars of Hermes, and the apex of the Triangle should touch the Circle of RAPHAEL. The area between the inner pair of concentric triangles should be yellow, and inscribed in purple Enochian letters with the Three Great Secret Names of God borne on the Banners of the East. In each angle should sit a yellow lamp. The Area between the outer pair of triangles should be white, and inscribed in black Greek letters with the three Holy Words PRIMEUMATON, ANEPHEXETON, and TETRAGRAMMATON. The area in the parallelograms located at the angles of the Triangle should be sky-blue and the letters of the name RAPHAEL therein should be dark orange. In the midst of the innermost Triangle should stand a Tripod to elevate the Material Basis.

Before beginning the Evocation, the Magician places the Material Basis in the Triangle with the Assiatic Pantacle planted in the front top of the Material Basis so that it will be clearly visible to him from the Circle. He then places the Yetziratic Pantacle on the Altar.

Finally he should be absolutely certain that all that he will need is in the Magic Circle, for once he begins the actual Evocation, he MUST NOT leave the Circle until the working is completed.

Now may the Magician begin the Evocation of the Angel CHASSAN to Visible Appearance.

(N.B. Those NAMES which are rendered in all capital letters are to be vibrated according to the Vibratory Formula of the Middle Pillar.)

THE WORKING

(The Magician opens by Watchtower, taking care that he not proceed until each portion of the Opening is successful, for without a proper Opening, the remainder of the Ritual is at best useless and at worst dangerous. He then faces East and states the Purpose of the Ceremony.)

The purpose of this Operation of the Theurgic Arts is four fold. One (knock): that there may be enhanced within me the virtues governed by the Powers of Air - keenness of mind, clearness of perception in intuition and psychism, and accuracy in divination - that 1 may better labour in the Great Work.

Two (knocks): That 1 may be strengthened in the Power NOSCERE that 1 may have knowledge to aid the ignorant.

Three (knocks): That I may receive guidance to further the Work of the Order in the Aquarian Age.

Four (knocks): That I may obtain the obedient service of that worthy and laudable Angel CHASSAN, that there may be peace between him and me, and that he may always come promptly to my call when summoned. So mote it be! (Knocks).

In the name of the Lord of the Universe Who works in Silence and whom naught but Silence can express, I declare this Temple of the Magic of Light duly open. (A battery of knocks 4, 3, and 3.)

(The Magician assumes the Sign of Osiris Slain.)

I invoke Thee, the great avenging Angel HU A to confirm and strengthen me during the ensuing Ritual, to keep me steadfast in the Path of the Magic of Light, and to confer upon me the Power of Discernment, that 1 may choose between the evil and the good, and try all things of doubtful or fictitious seeming with sure knowledge and sound judgment.

VOLUME EIGHT

(The Magician circumambulates three times deosil, vibrating HU A and saluting in the East. He then returns West of the Altar, faces East and assumes the Sign of Osiris Risen.)

I invoke Thee, HRU, Thou great Angel who art set over the Operations of this Secret Wisdom, to strengthen and establish me in my search for the Mysteries of Divine Light. Increase my spiritual perception and enable me to rise beyond that lower selfhood which is nothing unto that highest Selfhood which is in God the Vast One.

(The Magician circumambulates three times deosil, vibrating HRU and saluting in the East. He then returns to the West of Altar and faces East.)

Be my mind open to the Higher.

Be my heart a centre of the Light.

Be my body a Temple of the Rosy Cross.

(The Magician performs the Qabalistic Cross. He then assumes the Sign of Osiris Slain, maintaining a firm formulation of a sphere of brilliant white Light overhead.)

O Thou great and blessed Augueides, mine own Angelic Guardian vouchsafe to descend from Thy lofty Sanctum of Light, bringing Thy holy influence and presence into this magical Temple, that I may behold Thy glory and enjoy Thy society and aid both now and evermore. O Thou that resides in the holy Palace of the Neschamah, Thou who knowest the innermost truths of my soul, Thou art my true link with the Divine, do Thou descend and be present. Indwell this my body that I have dedicated as a Temple unto Thee. O thou inner Sun that illumines all my being, Thou sacred Star that has guided my steps through the centuries, if ever I have merited Thy society, if ever my Work has found favor in Thy sight, bring hither Thy resplendent presence, O my beloved eternal Companion, Guardian of my sacred birthright I beseech Thee in the Great Name YEHESHUAH: Move! Descend! And fill this Vessel with Thy manifest Light. Let the white Brilliance of the Divine Spirit descend!

(The Magician then perforins the Middle Pillar. If he has entered the Collegium Spiritus Sancti, he assumes the Form of his Genius; if not, he assumes the generic Form of a Mighty Angel in white and gold robes wearing a hexagram crown. The Magician reaches both hands towards the East, saying:)

Stretch unto Me your Hands, O Ye Divine Ones, for I am transformed to a God in Your midst. (The Magician assumes the Sign of Osiris Risen.)

I am the First and the Last. I am He thatliveth and was dead, and behold! I am alive for evermore, and hold the Keys of Death and of Hell. I am the Sun in His rising I have passed through the Gates of Darkness unto the Golden Dawn of Light. I am He who liveth and triumpheth, Whose beginning is not nor end cannot be, Who shineth as a flame in the midst of your palaces and reigneth amongst you as the balance of righteousness and truth. I am enthroned in the Neschamah where the mortal and immortal are united in the Presence of the Ancient of Days. I have passed the Eternal Gate to the marriage of Heaven and Earth.

I am Truth and I am Life; through Me Man liveth. I am Father and Mother, the Father of Fathers, the Mother of Mothers. I am AMOUN, the Concealed One, the Opener of the Day. I am ASAR-UN-NEFER, the Justified One. I am He Who is clothed with the Body of Flesh yet in Whom is the Spirit of the Great Gods. I am the Lord of Life triumphant over Death. There is no part of Me which is not of the Gods. I am the Preparer of the Way, the Rescuer unto the Light.

(The Magician circumambulates deosil vibrating KHABS AM PEKHT. He circumambulates a second time vibrating KONX OM PAX. He circumambulates a third time vibrating LIGHT IN EXTENSION. He returns to the West of the Altar, faces East, and makes the LVX signs in silence. The Magician elevates the Fan in his left hand and the Dagger in his right.)

Let the Names and Symbols of the Powers of Air be proclaimed, that these Powers may be re-awakened in the Spheres of those present and in the Sphere of this Order - for by Names and Images are all Powers awakened and re-awakened. (Trace Invoking Pentagrams of Spirit Active and of Air to the East.) YHVH. the Vast and Mighty One, (Inscribe Sigil from the Rose to the East.) Thy Glory flows out rejoicing to the ends of the Universe.

SHADDAI EL CHAI, Almighty and Everlasting God. (Inscribe Sigil from Rose to the East.)

Everliving be Thy Name, ever magnified in the Life of All.

RAPHAEL, Healing Hand of God. (Inscribe Sigil:) Blessed be Thy Name unto the countless Aeons.

ARIEL, noble Lion of God. (Inscribe Sigil:) Ruler of the Winds and of the Angels of the Air.

CHASSAN, worthy Angel of the Orders of the Air. (Inscribe Sigil:) Who ridest upon the Zephyr.

PARALDA, King of the Elementals of Air. (Inscribe Sigil:) Majestic Master of the aerial hosts of the Sylphs.

RUACH, Element of Air. (Inscribe Sigil:) Thou Wind, Spirit, and Breath of Life.

HIDDIKEL, River of Wisdom. (Inscribe Sigil:) Rushing Torrent of Paradise.

MIZRACH, the Eastern Quarter. (Inscribe Sigil:) The Place of the Powers of Air. (The Magician circumambulates thrice deosil, while invoking:)

Come near, ye Gods, to hear; and hearken, ye Angels and Spirits. Let the Heavens hear, and all that are therein. I invoke ye, Ye Powers of Air, in the mighty names YHVH and SHADDAI EL CH AI, to lend Your aid to the servant of the Highest in this Evocation of the Angel CHASSAN to Visible Appearance. (The Magician returns to the West of the Altar, faces East, and assumes the Sign of Osiris Slain.)

I, E CINEREPHOENIX, a Frater of the Rose of Ruby and the Cross of Gold, a faithful and devoted servant of that blessed Order which extends even unto the foot of the Throne of the Highest, do before Ye all bind myself by this my Oath, that Ye may know my purpose to be worthy.

I swear that this Work of Evocation is not undertaken for the purposes of evil or self-seeking, nor low material gain, nor earthly pleasure, but is undertaken as a joyous labour in that Great Work to which I am most solemnly pledged. I swear and affirm that 1 shall evoke the Angel CHASSAN for the purposes of enhancement of the Virtues of Air, strengthening of the Power NOSCERE to aid the ignorant, reception of guidance to further the Work of the Order in the Aquarian Age, and retention of the service of the Angel for the future workings of a kindred nature.

So do I swear by the Firmament of Heaven. Let the Powers of Air witness my pledge.

(Continuing to be aware of the energies invoked into the vortex of the Circle, the Magician faces the Quarter in which the Triangle of Evocation is located. In his left hand he holds the Yetziratic Pantacle of CHASSAN, and in his right hand the open Fan. With the Fan, he wafts the billows of incense towards the East between the Pillars.)

CHASSAN, CHASSAN, CHASSAN.

I seek Thee, CHASSAN, Thou Angelic Dweller in the sphere of Elemental Air. (Close the Fan, and with it trace a deosil circle of yellow light to the East.)

I seek Thee by the mighty Tetragrammaton, in the Most Holy Name YHVH. (In the Circle, trace the equilibriating Pentagram of Spirit Active:)

I seek Thee in the Everliving Name of SHADDAI EL CHAI (Trace the Invoking Pentagram of Air. Raise the Fan on high and open it.)

I seek thee CHASSAN, in Thy Yetziratic abode in the Names of Those who govern Thy Works - in the name of the blessed Archangel RAPHAEL, (Shake Fan towards the East.) and of the Ruler of the Angels of the Air, the mighty ARIEL. (Shake Fan once towards the East.)

I seek Thee, O Angel CHASSAN, by the power symbolized in the Sign of Kerubic Air, the ancient Glyph named in Hebrew ADAM and in Coptic PHRITITHI.

(With closed Fan, trace the Kerubic Sign of Aquarius in yellow light in the circled Pentagram. At this point, the Magician should visualize the area of the Gateway between the Pillars growing dark and cloudy with swirling mists. Replace the Fan on the Altar, and hold the Yetziratic Pantacle in both hands. Look into the swirling mists of the Gate and focus your Will on the purpose of the Evocation. Charge your Middle Pillar Centres once more with a ray of Kether brilliance. Visualize and feel the deosil current of yellow-glowing energy throbbing in the Magic Circle.)

I have sought Thee CHASSAN, and by virtue of this consecrated Pantacle (Hold the Yetziratic Pantacle on high in both hands. See the yellow Light playing about it.) and by virtue of this Thy Sigil, (With the Pantacle trace the Sigil from the Rose of CHASSAN in the Circled Pentagram to the East. The swirling mists between the Pillars should grow lighter.) and by virtue of Thine own true Name which I vibrate through the Gate of the East into the Yetziratic Realm of RUACH, 1 have found Thee CHASSAN! (Make Projecting Sign.) CHASSAN! (Projecting Sign.) CHASSAN! (Projecting Sign.)

(Make Sign of Silence. The three projections of force from the highly charged Magic Circle will disperse the mists and a landscape will become visible through the Gateway. The Magician assumes the Sign of Osiris Risen.)

O Lord of the Universe-Thou art above all things
And Thy Name is in all things; and before Thee,
The Shadows of the Night roll back and the Darkness hasteth away.

(The landscape through the Gate should now be clearly visible. It is a hilly countryside beneath a sky of scudding clouds lit from beneath with the rosy and golden tints of dawn. The hill in the foreground is surmounted by an ivy-decked tower rising above the evergreens. High on a tower, a large cut-glass window bearing the Air Glyph catches and reflects the light of dawn. On closer inspection, one sees that several hills in the distance are also crowned with towers, and one sees against the sky the silhouettes of large birds - no, they are Angels and Sylphs - flying gracefully from tower to tower. The Magician should have a strong sense that the tower in the foreground is the abode of CHASSAN. The Magician should now test the Vision with the Signs of the Lords who Wander. Once sure of contact, the Magician wraps the Yctziratic Pantacle in black cloth, binds it with a white cord passed around it thrice, and places it on the white triangle on the Altar.)

O Thou Angel CHASSAN, in the Names of SHADDAI EL CHAI and YHVH, I wrap Thee in Darkness and bind Thee with bonds of Light. Thine eyes are blind save to this Gate to the Hall of Maat. Thine ears are deaf save to my Call. Thy tongue is mute save to answer this Evocation. Thy feet are lame save to bear Thee to the Triangle of Art prepared to receive Thee. By all the Powers of Air, 1 evoke Thee, Thou mighty Angel CHASSAN, to manifest in a physical form in the Triangle without this Magic Circle! SHADDAI EL CHAI! SHADDAI EL CHAI! SHADDAI EL CHAI!

Spirit of Life. Spirit of Wisdom, Whose breath giveth forth and withdraweth the form of all things. Thou Who before Whom the life of beings is but a shadow which changeth and a vapour which passeth. Thou, who mountest upon the clouds and who walkest upon the wings of the Wind. Thou, Who breathest forth Thy breath and endless space is peopled. Thou, Who drawest in Thy breath and all that cometh from Thee returneth unto Thee. Ceaseless Motion in eternal Stability, be thou eternally blessed!

We praise Thee and we bless Thee in the changeless empire of created light, of shades, of reflections, and of images. And we aspire without cessation unto Thine immutable and imperishable brilliance. Let the ray of Thine intelligence and the warmth of Thy love penetrate even unto us! Then that which is volatile shall be fixed; the shadow shall be a body; the Spirit of Air shall be a soul; the dream shall be a thought. And no more shall we be swept away by the tempest, but we shall hold the bridles of the winged steeds of dawn. And we shall direct the course of the evening breeze to fly before Thee! O Spirit of Spirits! O Eternal Soul of Souls! O imperishable Breath of Life! O creative Sign! O Mouth which breathest forth and withdrawest the life of all beings, in the flux and reflux of Thine eternal Word, Which is the divine Ocean of movement and of truth!

(The Magician circumambulates thrice deosil while saying:)

In Thy most Holy Name of SHADDAI EL CHAI, I invoke and beseech Thee to look with favour upon this Work of Sacred Magic and to grant Thine aid unto the higher aspirations of my soul. I beseech Thee to charge Thy great Archangel RAPHAEL, and the Ruler of the Angels of Air, ARIEL, to aid in the successful culmination of this work that I may, with the Divine aid, truly evoke Thine Angel CHASSAN to visible manifestation.

(The Magician stands West of the Altar, and performs the Qabalistic Cross. He then strikes the Pantacle with the flat of the blade of the Dagger, and speaks toward the Tower visible beyond the Gate.)

O CHASSAN! I evoke Thee in the most Puissant Name SHADDAI EL CHAI! Move! Appear and show Thyself!

(It is possible that CHASSAN may begin to manifest at this point. Regardless, the Magician must continue. He should also bear in mind that the appearance of CHASSAN beyond the Gate does not fulfil the conditions of the Evocation. The Angel must pass through the Gate and manifest physically in the Triangle.)

RAPHAEL! RAPHAEL! RAPHAEL!

(The Magician circumambulates once deosil while saying:)

O Thou sublime and resplendent Archangel RAPHAEL, I invoke Thee in the Everliving Name SHADDAI EL CHAI to send a ray of Thy Briatic Glory into this Circle, that I may be empowered to compel Thine Angel CHASSAN to visible appearance. I invoke Thee also to charge ARIEL, Angelic Ruler of Air, to aid in this Work of the Evocation of CHASSAN.

(The Magician stands West of the Altar and faces East. He strikes the Pantacle with the flat of the Dagger blade and speaks towards the tower.)

O CHASSAN! In the Name of the Blessed Archangel of Air,- RAPHAEL, 1 evoke Thee into this Triangle of Art which awaits Thee! Move! Appear and show Thyself!

ARIEL! ARIEL! ARIEL!

(The Magician circumambulates once deosil while saying:)

O Thou illustrious Ruler of Air. I invoke Thee in the sacred Name SHADDAI EL CHAI and in the Archangelic Name RAPHAEL, to uphold this Work and to grant unto Thine Angel CHASSAN the Power of perfect physical manifestation in the Evocatory Triangle.

(The Magician stands West of the Altar, faces East, and strikes the Pantacle with the flat of the Dagger blade. He then speaks towards the tower.)

O CHASSAN! In the Name of Thine Angelic Ruler, ARIEL, I evoke Thee to true and perfect manifestation in the Triangle without this circle of Art! Move! Appear and show Thyself!

CHASSAN! CHASSAN! CHASSAN!

(The Magician circumambulates once deosil while saying:)

O Thou potent Angel of Air, I evoke Thee in the mighty Names of the Powers of Air, SHADDAI EL CHAI, RAPHAEL, ARIEL!

(The Magician stands West of the Altar and Faces East. He then strikes the Pantacle with the flat of the Dagger blade, and speaks towards the tower.)

O CHASSAN! Move! Appear and show Thyself!

(The wrapped Pantacle is now borne to the Four Quarters and barred, purified, and consecrated as in the Neophyte Ritual. During this procedure, the Angel will become visible through the Gate if He has not appeared previously. When the Pantacle is returned to the Altar, the blackcloth is removed, as the Magician says:)

Too long hast Thou dwelt in Darkness - Quit the Night and seek the Day.

(This is a very likely point for the physical manifestation in the Triangle to begin. The Magician stands West of the Altar facing East, taking the Fan in his left hand and the Dagger in his right.)

O CHASSAN, Thou Mighty Angel, I call Thee - I adjure Thee - 1 evoke Thee! Come Thou forth from Thine Airy abode in the Yetziratic Realm of Ruach! Come Thou forth and assume a physical form! The Material Basis hath been prepared and consecrated for Thee in the Triangle of Evocation without this Magic Circle. I evoke Thee CHASSAN in the Names and letters of the Great Eastern Quadrangle revealed unto Enoch by the Great Angel Ave!

(The Magician uses the Projecting Sign to focus a projection of his Will and of the energies in the Circle on the Material Basis and the Assiatic Pantacle in the Triangle. He then makes the Sign of Silence.)

I evoke Thee CHASSAN in the Three Great Secret Holy Names of God borne on the Banners of the Watchtower of the East: ORO IBAH AOZODPI!

(Projecting Sign followed by Sign of Silence. The Magician should be reaching a level of ekstasis by this point.)

I evoke Thee CHASSAN, in the name of BATAIVAH, great King of the East!

(Projecting Sign, and then Sign of Silence. The area defined by the Triangle should, to the clairvoyant eye, be pulsating with yellow light.)

I evoke Thee CHASSAN, by virtue of this Pantacle consecrated in thy Name according to the Hermetic Formula of the Enterer!)

(The Magician strikes the Pantacle with the flat of the dagger blade.)

And by my knowlege of Thine own true Name whose number is one thousand and eight, I evoke Thee

CHASSAN! CHASSAN! CHASSAN!

(Projecting Sign, and then Sign of Silence.)

In the name of YHVH! In the name of SHADDAI ELCHAI! (Projecting Sign, and then Sign of Silence.)

In the Names of RAPHAEL and ARIEL! (Projecting Sign, and then Sign of Silence.)

In the names of RUACH, HIDD1KEL, and MIZRACH! (Projecting Sign and then Sign of Silence.)

In the name of PARALDA, King of the Sylphs! (Projecting Sign, and then Sign of Silence.)

In the name of CHASSAN, Angel of Air! (Projecting Sign, and then Sign of Silence.)

ZODACARE OD ZODAMERANU! ZODAMERANU! ZODAMERANU! (Projecting Sign and Sign of Silence.)

CHASSAN! CHASSAN! CHASSAN! (Projecting Sign, and then Sign of Silence.)

(If the Angel has not attained complete manifestation at this point, the Magician should repeat the Invocation of SHADDAI EL CHAI up to three times, if necessary. Once CHASSAN is fully materialized, the Magician should test the manifestation with the Signs of the Lords

47

who Wander and with the LVX Signs. If it is truly CHASSAN who has appeared, He will return the LVX Signs. If it is not, the manifesting Spirit will vanish, flee, or metamorphose into another form. If any of these results occur, banish the Spirit thoroughly and begin again. If the Angel responds correctly with the LVX Signs, the Magician should greet Him with:)

In the Grand Word YEHESHUAH, by the Key Word INRI, and through the concealed Word LVX, I greet and salute Thee, O CHASSAN; and by those same words of Power I require Thee to bind Thyself by this Oath. (In an Evocation, do not hold conversation with any Spirit until he has pledged himself to the Oath prepared for him.)

I, CHASSAN, an Angel of Air, in the Presence of the Lord of the Universe Who Works in Silence and Whom naught but Silence can express, do solemnly swear to do naught to harm E CINERE PHOENIX nor any other Man, nor this Temple of the Magic of Light. I undertake to answer any questions put to Me truthfully and without deception. I pledge to do all in my power to aid the Magician that the Virtues of Air may be enhanced within him that he may better labour in the Great Work. I vow to strengthen the Magician in the Power NOSCERE that he may have knowledge to aid the ignorant. I promise that I shall guide him to further the Work of the CHEVRAH ZERACH AUR BOQER and the Ordo Rosae Rubeae et Aureae Crucis in the Aquarian Age. Further, I pledge to serve this Son of the Lineage of Adam faithfully, and that I shall always come promptly to his Call when summoned. I swear to uphold all these things without evasion, reservation, or equivocation. Such is my Oath, whereunto I pledge Myself in the Presence of the most High YHVH and the Everliving SHADDAI EL CHAI; in the Presence of the wise and puissant Archangel RAPHAEL; and in the Presence of the Angelic Ruler of the Sphere of Ruach, ARIEL. So mote it be! (The Magician replies:) So mote it be.

(The Magician may then converse with the Angel. When all is concluded, the Magician should address the Angel thus:)

O Thou true and faithful Angel CHASSAN, Thou hast complied with the charge set before Thee and pledged Thyself to the Oath prepared for Thee. Therefore I pray that Thou mayest be nourished and elevated by that ray of the Divine Power which thou hast borne as messenger to me this day.

(With the Dagger, the Magician inscribes a Cross before CHASSAN and draws a ray of the White Brilliance down on the Angel in the Triangle. The Magician allows the Angel to experience the Light for a few moments, then grants Him license to depart.)

O CHASSAN, I now bid Thee depart in peace unto Thine Abode, and may the blessing of SHADDAI EL CHAI go with Thee. Be there always peace between Thee and me, and be Thou ready to come when Thou art called unto me by Word or Will.

(The Magician inscribes the Banishing Pentagrams of Spirit Active and Air to the East while vibrating YHVH and SHADDAI EL CHAI, then inscribes in the midst of the Pentagram the Sigil of CHASSAN while vibrating the name CHASSAN. The Magician then circumambulates once widdershins, returns to the West of the Altar and faces East. Knocks) So mote it be.

Ye Powers of Air, Who have lent Your aid unto this Working, depart Ye in peace unto Your Abodes and Habitations, and go with my humble gratitude and with the blessings of YHVH.

(The Magician inscribes the Banishing Pentagram of Spirit Active and Air to the East while vibrating YHVH and SHADDAI EL CHAI, then inscribes in the midst of the Pentagram the Glyph of Aquarius, vibrating RUACH. The Magician circumambulates once widdershins, returns to the West of the altar, and faces East. Knocks). So mote it be.

I now release any spirits that may have been accidentally imprisoned by this ceremony. Depart in peace to your Abodes and habitations, and go with the blessings of YEHESHUAH YEHOVASHAH.

(The Magician performs the Banishing Rituals of the Pentagram and Hexagram. Knocks). So mote it be.

(The Magician faces East and assumes the Sign of Osiris Slain.)

Unto Thee, sole wise and eternal One, be the praise and the glory forever, Who hath permitted me to enter thus far into the Sanctuary of Thy Sacred Mysteries. Not unto me but unto Thee be the Glory.

(The Magician performs the Qabalistic Cross.)

TETELESTAI! It is finished.

(The Magician gives one knock and concludes with:)

I now declare this Temple of the Magic of Light to be duly closed.

THE COMPLETE GOLDEN DAWN SYSTEM OF MAGIC

THE CANOPIC GODS
THE SYMBOLISM OF THE FOUR GENII OF
THE HALL OF THE NEOPHYTES

By

G.H. FRATER SUB SPE

In a Temple of the Grade of Neophyte, the Four Gods, Ameshet, Ahephi, Tmoumathph, Kabexnuf, said also to be Vice-gerants of the Elements, and answering to the Rivers of Eden as drawn in the Warrant of the Temple, are said to rule in the four Corners of the Hall between the Stations of the Kerubim.

In Egyptian mythology, these Gods are also said to be the Children of Horus, and to partake of his symbolism. If now, we regard the Neophyte Ceremony as representing the entrance into a new life, Regeneration - Mors Janua Vitae - the Egyptian symbolism wherein that idea was so clearly and exactly worked out becomes important. Bear in mind that a new life means a new plane or a higher world, a passing, say, from the Kether of Assiah to the Malkuth of Yetzirah.

Now as behind Kether depend the Veils of the Negative Existence, Ain, Ain Soph and Ain Soph Aour, so through Negative Existence must pass the Soul that goes from Assiah to Yetzirah, or vice-versa. This process is illustrated by the Neophyte Ceremony as described in Z-3, and as seen by the clairvoyant eye. In Egyptian mythology, the Dead, when the Ceremonies are complete, the Soul weighed and passed, the Body mummied and preserved from corruption, became one with Osiris, and is called an Osirian. Hence, the Hierophant, who represents Osiris when the Candidate is placed in the North, speaks to him in the character of his Higher Soul - "The Voice of my Higher Self said unto me" etc.

Osiris, however, is a mummied form, and the body of the Egyptian dead was mummied at this part of the Ceremony. Let us now consider the nature of the body which is mummied. The body itself may be considered as a vehicle whereby the life forces act, and the medium whereby these life-forces act is what are termed the Vital organs. Withdraw or destroy any of these, and the life ceases to function in that body. Not less important, then, than the body itself, the vehicle of the Soul, are the Organs, the media for the action of organic life, and it is equally important to preserve these from corruption, yet not together with the body. For as the body of Osiris was broken up, so must the body of the Osirian be divided. This is the meaning of the viscera being preserved apart from the body.

The death and resurrection of Christ has other symbolisms and the teachings belong to a higher Grade. Let none therefore object that His Body was laid in the Tomb entire.

The Body of Osiris was first laid in the Chest or Pastos whole. The division into 14 parts was subsequent. Note that 1 plus 4 equals 5, the five wounds.

For even as Yod Heh Vav Heh must be known before Yod Hell Shin Vav Heh can be comprehended, and as Moses must precede Christ, so must the Mysteries of Osiris first be known.

Now the Guardian of the Hall and of the Neophytes against the Qlippoth (whose Kether is Thaumiel, the Dual or Two-headed One, the Demons of corruption and disintegration) is the Hiereus or Horus, and to the Children of Horus, who partake of his symbolism, are the viscera committed, to guard them against the demons of disintegration and corruption. As the elements and the forces of the Elements are to the world, so are the vital organs and the Life which animates them to the human body. Appropriately, then, are the vital organs and the life which animates them, placed under the charge of the Vice-gerents of the Elements, the Children of Horus, the Great Gods Ameshet, Ahephi, Tmoumathph and Kabexnuf, who regulate their functions in material life, and guard them after so-called death, when the man that was has become an Osirian.

Consider then, what are these vital organs and their functions. Broadly they may be divided into the alimentary system and the circulatory system, for in this classification we take no account of the brain or reproductive organs which belong to another classification, and are not Elemental nor concerned in the maintenance of the life of the material body.

Each of these divisions may be further divided into that which divides or distributes to the body - that which is needed for life, and that which casts out from the body and renders to the Qlippoth that which is unnecessary or pernicious. From this arises a four-fold division as in the following:

> **A. is the receptive aspect of the Alimentary system.**
> **B. is the excretory aspect of the Alimentary system.**
> **C. is the receptive aspect of the Circulatory system.**
> **D. is the excretory aspect of the Circulatory system.**

With this Key, the division becomes easy, for in the Alimentary System, the stomach and the upper intestines divide the food taken into the system by a process called digestion, and by assimilation retain what is necessary. This therefore is "A" in the above. But the lower intestines receive and cast out that which is rejected. These therefore will be represented by "B." In the circulatory system, the heart is the organ which distributes the blood which it receives washed and purified by the lungs. Hence the lungs and heart are represented by "C." The matter rejected from the circulatory system is rejected and cast forth by the liver and gall-bladder, which therefore will be represented by "D."

Now as to the treatment of these vital organs in the process of mummification. Insofar as during life they were under the guardianship of the Great Gods mentioned, so in death they were dedicated each to one of these, who were the four Genii of the Underworld or the Lesser Gods of the Dead.

These vital organs then, being taken out and separately embalmed, were placed in egg-shaped receptacles, symbolic of Akasa. They were under the care of Canopus, the Pilot of Menelaus, and the God of the Waters of Creation, the Eternal Source of Being, whose symbol was a jar. These were under the protection of that one of the Genii of the Underworld or Vice-gerents of the Elements to whom that particular organ was dedicated. Hence each egg-shaped package was enclosed in a jar whose lid was shaped like the head of that God.

Now Ameshet was also termed "The Carpenter" for he it is who by the medium of his organ, the Stomach, frames the rough materials and builds up the structure of the body; to him the Stomach and Upper Intestines were dedicated (A).

Ahephi was also termed "The Digger" or "Burier" for he puts out of sight or removes that which is useless or offensive in the body, and to him the Lower Intestines or Bowels were dedicated (B).

Tmoumathph was also called "The Cutter" or "Divider" for he divides and distributes the blood bearing with it the Prana and the Subtle Ether by the Holy Science of Breath brought into the body, and to him were the lungs or heart dedicated (C).

Kabexnuf was termed "The Bleeder" for as a stream of blood is drawn from the body, so is a stream of impurity drawn from the blood, and cast out into the draught by the action of the Liver and Gall-Bladder. To him therefore, these organs were dedicated (D).

These jars were called Canopic Jars and were arranged in a certain order round the Mummy. Consider now, the points of the compass to which they would naturally be attributed. Reason itself will insist that the organs of the Alimentary System, the most material and earthy, should be in the North. The warm and vital heat of the Circulatory System should be to the South. In the following tables, the Receptive and Distributive organs should be placed to the East, the source of Life and Light, and the organs that purify and cast out should be to the West that borders on the Qlippoth.

This gives us the following arrangement:

Ameshet — Northeast quadrant. (Stomach and Upper Intestines).
Ahephi — Northwest quadrant. (Bowels).
Tmoumathph — Southeast quadrant. (Heart and Lungs).
Kabexnuf -- Southwest quadrant. (Liver and Gall-Bladder).

Yet this arrangement, would, as it were, symbolise the entire separation of the Alimentary System and the Circulatory System, which is contrary to Nature, for they continually counterchange, and thus arises Life. Wherefore in the Hall of the Two Truths, the portions of Ahephi and Kabexnuf are reversed, and the order becomes.

EAST — Ameshet.
SOUTH — Tmoumathph.
NORTH - Kabexnuf.
WEST — Ahephi.

Now these, being thus arranged, do partake of the symbolism of the elements to which they belong. For Ameshet being to the East, the quarter of Air, has the head of a Man. Tmoumathph, to the South, has the head of a Jackal who is the purveyor of the Lion (for these are the Vice-Gerents of the Elements, while the Kerubim are the Lords thereof); so Tmoumathph is properly a jackal. Kabexnuf in the West, in the region of Water, has the form of a Hawk, the subordinate form to the Alchemic Eagle of Distillation, and the form also, of Horus, the Hiereus, beside whom is his station, and of whose symbolism he partakes.

Ahephi in the North, has the head of an Ape. The symbolism of the Ape in ancient Egypt is very complex. Here it may be taken that while Apis, the Bull, represents the Divine Strength of the Eternal Gods, the Ape represents the Elemental Strength which is far inferior and blended with cunning. Ahephi, however, has other symbolism and other attributes. For by reason of the fertilising qualities of the Nile and of the fact that what is brought down by the Nile as refuse from the Land of the Sacred Lakes is, to Egypt, its life and the source of its fertility, so there arises a correspondence between the Nile and the lower intestines. Both are under the care of Ahephi (Hapi) who thus was worshipped as Nilus, and in this connection he has for his symbol, a head-dress of Lotus Flowers.

Now, further, the Alimentary System is under the special guardianship of Isis and Nephthys. Isis who conquers by the power of Wisdom and the forces of Nature, guards Ameshet. And Nephthys who hides that which is secret, guards Ahephi - whence also, until recent days, in the fulness of Time, the sacred sources of Ahephi, the Nile, were kept secret from the whole world.

Tmoumathph is under the guardianship of Neith. the Dawn. This is the Celestial Space, who makes the Morning to pass and awakes the Light of a Golden Dawn in the Heart of Him whom the Eternal Gods shall choose, by the Sacred Science of the Breath.

Kabexnuf is guarded by Sekhet, the Sun at the Western Equinox, the Opening of Amenti, who wears the Scorpion on her head. These guardianships were often painted on the Canopic jars.

When, therefore, the Candidate kneels at the foot of the Altar, or where the Corpse lies on the Bier preparatory to the passing over the River towards the West, there the Soul stands before Osiris, and the Goddesses stand by and watch while the Beam sways and the decision is taken. Then, the body of the Candidate is, as it were, broken up as the body of Osiris was broken, and the Higher Self stands before the place of the Pillars, but the lower self is in the invisible station of the evil persona. Then is the Candidate nigh unto death, for then, symbolically, his Spirit passes through the Veils of the Negative Existence, passing from the Kether of Assiah to the Malkuth of Yetzirah. Therefore, unless the Genii of the Underworld were then present and directing their forces on the vital organs, he must inevitably die.

Let their symbols then be represented in all operations and formulae drawn from the symbolism of the Hall of the Two Truths, for they are of the utmost importance, but as their stations are Invisible, so shall their symbols be astral and not material.

Thus shall perfect health of body be preserved, which is of utmost importance in all magical working, and thus shall the lessons of the Hall of the Neophytes be duly carried out in our daily life.

THE EGYPTIAN GOD-FORMS OF THE NEOPHYTE GRADE

The stations of the God-forms used in our symbolism come under two heads:

1. Visible Stations.

2. Invisible Stations.

The Visible Stations are the places of the Officers, each of whom has a special astral shape suitable to the forces he represents.

On the Dais are places for the Three Chiefs, the Past Hierophant and the Hierophant. The order in which they sit (as you face East) is:

Imperator-Nephthvs

Cancellarius-Thoth

Hierophant-Osiris

Past Hierophant-Aroueris

Praemonstrator-Isis

These names are those of the God-forms they represent. The following are the descriptions of the God-forms of the seven Officers of the Neophyte Grade.

Hierophant: Osiris in the Underworld. Expounder of the Mysteries in the Hall of the Dual Manifestation of the Goddess of Truth.

Hierophant is represented by two God-forms, the passive and active aspects of Osiris. Seated on the Dais as Hierophant, he is clothed in the God-form of Osiris. He wears the tall white crown of the South, flanked by feathers striped white and blue. His face is green, the eyes blue, and from his chin hangs the royal beard of authority and judgment, blue in colour and gold tipped. He wears a collar in bands of red, blue, yellow, and black - and on his back is a bundle strapped across his chest by scarlet bands. He is in mummy wrappings to the feet, but his hands are free to hold a golden Phoenix Wand, a Blue Crook and Red Scourge. The hands are green. His feet rest on a pavement of black and white.

The God-form of Osiris never moves from the Dais. When the Hierophant has to move from the Dais, he is covered by the form of Osiris in action - Aroueris, which is built up by the Past Hierophant, seated on Hierophant's left. If no one is seated as Past Hierophant, then inner Order Members help the Hierophant to formulate the second God-form.

Aroueris, Horus the Elder, is very lively to look upon - like pure flames. He wears the Double Crown of Egypt, the cone shaped crown in red inside the white crown of the North, with a white plume. His nemyss is purple banded with gold at the edges. His face and body are translucent scarlet. He has green eyes and wears a purple beard of authority. He wears a yellow tunic with a waist cloth of yellow striped with purple, from which depends a lion's tail. In common with all Egyptian Gods, he has a white linen kilt showing like an apron under the coloured waist cloth.

His armlets and anklets are of gold. He carries in his right hand, a blue Phoenix Wand and in his left, a blue Ankh. He stands on a pavement of purple and gold.

Hierus: Horus in the Abode of Blindness unto and Ignorance of the Higher. Avenger of the Gods.

He wears the Double Crown of the South and North, red and white, over a nemyss of scarlet banded with emerald green. His face is that of a lively hawk - tawny and black with bright piercing eyes, his throat is white. His body, like that of Aroueris, is entirely scarlet. He wears collar, armlets, and anklets of emerald; a waist cloth of emerald striped red, from which depends a lion's tail. He carries in his right hand an Emerald Phoenix Wand, and in his left a blue Ankh. He stands on a pavement of emerald and scarlet.

Hegemon: Thmaa-Est "Before the Face of the Gods in the Place of the Threshold."

Thmaa-est wears a black nemyss bound at the brow with a purple band from which rises, in front, a tall ostrich feather of green striped with red in equal bands. She wears a banded collar of red, yellow, blue and black. Her tunic is emerald green reaching to the feet where it is banded to match the collar. She has purple and green shoulder straps and a purple girdle also bordered in the colours mentioned above. Her face and body are natural colour - i.e., a light Egyptian red-brown. She wears armlets of emerald and red, and carries a combined form of Lotus ar.d Phoenix Wand. It has an orange flower - a blue stem, and ends in an orange Sign of the Binary. In her left hand she carries a blue Ankh, and she stands on a pavement of yellow and purple, bordered with blocks of red, blue, yellow, black, in succession.

Kerux: Anubis of the East. Watcher of the Gods.

Anubis has the head of a black jackal, very alert, pointed ears well pricked up. His nemyss is purple banded with white; he wears a collar of yellow and purple bands, and a tunic of yellow flecked with tufts of black hair. His body is red. His waist cloth is yellow striped with purple and from it hangs a lion's tail. His ornaments are purple and gold. His Phoenix Wand and Ankh are blue. He stands on a pavement of purple and yellow.

Stolistes: Auramo-ooth: "The Light shining through the Waters upon Earth.""Goddess of the Scales of the Balance at the Black Pillar."

Auramo-ooth is mainly in blue. Her face and body are natural. She wears a blue Crown of the North from which springs a delicate gold plume, over a vulture head-dress of orange and blue. Her collar is orange and blue also. She carries a blue Ankh and a Lotus Wand, having an orange lotus on a green stem. Her plain blue tunic reaches to the feet. She stands on black.

Dadouchos: Thaum-Aesch-Niaeth. "Perfection through Fire manifesting on Earth." "Goddess of the Scales of the Balance at the White Pillar."

Thaum-aesch is mainly in red. Her face and body are natural. She wears a red Crown of the South, flanked by two feathers in green barred black, over a vulture head-dress in red and green. Her collar is red and green and she carries a green Ankh and a Lotus Wand with a red flower and a green stem. Her simple red tunic reaches to the feet and she stands on black.

Sentinel: Anubis of the West.

His form is the same as that of Kerux but his nemyss, ornaments, and dress are black and white. He has a lion's tail and carries a black Phoenix Wand and Ankh. He stands on black.

THE THREE CHIEFS

Imperator: Nephthys.

Nephthys has a face and body of translucent gold. She is crowned with a Cap over a vulture head-dress of black and white, the vulture head being red. Her collar and ornaments are black and white, and she wears a black robe to the feet. It is bordered in black and white. She carries a blue Ankh and a Lotus Wand with a green flower and a blue stem. She stands on black and white pavement.

Praemonstrator: Isis.

Isis has a face and body of translucent gold. She is crowned with a Throne over a vulture head-dress of blue and orange. The vulture head is red. Her robe is of blue bordered with gold. Her ornaments are blue and orange, and she carries a blue Ankh and a Lotus wand with a green flower and a blue stem. She stands on blue and orange.

Cancellarius: Thoth.

The God-form of Thoth is built up by the Cancellarius or the officer seated on the right of Hierophant. This is his visible station, but during a Neophyte Grade, he also has an invisible station in the East w'hile the Obligation takes place.

He has an Ibis head, black beak and white throat. His nemyss is yellow bordered with mauve. His collar yellow with a middle band of squares in mauve and green. His tunic is mauve with yellow stripes, and he has a lion's tail. His limbs are natural colour, his ornaments are red and green. He carries a blue Ankh, and a stylus and writing tablet. He stands on mauve and yellow.

THE INVISIBLE STATIONS

These fall naturally into four groups given below in order of their importance.

1. **Stations in the Path Samekh in the Middle Pillar - Hathor - Harparkrat - Evil Persona.**
2. **Kerubim.**
3. **Children of Horus.**
4. **The Forty-Two Assessors.**

First, Hathor: This Great Goddess formulates behind Hierophant in the East. Her face and limbs are of translucent gold. She wears a scarlet Sun Disc, resting between black horns from the back of which rise two feathers in white, barred blue. She has a black nemyss - a collar of blue, red, blue; and blue bands which support her robe of orange, bordered with blue and red. Her ornaments are blue and orange. She carries a blue Ankh and Lotus Wand with a green flower and a blue stem. She stands on black bordered with blue.

Harparkrat: He formulates in the centre of the Hall between Hegemon and the Altar, where he sits or stands on a Lotus, facing East. His face and body are translucent emerald green. He has blue eyes, and a curl of blue hair, denoting youth, comes round his face on the right side. He wears the double crown, red and white. His collar is yellow and blue; his waist cloth is yellow and blue with a mauve girdle, whence depends a lion's tail. His Lotus has leaves alternately blue and yellow, and rests on a pavement of mauve and orange. He has no insignia. His left forefinger is on his lips.

Omoo-Sathan. Typhon, Apophis, Set. The Evil Persona is a composite figure of the powers arising from the Qlippoth. It rises from the base of the Altar standing East of the Altar facing West, in the Sign of Typhon. He is black, and has an animal, somewhat lizard-like, head, a black body and tail, and he stands on black. His nemyss is of olive green decorated with russet, his collar of russet and citrine. He has a white apron and a waist cloth of dull red striped with russet. He has no ornaments.

Second, the Kerubim. The Kerub of Air is formed behind Hathor and she is a pow'er of Hathor, and has the same general colouring. She has a young girl's countenance and behind her are spread large and shadowing wings.

The Kerub of Fire is in the South beyond the seat of Dadouchos. It is a power of the great Goddess Tharpesh, and has the face and form of a Lion with large and clashing wings. The colouring is very lively and flashing Leo green with ruby and flame-blue and Emerald green.

The Kerub of Water is formed behind Hiereus and is a power of the great God Toum or Tmu. It has the face and form of a great Eagle with large and glistening wings. The colours are mostly blue and orange with some green.

The Kerub of Earth is in the North behind the Seat of Stolistes. It is a power of the great God Ahapshi and has the face and form of a Bull with heavy darkening wings, and the colours are black, green, red, with some white.

These forms are not described in detail, but see the paintings in the colour plate section. We are to imagine them there as great stabilising forces whose forms vary according to circumstances.

Third, the Children of Horus. These have their invisible stations in the corners of the Hall. They are the guardians of the viscera of the human being - every part of whom comes up for judgment in its right time and place.

Ameshet: The man-faced is in the North East. He has a blue nemyss banded with red, blue and black. His face is red and he has a black ceremonial beard. Round the shoulders of his white mummy shape are bands of red, blue and black, three times repeated. He stands on red, blue and black with a border of green, white and yellow.

Tmoumathph: The Jackal-faced, is in the South East. He has a black face with yellow linings to his pointed ears. He wears a blue nemyss with borders of black, yellow and blue the same colours appearing threefold at his shoulders. He has a white mummy shape and stands on blue, yellow and black, with a border of green, yellow, mauve.

Kabexnuv: The Hawk-faced, is in the North West. He has a black and tawny face, and a nemyss of black bordered with red, yellow, black. The same colours appear three fold, at his shoulders. He has a white mummy shape and stands on red, yellow, and black with a border of green, mauve, white.

Ahephi: The Ape-faced, is in the South West. He has a blue nemyss bordered with red, blue and yellow bands. These colours appear on his shoulders in the same order. His face is red; and he stands on red, blue, and yellow, with a border of green, orange, and mauve.

Tmoumathph is sometimes written Duamutef. Kabexnuv is sometimes written Qebhsenef. Ahephi is sometimes written Hapi. Ameshet is sometimes written Mesti.

Fourth, the Forty-Two Assessors. These are not described at all save to say that they make the Sign of the Enterer as the Candidate is passed by them. They are Witnesses in the Judgment Hall of Osiris. (This paper originated in the early days of the Stella Matutina. I.R)

LAMENS AND EXAMINATION FOR THE GRADE OF PRACTICUS ADEPTUS MINOR

By

G.H. FRATER D.D.C.F.

(The Opening of this document was addressed originally to four T.A.M.'s dated 1st of November 1894 by Mathers. It includes an instruction on some Lamens of Egyptian Gods. Following this there is a paper describing the content of an examination to be taken by the T.A.M. before the next sub-grade of Practicus Adeptus Minor Grade could be attained. I.R.)

As shown in the one of the Flying Rolls addressed to members of the Second Order, you were appointed under the symbols of certain Egyptian Divinities to exercise certain authority as laid down in the aforesaid notice. Herewith I give you the necessary instructions for properly employing those particular symbols.

The Lamen of the God or Goddess in question is to be of any convenient or preferred size, and is to worn suspended from a Ribbon of the colour of the element required.

The figure of the Divinity is to be painted thereon in any convenient colours (not **necessarily** those of its element, as the Gods contain many of its correspondences in their formula, but copied from any good Egyptian representation.)

The figure is to be within a double circle of the colour of the element and on a white ground. It may be represented either standing or seated. Within the double circle its name is to be written in Coptic letters. This is to be worn at all meetings with other Regalia.

When the member in question is exercising his or her authority or judgement in the matter pertaining to the God or Goddess, let him or her, keeping the mind as pure as possible, assume the colossal form of the God or Goddess as taught in the Ritual Z and vibrate its name.

Thus let him or her judge the question as detached from his ordinary human personality. To this end let him be sure to formulate himself as the figure of the God as colossal and not simply as an ordinary size figure. Though this at first might be difficult it will gradually become easier of performance.

These symbols of the Gods are given to you that you may have greater wisdom and power in the resolution of difficult matters, than the symbols of the Theoricus grade could give you.

RITUAL B

Each T.A.M. shall make or adapt and consecrate for himself unassisted the Ring and the Disc of a Theoricus for use in divination and consultation. The same Ring or a similar one is to be worn as badge of his grade suspended from a collar of one or all colours of Malkuth.

He should carefully study and practice himself with the following subjects in which a rigid examination will have to be passed before the grade of P.A.M. can be attained.

1. Careful study of the symbolism contained in the Zelator ritual of the first Order so as to be able to explain any part thereof. A lecture on this subject will be available.
2. Development of the sense of Clairaudience in the Spirit Vision.
3. The knowledge of the Ritual of the 12 Gates in Astral Projection. Skrying and travelling in the Spirit Vision answering to the diagram of the Table of Shew Bread.
4. The method of bringing the Divine White Brillance into action by a certain ritual of Ascent and Descent.
5. Careful and elaborate Clairvoyant study and analysis of the four squares above the Calvary Crosses in each lesser angle of the Four Enochian Tablets, and of their influence when combined with a Servient Squares in each lesser angle.

6. Development of the employment and uses of Telesmata and Symbols.
7. Of the combination of various forces so as to reconcile their action in the same symbol or Telesma.
8. The Egyptian art of the formation of a combined series of images of Gods or Forces so as to have the effect of a continuous prayer or invokation for the Power desired.
9. The knowledge of SHADDAI ELCHAI in the art of taking in any working, the God Form which would govern the same by means of identification with a Telesmatic figure.
10. The true system of astrological divination.
11. Of the correspondences existing between each of the 16 geomantic figures and each of the 16 lesser angles of the Enochian Tablets treated as a whole.
12. Tarot divination translated into magical action.
13. The knowledge of the secret ntuals of the symbolism of the order of the Week of Creation answering to the diagram of the 7 branched Candlestick.
14. The thorough elementary knowledge of the formulae of Awakening of the Abodes by means of the playe or raying of the chequers of the lesser angles of the Enochian Tablets. (Chess).
15. The opening of the knowledge of the masculine and feminine potencies necessary unto the manifestation of all things, as symbolized in the diagram of the Flaming Sword between Metatron and Sandalphon.

THE COMPLETE GOLDEN DAWN SYSTEM OF MAGIC

THE RING AND THE DISC WITH THE WORKING
OF THE TRIPOD
(Taken from Liber Hodos Chamelionis)

By

G.H. FRATER D.D.C.F.

The especial magical implements of a Theoricus Adeptus Minor are the Ring and the Disc. Of these, the Ring should be worn in all second Order meetings in the manner of a Jewel, as a badge of rank, suspended by a ribbon either of citrine, olive, russet, or black color, or of all four colours combined. Also this Ring may be used for the purpose of decoration only, reserving another Ring for practical use.

The Ring, represented in the diagram below is shown as somewhat larger than is convenient for practical work.

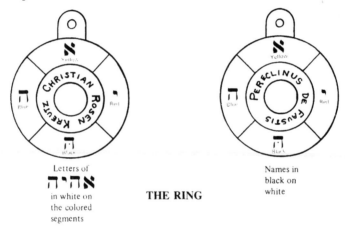

Letters of
אהיה
in white on
the colored
segments

THE RING

Names in
black on
white

The Disc should be of fair size, somewhat larger than the diagram, but not too large. It can be classified in three parts:

1. The White Center.
2. The Coloured Rays.
3. The Letters.

The White Center hath upon it in black the Letters of the name YHShVH arranged as shewn, and also the Motto of the Theoricus Adept. The first is to keep the working pure and to control astral action. The second is to identify the Theoricus with the working.

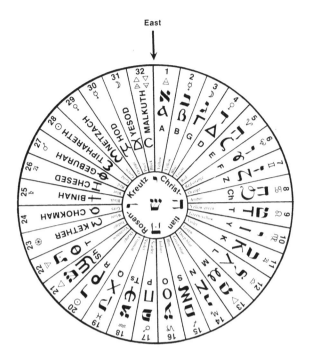

THE DISK

The Rays should be of the colours of the letters to which they are attributed, as to represent the White Light of the Center operating through the colours.

The Letters may be of one or of several Alphabets, and the numerical values and Yetziratic attributions may be also added. In all cases care should be taken that the proper coloured Ray leads from the White Center to the Letter to which that colour is attributed.

The Ring should be made of convenient size, and may be made (like the Disc) of any convenient material; thick pasteboard will do. It should not be too light, or the elasticity of the thread employed may vitiate its action. In the diagram the Ring is represented too large. It should be coloured appropriately, having the letters of EHEIEH in White upon both sides. Within the inner circle upon one side should be written in black upon the white ground the Motto of the Theoricus, and on the other side the title "Pereclinus de Faustis." The thread may be of linen, silk, or of cotton, and preferably White, though for a particular purpose a special colour may be used, as for working a Fire invocation, Red thread may be used. (Hair is too springy and has a personal element. Iron or steel wire for Martial purposes. Brass or Copper wire for Venusian purposes. N.O.M.) But usually white answers all purposes.

The part of the Ring to which the thread is fastened should be white, and is considered as the top of the Ring. The left hand line of the "A" ray of the Disc is considered as the top of the Disc, and not the Kether segment, because this working is more naturally allied to the Paths than to the Sephiroth.

OF THE METHOD OF WORKING

Now when the Theoricus Adept shall desire to employ the Disc and Ring for the purposes of Divination or of Consultation, let him - wearing the Insignia and having his necessary magical implements at hand - invoke in the ordinary manner the particular Spirit, Force or Elemental whom he wisheth to consult. (Note by N.O.M. "By means of a Telesma if desired. Put names, seal and sigil of Force on one side, and the name of THMAH [spelled in Coptic] on the other.")

Let him place the Disc flat upon the table before him. The Top thereof, i.e., the left hand line of the "A" ray being always opposite to him, then, leaning the elbow of the arm of the hand, by which he holds the thread attached to the Ring, upon the table for the sake of steadiness, let him so hold the Ring as to be suspended exactly above the White Center of the Disc, directing his gaze to the same point.

The thread by which the Ring is suspended should be passed immediately across the exact center of the ball of the first joint of the thumb, (and this is most important) being there retained by the pressure thereon of the center of the ball of the first joint of the finger selected to hold it with; (the first or the second finger will be found most convenient). The Ring will soon commence to oscillate and to vibrate.

The mode of receiving a communication thereby is as follows. No notice is to be taken of a short oscillation that does not pass completely beyond the circle of colored rays on to the circle of letters. But if it goeth clearly onto the circle of letters, such letters are to be taken in order, as spelling out a word or a sentence. When the Ring circleth, or oscillateth to the right hand (or with the Sun's course) it meaneth "Yes"; but if it circleth to the left hand (against the course of the Sun) it meaneth "No": and if it continueth to oscillate vaguely it meaneth "Doubtful".

The point of suspension of the Ring must be carefully maintained exactly above the center of the Disc. To avoid self-deception, and until facility of action be attained, care should be taken that the hand should be kept as steady as possible; and every communication should be carefully tested (as in Skrying) to avoid either automatic self-deception or wilful deception, by either the Force invoked, or by a hostile Force endeavoring to cut between, and thus to vitiate the operation.

Also, it should be clearly understood beforehand what language is being employed, and if a numerical value be intended instead of the Letter thereto belonging. And it is for the purpose of protecting against deception, and of identifying the Operator with the operation, that the Divine Names and the Motto of the Theoricus are placed upon the Disc and the Ring.

OF THE CONSECRATION OF THE DISC AND THE RING

A Golden Dawn Altar being prepared in the usual way, the Cross and Triangle upon it arranged with the Cross within the Triangle as in the Grade of Zelator, the room is purified and consecrated, etc. (Note by N.O. M. "Fire, Air, Water, three circles on altar, or the three elements. Open as in the 1-10 Grade; or in the full consecration formula as given in the Rituals of the Rose-Cross, the Lotus Wand and Elemental Implements. Use both Lesser Banishing Rituals of both the Pentagram and Hexagram. The four magical implements might be put on the Altar. The Pentacle is placed in the middle as the synthesis with Dagger, Cup and Wand around it.) Lay the Disc upon the Cross and Triangle, the left hand line of the Segment corresponding with the Eastern Arm of the Cross; lay the Ring upon the exact center of the Disc, its point of suspension (where the thread is attached) corresponding with the left hand line of the "A" segment of the Disc. Coil the thread around it in a spiral form in the direction of the course of the Sun, laying upon the coloured parts of the Disc. Place the Lesser Magical Implements around it at the usual angles or sides.

Stand at the West of the Altar. The Altar and places of the Pillars should be arranged as for the 1-10 Grade of Zelator. Hold the Magical Sword in the left hand and the Lotus Wand by the black part in the right hand, so that the pommel of the Sword and the black part of the Wand shall be immediately above the left and right hand outer edges of the Disc respectively. The point of the Sword and the Lotus end of the Wand shall be joined together perpendicularly above the centers of the Ring and the Disc. In this position, rehearse any convenient Oration to the Divine Powers ruling the Paths and the Sephiroth, asking that the Power of Truth may be conferred upon the Disc and the Ring.

Lay down the Lotus Wand on the right side of the Disc, and lay the Sword down upon the left of the Disc and Ring. Give then the Sign of the Interposer, namely that of a Zelator, and then invoke the Great Goddess THMAH to manifest the forces of Truth therein by the virtue of:

and concluding with the Threefold Name of the Goddess:

THMA-ESH   **THMA-ETH**   **THMA-EST**

When the ceremony is completed, and when the Disc and the Ring are not in use, wrap them up in a clean covering of White Silk or White Linen, as in the cases of the Rose-Cross and the Lotus Wand.

THE PHILOSOPHICAL EXPOSITION OF THE WORKING OF THE RING AND THE DISC

Let the Theoricus Adeptus Minor recall that which was said in the lecture on the Microcosm, under the headings of "How the Spiritual Consciousness can act around and beyond the Sphere of Sensation," and "Of Travelling in the Spirit Vision."

In the working by the Ring and Disc then, the Operator buildeth up partly from his own Nephesch and partly from the surrounding atmosphere a species of truncated cone of astral light. The Disc is its base, while the truncated summit thereof is at the point of suspension of the Ring where the thread thereof passeth between the thumb and finger of the Operator. The action of the Will of the Operator in formulating his desire of communication buildeth up the symbol of a receptacle of impressions. This will take the form of another inverted cone rising from the point of suspension of the Ring. So that upon the Disc as a base there will be built up in the astral light a form somewhat resembling an hourglass of which the center will be the place of the finger and the thumb of the Operator, holding the thread of suspension of the Ring. And from the impressions received by the conical receptacle, the hand will translate into action in the lower cone the expression of these ideas, in words and sentences spelled out by the movements of the Ring over the letters of the Disc.

But were it an uninitiated person who attempted this form of Divination or of consultation, he or she, being ignorant of the formulas involved, would almost to a certainty open a conical receptacular funnel in the sphere of sensation (of him or her) thus preparing a ready path unto obession. Therefore, it is not entirely the Force invoked which actually spells out the words, but to a great extent **it is the Operator himself who translates his own impressions thereof.** And for this reason it is that this form of Divination is not taught unto the Zelator Adept, self-deception therein being so extremely easy, and the hand being liable to translate that which the heart wisheth.

Therefore it is also that the language wherein the communication is received need not necessarily be that in which the Force invoked would speak, supposing it to be endowed with the human organs of speech, but the impression received by the Operator is translated according to the understanding of the Operator. And all this is in accordance with the degree of Force respectively exercised in the Upper or in the Lower Cone.

CONCERNING THE USE OF THE FORMATION OF A VACUUM IN THE ATMOSPHERE TO AID SKRYING AND RECEIVING OF IDEAS IN MAGICAL WORKING

The first and most important point is the formation of a cone, and from that a vortex, the center of which is then first to be extended upwards and downwards, thus forming the outline of a sphere enclosed by a Whorl, increasing at the circumference, diminishing towards and terminating at the Poles:

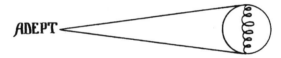

From the Poles, two rays of communication converge to a focus on the Sphere of Sensation. This Sphere thus artificially constructed enclosing a vacuum becometh naturally a reflection of the Universe. Therefore, anything that the Operator may will to see clearly is sympathetically reflected therein.

Therefore, let the Adept then command that which he is to see, to manifest therein. But if it be an Elemental or Spirit of a material or of an evil nature, let him guard carefully against being obsessed thereby seeing that the entering of it into that Sphere may give it a certain hold upon his own Sphere of Sensation, and when he hath gained his end, let him banish, command or license the Force summoned to depart, then reverse the process of construction and withdaw the Whorl into his Sphere and carefully close the latter at that point.

OF THE OPERATION KNOWN ANCIENTLY AS THE MAGICAL CONSULTATION BY MEANS OF THE TRIPOD (AND WITHIN RECENT YEARS REVIVED IN A MISTAKEN FORM AMONG THE UNINITIATED UNDER THE TITLES OF SPIRITUALISM AND TABLETURNING)

Now if the Theoricus Adeptus Minor shall wish to employ the Magical Consultation with the Tripod or table with three feet, let him know that the model thereof is the circular Altar of the Vault of Christian Rosenkreutz. One leg of the table should coincide with the Eastern point of the top which later should be coloured in exact representation of the Altar, and the legs should be black. (A table may have the regular painted top, and others removable, painted for special purposes. N.O.M.) If desired, the magical Operator, the better to isolate him or herself, may trace any convenient magical circle of defence upon the floor (consonant with the force he desires to invoke) wherein to sit while employing the working of the Tripod. (Note: A circle may consist of a tape and on it at certain places, Telesma or pentacles may be placed. N.O.M.) The mode of Operation is as here followeth.

The table should be placed with the same orientation as the Altar in the Vault; one leg, which we will call the apex of the triangle formed by the legs, being placed at the Eastern point as regards the design upon the top thereof. The Operator will usually, if working alone, find it best to be seated either at the Western part of the table, or at the point immediately opposite to that of the Force to be evoked. Let him then place his hands on the top of the table towards each side thereof. After a certain time, the length of which will depend upon varying conditions, the Tripod will begin to tilt up and down; and in some cases even a species of explosive knocks may be heard, which ariseth from a more sudden transmission of astral force from the cone of reception to the table. Now remember that the movements of the table should be really the combined product of the Operator and the communicating Force, always supposing that the Operator be not obsessed by the Force invoked, nor voluntarily self-deceiving. And the philosophical explanation is of a similar principle to that of the Disc and Ring: only that in this instance self-deception is even yet more easy.

For the reception of communications by the Tripod some convenient preconceived plan of correspondences between the tilts of the table and the letters of the alphabet or simple words should be employed.

This form of magical operation is usually found to be more exhausting than the employment of the Ring and Disc, seeing that a greater amount of astral Force has to be employed in the operation. Not only one but several persons may take part in this operation by the Tripod, but in such cases they should partition among them the points of the table corresponding either to their natures, or to the Forces with which each intendeth to ally himself. If there be three persons, let them take Air, Fire and Water, leaving Earth vacant. If five persons, the Spirit and the four elements, the Spirit being at the point of the East. If six or seven persons the points of the hexagram and so on, according to the quarters that they occupy, so as always to form some intentionally and not accidentally equilibriated symbol. Now in the case of several persons taking part, each one will form his own cone. The synthesis will form together another Great Cone enclosing the whole, and so a large amount of force may be thus obtained. But also, careful watch should be kept against both obsession and self-deception.

The greatest harmony should prevail among the Operators for the least discordant feeling will produce some error or disruption. And remember that in working with the Tripod the cone of reception will attract any passing Intelligence or Force. Thus, without the greatest care, much deception could arise, and even against the intention of the communicating Intelligence deception may result through confused mistranslations by the Operator or Operators.

Results may be obtained from tables not circular in form, and having four or more legs. But the Tripod is the best form. Also the Ring and the Disc may be used in conjunction with the Tripod. In invocation, a flashing Tablet or Tablets of the nature of the Force to be invoked may be placed upon the table. Also by using the table as a physical basis of strength, and sitting thereat, even physical appearances and manifestations may be produced. In such a case it may advantageous to have black drapery fastened around the edge of the table (not covering the table top, for this would hide the symbols. S.R.M.D.) and reaching to the ground, so as to form, as it were a cylindrical receptacle of force extending from the top of the table to the floor. Such drapery should be in three divisions. Or three slits may be cut, one by each leg from the top of the table to the floor, so that the three are united only along the edge of the table top.

In all such operations let the greatest care be taken to combat obsession, for in case of this arriving, although occasionally striking physical results may ensue, yet there will be danger therewith. And the result of such obsession will always be to make the Operator personate and imitate the action of the Force evoked, even to the extent of attempting to deceive both himself and those who may be with him.

But the Theoricus Adeptus Minor hath sufficient knowledge to know what to do, and what to avoid herein, and when.

Now the Formula of this operation by the Tripod will be closely similar to that contained in the Pyramid and Sphynx Formula of the Enochian Tablets. The truncated cone will answer to the Pyramid, with a cone of reception above opening therefrom to attract the Force which shall act through the top thereof. The surface of the table will answer to the place of the Sphynx.

And thus thou wilt easily see how particular the Operator must always be in discerning the Force which is acting through the vortex above.

VOLUME NINE

THE TAROT

VOLUME NINE

THE TAROT

TABLE OF CONTENTS

IMPORTANT TABLES AND ILLUSTRATIONS

VOLUME NINE

THE TAROT

THE COMPLETE GOLDEN DAWN SYSTEM OF THE TAROT

This includes Documents N, O, P, Q, R, and an Unlettered Theoricus Adeptus Minor Paper

THE GREAT ANGEL HRU IS SET OVER THE OPERATION OF THIS SECRET WISDOM

"What thou seest write in a Book, and send it unto the Seven Abodes that are in Assiah."
"And I saw in the right hand of Him that sat upon the Throne a book sealed with Seven Seals. And I saw a strong Angel proclaiming with a loud voice, 'Who is worthy to open the Books and to loose the seals thereof?'"

ANKH OF THE TAROT

THE TITLES OF THE TAROT CARDS

1. Ace of Wands is called the Root of the Powers of Fire.
2. Ace of Swords is called the Root of the Powers of Air.
3. Acc of Pentacles is called the Root of the Powers of Earth.
4. Ace of Cups is called the Root of the Powers of Water.
5. The King of Wands is called the Lord of Flame and Lightning.The King of the Spirits of Fire.
6. The Queen of Wands is The Queen of the Thrones of Flames.
7. The Knight of Wands is The Prince of the Chariot of Fire.
8. The Knave of Wands is The Princess of the Shining Flame, and The Rose of the Palace of Fire.
9. The King of Cups is The Lord of the Waves and the Waters, and The King of the Hosts of the Sea.
10. The Queen of Cups is The Queen of the Thrones of the Waters.
11. The Knight of Cups is The Prince of the Chariot of the Waters.
12. The Knave of Cups is The Princess of the Waters and the Lotus.
13. The King of Swords is The Lord of the Wind and the Breezes, The Lord of the Spirits of the Air.
14. The Queen of Swords is The Queen of the Thrones of the Air.
15. The Knight of Swords is The Prince of the Chariots of the Wind.
16. The Knave of Swords is The Princess of the Rushing Winds, The Lotus of the Palace of Air.
17. The King of Pentacles is The Lord of the Wide and Fertile land. King of the Spirits of the Earth.
18. The Queen of Pentacles is The Queen of the Thrones of Earth.
19. The Knight of Pentacles is The Prince of the Chariot of Earth.
20. The Knave of Pentacles is The Princess of the Echoing Hills, The Rose of the Palace of Earth.

THE FOLLOWING ARE THE NAMES AND ATTRIBUTIONS OF THE TAROT TRUMPS

NAMES	TITLES	HEBREW	SIGNS
Fool	The Spirit of Ether.	Aleph	Air
Magician	The Magus of Power.	Beth	Mercury
High Priestess	Priestess of the Silver Star.	Gimel	Moon
Empress	Daughter of the Mighty Ones.	Daleth	Venus
Emperor	Son of the Morning, Chief among the Mighty.	Heh	Aries
Hierophant	Magus of the Eternal Gods.	Vau	Taurus
Lovers	Children of the Voice Divine, The Oracles of the Mighty Gods.	Zayin	Gemini
Chariot	Child of the Power of the Waters, Lord of the Triumph of Light.	Cheth	Cancer

THE COMPLETE GOLDEN DAWN SYSTEM OF MAGIC

NAMES	TITLES	HEBREW	SIGNS
Fortitude	Daughter of the Flaming Sword, Leader of the Lion.	Teth	Leo
Hermit	The Magus of the Voice of Light, The Prophet of the Gods.	Yod	Virgo
Wheel of Fortune	The Lord of the Forces of Life.	Caph	Jupiter
Justice	Daughter of the Lord of Truth, The Holder of the Balances.	Lamed	Libra
Hanged Man	The Spirit of the Mighty Waters.	Mem	Water
Death	The Child of the Great Transformers, Lord of the gates of death	Nun	Scorpio
Temperance	Daughter of the Reconcilers, The Bringer Forth of Life.	Samekh	Sagittari
Devil	Lord of the Gates of Matter, Child of the Forces of Time.	Ayin	Capricor
Blasted Tower	Lord of the Hosts of the Mighty.	Peh	Mars
The Star	Daughter of the Firmament, Dweller between the Waters.	Tzaddi	Aquarius
The Moon	Ruler of Flux and Reflux, Child of the Sons of the Mighty.	Qoph	Pisces
The Sun	Lord of the Fire of the World.	Resh	Sun
Judgment	The Spirit of the Primal Fire.	Shin	Fire
Universe	The Great One of the Night of Time.	Tau	Saturn

THE FOLLOWING IS A FULL LIST OF THE NAMES AND ATTRIBUTIONS OF THE REMAINING MINOR ARCANA

Card	Lord of	Decan	Sign
5 Wands	Strife	Saturn	Leo
6 Wands	Victory	Jupiter	Leo
7 Wands	Valour	Mars	Leo
8 Pentacles	Prudence	Sun	Virgo
9 Pentacles	Material Gain	Venus	Virgo
10 Pentacles	Wealth	Mercury	Virgo
2 Swords	Peace Restored	Moon	Libra
3 Swords	Sorrow	Saturn	Libra
4 Swords	Rest from strife	Jupiter	Libra
5 Cups	Loss in Pleasure	Mars	Scorpio
6 Cups	Pleasure	Sun	Scorpio
7 Cups	Illusionary success	Venus	Scorpio
8 Wands	Swiftness	Mercury	Sagittarius
9 Wands	Great Strength	Moon	Sagittarius
10 Wands	Oppression	Saturn	Sagittarius

Card	Lord of	Decan	Sign
2 Pentacles	Harmonious Change	Jupiter	Capricorn
3 Pentacles	Material Works	Mars	Capricorn
4 Pentacles	Earthy Power	Sun	Capricorn
5 Swords	Defeat	Venus	Aquarius
6 Swords	Earned Success	Mercury	Aquarius
7 Swords	Unstable Effort	Moon	Aquarius
8 Cups	Abandoned Success	Saturn	Pisces
9 Cups	Material Happiness	Jupiter	Pisces
10 Cups	Perpetual Success	Mars	Pisces
2 Wands	Dominion	Mars	Aries
3 Wands	Established Strength	Sun	Aries
4 Wands	Perfected Work	Venus	Aries
5 Pentacles	Material Trouble	Mercury	Taurus
6 Pentacles	Material Success	Moon	Taurus
7 Pentacles	Success Unfulfilled	Saturn	Taurus
8 Swords	Shortened Force	Jupiter	Gemini
9 Swords	Despair and Cruelty	Mars	Gemini
10 Swords	Ruin	Sun	Gemini
2 Cups	Love	Venus	Cancer
3 Cups	Abundance	Mercury	Cancer
4 Cups	Blended Pleasure	Moon	Cancer

THE 78 TAROT CARDS THEIR DESCRIPTION AND MEANING

THE ACES

The first in order and appearance are the four Aces, representing the force of the Spirit acting in, and binding together the four scales of each element and answering to the Dominion of the Letters of the Name in the Kether of each. They represent the Radical or Root-Force and are said to be placed on the North Pole of the Universe, wherein they revolve, governing its revolution, and ruling as the connecting link between Yetzirah and Assiah.

THE RADIX OF THE POWERS OF FIRE

ACE OF WANDS

A white radiating Angelic Hand issuing from Clouds and grasping a heavy Club which has three branches in the colours and with the Sigils of the Scales. The right and left hand branches end respectively in three Flames and the centre one in four Flames, thus yielding Ten the number of the Sephiroth. Twenty two leaping Flames or Yods surround it, answering to the Paths. Three fall below the right branch for Aleph, Mem and Shin. Seven above the central branch for the double letters. And between it and that on the right, are twelve -- six above and six below -- about the left hand Branch. The whole is a great and Flaming Torch, symbolising force, strength, rush, vigour, energy, and it governs according to its nature various works and questions. It implies natural as opposed to Invoked Force.

THE RADIX OF THE POWERS OF THE WATERS

ACE OF CUPS

A Radiant white Angelic Hand issuing from clouds and supporting on its palm a Cup, resembling that of the Stolistes. From it rises a fountain of clear and glistening Water; and spray falling on all sides into clear calm water below, in which grow Lotus and water lilies. The great letter Heh of the Supernal Mother is traced in the spray of the Fountain. It symbolises Fertility, Productiveness, Beauty, Pleasure, Happiness, etc.

THE RADIX OF THE POWERS OF AIR

ACE OF SWORDS

A white radiating Angelic Hand, issuing from clouds, and grasping the hilt of a Sword, which supports a white radiant celestial Crown from which depend, on the right, the olive branch of Peace, and on the left, the Palm branch of suffering. Six Vaus fall from its point.

It symbolises invoked as contrasted with natural Force; for it is the Invocation of the Sword. Raised upward, it invokes the Divine Crown of Spiritual Brightness. Reversed it is the invocation of demoniac force, and becomes a fearfully evil symbol. It represents therefore very great power for good or evil, but **invoked.** And it also represents whirling force, and strength through trouble. It is the affirmation of justice, upholding Divine authority; and it may become the Sword of Wrath, Punishment and Affliction.

THE RADIX POWERS OF THE EARTH

ACE OF PENTACLES

A white radiant Angelic Hand, holding a branch of a Rose Tree, whereon is a large Pentacle, formed of five concentric circles. The innermost Circle is white, charged with a red Greek cross. From this white centre 12 white rays issue. These terminate at the circumference, making the whole something like an astrological figure of the Heavens.

It is surmounted by a small circle, above which is a large Maltese Cross, and with two white wings; four roses and two buds are shewn. The hand issueth from the clouds as in the other three cases. It representeth materiality in all senses, good and evil, and is therefore in a sense illusionary. It shows material gain, labour, power, wealth, etc.

THE SIXTEEN COURT CARDS

THE FOUR KINGS

The Four Kings or Figures mounted on Steeds. (This is very important due to the general confusion even in these papers between Kings and Knights; all Kings should be on horses and all Knights should be on thrones or chariots.) They represent the Yod forces of the Name in each suit, the Radix, Father, and commencement of Material Forces. A Force in which all the others are implied and of which they form the development and completion. A force swift and violent in action, but whose effect soon passes away, and therefore symbolised by a figure on a steed riding swiftly, and clothed in complete armour.

Therefore is the knowledge of the scale of the King so necessary for the commencement of all magical working.

THE FOUR QUEENS

Are seated upon Thrones, representing the Forces of Heh of the Name in each suit, the Mother, and bringer forth of material Force, a Force which develops, and realises the Force of the King. A force steady and unshaken, but not rapid though enduring. It is therefore symbolised by a figure seated upon a Throne but also clothed in armour.

THE FOUR KNIGHTS

These Knights (sometimes called Princes) are figures seated in chariots, and thus borne forward. They represent the Vau forces of the Name in each suit; the Mighty son of the King and the Queen, who realises the influence of both scales of Force. A prince, the son of a King and Queen, yet a Prince of Princes, and a King of Kings. An Emperor, whose effect is at once rapid (though not so swift as that of a king) and enduring (though not as steadfast as that of a queen). It is therefore symbolised by a figure borne in a chariot, and clothed with armour. Yet is his power illusionary, unless set in motion by his Father and Mother.

THE FOUR PRINCESSES

These are also known as the Knaves. The Four Princesses or Figures of Amazons standing firmly by themselves, neither riding upon Horses, nor seated upon Thrones, nor borne on Chariots. They represent the forces of Heh final of the Name in each suit, completing the influences of the other scales. The mighty and potent daughter of a King and Queen: a Princess powerful and terrible. A Queen of Queens, an Empress, whose effect combines those of the King, Queen and Prince. At once violent and permanent, she is therefore symbolised by a figure standing firmly by itself, only partially draped and having but little armour. Yet her power existeth not save by reason of the others, and then indeed it is mighty and terrible materially, and is the Throne of the forces of the Spirit. Woe unto whomsoever shall make war upon her when thus established!

WHERE THE COURT CARDS OPERATE

The Princesses rule over the Four Parts of the Celestial Heavens which lie around the North Pole, and above the respective Kerubic Signs of the Zodiac, and they form the Thrones of the Powers of the Four Aces.

The Twelve Cards, 4 Kings, 4 Queens, and 4 Knights rule the Dominions of the Celestial Heavens between the realm of the Four Princesses and the Zodiac, as is hereafter shewn. And they, as it were, link together the signs.

WANDS

THE LORD OF THE FLAME AND THE LIGHTNING
KING OF THE SPIRITS OF FIRE

KING OF WANDS

A winged Warrior riding upon a black horse with flaming mane and tail. The horse itself is not winged. The Rider wears a winged Helmet (like an old Scandinavian and Gaulish Helmet) with a royal Crown. A corselet of scale-mail and buskins of the same, and a flowing scarlet mantle. Above his Helmet, upon his cuirass, and on his shoulder pieces and buskins he bears, as a crest, a winged black Horse's head. He grasps a Club with Flaming ends, somewhat similar to that in the symbol of the Ace of Wands, but not so heavy, and also the Sigil of his scale is shewn.

Beneath the rushing feet of his steed are waving flames of Fire. He is active, generous, fierce, sudden and impetuous. If ill-dignified he is evil-minded, cruel, bigoted, brutal. He rules the celestial Heavens from above the 20th degree of Scorpio to the first two Decans of Sagittarius and this includes a part of the constellation Hercule (who also carries a club). Fire of Fire. King of the Salamanders.

QUEEN OF THE THRONES OF FLAME

QUEEN OF WANDS

A crowned Queen with long red-golden hair, seated upon a Throne, with steady Flames beneath. She wears a corselet and buskins of scale mail, revealed by her robe. Her arms are almost bare. On the cuirass and buskins are leopards' heads winged. The same symbol surmounteth her crown. At her side is a couchant Leopard on which her hands rest. She bears a long Wand with a very heavy conical head. The face is beautiful and resolute.

Adaptability, steady force applied to an object. Steady rule; great attractive power, power of command, yet liked notwithstanding. Kind and generous when not opposed. If ill-dignified, obstinate, revengeful, domineering, tyrannical and apt to turn suddenly against another without a cause. She rules the Heavens from above the last Decan of Pisces to above the twentieth degree of Aries, including a part of Andromeda. Water of Fire. Queen of the Salamanders or Salamandrines.

THE PRINCE OF THE CHARIOT OF FIRE

KNIGHT OF WANDS

A Kingly figure (but **not** a King) with a golden winged Crown, seated on a Chariot. He has large white wings. One wheel of his Chariot is shewn. He wears corselet and buskin of scale armour, decorated with winged Lions' heads, which symbol also surmounts his crown. His chariot is drawn by a lion. His arms are bare, save for the shoulder pieces of the corselet, and he bears a torch or firewand, somewhat similar to that of the Z.A.M. Beneath the Chariot are flames, some waved, some salient.

Swift, strong, hasty, rather violent, yet just and generous, noble and scorning meanness. If ill-dignified, cruel, intolerant, prejudiced, and ill-natured. He rules the Heavens from above the last decan of Cancer to the 2nd decan of Leo. Hence he includes most of Leo Minor. Air of Fire. Prince and Emperor of Salamanders.

8

VOLUME NINE

PRINCESS OF THE SHINING FLAME -- THE ROSE OF THE PALACE OF FIRE

KNAVE OF WANDS

A very strong and beautiful woman, with flowing red-golden hair, attired like an Amazon. Her shoulders, arms, bosom and knees are bare. She wears a short kilt, reaching to the knees. Round her waist is a broad belt of scale mail, narrow at the side, broad in the front and back, and having a winged tiger's head in front. She wears a Corinthian shaped helmet, and Crown with a long plume. It also is surmounted by a tiger's head, and the same symbol forms the buckle of her scale-mail buskins.

A mantle lined with tiger's skin falls back from her shoulders. Her right hand rests on a small golden or brazen Altar, ornamented with Ram's heads, and with Flames of Fire leaping from it. Her left hand leans on a long and heavy club, swelling at the lower end, where the sigil is placed. It has flames of fire leaping from it the whole way down, but the flames are ascending. This Club or torch is much longer than that carried by the King or Queen. Beneath her firmly placed feet are leaping Flames of Fire.

Brilliance, courage, beauty, force, sudden in anger or love, desire of power, enthusiasms, revenge.

Ill-dignified, superficial, theatrical, cruel, unstable, domineering. She rules the heavens over one quadrant of the portion round the North Pole. Earth of Fire. Princess and Empress of the Salamanders. Throne of the Ace of Wands.

CUPS

LORD OF THE WAVES AND THE WATERS KING OF THE HOSTS OF THE SEA

KING OF CUPS

A beautiful youthful winged Warrior, with flying hair, riding upon a white horse, which latter is not winged. His general equipment is similar to that of the King of Wands, but upon his helmet, cuirass and buskins is a peacock with opened wings. He holds a Cup in his hand, bearing the sigil of the Scale. Beneath his horses' feet is the sea. From the cup issues a crab.

Graceful, poetic, venusian, indolent, but enthusiastic if roused. Ill-dignified, he is sensual, idle, and untruthful. He rules the heavens from above 20° of Aquarius to 20° Pisces including the greater part of Pegasus. Fire of Water. King of Undines and of Nymphs.

QUEEN OF THE THRONES OF THE WATERS

QUEEN OF CUPS

A very beautiful fair woman like a crowned Queen, seated upon a Throne, beneath which is flowing water, wherein Lotuses are seen. Her general dress is similar to that of the Queen of Wands, but upon her Crown, Cuirass and Buskins is seen an Ibis with opened wings, and beside her is the same Bird, whereon her hand rests. She holds a Cup, wherefrom a cray fish issues. Her face is dreamy. She holds a Lotus in the hand upon the Ibis.

9

She is imaginative, poetic, kind, yet not willing to take much trouble for another. Coquettish, good-natured, underneath a dreamy appearance. Imagination stronger than feeling. Very much affected by other influences, and therefore more dependent upon good or ill-dignity than upon most other symbols. She rules from 20° Gemini to 20° Cancer. Water of Water. Queen of Nymphs and Undines.

PRINCE OF THE CHARIOT OF THE WATERS

KNIGHT OF CUPS

A winged Kingly figure with a winged crown, seated in a chariot drawn by an Eagle. On the wheel is the symbol of a Scorpion. The Eagle is borne as a crest upon his crown, cuirass and buskins. General attire like Knight of Wands. Beneath his chariot is the calm and stagnant water of a lake. His scale armour resembles feathers more than scales. He holds in one hand a Lotus, and the other a Cup, charged with the Sigil of his scale. A serpent issues from the Cup, and has its head tending down to the waters of the Lake.

He is subtle, violent, crafty and artistic. A fierce nature with calm exterior. Powerful for good or evil, but more attracted by the evil, if allied with apparent Power or Wisdom. If ill-dignified he is intensely evil and merciless. He rules from 20° of Libra to 20° Scorpio. Air of Water. Prince and Emperor of Nymphs and Undines.

PRINCESS OF THE WATERS AND LOTUS OF THE PALACE OF THE FLOODS

KNAVE OF CUPS

A beautiful Amazon-like figure, softer in nature than the Princess of Wands. Her attire is similar. She stands on a sea with foaming spray. Away to her right is a Dolphin. She wears as a crest on her Helmet, belt and buskins, a Swan with opening wings. She bears in one hand a Lotus, and in the other an open Cup from which a Turtle issues. Her mantle is lined with swans-down, and is of thin floating material.

Sweetness, poetry, gentleness, and kindness. Imagination, dreamy, at times indolent, yet courageous if roused. Ill-dignified she is selfish and luxurious. She rules a quadrant of the Heavens around Kether. Earth of Water. Princess and Empress of Nymphs and Undines. Throne of the Ace of Cups.

SWORDS

LORD OF THE WINDS AND BREEZES
KING OF THE SPIRIT OF AIR

KING OF SWORDS

A winged Warrior with crowned and winged Helmet, mounted upon a brown steed, his general equipment is as that of the King of Wands, but he wears as a crest a winged six-pointed star, similar to those represented on the heads of Castor and Pollux, the Dioscuri, the Twins Gemini (a part of which constellation is included in his rule). He holds a drawn sword with the Sigil of his Scale upon its pommel. Beneath his horse's feet are dark, driving, stratus clouds.

He is active, clever, subtle, fierce, delicate, courageous, skillful, bit inclined to domineer. Also to overvalue small things, unless well-dignified. Ill-dignified, deceitful, tyrannical and crafty. Rules from 20° Taurus to 20° Gemini. Fire of Air. King of Sylphs and Sylphides.

QUEEN OF THE THRONES OF AIR

QUEEN OF SWORDS

A graceful woman with curly waving hair, like a Queen seated upon a Throne, and crowned. Beneath the Throne are grey cumulous clouds. Her general attire is similar to that of the Queen of Wands. But she wears as a crest a winged child's head (like the head of an infantile Kerub seen sculptored on tombs.)

A drawn sword in one hand, and in the other a large bearded newly-severed head of a man.

Intensely perceptive, keen observation, subtle, quick, confident, often perseveringly accurate in superficial things, graceful, fond of dancing and balancing. Ill-dignified, cruel, sly, deceitful, unreliable, though with a good exterior. Rules from 20° Virgo to 20° of Libra. Water of Air. Queen of the Sylphs and Sylphides.

PRINCE OF THE CHARIOTS OF THE WINDS

KNIGHT OF SWORDS

A Winged Knight with a winged Crown, seated in a chariot drawn by Arch Fays, archons, or Arch Fairies, represented as winged youths very slightly draped, with butterfly wings, heads encircled with a fillet with Pentagrams thereon, and holding wands surmounted by Pentagram shaped stars. The same butterfly wings are on their feet and fillet. General equipment is that of the Knight of Wands, but he bears as a crest, a winged Angelic Head, with a Pentagram on the Brow. Beneath the chariot are grey rain clouds or nimbi. His hair long and waving in serpentine whirls, and whorl figures compose the scales of his armour. A drawn sword in one hand, a sickle in the other. With the sword he rules, with the sickle he slays.

Full of ideas and thoughts and designs, distrustful, suspicious, firm in friendship and enmity, careful, slow, over-cautious. Symbolises Alpha and Omega, the Giver of Death, who slays as fast as he creates. Ill-dignified harsh, malicious, plotting, obstinate, yet hesitating and unreliable. Ruler from 20° Capricorn to 20° Aquarius. Air of Air. Prince and Emperor of Sylphs and Sylphides.

PRINCESS OF THE RUSHING WINDS - LOTUS OF THE PALACE OF AIR

KNAVE O SWORDS

An Amazon figure with waving hair, slighter than the Rose of the Palace of Fire, Knave of Wands. Her attire is similar. The feet seem springy, giving the idea of swifness. Weight changing from one foot to another, and body swinging round. She resembles a mixture of Minerva and Diana, her mantle resembles the Aegis of Minerva. She wears as a crest the head of Medusa with Serpent hair. She holds a sword in one hand and the other rests upon a small silver altar with grey smoke (no fire) ascending from it. Beneath her feet are white cirrous clouds.

Wisdom, strength, acuteness, subtleness in material things, grace and dexterity- If ill-dignified, she is frivolous and cunning. She rules a quadrant of the Heavens around Kethei.

Earth of Air. Princess and Empress of the Sylphs and Sylphides. Throne of the Ace of Swords.

PENTACLES

LORD OF THE WILD AND FERTILE LAND
KING OF THE SPIRITS OF EARTH

KING OF PENTACLES

A dark winged Warrior with winged and crowned helmet; mounted on a light brown horse. Equipment as of the King of Wands. The winged head of a stag or antelope as a crest. Beneath the horse's feet is fertile land, with ripened corn. In one hand he bears a sceptre surmounted with a hexagram, in the other a pentacle like a Z.A.M.'s.

Unless very well dignified, he is heavy, dull, and material. Laborious, clever and patient in material matters. If ill-dignified he is avaricious, grasping, dull, jealous, not very courageous, unless assisted by other symbols. Rules from above 20° of Leo to 20° of Virgo. Fire of Earth. King of the Gnomes.

QUEEN OF THE THRONES OF EARTH

QUEEN OF PENTACLES

A woman of beautiful face with dark hair, seated upon a throne, beneath which is dark sandy earth. One side of her face is dark, the other light, and her symbolism is best represented in profile. Her attire is similar to that of the Queen of Wands. But she bears a Winged goat's head as a crest. A goat is by her side. In one hand she bears, a sceptre surmounted by a cube, and in the other an Orb of gold.

She is impetuous, kind, timid, rather charming, greathearted, intelligent, melancholy, truthful, yet of many moods. Ill-dignified, she is undecided, capricious, foolish, changeable. Rules from 20° Sagittarius to 20° Capricorn. Water of Earth. Queen of Gnomes.

PRINCE OF THE CHARIOT OF EARTH

KNIGHT OF PENTACLES

A winged kingly figure seated in a chariot drawn by a bull. He bears as a crest the symbol of the head of a winged bull. Beneath the chariot is land with many flowers. In one hand he bears an orb of gold held downwards, and in the other a sceptre surmounted by an Orb and cross.

Increase of matter, increase of good and evil, solidifies, practically applies things, steady, reliable. If ill-dignified, animal, material, stupid. Is either slow to anger, but furious if roused. Rules from 20° Aries to 20° of Taurus. Air of Earth, Prince and Emperor of the Gnomes.

PRINCESS OF THE ECHOING HILLS— ROSE OF THE PALACE OF EARTH

KNAVE OF PENTACLES

A strong and beautiful Amazon figure with red brown hair, standing on grass and flowers. A grove of trees near her. Her form suggests Hera, Ceres, and Proserpine. She bears a winged ram's head as a crest, and wears a mantle of sheep's skin. In one hand she carries a sceptre with a circular disc, in the other a Pentacle similar to that of the Ace of Pentacles.

She is generous, kind, diligent, benevolent, careful, courageous, preserving, pitiful. If ill-dignified, she is wasteful and prodigal. Rules over one Quadrant of the Heavens around the North Pole of the Ecliptic. Earth of Earth. Princess and impress of the Gnomes. Throne of the Ace of Pentacles.

THE THIRTY-SIX DECANS

Here follow the descriptions of the smaller cards of the 4 Suits, thirty-six in number, answering unto the 36 Decans of the Zodiac.

Commencing from the sign Aries, the **Central** Decans of each sign follow the order of the Days of the Week.

CARD	DECAN	MEANING	DAY
3W	Aries	Established Strength	Sunday
6P	Taurus	Material Success	Monday
9S	Gemini	Despair and Cruelty	Tuesday
3C	Cancer	Abundance	Wednesday
6W	Leo	Victory	Thursday
9P	Virgo	Material Gain	Friday
3S	Libra	Sorrow	Saturday
6C	Scorpio	Pleasure	Sunday
9W	Sagittarius	Great Strength	Monday
3P	Capricorn	Material Works	Tuesday
6S	Aquarius	Earned Success	Wednesday
9C	Pisces	Material Happiness	Thursday

There being 36 Decanates and only seven Planets, it follows that one of the latter must rule over one more decanate than the others. This is the Planet Mars which is allotted the last decan of Pisces and first of Aries, because the long cold of the winter requires a great energy to overcome it and initiate spring.

THE COMPLETE GOLDEN DAWN SYSTEM OF MAGIC

The beginning of the decanates is from the Royal King Star of the Heart of the Lion, the great star Cor Leonis, and therefore is the first decanate that of Saturn in Leo.

Here follow the general meanings of the small cards of the Suits, as classified under the Nine Sephiroth below Kether.

CHOKMAH

The Four Twos symbolise the Powers of the King and Queen; first uniting and initiating the Force, but before the Knight and Knave are thoroughly brought into action. Therefore do they generally imply the initiation and fecundation of a thing.

BINAH

The Four Threes, generally, represent the realisation of action owing to the Prince being produced. The central symbol on each card. Action definitely commenced for good or evil.

CHESED

The Four Fours. Perfection, realisation, completion, making a matter settled and fixed.

GEBURAH

The Four Fives. Opposition, strife and struggle; war, obstacle to the thing in hand. Ultimate success or failure is otherwise shown.

TIPHARETH

The Four Sixes. Definite accomplishment, and carrying out of a matter.

NETZACH

The Four Sevens. Generally shows a force, transcending the material plane, and is like unto a crown which is indeed powerful but requireth one capable of wearing it. The Sevens then show a possible result which is dependent on the action then taken. They depend much on the symbols that accompany them.

HOD

The Four Eights. Generally show solitary success; i.e., success in the matter for the time being, but not leading to much result apart from the thing itself.

YESOD

The Four Nines. Generally they show very great fundamental force. Executive power, because they rest on a firm basis, powerful for good or evil.

MALKUTH

The Four Tens. Generally show fixed culminated completed Force, whether good or evil. The matter thoroughly and definitely determined. Similar to the force of the Nines, but ultimating it, and carrying it out. These are the meanings in the most general sense.

Here follow the more particular descriptions and meanings. **Decan cards are always modified by the other symbols with which they are in contact.**

VOLUME NINE

SATURN IN LEO, 1°-10°. THE LORD OFSTRIFE

FIVE OF WANDS

Two white radiant angelic hands issuing from clouds right and left of the centre of the card. They are clasped together as in the grip of the First Order, i.e. the four fingers of each right hand crooked into each other, the thumbs meeting above; and they hold at the same time by their centres Five Wands, or torches, which are similar to the wand of a Z.A.M. Four Wands cross each other, but the Fifth is upright in the centre. Flames leap from the point of junction. Above the central Wand is the symbol Saturn and below it that of Leo, representing the Decanate.

Violent strife and contest, boldness, rashness, cruelty, violence, lust and desire, prodigality and generosity, depending on well or ill dignified.

Geburah of Yod. (Quarrelling and fighting.) This decan hath its beginning from the Royal Star of Leo. and unto it are allotted the two Great Angels of the Schem- hamephoresch, Vahaviah and Yelayel.

JUPITER IN LEO, 10°-20°. LORD OF VICTORY

SIX OF WANDS

Two hands in grip, as in the last, holding six Wands crossed, 3 and 3. Flames issuing from the point of junction. Above and below are two short wands with flames issuing from a cloud at the lower part of the card, surmounted respectively by the symbols of Jupiter and Leo, representing the Decanate.

Victory after strife, success through energy and industry, love, pleasure gained by labour, carefulness, sociability and avoiding of strife, yet victory therein. Also insolence, pride of riches and success, etc. The whole depending on dignity.

Tiphareth of Yod. (Gain.) Hereunto are allotted the Great Angels from the Schem- hamephoresch, Saitel and Olmiah.

MARS IN LEO, 20°-30°. LORD OF VALOUR

SEVEN OF WANDS

Two hands holding by grip, as before, 6 Wands, three crossed by three, a third hand issuing from a cloud at the lower part of the card holding an upright wand, which passes between the others. Flames leap from the point of junction. Above and below the central wand are the symbols Mars and Leo, representing the Decan.

Possible victory, depending upon the energy and courage exercised; valour, opposition, obstacles, difficulties, yet courage to meet them, quarrelling, ignorance, pretence, wrangling and threatening, also victory in small and unimportant things, and influence over subordinates. Depending on dignity as usual.

Netzach of Yod. (Opposition yet courage.) Herein rule the two great Angels Mahashiah and Lelahel.

SUN IN VIRGO, 1°-10°. LORD OF PRUDENCE

EIGHT OF PENTACLES

A white radiating Angelic hand issuing from a cloud and grasping a branch of a Rose tree, with four white roses thereon which touch only the four lowermost pentacles. No rosebuds seen, but only leaves touch the four uppermost disks. All the Pentacles are similar to that of the Ace, but without the Maltese cross and wings. These are arranged as in the Geomantic figure Populus.

Above and below them are the symbols Sol and Virgo for the Decan. Over-careful in small things at the expense of the great. "Penny-wise and pound-foolish." Gain of ready money in small sums. Mean, avariciousness, Industrious, cultivation of land, hoarding, lacking in enterprise.

Hod of Heh. (Skill, prudence, cunning.) Here rule those mighty angels Akaiah and Kehethel.

VENUS IN VIRGO, 10°-20°. LORD OF MATERIAL GAIN

NINE OF PENTACLES

A white radiating angelic hand as before holding a Rose branch with nine white roses, each of which touches a Pentacle. (See the Golden Dawn Tarot Deck by Wang and Regardie, U.S. Game Systems, 1978-9 for the various arrangements indicated in these descriptions.)

There are more buds arranged on the branches as well as flowers. Venus and Virgo above and below.

Complete realisation of material gain, inheritance, covetousness, treasuring of goods and sometimes theft, and knavery. All according to dignity.

Yesod of Heh. (Inheritance, much increase of goods.) Herein rule the mighty angels Hazayel and Aldiah.

MERCURY IN VIRGO, 20°-30°. LORD OF WEALTH

TEN OF PENTACLES

An Angelic hand holding a branch by the lower extremity, whose roses touch all the pentacles. No buds however are shown. The symbols of Mercury and Virgo are above and below Pentacles.

Completion of material gain and fortune, but nothing beyond, as it were, at the very pinnacle of success. Old age, slothfulness, great wealth, yet sometimes loss in part, and later heaviness, dullness of mind, yet clever and prosperous in money transactions.

Malkuth of Heh. (Riches and wealth.) Herein rule the Angels Hihaayah and Laviah.

MOON IN LIBRA, 1°-10°. LORD OF PEACE RESTORED

TWO OF SWORDS

Two crossed swords, like the air dagger of Z. A. M., each held by a white radiating angelic hand. Upon the point where the two cross is a rose of five petals, emitting white Rays, and top and bottom of card are two small daggers, supporting respectively the symbols of Luna (in horizontal position) and Libra, representing the Decan.

Contradictory characteristics in the same nature. Strength through suffering. Pleasure after Pain. Sacrifice and trouble yet strength arising therefrom symbolised by the position of the rose, as though the pain itself had brought forth beauty. Peace restored, truce, arrangement of differences, justice. Truth and untruth. Sorrow and sympathy for those in trouble, aid to the weak and oppressed, unselfishness. Also an inclination to repetition of affronts if once pardoned, of asking questions of little moment, want of tact, often doing injury when meaning well. Talkative.

Chokmah of Vav. (Quarrels made up, but still some tension in relationships. Actions sometimes selfish and sometimes unselfish.) Herein rule the great Angels Yezalel and Mebahel.

SATURN IN LIBRA, 10°-20°. LORD OF SORROW

THREE OF SWORDS

Three white radiating angelic hands issuing from clouds and holding three swords upright (as if the central sword had struck apart from the two others which were crossed in the preceding symbol.) The central sword cuts asunder the Rose of Five Petals (which in the preceding symbol grew at the junction of the swords). Its petals are falling, and no white rays issue from it. Above and below the central Sword are the symbols of Saturn and Libra, referring to the Decanate.

Disruption, interruption, separation, quarrelling, sowing of discord and strife, mischief-making, sorrow, tears, yet mirth in evil pleasures, singing, faithfulness in promises, honesty in money transactions, selfish and dissipated, yet sometimes generous, deceitful in words and repetition. The whole according to dignity.

Binah of Vau. (Unhappiness, sorrow, tears.) Therein rule the Angels Harayel and Hoqmiah.

JUPITER IN LIBRA, 20°-30°. THE LORD OF REST FROM STRIFE

FOUR OF SWORDS

Two white angelic radiating hands, each holding two swords, which four cross in the centre. The rose of five petals with white radiations is reinstated on the point of intersection. Above and below, on the points of two small daggers are the symbols of Jupiter and Libra representing the Decan.

Rest from sorrow, yet after and through it. Peace from and after war. Relaxation of anxiety. Quietness, rest, ease and plenty, yet after struggle. Goods of this life, abundance. Modified by the dignity as in the other cases.

Chesed of Vav. (Convalescence, recovery from sickness, change for the better.) Herein rule Laviah and Kelial.

MARS IN SCORPIO, 1°-10°. LORD OF LOSS IN PLEASURE

FIVE OF CUPS

A white radiating angelic hand as before holding Lotuses or water lilies of which the flowers are falling right and left. Leaves only and no buds surmount them. These lotus stems

17

ascend between the cups in the manner of a fountain, but no water flows therefrom, neither is there water in any of the Cups, which are somewhat of the shape of the magical implement of the Z.A.M. Above and below are the symbols of Mars and Scorpio, representing the Decan.

Death or end of pleasures: disappointment, sorrow and loss in those things from which pleasure is expected. Sadness, deceit, treachery, ill-will, detraction, charity and kindness ill-requited. All kinds of anxieties and troubles from unexpected and unsuspected sources.

Geburah of Heh. (Disappointments in love, marriage broken off, unkindness from a friend, loss of friendship.) Therein rule Livoyah and Pehilyah.

SUN IN SCORPIO, 10°-20#. LORD OF PLEASURE

SIX OF CUPS

An angelic hand as before, holds a group of stems of Lotuses or water lilies from which six flowers bend, one over each cup. From these flowers a white glistening water flows into the cup as from a fountain, but they are not yet full. Above and below are the symbols of Sun and Scorpio, representing the Decanate.

Commencement of steady increase, gain and pleasure, but commencement only. Also affront, detection, knowledge, and in some instances, contention and strife, arising from unwarranted self-assertion and vanity. Sometimes thankless and presumptuous. Sometimes amiable and patient, according to dignity.

Tiphareth of Heh. (Beginning of wish, happiness, success or enjoyment.) Therein rule Nelokhiel and Yeyayel.

VENUS IN SCORPIO, 20°-30°. LORD OF ILLUSIONARY SUCCESS

SEVEN OF CUPS

A hand as usual holds the lotus stems which arise from the central lower cup. The hand is above this cup and below the middle one. With the exception of the central lower cup, each is overhung by a lotus flower, but no water falls from them into cups which are quite empty. Above and below are the symbols of the decanate, Venus and Scorpio.

Possibly victory, but neutralized by the supineness of the person. Illusionary success. Deception in the moment of apparent victory. Lying, error, promises unfulfilled. Drunkenness, wrath, vanity, lust, fornication, violence against women. Selfish dissipation. Deception in love and friendship. Often success gained, but not followed up. Modified by dignity.

Netzach of Heh. (Lying. Promises unfulfilled. Illusion. Error. Deception, slight success at outset, but want of energy to retain it.) Therein rule Melchel and Chahaviah.

MERCURY IN SAGITTARIUS, 1°-10°. THE LORD OF SWIFTNESS

EIGHT OF WANDS

Four white Angelic Hands radiating (two proceeding from each side) from clouds, clasped in two pairs in the centre with the grip of First Order. (See description above.) They hold 8 wands crossed four and four. Flames issue from the point of junction. Surmounting two small wands with flames issuing down them. Placed in the centre at top and bottom of card are the symbols of Mercury and Sagittarius, representing the Decan.

Too much force applied too suddenly. Very rapid rush, but too quickly passed and expended. Violent but not lasting. Swiftness. Rapidity. Courage, boldness, confidence, freedom, warfare. Violence, love of open air, field sports, garden, meadows. Generous, subtle, eloquent, yet somewhat untrustworthy. Rapacious, insolent, oppressive. Theft and robbery, according to dignity.

Hod of Yod. (Hasty communication and messages. Swiftness.) Therein rule Nithahiah and Haayah.

MOON IN SAGITTARIUS, 10°-20°. THE LORD OF GREAT STRENGTH

NINE OF WANDS

Four Hands as in the previous symbol holding eight wands crossed four and four, but a fifth hand at the foot of the card holds another wand upright, which traverses the point of junction with the others. Flames leap therefrom. Above and below the symbols Luna (depicted horizontally) and Sagittarius.

Tremendous and steady force that cannot be shaken. Herculean strength, yet sometimes scientifically applied. Great success, but with strife and energy. Victory preceded by apprehension and fear. Health good and recovery, yet doubt. Generous, questioning and curious, fond of external appearances, intractable, obstinate.

Yesod of Yod. (Strength, power, health. Recovery from sickness.) Herein rule Yirthiel and Sahiah.

SATURN IN SAGITTARIUS, 20°-30°. THE LORD OF OPPRESSION

TEN OF WANDS

Four hands upholding 8 wands crossed as before. A fifth hand at foot of card holding two wands upright which traverse the junction of the others. Above and below the symbols Saturn and Sagittarius. Flames issue therefrom.

Cruel and overbearing force and energy, but applied only to selfish and material ends. Sometimes shows failure in a matter, and the opposition too strong to be controlled arising from the person's too great selfishness at the beginning. Ill-will, levity, lying, malice, slander, envy, obstinacy, swiftness in evil, if ill-dignified. Also generosity, self-sacrifice, and disinterestedness when well-dignified.

Malkuth of Yod. (Cruelty, malice, revenge and injustice.) Therein rule Reyayel and Avamel.

JUPITER IN CAPRICORN, 1°-10°. LORD OF HARMONIOUS CHANGE

TWO OF PENTACLES

Two wheels, discs or Pentacles similar to that of the Ace. They are united by a green and gold Serpent, bound about them like a figure of Eight. It holds its tail in its mouth. A white radiant angelic hand grasps the centre or holds the whole. No roses enter into this card. Above and below are the symbols Jupiter and Capricorn. It is a revolving symbol.

The harmony of change. Alternation of gain and loss, weakness and strength, ever varying occupation, wandering, discontented with any fixed condition of things; now elated, now melancholy, industrious yet unreliable, fortunate through prudence of management, yet sometimes unaccountably foolish. Alternately talkative and suspicious. Kind yet wavering and inconsistent. Fortunate in journeying. Argumentative.

Chokmah of Heh final. (Pleasant change, visit to friends.) Herein rule Lekabel and Veshiriah.

MARS IN CAPRICORN, 10°-20°. THE LORD OF MATERIAL WORKS

THREE OF PENTACLES

A white rayed angelic hand as before, holding a branch of a Rose-tree, of which two white rose-buds touch and surmount the topmost pentacle. The latter are arranged in a Triangle

Above and below are symbols of Mars and Capricorn. Working and constructive force, building up, erection, creation, realisation, and increase of material things, gain in commercial transactions, rank, increase of substance, influence, cleverness in business, selfishness, commencement of matter to be established later. Narrow and prejudiced, keen in matter of gain. Modified by dignity. Sometimes given to seeking after the impossible.

Binah of Heh final. (Business, paid employment, commercial transactions.) Therein rule Yechavah and Lehachiah.

SUN IN CAPRICORN, 20°-30°. THE LORD OF EARTHLY POWER

FOUR OF PENTACLES

A hand holding a branch of a Rose-tree, but without flowers or buds, save that in the centre is one fully blown white rose. Four pentacles with Sun and Capricorn above and below. Assured material gain, success, rank, dominion, earthly power completed, but leading to nothing beyond. Prejudiced, covetous, suspicious, careful and orderly, but discontented.

Little enterprise or originality. Altered by dignity as usual. Chesed of Heh final. (Gain of money or influence. A present.) Therein rule Keveqiah and Mendial.

VENUS IN AQUARIUS, 1°-10°. THE LORD OF DEFEAT

FIVE OF SWORDS

Two rayed hands each holding two swords nearly upright, but falling apart from each other, right and left of card. A third hand holds a sword upright in centre as if it had separated them. The petals of the rose (which in the four of Swords had been reinstated in the centre) are torn asunder and falling. Above and below the symbols of Venus and Aquarius.

Contest finished, and decided against the person, failure, defeat, anxiety, trouble, poverty, avarice, grieving after gain, laborious, unresting, loss and vileness of nature. Malicious, slandering, lying, spiteful and talebearing. A busybody and separator of friends, hating to see peace and love between others. Cruel yet cowardly, thankless, and unreliable. Clever and quick in thought and speech. Feelings of pity easily roused but unenduring. As dignity.

Geburah of Vav. (Defeat, loss, malice, spite, slander, evil-speaking.) Herein rule Aniel and Chaamiah.

VOLUME NINE

MERCURY IN AQUARIUS, 10°-20°. THE LORD OF EARNED SUCCESS

SIX OF SWORDS

Two hands as before, each holding three swords which cross in centre. Rose re established hereon. Mercury and Aquarius above and below, supported on the points of two short daggers or swords.

Success after anxiety and trouble. Selfishness, beauty, conceit, but sometimes modesty therewith, dominion, patience, labour, etc., according to dignity.

Tiphareth of Vav. (Labour, work, journey by water.) Herein rule Rehaayaland Yeyeziel.

MOON IN AQUARIUS, 20°-30°. THE LORD OF UNSTABLE EFFORT

SEVEN OF SWORDS

Two hands as before, each holding swords. A third hand holds a single sword in the centre. The points of all the swords do just touch one another, the central sword not altogether dividing them. The rose of the previous symbols of this suit is held by the hand which holds the central Sword, as if the Victory were at its disposal. Above and below Luna and Aquarius. (In the small cards, the Lunar Decans are always represented by a crescent on its back.)

Partial success, yielding when victory is within grasp, as if the last reserves of strength were used up. Inclination to lose when on the point of gaining though not continuing the effort. Love of abundance, fascinated by display, given to compliment, affronts and insolences, and to detect and spy on another. Inclined to betray confidences, not always intentional. Rather vacillating and unreliable, according to dignity as usual.

Nt tzach of Vav. (Journey by land, in character untrustworthy.) Herein rule Michael and Hahihel.

SATURN IN PISCES, 1°-10°. THE LORD OF ABANDONED SUCCESS

EIGHT OF CUPS

A hand holding a group of stems of Lotuses or water lilies. There are only two flowers shown which bend over the two center cups pouring into them a white water. The cups are not yet filled. The three upper cups are empty. At top and bottom are Saturn and Pisces.

Temporary success, but without further result. Things thrown aside as soon as gained. No lasting even in the matter in hand. Indolence in success. Journeying from place to place. Misery and repining without cause. Seeking after riches. Instability according to dignity.

Hod of Heh. (Success abandoned, decline of interest in anything.) Herein rule Vavaliah and Yeihiah.

JUPITER IN PISCES, 10°-20°. THE LORD OF MATERIAL HAPPINESS

NINE OF CUPS

Hand from cloud holding Lotuses or water lilies, one flower of which overhangs each cup, and from which water pours. All the cups are full and running over. Above and below are the symbols of Jupiter and Pisces representing the Decan.

Complete and perfect realisation of pleasure and happiness almost perfect. Self-praise, vanity, conceit, much talking of self, yet kind and lovable, and may be self-denying therewith. Highminded, not easily satisfied with small and limited ideas. Apt to be maligned through too much self-assumption. A good, generous, but, maybe, foolish nature.

Yesod of Heh. (Complete success, pleasure, happiness, wish fulfilled.) Therein rule Saliah and Aariel.

MARS IN PISCES, 20°-30°. THE LORD OF PERFECTED SUCCESS

TEN OF CUPS

Hand holding bunch of Lotuses or water-lilies whose flowers pour a pure white water into all the cups, which all run over. The top cup is held sideways by a hand and pours water into top left hand cup. A single lotus flower surmounts top cup and is the source of the water that fills it. Above and are below Mars and Pisces.

Permanent and lasting success, happiness because inspired from above. Not sensual as Nine of Cups, The Lord of Material Happiness, yet almost more truly happy. Pleasure, dissipation, debauchery.

Pity, quietness, peacemaking. Kindness, generosity, wantonness, waste, etc., according to dignity.

Malkuth of Heh. (Matters definitely arranged as wished, complete good fortune.) Herein rule Aasliah and Mihal.

[This is not such a good card as stated above. It represents boredom and quarrelling arising therefrom; disgust springing from too great luxury. In particular it could represent drug habits, the sottish excess of pleasure and the revenge of nature.]

MARS IN ARIES, 1°-10°. THE LORD OF DOMINION

TWO OF WANDS

Hand grasping two Wands crossed. Flames issue from the point of junction. On two small wands, above and below, with flames issuing from them, are Mars and Aries.

Strength, dominion, harmony of rule and justice. Boldness, courage, fierceness, shamelessness, revenge, resolution, generous, proud, sensitive, ambitious, refined, restless, turbulent, sagacious withal, yet unforgiving and obstinate, according to dignity.

Chokmah of Yod. (Influence over others. Authority, power, dominion.) Rule therein Vehooel and Deneyal.

VOLUME NINE

SUN IN ARIES, 10°-20#. THE LORD OF ESTABLISHED STRENGTH

THREE OF WANDS

Hand issuing from clouds holds three wands in centre. Two crossed and one upright. Flames from point of junction. Above and below are Sun and Aries.

Established force and strength. Realisation of hope. Completion of labour, success of the struggle. Pride, nobility, wealth, power, conceit. Rude self assumption and insolence. Generosity, obstinacy according to dignity.

Binah of Yod. (Pride, arrogance and self-assertion.) Herein rule Hechashiah and Aamamiah.

VENUS IN ARIES 20°-30N. LORD OF PERFECTED WORK

FOUR OF WANDS

Two hands as before, issuing from clouds each side of card, and clasped in centre with First Order grip, holding four wands crossed. Flames issue at point of junction. Above and below are two small flaming wands with Venus and Aries, representing the Decan.

Perfection, a completion of a thing built up with trouble and labour. Rest after labour. Subtlety, cleverness, beauty, mirth, success in completion. Reasoning faculty, conclusions drawn from previous knowledge. Unreadiness, unreliable, and unsteady, through over anxiety and hurriedness of action. Graceful in manners. At times insincere, etc.

Chesed of Yod. (Settlement, arrangement, completion.) Herein rule Nanael and Nithal.

MERCURY IN TAURUS, LORD OF MATERIAL TROUBLE

FIVE OF PENTACLES

Hand holding a branch of White Rose Tree, from which roses are falling, leaving no buds behind. Five pentacles similar to Ace: Mercury and Taurus for Decan.

Loss of money or position. Trouble about material things. Toil, labour, land cultivation, building, knowledge and acuteness of earthly things, poverty, carefulness. Kindness, sometimes money regained after severe toil and labour. Unimaginative, harsh, stern, determined, obstinate.

Geburah of Heh final. (Loss of profession, loss of money, monetary anxiety.) Therein rule Mibahiah and Pooyal.

MOON IN TAURUS, 10⁰-20°. LORD OF MATERIAL SUCCESS

SIX OF PENTACLES

Hand holding a rose branch with white roses and buds, each of which touch a pentacle. Above and below Luna and Taurus represent the Decanate.

Success and gain in material undertakings, power, influence, rank, nobility, rule over the people. Fortunate, successful, just and liberal. If ill-dignified, may be purse-proud, insolent from success, or prodigal.

Tiphareth of Heh final. (Success in material things. Prosperity in business.) Herein rule Nemamiah and Yeyelal.

SATURN IN TAURUS, 20°-30°. THE LORD OF SUCCESS UNFULFILLED

SEVEN OF PENTACLES

Hand from a cloud holding rose branch of seven pentacles arranged as in Rubeus. Only five of which overhang but do not touch the five upper pentacles. No other buds shown, and none are near or touch the two lower pentacles. Above and below are Saturn and Taurus.

Promises of success unfulfilled. (Shown in the symbolism of the rosebuds, which do not as it were come to anything.) Loss of apparently promising fortune. Hopes deceived and crushed. Disappointment. Misery, slavery, necessity and baseness. A cultivator of land, and yet is loser thereby. Sometimes it denotes slight and isolated gains with no fruits resulting therefrom, and of no further account, though seeming to promise well. According to dignity.

Netzach of Heh. (Unprofitable speculation and employment. Little gain for much labour.) Therein rule Herochiel and Mitzrael.

JUPITER IN GEMINI, 1°-10°. LORD OF SHORTENED FORCE

EIGHT OF SWORDS

Four hands as usual, each holding two swords, points upwards, touching near top of card, two hands lower on left, two on right of card. The rose of other sword symbols re-established in centre. Above and below are Jupiter and Gemini.

Too much force applied to small things, too much attention to detail, at expense of principle and more important points. Ill-dignified, these qualities produce malice, pettiness, and domineering qualities.

Patience in detail of study, great ease in some things, counter-balanced by equal disorder in others. Impulsive, equally fond of giving or receiving money, or presents. Generous, clever, acute, selfish, and without strong feeling of affection. Admires wisdom, yet applies it to small and unworthy objects.

Hod of Vav. (Narrow, restricted, petty, a prison.) Herein rule Vemibael and Yehohel.

MARS IN GEMINI, 10°-20°. THE LORD OF DESPAIR AND CRUELTY

NINE OF SWORDS

Four hands (somewhat as in preceding symbol) hold eight swords upright but with the points falling away from each other. A fifth hand holds a ninth sword upright in the centre, as if it had disunited them, and struck them asunder. No rose at all is shown (as if it were not merely cut in pieces but completely and definitely destroyed). Above and below Mars and Gemini.

Despair, cruelty, pitilessness, malice, suffering, want, loss, misery. Burden, oppression, labour, subtlety and craft, lying, dishonesty, slander. Yet also obedience, faithfulness, patience, unselfishness, etc., according to dignity.

Yesod of Vau. Therein rule Aaneval and Mochayel.

VOLUME NINE

SUN IN GEMINI, 20°-30°. LORD OF RUIN

TEN OF SWORDS

Four hands (as in previous symbol) hold eight swords with points falling away from each other. Two hands hold two swords crossed in the centre (as if their junction had disunited the others). No rose, flower or bud is shown. Above and below are Sun and Gemini.

(Almost a worse symbol than Nine of Swords.) Undisciplined warring force, complete disruption and failure. Ruin of all plans and projects. Disdain, insolence and impertinence, yet mirth and jolly therewith. A Marplot, loving to overthrow the happiness of others, a repeater of things, given to much unprofitable speech, and of many words, yet clever, acute, and eloquent, etc., depending on dignity.

Malkuth of Vav. (Ruin, death, defeat, disruption.) Herein rule Dambayah and Menqal.

VENUS IN CANCER, 1°-10. LORD OF LOVE

TWO OF CUPS

Hand at lower part from cloud holds lotuses. A Lotus flower rises above water, which occupies the lowest part of card, and rises above the hand holding the Lotus. From this Lotus flower a stem rises, terminating nearly at the top of the card in another Lotus or water-lily flower, from which a white water gushes like a fountain. Crossed on the stem just beneath are two Dolphins, Argent and Or, on to which the water falls and from which it pours in full streams, like jets of gold and silver, into two cups, which in their turn overflow, flooding the lower part of the card. Above and below Venus and Cancer.

Harmony of masculine and feminine united. Harmony, pleasure, mirth, subtlety, sometimes folly, dissipation, waste, and silly action, according to dignity.

Chokmah of Heh. (Marriage, home, pleasure.) Herein rule Ayoel and Chabooyah.

MERCURY IN CANCER, 10°-20°. LORD OF ABUNDANCE

THREE OF CUPS

Hands as before holds group of Lotuses or Water-lilies, from which two flowers rise on either side of, and overhanging the top cup, pouring into it the white water. Flowers in the same way pour water into the lower cups. All the cups overflow, the topmost into the two others, and these upon the lower part of the card. Above and below Mercury and Cancer.

Abundance, plenty, success, pleasure, sensuality, passive success, good luck and fortune. Love, gladness, kindness and bounty. According to dignity.

Binah of Heh. (Plenty, hospitality, eating and drinking, pleasure, dancing, new clothes, merriment.) Herein rule Rahael and Yebomayah.

MOON IN CANCER, 20°-30°. THE LORD OF BLENDED PLEASURE

FOUR OF CUPS

Four cups, the two upper overflow into the two lower, which do not overflow. A hand grasps a bunch of lotuses from which ascends a stem bearing one flower at the top of the card, from which water issues into two top cups. From the centre two leaves pass right and left, making as it were a cross between the four cups. Luna and Cancer are above and below.

Success or pleasure approaching their end. A stationary period in happiness which may or may not continue. It does not show marriage and love so much as the previous symbol. It is too passive a symbol to represent perfectly complete happiness. Swiftness, hunting and pursuing. Acquisition by contention; injustice sometimes. Some drawbacks to pleasure implied.

Chesed of Heh. (Receiving pleasure, but some slight discomfort and anxieties, therewith. Blended pleasure and success.) Therein rule Hayayel and Mevamayah.

NOTE

By

G.H. FRATER D.D.C.F.

Here finishes the description of the 36 smaller cards, referring to the 36 Decanates of the Zodiac. Although the Angels of the Schem ha-mephoresch have been linked with the Decanates, yet their dominion is far more exalted, extended, and important than this would at first sight seem to imply. In all of this I have not only transcribed the symbolism, but have tested, studied, compared, and examined it both clairvoyantly and in other ways. The result of these has been to show me how absolutely correct the symbolism of the Book T is, and how exactly it represents the occult Forces of the Universe.

TAROT DIVINATION

This form is especially applicable to Divination concerning the ordinary material events of daily life.

It is a mode of placing the cards based upon the scheme of the dominion of the Tarot Symbols. **The more rigidly correct and in harmony with the scheme of the Universe is any form of Divination, so much the more is it likely to yield a correct and reliable answer to the enquirer.** For then and then only is there a firm link, and bond of union, established between it and the Occult forces of Nature. The moment the correct correspondence of the Symbols employed ceases to be observed, the link between them and the inner Occult forces is strained, and in some cases broken. For this cause, therefore, is it that the same mode of Divination will sometimes yield a true and sometimes false answer, and at other times a partly true and partly false; because the correspondences are either not rigidly observed or else made use of by an ignorant and uninitiated person.

Therefore the Diviner should enter upon the Divination with a mind clear and unprejudiced, neither disturbed by anger, fear, nor love, and with a sound knowledge of the correspondences of the symbols which he employs. Also he should be able to employ his clairvoyant and intuitive faculties therein when necessary and should avoid as much as possible a warped or strained decision. Also it is not well to divine repeatedly concerning the same matter; and the Diviner should also recognise that even the material occult forces do not act as the instruments of a blind fatality, but rather in accordance with the will of the more spiritual powers which are behind them.

Also it may be well for the Diviner to put on his insignia, and make over the pack any invoking hexagram or pentagram, either with the hand alone, or with convenient magical instruments. And it may also be advisable in some instances to invoke an elemental force consonant with the matter, to aid in the divination.

VOLUME NINE

And let it not be forgotten that in working with the lesser magical implements all four should be at hand, even though only one be actually employed. For if this be not done, it will give undue force to the suit corresponding to the Element invoked, and instead of being an aid in the matter, it will be a hindrance to correct reading.

THE OPENING OF THE KEY

The mode of performing the Divination called "The Opening of the Key" is by five consecutive operations of laying out the cards, they having been previously well shuffled, and, in addition in the first and fourth cases, having been cut as well, and in a certain manner. These five operations answer respectively, the first to the Dominion of the Four Knaves under the presidency of the Four Aces; the Second to that of the Kings, Queens and Knights, referred to the Twelve Houses; the Third to that of the Twelve Keys attributed to the Signs; the Fourth to that of the smaller cards answering to the 36 Decanates; and the Fifth and last to the rule of the Sephiroth in the Celestial Heavens.

These are five distinct operations, consecutively executed from the mode of Operation called the "Opening of the Key," which, as has been before said, is especially applicable to the daily events of life. The first of these methods shows the opening of the matter as it then stands. The 2nd, 3rd, 4th, its consecutive development, and the 5th its termination.

Before commencing the Divination, one of the sixteen court cards should be selected to represent the significator of the enquirer, and should answer as nearly to his description.

> **WANDS generally - very fair-haired and red-haired persons with fair complexion.**
> **CUPS generally - moderately fair persons.**
> **SWORDS generally - dark persons.**
> **PENTACLES generally - very dark persons.**
> **KINGS - Generally men.**
> **QUEENS - Generally women.**
> **KNIGHTS - Generally young men.**
> **PAGES (KNAVES) - generally young women.**

Of these the Queens and Knights in reading the cards during the processes almost always represent persons connected with a matter under consideration. The Kings, if looking against the direction of the reading, or if meeting it, represent the coming of a person or event, or phase of an event, but if looking with the direction of the reading represent the departure of a person or the going off or wane of some event.

The Pages (Knaves) if looking with the direction of the reading, represent general opinion in harmony with, and approving of the matter; but if looking against the direction of the reading the reverse.

If the Diviner be performing the Divination for a person at a distance and of whose general description he is ignorant, he can select the significator by cutting the pack, and taking one of the court cards of that suit, cut to represent him, of course earnestly thinking of the person at the time.

It is usually much better for the Enquirer to shuffle or cut the cards himself; but if the Diviner should have to do this himself, he must, while doing so, earnestly think of the person enquiring, or concerning whom the Divination is performed. In all cases of shuffling and cutting, the person doing so should think earnestly of the matter in hand. In cutting, if a false cut be made, that is to say if one or more cards should drop in the process, the cards should be at once reshuffled, and again cut clearly, otherwise it is probable that the answer will be unreliable. If the matter be important, he should wait twelve hours before reshuffling.

In the laying out of the Cards, if any are inverted, they must remain so and must not be turned round, as that would alter the direction in which they would be looking. A card has the same meaning and forces, whether right side up or inverted, so that no particular attention need be paid to the circumstances.

The order of the cards as laid down must also not be interfered with. In the reading of the cards when laid out, the Significator of the Enquirer is the starting point, and reading proceeds by counting over certain cards in the direction in which the face of the Court card chosen as Significator of the Enquirer is turned.

AN ALTERNATIVE METHOD OF SELECTING THE SIGNIFICATOR

By

C.S. HYATT

(In 1963 by chance I met a lady who sought employment as a part-time baby sitter. After a few months of employment she introduced me to the Tarot system, which from this point of time seems similar to if not identical with the Golden Dawn System herein described. However she used a different method of determining the significator, using both astrology and numerology.

First she requested the birth data. From this she determined if the sign was either Fire, Water, Air or Earth. She attributed Wands to Fire, Cups to Water, Swords to Air, and Pentacles to Earth. For example, November 17, 1907, would be (11-17-1907). First this querent would be a Cup since Scorpio is the Sun sign in early November. Next she would simply add the numbers together giving a total of 45. This number would be reduced to a number from two to ten (excluding the number one) in this case giving the number 9. So that the significator is the 9 of Cups which is the Lord of Material Happiness.) Now we may return to the official document of D.D.C.F.

The mode of counting is as follows, recognising the card from which one starts as the No. 1.

From every Ace - Count five cards (spirit and four elements).

Princess (Knave) Seven cards (seven palaces of Malkuth).

King, Queen, Knight - Count four cards, (letters of Tetragrammaton).

Smaller cards - Count its own number (a Sephirah).

Key of Aleph - Mem - Shin - Count three cards (number of the Mother letters).

Key of double letters - Count nine cards (number of planets and Caput and Cauda Draconis).

Key of single letters - Count twelve cards (number of signs).

The counting is continued till one alights on a card which has already been read.

Thus, in the following example, we will suppose that the significator is the Queen of Cups, and that she is looking to the left. We should read as follows: Queen of Cups - a fair woman; counting four, we come to Five of Pentacles, i.e. "Loss of money"(and as it has on one side the Moon and on the other a card of Pentacles, it shows that it is through deception in business matters). We then count 5, (the number of the card) from the 5 of Pentacles. This falls on the 6 of Cups "Success." But as this has on one side the Foolish Man, and on the other the Ace of Wands, this will not be great owing to unwise conduct. Then we count six from the 6 of Cups, still going in the same direction which brings us to the Queen of Cups, a card we have already read, so we finish there.

SIGNIFICATOR - QUEEN OF CUPS

Thus the reading will be "A rather fair woman has lost money through some cheating in business, and though she is again beginning to succeed, this success is liable to be damaged by unwise conduct on her part for which she will have herself to thank."

If the significator were the Knave of Wands, and (looking towards the right) we should count seven to the 2 of Pentacles, then two from that to the 5 of Pentacles. Then five from that to the Hierophant, twelve from that to the Queen of Cups, four from that to the King of Pentacles. Then four to the Foolish Man, and thence three to the 2 of Pentacles, where we stop, having read that card already. The interpretation given is: "A young woman is just making a change in her business, which brings her loss of money through some deceit on the part of a fair woman and a dark man whose foolish advice has led to the change." The cards would then be paired two by two. from opposite ends as hereafter shown, (as in a horseshoe) thus: Moon and Tower, etc.

From the Moon and the Tower, "The deceit is discovered." 3 of Pentacles and Queen of Cups, "On the part of this person who has brought about her loss." 2 of Pentacles and Hierophant, "by advising the change." Knight of Cups and Knight of Wands, "for the young woman meets an older man," King of Pentacles and Fool "who counteract the foolish advice of the dark man." Ace of Wands and 6 of Cups "and she in consequence succeeds better, but only by the dint of energy and hard work."

The scheme of Divination called "The Opening of the Key" is worked out in the following manner. I adjoin an example carried carefully through the five stages for the instruction of the Z.A.M. The complete pack of 78 cards is employed.

FIRST OPERATION

REPRESENTING THE OPENING OF THE QUESTION

The significator being chosen, the enquirer shuffles the cards, thinking earnestly of the matter under consideration. He then places the cards in a single packet on the table before him, face downwards. This represents the Name YHVH, which is now to be separated into the component letters. He therefore is to cut the pack as nearly in the middle as his eye can direct, and to face the uppermost portion to the right of the lowermost; the former will represent YH and the latter VH (final). He again is to cut the right hand packet into two parts, as nearly in the centre as he can, and place the uppermost part to the right again. This will represent Y and the lower part the remaining H. He is now to cut the left hand packet to the left, its uppermost part will represent V and its lower part H (final). So that he will now have four packets nearly equal in size, answering from **right to left** to the name YHVH under the presidency of the Four Princesses (knaves) and through them to the four radical forces (Aces). These four packets are then turned face upwards without altering their relative position, and the meaning of their four bottom cards (which are now uppermost) thus shown may be read as an indication of the matter. Each packet is now examined to find where the Significator of the Enquirer is, being careful not to alter the order of the Cards. The packet containing the Significator is retained for reading, and the others are put aside and not used in this particular reading (operation). Carefully note to which of the Four letters the packet containing the significator of the Enquirer corresponds. If to Y and Wands, energy and strife. If to H and Cups, pleasure. If to V and Swords, sickness and trouble. If to H final and Pentacles, business and money. The packet containing the significator is now spread out face upwards in the form of a horseshoe (count in the way the Significator looks) and its meaning is read in the manner previously described.

First by counting to certain cards until one alights upon that which has been previously read; and then by pairing them together in succession from opposite ends of the horseshoe. (You do not miss the significator.)

Before commencing counting from the Significator, the Diviner should first notice what suit predominates in the number of cards. In this a majority of Wands would signify energy, quarrelling, opposition. Of Cups, pleasure and merriment. Of Swords, trouble and sadness, sometimes sickness and death. Of Pentacles, business, money, possession, etc. Also if in the cards laid out there should be either three or four cards of a sort, such as 3 Aces. 4 Fives, etc., their meaning should be noted according to the table hereafter given. A majority of the Trumps (Major Arcana) shows forces beyond one's control.

Supposing that a young man asks the question "Shall I succeed in my present affairs?" His complexion is fair, and his hair light brown. The Diviner therefore takes the Knight of Cups for Significator. (Had he been an older man he would have selected the King of the same suit instead) and requests Enquirer to carefully shuffle the pack and place it face downwards on the table before him. He then instructs him to cut the pack as nearly in the centre as possible, and to place the uppermost half well to the right. Then to cut each of the packets as nearly in the centre as possible, putting each uppermost half to the right of and beside the lower half, thus yielding four packets of nearly equal dimensions.

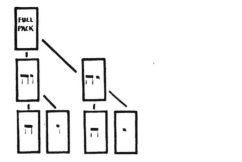
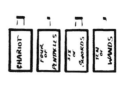

Here the 10 of Wands is strong, being in the place of Yod which governs Wands - Fire. The Six of Swords is moderately strong, being in the place of Heh which rules Cups - Water, which is not a hostile and contrary element to Air; the 4 of Pentacles is weak because it is in the place of Vau which rules the contrary element to Earth, viz. Air; and the Chariot, Cancer, a watery sign, is fairly strong, being in the place of Heh final, which rules Earth, a friendly element to Water.

The Diviner then reads these 4 Cards as a preliminary thus: "The Enquirer works very hard and gains but little money, yet matters are beginning to improve." This is based on the 10 of Wands showing cruelty, harshness, etc. 6 of Swords labour and work. 4 of Pentacles gain of money, and the Chariot success.

The Diviner then examines the Four Packets to find where the Significator is. It proves to be in the one of which the 6 of Swords is the bottom card. This is in the place answering to the letter Heh, which represents pleasure and rules Cups. This is so far a good omen, as it shows society and merriment. This pack of cards is retained for reading, the others are put aside as not bearing on the question.

Let us suppose that this packet consists of 20 cards, and that they are in the following order. The Diviner spreads them out in the form of a horseshoe:

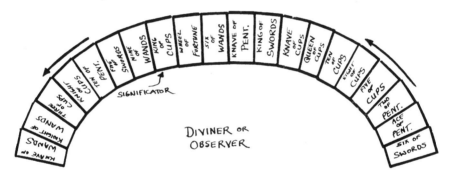

The suit of Cups is distinctly in the majority - pleasure, visiting friends, love-making, etc. There are 3 Knaves which indicates society of the young. From which the Diviner reads that the Enquirer is fond of young people and of flirting, etc. There being no other set of 3 or 4 cards of a sort, the Diviner proceeds to read by counting from the Significator, whose face is turned towards the 9 of Wands.

The counting therefore proceeds in the direction of the arrow, thus: 4 from the King of Cups, 10 of Pentacles, 10 from this, 8 of Cups. 8 from this, Wheel of Fortune. 9 from this, Knave of Wands, 7 from this, 10 of Cups. 10 from this, 5 of Swords. 5 from this, Knight of Wands. 4 from this, Ace of Pentacles. 5 from this, 10 of Cups. And as this card has already been taken, this form of reading finishes here.

In this reading as hereafter explained, each card is modified by the card on either side of it. If it be an end card, such as the 6 of Swords, in this case it is modified not only by the card next to it, Ace of Pentacles, but also by the card at the opposite end, Knave of Wands.

If these cards are of a contrary element to the card itself, they very much weaken and neutralize its force, but if the contrary element is only in one card, and the other is of a connecting nature, it does not much matter. This is explained later among the tabulated rules. The King of Cups is between the 9 of Wands and the Wheel of Fortune, both of which cards are of a fiery nature, and therefore contrary to Cups which is Water, and therefore it shows that the Enquirer is rather lacking in perseverance and energy. 10 of Pentacles, "His business will begin to prosper," 8 of Cups, "but yet he will lose interest in it, owing to his love of pleasure and society" (shown by 8 of Cups having the suit on each side of it). Wheel of Fortune, "and through his fortune changing for the better." Knave of Wands (Knight of Wands on one side and 6 of Swords on the other), "He yet is anxious through falling in love with a graceful and sprightly girl with chestnut hair and fair complexion whom he has recently met: (shown by Knight of Wands turned contrary to the course of the reading). 10 of Cups, "His suit is at first favourably received." 5 of Swords, "but some slanderous reports and mischief making" (not altogether without foundation) "come to her knowledge." Ace of Pentacles, "though his increasing prosperity in business." 10 of Cups, "had lead her to regard him with favour."

The Diviner now pairs the cards from opposite ends of the horseshoe, as in the following example.

Knave of Wands - 6 of Swords

"She is anxious about this."

Knight of Wands - Ace of Pentacles

"And he begins to neglect his business which yet is fairly good."

3 of Cups - 2 of Pentacles

"And instead throws aside his business for pleasures."

Knight of Cups - 5 of Cups

"The consequence of this is that the engagement between them is broken off, shown by Knight being turned in opposite direction."

10 of Pentacles - 8 of Cups

"Still his business does fairly well though he is losing interest in it.

5 of Swords - 10 of Cups

"The matter is the subject of much gossip.

9 of Wands - Queen of Cups

These two cards of contrary suits are therefore of little importance. "Among their acquaintances."

King of Cups - Knave of Cups

"He moreover begins to pay attention to another girl of not quite so fair complexion."

Wheel of Fortune - King of Swords

"Who however prefers a dark man, who is much admired by the fair sex (shown by his being next to two Knaves and a Queen.)

6 of Wands - Knave of Pentacles

"But he has already gained the affection of a girl with dark brown eyes and hair. " (This description is obtained by mixing the effect of the Wands with Pentacles.)

VOLUME NINE

This concludes the reading in the First Operation, which may be thus resumed:

"The enquirer is a fair young man who works very hard, and has hitherto gained but little money, yet matters are beginning to improve. He is fond of society, and of visiting friends. He is rather lacking in perseverance and energy. Notwithstanding this, his business and money transactions will begin to prosper. But yet he will lose interest in it owing to his love of pleasure and society, and though his fortune is changing for the better he has yet much anxiety through falling in love with a graceful and sprightly girl with chestnut hair and fair complexion whom he has recently met. His suit is at first favourably received, but some slanderous tales and mischief-making not altogether without foundation, come to her knowledge, though his increasing prosperity in business has led her to regard him with favour. She is made anxious by this, and he begins to neglect his business which yet is fairly good, and instead abandons it for pleasure and merry-making."

"The consequence of this is that the engagement is broken off. Still his business does fairly well though he has lost interest in it. The whole affair is the subject of much gossip among their mutual acquaintances. (One of the chief mischief-makers is a fair middle-aged woman shown by the Queen of Cups.) He, however, soon begins to pay attention to another girl of not quite so fair a complexion. She, however, prefers a dark young man who is much admired generally by the fair sex, but he has already gained the affection of a young woman with dark brown hair and blue eyes."

SECOND OPERATION

REPRESENTING THE DEVELOPMENT OF THE MATTER

The Enquirer again carefully shuffles the cards, and places the Pack on the table face downwards, but he is **not to cut them.** The Diviner now takes the Pack and deals it round card by card in 12 Packets face downwards in rotation as in the following diagram:

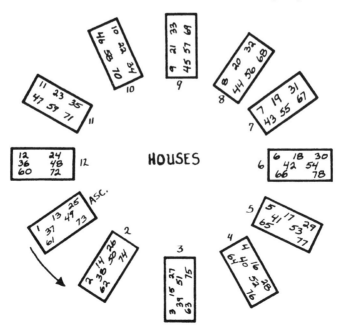

(Deal and read in order of Houses against the direction of the Sun.) So that the first packet answering to the Ascendant will consist of the 1st, 13th, 25th, 37th, 49th, 61st, 73rd cards as shown, and so on.

This Operation is under the presidency of the Court Cards, whose dominion in the Celestial Heavens falls immediately between that of the 4 Knaves and that of the Keys answering to the 12 Signs of the Zodiac. It represents the 12 Astrological Houses of Heaven, as shown.

Without altering the relative order of the packets, or of the cards in the packets, the Diviner examines each in succession, till he finds the one which contains the Significator. This he retains for reading, noting carefully to which astrological house it corresponds and gathers up the other packets, and puts them aside, as they are not of any further use in this operation.

As before, the Diviner reads the packet containing the Significator, by spreading them out in the form of a horseshoe, first reading by counting the cards in order from the Significator in the direction in which the face of the figure on the card is turned, and next by pairing the cards together from the opposite ends of the horseshoe. It is hardly likely that in so small a packet there will be either 3 or 4 cards of a sort, but if there be, the Diviner takes note of the same, and also observes which suit predominates. I now continue the examples commenced in the previous operation. I must here observe that the example is purely of my own invention, and of course is not contained in the Book T, wherein only the mode of working is given. I have purposely taken a commonplace, trivial, and material question for elucidation.

We will suppose the Enquirer to have duly and carefully shuffled the Cards, thinking of his affairs, and that the Diviner has dealt them round into 12 packets as above shown. The packet containing the Significator is located in the Ascendant, and it contains the following cards in the order given.

This mode of reading shows that as the Significator is in the Ascendant it will principally relate to the Enquirer's manner of living at this point.

The Significator is in this case right side up, whereas in the previous reading it was inverted and is looking towards the 9 of Swords, which direction therefore the reading proceeds, counting thus: 4 from King of Cups - Knave of Pentacles; 7 from this - Sun; 9 from this; - Knave of Pentacles; 7 from this - Sun; where the reading ends.

King of Cups - Knave of Pentacles

"The enquirer is unhappy"(looking to 9 of Swords) "and makes the acquaintance of the girl with the dark hair and blue eyes with whom the dark young man (his rival) is in love. (She is artistic and well-mannered; and hopes to carry out her wishes, i.e. to marry the dark man with whom the fair girl, to whom the Enquirer has transferred his affection, is now in love.) For she is beginning to be apprehensive regarding her success, and is jealous in consequence."

Pairing the cards from opposite ends of the horseshoe the Diviner proceeds:

King of Cups - 9 of Swords

"The Enquirer is anxious, and his health begins to suffer."

8 of Pentacles - Sun

"But hopes ultimately to succeed through skillful action in the matter."

4 of Swords - Knave of Pentacles

"He therefore endeavours to make a friend of the dark girl."

Temperance

"As he expects to realize his wishes by her means in the end." (This is shown by the card being single in the end.)

THIRD OPERATION

CONTINUING THE DEVELOPMENT OF THE QUESTION

The Enquirer again carefully shuffles the cards, while thinking earnestly on her affairs. The pack is **not cut.** The Diviner deals out the cards into 12 Packets in precisely the same manner as in the Second Operation. Only instead of being referred to the 12 Astrological Houses, these 12 Packets are under the presidency of the 12 Keys of the Tarot attributed to the 12 Signs of the Zodiac. The first packet, Emperor - Aries, the 2nd, Hierophant - Taurus, the 3rd, Lovers - Gemini, and so on. As before the Diviner selects the packet which contains the Significator for reading, and rejects the rest. He notes also the meaning of the Trump answering to the Sign of the Zodiac, under which the Packet falls. He spreads the cards out in the form of a horseshoe, exactly as before. I now continue the example before commenced:

EXAMPLE

We will suppose that the Packet containing the King of Cups is that whose position answers to the Hierophant - Taurus and that it consists of the following cards, arranged as in the diagram.

The Hierophant and the majority of the cards in this packet being Keys alike show that the forces at present at work are ceasing to be under the control of the Enquirer. The reading proceeds according to the usual order of counting, as follows: King of Cups, 2 of Wands. Magician - Queen of Wands; Universe - Tower; 2 of Wands again.

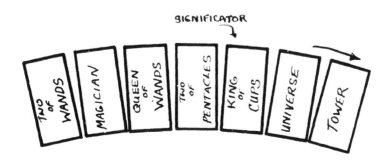

It may be mentioned that supposing a packet to consist of six cards, and the Significat or to be a Knave, or counting 7 from it, it would come back to the Knave again, this would show that the Enquirer would act according to his own ideas in this point of question, and would not let his line of action be influenced by the opinion of others. (The reading would then proceed by the pairing of the cards as usual:)

King of Cups - 2 of Wands

"Though anxious concerning several matters, he (the Enquirer) is beginning to succeed better by this line of action."

Magician - Queen of Wands

"Which seems to be quite the best. But the older woman (who previously made mischief and was represented by the Queen of Cups in the 1 st Operation) who is artful and a gossip,"

Universe - Tower - 2 of Wands

"Again injures the matter because she wishes to get an influence over the Enquirer herself. " Pairing the cards, the Diviner proceeds:

2 of Wands - Tower

"Her influence cunningly exercised, brings about a complete disruption of the whole matter.

Universe - Magician

"The entire matter becomes invested with trickery and glamour."

Queen of Wands - King of Cups

"As she herself pays him a good deal of attention and sympathy."

2 of Pentacles

"Which furthers her plans by bringing about a friendship between them."

FOURTH OPERATION

THE FURTHER DEVELOPMENT OF THE QUESTION

As before the Enquirer is instructed to shuffle the pack and place it on the table but **not to cut it.**

The Diviner takes the Pack, turns it face upwards, and goes through it, being careful not to disarrange the order of the cards, till he finds the Significator. At this point he cuts the Pack, that is to say, he takes the Significator and the cards which had been beneath it and places them on the top of the remainder, turning the whole face downwards again, ready for dealing out. **(Be very careful here: S.A.)**

The consequence of this Operation is that the Significator becomes the top card of the pack (bottom, really; face on table). The Diviner takes off the Significator, places it face upwards on the middle of the table and then the following 36 cards laid out in the form of a circle round it, face upwards, answering to the 36 Decanates of the Zodiac, and showing the further development of the Question. These are dealt round in the order and direction of dealing as the 12 packets in the two previous operations.

The reading proceeds by the same law of counting, but instead of counting from the Significator itself, it begins from the first card of the 36, and always goes in the direction of dealing. The suit which is in the majority and the circumstances of either 3 or 4 cards of a sort being found in the 36 Decanates are also noted. When the reading by counting is finished the cards are paired together; 1st and 36th; 2nd and 35th; 3rd and 34th; and so on, placed in order successively upon the Significator. I now continue the example before commenced.

We will suppose the Enquirer to have shuffled the pack, and that the Diviner takes it in his hands, and in turning it up finds the bottom card to be Temperance. On going through it he comes to the Significator, thus:

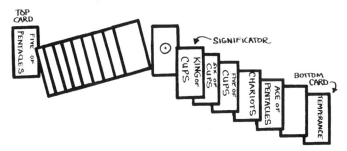

He therefore takes the cards from King of Cups to Temperance included and places them above (or behind, S. A.) the 5 of Pentacles, being careful not to disturb their relative order. This has really the effect of cutting the pack between the Queen of Wands ond the King of Cups.

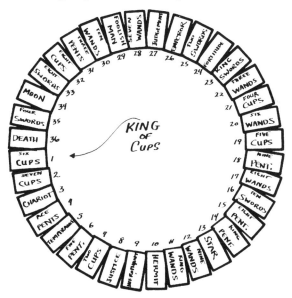

Of course when he again turns them face downwards for dealing, the King of Cups will necessarily be the top card and the Queen of Wands the bottom card; Temperance being immediately above the 5 of Pentacles, the former top card. The Diviner takes the top card, the Significator and places it face upwards in the centre, and then deals round in succession 36 cards, face upwards in the order shown in the above Diagram.

Let us suppose them to be thus arranged. The reading always proceeds in the same direction as the dealing in this form of operation, commencing the counting from the 1st card dealt.

We here find 12 out of the 22 keys; 7 of Wands; 7 of Cups; 5 of Swords; 6 of Pentacles; total 37 including Significator. The preponderance of the Keys represent "Influences beyond the control of the Enquirer." There are four Kings - "Meetings with influential persons," and four Eights, "Much news and correspondence."

The counting proceeds as follows from the first card dealt. King of Cups - Six of Cups - 5 of Pentacles - Hermit - 4 of Cups - Fortitude -4 of Swords - 7 of Cups - Justice - 5 of Cups King of Swords - Emperor - 6 of Cups again.

King of Cups - 6 of Cups

"The Enquirer's love of pleasure-going,"

5 of Pentacles

"Brings about loss of money and business."

Hermit

"And he is forced to be more prudent,'

4 of Cups

"And not go into the society of others so much, which has already brought him anxiety (shown by 4 Cups between 2 Wands, contrary elements weakening effect on this card.) Fortitude "He works more closely,"

4 of Swords

"And begins to get better."

7 of Cups

"Yet he has not sufficient energy in his nature to stick to work for long."

Justice

"The retributive effect of this is."

5 of Cups

"That he loses his friends."

King of Wands

"And his former rival who, though rather a vain man, is energetic and hard working."
Emperor - 6 of Cups
"Replaces him in popularity and esteem."
Pairing them now the diviner proceeds:

King of Cups - Death - 6 of Cups

"The enquirer loses pleasure in consequence."

4 of Swords - 7 of Cups

"And becomes less energetic even then before, and more anxious for pleasure-going than ever."

Moon - Chariot

"Yielding to the tempation of idleness and vanity by means of fraud."

8 of Swords - Ace of Pentacles

"He embezzles the money of his employer, and sees prison staring him in the face."

8 of Cups - Temperance

"The result of this is the loss of good name."

3 of Pentacles - 5 of Pentacles

"And of his situation of trust."

10 of Wands - 2 of Cups

"His former friends and admirers turn a cold shoulder to him."

Fool - Justice

"And the result of this folly is that he is arrested and brought before a court of law."

7 of Wands - Hierophant

"The decision is adverse."

Judgment - Hermit

"And judgment very justly given against him."

Emperor - King of Wands

"But his employer, though stern, is a kind hearted man,

2 of Swords - 9 of Swords

"Offers to take him back and overlook the past.

Star - Fortitude

"As he hopes this will have proved a lesson to him,

King of Swords - King of Pentacles

"And points out to him that his former rival,

3 of Wands - 8 of Pentacles

"Though perhaps vain, was yet a hard-working and good man of business.

4 of Cups - 10 of Swords

"The Enquirer in consequence of this determines to completely give up his former mode of life which had brought him to the brink of ruin, and becomes a steady man.

8 of Wands - 6 of Wands

"After this he suddenly receives a hasty message which gives him much pleasure,

3 of Cups - 9 of Pentacles

"Stating that owing to the loss of a relative he is the inheritor of a legacy."

This concludes the Fourth Operation.

It is always necessary for the Diviner to employ his intuition in reading, and sometimes he may have to clairvoyantly "go through" a card of doubtful signification. Thus in the reading just given it is only the circumstance of the Moon, Chariot, 8 of Swords, Ace of Pentacles being followed by other confirmative cards which justifies such an evil meaning of them.

FIFTH OPERATION

CONCLUSION OF THE MatTER

The cards are to be again carefully shuffled by the Enquirer but **not cut.** The Diviner then takes the Pack, and deals it card by card in rotation into ten answering to the Tree of Life. This refers to the rule of the 10 Sephiroth in the Celestial Heavens.

This being done, the Diviner selects the packet containing the Significator for reading, noting carefully under which Sephirah it falls, and taking this as a general indication in the matter. This packet is then spread out in a horseshoe form, and read in the usual way, counting from the Significator and this time in the direction in which the face of the figure looks. The cards are finally paired together as in the previous Operation. This completes the Mode of Divination called "The Opening of the Key." I now give the conclusion of the example.

We will suppose that the cards have been shuffled and dealt in the following manner into 10 packets answering to the Sephiroth in the Tree of Life:

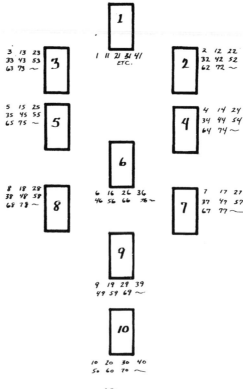

The packet containing the Significator falls under Binah, containing the 3, 13, 23, 33, 43, 53, 63, and 73rd cards dealt. This is an argument of sadness and trial. The cards are spread as follows:

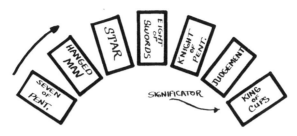

The counting proceeds as follows: King of Cups - Star - Judgment - King of Cups again. Evil cards are in the majority, another argument of loss and trouble.

King of Cups - Star - Judgment

"He has hopes of thus establishing his fortunes and that a favourable result will ensue for him."

The Diviner then pairs them thus:

King of Cups - 7 of Pentacles

"He plunges therefore into speculation by which he loses heavily (indicated by 7 Pentacles near Hanged Man.)

Knave of Cups - Hanged Man

"And his love affair comes to nothing."

Star - Judgment

"All his expectations are disappointed,"

Knight of Pentacles - 8 of Swords

"And his life for a time is arduous, petty, and uninteresting."

(The coming of trouble is here shown by the Knight of Pentacles looking against the direction of the reading. If it were turned the other way it would show that his troubles were quitting him and that matters would improve.) This completes the operation, and shows the general development and result of the question.

TABULATED RULES

SHUFFLING, CUTTING, DEALING AND EXAMINING

In shuffling, the mind of the Enquirer should be earnestly fixed on the matter concerning which he desires information. If any cards fall in the process, they should be taken up without being noticed and the shuffling resumed. The shuffling being concluded, and the pack placed upon the table, if any cards fall to the ground, or become turned in a different direction, the shuffling should be done again, in less important matters. In more important matters see previous instructions.

A cut should be clean and decided. If any cards fall from the hand in the performance, the operation of shuffling should be repeated before they are again cut. In dealing, care should be taken not to invert the cards, and their relative order should be strictly maintained. In examining a pack of cards, their relative order should be rigidly maintained, as without care in this respect, one may be easily pushed under or over another, which would of course have the effect of completely altering the counting in the Reading.

THE SELECTION OF THE SIGNIFICATOR AND OF THE COMPLEXION ASSIGNED TO THE COURT CARDS

Wands generally	**Fair and red-haired person**
Cups generally	**Moderately fair**
Swords generally	**Moderately dark**
Pentacles generally	**Very dark**
Kings	**Men**
Queens	**Women**
Knights	**Young men**
Princesses (Knaves)	**Young women**

Therefore the Significators are to be thus selected. For example, a dark complexioned middle-aged man, King of Pentacles. A fair young woman. Princess (Knave) of Cups, etc.

In the actual reading of the cards, these descriptions can be modified by those which are on either side of them, thus: The Queen of Cups, which indicates a fair woman with golden brow n hair, if between cards of the suits of Swords and Pentacles. would show a woman with rather dark brown hair and dark eyes. As before stated, the Knights and Queens almost invariably represent actual men and women connected with the subject in hand. But the Kings sometimes represent either the coming on or going off of a matter, arrival, or departure, according to the way in which they face. While the Knaves show opinions, thoughts, or ideas, either in harmony with or opposed to the subject.

THE GENERAL SIGNIFICATION OF THE MAJORITY OF A PARTICULAR SUIT AND OF THE PARTICULAR SIGNIFICATION OF EITHER 3 OR 4 CARDS OF A SUIT IN A READING

A	majority of Wand	**Energy, quarrelling, opposition**
A	majority of Cups	**Pleasure and merriment**
A	majority of Sword	**Trouble and sadness, sickness, or death**
A	majority of Pentacle	**Business, money, possessions, etc.**
A	majority of Key	**Forcees of considerable strength, but beyond the Enquirer's control**
A	majority of Court Cards	**Society, meeting with many persons**
A	majority of Ace	**Strength often; aces are always strong cards**

4	Aces	Great power and Force
3	Aces	Riches and Success
4	Kings	Great swiftness and rapidity
3	Kings	Unexpected meetings, generally shows news
4	Queens generally	Authority and influence
3	Queens generally	Powerful and influential friends
4	Knights	Meetings with the great
3	Knights	Rank and honour
4	Knaves	New ideas and plans
3	Knaves	Society of the young
4	Tens generally	Anxiety and responsibility
3	Tens generally	Buying, selling, commercial transactions
4	Nines generally	Added responsibility
3	Nines generally	Much correspondence
4	Eights generally	Much news
3	Eights generally	Much journeying
4	Sevens generally	Disappointments
3	Sevens generally	Treaties and compacts
4	Sixes generally	Pleasure
3	Sixes generally	Gain and Success
4	Fives generally	Order, regularity
3	Fives generally	Quarrels, fights
4	Fours generally	Rest and Peace
3	Fours generally	Industry
4	Threes generally	Resolution and determination
3	Threes generally	Deceit
4	Deuces generally	Conference and conversations
3	Deuces generally	Reorganization and restarting of a thing.

The Keys are not noticed as above, by threes and fours.

EXTRA AND BRIEF MEANING OF THE 36 SMALLER CARDS

WANDS

Deuce	Influence over another. Dominion.
Three	Pride and arrogance. Power sometimes.
Four	Settlement. Arrangement completed.
Five	Quarrelling. Fighting.
Six	Gain and success.
Seven	Opposition; sometimes courage therewith.
Eight	A hasty communication, letter or message. Swiftness.
Nine	Strength. Power. Health. Energy.
Ten	Cruelty and malice towards others. Overbearing strength. Revenge. Injustice.

CUPS

Deuce	Marriage, love, pleasure. Warm friendship.
Three	Plenty. Hospitality, eating, drinking. Pleasure, dancing, new clothes and merriment.
Four	Receiving pleasures or kindness from others, yet some discomfort therewith.
Five	Disappointment in love. Marriage broken off, etc. Unkindness from friends. (Whether deserved or not is shown by the cards with it, or counting from or to it.) Loss of friendship.
Six	Wish, happiness, success, enjoyment.
Seven	Lying, deceit, promises unfulfilled, illusion, deception. Error, slight success, but not enough energy to retain it.
Eight	Success abandoned, decline of interest in a thing. Ennui.
Nine	Complete success. Pleasure and happiness. Wishes fulfilled.
Ten	Matters definitely arranged and settled in accordance with one's wishes. Complete good fortune.

SWORDS

Deuce	Quarrel made up, and arranged. Peace restored, yet some tension in relations.
Three	Unhappiness, sorrow, tears.
Four	Convalescence, recovery from sickness, change for the better.
Five	Defeat, loss, malice. Slander, evil-speaking.
Six	Labour, work; journey, probably by water. (Shown by cards near by.)
Seven	In character untrustworthy, vacillation. Journey probably by (Shown by cards near, etc.)
Eight	Narrow or restricted. Petty. A prison.
Nine	Illness. Suffering. Malice. Cruelty. Pain.
Ten	Ruin. Death. Failure. Disaster.

PENTACLES

Deuce	Pleasant change. Visit to friends, etc.
Three	Business, paid employment. Commercial transactions.
Four	Gain of money and influence. A present.
Five	Loss of profession. Loss of money. Monetary anxiety.
Six	Success in material things; prosperity in business.
Seven.	Unprofitable speculations, employments; also honorary work undertaken for the love of it, and without desire of reward.
Eight	Skill, prudence, also artfulness, and cunning. (Depends on cards with it.)
Nine	Inheritance. Much increase of money.
Ten	Riches and Wealth.

BRIEF MEANINGS OF THE 22 TRUMPS

0. Fool.

Idea, thought, spirituality, that which endeavours to rise above the material. (That is, if the subject which is enquired about be spiritual.) But if the Divination be regarding a material event of ordinary life, this card is not good, and shows folly, stupidity, eccentricity, and even mania, unless with very good cards indeed. It is too ideal and unstable to be generally good in material things.

1. Magician or Juggler.

Skill, wisdom, adaptation. Craft, cunning, etc., always depending on its dignity. Sometimes occult Wisdom.

2. High Priestess.

Change, alteration, Increase and Decrease. Fluctuation (whether for good or evil is again shown by cards connected with it.) Compare with Death and Moon.

3. Empress.

Beauty, happiness, pleasure, success, also luxury and sometimes dissipation, but only if with very evil cards.

4. Emperor.

War, conquest, victory, strife, ambition.

5. Hierophant.

Divine Wisdom. Manifestation. Explanation. Teaching. Differing from though resembling in some respects, the meaning of The Magician, The Hermit, and The Lovers. Occult Wisdom.

6. The Lovers.

Inspiration (passive and in some cases mediumistic, thus differing from that of the Hierophant and Magician and Hermit.) Motive, power, and action, arising from Inspiration and Impulse.

7. The Chariot.

Triumph. Victory. Health. Success though sometimes not stable and enduring.

8. Fortitude or Strength.

(In former times and in other decks 8 Justice and 11 Fortitude were transposed.) Courage, Strength, Fortitude. Power not arrested as in the act of Judgment, but passing on to further action, sometimes obstinacy, etc. Compare with 11 - Justice.

9. The Hermit.

Wisdom sought for and obtained from above. Divine Inspiration (but active as opposed to that of the Lovers). In the mystical titles, this with the Hierophant and the Magician are the 3 Magi.

10. Wheel of Fortune.

Good fortune and happiness (within bounds), but sometimes also a species of intoxication with success, if the cards near it bear this out.

11. Justice.

Eternal Justice and Balance. Strength and Force, but arrested as in the act of Judgment. Compare with 8 - Fortitude. Also in combination with other cards, legal proceedings, a court of law, a trial at law, etc.

12. Hanged Man or Drowned Man.

Enforced sacrifice. Punishment, Loss. Fatal and not voluntary. Suffering generally.

13. Death.

Time. Ages. Transformation. Change involuntary as opposed to The Moon. Sometimes death and destruction, but rarely the latter, and the former only if it is borne out by the cards with it. Compare also with High Priestess.

14. Temperance.

Combination of Forces. Realisation. Action (material). Effect either for good or evil.

15. Devil.

Materiality. Material Force. Material temptation; sometimes obsession, especially if associated with the Lovers.

16. Tower.

Ambition, fighting, war, courage. Compare with Emperor. In certain combinations, destruction, danger, fall, ruin.

17. Star.

Hope, faith, unexpected help. But sometimes also dreaminess, deceived hope, etc.

18. Moon.

Dissatisfaction, voluntary change (as opposed to Death). Error, lying, falsity, deception. (The whole according to whether the card is well or ill-dignified, and on which it much depends.)

19. Sun.

Glory, Gain, Riches. Sometimes also arrogance. Display, Vanity, but only when with very evil cards.

20. Judgment.

Final decision. Judgment. Sentence. Determination of a matter without appeal on its plane.

21. Universe.

The matter itself. Synthesis. World. Kingdom. Usually denotes the actual subject of the question, and therefore depends entirely on the accompanying cards.

THE SIGNIFICATION OF THE CARDS

A card is strong or weak, well-dignified or ill-dignified, according to the cards which are next to it on either side. Cards of the same suit on either side strengthen it greatly either for good or evil, according to their nature. Cards of the suits answering to its contrary element, on either side, weaken it greatly for good or evil. Air and Earth are contraries as also are Fire and Water. Air is friendly with Water and Fire, and Fire with Air and Earth.

If a card of the suit of Wands falls between a Cup and a Sword, the Sword modifies and connects the Wand with the Cup, so that it is not weakened by its vicinity, but is modified by the influence of both cards; therefore fairly strong. But if a card pass between two which are naturally contrary, it is not affected by either much, as a Wand between a Sword and a Pentacle which latter, being Air and Earth, are contrary and therefore weaken each other.

Here the question being of the Wand, this card is not to be noticed as forming a link between the Sword and Pentacle.

A FEW EXAMPLES
By
G.H. FRATER S.R.M.D.

9 SW. 10 SW. 5 SW.

Very strong and potent in action. Very evil.

10 W. 10 SW. 2 W.

Not quite so strong. Ruin checked and perhaps overcome.

6 C. 10 SW. 10 C.

Rather good than otherwise. It is bounty overcoming loss, like a piquant sauce which adds to pleasure.

9 P. 10 SW. 10 C.

Very weak, evil, slight loss in material things, but more anxiety than actual loss.

5 SW. 2 W. 9 SW.

Moderately strong. Rashness which brings evil in its train. Evil.

9 P. 2 W. 6 P.

Fairly strong. Good. Considerable gain and victory.

10 C. 2 W. 6 C.

Weak, evil. Victory which is perverted by debauchery and evil living. But other cards may mitigate the judgment.

9 SW. 10 C. 5 SW.

Medium strong. Evil. Sorrow arising from pleasure and through one's own pleasures.

9 P. 10 C. 6 P.

Perfect success and happiness.

10 W. 10 C. 5 SW.

Rather evil. Pleasure that when obtained is not worth the trouble one has had in obtaining it.

10 SW. 6 C. 9 P.

Fairly strong and good. The Sw. and P. being opposite elements counteract each other. Therefore is it as if they were not there.

10 SW. 6 C. 10 W.

Fairly good. Some trouble, but trouble which is overcome. If 6 C. were a bad card the evil would carry the day.

9 SW. Death. 3 SW.

Death accompanied by much pain and misery.

9 W. 9 SW. High Priestess.

Recovery from sickness.

6 W. Q W. King of Pentacles.

An active woman, courageous and reliable with dark chestnut hair, and open fearless expression.

7 C. King Cups. 5 SW.

A rather fair man but very deceitful and malicious.

PAIRING THE CARDS IN READING

On pairing the cards each is to be taken as of equal force with the other. If of opposite elements they mutually weaken each other. If at the end of the pairing of the cards in a packet, one card remains over, it signifies the partial result of that particular part of the Divination only. If an evil card and the other good, it would modify the good:

If it be the Significator of the Enquirer, or of another person, it would show that matters would much depend on the line of action taken by the person represented. The reason of this importance of the single card is, that it is alone and not modified. If two cards are at the end instead of a single one, they are not of so much importance.

THE EXERCISE OF CLAIRVOYANCE AND INTUITION

In describing any person from a Significator in the actual reading, the Diviner should endeavour, by Clairvoyance and using the card in question as a symbol, to see the person implied using the rules to aid, and restrict, his vision. In describing an event from the cards in the reading, he should employ his intuition in the same manner. Personal descriptions are modified by the cards next to them; e. g., the Knave of Wands represents usually a very fair girl, but if between cards of the suit of Pentacles, she might be even quite dark, though the Wands would still give a certain brightness to hair, eyes, and complexion.

VOLUME NINE

COUNTING

In all cases of counting from the card last touched, the card itself is 1, that next it is 2, and so on.

> **From every Ace count 5.**
> **From every Knave count 7.**
> **From every other Court card 4 is counted.**
> **From every small card the number of its pips.**
> **From every Key answering to an Element (Aleph, Mem, Shin) 3 is counted.**
> **From every Key answering to a Sign 12 is counted.**
> **From every Key answering to a Planet 9 is counted.**

UNOFFICIAL

UNOFFICIAL DESCRIPTION OF THE TAROT TRUMPS
By

G. H. SOROR Q. L.

The cards of the Lesser Arcana present to us the vibrations of Number, Colour and Element - that is, the plane on which number and colour function. Thus, in the Ten of Pentacles we have the number Ten and tertiary colours, citrine, olive, and russet, working in Malkuth, the material plane. In the Ten of Wands we have the number Ten and the tertiaries working in pure energy. In these cards, the Sephirah is indicated by the colouring of the clouds; the plane by the colouring of the symbols.

The four Honours of each suit taken in their most abstract sense may be interpreted as:

> **Potential Power is the King**
> **Brooding Power is the Queen**
> **Power in action is the Knight**
> **Reception and Transmission is the Knave.**

All these cards are coloured according to their elements plus the Sephirah to which they are attributed. With the Greater Arcana, however, we are given the Keys to divine manifestation, each one an individual force to be considered independently. It must never be forgotten that the Trumps are, intrinsically, glyphs of cosmic not human forces.

TRUMPS

0. The Fool.

This card as usually presented shows a man in motley striding along heedless of the dog which tears his garments and threatens to attack him. In this is seen only the lower aspect of the card, giving no hint to the Divine Folly of which St. Paul speaks. But in the Order pack, an effort is made to reveal the deeper meaning. A naked child stands beneath a rose-tree bearing yellow roses - the golden Rose of Joy as well as the Rose of Silence. While reaching up to the Roses, he yet holds in leash a grey wolf, worldly wisdom held in check by perfect innocence. The colours are pale yellow, pale blue, greenish yellow - suggestive of the early dawn of a spring day.

1. The Magician.

It represents the union and balance of the elemental powers controlled by mind. The Adept dedicating the minor implements on the Altar. The paths of Beth and Mercury link Kether the Crown with Binah, the Aimah Elohim. The Magician, therefore, is reflected in the Intellect which stores and gathers up knowledge and pours it into the House of Life, Binah. The number of the Path, 12, suggests the synthesis of the Zodiac, as Mercury is the synthesis of the planets. The colours yellow, violet, grey and indigo, point to the mysterious astral light surrounding the great Adept. It is a card linked with the name Tahuti and Hermes as the previous one is with Krishna and Harparkrat or Dionysius.

2. The High Priestess.

She rules the long path uniting Kether to Tiphareth, crossing the reciprocal Paths of Venus and Leo. She is the great feminine force controlling the very source of life, gathering into herself all the energising forces and holding them in solution until the time of release. Her colours, pale blue, deepening into sky blue, silvery white, and silver, relieved by touches of orange and flame, carry out these ideas.

3. The Empress.

She is an aspect of Isis; the creative and positive side of Nature is suggested here. The Egyptian trilogy, Isis, Hathor and Nephthys, symbolised by the crescent, full moon, and gibbous moon are represented in the Tarot by the High Priestess, Hathor. The Empress, Isis, takes either the crescent moon or Venus as her symbol. Justice, Nephthys, takes the gibbous moon.

Isis and Venus give the aspect of Love, while Hathor is rather the Mystic, the full moon reflecting the Sun of Tiphareth while in Yesod, transmitting the rays of the Sun in her path Gimel. In interpreting a practical Tarot it is often admissable to regard the Empress as standing for Occultism. The High Priestess for religion, the Church as distinguished from the Order.

The Empress, whose letter is Daleth, is the Door of the inner mysteries, as Venus is the door of the Vault. Her colours are emerald, sky-blue, blue-green and cerise or rose-pink.

4. The Emperor.

Here we have the great energising forces as indicated by the varying shades of red. It may be noted here that the red paths remain red in all planes, varying only in shade. Thus Aries, the Emperor, the Pioneer, the General, is blood and deep crimson, red, pure vermillion or glowing fiery red. He is Ho Nike the Conqueror, hot, passionate, impetuous, the apotheosis of Mars, whether in love or in war. He is the positive masculine as the Empress is the positive feminine.

5. Hierophant.

The High Priest is the counterpart of the High Priestess. As Aries is the house of Mars and the exaltation of the Sun, so Taurus is the house of Venus and exaltation of the Moon. He is the reflective or mystical aspect of the masculine. He is the thinker as the Emperor is the doer.

His colours unlike those of the Emperor vary considerably. Red, orange, maroon, deep brown, and chestnut brown, suggest veiled thought, interior power, endurance, contemplation and reconciliation. This card frequently indicates the hidden guardianship of the Masters.

6. The Lovers.

The impact of inspiration on intuition, resulting in illumination and liberation - the sword striking off the fetters of habit and materialism, Perseus rescuing Andromeda from the Dragon of fear and the waters of Stagnation. (Consult the Golden Dawn Tarot Deck, Wang & Regardie, U.S. Games Systems.)

The colours are orange, violet, purplish grey and pearl grey. The flashing colour of orange gives deep vivid blue while the flashing colour for violet is golden yellow. The flashing colours may always be introduced if they bring out the essential colour meaning more clearly. In practise this card usually signifies sympathetic understanding.

7. The Chariot.

Here we have a symbol of the spirit of man controlling the lower principles, soul and body, and thus passing triumphantly through the astral plane, rising above the clouds of illusion and penetrating to the higher spheres.

The colours amber, silver-grey, blue-grey, and the deep blue violet of the night sky elucidate this symbol. It is the sublimation of the Psyche.

8. Strength.

This also represents the mastery of the lower by the higher. But in this case it is the soul which holds in check the passions, although her feet are still planted on earth, and the dark veil still floats about her head and clings around her. The colours, pale greenish yellow, black, yellowish grey and reddish amber, suggest the steadfast endurance and fortitude required, but the deep red rose which is the flashing colour to the greenish yellow, gives the motive power.

9. The Hermit.

Prudence. These three trumps should be collated in studying them for they represent the three stages of initiation. The man wrapped in hood and mantle, and carrying a lantern to illuminate the Path and a staff to support his footsteps. He is the eternal seeker, the Pilgrim soul. His hood and mantle are the brown of earth, and above him is the night-sky. But the delicate yellow-greens and bluish greens of spring are about him, and spring is in his heart.

10. Wheel of Fortune.

In the Tree of Life, the Wheel is placed on the Pillar of Mercy, where it forms the principal column linking Netzach to Chesed, Victory to Mercy. It is the revolution of experience and progress, the steps of the Zodiac, the revolving staircase, held in place by the counter-changing influence of Light and Darkness, Time and Eternity - presided over by the Plutonian cynocephalus below, and the Sphinx of Egypt above, the eternal Riddle which can only be solved when we attain liberation. The basic colours of this Trump are blue, violet, deep purple, and blue irradiated by yellow. But the zodiacal spokes of the wheel should be in the colours of the spectrum, while the Ape is in those of Malkuth, and the Sphinx in the primary colours and black.

11. Justice.

Nephthys, the third aspect of Luna, the twin sister of Isis. Justice as distinguished from love. Her emblems are the Sword and the Scales. Like her sister, she is clothed in green, but in a sharper colder green than the pure emerald of Isis. Her subsidiary colours are blue, blue-green, pale green. It is only by utilising the flashing colours that we can find the hidden warmth and steadfastness.

12. The Hanged Man.

An elusive, because a profoundly significant symbol. It is sacrifice - the submergence of the higher in the lower in order to sublimate the lower. It is the descent of the Spirit into Matter, the incarnation of God in man, the submission to the bonds of matter that the material may be transcended and transmuted. The colours are deep blue, white and black intermingled but not merged, olive, green and greenish fawn.

13. Death.

The sign of transmutation and disintegration. The skeleton which alone survives the destructive power of time, may be regarded as the foundation upon which the structure is built. The type which persists through the permutations of Time and Space, adaptable to the requirements of evolution and yet radically unchanged. It is the transmuting power of Nature working from below upwards, as the Hanged Man is the transmuting power of the spirit working from above downwards. The colours are blue-green, both dark and pale, the two dominant colours of the visible world, and the flashing colours of orange and red-orange.

14. Temperance.

This is the equilibrium not of the balance of Libra but of the impetus of the Arrow, Sagittarius, which cleaves its way through the air by the force imparted to it by the taut string of the Bow. It requires the counterchanged forces of Fire and Water, Shin and Qoph, held by the restraining power of Saturn, and concentrated by the energies of Mars to initiate this impetus. All these are summed up in the symbolism of the figure standing between Earth and Water, holding the two amphorae with their streams of living water, and with the volcano in the background. The colours are bright-blue, blue-grey, slate-blue, and lilac-grey.

15. The Devil.

This card should be studied in conjunction with No. 13. They are the two great controlling forces of the Universe, the centrifugal and the centripetal, destructive and reproductive, dynamic and static. The lower nature of man fears and hates the transmuting process; hence the chains binding the lesser figures and the bestial forms of their lower limbs. Yet this very fear of change and disintegration is necessary to stabilise the life-force and preserve continuity. The colours are indigo, livid brown, golden brown and grey.

16. The Tower.

As always red remains persistent throughout the four planes, although modified in tone. Thus we find vivid scarlet shading into deep sombre red and vermillion shot with amber. The contrasting shades of green serve to throw the red into relief. The tremendous destructive influence of the lightning, rending asunder established forms to make way for new forms to emerge. It is revolution as distinguished from transmutation or sublimation. Destructive as opposed to the conservative, energy attacking inertia. The impetuous ejection of those who would enclose themselves in the walls of ease and tradition.

17. The Star.

This shows the seven-pointed Star of Venus shining above the Waters of Aquarius, the guiding force of love in all its forms and aspects, illuminates the soul during her immersion in Humanity. Thus bonds of Saturn are dissolved in the purified Waters of Baptism. The dove of the Spirit hovers above the Tree of Knowledge giving the promise of ultimate attainment - and on the other side gleams of the Tree of Life.

Pale colours suggest dawn and the morning Star - amethyst, pale grey, fawn, dove colour and white, with the pale yellow of the Star.

18. The Moon.

Here also is a river but it is the troubled waters of Night, wherein is to be descried a crayfish, counterpart of the Scarabeus. From the water's edge winds the dark path of toil, effort and possible failure. It is guarded by the threatening watch-dogs, seeking to intimidate the wayfarers, while in the distance the barren hills are surmounted by the frowning fortresses still further guarding the way to attainment. It is the path of blood and tears in which fear, weakness, and fluctuation must be overcome. The colours are dark crimson, reddish brown, brownish crimson and plum colours - but their sombre hues are lightened by the translucent faint greens and yellows to be found in their counterparts.

19. The Sun.

The Watery Paths of trial and probation are counterbalanced by the fiery paths of Temperance, Judgment, and Decision. In violent contrast to the sombre colouring of Aquarius and Pisces, we are confronted by the flaring hues of the Sun and Fire. The too-aspiring Icarus may find his waxen wings of Ambition and Curiosity shrivelled and melted by the fiery rays of the Sun and the heat of Fire. Approached with humility and reverence, the Sun becomes the beneficent source of life.

Protected by an enclosing wall, standing by the Waters of repentance, the Pilgrim may submit himself humbly but without fear to the searching Light and absorb warmth and vitality from it for the struggle before him. The colours are clear-orange, golden-yellow, amber shot with red, and the contrasting blue and purple.

20. The Last Judgment.

The three trumps attributed to the Elemental Paths are perhaps the most difficult to understand. They represent the action of forces exterior to the experience of humanity, not the influence of environment but the impact of the Supernals upon the sublunary.

In the Air we have pure spirit holding in leash the lust of the flesh. In water, the sublimating power of sacrifice. Here in Fire, we are shown the cosmic forces concentrating on the pilgrim from all sides. Judgment is pronounced upon him. He is not the judge nor does decision rest in his hands. Lazarus cannot emerge from the Sepulchre until the voice cries out, "Come forth!" Nor can he cast aside the conflicting grave-clothes until the command, "Loose him!" is given. Man of himself is helpless. The impulse to ascend must come from above, but by its power he may transcend the sepulchre of environment and cast aside the trammels of desire. Here once more, the fiery energy of red burns through the planes. Fiery scarlet, glowing crimson, burning red are emphasized by passive greens.

21. The Universe.

Observe that this represents not the World but the Universe. It should be remembered that to the ancients, Saturn represented the confines of the Solar system. They had no means of measuring either Uranus or Neptune. To them, therefore, Saturn passing through the spiral path of the Zodiac, marked at its cardinal points by the symbols of the Kerubim forming the Cross, was a comprehensive glyph of the whole.

Thus, in this card we find a synthesis of the whole Taro or Rota. The central figure should be taken as Hathor, Athor, or Ator, rather than Isis, thus indicating the hidden anagram which may perhaps be translated thus: ORAT - man prays. ATOR - to the Great Mother, TARO - who turns, ROTA - the wheel of Life and Death.

The colours like those of the Wheel of Fortune include the colours of the Spectrum and those of the elements, but they are placed against the indigo and black of Saturn, with the white gleam of the Stars shining in the darkness and the misty figure of the Aimah Elohim in the midst. In the practical Tarot, this card is taken to signify the matter in hand, that is the subject of any question that has been asked.

Having now reviewed the 22 Atous or Trumps in succession, it will be wise for the Student to reverse the process and seek to follow the Path of the Pilgrim from below upwards, thus seeking to comprehend the interior process of Initiation and Illumination. It is a process in which the whole Universe does not disdain to take part, for Man is himself the Microcosm of the Macrocosm and the Child of the Gods. And again, the Macrocosm must itself be undergoing a corresponding process in which the experience not only of humanity but of each individual must be an integral part. The fragments are gathered up into the baskets, that nothing may be lost; and from the feeding of the multitude there remains not less but more than the unbroken bread and fish - fit emblems of Earth and Water.

Cease not to seek day and night the Purifying Mysteries

THE TREE OF LIFE AS PROJECTED IN A SOLID SPHERE
By
V.H. FRATER S.R.M.D.

The Planets'sphere which illustrates this manuscript, as part of the Z. A. M.'s Abstract of the Tarot, has been drawn by S.R.M.D. as instructed. It represents the Heavens polarized on the plane of the Ecliptic, not on the plane of the Equator of our Earth, so that its North Pole is the veritable North Pole of our Heavens and not merely that part of them to which the North Pole of our Earth now points.

Another very important difference is that, throughout the true Tarot, the teaching assigns the commencing Point of the Zodiac to the bright Star "Regulus" which is in Leo. And it measures Right Ascension and Longitude from that point, and not from a suppositious point divided by the Equinox and called the 0° of Aries (though in reality now far removed from the constellation of that name), which has been adopted by modern or wetern astronomy and astrology.

By this now usual way of reckoning, and the Procession of the Equinoxes, it has gradually come to pass that the signs (or divisions, each of 30°, of the Zodiac) no longer coincide with the constellations of the same name, and each decade shows them slowly but surely receding.

But the Tarot method of reckoning from the star named Regulus has, it will be seen, the effect ol making the Signs and the Constellations coincide.

"Regulus" is also named Cor Leonis - "The Heart of the Lion."

"Regulus" means "Star of the Prince." "Regulus" coincides with the position of the "heart" in the figure of Leo upon the Star Maps.

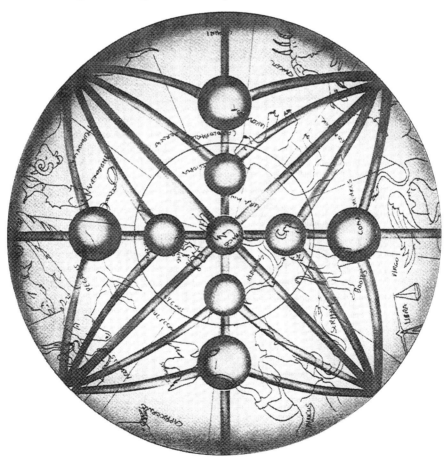

THE NORTHERN HEMISPHERE

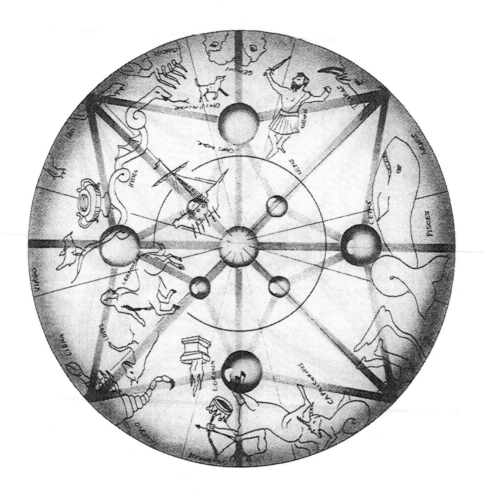

THE SOUTHERN HEMISPHERE

TABULAR VIEW OF THE DOMINION OF THE SYMBOLS OF THE TAROT IN THE CELESTIAL HEAVENS.

The Zelator Adeptus Minor shall know that the great "King Star" or "Heart of the Lion," which is in Leo upon the path of the Ecliptic and one of the "Four Tiphareth Points" (see later) of the Celestial Heavens, is the commencement and Ruler of all our reckoning of Longitude (or Ecliptic). The Path of the Sun itself is the commencement of our reckoning of the Latitude in the searching out of our Hidden Wisdom.

Also the Dragon, the constellation Draco, surroundeth the Pole Kether of our Celestial Heavens.

But the Northern Pole and Kether of the Material Planet (even of our Erthe, earth) looketh constantly unto Binah, for as much as she is under sorrow and suffering. When, oh Lord of the Universe, shall she turn from her evil ways so that she shall again behold Kether? Wherefore she is now a place of trial. For each thing in this world of Assiah looketh towards that which is its Natural Governor. To what part of the Celestial Heavens the Kether of a Planet constantly looketh, by that part is that Planet ruled. For in all things shine the Sephiroth even as hath been sufficiently said.

The Four Knaves rule the celestial Heavens from the North Pole of the Zodiac to the 45° of Latitude North of the Ecliptic. They form the Thrones of the Four Aces, who rule in Kether. The Four Kings, 4 Queens, 4 Knights rule the Celestial Heavens from the 45° of North Latitude down to the Ecliptic. The 12 Tarot Keys attributed to the 12 Signs of the Zodiac rule the Celestial Heavens from the Ecliptic down to the 45° of South Latitude. The 36 smaller cards of the Suits (from two to ten) rule the Celestial Heavens from the 45° South of the Ecliptic to the South Pole, or the Malkuth place therein. All calculation arises from the Star "Regulus," the 0° of our Leo.

SYMBOLS

These Four Aces revolve in Kether, their Thrones are the central portion of 45⁰ of Longitude in extent in the dominions of the Knaves of their respective suits.

STAR GROUPS

Ace of Wands

A part of the tail of Draco, fore-feet of Ursa Major, tail of Ursa Major, and of the Northern dog of Canis Venatici.

Ace of Cups

Head of Draco, body and legs of Hercules.

Ace of Swords

Body of Draco. Right arm of Orpheus, head and body of Lacerta. Body of Cygnus.

Ace of Pentacles

Body of Draco. Legs of Cepheus. Tail of Ursa Minor, and the Pole Star. Legs of Cassiopeia. Head and neck of Camelopardus.

Knave of Wands

Rules from North Pole to 45° and from 0° of Cancer to 30° of Virgo, the end of Virgo. The Throne of the Ace of Wands extends 45° from 22° - 30' of Cancer to 7° - 30' of Virgo within the limits of 45° Latitude.

Star groups corresponding to above.

Tail of Draco, Head and forepart of Ursa Minor, left arm and part of head and chest of Bootes. The greater part of the Northernmost dog of Canis Venatici. Tail and Back of Ursa Major, (ancient Italian name was Septemtriones, the 7 Ploughing Oxen). This includes the celebrated Seven stars of the constellation called "Charles Wain" by the English; "Seven Rishis" by the Hindus, and in the Egyptian Book of the Dead, Ch. XVII, "The Seven bright ones who follow their Lord, the Thigh of the Northern Heaven." In the Zodiac of Denderah, and in the Tablet of Edfus, that Ursa Major is represented as the thigh of an Ox.

Knave of Cups

Rules from North Pole to 45° of Latitude and from 0° of Libra to 30° of Sagittarius in Longitude. The Throne of the Ace embraces from 22° - 30° of Libra to 7° - 30° of Sagittarius within the above limits of Latitude.

Star Group

Head of Draco. Left arm, body and legs of Hercules, part of head, right shoulder and club of Bootes.

Knave of Swords

Rules from North Pole to 45° Latitude and from 0° of Capricorn to 30° of Pisces Longitude. The Throne of the Ace extends from 22° - 30° of Capricorn to 7° - 30° of Pisces as before.

Star Group

Body of Draco, part of Lyra. Head, body and right arm of Cepheus, the King and Father of Andromeda, the whole of Cygnus, head and body of Lacerta, back and part of head of Vulpecula the Fox.

Knave of Pentacles

Rules from North Pole to 45° Latitude, and from 0° of Aries to 30° of Gemini Longitude. The Throne of the Ace embraces from 22° - 30° of Aries to 7° - 30° of Gemini within the Latitude as above.

Star Group

Body of Draco, legs and part of right arm and Sceptre of Cepheus, tail and hind quarters of Ursa Minor, with the Pole Star of our Earth, head and neck of Camelopardalis (Giraffe), body and right arm, throne and legs of Cassiopeia, the Queen of Cepheus and Mother of Andromeda, head of Ursa Major.

Prince of Wands

Rules from Ecliptic to 45° North Latitude and from 20° Cancer to 20° Leo in Longitude.

Star Group

Head, body, and tail of Leo, body and tail of Leo Minor, hind quarters and legs of Ursa Major, head and fore-quarters of Southern dog of Canis Venatici.

King of Pentacles

Rules from Ecliptic to 45° North Latitude and from 20° of Leo to 20° of Virgo.

Star Group

Head and body of Virgo, left arm of Bootes, hair of Berenice. Body and hind quarters of Southern dog of Canes Venatici, hind feet of Northern dog of Canis Venatici.

Queen of Swords

Rules from Ecliptic to 45° and from 20° of Virgo to 20° of Libra.

Star Group

Right leg of Virgo, body and right arm and right leg of Bootes. Beam and part of Scales of Libra.

Knight of Cups

Rules from Ecliptic to 45° and from 20° of Libra to 20° of Scorpio.

Star Group

Part of Scales of Libra, left claws of Scorpio, body and legs of Ophiucus, the holder of the Serpent. Front half of Serpent's head, right arm and club of Hercules.

The King of Wands

Rules from Ecliptic to 45° North Latitude and from 20° of Scorpio to 20° of Sagittarius.

Star Group

Top of head and bow of Sagittarius, head and right arm of Ophiucus, rear half of Serpent.

Queen of Pentacles

Rules from Ecliptic to 45° North Latitude and from 20° of Sagittarius to 20° of Capricorn.

Star Group

Top of head, neck and horns of Capricorn, left hand of Aquarius, the man who carries the Water, the whole of Aquila. the Eagle, the greater part of Delphinus, whole of Sagitta. the Arrow, forefeet and body of Vulpecula the Fox, and the tail of the Cygnet which he seizes.

Knight of Swords

Rules from Ecliptic to 45° North Latitude, and from 20° of Capricorn to 20° of Aquarius.

Star Group

Tail of Capricornus, head and body of Aquarius, head and forelegs of Pegasus, the winged horse who sprang from the blood of Medusa near the sources of the ocean, the whole of Equilaus, the lesser horse, part of head of Dolphin, tail and hind quarters of Vulpecula, part of wing of Cygnus, the swan, part of head of Pisces.

King of Cups

Rules from Ecliptic to 45° of North Latitude and from 20° of Aquarius to 20° of Pisces.

Star Group

Body and tail of one of the Pisces, and part of the band. Body and wings of Pegasus, head and arms of Andromeda, chained to the rock, tail of Lacerta.

Queen of Wands

Rules from Ecliptic to 45° North Latitude and from 20° of Pisces to 20° of Aries.

Star Group

The other Fish and part of Band of Pisces, head and back of Aries, body and legs of Andromeda, the Triangle, hand left arm of Cassiopeia, the winged instep of Aries.

Knight of Pentacles

Rules from Ecliptic to 45° North Latitude and from 20° of Aries to 20° of Taurus.

Star Group

Tail of Aries, one horn and shoulder and back of Taurus, whole of Perseus, and the head of Medusa, hind quarters and legs of Camelopardalis, left leg of Auriga, Charioteer, and part of Capella, the she-goat which bears kids in her arms.

King of Swords

Rules from Ecliptic to 45° North Latitude from 20° of Taurus to 20° Gemini in Longitude.

Star Group

Head and body of Castor, one of the Gemini, greater part of Auriga and Capella, head and forepart of Lynx, forefeet of Camelopardalis.

Queen of Cups

Rules from Ecliptic to 45° North Latitude, and from 20° Gemini to 20° of Cancer in Longitude.

Star Group

Head and body of Pollux, the other of the Gemini; greater part of Cancer, crab; face of Leo; head and face of Ursa Major.

THE TWELVE KEYS WHICH GOVERN THE CELESTIAL HEAVENS FROM THE ECLIPTIC TO 45° OF SOUTH LATITUDE

Fortitude

Rules the whole of Leo, from the point of Regulus or Cor Leonis.

Stars

The fore-legs and hind-feet of Leo, greater part of the Sextans and of Crater, the cups, part of the body of Hydra, the great Water serpent, greater part of Antlia Pneumatica, the air Pump, greater part of Pisces Nautica, a small part of the ship Argo.

Hermit

Rules the whole of Virgo.

Stars

Left arm, hand, and arm of Virgo, and her ear of Corn; part of the body of Hydra, Corvus, the Crow, part of Crater, tail and right hand of Centaurus, the man horse, small part of Air Pump and of Argo.

Justice

Rules the whole of Libra.

Stars

Part of the South Scale of Libra, tail of Hydra, head, body, arms and forefeet of Centauri. Legs, body and tail of Lupus, the Wolf which he is killing. Right claw of Scorpio.

Death

Rules the whole of Scorpio.

Stars

Body and tail of Scorpio, head and neck of Lupus, whole of Ara - Altar, two feet of Ophiucus, point of arrow of Sagittarius, part of Norma, Mason's square.

Temperance

Rules the whole of Sagittarius.

Stars

The whole of Sagittarius, the Archer, except right hind leg, the tail, the crown of the head, extreme points of Bow and Arrow, Corona Australis, Telescope, Pavo - Peacock.

The Devil

Rules the whole of Capricorn.

Stars

Whole lower half of Capricornus. the he-Goat, part of Piscis Australis, Southern Fish, Microscope Part of Grus, the Crane. Part of Indus.

The Star

Rules the whole of Aquarius.

Stars

Legs of Aquarius, and the issuant water head of Piscis Australis, part of Grus, part of Phoenix, part of apparatus Sculptorum, part of Cetus.

The Moon

Rules the whole of Pisces.

Stars

The connecting band of Pisces, the body of Cetus, the sea Monster to which Andromeda was exposed, part of Apparatus Sculptorum. Part of Phoenix, part of Fornax.

The Emperor

Rules the whole of Aries.

Stars

Legs of Aries, part of body of Taurus, head and fore-part of Cetus, part of Fornax and of Eridanus.

The Hierophant

Rules the whole of Taurus.

Stars

Head and forepart of Taurus the Bull. The Bull sent by Neptune to frighten the horses of Sol and those of the Hippolytus. The greater part of Orion the Giant, and hunter. The beginning of the River Eridanus into which Phaeton was hurled when attempting to drive the horses of the Sun, greater part of Lepus, the Hare.

The Lovers

Rule the whole of Gemini.

Stars

Legs of Castor and Pollux, the Gemini, Canis Minor, a small part of Cancer. The whole of Monoceros, the Unicorn, except the hind-quarters. Head and fore-part of Canis Major, the greater Dog.

The Chariot

Rules the whole of Cancer up to Regulus in Leo.

Stars

One claw and part of the body of Cancer, forepaws of Leo, head and part of Hydra, part of Sextans, part of Pisces Nautica, hind legs and tail of Monoceros, part of the mast, rigging, and prow of the ship Argo.

IN CONCLUSION

The Keys answering unto the Seven Lords who wander (planets) and the Three Spirits (the elements) are not assigned any fixed dominion. The following 36 small cards (2's to 10's) rule the decans of the signs in the Celestial Heavens and their Dominion extendeth from 45° South of the Ecliptic unto Malkuth at the Southern Pole.

5 of Wands
0° - 10° of Leo, Saturn, Part of Argo, part of Pisces Volcun.

6 of Wands
10° - 20° of Leo, Jupiter, Part of Argo, part of Pisces Volcun.

7 of Wands
20° - 30° of Leo, Mars, Part of Argo, part of Pisces Volcun.

8 of Pentacles
0° - 10° of Virgo, Sun, Part of Argo, part of Pisces Volcun.

9 of Pentacles
10° - 20° of Virgo, Venus, Hind feet of Centauri, part of Pisces Volcun.

10 of Pentacles

20ⁿ - 30° of Virgo, Mercury, Hind legs of Centauri, part of Chameleon.

2 of Swords

0° - 10° of Libra, Moon, Hind legs of Centauri, pt. Crux, pt. Musea and Chameleon.

3 of Swords

10 - 20° of Libra, Saturn, Pt. of Crux, Musea and Chameleon.

4 of Swords

20° - 30° of Libra, Jupiter, Pt. of Musea, Circinus, Compasses, and Chameleon.

5 of Cups

0° - 10° of Scorpio, Mars, Pt. Circinus, Chameleon and of Triangulum Australis.

6 of Cups

10° - 20° of Scorpio, Sun, Pt. Triangulum Australis, Apus the Swallow and Octano.

7 of Cups

20° - 30° of Scorpio, Venus, Part of Pavo, Apus, Octano.

8 of Wands

0° - 10° of Sagittarius, Mercury, Part of Pavo, Apus, Octano.

9 of Wands

10° - 20° of Sagittarius, Moon, Part of Pavo, Apus, Octano.

10 of Wands

20° - 30° of Sagittarius, Saturn, Pt. of Pavo, pt. Hydra, watersnake.

2 of Pentacles

0° - 10° of Capricorn, Jupiter, Part of Pavo, part of Hydra.

3 of Pentacles

10° - 20° of Capricorn. Mars, Part of Toncan, part of Hydra.

4 of Pentacles

20° - 30° of Capricorn, Saturn, Part of Toncan, part of Phoenix.

5 of Swords

0° - 10° of Aquarius, Venus, Part Phoenix, end of Eridanus.

6 of Swords

10° - 20° of Aquarius, Mercury, Parts Hydrus, Reticulus, Rhombus.

7 of Swords

20° - 30° of Aquarius, Moon, Parts Phoenix, Hydra, Reticulum and Eridanus.

8 of Cups

0° - 10° of Pisces, Saturn, Part Phoenix, Eridanus, Reticulum.

9 of Cups

10° - 20° of Pisces, Jupiter, Part Phoenix, Eridanus, Reticulum.

10 of Cups

20° - 30° of Pisces, Mars, Part Phoenix, Dorado, Reticulum.

2 of Wands

0° - 10° of Aries, Mars, Part Phoenix and Dorado.

3 of Wands

10° - 20° of Aries, Sun, Part Coelum Sculptori, and Dorado.

4 of Wands

20° - 30° of Aries, Venus, Part Coelum Sculptori (Engraver's Burin).

5 of Pentacles

0° - 10° of Taurus, Mercury, Part Eridanus, Columba, Naochi, Dorado, Equilaus, Pictoris.

6 of Pentacles

10° - 20° of Taurus, Moon, Forepart of Lepus, Tail and Wing of Columba, part of Equilaus.

7 of Pentacles

20° - 30° of Taurus, Saturn, Part Equilaus and Lepus, Body of Columba.

8 of Swords

0° - 10° of Gemini, Jupiter, Feet of Canis Major, Prow Argo, part Equilaus Pictoris.

9 of Swords

10° - 20° of Gemini, Mars, Legs of Canis Major, Part of Prow of Argo.

10 of Swords

20° - 30° of Gemini, Sun, Hind quarters of Canis Major, part of Prow of Argo.

2 of Cups

0° - 10° of Cancer, Venus, Prow Argo, Tail Canis Major.

3 of Cups

10° - 20° of Cancer, Mercury, Prow of Argo.

4 of Cups

20° - 30° of Cancer, Moon, Prow of Argo.

While the greater number of the Northern Constellations are connected with classical mythology, the titles of many of the Southern Constellations, and especially of those near the South Pole, are of more or less recent nomenclature, and bear witness to absence of reference to Occult Knowledge, such names for instance as Reticulum, and Coelum Sculptores, Octanus, etc.

RECAPITULATION

In the dominion of the various forces, the rule of each may be divided into three portions. The centre is the most pronounced in its accord with the nature of its Ruler, and the two outer portions are tinged with the nature of the Ruler of the dominion bordering thereon. For example, in the case of Leo, the Dominion of Fortitude, the central 10 degrees will have most of this nature. For the beginning 10 degrees are tinged with the nature of Cancer, and the last ten degrees with the nature of Virgo, the nature of Leo however predominating the mixture.

The whole Heavens then, are thus divided into Four Great Belts or Zones:

The Uppermost

Is the Dominion of the Knaves like a Cross within a Circle.

The Second Belt

Under the Dominion of the other Court cards represents a Belt of Influence descending vertically.

The Third Belt

Is under the Dominion of the 12 Keys related to the Signs of the Zodiac, represents a Belt of influence acting horizontally. This Zone in union with the second Belt will therefore yield a great Zone of 12 Crosses encircling the heavens.

VOLUME NINE

The Fourth Belt

Consists of 36 Decans under the Dominion of the 36 small cards of the four suits, the numbers 2-10 of each suit. In each of these sets of 3 parts of a Sign, the central one will be more pronounced in effect than the lateral parts.

Therefore the 3 Decanates of each of the Signs will be symbolised by a triangle. Thus are yielded twelve Triangles surrounding the lower heavens, and therefore there will ultimate twelve Crosses surmounting 12 Triangles surrounding the heavens. In other words, the symbol of the G.D. in the Outer, 12 times repeated.

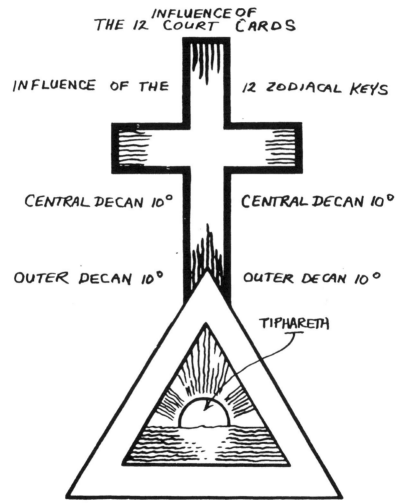

THE HIDDEN SUN OF TIPHARETH OPERATING AND RISING ABOVE THE WATERS OF SPACE.

The central Rising Sun will represent the hidden influence of Tiphareth in the centre of the Sphere, as will be hereafter explained, rising above the waters of Space (the ethereal expanse of the Sky called by the Egyptians "The Waters of Nu which are the parents of the Gods," The Shoreless Ocean of Space).

In the Golden Dawn initiation, the Cross surmounting the Triangle is preferably represented by a Calvary Cross of 6 Squares, as still more allied to Tiphareth.

ON THE OPERATION AND RULE OF THE TREE OF LIFE IN THE CELESTICAL HEAVENS PROJECTED AS IF IN A SOLID SPHERE

When the Tree of Life is considered not as being a plane but as a solid figure, and when it is projected in the Sphere, the North Pole of the Sphere will coincide with Kether, and the South Pole with Malkuth.

As we have before sufficiently learned the Ten Sephiroth are repeated not alone in each whole figure, but also in the parts thereof, so that every material thing created, will have its own Sephiroth and Paths.

Now as the North Pole corresponds with Kether, and the South Pole corresponds with Malkuth, the central Pillar of the Sephirotic Tree will form the invisible Axis of the Sphere, the Central point coinciding with Tiphareth. This latter Sephirah together with that of Yesod will be completely hidden from view, so that Tiphareth will be the exact centre of the Sphere.

Also the Sephiroth Chokmah, Binah, Chesed, Geburah, Netzach and Hod will be duplicated. As also the Paths, Aleph, Beth, Gimel, Vau, Cheth, Caph, Mem. Qoph, and Shin, and so many of the others will be even quadrupled. But although Tiphareth and Yesod will be concealed, there will be four especial points on the sphere where the influence of each will be indicated.

As projected in the before-described Celestial Sphere, Kether will govern a Radius of 10° around the North Pole, thus embracing the whole body of the Constellation Draco. Chokmah will be on the 60° North Latitude; embracing a radius of 10^n. the right foot of Hercules, the left arm, hand, and part of head of Bootes. Also on the other side of the Heavens, a radius of 10° including the head and shoulders of Cephus. and the head of Lacerta.

Binah, has a similar radius and is posited on the same parallel of Latitudes, and includes the pole Star of the Earth, the head of Camclopardelus, the tip of the tail of Draco; also Lyra and left knee of Hercules in the opposite side of the Heavens.

Chesed with a similar radius, and posited in the 30° of North Latitude, will include part of Coma Berenices, of Bootes, and of Virgo, and parts of Andromeda and of Pegasus.

And so with the other Sephiroth of the outer Pillars, each being 30° distant from the line of the Sephiroth above and below it, and having a radius of 10°.

The central line of the Two Pillars of Mercy and Severity will respectively traverse that of Mercy the 15° of Virgo and 15° of Pisces; that of Severity the 15° of Gemini and the 15° of Sagittarius. The four Yesod points will be on the line of the 60° of South Latitude, and at similar Zodiacal points. From which circumstances the path of Influence or nature of the Sun will be along the line of the Ecliptic, coinciding with Tiphareth, and that of the Moon will be on the 60° of South Latitude answering to the Yesod points on that line.

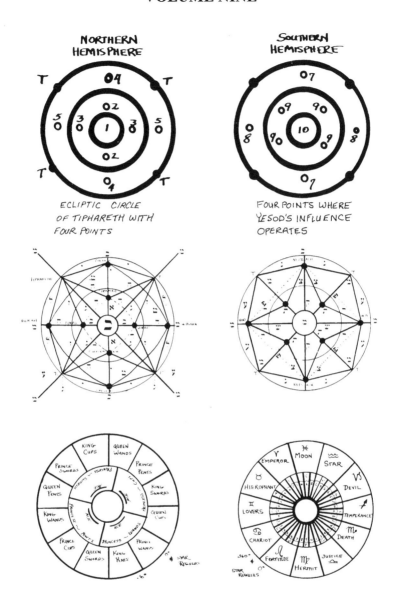

NORTHERN HEMISPHERE

SOUTHERN HEMISPHERE

ECLIPTIC CIRCLE
OF TIPHARETH WITH
FOUR POINTS

FOUR POINTS WHERE
YESOD'S INFLUENCE
OPERATES

THE LAW OF THE CONVOLUTED REVOLUTION OF
THE FORCES SYMBOLISED BY THE FOUR ACES
ROUND THE NORTH POLE

In the Book "T," it is written: "Also the Dragon (i.e. Draco, the constellation at the Northern pole of the Heavens) surroundeth the Pole Kether of the Celestial Heavens." It is further laid down that the Four Aces, (symbolised by the Knaves), rule the Celestial Heavens from the Northern Pole of the Zodiac unto the 45th Degree of Latitude North of the Ecliptic, and from the Thrones of the Four Aces which rule in Kether.

And again it is stated that:

> **The Throne of the Ace of Cups is the head of Draco.**
> **The Throne of the Ace of Swords is fore part of body.**
> **The Throne of the Ace of Pentacles is the hind part of body.**
> **The Throne of the Ace of Wands is the tail of Draco.**

Regard thou then the form of this Constellation of the Dragon. It is convoluted in the four places answering unto the rule of the Aces.

> **Head, First convolution is the Ace of Cups.**
> **Second convolution is the Ace of Swords.**
> **Third convolution is the Ace of Pentacles.**
> **Fourth convolution is the Ace of Wands.**

This convoluted course will represent the Law of the Aces.

Now in the Four Faces of YHVH, Fire and Water be contrary, and also Earth and Air be contrary. The throne of the Element will attract and seize, as it were, the Force of that element, so that herein be the Forces of Antipathy and of Sympathy, or what are known chemically as attraction and repulsion.

Recall also the allotment of the Triplicities:

> **Aries, Leo, Sagittarius is Fire, Wands of the Tarot.**
> **Cancer, Scorpio, Pisces is Water, Cups of the Tarot.**
> **Gemini, Libra, Aquarius is Air, Swords of the Tarot.**
> **Taurus, Virgo, Capricorn is Earth, Pentacles of the Tarot.**

Now the order of the Knaves, and consequently of the Thrones, is formed from right to left:

Yod

Knave of Wands is Leo and Fire.

Heh

Knave of Cups is Scorpio and Water.

Vau

Knave of Swords is Aquarius and Air.

Heh (final)

Knave of Pentacles is Taurus and Earth.

The order of the Aces is formed from left to right, though their motion is from right to left:

Yod

Ace of Wands.

Heh

Ace of Cups.

Vau

Ace of Swords.

Heh (final)

Ace of Pentacles.

This, then will be the order of their movement. Let us first suppose the Aces on the following stations:

Station 2

Ace of Wands.

Station 1

Ace of Cups.

Station 12

Ace of Swords.

Station 11

Ace of Pentacles.

Now the Station 2 is the Throne of the Ace of Wands, while the movement of the Aces is steadily from right to left in the direction of the numbering of the stations. In the ordinary course the Ace of Wands would pass to Station 3; the Ace of Cups to Station 2; the Ace of Swords to Station 1; the Ace of Pentacles to Station 12.

But the Station 2, being the Throne of the Ace of Wands, attracts and arrests the movement of that Force so that instead of passing into Station 3, it remains on Station 2 until the other Aces have passed over it in turn.

Ace of Wands remains on Station 2.

Ace of Cups passes also on to Station 2,

Ace of Swords passes on to Station 1,

Ace of Pentacles passes on to Station 12.

Ace of Cups passes to Station 3,

Ace of Wands remains at Station 2,

Ace of Swords passes also onto Station 2,

Ace of Pentacles passes also on to Station 1.

Ace of Cups passes on to Station 4,

Ace of Swords passes on to Station 3,

Ace of Wands remains at Station 2,

Ace of Pentacles passes also on to Station 2.

Ace of Cups passes to Station 5,

Ace of Swords passes to Station 4,

Ace of Pentacles passes on to Station 3,

Ace of Wands still remains on Station 2.

But Station 5 is the Throne of the Ace of Cups. Therefore it attracts and arrests that Force, in the same manner that the Throne of the Ace of Wands acted previously in attracting and arresting the Ace of Wands, the result of which has been to make that Force which previously was leading become the last of the Four.

> **Ace of Cups remains on Station 5,**
> **Ace of Swords passes also on to Station 5,**
> **Ace of Pentacles passes also on to Station 4,**
> **Ace of Wands, now at last passes into Station 3.**

For it has now become the last of the Four, and the Ace of Cups has commenced to act through its Throne. The Ace of Pentacles, moving to Station 4, would create a hiatus in the movement of the Aces, if the Ace of Wands did not move forward to Station 3. Also there is the attraction of the motion of those Aces in front of it. Wherefore all these Forces combining, at length cause it to move forward.

The movement then continues, thus:

> **The Ace of Swords passes on to Station 6,**
> **The Ace of Cups remains on Station 5,**
> **The Ace of Pentacles passes also on to Station 5,**
> **The Ace of Wands passes also on to Station 4.**
> **The Ace of Swords passes on to Station 7,**
> **The Ace of Pentacles passes on to Station 6,**
> **The Ace of Cups still remains on Station 5,**
> **The Ace of Wands passes also on to Station 5.**
> **The Ace of Swords passes on to Station 8, its Throne,**
> **The Ace of Pentacles passes on to Station 7,**
> **The Ace of Wands passes on to Station 6,**
> **The Ace of Cups still remains on Station 5.**
> **The Ace of Swords remains on Station 8,**
> **The Ace of Pentacles passes also on to Station 8,**
> **The Ace of Wands passes on to Station 7,**
> **The Ace of Cups now at length passes on to Station 6, and so on.**

The movement of the Aces will be very similar to the convolutions of Draco thus: The Course of the Aces:

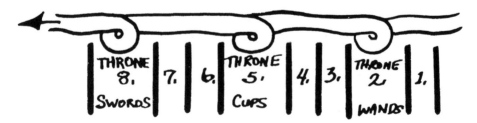

This will imply a much more sustained exercise of force through the Thrones than elsewhere. So that the generic effect of the Thrones will be that of the seasons, while the other stations will give the variations thereof accordance with their natures and with the order the movment the aces in them.

	SIGN	THRONE OF	FIRST IN ORDER	SECOND IN ORDER	THIRD IN ORDER	FOURTH IN ORDER
MOVEABLE	♈		▽	△	▽	△
FIXED	♉	ACE OF PENTACLES	▽	△	▽	△
COMMON	♊		△	▽	△	▽
M.	♋		△	▽	△	▽
F.	♌	ACE OF WANDS	△	▽	△	▽
C.	♍		▽	△	▽	△
M.	♎		▽	△	▽	△
F.	♏	ACE OF CUPS	▽	△	▽	△
C.	♐		△	▽	△	▽
M.	♑		△	▽	△	▽
F.	♒	ACE OF SWORDS	△	▽	△	▽
C.	♓		▽	△	▽	△

Order of Movement of Elements

And as Kether acted directly upon Tiphareth which is, as it were, the centre and focus of the Sephiroth when projected in a sphere, so do the Aces act upon the Sun as the centre and focus of the Solar System. So that the Sun, according to his position with regard to the Equinox and the Earth's surface will translate the effect of the seasons, he being the translator of the force of heat thereto, whether the then position of the Equinoctial points coincide with what we call 0° Aries, and 0° Libra (reckoning from Regulus) or not. So that his effect North of the Equator shall produce when just leaving the Equinoctial point, the effect of Aries, whether he be with that constellation actually in the heavens or not.

Conversely also, for the South of the Equator (as in the country of Australia) his quitting the Equinoctial point southward will translate the same effect of Aries.

But this rule shall not for one moment affirm that Aries and Libra are identical in nature. Nor that the Zodiac proper is inoperative. Nor that the nature of the Sun is not modified by the constellation in which he is. But only that the direct effect of the physical impact of his rays falling upon a certain portion of the Earth's surface, will be in proportion to the duration of their action, in the excitement they produce in the terrestrial forces.

And now as the Forces symbolized by these Aces, pass in succession over these stations, so will they awake certain terrestrial action according unto the sign of the division of the Zodiac above which they pass in the domain of the Knaves and according unto the nature thereof. Nevertheless, the force roused by the Ace when on its Throne will be of longer duration than at other points.

And hence it is that the Signs of the Zodiac be divided into Fixed or Kerubic, Moveable or changing, and Common or fluctuating, according unto the nature of the power which can be awakened therein. And again, these will be varied according unto their Elements, for the Elements have a various classification.

NOTE

By

G.H. FRATER S.R.M.D.

It is here advisable to transcribe the following from Cornelius Agrippa:

Of The Four Elements and Their Natural Qualities:

"It is necessary that we should know and understand the nature and quality of the Four Elements, in order to our being perfect in the principles and groundwork of our studies in the Talismanic or Magical Art.

"Therefore, there are four Elements, the original grounds of all corporeal things, viz.: Earth, Air, Fire, and Water, of which elements all inferior bodies are compounded, not by way of being heaped up together, but by transmutation and union; and when they are destroyed, they are resolved into elements.

"But there are none of the sensible elements that are pure. They are more or less mixed, and apt to be changed into one into the other, even as earth being moistened and dissolved becomes water, but the same being made thick and hard becomes earth again, and being evaporated through heat it passes into air, and that being kindlcd into fire; and this being extinguished into air again; but being cooled after burning becomes water again, or else stone or sulphur, and this is clearly demonstrated by lightning.

"Now every one of these Elements has two specific qualities: the former whereof it retains as proper to itself; in the other as a mean, it agrees with that which comes directly after it. For Fire is hot and dry; Water cold and moist; and Air hot and moist; and so in this manner, the Elements, according to two contrary qualities are opposite one to the other, as Fire to Water, and Earth to Air.

"Likewise the Elements are contrary one to the other on another account. Two are heavy, as Earth and Water; and the others are light, as Fire and Air.

TABLE SHOWING QUALITIES OF ELEMENTS

Fire

Heat, dryness, excessive lightness, brilliance, excessive subtlety, motion rapid.

Water

Cold, moisture, weight, obscurity, solidity, motion.

Air

Heat, moisture, lightness, slight obscurity, subtlety, excessive motion.

Earth

Cold, dryness, excessive weight, excessive obscurity, excessive solidity, rest.

TABLE SHOWING THE QUALITIES OF THE ELEMENTS WHEN MIXED IN PAIRS

Fire and Water.

Slight weight, some subtlety, intense and rapid motion.

Fire and Air.

Great heat, intense lightness, slight brilliance, intense subtlety, intense motion.

Fire and Earth.

Great dryness, slight obscurity.

Water and Air.

Great moisture, intense motion.

Water and Earth.

Great cold, intense weight, intense obscurity, intense solidity.

Air and Earth.

Some weight, intense obscurity, little solidity, little motion.

Therefore the Stoics called the former 'passives,' but the latter 'actives.' And Plato distinguishes them after another manner, and assigns to each of them three qualities, viz.: To the Fire brightness, thinness and motion. To the Earth, darkness, thickness, and quietness. And according to these qualities the Elements of Fire and Earth are contrary. Now the other Elements borrow their qualities from these, so that the Air receives two qualities from the Fire, thinness and motion, and from the Earth one, darkness. In like manner, Water receives two qualities from the Earth, darkness and thickness; and from the Fire one, motion. But Fire is twice as thin as Air, thrice more moveable, and four times lighter. The Air is twice more bright, thrice more thin, and four times more moveable than Water. Therefore, as Fire is to Air, so is Air to Water, and Water to Earth. And again, as the Earth is to the Water, so is Water to Air, and Air to Fire. And this is the root and foundation of all bodies, natures, and wonderful works. And he who can know and thoroughly understand these qualities of the Elements and their mixtures shall bring to pass wonderful and astonishing things in Magic.

"Now each of these Elements has a threefold consideration, so that the number of four may make up the number of twelve; and by passing by the number of seven into ten, there may be a progress to the Supreme Unity upon which all virtue and wonderful things do depend. Of the first Order, are the pure Elements, which are neither compounded, changed, nor mixed, but are incorruptible and not of which but through which the virtues of all natural things are brought forth to act. No man is fully able to declare their Virtues, because they can do all things upon all things. He who remains ignorant of these, shall never be able to bring to pass any wonderful matter.

"Of the second order are Elements that are compounded, changeable and impure, yet such as may, by art, be reduced to their pure simplicity, whose virtue, when they are thus reduced, doth above all things perfect all occult and common operations of Nature; and these are the foundations of the whole of natural Magic.

"Of the third Order are those elements which originally and of themselves are not elements, but are twice compounded, various, and changeable unto another. These are the infallible medium, and are called the Middle Nature, or Soul of the Middle Nature; very few there are that understand the deep mysteries thereof. In them is, by means of certain numbers, degrees and orders, the perfection of every effect in what thing soever, whether natural, celestial, or super-celestial. They are full of wonders and mysteries, and are operative in Magic, natural or divine. For, from these, through them, proceeds the binding, loosing, and transmutation of all things - the knowledge and foretelling of things to come, also the expelling of evil and the gaining of Good Spirits. Let no one, therefore, without these three sorts of Elements, and the true knowledge thereof, be confident that he can work anything in the occult science of Magic and Nature.

"But whosoever shall know how to reduce those of one order into another, impure into pure, compounded into simple, and shall understand distinctly the nature, virtue, and power of them, into number, degrees and order, without dividing the substance, he shall easily attain to the knowledge and perfect operation of all natural things, and celestial secrets likewise; and this is the perfection of the Qabalah, which teaches all these before mentioned; and by a perfect knowledge thereof, we perform many rare and wonderful experiments. In the original and exemplary world all things are all in all. So also in this corporeal world. And the elements are not only in these inferior things; but are in the Heavens, in stars, in devils, in angels, and likewise in God Himself, the maker and original example of all things.

"Now it must be understood that in these inferior bodies the elements are gross and corruptible, but in the heavens they are, with their natures and virtues, after a celestial and more excellent manner than in sublunary things. For the firmness of the celestial earth is there without the grossness of water, and the agility of Air without exceeding its bounds. The heat of fire without burning, only shining, giving light and life to all things by its celestial heat."

Now the successive effect of the passage of the Aces over the Stations above the place of a sign in the excitement of the Forces of that Sign may be readily calculated by the tables of the qualities of the elements simple and mixed, always being careful to take also into account the effect of the Throne upon the Season as well, and the nature of the Sign.

It is said that Kether is in Malkuth, and again, that Malkuth is in Kether but after another manner.

For downwards through the Four Worlds the Malkuth of the less material will be linked unto the Kether of the more material. From the Synthesis of the Ten corruscations of the AOUR (Light) proceedeth the influence unto EHEIEH, the Kether of Atziluth. And the connecting thread of the AIN SOPH is extended through the worlds of the Ten Sephiroth and is in every direction. As the Ten Sephiroth operate in each Sephirah, so will there be a KETHER in every MALKUTH, and MALKUTH in every KETHER. Thus:

Adonai Melekh

This will be the Malkuth of Atziluth.

Metatron

This will be the Kether of Briah.

Sandalphon - Metraton - Nephesch ha-Messiah

These will be the Malkuth of Briah.

Chaioth ha-Qadesh

This will be the Kether of Yetzirah.

Aschim

This will be the Malkuth of Yetzirah.

Rashith ha-Gilgalim

The Kether of Assiah.

Cholem Yesodoth

The Malkuth of Assiah.

Thaumiel

The Kether of the Qlippoth.

The symbol of the connection between MALKUTH of YETZIRAH and KETHER of ASSIAH will be of a form somewhat resembling that of an hour glass. The thread of the AIN SOPH before alluded to, traversing the centre thereof, and forming the AIN SOPH connection between the Worlds:

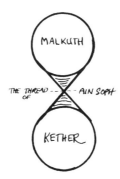

So that the symbol of the connection between the two planes is this. And also the modus operandi of the translation of force from one plane into another is in this, and hence doth the title of the Sphere of Kether of Assiah signify the commencement of a whirling motion.

Now also, in the diagram of Minutum Mundum, there be four colours attributed unto Malkuth. Citrine, russet, olive, and black. And if we consider them as in a vertical sphere, we shall find citrine uppermost and horizontal, russet and olive midmost and vertical, black lowermost and horizontal.

And again, these four represent in a manner the operation of the four elements in Malkuth; for example:

Citrine

Air of Earth.

Russet

Fire of Earth.

Olive

Water of Earth.

Black

Earth of Earth.

From the diagram of the hour glass symbol it will be manifest then that MALKUTH of YETZIRAH will be the transmitter of the Yetziratic forces unto KETHER of ASSIAH, and that the latter will be the recipient thereof, and that the Hour-glass symbol or double cone, will be the translator from the one plane unto the other. Here, therefore, let us consider the Yetziratic nomenclature of the Tenth Path answering unto Malkuth, and of the First Path answering unto Kether.

The Tenth Path: It is called the Resplendent Intelligence and it is so-called because it is exalted above every head, and sitteth on the Throne of Binah. and it illuminateth the splendour of all the Lights, and it causeth the current of Influence to flow from the Knight of Countenances, i.e. Metatron.

The First Path: It is called the Wonderful or Hidden Intelligence (The Highest Crown) for it is the Light to cause to understand the Primordial without commencement, and it is the Primal Glory, for nothing created is worthy to follow out its essence.

Whence it is plain that MALKUTH is, as it were, the collector together and synthesis of all the forces in its plane or world. While KETHER being superior unto all else in its plane or world, will be the recipient and arranger of the forces from the plane beyond, so as to distribute them unto its subordinate Sephiroth in a duly ordered manner.

And therefore any force of the multitudinous and innumerable forces in Malkuth may act through the upper cone of the hour glass symbol, and by means of the lower one translate its operation into KETHER below, but its mode of transmission will be through the cones by the thread of the Ain Soph, or of the Unformulated.

So that in the transmission of force between two worlds the Formulate must first become Unformulate, ere it can reformulate in new conditions. **For it must be plain that a force formulated in one world, if translated into another will be unformulated, according to the laws of a plane different in nature.** Even as water in its fluid state will be subject to different laws to those governing it when in the conditions of either ice or steam.

And as before said, there being in the Minutum Mundum diagram four chief elemental divisions of the Sephira MALKUTH, each of these will have its correlative formula of transmission unto the succeeding Kether. Hence also in the Order Tarot teaching is there the Dominion of the four Knaves of the Tarot pack around the North Pole. Why then is it that it is the Four Knaves answering unto the final Heh of YHVH, that are here placed, rather than the Four Kings, Queens or Knights, or one of each nature?

We are taught that these are the Vice Regents of the Name in the Four Worlds, and that they are thus attributed among the Sephiroth.

Yod

Chokmah and King.

Heh

Binah and Queen.

Vau

Tiphareth and Knight.

Heh (final)

Malkuth and Knave.

Now as Kether of Assiah is to receive from Malkuth of Yetzirah, it is necessary that in and about Kether there should be a force which partaketh of the nature of Malkuth, though more subtle and refined in nature. And therefore is it that the final Heh, or Knave force, has its dominion placed about Kether. They are so placed that they may attract from the Malkuth of the Higher and form the basis of action for the Aces. So that a refined matter may attract its like, and the spiritual forces may not lose themselves in the void, to produce but a mistaken and whirling destruction for want of a settled basis. And herein is the mutual formula in all things, of a spirit and of a body, seeing that each supplies unto each that wherein the other is lacking, yet herein also must there be a certain condition, otherwise the harmony will not be perfect. For unless the body be refined in nature, it will hinder the action of a spirit cognate unto it. And unless the spirit be willing to ally itself unto the body, the latter will be injured thereby and each will mutually react on the other.

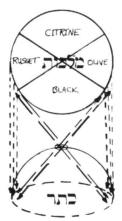

Hourglass Connection of Malkuth and Kether.

Therefore, also, let the Adeptus Minor understand that there may be fault of the spirit as well as of the body, and that **there is little difference between the material and sensuous person, and the envious, malicious and self-righteous person** - save that from their being more subtle and less evident, the sins of the latter are more insidious than those of the former, though both are alike evil. But **it is as necessary to govern the Spirit as to refine the body,** and of what use is it to weaken the body by abstinence, if at the same time uncharitableness and spiritual pride are encouraged! **It is simply translating one sin into another.**

And therefore are the final Heh forces so necessary in Kether, as it is said in the Tenth Path of the Scpher Yetzirah: "It is so called because it is exalted above every head, and sitteth on the Throne of Binah." Now, in the Tree, the two Sephiroth, Chokmah and Binah, are referred unto the Briatic World which is also called the Throne or vehicle, that is of the Atzilutic World unto which latter Kether is referred on the Tree. And referring unto the dominions of the Four Knaves, thou shalt find that in the sphere they include Chokmah and Binah as well as Kether.

Now there will be, not one, but four formulae of the application of the Four Forces of Malkuth, unto the revolution of the Aces in Kether, and these acting not singly but simultaneously and with a different degree of force.

Were Malkuth or Kether in the same plane or world the transmission of these forces from the one unto the other would proceed more or less in direct lines. In this case, seeing that Malkuth and Kether be in different planes or worlds, the lines of transmission of these forces are caught up and whirled about by the upper cone of the hour glass symbol into the vortex wherethrough passeth the thread of the unformulated, i.e. the Ain Soph. Thence they are projected in a whirling convolution (yet according unto their nature) through the lower cone of the hour glass symbol unto Kether.

Whence it resulteth that these formulae are of the nature of the Dragon, that is to say, moving in convolutions, and hence they are called the Dragon or Serpent Formulae.

Now imagining MALKUTH of Yetzirah to be in a vertical position above KETHER of Assiah, it will be plain that the whole of the black part of Malkuth will be towards Kether, but only a portion of the russet and olive parts, and that the citrine parts will be entirely removed and on the further side. Wherefore the natural operation of these four forces towards Kether will be: black, rather horizontal than vertical, and acting fully.

Citrine rather horizontal than vertical but acting at the edge of the circumference of Kether, and slightly rather than strongly. Russet and olive rather vertical than horizontal, and acting moderately.

Now these four formulae will imply four simultaneous movements in the revolution of the forces symbolised by the four Aces round the Northern Pole.

The first and most forcible in its immediate action will be that answering unto the Earth of Malkuth of Yetzirah, transmitting unto Kether of Assiah, and following the convolutions of the Constellation Draco. It is called the Direct or Creeping Formula and

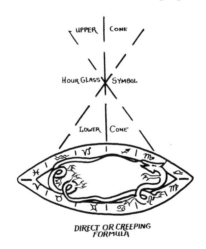

DIRECT OR CREEPING
FORMULA

for this reason the Dragon may be wingless and footed as regards its symbolic representation. This formula has been throughly explained in the beginning of this section on the revolution of the Aces. In the expressions Earth of Malkuth, etc., it should be remembered that these do not imply pure but mixed elemental natures, seeing that Malkuth receiveth the ultimate effect of all the forces in the Tree of Life, even as the colours which be attributed thereto be not primaries, but tertiaries. Therefore each element in Malkuth will be counter-changed with others, even as the Kerubim in the Vision of Ezekiel have each, not one but four heads and counterchanged.

The second and least forcible in its immediate action will be the Dragon formula answering unto the Air of Malkuth of Yetzirah, transmitting unto Kether of Assiah, and following the convolutions of four serpents upon the four triplicities of the elements in the Zodiac or more properly speaking, upon the stations in the Dominions of the Knaves above them.

Now also the Throne in each Dominion is marked in the Book T as embracing more than a third of each dominion, because of the enduring effect of its force. This formula is also called the looped or Flying Formula, and hence the serpents may be represented footless, but winged. Its action is more round the circumference at its edge, than that of the other formulae. This formula of operation will be readily understood on reference to the diagram thereof, but more especially from the four diagrams showing the change of order and course of the aces. In this formula the heads of the four serpents will be above the four cardinal signs.

The Third Dragon Formula, moderately forcible in its immediate action, is that answering unto the Fire of Malkuth of Yetzirah, transmitting unto Kether of Assiah, and following the law of the attraction and repulsion of the elements of the triplicities of the Zodiac. This is also called the Leaping or Darting Formula, and its serpents may be represented both footed and winged - footed to represent the attraction of the elements, winged to represent the repulsion by the contrary elements. This formula is more vertical in action, while the preceding two are more horizontal as before shown.

LOOPED OR FLYING FORMULA

This formula will be readily understood from the four diagrams thereof and also from those showing the change of order in the course of the Aces. As before the heads of the serpents rest upon the Stations above the Cardinal Signs.

The explanation of the course of one of the four serpents will be sufficient to explain the whole. Let us take that of Fire:

Fire is strongly attracted by the Station above Fire,
Fire is strongly repelled by the Station above Water,
Fire is slightly attracted by the Station above Air,
Fire is slightly repelled by the Station above Earth.

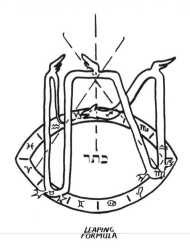

LEAPING
FORMULA

> **The Head rests on the Station above Aries.**
> **The Serpent s repelled into the lower Cone by Pisces,**
> **The Serpent slightly attracted by Aquarius,**
> **The Serpent slightly attracted by Capricorn,**
> **The Serpent strongly attracted by Sagittarius,**
> **The Serpent strongly repelled by Scorpio,**
> **The Serpent slightly attracted by Libra,**
> **The Serpent slightly attracted by Virgo,**
> **The Serpent strongly attracted by Leo,**
> **The Serpent strongly repelled by Cancer,**
> **The Serpent slightly attracted by Gemini and Taurus.**

The tail is strongly attracted by Aries, where it is united with the head again. (The course of the Four Serpents is shown in four different diagrams to avoid confusion.)

REVOLVING OR FLOWING
FORMULA

The fourth Dragon Formula and moderately forcible, is that answering unto the Water of MALKUTH of Yetzirah, transmitting into the KETHER of Assiah, and following the Law of the Zodiacal succession of the Signs in gradual Osented neither winged nor footed, but with fins to symbolise its flowing movement. This formula will be more vertical in action, and can be readily understood from the diagram thereof, and from those showing the change of order in the course of the Aces.

This formula may be best symbolically represented by the four Aces revolving as in a smaller wheel upon a great circle whose body is composed of the powers of the twelve Signs, so that this latter in its turn revolves upon the stations above the Zodiac. The effect of the revolution of the Wheel of the Aces will be to excite by the Ace of Wands the Fiery Signs, by the Ace of Cups the Watery Signs, by the Ace of Swords the Airy Signs, and by the Ace of Pentacles the Earthy Signs. Yet through the forces of the revolution of the Serpent as well, the forces of the Aces will be in their turn modified by the zodiacal natures in the body of the Serpent.

And as before said the action of these formulae will be simultaneous though differing in degree, and of them all that first explained which followeth the convolutions of the Constellation Draco is the strongest in operation. And it is to be noted that in two of these formulae, the heads of the Serpents are with the Order of the Signs, and in the other two against the natural order of succession of them in the Zodiac.

Also the action of the Spirit of Malkuth of Yetzirah transmitting unto Kether of Assiah will equal that of continued vibratory rays, acting from the centre to the circumference, and thus bringing into action the force from the "Thread of the Unformulate" MEZLA.

Recall that which is written in the Chapter of the Chariot - (Ezekiel, 1.45.)

"And I beheld, and lo! a tempestuous whirlwind came out from the North, a mighty cloud, and a fire violently whirling upon itself, and a splendour revolving upon itself, and from the midmost as an eye of brightness from the midst of the fire. And from the midmost the forms of the Four Chaioth."

THE TRUE SYSTEM OF ASTROLOGICAL DIVINATION

By

G.H. FRATER D.D.C.F.

(N.B. This paper belongs to the subgrade of Theoricus Adeptus Minor. It is mentioned in the preface to the document relating to the Ring and the Disc. Six diagrams accompany this document, and all relate to the various signs of the Grades - primarily to the Portal grade and the LVX Signs of the Adeptus Minor grade. These signs will be found in the drawings of the Signs of the Grades in this work. I.R.)

It is written: "His Father was the Sun, his Mother was the Moon, the Air carried him in her bosom, his nurse was the Earth." (The Smaragine or Emerald Tablet of Hermes.) Recall the analysis of the Keyword of the Adeptus Minor Grade.

I.N.R.I. is Yod, Nun, Resh, Yod.

The first "I" is Virgo, Isis, Mighty Mother - in this sense "Mother" being the producer of seeds and fruit on the Earth when the Sun is therein.

"N" is Scorpio, Apophis, Destroyer - the Destructive Force which is brought into play, to check or restrict the continuation of the action of Regenerative Force.

"R" is Sol.

The final "I" is Osiris Slain and Risen - the Sun in the Decadence of Force from the Autumnal, and his Increase of Force from the Vernal Equinox.

The Isis, Apophis, Osiris is I.A.O. The initials of these three produce the synthetical name IAO. This giveth a fresh Triad, of which again the beginning is Virgo, namely Air, TIPHARETH.

Now as the Adeptus Minor vibrateth these Names and maketh these Signs, he affirmeth certain correspondences in his own Atmosphere. That is to say that:

The Sign of Osiris slain: representeth the Equinoctial Forces.

The Sign of the Mourning of Isis: the Force of Light illumining at its greatest pitch. Wherefore the space included between the hands is the "Semi Arc" of the Sun at the Summer Solstice, which she thus recalleth as the affirmation of the Life Force of Osiris.

The Sign of Typhon and Apophis: the space between the hands above the head will mark the diminished extent of the whole "Arc" of the Sun and his Winter Solstice, thus representing the corresponding excess of the Darkness over the Light.

The Signs of the Rending asunder, and of the Closing of the Veil: mark the Arcs of Light midway between the Equinoxes and the Solstices.

The Sign of Osiris Risen: representeth the Synthetical extent of the variation between the utmost extent of the Light of the Solstices and the Equinoxes, as thus affirming that the power of the governance of these Forces may be found in the Self when depending on the higher illumination, as the New Name is found from the initials of the others.

In the diagrams the Light is therefore shewn as coming from above the figure; thus affirming its descent from, and also the Solar course of the Seasons dependeth from the movement of the Forces symbolized in the Book T, by the 4 Aces at the North Pole of the Universe, and their convoluted revolution.

VOLUME TEN

THE ENOCHIAN SYSTEM

VOLUME TEN

THE ENOCHIAN SYSTEM

TABLE OF CONTENTS

IMPORTANT TABLES AND ILLUSTRATIONS

THE ENOCHIAN SYSTEM

AN INTRODUCTION TO THE ENOCHIAN TEACHING AND PRAXIS

By

THOMAS HEAD, PH.D. (OXON)

Gabriel . . .Every Letter signifieth the Member of the substance whereof it speaketh. Every word signifieth the quiddity of the substance. The Letters are separated, and in confusion: and therefore, are by numbers gathered together: which also gathered signifie a number: for as every greater containeth his lesser, so are the secret and unknown forms of things knit up in their parents: Where being known in number they are easily distinguished, so that herein we teach places to be numbered: letters to be elected from the numbered, and proper words from the letters.[1]

With Enochian magic the reader arrives at the unifying system that underlay all the practical work of the Golden Dawn as originally constituted in 1887. All the initiation ceremonies of the Order, from the grade of Zelator to that of Philosophus, contained references to Enochian; but not until the level of Zelator Adeptus Minor did it become a subject of regular instruction and methodical investigation. The Order's interest in Enochian became semi-public in 1912, when Aleister Crowley issued a two-part precis of its material in the seventh and eighth numbers of The Equinox. As an historical document Crowley's account was badly flawed: in the first place by his lumping together the materials pertaining to the Order with those pertaining to his personal research; and in the second place by his trick of supplying verbose commentaries to everything that is obvious, while passing over the real obscurities as though they were self-evident. As a piece of instruction the thing is even worse - for nobody would be able to deduce from Crowley's essay alone how the Enochian system, or any part of it, functions as a definite practical scheme. Consequently it was not until 1940, when Israel Regardie published the fourth volume of the Golden Dawn, that a clear and accurate record of the Order's Enochian teachings and magical techniques became available to the public.

It should be noted in passing that Regardie paid a heavy price for his candour and his labours. His book was greeted with an outpouring of negative criticism, and a frenzy of chattered personal derision, which in their inarticulate fury were quite exceptional even for a milieu so full of touchy egos as the Anglo-American world of the occult. Viewed in retrospect these "book reviews" are often masterpieces of unintended comedy. Most of them, indeed, give the impression that they were written while their authors were frothing at the mouth and pawing the air with their left hands. But for a dedicated and sensitive young author - and Regardie was scarcely thirty when he began to publish the Golden Dawn - it must have been extremely painful to be the target of such unremitting vilification.

The gravamen of all this abuse was that Regardie had broken the oaths of secrecy by which he had bound himself as an Adept in the Hermes Temple. Regardie's defence - which was actually printed two years before he began to make the Order material public - rested on three claims: first, that the Temple had itself so far degenerated that its Hierophants could no longer initiate effectively; second, that as a further consequence the teaching had become so distorted that there was clear and present danger or its being lost altogther; and, third, that while vows of occult secrecy are certainly meant to protect the names of the members and the whereabouts of the organization, they do not in principle extend to the substance of the teaching itself2, which is implicitly addressed to whom it may concern. Today, after the passage of some forty years, it is abundantly clear the Regardie was entirely right and his detractors entirely wrong. The central position that the Golden Dawn material occupies in modern esoteric studies and its far-reaching influence across organizational lines are due, not at all to the wisdom of its titular guardians, but simply and solely to Regardie's act of preservation. Of this fact the Enochian teachings, with which alone we are here concerned, are quite possibly the best case in point. These, in the Temple to which Regardie belonged, were almost completely ignored. Today they are so far from being ignored that two Enochian dictionaries are currently in print, a third is on the way, and in both the United States and England there are several groups which (with varying results) are endeavouring to conduct serious research into both the language and the magic.

ENOCHIAN SOURCES

The Enochian system originated through the ceremonial skrying of Dr. John Dee and Edward Kelley, whose sittings took place over a period of seven years beginning in 1582, when Dee was 54 years old and Kelley 27. Dee was a polyhistor, and his erudition was like an imperial tureen - wide and deep and almost unbelieveably capacious. By the standards of his day he had valid claims to expert knowledge of mathematics, languages, geography, astronomy, mechanics, architecture, navigation, theology, cryptology, poetry, painting, drama, optics, music, philosophy, genealogy, medicine - and the Hermetic sciences. With the possible exception of Roger Bacon in the thirteenth century, Dee came nearer than any other Englishman to embracing all the knowledge of his age. His library, which by 1583 contained about 2500 books and 170 manuscripts, was the largest in England and a rival to almost all the private Continental collections. His physical appearance was striking, This is Aubrey's description: "Hee had a very faire cleare rosie complexion; a long beard as white as milke; he was tall and slender; a very handsome man."[3]

Less is known of Kelley, for he was not a public figure, and much of what was written about him is not well documented. The portrait that emerges from the record of his sittings with Dee is of a highly ambiguous personality, wary and mistrustful, unstable and picric, prone on the one hand to terrifying fits of anger accompanied by physical violence, and on the other hand to sudden spiritual conversions from which he promptly relapsed. Before attaching himself to Dee's household, Kelley had served as secretary to the mathematician and Hermetic scholar Thomas Allen, from whom he may have acquired his knowledge of occult philosophy. He possessed a number of old books, some pertaining to alchemy (in which he was passionately interested), but most of them apparently having to do with the recovery of buried treasure through the help of evil spirits. If Dee's mind was the tureen, Kelley's was the soup plate - somewhat shallow, but wide enough to hold a little bit of almost anything. Certainly he was intelligent and not uneducated; he had been an undergraduate at Oxford under the (false) name of Edward Talbot, though it appears he was sent down after some sort of trouble. A few years later he was pilloried at Lancaster for forgery. No evidence has survived bearing on his guilt or innocence, but it should be borne in mind that in Elizabethan England the administration of justice - at least where the poor and the unpopular were concerned - was no less rough and ready than the American Wild West.

Kelley presented himself at Dee's house in Mortlake on Thursday, 8 March 1582, and offered his services as a skryer. Two days later Dee was giving him a trial. Their preparations were of the simplest, consisting merely of setting up the shewstone or crystal on the table of practice and of a short prayer spoken by the Doctor. The result was that Kelley received, on that first day, a vision of the angel Uriel, who revealed his secret signature and issued preliminary directions for the construction of two magical talismans: (1) the Sigillum Dei Aemeth, a pentacle nine inches in diameter, to be made of purified wax; and (2) the Tabula Sancta, a table to be made of sweet wood two cubits high and two cubits square, on which a large rectangular seal containing twelve Enochian letters was to be surrounded with seven circular seals attributed to the planetary powers. The two talismans - which were in fact the first two Enochian documents - were to be employed together, the pentacle being placed on the Holy Table while in use.

Now events moved swiftly. On 14 March a spirit identified as the angel Michael gave instructions for making a magic ring of gold bearing a seal said to be identical to that "wherewith all miracles and divine works and wonders were wrought by Solomon."[4] This is the design:

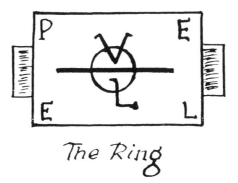

The Ring

Six days later Uriel dictated a square of 49 characters containing seven angelic names, thus:

Z	l	l	R	H	i	a
a	Z	C	a	a	c	b
p	a	u	p	n	h	r
h	d	m	h	i	a	i
K	K	a	a	e	e	e
i	i	e	e	l	l	l
e	e	l	l	M	G	✝

Starting with the left-hand column and reading from the top downwards, the following names are produced: Zaphkiel. Zedekiel, Cumael, Raphael, Hanael. Michael, and Gabriel - with the sign of the cross employed to close the last place. On the following day, 21 March, a second square was supplied by Uriel.

S	A	A	I²¹₈	E	M	E	VENIT IN COELIS
B	T	Z	K	A	S	E	DUES NOSTER
H	E	I	D	E	N	E	DUX NOSTER
D	E	I	M	O	30	A	HIC EST
I²⁶	M	E	G	C	B	E	LUX IN AETERNUM
I	L	A	O	I²¹₈	V	N	FINIS EST
I	H	R	L	A	A	²¹₈	VERA EST HAEC TABULA

Now the method of interpretations begins to wax complicated. The number 21 is here to read as the letter E while 8, 26 and 30 are to be read as L. Starting from the S at the upper left-hand corner one reads successive diagonal lines in a southwesterly direction (downward and to the left), thus producing the following angelic names: Sabathiel, Zedekiel (sic), Madimiel, Semeliel, Nogabel, Corabiel, and Levanael. Then, reading in still different directions along the diagonals, one obtains the names of another twenty-eight spirits - seven each of Daughters of Light, Sons of Light, Daughters of the Daughters of Light, and Sons of the Sons of Light. For the sake of simplicity and because the names in question appear on the Sigillum Dei Aemeth, I give all these results in tabular form.

Planet	Angel	Filiae Lucis	Filii Lucis	Filiae Filiarum Lucis	Filii Filiorum Lucis
Mercury	Corablel*	Azdobn	Beigia	Madimi	Hagonel
Luna	Levanael	Me	Ih	Ab	An
Venus	Nogahel	Ese	Hr	Ath	Ave
Jupiter	Zedekiel	Iana	Dmal	Ized	Liba
Mars	Madimiel	Akele	Heeoa	Ekiei	Rocle
Sol	Semeliel*	El	I	S	E
Saturn	Sabathiel	Stimcul	Stimcul	Esemeli	Ilemese

VOLUME TEN

*In line 1 the angelic name should be Kokabiel, and in line 6 it should be Semesiel - to agree with the Hebrew names of Mercury and Sol. But I give the names as Kelley wrote them since the change of a single letter on the square necessitates changing many other names obtained through alternative modes of permutation.

Shortly after the transcription of these squares Kelley began to produce a copious amount of material concerning an angelical language. The Enochian alphabet appeared first - twenty-one characters, somewhat like Ethiopic in styling though not in formation, and written like all Semitic languages from right to left. This was followed by a book containing almost one hundred squares, many of them as large as 2,401 characters (49x49), whose dictation became the principal business of all the sittings for nearly fourteen months. And the material continued to pile up, page after page, book after book, until the final parting between Dee and Kelley in 1589.

What are we to make of these angelic conferences?

The classic answer, of course, takes a tripartite form. First it is suggested that Dee was a sincere and pious but rather silly old man who from first to last was thoroughly cozened and deluded. Next it is alleged that Kelley was a liar and a charlatan whose "revelations" were a conscious exercise in forgery, a forgery which had, moreover the advantage of being fool-proof since it appears from Dee's spiritual diary that he himself rarely, if indeed ever, claimed to see or hear the angelic visitants. Third and finally, it is concluded that the spirits answering to the stone were either (a) Satanic imposters or (b) figments of Kelley's fertile invention. Such, in bald outline, is the answer proposed by Casaubon in his 54-page preface to *A True and Faithful Relation.*[5] And since Thomas Smith, in the book that for more than two hundred years stood as the standard biography of Dee followed Casaubon's lead and dismissed the angelic conferences as "execrable insanity," such in essence is the view that prevails today.

Having studied off and on for seventeen years the records of the conferences, I find all this a gross distortion of the evidence. There is no question that Kelley had a broad streak of opportunism: but almost from the beginning we find him openly doubting the nature of his spiritual contacts, protesting that their nature is diabolical and not angelic. He tells Dee that they are deluders, that his "heart standeth against them," that their promises cannot be relied upon. During the sittings he is constantly on the alert to catch the spirits out and embarrass them. On one occasion he convicts them of plagiarising from Cornelius Agrippa. To adopt the view, as the devotees of the fraud theory have done, that Kelley's constant endeavour to break off the conferences at almost any cost was merely a clever way of titillating Dee's enthusiasm is to ignore the obvious. For the one thing more likely than any other to make Dee abandon the conferences would have been a genuine doubt as to the nature of the spirits. And if one thing is clear from the thousands of pages of manuscript records, it is that Kelley was deeply frightened and intimidated by the spiritual forces he felt to be arrayed against him. For all his vacillation and instability, he was never really dissuaded from his conviction that they were too dangerous to meddle with. As for Dee himself, it is simply not the case that he meekly accepted everything he was told. Most of the time he is a model of caution. He notes every question and every answer; and if a discrepancy appears, he demands that it be explained before going on. He is all humility when praying to God - but in the matter of revelation he is more than ready to "try the spirits whether they are of God."

Paradoxically enough, however, the most substantial and convincing proof of the **essential genuineness of both Dee and Kelley is their monumental ignorance of what to do with the material they have accumulated.** The thing that distinguishes Enochian magic as taught by the Golden Dawn is that it makes possible an astonishingly effective

5

and powerful synthesis of both theoretical and practical occult philosophy. In the hands of Dee and Kelley the Enochian material remained a useless mass of letters and squares; and if Kelley feared it and Dee revered it, the salient fact is that neither of them ever accomplished anything with it. But in the hands of Macgregor Mathers and his colleagues the Enochian system stood revealed as a true concourse of all the forces in the macrocosm Sephirotic, elemental, planetary and astral. It fused Kabbalah, tarot, astrology, and geomancy into a unified psychological field. Its map of the planes is the most comprehensive, and at the same time the most practical, that I have ever encountered. In short, the method works: it unlocks the secret doors of the mind as no other published system has ever done.

ENOCHIAN POSSIBILITIES

At the same time, I do not wish to suggest that the Enochian system as organised by the Golden Dawn founders is complete and perfect beyond all possibility of improvement.

That, I am respectfully convinced, is not the case. Over and beyond the forty-eight Angelic Keys, the four Watchtowers, and the Tablet of Union there is a substantial body of Enochian documents whose investigation will greatly repay the student who has already assimilated and understood the available Golden Dawn material. These documents are:

1. **Sigillum Dei Aemeth.**
2. **Tabula Sancta.**
3. **The Round Tablet of Nalvage.**
4. **De Heptarchia Mystica**
5. **Liber Scientia Auxilii et Victoria Terrestris.**
6. **Liber Mysteriorum Sextus et Sanctus.**
7. **Tabula Bonorum Angelorum Invocationes.**

A few words in description of these may be found useful.

The Sigillum Dei Aemeth, which I reproduce below, is a magical synthesis of ideas of a purely spiritual nature with regard to the divine, archangelic, and angelic names associated with the celestial spheres wherein the planetary forces operate. The operation of the Sigillum occurs in the worlds of Yetzirah and Briah. Moreover, the four small sigils attributed to the Tablets of the Watchtowers receive their elucidation from this Sigillum, whence they are resolved into the names of four great Overseer Angels of these tablets.

VOLUME TEN

The Tabula Sancta or Holy Table is designed to be used with the Sigillum. It operation occurs in the world of Assiah and the lower planetary forces, rendering them open to the operation of forces in higher worlds. I have not been able to find a copy of the Tabula suitable for sending to the printer, but readers with access to Casaubon will find a magnificent reproduction included just before the beginning of the main text. The seven small sigils, reading clockwise from the top, are associated with Luna, Saturn, Jupiter, Mars, Sol, Venus, and Mercury.

Students of the Angelic Keys will recall that of the nineteen calls the first is unexpressed, being attributed to the Godhead. The Round Tablet of Nalvage, while not identical with the unexpressed call, is nevertheless associated with it. This tablet is reproduced below, together with a diagram showing how it is to be read.

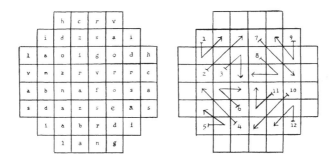

The book entitled Liber Scientia Auxilii et Victoria Terrestris shows how to extract from the Tablets of the Watchtowers the names of 91 Angelical Princes whose rule is in the Thirty Aethyrs of the Macrocosm. It further attributes each of these Angelic Princes to the governance of one of the archangels ruling the signs of the Zodiac. They are given in a special order corresponding to that of the degree of the Golden Dawn. The book also shows how to draw the sigils of these Angelical Princes. The forces described in the Liber Scientia operate in the world of Atziluth.

The Liber Mysteriorum Sextus et Sanctus exists only in manuscript form in the British Library; and the manuscript is in such poor condition that many of the pages will not reproduce legibly. It contains a large number of angelic squares - some of which I have been able to solve, some of which require further work, and many of which I cannot begin to read. It also contains a very large number of words in the angelic language, some of which I have been able to translate in a tentative way. The forces that are described operate in all four worlds.

Finally, the Tabula Bonorum Angelorum Invocationes describes angelic and archangelic operations that take place in the world of the macrocosm. The book is relevant both to the operations of the Four Watchtowers and to the Liber Scientia Auxilii, previously described.

ENOCHIAN NUMBERS

Having associated myself with Israel Regardie's call for greater openness with occult teaching material, I now wish to share with readers of this book some of the results of my own research. The quotation from John Dee's spiritual diaries with which I headed up this paper was written at the time the Angelic Keys were being dictated. Closely read and taken in context, it suggests not only that the Keys may involve more than one numbering system, but also that "the Letters" i.e., the characters of the Enochian alphabet, may be "in confusion"in the sense that the traditional order may not be correct. Much more plainly, in part three of "The Concourse of the Forces" MacGregor Mathers states: "The numbers such as 456 and 6739, etc. which occur in some of the Calls contain mysteries not here to be explained."

Following these and similar hints throughout Dee's diaries, as well as some of the manuscript books discussed above, I have been able to establish three conclusions with a rather high degree of rigour: first, that there are in fact two numbering systems in Enochian, of which one is used for gematria and the other only for translating letters into single digits; second, that the correct order of characters in the Enochian alphabet resembles that in Greek and Coptic; and, third, that the Gematric Code (as I propose to call it) follows a pattern rather more like Hebrew. Since this is not the place to recapitulate my reasoning, I will say only that after checking it several times and having it checked for me on an IBM 370 using a program written in LISP - I think it is right. Here are my results.

Characler	Gematric Code	Digital Code
A	1	1
B	2	2
G	3	3
D	4	4
K	5	5
K	6	6
Z	7	7
H	8	8
I	10	1
K	20	2
L	30	3
M	40	4
N	50	5
X	60	6
0	70	7
P	80	8
Q	90	9
R	100	1
S	200	2
T	300	3
U	400	4

The next step of course is to follow Mathers's lead, enter the Angelic Keys with the Digital Code, and translate the numbers into their correct values. Here is the result.

VOLUME TEN

Letters	Uncorrect Value	Correct Value
A* F	19	16
A C A M	7699	1214
C I A L	9996	2113
C L A	456	231
D	3	4
D A O* X	5678	4176
D A R G	6739	4113
E M O D	8763	5474
E R A N	6332	5115
G* A*	31	31
L	1	3
M	9	4
M A P M	9639	4184
M A T B	1000	1000
M I A N	3663	4115
N	6	5
N I	28	51
N O R Z	6	6
O	5	7
O B	28	72
O P	22	78
O S	12	12
O X*	26	76
P*	8	8
P D	33	84
P E O A L	69636	85713
Q U A R	1636	9411
S	4	2
T A X S	7336	3162
V	2	4
V* X	42	46

The seven letters with asterisks are the only ones for which correct values were given in the text and were presumably left there to serve as clues of a sort. Very helpful.

IN CONCLUSION

It is a joy to welcome *The Complete Golden Dawn System of Magic* into the world. With its rich treasure trove of new material, and illuminated by the ever vigorous and sapient writing of Israel Regardie, the book is clearly destined to attain the stature of a classic. May it outstrip its predecessor in success and be rewarded lavishly.

NOTES

[1]Meric Casaubon, *A True and Faithful Relation of What passedfor many years Between Dr. John Dee and Some Spirits.* London, 1659, p. 92.

[2]Some readers will challenge this; but it is a fairly common *viewpont* among esoteric teachers. In another tradition George Gurdjieff, at his first meeting with P.D. Ouspensky, stipulated that the latter's pledge of secrecy meant only that he would not write about Gurdjieff's ideas until he understood them clearly. And in still another context I myself, though not a member of any Masonic Order, have been given access on several occasions to material pertaining to the higher degrees. The men who supplied the material **knew** I would write about it. They made it available because they judged I would write accurately.

[3]John Aubrey, *Minutes of Lives*, essay on Dee.

[4]British Library, Sloane MS 3677.

[5]As the Puritan divine John Webster pointed out in *A Displaying of Supposed Witchcraft* (London, 1677) Casaubon's *True & Faithful Relation* was anything but an unbiassed account. To the contrary, Casaubon had deliberately set out to "register Dee among the damned" and for a perfectly logical if self-serving reason. A few years earlier he had argued in print that all divine inspiration (so called) was nothing "but imposture or melancholy or depraved phantasie, arising from natural causes." Cromwell's government took a dim view of that suggestion, and Casaubon found himself charged with atheism; whereupon he decided to "leap to the other end" by publishing some sensational text that would proclaim the existence of good and bad spirits alike. He did not, as Webster carefully notes, endeavour to destroy Dee's reputation out of personal malice or even out of personal conviction. For the true and faithful Casaubon the whole point was merely to bolster his own position as a good Christian.

Thomas Head
Box 675 , Atlanta, Georgia 30301

THE ENOCHIAN LANGUAGE

By

V.H. FRATER A.M.A.G.

Our earliest knowledge of this alphabet and language is derived from the skrying of Sir Edward Kelley and Dr. John Dee towards the end of the sixteenth century. This was in the time both of Mary Queen of Scots and Queen Elizabeth the First of England. In point of fact, Dr. John Dee became Queen Elizabeth's friend, astrologer and confidante. According to some of the latest research, Dr. John Dee was not the gullible, credulous spiritualist as some critics have alleged, but was in fact a true man of the Renaissance - a competent scientist, geographer and interestingly enough, a secret agent under the tutelage of Sir Francis Walsingham.

This alphabet and language is called Angelic or Enochian, as the Angels who instructed both Dee and Kelley claimed to be those who had once conversed with the patriarch Enoch of the Bible. Kelley was the skryer and used a shewstone or crystal ball, which is now in the British Museum. In this ball he saw Angels who instructed him to make large charts and designs which Dr. Dee would have before him on a desk, while Kelley was skrying. When an Angel in the shewstone would point to a certain letter on one of his charts, Kelley, in his turn, would pass the information on to Dr. Dee as for example: Tablet B, Column 7, Rank 11, etc. Dr. Dee would locate the letter and write it down, awaiting the next.

This was a slow and tedious method of gaining information. All of these conversations and instructions were recorded by Dr. Dee in diaries, still to be found in the British Museum in the Sloane and Harleian collection of manuscripts. In the year 1659, Meric Casaubon published a large tome reproducing the details of some of these conversations and instructions. In this book are to be found dozens of prayers offered humbly by Dee that he be guided in the right direction; many are beautiful, others are long and tedious.

From this basic material has grown one of the most complete systems of magical endeavor that was ever so beautifully and systematically organized, beyond even the wildest dreams of Dee and Kelley, by the Hermetic Order of the Golden Dawn towards the end of the nineteenth century.

As can be seen when consulting Meric Casaubon, many of the invocations - or Calls as they are named, dictated by the Angels, were given in reverse. It was felt that the Enochian words were so powerful that direct dictation would call forth powers and forces not then desired. The present dictionary in this Volume of the Enochian language has been complied from words used in the nineteen invocations that were given to Dee and Kelley. Over a period of time, it has become possible to separate the prefixes and suffixes from the basic Enochian words. Since I am no philologist this was no easy task, especially as it was soon recognized that in the process of repeated copyings, by uninformed members of the Golden Dawn, many errors had crept into the text. Words in one invocation had to be checked against similar words in another invocation to arrive at some semblance of accuracy.

Recently the words in this dictionary have been checked against those found in Casaubon's enormous tome. Even here, a fantastic number of errors were perceived and I became aware of what a momentous task it had been to compile this dictionary in the mid-thirties.

Though ordinarily I have assiduously avoided self-praise, I must confess, as I examine this dictionary after a time interval of nearly fifty years, that as simple dictionaries go, this is not such a bad job after all. The separation of the suffixes and prefixes from the proper root words was, in itself, no mean accomplishment, especially when one considers that no clue is to be found either in the Golden Dawn documents or in Crowley's renditions of the Calls in *Equinox I, #8*. Languages are not amongst my few accomplishments. My English is good, my French is execrable (as the maitre d' of a French restaurant I used to frequent can testify), I know but little Latin and Greek. So far as Hebrew is concerned, though I did study that intensively years ago, with the intent of translating some old Qabalistic texts, that project vanished into thin air before my second decade was out.

The Enochian language is not just a haphazard combination and compilation of divine and angelic names drawn from the Tablets. Apparently, it is a true language with a grammar and syntax of its own. Only a superficial study of the invocations suffice to indicate this to be a fact. The invocations are not strings of words and barbarous names, but are sentences which can be translated in a meaningful way and not merely transliterated.

The Enochian language is without any history prior to the skrying of Edward Kelley and John Dee. There is no record of its prior existence, regardless of some fanciful theories which have been invented to account for it. Many present-day philologists have often pointed out that it is impossible for any single human being to invent a language of his own, complete with errors, such as we find in the transcribing in Dr. Dee's diaries. Any inventor today would be careful enough to be more thorough in the construction of his language than were Dee and Kelley, or the Angels who originally dictated the Calls.

The Enochian alphabet consists of twenty-one letters which can be transposed into English. The individual letters are known to us in both the printed or elaborate style and also in a script or cursive form.

THE COMPLETE GOLDEN DAWN SYSTEM OF MAGIC

One of the curious anomalies about this Enochian alphabet is that each letter has a name, as in other languages, such as in Greek: Alpha, Beta, Gamma, etc., but this Enochian name bears absolutely no relationship to the **sound** value of the letter itself. Alpha in Greek is given the sound value of A; in Hebrew Gimel is given the sound value of G, etc.: but in Enochian, Veh, has the sound value of C or K, not of V, as one might at first have supposed.

Since the names of the letters are not commonly used, the use of the English alphabetical order and pronunciation is recommended in order to avoid confusion or unnecessary complication. In the text is shown the Enochian alphabet in both the elaborate and cursive style and also in the order given us by tradition. In passing, I should note that the cursive style is used but rarely, and for that reason is not worth committing to memory.

In the original **Golden Dawn** papers written by MacGregor Mathers and William Wynn Wescott, certain rules were laid down for the pronunciation of the Enochian words. Mathers advised that the consonants should be followed by the vowel which obtains in the corresponding Hebrew letters. For example: the word "sobha" could be pronounced soh-bay-hah. The god-names, like MPH ARSL GAIOL, to be found in the Water Tablet, are pronounced as: Em-pay-hay Ar-sel Gah-ee-Ohl. The one major exception to all rules is that the letter Z is always pronounced as zoad. So that the word Zamran is pronounced as Zoad-ah-mer-ah-noo.

Dr. Wescott laid down similar rules in another document he wrote for the Adeptus Minor, but his version gives several variations which should be noted. I have found these latter to be valid, making for greater euphony and ease in handling. He said: "M is pronounced em; N is pronounced en (also Nu or Noo - since in Hebrew the vowel following the equivalent letter Nun is used); A is pronounced ah; P is peh; S is ess: D is delhi." This rule, in fact, simplifies the entire procedure, If one had no further rules than these, the entire matter of Enochian pronunciation, which has been unnecessarily obscured and rendered so difficult, could then be handled with ease.

Another variation is that Y, J and I are similar to the Yod in Hebrew - as U and V are similar to the Vau in Hebrew. X has sometimes the value of Samekh and at others of Tzaddi, though there is no reason not to use it as in English.

Usage and experience will ultimately dictate which one is to be employed. Let me give several examples of words chosen relatively at random in order to exemplify the simplicity of the process of pronunciation. These names are to be found in the Tablet of Union:

EXARP	**Ex-ar-pay**
HCOMA	**Hay-coh-mah**
NANTA	**En-ah-en-tah**
BITOM	**Bay-ee-toh-em**

Though it has been suggested by Wescott that *every* letter should be pronounced separately, this idea makes for clumsiness, lack of euphony and unnecessary length, which creates fatigue and monotony. Further examples are:

CHIS	**Cah-hee-sah**
CHISGE	**Cah-his-jee**

The student must use not merely these rules but his own sense of euphony and intuition in dealing with this matter. Remember, there is no final version which is absolutely authoritative.

In the Portal grade of *The Complete Golden Dawn System of Magic* (Falcon Press, Phoenix 1983) there is a very short Enochian invocation which is abbreviated from the First Call, but also contains the names of three Archangels drawn from the Tablet of Union. I give the invocation first, followed by its transliteration in pronunceable phrases.

"OL SONUF VAORSAGI GOHO IADA BALTA. LEXARPH, COMANAN, TABITOM. ZODAKARA EKA ZODAKARE OD ZODAMARAN. ODO KIKLE QAA, PIAPE PIAMOEL OD VAOAN."

This means, "I will reign over you, saith the God of Justice. Lexarph, Comanan, Tabitom. Move therefore. Show yourselves forth and appear. Declare unto us the mysteries of your creation, the balance of righteousness and truth."

The pronunciation of these few lines of Enochian language is nowhere near as formidable as may appear at first sight. The following is the pronunciation I use. I might add in passing that this is an Invocation I have used frequently over the last forty-odd years, primarily in relationship to the practice of the Middle Pillar technique (which I have improved and enhanced, to be published by Falcon Press under the title The Sceptre of Power) and the Ritual of the "Watch Tower Ceremony" in this volume.

> **"Oh-el Soh-noof Vay-oh-air-sah-jee, Goho Ee-ah-dah Baltah. El-ex-arpay-hay. Cohmah-nah-noo. Tah-bee-toh-em. Zoad-a-kah-rah ay-kah zoad-a- kah-ray oh-dah Zoad-a-mer-ah-noo. Oh-dah kee-klay kah-ah, Pee-ah-pay pee-ah-moh-el oh-dah vay-oh-ah-noo."**

Using these as an example, the enterprising student should experience very little difficulty in handling any words or phrases to be found in the various Calls or in this dictionary. The major obstacle at first encountered is simply the strangeness of the appearance of the words and the lack of experience in pursuing the rules laid down. The sounds may seem very much like pure gibberish at the outset. If he persists, however, the student will soon learn to disentangle the sounds from apparent chaos and find himself confronted by a meaningful language and a meaningful set of invocations. In any event, do remember there is no absolute or final rendition of the way to pronounce these Calls. If he can approximate the instructions laid down here, his own version will be as authoritative as any.

In 1976, an Enochian Dictionary was published by Leo Vinci entitled **GMICALZOMA** through the Regency Press in England. I have no comments to make about it, other than that it is a workable and usable dictionary. It post-dates my Dictionary by many years, mine having begun to circulate in the U.S. and the United Kingdom a score of years earlier.

Not too long after that, Askin Publishers in England became interested in my dictionary and a correspondence ensued relative to having them publish mine. A friend, a philologist, promised to write an Introduction to it with a view to elucidating the origins of the Enochian language. Again, a series of mishaps occurred which prevented the Introduction from being written. It resulted in Askin Publishers taking the lead, and offering to get Dr. Laycock (an Australian philologist who had been in touch with me sometime before this) to do an Introduction for it. When the Introduction arrived, I was most disappointed in it, feeling that it exuded contempt and ridicule.

My next step was to telephone Askin Publishers in London to confess my total disappointment and stating that if they insisted on publishing Laycock's Introduction with my Dictionary, I would withdraw the latter. So it came to pass that Askin Publishers returned my Dictionary at my request. Sometime in the next immediate period they must have formulated a Dictionary which they published with the Laycock Introduction.

These facts need to be mentioned solely to establish the priority of my Dictionary. Not that that matters very much. There was a need for this Dictionary amongst students of Magic, and someone got there first.

The history of the Enochian Dictionary that is being published here should not be without interest.

Shortly after having benn elevated to the Adeptus Minor Grade, I began an intensive study of the Enochian system, including the beginning of a Dictionary. The study of the system resulted in my writing a paper entitled *An Addendum to the Book of the Concourse of Forces,* included in this volume. Within a couple of years, the Dictionary had achieved a well-defined form — that is by 1940-41. Then World War II intervened, when it was put aside with a number of other similar projects until the 1950's. During that time, the Dictionary was loaned to a number of different people on both sides of the Atlantic. Ordinarily I would not use names, but in this instance I feel it is incumbent upon me to do so.

There was a young man in Surrey, a protege of an osteopathic friend of mine A.E. Charles, to whom I lent it early in the 1950's -- altogether apart from a handful of students here in the U.S. Somewhere around 1956, I was visited in Los Angeles by Miss Tamara Bourkoun, a very ardent and knowledgeable student of Co-Masonry and the occult. Amongst other things, including the *Golden Dawn Tarot Deck,* I loaned her the *Enochian Dictionary* with my permission to copy it for her use if she so willed. From then on, it had some kind of circulation here and there among the more serious students of Magic who took the Enochian system seriously.

Early in the 1970's **Sangreal Foundation,** who had already published several of my things, were toying with the idea of seeing that the *Enochian Dictionary* was finally published. However again some unforeseen events occurred which precluded the possibility of that happening.

Now under the direction of the **Israel Regardie Foundation** and Falcon Press, this long awaited work has found itself in print, in this particular volume.

THE ENOCHIAN SYSTEM

A PREFATORY NOTE

By

V. H. FRATER, S.I.A.

(Note: Official documents H and S are omitted here by reason of their redundancy and obscurity, to be replaced by this more modern precis. I.R.)

To the First Order little is said of the Tablets of Enoch. They are mentioned in the Rituals, but do not enter into the Knowledge Lectures. But the detailed study of the Tablets and their attributions and the method of using them for vision forms a definite part of the course of work prescribed between 5 - 6 and the T.A.M. degree.

The Order has in its possession a considerable mass of detailed instruction on this subject, but as it is contained in a number of papers, some of considerable antiquity and others modern, wherein part of the ground is covered two or three times over, while other parts are by no means clearly explained, it has been felt that a paper attempting to cover the whole ground in logical sequence may be of assistance to those beginning the study of Enochiana before they go on to the more elaborate and intricate papers on special branches of the subject.

It is to be understood that this lecture does not claim to say anything new. It is a rearrangement and, I hope, a rather clearer explanation of information already in possession of the Order, and is intended to be w'hat it is called - an Introduction to, not a substitute for, the other Enochian literature.

The Order possesses a set of the Tablets completely worked out in detail, which can be consulted to illustrate the text where necessary. It is not necessary to make a copy of it, which would take some months, but it is strongly recommended that every Adeptus should make him or herself a set of the four Elemental Tablets as shown in the Temple, and a Tablet of Union, and have them by him when reading what follows. They may be made of coloured paper or painted in water colours. The lettering should be accurately copied and in the correct colouring. Half-inch squares make a very convenient size, the whole Tablet being then 6 ½ in.

CHAPTER ONE

THE ANGELIC SECRET LANGUAGE
THE CONSTRUCTION OF THE TABLETS

It is stated in the 1 - 10 Ritual that the Tablet of Earth, (and of course it applies to the others) "is written in what our tradition calls the Angelic Secret Language." The Tablets in use in the Outer Temple are lettered with English letters, but these are in fact a translation, or rather a transliteration, of very ancient characters belonging to what is known as the Theban Alphabet. There are two forms of the letters, the elaborate and the cursive. The Alphabet is as follows:

THE ENOCHIAN ALPHABET

Elaborate	Cursive	Title	Power
V	V V	Pe	B
ꞵ	К	Veh	C or K
ꞇ	ꞇ	Ged	G
ꭗ	ꭞ	Gal	D
ꭚ	ꭚ	Orth	F
ꭤ	ꭞ	Un	A
ꓶ	ꓶ	Graph	E
Ɛ	Ɛ	Tal	M
ꞇ	ꞇ	Gon	1, Y, or J
ꭥ	ꞃ	Na-hath	H
ꞔ	ꭤ	Ur	L
ꞛ	ꞯ	Mals	P
Ц	ꭖ	Ger	0
ꭢ	ꭟ	Drun	N
ꭓ	ꭣ	Pal	X
ꭞ	ꭝ	Med	0
ꭇ	ꭗ	Don	R
ꭓ	ꭓ	Ceph	Z
ꭓ	2	Vau	U or V
ꭓ	ꭥꭧ	Fam	S
ꭡ	)	Gisa	T

Whether its origin is now known is extremely doubtful, but it is possibly of great antiquity.

Every letter on the English tablets, therefore, may be replaced by the corresponding letter of this alphabet. These letters are reputed of greater magical force than Hebrew or English Letters and partake of the nature of sigils rather than simple letters.

But this Angelic secret language, whatever its origin, was a true language. In addition to the "numberless Divine and Angelic Names" drawn from the Tablets, according to rules some of which will be dealt with later, there are extant in this language a number of "Enochian Calls," or invocations of the Forces of the Tablets. These are not mere strings of Names, but can be translated, not merely transliterated into English. For example, the Call in the opening of the Portal Ceremony:

OL SONUF VA-ORSAGI GOHO IADA BALATA ELEXARPEH COMANANU TABITOM: ZODAKARA EKA ZODAKARE OD ZODAMRANU: ODO KIKLE QAA PIAPE PIAMOEL OD VAOAN.

This means: "1 will reign over you, saith the God of Justice, O Lexarph, Comananu, Tabitom. Move, therefore, and show yourselves forth and appear; declare unto us the mysteries of your Creation, the Balance of Righteousness and Truth."

It is stated in the 5-6 Ritual that some of our early brethren compiled a dictionary of this language; whether it now survives, I do not know. (In more recent years I have compiled a dictionary which will be found towards the end of this volume. I.R.) The language is pronounced by taking each letter separately, whenever a lack of vowels renders it necessary; but the pronunciation seems to come to one instinctively when one wants it. Thus m, p, h is pronounced Em-peh, Hctga He-C-Te-Ga. Z is always pronounced ZOD (o as in bone). Thus in the Name Ic Zod Heh Chal, Great King of the North, the "Zod" is represented only by a single Z on the Tablet of Earth.

Let us now analyse the form and arrangement of the elemental Tablets. You may have noticed in the Outer Order Rituals that the Tablet of Earth was called the Third or Great Northern Quadrangle, Air the First, Water the Second and Fire the Fourth, and possibly wondered why this order, and why the Third was given in the First Grade. Put your four Tablets together in two pairs, thus:

**Basic Arrangement
of the Four Tablets**

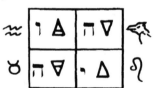

And you will then see that they thus correspond to the four elemental angles of the Pentagram, the angle of Spirit answering to the Tablet of Union. Also this is the order of the four lesser angles of each separate Tablet, and the four together form a sort of super-Tablet with the elements similarly arranged.

Now let us take one of the Tablets, and examine it more closely. To avoid confusion, I will refer throughout to the Tablet of Air, it being understood that my remarks apply, mutatis mutandis, to the others, unless they are specially mentioned.

First you will notice that there are twelve squares horizontally, and thirteen vertically, making 156 in all, or 624 in the four Tablets altogether. Of these 156, 76 are white, and 80 are coloured. The two groups must be separately considered. Each is divisible into two other groups.

(A) The White Squares into the Great Cross and the Four Sephirotic Crosses.
(B) The Coloured Squares into Kerubic and Servient Squares.

The White Squares.

These are always lettered in black.

The Great Cross. This consists of the two central vertical lines, and the central horizontal line - total, 36 squares. The two vertical lines are called the "Linea Dei Patris Filiique,"and the horizontal line as the "Linea Spiritus Sancti," thus referring to the Divine Triad, and also to the Spirit controlling the four elements in the lesser angles which are separated from each other by the Great Cross.

The Four Sephirotic Crosses. These are formed of the central vertical line and the second horizontal line in each lesser angle. Some confusion has been introduced into their attributions in some of our literature, by Chesed and Geburah being placed at the extremities of the cross-piece instead of Chokmah and Binah. The latter form, which is that given in Azoth, is believed to be correct.

The Coloured Squares.

The letters on these are coloured as follows:

(a)   In the lesser angle corresponding to the Element of the Tablet itself, in the complementary colour to the ground work - i.e. purple on the airy quarter of Air, orange on the watery quarter of Water; green is taken as the colour for the earthy quarter of Earth (black having strictly no complementary colour), and green on the fiery quarter of Fire.

(b)   In the other three lesser angles of each Tablet, in the colour of the element of the lesser angle. The King's Scale is used, Air being yellow; Water, blue; Earth, black; and Fire, red.

Kerubic Squares. These are the four squares above the Cross-bar of the Sephirotic Cross in each lesser angle. The order of their attribution to the Kerubim varies according to the lesser angle, in a manner presently to be explained.

The sixteen Servient Squares. These are the remaining coloured squares below the Cross-bar of the Sephirotic Cross in each lesser angle, and their attribution is dependent on that of the Kerubic squares.

These four distinct groups will require to be separately treated throughout, and in each Chapter I shall deal with them in this Order. In general it may be remembered that the white squares always have Spirit as one of their attributions, the coloured squares never: they are always elemental.

The Tablet of Union

Is shown in the Portal Ceremony consisting of 20 white squares, arranged in 4 horizontal rows of 5, and thus attributed, coloured and lettered as follows:

1st Line.

Air - Yellow letters - E X A R P

2nd Line.

Water - Blue letters - H C O M A

3rd Line.

Earth - Black letters - N A N T A

4th Line.

Fire - Red letters - B I T O M.

All are attributed to Spirit in part, and the letters are used in combination with those of the other four tablets in the formation of certain Names as explained in the next chapter.

CHAPTER TWO

THE FORMATION OF DIVINE AND ANGELIC NAMES FROM THE TABLETS

We now consider the mode of forming the more important of the "numberless Divine and Angelic Names" from the Tablets.

The White Squares.

1. The Great Cross. From the Great Cross of each Tablet are formed ten Names of importance for present purposes. 1.2.3. The "Three Great Holy Secret Names of God" occupy the whole of the Linea Spiritus Sancti, reading from left to right. They consist in each Tablet of a Name of 3 letters, one of 4 letters, and one of 5 letters, thus: *ORO IBAH AOZPI*, answering to I.A.O.

These are the Names borne on the Three Banners carried before the face of 4, the "Great King" of each quarter. This is always a Name of eight letters, and occupies the centre of the Cross, beginning at the 5th letter of the Linea Spiritus Sancti, and reading in a spiral through the two letters of the Linea Dei Patris Filiique immediately above the Linea Spiritus Sancti to the 8th letter of the Linea Spiritus Sancti, through the letters of the Linea Dei immediately below the Linea Spiritus Sancti, and ending with the 6th and 7th letters of the Linea Spiritus Sancti. Thus:

The King is a very powerful force, to be invoked with due care. 5.6.7.8.9.10. The Six Seniors, whose Names begin from the 6th and 7th squares of the Linea Spiritus Sancti, and read outwards along the three lines in each direction to the edge of the Tablet. Each is a Name of seven letters. Of the two formed in the Linea Spiritus Sancti, one will therefore be the first two Names of God reversed, thus ORO IBAH; Senior, H ABIORO. The other will be the third Deity Name, prefixed by the last two letters of the second, thus: ORO IBAH AOZP1, where AHAOZPI is the Name of a Senior.

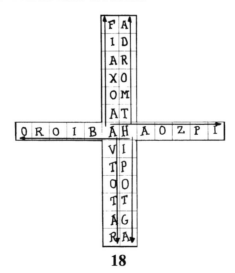

All these Names belong to a different and higher plane than those of the elemental squares, and are invoked by the Hexagram, not the Pentagram. The King and Six Seniors are attributed to the Sun and Planets.

2. The Sephirotic Crosses.

The Vertical line read downwards gives a Deity Name of six letters, used to call forth the angels and spirits of the lesser angle. The cross-bar from left to right gives a Deity Name of five letters which is used to command the spirits called forth by the first Name. These two Names should be used in a preliminary invocation when working with a square of the lesser angle. If we reverse the Names, reading them upwards and from right to left, we get those of the evil forces calling forth and controlling the evil angels of the lesser angle, which needless to say, should not be done - by the Z.A.M. at any rate.

3. The coloured squares.

From each square a Name is formed by taking the four letters in the four coloured squares of one horizontal row of the lesser angle, beginning with the letter in the square whose Name is desired, and reading left to right. In the Kerubic squares of the airy Angle of Air we have RZLA for the first; ZLAR for the second, LARZ for the the third; ARZL for the fourth. Remembering the rule as to pronunciation, these will be ERZODELAH, ZODELARE, LARZOD, ARZODEL.

From each of these four-letter Names is formed a more powerful Name of five letters which rules it, by prefixing a letter from the Tablet of Union as follows:

1. Kerubic Squares. Always (whatever the lesser angle) the first letter of the appropriate line of the Tablet of Union: thus from RZLA we shall form ERZLA, from DOPA in the Tablet of Fire BDOPA. These Names from the Kerubic squares rule those in the servient squares, and the first, i.e. that of the left-hand Kerubic square, is the chief of them.

2. The Servient Squares. The remaining letters of the Tablet of Union are thus allotted: The second letter of each line to the 16 squares of the angle of Air. The third letter of each line to the 16 squares of the angle of Water. The fourth letter of each line to the 16 squares of the angle of Earth. The fifth letter of each line to the 16 squares of the angle of Fire.

Evil names are formed by taking two adjoining letters instead of four, prefixing the appropriate Tablet of Union letter and reading from right to left, or left to right.

The formation of these Names is dealt with much more fully in the "Clavicula Tabularum Enochi," one of the more ancient of our documents on the Tablets.

CHAPTER THREE

THE ATTRIBUTION TO THE NAME YHVH

The Great Name YHVH is the Key to the whole system of Enochian attribution of the squares to the elements. The letters of the Name are thus attributed:

Yod to Fire and Wands;
Heh to Water and Cups;
Vau to Air and Swords;
Heh (final) to Earth and Pentacles.

Once more put your Tablets together as in Chapter One. Put the appropriate letter at the outside corner of each, and you will find the Name YHVH reads round counter-clockwise, beginning with the fiery angle of Fire, and taking in each tablet the lesser angle of its own element. Then fill in the letters appropriate to the lesser angles of each tablet and you will find them also forming the Name in the same way, while in the middle of the Four Tablets is the Name again, beginning with the fiery lesser angle of Air. So much for its general attribution. We now consider it in detail.

The White Squares.

1.   The Great Cross. Divide each vertical and horizontal line into four groups of three adjoining squares. Against the two top groups and the left hand group put the letter of the Name corresponding to the element of the Great Tablet. In the case of Air this will be Vau. The name reads upwards and from right to left, so below Vau and to its right we put Heh; below that and on its right Yod, leaving Heh Final for the bottom and right hand groups. Thus:

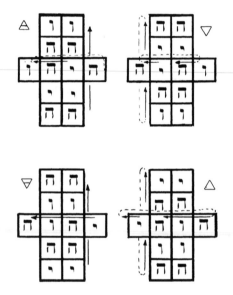

Each square represents **three** squares on the Tablets. This attribution is perfectly simple if it be remembered that the letter consonant to the Tablet always comes to the top and left.

2.   The Sephirotic Crosses represent the Sephiroth modified by the letter of the lesser angle. Thus they will be Kether of Vau in the airy lesser angle, of Heh in the watery, and so on. The attributions of these Crosses otherwise are constant in all angles of all tablets.

The coloured Squares.

I. The Kerubic Squares. The Attribution of the Letters of the Name to the Four Kerubic Squares of each lesser angle is a little more complicated, but is still quite easy if the following rules are remembered.

(a)   The outside square is always attributed to the letter corresponding to the element of the lesser angle. Thus in the four airy lesser angles the left hand square is attributed to Vau, in the four watery the right hand square always to Heh; in the four earthy the left-hand square always to Heh (final); in the four fiery the right hand square always to Yod.

(b)   In the Tablets of Air and Water the Name reads right to left in the two upper quarters, left to right in the two lower. In the Tablets of Earth and Fire, it reads left to right in the two upper quarters, right to left in the two lower. Thus if the four tablets are placed together, we have four rows, running thus:

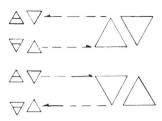

Applying these rules to the four lesser angles of Air, we get:

> **Airy quarter: Vau placed on the left, by rule (a) in that order in the other three, by rule (b).**
> **Watery quarter: Heh placed on the right by rule (a) on its left in that order, by rule (b).**
> **Earthy quarter: Heh (final) placed on the left by rule (a) on its right in that order by rule (b).**
> **Fiery quarter: Yod placed on the right, by rule (a) on its left in that order by rule (b).**

In the Earth and Fire Tablets a curious result follows. Take the airy and watery angles. In Air, Vau, on the left followed by Heh, Yod, Heh, brings Heh on the right; and in water, Heh, on the right similarly brings on the left, so that the attribution of the Kerubic squares (and hence, as we shall see, of the servient squares) is alike in the upper pair of angles and in both Tablets. The same thing happens in the earthy and fiery angles. Heh on the left brings Yod on the right, and vice versa. So the attributions of the Kerubic squares of the right lesser angles of the two lower tablets have only two arrangements, viz: for the upper and for the lower angles. This does not mean that the squares will be identical; as we shall see later, their elemental composition will differ in each lesser angle.

1. The Servient squares.

These, it will be remembered, are in four vertical columns of four squares, or four horizontal ranks of four squares. **To avoid confusion the word "column" will be used to denote vertical, and the word "rank" to denote horizontal rows invariably.**

The four columns follow the order of the four Kerubic squares always. The four squares under Heh are also attributed to Heh and so forth. The four ranks are also dependent on the four Kerubic squares, and whatever order these are in, right to left is the order of the servient ranks downwards. This rule is invariable, and does NOT depend on whether the Name reads right to left or left to right. Examples:

Air of Air	Air of Fire
Heh (f) Yod Heh Vau	**Heh Yod Heh (f) Vau**
Heh (f) 1st Rank	**Heh 1st Rank**
Yod 2nd Rank	**Yod 2nd Rank**
Heh 3rd Rank	**Heh (f) 3rd Rank**
Vau 4th Rank	**Vau 4th Rank**

Thus each servient square has a double attribution, by column and rank, no two being alike in the same lesser angle. We may get Heh, Heh column and Vau, Vau Rank, or Vau, Vau Column and Heh, Heh Rank. The other attributions will be quite different in the two cases (in one case to Pisces, the Moon of the Tarot Trumps; Qoph and Laetitia; in the other to Aquarius, the Star; Tzaddi and Tristitia.)

But these other attributions are dependent on those to the Name, which are, as has been said, the key to the system, and should be thoroughly mastered before going on to work out the corresponding Astrological, Tarot, and Geomantic attributions as explained in the next chapter.

CHAPTER FOUR

THE ASTROLOGICAL, TAROT, HEBREW AND GEOMANTIC ATTRIBUTIONS

The White Squares.

1. The Great Crosses refer to the 36 Decans of the Zodiac. The squares allotted to Yod will be fiery signs, those to Heh watery signs, those to Vau airy, those to Heh final earthy.

It will be remembered that in attributing the letters of the Name we took groups of three squares. Each group of three represents one sign, the separate squares being allotted to the three Decans as ruled by the Planets. The Decans of each sign go downwards or from left to right in order. The four Kerubic signs and their Decans occupy the Linea Spiritus Sancti, the four Cardinal signs the left side of the Linea Dei Patris Filiique, and the four mutable the right side. Those familiar with the Tarot papers will remember that the Decans start with the first Decan of Leo ruled by Saturn, the planets following in their order, except that Mars rules the last decan of Pisces and the first of Aries. The 36 smaller cards of the Tarot are also allotted to these squares, each in that of its own decan; note that the 2, 3, and 4 of each suit go with the Cardinal sign; 5, 6, 7 with the Kerubic; and 8, 9, and 10 with the Mutable.

Thus in the Air Tablet we get:

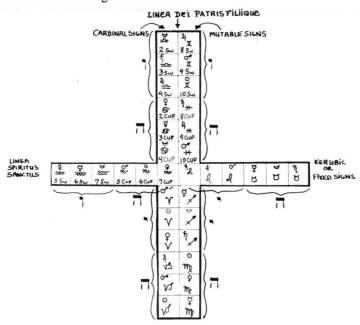

THE GREAT CROSS OF THE AIR TABLET

2. The Sephirotic Crosses.

The top square, and the five squares of the Cross-bar are allotted to six of the seven planets, excluding Saturn. The arrangement is constant, but is not the usual attribution of the Planets to the Sephiroth as on the Hexagram. It is as follows:

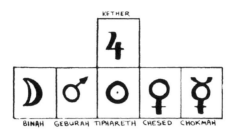

The corresponding Hebrew letters and Tarot Trumps are allotted to these squares.

The remaining four squares have no astrological attribution, but in addition to the six trumps the ten squares of each Cross are allotted to the Ace and small cards of the suit attributed to the element of the lesser angle.

The Coloured squares.

1. The Kerubic squares. These are allotted, as their Name implies to the four Kerubim whose emblems follow the order of the Letters of the Name: to Yod; to Heh; to Vau; to Heh (final) in each lesser angle. They are also allotted to the four Court Cards of the Tarot suit which corresponds to the lesser angle, Swords to Air, Cups to Water, Pentacles to Earth and Wands to Fire on each Tablet. Of the four Court Cards themselves the King is attributed to Yod, the Queen to Heh, the Knight to Vau, and the Knave to Heh (final).

2. The Servient Squares.

    These are allotted as follows: to the Twelve Signs of the Zodiac, with the symbols of Air, Water and Fire, and Saturn which is also Earth and to the corresponding 16 Trumps, Hebrew Letters and Geomantic figures.

    (a) The Columns go by triplicity according to the element of the Kerubic square at the head of the column, e.g. under Yod and Leo will be Aries, Leo, Sagittarius and Fire, with Heh, Tau, Samekh, and Shin, Emperor, Strength, Temperance, and Last Judgment, and so with the other columns.

    (b) The ranks go by Quality:

    To Yod and Fire are allotted the four Cardinal Signs;
    Heh and Water are allotted the four Kerubic Signs
    Vau and Air are allotted the four Mutable Signs
    Heh (final) and Earth are allotted the four Elemental symbols.

Thus under Heh in the Yod rank will be, Cancer, the Chariot, Cheth, and Populus.
Thus under Heh in the Heh rank will be, Scorpio, Death, Nun, and Rubeus.
Thus under Heh in the Vau rank will be, Pisces, the Moon, Qoph, and Laetitia.
Thus under Heh in the Heh (final) rank will be, Water, Hanged Man, Mem, Via and so on.

I work out the Water Angle of Air as an example:

♌ KNIGHT (KING) OF CUPS	♉ PRINCESS OF CUPS	♃ ACE OF CUPS	♒ KING (PRINCE) OF CUPS	QUEEN OF CUPS
☽ 3 OF CUPS	♂ 5 OF CUPS	☉ 6 OF CUPS	♀ 4 OF CUPS	☿ 2 OF CUPS
♌ STRENGTH	♉ HIEROPHANT	7 OF CUPS	STAR	♏ DEATH
♐ TEMPERANCE	♍ HERMIT	8 OF CUPS	♊ LOVERS	♓ MOON
△ LAST JUDGMENT	♄ UNIVERSE	9 OF CUPS	△ FOOL	▽ HANGED MAN
♈ EMPEROR	♑ DEVIL	10 OF CUPS	♎ JUSTICE	♋ CHARIOT

The following Table of Attributions, repeated though it is for the most part from earlier knowledge which should be familiar, may be useful for reference in working out the Squares.

In the following Table the Column will be in bold type, under which will follow in order, the Rank, the Letter, the Trump, Astrological symbol and finally the Geomantic figure.

BASIC ATTRIBUTIONS

Vau.

Heh (f), Aleph, Fool, Air, Fortuna Minor.

Sephirotic Cross (S.C.)

Chokmah, Beth, Magician, Mercury, no figure.

S. C.

Binah, Gimel, High Priestess, Moon, no figure.

S. C.

Chesed, Daleth, Empress, Venus, no figure.

Yod.

Yod, Heh, Emperor, Aries, Puer.

Heh (final).

Heh, Vau, Hierophant, Taurus, Career.

Vau.

Vau, Zayin, Lovers, Gemini, Albus.

Heh.

Yod, Cheth, Chariot, Cancer, Populus.

Yod.

Heh, Teth, Strength, Leo, Fortuna Major.

Heh (final).

Vau, Yod, Hermit, Virgo, Conjunctio.

S. C.

Kether, Caph, Wheel of Fortune, Jupiter, no figure.

Vau.

Yod, Lamed, Justice, Libra, Puella.

Heh.

Heh (f), Mem, Hanged Man, Water, Via.

Heh.

Heh, Nun, Death, Scorpio, Rubeus.

Yod.

Vau, Samekh, Temperance, Sagittarius, Acquisitio.

Heh (final).

Yod, Ayin, Devil, Capricorn, Career.

S. C.

Geburah, Peh, Tower, Mars, no figure.

Vau.

Heh, Tzaddi, Star, Aquarius, Tristitia.

Heh.

Vau, Qoph, Moon, Pisces, Laetitia.

S.C.

Tiphareth, Resh, Sun, no figure.

Yod.

Heh, Shin, Last Judgement, Fire, Cauda Draconis.

Heh (final).

Heh (f), Tau, Universe, Saturn (Earth), Caput Draconis.

GENERAL NOTE ON THE TAROT ATTRIBUTIONS.

Since 156 equals 78 × 2, it might have been expected that each Tarot card would come twice on each Tablet and no more, but it will be seen that this is not so, for:

(a) The 22 Trumps occur 4 times, once in each lesser angle. The 12 allotted to Simple Letters, the 3 allotted to the Three Mothers, and the Universe allotted to Tau and Saturn, come in the Servient squares, and the other six of the Double Letters on the six uppermost squares of the Sephirotic Cross. The apparent anomaly of the position of Saturn is thus explained in the "Book of the Concourse of Forces". "Now in the attribution of the Tarot Keys hereunto, Universe is attributed to Earth and Saturn though one of the seven 'Lords who wander' is yet here classed with those who abide, because he is the heaviest of the seven, and thus formeth a link between the Wanderers and the Abiders."

The reason for the other attributions are also given at some length in the same paper, and it is not worth-while to copy them here.

(b) The Aces and Court Cards occur once only, on the Kether squares of the Sephirotic Cross, and the four Kerubic squares of each lesser Angle.

(c) The 36 small cards occur twice each, on the Great Cross, and on the nine lower Sephiroth of the Sephirotic Crosses.

TABLET of UNION

E	X	A	R	P
H	C	O	M	A
N	A	N	T	A
B	I	T	O	M

The Tablet of Union.

Is allotted to the Aces and Court Cards thus:

	ACE	PRINCE	QUEEN	PRINCESS	KING
	SWORDS	SWORDS	SWORDS	SWORDS	SWORDS
	ACE	PRINCE	QUEEN	PRINCE S	KING
	CUPS	CUPS	CUPS	CUPS	CUPS
	ACE	PRINCE	QUEEN	PRINCESS	KING
	PENTS	PENTS	PENTS	PENTS	PENTS
	ACE	PRINCE	QUEEN	PRINCESS	KING
	WANDS	WANDS	WANDS	WANDS	WANDS

The foregoing methods of attributing the Enochian squares should be thoroughly grasped before proceeding further, as it is essential to understand the principles before beginning the working out of the Pyramids of each square.

CHAPTER FIVE
THE PYRAMIDS OF THE SQUARES

We have hitherto treated each square as a single whole and flat, but in reality it represents a Pyramid, shaped like the Pyramid of the elements in the Philosophus Grade with a square base and four sides composed of equilateral triangles truncated or cut off so as to leave a flat top. We have now to consider the attribution of the sides of these Pyramids. They will, among them, include all the attributions of the square already worked out in the previous chapter (save that the Letter of the Name on which the rest depend does not actually appear); in addition, each side of the Pyramid is coloured according to its own appropriate element, or left white for Spirit. Hence it by no means follows that a square from the airy angle of Air will have an all yellow pyramid - only two (one Kerubic and one Servient) in fact, do so. But every square of the Air Tablet has at least one airy side to its Pyramid; and every square of the Airy Angle of any Tablet has at least one airy side; every square in Air of Air having at least two airy sides (similarly in Water of Water, Earth of Earth, and Fire of Fire). The elements of the Tablet and of the Lesser Angle, therefore, always predominate over the others.

For example, in the airy angle of Air, out of 30 pyramids, with 120 sides: (This Schema applies mutatis mutandis to the lesser angle corresponding to the Element of the Tablet itself. Also note that the Earthy sides may be coloured in the four colours of Malkuth, Queen scale, if preferred.)

> **70 sides are yellow for Air**
> **10 sides are blue for Water**
> **10 sides are black for Earth**
> **10 sides are red for Fire**
> **10 sides are white for Spirit**
> **10 sides are either white or in the Sephirotic colours from the Minutum Mundum.**

In Water of Air:
> **40 sides are yellow for Air**
> **40 sides are blue for Water**
> **10 sides are black for Earth**
> **10 sides are red for Fire**
> **10 sides are white for Spirit**
> **10 are either white or in Sephirotic colour.**

On a flat surface, the Pyramid is represented by dividing the square into four triangles, leaving a small square in the centre to represent the flat top. On this, if desired, the appropriate Theban letter may be placed.

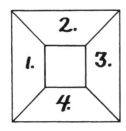

The Pyramid is supposed to be in position on the Tablet, so that Triangle No. 2 is towards the top of the Tablet. To work out the pyramid of any square completely, it is necessary to know the attributions of the four Triangles and the element of each. They are usually given in the order shown.

The White Squares. No. 2 is always Spirit, and white.

The Great Cross.

> No. 1. **Sign of Zodiac, small card of Tarot.**
> No. 2. **Spirit.**
> No. 3. **Planet of Decan.**
> No. 4. **Elemental Symbol of the Great Tablet concerned.**

I give the three left hand squares of the Linea Spiritus Sancti of the Air Tablet:

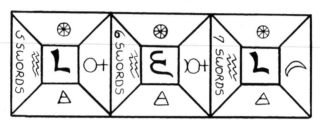

The Colouring of the Triangles.

For the Great Cross there are two alternative methods; for both of which there is high authority.

In both No. 2 is left white, and No. 4 coloured according to the element of the Tablet. It is only in the two side triangles that they differ.

(a) No. 1 may be coloured in the elemental colour of the Triplicity to which the sign belongs, and No. 3 in that of the Triplicity ruled by the Planet i.e., Saturn, Mercury for Air; Jupiter, Sun for Fire; Venus, Moon for Earth, and Mars for Water.

This method keeps the colouring throughout the Tablets to the elemental colours of the King's Scale, the attributions being always painted in the complementary colour to the ground.

(b) No. 1 may be coloured in the colour of the Sign itself, and No. 3 in that of the Planet itself, according to the Minutum Mundum diagram. In the set of Tablets worked out for reference, I adopted (a) but give here one square worked out in both ways for comparison. 1 take the second decan of Libra on the Air Tablet.

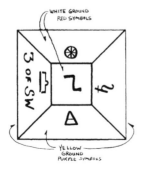
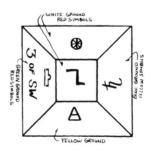

The Sephirotic Crosses:

No. 1. Elemental Emblem of Great Tablet

No. 2. Emblem of Spirit

No. 3. Elemental Emblem of lesser angle.

No. 4. Name of Sephirah, modified by letter of Name in lesser Angle. Tarot Ace or small card of suit. In first 6 only Planet, Hebrew Letter, and Tarot Trump.

Colouring:

No. 1. Elemental colour of Great Tablet.

No. 2. White.

No. 3. Elemental colour of Lesser Angle.

No. 4. Either white or in colour of Sephirah from Minutum Mundum.

Square of Chesed in Fiery Lesser Angle of Air.

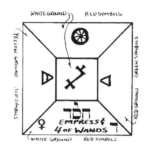

The bottom Triangle may be coloured blue and lettered in orange if preferred.

The Coloured Squares including the Kerubic and Servient squares.

No. 1. Tarot Court Card of appropriate suit of lesser angle. Card will correspond with Kerubic Emblem in 3.

No. 2. Elemental Emblem of Great Tablet.

No. 3. Kerub answering to Letter of Name to which the square is attributed.

No. 4. Elemental emblem of lesser angle.

Colouring.

No. 1. Agrees with No. 3. (This appears to be correct; in working out the Tablets for the Order 1 coloured No. 1 of the Kerubic Squares according to Element of Suit, instead of Element of Court Card corresponding to Kerub. This is probably wrong, and the diagrams are incorrect in this respect.)

No. 2. Elemental Colour of Great Tablet.

No. 3. Elemental Colour of Kerub.

No. 4. Elemental Colour of Lesser Angle.

The Square of Eagle Kerub in watery lesser Angle of Air:

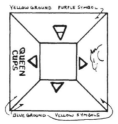

The Servient Squares:

No. 1. Elemental Emblem of Great Tablet. Astrological attribution.
No. 2. Elemental Emblem of letter ruling Column. Tarot Trump.
No. 3. Elemental Emblem of Lesser angle. Geomantic Figure.
No. 4. Elemental Emblem of Letter ruling Rank. Hebrew letter corresponding to Trump in 2.

Each triangle is coloured according to its elemental emblem. This method may sound fearfully complex, but it is actually much easier than it sounds. It takes far less time to work out a square than to describe how it is done.

Let us take at random the 3rd square in the 3rd rank of the 2nd Lesser angle of Air. (I have not at this moment the slightest idea what it is.)

Air Tablet - therefore No. 1. Yellow
Water angle - therefore No. 3. Blue. Heh on right of Kerubim, therefore Vau at head of our column, and Heh (final) for 3rd rank.
Therefore No. 2. Yellow, No. 4. black or citrine. Air column, earth rank, therefore Air, Fool, Aleph, and Fortuna Minor and we can put the square together thus:

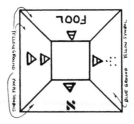

By pure accident I lit on a square which illustrates a doubtful point, viz: whether black should be used throughout for earth, or whether the four colours of Malkuth from the Minutum Mundum are more correct. It introduces the Queen's Scale, which seems against it, but they are used in the Sigil of the Earth Tablet, and I have used them in working out the complete Tablets. If they are used, citrine should be used for the lesser angle of earth in the Air Tablet wherever the lesser angle Element determines the colour. Also wherever in any angle Earth column crosses Air rank or vice versa. So with the olive, russet and black.

The Tablet of Union.

Nos. 2 and 4 always Spirit.
No. 1. Element of column (Spirit in first column)
No. 3. Element of rank and so coloured.

SQUARE A
of EXARP

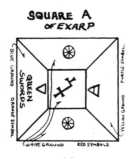

In the first part of Examination F the Candidate may be required to work out all the attributions of any lesser angle or squares selected by the Examiner. It is hoped that the foregoing will be sufficient to enable him to do so.

THE BOOK OF THE CONCOURSE OF THE FORCES
By

G.H. FRATER D.D.C.F.

It is demonstrated in the book called "T" that when the 10 Sephiroth in their grouping which is called the Tree of Life are projected in a Sphere (Kether coinciding with the North Pole, Malkuth coinciding with the South Pole, the Pillar of Mildness with the Axis), then the Pillars of Severity and of Mercy are quadrupled, i.e. there are 5 Pillars instead of 3 Pillars.

The same scheme is therefore applicable to the Celestial heavens, and the mode of the governance of these Tablets in the Heavens is also set forth in the Book "T." But as before and there is said, the rule of these Four Tablets, Terrestrial as well as in the Heavens, is in the Spaces between the 4 Pillars. That is between the double Pillars of Severity and Mercy. In these vast spaces at the ends of the Universe are these Tablets placed as Watch-Towers, and therein is their dominion limited on either side by the Sephirotic Pillars, and having the great central cross of each Tablet coinciding with one of the 4 Tiphareth points in the Celestial Heavens. Therefore even in the small squares into which each Tablet is divided, each represents a vast area of dominion, having the correlation therefore in the Universe, in the Planets, in our Earth, in the Fixed Stars, and even in Man, in animals, vegetables, and minerals.

A knowledge of these tablets will then, if complete, afford an understanding of the Laws which govern the whole creation. The dominion of the Tablet of Union is above that of the 4 Terrestrial Tablets and towards the North of the Universe.

The difference between the mystical names of the Angels of the Tablets and the Hebrew Names such as Kerub, Auriel, and Michael, etc. are here explained. Those Hebrew Angel Names which have been taught unto the First Order are rather general than particular, attending especially to an office or rule whereunto such an Angel is allotted. As it is written: "One Angel doth not undertake two messages." For these mighty Angels do rather shew forth their power in the governance of the 4 Great Sephirotic Columns as aforesaid, viz: the double columns of Severity and Mercy when projected in a sphere, and this also is under the Presidency of the Sephiroth. But the Names of the Angels of the Tablets do rather express particular adaptations of Forces shewing forth all variations and diverse combinations of those which are in the other case manifested in a more general way.

Notanda. Of the letters of the Tablets, some be written as capitals. These are the initial letters of certain Angels names drawn forth by another method, not now explained, and the offices of these do not concern a Z.A.M. The mystical meaning of certain letters which are reversed is also not now declared.

Some squares have more than one letter. In these cases, either letter characterises the Square. The higher one is preferable. The lower is weaker. If two letters are side by side, the presumption is in favour of equality. Where two letters are in one square, the best plan is to employ both. But one alone may be used with effect.

OF THE FOUR MIGHTY AND VAST OVERSEER ANGELS OF THESE TABLETS

It will be found written in the Clavicula Tabularum Enochi:
"Now we are to understand that there are 4 Angel overseers, each one of these Angels is a mighty Prince, a Mighty Angel of the Lord and they are of Him. They are as chief Watchmen and Overseers, set over several and respective parts of the World, viz: East, West, North, South, as under the Almighty, their Governor, Protector, Defender. And the seals and authority of whom are confirmed in the beginning of the world. To them belong Four Characters being tokens of the Son of God, by whom all things are made in the Creation and are the natural marks of his Holiness."

Now thou shalt observe in the Book of the Concourse of the Forces that unto each of the 4 Tablets of the Elements is there a sign annexed; i.e.: Unto the Tablet of Air a symbol of a T having four Yods above it.

Unto the Tablet of Water being a Cross Potent, having two letters b.b., a figure 4 and a figure 6, in the angles thereof.

Unto the Tablet of Earth, a simple Cross Potent without additions.

Unto the Fire Tablet there is a circle having 12 rays allotted.

These be the sacred seals or characters alluded to in the preceeding quotation. Now thou shalt know that these 4 seals be taken from the "Sigillum Dei Ameth" after and according unto "one certain guidance and letters which is there set forth, and this 'Liber Ameth vel

Sigillum Dei' that is the Book of Truth, or the Seal of God"entereth not into the knowledge of a Z.A.M.

The letters of the Word Ameth, Truth, are the three Elements, Earth, Water and Air for Tau is Earth, as Aleph, Mem, Shin, are Air, Water, and Fire.

These three letters or Elements are disposed together for the receiving of that Divine Fire which should enlighten them when thus harmonised so that therein may be manifested which is Emethsh or Amethsh, herein as the Shin of the Fire Divine entered, and this order of the Letters is that of the Angles of the Tablets, and of the 4 Tablets themselves, viz:

> **First - is Air and Aleph.**
> **Second - is Water and Mem.**
> **Third - is Earth and Tau.**
> **Fourth - is Fire and Shin.**

This again is the Order of the Elements in the Sepher Yetzirah of the Qabalah. From these 4 Sigils there are the 4 Names drawn forth as may follow in order.

From the Tau with 4 Yods or a (T) surmounted by four Yods of the Sigillum Ameth, (T) and 4 other letters counting by the rule of 4, 22, 20, 18: this yields Thaolog - Tahaoelog, for the Air Tablet. (The 4th Square each time from the last will shew the letter and figure given. You are not to count, say 22 or 20 or 18, but 4 only. N.O.M.)

These names are not to be lightly pronounced.

From the cross in whose angles are 2 (b's) a 6 and a 4 - see previous diagram, note that (T) equals a (t), while the cross equals (th).

The counting goes from Cross to (h), then b4, then 6b, and continues by six. 4 is Th, 22 is (h), (b) is 4, (y) is 14, 6 is (b), 6 is (A), (a) is 5, (t) is 9, (n) is 14. then (n) finishing the counting, yielding the name Thahebyobeaatanun for the Water Tablet.

To explain further, four moves from (T) yields 22. (h) (b) 4 is specially put; (y) 14 moves to 22, from (t). Then 6 (b) is special. From 6 (b) it is all plain moving by 6 to right.

From the Cross equals (th) 4, and proceed counting in each case forwards as by numbers, and proceed counting in each case forwards. 4 is (Th), 22 is (h), 11 is (a), (a) is 5, (o) is 10, (t) is 11, with a final letter of (h) which yields the name Thahaaothe, for the Earth Tablet.

(Count here not by 4 or 6, but by numbers given to right if over; to left if under.)

From the Fire Tablet Sigil count to the middle circle which is the Greek Omega, the long (o), and proceed in the Sigillum Ameth counting 12 in each case, for the number of rays is 12 around the circle. 6 is Omega, 12 is (h), (o) is 8, (o) is 17, (o) is 20, (h) is 12,6 is (A), (t) is 9, ending with an (n), which yields the name Ohooohaatan for the Fire Tablet.

(Count 12 in any case neglecting the numbers over or under, always forward. S.A.)

THE LAW OF THE ALLOTMENT OF THE ANGLES, CROSSES AND SQUARES OF THESE TABLETS.

The key of all and every allotment and combinations of the various subdivisions of the 4 Terrestrial Tablets is to be found in the transposition of the Letters of the Great Name. For the position of these Tablets together with the Tablet of Union in the midst and governing them, recalleth the Pentagram with the allotment of its angles under the presidency of the Great Name Yeheshuah. (The colours in the King Scale are White, Red, Blue, Yellow, and Black.)

Each Colour is again subdivided into its 4 Lesser Angles, representing the other 3 elements mingled with and differentiating the Elements of the Tablet itself under the Presidency of the 5 Crosses therein thus:

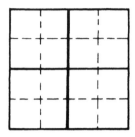

Also the word Aemeth is compounded of the 1st letter of the Alphabet and the last letter, and of a middle one, as though we affirm that Truth is to be found by the reconciliation of the extremes through the knowledge of the means.

Forget not that this Aleph is the Spiritual and Etherial, and Tau is the Universe, and Mem is the Sacrificial Man, placed between them so as to affirm the Reconciliation of the Natural to the Spiritual through self-sacrifice. And lastly that when Shin is added, there is an affirmation of the judgment set and the Book of Life opened which is in YHVH and that the Keys answering unto these 4 letters are:

> **Aleph is the Spirit of Aether**
> **Mem is the Spirit of the Mighty Waters.**
> **Tau is The Great One of the Night of Time.**
> **Shin is the Spirit of Primal Fire.**

As it would affirm firstly, the Aetherial and Divine Spirit brooding over the mighty Waters in the Silence of the Abyss of the Night of that Great One, before Creation, and before Time. And lastly, the Judgment of the Universe through Fire, when the End of the Ages shall be. Therefore is it that the numbering of the Angles followeth this order of:

> **Shin is Fire.**
> **Tau is Earth.**
> **Mem is Water.**
> **Aleph is Air.**

The above is the correct order and not the order of the attribution of the Elements to Tetragrammaton.

Yet perchance thou mayst say, wherefore are the letters of the name allotted as in the usual attribution to YHVH, since its letters are applied in a different manner in the Rose and in the Sepher Yetzirah, YHVH is equal to Aries, Taurus, Aries, Virgo.

Now the reason is this. It is true that Aleph, Mem, Tau, Shin equal Air, Water, Earth, and Fire, the purely terrestrial action, but YHVH is a certain Name added unto them to control their vehemence. So that over the violent Element Fire is placed the gentle letter of Yod - Virgo to calm and purify its raging. Over the quiet and peace loving element Water is placed the strong letter Heh - Aries to awaken it unto a fitting display of energy. Over the changing and whirling element of Air is placed the firm and resolute Vau, - Taurus. Over the stable and abiding earth is placed the exciting force of Heh - Aries.

So that with these letters from among the 12 Simple Letters hath the Almighty administered the government and combination of the Elements. Therefore is it that in these Tablets sheweth the law of their combination, and not Aleph, Mem, Tau, and Shin. Therefore is it that the name YHVH is a name of vehemence of all the Elements and this vehemence is held bound by it. But when the holy letter Shin of the Divine Spirit is placed therein it is rendered calm, seeing that the judgment is then set and the Book of Life opened. Herein also is a great Arcanum for it is a knowledge of the mystery of life.

Now each of these Terrestrial Tablets of the Elements is divided into 4 Lesser Angles by the Great Central Cross which cometh forth as from the Gate of the Watch Tower of the Element itself. The Horizontal Line of each of these Three Great Crosses is named "Linea Spiritus Sancti." The Perpendicular is called "Linea Dei," the Line of God, of Father and Son, the "Patris Filiique," Macroprosopus and Microprosopus combined. For these 4 Vertical lines resemble 4 mighty Pillars each divided into twain by a light line shewing this forth; The Father Himself, in the absence of the line. And in its presence shewing the Son. And as aforesaid the central points of these 4 Great Crosses do shew in the Celestial Heavens, and do correspond unto the 4 Tiphareth points referred to in the Book of the Astronomic view of the Tarot. Naturally then the Linea Spiritus Sancti coincides with the Zodiacal Belt wherein is the Path of the Sun who is the administrant of The Spirit of Life, and "The Lord of the Fire of the World." The Four Linea S. S. then form the complete circle of the Ecliptic, a circle at the centre of the Zodiacal Circle.

Therefore do the 4 Perpendicular or Vertical Lines of the 4 Crosses represent 4 Great Currents of Force passing between North above and South below, intersecting the Tiphareth points and thus affirming the existence of the Hidden Central Pillar of the Tree of Life forming the Axis of the Sphere of the Celestial Heavens.

Therefore are these Linea which are vertical called Linea Dei Patris Filiique, as manifesting that Central Column wherein are Kether and Tiphareth, Macroprosopus and Microprosopus. The Calvary Cross of 10 Squares which are in each of the 4 Lesser Angles of each Tablet are attributed unto the action of the Spirit through the 10 Sephiroth herein.

This Cross of 10 squares is the admission badge of the 27th Path leading unto the Grade of Philosophus, the only Grade of the First Order in which all the Tablets are shewn. It represents the Sephiroth in balanced disposition, before which the Formless and Void rolled back. It is the form of the opened out double cube and altar of incense. Therefore it is placed to rule each of the Lesser Angles of each Tablet.

THE KEYS OF THE GOVERNANCE AND COMBINATIONS OF THE SQUARES OF THE TABLETS.

They are the Sphynx and the Pyramid of Egypt, that is the combination of the Keruhs being the Sphynx. The combination of the Pyramid being the Elements.

Now learn a mystery of the Wisdom of Egypt: "When the Sphynx and the Pyramid are united, thou hast the formulae of the Magic of Nature."

"These are the keys of the wisdom of all Time and its beginnings - who knoweth it? In their keeping are the sacred mysteries and the knowledge of Magic and all the Gods."

In the Ritual of the 32nd Path leading unto the Theoricus Grade, it is thus written: "The Sphynx of Egypt spake and said: I am the synthesis of the Elemental Forces. I am also the symbol of Man. I am Life. I am Death. I am the Child of the Night of Time."

The solid Pyramid of the Elements again is the Admission Badge of the 28th Path leading to the Philosophus Grade. It is attributed to the Four Elements. Therefore on its base is the word Olahm, meaning World, and upon its sides are the names of the Elements: Aesh, Ruach, Mayim, Aretz or Ophir. Yet the Apex is not allowed to remain vacant, not quite acute in shape, but is cut off and so a small square is formed at the Apex, and the Letters Eth, meaning Essence are placed therein.

This small square maketh of the pyramid a certain Throne or shrine. On this throne a certain ruling force is seated. Within the Throne is a sacred Symbol. Place then its Sphynx within each Pyramid, and the image of its God above. Take thou each Pyramid as the key of the nature of each Tablet Square. The sphynx of each will vary in form according to the proportion of the Elements comprising the Square, and the God of Egypt whose image is to be placed above each Pyramid shall represent the force ruling under the direction of the Great Angel of the Square. This Angelic Name may be typified by the correspondences of the four letters of the Angel's Name, adding AL to the end of the Name - the letters of the Name standing for head, bust, and arms, body, lower limbs. Place the Name in Theban letters on the girdle.

This God shall be the symbol of the Power of the Light acting therein, as the Angel shall be the descent of that Light itself. The Four forms of the Sphynx are:

> **The Bull - Wingless**
> **The Eagle or Hawk - Winged**
> **The Angel - Winged**
> **The Lion - Wingless**

This variation as to wings is another reason why in grouping the Tablets and the lesser angles of the same, the two forms of Air and Water are placed above the two Tablets of Earth and Fire.

The symbolic form of each Sphynx is thus formed from the Pyramid of the Square.

The upmost of 4 triangles (into which a square falls when the diagonals are inscribed) sheweth the Head and neck, and if it is to be Angel or Eagle, these are unto the form of the Sphynx. The two triangles right and left show the Body with the arms or fore limbs here also. If Angel or Eagle there are Wings added unto the representation of the Figure. The lowest triangle adds the lower limbs and the tail of the Bull, Hawk and Lion.

When Air and Fire predominate there is a male tendency. When Water and Earth the type tendeth to female. Then as the symbolic forms of the Egyptian Gods who rule above the Pyramid, it is to be understood that what is here written regarding the Sphynx of the Pyramid and the God of Egypt ruling above is applicable especially unto the 16 squares of the Servient Angels in each lesser angle.

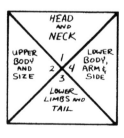

VOLUME TEN

TWO EXTRACTS FROM THE BOOK OF
THE CONCOURSE OF THE FORCES

I. Of squares marked by reversed letters, the full understanding hereof belongeth unto a more advanced grade than that of Z.A.M. Wherefore in this place it is enough to say that a reversed Letter signifieth that a certain more isolated action of the square is distinguished, so that it doth as it were not so much complete and harmonise with the other squares about it, as that it expresseth a certain faculty or faculties which do not entirely harmonise with them, and which for this reason are kept apart. They do not necessarily represent an evil form of action, though in one sense the evil forces grasp them more readily than through their lesser harmony with the other surrounding squares of the Tablet, that is in what are termed the "Battle Formulae."

II. Of the skrying of the squares servient in the spirit vision. Having in readiness the necessary implements and insignia, and the symbol of the Pyramid of the Square, having rehearsed the Angelic calls appropriate thereunto, and having invoked the appropriate names governing the Plane and division thereof in question, let the Z.A.M. imagine unto himself that he is enclosed within, or believe that he is voluntarily standing within an atmosphere corresponding unto that symbolised by the Pyramid of the Square, whether of Heat or Moisture, of Cold or Dryness, or of combinations of these.

Let him endeavour to follow the Ray therefrom unto the limits of the Macrocosmic World and to find himself in a scene corresponding unto the nature of the Pyramid Square. That is, either of landscape, or clouds, or water or Fire, or Ether, or vapour, or mist, or raying light, or a combination or combinations of these, according unto the nature of the Plane.

For the Pyramids of the Squares are not solid pyramids of brick or stone, built by the hand of man. But rather the symbolical representation of the Elemental formula governing the plane of that particular square.

Having arrived at the plane required, let the Z. A.M. invoke the God of Egypt who ruleth above the Pyramid by the power of the Angel of the Square, especially vibrating at the same time, the Egyptian name of the God or Goddess. Then he shall perceive before him the colossal symbolic form of the God or Goddess. Let him again use the Angelic formulae, and test it by the power of symbols and signs. If it abide these tests, thus shewing that it is a true image, let him then request it to make manifest before him the Sphynx of its power.

This shall also appear in a colossal figure and shape, and should be tested by the proper formula. He shall continue his invocations, until he can behold it clearly, ever invoking the Angel of the Plane by the Superior names, and the God of Egypt, by the name of the Angel, and by his own name, and by the knowledge of his symbolic image, and the Sphynx and by the name of the God of Egypt, and by his own particular symbolic form, according to the formula of the Square. Thus, therefore in this manner only, if thou wishest to escape from delusion shalt thou be able to discern truly by skrying, the nature of the Plane and of its operation, for standing before the Sphynx and saluting it with the proper signs and invoking the God of Egypt by his proper and true names, shalt thou ask by the virtue and power of those symbols and names, for the true knowledge of the operations and influences of that Plane.

Such as the special attributes of that vast portion of the confines of the universe included in that sphere; of its varying natures; of its elemental nature; of its inhabitants, elemental and spiritual, etc; of the operation of its rays through the Greater World; i.e., the Universe;

of its influence upon this particular planet; upon animals, plants, minerals; lastly upon man the microcosm.

And when thou shalt have obtained all this reflect that even then it is but a small part of the knowledge of the Wisdom of the Formulae contained in the plane, even of that one Square.

DIRECTIONS FOR MAKING THE PYRAMID

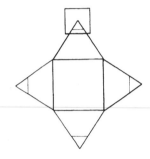

1. The Pyramid should be of white card-board, fairly strong and having about a 4 inch base.
2. In the centre of the cardboard describe a square for the base.
3. On each side, draw an equilateral triangle and from the apex of each triangle mark off a small portion.
4. On one of these apex lines draw a small square and mark a place for a slot to receive the foot of the God-form.
5. Cut the figure out and then half-cut the square base, so that the card-board will fold without breaking. Bind the edges with strips of paper except one side and fix the square top to three sides, leaving one to fall down as a door, inside which you place your Sphynx.

NOTES

By

S.R.M.D.

For quick working, make 16 triangles: 4 - red; 4 - blue; 4 - yellow; 4 - black.

1. Make a shallow inverted pyramid of card-board. Fill the sides as required with coloured triangles for the several squares. Let it be shallow enough to show all four sides at once.
2. Make a Red Lion - Black Bull - Blue Eagle - Yellow Angel. Divide each into three; the centre being halved. From these make composite sphynxes to lay under the pyramid.
3. Make small Egyptian Gods to put standing on cork above the Pyramid.

THE ENOCHIAN TABLETS

By

G. H. FRATER, S. A.

1. Prepare for private use Four Tablets with correct lettering as given in Official Lecture; and a Tablet of Union.
2. Make four Tablets coloured as brilliantly and as flashingly as possible, and in proportion; this should be done with coloured papers. They may be done in water-colours, but this is not so good.
3. The Four minor implements are to be used with the Enochian Tablets, and a small Altar should be arranged in the room at the time of working, draped with Black cloth, with a lighted candle by the wand, incense burning by the dagger, gold and silver or salt with the Pentacle, and Water in the Cup.
4. Use the Ritual of the Hexagram for the Invocation of the King and the Six Seniors.
5. Use the Ritual of the Pentagram for the Spirit and the Four Elements.
6. In pronouncing the Names take each letter separately: M is pronounced EM; N is pronounced EN; A is AH; P is PEH; S is ESS; D is DEH. NRFM is pronounced EN-RA-EF-EM or EN-AR-EF-EM. Z IS PRONOUNCED ZOD. Z1ZA is pronounced ZOD-EE-ZOD-AH. ADRE is AH-DEH-REH or AH-DEH-ER-REH. SISP is ESS-EE- ESS-PEH. GMNM, GEH-EM-EN-EM. TAAASD, TEH-AH-AH-AH-ESS-DEH. A1A- OAL AH-EE-AH-OH-AH-EE. BITOM, BEH-EE-TO-EM or BEH-EE-TEH-OO-EM. NANTA, EN-AH-EN-TAH. HCOMA, HEH-CO-EM-AH. EXARP, EX-AR-PEH.

PSAC RULED BY BPSAC	SACP RULED BY BSACP		ACPS RULED BY BACPS	CPSA RULED BY BCPSA
DATT RULED BY IDATT	ATTD		TTDA RULED BY ITTDA	TDAT
DIOM RULED BY IDIOM	I		O	M
O OOPZ	O		P PZOO RULED BY OPZOO	Z
R RGAN RULED BY MRGAN	G		A ANRG RULED BY MANRG	N

7. The Lesser Angle of Earth in the Southern or Fire Quadrangle. Each of the Lesser Angles may be thus divided. The foregoing analysis will require careful study with the Tablets before it is fully understood. It will be observed that the Elements are arranged in blocks of four words of four letters each. The Spirit names consist each of five letters, the fifth being taken from the Tablet of Union.

Thus in the Quadrangle of Fire, or Great Southern Quadrangle, we have BEH-EE-TO- EM from the Tablet of Union, BITOM. BEH-DEH-OH-PEH-AH from Top of Calvary Cross is B, 1st Angle, Bdopa. BEH-AH-EN-AH-AH from Top of Calvary Cross is B, 2nd Angle, Banaa. BEH-PEH-ESS-AC from Top of Calvary Cross is B, 3rd Angle, Bpsac. BEH-ZOD-EE-ZOD-AH from Top of Calvary Cross is B, 4th Angle, Bziza.

8. The Calvary Cross Names call forth with a word of Six letters and command with a Word of Five. They rule the Lesser Angles in which they are situated, and should be used in the preliminary Invocation.

9. The Six Seniors and the King are on a higher plane and should be invoked with the Hexagram Ritual. The Names of the Six Seniors are each of Seven Letters, that of the King 8.

10. The Deity names consist of a Name of Three Letters, Four letters, and Five letters, respectively. The Supernal Triad, IAO. YHVH, YHShVH, YHVShH.

11. The Name of the King and the Letters from the centres of the Crosses initiate the Whirl, and should not be used by those who do not understand its action.

With these elements of knowledge the intellect alone tells one much, though the intuitional and clairvoyant faculties are of course absolutely essential in working.

The following is an example of working:

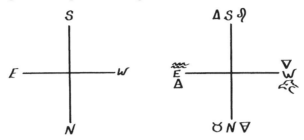

When, you go to seek Spirits or Forces on their own planes, the attribution of the Elements to the Cardinal Points is as follows:

As in the Zodiac.

Bearing this in mind, place yourself in the centre of a hollow cube, standing in the centre of the Tablet of Union between the O of HCOMA and the second N of NANTA, thus:

EXARP

HCOMA

Imagine yourself standing under (O).

NANTA

BITOM

Now imagine the Four Elemental Tablets standing round you like the four walls of a room, at the four cardinal points. This is subjective working.

Another method is to imagine a moonstone spheroid, containing the Universe, yourself standing as it were in the centre, and the Spirit Tablet or the Tablet of Union at the North and South Poles, at the same time dividing the surface into four quarters, imagining yourself outside the spheroid. This is objective working.

These Tablets can be applied to the Universe, to the Solar System, to the Earth, or to Man himself. "As above, so below."

Perhaps the most convenient method for a beginner to adopt is to apply this scheme to the Earth, treating the Three Deity Names as the Three Signs of the Zodiac in one quarter. Thus: take the Fire Tablet and place OIP on Leo, TEAA on Virgo, PDOCE on Libra, and so on w ith the other God Names, treating the Kerubic Sign as the "point de depart," one quarter of a House in Astrology will also be roughly equal to the square of each letter.

Each of these spaces would, under these circumstances, appear to be governed by a heroic figure of say twelve feet high, not winged. But the Spirit Names and the Names above the Calvary Cross, even on the Earth plane, bring forth Figures of tremendous size and beauty, which could easily lift a human being in the palm of the hand. I have seen from the fiery lesser angle of Fire AZOD1ZOD, the Figure being fiery red with emerald green flaming wings and hair. ZODAZODEE, Black and white, flashing and flaming. EEZODAHZOD, Blue and Orange, with a mist of flame. ZODEEZODAH, Orange, hazy gold wings like gold gauze, and nets of gold around him.

Having selected one of the methods given, perform the Lesser Banishing Ritual with the Sword.

Invoke with Minor Implement the Element required.

Our example being the Square of OMDI, a watery and earthy square in the lesser Angle of Earth in the Great Southern or Fire Quadrangle, we take the Fire Wand, and in the four Quarters invoke with the equilibriating Pentagram for Actives, and the Fire Pentagram using only the Tablet names, saying: EDEL PERNA - VOLEXDO and SIODA. "I command ye in the Divine Name OIP TEEA PEDOCE and BITOM that the Angel that governs the Watery and Earthy Square of OMEDEHEE shall obey my behest and submit to me when I utter the Holy Name TEHOMEDEHEE."

Having repeated this Invocation in the Four Quarters, turn to the East if you wish to go to the plane, or to the South if you wish to invoke the Spirits to come to you. Look at the painted Tablet which you have prepared until you can carry it in your mind, then close the eyes and vibrate the names OMEDHEE OEMDEHEE until your whole body trembles and you almost feel a sensation of burning. The items which follow are quite open to discussion and are simply my own personal experience. Then pass through the Tablets and try to see some sort of landscape. My experience of this particular plane was a dull red crumbling earth. I first found myself in a Cave. As a symbol I was told that this Square of OMDI was like the roots of a tiger lily; the Square MDIO, to the right, representing the Life working in it; the Square IOMD to the left, the sap flowing through the stalk and leaves; the Square DIOM, to the left of that, the Orange flower with the black spots upon it, fitly representing Air, Fire, and Earth, Yellow, Red and Black.

Afterwards I invoked the King and Six Seniors to explain the general bearings of the Quadrangle. After passing through several fire planes, each of them of greater Whiteness and Brilliance than the last, I seemed to be stationed on a high tower situated in the centre of the Quadrangle between the two A's around the tower and I was told by the Six Seniors that they were partly representative of the Planets, but that their Names should really be read in a circle, in a way we shall be taught later. At present, all I could gather was, that the Greek Cross was allotted somewhat in the way represented here, and the centre was the King.

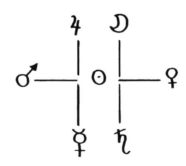

I also got an idea that the letters on the Crosses were opposed in power, positive or negative, as the case might be, to the letters in the Squares. From the Lectures circulated among the Adepts, I have gathered that the Angels placed over the Lesser Angles of the Great Quadrangle have the following properties:

Knitting together

Fire - Centrifugal and centripetal forces.

Destruction

Expansion and contractive, etc.

Moving from place to place.

Water - Motion, vibration, changing of forms.

Mechanical crafts

Earth - Creative, or productive of results on the material plane.

Secrets of Humanity

Fire - Controlling human nature, clear vision, etc.
That the subservient Angels of these Angles rule:

Elixirs

Air - Purification from illusions, diseases, sins by sublimation.

Metals

Water - The right methods of polarising the Soul so as to attract the LVX.

Stones

Earth - The fixing of the Higher Self in the purified body.

Transmutation

Fire - The consecration of the body, and the transmutation brought about by consecration.

THE COMPLETE GOLDEN DAWN SYSTEM OF MAGIC

THE FORTY-EIGHT ANGELICAL KEYS OR CALLS
By.

G.H. FRATER D.D.C.F.

These Calls or Keys which follow are only to be made use of with the greatest care and solemnity; especially if they be pronounced in the Angelical Language as given. Anyone profaning them by using them with an impure mind, and without a due knowledge of their attribution and application, shall be liable to bring serious spiritual and physical harm unto himself. The first Nineteen Calls or Keys, of which 18 alone are expressed, are attributed unto, and to be used with, The Tablet of Union and the Four other Terrestrial Enochian Tablets. The first Key hath no number and cannot be expressed., seeing that it is of the God-Head. And therefore it hath the number of O with us, though in the Angelic Orders it is called First. Therefore, their Second Key is with us the First. Unto the Tablet of Union are attributed Six Calls, of which the First is the highest and above the other five. The remaining Twelve Calls, together with Four of those belonging unto the Tablet of Union, are allotted unto the Four Tablets of the Elements.

The First Key governeth generally, that is as a whole, the Tablet of Union. It is to be used first in all invocations of the Angels of that Tablet but not at all in the invocations of the Angels of the other four Tablets. The Second Key is to be used as an invocation of the Angels of the Letters E.H.N.B. representing the especial governance of the Spirit in the Tablet of Union. It is also to precede in the second place all invocations of the Angels of that Tablet. Like the First Key it is not to be employed in the invocations of the Angels of the four other Tablets. (The Numbers such as 456 and 6739, etc. which occur in some of the Calls contain mysteries which are not here to be explained.) The next Four Keys or Calls are used both in the Invocations of the Angels of the Tablet of Union, and in those of the Angels of the Four Terrestrial Tablets as well. Thus: The Third Key is to be used for the invocation of the Angels of the letters of the line EXARP, for those of the Air Tablet as a whole, and for the Lesser Angle of this Tablet which is that of the Element itself - Air of Air. The Fourth Key is to be used for the Invocation of the Angels of the letters of the line HCOMA, for those of the Water Tablet as a whole, and for the Lesser Angle of this Tablet - Water of Water. The Fifth Key is to be used for the Invocation of the Angels of the letters of the line N ANTA, for those of the Tablet of Earth as a whole, and for the Lesser Angle of this Tablet - Earth of Earth. The Sixth Key is to be used for the Invocation of the Angels of the letters of the line BITOM, for those of the Tablet of Fire as a whole, and for the Lesser Angle of this Tablet - Fire of Fire. This finishes the employment of the Keys of the Tablet of Union. The remaining Twelve Keys refer to the remaining Lesser Angles of the Four Terrestrial Tablets, as hereafter set forth in the following Table.

FIRST KEY

I reign over you, saith the God of Justice. This is for the Tablet of Union as a whole.

SECOND KEY

Can the Wings of the Winds understand your Voices of Wonder. This is for the line EHNB.

VOLUME TEN

THIRD KEY

Behold, saieth your God, I am a Circle, on whose hands stand Twelve Kingdoms. This is for the line EXARP and for the Tablet of Air, IDOIGO, Air of Air.

FOURTH KEY

I have set my feet in the South and have looked about me, saying. This is for the line HCOMA and NELGPR, Water of Water.

FIFTH KEY

The Mighty Sounds have entered into the Third Angle. This is for the line NANTA and the Tablet of Earth, CABALPT.

SIXTH KEY

The Spirits of the Fourth Angle are Mine, Mighty in the Firmament of Waters. This is for the line BITOM and Tablet of Fire. RZIONR, Fire of Fire.

SEVENTH KEY

The East is House of Virgins singing praises amongst the Flames of First Glory. This is for the line of Water of Air, LILACZO.

EIGHTH KEY

The mid-day, the First, is as the Third Heaven made of Hyacinthine Pillars. This line is for Earth of Air, AIAOAI.

NINTH KEY

A mighty God of Fire with two edged Swords Flaming. This line is for Fire of Air, OAUVRRZ.

TENTH KEY

The Thunders of Judgement and Wrath are numbered and are harboured in the North in the likeness of an Oak. This line is for Air of Water, OBLGOTCA.

ELEVENTH KEY

The Mighty Seats groaned aloud and there were five thunders which flew into the East. This line is for Earth of Water, MALADI.

TWELFTH KEY

O you that reign in the South and are 28, the Lanterns of Sorrow. This line is for Fire of Water, IAAASD.

THIRTEENTH KEY

O you Swords of the South which have 42 eyes to stir up the Wrath of Sin. This line is for Air of Earth, ANGPOI.

FOURTEENTH KEY

O you Sons of Fury, the Children of the Just which sit upon 24 Seats. This line is for Water of Earth, ANAEEM.

FIFTEENTH KEY

O Thou, the Governor of the First Flame, under whose Wings are 6739 which weave. This line is for Fire of Earth, OSPMNIR.

SIXTEENTH KEY

O Thou, Second Flame, the House of Justice, which hath thy Beginnings in Glory. This line is for Air of Fire, NOALMR.

SEVENTEENTH KEY

O Thou, Third Flame, whose Wings are Thrones to stir up vexations. This line is for Water of Fire, VADALI.

EIGHTEENTH KEY

O Thou Mighty Light, and burning Flame of Comfort. This line is for Earth of Fire, UVOLBXDO.

And unto the Tablet of FIRE, the 6th, 16th, 17th and 18th KEYS. So that, to invoke, for example, the Angels of the Line NANTA of the Tablet of Union, thou shalt first read the First and Second Keys, and then the 5th key, and them employ the necessary Names. And to invoke the Angels of the Lesser Angle IDOIGO, Air of Air of the Tablet of Air, thou shalt read the Third Key only, and then employ the necessary Names. But to invoke the Angels of the lesser Angle CADALI, Water of FIRE of the Tablet of FIRE, thou shalt first read the sixth Key, and then the 17th Key, and after that use the necessary Names. Whereas, for the Angle of FIRE OF FIRE therein, the 6th Key alone would suffice, as also for the King and Angelical Seniors of that Tablet. And so of the other Angles of the other Tablets, these rules shall suffice. Now, though these CALLS are thus to be employed to aid thee in the Skrying of the Tablets in the Spirit Vision, and in magical working therewith, yet shalt thou know that they be allotted unto a much higher plane than the operation of the Tablets in the Assiatic World. And, therefore, are they thus employed in bringing the Higher Light and the All-Potent Forces into action herein; and so also, are they not to be profaned, or used lightly with an impure or frivilous mind as before said.

THE FIRST KEY ENGLISH

I reign over you Saith the God of Justice. In power exalted above the firmament of Wrath. In Whose hands the Sun is as a sword and the Moon as through-thrusting fire:

Who measureth your garments in the midst of my vestures and trussed you together as the palms of my hands:

Whose seats I garnished with the fire of gathering:

Who beautified your garments with admiration:

To Whom I made a law to govern the Holy Ones: Who delivered you a rod with the Ark of Knowledge.

Moreover Ye lifted up Your voices and sware obedience and faith to Him that liveth and triumpheth:

Whose beginning is not nor end cannot be: which shineth as a flame in the midst of your Palaces and reigneth amongst you as the balance of righteousness and truth.

Move therefore and show yourselves: open the mysteries of your creation. Be friendly unto me. For I am the servant of the same your God, the true worshipper of the Highest.

THE FIRST KEY ENOCHIAN

Ol Sonf Vorsag Goho lad Balt, Lonsh Calz Vonpho Sobra Z-O! Ror I Ta Nazps Od Graa Ta Malprg Ds Hol-Q Qaa Nothoa Zimz Od Commah Ta Nobloh Zien. Soba Thil Gnonp Prge Aldi Ds Vrbs Oboleh G Rsam; Casarm Ohorela Taba Pir Ds Zonrensg Cab Erm Iadnah Pilah Farzm Znrza Adna Gono Iadpil Ds Hom Od To h Soba Ipam Lu Ipamis Ds Loholo Vep Zomd Poamal Od Bogpa Aai Ta Piap Piamol Od Vaoan Zacare Eca Od Zamran Odo Cicle Qaa Zorge Lap Zirdo Noco Mad, Hoath Iaida.

THE FIRST KEY PHONETIC

Oh-el Soh-noof Vay-oh-air-sahjee Goh-hoh Ee-ah-dah Bahl-tah, Elon-shee Kahl-zoad Von-pay-hoh:

Soh-bay-rah Zoad-oh-lah.

Roh-ray Ee Tah Nan-zoad-pay-ess, Oh-dah Jee-rah-ah Tah Mahl- peer-jee:

Dah-ess Hoh-el-koh Kah-ah No-thoh-ah Zoad-ee-mah-zoad Oh-dah Koh-mah-mah- hay Tah Noh-bloh-hay Zoad-ee-aynoo;

So-bah Tah-heelah Jee-noh-noo-pay Peer-jee Ahl-dee; Dah-ess Ur-bass Oh-boh-lay Jee Rah-sah-may;

Cahs-armay Oh-hor-raylah Tah-bah Peer; Dah-es Zoad-oh-noo-ray-noo-sah-jee Kah- bah Air-may Ee-ad-nah.

Peelah-hay Far-zoad-mee Zoad-noo-ray-zoad-ah Ahd-nah Goh-noh Ee-ah-dah-pee-ayl Dah-ess Hoh-may Oh-dah Toh hay;

Soh-bay Ee-pah-may Loo Ee-pah-mees; Dah-ess Loh-hoh-loh Vay-pay Zoad-oh-May-dah Po-ah-may-ell, Oh-dah Boh-jee-pay Ah-ah-ee Tay-an Pee-ah-pay Pee-ah-moh-ayl Oh-dah Vay-oh-ah-noo.

Zoad-a-kah-ray Ay-kah Oh-dah Zoad-a-mer-ahnoo. Oh-dah Kee-klay kah-ah. Zoad-orjee Lah-pay Zoad-eer-raydoh Noh-koh Mahdah, Hoh-ah-tah-hay Ee-ah-ee-dah.

THE SECOND KEY ENGLISH

Can the Wings of the Winds Understand your voices of wonder. O You the Second of the First, Whom the burning flames have framed within the depth of my jaws;

Whom I have prepared as cups for a wedding or as the flowers in their beauty for the Chamber of the Righteous.

Stronger are your feet than the barren stone and mightier are your voices than the manifold winds.

For ye are become a building such as is not save in the mind of the All-Powerful.

Arise, saith the First. Move, therefore, unto thy servants. Show yourselves in power and make me a strong seer of things, for I am of Him that liveth forever.

THE SECOND KEY ENOCHIAN

Adgt Vpaah Zong Om Faaip Sald Vi-I-V L Sobam Ial-Prg I-Za-Zaz Pi-Adph.
Casarma Abrang Ta Talho Paracleda Q Ta Lorslq Turbs Ooge Baltoh.

Givi Chis Lusd Orri Od Micalp Chis Bia Ozongon.
Lap Noan Trof Cors Ta Ge O Q Manin Ia-Idon.
Torzu Gohe L Zacar Eca C Noqod Zamran Micalzo Od Ozazm Vrelp Lap Zir Io-Iad.

THE SECOND KEY PHONETIC

Ahd-gee-tay Oo-pah-hay Zoad-oh-noo-jee Oh-mah Fah-ah-ee-pay Saldah, Vee-ee-vee Ayl, Soh-bah-may Ee-ahl-peer-jee Ee-zoad-ah-zoad-ah-zoad Pee-ahd-pay-hay;

Cah-sarmah Ah-brahn-jee Tah-hoh Paraclaydah, Koh Tah Lor-es-sel-koh Toor-bay-ess Oh-oh-jee Bahl-toha.

Jee-vee Kah-hee-sah Loos-dah Ohr-ree Oh-dah Mee-cal-pah Kah-hees-ah Bee-ah Oh-zoad-oh-noo-goh-noo.

Lah-pay Noh-ah-noo Troh-eff Corsay Tah Jee Oh Koh Mah-nee-no Ee-ah-ee-doh-noo.

Tohr-zoad-oo Goh-hay Ayl. Zoad-a-kar-ray Ay-Kah Kah Noh-Kwoh-dah. Zoad-amer-ah-noo. Me-kah-el-zoad-oh Oh-dah Oh-zoad-ah-zoad-may Oo-rel-pay, Lah-pay Zoad- ee-ray Ee-oh Ee-ah-dah.

THE THIRD KEY ENGLISH

Behold saith your God. I am a Circle on whose hands stand Twelve Kingdoms. Six are the seats of Living Breath, the rest are as sharp sickles or the horns of Death, wherein the creatures of Earth are and are not, except Mine own hands which also sleep and shall rise.

In the first I made you stewards and placed you in the seats Twelve of Government, giving unto every one of you power successively over Four, Five and Six, the true Ages of Time: to the intent that from the highest Vessels and the corners of your governments ye might work My power: Pouring down the Fires of Life and increase continually upon the Earth.

Thus ye are become the Skirts of Justice and Truth.

In the Name of the same your God lift up, I say yourselves. Behold, His mercies flourish and His Name is become mighty amongst us, in Whom we say: Move, Descend and apply your selves unto us, as unto the Partakers of the Secret Wisdom of your creation.

THE THIRD KEY ENOCHIAN

Micma Goho Mad Zir Comselha Zien Biah Os Londoh Norz Chis Othil Gigipah Vnd-L Chis ta Pu-Im Q Mospleh Teloch Qui-I—N Toltorg Chis I Chis-Ge In Ozien Ds T Brgdo Od Torzul

VOLUME TEN

I Li E Ol Balzarg Od Aala Thiln Os Netaab Dluga Vonsarg Lonsa Cap-Mi Ali Vors CLA Homil Cocasb Fafen Izizop Od Miinoag De Gnetaab Vaun Na-Na-E-El Panpir Malpirg Pild Caosg.

Noan Vnalah Balt Od Vaoan. Do-O-I-A p Mad Goholor Gohus Amiran. Micma Iehusoz Ca-Cacom Od Do-O-A-In Noar Mica-Olz A-Ai-Om, Casarmg Gohia. Zacar Vniglag Od Im-Va-Mar Pugo Plapli Ananael Qa-A-An.

THE THIRD KEY PHONETIC

Meek-mah! Goh-hoh Mah-dah. Zoad-eeray Kohm-sayl-hah Zoad-ee-ay-noo Be-ah-hay Oh-ess Lon-doh-hah. Nohr-zoad Kah-heesah Otheelah Jee-jee-pay-hay, Oon-dah-lah Kah-heesah Tah Poo-eem Kwo-Mohs-play Taylohk-hay, kwee-eenoo Tohl-torjee, Ka- hees Ee Kah-hees-jee Ee-noo Oh-zoad-ee-ay-noo, Day-ess Tay Bray-jee-dah Oh-dah Tor-zoad-oo-lah.

Ee-Lee Ay Oh-Lah Bahl-zoad-ahr-jee Oh-dah Ah-ah-lah, Tay-heelnoo Oh-ess Nay-tah-ah-bay, Dah-loo-gahr Vohn-sahrjee Lohn-sah Cahpeemee-ahlee Vor-sah Cah Ayl Ah, Hoh-meel Koh-kahs-bay; Fah-faynoo Ee-zoad-ee-zoad-oh-pay Oh Dah Mee-ee-noh-ahjee Day Jee-nay-tah-ah-bah Vah-oo-noo Nah-nah-ay-ayl; Pahn-peer Mahl-peerjee Pee-el-dah Kah-ohs-gah.

Noh-ah-noo Oo-nah-lah Baltah Oh-dah Vay-oh-ah-noo.

Doo-oh-ee-ah-pay Mah-dah, Goh-hoh-lor Goh-hoos Ah-mee-rah-noo. Meek-mah Yeh-hoo-soh-zoad Kah-Kah-komah Oh-dah Doh-oh-ah-ee-noo Noh-ahr Mee-kah-ohl-zoad Ah-ah-ee-oh-mah, Kah-sarmjee Goh-hee-ah;

Zoadah-kah-ray Oo-nee-glah-jee Oh-dah Eem-vah-mar Poojoh, Plahplee Ah-nah-nah-ayl Kah-ah-noo.

THE FOURTH KEY ENGLISH

I have set my feet in the South and have looked about me saying:

Are not the Thunders of Increase numbered thirty-three which reign in the Second Angle?

Under Whom I have placed Nine Six Three Nine, Whom None hath yet numbered but One:

In Whom the Second Beginning of things are and wax strong, which also successively are the numbers of Time, and their powers are as the first.

Arise ye Sons of Pleasure and visit the Earth: For I am the Lord your God which is and liveth for ever.

In the Name of the Creator, move and show yourselves as pleasant deliverers that you may praise Him amongst the Sons of Men.

THE FOURTH KEY ENOCHIAN

Othil Lusdi Babage Od Dorpha Gohol

G-Chis-Gee Avavago Cormp P D Ds Sonf Vi-vi-Iv?

Casarmi Oali MAPM Soham Ag Cormpo Crp L

Casarmg Cro-Od-Zi Chis Od Vgeg, Ds T Capmiali Chis Capimaon Od Lonshin Chis Ta L-O CLA, Torzu Nor-Quasahi Od F Caosga Bagle Zire Mad Ds I Od Apila

Do-O—A—Ip Qaal Zacar Od Zamran Obelisong Rest-El-Aaf Nor-Molap.

THE FOURTH KEY PHONETIC

Oh-thee-lah Loos-dee Bah-bah-jee Oh-dah Dor-pay-hah Goh-hoh-lah:

Jee-kah-hees-jee Ah-vah-vah-goh Kohr-em-pay Pay-Dah Dah-ess Sohnoof Vee-vee-ee-vah Kas-ahrm-ee Oh-ah-lee Em-Ah-Pay-Em Soh-bah-mah Ah-gee Kohr-em-poh Kah-ar-pay Ayl:

Kah-sahrmjee Kroh-oh-dah-zoadee Kah-heesah Ohdah Vah-jeejee, Dah-ess Tay Kah-pee-mah-lee Kah-heesah Kapee-mah-ohnoo, Oh-dah Lon-sheenoo Kah-heesah Tay-ah Aylo-oh Kay-El-Ah.

Tor-zoad-oo Nohr-kwah-sahee, Oh-dah Eff Kah-ohs-gah; Bah-glay Zoad-eeray Mahdah Dah-ess Ee Ohdah Ahpeelah.

Doo-ah-ee-pay Kah-ah-lah, Zoad-a karah Oh-dah Zoadamerahnoo Oh-bayleesonjee, Raystellah Ah-ah-eff Nohr-moh-lahpay.

THE FIFTH KEY ENGLISH

The mighty sounds have entered in the Third Angle And are become as Olives in the Olive Mount, Looking with Gladness upon the Earth, and dwelling in the Brightness of the Heavens as continual comforters.

Unto Whom I fastened 19 Pillars of Gladness and gave them Vessels to water the Earth with all her creatures:

And they are the brothers of the First and the Second, and the beginning of their own Seats which are garnished with 69636 Continual Burning Lamps, whose numbers are as the First, the Ends, and the Contents of Time.

Therefore come ye and obey your creation. Visit us in peace and comfort.

Conclude us Receivers of your Mysteries, For why? Our Lord and Master is the All One.

THE FIFTH KEY ENOCHIAN

Sapah Zimii DUIV od noas ta quanis Adroch, Dorphal Caosg od faonts Piripsol Ta blior.
Casarm am-ipzi nazarth AF od dlugar zizop zlida Caosgi toltorgi:
Od z chis e siasch L ta Vi-u od Iaod thild ds Hubar PEOAL, Sobo-Cormfa chis Ta LA, Vis od Q Cocasb.
Eca niis, od darbs qaas. F etharzi od bliora. la-lal ednas cicles. Bagle? Ge-lad I L.

THE FIFTH KEY PHONETIC

Sah-pah-hay Zoad-ee-mee-ee Doo-ee-vay, Oh-dah Noh-ahs Tay-ah Kah-nees Ah-droh-kay, Dohr-pay-hal Kah-ohs-gah Oh-dah Fah-ohn-tay-ess Pee-reep-sohl Tay-ah Blee-ohr.

Kah-sarmay Ah-mee-eep-zoad-ee Nah-zoad-arth Ah-eff Oh-dah Dahloo-gahr Zoad-ee-zoad-oh-pay Zoad-leedah Kah-ohs-jee Tohl-torjee;

Oh-dah Zoad Kah-heesah Ay-See-ahs-kay Ayl Tah vee-oo-Oh-dah Ee-ah-ohdah Tayheeldah Dah-ess Hoobar Pay Ay Oh Ah Ayl.

Soh-bah Kohr-em-fah Kah-heesah Tay-ah El-ah Vah-less Oh-dah Koh-Koh-Kahs-bay. Ag-kah Nee-ee-sah Oh-dah Dahr-bay-ess.

Kah-ah-sah Eff Aythar-zoadee Oh-dah Blee-ohr-ah. Ee-ah-ee -ah-ayl.

Ayd-nahss Keeklay-sah. Bah-glay? Jee-Ee-Ahdah Ee-el!

THE SIXTH KEY ENGLISH

The Spirits of the Fourth Angle are Nine, mighty in the firmament of waters: Whom the First hath planted a torment to the wicked and a garland to the Righteous:

VOLUME TEN

Giving unto them fiery darts to Vanne the Earth, and 7699 Continual workmen whose courses visit with comfort the Earth, and are in government and continuance as the Second and the Third.

Wherefore, hearken unto my voice. I have talked of you and I move you in power and presence; Whose works shall be a Song of Honour and the Praise of your God in your Creation.

THE SIXTH KEY ENOCHIAN

Gah S diu chis Em micalzo pilzin: Sobam El harg mir Babalon od obloc Samvelg:

Dlugar malprg Ar Caosgi od AC A M Canal sobol zar f bliard Caosgi, od chisa Netaab od Miam ta VIV od D.

Darsar Solpeth bi-en. Brita od zacam g-micalza sobol ath trian lu-Ia he od ecrin Mad Qaaon.

THE SIXTH KEY PHONETIC

Gah-hay Ess Dee-oo Kah-heesah AY-Em, Mee-kahl-zoadoh Peel-zoadeenoo; Soh-bah-may Ayl Harjee Meer Bah-bah-lohnoo Oh-dah Oh-bloh-kah Sahm-vay-lanjee:

Dah-loogar Mah-lah-peerjee Ahray Kah-ohsjee, Oh-dah Ah Kah Ah Em Kah-nahl So-bolah Zoad-ah-ray Eff Blee-ahr-dah Kah-ohs-jee, Oh-dah Kah-heesay Naytah-ah-bay Oh-dah Mee-ah may Tay-ah Vee-ee-vah Oh-dah Dah.

Dahr-sahr Sohl-pet-hay Bee-aynoo. Bay-reetah Oh-dah Zoad-ah-kahmay Jee-meekah-el-zoadah So-boh-lah Aht-hay Tre-ah-noo Loo -EE-ah Hay Oh-dah Aykreenoo Mahdah Kah-ah-ohnoo.

THE SEVENTH KEY ENGLISH

The East is a House of Virgins singing praises amongst the Flames of First Glory, wherein the Lord hath opened His mouth and they are become 28 Living Dwellings in whom the strength of man rejoiceth, and they are apparelled with Ornaments of brightness such as work wonders on all Creatures.

Whose kingdoms and continuance are as the Third and Fourth, strong towers and places of comfort, the Seat of Mercy and continuance.

O ye servants of Mercy, Move, Appear, Sing praises unto the Creator! And be mighty amongst us! For to this remembrance is given power, and our strength waxeth strong in our Comforter!

THE SEVENTH KEY ENOCHIAN

Raas i salman paradiz oecrimi aao Ialpirgah, quiin Enay Butmon od 1 Noas N1 Paradial casarmg vgear chirlan od zonae Luciftian cors ta vaul zirn tolhami.

Sobol londoh od miam chis ta I od ES vmadea od pibliar, Othil Rit od miam.

C noqol rit, Zacar zamran oecrimi Qaada! od O micaolz aaiom! Bagle papnor i dlugam lonshi od vmplif vgegi Bigl IAD!

THE SEVENTH KEY PHONETIC

Rah-ahs Ee Salmahnoo Pahr-ahdeezoad, Oh-ay Kah-reemee Ah-ah-oh Ee-ahl-peer- gah, Kwee-ee-ee-noo Ayn-ah-yee Boot-mohnah Oh-dah Ee Noh-ah-sah Nee Pahr-ah-dee-ahlah

Kah-sahr-emjee Vay-jee-ahr Kah-heer-lahnoo Oh-dah Zoad-oh-nah-kah Loo-keef- tee-ahnoo Kohr-say Tay-ah Vah-oo-lah Zoad-ee-raynoo Tohl-hahmee.

Soh-boh-lah Lohn-d-do-hah Oh-dah Mee-ahmay Kah-heesah Tay-ah Dah-Oh-dah Ay-ess, Oomah-day-ah Oh-dah Pee-blee-ahray Otheelah, Reetah Oh-dah Mee-ahmay.

Kah-noh-kolah Reetah, Zoadakahray Mee-kah-ohl-zoad Ah-ah-ee-ohm! Bahglay Pahp-nohr ee Day-loo-gahm Lon-shee On-dah Oomplee-fah Oo-gay-jee Beeglah Ee- ah-dah.

THE EIGHTH KEY ENGLISH

The mid-day, the First, is as the Third Heaven made of hyacinthine Pillars 26, in whom the Elders are become strong, which I have prepared for my own Righteousness, Saith the Lord.

Whose long continuance shall be as buckles to the Stooping Dragon and like unto the Harvest of a Widow.

How many are there which remain in the glory of the Earth, which Are, and Shall not see Death until this house fall, and the Dragon sink?

Come away! For the Thunders have spoken!

Come away! For the Crown of the Temple and the robe of Him that Is, Was, and Shall be Crowned are divided.

Come! Appear unto the terror of the earth and unto our comfort and of such as are prepared.

THE EIGHTH KEY ENOCHIAN

Bazm ELO i ta Piripson oln Nazavabh OX casarmg vran chis vgeg ds abramg baltoha goho lad,

Soba mian trian ta lolcis Abaivovin od Aziagiar rior. Irgil chis da ds paaox busd caosgo, ds chis, od ipuran teloch cacrg oi salman loncho od voviva carbaf?

Niiso! Bagle avavago gohon!

Niiso! Bagle momao siaion od mabza IAD OI as Momar Poilp.

Niis! Zamran ciaofi caosgo od bliors od corsi ta abramig.

THE EIGHTH KEY PHONETIC

Bah-zoad-em Ayloh, Eetah Peeripsohnoo Ohlnoo Noh-zoad-ah-vah-bay-hay Oh-Ex, Cah-sarm-jee Oo-rahnoo Kah-heesah Vah-jeejee, Dah-ess Ah-brahmjee BaLl-toha Goho Ee-ah-dah, Soh-bah Mee-ahnoo Tree-ahnoo Tay-ah Lohl-kees Ah-bah-ee-voh-veenoo Oh-dah Ah-zoadee-ahjee-ahr Ree-ohray.

Eer-jeelah Kah-heesah Day-ah Dah-ess Pa-ah-Oh-Ex Boos-dah Kah-ohs-goh, Dah-ess Kah-heesah, Oh-dah Ee-poor-ahnoo Tay-lohk-ah Kah-karjee Oh-ee Sahl-mahnoo Lohn-kah-hoh Oh-dah Voh-vee-nah Kar-bahfay.

Nee-eesoh! Bahglay Ah-vah-vah-goh Goh-hoh-noo.

Nee-ee-soh! Bahglay Moh-mah-oh See-ah-see-ohnoo Oh-dah Mahb zoad-ah Ee-ah-dah Oh Ee Ahsah Moh-maray Poh eelahpay.

Nee-ee-sah, zoadamerahnoo Kee-ah-oh-fee Kah-ohs-goh Oh-dah Blee-ohr-sah, Oh-dah Kor-see Tay-ah Ah-brah-meejee.

THE NINTH KEY ENGLISH

A mighty guard of fire with two-edged swords flaming, which have eight Vials of Wrath for two times and a half, whose wings are of wormwood and of the marrow of Salt, have settled their feet in the West and are measured with their 9996 Ministers.

These gather up the moss of the earth as the rich man doth his treasures.

VOLUME TEN

Cursed are they whose iniquities they are. In their eyes are millstones greater than the Earth, and from their mouths run seas of blood.

Their heads are covered with diamonds and upon their hands are marble sleeves.

Happy is he on whom they frown not! For Why? The God of Righteousness rejoiceth in them. Come away! And not your vials, for the time is such as requireth comfort.

THE NINTH KEY ENOCHIAN

Micaolz bransg prgel napea Ialpor, ds brin P Efafage Vonpho olani od obza, sobol vpeah chis tatan od tranan balie, alar lusda soboln od chis holq c Noquodi CIAL.

Unal alson Mom Caosgo ta las ollor gnay limlal. Amma chis sobca madrid z chis ooanoan chis aviny drilpi caosgin, od butmoni parm zumvi cnila.

Dazis ethamza childao, od mire ozol chis pidiai collal. Vlcinina sobam vcim.

Bagle? IAD Baltoh chirlan par. Niiso! Od ip efafafe bagle a cocasb i cors ta vnig blior.

THE NINTH KEY PHONETIC

Mee-kah-ohl-zoad Brahn-sahjee Peer-jee-lah Nah-pay-tah Ee-ahl-poh-ray Dah-ess Bree-noo Pay Ay-fah-fah-fay Vohn-pay-ho Oh-lah-nee Oh-dah Ohb-zoad-ah, Soh-boh- lah Oopah-ah Kah-heesah Tah-tahnoo Oh-dah Trah-nah-noo Bah-lee-ay, Ah-laray Loos- dah Soh -bohlnoo Od-dah Kah-heesah Hohl-kew Kah Noh-koh-dee Kah-ee -ah-lah.

Oo-nahl Ahl-dohnoo Moh-mah Kah-ohs-goh Tay-ah Lah-sah Ohl-loray Jee-nayoh Lee-may-lah-lah.

Ahm-mah Kah-heesah Soh-bay-kah Mah-dreedah Zoad Kah-heesah. Oo-ah-noh- ahnoo Kah-heesah Ah-veenee Dree-lahpee Kah-ohs-jeenoo Oh-dah Boot-mohnee Parmay Zoad-oomvee Kah-neelah.

Dah-zoad-eesah Ayt-hahm-zoadah Kah-hil-dah-oh Oh-dah Meer-kah Oh-zoad-ohlah Kah-hees-ah Pee-dee-ah~ee Kohl-lah-lah.

Vahl-kee-neenah Soh-bahmay Ookeemay. Bahglay? Ee-ah-dah Bahl-toha Kar-heerlahnoo Pahray. Nee-ee-soh! Oh-dah Ee-pay Ay-fah-fah-fay Bahglay Ah Koh-Kahs-bay Ee Korsay Tay-ah Oo-neegay Blee-ohrah.

THE TENTH KEY ENGLISH

The thunders of Judgment and Wrath are numbered, and are harboured in the North in the likeness of an oak whose branches are 22 nests of Lamentation and Weeping laid up for the Earth, which burn night and day.

And vomit out the heads of scorpions and live sulphur, mingled with Poison.

These be the thunders that 5678 times (in ye 24th part of a moment) roar w'ith an hundred mighty earthquakes and a thousand times as many surges, which rest not, neither know any echoing time herein.

One rock bringeth forth a thousand, even as the heart of man doth his thoughts.

Woe! Woe! Woel Woe! Woe! Woe! Yea Woe! be to the earth, for her iniquity is, was, and shall be great.

Come away! But not your mighty sounds.

THE TENTH KEY ENOCHIAN

Coraxo chis cormp od blans lucal aziazor paeb sobol ilonon chis OP virq eophan od raclir. maasi bagle caosgi, di ialpon dosig od basgim;

53

Od oxex dazis siatris od salbrox, cinxir faboan.

Unal chis const ds DAOX cocasg ol oanio yorb voh m gizyax, od math cocasg plosi molvi ds page ip, larag om dron matorb cocasb emna.

L Patralx yolci matb, nomig monons olora gnay angelard.

Ohio! Ohio! Ohio! Ohio! Ohio! Ohio! Noib Ohio! Casgon, bagle madrid i zir, od chiso drilpa.

Niiso! Crip ip Nidali.

THE TENTH KEY PHONETIC

Koh-rahx-oh Kah-heesah Kohr-em-pay Oh-dah Blah-noos Loo-kahlah Ah-zoad-ee-ah-zoad-ohra Pah-ay-bah Soh-bohlah Eeloh-nohnoo Kah-heesah Oh-pay Veer-kwoh Ay-oh-fahnoo Oh-dah Rah-cleerah, Mah-ahsee Bahglay Kah-ohs-jee, Dah-ess Ee-ah-la-pohnoo Doh-seejee Oh-dah Bahs-jeemee.

Oh-dah Oh Ex-Ex Dah-zoadeesah See-ah-treesah Oh-dah Sahlbrox, Keenoo-tseerah Fah-boh-ahnoo.

Oo-nah-lah Kah-heesah Koh-noo-stah Dah-ess Dah-Ox Koh-kasjee Oh-ell Oh-ah-nee-oh Yohr-bay Voh-heemah Jee-zoad-ee-ax Oh-day Ay-orsah Koh-kasjee Pay-loh-see Mohl-vee Dah-ess Pah-jay Ee-pay, Lah-rah-gee Oh-em Dah-rohl-noo Mah-tor-bay Koh- kasjee Em-nah.

Ell Pah-trah-laxa Yohl-kee Maht-bay, Noh-meegee Moh-noh-noos Oh-loh-rah Jee- nah-yee Ahn-jee-lar-dah.

Oh-hee-oh! Oh-hee-oh! Oh-hee-oh! Oh-hee-oh! Oh-hee-oh! Oh-hee-oh! Noh-eebay Oh-hee-oh! Kah-ohs-gohnoo, Bah-glay Mah-dree-dah Ee, Zoadeerah, Oh-dah Kah-heesoh Dah-recl-pah.

Nee-eesoh! Kah-ahr-pay Ee-pay Nee-dah-lee.

THE ELEVENTH KEY ENGLISH

The mighty seat groaned aloud, and there were five thunders which flew into the East, and the Eagle spake and cried with a loud voice.

Come away! And they gathered themselves together and became the House of Death, of whom it is measured, and it is 31.

Come away! For I have prepared for you a place.

Move therefore and show yourselves. Open the mysteries of your creation! Be friendly unto me, for I am the servant of the same your God, the true worshiper of the Highest.

THE ELEVENTH KEY ENOCHIAN

Oxyiayal holdo, od zirom O coraxo dis zildar Raasy, od Vabzir camliax, od bahal.

Niiso! Salman teloch, casarman holq, od t i ta Z soba cormf I GA.

Niiso! Bagle abrang noncp.

Zacar ece od zamran. Odo cicle qaa! Zorge lap zirdo noco Mad, hoath Iaida.

THE ELEVENTH KEY PHONETIC

Ohx-ee-ah-yah-lah Hol-doh Oh-dah Zoad-eer-oh-mah O Kohr-ahxo Dah-ess Zoad-eel-dar Rah-ahs-ee Oh-dah Vahb-zoad-eer Kahm -lee-ahx Oh-Dah Bah-hahl.

Nee-ee-soh! Sahl-mah-noo Iay-loh-kah Kah-sahr-mahnoo Hohel-koh Oh-dah Tay Ee Tay-ah Zoad Soh-bah Kohr-em-fah Ee Gee-ah!

Nee-ee-soh! Bah-glay Ah-brahn-jee noh-noo-kah-pay.

Zoad-akarah Ay-kah Oh-dah Zoadamerahnoo. Oh-doh Kee-klay Kah-ah. Zoad-orjee Lah-pay Zoadeereedoh Noh-koh Mahdah, Hoh-ah-tah-hay Ee-ah-ee dah.

THE TWELFTH KEY ENGLISH

O You that reign in the South, and are the 28 Lanterns of Sorrow, bind up your girdles and visit us.

Bring down your train 3663, that the Lord may be magnified. Whose Name amongst you is Wrath.

Move, I say, and show yourselves. Open the mysteries of your creation.

Be friendly unto me! For I am the servant of the same your God, the true Worshipper of the Highest.

THE TWELFTH KEY ENOCHIAN

Nonci ds sonf babage, od chis OB Hubardo tibibp, allar atraah od ef!

Drix fafen MIAN, ar Enay ovof, sobol ooain vonph.

Zacar gohus od zamran. Odo cicle qaa.

Zorge lap zirdo noco Mad, hoath Iaida.

TWELFTH KEY PHONETIC

Noh-noo-kee Dah-ess Soh-noof Bah-bah-jee, Oh-dah Kah-heesah Oh-bay Hoo-bardoh Iee-bee-bee-pay, Ah-lah-lahr Ah-trah-ah-hay Oh-day Ay-eff. Dah-reex Fah-fah-aynoo Meeah-noo Ah-ray Ay-nah-ee Oh-voh-fah, Soh-oh-lah Doo-ah-ee-noo Ah-ah Von-pay- hoh. Zoad-ah-kahray Goh-hoo-sah Oh-dah Zoad-ah-mer-ahnoo, Oh-doh Kee-klay Kah- ah.

Zoadorjee Lahpay Zoadeereedoh Noh-koh Mah-dah. Hoh-ah-tah-hay Ee-ah-ee-dah.

THE THIRTEEN KEY ENGLISH

O you Swords of the South, which have 42 eyes to stir up the Wrath of sin: making men drunken, which are empty.

Behold the promise of God and his power, which is called amongst you a Bitter Sting!

Move and show yourselves. Open the mysteries of your creation.

Be friendly unto me! For I am the servant of the same your God, the true worshipper of the highest.

THE THIRTEENTH KEY ENOCHIAN

Napeai babage ds brin VX ooaona lring vonph doalim: eolis ollog orsba, ds chis affa.

Micma Isro Mad od Lonshi Tox, ds i vmd aai Grosb.

Zacar od zamran. Odo cicle qaa.

Zorge lap zirdo noco Mad, hoath Iaida.

THE THIRTEENTH KEY PHONETIC

Nah-pay-ah-ee Bah-bah-jee Dah-ess Bay-ree-noo Vee Ex Oo-ah-oh-nah Lah-reen-gee Vohn-pay-hay Doh-ah-leem; Ay-oh-leesah Oh-loh-jee Ohrs-bah, Dah-ess Kah-heesah Ahf-fah. Meek-mah Ees-roh Mahdah Oh-dah Lohn-shee Toh-tza.

Dah-ess Ee-Vah-mee-dah Ah-ah-ee Grohs-bay!
Zoad-a-kah-rah Oh-dah Zoad-a-mcr-ahnoo. Oh-doh Kee-klay Kah-ah.
Zoad-orjee Lah-pay Zoad-eer-eedoh Noh-koh Mah-dah, Hoh-ah-tah-hay Ee-aa-ee-dah.

THE FOURTEENTH KEY ENGLISH

O you Sons of Fury, the Child of the Just, which sit upon 24 seats, vexing all creatures of the earth with age, which have under you 1636.

Behold the Voice of God! The promise of Him who is called amongst you Fury or extreme Justice.

Move therefore and show yourselves. Open the mysteries of your creation! Be friendly unto me, for I am the servant of the same your God, the true worshipper of the Highest.

THE FOURTEENTH KEY ENOCHIAN

Noromi baghie, pashs O lad, ds trint mire OL thil, dods tol hami caosgi homin, ds brin oroch QUAR.

Micma bialo lad! Isro tox ds I vmd aai Baltim.

Zacar od zamran. Odo cicle qaa.

Zorge lap zirdo noco Mad, hoath Iaida.

THE FOURTEENTH KEY PHONETIC

Noh-roh-mee Bahg-hee-ay, Pahs-hay-sah Oh-ee-ah-dah, Dah-ess Tree-noo-tay Meer-kay Oh-el Tah-heelah, Doh-dah-sah Tol-hah-mee Kah-ohs-jee Hoh-mee-noo, Dah-ess Bay-ree-noo Oh-roh-chah Kwah-ah-ray, Meek-mah Bee-ah-loh Ee-ah-dah!

Ees-roh Tohx Dah-ess Ee Va-mee-dah Ah-ah-ee Bahl-tee-mah.

Zoad-a-kah-rah Oh-dah Zoad-a-mer-ahnoo. Oh-doh Kee-klay Kah-ah.

Zoad-orjee Lah-pay Zoad-eer-eedoh Noh-koh Mah-dah, Hoh-ah-tah-hay Ee-aa-ee-dah.

THE FIFTEENTH KEY ENGLISH

O Thou, the Governor of the First Flame under whose wings are 6739 which weave the earth with dryness;

Which knowest the great name Righteousness and the Seal of Honour!

Move and show yourselves! Open the mysteries of your Creation.

Be friendly unto me, for I am the servant of the same your God, the true worshipper of the Highest.

THE FIFTEENTH KEY ENOCHIAN

Ils tabaan L lalpirt, casarman vpaachi chis DARG ds oado caosgi orscor:

Ds oman baeouib od emetgis Iaiadix!

Zacar od zamran. Odo cicle qaa.

Zorge lap zirdo noco Mad, hoath laida.

THE FIFTEENTH KEY PHONETIC

Ee-lah-sah Tah-bah-ah-noo Ayl Ee-ahl-peer-tah, Kas-ahr-mah-noo Oo-pah-ah-chee Kah-heesah Dahr-jee Dah-ess Oh-ah-doh Kah-ohs-jee Ohrs-koh-ray: Dah-ess Oh-Mahnu Bah-ay-oh-oo-ee-bay Oh-dah Ay-mayt-gees Ee-ah-ee-ah-dix.

Zoad-a-kah-rah Oh-dah Zoad-a-mer-ahnoo. Oh-doh Kee-klay Kah-ah.
Zoad-orjee Lah-pay Zoad-eer-eedoh Noh-koh Mah-dah. Hoh-ah-tah-hay Ee-aa-ee-dah.

THE SIXTEENTH KEY ENGLISH

O Thou of the Second Flame, the house of Justice, Who hast Thy Beginning in glory, and shall comfort the Just, Who walkest on the Earth with 8763 feet, which undertand and separate creatures.

Great art Thou in the God of Conquest.

Move therefore and show yourselves. Open the mysteries of your creation! Be friendly unto me, for I am the servant of the same your God, the true worshipper of the Highest.

THE SIXTEENTH KEY ENOCHIAN

Ils viv Ialprt, Salman Balt, ds a croodzi busd, od bliorax Balit, ds insi caosgi lusdan EMOD, ds om od tliob.

Drilpa geh ils Mad Zilodarp.

Zacar od zamran. Odo cicle qaa.

Zorge lap zirdo noco Mad, hoath Iaida.

THE SIXTEENTH KEY PHONETIC

Ee-lah-sah Vee-ee-vee Ee-ahl-peert, Sahl-mahn-oo Bal-toh, Dah-ess Ah Cro-oh-dah-zoad-ee Boosdah, Oh-Dah Blee-ohr-ahx Bah-lee-tah, Dah-ess Ee-noo-see Kah-ohs-jee Loos-dah-noo Ah-Em-Oh-Day, Dah-ess Oh-Em Oh-dah Tah-lee-oh-bah.

Dah-reel-pah Gay-hah Ee-lah-sah Mah-dah Zoad-ee-loh dahr-pay. Zoad-a-kah-rah Oh-dah Zoad-a-mer-ahnoo. Oh-doh Kee-klay Kah-ah.

Zoad-orjee Lah-pay Zoad-eer-eedoh Noh-koh Mah-dah, Hoh-ah-tah-hay Ee-aa-ee-dah.

THE SEVENTEENTH KEY ENGLISH

O Thou third Flame whose wings are Thorns to stir up vexation.

And who has 7336 living lamps going before Thee.

Whose God is Wrath in Anger.

Gird up thy Loins and hearken.

Move therefore and show yourselves. Open the mysteries of your creation! Be friendly unto me, for 1 am the servant of the same your God, the true worshipper of the Highest.

THE SEVENTEENTH KEY ENOCHIAN

Ils D ialpirt, soba vpaah chis nanba zixlay dodseh, od ds brint TAXS Hubardo tastax ilsi.
Soba lad i vonpho vonph.

Aldon dax il od toatar.

Zacar od zamran. Odo cicle qaa.

Zorge lap zirdo noco Mad, hoath Iaida.

THE SEVENTEENTH KEY PHONETIC

Ee-loh-sah Dah Ee-ahl-peer-tah Soh-boh Oo-pah-ah-hay Kah-heesah Nah-noo-bah Zoad-eex-lah-yoh Dohd-say-hah: Oh-dah Dah-ess Bay-rccn-tah Tah-ah-ex-sah Hoo- bahr-doh Tahs-tax Ee-lah-see. Soh-bah Es-ah-dah Ee Von-pay-hoh Oon-pay-hoh.

Ahl-doh-noo Dahx Eelah Oh-dah Toh-ah-tahray.

Zoad-a-kah-rah Oh-dah Zoad-a-mer-ahnoo. Oh-doh Kee-klay Kah-ah.
Zoad-orjee Lah-pay Zoad-eer-eedoh Noh-koh Mah-dah, Hoh-ah-tah-hay Ee-aa-ee-dah.

THE EIGHTEENTH KEY ENGLISH

O Thou mighty Light and burning Flame of Comfort which openest the Glory of God unto the centre of the Earth.

In Whom the 6332 secrets of Truth have their abiding, which is called in Thy Kingdom Joy, and not to be measured.

Be Thou a window of comfort unto me.

Move therefore and show yourselves. Open the mysteries of your creation! Be friendly unto me, for I am the servant of the same your God, the true worshipper of the Highest.

THE EIGHTEENTH KEY ENOCHIAN

Ils micaolz Olprt od lalprt, bliors ds odo Busdir O lad ovoars caosgo, casarmg ERAN la lad brints cafafam, ds I vmd Aqlo Adohi Moz od Maoffas.

Bolp como bliort pambt.

Zacar od zamran. Odo cicle qaa.

Zorge lap zirdo noco Mad. hoath Iaida.

THE EIGHTEENTH KEY PHONETIC

Ee-loh-sah Mee-kah-ohl-zoad Ohl-peertah Oh-dah Ee-ahl-peertah Blee-ohr-sah Dah- ess Oh-doh Boos-dee-rah Oh-ee-ah-day Oh-voh-ahrsah Kah-ohs-goh, Kass-armjee Ay- rahnoo Lah ee-ahdah Breen-tas Kah-fah-fay-may Dah-ess EE Oo-may-day Ahk-loh Ah-doh-hee Moh-zoad Oh-dah Mah-oh-fah-fah-sah.

Boh-lah-pay Koh-moh Blee-ohrta Pahm-bay-tay.

Zoad-a-kah-rah Oh-dah Zoad-a-mer-ahnoo. Oh-doh Kee-klay Kah-ah.

Zoad-orjee Lah-pay Zoad-eer-eedoh Noh-koh Mah-dah, Hoh-ah-tah-hay Ee-aa-ee-dah.

TITLES OF THE 30 AETHYRS

1	LIL	16	LEA
2	ARN	17	TAN
3	ZOM	18	ZEN
4	PAZ	19	POP
5	LIT	20	KHR
6	MAZ	21	ASP
7	DEO	22	LIN
8	ZID	23	TOR
9	ZIP	24	NIA
10	ZAX	25	VTI
11	ICH	26	DES
12	LOE	27	ZAA
13	ZIM	28	BAG
14	UTA	29	RII
15	OXO	30	TEX

VOLUME TEN

THE CALL OF THE THIRTY AETHYRS ENGLISH

The heavens which dwell in the (First Aire), (or name the Aire required) are mighty in the Parts of the Earth, and execute the judgment of the Highest!

Unto you it is said: Behold the Face of your God, the beginning of Comfort, whose eyes are the Brightness of the Heavens, which provided you for the Government of Earth and her Unspeakable Variety, furnishing you with a Power Understanding to dispose all things according to the Providence of Him that sitteth on the Holy Throne, and rose up in the beginning saying:

The Earth, let her be governed by her parts and let there be division in her that trie glory of her may be always drunken and vexed in itself.

Her course, let it round (or run) with the heavens, and as an handmaiden let her serve them.

One season, let it confound another, and let there be no creature upon or within her one and the same. All her members let them differ in their qualities, and let there be no one creature equal with another.

The reasonable creatures of Earth, or Man, let them vex and weed out one another; and their dwelling places, let them forget their names.

The work of Man and his pomp, let them be defaced. His buildings, let them become caves for the beasts of the field! Confound her understanding with Darkness.

For why? It repenteth Me that I have made Man.

One while let her be known, and another while a stranger. Because she is the bed of an harlot, and the dwelling place of Him that is Fallen.

O ye Heavens, Arise! The lower Heavens beneath you, let them serve you! Govern those that govern. Cast down such as Fall. Bring forth with those that increase, and destroy the rotten.

No place, let it remain in one number. Add and diminish until the Stars be numbered.

Arise! Move! And appear before the Covenant of His Mouth which He hath sworn unto us in His justice. Open the Mysteries of your creation, and make us partakers of the Undefiled Knowledge.

THE CALL OF THE THIRTY AETHYRS ENOCHIAN

Madriaax ds praf LIL (or name the Aethyr required) chis micaolz saanir caosgo od fisis balzizras laida!

Nonca gohulim: Micma adoian Mad, laod bliorb, soba ooaona chis Lucifitias Piripsol, ds abraassa noncf netaaib caosgi od tilb adphaht damploz, tooatnoncfg Micalz Oma Irasd tol glo marb Yarry Idoigo od torzulp Iaodaf gohol:

Caosga tabaord saanir od christeos yrpoil tiobl busdir tilb noaln paid orsba od dodrmni zylna.

Elzap tilb parm gi Piripsax, od ta qurlst booapis.

L nibm ovcho symp od christeos ag toltorn mirc q tiobl 1 el. Tol paomd dilzmo as pian od christeos ag L toltorn parach asymp.

Cordziz, dodpal od fifalz L smnad: od fargt bams omaoas.

Conisbra od avavox, tonug. Orsca tbl noasmi tabges levithmong. Unchi omp tibl ors.

Bagle? Modoah ol cordziz. L capimao izomaxip, od cacocasb gosaa. Baglem pii tianta a babalond, od faorgt teloc vovim.

Madriiax, torzu! Oadriax orocho aboapri! Tabaori priaz ar tabas. Adrpan cor.s ta dobix. Iolcam priazi ar coazior, od Quasb Qting.

Ripir paoxt sa la cor. Vml od prdzar cacrg aoiveae cormpt.

Torzu! Zacar! Od zamran aspt sibsi butmona, ds surzas tia balta.

Odo cicle qaa, Od ozozma plapli Iadnamad.

THE CALL OF THE THIRTY AETHYRS PHONETIC

Mah-dree-ahx dah-ess pay-rah-fay (NAME AETHYR) Kah-hees mee-kah-ohl-zoad sah-ah-neer kah-ohs-goh oh-dah fee-see-sah bahl-zoad-ee-zoad-rah-sah Ee-ah-ee-dah!

Noh-nooh-kah goh-hoo-leem; mee-kah-mah ah-doh-ee-ah-noo Mah-dah; Ee-ah-oh-dah blee-ohr-bay, soh-bah oo-ah-oh-nah kah-hees Loo-kif-tee-ahs Pee-rip-soh-lah, dah-ess ah-brah-ahs-sah noh-noo-kah-fay nay-tah-ah-ee-bay kah-ohs-jee oh-dah tee- lah-bay ahd-phah-hay-tah dah-mah-ploh-zoad, too-ah-tah noh-noo-kah-fay, jee mee- kahl-zoad oh-mah ayl-rah-sahd toh-lah jee-loh-hah em-ah-bay yah-ree Ee-doh-ee-goh oh-dah tor-zoad-ool-pay Ee-ah-oh-dah-eff goh-hol; Kah-ohs-gah tah-bah-ohr-dah sah-ah-neer oh-dah krees-tee-ohs eer-poh-eelah tee-oh-bel boos-deer teel-bay noh-ahl-noo pah-ee-dah ohrs-bah oh-dah doh-dahr-mee-nee zoad-ee-Iah-nah.

Ayl-zoad-ah-pay teel-bay pahr-may jee Pee-reep-sax, oh-dah tah kew-rel-saht boo-ah-pees.

Ayl nee-bah-may oh-vah-choh see-mah-pay oh-dah krees-tee-ohs ah-jee tohl-tor-noo mee-rah-kah goh tee-oh-bel Ayl ay-lah, toh-lah pah-ohm-dah deel-zoad-moh Ah-ess pee-ah-noo oh-dah krees-tee-ohs ab-jee Ayl tol-tornoo pah-rah-chah ah-seem-pah.

Kohr-dah-zoad-ee-zoad, doh-dah-pah-lay oh-dah fee-fahl-zoad Ayl ess-mah-noo-ahd; oh-dah fahr-gee-tah bah-em-sah ohm-ah -oh-ah-sah.

Koh-nees-brah oh-dah ah-vah-vah-ohtza, toh-noo-gee. Ohrs-kah tee-bay-ayl noh-ahs-mee tah-bay-jee-sah lev-ee-thah-moh-noo-jee, oo-noo-chee oh-may-pay tee-bay-ayl ohr-sah.

Bah-glay? Moh-doh-ah oh-el kohr-dah-zoad. Ayl kah-pee-mah-oh ee-zoad-ee mahx-ee-pay, oh-dah kah-koh-kahs-bay goh-sah-ah. Bah-glay-noo pee-ee tee-ahnoo-tah ah bah-bah-loh-noo-dah, oh-dah fah-ohr-jee-tay tay-lohk-voh-veem

Mah-dree-ahx, tor-zoad-oo! Oh-ah-dree-ahx ohr-ochoh ah-boh-ah-pree! Tah-bah- ohree pree-ah-zoad ah-ray tah-bah-sah. Ahd-ray-pahnoo Kohr-sah tay-ah doh-beex. Ee-ohl-kah-mah pree-ah-zoad-ee-ah-ray koh-ah-zoad-ee-ohr-ray, oh-dah kew-ahs-bah kew-tee-noo-gah.

Ree-pee-rah pah-ohx-tay essah ayl-ahkohr. Oo-may-lah pray-dah-zoad-ah-ray kah- kahr-jee ah-oh-ee-vay-ah-ay koh-em-pay-toh.

Tohr-zoad-oo! Zoad-ah-kah-ray! Oh-dah zoad-ah-mer-ah-noo ahs-pay-tah see-bay-see boot-moh-nah, dah-ess soo-ray-zoad-ahs tee-ah bahl-toh-noo.

Oh-doh kee-klay kah-ah. Oh-dah Oh-zoad-oh-zoad-mah plah-plee Ee-ahd-nah-mah-dah.

VOLUME TEN

AN ADDENDUM TO THE BOOK OF THE CONCOURSE OF THE FORCES POSTSCRIPT TO ENOCHIANA
By

V.H. FRATER A.M.A.G.

(This thesis was written in 1935 following an intensive study of the Golden Dawn documents on the Enochian system. It has been left virtually in the same form it had at that time.)

That the Enochian scheme is a vast and extensive one is well known to the Zelator Adeptus Minor. But that it is as extensive as actually it is, is suspected I am sure by few. For the complete system of the Enochian Tablets comprises, in reality, several apparently disconnected schemes - most of which are not even known to the average Z.A.M. Though they are unknown is not to say that they are unimportant, for it requires but little perspicacity to realize that the Enochian system underlies a large part of the important work of the Order.

There are many hints to indicate that the Z.A.M. is not in full possession of all the Enochian knowledge. As the Adeptus Minor ritual so eloquently observes of but one of the parts of the system: "Before the Door of the Tomb, as symbolic Guardians, are the Elemental Tablets and the Kerubic Emblems, even as before the mystical Gate of Eden stood the watchful Kerubim and the Sword of Flame. Do not therefore forget that the Tablets and the Kerubim are the Guardians of the Tomb of the Adepti.

The whole system comprises the following segments:

1. Liber Enoch - (Liber Logaeth), these are the Enochian Tablets.
2. The Claves Angelicae.
3. Liber Scientiae Auxiliis et Victoriae Terrestris.
4. Sigllum Dei Aemeth.
5. Heptarchia Mystica.
6. The Round Tablet of Nalvage.

The first two items above have been dealt with very adequately in the routine instructions provided for the Zelator Adeptus Minor in such documents as The Book of the Concourse of the Forces, as well as in the various introductions and digests made of that book, and also in the Ritual "T" known as The Book of the Forty Eight Angelical Keys or Calls.

The remaining schemes are not dealt with at all in the study programme of work prescribed for the Z.A.M. In various places of those manuscripts there are deliberate gaps, indicating that such and such an item of knowledge does not come within the sphere of knowledge of the Z.A.M.

Nonetheless a certain amount of light can be thrown without too much difficulty upon these deliberate gaps, though whether or not they will be considered important depends wholly on how much of the ordinary Enochian material already available has been assimilated and appreciated by the Z.A.M.

Although in this paper I propose to concern myself almost exclusively with the third of the foregoing schemes, to show its relation to the previous two which are summarized in the material freely circulated within the Order, a few words in description of the others may be found useful.

The Sigillum Dei Aemeth consists of a highly elaborate Pentacle, said to be a magical synthesis of ideas of a purely spiritual nature with regard to Divine, Archangelic and Angelic Names concerned with the celestial spheres wherein operate the planetary forces. The latter are but the palaces or thrones of the forces depicted by the Sigillum. That this is so maybe gathered from a statement uttered by the Angel MICHAEL in his communications to the skryers - Dr. John Dee and Sir Edward Kelley - who were responsible for the recording of this system:

"When thou wilt have anything to do in the world, in human affairs, seek nothing in Sigillo Aemeth. Enoch, his book, is a wordly book. Veritas in Coelo, Imago veritatis, in herra homini, Imago imagini respondet. Coelestia autem petuntur a Coelo."

In Ritual "T,"' it is mentioned that Irwin's manuscript gave certain names after the first 18 Keys. Most of these names appear on the enclosed Heptagrams of the Sigillum.

(The Order documents do not explain who this mysterious Irwin is, though his name is used several times. However, Waite in his Brotherhood of the Rosy Cross refers to him and clears up the mystery, though in his usual sarcastic way it seems as if he had no use for Major Irwin.)

Moreover, it must be noted that the Sigils attributed to the four Enochian Tablets - a Cross, a Sun with 12 Rays, and a Cross in whose angles are b4, 6b and a (T) with 4 Yods, above it, receive their elucidation from this Sigillum, being resolved into the names of the so-called Four Great Overseer-Angels of these Tablets.

The Heptarchia Mystica is very closely related to the former system, for it gives the names and sigils and invocations of the Angels and the lesser Spirits of the Planets. It touches a much lower plane than the Sigillum, the heavens of Assiah as it were, while the Sigillum soars to the worlds of Briah and Yetzirah. The world of Atziluth is touched through the system of Liber Scientiae Auxiliis et Victoriae Terrestris. Moreover, the Heptarchical Mystery gives an additional seven Tablets which are rather different in content and structure from the four Elemental Tablets we know already.

The schemes numbered 1-5 are very intimately related to the Enochian system and one to another. Item 6, the Round Table of Nalvage, however, is a magical Tablet which for the moment I have been unable to relate to the others. The communicating Angel NALVAGE dictated, in much the same way as did Ave and Michael in other connections, a series of letters and words which were to be arranged in a certain manner. They begin ZIR MOZ IAD - Zodireh Mozod Iada -"I am the Joy of God." etc. What the practical application of this Tablet is remains yet to be discovered. It consists of four very small Tablets, each of nine letters, in all of which the word IAD figures in four distinct permutations, surrounded by four words of five letters each, making 32 letters. Whether this fact connects it with the four Terrestrial Tablets and the Tablet of Union I can hardly say at this time. Of this Tablet, NALVAGE stated: "The substance is God the Father. The circumference is God the Son. The order and knitting together is God the Holy Ghost." etc. This does suggest the three columns or the cross bar and double Pillars of the Central Cross of the Tablets - Linea Spiritus Sancti, Linea Dei Patris Filiique.

To refer back to Liber Scientae Auxiliis, as a preliminary point, let it be noted that in Ritual "T," the following passages occur: "The application of the Keys of the 30 Aethrys does not come into the knowledge of the Z.A.M. Now although these Keys are thus to be employed to aid thee in the Skrying of the Tablets in the Spirit Vision, and in magical working therewith, yet shalt thou know that they be allotted unto a much higher plane than the operation of the Tablets in the Assiatic World. And therefore are they thus employed in bringing the Higher Light and the All-potent Forces into action herein. And so also, they are not to be profaned, or used lightly with an impure or frivolous mind."

In other words, it relates to the schema described in the Order manuscript entitled. The Microcosm which lays down the philosophical dictum that the Kether of Man, "his Yechidah is his Divine Consciousness because it is the only part of man which can touch the All-potent Forces. Behind Yechidah are the Angelic and Archangelic Forces of which the Yechidah is the manifestos. It is therefore the lower Genius or Viceroy of the Higher Genius which is beyond, and which is an Angel Mighty and Terrible. This Great Angel is the Higher Genius, beyond which are the Archangelic and Divine."

What is to be observed from this is, that of the same nature as the Higher Genius are the all-potent macrocosmic forces called forth by the Keys of the Aethyrs, as shown by the fact that though 91 in number, which equals AMN, the latter has a gematria of 741 which reduces to 12. And 12 is the gematria of HUA, the great Avenging Angel, the holy and divine Genius in KETHER. And the invocation of these forces is to be undertaken in fulfillment of the Obligation wherein the 5-6 initiate swore on the Cross to apply himself to the Great Work so that, one day, he might become more than human, etc. Thus no frivolous or ignorant mind could invoke these divine forces without bringing serious spiritual and physical harm to himself, as the Ritual "T" duly and rightly warns.

The second point to be noticed is that to construct the Enochian Tablets entirely with capital letters is a serious mistake. It may be useful to do so for the sake of convenience or of increased legibility. But so doing obscures one of the several important functions of the Tablet. Certain letters thereon should appear in lower case letters and others in capitals. It is from these latter capital letters that are constructed the names of mighty Angelical Princes who rule in each of the thirty Aethyrs. To each of the Aethyrs there are attributed three Governors or Angelical Princes, with the exception of the thirtieth Aethyr named TEX, in which there are four.

Thus, the Tablets enshrine, in addition to those names already described by The Book of the Concourse of the Forces, the names of Ninety One Angelical Princes whose rule is in the Thirty Aethyrs of the Macrocosmic World.

91 equals the Gematria of Aleph Mem Nun which equals Amen, as mentioned previously. And Amen equals Amoun, the concealed One, the Opener of the Day. Hence also are the names of these 91 Princes opened up and yet concealed in all secrecy in the Four Terrestrial Tablets and the Mystical Tablet of Union. Note that Amoun is concealed within the heart of the God-Man YSHhVH (whose Gematria is 326.) 91+326 equals 417 equals 12. And twelve is the Gematria of the great Angel HUA.

The scheme delineated at length in the book entitled Liber Scientiae Auxiliis et Victoriae Terrestris, further conceives that each of these Angelic Princes is under the governancy of some one of the mighty Archangels ruling the mystical twelve Tribes of Israel together with the twelve Signs of the Zodiac. They are given in a special order which corresponds to the order of the Archangels depicted in the Zelator diagram of the Shewbread. There is, nevertheless, a slight discrepancy in the order of the Names of the Tribes as related to the Archangels. Rectified, the attribution may be noted as below:

Aries

The Tribe is Gad, the Deity name AOZPI, the Archangelic name is M ALCHIDAEL and the Governing Angelic name is OLPAGED.

Taurus

The Tribe is Ephraim, the Deity name MOR, the Archangelic name is ASMODEL and the Governing Angelic name is ZIRACAH.

Gemini

The Tribe is Manasseh, the Deity name is DIAL, the Archangelic name is AMBRIEL and the Governing Angelic name is HONONOL.

Cancer

The Tribe is Issachar, the Deity name HCTGA, the Archangelic name is MURIEL and the Governing Angelic name is ZARNAAH.

Leo

The Tribe is Judah, the Deity name is OIP, the Archangelic name is VERCHIEL and the Governing Angelic name is GEBABAL.

Virgo

The Tribe is Naphthali, the Deity name is TEAA, the Archangelic name is H AMALIEL and the Governing Angelic name is ZURCHOL.

Libra

The Tribe is Asshur, the Deity name PDOCE, the Archangelic name is ZURIEL and the Governing Angelic name is ALPUDUS.

Scorpio

The Tribe is Dan, the Deity name MPH, the Archangelic name is BARACHIEL and the Governing Angelic name is CADAAMP.

Sagittarius

The Tribe is Benjamin, the Deity name ARSL, the Archangelic name is ADVACHIEL and the Governing Angelic name is ZARZILG.

Capricorn

The Tribe is Zebulun, the Deity name GAIOL, the Archangelic name is HANAEL and the Governing Angelic name is LAVAVOTH.

Aquarius

The Tribe is Reuben, the Deity name ORO, the Archangelic name is CAMBRIEL and the Governing Angelic name is ZINGGEN.

Pisces

The Tribe is Simeon, the Deity name IBAH, the Archangelic name is AMN1TZIEL and the Governing Angelic name is ARFAOLG.

In classifying these names I have arranged the appropriate Great and Secret Holy Names of God as they appear on the Elemental Tablets following the suggestion made in S.A.'s Ritual where this passage occurs:

"Apply this scheme to the Earth treating the Three Deity Names as the Three Signs of the Zodiac in one quarter. Thus, take the Fire Tablet and place OIP in Leo, TEAA in Virgo, PDOCE in Libra, and so on with the other God-names, treating the Kerubic signs as the "point-de-depart"; one quarter of a House in Astrology will also be roughly equal to the square of each letter."

The above classification provides a comprehensive scheme to be used by itself, alone, or in collaboration with the Angelic Names of the Schem-hamphoresch, of great value in the art of invocation. In invocation, the two sets of names could be used conjointly to generate a good deal of power. The Pentagram could be used with the Archangelic name, together with the appropriate permutations of Tetragrammaton, as indicated by the Sepher Yetzirah. The Governing Angelic Name could be used with the Hexagram, using the appropriate figure of the planet ruling the Sign - Mars for Aries, and Jupiter for Pisces, etc., using not the Sigil of the planet but the Sigil of the Zodiacal Sign.

VOLUME TEN

The tabulation of the Names which now follow provides the names of:

The Aire or Aethyr itself.
The Name of the Angelical Governor of the Division.
The Number of the Tribe of Israel and its Presiding Archangel.
The Number of ministers and attendants.

Before proceeding to this classification, the Z.A.M. may recall that in Ritual "T" the following passage occurs: "The Numbers 456 and 6739 etc., which occur in some of the Calls contain Mysteries which are not now to be explained."

These unexplained Mysteries will be found to be self-explanatory by referring to the final column of the following Table which classifies in systematic order the Aethyrs, their Governors and their Angels, together with the number of subservient attendants.

1st LIL

OCCODON Ninth, 7209, PASCOMB Eleventh, 2360, VALGARS Seventh, 5562.

2nd ARN

DOAGNIS Fourth, 3636, PACASNA Second, 2362, DIALIVA Second, 8962.

3rd ZOM

SAMAPHA Ninth, 4400, VIROOLI Seventh, 3660, ANDISPI Tenth, 9236.

4th PAZ

THOTANF Tenth, 2360, AXZIARG Tenth, 3000, POTHNIR Twelfth, 6300.

5th LIT

LAZDIX1 First, 8630, NOCAMAL Seventh, 2306, TIARPAX Eleventh, 5802.

6th MAZ

SAXTOMP Fifth, 3620, VAVAAMP Twelfth, 9200, ZIRZIRD Fifth, 7220.

7th DEO

OBMACAS Fourth, 6363, GENADOL Third, 7706, ASPIAON Eleventh, 6320.

8th ZID

ZAMFRES Fifth, 4362, TODNAON First, 7236, PR1STAC Ninth, 2302.

9th ZIP

ODDIORG Third, 9996, CRALPIR Tenth, 3620, DOANZIN Ninth, 4230.

10th ZAX

LEXARPH Eleventh, 8880, COMANAN Seventh, 1230, TABITOM Ninth, 1617.

11th ICH

MOLPAND Tenth, 3472, VANARDA Sixth, 7236, PONODOL Third, 5234.

12th LOE

TAPAMAL Sixth, 2658, GEDOONS Eighth, 7772, AMBR1AL Second, 3391.

13th ZIM

GECAOND Tenth, 8111, LAPAR1N First, 3360, DOCEPAX Seventh, 4213.

14th VTA

TEDOOND Fifth, 2673, VIVIPOS Seventh, 9236, OOANAMB Twelfth, 8230.

15th OXO

TAHANDO Ninth, 1367, NOC1ABI Tenth, 1367, TASTOXO Twelfth, 1886.

16th LEA

COCARPT Second, 9920, LANACON Third, 9230, SOCHIAL Twelfth, 9240.

17th TAN

SIGMORF Second, 7623, AYDROPT Fifth, 7132, TOCARZI Ninth, 2634.

18th ZEN

NABAOM1 Fifth, 2346, ZAFASAI Seventh, 7689, YALPAMB Twelfth, 9276.

19th POP

TORZOXI Twelfth, 6236, ABAIOND Eighth, 6732, OMAGRAP Eleventh, 2388.

20th KHR

ZILDRON Fifth, 3626, PARZIBA Third, 7629, TOTOCAN Seventh, 3634.

21st ASP

CHIRSPA Twelfth, 5536, TOANTOM Eighth, 5635, VIXPALG Sixth, 5658.

22nd LIN

OXIDAIA Twelfth, 2232, PARAOAN First, 2326, CALZIRG Twelfth, 2367.

23rd TOR

RONOAMB Seventh, 7320, ON1Z1MP Seventh, 7262, ZAXANIN Eighth, 7333.

24th NIA

ORCAMIR Fourth, 8200, CHIALPS Tenth, 8360, SOAGEEL Twelfth, 8236.

25th VTI

MIRZIND Fourth, 5632, OBVAORS Second, 6333, RANGLAM Twelfth, 6236.

26th DES

POPHAND Twelfth, 9232, NIGRANA Eighth, 3620, BAZCHIM Twelfth, 5637.

27th ZAA

SAZIAMA Second, 7220, MATHULA Fourth, 7560, ORPAMB Fifth, 7263.

28th BAG

LABN1XP Tenth, 2630, FOCISNI Ninth, 7236, OXLOPAR Sixth, 8200.

29th RII

VASTR1M Third, 9632, ODRAXTI Fourth, 4236, GOMZIAM Fifth, 7635.

30th TEX

TAOAGLA Twelfth, 4632, GEMNIMB Fourth, 9636, ADVORPT Third, 7632, DOZiNAL Sixth, 5632.

From these names magical Sigils are formed. But it is extremely difficult adequately to describe how the names of these 91 Princes are formed and how their Sigils are drawn. In order to avoid excessive verbiage, the following four diagrams will demonstrate clearly their Sigils drawn on the Enochian Tablets. By comparing these diagram with the

SIGILS OF GOVERNORS

Enochian Tablets, it should be simple for the Z.A.M. to trace out these names and work out for himself the method by which they are formed from the letters of the Tablets. The customary division of Air, Fire, Water and Earth sub-elements or Lesser Angles does not enter into this matter, the Names and Sigils of the Princes, in any way whatsoever.

I stumbled on this formula accidentally. Later, I discovered that Crowley had worked them out years earlier, and published the Sigils in one of the Equinox volumes. I had seen this many years before my own discovery, but at that time his sigils and findings meant little to me. There are some discrepancies between Crowley's versions of the sigils and my own. Whose are more accurate, I cannot determine at this time. Nearly 50 years have elapsed since I worked on this particular problem, and my memory does not tell me much at present.

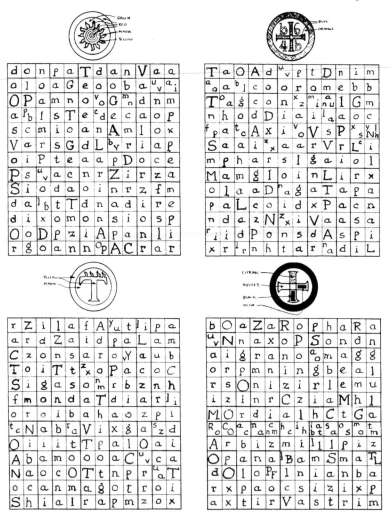

TABLETS WITH SIGILS

There is very little that actually can be said about this additional tabulation which will be of any immediate practical value to the Z.A.M. If the whole scheme of the Enochian Tablets is studied in all its innumerable ramifications and an earnest endeavour made to correlate the information given here to those Tablets, then the student will discover for himself many facts of tremendous importance and significance. Unless one is well-versed in this subject, any of these matters described at greater length could appear as trivial.

But this much may be said. By studying the classical attributions of the Egyptian Gods to the squares, and by taking the Gods which are allocated to the several squares to which the Names of any of the above mentioned Governing Princes are attributed, it is possible to construct an invocation composed of the formulae of these Gods. It will comprise a species of continuous invocation of the forces of the Atziluthic world.

For example, one of the Sigils of these Princes may pass through several letters, to which squares are attributed the Goddess Isis, Nephthys, Osiris two times, Kabexnuv and Horus two times, and Hathor. An invocation of these mighty forces, vibrating their names in their Coptic attributions will serve as a most potent conjuration of the Angel whose Sigil is thus being traced.

Again, the transliteration of the letters of these Names into Hebrew makes it possible to give the correct colours from the Rose to the depicted Sigils. It will also result, by the application of conventional Order methods, in the formation likewise of Telesmatic figures of great beauty and power. All of this must be worked out personally by the Z.A.M. who finds himself interested in this system. He will be amply repaid by any expenditure of time and energy in this direction.

The Thirty Aethyrs themselves represent a scheme considerably different from what we have been able to conceptualize through the Qabalah and its major glyph of the Ten Sephiroth. It is a more primitive scheme and, bluntly, it requires a good deal of manipulation to make attributions to the Tree.

The method of application of these Keys of the Thirty Aethyrs, together with the names of their Governing Princes is extremely simple, and in part has already been shown in Ritual "T."

Let the Z.A.M. prepare the Temple as in all his ceremonies of consecration and proper working. That is, wearing his Rose-Cross lamen, with Sword and Lotus Wand at hand, implements on the altar, let him thoroughly banish all forces from his chamber, purify with water, consecrate with fire - or use the method of Opening by Watchtower. Circumambulate, and adore the Lord of the Universe. Then let the invoking Lesser Ritual of the Hexagram be performed, preceded by the Qabalistic Cross and followed by the analysis of the Key-word I.N.R.I. Then let him to go to the West of the Altar, and facing East, recite the words of the Call of the 30 Aethyrs inserting the name of whichever Aethyr he proposes to deal with.

I feel I should mention, while on this topic, that Crowley discovered, when using these Calls to cross the Abyss, that this Call which seemed a curse turns out to be - seen from the "other side of the Abyss" - a glorious paean of praise and blessing.

In the event that the Z.A.M. proposes in his skrying in the Aethyrs, to deal with the Governing Princes and Archangels, let him follow the general invocation with a particular conjuration of the Names. A slight variation could be used of the Exhortation in the Portal Grade which invokes Lexarph, Comananu and Tabitom (who are the Three Ruling Angels of the Tablet of Union as well as the 10th Aethyr ZAX) inserting in their place the Names required.

Following his skrying in the Aethyr, let the Z.A.M. reconsecrate his Temple with Fire and Water, reverse circumambulate, Adoration, and the Banishing Ritual of the Pentagram.

With regard to the Sigils that occur let it be noted that the name LAZDIXI is the only one of the 91 Names that may be attributed to the squares or letters of the Tablets, in the formation of the appropriate Sigils, in two different ways. Both are correct; the original manuscripts are silent on this matter.

Likewise, it should be noted, when the Z.A.M. works out the Sigils for himself, that the name PARAOAN forms no Sigil. and actually does not appear on any of the Tablets. I can offer no suggestion or reason why this should be so. It seems that on each of the four Tablets, there are one or two squares left over, as it were, that is, left blank after all the Sigils of the other Names have been duly drawn. The name PARAOAN is drawn from all the Tablets, and is an Angel combining the qualities of all Four Terrestrial Tablets, or synthesizes them in some way.

Moreover, be it noted that the three Angels or Princes who are shown to be the Ruling Angels over the three Divisions of the Tenth Aethyr of ZAX are also the Angels who are given as the mighty Archangels ruling over the Mystical Tablet of Union.

It is also to be noted that in invoking the Aethyr itself, the name may be transliterated into Hebrew, and vibrated while tracing its Sigil on the Rose.

PART TWO OF THE ADDENDUM TO THE BOOK OF THE CONCOURSE OF THE FORCES

(Being an exposition of the third section of the Enochian system - the Sigillum Dei Aemeth.)

One of the first important results of the ceremonial skrying of Sir Edward Kelley and Dr. John Dee was the obtaining and construction of the SIGILLUM DEI AEMETH. In this connection it is interesting to note that of these words of The Seal of the God of Truth, the word Aemeth equals the Hebrew word for Truth. And these letters reversed give us the word Thmaa (Themis), which is the name of Her who stands before the Face of the Gods in the place of the Threshold. She is the Guardian of the Hall of the Dual Manifestation of Truth. Hence, this Sigillum Dei Aemeth is one especially under her guidance and presidency.

Aleph, Mem and Tau, are the three letters representing the three elements of Air, Water, and Earth. Shin representing Fire the holy spirit, is not represented directly in the name of this Sigil. However, it is implicit for the Holy spirit is Truth and overshadows the other elements of the Sigil like the brooding Spirit of God. And when the truth of the Sigil dawns on the mind, the Fire of the Spirit breaks through and illuminates the mind.

The Seal itself is a highly complex pantacle, which Dee and Kelley were instructed to make of pure wax, about 27 inches in circumference. It bears what is, at first sight, a confused medley of heptagons and heptagrams thrown in juxtaposition with innumerable crosses, numbers and letters, and a pentagram. It requires only a little attention to realize that this chaos is but a seeming one, though a good deal of careful attention is required in order to disentangle the secret of its formation. For the whole ensemble is a brilliant and highly ingenious piece of synthesis, combining diverse ideas in which all the rules of acrostics, permutations, and magical squares are alternately employed.

In the following description in these pages, it would be well to glance periodically at the Sigillum so as to be able to follow intelligently. Each step of deciphering should be referred to the reproduction of the Sigillum so that each step may be clearly understood.

Moreover, let it be remembered that the description which here follows is but a surface view of the whole, and that further meditation could disclose many other interesting and significant facts.

Around the extreme edge of the Seal's circumference is a series of numbers and letters. From these numbers,.the hieroglyphs or sigils which are attributed to the Enochian Tablets may be deciphered, as shown in Ritual X. They yield the names of the Great Elemental Kings or Angel Overseers who keep guard over the Watch-Towers.

VOLUME TEN

Within this circle of letters and numbers, occur seven symbols with other letters and numbers. Giving them with their formal astrological significance and Enochian names they are as follows:

1.	**Galas - Saturn**	♄ 5.
2.	**Gethog - Jupiter**	♃ 24.
3.	**Thaoth - Mars**	♂ 30.
4.	**Horlwn - Sun**	☉ 2/.
5.	**Innon - Venus**	♀ 9.
6.	**Aaoth - Mercury**	☿ /4.
7.	**Galethog - Luna**	☽ ☿

It was after these seven planetary symbols had been dictated that one of the communicating Angels remarked significantly: "Seven rest in seven; and the seven live by seven. The seven govern the seven, and by seven all government is."

In short, this Sigillum Dei Aemeth is essentially a synthetical glyph of the septenary forces of the planets, which it analyzes at great length and with much detail in each of its several planes. The application of Order teaching - Hebrew letters, names, geomantic symbols and sigils, Tarot cards and their Dominion in the Heavens in the appropriate colours - to the skeletal form of the Dee-Kelley skrying expands it into a much more coherent and workable system. After all, precisely this was done by the original founders of the Order to the bare bones of the Four Elemental Tablets, which in their original form in the British Museum Manuscripts bear only the faintest resemblance to the comprehensive and magnificent system as developed by the Order. In providing this analysis, I shall quote from some of the alleged speeches of the communicating Angels, as some of them are of great beauty and power.

Continuing the description of the letters of the Sigillum, and working inwards from the circumference to the centre, we next find a double Heptagon, each facet of which is divided into seven compartments, each containing a letter. The point of this Heptagon is uppermost. From the diaries of Dr. Dee, it would appear that these were dictated line by line, and Kelley, the seer, would report that these letters were manifested to his vision as baskets of letters by the great Archangel Uriel. They appeared in this order:

> **Z l l R H I a**
> **a Z C a a o b**
> **P a u p n h r**
> **h d m h i a i**

The next line was communicated by putting them in this order

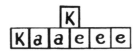

The sixth basket was seen thus:

And the seventh basket in this circular form:

Now this final line or basket of letters was deemed to be of such lofty significance that Uriel uttered this fine passage: "Those seven letters are the seven Seats of the One and Everlasting God. His seven secret Angels proceeding from every letter and cross so formed; referred in substance to the Father; in forme to the Sonne; and inwardly to the Holy Ghost."

Incidentally, note the description of these names having reference, in the case of the substance to the Father, the form to the Son, and the inward essence to the Holy spirit, and compare it with an almost identical description given by NALVAGE in the first part of this Addendum, with reference to the Round Table which commenced "Zodire Mozod lada." It seems a characteristic of all Enochiana as it were.

"Look upon it. It is one of the Names which thou hast before; every letter containing an Angel of Brightness; comprehending the seven inward powers of God, known to none but Himself. A sufficient BOND to urge all creatures to Life or Death, or anything else contained in this world. It banishes the wicked, expelleth evil spirits, qualifieth the Waters, strengtheneth the Just, exalteth the righteous, and destroyeth the wicked. He is One in Seven. He is twice Three. He is Seven in the whole. He is almighty. His name is everlasting; His truth cannot fail. His glory is incomprehensible. Blessed be His name. Blessed be Thou, O God, for ever."

By putting the above letters together in seven ordered lines, in the form of a square, we obtain the following figure. The Angel further remarked of this arrangement that "every letter containeth or comprehendeth the number of 72 virtues." It is important to recall that 72 equals the number of Angels of the Quinaries, the Shem-hamphoresh.

Z	l	l	R	H	i	a
a	Z	C	a	a	c	b
P	a	u	P	n	h	r
h	d	m	h	i	a	i
K	K	a	a	e	e	e
i	i	e	e	l	l	l
e	e	l	l	M	G	✛

For convenience sake, we will label this figure as the Archangelic Square.

Beginning with the letter Z in the upper left hand corner and reading all the way down the file, and including the first letter of the second horizontal file, we find spelled the name of Zaphkiel the Archangel of Binah and the Sphere of Saturn. Beginning with the Z on the second line and following a similar procedure, the result turns out to be Zadkiel, the Archangel of Chesed, and the Sphere of Tzedek or Jupiter. Then follow, commencing in each instance with an upper case letter, Camael, the Archangel of Geburah and the Sphere of Madim, Mars; Raphael the Archangel of Shemesh, Sun; Haniel the Archangel of Netzach and the sphere of Nogah, Venus; Michael the Archangel of Hod, and the sphere of Kokab, Mercury; and Gabriel, the Archangel of Yesod, and the sphere of Levanah, the Moon.

Malkuth is symbolized, without any other attribution or description, by the concluding Cross, and in Enochian symbolism, as Ritual X testifies, the Cross is always read as "th"as Tau the letter of Earth. And the idea of Earth as the epitomization of the foregoing names is further suggested by the fact that the whole figure is to be constructed of wax. Moreover, on the reverse side of the Sigillum Dei Aemeth, Malkuth is further summarized by this figure:

AGLA, a notariqon of "Thou art mighty forever, O Lord." And AGLA, be it noted, is the Name of Power vibrated to the North in the Lesser Ritual of the Pentagram.

This completes one way of reading the letters in the Square. As the archangel Uriel said, however, in the above-mentioned quotation, there are several ways of viewing these letters in the formation of Names. I content myself for the moment with the above, leaving to the Z.A.M. the task of further working out these mysteries in the light of what has already been stated.

Before proceeding to the next part of the Sigillum, I must record another Angelic speech, this time made by Michael: "Mark this Mystery. Seven comprehendeth the Secrets of Heaven and Earth. Seven knitteth man's soul and body together (three in Soul and four in body.) In seven thou shalt find the Unity. In Seven thou shalt find the Trinitie. In seven thou shalt find the sum and proportion of the Holy Ghost. O God, O God, O God. Thy Name, O God, be praised ever, from Thy seven thrones, from Thy seven trumpets, and from Thy Seven Angels, Amen, Amen, Amen!"

Immediately under the Heptagon described above, there will be seen on the Sigillum seven sets of upper-case letters and figures.

These figures and letters are organized in a square on a later page.

These names comprise, according to the Angel "seven names of God, not known to the angels, neither can they be spoken of or read of man. These Names bring forth Seven Angels (1), the governors of the heavens next unto us. Every letter of the Angels' names bringeth forth seven daughters (2). Every daughter bringeth forth her daughter (3); every daughter her daughter bringeth forth a son (4). Every son hath his son (5)." This would apparently indicate that there are five sets of hierarchical names. In the Order system, five relates to the letters of the Pentagrammaton, Yod Heh Shin Vau Heh equals the five elements. Each set of names therefore is attributable to the five elements, ruling the four Elemental Tablets and the Tablet of Union.

In the form above given, certainly it would appear that as names they cannot be spoken of or read by man. But by reference to the letters on the extreme circumference of the Sigillum, we find that 21 is E, 8 is L; also 30 is L. Thus by interpolating these letters instead of keeping the numbers, we acquire SAAIELEMEL, and BTZKASEL, etc. This makes the names a little less impossible to use, and by employing the now familiar rules of Enochian pronunciation, that is of vibrating each letter separately, a fairly sonorous vibration is obtained. These are the Divine Names ruling the spheres of the planets.

By treating these letters in much the same way as the former series, a similar square is obtained. This we shall call the Angelic Square to differentiate it from the Archangelic.

S	A	A	I²¹₈	E	M	E	VENIT IN COELIS
B	T	Z	K	A	S	E	DUES NOSTER
H	E	I	D	E	N	E	DUX NOSTER
D	E	I	M	O	30	A	HIC EST
I²⁶	M	E	G	C	B	E	LUX IN AETERNUM
I	L	A	O	I²¹₈	V	N	FINIS EST
I	H	R	L	A	A	21/8	VERA EST HAEC TABULA

The mode of reading these letters is slightly different from that previously demonstrated. It is easier to describe it by tracing a Sigil than to use a large number of words, and I again give the square below with a line drawn in ink to show the procedure to be adopted.

If the same process is continuously followed, commencing immediately after each number, the Z.A.M. will obtain the following:

> **Sabathiel - the Angel ruling the sphere of Saturn.**
> **Zedekiel - the Angel ruling the sphere of Jupiter.**
> **Madimiel - the Angel ruling the sphere of Mars.**
> **Semeliel - the Angel ruling the sphere of Sol.**

There is an undoubted mistake occurring at this juncture. If these letters and names were dictated, then Kelley must have wrongly heard and written an L where S was intended in last name. The name involved is actually Semesiel - since Semes or Shemesh is the Hebrew word for Sun. However, if one changes this letter on the square, the effects obviously are far-reaching, for it changes also many other names obtained by means of other modes of permutation. This I have not cared to do, beyond noting the existence of the error.

> **Nogahiel - the Angel ruling the sphere of Venus.**
> **Korabiel - the Angel ruling the sphere of Mercury.**

Here again is an error, one no doubt more of vision than of hearing, in this instance. R is recorded where K is quite evidently intended. The name of Mercury in Hebrew is Kokab nor Korab - therefore the angelic name should be Kokabiel.

Levanael - the Angel of the sphere of the Moon.

Here clearly we have the beginning of a hierarchical system. God names have already been given, together with symbols of planets and the Enochian names of these spheres. Now we have Archangels and Angels, with servient hierarchies hereafter to be noted.

Referring back to the Angelic Square again, let me demonstrate a second method of permutation. Below I give the square again, with a line drawn diagonally from top left to bottom right to indicate the procedure to be followed. This yields the name STIMCUL.

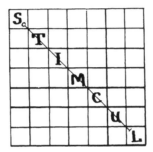

A similar process is to be employed for all other squares that is by drawing diagonal lines on the left of our first diagonal Name. This then yields BEIGIA, HEEOA, DMAL, ILI, IH, I. On the right of the first name, you will find AZDOBN, AKELE, IANA, ESE, ME, EL.

Should we refer to the Rose of the Z.A.M., we can make formal Sigils of their power in their true magical colours, as follows:

ANGELIC SIGIL

By referring to the Order document on Telesmatic Images, it will become evident that these letters may be used to call up telesmatic figures of no little beauty. Another mode of analysis can be pursued by taking the Gematria of the name AZDOBN, which in this case equals 720, (72x10) and by subjecting it to the Qabalah of Nine Chambers, as shown by a very similar technique with regard to the Sephiroth in Ritual "M" we obtain Gemini and Mercury. The name is thus clearly of a mercurial nature, with an octagram as its lineal figure, attributed to the Sphere of Hod, under the presidency of ELOHIM TZABAOTH, and in forming a telesmatic image, this idea should be carried into practice. Note too that its first two letters AZ are those of AZBOGAH, one of the Mercury Names.

Leaving these names for a moment, and referring back once more to the diagram of the Sigillum Dei Aemeth, we see that after the Unpronounceable Names of God which we obtained and formed into a square, there appears next a double Heptagram, point upwards, and inside this a double Heptagon with a facet upwards and point down. Within the points and borders of these lineal figures are further names and letters - four lines or separate divisions, in fact. If the Zelator Adeptus Minor refers to these, he will find around the seven-pointed figures, beginning with the uppermost names as follows: EL. ME, ESE, IANA, AKELE, AZDOBN, STIMCUL. (These should be written in both upper and lower case letters, though for legibility here I am using capitals only.) The second set of names beginning from the top is: I, HEEOA, IL, BEIGIA, I LI, STIMCUL, DMAL.

Quite clearly these are the names derived from the square by the second method of permutation, and we have now shown how these names were obtained, and whence they derive.

Let us apply a third method of permutation. This mode is similar to the second, except that it works from right top downwards to bottom left. The square is as below, and a diagonal line shows the name ESEMELI.

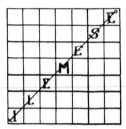

The names yielded by this method are, on the left: MADIMIEL, EKIEI, IZED, ATH, AB, S. This set of seven names are the third series within the Heptagon on the Sigillum, immediately beneath or within those listed before.

Going back to our method of presenting the diagonal permutations of the Square, but this time working from the bottom upwards, we obtain on the right side: ILEMESE, HAGONEL, IOCLE, LIBE, AVE, AN, EL. These also will be found to be the final set of names enclosed by the Heptagon.

Two things should here be noted. The first is, that in Ritual "T," which is the Book of the 48 Calls, there is a reference to Irwin's manuscript which was alleged to have given certain names. Reference to the page whereon this occurs, will disclose the fact that some of the above-mentioned names are those referred to. Some of the others, however, I cannot place, such as GALVAH, MURFIRI, NAPSAMA, NALVAGE. I am not able to work out whence they derive, though all are names which figure prominently in the record of the Dee-Kelley skrying. Evidently they belong to one of the other systems - to the Round Table of Nalvage, or the Heptarchia Mystica.

Incidentally, note that the name Ave occurs, and that our tradition asserts that the Terrestrial or Elemental Tablets were delivered unto Enoch by the great Angel Ave.

Secondly, it will now fully be understood why I have not ventured to correct what appeared to be two mistakes. If on the big Angelic Square I had altered certain letters so as to produce accuracy in the spelling of KORABIEL and SEMELIEL, which are obviously incorrect, the alteration would entail similar changes in the names of at least four other angelic names. And the responsibility for doing this is too great for me to assume. It does suggest however a profitable and worthwhile field of research for the Z.A.M. who has more experience in skrying and astral projection.

To complete the analysis of the Sigillum, let it be noted that the centre consists of a double Pentagram, enclosing a cross. The letters there will be seen to be the hierarchical names obtained from the Angelic Square by the first mode of permutation. They are names of the Angels of the Planets with the Angel of Saturn, SABATHIEL, enclosing the others, as though to affirm the supernal and general nature of Saturn, as corroborated by the Ritual of the Hexagram, where the Saturn Hexagram is said to call forth the general powers of the

Macrocosm. Within the enclosing sphere of Sabathiel, are the Angels of Tzedek, Madim, Shemesh, Nogah, and Kokab, arranged about the points of the Pentagram. The initial capital letters of these five planets are placed within the point or angle itself, the remaining letters being spaced out from point to point. In the centre, placed about the arms of the Cross, receiving the influence of all, is the name of Levanael, the Angel of the Moon. The synthesis of them all is the Earth.

Enough now has been stated concerning this matter of Names, and the Z.A.M. with a little application can work out other series of names, in various combinations, for himself.

One more important point should be noticed. Inasmuch as the Book of the Concourse of the Forces states that the names of the Six Seniors and the King of each Tablet, attributed to the points of the Hexagram, represent the operation of the Planets through the elemental world, the Z.A.M. should employ, when working with the names of the Archangels and Angels from the Sigillum, the names of the King and Six Seniors. For this reason, that the names on the Sigillum represent the root and source of the forces which in the Terrestrial Watch-Towers are mixed and compounded with the elements. And the true attribution of the names of the King and Six Seniors to the planets is:

King, the central whorl on the Cross, to the Sun.

The names on the left half of the Linea Spiritus Sancti to Mars.

The names on the right half of the Linea Spiritus Sancti to Venus.

The name on the upper half of the Linea Dei Patris to Jupiter.

The name on the lower half of the Linea Dei Patris to Mercury.

The name on the upper half of the Linea Dei Filiique to Moon.

The name on the lower half of the Linea Dei Filiique to Saturn.

This completes the description of the form of, and the names upon, the Sigillum Dei Aemeth. The Heptarchia Mystica continues the same magical theme, as it were, by listing the 49 Angelorum Bonorum, and their servient ministers, who are under the governance of the Angels whose Names are shown in the Heptagon of the Sigillum. For instance, HAGONEL, is described as presiding over, within his particular sphere of government, a King named CARMARA and a Prince named BAREES, under whom are 42 ministers, to whose commandment the Sons of Light are subject. And the invocation of these 49 Good Angels are the contents of Liber Logaeth, a description of which, together with a summary of the Heptarchical Mystery, will comprise the third section of this Addendum, (which I have not had the time to finish.)

There appears, on the surface, to be no relationship existing between the names given in Part I of this Addendum and those on the Sigillum and those on the Tablets comprising the Round Table of Nalvage. They occupy different planes, with different characteristics.

THE PYRAMID GODS AND THEIR ATTRIBUTION
By
G.H. FRATER D.D.C.F.

(Note: The God-forms of CANCELLARIUS, HEGEMON, STOLISTES and DAD-OUCHOS are not used in the ENOCHIAN PYRAMIDS. The addition of the final Coptic (st) in a NAME indicates the more spiritual force, since it is attributed to KETHER. I.R.)

The colouring represents the synthesis of the attributions, and should be studied very carefully. They will be found complete in the colour plate section of this work.

The words appearing in dark type in the following table relate to the Elements and that which follows are the God Names and Neophyte Grade officers.

Spirit. Or one triangle of each element.

Osiris - Hierophant on Throne.

Water. Or three out of four. Water.

Isis - Praemonstrator.

Earth. Or three out of four. Earth.

Nephthys - Imperator.

Fire. Or three out of four. Fire.

Horus - Hiereus.

Air. Or three out of four. Air.

Aroueris - Past Hierophant. The Hierophant when off the Throne.

2 Water. 2 Earth.

Athor - Invisible station, Kerub of East.

2 Fire. 2 Water.

Sothis - Invisible station, Kerub of West.

2 Air. 2 Water.

Harpocrates - Invisible station between Altar and Hegemon.

2 Fire. 2 Earth.

Apis - Invisible station. Kerub of North.

2 Air. 2 Earth.

Anubis - Kerux.

2 Fire. 2 Air.

Pasht or Sekhet - Invisible station Kerub of South.

Fire. Water. Earth.

Ameshet - Invisible station N.E. Child of Horus.

Fire. Water. Air.

Ahephi - Invisible station S.W. Child of Horus.

Earth. Water. Air.

Tmoumathph - Invisible station S.E. Child of Horus.

Earth. Air. Fire.

Kabexnuv - Invisible station N.W. Child of Horus.

THE PYRAMID GODS

First. OSIRIS. Aeshoori. Ruleth above when of the Four Triangles each is a different Element. So that all four elements are united in one square, for he representeth the Spirit ruling in the Four Elements equally balanced. That is when Shin entereth, forming Yeheshuah. Shape: A Mummied God with winged mitre, scourge and phoenix wand.

Second. ISIS. Aeisch. Ruleth above when of the Four Triangles of the Pyramid, each is of the Element of Water, or when three out of the four are water. For she representeth that watery and moist nature which is the Throne of the Spirit. This is the Heh of YHVH, the Mother and Beginning. Shape: Goddess with Throne headdress. Lotus wand, and crux Ansata.

Third. NEPHTHYS. Nephthuseh. Ruleth above when of the Four Triangles of the Pyramid each is of the element of Earth, or when three out of the four are of Earth. For she representeth the final Heh of YHVH, that is the Bride and end. Shape: Goddess on an altar with headdress surmounted by a bowl. Bears Lotus Wand and Crux Ansata.

Fourth. HORUS. Hoor. Ruleth above when the Four Triangles of the Pyramid or three out of the Four are of the Element of Fire. For he representeth the letter Yod of YHVH, the fiery and avenging force of the Spirit, the opposer of the infernal and devouring fire. Shape: God with Hawk's head and double mitre. Phoenix wand and Crux Ansata.

Fifth. AROUERIS. Araoueri. Ruleth above when of the Four Triangles of the Pyramid each is of the element of Air or three out of the Four. For he representeth the Vau of YHVH, and is as it were the Prince and Regent for Osiris. Shape: A God with double mitre, bearing Phoenix wand and Crux Ansata.

Sixth. ATHOR. Ahathoor. Ruleth above when of the Four Triangles of the Pyramid two be of Earth. She therefore representeth the first Heh and final Heh of YHVH, and uniteth the rule of Aeisch and Nephthuseh, Isis and Nephthys. Shape: A Goddess with disc and plumes between horns surmounting headdress. Bears Lotus Wand and Crux Ansata.

Seventh. SOTHIS. Shaeoeu. Ruleth above when of the Four Triangles of the Pyramid two be of Water and two of Fire. She therefore representeth Yod Heh of YHVH, and uniteth the rule of Aesisch and Hoor, Isis and Horus. Shape: Goddess with a Cow's head, disc, and plumes between horns. Lotus Wand and Crux Ansata.

Eighth. HARPOCRATES. Hoorpokrati. (This is Harpocrates, who is the younger Horus, the Lord of Silence.) Ruleth above when of the Four Triangles of the Pyramid, two be of Water and two of Air. He therefore representeth Vau Heh of YHVH, and uniteth the rule of Aeisch and Aroueri, Isis and Aroueris. Shape: Youthful God with double mitre, long curling tress of hair with left forefinger on lip.

Ninth. APIS. Ahapshi. Ruleth above when of the Four Triangles of the Pyramid two be of Earth and two of Fire. He therefore representeth Yod Heh of YHVH, and uniteth the rule of Nephthusch and Hoor, Nephthys and Horus. Shape: God with Head of Bull and disk between the Crook and scourge in hand.

Tenth. ANUBIS. Anoubi. Ruleth above when of the Four Triangles of the Pyramid two be of Earth and two of Air. He representeth Vau Heh of YHVH, and uniteth the rule of Nephthusch and Aroeouri, Nephthys and Aroueris. Shape: Goddess with Lioness' head, crowned with the disc and with Lotus Wand and Crux Ansata.

Eleventh. THARPESH. Ruleth above, when of the Four Triangles of the Pyramid two be of Fire, and two of Air. She therefore representeth Yod Vau of YHVH, and uniteth the rule of Horus and Aroueris. Shape: Goddess with Lioness head, crowned with disc and with Lotus Wand and Crux Ansata.

Twelfth. AMESHET or Emsta Ameshet. Ruleth above when of the Four Triangles of the Pyramid there be of these three elements partaking in any proportion, viz: Fire, Water and Earth. He therefore representeth Yod Heh Heh (f) of YHVH, and uniteth the rule of Horus, Isis, Nephthys, Sothis and Apis. Shape: A mummied God with human head.

Thirteenth. HAP1. Ahephi. Ruleth above when of the Four Triangles of the Pyramid, there be these three elements partaking in any proportions, viz: Fire, Water, and Air. He therefore representeth Yod Heh Vau of YHVH, and uniteth the rule of Horus, Isis, Aroueris, Sothis, Harpocrates, Tharpesh. Shape: A God, male, with an Ape head.

Fourteenth. TMOUMATHPH. Ruleth above, when of the Four Triangles of the Pyramid, there be these three elements, partaking in any proportion; Water, Air, Earth. He therefore representeth the rule of Isis, Aroueris, of Nephthys. He represeneth Heh Vau Heh (f) of YHVH, and uniteth the rule of Hoorpokrati, Ahathoor, and Anoubi. Shape: A God mummied with head of dog or jackal.

Fifteenth. KABEXNU V. Ruleth above when of the Four Triangles of the Pyramid, there be these three elements; Fire, Air, Earth, partaking in any proportion. He therefore representeth Yod Vau Heh (f) of YHVH, and uniteth the rule of Hoor, Aroueris, and Nephthys, of Tharpesh, Ahephi and Anubis. Shape: A God mummied, with hawk's head.

These be the Gods of Egypt who rule above the Pyramids of the Sixteen servient Angels and squares of each Lesser Angle, and in the middle of each pyramid is the sphynx of its power.

Revere then the sacred symbols of the Gods, for they are the Word manifested in the Voice of Nature.

These be the Elohim of the Forces, and before their faces the forces of Nature are prostrate.

GODS OF EGYPT AND THE ENOCHIAN TABLETS (CIRCA 1895)

By

V.H. FRATER A.P.S.

To study the rule of the GODS OF EGYPT over the subservient squares of the ENOCHIAN TABLETS, I have drawn two diagrams showing:

On the first, the 1 12 squares governed by the 11 GODS given first in order in The Book of the Concourse of the Forces.

On the Second, the 144 squares ruled by the last four there mentioned. (Both diagrams are now missing owing to the passage of time, but the enterprising student can, with close attention to the text reconstruct these drawings by himself. I.R.).

In the first diagram, the squares are coloured appropriately to the Element - ruling Powers of their respective Gods and Goddesses. Thus, squares ruled by OSIRIS are shown with an equilibriated cross of the elements in gold, traced upon them on a white ground.

Squares ruled by ISIS are blue - Water
Squares ruled by NEPHTHYS are black - Earth
Squares ruled by HORUS are red - Fire
Squares ruled by AROUERIS are yellow - Air
Squares ruled by AHATHOR are olive - Water and Earth
Squares ruled by SOTHIS are violet - Water and Fire
Squares ruled by HARPARCRAT are green - Water and Air
Squares ruled by APIS are russet - Earth and Fire
Squares ruled by ANUBIS are orange - Air and Fire.

In the second diagram, the rule of the other four Gods is shown in a similar way; but the colour used is that of the Element unequilibriated, in the square over which the God rules, thus:

AMESHET squares are BLACK because EARTH is unequilibriated, Water, Fire, Earth.
AHEPHI squares are YELLOW because AIR is unequilibriated, Water, Fire, Air.
TMOUMATHPH squares are BLUE because WATER is unequilibriated, Earth, Air, Water.
KABEXNUV squares are RED because FIRE is unequilibriated, Earth, Air, Fire.

To have shown all these squares thus coloured in the same set of Tablets would have created considerable confusion, and have rendered it impossible to grasp the detail in what may be perhaps called a "coup d'oeuil." The same result would follow had one endeavoured even to colour the 144 squares governed by the above four Gods, in tints appropriate to the mixture of the Elements.

At a glance, what strikes the attention on looking at the first diagram, is the general harmony and balance of colour in the four angles. Now turn the diagram through an arc of 45° against the Sun, and you have a map of the Elemental Empire - for each quadrangle there naturally falls to the point of the compass which is the habitation of its Element:

The Fiery Quadrangle is to the right or EAST
The Airy Quadrangle is to the left or WEST
The Earthy Quadrangle is to the bottom or SOUTH
The Watery Quadrangle is to the top or NORTH.

Hence we may speak of the following lesser angles as CARDINAL, viz: AIR OF AIR WATER OF WATER - FIRE OF FIRE - EARTH OF EARTH; and in the Cardinal lesser angles do the FOUR GREAT GODS hold their prime sway.

In the WEST - AROUERIS
In the NORTH - ISIS
In the EAST - HORUS
In the SOUTH - NEPHTHYS.

In every lesser angle, there is one square that may be termed the 'PRIME' Square of the Lesser Angle. This Prime Square is always the same in any of the four sets of lesser angles of the same element: as AIR OF AIR - AIR OF WATER - AIR OF EARTH - AIR OF FIRE. It is the right hand upper square in the watery and fiery lesser angles and the left hand square in the airy and earthy lesser angles.

This Prime Square is always ruled by the God of the Element of the Lesser Angle. Hence AROUERIS rules the Prime Square of the AIR lesser Angle of every quadrangle - ISIS of the Watery Lesser Angles - HORUS of the four fiery Lesser Angles - and NEPHTHYS governs the Prime Square of every earthy lesser Angle.

Which is the Prime Square of every lesser angle is determined by the horizontal and vertical forces corresponding to the element of the lesser angle. It is determined by the vertical fiery Kerubic Force, and the horizontal rank of Cardinal or Fiery Signs. It is therefore the FIRE of FIRE of the element of the quadrangle to which it belongs.

In the Cardinal Lesser Angles, the Cardinal Gods rule every square in both the column and the rank corresponding to the element of the Tablet. Thus, of the 16 squares, they rule no less than seven and enclose two sides of the Square. Note, too, that in each Cardinal Lesser Angle, a diagonal line of squares governed by three Gods of the second category proceeds from the 'Prime Square.' These three Gods are those which unite the rule of the God of the Prime Square with that of the God of the other elements.

There is in this a strange point worth noticing. Take the West and North lesser angles and you will observe that the Element hostile to each is only shown in the square opposed to and furthest from the prime square. Thus, in AIR, the hostile element EARTH is only seen in the ANUBIS square - Citrine; and in the Watery Lesser Angle, the hostile FIRE is only seen in the violet SOTHIS square. It is as though the AIR and the WATER, even when preponderating, made use of their mobility and volatility to escape from their respective enemies! AIR from EARTH - WATER from FIRE.

With the lower Elements, it is otherwise. In the South, we see the NEPHTHYS squares endeavouring to envelope ANUBIS, while in the East, the squares of HORUS strive to overwhelm the SOTHIS squares. It is as if these elements by their respective ponderosity and violence strove to wipe out an inimical nature. Is not this a natural and observable truth?

These four Cardinal Angles alone, of the whole 16, contain no square ruled by OSIRIS. That even and equilibriated force is there nowhere to be found. Unbalanced force is at its utmost violence, and the rule of the Four Great GODS is concentrated there where greatest power is needed. It is as if the Prime Squares of these Cardinal Angles were the sources of their respective elemental forces, whence they issue to continue in varying proportions one with another until they result in producing Osirian molecules of WATER, EARTH, FIRE, and AIR.

Passing to the other lesser angles of the Tablets, we find various pairs and quaternions resembling one another more or less completely until we find absolute identity in EARTH of FIRE and FIRE of EARTH, which only differ in having opposite squares for their Prime Squares - thus making a difference of right and left when viewed from that spot as a point of vantage.

Arranged as quaternaries beginning with the least equilibriated we get:

1. WATER of AIR - AIR of WATER - AIR of EARTH - WATER of FIRE
2. EARTH of AIR - FIRE of WATER - FIRE of EARTH - EARTH of
   FIRE
3. FIRE of AIR - EARTH of WATER - WATER of EARTH - AIR of FIRE

The last of these quaternions is composed of the four central lesser angles, placed around the Tablet of Union. They join, as it were, a Macrocosm of which an Osiris pyramid is the symbol - and a Microcosm to which the whole diagram acts as Macrocosm.

VOLUME TEN

THE RULE OF OSIRIS

We know that OSIRIS governs those Pyramids or Squares which contain all the Elements. From this it follows that He cannot have rule in the lesser angle of any Tablet which is attributed to the Element of the Tablet itself. It also follows that He cannot have rule in any square of ARIES, for he is the Fire of Fire - nor of GEMINI which is Air of Air, nor of SCORPIO which is Water of Water, nor of TAU which is Earth of Earth. But he rules two squares in every other lesser angle, and two squares of the other nine Signs and three Elements.

OSIRIS further rules six squares under each Kerub; but he governs no square in the Airy Tablet under the MAN; none in the EARTH Tablet under the BULL; nor in the WATER Tablet under the EAGLE; nor in the FIRE Tablet under the LION. Similarly OSIRIS rules no square in the AIR Tablet in the rank of Common Signs; in the WATER Tablet in the Kerubic rank; and in the Cardinal Rank of the FIRE Tablet.

Let us now consider this OSIRIAN rule as it affects the whole set of Tablets. We have seen that the Cardinal Quaternion of lesser angles contains no sign of OSIRIS. Of the other three sets, those numbered 1 and 2 form a sort of ring round the central number 3 -intermediate in position between this last and the Cardinal Four; and as we shall see, intermediate, also, in the state of balance. In Quaternion number 1, we see the OSIRIS squares close together as if entering into the lesser angle at a point opposite to the Prime Square - as if advancing against it side by side. This is the Dawn of Light.

In Quaternion number 2, the OSIRIAN Light has advanced to the centre and dispersed the inferior lights to the corners of the lesser angles. But they are not yet balanced. There is greater apparent equilibrium - it is the beginning of the end, the turning point.

In Quaternion number 3, OSIRIS has conquered the square and established his sway more completely. He has disseminated his Light throughout and has established a peace with the ruler of the Prime Squares.

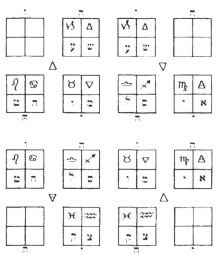

This presumption is still further borne out by a further analysis of the squares governed by OSIRIS in the lesser angles. In Quaternion number 1, which consists of the Airy and Watery lesser angles, the squares seized by the OSIRIS force are chiefly in the LION's column and in the elemental rank. That is to say, that the weakest force in the lesser angle is the one first subjugated.

Water of Air

Yod Heh (f) with Yod having Osiris square for the Element, and Osiris square under Heh (f) for the Cardinal sign.

Air of Water

Yod Heh (f) with Yod having Osiris square for the Element, and Osiris square under Heh (f) for the Cardinal sign.

Air of Earth

Yod Heh (f) with Yod having Osiris square for the Kerubic sign, and Osiris square under Heh (f) for the Cardinal sign.

Water of Fire

Vau Heh (f) with Vau having Osiris square for the Element, and Osiris square under Heh (f) for the Common sign.

The above tablet shows that eight OSIRIS squares are distributed thus among the Kerubic and horizontal influences.

Under YOD three, and in the Cardinal Rank, three.
Under HEH one, and in the Kerubic Rank, one.
Under VAU one, and in the Common Rank, one.
Under HEH (f) three, and in the Elemental Rank, three.

That is, that the fiery and earthy forces of these watery and airy lesser angles are the first to become equilibriated. Quaternion number 2 works out the exact converse of this. There, the watery and Airy forces of the fiery and earthy lesser angles are the first to be equilibriated. In Quaternion number 3, however, all this is rectified.

Fire of Air

Heh Heh (f) with Heh having Osiris square for the Element and Osiris square under Heh (f) for the Kerubic sign.

Earth of Water

Yod Vau with Yod having Osiris square for the Common sign, and Osiris square under Vau for the Cardinal sign.

Water of Air

Vau Yod with Vau having Osiris square for the Cardinal sign, and Osiris square under Yod for the Common sign.

Air of Fire

Heh (f) Heh with Heh (f) having Osiris square for the Kerubic sign, and Osiris square under Heh for the Element.

Under YOD two, and in the Cardinal Rank, two.
Under HEH two, and in the Kerubic Rank, two.
Under VAU two, and in the Common Rank, two.
Under HEH (f) two, and in the Elemental Rank, two.

The balance here, is nearly perfect; active forces ruling in passive lesser angles and passive forces in active.

The Zodiacal and Elemental emblems of the OSIRIS squares give the following figure:

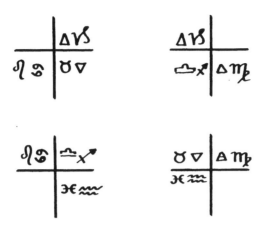

THE RULE OF ISIS - NEPHTHYS - HORUS - AROUERIS

Each of these four GODS rule a total of 13 squares, of which number more than half are concentrated in the appropriate Cardinal lesser angles. No less than seven squares of each of these Cardinal letter squares are ruled by the appropriate GOD. Thus in the Western lesser angle are seven AROUERIS squares; in the North, seven ISIS squares; in the East seven of HORUS and in the South, seven of NEPHTHYS.

This leaves six of each distributed over the whole of the other lesser angles. These sets of six contain each two sets of three - and each set is distributed in a similar manner, so that if we describe the two AROUERIS sets, the other three pairs will be easily grasped.

The first set of AROUERIS is distributed to the other three lesser angles of the AIR tablet, one to each - and they will be found at the points of intersection of the column and rank corresponding to AIR. The second set is distributed to the other three Tablets, one to each. They will be found in the lesser angles of AIR and at the points where the corresponding rank and column meet. They are the Prime Squares of these lesser angles.

This represents the organisation of the supreme authority of the Element of AIR throughout the Universe; the Supreme Power being concentrated in the AIRY Lesser

Angle of the AIR Tablet; with viceroys in each division of its kingdom, and embassies established in each of the other kingdoms. AROUERIS will be found to rule in no square allotted to a Sign that does not belong to the AIRY Triplicity, to the category of Common Signs and in no square allotted to Water, Earth, or Fire.

In the Western Lesser Angle, he rules the following squares:

AIR
LIBRA
AQUARIUS
GEMINI - PISCES - SAGITTARIUS - VIRGO
GEMINI being the PRIME SQUARE.

In all the other six lesser angles in which AROUERIS is found, he also rules the GEMINI Square. Hence, too, GEMINI is the Prime Square in all Airy Lesser Angles.

AROUERIS rules seven GEMINI squares altogether.

Similarly SCORPIO is the Prime ISIS Square, of which Sign she rules seven squares.

Similarly ARIES is the Prime HORUS Square, of which Sign he rules seven squares.

Similarly EARTH is the Prime NEPHTHYS Square, of which Sign she rules seven squares.

It will be noticed that there are 16 squares undereach Sign, and that almost half of those allotted to these four signs are governed by these Great GODS. They are further the Signs of which OSIRIS rules not a single square.

The whole of the Signs of the Squares ruled by these four Gods are shown below:

ISIS - SCORPIO - 7

NEPHTHYS - EARTH - 7

HORUS - ARIES - 7

AROUERIS - GEMINI - 7

TAURUS, CANCER, LEO, AQUARIUS, PISCES, WATER - 13 TAURUS, VIRGO, CAPRICORN, WATER, AIR, FIRE - 13 CANCER, LEO, LIBRA, SAGITTARIUS, CAPRICORN, FIRE - 13 VIRGO, LIBRA, SAGITTARIUS, AQUARIUS, PISCES, AIR - 13

THE RULE OF AHATHOOR - SHEOEU - ANOUBIHOORPARKRATI - AHAPSHI - THARPHESH

The GODS who rule only those squares in which two elements appear, and then in equal degree, have but a small dominion in the elemental Tablets. Each GOD rules only six squares, and in only two Tablets; three in each.

Every Tablet has nine squares ruled by one of these GODS. Every Cardinal Lesser Angle contains three such squares arranged diagonally from the Prime Square. Every other lesser angle has two squares ruled by the same GOD, while the squares of the Cardinal Lesser Angles are ruled each by a different GOD.

Each of these GODS, says The Book of the Concourse of the Forces, unites the rule of a pair of those in the preceding category.

Suppose we draw a line joining the West Lesser Angle to the North, that is, from the AROUERIS Lesser Angle to the ISIS Lesser Angle; it may be said to unite those two GODS. And the lesser angles through which it passes will be those which contain Harpocrates' squares, the GOD which unites the rule of ISIS and AROUERIS.

Along the bottom, AHAPSHI unites HORUS and NEPHTHYS and on the left, ANUBIS unites AROUERIS and NEPHTHYS. Then draw two diagonals, and the line joining AROUERIS and HORUS will cut the lesser angles containing THARPESH squares; while the other diagonal will show AMESHET uniting ISIS and NEPHTHYS.

The same uniting of the forces is shewn in another way. Take any lesser angle not Cardinal, and it will be seen that the two squares ruled by one of these six GODS is the synthesis of the other two. Thus in WATER of AIR, we get the blue Prime Square of ISIS and the yellow viceroyal square of AROUERIS and the two green squares of HARPOCRATES. Or take AIR of FIRE and we get the red vice-regal square of HORUS. the yellow embassy or Prime Square of AROUERIS, and the orange square of THARPESH.

Next we consider the signs of the squares ruled by these GODS and we get the following arrangement shewing the same point again:

AHATHOR will be found to rule EARTH TAURUS 2; WATER 2; SCORPIO.
SHEOEU will be found to rule ARIES CANCER 2; LEO 2; SCORPIO.
HOORPARKRATI will be found to rule GEMINI PISCES 2; AQUARIUS
2; SCORPIO.
AHAPSHI will be found to rule ARIES CAPRICORN 2; FIRE 2; EARTH.
ANOUBI will be found to rule GEMINI AIR 2; VIRGO 2; EARTH.
THARPHESH will be found to rule ARIES LIBRA 2; SAGITTARIUS 2; GEMINI.

This also shows that this group has the same rule as OSIRIS, and in addition 3 squares of those signs over which OSIRIS has no rule at all, viz: ARIES 3; GEMINI 3; SCORPIO 3; EARTH 3. This is a much better state of affairs than is shown in the squares under the ISIS class. It shows that the states symbolised by these pyramids are a step nearer Osirification than the former, and the GODS of less Elemental Power are needed for their governance.

THE RULE OF AMESHET - AHEPHI - TMOUMATHPH - KABEXNUV

These four Gods who rule squares in which three diverse elements occur, rule 144 out of the 256 subservient squares, having an individual rule over 36 each. Every GOD rules 12 squares in each of Three Tablets, but does not appear in the Tablet of the Element hostile to its own unequilibrated one.

Thus AHEPHI rules squares of WATER, FIRE, AIR, and therefore is not met with in the EARTH Tablet. If we take, as I think we are right in taking, these GODS' rule to be rather of the nature of the unbalanced Element, than of either of the others, then AHEPHI is more airy and corresponds to AROUERIS - AMESHET to NEPHTHYS - TMOUMATHAPH to ISIS - and KABEXNUV to HORUS - and they may be looked upon as governing forces more particularly derived from the appropriate lesser angles. If so, we find AHEPHI's subject-force derived from the AIR Tablet passing to the Watery and to the Fiery - KABEXNUV's rule from the Fiery through the Earthy to the Airy, establishing a right hand whorl of the masculine forces. If the rule of the other two GODS is similarly examined, a left hand whorl of the female forces is discovered.

Every Cardinal Lesser Angle contains three pairs of squares ruled by these GODS, but every other lesser angle contains two sets of five ruled each by one of them, by the GOD corresponding to the Lesser Angle, except in the case of the Lesser Angle of the opposing Element, where the GOD of the Tablet is absent and the ruling GODS are those of the opposite hostile Elements.

Thus take the Earthy Tablet of Nephthys - AHEPHI, WATER, FIRE and AIR, is absent. In FIRE of EARTH, we find AMESHET, WATER, FIRE, and EARTH, ruling 55 squares, and KABEXNUV, EARTH, AIR, AND FIRE, ruling the otherfive. In WATER of EARTH, we find AMESHET, WATER, FIRE, and EARTH-and TMOUMATHAPH, EARTH, AIR and WATER, while in the AIR of EARTH we get the GODS TMOUMATHAPH and KABEXNUV of watery and fiery rule respectively - and so with all the others.

Each of these Gods is said to unite the rule of a certain three of the ISIS category. Let us examine this by the light of these diagrams, taking the GOD KABEXNUV for our illustration. KABEXNUV unites the rule of HORUS, NEPHTHYS, and AROUERIS, and here we find him ruling 12 squares in the Tablet appropriate to each of these three GODS. But not only so, he is also found in the three corresponding lesser angles of each of these Tablets - thus binding together the forces of those GODS in the Lesser Angles of each Tablet, and also in the Tablets as a whole.

KABEXNUV further unites the rule of AHAPSHI, ANUBIS and THARPHESH. This too is shown on the Tablets, for the nine Lesser Angles in which alone KABEXNUV squares are formed from the three lines of squares which respectively contain the squares of those GODS, ANUBIS on the left, AHAPSHI at the bottom and THARPHESH diagonally. The disposition of the squares in the given lesser angle, other than the Cardinal ones, is by this rule. Every GOD rules three squares in a column and three squares in the corresponding rank. Two GODS in one lesser angle, and the ranks and columns ruled over those of the elements not in the title of the lesser angle. Thus in the lesser angle FIRE of WATER, the VAU and HEH (final) columns and ranks will be occupied.

The central quaternion of lesser angles shews the concentration of male and female agencies in perfect equilibriation round the Tablet of Union. Every other quaternion shews dispersion of force - not its concentration.

We now come to the analysis of Signs ruled by these four GODS. They give a very peculiar table, and show how much nearer Osirification they are than any others. This shews that each of these GODS rules 30 squares of those Signs in which OSIRIS holds sway against six of those in which he does not. If we contrast the classes of squares for the purpose of considering this Osirification, we get below, in tabular form, a comparison:

The ISIS Class rules 52 squares - 28 non OSIRIS. Percentage of latter 53.8.
The ATHOR Class rules 36 squares - 12 non OSIRIS. Percentage of latter 33.3.
The AMESHET Class rules 144 squares - 24 non OSIRIS. Percentage of latter 16.6.
The OSIRIS Class rules 24 squares - 0 non OSIRIS. Percentage of latter 0.0.

From these considerations of the signs of the squares governed by the respective GOD, we find the signs grouped in pairs, except the non-OSIRIS squares. The same GOD always governs both members of these pairs in the same lesser angle, no matter to which class of GODS he may belong - that is. if you take any one member of any of these pair squares and notice by which GOD it is governed, you know that the other member of the pair is governed by the same GOD in the same lesser Angle.

Thus LEO - if you find a LEO square governed by ISIS, the CANCER square in the same lesser angle is also governed by ISIS and it further follows that the same set of GODS which rules one member of one of these pairs throughout the Tablets also rules the others.

Thus, TAURUS and WATER form a pair. The 16 TAURUS squares are thus ruled -OSIRIS 2 - ISIS 1 -NEPHTHYS 1 - ATHOR 2 - AMESHET 5 - TMOUMATHAPH 5: therefore the 16 water squares are ruled by the same set of GODS and in the same lesser angles.

The table below shows the GODS ruling in every Sign, and the Signs ruled by every God.

GODS RULING SIGNS AND SIGNS RULED BY EVERY GOD

Osiris

There are 2 squares in each of the following signs or elements, Taurus, Cancer, Leo, Virgo, Libra, Sagittarius, Capricorn, Aquarius, Pisces, Fire, Water, Air, yielding a total of 24.

Isis

There is 1 square in each of the following signs or elements, Taurus, Cancer, Leo, Aquarius, Pisces, Water, and 7 in Scorpio, yielding a total of 13.

Nephthys

There is 1 square in each of the following signs or elements, Taurus, Virgo, Capricorn, Fire, and 7 in Earth yielding a total of 13.

Horus

There is 1 square in each of the following signs or elements. Cancer, Leo, Libra, Sagittarius, Capricorn, Fire, and 7 in Aries, yielding a total of 13.

Aroueris

There is 1 square in each of the following signs or elements, Virgo, Libra, Sagittarius, Aquarius, Pisces, Air, and 7 in Gemini, yielding a total of 13.

Ahathoor

There are 2 squares in each of the following signs or elements, Taurus and Fire, and one each in Scorpio and Earth, yielding a total of 6.

Sothis

There are 2 squares in each of the following signs or elements. Cancer and Leo, and one each in Aries and Scorpio, yielding a total of 6.

Harparcrat

There are 2 squares in each of the following signs or elements, Aquarius and Pisces, and one each in Gemini and Scorpio, yielding a total of 6.

Ahapshi

There are 2 squares in each of the following signs   or elements, Capricorn and F i r e , and one each in Aries and Earth, yielding a total of 6.

Anubis

There are 2 squares in each of the following signs or elements, in Scorpio and Air. and one each in- Gemini and Earth, yielding a total of 6.

Tharpesh

There are 2 squares in each of the following signs or elements, in Libra and Sagittarius, and one each in Aries and Gemini, yielding a total of 6.

Ameshet

There are 5 squares in each of the following signs or elements, Taurus, Cancer, Leo, Capricorn, Fire, Water, and 2 in each of Aries, Scorpio and Earth, yielding a total of 36.

Ahephi

There are 5 squares in each of the following signs or elements, Cancer, Leo. Libra, Sagittarius, Aquarius, Pisces and 2 each in Aries, Gemini and Scorpio, yielding a total of 36.

Tmoumathaph

There are 5 squares in each of the following signs or elements, Taurus, Virgo, Aquarius, Pisces, Water, Air, and 2 each in Gemini, Scorpio, and Earth, yielding a total of 36.

Kabexnuv

There are 2 squares in each of the following signs or elements, Aries, Gemini, Earth, and 5 each in Virgo, Libra, Sagittarius, Capricorn, Fire and Air, yielding a total of 36.

INSTRUCTION ON CHESSMEN
By
G.H. FRATERS D.D.C.F. AND N.O.M.
CHATURANGA AND SHATRANJ

The present European game of chess has been gradually developed from the more primitive form in which it reached Western civilisation. It came to us from the Arabs or Saracenic races who over-ran Spain in the eighth century.

These Arab races had a knowledge of the game for many centuries, and they are believed to have received it from the Persians and from ancient Egypt. The game in its essentials is found to exist in descriptions by the oldest poets of India.

In its oldest form traceable in literature its name is found in Sanskrit works as Chaturanga, from Chatur which is Four, and Ranga is members. Among the Saracens and Arabs, the name became Shatrangi. Introduced in Europe we find:

> **In France - Echecs**
> **In Italy - Seacci**
> **In England - Chess (perhaps from Chequered board on which it is played.)**
> **In Germany - Seach.**

In all forms the Board used is quite similar, being Square and divided into 8 x 8 or 64 squares.

The chess men too have not varied in number. 16 major pieces and 16 minor pieces or pawns.

In the Chaturanga these 32 men were divided equally between 4 players; two partners against two, generally green and black, against red and yellow. Each player had four pieces and four pawns. Dice were cast to determine which piece or pawn should be played. The earliest important change in the Game was the alteration made by combining the forces of the partners.

From that time, the Chaturanga out of India lost its chatur character, and was played by two persons, each with 16 pieces and pawns. This change brought in other changes, for whereas each partner used to have a King, when the two forces were combined one King had to be converted into a Minister or Vizier, who, in later times, became the Queen. In India, the names and titles of the pieces suggest a military ideal.

In Egypt the tendency was rather to look upon the pieces as Gods of various forces or natural powers.

Ancient Chaturanga. Four players, in pairs. Pieces and pawns arranged thus: King on the right, then Elephant, then a Horse, then Ship, and the Pawns were infantry. The Moves of the Element, with castle and Houdah on its back, and of the Knight, were unaltered for ages. Castling was unknown. Pawns moved one square forward only, but took diagonally. Dice were thrown to decide moves. Dice had four sides, marked on opposite sides with 4 and 3, or 5 and 2, making in each case 7.

The Brahmins abolished the use of dice.

Chaturanga is referred to in *Valurika's Ramayana*, Book 4, Chapter 51. It is also mentioned in one of the Sanskrit Puranas, where it is said that it was invented in the second age by the wife of Rawan, King of Lanka, that is Ceylon.

> **The Chaturanga Elephant has become our Castle,**
> **The Chaturanga Ship has become our Bishop,**
> **The Chaturanga Horse has become our Knight,**
> **The Chaturanga King remains King.**

But the second King has become our Queen. The Elephant and Ship, Castle and Bishop have exchanged places.

Perhaps the Elephant became Castle from the Houdah on its back. The ship was also formerly a chariot in some places.

In the oldest Chaturanga, Dice throwing:

> **If 2 were thrown, the player had to move the Ship.**
> **If 3 were thrown, the player had to move the Horse.**
> **If 4 were thrown, the player had to move the Elephant.**
> **If 5 were thrown, the player had to move the King or Pawn.**

Shatranji of Persia and Araby appears to have become well known in Persia about 1500 A.D. We then find that the game has become a contest between two players and 2 of the 4 Kings have become Ministers or Queens. The early title was Mantri or Farzin or Firz, hence it is supposed comes Vierge for Queen. The Castle and Bishop changed places.

This game is described by the Persian poet Firdansi; a copy of his book extant is dated 1486.

The Persians introduced the change of rank in a Pawn by reaching its eighth square.

In the third or European epoch, the modern game of chess was developed. The players being 2 only became quite defined.

It was laid down that the Queen should stand on her own colour, and that each player should have a white square at his right hand. Castling has been introduced, and each Pawn has been permitted to more either one or two squares at the first move.

The queening of a Pawn at the 8th square has been finally settled. The moves of the Queen and Bishop were much altered. Formerly the Queen could only move diagonally on her own colour, and the Bishop moving diagonally could only attack the next square but one. The Castles or Rooks were definitely placed at the extreme right and left.

The present moves are:

> **Pawns: 1 or 2 squares forward first move, one square only after, take diagonally forward, and never move back.**
> **King moves one square only in any direction.**
> **Bishop diagonally on his own colour only any number of squares if empty, forwards or backwards.**
> **Castle or Rook moves always in straight lines, not diagonally, and so moves over squares of both colours forwards and backwards and any distance if the squares are unoccupied.**

Queen moves in straight and diagonal lines, any distance over vacant squares, forward, or backwards, or laterally.

Knight moves in any direction but always to the square which may be described as two forward and one to side; or one diagonally and one forward or sideways so long as the designed place be vacant. It is immaterial whether the adjoining squares are occupied or not.

UPON THE ROSICRUCIAN RITUAL OF THE RELATION BETWEEN CHESS AND TAROT

By

G.H. FRATER S.R.M.D.

The modern game of Chess is derived from the scheme which follows; whence its name chess, from chequers. And like Tarot, originally the chess pieces were anciently small figures of the Egyptian Gods presenting the operation of the Divine Forces in Nature.

The chess pieces correspond to the Tarot Aces and Honours, thus, for the Chessmen, Tarot card, and Element:

> **King - Ace - Spirit**
> **Queen - Queen - Water**
> **Knight - King - Fire**
> **Bishop - Knight - Air**
> **Rook or Castle - Knave - Earth.**

Pawns, the potencies of the Ace combined with each of the other forces, the servant or viceroy of that force.

The pawns can only move one square at a time, and not two at the first move as in modern chess. The moves of the other pieces excepting the Queen are the same as those of modern chess. The move of the Queen in this scheme is unlike that of any piece in modern chess, for she controls only the 3rd square, from herself, in any direction - perpendicularly, horizontally, or diagonally, and can leap over any intervening piece. From which it results that she can check or control only 16 out of the 64 squares, including the one on which she stands, and these squares to which she can move are all of her own colour. Each elemental set of pieces then consists of: King, Queen, Knight, Bishop, Rook, and four pawns.

OFFICIAL RITUAL

The Correct Application of the Action of the Moveable Images Representing the Motion of The Ruling Angels Over the Servient Squares is Called The Plays or Raying of the Chequers of The Tablets.

Of the Chess King and the Tarot Ace. The move of this piece is one square every way, and answereth to the action of the Spirit wherever it goeth, commencing and initiating a fresh current. Whence represented by the motion of only one square in any direction and there staying for this purpose before moving onward. So that his action is not hurried, but represents a balanced movement. Yet in his beginning of action is he at first a mute force, and throned upon the water; as in the end of his action he is a life manifested and throned upon the earth. And herein is a mystery of the Lord Aeshoori when enthroned between Isis and Nephthys, thus representing the beginning and end of the action of him in whom end and beginning are not, but rather concealment and then manifestation. Herein is a great mystery of life,. for His Thrones are not in the two active elements, seeing that these are his horse and chariot of transition in the passage from concealment unto manifestation. This piece, then, is the symbolizer of the action of the potencies of the crosses on the Servient Squares.

Of the Chess Knight, the Tarot King. The move of this piece is three squares cornerwise every way and representeth the leaping motion of the flickering flame. Wherefore also is he not stopped in his course by a piece or an intervening square, even as Fire seizing on a matter speedily rendereth it transparent. This piece representeth the action of Fire as the Revealer of the strength of the Spirit, even as Hoor is the avenger of Aeshoori. It is a force potent and terrible, the King in the elemental operations.

Thus is opened the locked doors of matter and sheweth forth the treasure hidden therein. Therefore hath all life its beginnings in a Fire Celestial. And the number of squares covered by the move of the King in the midst of the Board (reckoning from the Square on which he standeth, but not including it) is 16 squares of which 8 are checked, and 8 are passed over.

Of the Chess Queen, the Tarot Queen. The move of this piece is unto every third square from her (reckoning the square whereon she standeth as the first) as well cornerwise, as well perpendicular, as horizontal. Thus again covering 16 squares out of a square of 25 squares, of which 8 are threatened, and 8 are passed over. But she threateneth not a piece upon the intervening square of her move. And her movement is as that of the waves of the sea, and (like the Knight) she is not hindered in her motion by a piece on an intervening square. This piece representeth the undulating action of water and of the sea, and she is ascribed unto the Great Goddess Isis, who is the Cherisher of Life.

The Chess Bishop or Fool, the Tarot Knight. The move of this piece is any number of squares cornerwise in any direction even unto the limits of the Tablet. He representeth the keen and swift wind, and he is ascribed unto Aroueris the God. He is stopped by any piece in his way, even as the wind is stopped by a material barrier. He representeth the swift vehicle of the Spirit.

The Chess Castle or Rook, the Tarot Knave. The move of this piece representeth the ponderous and formidable force of earth and its motion is any number of squares in a square direction, perpendicular or horizontal (but not cornerwise) even unto the limits of the boards.

It is ascribed unto Nephthys the Goddess. It representeth the completed action of the Spirit in matter, therefore is its movement square, and also stopped by intervening pieces, yet powerful from the length and breadth of its range.

The Pawns. The four pawns represent certain forces formed by the conjunction of the Spirit with each of the four elements severally, and they are severally ascrihed unto Ameshet, Ahephi, Tmoumathph, and Kabexnuv, who stand before the face of Aeshoori. And their movement is but one square forward, perpendicular, and they threaten one square forward diagonal on each side, thus formulatmg the symbol of the Triangle, for they each represent a mixture of three elements under the presidency of the Spirit. Therefore, each is as it were the servant of the God or Goddess, before whom he standeth yet they be all in a manner alike in action, although their Lords be different and each is the servant of the God or Goddess whose element is expressed in his symbol, without its contrary.

For in each set of 3 elements, taken together, two are contrary. Wherefore Ameshet (Water, Fire, Earth) is the servant of Nephthys, whose element Earth is expressed in his attribution without the contrary of Air.

Ahepi (Air, Fire, Water) equals Aroueris.
Tmoumathph (Water, Air, Earth) equals Isis.
Kabexnuv (Fire, Air, Water) equals Hoor.

Below is a further description of the Chess pieces. The pertinent element will be described in bold type, followed by the chess name, title and description.

Air

King, Socharis, Hawk with Osiris head dress.
Knight, Seb, Human head; Goose.
Bishop, Shu, Human head with feather.
Queen, Knousou, Goddess, human with vase.
Castle, Tharpesht, Lioness head with disc.

Water

King, Osiris, God with double crown - three weapons over chest.
Knight, Sebek, Crocodile headed.
Bishop, Hapimon, Fat God with water plants.
Queen, Thouerist, Hippopotamus' body crocodile head.
Castle, Shu, Cow head, disc horns.

Fire

King, Kneph, Ram-headed God, crowned.
Knight, Ra, Hawk disc.
Bishop, Toum, Human head, double crown.
Queen, Sati-Ashtoreth, Goddess.
Castle, Anouke, Goddess with crown.

Earth

King, Aeshoori, Mummied God, crook, scourge, Phoenix wand, whinged mitre.
Knight, Hoori, Hawk's head. Double mitre.
Bishop, Aroueris, Human, double mitre.
Queen, Isis, Throne head dress.
Castle, Nephthys, Altar head dress.
What follows is a description of the pawns.

Knight's Pawn

Kabexnuv, Mummy, hawk's head.

Bishop's Pawn

Ahephi, Mummy, ape's head.

Queen's Pawn

Tmoumathph, Mummy, dog's head.

Castle's Pawn

Ameshet, Mummy, human head.

What follows is a description of the chessmen with their Tarot, Element and Hebrew letter attribution.

King

Ace, Spirit, Shin.

Queen

Queen, Water, Heh.

Knight

King, Fire, Yod.

Bishop

Knight, Air, Vau.

Rook

Knave, Earth, Heh (f).
Differences from normal chess moves:

The pawns move one square only. No taking en passant.
No castling.
The Queen controls 3rd square in any straight line, counting square on which she stands as 1, and may jump over pieces.

AWAKENING OF THE ABODES

Four Players, two against two.
Partners. Fire, Air - Water, Earth.
The First player is the Querent. The first player chooses angle and sets the pieces in order of the Kerubic line, other players follow the first player's setting.

The corner square always has King in addition to other pieces. Both Kings must be checkmated. A pawn on the 8th square becomes the piece of which it is the vice-regent.

PTAH

The Ptah used for divination - set by first player on any square in his own Lesser Angle the King to reach and remain on the square of Ptah for one round of game undisturbed and unchecked.

The pieces should (if four players) be coloured Red, Black, Blue and Yellow.

THE BOARDS

The Four Boards of the Rosicrucian game, although different, nevertheless agree in certain particulars. In each board it is convenient to speak of the arrangement of the Lesser Angles as an Upper and Lower Rank - Air and Water forming the Upper Rank, and Earth and Fire the Lower.

It is evident that the columns of the one rank are continuous with those of the other; and in this continuity a certain regular rule is observable. Every column of eight squares in the Upper Rank is continued below by a column of the opposite Element.

Thus the Fiery columns invariably stand on the Watery columns below; the Watery on the Fiery; the Airy on the Earthy; and the Earthy on the Airy.

A different arrangement of the Ranks of Squares is observable, and a difference is seen in this in the Upper and Lower Tablets.

In the Upper Tablets the Kerubic Rank of squares is continuous with the Elemental Rank; and the Cardinal is continuous with the common sign Rank, whereas in the Lower Tablets the various Ranks - Kerubic, Cardinal, etc., are continuous right across the boards.

The diagonal lines or Bishop's move present pecularities. Every Lesser Angle throughout the Tablets has a diagonal line of four squares starting from its prime square; which are allotted respectively to Aries, Gemini, Scorpio and Earth (the non Osiris Squares). From these four squares the Bishops can move one square into a square of Libra, Sagittarius, Taurus or Water, these completing the series of squares in that Lesser Angle in which a Bishop can move. Let us call this the Aries System of diagonal squares.

This diagonal is crossed by another which in the Airy and Watery boards is composed of Cancer, Leo, Virgo and Air Squares, having as subsidiaries, squares of Aquarius, Pisces, Capricorn and Fire. In the Earthy and Fiery board the second series of four form the diagonal, and the first the subsidiaries. Let us call this the Cancer series.

If we now examine the Boards we shall see that the Aries system of any Lesser Angle is joined diagonally to the Aries system of the other three Lesser Angles; and that the Cancer also is similarly joined to every other Cancer system. So that we have two systems of squares; the Aries and the Cancer; of the whole, each containing four squares allotted to every sign it contains. This resembles the black and white systems of squares of the ordinary board; and it is as if we allotted the White to Aries, and the Black to Cancer.

AIRY & FIERY BOARDS

PLACING THE MEN

The yellow and red men are so placed that they advance to the attack of the black and the blue respectively by the columns; while the latter advance by the ranks. That is, the actives are shown as a vertical force, while the passives are shown as operating horizontally.

Shewing the Cross of life, corresponding to the forces of the Court Cards and the Zodiacal Trumps.

The central squares of the board contain the 16 signs that are allotted to each Lesser Angle. And it is only from these 16 squares that the pieces - except the Rook and the King develop their full influence or defensive force.

The Watery and Airy Boards are counterparts of each other, so far as the arrangement of the signs, etc., of the squares are concerned. And the same is true as regards the Earth and Water Boards. Every Board has its uppermost and lowermost ranks of the passive or female element; and its two central ranks are of the active or male element.

The most striking difference between the Air and Water, and the Earth and Fire boards is in the fact that in the former the ranks are broken; whereas in the latter they are not only continuous across each board, but they are continuous right across both boards when in situ. To this is due the greater balance and evenness seen in the play of the pieces in the lower boards.

The Aries and Cancer systems are composed respectively of naturally allied pairs of Signs.

The Aries System consists of Aries, Gemini, Scorpio and Earth, the non-Osiris Squares and Taurus and Water, Libra and Sagittarius, two natural pairs.

The Cancer system consists of Cancer, Leo; Virgo, Air; Capricorn, Fire; Pisces and Aquarius, for natural pairs.

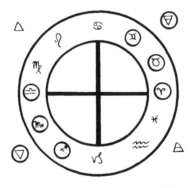

SYMBOLS CIRCLED - ARIES SYSTEM
SYMBOLS NOT CIRCLED - CANCER SYSTEM

EARTH of FIRE setting. EARTH Prime Player.

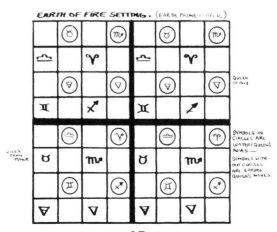

EARTH OF FIRE SETTING. (EARTH PRIME PLAYER)

Showing the Queens of Prime Player and his Ally governing all the Squares of the Aries System.

Blue - Watery Queen's move.
Brown - Earthy Queen's move.

THE QUEEN

The four Queens, the Watery portion of their respective Elements govern between them every Square of every board. But a Queen can never check another Queen for the following reasons.

Each of these pieces govern 16 Squares on the board, four in each Lesser Angle; and they are so placed as to divide the 64 squares equally between them.

It follows, therefore, that there is only one of them that can check the Ptah square.

The 16 squares governed by any Queen are allotted to eight Signs, two Squares of each Sign to every Queen. And the remaining two squares of the same 8 Signs are governed by the friendly Queen.

And the other pair of Queens govern the 32 other Squares similarly. The Queen of the Prime Player always governs the Water, Earth, Taurus, and Scorpio squares of its own lesser Angle, and also of the Lesser Angle of the same rank.

In each of the other two Lesser Angles the Queen of the Prime Player governs the Sagittarius, Gemini, Libra, and Aries squares.

The allied Queen governs the same squares in the opposite ranks of the Lesser Angles.

Thus the Prime Player's Queen and his ally together govern the Aries system of squares. And this is equally true of every Board.

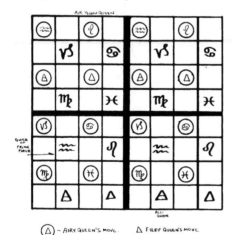

OPPOSING QUEENS GOVERN
SQUARES OF THE CANCER SYS
A PASSIVE PRIME PLAYER.
△ FIRE - PRIME PLAYER

(△) ~ AIRY QUEEN'S MOVE.   △ FIERY QUEEN'S MOVE.

Showing the variation against an active Prime Player.

Blue - Watery Queen's move.
Brown - Earthy Queen's move.

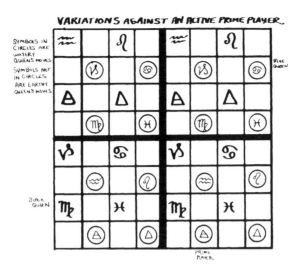

VARIATIONS AGAINST AN ACTIVE PRIME PLAYER

Green - Airy Queen's move.
Red - Fiery Queen's move.

Showing the opposing Queens governing all the Squares of the Cancer System, against a passive prime player.

Fire - Prime Player.

The opposing Queens govern the squares of the Cancer System in a similar manner. But there is a slight variation dependent on the position of the Prime Player. They together govern the Cancer system.

If Water or Earth be the Prime Player, the opposing Queens govern the Air, Fire, Leo and Aquarius squares in their own lesser Angles and in the others of the same rank; while in the other rank they govern Virgo, Pisces, Cancer and Capricorn squares.

If Air or Fire be the Prime Player these two sets of squares are reversed.

The Queen of the Prime Player, and, therefore, of the attacked Lesser Angle, invariably governs therein the passive Kerubic and Elemental squares.

The attacking Queens govern and have for their bases, when active Elements attack - the active Kerubic and Elemental squares.

When passive elements attack, the passive Cardinal and Common Sign squares.

The allied Queen, supporting the defence, has for base the squares corresponding to those of the Prime Player, the passive Kerubic and Elemental squares.

It also falls out that no Passive Queen can, under any circumstances of Board or setting, check an active Kerubic, Cardinal; Common or Elemental square in her own rank of Lesser Angles, nor a similar passive square in the other rank.

It is to be seen that there are certain Signs whereon the Queens are strong and others whereon they are weak.

In defence the Queens, or Watery Forces of each Element, are strong in the Water. Earth, Scorpio and Taurus squares of their respective domains. But in attacking the vulnerable points of the hostile domain depends on which Elements are in operation.

If Water be the Prime Player, and hence the point of attack, the Watery Queen can deliver a strong counter attack on Water, Earth, Scorpio and Taurus of yellow (being in the same rank), and on Aries, Gemini, Sagittarius and Libra of red. While the friendly Water of Earth delivers attack on Aries, Gemini, Sagittarius, and Libra of yellow and Water, Earth, Scorpio, and Taurus of Red.

The Aries System then offers the strong points for the Airy portion of an Elemental Force in defence; and the Cancer System in offence.

The Watery Forces of the Elements never oppose one another, nor clash in their action. Each undulates onwards unaffected by and unaffecting the undulations of the others. Each Queen will swamp opposing force only when that force encroaches on the domain of the particular Queen.

Every Queen has to fear the attack of the opposing Airy forces. But as the latter develop force as the matter proceeds towards ultimation, the Queen when protected is not likely to be destroyed by an opposing and threatening Bishop. The same is true as regards the hostile Knight's attack.

This rule of play is generally sound except in the case of a Queen that can check the Ptah Square; which ability greatly enhances her value.

THE BISHOP

The Bishops of Partners alw ays govern the same set of squares ; and the Bishops of the opposing sides govern opposite sets of squares. These sets are the same as those before mentioned as the Aries and Cancer Systems.

The Bishops of the Prime Player and his ally always govern the Cancer system; and those of the opponent always act in the Aries System.

Hence if the Ptah square be of the Aries system, the airy parts of the opposing forces have great power; but if it be of the Cancer System the opposing aerial forces are impotent in direct attack, and can only be operative secondarily. It follows, too. that the Bishops and Queens are great opponents, since the Bishops operate over the same system as their opposing Queens. The Queens can only touch 16 squares, while the Bishop can touch 32, giving the latter a great superiority in this respect. But the Queen must be considered the equal of the Bishop from the power she possesses to hop over an intervening piece, which would arrest the approach of the Bishop.

And further, the Watery piece is not hampered by the pawns in opening, whereas the Bishop as a rule cannot act at all until at least one pawn has been moved.

THE KNIGHT

The Knights can all reach every square on the Boards, and, therefore, operate over both the Aries and Cancer Systems.

The Knight moves from one of these Systems into the other every time he is played. If he starts on a square of the Aries, his first, third and fifth, etc., moves will bring him on to squares of the Cancer System. And in his first, third or fifth moves he can get to any Cancer system square on the board.

His second, fourth and sixth moves will equally bring him to any Aries System square. There appears to be only one square on the board that requires six moves to reach That is, if the Knight be in one of the corner squares he cannot cross the board diagonally into the opposite corner square in less than six moves.

This results in some peculiarities as shown in the diagrams on the following pages:

VOLUME TEN

ARIES SYSTEM — **THICK**   CANCER SYSTEM — THIN

6	5	4	5	4	5	4	5
5	4	5	4	3	4	3	4
4	5	4	3	4	3	4	3
5	4	3	4	3	2	3	2
4	3	4	3	2	3	2	3
5	4	3	2	3	4	1	2
4	3	4	3	2	1	4	3
5	4	3	2	3	2	3	KT

4	5	4	3	4	3	4	3
5	4	3	4	3	4	3	4
4	3	4	3	2	3	2	3
3	4	3	2	3	2	3	2
4	3	2	3	4	1	2	1
3	4	3	2	1	4	3	2
4	3	4	3	2	3	KT	3
3	4	3	2	1	2	3	4

4	3	2	3	2	3	2	3
3	2	3	2	3	2	3	2
2	3	4	1	2	1	4	3
3	2	1	2	3	2	1	2
2	3	2	3	KT	3	2	3
3	2	1	2	3	2	1	2
2	3	4	1	2	1	4	3
3	2	3	2	3	2	3	2

AIRY AND WATERY BOARDS

The various Signs can be moved as follows:

In the Aries System	In the Cancer System
Knight Can Move	**Knight Can Move**
On to Sagittarius 24 times	On to Pisces 23 times
On to Aries 23 times	On to Cancer 22 times
On to Libra 23 times	On to Capricorn 22 times
On to Gemini 22 times	On to Leo 21 times
On to Water 20 times	On to Virgo 21 times
On to Scorpio 19 times	On to Air 21 times
On to Earth 19 times	On to Water 20 times
On to Taurus 18 times	On to Aquarius 18 times

EARTHY AND FIERY BOARDS

The various Signs can be moved as fellows:

In the Aries System	In the Cancer System
Knight can Move	**Knight can Move**
On to Sagittarius 23 times	On to Virgo 23 times
On to Libra 23 times	On to Cancer 22 times
On to Aries 22 times	On to Capricorn 22 times
On to Gemini 22 times	On to Pisces 22 times
On to Scorpio 20 times	On to Leo 20 times
On to Earth 20 times	On to Aquarius 20 times
On to Water 19 times	On to Fire 20 times
On to Taurus 19 times	On to Air 19 times

The Knight when placed in the corner square can only move to 2 others.

The Knight when placed in two adjacent squares can only move to 3 others.

The Knight when placed in any other outside square can only move to 4 others.

The Knight when placed in the corner square of the second row can only move to 4 others.

The Knight when placed in any other second row square can only move to six others.

But in the central 16 its full power is developed and it can move to eight others. This gives the possible moves of a Knight as 336.

There is a curious difference between the details of these 336 moves in the upper and lower Ranks of Tablets.

The Air Board will be identical with the Watery.

The Earthy Board will be identical with the Fiery.

It will be seen by the annexed table that the squares of certain signs are more often attacked by the Knight than others; for instance in the first column it is shown that the four Sagittarius squares in the Air and Watery Boards are attackable from no less that 24 squares: while the four Taurus squares are only attackable from 18 squares.

VOLUME TEN

When playing from the 16 central squares, each Knight governs 8 squares. These 8 squares, however, are not promiscuously arranged, but follow one rule in the Air and Watery boards, and another in the Earth and Fire.

In the former the 8 squares are allotted always to 6 signs, 2 of which are moved to twice. Thus from the Earth square of the Water Tablet, the Knight moves to the following Squares: Virgo, Leo, Capricorn 2, Cancer 2, Pisces, Aquarius, duplicating Capricorn and Cancer, and missing Fire and Air of the Cancer System.

Or again from the Aries square, the Knight moves to Pisces, Aquarius, Air 2. Capricorn 2, Virgo and Leo, duplicating Air and Capricorn, and missing Fire and Cancer.

But in the Earth and Fire Boards it is different. There the Knight only moves to squares of 5 signs of its system, triplicating 1, duplicating 1, and missing three.

Thus from the Earth square the Knight moves to: Pisces 2, Capricorn, Cancer 3, Leo. and Aquarius; triplicating Cancer, duplicating Pisces, missing Fire, Air, and Virgo.

And from the Aries Square: Aquarius 2, Pisces, Virgo 3, and Air, Fire; triplicating Virgo, duplicating Aquarius, missing Cancer, Capricorn, and Leo.

WATER AND AIR BOARDS

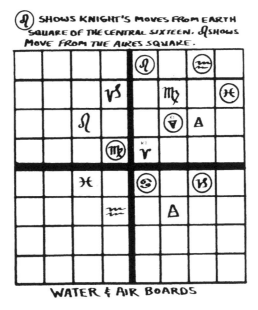

WATER & AIR BOARDS

Green shows the Knight's moves from the Earth square of the central Sixteen. Crimson shows move from Aries Square.

EARTH AND WATER BOARDS

WATER & AIR BOARDS

Ⓠ SHOWS KNIGHTS MOVES FROM EARTH SQ. OF THE CENTRAL 16. ♌ = MOVES FROM ARIES SQ.

Green as before.

Crimson as before.

From the central 16 squares an attack is made on the Cardinal and Common Signs 10 times each; but on the Kerubic and Elemental Squares 6 times each. This is true of every board, and the reason is to be found in the position of the ranks; which in every case are disposed so that the uppermost and lowermost ranks are Kerubic and Elemental, while the two central ranks are Cardinal and Common. The same reason will explain the peculiarities of the curious difference between the columns "No. of times the Sign is duplicated," "triplicated," and "missed."

This analysis of the moves from the 16 central squares seems to show a certain steadiness in the Earth and Fire Tablets, and is less seen in the Water and Air.

The same increase of steadiness is shown in the tablet at the foot of the diagrams on the Boards.

In Air and Water the extreme numbers are 24 and 18.

In Earth and Fire the extreme numbers are 23 and 19.

The moves of the Knight referred in a similar way to the remaining 48 Squares show the same point, a greater steadiness in the Earth and Fire boards than in the Water and Air. And this difference is seen in the outer row and not in the inner one.

The 28 outside squares are attacked by 96 possible moves.

The 20 next squares are attacked by 112 possible moves.

The 16 central squares are attacked by 128 possible moves.

The Knights or Fiery forces of the Elements meet and clash violently in all parts, and are strong in attack against everything and everywhere. Their moves, like Fire pass unarrested through the other elements in irregular courses like the lambent flame, leaping both diagonally and square-wise at every move. They contain the potential forces of the other pieces. Their force is similar to the Tarot King, and to Chokmah. They are the ABBA forces, and with the Queens represent the Briatic forces of the scheme.

VOLUME TEN

The Queens or Watery forces of the Elements never clash with one another, but ever undulate onwards each in its own course unaffected by opposing or crossing waves. But the Watery forces only move in their respective pre-ordained courses; they cannot leave their limits and enter upon the domain of others. Water, like Fire, is unarrested and undulating, and like Air and Earth it can act diagonally or square-wise containing the potential force of Air and Earth. They are the Queen of the Tarot, and Binah. They are the AIM AH, and are of Briah.

The Bishops are subtle and sharp, moving rapidly, but are easily arrested in their course. They clash not with opposing Bishops, and friendly Airs support each other in attack and defence; where the active Airs whirl the passive cannot come. They are the forces of the Knights, and of Yetzirah, the SON.

The Rooks are the heavy resisting powers of the Knave, mighty indeed in action when preceded by the action of the other three. That is, when in any matter the forces of Fire, Water, and Air have been absorbed and equilibriated, i.e., removed from the board, the mighty powers of the Castles come into play. But woe to him who too early calls these ponderous forces forth.

THE ROOK

This piece moves through columns as through ranks. He is able, therefore, to reach every square on the board, and is very powerful. But his movement is very ponderous, and it is a piece that is not moved many times in a game unless the forces of the other Elements have been absorbed in its working out. While the Aleph, Mem, and Shin forces are in full operation the Rook is easily attacked and with difficulty defended, unless he remain quiet, and act as a firm basis of support and defence to the side. If he however, make the mistake of entering early into action he is nearly sure to fall a prey to the more subtle forces whose proper sphere is attack.

If the more subtle forces do not bring about a solution of the question, and the matter has to be fought out to the bitter end, that is, if the Yetziratic and Briatic forces are absorbed and balanced in the matter, then do the ponderous forces of Assiah, the Knave, engage in powerful combat.

THE KINGS

The Kings of Water and Earth stand in squares of the Aries System. The Kings of Air and Fire stand in squares of the Cancer System.

If Water or Earth be the Prime player the opposing Bishops attack the squares on which they stand. If Air or Fire be the Prime Player they do not.

The King is the Ace, and the King of the Prime Player being the piece on whose action that of all the forces depends, it is this King that, at every move he makes, causes a new whirl to be set up in the other forces.

NOTES CONCERNING THE PLAY.

See to which system the Ptah square belongs. Because if it be a square of the Aries system the attack of the opposing Queens is insignificant, while that of the Bishops is strong. In such a case the number of pieces is 6; 2 Bishops, 2 Knights and 2 Rooks. That is, in these matters the Airy attack is strong, and the Watery weak.

If the Ptah be on a square of the Cancer System, one opposing Queen directly attacks this Square, but the Bishops do not. In this case the number of attacking pieces is 5; one Queen,

2 Knights, and 2 Rooks. That is, in these matters the Airy attack is insignificant, while the Watery is strong.

If an opposing Queen can attack the Ptah, the defence should note well which Queen it is and should remember that this fact greatly enhances her power. He should thereupon not hesitate to exchange what might otherwise be considered a more powerful piece for her. She should certainly be exchanged for a Bishop, and probably also for a Knight.

THE ARIES SYSTEM OF TRUMPS

Aries - Emperor.	The Chief Among the Mighty
Taurus - Hierophant.	Magus of the Eternal Gods.
Gemini - Lovers.	Oracles of the Mighty Gods.
Libra - Justice.	Holder of the Balance.
Scorpio - Death.	Child of the Great Transformer.
Sagittarius - Temperance.	Daughter of the Reconciler.
Saturn - Universe.	Great One of the Night of Time.
Water - Hanged Man.	Spirit of the Mighty Waters.

THE CANCER SYSTEM OF TRUMPS

Cancer - Chariot.	Child of the Powers of the Waters.
Leo - Strength.	Daughter of the Flaming Sword.
Virgo - Prudence.	Prophet of the Gods.

Capricorn - Devil.	Lord of the Gates of Matter.
Aquarius - Star.	Daughter of the Firmament.
Pisces - Moon.	Ruler of the Flux and Reflux.
Fire - Judgment.	Spirit of the Primal Fire.
Air - Fool.	Spirit of Ether.

The YHVH order of the pieces corresponds with their respective offensive and defensive powers, thus:

> **Most offensive - Knight.**
> **More offensive - Queen, than defensive.**
> **More defensive - Bishop, than offensive.**

The Rook, most defensive, i.e., in a general sense. Because every piece assumes both roles according to circumstances.

THE NUMERICAL STRUCTURE OF ENOCHIAN
By
DAVID ALLEN HULSE

I. THE ENOCHIAN NUMBERS WITHIN THE CALLS

Enochian is an isosephic language, that is a language whose alphabet serves both as phonemes and numbers. The esoteric structure of the Enochian alphabet is based on phonetic sounds resembling Greek, modeled on the alphabetical order of Hebrew and numbered digitally like Sanskrit. The language itself seems to be an amalgamation of Hebrew, Greek, English and Latin, with a sprinkling of esoteric languages such as Egyptian, Coptic, and Sanskrit. Above all, it is an artificial language, suggesting a grammatical structure but in reality containing no logical syntax. The number system of John Dee's Enochian Language can be seen in the Golden Dawn System of 48 calls derived from Dee's writings. The code is blinded in the sense that most use of the letters as numbers are erroneous, but there are clues within this code to allow its decipherment.

Within the 48 Calls the letters are employed as numbers sixty-three times, from which thirteen keys can be found which allow the decoding of Enochian. Eight keys clarify the correct allocation of numbers to letters. The ninth key shows the end or last letter of the Enochian alphabet. The tenth key details the empty or invisible letter in the Enochian system, corresponding to the 19th unlettered Enochian Call, the Call utilized to explore the 30 Aethyrs. The eleventh key reinforces the tenth key concerning the missing Enochian letter. The twelfth key alludes to the basic division of the Tarot which is the model for the number of letters in the Enochian system. The thirteenth key shows the Hebraic influence in blinding **L** as one in value.

The sixty-three codes using Enochian letters as numbers within the 48 Calls are as follows:

First Call
no appearance of numbers

Second Call
VIU - second
L - first
L - first

Third Call
OS - twelve
NORZ - six
LI - first
OS - twelve
CLA - four, five and six

Fourth Call
PD -33
VIU - second
MAPM - 9639
L - 1
LO - first
CLA - four, five and six

Fifth Call
D - third
AF - nineteen
L - first
VIU - second
PEOAL - 69636
LA - first
ULS - the ends
L - one

Sixth Call
S - fourth
EM - nine
ACAM - 7, 6, 9, 9
VIU - second
D - third

Seventh Call
NI - 28
D - third
ES - fourth

Eighth Call
LO - first
PI - third
OX - 26

Ninth Call
P - eight
OLANI - two
OBZA half
CIAL - 9996

Tenth Call
OP - 22
DAOX - 5678
OL - 24th
EORS - hundred
MATB - thousand
L - one
MATB - thousand

Eleventh Call
O - five
GA - 31

Twelfth Call
OB - 28
MIAN - 3663

Thirteenth Call
UX - 42
AFFA - empty

Fourteenth Call
OL - QUAR - 1636

Fifteenth Call
L - first
DARG - 6739

Sixteenth Call
VIU - second
EMOD - 8763

Seventeenth Call
D - third
TAXS - 7336

Eighteenth Call
ERAN - 6332

Nineteenth Call (the unnumbered Call, the Call of the 30 Aethyrs)

    L - one
    AG L - no one
    L - one
    SAGA - one

In these examples two major methods of representing numbers within the calls can be seen.

(a) **letters employed as numbers in which each letter of the alphabet corresponds to a number, and**

(b) **words employed as numeral names.**

The unique use of letters as numbers in these Calls is modeled directly upon the Sanskrit alphabet. The alphabets of Hebrew, Greek, Arabic, Coptic, and Latin are additional; the value of any given word is the sum total of the letters composing that word. But with Sanskrit the alphabet becomes positional, and every letter of a word becomes the digit of a number. The Hindu mathematician Aryabhata in his work *Dasagitka*, published in 499 A.D., details a system of substituting numbers for letters of the Sanskrit alphabet. In this system each letter of a word is a separate digit of a number; thus a word composed of three letters would represent a number composed of three digits. This code was Ka-Ta-Pa-Ya, the most poetical and complex allocation of numbers to letters for the Sanskrit alphabet. (For a description of this number system refer to the third section of this essay.) This same method of numerical notation is used in the 48 Enochian Calls.

Of the sixty-three times numbers are mentioned in the Calls, this digital system is used 32 times:

    L - 1 (Calls 4, 5, 10, 19 twice)
    OS - 12 (Call 3 twice)
    CLA - 456 (Calls 3 and 4)
    PD - 33 (Call 4)
    MAPM - 9639 (Call 5)
    AF - 19 (Call 5)
    PEOAL - 69636 (Call 5)
    ACAM - 7699 (Call 6)
    NI - 28 (Call 7)
    OX - 26 (Call 8)
    P - 8 (Call 9)
    CIAL - 9996 (Call 9)
    OP - 22 (Call 10)
    DAOX - 5618 (Call 10)
    O - 5 (Call 11)
    GA - 31 (Call 11)
    OB - 28 (Call 12)
    MIAN - 3663 (Call 12)
    UX - 42 (Call 13)
    OL - 24 (Calls 10 and 14)
    QUAR - 1636 (Call 14)

DARG - 6739 (Call 15)
EMOD - 8763 (Call 16)
TAXS - 7336 (Call 17)
ERAN - 6332 (Call 18)

The majority of the above attributions are blinded, for many values are given to one letter. For example, let us look at the use of "A" (the letter Un) as a number:

A is 1 in **AF** and **GA,**
A is 3 in **ERAN, TAXS, PEOAL,** and **QUAR,**
A is 6 in **CLA, MAPM, DAOX,** and **MIAN,**
A is 7 in **ACAM** and **DARG,** and
A is 9 in **CIAL** and **ACAM.**

The correct allocation is A as in 1 in **AF** and **GA,** the other nine examples being blinded values. There are eight correct attributions in the 32 uses of the letters as digital numbers.

These eight keys will enable us to reconstruct the proper number code for Enochian. Correctly analyzed they disclose the following information.

1) **AF** = 19 (Call 5)
AF, which is the number 19, assigns the letter A correctly to 1, bringing to mind the Hebrew Aleph and the Greek Alpha. This clue discloses the beginning of the Enochian alphabet, not Pe (B) as Mathers premised, but rather Un (A). [Note that Un is the Latin root for One (as in **UNUS, UNA, UNUM.**] Although **A** is numbered correctly as 1, **F** is blinded as the number 9. Looking at every use of letters as numbers in the Calls it is apparent that the "O" is never used. Therefore F blinded as 9, next to the correct allocation of A as 1 indicated the limit of this number code, not 1 through (1)0, but 1 through 9. This will be reinforced by the clue **AFFA** which means empty.

2) **GA** = 31 (Call 11)
GA as the number 31 is the only correct pair of letters used as digital numbers appearing in 48 Calls. This allocation indicates that the alphabet is numbered in the Hellenistic-Semitic order in which G is the third position (Gamma, Gimel = 3) rather than the seventh position of the alphabet as in Latin and most European languages. The allocation of A to 1 in GA reinforces the use of A as 1 which appears in **AF.**

3) **OS** = 12 (Call 3)
OS, which appears twice in the third call as 12, correctly allocates S to the number 2. This is highly informative for by this clue it can be seen that the Enochian letter "S" is modeled on the Greek Sigma, which is valued at 2 (00), rather than the Hebrew Shin, valued at 3(00), or the Hebrew Samekh, valued at 6(0).

4) **OX** = 26 (Call 8)
OX, which is valued at 26, correctly assigns "X" to 6, although "O" is blinded as 2 (resembling "OS" which also blinds "O" as 2). If the Enochian alphabet is numbered as Hebrew this number position would be S as Samekh, valued at 6(0). However since it is "X", this clue indicated that the phonetic model for Enochian is Greek, where X is Xi, valued at 6(0).

5) **DAOX** = 5678 (Call 10)
DAOX as the number series 5678, in conjunction with **OS** and **OX,** clarifies the numerical correspondence of 0. For by **DAOX,** 0 is valued at 7, which is its correct value, and not 2 as

in **OS** and **OX**. Therefore the model for 0 is the Greek Omicron, valued at 7(0), as well as the Hebrew Ayin also valued at 7(0).

6) U̲X - 42 (Call 13)

UX, which is the number 42, establishes the end of the Enochian alphabet. As **AF** indicated the beginning point of Enochian as " A", **UX** indicates that U as 4 is the true end of the Enochian alphabet. U as 4 is modeled on the Greek Upsilon valued at 4(00), which is the Hebraic position for the end of the alphabet (Tav as 400). From this clue the true model for Enochian can be seen; it is patterned on the phonetic sounds of Greek based on the Hebraic order of the alphabet. Therefore U as Upsilon, corresponding to the letter Tav of Hebrew, is the model for the end of the alphabet rather than the Greek Omega. This is further supported by the letter X appearing in **UX**. Although X is blinded as 2 (its true value being "6" as shown in **OX**), its shape as the English X suggests the rock Hebrew form for Tav as a cross. The association to U as 4 hints that U is in the position of Tav, as the last or 21st Enochian letter. Note also that Tav is assigned to the 21st Tarot Key.

7) P̲ = 8 (Call 9)

P, which is the number 8, is the only isolated letter correctly used as a number. In conjunction with X as 6 (from **OX**) and O as 7 (from **DAOX**), the phonetic model of Greek is again reinforced, for X as 6 is Xi, O as 7 is Omicron and **P** as 8 is Pi.

8) O̲P = 22 (Call 10)

OP, which is the number 22 is an example of a blinded number. Neither "O" nor "P" is valued at 2. However from **DAOX** as 5678, O is correctly numbered as 7 and from **P** as 8, P is correctly numbered as 8. Thus **OP** blinded is 22, while **OP** corrected is 78. There are 78 total Tarot cards of which 22 are symbolic-Qabalistic pictures of the Hebrew alphabet. These two correspondences of 22 and 78 are the blinded and correct numbering of **"OP"**. By suggesting the Tarot, the number series 0 through 21 is brought to mind, for the 22 cards composing the Major Arcana of the Tarot are numbered in this order. This is the esoteric basis of the Enochian alphabet, 22 letters, 21 represented and 1 unwritten. The Tarot assignment, brought out by the clues for Enochian, parallels the Enochian letter Un (A) to Key 0, The Fool and the Enochian letter Vau (U) to Key 21, The World. The missing or unwritten Enochian letter is the Greek model Theta, corresponding to Teth in Hebrew, and Key 8, Strength in the Golden Dawn Tarot.

(See the comment below on the clue **AFFA** for further clarification of this missing unwritten letter.)

In addition to the use of the alphabet as the digits of numbers, Enochian also contains descriptive names for numbers. Within the 48 Calls the appearance of words describing number concepts occurs 31 times. They are:

> **VIU** - second (Calls 2, 4, 5, 6, 16)
> **L** - first (Calls 2 twice, 5, 15)
> **NORZ** - six (Call 3)
> **LI** - first (Call 3)
> **LO** - first (Calls 4, 8)
> **D** - third (Calls 5, 6, 7, 17)
> **LA** - first (Call 5)
> **ULS** - the ends (Call 5)
> **S** - fourth (Call 6)
> **EM** - nine (Call 6)

ES - fourth (Call 7)
PI - third (Call 8)
OLANI - two (Call 9)
OBZA - half (Call 9)
EORS - hundred (Call 10)
MATB - thousand (Call 10 twice)
AFFA - empty (Call 19)
AG L - no one (Call 19)
SAGA - one (Call 19)

Four major keys and one additional clue can be gleaned from these 31 descriptive terms. The four major keys are as follows:

1) **ULS** - the ends (Call 5)

ULS, a word meaning the ends reinforces the establishment of the Enochian U (Vau) as the end of the Enochian alphabet. For **ULS** begins with the letter U (Vau) which is the "Omega" of the Enochian language. From the clue **UX**, the model for this letter U was discovered to be the Greek Upsilon. Although its Enochian name or title of Vau suggest the Hebrew Vav, the true model for the Enochian Vau is the Greek Upsilon. This Enochian letter U is also transliterated as V or W. However, in both the clues **UX** and **ULS** Dee chose to transliterate this letter as a U to further establish the correspondence of Upsilon.

Another Enochian number name can help support this theory, and this name is **VIU**, meaning second, which appears in the second, fourth, fifth, sixth and sixteenth call. In this name Dee transliterates the Enochian Vau as both V and U. Symbolically the term second can be seen as that which is not first, i.e. last. Therefore the double transliteration of Vau as V and U within the word for second suggests that the Enochian Vau is the last letter of the alphabet.

2) **AFFA** - empty (zero, nothing) (Call 13)

AFFA appears in the 13th Call as a term for that which is empty. It is composed of the clue **AF** (described above) written forward and backwards. **AF** is numbered as 19 by Enochian, though F as 9 is a blinded attribute. However in the light of **AFFA** as empty, the allocation of F to 9 in **AF** implies that the 9th position of the Enochian alphabet is empty. And this 9th position in our Hellenistic-Semitic model is Theta, or Teth, valued at 9 (and assigned to the 19th path on the Tree of Life).

Now in the Greek alphabet the number 5 progresses to 7, Epsilon followed by Zeta, with the number 6 missing or empty. This 6th position is assigned to the archaic letter Stau (or Digamma) which is valued at 6. Christian tradition relates that this 6th missing letter Stau is the mark of both Qain and the Beast of Revelations. This is supported by Revelation 13:18. the only instance when Stau appears in the New Testament as the number 6 in the number letters 666 (Chi Xi Stau).

While the Enochian alphabet has a letter for 6 (F found in **AF** and **AFFA**), it has no corresponding letter for the 9th position of its alphabet. This missing Enochian letter corresponds to the Greek letter Theta, valued at 9.

Why would Enochian have a missing letter valued at 9 and corresponding in its Greek model to the letter Theta? First, to allow 22 letters in all for its alphabet, permitting a correspondence to the 22 Major Keys of the Tarot. And second, out of respect and fear of God, honor was given to an invisible letter, corresponding to the unnumbered 19th Call which represents the God-head. For the angels instructed Dee that the 21 Enochian letters represent the servants of the king and not the king himself. This corresponds to the Jewish reverence for the Tetragrammaton, for Theta, as the empty 9th Enochian alphabet position, represents the initial for God in Greek: **Th EOS.** Therefore the initial for God, Theta, can be seen as the unsounded, unwritten and unthinkable concept within Enochian.

3) **EM** - nine (Call 6)

EM is the numeral name for nine. By the Greek phonetic order E is valued at 5 while M is valued at 4(0). Though EM is 54 as a digital number, by addition 5 +4 = 9. Nine is the missing Enochian letter corresponding to Theta and Teth, and nine of the Tree of Life as the letter Teth is the 19th path which connects the 4th and 5th Sephiroth (4 = M, and 5 = E).

4) **D** - third (Calls 5, 6, 7, 17)

D represents the numeral name for third. Though **D** is valued at 4 in Enochian (based on Delta and Daleth), it corresponds to the third Tarot Key, The Empress. Therefore by **D** as third, the Enochian parallel to the Tarot is established. This is further evidence for the clue supplied by **OP** as 22 and 78.

In addition to the above 12 keys concerning the Hellenistic-Semitic structure of Enochian one final key concerns the blinded use of the Enochian Letter "**L**" as the number one. L appears 16 times in the 48 Calls to designate one:

L - 1 (Calls 4, 5, 10, 19 twice)
L - first (Calls 2 twice, 5, 15)
LI - first (Call 3)
LO - first (Calls 4, 8)
LA - first (Call 5)
EL - first (Call 6)
AG L - no one (Call 19)
LIL - the call of the first Aire

Though **L** is valued at 3 by the digital code for Enochian (based on the Greek Lamda and the Hebrew Lamed, valued at 3(0), its blinded value of 1 in the Calls points to various Qabalistic formulae for the number 1.

For in Hebrew **L** refers to:

(A)**L** - the one law, power, might
L(A) - not, nothing, the void
(A)**L**(P) - Aleph, the first letter
(A)**L**(HIM) - Elohim, the first name for God in the Torah
L(ILITh) - Lilith, Adam's first mate

And in Greek L refers to:

L(OGOS) - the word which was sounded at the beginning of Creation.

Therefore the use of L as one (though blinded) points to the Greek and Semitic model for Enochian.

Now from these 13 keys the complete number structure of Enochian can be detailed:
1) The 21 Enochian alphabet letters must be arranged as the Greek phonetic order.
2) This arrangement must be qualified by the 22 Hebrew letters ranging from 1 (which is Aleph, Alpha and Un) to 400 (which is Tav, Upsilon, and Vau).
3) The one place in this order of 22 which must be left empty is the 9th place, or place of the Greek letter Theta.
4) The number values of the Enochian alphabet based on the corresponding values of the Greek- Hebrew model must be reduced to the number series 1 to 9. This is accomplished by placing the Enochian alphabet on the Qabalah of 9 chambers (AIQ BKR), which will

remove all zeros. The Enochian letters can then be used as digits of a composite number. Thus the 21 Enochian characters are numbered as follows.:

1	2	3	4	5	6	7	8	9
A	B	G	D	E	F	Z	H	
I	C	L	M	N	X	O	P	Q
R	S	T	U					

The letters which are underscored are derived from the clues in the 48 Calls. Note that the word "AIR" from Aethyr is the first column of our alphabet code.

A second number code for Enochian can be derived from the above table of correspondence. The 21 Enochian letters can also be given the number value of their corresponding Greek-Hebrew model. With this value any Enochian word can be given a number value by totalling the number value of the letters of any word. The table below will detail the two Enochian number codes, their parallel Greek, Hebrew and Tarot models, as well as their astrological attributes derived from these models.

Enochian Alphabet	Transliteration of Enochian	Digital Code	Additional Code	Greek Model	Tarot Key	Hebrew Model	Astrological Attribute
Un	A	1	1	Alpha	0	Aleph	Air
Pe	B	2	2	Beta	1	Beth	Mercury
Ged	G	3	3	Gamma	2	Gimmel	Moon
Gal	D	4	4	Delta	3	Daleth	Venus
Graph	E	5	5	Epsilon	4	Heh	Aries
Orth	F	6	6	Stau	5	Vav	Taurus
Ceph	Z	7	7	Zeta	6	Zain	Gemini
Na-hath	H	8	8	Eta	7	Cheth	Cancer
The missing or empty Enochian letter				Theta	8	Teth	Leo
Gon	I,J,Y	1	10	Iota	9	Yod	Virgo
Veh	C,K	2	20	Kappa	10	Kaph	Jupiter
Ur	L	3	30	Lambda	11	Lamed	Libra
Tal	M	4	40	Mu	12	Mem	Water
Drun	N	5	50	Nu	13	Nun	Scorpio
Pal	X	6	60	Xi	14	Samekh	Sagittarius
Med	o	7	70	Omicron	15	Ayin	Capricorn
Mals	p	8	80	Pi	16	Peli	Mars
Ger	Q	9	90	Koppa	17	Tzaddi	Aquarius
Don	R	1	100	Rho	18	Qoph	Pisces
Fam	S	2	200	Sigma	19	Resh	Sun
Gisa	T	3	300	Tau	20	Shin	Fire
Vau	U,V,W	4	400	Upsilon	21	Tav	Saturn (Earth)

As well as the numerical clues given in the Calls, Dee, in his own writings, supplies additional proof in support of a Hellenistic-Semitic model for the Enochian language:

1) The abbreviation Dee uses in his diary to designate himself is Delta, the fourth letter of the Greek alphabet.

2) Enochian reads from right to left resembling Hebrew (as well as Greek prior to 800 B.C.). This does not imply a demonic influence; rather it is an indication that John Dee attempted to create an Angelic language patterned upon Hebrew. The *Talmud* relates that the angels only speak Hebrew, while the *Zohar* states that when we die, there is only one angelic language we all speak.

3) One of Dee's Enochian Holy Books was titled, *The Book of SOYGA*. The communicating angel indicated that SOYGA is not the reversal of the Greek word (Holy). However, this is a blind. In reality this name SOYGA as a mirror of the Greek AGIOS is a clue to the true model for Enochian: Greek.

4) The Enochian Cosmology is composed of 30 Aethyr or Aires. This is undoubtedly patterned on the 30 Aeons or Worlds of the Coptic-Gnostic cosmology, which was also explored by the Renaissance Magus Giordano Bruno.

5) The name Enochian is obviously derived from the Hebrew "Enoch," which literally means to initiate. The *Zohar* relates that Adam was given the Book of Enoch in the Garden of Eden: but after the fall of Adam and Eve it was removed from mankind and only redeemed and brought back to earth by Enoch. Dee's own magical work was an attempt to redeem mankind again and bring this pristine Enochian wisdom back to earth.

6) The Enochian angel Madimi communicating to John Dee through the skrying of Edward Kelley, sent on June 29, 1583, a warning to Dee concerning Kelley which was expressed in Greek characters (supposedly a tongue Kelley did not understand). Recorded beside this warning in Dee's diary is a comment from Kelley to Dee concerning this cryptic warning: ' 'It is the Syrian Tongue you do not understand it." Now this is the exact model for the esoteric structure of Enochian, the combination of Hellenistic and Semitic Qabalahs.

7) John Dee numbered his own name as a transliteration of Hebrew using the Enochian alphabet of Pantheus recorded in the *Voarchadumia*. This earlier Enochian alphabet may have served as a model of Dee's own Enochian script; it is an angelic script based totally on Hebrew. With this Hebraic code, John Dee transformed his name into the Hebrew IAHN DAA. IAHN for John is valued at 66, while DAA for Dee is valued at 6. By this code Dee was able to transform his own name into the number of the beast: 666. This is probably the reason for the vast amount of magic squares appearing in John Dee's Holy Table which are composed of groups of 666. (Refer to Crowley's *The Equinox,* Vol. I, No. 7, for an illustration of this table.)

8) The grand name given to the angelic tablets which contain the Enochian system of John Dee is Liber LOGAETH, or *The Book of Speech from God.* This Enochian name of LOGAETH is a perfect description of the dual model of Greek and Hebrew. For LOG (or LOG A) is derived from the Greek LOGOS, meaning "the creative word," while AETH (or ETH) is the Hebrew AVTh, meaning "letter of the alphabet." Thus LOGAETH is a symbolic name for the Greek phonetic sounds (LOGA) modeled on a Hebraic alphabetical order (AETH).

II. THE GOLDEN DAWN SYSTEM FOR NUMBERING ENOCHIAN

A second method can be used for deciphering Enochian as numbers. This is the Golden Dawn system of allocations found in *The Book of Concourse of Forces* and used by Aleister Crowley in exploration of the 30 Aethyrs of the Enochian cosmology (recorded in his *The Vision and The Voice*).

In Crowley's *The Vision and The Voice*, the Enochian for the 30 Calls of the Aethyrs is given Hebrew and astrological equivalents. Crowley, in commenting on his vision of the 29th aethyr states that "the geomantic correspondences of the Enochian alphabet form a sublime commentary." This is the Golden Dawn basis for the allocation of Hebrew to the Enochian alphabet. In the Golden Dawn essay on *Talismans and Sigils* a table is given allocating 16 select Enochian letters to the 16 geomantic figures. These correspondences are as follows:

Enochian Letter	Transliteration	Geomantic Figure
MALS	P	POPULUS
UR	L	VIA
GED	G	FORTUNA MAJOR
CEPH	Z	FORTUNA MINOR
FAM	S	CONJUNCTIO
MED	O	PUELLA
DRUN	N	RUBEUS
GON	I,J,Y	ACQUISITIO
VAU	U,V,W	CARCER
TAL	M	TRISTITIA
DON	R	LAETITIA
ORTH	F	CAUDA DRACONIS
GISA	T	CAPUT DRACONIS
PE	B	PUER
UN	A	AMISSIO
GRAPH	E	ALBUS

By this table the Golden Dawn system of magic equated 16 of the 21 Enochian letters to the 16 geomantic shapes. Another Golden Dawn table of correspondences, *The Notes to the Book of the Concourse of the Forces,* was then used to equate a Hebrew letter, Tarot Trump and astrological symbol to each of these 16 geomantic Enochian letters:

Enochian Letter	Geomancy	Zodiac	Hebrew Letter	Number Value
P	POPULUS	Cancer	Cheth	8
L	VIA	Water	Mem	40
G	FORTUNA MAJOR	Leo	Teth	9
Z	FORTUNA	Air	Aleph	1
S	CONJUNCTIO	Virgo	Yod	10
O	PUELLA	Libra	Lamed	30
N	RUBEUS	Scorpio	Nun	50
I,J,Y	ACQUISITIO	Sagittarius	Samekh	60

116

U,V,W	CARCER	Capricorn	Ayin	70
M	TRISTITIA	Aquarius	Tzaddi	90
R	LAETITIA	Pisces	Qoph	100
F	CAUDA			
	DRACONIS	Fire	Shin	300
T	CAPUT			
	DRACONIS	Earth	Tav	400
B	PUER	Aries	Heh	5
A	AMISSIO	Taurus	Vav	6
E	ALBUS	Gemini	Zain	7

Unlike the digital code concealed in the 48 Calls, the Golden Dawn parallel between Enochian and Hebrew is not phonetic in basis but rather elemental as defined by the attributes of geomancy.

However, if the zeros in this code are removed, and this number code is then applied to the digital number codes in the Enochian Calls the following harmonies can be found:

1) **CLA** = (Calls 3, 4); in this number A = 6 is correct,
2) **MAPM** = 9639 (Call 5); in this number A = 6 and M = 9 are correct,
3) **ACAM** = 7699 (Call 6); in this number M = 9 is correct,
4) **P** = 8 (Call 9); this isolated number as 8 is correct,
5) **OL** = 24 (Calls 10, 14); in this number L = 4 is correct,
6) **MIAN** = 3663 (Call 12); in this number both 1 = 6 and A = 6 are correct,
7) **DARG** = 6739 (Call 15); in this number G = 9 is correct.

Crowley in his use of the above Golden Dawn Enochian Table of Attributions deviated in two main attributions. He often interchanged Leo with Cancer (both ruled by the luminaries), and Virgo with Gemini (both ruled by Mercury).

The Golden Dawn system does not number the complete Enochian alphabet. In this system 5 Enochian letters are excluded. Crowley realizing this disparity, developed 5 additional allocations based on the logic of *The Notes of the Book of the Concourse of Forces*. Since the geomantic attributes for Enochian are ultimately elemental in nature Crowley premissed that the five excluded Enochian letters must correspond to the five points of the elemental pentagram. These additional five Enochian letters and their Hebrew parallels are as follows:

Excluded Enochian Letter	Element	Hebrew Letter	Number Value
C(K)	Fire	Shin	300
D	Spirit	Daleth or	4 or
		Aleph Lamed	31
H	Air	Aleph	1
Q	Water	Mem	40
X	Earth	Tav	400

Thus with the addition of Crowley's five letters the complete Enochian alphabet can be numbered in line with their Hebrew model. This numerical rectification is as follows:

CROWLEY'S ATTRIBUTION

Enochian Letter	Number Value	Enochian Letter	Number Value
B	5	P	8
C(K)	300*	Q	40
G	9	N	50
D	4 (or 31)*	X	400*
F	300	O	30
A	6	R	100
E	7	Z	1
M	90	U (V,W)	70
I (J,Y)	60	S	10
H	1*	T	400
L	40	*Crowley variant	

III. THE SANSKRIT DIGITAL NUMBER CODE

The Sanskrit source for the Enochian code appearing in the Calls is known as the Vedic Number Code or Ka-Ta-Pa-Ya-Dhi, (Ka, Ta, Pa, and Ya all being valued at one in this code). It is this code which serves as a key to unlocking the allocation of the 50 letters of the Sanskrit alphabet to the 50 petals of the chakra system. The rules for the Katapayadhi Number Code are as follows:

1) The 34 consonants of the Sanskrit Alphabet represent the numbers 0 through 9 as digits within a number.
2) The 16 vowels receive no number value or place value.
3) Each consonant of a word is a place value (digit) of the resultant number.
4) When two consonants are conjoined in a word the last consonant receives the number value.
5) The number of consonants (or conjoined consonants) in a word determines the number of digits which compose the number value of that word. Thus all one consonant words will be valued between 0 and 9; all two consonant words will be valued between 10 and 99; all three consonant words will be valued between 100 and 999, etc.

The number values for the 34 consonants and the 16 vowels are as follows:

THE 34 CONSONANTS

Number Value	Sanskrit Letter	Petal of Chakra
1	Ka	1st petal - Anahata
1	Ṭa	11th petal - Anahata
1	Pa	9th petal - Manipuraka
1	Ya	4th petal - Svadisthana
2	Kah	2nd petal - Anahata
2	Ṭha	12th petal - Anahata
2	Pha	10th petal - Manipuraka
2	Ra	5th petal - Svadisthana
3	Ga	3rd petal - Anahata
3	Ḍa	1st petal - Manipuraka
3	Ba	1st petal - Svadisthana
3	La	6th petal - Svadisthana
4	Gha	4th petal - Anahata
4	Dha	2nd petal - Manipuraka
4	Bha	2nd petal - Svadisthana
4	Va	1st petal - Muladhara
5	Ṅa	5th petal - Anahata
5	Ṇa	3rd petal - Manipuraka
5	Ma	3rd petal - Svadhisthana
5	Śa	2nd petal - Muladhara
6	Ca	6th petal - Anahata
6	Ta	4th petal - Manipuraka
6	Sa	3rd petal - Muladhara
7	Cha	7th petal - Anahata
7	Tha	5th petal - Manipuraka
7	Sa	4th petal - Muladhara
8	Ja	8th petal - Anahata
8	Da	6th petal - Manipuraka
8	Ha	1st petal - Ajna
9	Jha	9th petal - Anahata
9	Dha	7th petal - Manipuraka
0 (as a place value)	Ña	10th petal - Anahata
0 (as a place value)	Na	8th petal - Manipuraka
0 (as a place value)	Ksa	2nd petal - Ajna

THE 16 VOWELS
(No place value or number value)

SanskritLetter	Petal of Chakra
A	1st petal - Visuddha
Â	2nd petal - Visuddha
I	3rd petal - Visuddha
Î	4th etal - Visuddha
U	5th petal - Visuddha
Û	6th petal -Visuddha
Ri	7th petal - Visuddha
Rî	8th petal - Visuddha
Li	9th petal - Visuddha
Lî	10th petal - Visuddha
E	11th petal - Visuddha
Ai	12th petal - Visuddha
O	13th petal - Visuddha
Au	14th petal - Visuddha
Am	15th petal - Visuddha
Ah	16th petal - Visuddha

The above allocation of the 50 Sanskrit alphabet letters to the 50 petals of the chakra system is derived from Arthur Avalon's *The Serpent Power*. The number code itself is derived from Jagadguru Swami Sri Bharati Krshna Tirthaji's *Vedic Mathematics*.

Sobam Ag Cormpo Crp L

VOLUME TEN

ENOCHIAN DICTIONARY

A

WORDS	PHONETIC	ENGLISH
Aaf	(Ah-ahff)	Amongst
Aai (AAo)	(Ah-ah-ee)	Amongst
Aaiom	(Ah-ah-ee-ohm)	Amongst us
Aala	(Ah-ah-lah)	Placed you
Abaivonin	(Ah-bah-ee-voh-nee-noo)	Stooping Dragon
Abila (Apila)	(Ah-bee-lah)	Liveth forever
Aboapri	(Ah-boh-ah-pay-ree)	Let them serve you
Abraassa	(Ah-brah-ah-ess-sah)	Provided
Abrang	(Ah-brah-noo-gee)	I have prepared
ACAM	(Ah-kahm)	7,6,9,9
Adgt	(Ah-dah-gee-tay)	Can
Adna	(Ah-dah-nah)	Obedience
Adohi	(Ah-doh-hee)	Kingdom
Adoian	(Ah-doh-ee-ah-noo)	Face
Adphaht	(Ah-dah-pay-hah-tay)	Unspeakable
Adroch	(Ah-dah-rohk-hay)	Olive Mount
Adrpan	(Ah-dah-ra-pahn-noo)	Cast down
Af	(Ah-eff)	Nineteen
Affa	(Ah-eff-fah)	Empty
Ag	(Ah-gee)	None, No
Aglo	(Ah-gloh)	In Thy
Alar	(Ah-lahr)	Have set
Aldi	(Ah-el-dee)	Of gathering
Aldon	(Ah-el-doh-noo)	Gather up, Gird
Allar	(Ah-el-lahr)	Bind up
Am	(Ah-em)	Beginning
Amipzi	(Ah-mee-pay-zoad-ee)	I fastened
Amiram	(Ah-mee-rahm)	Yourselves
Amis	(Ah-meess)	End
Amma	(Ah-em-mah)	Cursed
Ananael	(Ah-nah-nah-el)	Secret Wisdom
Anetab	(Ah-nay-tahb)	In government
Angelard	(Ah-nu-gee-lahr-dah)	His Thoughts
Aoiveae	(Ah-oh-ee-vay-ah-ay)	Stars
Ar	(Ah-ray)	To Vanne
Ar	(Ah-ray)	hat (in order)

(Ar) Tabas	(Tah-bahs)	That Govern
ARN	(Ah-rah-noo)	2nd Aethyr
As	(Ah-ess)	Was
ASP	(Ah-ess-pay)	21st Aethyr
Aspt	(Ah-ess-pay-tay)	Before
Ath	(Ah-tay-hay)	Works
Atraah	(Ah-tay-rah-ah)	Your Girdles
Audcal	(Ah-vah-dah-kahl)	Mercury
Avavaco	(Ah-vah-vah-koh)	Thunders of increase
Avavox	(Ah-vah-vohx)	His pomp
Aviny	(Ah-vee-nee)	Millstones
Aziagier	(Ah-zoad-ee-ah-gee-ayr)	Harvest
Aziazor	(Ah-zoad-ee-ah-zoad-ohr)	Likeness
Azieh	(Ah-zoad-ee-ay)	Whose hands

B

Babage (n)	(Bah-bah-gay)	South
Babalon (d)	(Bah-bah-Iohn)	Wicked (harlot)
Baeouib	(Bah-ay-oh-veeb)	Righteousness
BAG	(Bah-gee)	28th Aethyr
Baghie	(Bah-gee-hee-ay)	Fury
Bable (r)	(Bah-bay-lay)	For, Because, For Why?
Bahal	(Bah-hah-lah)	Cried loudly
Balit	(Bah-leet)	The Just
Balt (an)	(Bah-Iay-tay)	Justice
Baltim	(Bah-lay-teem)	Extreme Justice
Baltoh	(Bah-lay-toh)	The Righteous
Baltoha	(Bah-lay-toh-hah)	For my own righteousness
Balye	(Bah-lee-ay)	Salt
Balzarg	(Bah-lay-zoad-ar-gee)	Stewards, Presidents
Bal -zizras	(Bah-lay Zoad-ee-zoad-rahs)	Judgement
Bams	(Bahm-ess)	Let them forget
Basgim	(Bahs-geem)	Day
Bazm (elo)	(Bah-zoad-em)	Mid-day
Bia (I)	(Bee-ah)	Voices
Biah	(Bee-ah)	Stand
Bien	(Bee-ay-nu)	My voice
Bigliad	(Beeg-lee-ah-dah)	In our comforter
Blans	(Blah noo-ess)	Harboured

Blior	(Blee-ohr)	Continual comforters
Bliora	(Blee-oh-rah)	Comfort
Bliorax	(Blee-oh-rahx)	Shall comfort
Bliors	(Blee-oh-ray-ess)	Our comfort
Bogpa	(Boh-gee-pah)	Reigneth
Bolp	(Boh-lah-pay)	Be thou
Booapis	(Boh-oh-pees)	Let her serve them
Bramg	(Bay-ray-mee-gee)	Are prepared
Bransg	(Bay-ray-ness-gee)	Guard
Brgow	(Bay-rah-goh-vah)	Sleep
Brin	(Bay-reen)	Have
Brint	(Bay-reen-tay)	Hast
Busd	(Boos-dah)	Glory
Busdir	(Boos-dee-ray)	Glory
Butmon	(Boot-tay-mohn)	His mouth hath opened
Butrnoni	(Boot-tay-moh-nee)	Their mouths

C

C	(Kah)	Unto, with
Cab	(Kah-bay)	Rod
Cacacom	(Kah-kah-cohm)	Flourish
Cacocasp	(Kah-koh-cahs-pay)	Another while
Cafafm	(Kah-fah-fahm)	Their abiding
Calz	(Kah-lah-zoad)	The firmament
Cam(piao)	(Kah-em)	While
Camliax	(Kah-em-lee-ahx)	Spake
Canal	(Kah-nah-lah)	Workmen
Caosg (o)	(Kah-oh-ess-gee)	The Earth
Capimaon	(Kah-pee-mah-oh-nu)	Numbers of Time
Capimi-ali	(Kah-pee-mee ah-lee)	Successively
Carbaf	(Kah-ray-bahf)	Sink
Cars (Cors)	(Kah-ress)	Such
Casarm	(Kah-sah-raym)	To Whom
Casarman	(Kah-sah-ray-mah-nu)	Under whose
Casarmg	(Kah-sah-ray-em-gee)	To Whom
Ceph	(Kay-pay-hay)	Title of (z)
Chirlan	(Kah-hee-ray-Iah-nu)	Rejoiceth
Chis (or Chris)	(Kah-hees)	Are
Chisdao	(Koh-hees-dah-oh)	Diamonds
Chiso	(Kah-hee-soh)	Shall be

CHR	(Kay-hay-ray)	20th Aethyr
Cial	(Kee-ah-lah)	9, 9, 9, 6
Ciaosi	(Kee-ah-oh-see)	Terror
Cicle	(Kee-kah-lay)	Mysteries of Creation
Cla	(Kee-lah)	4, 5, 6.
Cnila	(Kee-nu-lah)	Blood
Caozior	(Koh-ah-zoad-ee-ohr)	Increase
Cocasb	(Koh-kah-see-bay)	Time
Colis	(Koh-lees)	Making
Collal	(Koh-lay-lahl)	Stones
Commah	(Kohm-mah)	Bindeth, trussed together
Como	(Koh-moh)	A window
Comselh	(Kohm-say-lay-hay)	A circle
Conisbra	(Koh-nees-bay-rah)	The work of man
Const	(Kohn-ess-tay)	Thunders
Cophan	(Koh-pay-hah-nu)	Lamentation
Cor	(Koh-ray)	Number
Coraxo	(Koh-rah-x-oh)	Thunders of judgement
Cordiziz	(Koh-ray-dee-zoad-ee-zoad)	Reasonable creatures of earth, men
Cormp	(Koh-ray-em-pay)	Numbered
Cormp	(Koh-ray-em-pay)	Hath yet numbered
Cormpt	(Koh-ray-em-pay-tay)	Be numbered
Crcrg	(Kah-ray-kah-ray-gee)	Until
Cri-mi	(Kah-ree mee)	Praises
Cro-od-zi	(Koh-roh oh-dah zoad-ee)	The 2nd Beginning
C-rp (crip)	(Kah Ar-pay)	But

D

D (Dial)	(Dah)	Third
Da	(Dah)	There
Damploz	(Dah-me-pay-loh-zoad)	Variety
DAOX	(Dah-oh-x)	5, 6, 7, 8
Darbs	(Dah-ray-bah-ess)	Obey
DARG	(Dah-ray-gee)	6, 7, 3, 9
Darr	(Dar-ray-ray)	Philosopher's Stone
Darsar	(Dah-ray-sahr)	Wherefore
Dax	(Dahx)	Loins
Dazis	(Dah-zoad ees)	Their Heads
De	(Day)	Of
DEO	(Day-oh)	7th Aethyr

DES	(Day-ess)	26th Aethyr
Diu	(Dee-vah)	Angle
DIafod	(Dah-lah-foh-dah)	Sulphur
Dluga (Dlagar)	(Dah-loo-gah)	Giving
Dlugam	(Dah-loo-gahm)	Given
DIugar	(Dah-loo-gahr)	Gave them
Do	(Doh)	In
Doalim	(Doh-ah-leem)	Sin
Dobix	(Doh-beex)	Fall
Dodpal	(Doh-dah-pah-el)	Let them vex
Dods	(Doh-dahs)	Vexing
Dodseh	(Doh-dah-say-hay)	Vexation
Dooain (or p)	(Doh-oh-ah-ee-noo)	His name
Don	(Doh-noo)	Title of letter E (r)
Dorpha	(Doh-ray-pay-hah)	Have looked about me
Dorphal	(Doh-ray-pay-hahl)	Looking with gladness
Dosig	(Doh-see-gee)	Night
Drilpi (a)	(Dah-ree-lah-pah)	Great
Drix	(Dah-ree-x)	Bring down
Droln	(Dah-roh-lah-noo)	Any
Ds	(Dah-ess)	Who, that or which
Du-i-b (Duiv)	(Doo-ee-bay)	Into the third angle
Drun	(Dah-roo-noo)	Title of letter

E

E	(Ay)	I
Eca	(Ay-kah)	Therefore
Ecron	(Ay-kah-roh-noo)	Praise
Ed-nas	(Ay-dah Nah-ess)	Receivers
Ef	(Ay-eff)	Visit us
Efafage	(Ay-fah-fah-gay)	Vials
El	(Ay-lah)	The same
Elzap	(Ay-lah-zoad-ah-pay)	Course
Em	(Ay-mee)	Nine
Emod	(Ay-moh-dah)	8, 7, 6, 3
Emetgis	(Ay-may-tay-gees)	Seal
Emna	(Ay-mee-nah)	Herein
Enay	(Ay-nah-ee)	The Lord
Eors	(Ay-oh-ray-ess)	Thousand
Eran	(Ay-rah-noo)	6332 (6322)
Erm	(Ay-ray-mee)	Ark

Es	(Ay-ess)	Fourth
Esiasch	(Ay-see-ar-ess-cha)	Brothers
Ethamz	(Ay-tay-hah-me-zoad)	Are covered
Etharzi	(Ay-tay-hah-ray-zoad-ee)	Peace

F

F (also EF)	(Eff)	Visit
Fa-a-ip	(Fah ah ee-pay)	Your voices
Faboan	(Fah-boh-ah-noo)	Poison
Fafeh	(Fah-fay-hay)	Intent
Fafen	(Fah-fay-noo)	Your train
Fam	(Fah-mee)	Title of S
Faod	(Fah-oh-dah)	The Beginning
Faonts	(Fah-oh-nu-tay-ess)	Dwelling (verb)
Faorgt	(Fah-ohr-gee-tay)	Dwelling place
Fargt	(Fah-ray-gee-tay)	Their dwelling places
Farmz	(Fah-ray-mee-zoad)	Ye lifted up your voices
Faxs	(Fahx-ess)	7336
Fifalz	(Fee-fah-Iah-zoad)	Weed out
Fifis	(Fee-fee-ess)	Execute

G

G	(Gee)	(With)
GA	(Gah)	31
Gah	(Gah-hay)	Spirits
Gal	(Gah-lah)	Title of D
G-chis-ge	(Gee Kah-hee-ess gay)	Are not the
Ge	(Gee)	Is not
Ged	(Gay-dah)	Title of G
Ge-lad	(Gay Ee-ah-dah)	Our Lord and Master
Geobofal	(Gay-oh-bah-fah-lah)	Great Work
Ger	(Gay-ray)	Title of Q
Gigipah	(Gee-gee-pah-hay)	Living Breath
Gisa	(Gee-sah)	Title of T
Givi	(Gee-vee)	Stronger
Gizyaz	(Gee-zoad-ee-ah-zoad)	Mighty Earthquakes
Gnay	(Gee-nah-ee)	Doth
Gnetaab	(Gee-nay-tah-ah-bay)	Your Governments
Gnonp	(Gee-noh-nu-pay)	I garnished

Gohe (or Goho)	(Goh-hay)	Saith
Gohia	(Goh-hee-ah)	We say
Gohol	(Goh-hoh-el)	Saying
Goholor	(Goh-hoh-lohr)	Lift up
Gohulim	(Goh-hoo-leem)	It is said
Gohus	(Goh-hoos)	I say
Gon	(Goh-noo)	Title of I
Gono	(Goh-noh)	Faith
Gosao	(Goh-sah-oh)	Stranger
Graa	(Gee-rah-ah)	Moon
Graa	(Gee-rah-ah)	Marquises
Graph	(Gee-rah-pay-hay)	Title of E
Grosb	(Gee-roh-ess-bay)	Bitter Sting

H

Hami	(Hah-mee)	Creatures
Harg	(Hah-ray-gee)	Hath planted
Hoath	(Hoh-ah-tay-hay)	True Worshipper
Holdo	(Hoh-lah-doh)	Groaned aloud
Hol-q	(Hoh-lah Koh)	Measureth (ed)
Horn	(Hoh-mee)	Liveth
Homil	(Hoh-mee-el)	True Ages
Homin	(Hoh-mee-noo)	Age
Hubai	(Hoo-bah-ee)	Lanterns
Hubar	(Hoo-bah-ray)	Ever burning lamps
Hubard	(Hoo-bah-ray-dah)	Living lamps

I

I	(Ee)	Is
Iad	(Ee-ah-dah)	God
Iadnah	(Ee-ah-dah-nah-hay)	Knowledge
Iadnamad	(Ee-ah-dah-nah-mah-dah)	The undefiled knowledge
Iadpil	(Ee-ah-dah-pee-el)	Him
Iaiadix	(Ee-ah-ee-ah-deex)	Honour
Ia-ial	(Ee-ah ee-ah-el)	Conclude us
Iaida	(Ee-ah-ee-dah)	The highest, most high
Iaidon	(Ee-ah-ee-doh-noo)	All-powerful
Ial	(Ee-ah-el)	Burning

Ialpirgah	(Ee-ah-el-pee-ray-gah)	Flames of first glory
Ialpon	(Ee-ah-el-poh-noo)	Burn
Ialpor	(Ee-ah-el-poh-ray)	Flaming
Iaod (of)	(Ee-ah-oh-dah)	Beginning
Iarry	(Ee-oh-ray-ree)	Providence
ICH	(Ee-kah-hay)	11th Aethyr
Id	(Ee-dah)	Always
Idoigo	(Ee-doh-ee-goh)	Him that Sitteth on the Holy Throne
Ieh	(Ee-ay-hay)	Art
Iehusoz	(Ee-ay-hoo-soh-zoad)	His mercies
Iisonon	(Ee-ee-soh-noh-noo)	Branches
Ils	(Ee-el-ess)	O Thou
Ilsi	(Ee-el-see)	Thee
Im-va-mar	(Ee-mee vah mah-ray)	Apply yourselves
Insi	(Ee-noo-see)	Walkest
Iod	(Ee-oh-dah)	Him
Ioiad	(Ee-oh-ee-oh-dah)	Him that liveth forever
Ip	(Ee-pay)	Not
Ipam	(Ee-pah-mee)	Beginningless
Ipamis	(Ee-pah-mees)	Endless
Ipuran	(Ee-poo-rah-noo)	Shall not see
Yolcam	(Ee-oh-ol-kah-mee)	Bring forth
Yolci	(Ee-oh-el-kee)	Bringeth forth
Yor	(Ee-oh-ray)	Roll
Yrpoil	(Ee-ar-poh-ee-lah)	Division
Irgil	(Ee-ar-gee-lah)	How many
Isro	(Ee-ess-roh)	Promise
Ixomaxip	(Ee-x-oh-mohx-ee-pay)	Let her be known
Iza-zaz	(Ee-zoad-ah zoad-ah-zoad)	Have framed within
Izizop	(Ee-zoad-ee-zoad-oh-pay)	From the highest vessels

L

L	(Lah)	The first
L (o) (a)	(Lah)	The first one
Laiad	(Lah-ee-ah-dah)	The Secrets of Truth
Lap	(Lah-pay)	For
Larag	(Lah-rah-gee)	Neither
Las	(Lah-ess)	Rich
LEA	(Lah-ay-ah)	16th Aethyr

Lei	(Lay-lah)	The same
Levithmong	(Levee-tha-mon-gee)	The Beasts of the Field
LIL	(Lee-lah)	1st Aethyr
Limlal	(Lee-em-lah-lah)	His Treasure
LIN	(Lee-noo)	22nd Aethyr
LIT	(Lee-tay)	5th Aethyr
LOE	(Loh-ay)	12th Aethyr
Loholo (Sobolo)	(Loh-hoh-loh)	Shineth
Lolcis	(Loh-Iah-kee-ess)	Bucklers
Loncho	(Loh-nu-kah-hoh)	Fall
Lon-doh	(Loh-noo doh)	Kingdoms
Lonsa (Lonshi)	Loh-noo-sah)	Power
Lonsh	(Loh-noo-ess-hay)	In power exalted
Lonshin	(Loh-noo-ess-hee-noo)	Their powers
Lors-l-q	(Loh-ray-ess el koh)	Flowers
Lrasd	(El-rah-ess-doh)	To dispose
Lring	(El-ree-nu-gee)	To stir up
Lu	(Loo)	Not or nor
Lucal	(Loo-kah-lah)	The North
Luciftian	(Loo-kee-eff-tee-ah-nu)	Ornaments of brightness
Luciftias	(Loo-ku-eff-tee-ah-ess)	Brightness
Lu-ia-he	(Loo ee-ah hay)	A Song of Honour
Lulo	(Loo-loh)	Tartar of Wine
Lusd (an)	(Loo-ess-dah)	Feet
Lusda	(Loo-ess-dah)	Their feet
Lusdi	(Loo-ess-dee)	Mv feet

M

Maasi	(Mah-ah-see)	Laid up
Mad	(Mah-dah)	The same your God
Madrid	(Mah-dah-ree-dah)	Iniquities
Madriiax	(Mad-dah-ree-ee-ahx)	O Ye Heavens
Malpirgi	(Mah-lah-pee-ar-gee)	Fires of life & increase
Malprg	(Mah-lah-pee-ar-gee)	Through-thrusting fire (Or Fiery Darts)
Mals	(Mah-lah-ess)	Title of P
Manin	(Mah-nu-nu)	In the Mind
Ma-of-fas	(Mah ohff fahs)	Not to be measured
Mapm	(Mah-pay-mee)	9639
Marb	(Mah-ah-bay)	According

Matorb	(Mah-toh-ar-bay)	Echoing
MAZ	(Mah-zoad)	6th Aethyr
Med	(May-dah)	Title of O
Miam	(Mee-ah-mee)	Continuance
Mian	(Mee-ah-nu)	3663
Micalp	(Mee-kah-el-pay)	Mightier
Micalzo	(Mee-kah-el-zoad-oh)	In Power
Micaolz	(Mee-kah-oh-el-zoad)	Mighty
Micma	(Mee-kah-mah)	Behold
Miinoag	(Mee-ee-noh-ah-gee)	Corners
Mir	(Mee-ray)	A torrent
Mire	(Mee-ar-kah)	Upon
(z)Mnad	(Mee-nah-dah)	Another
Molap	(Moh-lah-pay)	Men
Molvi	(Moh-lah-vee)	Surges
Mom	(Moh-mee)	Moss
Momao	(Moh-mah-oh)	The Crowns
Momar	(Moh-mah-ray)	Shall be crowned
Monasci	(Moh-nah-ess-kee)	The Great Name
Monons	(Moh-noh-noo-ess)	Heart
Mooab	(Moh-oh-ah-bah)	It repenteth me
Mospleh	(Moh-ess-pay-lay-hay)	The Horns
Moz	(Moh-zoad)	Joy

N

Na	(Nah)	Your
Na-hath	(Nah Hah-tay-hay)	Title of H
Nana-e-el	(Nah-nah ay ay-lah)	My Power
Nanba	(Nah-noo-bah)	Thorns
Napeai	(Nah-pah-ay-ee)	Oh you swords
Napta	(Nah-pay-tah)	Two edge swords
Nazarth	(Nah-zoad-ahht)	Pillars of gladness
Nazavabb	(Nah-zoad-ah-vah-bay-bay)	Hyacinthine Pillars
Nazps	(Nah-zoad-pay-ess)	Sword or Earls
Netaab	(Nay-tah-ah-bay)	Government
NI	(Nee)	28
NIA	(Nee-ah)	24th Aethyr
Nibm	(Nee-bah-mee)	Season
Nidali	(Nee-dah-lee)	Mighty Sounds
Niis	(Nee-ee-ess)	Come Ye

Niiso	(Nee-ee-soh)	Come Away
Noaln	(Noh-ah-lah-noo)	May (be)
Noan (Noas)	(Noh-ah-noo)	Ye are become
(i) Noar	(Noh-ah-ray)	Become
Noasmi	(Noh-ah-ess-mee)	Let them become
Nobloh	(Noh-bay-loh)	The Palms
Noco	(Noh-koh)	Servant
Nocod	(Noh-koh-dah)	Thy servants
Noib	(Noh-ee-bay)	Yea!
Nonig	(Noh-mee-gee)	Even
Nonca	(Noh-noo-kah)	Unto You
Nonci (f)	(Noh-noo-kee)	O You (ye)
Noncp	(Noh-noo-kah-pay)	For You
Noquodi	(Noh-koo-oh-dee)	Their Ministers
(c) Noquol	(Noh-koo-oh-lah)	O Ye Servants
Nor	(Noh-ray)	Sons
Noromi	(Noh-roh-mee)	O Ye Sons!
Nor-molap	(Noh-ray moh-lah-pay)	Sons of Men
Nor-quasahi	(Noh-ray koo-ah-sah-hee)	Ye Sons of pleasure
Norz	(Noh-ray-zoad)	Six
Nothoa	(Noh-tay-hoh-ah)	In the midst (?)

O

O	(Oh)	5
O	(Oh)	Be
Oado	(Oh-ah-doh)	Weave
Oadriax	(Oh-ah-dah-ree-ahx)	Lower Heavens
Oali	(Oh-ah-lee)	I have placed
Oanio	(Oh-ah-nee-oh)	Moment
OB	(Oh-bay)	28
Obelisong	(Oh-bah-lee-soh-noo-gee)	Pleasant deliverers
Obloc	(Oh-bay-loh-kah)	A Garland
Oboleh	(Oh-boh-lay-hay)	Your Garments
Obza	(Oh-bay-zoad-ah)	Half
Od	(Oh-dah)	And
Odo	(Oh-doh)	Open or Openest
Odzi	(Oh-dah-zoad-ee)	Beginning
Oe	(Oh-ay)	Sing (ing)
O-q	(Oh koh)	But
Ohio	(Oh-hee-oh)	Woe

Ohorela	(Oh-ho-ray-lah)	I made a Law, Dukes
Oi	(Oh-ee)	This (or that is)
Oiad	(Oh-ee-ah-dah)	Just or God
Oiap	(Oh-ee-ah-pay)	The same
OL	(Oh-lah)	24th part
Ol	(Oh-lah)	I made you (I have made)
Olani	(Oh-lah-nee)	Two Times
Ollor	(Oh-lah-loh-ray)	Man
(Ollora, Ollog)	(Oh-lah-loh-rah)	Same
Oln	(Oh-lah-noo)	Made
Olpirt	(Oh-lah-pee-ray-tay)	Light
Om	(Oh-mee)	Know or Understand
Omoas	(Oh-mah-ah-ess)	Their Names
Oma (p)	(Oh-mah)	Understanding
Omax	(Oh-mahx)	Knowest
Ooa	(Oh-oh-ah)	Their
Ooaona	(Oh-oh-ah-oh-nah)	Eyes, visible appcarance
Ooge	(Oh-oh-gay)	Chamber
Op	(Oh-pay)	22
Oroch (a)	(Oh-roh-kah-hay)	Under you (beneath
Orri	(Oh-ray-ree)	Barren Stone
Ors	(Oh-ray-ess)	(with darkness)
Orscor	(Oh-ray-ess-koh-ray)	Dryness
Orsca	(Oh-ray-ess-kah)	Building
Orsha (Orsba)	(Oh -ray-ess-hah)	Drunken
Orth	(Oh-ray-tha)	Title of F
Os	(Oh-ess)	Twelve
Othil	(Oh-tay-hee-Iah)	I have set
Ovcho	(Oh-voh-kah-hoh)	Let it confound
Ovof	(Oh-voh-eff)	May be magnified
Ovoars	(Oh-voh-ah-ar-ess)	The Center
Ox	(Ohx)	26
Oxex	(Ohx-ayx)	Vomit out
Oxiayal	(Ohx-ee-ah-yahl)	Mighty Seat
OXO	(Ohx-oh)	15th Aethyr
Ozazm	(Oh-zoad-ah-zoad-mee)	Make me
Ozol	(Oh-zoad-oh-lah)	Their heads
Ozongon	(Oh-zoad-oh-nu-goh-nu)	Manifold Winds
Ozozma	(Oh-zoad-oh-zoad-mah)	And make us

P

P	(Pay)	8
Pa	(Pah)	Be
Pa-aox (t)	(Pah-ahx)	Remain
Paeb	(Pah-ay-bay)	An Oak
Page	(Pah-gay)	Rest
Paid	(Pah-ee-dah)	Always
Pal	(Pah-lah)	Title of X
Pambt	(Pah-mee-bay-tay)	Unto me
Panpir	(Pah-noo-pee-ray)	Pouring down
Paombd	(Pah-oh-mee-bay-dah)	Her members
Papnor	(Pah-pay-noh-ray)	This remembrance
Par	(Pah-ray)	In Them
Parach	(Pah-rah-kah-hay)	Equal
Paracleda	(Pah-rah-kah-lay-dah)	A wedding
Paradial	(Pah-rah-dee-ah-lah)	Living dwellings
Paradizod	(Pah-rah-dee-zoad-oh-dah)	Virgins
Parm	(Pah-ray-mee)	Run
Parmg	(Pah-ray-mee-gee)	Let it run
Pashs	(Pah-ess-hay-ess)	Children
Patralx	(Pah-tay-rah-layx)	Rock
PAZ	(Pah-zoad)	4th Aethyr
Pd	(Pah-dah)	Thirty-three
Pe	(Pay)	Title of B
PEOAL	(Peh-oh-ah-lay)	5, 9, 6, 3, 6
Pi	(Pee)	Places (Bed)
Piad	(Pee-ah-dah)	Your God
Pi-adph	(Pee ah-dah-pay-hay)	Depths of my Jaws
Piamo-1	(Pee-ah-moh-ell)	Righteousness
Piap	(Pee-ah-pay)	Balance
Pidiai	(Pee-dee-ah-ee)	Marble
Pii	(Pee-ee)	Bed (or She is a place)
Pilah	(Pee-lah)	Moreover
Pild	(Pee-lah-dah)	Continually
Pilzin	(Pee-Iah-zoad-ee-nu)	Firmament of Waters
Pir	(Pee-ray)	Holy Ones
Piripsax	(Pee-ree-pay-sahx)	With the Heavens
Piripsol	(Pee-ree-pay-sohl)	The Heavens
Plapli	(Pay-lah-pay-lee)	Partakers
Plosi	(Pay-loh-see)	As many

Poamal	(Poh-ah-mah-lah)	Your Palace
Poilp	(Poh-ee-lah-pay)	Are divided
Pop	(Poh-pay)	19th Aethyr
Praf	(Pay-rah-eff)	Dwell
Prdzar	(Pay-ray-dah-zoad-ahr)	Diminish
Prg	(Pay-ray-gee)	Flames
Prge	(Pay-ray-gay)	With the Fire
Prgel	(Pay-ray-gay-lah)	Of Fire
Priaz (i)	(Pay-ree-ah-zoad)	Those
Prt	(Pay-ray-tay)	Flame
Pugo	(Poo-goh)	Unto
Pu-im	(Poo-eem)	Sharp sickles (Knights)

Q

Q	(Koh)	Or
Q (Cocasb)	(Koh)	Content of Time
Qaa	(Kah-ah)	Your Garments
Qaaon (s)	(Kah-ah-oh-noo)	In Your Creation
Qanis	(Kah-nee-ess)	Olives
Qting	(Koh-tee-noo-gee)	The Rotten
Quaal (Quaadah)	(Koo-ah-ah-lah)	The Creator
Quar	(Koo-ah-ray)	1636
Quasb	(Koo-ah-ess-bay)	Destroy
Quasahi	(Koo-ah-sahee)	Pleasure
Qui-i-n	(Koo-ee ee noo)	Wherein
Qurlst	(Koo-arel-ess-tay)	As an handmaid

R

Ra-as (y)	(Rah ah-ess)	The East
Raclir	(Rah-kah-lee-ray)	Weeping
Restel	(Ray-ess-tay-lah)	That you may praise Him
RII	(Ree-ee)	29th Aethyr
Rior	(Ree-or-rah)	Widow
Ripir	(Ree-pee-rah)	No place
Ripson	(Ree-pay-soh-noo)	Heaven
Rit	(Ree-tay)	Mercy
Rlodnr	(Ree-loh-dah-noo-ar)	Mercury
(Ror)	(Roh-ray)	Sun, Kings
Roxtan	(Rohx-tah-nu)	Wine
Rsam	(Rah-sah-em)	Admiration

S

S	(Ess)	Fourth
Sa	(Sah)	In
Saanir	(Sah-ah-nee-ray)	Parts
Salbrox	(Sah-lah-brohx)	Sulphur
Said	(Sah-lah-dah)	Wonder
Salman	(Sah-lah-mah-nu)	A house
Samvelg	(Sahm-vay-lah-gee)	To the Righteous
Sapah	(Sah-pah)	Mighty Sounds
Sision	(See-see-oh-noo)	Temple
Siatris	(See-ah-tay-ree-ess)	Scorpions
Sibsi	(See-bay-see)	The Covenant
So	(Soh)	In
Sobam	(Soh-bah-mee)	Whom
Sobha	(Soh-bay-hah)	Whose
Sobra	(Soh-bay-rah)	In whose
Solpeth	(Soh-lah-pay-tay-hay)	Hearken
Sonuf	(Soh-noof)	Reign
Surzas	(Soo-ray-zoad-ah-ess)	He hath sworn
Symp	(See-mee-pay)	Another

T

T	(Tay)	Also
Ta	(Tah)	As
Taba	(Tah-bah)	To Govern
Tabaame	(Tah-bah-ah-may)	Prelates (governors)
Tabaan	(Tah-bah-ah-nu)	Governor
Tabaord	(Tah-bah-oh-ray-dah)	Let her be governed
Tabaori	(Tah-bah-oh-ree)	Govern
Tabges	(Tah-bay-gay-ess)	Caves
Tal	(Tah-lah)	Title of M
Talbo	(Tah-Iah-boh)	Cups
TAN	(Tah-noo)	17th Aethyr
Tastax	(Tah-ess-tayx)	Going Before
Tatan	(Tah-tah-noo)	Wormwood
Teloah	(Tay-Ioh-ah)	Death
Teloc (Vovim)	(Tay-Ioh-kah)	Him that is fallen

Teloch	(Tay-loh-kah-hay)	Death
TEX	(Tayx)	30th Aethyr
Thild	(Tay-hee-lah-dah)	Their own
Thil (n)	(Tay-hee-lah)	Seats
Ti	(Tee)	It
Tia	(Tee-ah)	Unto us
Tianti	(Tee-ah-nu-tee)	She is (or bed)
Tibibf	(Tee-bee-bay-eff)	Sorrow
Tilb	(Tee-lah-bay)	Her
Tiobl	(Tee-oh-bay-lah)	In her
Tliob	(Tay-lee-oh-bay)	Separate, to
Toatar	(Toh-ah-tay-ray)	Hearken
Toh	(Toh-hay)	Triumpheth
Toglo	(Toh-gee-loh)	All things
Toibl	(Toh-ee-bay-lah)	Within her
Tonug	(Toh-nu-gee)	Let them be defaced
Tooart	(Toh-oh-oh-ray-tay)	Furnishing
TOR	(Toh-ray)	23rd Aethyr
Torg (i)	(Toh-ray-gee)	Creatures of Earth
Torzu	(Tor-zoad-oo)	Arise
Torzul	(Toh-ray-zoad-oo-lah)	Shall Rise
Torzulp	(Toh-ray-zoad-oo-Iah-pay)	Rose Up
Tox	(Tohx)	Of Him
Tranan	(Tay-rah-noh-noo)	Marrow
Trian	(Tay-ray-ee-ah-nu)	Shall Be
Trint	(Tay-ray-ee-nu-tay)	Sit
Trof	(Tay-roh-eff)	Building
Turbs	(Toor-bay-ess)	Their Beauty

V

Vabzir	(Vah-bay-zoad-ee-ray)	Eagle
Vaoan	(Vav-oh-ah-noo)	Truth (purified, glorified)
Vau	(Vah-oo)	Title of U or V
Vaul	(Vah-oo-Iah)	Work
Vaun	(Vah-oo-nu)	Ye might work
Vcim	(Vah-kah-ee-mee)	They frown not
Veh	(Vay-hay)	Title of C or K
Vap	(Vay-pay)	Flame
Vgear	(Vah-gay-ah-ray)	The strength of man

Vgeg (i)	(Vah-gay-gee)	Wax Strong
Vi	(Vee)	In
Vi-i-v	(Vee-ee-vah)	The second angle
Vin	(Vee-noo)	Invoke
Virq	(Vee-ray-koh)	Nests
Vi-v	(Vee vah)	The Second
Vlcinin	(Vah-lah-kee-nee-nu)	Happy is He
Vis	(Vah-lah-ess)	The Ends
V-ma-dea	(Vah-mah-day-ah)	Strong Towers
Vmd	(Vah-mee-dah)	Called
Vml	(Vah-mee-lah)	Add
Vmplif	(Vah-mee-pay-lee-eff)	Our Strength
Vnalah	(Vah-nah-lah)	Skirts
Vnas (Vnal)	(Vah-nah-ess)	These
Vnchi	(Vah-noo-kah-hee)	Confound
Vnd-1	(Vah-noo-dah-Iah)	The rest
Vnig	(Vah-nee-gee)	Requireth
Vniglag	(Vah-nee-gee-Iah-gee)	Descend
Vnph	(Von-pay-hay)	Anger
Vohim	(Voh-hee-mee)	Hundred
Vonpho	(Von-pay-hoh)	Wrath
Vonsarg	(Voh-nu-sah-ray-gee)	Everyone
Vooan	(Voo-ah-nu)	Truth, with them that fall
Vorsg	(Vor-sah-gee)	Over You
Vovina	(Voh-vee-nah)	The Dragon
Vp	(Vah-pay)	Not
V-pa-ah (i)	(Vah pay ah-hay)	Wings
Vran	(Vah-rah-noo)	The Elders
Vrbs	(Vah-ray-bay-ess)	Beautified
Vrelp	(Vah-ray-Iah-pay)	A Strong Seer of Things
VTA	(Vah-tah)	14th Aethyr
VTI	(Vah-tee)	25th Aethyr
VX	(Vah-ex)	42
Un	(Oo-noo)	Title of A
Ur	(Oo-ray)	Title of L
Uran	(Oo-rah-noo)	Shall see

Z

Z (od)	(Zoad)	They (as)
ZAA	(Zoad-ah-ah)	27th Aethyr

Zacar-e	(Zoad-ah-kah-ray)	Move
Zamran	(Zoad-ah-mer-rah-noo)	Show Yourselves
Zar	(Zoad-ah-ray)	(Courses)
ZEN	(Zoad-ay-noo)	18th Aethyr
ZID	(Zoad-ee-dah)	8th Aethyr
Zien	(Zoad-ee-ay-nu)	My hands
Zildar	(Zoad-ee-lah-dah-ray)	Flew
Zilodarp	(Zoad-ee-loh-dah-ray-pay)	Conquest
ZIM	(Zoad-ee-mee)	13th Aethyr
Zimii	(Zoad-ee-mee-ee)	Have entered
Zimz (a)	(Zoad-ee-mee-zoad)	My vestures
ZIP	(Zoad-ee-pay)	9th Aethyr
Zir	(Zoad-ee-ray)	I am
Zirdo	(Zoad-ee-ray-doh)	I am
Zirn	(Zoad-ee-ray-noo)	Wonders
Zirom	(Zoad-ee-roh-mee)	There were
Zirop	(Zoad-ee-roh-pay)	Was
Zixlay	(Zoad-ix-lay)	To stir up
Zizop	(Zoad-ee-zoad-oh-pay)	Vessels
Zilda	(Zoad-lee-dah)	To water
Znrza	(Zoad-nu-ray-zoad-ah)	Sware
Z-ol	(Zoad oh-lah)	Hands
ZOM	(Zoad-oh-mee)	3rd Aethyr
Zomd	(Zoad-oh-mee-dah)	In the midst of
Zonac	(Zoad-oh-nah-kah)	They are apparelled
Zongon	(Zoad-oh-nu-goh-nu)	The Winds
Zonrensg	(Zoad-on-raynu-ess-gee)	Delivered
Zorge	(Zoad-or-gee)	Be friendly unto me
Zumbi	(Zoad-oo-mee-bee)	Seas
Zylna	(Zoad-ee-lah-nah)	In itself

THE COMPLETE GOLDEN DAWN
SYSTEM OF MAGIC

GLOSSARY

GLOSSARY

A

Aatiq Yomin
(Aramaic) Macroprosopus or the Greater Countenance, referred to Kether and secondarily to Chokmah and Binah.

Abiegnus
The mystic mountain of the Rosicrucians, symbolizing Initiation.

Abba
Yod of Tetragrammaton. The Supernal Father (Aramaic) referred to Chokmah.

Aces (4)
The Tarot cards attributed to the four basic elements.

Acquisitio
A Jupiterian geomantic figure signifying good luck and gain.

Agni
The tattwic fire element; also named Tejas. A red equilateral triangle.

Aima
Heh of Tetragrammaton. The supernal Mother referred to Binah.

Aima Elohim
Mother of the Gods. Referred to both Y and H of Tetragrammaton.

Ain
Ain Soph
Ain Soph Aour
The three veils of the Absolute. Nothing, No Limit, Light without end.

Aiq Bkr
A qabalistic method of permutation.

Akasa
The first tattwa. Ether or Spirit, depicted as a black or indigo egg.

Albus
A Mercurial geomantic figure, representing gain.

141

Alembic
Alchemical distillation vessel.

Aleph
The first letter of the Hebrew alphabet. The first path on the Tree of Life uniting Kether with Chokmah.

Amissio
A Venusian geomantic figure representing loss.

Apas
Gustiferous ether. Element of Water. Silver crescent.

Ararita
A Hebrew notariqon comprised of the initials of a sentence: One is his beginning. One is his individuality. His permutation is One.

Aretz
Hebrew for the element Earth.

Ariq Anpin
The Ancient of Days. Another title of Kether.

Asch
Hebrew word for the element of Fire.

Assiah
The world of Form.

Athanor
An alchemical furnace.

Atziluth
The world of Archetypes.

Auriel
Literally the Light of God. The Archangel of Earth.

Ave
The Angel who allegedly communicated part of the Enochian system to John Dee.

B

Bataivah
Enochian. The Great King of the East, Air Tablet.

Binah
The third Sephirah on the Qabalistic Tree of Life.

Boaz
The black Pillar of the Temple, representing Severity.

Briah
The World of Creation.

C

Canopic Gods
The four Sons of Horus who rule over the viscera.

GLOSSARY

Caput and Cauda Draconis

Two geomantic fiqures representing the N. and S. nodes of the Moon, Caput being a beneficent Figure and Cauda unfavorable.

Carcer

A Saturnine geomantic figure representing delay and restriction.

Chesed

The fourth Sephirah on the Qabalistic Tree of Life, to which Jupiter is referred.

Chiah

A part of the soul, referred to Chokmah. Buddhi. The magical Will.

Chymical Marriage

One of the three Rosicrucian classics with an alchemical slant.

Confessio

One of the three Rosicrucian classics of the early 17th century.

Conjunctio

Mercurial geomantic figure, operating synergistically with other figures for good or ill.

Cucurbite

Glass boiling vessel used in Alchemy. Part of distilling apparatus.

D

Daath

An 11th Sephirah, not one of the basic Ten, added to the Tree of Life to account for a link between the human and the divine. A resultant of the "Union" of Chokmah and Binah.

Dadouchos

Officer in the Temple in charge of the Thurible, incense and lights.

Divination

Method of determining the outcome of life events, used as a means of developing intuition and the inner psychic sense.

E

Enochian

System of magic developed by Sir John Dee and Edward Kelley. The crown and jewel of the Order system, synthesizing all other systems.

Exordium

An Introduction, the beginning of a statement. E.G., the General and Particular Exordium opening the document Z-l, both of great magical import. They are dedicated to Thoth.

Edelperna

Enochian. The Great King of the South, Fire Tablet.

Emor Dial Hectega

Enochian. Three Deity Names abstracted from the Earth Tablet in North.

Empeh Arsel Gaiol

Enochian. Three Deity Names abstracted from the Water Tablet in West.

143

F

Fama Fraternatitas
One of the great Rosicrucian Classics of the early 17th century.

Fortuna Major and Minor
Two Solar geomantic figures indicative of good fortune and success.

G

Gabriel
Literally, Might of God. Archangel of Water.

Gematria
The art of manipulating letter-numbers to gain meaningful insights.

Geburah
The fifth Sephirah on the Qabalistic Tree of Life.
Geomancy, An archaic method of divination by means of the element of Earth.

Gihon
Referred to the element of Water. One of the four Rivers, the Waters of Mercy flowing from above into Chesed.

Gnomes
The Earth elementals.

H

Hegemon
The leader of the Soul. Represents equilibrium and harmony as a Temple Officer. Reconciles the offices of Hierophant and Hiereus.

Hekas
Hekas Este Bebeloi
Announcement that the place and the congregation are holy.

Hexagram
Powerful symbol representing the operation of the seven planets under the presidency of the Sephiroth and the name ARARITA.

Hiddikel
One of the four rivers flowing from above into Tiphareth, and represents Air.

I

Insignia
Worn by Officers in the Temple defining their function.

Ic Zod Heh Chal
Enochian. Great King of the North, Earth Tablet.

GLOSSARY

J

Jachin
The right sided Pillar in the Temple. White, representing Mercy as opposed to Boaz which is Black and Severity.

K

Kalah
Bride, referred to Malkuth, the final Heh of YHVH. The bride of Microprosopus.

Kamea
A magical square from which sigils may be drawn.

Kerub
The Four essential vice-regents of the Elements, corresponding to the letters of the Name YHVH.

Kerux
The Officer in the Temple who is the Guardian of the inner door and the Herald, leading circumambulations.

Kether
The first Sephirah on the Qabalistic Tree of Life.

L

Lamen
Badge worn by officers in the Temple denoting their function. Also a glyph relating to the Great Work.

Laetitia
A Jupiterian geomantic figure representing joy and happiness.

LVX
Light. Also represents the signs used by the Adepts in the Adeptus Minor grade. Since its gematria is 65 it also relates to the Higher and Divine Genius (Adonai).

M

Malkuth
The tenth and final Sephirah on the Tree of Life.

Malkah
Queen. One title of Malkuth considered as Bride of Microprosopus.

Mayim
Hebrew for Water.

Metatron
The great Archangel of Kether. Also the male Kerub of Brightness representing the White Pillar.

Michael
Literally, Who is like God. Great Archangel of Fire.

N

Nahar
River flowing from the Supernal Eden differentiating in Daath into four heads, the four elements.

Neophyte
First grade of the Order, not placed on the Tree.

Nephesch
Part of the Soul, sometimes referred to Yesod or to Malkuth. Described as the animal soul, or the automatic consciousness.

Neschamah
Part of the Soul, the higher aspiring Self, referred to Binah. Feminine and yearning.

Netzach
The seventh Sephirah on the Qabalistic Tree of Life.

Notariqon
Shorthand writing with Hebrew letters to gain meaningful insights. For example AGLA is a notariqon of four words meaning "Thou art mighty for ever O Lord."

O

Oip Teaa Pedoce
Enochian. Three Deity Names abstracted from the Fire Tablet in South.

Oro Ibah Aozpi
Enochian. Three Deity Names abstracted from the Air Tablet in East.

P

Pastos
The Tomb of our Father C.R.C.

Pentagram
A powerful symbol called the Signet Star of the Microcosm, representing the operation of the Spirit and the Four Elements under the presidency of YHShVH.

Pentacle
A symbol referred to the element Earth. Also a symbol of the initiate's understanding of the Universe.

Philosophus
The fourth grade of the Order, exclusive of Neophyte, attributed to Fire and Netzach, and Venus.

Phrath
Euphrates. One of the four rivers flowing into Malkuth the Earth.

Pison
One of the four rivers flowing into Geburah - Fire.

Populus
A Lunar geomantic figure, suggesting movement and change.

Practicus

The third grade of the Order, exclusive of Neophyte, attributed to Water and Hod, and Mercury.

Prithivi
One of the tattwas, Earth - a yellow square.

Puella
A Venusian geomantic figure suggesting art, love and peace.

Puer
A Martial geomantic figure for activity and energy.

Q

Qabalah
Early form of mysticism of the Hebrews, serving as the basis for Magic.

Qesheth
Rainbow of Promise. Veil separating the four lower Sephiroth from Tiphareth

Qliphoth
The world of shells or demons below Malkuth. (Yet this world also has its own ten Sephiroth.)

R

Ra Agiosel
Enochian. The Great King of the West, Water Tablet.

Ritual
A set of external events so designed as to energize an inner set of psychic responses related to them.

Ruach
Part of the Soul referred to the cluster of Sephiroth about Tiphareth. The mind, lower Manas. Also the Hebrew for Air and Spirit.

Rubeus
A Martial geomantic figure spelling out trouble and conflict.

S

Salamanders
The Fire elementals.

Sandalphon
The Archangel reconciler for Earth and its Celestial Soul. She is the female Kerub of the Ark.

Shem ha-Mephoresch
The undivided Name from which are derived the 72 angelic names attributed to the 36 Tarot pip cards.

Sephiroth
Term for the ten centers comprising the Qabalistic Tree of Life.

Sepher Yetzirah

The Book of Formation, one of the oldest texts of Qabalistic literature. The term Yetziratic refers to this book which gives the principal astrological values to the letters of the Hebrew Alphabet.

Serpent Formulae

A description of the magical forces of the four elements as they circulate around the North Pole or the Kether of our system to which the four Aces are attributed.

Sigil

Signature. Usually of a spirit or intelligence or Angel. Anciently derived from the Kameas, but in the Order traced on the Rose.

Skrying

Originally related to crystal gazing, but now refers to the development of the inner vision.

Stolistes

Officer in the Temple in charge of the gowns and robes, and the purifying Water.

Sylphs

The Air elementals.

T

Tarot

Set of 78 cards related to the Tree of Life. Origin more or less obscure.

Talisman

A dead or inert substance galvanized into life by magically charging it with a specific form of energy.

Tattwa

Hindu term for the five elements that issue from Swara the great Breath. Their symbols are used in the Order for skrying.

Tejas

The tattwic element of Fire. Synonym is Agni. A red triangle.

Telesmata

Refers to telesmatic images. These are built up in the imagination using the letters of the Divine or Archangelic Name to provide the character and nature of the Form. Sometimes, as a synonym of talisman.

Temurah

Permutation. A method of arranging Hebrew letters to gain meaningful insights.

Tetragrammaton

Latin for the four Letters of the divine name YHVH, the cornerstone of much if not all of the G.D. attributions to the Tree.

Theoricus

Second grade of the Order, exclusive of Neophyte. Attributed to Yesod, Luna and Air.

Tiphareth

The sixth Sephirah on the Tree of Life equidistant from Kether and Malkuth, representing harmony, beauty and equilibrium.

GLOSSARY

Torah
The Law. The first five books of the Bible.

Tree of Life
Etz Chayim. A geometrical glyph underlying most of the Golden Dawn teaching.

U

Undines
The Water elementals.

V

Vault
The seven-sided initiation chamber of the Adepti where C.R.C. was interred and resurrected.

Vayu
The tattwic element of Air, a blue sphere.

Via
A Lunar geomantic figure suggesting travel and change.

W

Watchtower
An Enochian term referring to one of the four cardinal quarters.

Y

Yachin
Also written as Jachin. The Right (white) Pillar of the Temple, representing Mercy.

Yesheshuah
The Pentagrammaton. The letter Shin representing the fire of the Holy Spirit, descending into and illuminating Tetragrammaton.

Yetzirah
The World of Formation.

Z

Zauir Anpin
Microprosopus, the Lesser Countenance, referred to Tiphareth.

Zohar
One of the major texts of the Qabalistic Literature.

Zelator
First grade of the Order, exclusive of Neophyte, attributed to Malkuth.

APPENDICES

APPENDICES

TABLE OF CONTENTS

APPENDIX I

THE PENTAGRAM RITUALS

By
ISRAEL REGARDIE

Edited by
David Cherubim, Israel
Regardie Foundation

THE PENTAGRAM RITUAL OF AIR

1. Perform the Lesser Banishing Ritual of the Pentagram.

2. Perform the Lesser Invoking Ritual of the Air Pentagram.

3. Face East. Feel breezes coming eastward or from the East, and feel that the breeze goes right through you, coming into the front and going out the back. After having got the wind through, try to feel the wind as yellow. See a stream of yellow light emanating from this particular cardinal point.

4. Vibrate each of the following Names as often as you feel inclined:
    SHADDAI EL CHAI (Divine Name)
    RAPHAEL (Archangelic Name)
    CHASSAN (Angelic Name)

5. Visualize Sylphs–little fairy-like figures. Let your imagination run away with you as with the Gnomes, but do not force it. Remember they are trying to subtilize, trying to eliminate the gross, and trying to make everything in which the Light can function. Let the cramp of the mind go and let the mind play with these fairy-like Sylphs. Feel that they are pouring through you.

6. Recite the Invocation. It is the Prayer of the Sylphs. REMEMBER YOUR IDEA OF GRATITUDE. You, too, must help them, even as they are helping you. They have no consciousness in our sense of the work. Having no consciousness, they have no sense of a goal, and we must give them a concept of goal. And for the benefit of all the Sylphs in our Nature, we recite the Invocation and we inspire them to our goal.

Holy art Thou, Lord of the Air,
Who has created the Firmament.
SHADDAI EL CHAI. Almighty and everlasting,
Ever-living be thy Name,
Ever-magnified in the life of all.
We praise Thee, and we bless Thee,
In the changeless empire of created Light;

1

And we aspire without cessation unto thine
Imperishable and Immutable Brilliance. AMEN.

7. Perform Banishing Ritual.

8. Perform meditation.

THE PENTAGRAM RITUAL OF FIRE

1. Perform the Lesser Banishing Ritual of the Pentagram.

2. Perform the Lesser Invoking Ritual of the Fire Pentagram.

3. Face South.

4. Vibrate each of the following Names as often as you feel inclined:

YHVH TZABAOTH (Divine Name)
MICHAEL (Archangelic Name)
ARAL (Angelic Name)

As you vibrate the Names, imagine a flame as coming into the room from the South, either as flame or as definite entities. See yourself as being licked by the flame, scorched by them, and see the elementals working upon you in the same way as the Gnomes, Sylphs, and Undines.

5. Visualize Salamanders.

6. Recite the Invocation. It is the Prayer of the Salamanders. REMEMBER YOUR IDEA OF GRATITUDE. You, too, must help them, even as they are helping you. They have no consciousness in our sense of the work. Having no consciousness, they have no sense of a goal, and we must give them a concept of goal. And for the benefit of all the Salamanders in our Nature, we recite the Invocation and we inspire them to our goal.

Holy art Thou, Lord of the Fire,
Wherein Thou hast shown forth
The Throne of thy Glory.
YOD-HEH-VAV-HEH TZABAOTH.
Leader of Armies is thy Holy Name.
O Thou flashing Fire,
Thou illuminest all things
With thine insupportable Refulgence
Whence flow the ceaseless streams of Splendour
Which nourisheth thine Infinite Spirit.
Help us, thy children, whom Thou hast loved
Since the birth of the Ages of Time. AMEN.

7. Perform Banishing Ritual.

8. Perform meditation.

THE PENTAGRAM RITUAL OF WATER

1. Perform the Lesser Banishing Ritual of the Pentagram.

2. Perform the Lesser Invoking Ritual of the Water Pentagram.

THE PENTAGRAM RITUALS

3. Face West. There must be relaxation of mind, relaxed enough to let the subtle currents flow through from the Undines in whom the force comes up. We assist the Undines by our Prayer for the elemental. We enable them to formulate in consciousness for what they unconsciously feel.

4. Vibrate each of the following Names as often as you feel inclined:

ELOHIM TZABAOTH (Divine Name)
GABRIEL (Archangelic Name)
TALIHAD (Angelic Name)

5. Visualize Undines.

6. Recite the Invocation. It is the Prayer of the Undines. REMEMBER YOUR IDEA OF GRATITUDE. You, too, must help them, even as they are helping you. They have no consciousness in our sense of the work. Having no consciousness, they have no sense of a goal, and we must give them a concept of goal. And for the benefit of all the Undines in our Nature, we recite the Invocation and we inspire them to our goal.

Holy art Thou, Lord of the Mighty Waters,
Whereon Thy spirit moved in the Beginning.
ELOHIM TZABAOTH.
Glory be unto Thee RUACH ELOHIM,
Whose Spirit hovered over the
Great Waters of Creation.
O Depth, O inscrutable Depth,
Which exhalest unto the height;
Lead Thou us into the true Life,
Through sacrifice, through Love,
So that one day we may be found
Worthy to offer unto Thee,
The Water, the Blood and the Tears,
For the remission of sins. AMEN.

7. Perform Banishing Ritual.

8. Perform meditation.

THE PENTAGRAM RITUAL OF EARTH

1. Perform the Lesser Banishing Ritual of the Pentagram.

2. Perform the Lesser Invoking Ritual of the Earth Pentagram.

3. Face North. Visualize lying on cool, black, rich earth. Visualize earth all around you, and penetrating right through your open pores to the center of your being.

4. Vibrate each of the following Names as often as you feel inclined:

ADONAI HA-ARETZ (Divine Name)
AURIEL (Archangelic Name)
PHORLAKH (Angelic Name)

5. Visualize Gnomes–on the earth, under the earth, on your body, in your body–myriads of them, and let your imagination (without forcing) see these Gnomes playing, working, doing whatever comes into your mind. Especially watch their actions in your body.

6. Recite the Invocation. It is the Prayer of the Gnomes. REMEMBER YOUR IDEA OF GRATITUDE. You, too, must help them, even as they are helping you. They have no consciousness in our sense of the work. Having no consciousness, they have no sense of a goal, and we must give them a concept of goal. And for the benefit of all the Gnomes in our Nature, we recite the Invocation and we inspire them to our goal.

Holy art Thou, Lord of the Earth,
Which Thou hast made for Thy footstool.
ADONAI HA-ARETZ, ADONAI MELEKH.
Unto Thee be the Kingdom, the Power, and the Glory.
MALKUTH-GEBURAH-GEDULAH, AMEN.
The Rose of Sharon, and the Lily of the Valley.
O Thou who hidest beneath the Earth,
In the Valley of Gems,
The marvelous seed of the Stars.
Live, reign, and be Thou the eternal
Dispenser of Thy treasures,
Whereof Thou hast made us
The wardens. AMEN.

7. Perform Banishing Ritual.

8. Perform meditation.

THE PENTAGRAM RITUAL OF SPIRIT

We are dealing with a subject which is considerably more complex to discuss than any which we heretofore had. It is the Fifth Element–Ether or Akasha. The ancients did not include this and we have to look to the Alchemists for whatever we are able to give out regarding it. As soon as we reach this Fifth Element, we have difficulty in understanding what they meant. We have no prayer for the Fifth Element; but that there is a Fifth Element is fairly obvious. This Element is half manifest, half concealed. The Alchemists pay attention to five Elements and to the manipulating of this Fifth Element of Ether. The Fifth Element synthesizes the Four Elements and yet, although a synthesis is an Element by itself, this Fifth Element is a duality.

We will use the truncated pyramid. A truncated pyramid is one whose vertex is cut off by a plane usually parallel to the base. (The vertex of a pyramid is the point of intersection of the generating lines or boundary planes respectively.) Each side of the truncated pyramid is considered to be one of the elements, Earth, Air, Fire and Water. The base is OLAHM (the World). The top is ALEPH TAU–the Alpha and Omega, Spirit, and Essence–and it is directly involved here as the Fifth Element.

Imagine, after thoroughly relaxing, that you have built up a huge pyramid. See that Pyramid built up with all the imagination you have. You have to build up that Pyramid with the truncated top, and see yourself standing at the top. The East side of the Pyramid is Yellow in color, the South is Red, the West is Blue, and the North is Green. Expand your consciousness. Here, however, we approach a different concept, not Elemental, but Spiritual. Up to now we have dealt with the elemental side, the Green Ray. That was to strengthen the interior basis of your nature, so that now it will have something interior to work on. Enlarge your body to fill infinite Space so the forces of God can pour through you.

Inasmuch as there are some of you who are able to do this Ritual twice a day, I am going to give you variations of this in two ways because I do not want it mixed up with other work–not even with the Middle Pillar. Simply do this one thing. Of course you do the relaxation. It is always a part of your formula and routine.

THE PENTAGRAM RITUALS

1. Perform the Lesser Banishing Ritual of the Pentagram.

2. Perform the Greater Invoking Pentagram Ritual of Spirit, Active and Passive.

3. Face East and trace the Sign of Aquarius with your hand outstretched, and vibrate the appropriate divine Names I gave you for the Element of Air:

    SHADDAI EL CHAI
    RAPHAEL
    CHASSAN

    Stand still and recite the prayer of Air, and at the same time imagine that the Sylphs are there and pouring through you:

    Holy art Thou, Lord of the Air,
    Who has created the Firmament.
    SHADDAI EL CHAI.
    Almighty and everlasting,
    Ever-living be thy Name,
    Ever-magnified in the life of all.
    We praise Thee, and we bless Thee,
    In the changeless empire of created Light;
    And we aspire without cessation unto thine
    Imperishable and Immutable Brilliance. AMEN.

4. Face South and trace the Sign of Leo. Then vibrate the appropriate divine Names of Fire:

    YOD-HEH-VAV-HEH TZABAOTH
    MICHAEL
    ARAL

    Stand still and recite the prayer of Fire, and at the same time imagine that the Salamanders are there and pouring through you:

    Holy art Thou, Lord of the Fire,
    Wherein Thou hast shown forth
    The Throne of thy Glory.
    YOD-HEH-VAV-HEH TZABAOTH.
    Leader of Armies is thy Holy Name.
    O Thou flashing Fire,
    Thou illuminest all things
    With thine insupportable Refulgence
    Whence flow the ceaseless streams of Splendour
    Which nourisheth thine Infinite Spirit.
    Help us, thy children, whom Thou hast loved
    Since the birth of the Ages of Time. AMEN.

5. Face West and trace the Sign of Scorpio. Then vibrate the appropriate divine Names of Water:

    ELOHIM TZABAOTH
    GABRIEL
    TALIHAD

    Stand still and recite the prayer of Water, and at the same time imagine that the Undines are there and pouring through you:

Holy art Thou,Lord of the Mighty Waters,
Whereon Thy spirit moved in the Beginning.
ELOHIM TZABAOTH.
Glory be unto Thee RUACH ELOHIM,
Whose Spirit hovered over the
Great Waters of Creation.
O Depth, O inscrutable Depth,
Which exhalest unto the height;
Lead Thou us into the true Life,
Through sacrifice, through Love,
So that one day we may be found
Worthy to offer unto Thee,
The Water, the Blood and the Tears,
For the remission of sins. AMEN.

6. Face North and trace the Sign of Taurus. Then vibrate the appropriate divine Names of Earth:

    ADONAI HA-ARETZ
    AURIEL
    PHORLAKH

    Stand still and recite the prayer of Earth, and at the same time imagine that the Gnomes are there and pouring through you:

    Holy art Thou, Lord of the Earth,
    Which Thou hast made for Thy footstool.
    ADONAI HA-ARETZ, ADONAI MELEKH.
    Unto Thee be the Kingdom, the Power, and the Glory.
    MALKUTH-GEBURAH-GEDULAH, AMEN.
    The Rose of Sharon, and the Lily of the Valley.
    O Thou who hidest beneath the Earth,
    In the Valley of Gems,
    The marvelous seed of the Stars.
    Live, reign, and be Thou the eternal
    Dispenser of Thy treasures,
    Whereof Thou hast made us
    The wardens. AMEN.

7. Return to the center of the Temple, and relax forthwith in the completest way possible.

8. Build up the Pyramid
    East side of Pyramid YELLOW
    South side of Pyramid RED
    West side of Pyramid BLUE
    North side of Pyramid GREEN
    Base side of Pyramid BLACK
    Truncated top of Pyramid WHITE

9. Then imagine that you are standing on the top of the Pyramid. You are a vast figure of enormous size perched on an equally large Pyramid, and feel that you are standing on that truncated peak.

10. Then vibrate the Names:

JEHESHUAH
JEHOVASHAH

and whilst vibrating the Names, feel yourself being bathed with Light, and that the power is coming through from every part of Space, making you glow with Light.

11. Get off the Pyramid. Wait of course on top, and when you get the impulse to do so, get down. This is a test. I am not telling you what side. You go down to the bottom of the inside of the Pyramid, and remember I am not telling you what side you go into the Pyramid, or what side you go out.

12. Inside the Pyramid you vibrate once more the Divine Names:

JEHESHUAH
JEHOVASHAH

and then four other additional Names. They are four words of five letters each:
EXARP (pronounced X-R-Pay)
HCOMA (pronounced Hay-Co-Mah)
NANTA (pronounced En-En-Tah)
BITOM (pronounced Bay-E-Toe-Em)
These are Enochian Spirit Names.

13. Then wait quietly inside. Do not try to make things happen or formulate things in your imagination. If you get ideas, feelings, or any other concepts, make a mental note of it, and record it in your own notebook or diary at the end of the ritual. Wait quietly for some time until you feel the Meditation has come to an end.

14. Then ascend once more to the top of the Pyramid and feel yourself once more bathed with Light.

15. Then as you stand on the top of the Pyramid, recite the Invocation:
JEHESHUAH, JEHOVASHAH.

I invoke ye, ye Angels of the Celestial Spheres
Whose dwelling is in the Invisible.
Ye are the Guardians of the Gates of the Universe.
Be ye also the Guardians of this Mystic Shrine.
Keep far removed the evil and the unbalanced.
Strengthen and inspire me so that I may preserve unsullied
This abode of the Mysteries of the Eternal Gods.
Let my Sphere be pure and holy,
So I may enter in and become a partaker
Of the secrets of the Light Divine. AMEN.

16. Then when you feel you have enough, draw in and perform the Greater Banishing Ritual of the Spirit Pentagram, Active and Passive.

17. Perform the Lesser Banishing Ritual of the Pentagram.

18. Record the result of your Meditation in your notebook or diary.

APPENDIX II

THE RE-AWAKENING OF OSIRIS

RECLAIMING THE GOD OF REINTEGRATION IN THE GOLDEN DAWN SYSTEM

By

CHARLES "CHIC" CICERO & SANDRA "TABATHA" CICERO

On August 17, 1984, Israel Regardie gave us two copies of his newly published book entitled *The Complete Golden Dawn System of Magic,* one personally signed for each of us. It was an impressive and valuable book—one which Regardie could rightly be proud of. Not only did the book contain much in the way of previously unpublished material, such as original Golden Dawn initiation ceremonies from the Yorke Collection, rituals from A. E. Waite's Fellowship of the Rosy Cross, and Regardie's own Enochian Dictionary, it also included new contributions from some members of our own Golden Dawn Order, bridging the gap between the Golden Dawn's past and its present. It was Regardie himself who first gave the book its long-standing nickname—the Doorstop Edition—because as he put it, "the damn thing is thick enough to stop a door with."

However, one of our fondest memories of "Francis" has to do with a typo in the book. While thumbing through the text, he stopped and grumbled, went over to his typewriter and clanged away at it. When he returned he brought with him a piece of paper, cut into two parts, which he attached directly into the text of our books with scotch tape. It read:

> *"Insert, page 4, Volume Six. Immediately after Hiereus states that all present have been so honored.*
>
> *(Hiereus and Kerux return to their places. Hierophant gives the Sign of the Enterer, but not the Sign of Silence.)*
>
> *Hiero: Let the number of Officers in this degree and the nature of their Offices be proclaimed once again, that the Powers whose images they are may be re-awakened in the sphere of those present and in the Sphere of this Order -- for by names and images are all Powers awakened and re-awakened. (He makes the Sign of Silence.)"*

Regardie grumbled, "I'm not the world's best proof-reader," he informed us. No matter: We were thrilled to have correction pages straight from Regardie's typewriter, plastered into our books. It just made them more special to us.

When we were recently asked to provide material for New Falcon's 2011 edition of Regardie's *The Complete Golden Dawn System of Magic,* we were very happy to oblige. Since 1984 several printings and editions of this book have been produced, often with new contributions

THE RE-AWAKENING OF OSIRIS

from authors from various spiritual paths within the wider magical community who have found wisdom within the curriculum of the Golden Dawn. This is a tribute to the inherent value of the Order's teachings as well as to the efforts of Israel Regardie—no other person has done more to make the teachings of the Golden Dawn available to practitioners of all esoteric traditions.

Adapting Golden Dawn teachings into other traditions such as Thelema or Wicca is simply the natural evolution of a successful system into other avenues of magical thought. But while other contributors emphasize how the Golden Dawn system can be utilized in the Thelemic New Aeon of Horus, we wanted to draw attention to the fact that many of today's Golden Dawn students, temples, and Orders, are focused on the Traditional Golden Dawn and the importance of the God Osiris to that tradition.

The Outer Order of the Golden Dawn has been described as "Osirian" in essence because the Egyptian God Osiris, embodied by the initiating Hierophant, plays a central, critical role in the magical, alchemical work of the Neophyte Hall and the Outer Order in general.

To the ancient Egyptians, Osiris (Coptic *Ousiri*) was the son of Geb and Nut. Osiris was revered as a God of vegetation and grain, and he was also associated with the annual flooding of the Nile river which nourished the fertile fields at the start of the Egyptian new year. He is usually portrayed as a green-skinned man with a Pharaoh's beard, dressed in mummy-wrappings on the lower half of his body. He wears the *Atef* crown, a high white miter or cone flanked by two large ostrich feathers at either side, and holding a symbolic crook and flail.

His name was inscribed on the Palermo Stone, making him one of the earliest known of the Egyptian Gods. The mysteries at Abydos commemorating the death of Osiris were celebrated on the 17th of Athyr (November 13), the same day that the Egyptians began planting their crops. Osiris, God and Pharaoh of Egypt, was associated with farming and civilization. Many of the stories of Osiris come from the Pyramid Texts and later sources such as Plutarch and Diodorus Siculus. Osiris became the preeminent God of the underworld, the afterlife, and of all life in general.

The name "Osiris" is the Greek rendition of the Egyptian name *Asar*. The origin of Osiris' Egyptian name seems to have been unknown even to the Egyptians. No one is certain as to the meaning of the name, but several possibilities have been suggested, including "the Strength of the Eye." The oldest and simplest form of the name is the hieroglyph of the Throne over an eye. He was also known by the title *Unnefer*, which comes from the roots *un* ("to open, to appear, to make manifest") and *neferu* ("good things"). This became the basis of the Greek title *Onnophris*, said to mean "the beautiful" or "the beneficent." Another epithet was Osiris *Khenti-Amenti* or "Lord of the Westerners," since the dead were thought to enter the underworld in the west, the direction of the setting sun. As the God of the dead, Osiris was also called "King of the Living," because the Egyptians regarded the blessed dead who had achieved eternal life as "the Living Ones."

There are different versions of the death of Osiris, murdered at the hands of his evil brother Set (called Typhon or Apophis by the Greeks), but it is usually recounted that the body of Osiris was torn to pieces and scattered to the winds. His resurrection was accomplished by his sister-wife, the Goddess Isis, who collected the scattered body parts and raised Osiris from the dead with a magic spell under the direction of Thoth. Thus Osiris was transformed into a God of resurrection from death. He came to symbolize rebirth, eternal life, and immortality. He also became the "Judge of the Dead" in the Underworld.

The kings of Egypt sought to acquire the mercies of Osiris in order to unite with him in an everlasting and glorious afterlife. The funeral rites of kings were designed to mimic the journey of Osiris from death to resurrection. By imitating the risen God, they aspired to join him in eternal life. Therefore they developed burial rituals based upon assimilation magic. The cult of Osiris grew in popularity during the Middle and New Kingdoms when the

9

prospect of eternal life with the God was offered not only to the royal kings of Egypt, but also to the average Egyptian man or woman if they could afford the cost of the funeral ceremonies.

Egyptians believed that the deceased would be brought to the "Hall of Judgment" as described in the 125th chapter of the Egyptian *Book of the Dead* to undergo a ceremony called the "Weighing of the Soul." This was a type of underworld trial wherein the deceased's life on earth was evaluated by a tribunal of forty-two judges. The heart of the deceased was weighed in a scale against the feather of Maat (Goddess of Truth). If the deceased had lived a virtuous life in accordance with the precepts of Maat, he or she would be deemed innocent and welcomed to join Osiris in eternal life. A person who had lived a corrupt life would be found guilty and devoured by a beast.

Osiris was revered by the Egyptians. He was a deity unlike all others, in that he was an accessible God whom people could strongly empathize with—they could identify with him as one of them. Thus did he become the beloved God of Resurrection and Eternal Life, for he set an example that the rest of humanity could follow. What the Gods did for Osiris, the Egyptians reasoned, they might be persuaded to do for ordinary mortals. Their ceremonies were designed to insure that after death the deceased would, like Osiris, rise again and inherit life everlasting.

It is easy to see why the Godform of Osiris became so strongly incorporated into the Golden Dawn's system of magic. Osiris, the God who died, was dismembered and resurrected, is an ideal model for the candidate of the Mysteries who "dies" to an old way of life, is symbolically "dismembered" by the initiatory process, and is "reborn" into a new spiritual existence. Osiris is the perfect deity to represent this three-fold process, because in addition to being a magical practice, this is also a psychological and alchemical process. Theurgy or "God-working" is a three-fold practice. In analytical psychology this "Osirian" process is called *analysis, confrontation* (with the shadow), and *self-realization*. In alchemy it is known as *separation, purification,* and *recombination*. In magic it is referred to as *purification, consecration,* and *union*. All of these terms are used to describe the same basic experience of spiritual growth. In the Outer Order of the Golden Dawn, the student must examine his or her own inner workings—separating or "dismembering" them by defining and analyzing the various components of the psyche. The initiatory process works to purify and consecrate these psychic components until at length they are recombined, reunited, and realized or "resurrected" in a more exalted or spiritualized Whole.

The results of theurgical practice, like the work of alchemy, is cyclical and so this process is repeated on a higher level in the more advanced grades of the Golden Dawn's Inner Order (the R.R. et A.C.). Here the Egyptian and Osirian paradigm remains, but it also morphs into the symbolism of Rosicrucianism and mystical Christianity. In the Second Order the Initiate is introduced to the legend of Christian Rosencreutz, which is itself an allegory of the life of Christ. Throughout the Golden Dawn system, the model of a dying and resurrected Deity takes precedence, precisely because it symbolizes the continual process of alchemical growth and spiritual evolution that marks the transformation of an Initiate of the mysteries. It is the alchemical formula of I.A.O., Isis, Apophis, Osiris, or birth, death, and resurrection. To the Golden Dawn magician, this represents a potent process of transmutation and the keys to the doors of magical power and immortality.

There is another reason why the Golden Dawn emphasized the God Osiris, and this had to do with the way the Thrones of Osiris and Horus were viewed by the Egyptians themselves. The Pyramid texts describe the dual nature of the Pharaoh in the two characters of Horus and Osiris. In life the Pharaoh was the physical incarnation of Horus—son of Osiris and rightful heir to the Throne of Egypt. Upon his death however, the Pharaoh left behind his association with Horus. Once his soul had passed through the Hall of Judgment, the God Horus would lead the Pharaoh to the Throne of Osiris. At that point, the Pharaoh ascended to the Throne and became united with Osiris for all eternity. The Pharaoh as Horus in life became the Pharaoh as Osiris in death. New incarnations of Horus succeeded the deceased Pharaoh on earth in the form of new Pharaohs. When a new Pharaoh took over the Kingdom and gained the Throne of Egypt, he was called by the title "the Living Horus."

Horus possessed the Throne of the Kingdom, the earthly realm of Egypt. The Throne of the Spiritual Realm belonged to his father Osiris. In the Hall of the Neophytes, as in the entire First Order of the Golden Dawn, both of these Thrones are represented. The Throne of Horus—the earthly Throne of the Kingdom—is located in the West of the Hall, in the darkest part of Malkuth (the "Kingdom"). Horus was a warrior and protector God. It was his duty, and the function of his Kingship, to protect the Kingdom from the forces that would attack it from without. This is also the function of the Hiereus in the Neophyte Hall: *"The Throne of the Hiereus at the Gate of the West is the Place of the Guardian against the multitudes that sleep through the Light and awaken at Twilight."* (See page 19, Volume Six.)

The second Throne, the Throne of Osiris—the Throne of the Spiritual Realm—is situated upon the Dais in the East of the Neophyte Hall, the place of "Light." Aaron Leitch has pointed out that this was exactly how the Egyptian Gnostics described the Spiritual Realm. In the Gnostic text known as the "Hymn of the Pearl," the *true self, living soul,* or *spirit* of the individual in the hymn "has come from" or "is sent from" the "Kingdom of Light in the East." The Hierophant's Throne in the East is described in similar terms: *"I am called Power and Mercy and Light and Abundance, and I am the Expounder of the Mysteries ... My Throne at the Gate of the East is the Place of the Guardian of the Dawning Sun."*

In the Neophyte Ceremony, the new Candidate is brought into the Hall from the West—the darkest place of Malkuth where the Throne of Horus is located. He is then led through the Hall until at length he reaches the Throne of Osiris in the East. (This journey is mirrored yet again by the Candidate's journey through the Grades and Offices—beginning with the Office of Phylax as a 0=0, ascending to the "highest Grade of the Outer" when taking the Throne of Hiereus in the West as a Philosophus, and finally becoming a Hierophant, after symbolically passing through the Veil into "the Tomb of Osiris Onnophris" (the Vault of the Adepti) when he or she symbolically becomes one with Osiris, as an Adeptus Minor.)

There is a vital difference between the two Thrones in the Neophyte Hall. The Golden Dawn system views the two Thrones much like the ancient Egyptians did. The Throne of the Hiereus is the Throne of Egypt, the Throne of the physical realm. In the opinion of traditional Golden Dawn magicians, it is not preferable to place the God Horus on the Hierophant's Throne, because it is based on the assumption that the Hierophant's Throne is like the Throne of Egypt, and Horus would naturally take over the Throne of Egypt, the Throne of the Kingdom, from his dead father Osiris. But the Throne of Hierophant is *not* the Throne of Egypt, but rather the Throne of the Spirit Realm. If Horus ascends to the Throne in the East, it means Horus is deceased. And in moving Horus to the Throne of the East, some have placed the God Set on the Throne of the West. This scenario simply does not work for traditional Golden Dawn magicians such as ourselves, because it means that the God Set rules the world and the Kingdom of Matter in Malkuth, having just waited for Horus to die so he could take the Throne of Egypt yet again.

Osiris and other deities associated with death, resurrection and rebirth were vitally important to what we know of the ancient mystery religions that flourished in the Hellenistic era. The Greek word *mysteria* or "mysteries" implied private or secret rites that were not intended for the general public. The deities invoked and worshiped by these religions varied. The Samothracian mysteries, possibly the oldest of these cults, centered around the Kabiri or "great Gods." The Orphic mysteries were said to have been founded by the Greek hero, Orpheus. These rites focused on the God Dionysos-Phanes, the creator of Heaven and Earth and the bringer of Light. The mysteries of Isis and Osiris were played out in Egypt, along with the cult of Serapis (another form of Osiris) in Alexandria. There were also the mysteries of Cybele and Attis, deities that were imported from Asia Minor, whose myths resembled those of the Babylonian divinities Ishtar and Tammuz. However, the most famous of the mysteries was centered at Athens—the Eleusinian mysteries—which focused on the deities of Demeter, Persephone, and Hades. Later the cult of Mithras, the Persian Sun God, sprang up at outposts of the Roman Empire. What little is known of the mysteries is that nearly all of them dealt with the ideas of death and resurrection—the death of one Kabir at the hands of the other three Kabiri, only to be brought back to life again; the many deaths and reincarnations of Dionysos; Persephone's descent into the underworld of Hades; the dismemberment of Osiris at the hands of the evil Set, and Osiris' resurrection at the hands of Isis through the magic power of Thoth. The theme of death and resurrection, so essential to the ancient mystery religions, also permeates the ritual dramas of the Golden Dawn's initiation rites and teachings.

Osirian imagery is extensively used on the Pillars of the Neophyte Hall. The Black Pillar of Boaz is painted with various diagrams taken from the 125th Chapter of the Egyptian *Book of the Dead*. It specifically refers to the "Formula of Coming Forth by Day." The 125th Formula is entitled "The Formula of Entering in the Hall of Two Truths: A Paean to Osir, the Chief of Amentet." The vignette is divided into five registers that illustrate the "Weighing of the Soul" in the underworld, wherein the deceased is judged to see if he or she is worthy of being united with Osiris in eternal life.

Jachin, the White Pillar, is decorated with diagrams from the 17th Chapter of the "Formula of Coming Forth by Day" from the *Book of the Dead*. This Formula bears a very long title relating to the "Beginning of the Exaltations and Enlightenments [...] Coming forth into Shining Nuterkheret (the divine underworld) [...] "Beautiful Amentet" [...] Coming Forth as a Living Soul." Brodie-Innes tells us that the scenes on the White Pillar are *"a pictorial synthesis of the gradual freeing of the soul from the body, left to be mummified and its union with Osiris, Lord and Judge of the Dead and of the resurrection, the sun in his rising."* (Page 13, Volume Three.)

The Black and White Pillars of the Hall represent two opposites, the two great "Opposing Forces" that *"express the interchange and reconcilement of opposing forces, and the Eternal Balance of Light and Darkness which gives form to the Visible Universe."* (Page 6, Volume Three.) They also symbolize the doorway to the mysteries, and the "symbolic gateway of occult wisdom." The area between the Pillars is known as "the Place of Balanced Power between the Ultimate Light and the Ultimate Darkness." It is also the gateway of initiation. Many important magical workings occur between the Pillars in the Neophyte Hall: it is to this location that the simulacrum or astral image of the Candidate is projected before taking the Obligation, signifying the commencement of the dismembering of the Initiate (like the symbolic dismembering of Osiris) into his or her component parts.

The process undertaken by an Initiate advancing through the grades is an alchemical one; the psychic mechanism of the candidate undergoes a kind of dissolution (death/dismembering) during the ceremony of the Neophyte. The integral elements are awakened and purified through the elemental grade ceremonies of the Outer Order, until at length all of the base components are consecrated (resurrection/*re*-membered) and reintegrated back into the psyche of the Initiate (rebirth/new life/wholeness). This entire alchemical-initiatory process is prefigured at the end of the Neophyte Ritual when all present partake in a type of Hermetic Eucharist properly called "the Mystic Repast" of the Four Elements, represented by a rose (Air), candle (Fire), cup of wine (Water), and bread and salt (Earth). These four elements symbolize the "inner elements" or distinct sections of the human psyche. The Z- Documents describe the Mystic Repast as *"a communion in the body of Osiris. Its mystic Name is 'The Formula of*

THE RE-AWAKENING OF OSIRIS

the Justified One.'" (Page 80, Volume Six.) The elements are ritually consecrated by the Hierophant with the "Prayer of Osiris" (page 57, Volume Six) as follows:

> *For Osiris Onnophris who is found perfect before the Gods, hath said: These*
> *are the Elements of my Body,*
> *Perfected through Suffering, Glorified through Trial.*
> *For the scent of the Dying Rose is as the repressed Sigh of my suffering: And*
> *the flame red Fire as the Energy of mine Undaunted Will:*
> *And the Cup of Wine is the pouring out of the Blood of my Heart:*
> *Sacrificed unto Regeneration, unto the Newer Life:*
> *And the Bread and Salt are as the Foundations of my Body,*
> *Which I destroy in order that they may be renewed.*
> *For I am Osiris Triumphant, even Osiris Onnophris, the Justified.*
> *I am He who is clothed with the Body of Flesh,*
> *Yet in whom is the Spirit of the Great Gods.*
> *I am the Lord of Life, triumphant over Death.*
> *Those who partaketh with me shall arise with me.*
> *I am the Manifestor in matter of Those Whose Abode is in the Invisible.*
> *I am purified. I stand upon the Universe.*
> *I am its Reconciler with the Eternal Gods.*
> *I am the Perfector of Matter,*
> *And without me, the Universe is not.*

In *The Tree of Life*, Regardie describes the magical process of a Eucharist (and the Mystic Repast) as a potent alchemical technique for achieving union with deity:

> *"A substance is ceremonially consecrated and named after a spiritual principle having a special affinity for it [...] the substance is charged by invocation with that divine presence, and being consumed it is anticipated that, through the assimilation of elements, the God or the divine essence invoked invariably incarnates in the Magician's being, by means of the consecrated substance. This incarnation is another form of the Union of the Theurgist with the God, which union by definition of those in authority among the ancients is one of the most important aspects of Magic. This particular species of Union, if continued in over a period of time, assists the communion with the divine Essences, as the vehicles become more refined and more highly sensitive to the presence of the God."*

Hermetic philosophy portrays the fourfold pattern as an important model or paradigm which defines the universe—both the greater universe or macrocosm of which we are a part, and the lesser universe or microcosm which is the individual human soul, reflecting the greater universe in miniature. Partaking of the four elements in the Mystic Repast is a foreshadowing of the equilibration process that the Initiate will undergo in the four Elemental grades of the Outer Order. Taken as a whole, the grades of the Outer Order represent the essential work of the Golden Dawn, which is to balance the elemental forces within the psyche of the Initiate. Osiris, the Lord of Life, sublimated through the alchemical process of death, resurrection and rebirth, is an archetypal symbol for spiritual balance.

This balanced and equilibrated aspect of Osiris is also shown in the Enochian system, often thought of as the pinnacle of the entire Golden Dawn system of magic. The various squares of the Enochian Watchtower Tablets are actually truncated pyramids with four sides. An Enochian pyramid that is completely balanced in its elemental composition is known as an "Osiris

Square." In his paper on "The Pyramid Gods and Their Attribution," Mathers describes Osiris as the God who: *"Ruleth above when of the Four Triangles each is a different Element. So that all four elements are united in one square, for he representeth the Spirit ruling in the Four Elements equally balanced."* (Page 96, Volume 10.) Within the Order's system of Enochian Chess, the name of Osiris is even used to describe the process of becoming elementally balanced— *Osirification.* (Page 107, Volume Ten.) Although this term was used to describe certain Enochian pyramids that are almost (but not quite) Osiris Squares, the term Osirification could well be used to describe the Initiate who is undergoing the process of elemental equilibration through the alchemical/theurgical work of the Golden Dawn. Osirification *is* the alchemical process of *separation, purification* and *recombination.* Osirification *is* the process of *purification, consecration* and *union.* It *is* the psychological process of *analysis, confrontation* (with the shadow) and *self-realization.* This process, if correctly undertaken, can lead to the psyche of the Initiate mirroring that of an Osiris Square, with the four elemental portions of the psyche in balanced disposition, ruled by the governing quintessence of Spirit. This was a point that Israel Regardie reiterated time and again. In *The Middle Pillar,* he stated:

> *"Analytical psychology and magic comprise in my estimation two halves or aspects of a single technical system. Just as the body and mind are not two separate units, but are simply the dual manifestations of an interior dynamic 'something' so psychology and magic comprise similarly a single system whose goal is the integration of the human personality. Its aim is to unify the different departments and functions of man's being, to bring into operation those which previously for various reasons were latent. Incidentally, its technique is such that neurotic symptoms which were too insistent upon expression either become eliminated or toned down by a process of equilibration."*

In his book *The Philosopher's Stone,* Regardie maintained that the true purpose of magic was to:

> *"...effect psychological integration, to bring about a psychic release from bondage to unconscious projection, and to produce an exaltation of consciousness to the Light, that any legitimate magical initiating system owes its existence. The function of every phase of its routine, the avowed intention of its principal rituals, and the explicit statement of its teachings is to assist the Candidate by his aspiration to find that unity of being which is the Inner Self, the pure essence of mind."*

As Traditional Golden Dawn Magicians, we embrace Osirification as the embodiment of the theurgic process of self-realization and wholeness. The Osirian-Rosicrucian Current is not some relic of a passing Aeon, but a herald (Keryx) of the New Aeon of Aquarius, combining the best of our spiritual heritage from previous Aeons with fresh insights and vibrant experiences of the present Age dawning about us like the rising sun breaking over the horizon, a worthy symbol of the "Kingdom of Light in the East."

The Hierophant of the Mysteries tells us: *"By names and images are all Powers awakened and re-awakened."* Many Golden Dawn magicians of the twenty-first century prefer not to leave Osiris out of the alchemical process of self-realization. By names and images, we choose to awaken and reawaken the God of Reintegration into the magical system which is his, and *our*, birthright. We choose to affix Osiris into our magical praxis.

With scotch tape if need be.

APPENDIX III

CONSECRATION OF A LUNAR TALISMAN

By

CHARLES "CHIC" CICERO & SANDRA "TABATHA" CICERO

For this ritual the Zelator Adeptus Minor will need the Lotus Wand. This ceremony would ideally be performed during the day and hour of Luna. Remember that the Moon in increase is favorable for magical working—likewise, the Moon in decrease is unfavorable. The Z. A. M. should be dressed in the regalia of the Second Order. Arrange the Temple in accordance with the Neophyte Hall. Outside the Temple, wrapped in a black piece of cloth and bound three times with a black cord, should be a talisman you want charged with the energies of Luna. This could be a piece of jewelry, a Lunar gemstone, or a piece of paper covered with symbols which relate to the Moon. Upon the Altar should be the Cross and Triangle, Tablet of Union, a chalice of Water, and a censer or stick of incense. A Sword for banishing should be close at hand. The position of Luna should be determined for the time of the ritual, and a symbol of the planet should be placed on the floor or hung on the wall corresponding to the direction noted. In addition to the Rose Cross Lamen, the Adept should wear a seal of Luna in the proper colors. A white cloth used to wrap the talisman after consecration is also required.

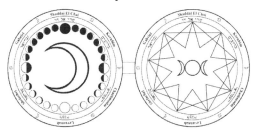

After a period of relaxation and meditation, give five knocks. Then go to the northeast and proclaim:

Hekas! Hekas! Este Bebeloi!

With the Sword, perform the *Lesser Banishing Ritual of the Pentagram* or LBRP (see pages 68-70, Volume Three). Perform the Lesser *Banishing Ritual of the Hexagram* or LBRH (see pages 26-28, Volume Four).

Take up the chalice of Water. Starting in the east, purify the Temple in all quarters by tracing a Cross and the Invoking Water Triangle ▽ Say:

15

All the fountains of the great deep were broken up, and the rain was upon the earth.

Replace the cup. Take up the incense. Consecrate the room with Fire in all quarters, starting in the east, tracing a Cross and *Invoking Fire Triangle* △. Then say:

The Voice of Tetragrammaton draws out Flames of Fire.

Replace the incense. Take up the Lotus Wand. Go to the east and perform the *Supreme Invoking Ritual of the Pentagram* or SIRP. (See pages 15-17, Volume Four). As you do this, hold the white portion of the Wand when performing the *Qabalistic Cross*. When invoking the elements, grasp the white band of the Lotus Wand when tracing the Spirit Pentagrams with the Wand-head. Grasp the Kerubic elemental bands of the Lotus Wand when tracing the elemental Pentagrams with the Wand-head:

Air—the violet band of Aquarius
Fire—the yellow band of Leo
Water—the blue-green band of Scorpio
Earth—the red-orange band of Taurus

(NOTE: If you are using a Phoenix Wand instead of a Lotus Wand, grasp the colored band of the planet that rules the Kerubic Sign of each specific element while invoking that element, and trace the pentagram with the head of the Phoenix: *Air*—the blue-violet band of Saturn, co-ruler of the Sign Aquarius. *Fire*—the orange band of Sol, ruler of the Sign Leo. *Water*—the red band of Mars, co-ruler of Scorpio. *Earth*—the green band of Venus, ruler of Taurus.)

Finish with the Qabalistic Cross, holding the white portion of the wand. Remain west of the Altar facing east. Make the Sign of the Rending of the Veil. (See page 16, Volume Six for all Grade Signs.) Visualize the Veil opening as you step through it. Say the following Enochian oration:

OL SONUF VAORSAGI GOHO IAD BALATA. ELEXARPEH. CO-MANANU. TABITOM. ZODAKARA, EKA ZODAKARE OD ZODAMERANU. ODO KIKLE QAA PIAPE PIAMOEL OD VAOAN. (Oh-ell son-oof vay-oh-air-sah-jee go-ho ee-ah-dah bahl-tah. El-ex-ar-pay-hay. Co-mah-nah-noo. Tah-bee- toh-em. Zohd-ah-kah-rah eh-kah zohd-ah-kah-ray oh-dah zohd-ah-mehr-ah-noo. Oh-doh kee-klay kah-ah pee-ah-pay pee-ah-moh-el oh-dah vay-oh-ah-noo.)

I invoke ye, ye Angels of the celestial spheres, whose dwelling is in the invisible. Ye are the guardians of the gates of the Universe, be ye also the guardians of this mystic sphere. Keep far removed the evil and the unbalanced. Strengthen and inspire me so that I may preserve unsullied this abode of the mysteries of the eternal Gods. Let my sphere be pure and holy so that I may enter in and become a partaker of the secrets of the Light Divine.

Go deosil to the northeast and say:

The visible Sun is the dispenser of Light to the Earth. Let me therefore form a vortex in this chamber that the Invisible Sun of the Spirit may shine therein from above.

CONSECRATION OF A LUNAR TALISMAN

Take the Lotus Wand by the white portion and circumambulate the Temple three times deosil, saluting with the Neophyte Signs when passing the east. Then stand west of the Altar facing east and perform the *Adoration to the Lord of the Universe*. Give the Projection Sign of a Neophyte (also called the Sign of Horus) while reciting the first three stanzas. Give the Sign of Silence (the Sign of Harpocrates) after the last verse:

> **Holy art Thou Lord of the Universe!** (Projection Sign)
> **Holy art Thou Whom Nature hath not formed!** (Projection Sign) **Holy art Thou the Vast and the Mighty One!** (Projection Sign)
> **Lord of the Light and of the Darkness.** (Sign of Silence)

Then go to the west of the Altar and face east. Say:

> **The Holy Guardian Angel of** (state magical name) **under the authority of the Concealed One is in command of those beings who have been summoned to this ceremony. I charge all ye Archangels, Angels, Rulers, Kings, and Elementals called to this place to witness and aid in this Rite. I call upon the Crown, EHEIEH, the One Source Most High, to look with favor upon me as I perform this ceremony. Grant me success in this, my search for the Hidden Wisdom and my aspiration towards the Light Divine. To the glory of the Ineffable Name and the completion of the Great Work. So mote it be!**

Still grasping the Wand by the white portion, go to the east and perform the *Qabalistic Cross*. Then draw an *Invoking Hexagram of the Supernals* and visualize it in a golden light while intoning "Ararita."

In the center of the figure place the sigil of Saturn ♄ in brilliant white. Vibrate "YHVH Elohim." Then draw the letter Aleph also in brilliant white and intone the name of the letter. Trace the same figures and intone the same names in the south, west, and north.

Upon returning to the east, repeat the *Analysis of the Keyword*, given as follows:

> ****[[**NOTE: *This is the "Analysis of the Keyword" for the Hexagram Ritual, as opposed to the version used in the Rose Cross Ritual:* Extend your arms out in the shape of the Tau Cross and say: "I.N.R.I." Then say: YOD NUN RESH YOD." As the names of the Hebrew letters are pronounced, trace them in the air before you, from right to left
>
> יהוה .
>
> Return to the Osiris Slain position and say, **"Virgo, Isis, mighty Mother! Scorpio, Apophis, Destroyer! Sol, Osiris, Slain and Risen! Isis, Apophis, Osiris!"** Through the previous oration, gradually raise the arms and lift the head upwards. Vibrate strongly, **"IAO."**
>
> Return to the stance of the Tau Cross saying, **"The Sign of Osiris Slain."**

17

Put your right arm straight up in the air from the shoulder. The left arm should be straight out from the left shoulder so that the position of the two arms together resemble the letter L. Hands are to be open flat with palms forward. Turn your head so that you are looking over your left arm. Say, **"L, the Sign of the Mourning of Isis."**

Raise the arms overhead to an angle of sixty degrees so that they form the letter V. Keep the arms straight and the palms facing forward. Throw the head back and say, **"V, the Sign of Typhon and Apophis."**

Cross the arms on the chest to form the letter X. Bow your head and say, **"X, the Sign of Osiris Risen."**
Say slowly and powerfully, **"L.V.X."** (Spell out each letter separately and give the sign of each as you do so.) Say **"LUX."** Remain in the Sign of Osiris Slain and say, **"The Light..."** (hold arms out in the Tau Cross position for a moment then recross them again on the chest)" ...**of the Cross!"** *This ends the Analysis of the Keyword.*]]**

Vibrate the name **"Eheieh"** four times using the *Vibratory Formula of the Middle Pillar* (see page 69 of Volume Six). Then say:

The changing God; Eternal, Infinite. Young and Old, of a spiral form.
And another fountainous, who guides the Empyreal Heaven.

Endeavor strongly to feel the divine presence. Then give the LVX Signs.
Hold the Wand high, grasping the white portion with both hands. Say:

For the Creator congregated seven firmaments of the world. Circumscribing Heaven in a round figure, he fixed a great company of inerratic Stars, and he constituted a Septenary of erratic Animals.

Placing Earth in the middle, and Water in the middle of the Earth. The Air above these. He fixed a great company of inerratic stars, to be carried not by laborious and troublesome tension, but by a settlement which hath not error. He fixed a great Company of inerratic Stars, Forcing Fire to Fire. To be carried by a Settlement which hath not Error.

He constituted them six; casting into the midst the Fire of the Sun, suspending their disorder in well-ordered Zones.

For the Goddess brings forth the great Sun, and the bright Moon. O Aether, Son, Spirit, Guides of the Moon and of the Air, and of the Solar Circles, and of the monthly clashings, and of the Aerial recesses. The Melody of the Aether, and of the passages of the Sun, and Moon, and of the Air; and the wide Air, and the Lunar Course, and the Pole of the Sun. Collecting it, and receiving the Melody of the Aether, and of the Sun, and of the Moon, and of all that are contained in the Air. Fire, the derivation of Fire, and the Dispenser of Fire; His hair pointed is seen by his native Light; Hence comes Saturn. The Sun Assessor beholding the

CONSECRATION OF A LUNAR TALISMAN

pure Pole; and the Aetherial Course, and the vast motion of the Moon, and the Aerial fluxions, and the great Sun, and the bright Moon.

Perform the *Lesser Invoking Hexagram Ritual of Luna*, commencing with the Qabalistic Cross. (Hold Wand by the white band and trace the figures with the Wand head.) Then trace the four Lesser Hexagrams of Luna in their respective Quarters, holding the Lotus Wand by the yellow-orange band of Cancer (which is both the Day and Night House of Luna) *or* by the band which represents the zodiacal sign that Luna is in at the time of the working . [NOTE: If using the Phoenix Wand, hold the blue (Luna) band of the Wand when tracing the hexagrams.] Intone **"Ararita"** as each figure is traced. Follow this with the *Analysis of the Keyword.*

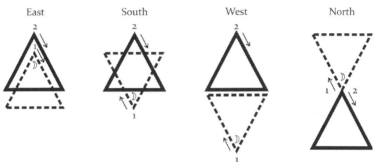

Turn to face the direction where you have determined Luna to be at the time of the working. Grasping the Wand by the same band used to invoke the Lesser Hexagrams, trace a large golden *Greater Invoking Hexagram of Luna*. Vibrate the name **"Ararita"** while drawing the Hexagram. Intone **"Shaddai EL Chai"** when tracing the Moon sigil ☽ in blue at the center. Trace the Hebrew letter Aleph א in blue and intone the name of the letter. Then say:

Thou Throne of the Almighty and Living One! Sphere of strength and foundation! Splendorous Vision of the Machinery of the Universe! Thou who wears as a diadem the crescent horns of LEVANNAH carved from pearl and moonstone! Ninth in number! Purifier of the Divine Emanations; Thou who proves and corrects the designing of their representations, disposing the unity with which they are designed without diminution or division. The keys of the mysteries of regeneration are in Thy grasp! The Astral Light is Thy abode! SHADDAI EL CHAI! Let a ray of Thy perfection descend upon me, to awaken within my being that which shall prove a channel for the working of Thine abundant power. May this Lunar talisman which I am about to consecrate be a focus of Thy light so that it may awaken within my soul a clear inner vision and enhanced intuition.

Trace the sigil and letters of Shaddai El Chai in the Air with the Wand. Then trace the sigil and the letters over your heart. Vibrate the name seven times using the Vibratory Formula.

Astrally formulate four pillars surrounding you. Then visualize clearly a large Banner of the East (see color plate 1). After the image is firmly within your mind, see it enveloping you like a cloak. Say:

> **In the Divine Name of SHADDAI EL CHAI, I command ye, O ye dwellers in the Invisible realms, that ye fashion for me a magical base in the Astral Light wherein I may invoke the Divine Forces to charge this talisman. Grant unto me the presence of GABRIEL, the Great Archangel of the sphere of Yesod.**

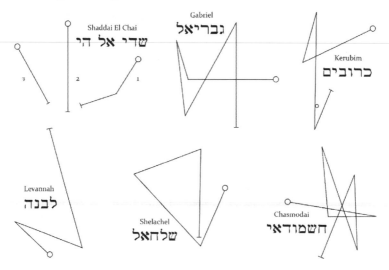

Hold the Wand by the same band used to invoke the lesser Hexagrams. Trace the *Greater Invoking Hexagram of Luna* and within it the sigil of Gabriel. Vibrate the name strongly. Then say:

> **O ye Strong Ones of Yesod, I conjure ye by the name of the Almighty One, and by the name of Gabriel, whose throne and seat ye are. KERUBIM! Come to me now! Be present at this ceremony and fill this sphere with your magic power!"** (Trace the sigil of the Kerubim and intone the name.)

> **Command unto me the presence of GABRIEL, the Angel of Levannah, and her intelligence SHELACHEL that they may consecrate this most powerful symbol. I conjure ye potently to make manifest your presence within my soul that this Lunar talisman may be charged. Come forth, all ye powers and forces of the realm of Yesod, obey ye now in the name of SHADDAI EL CHAI, the divine ruler of your kingdom, and GABRIEL, your Archangel, and the mighty KERUBIM!**

CONSECRATION OF A LUNAR TALISMAN

Put the Wand aside. Place the black-wrapped talisman at the edge of the circle to the west. Push it into the circle with the tip of the Sword. Then say:

> **Creature of Talismans, enter thou within this sacred circle, that thou mayest become a worthy dwelling place for the Forces of LEVANNAH.**

Consecrate the talisman with Water and Fire. (Dip your fingers into the Water and mark the talisman with a Cross. Sprinkle thrice in the form of the *Invoking Water Triangle* ▽. Wave the incense in the form of a Cross and give an additional three waves in the form of *the Invoking Fire Triangle* △). Then say:

> **In the Name of SHADDAI EL CHAI, I,** (give magical name), **proclaim that I have invoked ye in order to form a true and potent link between my human soul and the Light Divine. To this end I have brought into this circle a Talisman covered with a black veil and bound thrice with a cord, so that this creature of talismans shall not see the light nor move until it be duly consecrated unto me. I proclaim that this talisman shall be charged by the Archangel GABRIEL, so that through its use, I may increase my powers of clairvoyance and psychic awareness, so that I may be better enabled to perform the Great Work.**

Place the talisman at the foot of the Altar and say:

> **I,** (magical name), **do solemnly pledge to consecrate this talisman in due ceremonial form. I further promise and swear to use it to obtain only pure and clear mystical visions and insights. May the powers of Yesod, the sphere of Foundation, witness my pledge.**

Place the talisman upon the white Triangle on the Altar and stand west, facing the east. With Sword in hand, trace over the talisman the sigils of *Shaddai El Chai* and *Gabriel* while intoning their names. (Vibrate **Shaddai El Chai** a total of seven times according to the Vibratory Formula.) Then say:

> **I invoke the Great Angel of Yesod and Luna, GABRIEL, the Strong One of God! Lay Thy hand invisibly on this talisman and give it life.**
> **Anoint it, so that through its use I may increase my powers of astral perception and tread the path of the Seer, to the glory of Thine ineffable name. I also invoke the choir of angels known as the KERUBIM** (intone and trace the sigil), **the Strong Ones, that they may bind into this talisman the firm and sturdy Foundation of Yesod, which gives stability to the sphere of LEVANNAH. O ye Mighty Ones of Yesod, assist me in this my invocation of the Lunar powers! I command ye to send hither the Intelligence of the Moon, SHELACHEL, that he concentrate and bind into this talisman life and power. O ye divine Forces of Yesod, manifest yourselves through this Lunar Intelligence, to insure that this talisman give forth to me only true and correct impressions in the form of dreams and visions;**
> **not the false and distorted images that abound in the Akashic Record.**

21

Descend I command Thee, Mighty archangel GABRIEL, to charge this talisman aright, that it may become a powerful tool consecrated to the work of the Magic of Light.

Lift the talisman in the left hand, smite it thrice with the Sword, and raise both it and the Sword aloft, stamping the foot three times. Then take the talisman to the north and say:

The voice of the Exorcist said unto me, "Let me shroud myself in darkness, peradventure thus shall I manifest myself in Light. I am the only being in an abyss of Darkness. From an Abyss of Darkness came I forth ere my birth, from the silence of a primal sleep." And the Voice of Ages answered unto my soul, Creature of Talismans, the Light shineth in the Darkness, but the Darkness comprehendeth it not. Let the Mystic Circumambulation take place in the pathway of Darkness with the symbolic light of Occult Science to lead the way.

Visualize the light of a lantern held by an angelic hand before you. Circumambulate the Temple once with the talisman and the Sword, following the light. After going around once, stop in the south and lay the talisman on the ground. Bar it with the Sword, saying:

Unpurified and unconsecrated, thou canst not enter the Gateway of the West.

Purify the talisman with Water and consecrate with Fire as before. Lift it with the left hand, face the west and say:

Creature of Talismans, twice purified and twice consecrated, thou mayest approach the Gateway of the West.

Pass to the west with the talisman in the left hand. Partly unveil it, smite it once with the Sword and say:

Thou canst not pass from concealment unto manifestation, save by the virtue of the name "ELOHIM." Before all things are the Chaos and the Darkness, and the gates of the Land of Night. I am He whose Name is Darkness. I am the Great One of the Paths of the Shades. I am the Exorcist in the midst of the Exorcism. Take on therefore manifestation without fear before me, for I am he in whom fear is not.

Replace the veil over the talisman and carry it once more around the circle. Then stop in the north, place the talisman on the floor and say:

Unpurified and unconsecrated, thou canst not enter the Gateway of the East.

Purify and consecrate the talisman with Water and Fire as before. Lift it in the left hand and say:

Creature of Talismans, thrice purified and thrice consecrated, thou mayest approach the Gateway of the East.

Go to the east and partly unveil the talisman. Strike it once with the Sword and say:

CONSECRATION OF A LUNAR TALISMAN

> Thou canst not pass from concealment unto manifestation save by the virtue of the name YHVH. After the formless and the Void and the Darkness, then cometh the knowledge of the Light. I am that Light which riseth in darkness. I am the Exorcist in the midst of the Exorcism. Take on therefore manifestation before me, for I am the wielder of the forces of the Balance. Creature of Talismans, long hast thou dwelt in darkness. Quit the night and seek the Day.

Take the talisman to the west of the Altar. Place it again on the White Triangle. Hold the pommel of the Sword immediately over it and say:

> By all the names, powers and rites already rehearsed, I conjure upon thee power and might irresistible. KHABS AM PEKHT. KONX OM PAX. LIGHT IN EXTENSION. As the Light hidden in darkness can manifest therefrom, so shalt thou become irresistible.

Put aside the Sword and take up the Wand by the white portion. Remain west of the Altar facing east. Repeat the following invocation:

> SHADDAI EL CHAI! Oh thou Almighty and Living One! Supreme Lord of Life! Life-giver and Life-Creator! Thee do I invoke! Thou who activates the final manifestation of Form in the physical realm. Thee do I invoke! Thou Vision of the Inner Workings of the Universe. Thee do I invoke! Thou receptive Chalice that receives and purifies the influence of all the Emanations. Thee do I invoke! Thou whose image is that of a beautiful naked man, very strong. Thee do I invoke! Thou Mirror of Tiphareth, reflecting back the solar Light through the Luminary of the Moon. Thee do I invoke! Throne of the Aether of the Wise, the Akashic Light, realm of both mind and matter. Thee do I invoke! SHADDAI EL CHAI! (Vibrate powerfully seven times, employing the Vibratory Formula.)

> I INVOKE THEE! Administer your divine guidance over these proceedings to insure that this Lunar talisman be properly charged. Grant unto me that through its use, my powers of perception may be increased. May it aid me to comprehend visions that are occult in nature. Thus may my clairvoyant abilities be expanded and my inner sight elevated. Thus will I be better equipped to perform the works of divination, skrying, and godform assumption. SHADDAI EL CHAI! I also ask that you instill within this talisman the power to resist the false and deceptive images that reside in the Sphere of Illusion known as Maya.

> Grant that this Lunar talisman provide me only with true impressions, reflected from Tiphareth and ultimately from the Crown on High. I invoke thee, exalt my soul to the feet of thy glory. Hear me and manifest in splendor to one who aspires to the Light of the Hidden Wisdom.

Take up the talisman. Put it on the floor to the east of the Altar in the place between the Pillars of the Neophyte Hall. Stand just east of the talisman and face west. Holding the Wand by the colored band previously used to invoke Luna, trace the *Greater Invoking Hexagram of Luna* over the talisman. Vibrate "Ararita" while drawing the hexagram. Intone "Shaddai El Chai" when tracing the sigil of the Moon ☽. Finally vibrate the name of "Aleph" when drawing the letter א in the center.

Intone the following names and trace their corresponding sigils over the talisman:

> **Shaddai El Chai. Gabriel. Kerubim. Levannah. Schelachel Chashmodai.**

Then say:

> **I invoke into this talisman the Forces and Powers of LEVANNAH, the blue and silver crescent of the Moon. Thou Bright Lady of the night, Queen of dreams and visions, thee I invoke! Ruler of the Lunar tides and the currents of Flux and Reflux. Etheric partner of the Earth. Moonstone bride and Mother. The Mirror of Contemplation. Thou art a Goddess of many names: ISIS. DIANA. ARTEMIS. SELENE. HECATE. UMA. Shining One of the silver bow and the veil! Beautiful art thou in thy fullness! By seed and by root, and by bud and leaf, and by flower and fruit of my entire being, do I invoke thee! Bestow upon this talisman your powers of foresight and intuition. May the perfume of thy essence anoint this Lunar talisman so that through its use my precognitive abilities may be increased. Thus may I be better able to comprehend the Hidden Nature of the Universe.**

Focus the entire force of the will, and project it at the talisman using the Sign of the Enterer at least three times, or until you feel your energy begin to drain. When this happens, give the Sign of Silence at the end for protection. A light should be visualized flickering about the talisman. Return it to the white Triangle upon the Altar. Purify and consecrate it again. Remove the black cord. Strike the talisman three times again with the Sword and proclaim:

> **By and in the Name of SHADDAI EL CHAI, I invoke upon thee the Powers and Forces of LEVANNAH!**

Put aside the Sword and take up the Wand by the colored band previously used to invoke Luna. Trace over the talisman the sigils of *Shaddai El Chai, Gabriel, Kerubim, Schelachel*, and *Chashmodai*. (Vibrate the divine Hebrew name of Yesod seven times as before.)

Circumambulate the Temple thrice with the Wand and the talisman. Then go to the station of the Hierophant in the east. Unveil the talisman, placing it back upon the ground in front of you. Still grasping the Wand by the colored band previously used to invoke Luna, contemplate the various attributes of Luna. Make the Sign of the Rending of the Veil and say:

> **Let the white brilliance of the Divine Spirit, reflected through the silvery blue mirror of LEVANNAH, descend upon this talisman, to fill it with the splendor of Thy majesty, that forever it may be unto me an aid to aspire to the Great Work.**

CONSECRATION OF A LUNAR TALISMAN

Hold the Wand by the white portion and draw the Flaming Sword over the talisman. Take up the talisman and step between the pillars. Formulate an astral Banner of the East enveloping itself around the talisman. Hold it on high and say:

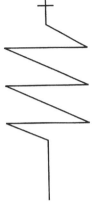

> **Behold, all ye powers and forces I have invoked. Take witness that I have duly consecrated this talisman with the aid of GABRIEL, great archangel of Yesod and LEVANNAH, that it may aid and improve my intuition. May it provide me with a sure footing whenever I tread the paths of the Astral Realm, giving me the ability to discern between the true and the untrue. And by the exaltation of my higher nature, may it assist me in my path to the Light Divine.**

Wrap the talisman in white silk or linen and place it upon the Altar. (NOTE: Never banish over a talisman when it is unwrapped.) Grasp the Wand with both hands by the white portion and raise it on high. Then say:

> **Not unto my name, O Adonai, but to Thy Name be ascribed the Kingdom, the Power and the Glory, now and forevermore! Amen!**

Give the LVX Signs. Purify and consecrate the Temple with Water and Fire as in the beginning of the ritual.

Perform the Reverse Circumambulation three times widdershins. Feel the energy that you have carefully built up throughout the ceremony begin to dissipate. Give the *Adoration to the Lord of the Universe:*

> **Holy art Thou Lord of the Universe!** (Projection Sign)
> **Holy art Thou Whom Nature hath not formed!** (Projection Sign) **Holy art Thou the Vast and the Mighty One!** (Projection Sign)
> **Lord of the Light and of the Darkness.** (Sign of Silence)

Return to the position of Luna in the Temple. Hold the Wand by the colored band previously used to invoke Luna, and point with the black end of the Wand. Draw the *Greater Banishing Hexagram of Luna* in that direction, vibrating the words "Ararita," **"Shaddai El Chai"** and **"Aleph."**

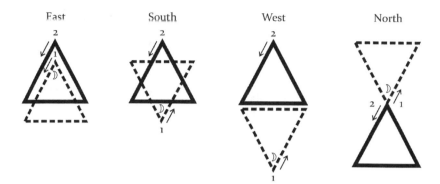

Perform the *Lesser Banishing Hexagram Ritual of Luna*, commencing with the *Qabalistic Cross* while holding the Wand by the white band. Then trace the Lesser Hexagrams of Luna (four forms) in their respective quarters, while holding the Wand by the colored band previously used to invoke Luna, and pointing with the black end. Intone **"Ararita"** as each figure is traced. Follow this with the *Analysis of the Keyword* given previously in this ritual. Say:

> **I now release any Spirits that may have been imprisoned by this ceremony. Depart in peace to your abodes and habitations. Go with the sanction of SHADDAI EL CHAI and the blessings of YEHESHUAH YEHOVASHAH.**

Perform the *Supreme Banishing Ritual of the Pentagram* (SBRP). Hold the white band of the Wand when giving the *Qabalistic Cross* and the Archangelic names. Trace the Banishing Pentagrams while grasping the appropriate colored bands (as in the SIRP at the beginning of the ceremony.) Be sure to point with the black end of the Wand for banishing.

Perform the LBRH. Perform the LBRP. Knock five times as in the beginning. Then say:

I now declare this Temple duly closed. So Mote it Be!

****

ASTROLOGICAL, ANGELIC AND DEMONIC FORCES RESIDENT IN THE LESSER ARCANA OF THE TAROT

By

LON MILO DUQUETTE

There is no question that the Tarot is one of the most important weapons in the magical arsenal of the Golden Dawn magician. Simply by examining its structure we come face to face with the rudiments of Qabalah and the basics of Hermetic thought. By meditating upon its images we learn the ineffable language of the soul and program ourselves to recognize the initiatory guide-posts that will eventually map our return journey to godhead. For the initiate of the Western Mystery Tradition, the Tarot is at once our encyclopedia, our dictionary, our telescope, our microscope, our history book, and oracle of the future.

Tarot is the near-perfect mirror of the living cosmos. As such, it teams with the forces that create, sustain, and destroy the universe. In magic, these forces are personified as gods, archangels, angels, intelligences and demons. Each of these spiritual "entities" has its unique role to play in the grand scheme of things. Each is the obedient servant of the greater force of which it is only a partial aspect, and lord of the lesser forces that are component aspects of itself.

There are other near-perfect mirrors of the cosmos. The *I Ching—the Book of Changes—* is perhaps the most sublime, dissecting all in heaven and earth and neatly categorizing the component parts in the images of 64 Hexagrams. Theoretically there are infinite ways we could divide the cosmos for examination, but no matter how we slice up the divine pie we are merely creating different ways of looking at (and thinking about) the same thing. Each new method of division creates a distinctive hierarchy of spiritual entities formed by the laws dictated by the dynamics of that particular mode of division.

For instance, it is very difficult for us to gain much hard information by contemplating the undivided, absolute and infinite *One*. In fact, about all we can say about the supreme monad is that it *is* absolute and infinite. We cannot even begin to speculate how it goes about exercising its infinite power to create, sustain and destroy the universe. Only when we divide the *One* in half do we start getting something we can wrap our minds around.

Now we have the concept of *duality*, a world of extremes. Now we have *something* and its opposite, positive-negative. Now we have up-down, yes-no, night-day, hard-soft, male-female, happy-sad, good-evil, pleasure-pain. We can even start to speculate about spiritual entities that might be created from this primal division and what kinds of forces they would manifest.

Perhaps at the very top end of the hierarchy there are two tremendous and eternally contending *gods* whose efforts respectively govern the pulse of an expanding-contracting universe.

Somewhere in the middle of the dualistic chain of command we might find pairs of *archangels* of polarity—of magnetism and electricity. Down here on the material plane we might dissect our computer and see that its brain ultimately functions through the agency of the either-or *demons* of binary logic.

The more we divide the *One* and consider its parts, the more food for thought we create. When we divide the *One* into three parts we discover even more. *Three* is such a sublime and unique number that, since prehistoric times, it has been held in supernatural reverence by cultures and religions arctand the world. With *Three* we transcend the *either-or* world of duality and are introduced to synthesis. *Three* sets the stage for all things that have a beginning, a middle, and an end—a birth, a life, and a death—a rising, a zenith, and a fall.

If we were to personify the sacred qualities of *Three* as gods, I don't think we could improve on the Hindu trinity of Brahma, the creator; Vishnu, the preserver; and Shiva, the destroyer. The Hindus also give us the concept of three Gunas—Sattvas, Rajas and Tamas, three forms of energy that govern the movement of everything in heaven and earth. Sattvas manifests the qualities of clarity, peacefulness, understanding, poise, and ecstasy. Rajas is the quality of animation. It is activity, agitation, inspiration, and brilliance. Tamas is denseness. It manifests as ignorance, sloth, and darkness. With *Three* the worlds begin to spin. Like the three beasts that occupy the rim of the Wheel of *Fortune* Tarot card, there is never a time when any one of these three qualities of energy can permanently prevail or be vanquished.

In the zodiac we will see the dynamics of this three-fold division as the cardinal, fixed, and mutable signs, and the *ascendant, succendent,* and *cadent* progression of decans. This pattern will be obviously important when we are introduced to the spiritual inhabitants of the Lesser Arcana of the Tarot.

The qualities of *One, Two,* and *Three* are very abstract and sublime, and without question set the primal patterns for the mysteries of the numbers to follow. But only when we divide the *One* into four parts do we bring our meditations solidly to bear upon our own lives and the world around us—a world of dimension—of north, south, east, and west—lines by which we measure the earth and, when extended, reach into space to fix the four kerubic signs of the zodiac—landmarks that define four seasons of the year.

The Hebrew mystics chose to consider the supreme force of the universe as a single deity that exercised its will through the agency of four fundamental levels of divine consciousness. These levels are identified by the four letters (actually three, because one letter is repeated) of the deity's name, יהוה —*Yod Heh Vau Heh.* These four 'worlds' are respectively: Atziluth, the archetypal world; Briah, the creative world; Yetzirah, the formative world; and Assiah, the material world.

Because, according to scripture, humans are made in the 'image' of deity, each one of us is a microcosmic reflection of this four-part macrocosmic arrangement. For each of us, *Yod Heh Vau Heh* manifests as the four parts of the human soul: Chiah, the life force; Neshamah, the soul intuition; Ruach, the intellect; and Nephesh, the animal soul. On the elemental end of the scale, *Yod He Vau Heh* manifests as the four elements of Fire, Water, Air, and Earth, and in the Tarot as the four suits; Wands, Cups, Swords, and Pentacles.

ה Heh (final)	ו Vau	ה Heh	י Yod	*Hebrew Letter*
Assiah—Material World	Yetzirah—Formative World	Briah—Creative World	Atziluth—Archetypal World	*Qabalistic World*
Nephesh Animal Soul	Ruach Intellect	Neshamah Soul Intuition	Chiah Life Force	*Part of Soul*
Earth	Air	Water	Fire	*Element*
Pentacles	Swords	Cups	Wands	*Tarot Suit*

Table 1

(Table reads from right to left.)

To better understand the mechanics of *Yod Heh Vau Heh*, the ancient adepts proceeded with anal-retentive precision to take each of these four great divisions of deity and divide it, subdivide it, and subdivide it again. In doing so they created legions of spiritual beings that execute their specific duties in the universe in strict obedience to a logical hierarchy. The 56 cards of the Lesser Arcana of the Tarot demonstrate these divisions and subdivisions of the Great Name and serve as residences for the various spiritual agencies those divisions and subdivisions host.

ASTROLOGICAL MATRIX OF THE 56 SMALL CARDS

THE FOUR ACES

We say that there are 56 cards in the Lesser Arcana, but ultimately there are only four: the four aces. The four Court Cards and the nine Small Cards of each suit (and the spiritual entities they represent) live inside their respective Ace.

The four Court Cards divide their Ace int four elemental subdivisions. The Kings are the *Fire* subdivisions, the Queens are the *Water* subdivisions, the Princes are the Air subdivisions, and the Princesses are the *Earth* Subdivisions of their respective Aces.

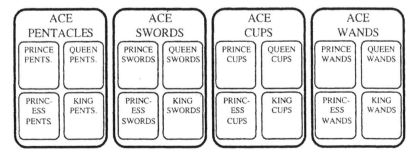

Table 2

Astrological Rulership of the Lesser Arcana of the Tarot. (Table reads from right to left).

ASTROLOGICAL, ANGELIC AND DEMONIC FORCES

THE ACES AND THE COURT CARDS

—The Princesses (See Table 2)

Each of the four Princesses enjoys a unique relationship with her Ace. In a very real sense, the Ace and the Princess represent the entire spectrum of meaning inherent in the suit. They are the *Alpha* and *Omega* of their suit. As such, the Princesses are called the "Thrones of the Aces." Instead of ruling certain 30 degree periods of the Zodiac (as do the Kings, Queens, and Princes), the Princess rules with her Ace an entire quadrant of space projected from the Earth's north pole. The midpoint of each quadrant is the Fixed sign of the Zodiac appropriate to the Element the Ace and Princess represent. For example: the Ace and Princess of Pentacles (Earth) rule the Aries/ Taurus/Gemini quadrant of space above the North Pole, Taurus being the fixed earth sign of the Zodiac. (See top line of Table 2.)

—The Kings, Queens and Princes

The 12 remaining Court Cards—the Kings, Queens and Princes of each suit—each rule 30 degrees of the Zodiac. They do not, however, rule a complete Zodiac sign. (That job is handled nicely by twelve of the twenty-two cards of the Greater Arcana.) Rather, to demonstrate the necessity for the elements to combine with each other, the Kings, Queens and Princes each rule from 20 degrees of one sign to 20 degrees of the next. (See second line from the top of Table 2.)

THE ACES AND THE SMALL CARDS

The nine Small Cards of each suit divide their Ace by three and then subdivide each of the three divisions by three.

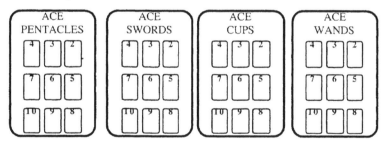

As we learned earlier in *The Complete Golden Dawn System of Magic*, the 12 signs of the zodiac are categorized first by element (Fire, Water, Air or Earth) then by 3 aspects of *cardinal* (the initial birth of the qualities of the element in question), *fixed* (the matured and definitive qualities of the element), and *mutable* (the element in its decline and readiness to change).

Mutable	*Fixed*	*Cardinal*	*Element*
Sagitarius	Leo	Aries	3 Fires signs
Pisces	Scorpio	Cancer	3 Water signs
Gemini	Aquarius	Libra	3 Air signs
Virgo	Taurus	Capricorn	3 Earth signs

Table 3

(Table reads from right to left)

The 36 Small Cards are ingeniously allotted to the 36 decans by applying impeccable qabalistic logic. The nine Wands represent the Fire signs of the zodiac; the nine Cups represent the Water signs; the nine Swords represent the Air signs; and the nine Pentacles represent the Earth signs.

The 2s, 3s & 4s, being the first series of 3 cards in each suit, are allotted to the *cardinal* signs. The 5s, 6s & 7s, being the second series, are allotted to the *fixed* signs. The 8s, 9s & 10s, being the third series, are allotted to the *mutable* signs. (See the bottom lines of Table 2.)

One of the seven planets of the ancients rules each of the 36 Small Cards. (See third line from the bottom of Table 2.) Starting with 0 degree Leo, the traditional Chaldean start of the year, the planets are assigned in the order they are attributed to the sephiroth of the Tree of Life: Saturn, Jupiter, Mars, Sol, Venus, Mercury, Luna. The series is repeated until all 36 decans are occupied by a planet. You will notice that Mars occupies both the last decan of Pisces and the first decan of Aries. The traditional explanation for this informs us that it is because the year needs an extra dose of Mars energy to jump start the beginning of Spring. (Hey! Don't blame me...blame the Chaldeans!)

The compatibility or incompatibility of planet and zodiac sign are important factors when determining the divinatory meanings of the Small Cards. It is easy to see how the 2 of Wands (Mars in the very compatible Aries) is *"Dominion"*—but that in the 5 of Wands (unyielding and brooding Saturn in boisterous and self-centered Leo) is *"Strife."*

ARCHANGELS, ANGELS, AND DEMONS OF THE 36 SMALL CARDS

Table 4 contains the names and Tarot addresses of 252 traditional archangels, angels, and demons. This is by no means an exhaustive list, but it is illustrative of how easily the hierarchies of the spirit world can be organized by the Tarot, and how marvelously alive with spiritual forces each card is.

- The top three lines divide the year into zodiac signs and decans and provide the approximate days of the years they rule.

- The next four lines begin a traditional Qabalistic hierarchy of Archangel, Angel, and two Lords (one for the day, one for the night) who rule the Zodiac sign.

- The next two lines splits each Zodiac sign into three decans and displays the names of the traditional Angel of each.

- The next two lines split each decan in two, forming 72 quinairies (periods of five degrees) and displays the names of the 72 Angels of the *Shem ha-Mephorash* resident in each quinairy.

- The next three lines indicate the suit, number, and traditional title of each Small Card.

- The next two lines display the names and day or night designation of the 72 Demons of the Goetia.

- The bottom two lines display the names of the twelve Qliphotic Genii, and the twelve orders of the Qliphoth.

ASTROLOGICAL, ANGELIC AND DEMONIC FORCES

Days of the year	Zodiac Sign	Archangel	Angel	Lord by Day	Lord by Night	Angel of the Decans	Decan	72 Angels of the Shem ha-Mephoorash	Tarot Suit	Tarot Card	Title of Small Card	Day Demon	Night Demon	72 Demons of the Goetia	Qliphotic Genus / Order of the Qlphoth
JUNE/JULY Jun 21–Jul 22	CANCER Cardinal Water	Muriel	Pakiel	Rasdar	Akel	Mathravash	0–10	Eiael / Habuiah	CUPS	2	LOVE	BUER	BIFRONS		Characith / SHICHIRIRON Black Ones
						Rahadetz	10–20	Rochel / Ilbamiah	CUPS	3	ABUNDANCE	GUSION	VUAL		
						Alinkir	20–30	Haiaiel / Mumiah	CUPS	4	BLENDED PLEASURE	SITRI	HAAGENTI		
JULY/AUGUST Jul 22–Aug 22	LEO Fixed Fire	Verkiel	Sharatiel	Sanahem	Zalbarhith	Losanahar	0–10	Vehuiah / Ieliel	WANDS	5	STRIFE	BELETH	CROCELL		Temphioth / SHALHEBIRON Flaming Ones
						Zachi	10–20	Sitael / Elemiah	WANDS	6	VICTORY	LERAJE	FURCAS		
						Sahiber	20–30	Mahashiah / Lelahel	WANDS	7	VALOUR	ELIGOS	BALAM		
AUGUST/SEPTEMBER Aug 23–Sep 22	VIRGO Mutable Earth	Hamaliel	Shelahbel	Lasiara	Sasia	Ananaurah	0–10	Aehaiah / Cahethel	DISKS	8	PRUDENCE	ZEPAR	ALLOCES		Yamatu / TZAPHIRIRON Scratchers
						Rayadyah	10–20	Haziel / Aladiah	DISKS	9	MATERIAL GAIN	BOTIS	CAMIO		
						Mishpar	20–30	Lauiah / Hahiah	DISKS	10	WEALTH	BATHIN	MURMUR		
SEPTEMBER/OCTOBER Sep 23–Oct 22	LIBRA Cardinal Air	Zuriel	Chedeqiel	Thergebon	Achohraon	Tarasni	0–10	Ieiazel / Mebahel	SWORDS	2	PEACE RESTORED	SALLOS	OROBAS		Lafcursiax / ABIRIRON Clayish Ones
						Saharnatz	10–20	Hariel / Hakamiah	SWORDS	3	SORROW	PURSON	GREMORY		
						Shachdar	20–30	Leviah / Caliel	SWORDS	4	REST FROM STRIFE	MARAX	OS		
OCTOBER/NOVEMBER Oct 23–Nov 22	SCORPIO Fixed Water	Barkiel	Saitzel	Bethchon	Sahaqnab	Kamotz	0–10	Leuuiah / Pahliah	CUPS	5	LOSS IN PLEASURE	IPOS	AMY		Nianiel / NECHESHTHIRON Brazen Ones
						Nundohar	10–20	Nelchael / Ieiaiel	CUPS	6	PLEASURE	AIM	ORIAS		
						Uthrodiel	20–30	Melahel / Hahuiah	CUPS	7	ILLUSIONARY SUCCESS	NABERIUS	VAPULA		
NOVEMBER/DECEMBER Nov 23–Dec 21	SAGITTARIUS Mutable Fire	Advakiel	Saritiel	Ahoz	Lebarmin	Mishrath	0–10	Nithhaiah / Haaiah	WANDS	8	SWIFTNESS	GLASYA-LABOLAS	ZAGAN		Saksaksalim / NACHASHIRON Snakey Ones
						Vehrin	10–20	Ieathel / Sahiiah	WANDS	9	GREAT STRENGTH	BUN	VALAC		
						Aboha	20–30	Reiiel / Amael	WANDS	10	OPPRESSION	RONOVE	ANDRAS		
DECEMBER/JANUARY Dec 31–Jan 19	CAPRICORN Cardinal Earth	Hanael	Samreqel	Sandali	Abyar	Misnin	0–10	Lecabel / Vasariah	DISKS	2	HARMONIOUS CHANGE	BERITH	HAURES		A'ano'nin / DAGDAGIRON Fishy Ones
						Yasyasyah	10–20	Iehuiah / Lehahiah	DISKS	3	MATERIAL WORKS	ASTAROTH	ANDREALPHUS		
						Yasgedibarodiel	20–30	Chavakiah / Monadel	DISKS	4	EARTHLY POWER	FORNEUS	CIMEIES		
JANUARY/FEBRUARY Jan 20–Feb 18	AQUARIUS Fixed Air	Kambriel	Tzakmiqel	Atnor	Polayan	Saspam	0–10	Aniel / Haamiah	SWORDS	5	DEFEAT	FORAS	AMDUSIAS		Hemethterith / BAHIMIRON Beastial Ones
						Abdaron	10–20	Rehael / Ihiazel	SWORDS	6	EARNED SUCCESS	ASMODAY	BELIAL		
						Gerodiel	20–30	Hahahel / Michael	SWORDS	7	UNSTABLE EFFORT	GAP	DECARBIA		
FEBRUARY/MARCH Feb 19–Mar 20	PISCES Mutable Water	Amnitzel	Vakabiel	Ramara	Nathdonnel	Bihelami	0–10	Vevaliah / Ielahiah	CUPS	8	ABANDONED SUCCESS	FURFUR	SEERE		Qulielfi / NASHIMIRON Malignant Women
						Avron	10–20	Saliah / Ariel	CUPS	9	MATERIAL HAPPINESS	MARCHOSIAS	DANTALION		
						Satrip	20–30	Asaliah / Mihael	CUPS	10	PREFECTED SUCCESS	STOLAS	ANDROMALIUS		
MARCH/APRIL Mar 21–Apr 20	ARIES Cardinal Fire	Malkidiel	Sharhiel	Saterion	Sapatavi	Zazer	0–10	Vehuel / Daniel	WANDS	2	DOMINION	BAEL	PHENEX		Tzuflifu / BEIRIRON The Herd
						Behahemi	10–20	Heahaziah / Amamiah	WANDS	3	ESTABLISHED STRENGTH	AGARES	HALPHAS		
						Satander	20–30	Nanael / Nithael	WANDS	4	PERFECTED WORK	VASSAGO	MALPHAS		
APRIL/MAY Apr 21–May 21	TAURUS Fixed Earth	Asmodel	Araziel	Raydel	Totath	Kedamidi	0–10	Mebahiah / Poiel	DISKS	5	MATERIAL TROUBLE	SAMIGINA	RUM		Urens / ADIMIRON Bloody Ones
						Minacharai	10–20	Nemamiah / Ieilael	DISKS	6	MATERIAL SUCCESS	MARBAS	FOCALOR		
						Yakasaganotz	20–30	Harahel / Mizrael	DISKS	7	SUCCESS UNFULFILLED	VALEFOR	VEPAR		
MAY/JUNE May 21–Jun 21	GEMINI Mutable Air	Ambriel	Sarayel	Sarash	Ogarman	Sagarash	0–10	Umabel / Iahhel	SWORDS	8	SHORTENED FORCE	AMON	SABNOCK		Zamradiel / TZELILIMIRON Clangers
						Shehadani	10–20	Annauel / Mekekiel	SWORDS	9	DESPAIR & CRUELTY	BARBATOS	SHAX		
						Bethon	20–30	Damabiah / Meniel	SWORDS	10	RUIN	PAIMON	VIN		

Table 4

Archangels, Angels, and Demons of the 36 Small Cards of the Tarot

MACGREGOR MATHERS AND THE SECRET CHIEFS

By

S. JASON BLACK

While there were many individuals involved in the evolution of the Golden Dawn, the person most instrumental in its development, as well as the name most associated with it, is MacGregor Mathers.

Mathers has a mixed reputation among historians of the magical revival. First, he is widely acknowledged to have been an indefatigable researcher in old libraries and collections such as the British Museum. Second, he is seen as the crank who implied (during his suit against Crowley for revealing Golden Dawn secrets), that he was the miraculously-surviving James the First of Scotland. This leaves his other remarkable claim—that he was repeatedly contacted and guided by superhuman intelligences—dismissed as a well-intentioned fraud. I must admit that until recently I was of this party. I am no longer so sure because the literature of living witnesses of apparitions is overwhelming.

He called these persons "Secret Chiefs." Mathers was, in many ways, a typical "English eccentric." Born in England, throughout his life he would fantasize himself a highland chieftain, marching around in kilts and other regalia. Far from looking ridiculous, being an athlete, he cut quite a dashing figure—although his friends wondered what in hell he was doing. He was far from lazy (as the material in this book demonstrates) and was capable of great effort in a field that interested him. The first of those was the Theosophical Society.

His involvement in Blavatsky's amazingly successful and widespread movement soon led him to become an officer in the sizable London branch leading to acquaintance with individuals he would never otherwise have met. Among these were a Mr. Woodman and a Dr. Westcott, both high-ranking Freemasons with a strong interest in the occult arts, an interest that they passed on to MacGregor like a bad cold. For those of you unfamiliar with Theosophy, then, as now, it does not approve of esoteric practice of almost any kind. It was, I think, over this attitude that Mathers resigned from the Society and threw in his lot with the other two gentlemen. Another life-changing event during this period was his courtship and marriage to Moina Bergson (the daughter of the famous philosopher Henri Bergson), who was to be his partner in the Golden Dawn work for the remainder of his life.

Around this time the first controversial (or at least ambivalent) event in the origins of the Order occurs: the discovery of the cipher manuscript. Dr. Westcott was strolling in an open-air book market when he comes across a hand-written document which (I suppose), attracts his attention because it contains occult symbols that he recognizes. He buys it. Over time, he succeeds in translating it into English—from a German cipher—

MACGREGOR MATHERS AND THE SECRET CHIEFS

Revealing it to be a set of Rosicrucian-like initiation rituals from a German secret society called the Golden Dawn. It contained the framework for many of the initiation rituals in this book and the address of an initiate named Fraulein Anna Sprengel.

From this point a conflagration of argument and counter-argument has ensued up to the present day. The first and most obvious one is that the manuscript disappeared soon after translation. This has been used, for good reason admittedly, to assume that it was trumped up by a group of intelligent initiates to create a myth to surround the Order that they were creating. This assumption is reasonable on its face and rather common. Theologians with an archaeological background have been long aware that the Pentateuch was forged long after it was supposed to have been written, and the Gospels are nothing more than Graeco-Egyptian initiation rituals turned into "history." Crowley's *Liber Al (The Book of the Law)* was considered to have also been lost in the same fashion. (It turned out that a few high-ranking O.T.O. initiates of the older generation had kept it for safekeeping, uncertain just what the fate of their brotherhood would be. This was revealed a number of years ago when I was an active member of this group.) It is not so easy to use this explanation for the Golden Dawn cipher, as the organization as a whole has been moribund since around 1917.

The second controversy is the insistence of the three men that they had actually corresponded with Fraulein Sprengel and had received permission to form their own order based on her material.

There have been claims that attempts have been made to establish the existence of Fraulein Sprengel. This may be so. I have only three words to say to this: Two World Wars. As far as any missing correspondence after nearly a century and a half goes, my remarks are the same as those about the cipher manuscript.

In addition to all of this, these were secret societies. I can tell you from personal experience that, over and above any mystical reasons, there is often hard, practical necessity for secrecy. It rarely appears in any histories of the O.T.O., but some time in the 1920s there was a police raid in London on a Gnostic Mass temple, with attendant publicity. It was, of course, advertised as a "devil worship cult."

One last, off-the-wall suggestion has been made about the origin of the cipher manuscript. It is that Westcott was a multiple personality and he wrote it himself and forgot. To begin with, contrary to popular belief, true multiples are extremely rare. A secondary personality so sophisticated as to produce German literature in code is likely to be noticed by his friends. I do not remember the name of the author who came up with this nonsense. I would be delighted to give him credit, but it is a magnificent example of the desire to believe, in this case, in fraud.

And so we must say that the Sprengel/cipher story remains unproven. Nothing more.

The more troublesome aspect of the story regards the "Secret Chiefs."

The most general, and usually wisest, response to the subject is not to discuss it. This is for two reasons: it is embarrassing, and it is considered unimportant. The first is true. The second is very far from true.

To be right up front, I am suggesting that Mathers' claim that he met these "Chiefs" in physical form in a London park may have literally occurred. This goes completely against the grain of the accepted wisdom, even of Golden Dawn aficionados, but I will present evidence from completely disparate sources that are so similar to what Mathers claimed to have experienced that the reader may be as startled as I was. The material applies not only to Mathers' "Secret Chiefs," but to Crowley's Aiwass, and even Joseph Smith's Moroni.

Admittedly, some of Mathers' claims, and indeed Crowley's, seem so politically motivated ("The chiefs speak through me! No they don't, *through me!*") that I do not intend to approach them except to say that such behavior on both their parts has been a primary cause of muddying the subject. I will concern myself only with the primary alleged initial encounters.

THE COMPLETE GOLDEN DAWN SYSTEM OF MAGIC

The clearest way in which I can state my thesis is by giving a brief quote from the veteran paranormal researcher John Keel:

> Paranormal phenomena are so widespread, so diversified and so sporadic yet so persistent that studying any single element is not only a waste of time but will also lead to the development of belief. Once you have established a belief, the phenomenon adjusts its manifestations to support that belief and thereby escalate it.

Dr. Israel Regardie, in *What You Should Know About the Golden Dawn* (New Falcon Publications, 1993), remarks that "It can confidently be asserted that these [attempts to contact ascended masters] have been among the most fruitful causes of the disruption of the order." Or, may *I* add, of any Order. Whatever "contacts" Mathers may have had, they did not tell him to start a world religion, but gave him instructions on the development of a system of self-development based on European magic intended for a small dedicated group of people. This, while not absolutely unique, is amazingly rare in the annals of what I hope I will be forgiven for calling "contactees."

In reference to the Keel quote above, the point is that almost no one in that subset of the esoteric community involved in magic (in the U.S. at least) has read anything about psychic research. I, on the other hand, began with years of reading such material and other, softer things (such as the Cayce material). It was only many years later that I encountered any material on Hermetic or Goetic magic in any form outside of fiction.

It would be best perhaps to begin with a brief comment on Mathers' initial inspiration: Blavatsky. Here we are only interested in her claim to be in contact with "Eastern Masters" who could appear and disappear at will, as well as cause physical letters to drop out of the air in front of witnesses in broad daylight. These persons follow the classic pattern of behavior toward their contacts by inspiring a new (in this case successful) religious movement; promising secrets, which they may have delivered in her books; and giving the appearance of dark-complected, eastern-looking men. This last is unexpectedly important. In addition, in spite of the committed attacks of the London Society of Psychical Research, these "masters" were seen to appear and disappear in front of multiple witnesses, with or without Blavatsky's presence, frequently in good light.

Now, Mathers claimed to have had multiple encounters, in daylight, in ordinary London surroundings (usually a park) with personages in physical form that he never ceased to insist were superhuman "masters" or, in his terms, "Chiefs." On one occasion he implied that one of his contacts may have been the Comte de St. Germain. This has been taken to have been a bit of show business on his part, but I now wonder if this "person" was not the one who suggested it to Mathers, and not the other way around. I say this because, through rather extensive reading, it has become an obvious pattern that these "beings" adopt names that, while they sound like they come from an old SciFi story upon examination, many, if not most, of the names are abbreviations of things with a previous association. Examples: Ashtar (founder of a UFO religion) Ashtoreth. Apol, Apollo and the list goes on.

Every primary source that I have ever read on the practice of magic tells the practitioner to consult spirits, but not to trust them. Modem occultists who have forgotten this universal rule, if they have the experience at all, often wind up as the butt of supernatural jokes or far worse.

Mathers reported physical sensations on encountering these "Chiefs" which are also held in common by others who have had such experiences. For example, an unreasonable desire to take a walk or drive someplace at an odd hour of the day or night. Or a "chance" encounter with a person or persons unknown who seem to know a great deal about you. An overwhelming physical sense of terror or some equally strong emotion not easily identified. In Mathers' case, he said he felt like he had stood near a lightning strike. In addition he remarked on bleeding from the nose and ears during and after the encounters. This also is remarkably common.

The second "contactee" associated with the Order is Aleister Crowley, famous for his bizarre experiences in Cairo in 1904, leading ultimately to his three-day dictation session with the entity "Aiwass" thus producing the notorious *Book of the Law*.

The events began with his ditzy wife Rose, who went into a spontaneous trance in their hotel room and said, "They are waiting for you." I have been in the presence of someone who went into such a trance once. By that time I had experienced a great deal of disturbing phenomena in connection with magic and I confess I was not happy. In light of this experience I wonder if Crowley's remark that he was "annoyed" may have been disguising more than a little unexpected fear.

When asked just exactly who it was that was waiting, she replied, "Horus, Horus." This caught his attention, as she knew nothing about the ancient Egyptian religion. He took her to the Boulak museum at Cairo and told her to show him Horus, confident that she would blow it and the episode would be over. To his surprise, she bypassed all the other exhibits and led him directly to a statue of the god Horus.

At this point he was understandably impressed. I will skip the details. What I will say, is that Crowley's description of the matter until this point, far from being unusual, is absolutely typical of this particular type of event.

The pattern usually goes something like this: A person, or small group, begins having odd "psychic" experiences, most of which can be explained away—at the beginning. These begin to escalate, usually in short order to "messages" that can may be received verbally (as in clairaudience, mediumship or automatic writing). In Crowley's case, it culminates in "The Encounter" and the subsequent delivery of a message or revelation of varying degrees of complexity.

The subject matter of *Liber Al* stands on its own. I like it and always have. There is one thing that needs to be pointed out in light of our subject: The fact that there are several prophecies in the book that, by almost any interpretation, have already come true, and on the schedule written in the book. This has been used as an argument that it is a "holy book." Routinely, messages are delivered with a limited number of predictions which do in fact come true. This can be something as small as a personal event, to something larger, like a plane crash or volcanic eruption, both of which have happened. So I find myself in the rather embarrassing position of, on the one hand, suggesting that the Aiwass encounter literally happened and on the other pointing out that it follows a pattern so common that I think it likely that something of the sort is happening to someone even as I write, and the claim to unique revelation, to be blunt, is "what they all say." In addition, the "greetings" from these beings from multiple sources are rife with references to "Adonai" and a host of Kabbalistic and Greek terms that the recipients, unlike Mathers and Crowley were utterly unequipped to even recognize, so the use of holy names means nothing.

Finally, I come to Aiwass himself, described by Crowley as a dark, Eastern-looking man, veiled, who stood behind him for a three-day session of divine dictation. This, too, has occurred many times, although rarely so gracefully as in *Liber Al*. Throughout the accounts that I have read, dealing with many countries and over many decades, these beings are, for whatever reason, almost, but not always, described as dark-complected Eastern looking people with high, graceful cheekbones and a very slight oriental caste to their features. Aiwass seems to have been no different. For Mathers' people we have no description.

REGARDIE AND ME

THE PLACE OF THERAPY IN THE GREAT WORK

By

JACK WILLIS, D.C.

I first met Francis Israel Regardie in 1972. It was the day that was to start an almost ten-year relationship and a day that began my introduction to the Great Work and, I would add, the great man. It was at Francis' suggestion that I went to chiropractic school and, when he retired, he turned over his practice to me.

What was Francis like as a person? From a first person perspective, what was the experience of seeing him weekly for almost ten years and, occasionally, personally outside his office? How does one paint a word picture of a man as complex and varied as was Francis? A novel, perhaps a short story. None would do him justice. He was, in a favorite phrase, *sui generis*, unique. In the heat of California, the days of tie-dye and hippy clothing, I never saw him without a vest. Insightful yet opinionated, flexible yet stubborn, of immense learning and phenomenal memory, he had little tolerance for foolishness. If he liked you, he invited you into his heart; if he did not like you or found you insincere, he was quick to dismiss you from his life. But, above all, running like a red thread (a favorite phrase of Wilhelm Reich) through his being was his commitment to the Great Work.

People came from around the world to learn the Golden Dawn from Dr. Regardie; but before he would consent to teach them they first had to have the required psychotherapy. Francis was quite clear both in his knowledge and his opinions. Jungian therapy was totally unacceptable, as were gestalt, transactional analysis, and psychosynthesis. Behavioral therapy was a phrase, knowing him, I would never have mentioned in his presence. Psychoanalytic therapy he approved of, except that it so seldom worked. For too many people, psychoanalysis was insight without awareness. He never quoted that old canard to me, but he well could have: "He's been through analysis and he's just as big a bastard as he ever was." For Regardie, there was only one real therapy: Reichian. It brought you alive, body and spirit. Whether you were using the thaumaturgy of the Golden Dawn, the tarot, the tree of life, the kaballah, or astrology—in all of which Francis was an adept—you first had to clean out your soul. Any technique in the hands of bad intent, though unconscious, would lead to bad results. Francis loved the Great Work too much, he was too committed to it, to let it become the unwilling or unintended host for (unconscious) bad intent.

Dr. Regardie's commitment to Reichian therapy began early. He got together with three other chiropractors and they pooled their resources to send one of them East to get therapy with Reich so that he could come back and train the others. Phillip Curcuruto, D.C. was chosen. After about three years, Dr. Curcuruto returned and trained Dr. Regardie and their colleagues. From then on, Dr. Regardie would train no one in the Great Work unless they had undertaken at least four years of Reichian therapy.

Isn't there a contradiction here? If Regardie demanded therapy before training, then why did he publish *The Complete Golden Dawn System of Magic*, thus letting anyone learn it? Yes, there is a contradiction, but only to those who did not know Francis. If he was intolerant of some types of therapy, he was positively livid with the people who posed as teachers of the Great Work but who knew little and yet pontificated from on high. If the Great Work was to be preserved in its proper form, it had to be documented so there was a canonical source of proper teaching. Better to let the unwashed masses, the mass of men who lead lives of quiet desperation, practice the proper form of the Great Work than to let it be distorted over time by equally pernicious (or worse) men who would pervert the very form of the practice in furtherance of their unconscious evil ends.

For both those familiar with, and for those unfamiliar with, Reichian therapy, let this serve both as an introduction to it and an explanation of why Dr. Regardie regarded it as an essential precursor to practice of the Great Work.

Reich's history is unremarkable. He was a relatively minor figure from the early 1920's up to about 1934 in Freud's group of students in Vienna. Based on some early work by Freud on character types and formation, the analyst Karl Abraham started to develop a theory of character and published his articles in the official journal of the psychoanalytic movement. Unfortunately, Abraham died very young with the theory not yet finished. Reich picked up the mantle and wrote of character as a central element in the individual and in the therapeutic process. Unfortunately, after some early valuable contributions to the theory of character, Reich's own character (unanalyzed) came to the fore and he began a long decline into what can only be called madness. But his contribution remained.

One day, while doing a then-conventional analysis of a patient, Reich made a comment on the patient's symptoms and noted that the patient responded with a wide range of body responses, many of which involved the autonomic (involuntary) nervous system. This, in itself, was not a new observation. The analyst, Franz Alexander, was already doing work in the area of psychosomatic illness. What was new—we now call it serendipitous—was that Reich made the connection: if I can get body changes by interpreting symptoms, why can't I accomplish the same thing (as it turned out, more) by working directly on the body. Thus began what Reich called vegetotherapy and what we now call Reichian therapy. So, in short (and we will return to it in more detail shortly), Reichian therapy is psychotherapy that works from the body instead of the mouth.

Before we continue, it is best to say specifically what character is and why it is an important issue for someone involved in the Great Work. I will approach the concept of character from two directions. First, I will distinguish between (1) behavior, (2) personality, and (3) character. Second, I will give you a specific definition of character.

Behavior is that which we observe a person doing at any given moment. Your reading this article is an example of behavior. In addition, your posture, your sitting arrangement, whether you are also playing music in the background (and the type of music), and so on are all examples of behavior. It is external, directly observable. Let me use another example. You are called upon to give a presentation—perhaps at work, at school, a toast at a party, even reading something out loud at a meeting. You become intensely nervous; you have performance anxiety. That is a behavior. Appearing before others to speak, other than just to present your own opinion on something, results in shaking of the voice, sweaty palms, perhaps a change in skin tone from pale to flushed with embarrassment.

Now we move up (really down, for it is more central to who you are) to personality. The same type of behavior seen in many different situations is personality. If you are nervous about a speech, it is one instance and it is behavior; if you are nervous in many situations, it is part of your personality. One would say of you, you are an anxious person. At least one component, or part, of your personality is anxiety. Usually, when we describe someone, we are describing his personality. Since, right now, your behavior is reading an article in *The Complete Golden Dawn System of Magic*, if you were observed over time one might say of you that you are an intellectual, or a student of the occult, or an inveterate reader, or someone in search of a new way of living. In any case, we would be talking of your personality.

If behavior is observed, and personality can be characterized as similar behavior observed in many situations over time, character is never seen. Character is inferred. Now, before we go further, we have to deal with an ambiguity of language. We use the word "character" in two different ways and it is important to clarify how we are using it here. In the one sense, character is used in a moral or normative sense. When we say of someone that he is "of good character" or "he is quite a character," we are using the term in its moral or normative sense. When a teacher (foolishly) gives a student a grade for character, she is behaving as a moral judge (for which she is not qualified). That is not how we are using the word here. Our use of the word is in its psychological sense, and that leads us to a specific definition.

Character is: my view of myself, the world, and the relationship between the two. This view is not the one consciously held (that is the part of the self-system or part of the personality); this view is held subconsciously. That is to say, it is the way we approach life and people. Do I regard people as basically good? Then trust is probably part of my character. Do I regard myself as basically competent? Then pride is probably part of my character. Let me emphasize once more—because it is central to Reichian therapy and to why Dr. Regardie regarded character restructuring as a prerequisite to the practice of the Great Work—that character is not known to us. Our character is buried deep in our being and is the base of everything else.

Character gives rise to personality and personality gives rise to behavior. We have to guard here against another danger: the danger of being Aristotelian. Aristotle developed and bequeathed to us a form of logic. This is the familiar syllogism:

I believe people are good

Tim is a person

Therefore Tim is good

Human psychology does not work by Aristotelian logic. I might believe people are basically good, but I feel toward Tim that he is dishonest. This might be because I have had experience with Tim or it might simply be, to paraphrase Shakespeare, that Tim has a lean and hungry look. Character need not be consistent, and while it gives rise to personality and thus behavior, it is not the sole determinant. Character, in the end, will out (that is, it will be the main determinant factor in who I am and how I act), but it is not the only thing which controls our personality and behavior. One can be over-tired and thus in a "bad mood." Hormones, age, life's circumstances, health and disease, trauma, disappointments, even good fortune all can, and do, play against our character to determine our behavior. With this understanding, we can return to why Francis Regardie took up the practice of Reichian therapy, and why he regarded such therapy as essential for practitioners of The Golden Dawn.

As is known to all students of the Great Work, Magick can be used for good or for ill. While one may intend the choice to be made by intentions, by one's will (to use William Jame's term not Crowley's where it is capitalized: Will) it will in fact be made by your character. If unrecognized hostility is a part of your character, that hostility will appear in your work with other members of the Golden Dawn and factions will develop within the temple. If you, unconsciously, as part of your character, are trying to get revenge on your mother or father for her or his failures, then you will bring that energy into the practice and it will affect others about you. Francis knew all too well that the history of Magick has been one of conflict, of factions, of plots, of dishonest dealing, of subterfuge. For the Great Work to do its work, it needs people of good character (using the word in both its psychological and normative sense).

Thus we return to why Regardie advocated, practiced, taught, and believed in Reichian therapy. When Reich made that serendipitous move from talking to working on the body, he also made the move from behavior and personality directly to character. That that was his intent does not matter; that he did it does matter. Reichian therapy works directly on the character. To see why, we must return once more to the issue of character, personality and behavior, and then we can examine Reichian therapy directly.

Let me illustrate with a simple example. It is not uncommon when a person crosses his legs that the free foot bounces up and down fairly constantly. In body language, this is a sign of anxiety (to be more accurate: a sign of agitation, anxiety, discomfort, or sometimes anger or annoyance). A psychotherapist, seeing this, would recognize that the person was anxious. Now, if it happened only occasionally (a behavior), then the therapist would know that the current topic was causing the reaction, that the current topic was emotionally charged. If it happened most of the time, then the therapist would know that it was part of the person's personality. Perhaps the person is uncomfortable talking about himself, perhaps he has high anxiety levels, perhaps he is an angry person and so is angry at having to be at the therapist's office. In any event the therapist would have some valuable knowledge. But what does he *do* with this knowledge? If he ignores the movement, he is dismissing a possibly important issue. If he calls the movement to the attention of his patient, the response might be that the person simply learns to inhibit the motion; or the therapist might add to the issue by making the person self-conscious and even more uncomfortable. In either event, all the therapist is doing is dealing with the behavior or the personality. He has not gotten to the character. But the character is the central issue.

So the therapist might, as Reich did in the mid 1920's, deal not with the motion of the foot but with the *meaning* of the motion. After deciding the cause (anxiety, discomfort, anger, etc.) the therapist then starts to address that issue directly. He might not, and probably would not, mention the motion; he will only discuss the character trait that is being made manifest by the motion. This was Reich's first contribution to analytic practice: character analysis. But there is a better way as Reich—and after him, Regardie—found out, and that is to work directly on the body. Mobilize the character trait directly by dealing with the leg muscles that are used to display that behavior and/or personality.

In Reichian therapy, the patient lies on a bed usually unclothed (it is impossible to work on the body if it can not be seen). In Reichian therapy, there are well over 100 different "exercises" (that is not a good word to use, but in English we have no better word) that have the effect of potentiating the character. We might have the patient first start by extending the legs and having both feet make that same up and down (really flex and extend) motion. At the same time, the patient would be instructed to breath deeply, using both the diaphragm and the chest. (Reichian breathing is NOT like yoga breathing; the purpose and the effect are quite different: yoga breathing is intended to *quiet* the emotions while Reichian breathing is intended to *facilitate* the emotions.) As the person continued the motion with the breathing, he would begin to directly experience the emotion which was being manifest in the foot motion. He would directly experience the anxiety or the anger or whatever was being displayed by the foot motion. This direct experience of the emotion brings the character trait into the open. We have gone directly from a body motion to a character trait (by way of the emotion).

In 1945, Reich made a change in his method of working. He dropped the verbal part of therapy and dealt only with the body. This was not a change with which Francis Regardie agreed. Francis recognized that man is a conceptual animal, a conceptual animal with passions and unconscious motivations (the character). To deal with a person we must deal with his life experience (what is the world—recalling the definition of character), with the view he has developed of himself in respect to those life experiences (who am I?), and with the techniques he has worked out when young and vulnerable to cope with his situation (what is the relationship between the world and me?). Contemporary cognitive neuroscience research has isolated a number of neural circuits that control, or cause, or mediate (it is hard to tell which) various emotional states. But what still remains beyond our grasp, and possibly always will, is the ineffable part of us which makes us who we are. To discover our true self—the self *we would have been* absent the disastrous effects of bad parenting, bad teachers, bad friends, bad relatives, or simple misfortune—we have to first undo ourselves (see *Undoing Yourself With Energized Meditation* by Christopher S. Hyatt, Ph.D., New Falcon Publications). For all the value of Dr. Hyatt's book and those like it, there will always be an inherent problem with their use. It is the YOU who are doing the correction, the undoing, and you can't step outside your skin (your character) to do that job.

As anyone who has worked with astrology or tarot or the kaballah or the tree of life knows, the answer lies not in the concretes of the practice, but in the interpretation. One astrologer can give accurate predictions, and another inaccurate predictions. One person can apply the middle pillar technique with illumination, another with the inability to go beyond a block at the throat. As you study and learn *The Complete Golden Dawn System of Magic*, as you delve deeper into the OTO or the Golden Dawn or any of the other branches of the Great Work, keep in mind that you need also to purify yourself not just with purification rituals, but from the inside out. Inner purity can not come from outer practice; it has its own path. And Francis Regardie found that path in his application of Reichian therapy.